SINATRA

SINATRA

The Chairman

JAMES KAPLAN

SPHERE

First published in Great Britain in 2015 by Sphere

A CIP catalogue record for this book
is available from the British Library.

HB ISBN: 978-1-84744-528-5
C Format ISBN: 978-1-84744-529-2

Printed and bound in Great Britain by
Clays Ltd, St Ives plc

Papers used by Sphere are from well-managed forests
and other responsible sources.

MIX
Paper from
responsible sources
FSC® C104740

Sphere
An imprint of
Little, Brown Book Group
Carmelite House
50 Victoria Embankment
London EC4Y 0DZ

An Hachette UK Company
www.hachette.co.uk

ww.littlebrown.co.uk

For K.A.C.

And to the memory of

P.W.K.

Rap Mr. Sinatra if you want to, buddy, but don't tell me you're not rapping him more out of envy than disapproval.

—LEO DUROCHER

If you want to know a man, give him power.

—MENACHEM MENDEL SCHNEERSON, A.K.A.
THE TZEMACH TZEDEK (1789—1866)

CONTENTS

———

Act One

THE
WHIRLWIND

I

||||||||||

leven days after winning the Oscar for *From Here to Eternity*, Frank Sinatra sat down and typed a note to a friend, clearly in response to a congratulatory letter or telegram. The note, on Paramount Pictures stationery and in Frank's customary, too-impatient-to-press-the-shift-key style, began,

april 5, 1954

dear lew—

my paisan mr sinatra is still on cloud nine and the bum refuses to come down . . .

That bum—"mr sinatra"—was so thrilled, the note continued (still all lowercase, still in the third person), that he was "ridiculous." And then, after a final thanks to the recipient, came the signature: "maggio."

It's a charming letter and a fascinating one.[*] Throughout his life, Sinatra employed secretaries who answered his voluminous mail, often signing his name themselves. From time to time, though, when the spirit moved him, he penned or typed his own missives, and the letters are *him*, revealing his restless intellect, his sense of humor (always more spontaneous in personal circumstances than onstage), even a literary sensibility. And why not? As a great singer, he was a great storyteller; why should that faculty switch off when he was away from a microphone? In this note, he is writing in character, as PFC Angelo Maggio, the role that won him that Academy Award, and the voice is perfect: "the bum refuses"; "he's so thrilled he is ridiculous." From

---

[*] All the more fascinating for the mystery of exactly whom the letter was sent to. Kitty Kelley asserts (*His Way*, p. 526) that the note read "Dear Leland" and was addressed to the producer Leland Hayward. She claims that the letter "is on file in the correspondence collection at the Performing Arts Research Center at the New York Public Library." A search of Hayward's correspondence at the NYPL yielded no such artifact. A scanned copy of the note provided by a Sinatra archivist appears authentic and clearly reads "Dear Lew." But which Lew? Perhaps the movie director Lewis Allen, with whom Sinatra would work shortly, or the director Lewis Milestone, who would nominally helm *Ocean's 11* several years thence, but almost certainly not MCA head Lew Wasserman, whose agency had unceremoniously dropped the down-on-his-luck Frank as a client in 1951 and whom the singer would not forgive for decades.

the moment he'd first picked up James Jones's blockbuster novel, Sinatra had completely identified with Maggio, the feisty little private from Brooklyn who speaks in a kind of Damon Runyon–ese. He had campaigned, hard, for the movie role by barraging the filmmakers—Columbia Pictures president Harry Cohn; producer Buddy Adler; director Fred Zinnemann; screenwriter Daniel Taradash—with telegrams touting his perfect suitability for the part, and he had signed every wire just as he'd signed this note: "Maggio."

Frank Sinatra had identified so powerfully with the character not only because Angelo Maggio was a skinny, streetwise Italian-American from Brooklyn—like Sinatra's native Hoboken, close geographically to Manhattan but oh so far away—but also because Maggio was one of the world's downtrodden, a little man who drank to ease his sorrows and spoke truth to power with wisecracks. When Sinatra first read *From Here to Eternity* in late 1951, he was feeling considerably downtrodden himself. His records were no longer selling; he was having vocal and financial problems; the IRS was after him. He had become infamous, pilloried in newspapers across the United States, after leaving his wife and three children for Ava Gardner. Metro-Goldwyn-Mayer had recently terminated his movie contract, and he would soon also be dumped by Columbia Records, as well as by his talent agency, the Music Corporation of America.

"He's a dead man," the talent agent Irving "Swifty" Lazar declared in 1952. "Even Jesus couldn't get resurrected in this town." Maybe not, but Frank Sinatra could. Literally overnight—after the Academy Awards ceremony on March 25, 1954—Sinatra brought off the greatest comeback in show-business history. And he had done it all in Hollywood, a ruthlessly Darwinian company town that reviles losers but has the sappiest of soft spots for a happy ending. His Oscar underlined the fact that he was also a freshly viable recording artist with a new contract at Capitol Records, where he and a brilliant young arranger named Nelson Riddle had begun creating the string of groundbreaking recordings that would revolutionize popular music in the 1950s.

And quite suddenly that spring, without a shred of embarrassment about its fickleness, the entire entertainment industry began throwing itself at his feet. "The whole world is changing for Frank Sinatra," Louella Parsons wrote in her syndicated column of April 19. "Today he has so many jobs offered him he can pick and choose."

Parsons was talking about movies, although television, radio, and nightclubs were also calling. Among the film possibilities offered to Sinatra: a supporting part alongside the hot-as-a-pistol young Robert Mitchum in the medical melodrama *Not as a Stranger;* the second lead in a Warner Bros. remake of *Four Daughters,* the picture that had catapulted John Garfield to fame; a co-starring role alongside Marilyn Monroe in the 20th Century Fox musical *Pink Tights,* even though Monroe soon dropped out when she heard how much more the studio was offering Sinatra than her. And, lo and behold, MGM—where Louis B. Mayer had personally fired Sinatra in 1950 after he made an impolitic joke about Mayer's mistress* (and where Mayer himself was now history)—wanted him back, for the long-discussed *St. Louis Woman,* alongside Ava Gardner.

This was distinctly problematic for several reasons. For one thing, Gardner, who'd been outraged that Metro had dubbed a professional singer's voice over hers in *Show Boat,* was determined never to make another musical. For another, she had come to hate Hollywood with a passion. She was living as an expatriate, cohabiting in Spain with the charismatic and brilliant bullfighter Luis Miguel Dominguín, the darkly handsome torero whose rivalry with his brother-in-law Antonio Ordóñez would later inspire Ernest Hemingway's long *Life* magazine piece *The Dangerous Summer.* Most important of all, however, she was about to file for divorce from Frank.

While the Hollywood of 1954 bore some similarities to today's entertainment capital, it was altogether a sleepier, more rustic town. Not a more virtuous one by any means, but more tightly bounded. The studios still held sway; their publicity departments controlled access to stars and information about them, even when it came to police matters. There was a certain code of conduct for the press and other prying outsiders when it came to celebrities.

It is, for example, impossible to imagine any major star today living, as Sinatra did in the spring of that year, in a garden apartment, albeit such a glamorous one as Frank's five-room bachelor pad in a redbrick complex at the corner of Wilshire Boulevard and Beverly Glen. A decade before, when he had first come to Hollywood, he had resided in a pink-walled stucco mansion in Toluca Lake. It was a mark of both his change of fortunes and his maturity (not to mention the change of times) that Sinatra no longer had to ward off hordes of bobby-soxers, or hordes of any kind. In the spring of 1954, he was approaching thirty-nine—lean and balding, not settled by any means (his defiant hedonism and overweening ego would guard against such a fate for a very long time), but grown up, in his own particular way. His oaken baritone on the Capitol recordings, rich with sad knowledge—or, on up-tempo numbers,

------

* A couple of months earlier, after a horseback-riding accident, the boss had been pushed into work in a wheelchair, a cast on his leg. While Sinatra sat with some pals at lunch in the MGM commissary, someone said, "Hey, did you hear about L. B.'s accident?" And Frank responded instantly, "Yeah, he fell off of Ginny Simms."

with swaggering authority—was a sea change from the tender Voice that had soothed America through the war.

But the secret was that he was still yearning. (He would always yearn, even after he had gained all the world had to offer.) He had spent the previous Christmas and New Year's in Rome, where Gardner was shooting Joseph L. Mankiewicz's *The Barefoot Contessa,* desperately trying to hold on to her, even as she was edging away, already in love with the bullfighter. Ava loved Frank too—she always would—but her passion for him had ebbed, diminished in good part by his plummet from success, which had coincided with her own rise to stardom. He had drained her scant reserves of patience and sympathy. Unknown to her, just before she left for Europe the previous November, he had made a serious suicide attempt, cutting his left wrist in the New York apartment of his close friend the songwriter Jimmy Van Heusen: he would have bled out had Van Heusen not returned and found him.

And Ava smelled his desperation and hated it even as she loved him. She was heedless and restless and easily bored, and she was in love with another man.

The gossip columnists (Sinatra read them as closely as any fan) cobbled up a sweet fantasy: Gardner would come to the Oscars that March—she herself was up for Best Actress, for *Mogambo*—and the couple would reunite. But she stayed with her lover in Spain.

If Frank himself had harbored any fantasy that his renewed fame would bring her back, he was rudely disappointed.

"One night we went to Frank's for a dinner party," recalled the lyricist and screenwriter Betty Comden, "and we saw that one of the rooms was filled with pictures of Ava, and around the pictures were lit candles. It was like the altar of a little church."

Yet another night, Gardner's biographer Lee Server writes, Swifty Lazar, who lived in the same apartment complex as Sinatra, came home late and saw that Frank's door was open.

> Wondering if there was a problem, he stuck his head through the doorway and saw Sinatra by himself, evidently very drunk, slumped in an armchair, holding a gun. Cautiously Lazar stepped inside and as he did he saw that Sinatra was aiming his gun—an air gun, it turned out to be—at three large portrait images of Ava he had propped up on the floor. The three faces of Ava were full of pellet holes where Sinatra had been shooting at them—all night long, as it appeared.

If Gardner had been Delilah to Frank's Samson while they were together, she would be his muse for years after they broke up—specifically and crucially, the great Capitol years. "Ava taught him how to sing a torch song," Nelson Riddle famously said. "She taught him the hard way." On May 13, 1954, Sinatra—with Riddle conducting a twenty-nine-piece orchestra—recorded three songs that could have been addressed directly to his wandering wife: "The Gal That Got Away," "Half as Lovely (Twice as True)," and "It Worries Me." On the last, Frank sang,

Just what did I do—was I mean to you?

Taken as autobiography (which to some extent it must be), the lyric may look disingenuous—of course he had been not just mean but brutal to her, and she to him, on innumerable occasions. But listened to, the line, sung with exquisite tenderness, is meltingly lovely. In fact, Frank in his new middle period was every bit the ballad singer that Frankie of the Columbia years had been—and then some. He had lived more, suffered more.

On June 12, 1954, Ava Gardner arrived in Lake Tahoe to begin the six-week Nevada residence required for her divorce from Frank Sinatra. Las Vegas, where she had sojourned while splitting from her first husband, Mickey Rooney, was out; Frank was in town, playing the Sands, and Vegas was a small place in those days. (And, extraordinarily enough, both Rooney and Gardner's second husband, Artie Shaw, were also appearing at casinos along the Strip: a constellation of exes.)

While in Tahoe, Ava and her maid, Reenie Jordan, stayed in a lakefront house provided by her inveterate suitor, the epically weird, immensely wealthy oil and aviation magnate Howard Hughes. Hughes, a control freak to the nth degree and a paranoiac master of intrigue, especially when it came to affairs of the heart, had a habit of installing girlfriends—both current and prospective—in rented houses, sometimes in proximity to each other, the better to monitor their comings and goings. For years, he had been trying to reel in Gardner, to bed or to wed, without success. He showered her with expensive gifts, jewels and fur coats and convertibles; she accepted his presents and laughed in his face.

Now he sensed an opening. Her marriage was ending; perhaps she needed a shoulder to cry on. But the emotionally tone-deaf Hughes needed data to press his campaign. He had the rented house bugged and retained a fancy Washington, D.C., investigator named Robert Maheu to surveil the premises while Ava was in residence.

Maheu, whose specialty was high-level cloak-and-dagger work (in later years, he would be intimately involved in a CIA-backed plot to assassinate

Fidel Castro), was understandably loath to make a long trip for what was plainly a jealous-boyfriend job. He subcontracted the work to a local private detective, who quickly ascertained that Hughes's competition was Ava's never-say-die, soon-to-be ex.

One afternoon that summer, Frank showed up at the Tahoe house, no doubt with reconciliation in mind, and managed to persuade Ava to take a boat ride with him. Unwisely, the local detective elected to follow them in another boat. Sinatra quickly spotted him and gave furious chase; the detective just managed to make it back to shore and hightail it into the woods. Any hint of romance thoroughly spoiled, Frank left Tahoe without swaying Ava.

Romantic history: first as tragedy, then as farce.

At the end of July, she failed to show up for her court date for the divorce. She had asked him to repay the not inconsiderable sums she'd lent him when he was down-and-out; he had bridled at the request. They were at an impasse: still legally married, though apart. He would never get her out of his system, nor would she ever truly get him out of hers.

———

And yet—to all appearances, at any rate—the bum was on cloud nine and refused to come down. If the middle-of-the-night Sinatra was tormented by Ava's abandonment, his daytime self seemed to have thoroughly forsworn the doubt and contemplation that dogged his days through much of the early 1950s. Now, like a king returned from exile, he took the world's measure and saw that it was good. He entered into a frenzy of personal and professional activity that would scarcely let up for the next dozen years.

Frank not only won an Academy Award in 1954 but also had his biggest hit record in eight years, "Young at Heart." He went into the recording studio nineteen times in 1954 and laid down thirty-seven tracks. He shot three movies. He played two two-week stands at the Sands in June and November and did three weeks at the Copacabana over Christmas and New Year's. He only dipped his toe into the still-youthful medium of television, making a mere four appearances (one of them the Oscars broadcast), but he was on the radio constantly: there was his twice-a-week, fifteen-minute show *To Be Perfectly Frank*; his weekly, semi-tongue-in-cheek detective series *Rocky Fortune* (he would quickly tire of the program, a less than dignified vestige of his hard-luck days, and wind it up in March); and later in the year, a series sponsored by Bobbi home permanents called *The Frank Sinatra Show*.

He worked hard, too, at distracting himself from Ava. Frank hadn't been much more than a boy when he married Nancy Barbato in 1939, and though he might have acted like a bachelor throughout his twelve-year first marriage, he hadn't been this free in a long time. In 1954, he would be linked romantically with, among others, the French actress Gaby Bruyère, the Swedish actress Anita Ekberg, and the American actresses Joan Tyler, Norma Eberhardt, Havis Davenport, and (perhaps) Marilyn Monroe. He also kept company with the singer Jill Corey and the heiress and would-be thespian Gloria Vanderbilt. There were probably numerous others. But more problematically, that spring he also seems to have begun a relationship with the not quite sixteen-year-old Natalie Wood.

Wood, whose early career was managed by her generalissimo-like stage mother, Maria Gurdin (Natalie called her Mud, short for Mudda; her alcoholic and feckless father was barely a presence in her life), had become a certifiable child movie star at age eight in 1947's *Miracle on 34th Street*. Now, however, she was in an awkward period, wishing to transition into grown-up movie roles before she was a grown-up, trying to look older by wearing heavy makeup and falsies. At fifteen, she was birdlike—barely five feet tall and physically undeveloped—but despite her youth and small stature she was a formidable presence, with huge, emotional dark eyes and a quick, intuitive intelligence. With film parts for teenagers scarce, Natalie was marking time by working on an ABC sitcom called *The Pride of the Family* and hating every minute. In May, however, she was cast in Warner Bros.' swords-and-sandals epic *The Silver Chalice* (in which Paul Newman, to his everlasting shame, made his movie debut in a brief toga). Wood had a small role, yet according to her biographer Suzanne Finstad, "Mud was scheming to upgrade that ranking."

> The two went to Warners off and on throughout May, fitting Natalie for her Grecian costumes . . . One day while they were at the commissary, Frank Sinatra walked in, preparing for his next picture, *Young at Heart*. Sinatra either approached Natalie, or her mother sent her over to introduce herself . . . Sinatra was taken with Natalie, and got "a kick" out of Maria, inviting them to a party at his house. Mud eagerly accepted, whispering to Natalie afterward that she would let her go alone, urging Natalie to get close to Sinatra "because it would be good for her career."

Youth and beauty—male and female—have always been fungible commodities in Hollywood, which has a long history of stage mothers who, in essence, pimp out their underage daughters for career advancement and profit. And so, at her mother's urging, Natalie went to the party, alone. There, Finstad writes, she "consumed quantities of wine . . . and in the course of the evening, told Sinatra about 'Clyde,' the code name for penis that Bobby [Hyatt, her teenage co-star on *The Pride of the Family*] had coined to fool Natalie's mother. Sinatra was so amused, he and his friends . . . incorporated 'Clyde' into their hipster slang." *

God alone knows what went on at that party. But Frank seems to have been touched by the young actress, who had precocious powers of empathy. (Not to mention a clear need for a father figure.) Perhaps he told her his troubles. In any case, Wood frequented his apartment that May and June, and her close friends at the time felt sure they were having an affair. Yet for all the unseemliness of the liaison, Wood appears to have been something more than a conquest where Frank was concerned. He was a man on the cusp of middle age, almost certainly nostalgic for the days when he had made all those bobby-soxers swoon. Surely on some level, Natalie Wood reminded him of those girls and their idolatry.

He was also a man in pain, and the vivacity and uncritical presence of a magically lovely young girl must have been balm to his soul, even if the liaison was, consciously or unconsciously, poison to hers. A complex emotional bond formed between them, one that would continue as Frank and Natalie stayed friends, and now and then lovers, until she died at age forty-three in 1981.

———

Still, the most important emotional connection in Frank Sinatra's life in the spring of 1954 was the one between him and his new arranger at Capitol Records, the sublimely gifted Nelson Riddle. The two had first struck gold together the previous spring, after Capitol vice president and creative head Alan Livingston, who felt Sinatra needed the kind of new sound that his previous arranger Axel Stordahl was unable to provide, cleverly introduced Riddle, in the guise of a substitute conductor. Sinatra had had no idea who Riddle was before their first recording session, but the moment he heard the playback of the Riddle-arranged "I've Got the World on a String," he knew his life had been altered as irrevocably as it had been the first time he laid eyes on Ava Gardner. This was the thunderbolt, musically speaking.

"I've Got the World on a String" was issued only as a single. Frank's first album for Capitol, *Songs for Young Lovers,* released in January 1954, contained just one tune orchestrated by Riddle, "Like Someone in Love." The second Capitol album, *Swing Easy!,* recorded in April, was a different ball game.

Swing Easy! was post-meridian Sinatra in every way: he had won the Oscar

---

* If true, this is a puzzling sidelight, since "clyde," in Rat Pack argot, came to be a kind of grab-bag code word with a multitude of meanings according to the context, as in "I don't like her clyde [voice]"—whereas "bird" meant just one thing: penis.

and crossed the shadow line; now he truly could swing easy. And Nelson Riddle was the genius who would take him where he wanted to go. *Young Lovers* had been beautiful, but in the sense that it had been almost entirely arranged by Frank's old-reliable up-tempo man George Siravo, it was fundamentally conservative: the most striking thing about the album was the voice singing the songs.

In Riddle, Frank Sinatra had met his musical match. Though the arranger hadn't had anything like Frank's early success—he played trombone and did some orchestration for the Charlie Spivak Orchestra in the early 1940s, then played third trombone for Tommy Dorsey after Sinatra's departure—the serious-minded New Jerseyan seems to have had, from the beginning, a head full of complex music and a deep ambition to hear it played and sung. In contrast to his bandmates, who spent most of their off-hours boozing and trying to get laid, Riddle devoted much of his spare time to listening to Ravel and Debussy and Jacques Ibert on his portable record player. The lushly romantic Ibert composition "Escales"—"Ports of Call," in English—was one of his holy grails. As was "Stomp It Off," arranged by the great Melvin "Sy" Oliver for the Jimmie Lunceford big band.

The common thread between the two compositions was sex—slow and sensual, in the case of the Ibert; rock 'n' roll, with the Oliver. Riddle was a sensualist with the demeanor of a scientist. And not a happy scientist. "Dad

In the genius arranger Nelson Riddle, Frank Sinatra had met his musical match—and a kind of dark double.

had a sadness about him," Riddle's daughter Rosemary Riddle Acerra recalls. "It was interpreted sometimes as sadness, where it might not have been in all cases. It was just this somber, serious mood. He was always thinking." Julie Andrews, who worked with Riddle on her TV variety series in the 1970s, called him Eeyore.

Two major subjects were inextricably intertwined in his mind. Once, during a marital spat, Riddle's wife, Doreen, accused him of only thinking about music and sex. The arranger later remarked to his son, with the glimmer of a smile, "After all, what else is there?" Riddle wrote of his work with Sinatra, "Most of our best numbers were in what I call the tempo of the heartbeat . . . Music to me is sex—it's all tied up somehow, and the rhythm of sex is the heartbeat."

He went on, "In working out arrangements for Frank, I suppose I stuck to two main rules. First, find the peak of the song and build the whole arrangement to that peak, pacing it as he paces himself vocally. Second, when he's moving, get the hell out of the way . . . After all, what arranger in the world would try to fight against Sinatra's voice? Give the singer room to breathe. When the singer rests, then there's a chance to write a fill that might be heard."

He had learned this lesson painfully, on an aborted early session with Frank: partway into a take of "Wrap Your Troubles in Dreams," Sinatra stopped the band and called Riddle into the recording booth, explaining heatedly to his ambitious young arranger (Nelson was five and a half years Frank's junior) that he was crowding the singer out, having simply written too many notes, beautiful as the notes might have been. Riddle never made the mistake again.

It was a critical moment. Sinatra, who was capable of firing associates at the drop of a Cavanagh fedora, could easily have axed Riddle then and there and returned to the comfort of Stordahl. But Frank was musically acute enough to realize that comfort was not what he needed at this point in his career. Nelson Riddle was taking him in new and daring directions: he just needed a little guidance in the art of arranging for Sinatra.

"I loved how Nelson used Ravel's approach to polytonality," Quincy Jones told Will Friedwald. "Nelson was smart because he put the electricity up above Frank . . . and gave Frank the room downstairs for his voice to shine, rather than building big lush parts that were in the same register as his voice."

"Dad evolved, with Frank's help, and some of his own," Rosemary Riddle Acerra says. "I think Frank was very astute and generous." At the same time, she says, her father was very clear about why he was there: not, like so many around Sinatra, as a mere employee, a hanger-on, or a supplicant, but as a musical collaborator of the first order. "Dad wanted to work with Frank because he saw something very special," Acerra says.

Swing Easy! had artistic energy in abundance, much of it brought along by the scholarly-looking arranger, who knew which players could give him the sound he wanted: not, as Friedwald writes, "the conservatory-trained studio staff musicians of the '30s and '40s but guys who had cut their teeth as teenagers in the touring swing bands." Guys like the reed players Arthur "Skeets" Herfurt and Mahlon Clark; the trombonists Milt Bernhart, George Roberts, and Juan Tizol; and, for the first time on *Swing Easy!*, the great minimalist trumpeter Harry "Sweets" Edison. The album was sheer grace; Riddle's spare and gleaming up-tempo arrangements brought out Sinatra at the very peak of his art and emotional complexity. It was to be a long peak. His voice had ripened from the boyish tenor of his Columbia days to a baritone with a faint husk—from violin to cello, in a famous formulation attributed to both Nelson Riddle and Sammy Cahn—and the voice had become rich with knowledge.

The album's first song, Cole Porter's great "Just One of Those Things," sums it up. It is a three-minute-fifteen-second symphony modulating from tenderness to bold defiance, with Ava in every breath. Sinatra's reading of a song that many singers give a breezy interpretation is quietly devastating. Witness the contrast between the first chorus's "So goodbye, dear, and amen," all soft ardor and delicate sadness, and the second's, a stammered mini-psychodrama of leave-taking: "So goodbye, goodbye, bye, bye, goodbye, baby, and amen . . ."

She taught him the hard way.

Even as Frank was recollecting emotion in the tranquillity of Hollywood's KHJ Radio Studios, he was synthesizing it in new and fascinating ways for the movie cameras. That April and May, in the dusty railroad-stop town of Newhall, forty miles north of Los Angeles, he shot a new film—not one of the glitzy studio projects that the gossip columns were talking about, but a black-and-white noir piece called *Suddenly,* in which Frank Sinatra played, of all things, a man out to assassinate the president of the United States with a telescope-equipped rifle.

He had been interested in Richard Sale's pulpy yet propulsive script from the moment he saw it, but since his grand new career plan—now that he could afford the luxury of having a career plan—called for him to alternate dramatic pictures with musicals, Frank had initially wanted to do *Pink Tights* at 20th Century Fox first. That idea went out the window when Marilyn Monroe, who'd finally become a big star the previous year in *Niagara,* decided (egged on by Joe DiMaggio, who knew a thing or two about negotiating contracts) that she was sick of dumb-blonde roles and refused to show up. Fox suspended her, and then, as big stars could, she simply went her merry way, marrying DiMaggio in January, then (to the Yankee Clipper's chagrin) flying off to entertain the troops in Korea in February. Fox tested a newcomer named Sheree North for the dumb-blonde role, and Frank decided to make *Suddenly* his first picture after *From Here to Eternity*.

The assassin, Johnny Baron, is the one out-and-out villain Sinatra ever portrayed on-screen, and it is at once a mesmerizingly effective performance and a very strange one. Frank comes on-screen twenty minutes into the picture, taking a family captive and cold-bloodedly killing a Secret Service agent, and he's the center of attention the rest of the way. As was the case with his first full-length role, in 1943's *Higher and Higher,* you can't stop looking at him— except that a decade later, his face has changed dramatically.

At thirty-eight, Sinatra was still a striking physical presence. He might have been approaching middle age, but he didn't seem to have gained an ounce since his teen-idol days: on-screen, his waist, in high-topped pleated pants, is almost alarmingly narrow; his butt is nonexistent. *Suddenly's* cinematographer, Charles G. Clarke, often shot Frank in tight, unnerving close-ups and amazingly frequently on his bad side—the left side of his face, the side deformed around the ear and neck by a forceps delivery at birth and a childhood mastoid operation.

Creepily effective as a presidential assassin in 1954's *Suddenly*. At thirty-eight, Sinatra was still a striking physical presence, his features cleanly sculpted, his eyes avid and riveting.

But his features are cleanly sculpted, his eyes avid and riveting: this is now a mature face, one in which liquor and cigarettes and heartbreak have made deep inroads. And fame. It's impossible not to notice that this would-be presidential assassin looks fresh from poolside in Palm Springs: he has a deep tan and a sleek, self-pleased aspect that a contract killer's backstory doesn't quite account for.

The sleekness—Frank's bad side notwithstanding—infuses his performance. Unlike, say, Richard Widmark in his noir roles or Humphrey Bogart in *The Desperate Hours,* Sinatra's psycho killer doesn't quite have the look of a man who can't help himself. He widens his eyes arrestingly when he threatens to slit the little boy's throat, then slaps him down; he introspects convincingly when he reflects on how his wartime combat experience made him a murderer (a theme that will be revisited, hauntingly, in *The Manchurian Candidate*). It's a solid, unsettling turn. Nevertheless, it feels controlled, tightly wound. There's never the sense that this guy might really go off the rails—the way the real-life Frank was wont to from time to time.

Burt Lancaster, Sinatra's co-star in *From Here to Eternity,* recalled that Frank's performance in that film displayed a fervor, an anger, and a bitterness that had as much to do with Frank's personal and professional travails in the preceding years as with the character of Maggio. "You knew this was a raging little man who was, at the same time, a good human being," Lancaster said.

You also sensed that these real-life factors heavily influenced the members of the academy to give him the Best Supporting Actor Oscar.

With *Suddenly,* Frank was suddenly in new territory. As Tom Santopietro writes in *Sinatra in Hollywood,* the movie "marked the start of Sinatra's dramatic career on film as a leading man; there was no Lancaster or Montgomery Clift in sight now. This was the Frank Sinatra show, pure and simple, a feature film that turned into a one-man showcase the second he appeared onscreen."

Now he had power, and power meant control. He didn't have to kiss up to anyone anymore. His role in *From Here to Eternity* had been the first and last in which Frank let himself be so emotionally naked. From *Suddenly* on, he would be an actor, acting—sometimes compellingly (how compellingly was almost always a function of how much he respected the director) and sometimes just going through the motions. With this movie, Sinatra had a point to prove, and he proved it: he was now a movie star as well as a recording star.

2

||||||||||||

Then we have Frank Sinatra. And Frank, who was in Young at
Heart, *he and I always got along beautifully. He was very protective, you know, and really dear to me. But he was late. Every
day . . . Everyone was ready at 9:00 and we would maybe shoot
at 11:00, and the studio was not too happy about that. Nobody
knew what the problem was, but he was always late, which was
not very professional . . . I'm a great admirer of his talents, but
he does do things like that . . . He's like a bad kid. He seems
to enjoy keeping people waiting and things, which is not very
attractive and annoys an awful lot of people. It's the bad boy.
It was a little bit of a macho image that I think he was putting
across. But other than that, I really liked him very much, and
still do, of course.*

—DORIS DAY, RADIO INTERVIEW

D oris Day's words, dripping with ambivalence about her co-star in Warner
Bros.' 1954 musical melodrama *Young at Heart*, remind us that human
beings are complicated creatures and that no human was more complicated than Frank Sinatra. In the comeback year of 1954, as Frank regathered
the vast power he'd lost, he also achieved new heights of arrogance. There was
Sinatra, and then there was everybody else. He knew it, and the world knew it.

Doris Day had first gotten to know Sinatra when they worked together in
1947 on *Your Hit Parade*. In her autobiography, she recalled that when Frank's
fortunes had dipped and he was working the nightclubs, her husband, Martin
Melcher, urged her to show her support by going to the Cocoanut Grove to
hear him sing. "The Cocoanut Grove was a cavernous place," Day recalled,
"and when it was only a third filled, as it was that evening, it had a melancholy
air. Frank's voice had changed. He wasn't singing the way he had sung before
or the way he sings now. He seemed uncertain . . .

"Frank came over to our table and sat with Marty and me for a while and
had a drink. He knew he wasn't singing the way he wanted to. Of course, we
didn't talk about that, but he seemed a little embarrassed. About the small
turnout, too."

Sinatra had bounced back, but American popular music was still hip-deep in schlock in 1954, with hits like "Sh-Boom" by the Crew-Cuts, Archie Bleyer's "Hernando's Hideaway," the Four Aces' "Three Coins in the Fountain," and Eddie Fisher's "Oh! My Papa" blaring from the nation's radios and jukeboxes. And Mitch Miller was still going strong at Columbia, still forcing great singers into recording mediocre material that, in the coercively conservative climate of the times, turned into popular hits. The bouncy, negligible R&B number "Make Love to Me," foisted by Miller on the sublime balladeer Jo Stafford, hit number 1 that year, as did "This Ole House," the hoedown-style monstrosity that he inflicted on Rosemary Clooney.

No one was telling Frank what to record at Capitol. Among the thirty-seven singles, soundtrack tunes, and album numbers he laid down in 1954, there were some interesting missteps, but they were *his* missteps. And Sinatra and Riddle were mostly making genius together. Especially on the albums. Continuing the prescient model he had initiated at Columbia with 1946's *Voice of Frank Sinatra,* Frank organized each of his Capitol compilations around a specific mood or mode: downbeat or upbeat, ballads or swingers. The term "concept album" wouldn't be coined until much later, but Sinatra invented the idea, and Riddle helped him perfect it. More than ever, he was far more than just a singer: he was an artist shaping his medium.

At the same time, there was always the dark undertow—the inner voices that told him that underneath it all he was nothing and nobody, a little street guinea from Hoboken. The furies that would frequently blind him when his vulnerabilities were touched. The terrible impatience—with the incompetence and stupidity that were so rife in the world, with things he needed to happen instantaneously, and so rarely did. The realization that he was like nobody else and therefore destined to be alone. His terrors: of aloneness itself; of sleep, the cousin to death. And always, always, the vast and ravening appetites.

When all these things are taken together, is it any wonder that he often showed up on the Burbank soundstage for *Young at Heart* two or three or four hours later than anyone else?

———

The director was an amiable hack named Gordon Douglas, whose chief claim to fame was shooting the *Our Gang* comedies for Hal Roach in the 1930s.[*] The production was overseen by Martin Melcher—a man who, despite his kindness toward Sinatra just a couple of years earlier (or perhaps because of it),

---

[*] And whom Sinatra would tap no fewer than three times to direct him again, in *Robin and the 7 Hoods, Tony Rome,* and *The Detective.*

almost instantly incurred Frank's wrath, apparently by trying to persuade him to sing inferior songs in the movie, songs to which Melcher controlled the publishing rights. Sinatra had him banned from the set. (The fatwa was enforced by Jack Warner himself.) Next to go was the Academy Award–winning cinematographer Charles Lang, a perfectionist who took forever with his lighting setups. "Of course Frank had no right to do what he did," Day writes, "but when a picture is in production with all of its overhead in operation, there is no right or wrong; there is only that old devil, expediency."

Sinatra would never in a million years have pulled such stunts with *From Here to Eternity*'s director, Fred Zinnemann. Not only had he been hungry and powerless then; he'd had great respect for Zinnemann, as well as his co-star Montgomery Clift.

But that had been a very different time. Frank knew that selling records was all well and good, but being a movie star would give him a worldwide presence second to none. (Not to mention a financial hedge against poor record sales.)

Sinatra knew he had acting talent and screen presence but was also wise enough to know where his main gifts lay. He had never taken an acting lesson; he had come to the craft when he was close to thirty. He was insecure the moment he walked onto a movie set. Everything took too long—much too long—and there were far too many variables: lighting, direction, co-stars, and eventually editing. In a recording studio, he was boss. On a movie set he was just talent, and knowing that led to self-doubt, which was usually followed by an explosion.

He could be set off in a recording studio, too, but between his fanatical preparation—which included everything from choosing the material to making sure he had the best arranger and musicians possible—and his control over the whole process, there were far fewer grounds for insecurity. He could be impatient in a recording studio but was also known to do twenty or thirty takes of a song (some of them, admittedly, partial takes) in order to get it just right.

Making movies, he had long had a deserved reputation as One-Take Charlie. But as with so many things about Sinatra, this cut two ways. It wasn't just his impatience and insecurity that made him work like this but the realization that his best and freshest acting would come in the first (or sometimes the second) take. "People think that because he would shoot only one or two takes he didn't take it seriously, but that wasn't the case at all," Frank's friend Robert Wagner wrote.

Spencer Tracy didn't like a lot of takes either, and nobody thought he was casual about the work. Frank was very conscious of his lack of training; he was never sure that he would be able to reproduce an effect more than once or twice because he had to rely on emotion more than craft. He was very serious about his work; he went over his wardrobe, the look of the film, the dramatic arc. He didn't just pick up a script, look at it, and shoot it. He prepared.

This would be less the case in the latter part of Sinatra's movie career. But in the mid- and late 1950s, the years just after *Eternity* and a few years past, he was still serious about reestablishing himself at the top of show business, which meant appearing to best effect in the movies he made. In this light, his expulsions of Melcher and Lang make perfect sense: Frank could only do good work if the conditions felt ideal to him. Powerless to some extent, he exerted his power in the only way he could, and it wasn't pretty. But the result was good work.

His character in *Young at Heart* was Barney Sloan, a moody, self-pitying, indeterminately ethnic musical arranger (it turns out he's an Italian-American who changed his name, as Frank in real life had once refused to) who finds himself plopped down amid a Waspy, musical Connecticut family with three blond daughters—played by Day, Dorothy Malone, and Elisabeth Fraser. Barney might be the glummest character Sinatra ever played, but he's far from the least interesting. With his pitiful backstory (orphaned as a child, deprived in the Depression, wounded in the war), he's all pouts and frowns, sitting at the piano with a cigarette hanging from that voluptuous lower lip while his unseen fingers form gorgeous, moody chords (Bill Miller did the actual playing); he never smiles, let alone utters a kind word, until the preternaturally cheery Laurie Tuttle (Day) starts to work her magic on him.

And magic it is. At thirty-two, Doris Day was a huge star (she had top billing on the film) and for good reason. As a singer, she'd broken out in 1945 with her recording of "Sentimental Journey" for Les Brown and His Band of Renown; as a movie actress, she'd been in the Box Office Top 10 since 1951. The year before *Young at Heart,* she'd scored the full parlay, starring in *Calamity Jane* and notching a number 1 record with a song from the picture, "Secret Love." And she wasn't just a movie and recording star but a full-fledged sex goddess, whose long legs and curvaceous figure, freckles and turned-up nose and thousand-watt smile, had stirred the loins of a million men, including the troops in Korea, who voted her their Favorite Star of 1950, and the young John Updike, who would obsess over her in poetry and prose for the rest of his life. Day was the stealth counterpart to Marilyn Monroe: her all-American features, bobbed blond hair, and sunny forthrightness made her look like a farm girl but hinted at an excellent roll in the hay.

She and Sinatra have a strange chemistry in *Young at Heart,* or rather lack thereof: they seem to be working on two separate planes. He sings, quite wonderfully, standards like the Gershwins' "Someone to Watch over Me," Cole Porter's "Just One of Those Things," and Mercer and Arlen's "One for My Baby"; she wastes her wonderful voice on nonentities like "Ready, Willing, and Able," "Hold Me in Your Arms," and "There's a Rising Moon." (Songs to which, no doubt, Marty Melcher controlled the publishing rights.) Frank looks middle-aged; Doris looks fresh as a daisy. He mopes; she grins, showing that enchantingly angled front tooth. And the more Barney mopes, the more Laurie sets her jaw and takes him on as a project, until—you guessed it.

In reality, Day's life story was far more like Barney's than Laurie's: a car wreck as a teenager that almost left her crippled; two bad marriages behind her and one in process; abiding panic attacks, depressions, and hatred of much about the movie business. *Young at Heart* was her last movie on a seven-year contract with Warner Bros., and she was itching to escape what she called "peonage." And in his own tortuous way, Frank seems to have felt a real affection and respect for her. Their characters in the picture might not have matched up, but he tried hard—one guesses for her sake as much as his own—to make his characterization work, and it did.

He also showed the unique brand of courtliness he would always extend to women he considered ladies (those he suspected of being otherwise got very different treatment). During the shoot, Ethel Barrymore, the grande dame of the American theater who played Laurie Tuttle's spinster aunt, celebrated her seventy-fifth birthday, and Frank threw her a surprise party on the set. "She was very touched," Day recalled.

Sinatra proposed a toast to her and she kissed him on the cheek. I knew that it was entirely possible that this might be her last birthday, and my emotions being what they are, my eyes filled with tears . . .

"Hey!" somebody called out. "Doris needs a Kleenex!"

From across the set, someone threw a box of Kleenex to me. I didn't see it coming and the box struck me in the forehead. It stung a little and I gasped, more in surprise than pain. Frank sprang at the man who had flipped the box at me and grabbed the front of his shirt, pulling the fabric up tight under his chin.

"Don't you ever do that!" he shouted at the man. "You don't throw things at a lady, you understand?"

"It's all right, Frank," I said. "I'm not hurt—"

"That's beside the point! You bring the box, you creep, and you *offer* a Kleenex—you got that? You *offer* a Kleenex!"

Frank let the man go and came over to me to be sure that I was all right. Often, over the years, whenever I pulled a Kleenex out of a box, I thought of Frank.

In all probability, the grip or gaffer who tossed the Kleenex box could have broken the five-foot-seven, 130-something-pound Sinatra in two like a stick—had the man not felt in the wrong, and had he not been surrounded by people far above him in the moviemaking hierarchy, and had his assailant not been the star of the show, who was, after all, Frank Sinatra. Or, more accurately, was Frank Sinatra again. For a couple of years, Sinatra had barely been himself. Now he was getting even bigger than the larger-than-life he already was. That was more than one man's shirtfront he was holding.

———

"I have never seen Frank in such form," Louella Parsons had written in July of Sinatra's June show at the Sands. "He sings and sings and sings, and jokes and jokes. Frank has gotten Ava completely out of his system, which now I'm sure of, after seeing how gay he is and apparently carefree."

The overbearing Hearst gossip columnist was fond of issuing chirpy, authoritative pronouncements about Sinatra, as a way of trying both to rein him in and to assert her own power, and now and then she was even right. But she'd written these words around the same time that Frank made the long, fruitless trek from Vegas to Lake Tahoe to try to woo his wife back. And for someone as resolutely assertive as Parsons, "apparently carefree" had a dangerously hedged look about it.

Something in Frank was bubbling ominously that fall. Perhaps he was feeling anxious about the not-so-distant horizon of middle age or the growing certainty that Ava wasn't coming back to him. Jule Styne, unable to abide his housemate's middle-of-the-night obsessing over his lost love, moved out in September. And the gossip columns, as they loved to, piled on. "Nancy Sinatra insists there's no chance of a reconciliation after Ava sheds the warbler in Nevada," one reported in August.

He was largely without Riddle that autumn, too. After a September 23 session in which Frank recorded a "Someone to Watch over Me" of aching tenderness and two other tunes of aching banality—the tootling, Pied Pipers–backed "Don't Change Your Mind About Me" and Mack Gordon and Jimmy Van Heusen's gloppy *Young at Heart* duet for Day and Sinatra, "You, My Love"—he and Nelson barely saw each other for the rest of the year.

As always, Sinatra's soul was divided. On the one hand, he must have realized how good—how great—Riddle was; at the same time, it was as though

Frank couldn't bear to settle into a committed relationship. And then there was his frantic schedule: throughout October and November, he was shooting another movie, a melodrama called *Not as a Stranger,* and in November and December he recorded the soundtrack songs for a planned (but never pro- duced) animated feature of the Broadway hit *Finian's Rainbow.* Lyn Murray, who'd arranged the vocals on Broadway, did all the conducting and most of the orchestrating, though Nelson dropped in to write the charts for two numbers, "Necessity" and "That Great Come-and-Get-It Day."

Finian, a fascinating failure, was a victim of the corrosive political climate. The Broadway production, lauded as a classic, had a great score by Yip Har- burg and Burton Lane; it had run all through 1947 and most of 1948. Six years later, the prospect of an animated adaptation generated great excitement. The producers raised $300,000 and recruited a stunning array of musical talent, including, besides Sinatra, Ella Logan (who starred in the original show), Louis Armstrong, Ella Fitzgerald, and the Jazz All-Stars (Oscar Peterson, Red Norvo, Herb Ellis, and Ray Brown, among others). But after the entire soundtrack had been recorded, the whole project fell apart when Harburg, an avowed leftist, and the director and chief animator, John Hubley, both refused to testify before the House Un-American Activities Committee and Chemical Bank withdrew the rest of the financing.

The songs are a tantalizing hint of what might have been. Particularly fine are the delightful "If This Isn't Love," on which Sinatra duets with Ella Logan, backed by a children's chorus; the great "Old Devil Moon," with Frank, Logan, and the Jazz All-Stars; and "Necessity," a gorgeous duet between Fitzgerald and Frank, backed by the Oscar Peterson Trio. (It must be said that "Ad-Lib Blues," a scat duet between Sinatra and Armstrong, reminds us how great a scat singer Satchmo was and how great Frank was at . . . other things.)

Sinatra's patent joy at performing superb material with great musicians shows what a refuge music was for him. A movie set where he was marking time, on the other hand, was a different matter entirely.

Not as a Stranger, Morton Thompson's multipage novel about the turbulent lives and loves of young interns, was a huge best seller in 1954 and therefore a natural to be adapted for the movies. But unlike that other popular doorstop, *From Here to Eternity,* Thompson's book lacked both literary quality and histor- ical resonance; it was merely a sexy melodrama and an odd choice as the first directing assignment for the successful young producer Stanley Kramer, who had a strong social conscience and an eye for good material. Kramer, who'd produced *The Men, Cyrano de Bergerac, Death of a Salesman, High Noon, The Wild One,* and *The Caine Mutiny,* all before turning forty, was a sharply intelli- gent, unapologetically earnest filmmaker. Unfortunately, as Robert Mitchum's biographer Lee Server writes, "Kramer had unwittingly loaded the picture with a number of Hollywood's most ferocious drinkers"—among them Mitchum, Broderick Crawford, Lee Marvin, Lon Chaney Jr., Myron McCormick, and, still in the apprentice phase but transitioning into the master category, Frank Sinatra. "It wasn't a cast so much as a brewery," recalled Mitchum, who became a good friend and drinking buddy of Frank's on the picture.

And with Kramer at the helm, the stage was set for mayhem. Server writes,

> The tippling would begin early, and by late afternoon the sets at the California Studios would become a full-blown bacchanal. Fights, with fists and food, erupted at a moment's notice . . .
>   One day Broderick Crawford went berserk. The scrawny but fearless Frank Sinatra enjoyed needling the huge, powerful Crawford, likening the actor to the retarded character, Lenny, in *Of Mice and Men* . . . Crawford . . . took all the needling he could stand one day and attacked Sinatra, holding him down, tearing off his hairpiece, and . . . *eating* it.

Probably not *literally* true. But a great story nonetheless, and indicative of the disorder that had taken over the shoot.

In between the bedlam, a movie somehow got made—more's the pity. With its strangely flat black-and-white cinematography and ham-handed direction, *Not as a Stranger* looks and plays like an excruciatingly long TV melodrama. Oddly, Sinatra, whose wisecracking (and, indeed, lushly bewigged) intern Al Boone carries a slight echo of *From Here to Eternity's* private Maggio, is the liveliest thing in the picture—although he disappears for most of the film's second half to make way for an uninteresting triangle between Mitchum, an achingly earnest Olivia de Havilland, and Gloria Grahame as the rich bitch who breaks them up.

If *Not as a Stranger* was an odd choice for Stanley Kramer, it was no less odd for the third-billed Sinatra. "Why did Frank Sinatra bother to make this movie?" Tom Santopietro asks. "Did he simply want to keep working continuously on A-list productions in order to build upon the success of *From Here to Eternity* and *Young at Heart*? Was it his well-known fear of being bored?"

Yes and yes are the answers, but the third and overarching answer is that he still wasn't as big a star in the movies as he was in popular music. He had yet to prove he could carry a big film. (He'd won critical raves for *Suddenly,* by no means a big film, but the picture had died at the box office.)

In the midst of a career comeback, momentum was everything. He couldn't afford to sit around and wait for the perfect movie role to pop up.

And momentum meant visibility. In December, Frank won *Billboard's* disc jockey poll for best single of the year, "Young at Heart," and best LP, *Swing Easy! Down Beat* and *Metronome* both named him the top male vocalist of 1954. To trumpet these honors and to boast about the movies he had in release (*Suddenly; Young at Heart*), in production (*Not as a Stranger*), and slated to start shooting soon (*Guys and Dolls*), he placed a full-page advertisement in *Billboard,* signing the ad "Busy, busy, busy—Frank."

He wasn't exactly whistling in the dark, but he remembered all too clearly what not-busy felt like. He remembered the demons to which idleness had introduced him. And even in the midst of bustle, idleness lurked, like death in Arcadia. Especially on a movie set. Especially on *Not as a Stranger*.

On Friday night, November 5, midway through the shoot, Frank and Lee Marvin went to a Hollywood restaurant to join Robert Mitchum and the film's co-screenwriter Edward Anhalt for dinner. The Villa Capri, just a few blocks from Capitol Records, was a dark, smoky, noisy Italian bistro with straw-bottomed wine flasks hanging from the ceiling; it was run by Patsy D'Amore, who had introduced pizza to Hollywood in the late 1930s and was a great fan of Sinatra's. By the mid-1950s, the restaurant had become a kind of clubhouse for Frank, who had a special booth in the back. Joe DiMaggio, another regular, was sitting at the bar that night, looking as though he had lost his best friend.

In fact, the Yankee Clipper was newly separated from Marilyn Monroe— their initial divorce hearing had been at the end of October—and he was as miserable about it as she apparently was not. A great deal of DiMaggio's unhappiness had to do with public humiliation: he was a retired superstar, his great deeds behind him, and he was just as famous in 1954 for having married the hottest actress in the movies as for his erstwhile athletic achievements. And as a proud, old-fashioned, and furiously private Italian-American male, he suffered at the world's perception that he was unable to control his mercurial and highly sensitive wife, who had never met a camera she didn't like.

After the initial sexual thrill, the marriage had been hollow from the beginning. DiMaggio seemed to want a woman who would have babies and stay busy in the kitchen; had he spoken to Marilyn about this? He was distant, uncommunicative, and pathologically possessive; hating her Hollywood friends, he tried to keep her cloistered. At times, he roughed her up. Worse, once the passion wore off, he bored her deeply: soon after the honeymoon (much of which she spent entertaining the troops in Korea while Joe cooled his heels in Tokyo), she announced to a dumbfounded friend that she planned to marry the playwright Arthur Miller.

And then there was the last straw, the famous skirt-blowing scene in Billy Wilder's *Seven Year Itch*. The scene, shot in midtown Manhattan in full view of a gaping public and press contingent, revealed Monroe's crotch, in filmy white panties, to the world. DiMaggio beat her up in their hotel room that night; she had to have powder applied to the bruises on her shoulders when she played her scenes the next day.

Now Joe was moping around Hollywood, trying to drown his sorrow. When Sinatra and Mitchum approached him and asked if he wanted to join them, DiMag was reluctant at first, but after gentle pressure from Frank—he and Joe were old pals from Toots Shor's joint in New York—and several more drinks all around, DiMaggio admitted he was desperate to find Marilyn but that she was giving him the slip. "A lot of drinks later," Lee Server writes,

> DiMaggio went off to the men's room and Sinatra said, "You know, we ought to do something for him. He really is in terrible shape. We got to help him get to Marilyn."
> "But she's hiding out," somebody said.
> Frank said, "I know where she is. We'll go over there and we'll tell her that she's got to talk to him."

From here on, accounts vary. Widely. Server had the advantage of interviewing Edward Anhalt, a direct participant in the evening's activities, but between the volume of alcohol consumed on that night and the number of years that had passed since 1954, it's safe to assume that elements of myth might have crept into his account.

Anhalt claimed that Frank knew where Monroe was because "he was balling Marilyn himself, but we didn't think of that at the time." DiMaggio's biographer Richard Ben Cramer never mentions this theory. Instead, he says that Barney Ruditsky, a detective he claims was working for Sinatra,

> had a man keeping tabs on Marilyn as a favor from Sinat [his old Toots Shor's nickname] to DiMag . . . If there was one man in the country who understood DiMaggio—understood what it was to be a Dago poor-boy who was (all of a sudden, the very next day) the toast of the nation and the target of a million eyes—that was Sinatra. Frank also understood how it was with Joe and broads. Frank had his own too similar troubles with Ava Gardner.

Sometime that evening, Ruditsky's man contacted Ruditsky, who phoned (or was phoned by) either Sinatra or DiMaggio.

Barney Ruditsky, a Jew born in England, was a legendarily tough and smart New York City police detective who, among other achievements, had helped bring in Louis "Lepke" Buchalter of Murder Incorporated. After retiring from the NYPD, he moved to L.A., where he opened a nightclub called Sherry's and a private-detective agency that would become the go-to firm for Hollywood. Unsurprisingly, most of his cases involved unfaithful spouses. Frank appears to have hired Ruditsky as a favor to DiMaggio. Ruditsky's "man" was a twenty-one-year-old rookie operative named Phil Irwin, who'd been tailing Monroe and on the night in question had spotted her white Cadillac convertible—not a hard car to spot—parked in front of a two-story Tudor-style house on the corner of Waring Avenue and Kilkea Drive, in a quiet middle-class neighborhood in Hollywood.

The house was actually a three-unit apartment, with two entrances on Waring, numbers 8120 and 8122, and one on Kilkea, at number 757. The addresses are key to the story. The building's landlady, a Mrs. Blasgen, lived at 757 Kilkea; 8120 Waring was occupied by a thirty-seven-year-old legal secretary named Florence Kotz; and the tenant of 8122 Waring was a friend of Marilyn Monroe's, a young actress named Sheila Stewart.

Sheila Stewart was a beard.

Although Kitty Kelley asserts in *His Way* that Monroe "was supposedly having a lesbian relationship" with Stewart, a relationship that Sinatra and DiMaggio were hoping to uncover as "evidence to use in the divorce [Marilyn] was seeking from DiMaggio," Monroe had in fact been granted an uncontested divorce the previous week, and Sheila Stewart had lent her apartment to Marilyn to use for an assignation with her voice teacher, who was not a woman but a man named Hal Schaefer.

Schaefer, twenty-nine, was a gifted jazz pianist, arranger, and composer who had orchestrated the music for the 1953 movie *Gentlemen Prefer Blondes* and coached Monroe for her celebrated performance in the film of "Diamonds Are a Girl's Best Friend." He was the precise opposite of DiMaggio—handsome but physically slight; an artistic, sensitive young man—and at some point, it's not clear when, Monroe sought him out as a port in a storm. Schaefer later claimed that the two of them fell deeply in love. He and Marilyn might have been spotted together by Ruditsky or Irwin: one account says that while DiMaggio was dining with Sinatra on the night of November 5, a detective told Joe that if he went to a certain apartment house on Waring Avenue in West Hollywood, he'd find Monroe "in the arms of another man."

What's not clear is whether Ruditsky knew the identity of the other man. Nor is it clear what exactly Sinatra and DiMaggio hoped to accomplish when they, along with a sizable group, converged on the Tudor house at the corner of Waring and Kilkea.

The screenwriter Anhalt played the entire episode for laughs when he recounted it to Lee Server many years later. It had all been a drunken escapade, he claimed—a very drunken escapade. The way Sinatra presented it, Anhalt claimed, Monroe just needed to be persuaded to talk to DiMaggio. "This didn't make a lot of sense at first," Anhalt said. "But the more we drank, the more it began to seem reasonable. And we got to the point where someone said, 'What if she won't open the door?' And Lee Marvin says, 'Well, we'll break it down.'"

It was decided that the only man for the job was the oxlike Broderick Crawford, who was drinking at another bar. Crawford was fetched, at which point, Anhalt continued,

> We all went back to our cars and drove off to this address Sinatra told us . . . And we got out. Everybody's staggering around on the sidewalk trying to stay upright, and we head into the building, Sinatra and his guys, DiMaggio, Mitchum, Lee Marvin, Brod [Crawford], everybody who was there. And I said, "What apartment is she in?" And Frank said, with great authority, "She's in 3A." And we all went upstairs, as many as could manage it. And Brod and some other guys leaned on the door and broke it open and went tumbling inside this apartment. And inside was a little old lady who looked nothing like Marilyn Monroe, and she started screaming. So everybody says, "Oh shit! Let's get outta here!" They're knocking each other over to get back out through the doorway. And everybody staggered back out on the street and got back into their cars and drove away. Somebody called the police, of course, and they reported it in the papers . . . and this woman said she had seen all these movie stars come breaking into her apartment, and I think maybe everyone thought she made it up, that she had had an attack of dementia.

Except that the little old lady in question, Ms. Kotz, was all of thirty-seven at the time, and the "building" Anhalt refers to (which had no apartment 3A) was in fact a nice house on a hitherto quiet street. As the *Los Angeles Times* later reported, Florence Kotz "was fast asleep about 11 p.m. when five or six men suddenly battered down the back door to her apartment, tearing it from its hinges and leaving glass strewn on the floor . . . A bright flash of light was shone in her eyes and she was confronted with a number of men, some of whom seemed to be carrying an instrument which at first sight she believed to be an ax."

In fact it was a flash camera.

Who were these men? In the end, the only people whose presence that night was definitely established were Sinatra and DiMaggio, along with

Ruditsky and his operative Irwin and—weirdly—Ruditsky's and Irwin's wives, who stayed in the car as this mob smashed into Florence Kotz's apartment (and as, in the apartment next door, a terrified Marilyn Monroe and Hal Schaefer hurriedly dressed and fled into the night). Besides Frank and Joe—and Mr. and Mrs. Ruditsky and Irwin, and Mitchum, Marvin, and Crawford—Frank's friend, music publisher, manager, and sometime bodyguard, Hank Sanicola, might also have been present, along with the Villa Capri's maître d', Billy Karen, as well as, perhaps, Patsy D'Amore himself. And then there was that unnamed photographer, there to catch Marilyn in the act, whatever the act might have been.

Quite a crowd.

The incident, which would become infamous as the Wrong-Door Raid, was all very humorous by some accounts—but not to Hal Schaefer, who, after being followed and threatened anonymously for the next six months, would attempt to commit suicide by swallowing sleeping pills and Benzedrine washed down by typewriter cleaning fluid. And not to Florence Kotz, who would pursue the matter with the Los Angeles Police Department until the case was closed for lack of evidence a year later. Nor to Frank himself, who would experience a strange kind of retribution when, as would happen again and again in his life, the world decided to take seriously what he had regarded as a moment of minor misbehavior.

———

On the night of November 19, 1954, Sammy Davis Jr., driving his new Cadillac DeVille convertible to Los Angeles from Las Vegas, swerved to avoid hitting a car that was making a U-turn and collided with another vehicle. His head snapped forward into a conical ornament in the center of the steering wheel, and the ornament struck Davis square in the left eye, nearly killing him and destroying the eyeball. As he lay in Community Hospital in San Bernardino, he despaired of ever performing again. Many of Hollywood's biggest stars made the sixty-mile drive to rally to his side—Jeff Chandler, Tony Curtis and Janet Leigh, Jack Benny, Eddie Cantor. "For years," Davis's biographer Wil Haygood writes, "Sammy had cheered Hollywood on, slavishly saluting stars, sidling up to them, snapping their photos, his adoration shameless. Now it was being returned."

The one notable absence was Frank Sinatra.

Looked at one way, the relationship between Sinatra and Davis was simple: Frank was the sun, and Sammy was the moon. Ten years younger, Sammy had idolized Sinatra from the moment he first heard his voice on the radio. Davis had been a teenager then, but he was already a veteran vaudevillian, having performed since the age of three with his father and uncle in the Will Mastin Trio. He was volcanically talented—as a singer, dancer, and impressionist— but Sinatra was the man he wanted to sound like, be like. He had the Voice, the style, the money, the women. And he was white. "He helped me overcome my greatest handicap, my inferiority complex about being a Negro," Davis said.

Practically from the moment they'd met, Frank, who on matters of racial tolerance was fervently liberal (on his own terms), had taken Sammy under his wing. In 1947, when Sinatra headlined at the Capitol Theater in New York, he demanded that the management hire the Mastin Trio to open for him, at five times their usual salary.

With the Mastin Trio and then as a solo act in the early 1950s, Davis frequently performed in Las Vegas, where his path often crossed with Sinatra's and their friendship deepened. Vegas was a remote outpost then, not far past the Old West days when cowboys and workers from the newly built Hoover Dam used to roll into town to get drunk, get laid, and gamble away their salaries. "On Fremont Street," recalled Jerry Lewis, who performed at the Flamingo with Dean Martin beginning in the late 1940s, "they had a place to *tie your horse!*" Out along Route 91, the two-lane blacktop that would eventually become the Strip, there were wide stretches of desert between the dozen or so casinos, punctuated by little besides tumbleweed and rattlesnakes.

And being a cowboy town, Las Vegas was also a racist town. When Sammy Davis Jr. performed at the Last Frontier Hotel & Casino, he couldn't stay in the hotel or eat in the establishment's restaurants. After his show was over, he had to go back to a rooming house in the black district on the run-down west side of Vegas. It was this way at every casino on the Strip. Frank Sinatra hated it and vowed to do something about it as soon as he was able.

Frank was a dyed-in-the-wool liberal, he thoroughly appreciated Sammy's whirlwind talents, and yet in crucial ways the friendship was asymmetrical. The stamp had been set from the beginning: Frank was the leader, the Chairman of the Board (the New York disc jockey William B. Williams might already have bestowed the title on him by 1954); Sammy was the acolyte. This had partly to do with Frank's age and his unexampled status in show business and partly to do with his domineering personality, but it was a function of Davis's personality as well. Throughout the civil rights movement and afterward, other African-American entertainers would come along showing pride and even defiance about their blackness, but such pride and defiance were not in Sammy's makeup. Along with the color of his skin, he was ashamed of his small stature (he was five four) and his crooked teeth. He knew how talented he was, but he was also a chameleon, hence his skill at impressions—which were almost always of white entertainers: Cary Grant, James Cagney, Humphrey Bogart. (His worst impression, make of it what you will, was of Frank Sinatra.)

"Sammy Davis was one of the great, great entertainers of the world," the comedian Shecky Greene said. "But there was also no Sammy Davis."

But it wasn't the asymmetry of Davis's friendship with Sinatra that kept Frank away from the hospital. It was Frank's dislike—fear—of hospitals.

Finally, a girlfriend at the time, a model named Cindy Bayes who was also a close friend of Sammy's, laid down the law to him.

I said, "You don't understand what you mean in this kid's life." He said, "I'll go tomorrow." But at five in the morning he comes back [home]. He was drunk. I came running out in a bathrobe. He started sobbing— not about Sammy, but about what a mess he had made of his life. I said, "I don't want to see you again, because you're so destructive." The next day about two hundred flowers arrived. But what did it mean?

It meant he felt, but would not say he was, guilty. About many things. The next day Frank went to the hospital and told Sammy that he would—not could, would—recuperate at his place in Palm Springs when he got out of the hospital.

Back on the upswing, covered with honors from *Billboard* and *Down Beat* and *Metronome,* Frank Sinatra truly seemed to have the world on a string. What was he doing sobbing to Cindy Bayes about the mess he had made of his life?

In the darkness of 5:00 a.m., he knew he was alone and always would be. "My father was a deeply feeling man who could not attain a meaningful intimate relationship," Sinatra's younger daughter, Tina, wrote in her memoir. "I don't know that he ever had faith in finding a soul mate, even during his pursuit of Ava. After that marriage imploded, he would hedge all emotional bets. He would keep a part of himself safe and shut off. As he once told me, 'I will never hurt like that again.'"

In protecting himself from hurt, he was only assuring himself another kind of pain, but one that was more easily anesthetized by ceaseless activity, by sex and romance, by alcohol. But that 5:00 a.m. moment always came, the moment when the anesthesia wore off.

Three weeks later, another mess.

Sammy, rested and reenergized thanks to his stay in the desert and wearing a jaunty-looking patch over his left eye, celebrated his twenty-ninth birthday with a party at his new house in the Hollywood Hills. He was excited—about his recovery, which was proceeding well; about the gig that Herman Hover, the owner of Ciro's, had promised the Mastin Trio as soon as Sammy was ready (Frank had leaned on Hover to make it happen); about the house, the first place he'd ever had to hang his hat in (although his white publicist Jess Rand had had to rent the place under his own name, for all too obvious reasons); about his birthday. The house was filled with friends—eating, drinking, smoking, laughing. Frank was there and a very pregnant Judy Garland. After a while Cindy Bayes arrived, escorted by Bob Neal, a dark-haired Texas playboy—in those days, there was still actually such a thing as a playboy—who had money to burn, being both an oilman and the heir to the Maxwell House coffee fortune.

After many drinks were consumed, Judy Garland and Cindy Bayes wanted to move the party along—they decided to go catch Mel Tormé at the Crescendo, a jazz club on Sunset. The agreeable Bob Neal was game; Frank, however, had no desire to go hear Mel Tormé. For one thing, Tormé was another singer, and a sublimely gifted one at that, capable of things even Sinatra couldn't do (scatting, for example). For another, Frank and Tormé had history: not only had Frank dated Mel's wife, Candy Toxton, before she married Mel, but he'd also shown up drunk at the couple's engagement party and chased Toxton up the stairs, forcing her to lock herself in a bathroom.

Finally, Cindy Bayes told Frank that she, Garland, and Neal were going to the Crescendo whether he went or not. Perhaps not wanting to be edged out by the wealthy Casanova, Frank grudgingly agreed to go. Not a good start.

The party proceeded to the club and listened to Tormé. Apparently, Frank behaved himself. But when the club closed at 2:00 a.m., the foursome, feeling no pain, walked into the foyer with drinks hidden under their overcoats. The headwaiter noticed and warned the group that what they were doing was illegal and that a couple of plainclothes policemen were standing nearby.

This alone would have irked Sinatra.

At that moment, however, Mel Tormé's press agent (as a publicist was called in those days), James Byron, who'd been standing nearby, either called out to the party or approached them and asked Bob Neal the name of his date. He might have put it more pungently, asking who the broad was. Byron almost certainly would have been inquiring about Cindy Bayes, although Sinatra, for reasons of his own, would later maintain that the press agent had failed to recognize Judy Garland—an unlikely possibility, no matter how pregnant she was. It was all very straightforward: filling out the names of the group would allow Byron to plant an item in the gossip columns about Sinatra and Garland coming to hear his client.

But Frank elected to take the inquiry amiss. According to Byron, "Sinatra said, 'What business is it of yours? You're probably a cop. I hate cops. You're either a cop or a reporter. And I hate cops and newspapermen.'"

According to Kitty Kelley, Frank's language was more pungent. According to Kelley, Sinatra lunged at Byron in the phone booth, shouting, "Get out of there, you bastard . . . You fucking parasite. You're nothing but a leech. You're a newspaperman. I hate cops and I hate reporters. Get out of there right now and take off your fucking glasses."

By all accounts, all parties proceeded to the parking lot, where Frank yelled at Byron, "Why don't you go out and make a decent living and not suck off other people? You leech."

"And who are you, Frank?" Byron said. "You're dependent on other people. You're dependent on the press and the public."

"I am not. I have talent and I am dependent only on myself," Frank said.

Accounts now diverge considerably. According to Byron, "Sinatra told me to take off my glasses and then he jumped me. He hauled off with his left and hit me on the side of the face. We exchanged several blows and I hit him in the nose a couple of times."

But years later, Cindy Bayes told her son, "The guy comes over to hit Frank and the guys from the parking lot were holding Frank's arms down stupidly thinking they were helping him. Frank did not make the first hit."

This jibes with Sinatra's account: "I went back to Byron and told him to take his glasses off. Then suddenly two guys held my arms and Byron tried to knee me. He succeeded in denting my shin bone and clawing my hand. I couldn't do anything because I was held by two men. I broke loose. It ended when I gave him a left hook and dumped him on his fanny."

Of course it didn't end there. Nothing with Frank ever ended anywhere near where he wanted it to end.

"I have talent and I am dependent only on myself." His restlessness and his impatience were of a piece with the emotional disconnect. His simple need for movement frequently trumped good sense. This even extended to his music. He would have seen from the beginning how deep his musical bond—and yes, therefore his emotional bond—with Nelson Riddle was, and some part of him might have resisted it. Riddle, a shy man who was in awe of Sinatra as both a musician and a star, would not, could not, have pressed the issue. And so just as he constantly looked for new lovers, Frank sought (and would continue to seek) other arrangers, even as some part of him must have known Riddle could give him all he needed, and more. There was some musical sense to this, but there was an emotional story behind it as well.

What else could account for the December 13 session with Ray Anthony and his orchestra, an outfit best known for "The Bunny Hop," "The Hokey Pokey," and the theme from *Dragnet*? Frank recorded two songs that day, both arranged by a former trombonist, not Nelson Riddle: his name was Dick Reynolds, and the tunes were "I'm Gonna Live till I Die," a fast-paced belter whose title said the little the song had to say, and "Melody of Love," a rather soppy waltz that, according to Will Friedwald, "may be the only Sinatra record completely bereft of anything resembling drama or even a climactic moment."

A large statement. And this in a life so filled with drama and climactic moments.

He was searching. And in some ways flailing.

————

A couple of days later, *Not as a Stranger* wrapped. Stanley Kramer swore he would never use Sinatra in a movie again, not even if he had to go begging with a tin cup. Kramer didn't mention Mitchum or Marvin or Broderick Crawford, only Frank.

3

||||||||||

I'm not going to get married. If I feel the need for company,
I call up for a date and go out somewhere.

—FRANK SINATRA, TO A NEWSPAPER COLUMNIST, APRIL 1955

You be nice to tender people.

—HAROLD ARLEN TO FRANK SINATRA

Maybe an angel could save him.

Frank had first met Gloria Vanderbilt in the summer of 1945, when her husband, Leopold Stokowski, was conducting at the Hollywood Bowl. When the singer went backstage after the concert to congratulate the maestro, he took admiring notice of the sixty-three-year-old conductor's swan-necked, ethereally lovely twenty-one-year-old wife, whose devotion to her husband bordered on worship.

Nine years later, the bicoastal gossip mill buzzed with the rumor that the role of handmaiden to a living legend was wearing on Madame Stokowski. The maestro toured frequently, while she stayed in New York caring for their two young sons. In the evenings, she was frequently out and about with starry company. An item in Dorothy Kilgallen's column that November noted, "Gloria Vanderbilt Stokowski, who was almost a recluse for so many weeks after her marriage to the maestro, has done the complete reversal. Now hangs out in Sardi's." (Another item higher in the column read, "Don't be surprised if Frank Sinatra and Ava Gardner decide they just can't resist giving it another whirl.") In private, Vanderbilt had asked her husband for a divorce; he had told her he would never let her go.

At thirty, the heiress was as famous as her husband, having first come to the world's attention at age seven, as the center of a sensational custody battle between her flighty and hedonistic mother and her aunt the philanthropist Gertrude Vanderbilt Whitney. Brought up by her aunt in luxury on Long Island and Fifth Avenue, Gloria blossomed into an exotic-looking, dark-haired beauty whose photograph first appeared in *Harper's Bazaar* when she was fifteen. At seventeen, she went to Beverly Hills to visit her mother and instantly fell under the spell of Hollywood, and Hollywood fell for her: stars like Errol Flynn, Van Heflin, and George Montgomery danced attendance. After a disastrous early marriage to an actor's agent named Pat DeCicco—a shady minion of Howard Hughes and probably a small-time hood—she met Stokowski, who seemed to promise an ideal life of artistic purity.

Gloria had long nourished artistic longings. She had studied acting; she also wrote poetry and had a gift for painting, avocations the possessive maestro liked better because they were solitary. Stokowski was far less pleased with his gregarious young wife's attraction to the glittering life he called Vanity Fair and a circle that included her best friends, Carol Marcus (who'd twice been married to the writer William Saroyan) and Oona O'Neill Chaplin, as well as the songwriters Harold Arlen and Jule Styne (who'd moved back to New York to pick up his Broadway career) and the ever-provocative Truman Capote, who encouraged her to get out and get around, with other men if need be.

In early 1954, after Vanderbilt and the theater producer Gilbert Miller acted together in a skit for a charity ball, Miller proclaimed her "a star in the making," citing her "electric presence, dignity, poise, intelligence, beautiful speech." That fall she was cast alongside Franchot Tone in a revival of Saroyan's *Time of Your Life,* to be produced at New York's City Center theater that coming January.

Then Jule Styne called and said that Sinatra was coming to town and wanted to take her out.

Frank was to begin a three-week stand at the Copa just before Christmas, and the gossip columns were reporting he'd be accompanied to New York by Miss Sweden of 1951, Anita Ekberg. Perhaps conversation with Ekberg was wearing thin; maybe he just wanted to cover his bases; in any case, he had suddenly conceived a desire to see Gloria Vanderbilt.

Harold Arlen, also a friend of Frank's, warned him, "You be nice to tender people."

Frank was fully capable of this. It wasn't falsity. In one part of his complex and contradictory soul, he was ever receptive to, even solicitous of, those who inspired his better angels.

Vanderbilt, for her part, was electrified by the call. "The phone can ring and your whole life can change," she wrote in a memoir.

> I'd met him once before . . . But that didn't count. It didn't count
> because he didn't exist for me, no one did then. I was veiled, and others
> existed in my thoughts only as people permitted to stand in Leopold's
> presence. Now it was different—in an instant everything had changed,

and all I could think of was whether I was thin enough, thin enough to meet him.

The date was made through Styne: 7:30 p.m. on Tuesday, December 21. There is a photograph of the two of them that night, at a performance of the new hit Broadway musical *The Pajama Game,*[*] seated—where else?—in the first row of the orchestra at the St. James Theater. Though photographers weren't allowed into the theater, one had somehow managed to sneak in and get a shot: Frank on the aisle, handsome in a dark suit—you can almost smell the bay rum on his cheeks—but appearing strangely disengaged with the glorious creature on his left, studiously examining his playbill and actually appearing to be chewing gum. He looks almost bored. Can this be? More likely, it is the look of a man, oversensitive to begin with, who has detected the photographer in his peripheral vision and who, though he strongly wishes not to be seen or bothered, is doing his best, in the dignified surroundings of the orchestra section of a Broadway theater, amid the ladies in their furs and pearls and the gents in their black tie, not to create the all too expectable incident.

On the face of it, they are a mismatch. Gloria Vanderbilt, a vision in white silk, her hair pulled back, a quadruple strand of freshwater pearls around her beautiful neck, diamond swags hanging from those lovely ears, fits far better with the tuxedoed toff seated on her other side, a blond hunk with a perfectly unreflective face and a no doubt irreproachable pedigree . . . But here she is with Sinatra, and this photographer, hoping to get the pair to look at his camera, has triggered his flash. Distracted from the playbill she holds in white-gloved hands, her head snapping up so quickly that the swag hanging from her left ear is a blur of motion, she shoots the man a look of cold fury. "She looks," a biographer wrote, "like a gorgeous cobra that could kill you with one swift glance." But her anger likely covers another, less imperious emotion; she is after all still a married woman, caught, if not quite in the act of betrayal, then well along in the intention.

Yet Sinatra meant more to her than sex or even love. "I'm seeing him again tonight," she wrote, breathlessly, of the morning after, "and all day, even though I got no sleep, instead of being tired I feel high, like I'm taking deep drafts of some kind of rare oxygen that connects not with another *person* but with an

---

[*] The very show in which, that June, a twenty-year-old Shirley MacLaine had become an instant sensation when she stepped out of the chorus and into the lead role after the star Carol Haney broke her ankle. By the time Frank and Gloria got to the St. James Theater, MacLaine was already in Hollywood with a movie contract from producer Hal Wallis. Sinatra probably hadn't heard of her yet but would soon.

Sinatra's affair with Gloria Vanderbilt was brief but fiery, the catalyst that loosed her from her marriage to the conductor Leopold Stokowski: "He is the bridge, the bridge to set me free," she wrote of Frank.

unknown place in myself . . . Because when I'm inside that place I have the courage to be free . . . He is the bridge, the bridge to set me free."

Less than a week after they met, Vanderbilt would move with her sons out of the Gracie Square penthouse they'd lived in with Stokowski to a hotel on Park Avenue. The papers would soon announce the couple's separation.

But what was she to Frank?

They would have just three weeks together, and then he was off to Australia, for concerts in Melbourne and Sydney. For those three weeks, they saw each other almost every night, for propriety's sake in the company of an older pair, Frank's friend the sports columnist Jimmy Cannon and the actress Joan Blondell, the four of them riding around Manhattan in a long black limousine. (A decade later, the weeks with Vanderbilt would find an unintentional echo in Ervin Drake's "blue-blooded girls of independent means" lyric for "It Was a Very Good Year.") Vanderbilt recalled that one night at dinner Frank "turned to me and said that he'd thought about me, wanted to see me again, ever since that night he'd watched me in the audience at the [Hollywood Bowl] concert, how I'd looked at Leopold as he conducted, my eyes never leaving him. I winced."

She winced because at the moment she felt disloyal, but could she also have been wincing at Sinatra's vision of the perfect handmaiden? A woman of rare sensibility, delicacy, and beauty who would speak softly and walk a step behind? She had been twenty-one then; now she was thirty. She was a caterpillar molting.

"At that point, I never thought I could be in love or involved with anyone again unless we could work together," Vanderbilt recalled, fifty-five years later. "That's what I really wanted."

But this was her dream, not his.

For Christmas, he gave her a Tiffany bracelet engraved "For Miracle and Me"—because, she remembered, "we both said that it was sort of a miracle that we had met." On New Year's Eve, there was a party in his penthouse suite at the Sherry-Netherland, and when the other guests left, Frank turned off the lights and took her to the window. "You looked down over the park, which was just beautiful, and it was snowing," she remembered. In the frost on the window he drew a heart and traced their initials inside: FS & GV.

In his fortieth year, he too was sweetly dreaming that he might find what he needed with her. "We talked about having children together," Vanderbilt said. "We talked a lot about places we'd like to go to together—the things that lovers talk about when they're fantasizing, you know.

"He never talked about Ava. He would drink Jack Daniel's, but I never saw him drunk once. And I never saw him belligerent; I never saw anything like that."

She told him about her affection-starved girlhood and how terrifying it had felt to be a child in the public eye. Oddly, he confided back something for which the public had long criticized him. "He was very open in talking about his relationship with the Mob," she recalled. "And how conflicted he was about it. He was drawn to it, he said."

He was stripping himself bare for her. But there were so many layers still beneath.

———

"The list of celebrities who can't get to see Sinatra is almost more glittering than the roster of those who make it," Dorothy Kilgallen reported a few days after New Year's. "Latest victims of the velvet rope include Zsa Zsa and Rubi [the international playboy Porfirio Rubirosa] . . . and Marlon Brando."

Maybe Frank slipped the Copa doorman a C-note to keep Brando out. But no doorman on earth would have stood in the way of Sinatra's January 7 visitor: on that night, Marilyn Monroe, newly platinum blonde and wearing a white ermine jacket, accompanied by the photographer Milton Greene and his wife, walked into the sold-out show and proceeded directly to a ringside table. Frank stopped the show and gave her a wink when she sat down.

On Tuesday night, January 11, between sets at the Copa, Frank whisked Gloria down to the Statler Hotel to attend a celebration for Tommy and Jimmy Dorsey, who twenty years or so earlier had gotten together to form the Dorsey Brothers Orchestra. The occasion was loaded with ambivalence: for one thing, the two brothers, who were famously hot-tempered and competitive, had split up to form separate bands almost immediately. For another, Frank Sinatra, who joined Tommy Dorsey's band in 1939 and left in 1942 to go out on his own as a singer, had parted with the domineering bandleader on acrimonious terms, amid furious recriminations and lawsuits from Dorsey and, probably, a threat of gangland violence against Dorsey by Frank's north Jersey godfather Willie Moretti.

During Sinatra's three years with the then-all-powerful Tommy Dorsey Orchestra, the spotlight had shifted from the charismatic bandleader to the even more charismatic singer. And in leaving Dorsey, Sinatra had, virtually single-handedly, ushered out the big-band era and ushered in the age of the vocalist as star. A dozen years on, he was the star of stars, and Dorsey was old news. Tommy, who with his prematurely white hair had once been nicknamed the Old Man by his musicians, really did look old, though he was not yet fifty. He would be dead within two years.

Yet all the past battles appeared to be forgotten at the anniversary gala, which proceeded amid affectionate speeches and a general haze of nostalgia. Frank had reminisced fondly to Gloria about his old days traveling with Dorsey—indeed, he would continue for the rest of his life to recall those days to friends, as though they had been the best of his life. That night at the Statler, he sang two of the songs most identified with him during the Dorsey years, Ruth Lowe's "I'll Never Smile Again" and Joe Bushkin and John DeVries's "Oh! Look at Me Now," laughingly making a hash of the latter's lyrics. After apologizing, he said, "Here's a song Tommy just asked me to do that I had the—I don't know whether you call it good fortune, whatever it was, I wrote the lyrics to this. Ha-ha-ha! Lyrics! Oh boy! I'm leavin'! I'm packin'!"

He was being genuinely self-deprecating, and the effect was utterly charming. (The fact that Gloria was beaming at him from the audience would have inspired him.) Then he began singing the tune, which he wrote in 1941 with Sol Parker and Hank Sanicola:

> *This love of mine goes on and on,*
> *Though life is empty since you have gone.*

Listening today, one is struck by the contrast between the Jersey boy who has just spoken and the nonpareil interpreter of the American popular song now singing with such beautiful tone and diction. (Gloria was probably still beaming, though listening carefully to the lyrics might have given her pause.) But to see the singer as somehow inauthentic to the speaker is to ignore the twenty years of very hard work the kid from Hoboken had put himself through. And at this moment, unbeknownst to all but a few people, he was working harder than ever.

In the second week of January, Gloria began rehearsals for *The Time of Your Life*. Frank came to watch and was impressed; at least that was what he told her. In a few months, he told her, his production company was going to make a movie called *Johnny Concho*, his first Western. There might be a role in it for her. She was thrilled. They had their farewell dinner at Le Pavillon, and then, after another apricot-and-aqua dawn, the gorgeous dream faded and he was off to Australia.

His last overseas tour, in Europe with Ava in the spring of 1953, had been up-and-down. He had begun recording with Riddle before he left, they were already making magic together, but the world didn't know it yet. Frank barely knew it himself. His down period was then entering its nadir: Ava had one foot out the door; his confidence was wobbling. He played to packed houses in northern Italy and Rome, but in Naples, where the promoter had taken it upon himself to advertise that Gardner would be appearing along with him, the crowds and the press were far more interested in the resplendent Ava, whose movie career was surging, than in her small, pale consort. The audience chanted her name—"Ah-va! Ah-va! Ah-va!"—and threw seat cushions when she wouldn't join him onstage. In Sweden, the small audiences barely applauded. One theater manager, alleging that Frank spent more time backstage checking his boat schedule than entertaining the public, refused to pay his fee. Claiming a nervous collapse, Sinatra ended the tour early.

Things were very different in January 1955. Sinatra landed in Sydney, his fourteen-year-old daughter, Nancy, in tow, and joked easily with the press, giving long interviews to radio and newspaper reporters before his first concert. He was scheduled to give fifteen shows over ten nights in Australia; for this, he would be paid $80,000—roughly the equivalent of $700,000 today.

He was worth every penny. The crowds were big and welcoming; they laughed at his jokes. And he sang magnificently, reveling in the incomparable vocal instrument that was—just then—at its peak: rich and feeling on the ballads, supple and athletic on the up-tempo numbers. In the closing song of his January 19 show at West Melbourne Stadium, "Ol' Man River," he flaunted his renowned breath control on the phrase "you get a little drunk and you lands in jail," holding the low note on the word "jail" until it seemed no human could hold it any longer, then dropping the tone a fifth, then dropping *again,* then moving seamlessly into "I gets weary and sick of tryin'," all on a single lungful of air, for an astonishing twenty seconds or more.

For comfort and solidity, Frank had brought along a small combo of his regular musicians: Bud Shank on alto sax, the guitarist Nick Bonney, the drummer Max Albright, and, playing piano and conducting Dennis Collinson's local orchestra, Bill Miller. In the three years he'd been working with Sinatra, Miller, a brilliant and inventive musician himself, had become, as Sinatra chronicler Richard Havers writes, "his musical confidant . . . Frank and Bill would work together on songs before going into the studio, teasing out the subtle nuances, working on the phrasing and slight shifts in the timing that gave Frank his unique approach to what were in many cases old songs, and in others already standards." Their complete ease with each other was especially evident on the beautiful duet of Sinatra's old 1940s chestnut "(I Got a Woman Crazy for Me) She's Funny That Way" and would reach its artistic apogee, of course, on their solo-piano-backed version of the great Johnny Mercer–Harold Arlen saloon song "One for My Baby," recorded in 1958 but not released until 1990.

The troupe also included a young vocalist named Ann McCormack, about whom Nancy junior, who was keeping a diary of the trip, made a sorrowful discovery. Needing some hotel stationery on which to write home, she looked in the desk drawer of her father's room and found, along with paper and envelopes, "some intimate ladies' apparel."

Nancy knew her father had been seeing one of the girls in the show, she writes; what she didn't know was that the girl had been with Frank next door. She was so upset that she stopped writing in her diary.

The incident rhymes oddly with another discovery Nancy writes about in *Frank Sinatra: My Father*—a time when, playing dress-up in her mother's dressing room as a little girl, she'd happened upon a stack of movie magazines hidden in the closet, fan magazines that contained photographs of the still-married Frank with girlfriends like Marilyn Maxwell and Lana Turner. "I was devastated," she wrote. Whatever she was looking for in that hotel desk drawer, the thing she actually found might have upset more than surprised her.

Bill Miller, Sinatra's musical right hand for forty years, a brilliant artist who chose to live in his boss's shadow. In tribute to the pianist's perpetual pallor, Frank called him Suntan Charlie.

Around 8:00 p.m. on Tuesday, February 8, Frank Sinatra walked into KHJ Radio Studios in Hollywood and greeted the small group already assembled there: the producer Voyle Gilmore and a handful of musicians—Bill Miller, the celesta player Paul Smith, the guitarist George Van Eps, the bassist Phil Stephens, the drummer Alvin Stoller. For the first four songs Frank would be recording for his new album—Rodgers and Hart's "Dancing on the Ceiling" and "Glad to Be Unhappy," Kay Swift's "Can't We Be Friends?," and Alec Wilder's "I'll Be Around"—there would be no strings, no horns. Nelson Riddle had written the minimalist arrangements but was not present to conduct that night; instead, Miller would lead the session from the piano. Frank had been preparing his new album, his third for Capitol, for months, meticulously planning the song list and the sequencing of the tunes and, collaborating closely with Bill Miller and Riddle—often at night at Sinatra's house—working out every note, phrase, and nuance.

The album, as Will Friedwald writes, "inaugurated [Frank's] tradition of using a title song to set the mood, something he continued doing off and on for the rest of his career." The song in this case was Bob Hilliard and Dave Mann's "In the Wee Small Hours of the Morning."

Hilliard and Mann had dashed the song off in a postmidnight session just a few months earlier. As befitted the hour of the composition, both music and lyrics were of an exquisitely gentle sadness—an emotion that, in Frank's post-Ava life, felt all too familiar. Yet it was a hallmark of Sinatra's resurgence that he could now alchemize his sadness into gold. Bill Miller told Friedwald that "both singer and pianist instantly realized that 'In the Wee Small Hours' was going to be an important number for them."

No Sinatra album to date had set an emotional ambience so strongly as this one would. The first two albums of his Capitol period, *Songs for Young Lovers* and *Swing Easy!*, had each sustained a mood, but more simplistically: you could call them concept albums, if you wanted to cite concepts like Romantic or Upbeat. *In the Wee Small Hours* was a far more complex piece of work. The disc jockey and Sinatra specialist Jonathan Schwartz has compared it to both a novel and a two-act play, writing, "Sinatra, a man who lived his life in italics, was a piece of high drama in many acts. The record album—with its first-act curtain, 'When Your Lover Has Gone,' and intermission as the disc was turned over, and the second act's opening number, 'What Is This Thing Called Love?'—helped create the perfect format for the dramatic figure Sinatra had become."

Besides the title song, the carefully worked-out song list, and the exquisite orchestrations, technology itself benefited—and shaped—*Wee Small*. Sinatra had seen a lot of recording history in his twenty-year career. In his first two years at Columbia Records, a record album, like the photograph album from which it took its name, was a large, heavy, object-containing book—the objects in this case being ten-inch 78 rpm shellac phonograph records, with one song of about three minutes' duration per side. Sinatra's first album, Columbia's 1946 release *The Voice of Frank Sinatra*, had contained four 78s, eight songs, and weighed a couple of pounds. When Columbia introduced the first 33 rpm long-playing album in 1948, it suddenly became possible to put eight songs on just one ten-inch vinyl disc: inside its cardboard sleeve, the album now weighed only a few ounces.

In the Wee Small Hours was Sinatra's first twelve-inch LP, a format that gave the singer the luxurious span of sixteen songs, more than forty-eight minutes of music, to weave his spell (to cover all bases commercially, Capitol also released the album in double-disc ten-inch and quadruple-disc 45 rpm extended-play formats). *Wee Small* is an amazingly integrated piece of work, both for its time and for all time, holding its mood of tender sadness through-out, amid the many somber colors of Nelson Riddle's musical palette. Frank so often sings in a kind of hush that when he momentarily switches gears from gentle to rascally, as in the cynical verse to "Can't We Be Friends?" ("I took each word she said as gospel truth/The way a silly little child would"), the effect is jarring. This is an album of capitulation, not retaliation—his "Ava album," as Frank would later call it.

Two of the songs that feel most naked in this regard are Hoagy Carmi-chael's exquisitely ironic "I Get Along Without You Very Well," with a lyric based on a poem by Jane Brown Thompson, and Cole Porter's towering "What Is This Thing Called Love?" On the latter, with its lyric equal to any Roman ode, Sinatra is in spine-chillingly peak vocal form; as he makes plunging melodic improvisations that flirt with basso territory, he sounds like a cave of the winds. But then, with one of his patented lyrical improvisations, he comes close to ruining this great rendition of a great song. Porter's superbly concise lines convey in absolutely minimal form all the soaring hope and crushing heartbreak of new love:

> *I saw you there one wonderful day,*
> *You took my heart and threw it away.*

Yet Frank, for reasons best known to himself, takes it upon himself to augment the second line:

> *But you took my heart and you threw my heart away.*

This was a very long way from the Frank Sinatra of twenty years earlier, who as a singing waiter at the Rustic Cabin in Englewood Cliffs, New Jersey, got so nervous at the sight of Cole Porter in the house one night that he forgot the words to "Night and Day"[*] and was reduced to singing the title phrase over and over again. This was an artist who now considered himself the equal, and the collaborator, of any of the great artists whose songs he was singing.

———————

The story goes that Sinatra was so thrilled with Riddle's arrangement of "What Is This Thing Called Love?" that after he had finally satisfied himself with

---

[*] Porter's biographer William McBrien says the song was "Let's Do It," although it seems unlikely that the twenty-year-old Sinatra would have hazarded that talky list song, with its "Lithuanians" and "Letts." *Cole Porter,* p. 371.

a perfect vocal (on the twenty-first take! small wonder that he was fooling around with the words), he turned to the arranger and said, "Nelson, you're a gas."

There was a pause while the serious, socially awkward Riddle came up with the best answer he could think of. "Likewise," Nelson said.

The musicians gave each other looks.

On the night of March 30, a year and five days after his Academy Award triumph, Frank stood once again on the stage of the Pantages Theater in Hollywood, once again in black tie—except that this time instead of accepting an award, he was presenting one: the Best Supporting Actress Oscar, to Eva Marie Saint for *On the Waterfront*. That movie, with twelve nominations and eight wins, was the big winner that night—the biggest since the year before, when *From Here to Eternity* had had thirteen nominations and won eight Oscars, including Sinatra's for Best Supporting Actor. Best Actor this year went to Marlon Brando for his role as the Christlike longshoreman Terry Malloy in *On the Waterfront*: an upset victory over the favorite, Bing Crosby in *The Country Girl*.

But the biggest upset in the Pantages Theater that night might have been in Frank Sinatra's stomach. He had badly wanted the role of Terry Malloy, which had seemed so perfect for him: the film was even to be shot in Hoboken. (Though as a teenager Frank had actually worked—briefly—on the Hoboken docks, he had not discovered in himself much of a taste for manual labor.) *On the Waterfront*'s producer, Sam Spiegel, had pursued Sinatra relentlessly for the role, promising it to him, declaring that no one else on earth was as qualified to play it, assuring him that it would win him a Best Actor Oscar to bookend that other statuette. In the end, though, it was a matter of pure economics where Sam Spiegel was concerned: Marlon Brando, one of the biggest box-office draws in the world, would simply put more asses in movie theater seats.

Where *On the Waterfront*'s director, Elia Kazan, was concerned, Brando—who had demonstrated astonishing craft and versatility in films like *A Streetcar Named Desire*, *Julius Caesar*, *Viva Zapata!*, and *The Wild One*—was the better artistic choice as well. "Frank Sinatra would have been wonderful, but Marlon was more vulnerable," Kazan later said. "He had this great range of violent emotions to draw from. He had more schism, more pain, and so much shame—the actor who played Terry had to have a lot of shame." As *From Here to Eternity* had shown, to the surprise of many, Frank could portray vulnerability wonderfully on-screen. Displaying shame, on-screen or off, was not his forte.

When Brando got the role, Frank "half destroyed" his living room in a fit of rage. Now Brando had the Oscar Sam Spiegel had promised to Sinatra.

And now history was about to repeat itself, this time as musical comedy.

In early 1954, after picking up the movie rights to Frank Loesser's smash Broadway musical *Guys and Dolls* (based on Damon Runyon's Times Square short stories) for $1 million, Samuel Goldwyn hired the renowned writer-director Joseph L. Mankiewicz to helm the film, then spent a very well-publicized half year trying to cast the four principals: the smooth-talking high roller Sky Masterson; the rough-hewn gambler Nathan Detroit; Nathan's long-suffering fiancée, the chorine Miss Adelaide; and the pious but sexy missionary Sergeant Sarah Brown.

As was (and still is) frequently the case in Hollywood, many casting permutations were bruited about, with stars as diverse as Gene Kelly, Bing Crosby, Bob Hope, Clark Gable, Robert Mitchum, Kirk Douglas, and Burt Lancaster (and for one mad moment Dean Martin and Jerry Lewis) mentioned as possibilities for the male leads. Betty Grable, Jane Russell, Debbie Reynolds, Grace Kelly, and Marilyn Monroe were all in the running at one time or another for the part of Adelaide or Sarah. A Hedda Hopper column of early May had Goldwyn asking Frank Sinatra to play the "Guy Madison" * role (Goldwyn, who was born in Poland and immigrated to America in his teens, had a notoriously interesting relationship with the English language). But soon afterward, word got out that Goldwyn and Mankiewicz were in hot pursuit of Marlon Brando to play Sky Masterson.

If it's true that Goldwyn had first approached Sinatra to play Masterson, then his initial instincts were good. On Broadway, Sky had been played by Robert Alda (the father of Alan), a handsome leading man with a pleasant voice. Alda sang several of the show's key songs, both solo and together with Isabel Bigley, who played Sarah Brown. Sam Levene, who was a wonderful actor but could barely carry a tune, played Nathan Detroit. To compensate for Levene's limited vocal abilities, Frank Loesser wrote Nathan's only solo, "Sue Me," in a single octave. Levene croaked the song out very effectively.

By June, Earl Wilson was reporting that Samuel Goldwyn wanted Frank Sinatra to play Nathan Detroit.

Thirty years later, in a talk at Yale Law School, Sinatra confessed to having been nonplussed by Goldwyn's apparent change of mind. "[My] agent said to me, 'Sam Goldwyn loves you, Frank, and I know you admire him and I love him.' I said, 'That's true, but I don't want to play Nathan because I don't know how to play him.' I meant it. I didn't know how to play him. I said, 'If it was the other way around, the role of Sky Masterson is a vocalist,' and I said that's

---

* Guy Madison was a television actor best known for the Wild Bill Hickok series.

what I thought should be the part I'd play. He said, 'But it may be [Goldwyn's] last film . . . You'd do a wonderful thing if you'd just play the role and make him happy.'"

Goldwyn's biographer A. Scott Berg tells a rather different story. "In the midst of negotiations, Frank Sinatra's agent got hold of the script," he writes.

> His client insisted on being in the picture. There would be no conflict in the fact that Goldwyn was about to sign Brando; Sinatra was desperate to play Nathan Detroit. Mankiewicz thought Sinatra was all wrong for the part; in fact, he still hoped to talk Goldwyn into signing Sam Levene . . . But he met the singer at the Beverly Hills Hotel and found that "Frank was just in love with it." Even though Brando and Sinatra were better suited for each other's roles, Goldwyn liked the ring of the stars' names.

Sinatra, his career still on the post-slump upswing, received third billing, after Brando and Jean Simmons, who played Sergeant Sarah.

Marlon Brando might have been the world's most brilliant movie actor, but there was this one small detail: he had never sung in a movie before. And another: Joseph L. Mankiewicz—who had directed Brando in *Julius Caesar*— had never written or directed a musical.

For the sake of getting on the picture, Frank had made no fuss about Goldwyn's signing Brando for a role Frank felt should have been his. This didn't mean he had reconciled himself to the situation.* In some ways, the slightly timid and awkward character of Nathan Detroit was a rehash of the timid and awkward Clarence Doolittle character Sinatra had played in *Anchors Aweigh* and more or less reprised in other roles of the 1940s. Goldwyn had given the Gene Kelly role to Brando.

Under the expert control of Mankiewicz, whom both Frank and Brando respected, the shoot of *Guys and Dolls* proceeded efficiently but with a certain amount of tension. "Brando's desire to continually rehearse wore on 'one-take Charlie' Sinatra," Tom Santopietro writes.

> Frank, fueled by instinct, not intellectual analysis, never did grow comfortable with cerebral actors and was not particularly circumspect in his critique of Brando's Method ways, referring to the estimable Brando as Mumbles. Or, as Sinatra pungently told director Mankiewicz, "Don't put me in the game, Coach, until Mumbles is through rehearsing." (Of

---

* In years to come, Sinatra would correct history by making "Luck Be a Lady"—a Sky Masterson song—one of his signature numbers.

course, Brando got his own back by proclaiming that when Sinatra dies, "The first thing he'll do will be find God and yell at him for making him bald.")

But if Frank was building up a head of steam about Brando, he might not have been eager to go up against a man who was eight years younger, muscular, and no shrinking violet himself when it came to physical confrontation. The production's single chronicled detonation occurred between Frank Sinatra and Frank Loesser.

Goldwyn and Mankiewicz had cut five of the Broadway show's key musical numbers, ordering Frank Loesser to write three new songs for the film—songs Loesser didn't like very much—including one, "Adelaide," specifically designed to beef up Sinatra's on-screen singing time. The skids were greased for a face-off between the two hot-tempered Franks.

"Sinatra apparently felt that Nathan's character should conform to his own well-established crooning style, whereas my father felt that Nathan should remain a brassy Broadway tough who sang with more grits than gravy," Frank Loesser's daughter wrote in a memoir.

I am told that my father conducted himself with uncharacteristic restraint for a time, watching Sinatra do his thing—until, finally, he could stand it no longer. After a rehearsal that left his blood boiling, he approached Sinatra with an offer to give him some help with "Sue Me," some tips on what he'd had in mind when he wrote the song . . .

"Why don't we meet in my bungalow and rehearse it?" he asked mildly through his clenched teeth.

"If you want to see me," Sinatra said, "you can come to my dressing room."

My father left the set to go outside and jump up and down and scream for a while. When he was calmer, he showed up at Sinatra's dressing room only to find it crowded with hangers-on and noisy with radio music.

"How the hell can we rehearse in this atmosphere?" he said, his blood resuming its full boil.

"We'll do it my way," Sinatra said, "or you can fuck off."

A contrapuntal duet of explosions swiftly followed, culminating in each man's avowal never to work with the other again.

Or as Wilfrid Sheed put it in his meditation on the great writers of the American popular songbook, *The House That George Built,* "Frank Sinatra . . . never forgave Frank Loesser for telling him how to play Nathan Detroit. The nerve of some people."

———————

Early in April, the syndicated columnist Bob Thomas had the temerity to ask Sinatra about the status of his marriage to Ava Gardner. Frank responded with what sounded like resignation. "It's a stalemate," he told Thomas.

> "She established residence in Nevada, but she never filed the papers for divorce. I don't know what she's going to do."
> He left no doubt that the marriage is over, but he's not concerned about a divorce.
> "I'm not going to get married," he said. "If I feel the need for company, I call up for a date and go out somewhere. I have no plans for anything serious."

Sinatra laughed, the columnist wrote, when asked if he had any plans to marry Gloria Vanderbilt.

> Frank cracked, "Sure—and what's the penalty for bigamy these days?"
> He pointed out that he was still legally wed to Ava and Miss Vanderbilt to Leo Stokowski.
> "I found Gloria delightful company," he said. "It was wonderful to hear a woman talk intelligently about music and books. Out here, the girls seem to limit their conversation to what's happening in Hollywood and at the race track."

Thomas reported that Frank had signed a five-year, five-picture deal with United Artists and was talking with other studios about various projects. "But the story he is most interested in is 'Teahouse of the August Moon,'" the columnist wrote. "He would like to play the Okinawan interpreter."

The role, of course, went to Marlon Brando.

———————

One night in the spring of 1955, Peggy Lou Connelly, an attractive twenty-three-year-old singer from Fort Worth, accompanied a girlfriend to the Villa Capri in Hollywood, where the friend, a model married to a jazz pianist, hoped to meet Sinatra. "I did everything to discourage her, because I liked her husband a lot, but I didn't think anything would come of it, so I let myself be dragged along," Connelly remembered more than fifty years later.

As it happened, Sinatra was at the Villa Capri that night, sitting with his close friend the songwriter Jimmy Van Heusen. And, Connelly recalled, the two young women had barely ordered their food when Van Heusen loomed up out of the smoky darkness and asked if they would mind if Mr. Sinatra came over and had coffee with them after they'd finished their dinner.

For an innocent girl from Fort Worth, the sight of Van Heusen was alarming, to say the least. "He had rather bulbous eyes and rather unattractive teeth, and he was balding," Connelly said. To her friend, though, it didn't matter what the emissary looked like—Sinatra was Sinatra. Of course they would have coffee with him, she said.

Connelly, for her part, was terrified by the prospect of meeting Frank. She was a young girl from the provinces, living at the Hollywood Studio Club, a chaperoned residence for aspiring actresses. "I had been in Hollywood for such a short time that I was impressed by bit players," Connelly recalled. "To meet one of the biggest stars in the world, I was not prepared for it. So I did not speak, really. I smiled, and when Frank asked me 'Where are you from?' I smiled and said my name and said, 'I'm from Texas, and I'm a singer.' That's really all I said."

The dark-haired, freckle-faced Connelly sat shyly while her gorgeous friend did all the talking, flirting aggressively with Sinatra. "And after ten minutes he stood up and he said to *me*—not my friend—'Miss Connelly, would you like to have dinner with me next Thursday?' He liked to be formal. And I said yes, and Jimmy took my phone number. And so it began."

What began that night for Peggy Connelly was a three-year relationship with Sinatra, one that would bring her into frequent contact with the man who would soon become the most important composer in Frank's life and was already his procurer in chief, Jimmy Van Heusen. She never got over her first impression. "I used to feel sorry for him because I thought he was so ugly," Connelly recalled. "I never saw him with a girl. I never even saw him get near the prostitutes that he used to bring around."

Van Heusen, born Edward Chester Babcock in Syracuse, New York, in 1913 (he invented the sporty pseudonym as a teenage disc jockey), was a paradox: foulmouthed, obsessed with sex and alcohol, but a songwriter of deep and delicate gifts, verging on genius. He and Sinatra had first met in Manhattan in the lean 1930s, when Van Heusen was plugging songs for the music publisher Remick and trying to sell a few tunes of his own and Frank, who had yet to meet Harry James or Tommy Dorsey, was still singing at the Rustic Cabin. The skinny Hoboken kid with the sublime voice used to gather up his pal Nick Sevano and ferry across the Hudson to hit the nightspots with Van Heusen and Hank Sanicola, who at the time was also plugging songs in Tin Pan Alley.

Another member of the posse was a fast-talking, wisecracking, breathtakingly talented little lyricist named Sammy Cahn, then working with a songwriter named Saul Chaplin.

From the beginning, Van Heusen's songs had a melodic subtlety that made him highly sought after by singers: in a historic sequence of New York recording sessions by Sinatra and the Dorsey band between February and August 1940, the first number Frank recorded was a Van Heusen tune, co-written with the lyricist Eddie De Lange, called "Shake Down the Stars." Another, "Polka Dots and Moonbeams," written with Johnny Burke, was one of Sinatra's loveliest early ballads.

It was Burke, Bing Crosby's lyricist (Crosby called him "the Poet"), who lured Van Heusen to Hollywood, in the summer of 1940, to help him write songs for Bing's movies. (Sammy Cahn would make a similar move not long afterward, to write motion-picture music with Jule Styne.) Jimmy, who'd used his first song royalties to take flying lessons and then bought his own plane, a two-seat Luscombe Silvaire, flew himself to Los Angeles. His last fuel stop before Van Nuys Airport was a dot on the map called Palm Springs. In the late summer of 1940, the airport there was nothing but a couple of adobe huts and a few fuel drums, and the incredible heat shimmered off the tarmac, yet the minute Van Heusen stepped out of his plane, he was happy. He had suffered all his life from sinus trouble; suddenly he could really breathe for the first time. He was in love with the desert. It was to be a lifelong affair and another of the passions he shared with Sinatra.

While Burke and Van Heusen turned out tunes for Crosby's movies, Frank Sinatra soared into stardom with Dorsey, then left the band and, in 1943, moved to California and began making movies. With his 4-F draft status, Frank was able to build his singing and film careers throughout World War II; Van Heusen did double duty, writing movie music with Burke by night and risking his life as a test pilot for Lockheed during the day.

But after the war, Burke became progressively more debilitated by alcoholism. "When I wrote 'But Beautiful' [in 1947], he was so sick that he couldn't pick up a cup of coffee off the table," Van Heusen recalled. "He had to put his face down and sip it."

Van Heusen's partnerships with lyricists had always been, in modern parlance, monogamish, but as Burke's health worsened, Jimmy was forced to branch out even more. There was also the fact that as Bing Crosby passed age fifty, he was contemplating retirement. Crosby had inspired a certain unsentimental edge in Burke and Van Heusen's work for him, specifically enjoining Johnny not to write the phrase "I love you" in any of the lyrics. Without the lodestars of Burke and Crosby to guide him, Van Heusen engaged in some sheerly commercial work that had a whiff of cynicism about it. What else would explain the soupy "You, My Love," the theme for *Young at Heart,* which Jimmy wrote with the frequent Harry Warren collaborator Mack Gordon; or the fittingly turgid theme song for *Not as a Stranger* ("I think of youuu, my love, not as a stranger"), composed with the lyricist Buddy Kaye?

Then Sinatra had an idea.

In the spring of 1955, he signed with MGM to co-star with Debbie Reynolds in a movie adaptation of a Broadway comedy called *The Tender Trap,* a very 1950s story about a confirmed bachelor and cynical ladies' man who finally gets reeled in by a dewy young thing. Metro wanted a theme song for the picture, one that Frank could sing over the titles, and Frank had just the writers in mind: Sammy Cahn and Jimmy Van Heusen.

It was perfect. Cahn too was in need of a new collaborator, his longtime partner Styne having decamped for Broadway. Like Van Heusen, Cahn had already done significant work for Sinatra, including (with Styne) the great songs "I Fall in Love Too Easily," "Guess I'll Hang My Tears Out to Dry," and "Time After Time." His lyrics, though never pedestrian, tended to have a heartfelt, almost coercively emotional quality. But he also had another side: after

Sinatra brought the songwriters Sammy Cahn and Jimmy Van Heusen together, giving each man a partner who could deliver him from schmaltz. They wrote some forty songs for Frank, including such enduring hits as "Come Fly with Me."

immigrating to Hollywood and before succumbing to the charms of Goldwyn Girl Gloria Delson, whom he married in 1945, Sammy had been part of
the poker-playing, skirt-chasing crew that frequented Sinatra's Sunset Tower
bachelor pad. Though he no longer alley-catted with Sinatra and Van Heusen,
he had long delighted in writing witty, often bawdy special lyrics for parties
and other occasions. He and Jimmy Van Heusen could each use a songwriting
partner capable of delivering the other from schmaltz. They were a musical
marriage waiting to happen, and Sinatra had made the match.

4

⫿⫿⫿⫿⫿⫿⫿⫿⫿⫿

Then all those hookers our boy met.
He had the kind of fun that no one could hardly rap
He banged the way you do on a tymp
And lived just like a musical pimp.

—SAMMY CAHN, SPECIAL-OCCASION LYRICS COMPOSED FOR
JIMMY VAN HEUSEN'S FIFTY-FOURTH BIRTHDAY

Something about Julius Epstein's script for *The Tender Trap* clearly spoke to
Frank—something beyond the chance to return to MGM, which had so
unceremoniously dumped him five years earlier; something even beyond
the prospect of being top billed for the first time in a film comedy. He would
play Charlie Reader, a thirty-five-year-old Manhattan theatrical agent who
leads the bachelor life of Riley, 1950s-style, traffic directing a steady stream
of gorgeous and compliant young women who show up at the door of his
gloriously panoramic Sutton Place apartment. Of course, because it is a story,
Charlie has to change in the third act, and change for a perennial bachelor
naturally means settling down. Will he choose Sylvia, the wry and sophisticated concert violinist with a few miles on her (played by the thirty-eight-year-
old Celeste Holm), or Julie (portrayed by the twenty-three-year-old Debbie
Reynolds), the theatrical ingenue so bent on marrying and making babies that
even a starring role in a Broadway musical barely appeals to her?

Seen today, the 1955 movie is a load of Technicolor hooey, scarcely spiced
up by the epic amount of smoking and drinking that goes on and the Feydeau-
esque comings and goings of Charlie's various luscious squeezes, their plen-
teousness and pulchritude helpfully underlined by the eye-popping double
takes of Charlie's best friend, the married but itchy Joe (David Wayne). Even
the title of the picture and its theme song seems like a joke, and a semi-dirty
one at that. "Every time Jack Benny sees me at a party," Sammy Cahn wrote
in his memoir, "before he even says hello, he will say, 'How could *anyone* . . .
write a song called "The Tender Trap"?'" Can anyone actually have bought any
of this malarkey?

Well, yes. For one thing, silly title or no, the theme, the first outing by the
new team of Cahn and Van Heusen, was just terrific: in a beautiful opening
sequence (the movie goes straight downhill from there), Sinatra sings "The

Tender Trap" as he struts toward the camera, all alone under a bright blue CinemaScope sky.

And *autres temps, autres mœurs,* as the French say. What feels appallingly outdated today seemed racy and fun in 1955. Even the *New York Times*'s ordinarily fusty Bosley Crowther, who'd never hesitated to stick it to Frank when he appeared in inferior pictures—and there had been a lot of inferior pictures, from *The Miracle of the Bells* to *The Kissing Bandit* to *Double Dynamite*—melted with delight. "This comical dissertation on the fun a bright fellow can have merely by remaining single in the glutted marriage market of New York is a vastly beguiling entertainment, even for guys who already are hooked and for ladies of desperate disposition who have their traps out for any fair game," he gushed.

Frank, of course, bought into the concept more than anyone. After all, he and Charlie were a lot alike—an idea that must have given the movie a lot of pop for mid-1950s audiences—except that Frank was a lot richer, the girls were more plentiful, and (the beauty part, at least in theory) he didn't have to get married at the end. Ever since Ava had all but divorced him, he had tried to get used to the idea of life without her the only way he knew how: singing sad songs (*In the Wee Small Hours*) or semi-defiant ones (in May, his recording of "Learnin' the Blues," a great swinger by an out-of-the-woodwork young songwriter named Dolores Vicki Silvers, hit number 2 on the *Billboard* singles chart); and through an incessant round of flings, affairs, and romances conducted both sequentially and, with a boldness that Charlie Reader might have envied but only Frank Sinatra could really bring off, simultaneously.

Around the same time (for example) that he was tracing his and Gloria Vanderbilt's initials on the window of his penthouse suite at the Sherry-Netherland, he was romancing the nineteen-year-old singer Jill Corey, who came to the Copacabana during that laden Christmas–New Year's stand of 1954–55. "I had a date with a singer by the name of Richard Hayes," Corey recalled. "He took me to see Sinatra at the Copa. And we were seated on the stage area, and in the middle of the show [Frank] discovered me. My cheeks began to warm, because he directed his view at me. Richard didn't seem to mind, because he was in awe of Sinatra. For a good twenty-five minutes, he was turning his head my way, then acknowledging somebody else, and then coming right back to me. I turned red; I was a nervous wreck."

There was no meeting that night, only heavy eye contact, and the next day Corey had to go to Pittsburgh for a club engagement. But two weeks later, she remembered, "I'm outside of the building, going down the steps, and the manager comes running after me: 'There's a phone call for you from New York.' I said, 'Who is it?' He said, 'It's Frank Sinatra.'"

Corey picked up the phone. "Where in the hell have you been?" barked

Sinatra, to whom she had never spoken before. "I had five people searching for you. When are you getting back to New York?"

Corey told Frank that she was headed back to New York the next day, to do a live television show called *Stop the Music*. He asked what time her show was over; eight o'clock, she said.

"I'll be onstage at the same time," Sinatra said. "Would you mind if my chauffeur came and picked you up? He'll have a little hat in his hand; you'll recognize him."

Like Gloria Vanderbilt, Corey was instantly almost incapacitated by the prospect of meeting Sinatra. "I get back to New York, and I spend the whole day not getting ready for the performance that night but trying to find the right dress," she recalled. "And all through my mind, I kept thinking, 'Do I call him Frankie or Frank?'

"I finish the show, and I see a man standing who looks like he's in chauffeur clothes. He said, 'Miss Corey? I'm here at Mr. Sinatra's request to pick you up and take you back to his show.'"

The rest played like a scene from *GoodFellas*. Jules Podell, the manager of the Copacabana, met Corey at the door to the club and escorted her to a ringside table. Sinatra's show was almost through. "He took his bow, then he came up the steps, grabbed me by the hand, took me through the doors, and into a kitchen. Now, I'm nineteen. I've worked many, many places from the time I was fourteen, singing with a dance band, but I had never entered or exited [a club] through a kitchen. I said nothing. And we get to an elevator that takes you to the second floor, where you go down a hallway, and there is the Hotel Fourteen. I watch him as he's helped change out of his tuxedo into street clothes. He said, 'I'm hungry. Are you?' I said yes. He said, 'Well, let's go for a drive through the park first.' So we went for a drive through the park with the chauffeur. And he said, 'Harwyn Club'—where Grace Kelly and Prince Rainier [had been] seen dancing. He said, 'We can eat there. Is that all right with you?' I said, 'Yes, it's all right with me.'"

Not long afterward—after spending more evenings with Vanderbilt—Frank was off to Australia, and his dalliance with Ann McCormack. He would phone Gloria Vanderbilt several times from Down Under and from Los Angeles when he returned home; he would phone Corey, too, promising to take a few days off from *Guys and Dolls* to fly to New York and catch her opening at the Blue Angel. (Though Frank, Corey insisted to a columnist, was "just a pal—not a romance.") He appears to have made good on his promise, even though he had just begun a new relationship with Peggy Connelly, was conducting an on-again, off-again intermezzo with Judy Garland, and, in his spare time, was spotted at a nightclub with one Ilsa Bey, identified in the papers as "the foreign beauty who owns a Texas oil well."

In June, Dorothy Manners, filling in for Louella Parsons, reported that the high-flying Frank had chartered not one but two planes to ferry a crowd of friends from Los Angeles to Las Vegas "to catch Rosemary Clooney's closing at the Sands, Noel Coward's opening at the Desert Inn, and the new 'Follies,' with Peter Lind Hayes, . . . at the Sands." According to Manners, the group included Humphrey Bogart and Lauren Bacall, Judy Garland and her husband, Sid Luft, the songwriter Sylvia Fine (Mrs. Danny Kaye), the Beverly Hills restaurateur Mike Romanoff and his wife, Jimmy Van Heusen, and the Peter Lawfords.

If the columnist's attendance roll is accurate—and as we'll soon see, there is reason to believe it is—the inclusion of the newlyweds Peter and Pat Lawford is a kind of minor major surprise. Conventional wisdom has it that as the result of an absurd misunderstanding or a baseless tantrum on Sinatra's part, or a little of both, Peter Lawford was in the midst of an epic freeze-out by Frank: in late 1953, while Sinatra was down on his luck and Ava Gardner had one foot out the door, Lawford and his manager had a drink with Ava and her sister Bappie; Frank read a gossip column that airbrushed out the manager and Ava's sister, and he predictably went ballistic. Several sources have claimed that Sinatra, who was notorious for being able to hold a grudge forever, didn't speak to his former MGM pal for almost five years, from late 1953 until the summer of 1958, and that Frank only let Peter off the hook then out of sheer opportunism: because Frank had just become interested in the fast-heating presidential prospects of Pat Lawford's brother John F. Kennedy.

But there is reason to believe that by the middle of 1955, the thirty-eight-year-old junior senator from Massachusetts, the second-youngest man in the U.S. Senate, was already on Sinatra's radar screen. Nancy Sinatra writes that her father told her he first met Kennedy soon after the senator's marriage to Jacqueline Bouvier in September 1953. Other sources claim that the two men met at a Democratic Party rally in 1955. Addressing the rally, Frank spoke passionately about the widely held idea that entertainers should stay out of politics. If it came to a choice, he said, he would give up his career for the cause in which he believed so deeply.

In addition, Jack Kennedy had long been a known quantity in Hollywood, having first cut a swath there before World War II as the glamorous and sought-after son of Joseph P. Kennedy—banker, co-founder of RKO Pictures, ambassador to England, and lover of Gloria Swanson—and having returned often as a rising politician and sun-loving sybarite, especially after acquiring a movie-star brother-in-law. Among his many West Coast liaisons in the late 1940s was a brief fling with Ava Gardner.

It was natural that he and Sinatra would gravitate to each other, for many reasons.

FBI files state that beginning in mid-1955, John Kennedy kept a suite on the eighth floor of Washington's Mayflower hotel—room 812—as his "personal playpen" and that Sinatra, among other luminaries, attended parties there.

Also by mid-1955, after John Kennedy's twenty-nine-year-old brother, Robert, was appointed chief counsel of the powerful Senate Permanent Subcommittee on Investigations (which under its previous chairman, Senator Joseph McCarthy, and his chief counsel, Roy Cohn, had gone after Communists and which under its new chairman, Senator John McClellan of Arkansas, would investigate organized crime), the Kennedy brothers were Democratic figures to conjure with in Washington and much in the headlines. For Sinatra, Jack Kennedy—a witty and articulate eastern patrician, fascinated with the acquisition, maintenance, and uses of power, and a hedonist to boot—would have had much of the same appeal as Frank's idol Franklin Delano Roosevelt, with the added charge of youth and sex appeal.

Clearly, Peter Lawford was worth reconciling with. And even though Frank had known almost from the start that his fury at Lawford was unfounded*— and despite the fact that as a rule his furies needed no rational fuel to keep them burning—a year and a half would have given even him enough time to cool down.

———

Summer of 1955: Louella Parsons is on vacation, leaving the writing of her column to Dorothy Manners. Earl Wilson is on a working holiday, leaving the scut labor to his assistants while he dispatches bons mots from Italy. Frank Sinatra doesn't do vacations.

Between the end of June and the end of August, he stopped moving only to sleep, and he didn't sleep much. Even as he started shooting *The Tender Trap* at MGM, he was signing (for $150,000) to star in *Carousel* for 20th Century Fox and a musical version of Thornton Wilder's *Our Town* on NBC television in September. On June 29, he broadcast the last of his twice-weekly *Frank Sinatra Show* for Bobbi home permanents and the next night, at Hollywood's KHJ Radio Studios, recorded a ravishing rendition of Johnny Mercer and Jimmy Van Heusen's "I Thought About You," with a hint of Hoboken ("I took a chrip on a chrain, and I thought about you") and a glorious Riddle arrangement.[†]

For a couple of weeks in late June and early July, he was actually shooting

———

* Lawford's manager Milt Ebbins had phoned Sinatra immediately after the incident to explain that drinks with Ava had been his, Ebbins's, idea; Frank had exploded anyway.
† Sinatra and Riddle would improve on this version, which was never officially released, the following January in one of the *Songs for Swingin' Lovers!* sessions.

two movies at once, shuttling back and forth between Goldwyn Studios, where he was finishing work on *Guys and Dolls,* and the *Tender Trap* set at Metro. On July 9 (the all-too-significant day Bill Haley's "Rock Around the Clock" displaced Frank's "Learnin' the Blues" at number 1 on the *Billboard* singles chart), *Guys and Dolls* wrapped, and on the eleventh Sinatra chartered a bus with a bar on board to take Bogart and Bacall, Dean Martin, Sammy Davis Jr., Van Johnson, June Allyson, Eddie Fisher, Debbie Reynolds, the Sands' general manager, Jack Entratter, and Michael Romanoff to a Judy Garland concert in Long Beach. The contingent arrived feeling no pain. Judy introduced Frank onstage and asked him to sing a song; for some reason, he declined. On July 15 and 27, he laid down vocal tracks for *The Tender Trap,* and on the twenty-ninth, again with Riddle arranging and conducting, he recorded a single, an irresistibly bouncy torch song called "Same Old Saturday Night" ("Went to see a movie show/Found myself an empty row"), credited to Sammy Cahn and the otherwise unheralded (or perhaps pseudonymous) Frank Reardon, who at the very least had taken careful notes at the School of Van Heusen.

In the meantime, Cahn and the actual Van Heusen, having clicked so well composing "The Tender Trap" for Sinatra, were now writing a mini-score of four tunes for the *Our Town* TV special. In his memoir, Cahn suggested that though it had been Frank's idea to put the two of them together, there was really a kind of kismet to it. "For years people had been saying that Sammy Cahn's meat-and-potatoes lyrics and Jimmy Van Heusen's polka-dot-and-moonbeams music made for a happy combination," he writes. Yes, but. The chemistry between lyricist and composer is a delicate one, and talent on both sides of the equation doesn't always equal felicity of product. All kinds of subtle factors come into play, and in the case of *Our Town,* the musical, an argument can be made that despite the noble intentions of all parties, and the immortal quality of Wilder's play, the project was misbegotten from the start, the central problem being Frank Sinatra.

The character of the Stage Manager, *Our Town*'s onstage narrator and the framer of the action, is a reasonably elastic one, having been played over the years by actors as diverse as Henry Fonda, Spalding Gray, and Paul Newman. The constant is that the character is a New Englander of a certain age, a calm and philosophical presence who must convey the life-cycle events of Grover's Corners, New Hampshire, whether mundane, amusing, or heartbreaking, with a wry stolidity and a humble simplicity. For all these reasons, Sinatra as the Stage Manager just didn't add up. The idea of converting part of his narration to song was a good one—on paper. As, in theory, was the hiring of Cahn and Van Heusen to write the songs.

Sammy and Jimmy had struck gold with "The Tender Trap" because it had a certain hard-hearted humor to it that played to both men's strengths. Van Heusen was a cynic, a soured romantic, capable of writing a beautifully romantic tune if the poetry of the lyric charmed away his defenses. Cahn was an extraordinarily clever lyricist, but when he aspired to poetry, bad things often happened. Sentimentality was his Achilles' heel (along with a certain didacticism), and when Van Heusen got anywhere near sentimentality (as we've seen with the songs he wrote for *Not as a Stranger* and *Young at Heart*), he tended to check out artistically and write merely serviceable music, far beneath what he was capable of.

"When you write lyrics to Broadway musicals with books by Broadway writers—well, that's one thing," Cahn tells us. "When you confront the genius of a Thornton Wilder, you must react more deeply, and react we did. I believe it is our best writing."

"A Thornton Wilder" being the problematic phrase in that statement.

On the night of August 15, Sinatra recorded all four songs, and three of them were pure Karo syrup. Faux-folksy sentimentality and didacticism washed over the lyric of the title number, "Our Town" ("You will like the folks you meet in our town/The folks you meet on any street in our town/Pick out any cottage, white or brown/They're all so appealin'—with that lived-in feelin'"), and despite Van Heusen's gifts, and Riddle's, the tune was solid but unmemorable. "Look to Your Heart" and "The Impatient Years" were equally unexceptional.

What, then, happened with "Love and Marriage"?

It is a thoroughly charming song, and a thoroughly memorable one: cheerful, winning, and utterly false. The irony of its being sung by Sinatra is transcendent. Can Cahn and Van Heusen possibly have meant it sincerely?

Will Friedwald writes that the two songwriters "wanted you to think of them as professionals first and artists second; to hear them tell it, they didn't write music to express anything like an aesthetic longing in their souls, but rather they were something akin to musical tailors, crafting product for the specific needs of artists, producers and the marketplace." He then goes on, however, to call "Love and Marriage" "wryly cynical in poking fun at the social conventions of the day."

There is no hint of irony in Cahn's description of the song's genesis. "We began by rambling around the room, thinking and talking about Mr. Thornton Wilder's play," he writes.

> As you may know, the first act is called "The Daily Life," the second act, "Love and Marriage," so at some point I turned to Jimmy and said, "Since we're doing a musical, Mr. Van Heusen, would you *please* . . . ?" Whereupon he went to the piano and started thumping out *oompah*,

oompah—which led to "Oom-pah, oom-pah, Love and marriage,/Go together like a horse and carriage."

The tale smacks of biopic inevitability, even though at least one source reports that Sinatra "didn't much care for" the song. On the other hand, we have Cahn's fascinating and entirely credible-sounding account of Frank's initial reaction to the mini-score:

> The first time we sat down with Sinatra to play him the *Our Town* songs was in the home of his ex-wife Nancy, where he'd gone, Sina- tra fashion, for a home-cooked meal. He kept following the songs intently—when Sinatra is in deep thought he has a habit of stroking his lower lip with the back of his thumb—and when we were finished he looked up and said, "Gee, it's good." For him, that's high praise.

Throughout his career, when considering whether or not to record a tune, Sinatra always gave first thought to business. From the 1940s to the 1990s, he was always on the lookout for hits. If he happened to like or even love a num- ber, all the better. Yet there is a famous, and famously long, list of great and good songs he never recorded for one reason or another, and in many cases the reasons were commercial. Conversely, there is a shorter but still substantial roster of tunes he didn't love but recorded anyway, with an eye to the charts: perhaps "Love and Marriage," that pluperfect hymn to 1950s hypocrisy which he sang so winsomely and convincingly, was one of them. In any case, the song would hit the *Billboard* charts at number 5 in November.

As for the real story of love and marriage in Frank Sinatra's life, the tale of the home-cooked meal at Nancy's house in the summer of 1955 certainly gives us one version of it in a nutshell.

———

Constant activity was a balm to Sinatra's ferocious impatience, his terror of boredom and solitude. After wrapping *The Tender Trap* at the end of July, he headed right over to 20th Century Fox to begin rehearsals and costume fit- tings for *Carousel*. If the part of the Stage Manager in *Our Town* was a misfit for him, the role of Billy Bigelow, the wastrel carousel barker in Rodgers and Hammerstein's towering musical fable, seemed made to order. "Frank Sinatra is more excited over this venture than any he's ever undertaken," Louella Par- sons had reported in July in a column announcing that twenty-one-year-old Shirley Jones, who'd just starred in the movie version of *Oklahoma!*, had been signed to play *Carousel*'s Julie Jordan, Billy Bigelow's sweetheart.

Louella could certainly be breathless, but in this case she was telling it straight: the role of Billy, a reprobate who works hard at reforming and in the process gets to sing some of the greatest songs of the American musical theater, seemed heaven-sent. Frank had been singing "Soliloquy," Billy's aria to fatherhood and the show's centerpiece, for years, trying to grow into the great song. Here was a chance to show the world that at almost forty he was finally ready to make it his.

Shirley Jones vividly recalls Sinatra's excitement about the film, and her own. "When they told me that I was going to play opposite him, I was thrilled," she said. "I was a little nervous, because I knew that he was a ladies' man, and I knew that I may have a little problem here every now and then . . . But this is the interesting thing: *he* was so thrilled about playing this role.

"We did all the costume fittings, all the pre-photography; we did some rehearsing at the studio. One day we finished rehearsing and I was about to leave the studio, and one of his henchmen came over to me and said, 'Shirley, Frank wants to see you in his dressing room.' I thought, 'Uh-oh.' Anyway, I went up there, and he was in the bathroom, taking a shower. I went in and I sat down—there was a piano there—on the piano stool. He came out with a towel wrapped around him, but just very nonchalant. [He said,] 'Oh, thanks for coming up, sweetheart. I just wanted to talk to you for just a few minutes.' He said, 'Do you know how excited I am to play Billy Bigelow?'

"I mean, he was genuine," Jones recalls. "I said, 'I know, Frank. It's only the best role for a male singer that was ever written. And you're so perfect for it.'"

After the twenty-one-year-old had sat for an awkward few minutes with the nearly naked thirty-nine-year-old star, Sinatra seemed to realize that *Carousel* was all Jones was interested in discussing. "He finally went in and put a robe on," she said. "And he came back out and said, 'Let's talk about [the movie] a little bit—do you think that this is the way they would want it played?' He was talking about Rodgers and Hammerstein, because he knew that I had already done *Oklahoma!* and that I was the only person ever put under personal contract to them. I said, 'Oh, God, Frank. Of course. It's a great role, and you'll be just sensational.' He gave me some compliments. He said, 'We need to work things out together. If I need your help, I'll ask, and if you need mine . . .' He went on like that. Just really excited about it. It was a great conversation."

On August 15, the same day he laid down the four *Our Town* tracks, Sinatra and Cameron Mitchell, who was to play Billy Bigelow's partner in crime Jigger Craigin, prerecorded the great chantey "Blow High, Blow Low." The song—unlike the *Our Town* numbers, which were to be issued as commercial recordings after Frank sang them live on the September broadcast of the play—was meant to be dubbed into the film of *Carousel*. And, as is the case with three of the four songs Sinatra recorded for the movie (a lovely duet of "If I Loved You," with Shirley Jones, remains), the master tape of "Blow High, Blow Low" has been lost to history, a victim of the controversy that surrounded his sudden withdrawal from the film a few days later.

Fox, which had introduced CinemaScope in 1953 in a 35-millimeter format, had recently developed a new 55-millimeter version that delivered a less grainy print. The studio had decided to break in the new format on *Carousel*, shooting some scenes in both CinemaScope and CinemaScope 55, presumably to deliver a better-quality print to those theaters that were equipped to project it.

Shirley Jones, who got to Maine a few days ahead of Sinatra, vividly remembers standing on a dock with the producers Phoebe and Henry Ephron, waiting for the star to arrive. "We had the two cameras there, which I knew about way ahead of time," she said. "I assumed everybody else did. [Frank] came right from the airport to the dock, got out of the car, and came over and looked at the two cameras. Didn't say hello to anybody. He said to Henry King, the director, 'Why the two cameras, Henry?' Henry said, 'Well, you know, Frank, we're doing two separate processes.' Frank said, 'Does that mean I'll have to do a scene twice?' Henry said, 'Not all of them. Every once in a while, you might have to, because the cameras aren't [always] on at the same time.' And Frank said, 'I signed to do one movie, not two.' Got back in the car, and went back to the airport."

Gordon MacRae, who'd co-starred with Jones in *Oklahoma!*, came east on a moment's notice from a Lake Tahoe nightclub gig to fill in for Sinatra. And 20th Century Fox sued Frank for $1 million. (Sinatra eventually settled with the studio by agreeing to do another film for it at an unspecified future date. And in a supreme irony, Fox wound up never releasing *Carousel* in Cinema-Scope 55.)

What accounted for Sinatra's abrupt departure? The mystery has echoed down through the decades, taking on a kind of haunted quality because of the magnitude of the missed opportunity: all the world seems to agree that Frank, with his real-life raffishness and existential doubts, not to mention his astounding voice, would have made an amazing Billy Bigelow. Could he have been scared? "How can I play Billy Bigelow?" Sinatra is reported to have asked a friend before going to Maine. "He's a big, strong guy with a big, strong voice, and look at me!"

"Through the years, some have muttered that Sinatra was actually more concerned about whether he had the tools to successfully pull off the role, utilizing the two cameras dustup as an excuse," Tom Santopietro writes.

This scenario is shot down by *Carousel* producer Henry Ephron, who years later recalled Sinatra bluntly telling him at the time: "Well, forget it, kid. It's me or the camera. One of us has to go. Listen, Henry. You know me. You've heard me say it—it's been printed a thousand times— I've only got one good take in me."

Even more interestingly, Ephron went on to state that while prerecording songs for the film before leaving for the location shoot, Sinatra turned in a brilliant recording of "If I Loved You" but had difficulty with Billy Bigelow's "Soliloquy," the eight-minute rumination by Bigelow about what sort of boy his son will be. The song represents the ultimate challenge for singing actors, and whatever the reason for Sinatra's difficulties, whether the song was beyond his range or, more likely, that it was just a night when he was not in good voice, Frank stopped the session, telling Ephron, "Let's try it another time. I've had it for tonight." *

But the story doesn't quite shoot down the possibility that Sinatra had serious misgivings. On the one hand, it seems highly unlikely that he wouldn't have wanted to take on the challenge of creating the definitive "Soliloquy"— and the definitive Billy Bigelow. On the other hand, it also seems at least mildly doubtful that as canny a movie actor as Frank wouldn't have known ahead of time, along with Shirley Jones and others, about the two cameras. Two other theories adduced by Friedwald—that "Sinatra beat it rather than being holed up in Maine for a whole summer" or "that the singer left because of Rodgers and Hammerstein themselves, who doubtlessly considered Sinatra too hip and too real to fit into one of their productions"—sound even more improbable.

Did Frank have doubts about being able to pull off the role? "I think he did," Shirley Jones said. "But it's the kind of doubt that everybody has when they're starting a new film. Because he was so excited about it. He said, 'This is the best opportunity I've ever had.' It was that kind of thing.

"Now, he may have got cold feet," she said. "I heard different stories. After that, I went to see Frank in Vegas, and I went to a party where he was, and I tried to get it out of him: 'What the hell happened, Frank?' 'I don't want to talk about it, Shirley. I-don't-want-to-talk-about-it-Shirley.' That's all I ever got from him.

"But you know what I think?" Jones said. "I've since heard it from several people. I was told just recently that Ava Gardner was doing a film, on location,

---

* In 1958, Frank would attempt Billy Strayhorn's masterpiece, the long and melodically tricky tone poem "Lush Life," with the same result.

and he thought she was having an affair, and she said, 'Get your ass down here, or I'm going to.' He was still trying to get her back. I mean, he never gave up on her. And I think something happened in the interim where he thought maybe he had a chance to get her back. And he left the movie to do so."

Letting his golden chances pass him by.

She—Ava—was the ground tone of his life, his late-night obsession and midday daydream, the receptacle of all the uncertainty that his mother, Dolly, had instilled in him. Wherever he was, whomever he was with, she was in the back of his mind, or the forefront. And all the success in the world was only a temporary solace to a mind as complex and fragile as his.

———

A week after he walked off the *Carousel* set, Frank appeared on the cover of *Time*. It was his first *Time* cover, a huge distinction in the days when Henry Luce's magazine empire dominated American culture and reverberated around the world. Yet despite Sinatra's staggering rate of productivity thus far in 1955—a great album (*Wee Small Hours*), a number 2 single ("Learnin' the Blues"), and two movies (*Young at Heart, Not as a Stranger*) released; two more films (*Guys and Dolls, The Tender Trap*) completed, as well as numerous recordings— and despite the comparative lack of brouhaha in his life in the recent past (the walk off excepted), the magazine chose to go with a strange, arrestingly dark cover image, a trompe l'oeil painting by Aaron Bohrod that depicted a menacing-looking Sinatra in a gangsterish outfit (black-banded fedora, big-collared, open-necked pink shirt, dark jacket) floating over a scattering of controversial newspaper clippings (SOCKS COLUMNIST AT CIRO'S, reads one headline; another says, AVA STAYS AWAY, above a picture of the actress) and a grotesque tragedy mask, all set against a black background.

Time was certainly looking to arrest attention and goose newsstand sales with the provocative cover; at the same time, there was a mean-spiritedness about the image that felt almost vindictive. There was also, in the white-bread Eisenhower 1950s, more than a hint of racism in depicting a Sinatra who, counter to his usual elegant turnout, had been made to resemble a street-corner goombah, if not a low-level mafioso.

The cover story, written in highly colorful, and occasionally overwrought, *Time*-ese by the magazine's man in Hollywood Ezra Goodman, was of a piece with the cover. The lead paragraph recounts an apocryphal-sounding tale of Sinatra's Hoboken boyhood; the story ends with Frankie, in a Little Lord Fauntleroy suit, chasing some boys who tried to bully him, cursing and waving a "jagged chunk of broken bottle." Having set this dubious foundation, the story intones,

TWENTY CENTS   AUGUST 29, 1955

TIME
THE WEEKLY NEWSMAGAZINE

Donno Why
Crazy Over Me

VOICES N.Y. OPENER
NEEDS 142 CUES
in QUELL MORS

ocks Columni
At Ciro's, Ch

Ava Stays Awa

Dramatic Role
Sinatra

FRANK SINATRA

$6.00 A YEAR   VOL. LXVI NO. 9

Aaron Bohrod's *Time* cover painting of Frank was both attention-getting and mean.
Depicting Sinatra as a street-corner goombah, if not a low-level hood, it slapped him on
the wrist for his bad behavior and comported with the facile racism of the era.

Thirty-odd years have passed over Hoboken since that day, but what
was true then still holds true. Francis Albert Sinatra, long grown out of
his Little Lord Fauntleroy suit, is one of the most charming children in
everyman's neighborhood; yet it is well to remember the jagged weapon.
The one he carries nowadays is of the mind, and called ambition, but
it takes an ever more exciting edge. With charm and sharp edges and a
snake-slick gift of song, he has dazzled and slashed and coiled his way
through a career unparalleled in extravagance by any other entertainer
of his generation.

He is childlike. He is serpentine. He is armed and dangerous. His gift of song
is a snake-oil trick. He first appears in the piece as a kind of megalomaniacal
Nathan Detroit: "Said Frank Sinatra last week, as he sat cockily in his ebony-
furnished, 'agency modern' offices in Los Angeles' William Morris Agency and
tilted a white-banded black panama off his forehead: 'Man, I'm buoyant. I feel
about eight feet tall.'"

Then, in case the reader didn't get the message, Goodman drives it home. "The man looks . . . like the popular conception of a gangster, model 1929," he writes. "He has bright, wild eyes, and his movements suggest spring steel; he talks out of the corner of his mouth. He dresses with a glaring, George Raft kind of snazziness—rich, dark shirts and white figured ties, with ring and cuff links that almost always match. He had, at last count, roughly $30,000 worth of cuff links."

Was this the same Frank Sinatra who was often photographed wearing beautiful conservative bespoke suits, white shirts, dark silk neckties, and white pocket squares? The same Sinatra who'd spoken so eagerly to Shirley Jones about the possibilities of *Carousel*? The same man who had sung "In the Wee Small Hours of the Morning" with the kind of tenderness that, Ava Gardner once said, "makes me want to cry for happiness, like a beautiful sunset or a boys' choir singing Christmas carols"?

Apparently, it was. *Time* quoted "one of his best friends," who said, sounding an awful lot like Sammy Cahn, "There isn't any 'real' Sinatra. There's only what you see. You might as well try to analyze electricity. It is what it does. There's nothing inside him. He puts out so terrifically that nothing can accumulate inside."[*]

Sammy, if it was Sammy, had a point: Frank was incomparably complicated, electric, mercurial. But he was also wrong: nobody who is not in a vegetative state has nothing inside. Sinatra's terrific output came straight from the formidable chaos brewing within.

He couldn't stay off the newsstands. On September 10, Frank reopened the Dunes in Vegas, riding into the casino on a camel. A widely printed Associated Press photograph showed the singer in a jeweled turban and a silk sultan's outfit and surrounded by young women dressed as harem girls. The caption: "He gets paid for this." In many papers, the photograph accompanied a Bob Thomas column in which Sinatra gave his version of the *Carousel* story: "When I got up to Maine, they spring this two-process gimmick on me. I just don't work that way . . . I have wanted to do 'Carousel' for seven years. It broke my heart not to." He also commented on 20th Century Fox's million-dollar lawsuit: "I would have been insulted if they had sued me for less."

The following week, the September issue of *Confidential* ("Tells the Facts and Names the Names") hit the stands with a cover story titled "From a Detec-

---

[*] Cf. Sammy Cahn's recollection of watching Sinatra sing with Dorsey: "Frank can hold a tremendous phrase, until it takes him into a sort of paroxysm—he gasps, his whole person seems to explode, to release itself." Cahn, *I Should Care*, p. 130.

tive's Report: The Real Reason for Marilyn Monroe's Divorce." The story, about the previous November's Wrong-Door Raid, alleged that Sinatra had been not a bystander, as he had told the police, but a full participant. In a subterranean way, the *Confidential* story was as significant as the *Time* cover: the bimonthly scandal sheet was said to have had a circulation of five million—bigger than *TV Guide, Look,* the *Saturday Evening Post, Time,* or *Life*. It was the forerunner of today's celebrity gossip industry, the equally influential underside of the straight American story of the 1950s. "Everybody reads it," Humphrey Bogart said, "but they say the cook brought it into the house." The *Confidential* piece would have further repercussions for Sinatra.

On Sunday, September 18, Frank's voice, but not Frank, joined Dean Martin and Jerry Lewis on a historic episode of *The Colgate Comedy Hour*. This was the show where Martin and Lewis, who were in the midst of epic battles and had less than a year to survive as a comedy team, seemed to declare an uneasy truce in a skit spoofing the popular quiz show *The $64,000 Question*.

The Wrong-Door Raid started out as a lark but wound up having serious repercussions for Frank.

When Dean, playing the emcee, pushes Jerry, as the contestant, underwater in a dunk-tank isolation booth, Jerry rises up and splutters, "Haven't you heard? The feud is over!" In a poolroom sketch later, Jerry, purporting to be a songwriter, tries to sell Dean a goofy tune called "Yetta, I Can't Forget Her." As delivered by Lewis in his Idiot Kid mode, the song is pure malarkey, but when he turns on a radio the next moment, lo and behold, there's Sinatra singing it, quite charmingly, showing the spell he can weave with even the lowliest material. At show's end, Dean thanks Frank for recording "Yetta" and says, "We'd like you all to join Jerry and myself in watching Frank Sinatra in *Our Town*, tomorrow night, on NBC color and black-and-white network!"

No official reproduction, no videotape or DVD, was ever made of that September 19 telecast (although a partial kinescope of the show exists) for one reason: Thornton Wilder, having somehow been talked into allowing a musical adaptation of his masterpiece, was so disgusted by the result that he wanted it swept under the rug of history.

He had a point. Though there is something to be said for the talent and good intentions of all involved, and something to be said, too, for using Sinatra's star power to bring Wilder's great play to a mass audience, it was clear from the moment Frank walked up to his mark in a 1950s suit and fedora and spoke, in an unreconstructed north Jersey accent, the words, "Mornin'. The name of our town is Grover's Corners, New Hampshire," that the enterprise was wrong, all wrong. Frank even gave a little tell about how out of place he felt—needlessly rubbing his right index finger alongside his nose between the town's two map coordinates, "Latitude forty-two degrees, forty minutes" and "longitude seventy degrees, thirty-seven minutes"—before launching into Cahn and Van Heusen's theme song ("You will like the folks you meet/In our town") and hitting a Freudian clam, on live national television, on the word "our."

The *New York Times* critic J. P. Shanley thought the show was just swell, pronouncing it "magnificent entertainment" and writing that though adding music to the story was an "extremely risky" gamble, the "tender narrative of joy and sorrow in the hearts of a group of unspectacular Americans lost none of its charm in the television adaptation . . . And it was complemented splendidly with songs by James Van Heusen and lyrics by Sammy Cahn."

"Complemented" is a strong word to use about a narrative that was arguably quite complete in the first place. "Ornamented" is more like it, and to a great degree one's taste for the production depended on one's liking for the ornaments hung on Wilder's great play. As for the show's most memorable song, even putting aside the discordance of Frank Sinatra's singing about love and marriage, the tune was jarringly bouncy and contemporary sounding in the solemn early-twentieth-century setting. As for the other numbers, Van Heusen could always write a beautiful melody, especially on the title song, but it's hard to believe that the man who had found Syracuse so stifling and provincial could be anything like sincere about glorifying small-town life. And as nimble a lyricist as Cahn was, Grover's Corners was way out of his wheelhouse.

Still, the team had delivered for Sinatra. And he would soon give them the chance for far more profitable occupation.

———

At the end of the month, Frank began a new daily commute, to RKO Studios in Culver City, to start shooting his fifth feature film of 1955, *The Man with the Golden Arm,* loosely adapted (by Walter Newman, Lewis Meltzer, and an uncredited Ben Hecht) from the 1949 Nelson Algren novel of the same name. Remarkably for that overdrive year, Sinatra worked on no other movies, television shows, or radio broadcasts during the six weeks of the shoot. He did do two nighttime recording sessions, only one of them a standard three-song date with Riddle; the other, with Elmer Bernstein, was to lay down the pretty corny Cahn–Van Heusen title song, which wound up not being used in the picture—a wise choice, given the movie's terrific jazz score by Bernstein, played by the trumpeter/bandleader Shorty Rogers and His Giants.

From the start, Frank's focus on *The Man with the Golden Arm* was absolute. The story was straight up his alley: the protagonist was the portentously named Frankie Machine, a hotshot Chicago card dealer and recovering heroin addict who comes back from a six-month prison term for drug possession and tries, against all odds, to stay on the straight and narrow. Like *From Here to Eternity*'s Angelo Maggio, Frankie Machine is a little man struggling to maintain his dignity; unlike Maggio, however, Frankie isn't a wiseacre but a figure of pure pathos, set against an unrelievedly gritty urban background.

The director Otto Preminger originally considered both Marlon Brando and Sinatra for the role, sending their agents about a third of the not yet completed script. Frank both desperately wanted the role and desperately wanted to beat out Brando. "I got a call the next day from Sinatra's agent, who said, 'He likes it very much,'" Preminger recalled. "I said, 'All right, I'll send him the rest of the script as soon as I have it.' He said, 'No, no. He wants to do it without reading the script.'"

He had beaten out Brando at last.

As we've seen (and will continue to see), Frank's commitment to a given film project depended not only on his connection to the material but on his respect for the director. If Sinatra smelled blood in the water—that is, if a filmmaker displayed any sign of weakness—he either absented himself (sometimes literally) or took over. With Otto Preminger at the helm of *The Man with the Golden Arm,* neither was a possibility.

Preminger was an Austro-Hungarian with a shaved head who, beginning in the 1940s, had made a lucrative sideline of playing sadistic Nazis in films. The fact that he was a Jew made this ironic, but his personality as a director was not dissonant with his movie roles: he was renowned for exerting a Prussian discipline on his sets. "I do not welcome advice from actors," he said. "They are here to act."

Yet if Hollywood expected an explosion between the whip-cracking director and his temperamental star, the town was to be disappointed. Tom Santopietro writes, "Although Preminger publicly stated that Sinatra 'has a chip on his shoulders all the time. He can be small in little things,' the director came to admire Sinatra's talent greatly. Each man had respect for the other, knowing that together they had the chance to create a uniquely powerful film within the controlled and controlling studio atmosphere of the mid-1950s."

Customarily impatient and demanding on movie shoots, Sinatra gave Otto Preminger his full cooperation on *The Man with the Golden Arm.* The result was one of his three best performances.

Frank's admiration for Preminger and his commitment to the role of Frankie Machine put him back in a frame of mind he hadn't experienced since working with Fred Zinnemann on *From Here to Eternity*. "Sinatra arrived for work each day at 8 a.m. on the dot," Daniel O'Brien writes in *The Frank Sinatra Film Guide*, "rarely departing until the previous day's rushes had been screened nearly twelve hours later . . . [his] energies entirely consumed by the *Golden Arm* production." Preminger recalled in his memoir that Sinatra "was surprised to discover that he loved rehearsals. He could not get enough. When I wanted to quit, he would ask, 'Let's do it again, just once, please!'"

The director also remembered Frank's solicitude to his inexperienced twenty-two-year-old co-star, Kim Novak: "She was terrified, and . . . sometimes we had to do even very short scenes as often as thirty-five times. Throughout the ordeal, Sinatra never complained and never made her feel that he was losing patience." At one point, the filming became too much for Novak, and she had to take a brief break. Frank sent her the complete works of Thomas Wolfe.

Of course he wasn't just thinking with his head. But the complete Wolfe, not to mention thirty-five takes, an amazing gesture for him, speaks well of his tenderness to a new lover—a kindness he later undercut by noting rather caddishly to his valet that Novak's "legs were too heavy for him, but her face more than made up for it."

Around that time, the trombonist Paul Tanner recalled, he got a phone call at close to 11:00 on a weeknight. It was Nelson Riddle, asking him if he could come down to the Capitol recording studios at 11:30. "What in the world for?" Tanner asked incredulously.

"Frank wants me to get the orchestra together," Riddle said.

"That means paying triple scale, you know," Tanner told him.

"Don't worry, you know he's good for it," the arranger said.

Tanner showed up at Capitol at the appointed time to find twenty-four other musicians, including Harry "Sweets" Edison. "There was no producer in the booth, but there was an engineer handling the microphones and the control panel," the trombonist recalled.

> We ran down about eight to ten tunes, but nothing was ever recorded. Kim Novak, his lady of the moment, was sitting in the rear of the studio with [the music publisher and Sinatra friend] Frank Military. Sinatra merely wanted to serenade her. At the end, he thanked everybody and told us we'd all get paid for our efforts. Then he took Kim's hand and with Military walked out the door and into the night.

Sinatra was enormously effective as Frankie Machine, a part that seemed to have been made for him and one that finally established him as a major dramatic star, against all logic and expectation. The movie holds up—despite the kitchen-sink creakiness of its black-and-white staging and the patent phoniness of its urban exteriors*—on the strength of his performance: you simply can't take your eyes off Sinatra.

It's hard to know what Brando would have done with Frankie Machine, but the great actor's physique and commanding presence would surely have turned the character into something other than a little man. Frank was powerfully drawn to the role not just because of the unforgettable withdrawal sequence, done in one take (in preparing for the part, he surreptitiously observed a heroin addict in withdrawal at a clinic and was shattered by the experience), but also because Frankie Machine's desperation spoke to Frank Sinatra in a deeper way than he might have been willing to let on. For all his bigness and all his greatness, he would always be a little man at heart.

"Frank Sinatra reports that he will take only a few days' rest at his Palm Springs home after finishing 'The Man With the Golden Arm,'" the Hollywood columnist Harrison Carroll reported on October 18. "Then he'll go to work on his own production, 'Johnny Concho.'" Frank, who had a way of ping-ponging between the sublime and the ridiculous, had decided to eschew recording for the rest of the year and—why not?—make a Western. His company, Kent Productions, would produce the picture; United Artists would distribute it; a member of his entourage, Don McGuire, would direct. In his characteristic slam-bang scheduling style of 1955, Frank would proceed more or less straight from Otto Preminger's Culver City set to Melrose Avenue's California Studios (where a new TV show called *Gunsmoke* was also shooting at the time) and jump on a horse. After that few days' rest.

It is doubtful that Frank rested alone, although it is certain that he didn't rest with Gloria Vanderbilt, with whom his relations had suddenly grown frosty. The announcement that Kent Productions had signed Vanderbilt to co-star in *Johnny Concho* (in which, Frank said, she would be "perfect for the romantic lead") hit the newspapers in late October, but in fact the signing had taken place earlier in the year, before Frank discovered that Vanderbilt had moved in with the director Sidney Lumet, whom she'd met in New York soon after

---

* Preminger told Peter Bogdanovich that he wanted to shoot on location in Chicago but that budgetary considerations made it impossible.

Sinatra left town for Australia.* Vanderbilt and Lumet, who would eventually marry, had also begun working together—her romantic dream—on a summer-stock production of *Picnic* and a television play.

On November 12, Vanderbilt arrived in Los Angeles, her two young sons and their nanny in tow, to start work on Sinatra's Western. The trip was a fiasco from start to finish. First, Frank failed to meet Vanderbilt at the airport—never a good sign with Frank—and though he did send flowers to her room at the Beverly Hills Hotel, he was "very cool" on the phone, she recalled. On the night of the fourteenth, Sinatra went to the Hollywood premiere of *Guys and Dolls*—with Deborah Kerr as his date. But the sensitive and patrician Vanderbilt's unpleasant interactions with *Johnny Concho*'s first-time director, the tough-talking Don McGuire, were what sealed the deal.

"I had sort of thought it was going to be a *High Noon* kind of movie," Vanderbilt remembered. "I mean, I was an intense, serious Method actress." But McGuire, a sometime actor and the not-so-stellar screenwriter of Sinatra's 1952 flop *Meet Danny Wilson* (as well as two Martin and Lewis movies, *3 Ring Circus* and *Artists and Models*, and the noir Western *Bad Day at Black Rock*), treated her like an heiress rather than an actress.

"Don McGuire said, 'Now, when you come out here it's blue-jean time.' And, 'When you come to rehearsals you don't have to dress up'—this kind of thing," Vanderbilt recalled. She returned to New York on November 17, five days after she'd arrived.

When Vanderbilt complained to Frank about McGuire, she recalled, "He said, 'I will deal with him in my own way.'" In truth, though, Sinatra dealt with Vanderbilt in his own way. After an approved spinmeister painted her to the press as a spoiled rich girl ("Heiress Gloria Vanderbilt pulled out of a costarring role in Frank Sinatra's first Western because her part wasn't big enough," the Associated Press reported), the part of Mary Dark, the town storekeeper's daughter who falls in love with Johnny Concho, quickly went to Phyllis Kirk, and Sinatra's first Western—though regrettably not his last—was shot in a fast five weeks. Gloria Vanderbilt wouldn't see Frank again for ten years.

———

Officially, Frank Sinatra celebrated his fortieth birthday on the set of *Johnny Concho,* cutting a cake while Don McGuire and Phyllis Kirk (and a wire-

---

* Vanderbilt maintains that Sinatra signed her at the same time to act in another film he planned to develop, a story Peter Lawford had recently brought him called *Ocean's 11*. This argues for a much earlier reconciliation between Sinatra and Lawford than other writers have claimed.

service photographer) looked on and the cast and crew sang him the Birthday Song. "He bowed and thanked the group, but shyly admitted he's getting to a point where he wants to forget birthdays," wrote the Hollywood columnist Jim Mahoney, who would later become Frank's publicist.

> He told me later in the day he's shopping around the Beverly Hills area for a piece of property on which to build a home.
> "I won't be able to do much about it until next year," he said, "since I've got another picture to do right after the first of the year and then another in Europe after that."

As usual, Frank wasn't letting the grass grow under his feet. The two pictures were *High Society*, which he would shoot in January in Newport, Rhode Island, with Bing Crosby and Grace Kelly, and *The Pride and the Passion*, with Cary Grant, which would start production in Spain in April. He was also scheduled to star in a biopic about the comedian Joe E. Lewis in the fall.

The newspapers seemed in a festive mood about Sinatra's big birthday. His old antagonists Westbrook Pegler and Lee Mortimer stayed mum. "Nothing has seemed impossible to Sinatra in his first two-score of years," the Associated Press's Bob Thomas bubbled. "He is now working on plans that extend to 1960." In expansive spirits between scenes on the *Johnny Concho* set, he told Thomas about his pet project, an international goodwill tour:

> "I've been wanting to do this for a long time," he said . . . "I'm trying to arrange it now so I'll have three weeks off between my next two pictures. I'd like to go out with two typically American stars—a name they all recognize like Gary Cooper and a girl like Marilyn Monroe. We'd put on a show in each of the world capitals for the benefit of children in that country. If it can be arranged, I'd like to do it in Moscow, too."

Taking advantage of the star's good mood, Thomas went for the big question. Since Frank was headed to Spain next year, would he be seeing Ava? There had been rumors that they might try to resume their rocky marriage.

Frank shook his head. "I don't know about that situation," he said.

He knew more than he was saying. Though Ava was now an expatriate and frequently filming overseas, there is evidence that Frank, an inveterate and free-spending long-distance dialer in the days when long-distance really meant something, had been in touch with her continually. "No matter what you read about his dates with Gloria Vanderbilt," columnist Erskine Johnson had written in March, "Frank Sinatra is still long-distancing Ava Gardner all over Europe. Night-after-night phone calls to the beauty who's still Mrs. Sinatra."

Over the spring and summer, Ava had returned to MGM to shoot interiors for her latest film, *Bhowani Junction,* and she and Sinatra were occasionally even seen in public together. According to her press agent Dave Hanna,

> Being in Hollywood reminded her of things about [Frank] she wanted to remember affectionately . . . She played his records constantly, and proclaimed to all and sundry that he was the greatest of the great . . . despite the split, the one dependable person in her life. Frank seemed to enjoy their new free-wheeling relationship and occasional displays of her dependence on him; he was known to instruct operators to get "Mrs. Sinatra" on the phone.

On the other hand, by November, according to Louella Parsons, Sinatra had told *The Pride and the Passion*'s director, Stanley Kramer (who had changed his mind about never working with Frank again), that if Kramer persisted in trying to get Mrs. Sinatra to play the female lead in the picture, he would quit. Parsons wrote,

> Considering that there has been talk that Frank and Ava were in communication about warming up their cold marriage, this comes as a bit of a surprise.
>
> It was believed that Ava was the one holding out against appearing with her ex-husband who is due in Madrid in April for the Kramer picture.

They fought when they were together, now they were fighting when they were apart: What else was new?

––––––––

Otto Preminger had sped up the production schedule of *The Man with the Golden Arm* so that the film and its star would be eligible to contend in the 1955 Academy Awards. The picture opened in New York on December 15. The *Times*'s Bosley Crowther, who just a month earlier had been so gaga for Sinatra in *The Tender Trap,* was underwhelmed. Having noted that Preminger's movie had been denied a Production Code seal because of its controversial content, the critic went on to say that "for all the delicacy of the subject and for all the pathological shivers in a couple of scenes, there is nothing very surprising or exciting about 'The Man With the Golden Arm.' It is a pretty plain and unimaginative looksee at a lower-depths character with a perilous weakness for narcotics that he miraculously overcomes in the end." As for Sinatra's performance, "plausible" was as far as the hard-to-please Mr. Crowther was willing to go.

But in truth, "plausible" spoke volumes where Frank's fast-growing ability as a dramatic actor was concerned. And remarkably, the critical acclaim for his performance was nearly universal this time around, despite a certain distaste for the movie itself. SINATRA'S ACTING REDEEMS SORDID FILM ON DRUG HABIT, read the headline in the then-staid *Los Angeles Times*. And the *Saturday Review*'s Arthur Knight was eloquent, referring to Frank as the

> thin, unhandsome one-time crooner who has an incredible instinct for the look, the gesture, the shading of the voice that suggests tenderness, uncertainty, weakness, fatigue, despair. He brings to the character much that has not been written into the script, a shade of sweetness, a sense of edgy indestructibility that actually creates the appeal and intrinsic interest of the role . . . a truly virtuoso performance . . . he is an actor of rare ability.

The only off note was calling Sinatra a "one-time crooner." Maybe Knight was referring to the change in Frank's singing style. Still, the fact that the man who had won both the *Down Beat* and the *Metronome* year-end polls as top male vocalist and the man who was Hollywood's newest dramatic star were one and the same was nothing short of miraculous. The fact that the same man had made *Johnny Concho* was, well, nothing short of Frank.

The Rat Pack was born in the middle of the 1950s, not the end, and Dean, Sammy, Joey, and Peter were nowhere near it. Frank was present at the creation. It all began in Holmby Hills, an exclusive enclave of West Los Angeles just off Sunset Boulevard, in the big white-brick house on South Mapleton Drive that belonged to the fifty-five-year-old Humphrey Bogart and his young wife, Lauren Bacall.

Bogart was a legendary consumer of alcohol ("I think the whole world is three drinks behind," he used to say, "and it's high time it caught up") and a notorious rebel when it came to all things Hollywood. Unlike most movie stars, he didn't like to go out, couldn't stand all the seeing-and-being-seen malarkey of Tinseltown, and so the world came to him—or at least that part of the world he considered amusing: such glittering old-Hollywood luminaries as Judy Garland and her husband, Sid Luft, the David Nivens, Spencer Tracy, Ira

Gershwin, the Rodeo Drive restaurateur Mike Romanoff and his wife, Gloria, Bogart's agent Irving "Swifty" Lazar, and Sinatra.

Frank, who was agonizingly insecure about many things, "craved class like a junkie craves the needle," in the words of his valet George Jacobs. And in Sinatra's eyes, Humphrey Bogart, who had grown up rich in Manhattan and then spent the rest of his life living it down, was pure class. Sinatra idolized everything about the wry, disaffected Bogart, from the way he dressed (custom-made suits, shirts, shoes; sport jackets with pocket squares; fedoras from Knox and Cavanagh to cover his receding hairline) to the way he drank and smoked, to the cool irony that colored his worldview. Cool looked good to Frank Sinatra. Unattainable, but good.

Sinatra had begun hanging around the Bogarts' house in the early 1950s, when he was down on his luck: Bogie and Bacall took him in; his disaffection with Hollywood matched theirs. As did his capacity for alcohol. Even after his miraculous comeback, Frank continued drinking: success held some demons at bay but also brought on new ones.

One late night when Bogart, Sinatra, and some of the other usual suspects were imbibing in the swank upstairs room at Romanoff's, Bacall, much younger than the rest and sharp-tongued, looked around and said, "I see the rat pack is all here."

Bogart liked that. In his usual spirit of irony, he proposed that those present form a semiofficial club under that name. "In order to qualify," Lauren Bacall wrote in her memoir, "one had to be addicted to nonconformity, staying up late, drinking, laughing, and not caring what anyone thought or said about us."

"The Holmby Hills Rat Pack held its first annual meeting last night at Romanoff's restaurant in Beverly Hills and elected officers for the coming year," the columnist Joe Hyams wrote in the December 15, 1955, *New York Herald Tribune*. "Named to executive positions were: Frank Sinatra, pack master; Judy Garland, first vice-president; Lauren Bacall, den mother; Humphrey Bogart, rat-in-charge-of public relations; Irving Lazar, recording secretary and treasurer."

"Remember, it was all a joke," Bogart later told Hyams. The club's officers and its "platform of iconoclasm—they were against everything and everyone, including themselves"—were, according to Bacall, "Bogie's way of thumbing his nose at Hollywood."

That was Bogie. Sinatra, who had been odd man out for so long but now found himself so very in, was going to have to recalibrate his position from here on.

———

Frank had spent very little time in any one place in 1955, let alone the house at 320 North Carolwood Drive—in Holmby Hills, just across Sunset from Bogie and Betty's place—occupied by his ex-wife and three children. But he did stop by for long enough to present his fifteen-year-old daughter, Nancy, with a gift-wrapped Chevrolet convertible for Christmas.

————

He threw a monster New Year's Eve party in Palm Springs, a brawl that extended well into the following day. Noël Coward, arriving with his partner—in those days he would have been called a boyfriend—Graham Payn, on New Year's Day, found the scene pleasant but chaotic. "It is enjoyable but not the acme of peace on account of people of all shapes and sizes swirling through this very small house like the relentless waves of the sea," he wrote in his journal.

> Their swirling is accompanied by a bongo drum band in the living-room . . . The Danny Kayes, the [Charles] Vidors, the Romanoffs, the Goldwyns, Lucille Ball, Mike Todd, etc., are all in and out and the noise is considerable. Bogey pushed Irving Lazar into the pool and Irving Lazar pushed Bogey into the pool and there is a great deal of "fucking" and "shitting" and other indications that the new year will be no less bawdy than the old one. The prevailing chaos is curiously domi-nated by Frankie, who contrives, apparently without effort, to be cheer-ful and unflagging and, at the same time, sees that everyone has drinks and is looked after. He is a remarkable personality—tough, vulnerable and somehow touching. He is also immeasurably kind.

In the same entry, Coward also wrote, "Frankie is enchanting as usual and, as usual, he has a 'broad' installed with whom he, as well as everyone else, is bored stiff. She is blonde, cute, and determined, but I fear her determination will avail her very little with Betty Bacall on the warpath."

That Sinatra and Bacall had eyes for each other was an open secret in Hol-lywood, one that Humphrey Bogart apparently chose to ignore. It was compli-cated. Though he and his young wife were a famously devoted couple, Bogart had only recently ended a long affair with his makeup woman and wig maker Verita Peterson, a relationship he'd begun when his previous marriage was breaking up. Bacall had been deeply wounded by the liaison but had looked the other way to save face. And she had long been drawn to Frank, who was much closer to her in age than Bogie. Bogart had also been unwell for some time, suffering from coughing fits and having difficulty eating.

That New Year's Day, "as dinner came to a close, Frank, looking sad, begged us to stay on," Bacall wrote.

> Not begging in the true sense, but begging in Frank's sense—looking very forlorn and alone. I thought, "Oh, the poor guy, we should stay." I looked at Bogie and he said, "Sorry, old pal, we've got to get back to town." In the car going home, I said, "We should have stayed." Bogie said, "No, we shouldn't. You must always remember we have a life of our own that has nothing to do with Frank. He chose to live the way he's living—alone. It's too bad if he's lonely, but that's his choice. We have our own road to travel, never forget that—we can't live his life."

5

||||||||||||

I want a long crescendo.

—FRANK SINATRA TO NELSON RIDDLE, JANUARY 1956

Frank carried the sheer exuberance of the previous year with him into KHJ Radio Studios on Monday night, January 9, 1956, when he arrived to record four songs for the album that would become *Songs for Swingin' Lovers!* The exclamation point was a fitting punctuation for his life at that moment. He was clicking on all cylinders—making great records, turning in memorable movie performances, earning serious money. *Time*'s cover story on him in August had estimated his income for that year at "something close to $1,000,000"—an astronomical number in the mid-1950s. The old days, the bad, poor days, were a blip in the rearview mirror; the limbo of his marriage to Ava was forgotten for the moment. "Swingin'" was the operative word.

He usually strolled into Studio A, upstairs at KHJ, at about 8:00 p.m. and always with an entourage: in this period, the group would have consisted of Jimmy Van Heusen (one of whose songs would be recorded on the night of January 9); Hank Sanicola; Don McGuire, who was directing Frank during the day in *Johnny Concho*; a prizefighter or two; sundry members of the Holmby Hills Rat Pack; and the blonde or brunette of the moment. The atmosphere crackled with excitement that night, as was usually the case at Sinatra recording sessions. "There was always a crowd at those Sinatra sessions on Melrose," the trombonist Milt Bernhart recalled.

> They should have charged admission! Because the studio had been a radio theater, it had an auditorium. And the place was packed to the back. You weren't just playing a record date, you were playing a performance. They took a great chance on the people applauding, because they could get caught up in the thing, and ruin a take . . . but believe me, they were sitting on the edge. And it was an "in" crowd: movie stars, disc jockeys. It was big, big . . . It was hard to get in, you had to be invited. But they'd fill the damn place!

For Nelson Riddle, the anticipation was less pleasurable. "At a Sinatra session the air was usually loaded with electricity," he remembered. But the thoughts that raced through my head were hardly ones to calm the nerves. On the contrary—questions such as: "Will he like the arrangement?" and "Is the tempo comfortable for him?" were soon answered. If he didn't make any reference to the arrangement, chances are it was acceptable. And as far as the tempo was concerned, he often set that with a crisp snap of his fingers or a characteristic rhythmic hunching of his shoulders.

The tempo that night was upbeat, in keeping with the album's preplanned scheme. (The one slower-paced number Frank recorded, Andy Razaf and Eubie Blake's "Memories of You," didn't make it onto *Swingin' Lovers*.) The other three songs on the roster were Sammy Fain, Irving Kahal, and Pierre Norman's "You Brought a New Kind of Love to Me," Johnny Mercer and Van Heusen's "I Thought About You," and Mack Gordon and Josef Myrow's "You Make Me Feel So Young," a song that had debuted, without much of a splash, in the 1946 musical film *Three Little Girls in Blue*. Riddle and Sinatra were about to turn it into an instant classic.

Songs for Swingin' Lovers! was dance music of the hippest kind: swinging, infectious, supremely listenable. Rock 'n' roll might have been on its way in— 1956 was the year it would land like a falling grand piano—but its appeal at first was merely visceral and primitive. Sinatra and Riddle had visceral and sophisticated locked up in a way that would last.

The key lay in the hand-in-glove development of Sinatra as a singer and Riddle as an arranger. It wasn't just that Frank's voice had deepened; it had also toughened, through time, heartbreak, cigarettes, and liquor. "I didn't care for his original voice," Riddle once said. "I thought it was far too syrupy. I prefer to hear the rather angular person come through . . . To me his voice only became interesting during the time when I started to work with him . . . He became a fascinating interpreter of lyrics, and actually he could practically have talked the thing for me and it would have been all right."

Interestingly, Sinatra had recently been quoted in Walter Winchell's column as saying, "Everything I learned I owe to Mabel Mercer." He was speaking of the trailblazing vocalist who began as an idiosyncratic chanteuse of the American popular song and eventually became a virtual diseuse, sitting in an armchair onstage and literally speaking the lyrics to piano accompaniment. Audiences hung on every syllable.

"I've always believed that the written word is first, always first," Frank once said. "Not belittling the music behind me, it's really only a curtain . . . you must look at the lyric, and understand it."

But of course there was more to it than that. A singer sings in tempo, and something about Sinatra's tempo had changed radically in just a couple of years. "During the Capitol period," Charles L. Granata writes, Frank "began to take more noticeable liberties with the rhythm and timing of his vocal lines."

The conductor Leonard Slatkin—both of whose parents played on the *Swingin' Lovers* sessions—said, "Imagine that you're delivering a sentence in a particular cadence, a particular rhythm, where the strong syllables come on strong beats and the weak syllables come on weak ones. When you listen to Sinatra's songs, even ones that are highly rhythmically charged, you'll find that often he'll delay that strong syllable. It may not occur right on the downbeat. It will be just that fraction late, giving a little more punch to the word itself. I'm sure he thought about it. I'm sure that this was not just improvisatory on his part."

It wasn't. "Syncopation in music is important, of course, particularly if it's a rhythm song," Sinatra said. "It can't be 'one-two-three-four/one-two-three-four,' because it becomes stodgy. So, syncopation enters the scene, and it's 'one-two,' then maybe a little delay, and then 'three,' and then another longer delay, and then 'four.' It all has to do with delivery."

And his delivery was now at its peak. Listen to Frank's version of "You Make Me Feel So Young" on *Songs for Swingin' Lovers!*, and you hear a great singer in joyous command of every component of his art—voice, tempo, lyrical understanding, expression. It is (imagine the seats in the radio theater, packed with rapt listeners) simply a magnificent performance. It is also a perfect union of singer, arrangement, and musicians. And the secret eminence behind it all was Tommy Dorsey.

Three powerful forces had come together in 1939 when the great bandleader hired the genius arranger Sy Oliver and then lured Frank Sinatra away from the Harry James orchestra. Oliver wrote charts that wedded strings to horns in a new and powerful way, and a Dorsey signature sound was born.

Sinatra mainly sang ballads when he was with Dorsey; still, he had ears—great ears—and he heard what Oliver could do with an up-tempo number. A couple of years after Frank went out on his own, Nelson Riddle joined the Dorsey band as third trombonist. Riddle was only a so-so horn player, but as a budding arranger he took careful note of Sy Oliver's writing. When it came time to write up-tempo charts for Sinatra, Riddle brought along not only his deep grounding in the complex orchestral textures of the French impressionist composers (Debussy, Ravel, Jacques Ibert) but also his big-band chops.

"In planning *Songs for Swingin' Lovers* [which Riddle called "perhaps the most successful album I did with Frank Sinatra"], Frank commented on 'sustained strings' as part of the background to be used," the arranger wrote.

Perhaps unconsciously, my ear recalled some of the fine arrangements Sy Oliver had done for Tommy, using sustained strings but also employing rhythmic fills by brass and saxes to generate excitement. The strings, by observing crescendos in the right places, add to the pace and tension of such writing without getting in the way. It was a further embroidery on this basic idea to add the bass trombone (George Roberts) plus the unmistakably insinuating fills of Harry "Sweets" Edison on Harmon-muted trumpet. I wish that all effective formulas could be arrived at so simply.

"All the preparation in the world, however," Peter Levinson wrote in his biography of Riddle, "couldn't replace the reality of having a core group of first-rate musicians challenged by having first-rate arrangements and interacting with a singer they respected who had emerged from the same big band background."

The musicians assembled on the stage in Studio A were truly a starry group, an amalgam of some of the finest classical string players and jazz instrumentalists around: Frank demanded no less. Besides the Slatkins, George Roberts, and Sweets Edison, the orchestra included trumpeter Zeke Zarchy, another Dorsey alumnus; the great Duke Ellington valve trombonist Juan Tizol (who was also the composer of "Caravan" and "Perdido"); alto saxophonist Harry Klee, who doubled on flute (he can be heard swinging beautifully on the outro of "Feel So Young"); and Sinatra's musical right hand, pianist Bill Miller. And then there was the sad-eyed trombonist with a jutting lower lip, Milt Bernhart, who played a crucial role in the most famous song Frank Sinatra ever recorded.

As Frank Sinatra Jr. tells the story, his father had finished the second recording session of the week in the early hours of Wednesday, January 11, 1956, and planned to go to Palm Springs first thing on Thursday. The final *Swingin' Lovers* session was set for Monday the sixteenth, and Frank wanted to rest up over the weekend.

Instead, though, producer Voyle Gilmore called him at 1:00 a.m. on Wednesday and said that because the album looked to be a big seller, Capitol's vice president Alan Livingston had made an executive decision to put three more songs onto the twelve-inch LP. This would necessitate an extra recording session on Thursday the twelfth. Frank was not pleased.

He phoned Riddle at home, waking him up, and told him that he had to arrange three more songs immediately. "Sinatra gave him three songs real fast. Either he had them already written down or he pulled them out of a hat," Frank junior said.

Nelson got out of bed and started writing. By seven o'clock the next morning he got two songs to the copyist. He then had a few hours sleep and started writing again at about one o'clock in the afternoon. Nelson knew that "you-know-who" wasn't going to be a very happy person that night because he did not want to be working . . . With [Riddle's wife] Doreen at the wheel of their station wagon, Nelson was in the back seat finishing the arrangement while holding a flashlight.

Rosemary Riddle Acerra notes that her father used a leaf from the dining-room table as a laptop desk.

When the Riddles arrived at the studio, according to Frank junior, Vern Yocum, the copyist, had several of his associates there. Sinatra recorded the first two tunes with Nelson and the orchestra while the copyists were writing down the last arrangement.

The first two songs were Mabel Wayne and Billy Rose's "It Happened in Monterey" and Isham Jones and Gus Kahn's "Swingin' down the Lane." Frank then shifted gears and, with a chorus, recorded a single called "Flowers Mean Forgiveness." Then he returned to the album, with Cole Porter's "I've Got You Under My Skin."

Sinatra's usual method with Riddle when planning out arrangements was to sketch out ideas verbally—"make it sound like Puccini"; "give me some Brahms in bar eight"—while Nelson took rapid notes. All this usually happened well in advance of recording. In this case, with one day's notice, Frank told Riddle about "I've Got You Under My Skin": "I want a long crescendo."

"I don't think he was aware of the way I was going to achieve that crescendo," Riddle later said, "but he wanted an instrumental interlude that would be exciting and carry the orchestra up and then come on down where he would finish out the arrangement vocally."

The arranger's mind turned immediately to one of his masters, Maurice Ravel, and the French composer's great and sensuous ballet, *Boléro*. Riddle has written of the piece's "absolutely tantalizing slow addition of instruments to this long, long crescendo, which is really the message of *Boléro* . . . [I]t is excruciating in its deliberately slow addition of pressure. Now that's sex in a piece of music."

His rough idea was to write a chart with an Afro-Cuban flavor—the mambo movement was then at its peak, with Cuban bandleaders like Pérez Prado, Machito, and the Spanish-born, Cuban-trained Xavier Cugat in the forefront—but with the clock ticking, he was stuck. He phoned George Roberts for advice. "Why don't you steal the pattern out of Kenton's '23 Degrees North, 82 Degrees West'?" the trombonist, an alumnus of Stan Kenton's big band, said.

Kenton's band had been incorporating Latin influences into its performances since the mid-1940s; the title of his 1952 hit "23 Degrees North, 82
Degrees West" referred to the map coordinates of Cuba. Riddle didn't steal the
pattern, but he got the message. He wrote a long, sexy crescendo for Roberts's
bass trombone and the string section, and at the bridge—the song's middle
section—he sketched out eight bars of chord symbols for the trombonist (and
fellow Kenton alumnus) Milt Bernhart to use as a framework. Bernhart's solo
itself was to be totally improvised, and it would have to be good.

"I've Got You Under My Skin" was the last song Sinatra recorded on the
night of January 12, which means that by the time the tape started rolling,
the clock might have ticked over into the early hours of Friday the thirteenth.
First, though, the band ran through the number once while Frank stood in the
control booth with Riddle, producer Voyle Gilmore, and recording engineer
John Palladino. Sinatra was listening carefully, making sure the recording balances were correct and the arrangement sounded right. Riddle's heart was in
his throat. Though he had dashed off the chart under maximum pressure, he
knew Frank expected nothing less than greatness. "There's only one person
in this world I'm afraid of," Riddle once confided to George Roberts. "Not
physically—but afraid of nonetheless. It's Frank, because you can't tell what
he's going to do. One minute he'll be fine, but he can change very fast."

When the run-through was finished, though, the battle-scarred studio
musicians stood as one and gave Riddle a warm ovation, "probably because
somebody knew that he wrote it in a hurry," Bill Miller recalled. Years later,
in an interview with Riddle, Jonathan Schwartz asked him if he hadn't said to
himself about the arrangement, "This is awfully good." "No, I probably said,
'Wow, isn't it nice that I finished it in time,'" Nelson answered.

But Frank knew it was awfully good. Though he was usually One-Take
Charlie on movie sets, in the recording studio he would spend as much time as
necessary to get a song right. Still, Milt Bernhart recalled, "it was unusual that
he would have to go past four or five takes." Accordingly, "I left the best stuff I
played on the first five takes," Bernhart said. But, the trombonist remembered,
Sinatra knew that something special was happening.

Frank kept saying, "Let's do another." This was unusual for Sinatra! I
was about ready to collapse—I was running out of gas! Then, toward
the tenth take or so, someone in the booth said, "We didn't get enough
bass . . . could we get the trombone nearer to a microphone?" I mean,
what had they been doing? There was a mike there for the brass, up on
a very high riser. "Can you get up to that one?" they asked. And I said,
"Well, no—I'm not that tall." So they went looking for a box, and I don't

know where he found one, but none other than Frank Sinatra went and got a box, and brought it over for me to stand on!

Eleven takes, twelve, thirteen—some of them would have been false starts, only seconds long, but some went on longer, until Frank raised a hand, shaking his head, stopping the music, and telling the band and the control booth what had to change.

Then take twenty-two. "Milt perspired a lot to start with," recalls guitarist Bob Bain, who played on the session. Now the trombonist was soaked through. "He looked at me and said, 'I don't have another one left.'"

The song starts at a lope, in 2/4 time, with a baritone sax or bass clarinet playing the now-famous repeating figure—bum-ba-dum-BOM ba-dum-BOM ba-dum-BOM—in the background. Despite the lateness of the hour and the number of takes, despite the number of unfiltered Camels he has smoked that day, Sinatra, under his Cavanagh fedora, is singing as easily and bell-clearly as if he had just stepped out of the shower and taken it into his mind to do a little Cole Porter. Perhaps, now and then, as he loses himself in the great song and the sound of the great band around him, he closes his eyes. The heavenly strings and the bright brass interplay effortlessly behind the first and second choruses, and then, as Frank caresses the last lines of the bridge—

But each time that I do, just the thought of you
Makes me stop before I begin . . .

—Roberts and the strings lift the long crescendo higher and higher and higher until it seems they can go no higher and then Milt Bernhart goes wild on his slide trombone, simply blowing his lungs out. It is to Sinatra's immense credit that his powerful final chorus, driving the song home, is as strong in its own right as Bernhart's historic solo.

"After the session, I was packing up, Frank stuck his head out of the booth, and said, 'Why don't you come in the booth and listen to it?'" the trombonist recalled.

So I did—and there was a chick in there, a pretty blonde, and she was positively beaming. He said to me, "Listen!" That was special! You know, it never really went past that. He never has been much for slathering around empty praise. He just doesn't throw it around very easily. If you weren't able to play like that, then why would they have called you? You knew that you were there—we all were there—at Frank's behest. Rarely, if ever, would he directly point something out in the studio.

Another time, Bernhart remembered, Sinatra praised the French horn player Vince DeRosa on executing a difficult passage by telling the band, "I wish you guys could have heard Vince DeRosa last night—I could have hit him in the mouth!"

"We all knew what he meant—he had loved it!" Bernhart said. "And believe me, he reserved comments like that only for special occasions. You see, it was very hard for him to say, 'It was the greatest thing I ever heard . . .' But that's Sinatra. He could sing with the grace of a poet, but when he's talking to you, it's Jersey!"

———

By the mid-1950s, when Frank had come back and pushed his career into overdrive, Bing Crosby was pondering retirement. He had turned fifty; he had recently lost his wife, the mother of their four young sons, to ovarian cancer. He had less hair than ever (he'd begun wearing a toupee onstage in his thirties), more padding around the waist. He had plenty of money. He also had family and kidney problems. The golf course looked tempting. "I've always said that my favorite kind of picture would be one that opened with a shot of me sitting in a rocking chair on a front porch," he told an interviewer in 1954. "The rest of the picture would be what I saw."

At that point, Bing had just finished making *The Country Girl,* a nonmusical adaptation of a Clifford Odets play about an alcoholic stage actor trying to make a comeback. His co-star (and offstage reputedly his paramour) had been the twenty-four-year-old Grace Kelly, somewhat implausibly playing his suffering young wife (but winning an Oscar for her troubles; Crosby was nominated). A year earlier, Kelly had with equal implausibility played Ava Gardner's competition for the fifty-two-year-old Clark Gable in *Mogambo,* the movie Ava shot on location in Africa while a down-on-his-luck Frank, who'd accompanied her, fretted and cooled his heels.

Despite Sinatra and Crosby's many radio shows together and even a couple of joint appearances on television, they'd never made a movie together. That changed in January 1956, when they teamed with Grace Kelly and Louis Armstrong (along with his All Stars) in MGM's *High Society,* a musical remake of *The Philadelphia Story,* with a score by Cole Porter.

Movie musicals were an endangered genre in the mid-1950s, quickly losing ground to TV, which not only gave audiences visual entertainment at home but also was bringing new visions of reality to daily life—visions that seemed to jibe less and less with the notion of characters' suddenly breaking into song. It was a time when the movie studios themselves were imperiled by television and the rise of independent producers, some of whom were powerful actors like James Stewart—and Bing Crosby and Frank Sinatra—who were putting together their own film projects. But some of the studios, mainly MGM and 20th Century Fox, were still turning out big musical entertainments, using Technicolor and wide-screen processes like Todd-AO, VistaVision, and CinemaScope to gain a visual edge on television while it was still possible.

High Society, in Technicolor and VistaVision, was to be a major production in every way. The project first began to coalesce after the producer Sol C. Siegel paid Cole Porter $250,000 to write his first movie score in a decade; Crosby, Sinatra, and Kelly were soon brought on board with similarly rich deals (Crosby's company co-produced, and Frank received the same fee as Porter). The great songwriter Johnny Green ("Body and Soul," "Out of Nowhere"), also an MGM conductor and arranger, was to supervise the music; Conrad Salinger, another Metro stalwart, would collaborate on the orchestrations with Riddle. The director was the likable journeyman Charles Walters, who had helmed the slick and uncompelling *The Tender Trap,* and some of the problems with the final film can be laid at his feet.

The Philadelphia Story had been a triumph of pre–World War II American movie comedy. Produced by Joseph L. Mankiewicz and brilliantly adapted from Philip Barry's play by Donald Ogden Stewart, the film sparkled in every way, from George Cukor's pitch-perfect seriocomic direction to the incomparable starring troika of Katharine Hepburn, Cary Grant, and James Stewart to the Franz Waxman score and beautiful black-and-white cinematography by Joseph Ruttenberg. As a comedy of manners, as a paragon of prewar American filmmaking, the movie remains magical in every detail. It has Shakespearean charisma.

High Society had big shoes to fill, and on paper it stood a fighting chance. Crosby and Sinatra were giants, Kelly was a dreamily beautiful screen presence, Louis Armstrong was not only a great musician but visual and vocal catnip, and composers didn't come any better than Cole Porter.

The Philadelphia Story benefited from all its brilliant elements and also from its elegiac feeling for the decline of a class, along with the powerful sense of romance that was still believable before the war, the Holocaust, and the bomb. (Just listen to a few bars of the Waxman score, and it all comes flooding back.)

High Society, set amid the majestic "cottages" of Newport, Rhode Island, rather than on Philadelphia's Main Line, tries for a sense of elegy—the grand old ways are giving way to the vulgar new ones; the rich are shuttering their mansions and selling them to save on taxes—but it doesn't try very hard. Mainly it proceeds amid the garish Technicolor light of the Eisenhower 1950s, and it's hard to care much about the goings-on: the peccadilloes of the wealthy; the culture clash between the proletarian reporters for the gossip magazine *Spy* (Sinatra and Celeste Holm) and the society toffs they envy and disdain. In the end, the only compelling things about the movie are its faces and moments and sounds. Fortunately, there are enough of all three to make *High Society* worth watching.

Frank is good as Macaulay "Mike" Connor, and he's fun to watch, especially when he breaks into one of Porter's terrific songs (although Bing gets the best solo number by far, the great "I Love You, Samantha"), but as is distinctly not the case with his portrayal of Frankie Machine, he isn't believable, not even for a second, as a hack writer aspiring to higher things, including Grace Kelly's Tracy Lord. He looks great with his Technicolor tan and his luxuriant toupee ("Frankie now looks positively furry—instead of fringey—on top," wrote Earl Wilson), and his snazzy sport coats and straw fedoras seem to have come straight from KHJ Radio Studios onto the MGM set, but strangely for a man who could act so wonderfully in dramatic roles and convey yearning so heartrendingly in torch songs, the quality of yearning that Jimmy Stewart projects with such absolute believability in his Oscar-winning turn in *The Philadelphia Story* is entirely lacking in Frank's Mike Connor.

The irony of Sinatra's playing a reporter, and a reporter for a gossip magazine at that, is delicious. But there was one thing Frank did bring convincingly to the role: in Philip Barry's play and in both movie adaptations, Macaulay Connor is an outsider, a bluish-collar trespasser in the world of the wealthy. In real life, Frank Sinatra, no matter how much wealth and fame accrued to him, always felt himself to be an outsider, an Italian-American kid from Hoboken who had crashed the big party. This is what put the chip on his shoulder, and there's a hint of that chip in his portrayal of the Anglo-Irish Mike Connor. (Shades of his father's prizefighting nom de ring, Marty O'Brien.) Sinatra emanates a street-kid defensiveness that's interesting to watch, if not necessarily apropos. That defensiveness might also have contained a germ of his real insecurity about Grace Kelly, bricklayer's daughter though she might have been.

The two don't entirely click together on-screen, which is a pity. This is partly the fault of John Patrick's merely serviceable re-adaptation of Barry's play—Mike's passionate speech to Tracy when they're in a clinch ("You've got fires banked down in you, hearth-fires and holocausts") is trimmed down to a few words and some stage business—and maybe the result of a slight lack of chemistry between Sinatra and Kelly, one of the few female co-stars who seem to have dodged his fabled checklist (but who seems to have had quite a checklist of her own). "Sinatra got a kick out of 'Gracie,' as he called her, but he had felt humiliated pining around the set of *Mogambo* over Ava in front of Grace," George Jacobs recalled. "He was certain she saw him as a major loser and he could not bring himself to make a play for her." Frank and Grace had reportedly gone on a date about a year earlier; he is said to have been drunk when he picked her up, to have sobbed to her about Ava, and then to have tried to manhandle her. A friend of Kelly's said that Frank phoned her the next day to apologize and the two of them laughed about it, but that was that for romance.

He also would have known that even as *High Society* was shooting, Kelly, enacting a sort of reverse version of her film role, had fallen deeply in love with—and would soon marry—Prince Rainier III of Monaco. Her destiny was to be a princess; this would be her last movie.

And Kelly's subtraction from motion pictures was a real loss. She was of course lovely to look at, but she could also act and was a beguiling screen presence when the material was right. It's a shame that *High Society* required her to follow in Katharine Hepburn's quicksilver footsteps, and a shame that the movie wasn't better: Kelly made a wonderful Tracy Lord, and even though she couldn't really hold up her end musically—nor was she required to; she only sang a little harmony with Crosby on "True Love" and warbled a bit in a drunk scene—she stood up strong alongside her formidable co-stars.

Bing Crosby is said to have been unrequitedly besotted by Kelly, and he brings the full force of his balked ardor to playing C. K. Dexter-Haven, the wastrel playboy who was once married to Tracy Lord and is still in love with her. The two of them have the on-screen chemistry that Sinatra and Kelly lack, a reaction made stranger and more poignant by Bing's age: while his hairpiece is as lush as Frank's, he looks a decade older than his fifty-three years, and in repose his face is sullen, even mean. But his Dexter lights up around Tracy, and even at the thought of her: his minor-key "I Love You, Samantha" (Tracy's middle name, and Dexter's pet name for her), sung as he dresses for a party celebrating her engagement to another man, is a tour de force of great vocalizing, great stage business—he winds his watch and self-consciously pats his tummy as he puts on his tux—and great acting. The song is one of the movie's three highlights, and Bing gets to share in the other two. There's his charming duet with Louis Armstrong on "Now You Has Jazz," and then there's the irresistible "Well, Did You Evah?" with Sinatra.

Crosby and Armstrong had sung together often, on the radio and on records, but Bing and Frank had never recorded before as a twosome; Sinatra said that the chance to duet with Crosby was his main reason for doing the movie. The song-and-dance routine takes place at a bachelor ball for George Kittredge (John Lund), the society stiff who is engaged to Tracy: as Dexter and

Mike get loaded on champagne in the mansion's library, they dish musically—
and to 1950s ears titillatingly—on the general stuffiness of the surroundings:

> MIKE (*singing*): Have you heard that Mimsy Starr, she got pinched in
> the Astor Bar?
> DEXTER: Sauced again, eh?
> MIKE: She was stoned!
> DEXTER: Well, did you evah!
> MIKE: Never!
> BOTH (*singing*): What a swell party this is!

The two play perfectly together, as though they'd been waiting their whole
lives to do this number. Neither man dominates; each brings his own genius
as a singing actor. It's a miraculously graceful scene, one of the greatest in
movie musicals (Charles Walters, who might not have been a brilliant director but sure knew how to choreograph, staged it). Sinatra and Crosby, Jeanine
Basinger writes in *The Star Machine,* had to

> sing, dance, hit their camera marks, respect the sophisticated Cole
> Porter lyrics, deliver scripted dialogue, stay within their characters, pre-
> tend to be slightly drunk, keep the beat of the orchestra playback, move
> around a specially designed library set with limited space while fol-
> lowing a specific choreography that had to look improvised, and never
> forget that they were rivals for the audience's affection . . . They had
> to watch out for each other in more ways than one. (Each was keenly
> aware of the other's star power.) . . . These men are what stars are,
> doing what stars do. They seem as if they're making it up right in front
> of you. (The illusion of stardom is always the illusion of ease.)

And part of the illusion was that Frank and Bing were pals. In fact, Sinatra was
intimidated by his onetime idol, who was so cool and aloof offstage that even
Crosby's longtime comedy partner Bob Hope would say after his death, "You
know, I never liked Bing. He was a son of a bitch."

Yet Frank really had been waiting his whole life to do this duet: the boy who
had dreamed of being Bing Crosby was now meeting him on—professionally,
at least—level ground.

———

During the filming of *High Society,* the crew nicknamed Crosby "Nembutal"
and Sinatra "Dexedrine." In 1956, as in the previous year, Frank continued to

live as though the devil himself were prodding him with a pitchfork. "So long as I keep busy, I feel great," he told a reporter. The problems occurred when he wasn't busy enough: sleep, solitude, and leisure did not sit well with him. He was like a whole-body case of restless leg syndrome. Though he would shoot only three movies in 1956, as compared with the five he made in 1955, he would travel to Spain to shoot *The Pride and the Passion;* play three three-week stands at the Sands while commuting back to L.A. to make records and attend to motion-picture business; sing "The Star-Spangled Banner" at the Democratic National Convention; return to the Paramount Theater in Times Square to do a week with the Tommy and Jimmy Dorsey Orchestra; and sign a $3 million television contract with ABC. For starters. But mainly, that year (if there could be such a thing as mainly with Sinatra), he would make records.

He went into the recording studio twenty-one times in 1956, the most sessions he had done since 1947. He was effervescing with musical ideas, and beginning in February he had a new laboratory in which to explore them. In 1955, Capitol Records, cash rich after its recent purchase by the British music publishing and recording colossus EMI, had broken ground for a monumental

Sinatra and Bing Crosby play perfectly together in their duet in *High Society.* In reality, Frank was intimidated by his onetime idol, who was cool and aloof offstage.

new headquarters at the corner of Hollywood Boulevard and Vine Street in downtown Hollywood; in February 1956, the new building opened: a cylindrical tower designed by the architect Welton Becket to replicate a stack of records. Atop the Capitol Records Tower, as the structure came to be called, stood a sixty-foot spire containing a blinking red light that spelled out "Hollywood" in Morse code.

The building's ground floor contained three recording studios. Studios A and B were built to accommodate full orchestras; the more intimate Studio C was designed for jingles, voice-overs, and smaller sessions. Naturally, everything in the facility was state-of-the-art, mid-1950s style, from the shock-mounted concrete echo chambers built deep below street level to the tube condenser microphones, speakers, and tape-editing equipment in the rooms above.

It was all pristine and beautiful, a kind of cathedral of sound, and Sinatra's first project there was appropriately high-minded and daringly ambitious: commercial considerations notwithstanding, Frank wanted to lead an orchestra once again.

He'd done so once before, back in the Columbia (and 78 rpm) days, with *Frank Sinatra Conducts the Music of Alec Wilder*. The 1946 album contained six of Wilder's meditative compositions, pieces with titles like "Air for English Horn," "Slow Dance," and "Theme and Variations," and while the enterprise was only possible because of the bushels of money Sinatra's popular records were bringing in to Columbia at the time, it proved to Frank and some small part of the world (including the orchestra players he conducted) that he was more than just a Voice.

Ten years on, Sinatra had the same kind of commercial power, and then some. In 1956, he was making real money for Capitol and from Capitol: "Young at Heart" was a million seller, and *In the Wee Small Hours* went gold, reaching number 2 on *Billboard's* 1955 album chart. He now had the leverage to renegotiate his original contract with the label, a four-year, lowball deal he'd signed (in 1953) with Capitol's vice president Alan Livingston when his career had been at a low ebb. His clout was increased considerably by interest from outside. "When we took him on two and a half years ago, Frank couldn't get a record," Livingston told *Down Beat*. "Now, every company in the business is after him, and it would be silly to deny that he has had generous offers from every quarter." RCA Victor, in particular, wooed him seriously when the negotiations stalled.

When Sinatra and Capitol finally came to terms, the label's premier artist scored an impressive seven-year contract, with an annual guarantee of $200,000 and virtual carte blanche to record whatever he pleased. The suits were happy enough with their star to grant him an indulgence or two, and the first was *Frank Sinatra Conducts Tone Poems of Color*.

The idea for the album originated with a series of twelve poems about colors by the radio writer Norman Sickel, who had worked on the *To Be Perfectly Frank* series. ("Orange is the gay deceiver," one began, "and I do deceive/but nicely./I am the daughter/of the yellow laughter/and the violent Red!") Sinatra, who would take up painting in his fifties, liked the verses so much that he commissioned a dozen original orchestral works based on them, from a brilliant group that included Nelson Riddle, Alec Wilder, the bandleader and arranger Billy May, and the movie orchestrators Jeff Alexander, Elmer Bernstein, and André Previn. Conspicuously absent was Axel Stordahl.* Sinatra assigned each writer a different tonal color and text and then assembled nearly sixty musicians in Capitol's new Studio A.

One of the first things Sinatra and the musicians discovered about the spanking-new facility was that despite Capitol's exhaustive efforts to duplicate the rich acoustics of KHJ Radio Studios, the sound in Studio A was miserable. A photograph taken during a break in recording shows Sinatra perched on a stool, looking over at the redoubtable cellist Eleanor Slatkin, who's leaning on her 1689 Andreas Guarnerius and grimacing as she apparently says something to him. She later remembered just what it was: "Frank asked me what I thought of the playback, and I said, 'I think it sounds like shit!' As the word came out, I heard the click of the camera as the photographer snapped the picture. I could get away with it—he just laughed!"

Frank adored the Slatkins, both Felix and Eleanor, as well as their two young sons, Leonard and Fred. The couple were brilliant, tough musicians who weren't afraid to call a spade a spade, and Sinatra revered them as kindred spirits. They had begun playing on Frank's Hollywood recording sessions for Columbia in the mid-1940s, but it was during the Capitol period, as Sinatra became increasingly fascinated with the Hollywood String Quartet, which Felix and Eleanor Slatkin had founded before World War II, that their friendship blossomed. "My dad and Frank became very, very close, and more reliance was placed on my father's opinions," Leonard Slatkin says. Felix Slatkin, Sinatra's first violinist—his concertmaster—quickly established himself as the de facto orchestra leader on many of the recording dates for which Riddle is listed as both arranger and conductor. Like many arrangers, Nelson Riddle, for all his towering brilliance, was an indifferent conductor at best. (Sina-

---

* Stordahl, who had incurred Sinatra's ire by going to work as the conductor on Eddie Fisher's TV show, might still have been on Frank's shit list. There is also the possibility that at this point Nelson Riddle had made Sinatra's first arranger look like old hat.

Frank in a rare role, on the album *Frank Sinatra Conducts Tone Poems of Color*. The cellist Eleanor Slatkin has just commented pointedly—and scatologically—about a playback in Capitol's sonically challenged Studio A.

tra biographer Arnold Shaw paints an unforgettable verbal picture of Riddle "conducting with the index finger of his right hand as if he were rhythmically pressing a bell-button.")

"Conducting is primarily about showing the passage of time," Leonard Slatkin says. "All music, at least [Sinatra's] kind, relies on some degree of steady rhythm as it progresses. It means that you have to, as a conductor, physically be able to keep steady time but at the same time be flexible enough to allow moments where a phrase might be stretched out a little longer or speed up just a little bit. This requires a degree of technical skill that goes beyond just intuitiveness."

Nevertheless, in the special context of the *Tone Poems* sessions—and with a little bit of help—Sinatra, who couldn't read music, got along surprisingly well. On a couple of the sessions, Eleanor Slatkin recalled, her husband "was damn near conducting [the strings] from his chair, but Frank was so gifted musically that he could bring it all off."

What he brought off was a pleasant and respectable album that was probably too highbrow for most of his audience and too lowbrow for classical listeners. "Interesting" is the adjective that mainly comes to mind. Sales were predictably light.

Tone Poems was a Capitol release, but the slipcover of the LP was also imprinted with the name of Essex Productions, a company Sinatra had recently formed and for which he held grand ambitions. "He informed the trade press," Friedwald writes, "that Essex was a 'full-fledged independent record company' and that he himself remained 'only nominally a Capitol artist,' claiming that all Sinatra product was merely distributed by Capitol."

Alan Livingston begged to differ, pointing out that Essex was "purely a paper deal for tax purposes. We still owned every Sinatra record made at Capitol, and in perpetuity."

From the mid-1950s on, Frank and his lawyer Milton "Mickey" Rudin, of the Los Angeles firm Gang, Kopp & Tyre, would form a number of corporations with British-y names—Essex, Bristol, Kent, Canterbury—ostensibly, and sometimes actually, for the purpose of co-producing Sinatra's movies and records but also (and arguably mainly) in order to lessen his personal income tax exposure. Essex might have started out as a dream of Frank's, but before long it would become a nightmare for Capitol.

———

On February 19, Frank was nominated for a Best Actor Academy Award for his performance in *The Man with the Golden Arm*. He was competing against Ernest Borgnine, who'd played Angelo Maggio's tormentor Sergeant Fatso Judson in *From Here to Eternity* and was now up for his performance as a lonely Brooklyn butcher in *Marty*; James Cagney (for *Love Me or Leave Me*); James Dean (*East of Eden*); and Spencer Tracy (*Bad Day at Black Rock*). Sinatra knew he'd given a great performance in *The Man with the Golden Arm*, the performance of his life. He didn't just hope to win; he expected it.

———

A week later, the first installment of "The Real Frank Sinatra Story," a syndicated Sunday series by the columnist Dorothy Kilgallen, ran in Hearst newspapers across the nation. The politically conservative Hearst papers had been on Frank's case since the early 1940s for his liberal stances, his infidelities, and his Mob ties, although it's hard to think there wasn't also an element of ethnic contempt, in that Waspocratic era, for an Italian-American who didn't know his place. The first Hearst columnist to go after Sinatra was the Red-baiting, Jew-hating Westbrook Pegler; next came the Hemingway wannabe Robert Ruark, who had the journalistic good fortune to chance upon Frank fraternizing with Lucky Luciano in February 1947 at the Mafia summit in Havana.

The New York–based Kilgallen, who had started out in a dither about Frank—in 1944, she wrote a fan-magazine piece titled "The Stars I'd Like to

Be Married to (If I Weren't Already Mrs. Richard Kollmar)"; Sinatra led the list—soon began toeing the Hearst company line. Now and then her columns had positive things to say about Frank, but the few compliments she doled out sounded grudging.

The Sunday series began with a bang. "Success hasn't changed Frank Sinatra," Kilgallen wrote. "When he was unappreciated and obscure he was bad-tempered, egotistical, extravagant and moody." He was, she said, "a Jekyll and Hyde dressed in sharpie clothes." The pieces were factually accurate but acidulous, especially on the subject of his many romances. She named names: famous ones like Ava, Lana Turner, Anita Ekberg, Gloria Vanderbilt, Kim Novak, and Jill Corey; lesser-known ones like pop singer Jo Ann Tolley, fashion model Melissa Weston, and actress Lisa Ferraday. "A few of the women, like Ava and Lana, were public idols themselves and priceless examples of feminine beauty," Kilgallen wrote.

> Many more, of course, have been the fluffy little struggling dolls of show business, pretty and small-waisted and similar under the standard layer of peach-colored Pan-Cake makeup—starlets who never got past first base in Hollywood, assorted models and vocalists, and chorus girls now lost in the ghosts of floor shows past. Others belonged to the classification most gently described as tawdry.

On balance, the worst that can be said about Kilgallen's characterization is that her feminist sympathies were somewhat muddled. Sure, Frank got around—a lot. His famous quotation of decades later—"If I had as many love affairs as you've given me credit for," he told reporters, "I'd now be speaking to you from a jar in Harvard Medical School"—was, as I wrote in *Frank: The Voice,* not just an evasion but the Big Lie:

> "Love affairs" was more than a euphemism, but less than the truth: Love was always what it was about, and never quite what it was really about. Love was the fleeting ideal, the thing to be sung about, to be dreamed of while he zipped his trousers on his way from one conquest to the next. In truth, there were probably even more affairs than the hundreds he'd been given credit for. For there always had to be someone. His loneliness was bottomless, but there was always someone to try to help him find the bottom.

And while this may be pitiable, is it reprehensible? Was he exploiting the many women he slept with? Though some of the girlfriends he wooed with lavish gifts and hearts-and-flowers declarations might have momentarily fantasized that they had his exclusive attention, the illusion couldn't have lasted long. He was *Frank Sinatra.* He was, Peggy Connelly recalled, "always on his way somewhere else in his mind, even while he was looking you in the eye. Someone once said he had no 'now.' He was never satisfied to be where he was."

And some*where* else was often some*one* else. In 2012, Jill Corey, finally beginning to process Frank's mid-1950s relationship with Connelly and others, said, "I suppose I can understand he probably could have been carrying on a relationship with both of us at the same time, or maybe four others. I have no idea."

Best for a woman's mental health was either to reject him outright—we've seen it happen, and we'll see it again; he wasn't universally irresistible—or to understand (or squint at the fact) that any serious relationship with him was a membership in a kind of harem, a group of shifting size and constitution that would cling around the singer over the next decade and a half. Many women shared this understanding. There were no formal requirements for membership, but it seemed to help a good deal if a young woman was fresh-faced, innocent to a degree, intelligent, talented as an actress or singer or both, and not aggressive, over-perfumed, or over-inquisitive about the exact contours of Frank's love life. In return, she could expect everything except intimacy: tenderness, respect, attentiveness, many Italian meals, travel, visits to historic recording sessions, lavish gifts, romance, good sex, the occasional proposal of marriage, and always that absolutely electrifying moment at a nightclub or recording session or in a casino showroom when he turned his startling blue eyes toward her and sang to her and her alone.

Not to mention stories to tell her grandchildren.

———

A biographer once asked Peggy Connelly, whose relatively serious relationship with Sinatra continued for several years, if he had been the love of her life.

"I said, 'Certainly not,'" she recalled. "Because there just finally wasn't enough of a human being. Frank had a public persona that took him over; everywhere he went he was the focus of attention. He couldn't switch gears very often. I think he was always on his guard.

"I mean, he did everything for me," Connelly said. "He was generous. He complimented me to everybody. I heard all kinds of compliments that came back to me from other people. And I was very aware that I had become known as Sinatra's steady, in a way—I don't know what you'd call it. He took me everywhere, and we met everybody. Cary Grant used to say, when there was a party, 'Oh, I hope Frank brings Peggy; he always behaves so much better.' But he just didn't have that cuddly, man-woman kind of need. You can only live without that for so long."

As for the Tawdry Ones about whom 1950s newspaper etiquette forbade Dorothy Kilgallen to be more specific, the story could now and then be a good deal darker. Sinatra had a way of disrespecting those he considered disrespectable, as a way of punishing the disrespectability he felt imbrued with. But it's unlikely Kilgallen's reporting took her there. What she was really doing in her big piece on Frank was chastising him for promiscuity, the vice that Eisenhower America felt compelled to condemn and the same one America, secretly or not so secretly, loved Sinatra for. She was being a prude and a scold, and she was violating Frank's intricate code for journalists, which allowed a reporter or columnist to now and then ask a personal question or two as long as Sinatra had met with him or her personally and assessed his or her bona fides and as long as he or she made sure to compliment Frank frequently and lavishly in print.

When Frank didn't like a piece, he usually sent a nasty telegram. (Sometimes he also threatened legal action.) In Dorothy Kilgallen's case, however, he decided to do something special: he sent her a tombstone with her name engraved on it.

To bring the perfectly ambivalent month of February to a terrible close, on leap day, the twenty-ninth, Humphrey Bogart was diagnosed with esophageal cancer. In those days, it was a death sentence. Frank was devastated.

———

With Frank Sinatra, the sublime and the ridiculous, the exquisite and the coarse, alternated so quickly and frequently that it's useless to try to reconcile them. He wasn't one thing or the other; he was both, and then a moment later he was something else again. The man who went to significant expense and effort to send a Sicilian-style message in granite to Dorothy Kilgallen, the man who, when human relations palled, periodically had his valet dial him up some professional company, was the same man who envisioned a new album that would combine Nelson Riddle's unparalleled arranging gifts and the rich and delicate sound of the classical string quartet Frank had come to revere.

"We became very close friends and saw a lot of him between the recordings in those days, and spent many weekends with Frank at his home in Palm Springs," Eleanor Slatkin recalled, when Sinatra was still alive.

As you know, he has a tremendous collection of classical records, and every time we were at his house, he had classical music playing . . . and a lot of opera too. He is very knowledgeable, and of course, he knew many of the artists. He fell in love with the Quartet . . . and he said, "You know, I think it would be a terrific idea to do an album with a string quartet . . ." and so came *Close to You*. Everything you did with Frank was Frank's idea.

The potential problem, however, was that the quartet alone "might not be enough to support a pop singer—even one who exceeded many classical voices in artistry and execution," Will Friedwald writes.

> And even if it could, the quartet alone might not sustain the attention of a pop audience. So . . . as [the HSQ second violinist] Paul Shure recalled, "Nelson decided to use a string quartet and [four rhythm], and each tune would have another instrument. He'd have string quartet and French horn . . . , string quartet and flute . . . , string quartet and trumpet . . . , string quartet and solo violin . . . It was all a core of string quartet writing with different instruments added."

The album was a brilliant meeting of minds between Sinatra and Riddle. It was also commercially problematic, to say the least. And coming on the heels of *Tone Poems of Color,* it gave pause to the men in the Capitol front office. "It was something that Capitol Records really didn't want to do," Leonard Slatkin said. "Using [the HSQ], putting their name on the cover. I think that was really the objection. Because it was before the time when we even used the word 'crossover.' They said, 'How can we sell this? What's our market? We have no idea.' But Frank insisted. He said, 'If you guys don't do this, I'm leaving.' Of course, this was a challenge that Nelson was so up to. I mean, those are just stunning arrangements all the way through. Like a lot of Frank's work of that period, it almost needs to be about two in the morning when you listen to it."

The challenge for Riddle was writing for so few instruments. "It's the most stunning thing that Nelson Riddle ever did," Paul Shure said.

> Using the string sound as a basis rather than a pad or an enhancement really was a turnaround for Nelson. String quartet writing is the hardest thing to do, because everything is so open. With a larger orchestra, you have a big palette to work with, and there are all kinds of things going on. You can use the orchestra to overcome melodic deficiencies, by using riffs and doing things with the woodwinds or brass over a string pad and get away with it. When you're writing for four, six, or eight instruments, it's another story.

On March 1, back at Capitol (where sound engineers had been laboring furiously to improve studio acoustics), Sinatra and Riddle, along with the Hollywood String Quartet and several other musicians, had a go at "Don't Like Goodbyes," a number from Harold Arlen and Truman Capote's Caribbean musical *House of Flowers*. Frank was bothered by something, either the acoustics or the arrangement; if it was the latter, there might have been a reshuffling of instrumentalists for the next studio date, a week later. This time—using the quartet plus a clarinet, a French horn, a flute, a harp, and an additional violin, along with a rhythm section of guitar, bass, drums, and piano—Nelson came up with the goods, and "Goodbyes," along with three other songs ("If It's the Last Thing I Do," "P.S. I Love You," and "Love Locked Out"), was laid down for posterity.

Close to You wasn't just a work of brilliance; it was hard work. Its making would span eight months on and off, more time than Sinatra would devote to any album until 1980's *Trilogy*.

———

For most of March, Frank played the Sands, commuting back and forth between the fleshpots of Vegas and the company town of Los Angeles. On the fifteenth, he conducted the last session for *Tone Poems of Color*. And on the night of the twenty-first, with Peggy Connelly on his arm, he was back at the Pantages Theater for the twenty-eighth annual Academy Awards, remembering keenly the heft of the eight-pound statuette he was all but certain he would hold again.

It wasn't to be. After presenting the Best Score award to Alfred Newman (for *Love Is a Many-Splendored Thing*), Frank had to sit and watch in disbelief as the Best Actor Oscar went to Ernest Borgnine for *Marty*. He was devastated. He had behaved for Otto Preminger on *The Man with the Golden Arm* as he had for Fred Zinnemann on *From Here to Eternity*: he had rehearsed, shown up at eight on the dot every morning, done every take that was asked of him. He had done the acting of his life. How could they begrudge him?

"I had wanted to go on to the parties they held afterwards," Connelly recalled, "but we walked out, got in the car, and went home. He went into his bedroom, didn't turn the light on, just sat down on the bed. I finally decided to go in.

"I kneeled down on the floor and put my arms around him. It's embarrassing now to remember what I said to him: 'It's terrible. But Ernie Borgnine is fat and ugly—think what it'll do for his career.' Frank said, 'Yeah, but think what it would've done for *mine*.' 'You don't need it,' I told him. 'You're Frank Sinatra.'"

In April, he did two more sessions for *Close to You:* on the fifth, he recorded, besides "The End of a Love Affair," "It Could Happen to You," and "With Every Breath I Take," a Johnny Burke–Jimmy Van Heusen number called "There's a Flaw in My Flue."* The song, on which Frank's vocal was as beautiful as any other on the album, contained lines such as

Now I try to remember and smoke gets in my nose

There are a couple of theories about why Sinatra laid down this parody, originally written by Burke and Van Heusen for a comedy segment on a wartime Bing Crosby broadcast. In *Frank Sinatra: My Father,* Nancy Sinatra claims that the tune was "a joke on the Capitol executives." When the demo album went out to the big brass, she writes, they all proclaimed it "beautiful!," and were ready to release it in its entirety—until Frank, shaking his head at the executives' denseness, had the number removed.

Nonsense, argues the Sinatra archivist Ed O'Brien, who claims that Frank "obviously viewed [the song] as a comedy piece . . . It was a throwaway meant to amuse his audience." O'Brien, who interviewed the former Capitol vice president Alan Livingston at length before Livingston's death, says that the label "never seriously considered" putting the song on the album.

And yet. Bing Crosby, a far cooler character than Sinatra (and an effortlessly funny one to boot), would have brought off the comedy of "Flaw" without breaking a sweat. Frank had a strange and uncertain sense of humor, usually too close to the bubbling caldron of his anger for comfort: his jokes, onstage or off, tended to throw menacing shadows. When he opened his mouth to sing, it was serious business, even if the song was joyous. (Over the years, when he sang the parodies Sammy Cahn now and then penned for him, his often hesitant delivery had a way of too obviously signaling the joke.) Couldn't his motives have been mixed where "Flaw" was concerned? Might he not have meant it both to amuse his pals and to nettle the suits? If it's true that his beloved *Close to You* had been a hard sell to Capitol and that Sinatra had threatened to walk unless the album was made, "There's a Flaw in My Flue" might have been the first volley in an incipient war between the singer and his record label.

---

* For whatever reason, "Flaw" was shelved at the eleventh hour. Also, because *Close to You* was running longer than the LP limit of forty-five-plus minutes, Capitol put aside two other songs, "Wait till You See Her" and "If It's the Last Thing I Do." All three numbers were included on the CD release *Close to You and More* in 1987.

On Monday night, April 9, Frank convened in Capitol Studio A with Riddle, a twenty-seven-piece orchestra, and a chorus to show his variety on a productive—if not great—non–*Close to You* session. Sans chorus, he recorded a good, straight-ahead blues called "No One Ever Tells You" and a pleasant enough John DeVries–Joe Bushkin ballad, "Something Wonderful Happens in Summer." With the singers, he laid down two charming if extremely white-sounding R&B-flavored singles, "Five Hundred Guys" (to which he devoted a laborious fourteen takes) and the much catchier "Hey! Jealous Lover" (with lyrics by Sammy Cahn and music by Kay Twomey and Bee Walker), which would go to number 6 on the *Billboard* chart in the fall.

The following night, Tuesday the tenth, in Municipal Auditorium in Birmingham, Alabama, several members of a group that called itself the North Alabama Citizens' Council (soon to change its name to the Original Ku Klux Klan of the Confederacy) attacked the stage while Nat King Cole, a friend to both Frank Sinatra and Nelson Riddle (and Riddle's frequent employer) was performing before an all-white audience. Three of the men stormed over the footlights while Cole was singing "Little Girl," knocking him down and roughing him up before police rushed from the wings and subdued them. The attackers had apparently intended to kidnap Cole, who, after he had been attended to by a doctor, did a brief second performance—for an all-black audience.

The moment Sinatra heard the news, he called Cole to console him as best he could, then phoned the singer's wife to assure her that Nat would be gotten safely out of Birmingham and flown home to Chicago. It happened the next morning (Cole biographer Daniel Mark Epstein says a commercial flight was diverted), just as Frank had said it would.

Sinatra tended to spend money whether he had it or not—like a drunken admiral, one of his friends once said. But with real money coming in, Frank took stock and decided to make a big change. He'd been renting the garden apartment on Wilshire and Beverly Glen since his down-at-heels days; it was a nice place, but now he wanted a Los Angeles base of operations all his own, one befitting his elevated station, and he didn't want anyone else's house—he wanted to build the bachelor pad of bachelor pads, from scratch, to his own specifications. He'd found the perfect site, an aerie on Bowmont Drive, high atop the Hollywood Hills, just east of Coldwater Canyon and overlooking what looked like all of creation: the San Fernando Valley to the north, the City of Angels to the south, the Pacific to the west. And he'd found the perfect man to design his dream home: the superstar (and, unusual for the time, African-

American) architect Paul Revere Williams, who'd created dozens of strikingly modern public buildings across Southern California, as well as numerous movie stars' houses.

Williams listened carefully to his new client's wishes and soon came back with a set of drawings that Frank loved. The house would be small (two bedrooms) but elegantly simple in its contours, with clean lines, plenty of big picture windows all around, built-in appliances, and what was then called an Oriental interior motif, with expanses of rich wood and surfaces painted in his favorite color, orange.

Ground had been broken at 2666 Bowmont early in the spring, and construction was proceeding apace, as things tended to proceed when Sinatra was involved. On Saturday, April 14, he awoke early, excited, and drove up to the site to watch the foundation being laid. The morning was cold and drizzly; the hopeful smell of freshly poured concrete hung in the misty air. Frank watched the workmen for a while, wide-eyed with pleasure. Afterward, he drove down to Columbia Pictures for a meeting with studio president Harry Cohn. Sinatra was slated to star in the musical *Pal Joey* in the spring of 1957, and there were several matters to discuss.

The last movie Frank had made for Columbia had been *From Here to Eternity,* and things had been very different then. Down on his luck, his movie and recording careers stalled, Sinatra had gone to Harry Cohn with hat in hand

Frank and his longtime valet George Jacobs at Sinatra's bachelor-pad aerie overlooking Coldwater Canyon. "Oh, man, I had a life with that poor man," Jacobs said.

and all but begged for the role of Angelo Maggio. This time, Frank was very far from down on his luck. His stride into Cohn's office would have been easy and graceful, his handshake firm, his smile broad. He now possessed power to intimidate even Harry Cohn.

The agents and lawyers had already worked out Sinatra's deal for *Pal Joey*, at a rate very far from the reported $8,000 to $10,000 he had earned for ten weeks of work on *From Here to Eternity*. Columbia had never been one of the richest studios, but with Frank's Essex Productions participating (and assuming part of the risk), the studio could afford to offer Sinatra a salary of $150,000 for *Pal Joey*, along with 25 percent of the net box-office receipts—the kinds of terms every star in Hollywood wanted but very few could demand. Frank walked into Harry Cohn's office with this deal already in his pocket. What he was there to discuss with Cohn and his minions was not money but the marketing of the movie.

Pal Joey was an adaptation of the 1940 Rodgers and Hart Broadway musical of the same name, which itself had been adapted from a series of *New Yorker* stories by John O'Hara. The main character was Joey Evans, a second-rate nightclub singer (he was a dancer in the original musical) who dreams of opening his own club; the action turns around Joey and the two women who come into his life: Vera, a bored socialite of a certain age with the power to bankroll his dream, and Linda, a naïve young secretary. For the two female leads, Columbia had signed Rita Hayworth, who was thirty-seven but still a knockout (and a box-office draw), and the twenty-three-year-old Kim Novak, with whom Frank was still involved, in his fashion.

"We talked things out," Sinatra recalled, "and then I saw an uneasy look coming into the faces of the Cohn braintrust and Harry himself. I don't like frightened people, and I don't like being frightened myself. So I asked, 'What's the trouble?' All were afraid to talk up. 'If it's billing,' I said, 'it's okay to make it Hayworth/Sinatra/Novak. I don't mind being in the middle of that sandwich.' Man, were they relieved!"

That night, Frank had dinner at 320 North Carolwood with Big Nancy and the kids—Nancy Sandra, who was almost sixteen; twelve-year-old Frank junior; and seven-year-old Tina. Dinner with his ex-wife and children was an almost weekly ritual for Sinatra when he was in town, and "there was something 'special event' about these occasions, like papal visits," George Jacobs writes, describing the first time he accompanied his boss to one of the dinners.

> Mr. S was very touchy and huggy with the kids. He truly loved them,
> and always arrived with either toys, gifts, or, as they got older, money.

But at the same time the situation was awkward, especially the goodbye part. The kids never begged him to stay, but their longing expressions conveyed the powerful message, and it hurt. Driving back to the apartment, Mr. S looked down. I told him how much I liked his family, and all he could say was, "I know, I know." He would call them every single day, wherever he might be, at six o'clock just before their dinner, and be the best telephone father there ever was.

Though Big Nancy had thrown Frank out and changed the locks the first time he allowed himself to be seen in public with Ava Gardner (early 1950), his former house, a sprawling, Spanish Mission–style ranch set on two and a half Beverly Hills acres, still bore his strong imprint. The interior color scheme was predominantly bright orange and black, and most of the many family photographs proudly displayed the paterfamilias, just as though he had never left.

In Frank's apartment, on the other hand, there were lots of pictures of his children and none at all of their mother. There was a weird asymmetry to Sinatra's relationship with Nancy Barbato Sinatra, the ex-wife who, George Jacobs writes, "didn't seem ex at all." There was something very Old World about it. She had even tutored Jacobs carefully about how to cook all of Frank's favorite dishes. He was the *padrone,* who did what he liked and came and went as he pleased. Big Nancy, on the other hand, didn't really even date, despite occasional excited reports in the gossip columns, and she would never marry again. "I married one man for life, and with my luck it had to be your father," she would later tell her younger daughter. Her steadiest companions in the mid-1950s were Barbara Stanwyck, whose ex-husband Robert Taylor had also left *her* for Ava Gardner, and the handsome Latin actor Cesar Romero, a closeted homosexual. It was as if she had entered a cloister when Frank left (complete with devotional images of him on all the walls).

Except.

Tina Sinatra, who as a little girl always hoped her father would come home for good, would discover years later that he "actually *was* coming home" to Nancy. "Sporadically, but very romantically. He'd encourage Mom just often enough to make waiting for him seem almost reasonable."

Il padrone.

After his home-cooked dinner that night, Frank popped over to Hedda Hopper's house for a last-minute interview: he was due to leave for Spain in three days to shoot *The Pride and the Passion.* They talked about the construction of his new house, his meeting at Columbia. He even gave the columnist his sandwich line about Hayworth and Novak. The two of them had a laugh over that. Then Hopper jumped right in with the unavoidable question: Would he see Ava in Spain?

"If I do meet Ava," Sinatra told her with a blue-eyed stare, "it will be in some public place. It will be a casual matter—hello, how are you, goodbye."

"No chance of a reconciliation?"

"There would have to be a complete change . . . But complete. I don't think that could happen."

———

He had written to her, according to a friend, asking when, if ever, she intended to pick up her divorce decree. They could discuss it, Ava replied, when Frank came to Spain.

6

||||||||||||

i guess i have finally reached the stage in life when work
becomes a labor of you know what, and man this aint it.

— FRANK SINATRA TO ALEC WILDER, APRIL 1956

Frank Sinatra was now a legitimate movie star, and his compensation confirmed it: for making *The Pride and the Passion,* a period epic to be shot in Spain over the spring and summer of 1956, he would earn $250,000, the equivalent of some $2 million today. His contract reflected his lofty standing, stipulating that "no other artist is to receive better living accommodations than those provided for Sinatra; that he is to be paid ten thousand dollars per week and supplied with twenty-five dollars per day for tips and incidentals, plus reasonable baggage allowance."

But the fame, the money, and the perks barely concealed one unchanging fact: no matter how big a movie star he became, motion pictures would never give Frank the kind of concentrated, almost fanatical control that he exerted over his music.

The Pride and the Passion was a misbegotten enterprise from the start; despite Sinatra's big salary, he was just along for the ride. The $4 million epic, produced and directed by Stanley Kramer, was based on the C. S. Forester novel *The Gun,* about the struggle of Spanish peasant fighters to deploy a giant cannon against the French army during the Napoleonic Wars. The title of the novel gives you the root of the movie's problems: the gun was the centerpiece of the story, making the doings of the three stars—Sinatra, Cary Grant, and, in her first American movie, the twenty-one-year-old Sophia Loren—pale by contrast. The film's silly title—it sounded as if it should be accompanied by the strum of a gypsy guitar—was a Band-Aid, a lackluster attempt to lend human interest to a narrative that was fundamentally inert.

Frank, a careful and intelligent reader and an incisive student of song lyrics, would have understood this from the moment he read the script. As the rebel leader Miguel, he would get plenty of action: he would command peons and jump into rivers and butt heads with Grant's character, the stodgy British navy commander Trumbull. Miguel and Trumbull would compete for the love of Loren's character, the lusty peasant girl Juana. But always, always, front and center in almost every scene, there was the giant gun, having to be dragged over hill and dale in order to besiege the French in the walled city of Ávila. Sinatra had characteristic confidence in his ability to portray a Spanish guerrilla fighter: he engaged a Spanish guitarist (who turned out to be Argentinean) as a dialogue coach, saying somewhat puzzlingly, "I want to play this role like a Spaniard trying to speak English—not like an American trying to talk like a Spaniard trying to speak English."

He *could* do the role, but did he want to? From the beginning, Frank's participation in the movie was a matter of pride without passion. Even worse. SINATRA DREADS TRIP TO SPAIN FOR FILM, read the headline of Louella Parsons's April 22 column. "Only Frank Sinatra's most intimate friends know that he cabled Stanley Kramer trying to get out of 'The Pride and the Passion' in Spain," Parsons wrote. But her take on Frank's reluctance had nothing to do with the movie itself. Rather, Louella felt that "he dreads a head-on meeting with Ava Gardner, who lives there."

She had a point. In going to Spain, Frank was sailing off into highly fraught, not to say incendiary, emotional territory. His companion on the trip (along with Jimmy Van Heusen) was Peggy Connelly. But as the newspapers had been pointing out delightedly for months, Spain was also the home of his not quite ex-wife. Despite the pronouncements both Frank and Ava had made to friends, columnists, and reporters, their feelings about each other continued to be volatile and unresolved. They talked on the phone every week, sometimes every day; they would continue to stay in close touch, as other lovers came and went, until the end of Gardner's life.

Ava had fallen for Spain a couple of years before, as she and Frank were breaking up, "all its from-the-blood passion and authenticity looming before her as the antithesis of Hollywood phoniness," her biographer Lee Server writes. "Her dream Spain overlooked the fears and treachery of a land under the yoke of the Franco fascists, but it was very real in her imagination."

And her imagination was vivid. "It was so unspoiled in those days, so dramatic, so historic—and so goddamn cheap to live in that it was almost unbelievable," Gardner wrote in her memoir.

> But there was more than dollars and sense involved in my decision. I fell in love with classic Castilian—when you hear it spoken and can understand it, it's so pure and musical that it's a delight to the senses. And I felt emotionally close to Spain—who can really say why?—and the Spanish people responded in kind, accepting me without question. Which couldn't have been easy for them. After all, I represented everything they disapproved of. I was a woman, living alone, divorced, a non-Catholic, and an actress.

With her characteristic creativity, Ava finalized the divorce that was still incomplete when she first moved to Spain. Nor was she alone at first. While shooting a movie there soon after *Mogambo,* her marital Waterloo with Sinatra, she had fallen in love with the great bullfighter Luis Miguel Dominguín, devilishly handsome and four years her junior. But that relationship soon fell victim to Ava's boredom and impatience, and in the spring of 1956 she was between lovers, at loose ends, and dangerous.

On some level—maybe more than she was willing to admit to herself or anyone else—she was waiting for Frank's arrival. She had bought a house in a suburb just outside Madrid; she was also driving a new convertible he had sent her after she'd casually mentioned to him in one of their periodic phone calls that she'd totaled her Mercedes while speeding to an appointment.

Sinatra, Van Heusen, and Connelly arrived in Madrid on April 18, the very day of Grace Kelly's wedding to Prince Rainier in Monaco. Though Frank had been invited to the ceremony, he gave it wide berth because he knew Ava would be there. Shooting on *The Pride and the Passion* was scheduled to start on the twenty-second in El Escorial, a hilly region thirty miles from Madrid, and after a warm-up quarrel with Stanley Kramer's people about having a hi-fi system installed in his huge hotel suite—the system was installed—Frank settled into the initially pleasant business of relaxing for a couple of days and getting acclimated. In a slightly peculiar but apparently characteristic arrangement, Van Heusen stayed in Sinatra and Connelly's suite, in a bedroom down the hall from Frank and Peggy's. One morning, Connelly remembered, "We had just awakened, and we were under the covers planning the day, and Jimmy came in and said, 'Please, please, there'll be no fucking in my presence.' It made Frank laugh."

A party given by a Spanish movie magazine brought Sinatra together with his two co-stars, Cary Grant and Sophia Loren. Frank knew Grant well from the Hollywood party circuit, but he was meeting the gorgeous, voluptuous Loren for the first time. Sparks did not fly. Frank smiled appreciatively, but Loren was painfully shy, and her English was terrible. (And truth be told, if the Italian starlet had eyes for anyone, it was the still-astounding-looking fifty-two-year-old Grant.) With Connelly at his side, Sinatra minded his manners.

It was the calm before the storm. Everyone in the world seemed aware that Ava was just a couple of miles away and that she and Frank "had not lived in such close proximity for this long in nearly two years," Lee Server writes. "But tempting as it was—grueling as it was—Sinatra stood his ground. In the end it was Ava who made the call, treating it as lightly as she might a ring-up to an uncle passing through from back home, though perhaps a bit less respectfully."

According to Richard Condon, who would later become a novelist and the author of *The Manchurian Candidate* but was then working as a unit publicist on *The Pride and the Passion,* he and a few others were in Frank's hotel suite when he took Ava's call.

"You goddamned jerk," she yelled so loudly that everyone in the room could hear. "You've been here how many days and you don't even call me."

"I've been busy," said Frank.

"What's happening?"

Peggy Connelly walked into the room and listened to Frank's end of the conversation. A few minutes later he hung up.

"Was that Ava?"

"Yes, it was."

"Are you going to see her?"

"Maybe."

"Well, I won't like it at all. I didn't come here so you could see Ava."

Frank looked at her for a few seconds and then very calmly told her to go back into the bedroom, pack her bags, and leave. Weeks later, he sent her a twenty-thousand-dollar grand piano and begged her to return.

The grand piano was the cherry on the sundae. Connelly might have been temporarily dismissed for insubordination, but as Dorothy Kilgallen noted in her column of May 30, Frank treated Peggy to stays in Paris and London on her way back to the States and, when she arrived in New York, put her up in an apartment at the Waldorf-Astoria and provided her "with two seats down front for all the best Broadway shows."

Just before Sinatra began the sixteen-week shoot—a period that had come to feel like a jail term—he sat down and wrote a letter to Alec Wilder ("professor") at the Algonquin Hotel, typing in his characteristic lowercase style and sounding as though he had a bottle of Jack Daniel's close by his side.

It was a letter of complaint, pure and simple, in the key of self-pity. ("j. christ four and a half months . . .") He'd never been accused of welshing, Frank wrote, but now he understood why some people ran out on deals. It was only his "dogged dago decency" that was keeping him from catching a plane home—and not just any plane but an overnight TWA flight, with a first-class sleeper berth and "some fine old cordon bleu" on hand.

"[S]eriously," he continued, "i guess i have finally reached the stage in life when work becomes a labor of you know what, and man this aint it."

He signed, in pencil: "Frank."

There's a strange hollowness to this longish letter: it's not quite clear what

Sinatra's beef *is*. He knew well when he signed the deal for *The Pride and the Passion* that the shooting schedule called for sixteen weeks (not four and a half months) of location work; now he was acting as though the fact has been foisted on him, poor him, much like that two-camera switcheroo on *Carousel*. The self-righteous claim that only his innate (and Italian) sense of decorum is keeping him from a sybaritic perch in a first-class berth on a transatlantic TWA flight is decidedly unsympathetic, as jarring as a wrong note in a Riddle arrangement. One wonders what Wilder thought.

On the other hand, Frank's realization that his work should be a labor of love packs true force. It was a principle that served him beautifully when he followed it, which he would continue to do only intermittently. He was only truly happy when he was singing—and not just singing, but singing well. But from the day he left for Spain, he wouldn't sing onstage for almost four months and would not set foot in a recording studio again for almost six months: factors that might have contributed to a vocal crisis he would suffer at the end of the year.

He suffered mightily on the Spanish movie, and therefore so did everyone around him. Though some detected high spirits in Frank as the shoot began, Sinatra biographer Arnold Shaw wrote, "it was not long before he became impatient and restless. 'This is something I can't help,' he once told director Vincente Minnelli. 'I have to go. No one seems able to help me—doctors, no one. I have to move.'"

"Sixteen weeks!" he exclaimed to Kramer one day. "I can't stay in one place sixteen weeks. I'll kill myself." And, "Let's get this circus on the road. Forget rehearsals. Just keep the cameras turning."

He was on a rolling boil. Frank's makeup man Bernard "Beans" Ponedel recalled, "He was always yelling at Kramer, 'Don't tell me. Suggest. Don't tell me. Suggest.'" One wonders whether Fred Zinnemann and Otto Preminger simply intuited that they needed to suggest, or whether Sinatra allowed them to tell him because he respected them more.

"When Sinatra walks into a room, tension walks in beside him," Stanley Kramer later said.

You don't always know why, but if he's tense, he spreads it. When we were shooting in Spain, he was impatient . . . He didn't want to rehearse. He didn't want to wait around while crowd scenes were being set up. He wanted his work all done together. He was very unhappy. He couldn't stand it, he wanted to break loose. Eventually, for the sake of harmony, we shot all his scenes together and he left early. The rest of the cast acquiesced because of the tension, which was horrific.

Kramer made it sound as though Sinatra's impatience were some mysterious natural force—which to a great degree it was. What he was leaving out was the personality clash between himself and his star, the alpha-dog head butting. Not to mention the utter crappiness of *The Pride and the Passion,* a fact that would have become even more apparent as the mammoth production, with its production crew of four hundred and its ninety-four hundred extras, got under way.

Decades later, the grand epic, shot in VistaVision and Technicolor, fails as spectacle; it lacks even nostalgia value. There are many shots of the cannon being dragged across the gorgeous landscape of the Escorial while George Antheil's bombastic score swells and pounds variations on "La Marseillaise" and "Rule, Britannia!" There is zero comic relief and no character development whatsoever. The sublime Cary Grant has to stand around looking stiff and annoyed, while Sinatra, who wears his most absurd wig to date—with bangs, yet—speaks terrible dialogue in a cheesy Spanish accent: "Chu vould like to see thees gun?" And, "Citizens of Delgado, I speet in your face." "It's no accident," Tom Santopietro writes, "that Frank Sinatra did not attempt to change his speaking voice for another movie until the equally misbegotten *Dirty Dingus Magee,* thirteen years later."

The one interesting note in Frank's performance—besides the startling blueness of his eyes in Technicolor—is an air of street-kid insolence that doesn't show up in his other movies and somehow feels true to life (and to his relationship with Stanley Kramer). Otherwise, this colossally dreadful, utterly charmless mess of a movie was a huge waste of the talents of Cary Grant and Frank Sinatra. At least Sophia Loren, looking improbably gussied up throughout—as though the peasant forces had included makeup artists and hairdressers—got to do a lusty flamenco dance.

While Stanley Kramer and his ten thousand lived in tents on the Escorial, Sinatra made the long, dusty commute to and from the location each day in a chauffeured Mercedes, building up a head of steam as he rode, stewing about the meaningless work he was doing and about Ava, who always tormented him but was now getting to do so at close range. He put off seeing her for as long as possible but finally went out to dinner with her one night, along with two beards, Richard Condon and a visiting Otto Preminger (whose presence must have been a sore reminder for Frank of what making a real movie was like).

"Throughout dinner Frank and Ava never spoke to us—not one word," Condon recalled. "They were holding hands all night long and gazing sappily at each other, and when the last course was over, they stood up and left the room, leaving Otto and me with each other."

Lee Server presents another version: "After dinner they parted respect-fully," he writes.

> Later in the night Frank had returned to his suite, and as assorted cronies and guests lay about having a nightcap, Frank got her on the phone. They were talking and then Frank began singing softly to her through the phone, one tune after another, a regular concert in sotto voce. Twenty minutes later guests saw Ava Gardner come through the door of the suite, and then she and Frank disappeared. Ava was wearing a mink coat and a negligee.
>
> It was a one-night stand, not a reconciliation.

But Server is probably conflating Condon's story with another incident. Frank and Ava's reunion seems to have been more than a one-night stand. Returning to Spain after a few weeks of luxurious exile, Peggy Connelly entered the suite at the Castellana Hilton and immediately realized she had come at an inopportune moment. "The first thing I saw was the unmade bed and the mess in the bedroom, and knew something had been going on," she recalled. "Then I caught a glimpse of Ava through the living room door. It was very obvious she had spent the night."

Sheer youthful nerve made Connelly walk in instead of running the other way. The twenty-four-year-old wanted to establish her presence as well as size up her thirty-three-year-old rival. "I went in because mail had piled up for me from home, and I wanted my mail," she said. "I didn't have to go in, but I wanted to, just from contrariness. I said, 'I'm sorry, this must be a very difficult situation.' [Ava] looked at me from under her eyebrows, didn't say anything. I just got my mail and walked out."

From the hotel, she headed to the location to meet Sinatra for lunch. "He couldn't have been cooler," she recalled. "A kiss, then he asked me, 'How were things at the hotel?'—a completely inane remark unless there was something wrong at the hotel. I said, just as cool, 'Crowded.' And he said, 'Oh, was she still there?' There was no drama.

"I agreed with people—I thought she was devastatingly beautiful," Connelly recalled. Was she aware of the torch Frank carried for his second wife? "At times," she said. "I didn't resent it, but I regretted it. He never made it obvious; it was just in the air. But the fact that he kept her perfume—it was a wonderful perfume, Jungle Gardenia; it wasn't expensive, but very exotic . . ." Her voice trailed off. "I used it in later years," Connelly said.

By the end of June—even with side trips to the Prado to take in the great paintings of Goya and Velázquez, which fascinated him—Frank had had it with

Spain. On July 1, he informed Kramer that he would be leaving on the twenty-fifth of the month, three weeks short of the sixteen for which he had contracted. "Hot or cold, Thursday I'm leaving," Sinatra told the director.* Kramer told Frank that he needed him until at least August 1. Frank told Kramer that he'd give him three more days, until July 28. A barrage of transatlantic cables between production headquarters and Stateside lawyers and agents ensued. No agreement having been reached, Frank left on the twenty-eighth, daring Stanley Kramer and United Artists to suspend him—and leaving the cast and crew much relieved. With so much film already in the can, the moviemakers were over a barrel. Sinatra's remaining scenes were shot months later at Universal Studios in Hollywood, "with potted palms," as Kramer put it, producing a noticeably phony effect that detracted little from a film that was already too lousy to get much worse.

―――――

On May 5, while Frank was in Spain, a new single hit number 1 on the *Billboard* chart, supplanting Les Baxter and His Orchestra's whistle-happy Muzak favorite "The Poor People of Paris." The new record was Elvis Presley's decidedly non-Muzak-y "Heartbreak Hotel," which had been released in January and quickly became a million seller. Presley had performed the song on national TV in February, backed by, of all outfits, the Tommy and Jimmy Dorsey Orchestra.

The television version of "Heartbreak Hotel" was a respectable enough synthesis of the Dorsey brothers' ever more old-fashioned-sounding big-band music and Elvis's brand-new R&B-tinged rockabilly; still, it was hard to escape the feeling that Presley had been defanged for adult consumption. But the single itself, which had been recorded in an echoey hallway at RCA Studios in Nashville and was roundly disliked at first by RCA executives, along with almost everyone who heard it except Presley, had an eerie presence that spoke powerfully both of blue-highway, backcountry America and of new changes coming. It was an enormously charismatic recording, and it reached across the Atlantic to the fifteen-year-old John Lennon, who, because the British Broadcasting Corporation didn't play rock 'n' roll in 1956, heard it on Radio Luxembourg. Lennon later recalled,

> When I first heard "Heartbreak Hotel," I could hardly make out what was being said. It was just the experience of hearing it and having my hair stand on end. We'd never heard American voices singing like that.

―――――

* The quotation is from Kramer; the twenty-fifth of that month fell on a Wednesday.

They'd always sung like Sinatra or enunciated very well. Suddenly, there's this hillbilly hiccupping on tape echo and all this bluesy stuff going on. And we didn't know what Elvis was singing about . . . It took us a long time to work [out] what was going on. To us, it just sounded like a noise that was great.

Both the thirteen-year-old George Harrison and the twelve-year-old Keith Richards had the identical experience at the same time. Frank didn't know it then, but "Heartbreak Hotel" would change his life too.

––––––––

"Frank Sinatra has been booked to sing the party's 1956 campaign song at the democratic national convention," read a newspaper squib in early August. "However, as far as we know, the G.O.P. hasn't planned to retaliate with Elvis Presley."

Satirical or not, the story was true: Frank had indeed been chosen to sing "The Democratic March" (to the tune of "The Yellow Rose of Texas") at the convention, which was to be held at the International Amphitheatre in Chicago in mid-August. Even more impressive, the party had asked him to kick off the event with "The Star-Spangled Banner"—a decision that caused amusement, disbelief, and consternation among some of the nation's editorial writers, especially Sinatra's old nemesis Westbrook Pegler.

Pegler, the first columnist to win a Pulitzer (in 1941, for his exposés on corruption in Hollywood unions) and one of the most disagreeable journalists ever to see print, had been rabidly anti–New Deal and anti-FDR in the 1930s and 1940s; after World War II, he'd moved ever rightward politically. In the late 1940s, in the wake of Sinatra's visit to the Mob summit in Havana, Pegler mounted a vigorous newsprint campaign against the singer, calling him out as a friend of organized crime and a Red sympathizer, and an adulterer to boot.

In the ensuing years, the columnist went back to castigating other old enemies (Jews, blacks, the Democratic Party, unions), but Sinatra's prospective appearance at the 1956 convention gave him fresh inspiration. On August 14, Pegler devoted his entire syndicated column to Frank, gleefully wielding a rake amid a whole field of old coals:

Sinatra . . . has a police record with two gun-raps, an old pinch in Jersey for an error which Dickens called "an amiable indiscretion," one assault job, and stacks of envelopes in the newspaper morgues about his panting pursuit of Ava Gardner while his wife and kiddies languished in Hollywood, his eventual espousal of that morsel and their ultimate, and inevitable, divorce.

The column proceeded, in Pegler's ever colorful and not particularly coherent style, to build an indictment by association, stringing together a series of reprehensible characters the columnist considered either tightly or loosely affiliated with Sinatra: from Frank's New Jersey godfather the late mobster Willie Moretti, who had supposedly gotten the singer out of the "Jersey rap," to the Democrats' prospective vice presidential nominee, the Tennessee senator Estes Kefauver, "who qualified as a statesman of majestic stature by impressing into his political service an old friend of Sinatra and the Moretti boys, the sinister Frank Costello." Pegler was referring to the New York mobster's televised testimony before Kefauver's Senate Special Committee on Organized Crime in Interstate Commerce in 1951, which had riveted the nation: unlike other gangsters who appeared before the committee, Costello refused to have his face shown on camera; instead, viewers saw a tight shot of his wringing hands as he continually pleaded the Fifth in a gravelly voice. The Kefauver hearings not only sent TV sales soaring but gave America a primer on organized crime.

And then there was Jimmy Tarantino, whom Pegler seemed to have dredged up largely because his name ended with a vowel: a petty thief and blackmailer who in the early 1950s had managed to persuade Sinatra to help bankroll the scandal sheet *Hollywood Nite Life* (a precursor of *Confidential*). Frank had soon written Tarantino off for the lowlife that he was. But for Pegler, Jimmy was a gift that kept on giving.

After going off on tangential diatribes about Harry Truman and Eleanor Roosevelt, both of whom were to make keynote speeches at the convention, the columnist seemed to remember that he was writing about Sinatra and came to the point, which appeared to have something to do with the severe north-south division in the Democratic Party over the issue of civil rights. The northern bloc, in the columnist's opinion, was "berating [the southerners] as ignorant, sub-human riff-raff on the 'integration' squabble and setting up Sinatra to challenge their primitive notions of good behavior and marriage."

In reality, of course, it was Pegler who was berating the northern majority, whom he hated, for its support of civil rights, which he hated, and integration, which he (along with much of the rest of the country) detested and belittled. If he could make his mini-diatribe part of a larger harangue about Frank Sinatra, and throw in for good measure the unions, Truman, and Mrs. Roosevelt, all the better.

Something happened on the speaker's platform at the International Amphitheatre on August 13, not long after Frank sang "The Democratic March": as Bill Davidson related the incident in a 1957 *Look* magazine cover story about the star, Sinatra was just turning away from the microphone when the seventy-four-year-old Speaker of the House, Sam Rayburn, put a friendly hand on his shoulder and said, "Aren't you going to sing 'The Yellow Rose of Texas'?" And Sinatra replied to the venerable man, the mentor of Lyndon Johnson and one of the most respected legislators ever to stride the floor of the U.S. Congress, "Take the hand off the suit, creep."

The story is deliciously awful; it is also apparently not true. Sam Rayburn even sent a supportive telegram to Frank when the singer denied the story (and brought a libel suit against *Look* for over $2 million). What may be true is that Sinatra made a similarly crude remark at the convention to *another* elderly lawmaker, Senator Theodore Green of Rhode Island.

It is true that Frank couldn't bear to be touched by strangers. "In bars or nightclubs where he was singing, people would get pally, say 'Have a drink' or something, and touch him on the shoulder," Peggy Connelly recalled. "He would freeze, look down at that hand on his arm and stare, and not move until the hand was taken off." It is also true that in the hot emotional atmosphere that almost always surrounded Sinatra, things frequently happened, and stories were told afterward, and the stories tended to pass through distorting lenses, bounce off mirrors, and turn strange corners.

Eleanor Roosevelt, Harry Truman, and Frank Sinatra weren't the only luminaries at the 1956 convention. The thirty-nine-year-old senator John F. Kennedy of Massachusetts, a rising political power widely considered a viable contender for the vice presidential nomination, had been picked by MGM's president, Dore Schary, to introduce and narrate a short film about the history of the Democratic Party. "When the lights came up after the film," biographer David Nasaw writes, "[Kennedy] was escorted onto the platform and given a standing ovation." "Senator John F. Kennedy of Massachusetts," the *New York Times* reported, "came before the convention tonight as a movie star."

Visibility and momentum aside, political pundits had misgivings about how Kennedy's Catholicism would affect his chances to get the nomination. Even JFK's own father wanted his son to give wide berth to the presumptive presidential candidate, Adlai Stevenson, because Dwight Eisenhower was seen as a shoo-in for reelection and Joe Kennedy hated losing battles.

Stevenson refused to name a running mate, throwing the decision to a ballot on the convention floor. After the presidential candidate asked Jack Kennedy to make his nominating speech, it was assumed as a customary procedural matter that Kennedy was officially out of the running, but Kennedy kept his hat in the ring anyway. The choice went to three tight ballots, and Estes Kefauver was selected to accompany Adlai Stevenson on the ticket whose landslide defeat in November was a foregone conclusion. Vacationing in the South of France, Joseph P. Kennedy was delighted: his son had lost a skirmish but avoided the taint of association with the loser Stevenson and established himself as a force to reckon with.

Frank Sinatra was with Jack and Bobby Kennedy and their families when Kefauver won the third ballot. As soon as the 1956 ticket was determined, Frank recalled, Bobby Kennedy said, "Okay. That's it. Now we go to work for the next one"—meaning the 1960 presidential election, and that there was no time to waste. Sinatra was impressed.

From Chicago, Frank headed straight to New York to play a weeklong stand at the Paramount with the Tommy and Jimmy Dorsey Orchestra. In between sets, Sinatra and the band would leave the stage, the curtains would open, and the audience would be treated to a viewing of *Johnny Concho*.

Frank had had a brief and casual reunion with his old boss at the tribute to the Dorsey brothers the year before, dropping by and singing a few songs before going back to his set at the Copacabana. But this August week at the Paramount was to be a real gig, Sinatra's first with Tommy since he'd left the band fourteen years earlier, and the power polarity had reversed: Frank was the boss now. He had come up with the idea of booking the Dorseys, and though the brothers "were still a hard-working act appearing on [*The Jackie Gleason Show*] every week and the original *American Bandstand*, as well as playing one-nighters," as Richard Havers writes, Sinatra had left one-nighters far behind. Tommy Dorsey, prematurely aged at fifty, was all too aware of his own eclipse. When he heard that Nelson Riddle, his former third trombonist, would be joining Sinatra in New York to supervise his arrangements, Dorsey bridled, telling his manager, Tino Barzie, "I conduct the orchestra. It's my orchestra."

At the same time, the white-haired bandleader was enormously proud of his two protégés. Barzie recalled "that often when [he was] driving with Dorsey in his Cadillac on the road, Tommy would flip the radio dial, eager to listen to his alumni Sinatra and Riddle's recordings of 'It Happened in Monterey,' or 'You Make Me Feel So Young,' which were then all over the airwaves. 'Tommy would say, "Listen to that son of a bitch—the greatest singer ever! He knows exactly where to go and what to do." '"

Dorsey's manager explained Tommy's sensitivities to Sinatra's manager Hank Sanicola, and all parties came to an accommodation: Riddle, who after all had little interest in conducting, would arrive in New York two days prior to the Paramount gig to run down his charts with the Dorsey band.

Riddle stayed at Dorsey's house in the New Jersey countryside. Early one morning, Dorsey's wife, Jane, found the arranger sitting on a log, tossing pebbles into the lake. "We looked up at Tommy's bedroom," Jane Dorsey recalled, "and [Nelson] said to me, 'Janie, do you have any idea how much that man taught me?'" She responded that she had a pretty good idea. Riddle said, "He taught me everything I know. Every note I write I learned from that man upstairs . . . People rave over my arranging today, and I just think to myself, God bless Tommy Dorsey. If it hadn't been for him, I never could have done this."

Over dinner the next night, "Tommy said to Nelson, 'I really like the things you've been doing with Frank,'" Dorsey's biographer Peter Levinson writes.

> Nelson then essentially repeated what he had told Janie, "I'll tell you the truth—much of the skill and ability to do these things came from my time with you," whereupon Dorsey began to cry. Nelson rushed over to embrace him . . .
>
> In his depressed state, Dorsey exclaimed, "Nelson, I don't want Frank to come down to rehearsal and give me any orders or cast any aspersions toward me or embarrass me in front of my boys. I couldn't stand that." Nelson said, "He won't do that. Don't worry, Tommy, he won't."

Dorsey, renowned during his heyday as a tough guy and a martinet who would physically throw musicians off the band bus if they gave him trouble, knew what Sinatra was capable of. During Frank's three-year tenure with the Tommy Dorsey Orchestra (1939–42), as he went from boy singer to national sensation, his ego had grown proportionately. "If Tommy Dorsey was late to a rehearsal," Sammy Cahn once recalled, "Frank Sinatra acted as substitute orchestra leader. When Dorsey arrived, Sinatra would fix him with a glare of 'Where the fuck you been?' Dorsey would apologize that he'd been tied up in this and that and Sinatra'd say something quaint like 'bullshit.'"

Then came Frank's downfall. (Had Dorsey secretly, or not so secretly, rejoiced?) The last time Sinatra had played the Paramount, in 1952, had been at the nadir of his career. Frank had had to personally call the theater's manager, Bob Weitman, and beg for a two-week booking. The seats were half-filled for many of his shows, and the papers were pronouncing him yesterday's news. The movie then had been the not-so-good *Meet Danny Wilson*.

Now the movie was the truly terrible *Johnny Concho*. "Mr. Sinatra, the actor, might mention to the producer, who happens to be Mr. Sinatra, that he needs better writing and direction than he gets here," sniffed Bosley Crowther in the *New York Times*. But it didn't matter: Frank himself was a smash hit. After the negative review, Crowther continued,

> For all that, it seemed like old times at the Paramount yesterday, when Mr. Sinatra appeared in person to entertain with songs and wisecracks from the stage. A capacity audience of loud enthusiasts, clearly reminiscent of those who gathered at the Paramount in the Forties when Mr. Sinatra appeared frequently as a soloist with Tommy Dorsey's band, was on hand to greet him. And the old familiar chorus of shrieks and squeals, especially from the feminine patrons, often responded to his vocal tricks.
>
> The patrons were lined on Forty-third Street west to Eighth Avenue and north to Forty-fourth Street when the doors of the theatre were opened at 9:50 a.m. A few placards, carried by teen-agers, proclaimed "We Love Frankie" and "Sinatra for President."

Just across town, at Radio City Music Hall, *High Society* was doing land-office business. These days, it seemed, Frank simply couldn't lose.

Yet a strange thing happened three nights into the Paramount run, where Sinatra's opening act was a young comedian named Joey Bishop. Maybe it was the constant shifts between air-conditioning and hot outdoor air (the weather was scorching in Chicago and New York that August), maybe it was all the late hours, or maybe it was the fact that he was doing four shows a day, twenty-four songs per show, but Frank came down with a bad case of laryngitis. Could the recent unpleasantness in Spain, the high jinks with Ava, have had anything to do with it? "Emotional tension absolutely destroyed him," his first publicist, the late George Evans, had once said. "You could always tell when he was troubled. He came down with a bad throat. Germs were never the cause unless there are guilt germs."

Evans had known his client well, better than almost anyone else knew Sinatra in the early days. But while Gardner, with her letters and late-night long-distance calls, kept a kind of pilot light of agitation burning in his life, why would whatever lingering guilt he might have felt over her have spiked in the late summer of 1956?

An alternate theory: in Los Angeles, Sinatra's idol and close friend Humphrey Bogart was desperately ill with esophageal cancer, his body wasted by the massive surgery his doctors had performed to try to keep the disease in check, and constant rounds of chemotherapy. Betty Bacall, depressed and terrified, would naturally have reached out to her closest friends that August. One of the closest of all was Frank.

"Frank Sinatra's Sands opening promises to be a gala affair," Louella Parsons wrote, breathlessly, on September 12. "Reservations have been made by Lauren Bacall, Kim Novak, the Leo Durochers, the Nelson Riddles, Jimmy Van Heusen and Mr. and Mrs. William Goetz."

Bill Goetz, an independent movie producer, and his wife, Edie, the daughter of Louis B. Mayer, the man who had fired Sinatra from MGM, were Hollywood royalty who had become close friends of Frank's as his star had risen again. He would have been thrilled to have them at his opening. The same was true of Leo Durocher, the former manager of the Brooklyn Dodgers and the New York Giants, who'd first met Sinatra at Toots Shor's saloon on Fifty-First Street; Durocher was someone Frank could be himself with.

And Kim Novak was the current leading lady of his harem, although he was equally attentive to all its members. Ever the gentleman, he sent a car to take Novak to Las Vegas—she refused to fly—even as he made plans for a thirty-second birthday party for Bacall on Sunday the sixteenth at the Sands. That same week, he phoned Peggy Connelly three times in New York and sent flowers in support of her opening at the Blue Angel. Less satisfyingly, Ava reported to Parsons that she would be spending Christmas with her family in North Carolina, then picking up her divorce papers from Frank in Reno.

To hold the demons at bay, he maintained a jam-packed schedule. The rest of America might have been getting back in gear after Labor Day, but Sinatra, who'd been running at top speed straight through the summer, just kept going. Now he was going to get to tell the television-watching public about it.

Edward R. Murrow had been trying for a couple of years to corral Frank for his big CBS interview show *Person to Person*, and he'd finally succeeded. The first show of the program's fourth season would be broadcast live on September 14 from Sinatra's recently completed Coldwater Canyon house, turning the place for fifteen minutes into the world's most public bachelor pad. It would be an unprecedented opportunity for the country to see America's swinger in chief in his natural habitat. "Hollywood people called [it] 'the Teahouse,' after the hit Broadway play *The Teahouse of the August Moon*," Frank's valet George Jacobs recalled, "and those who really knew what was going on called it the Whorehouse of the August Moon."

"When its owner is in a reflective mood," TV reporter Hal Humphrey wrote of Frank's home, "he has his choice of looking out over the blue Pacific, or the sun-drenched San Fernando Valley. On a clear day he can see Peggy Lee, who lives a piece down the hillside."

Peggy Lee, too, would soon beat a path to Frank's door.

Seen today, the black-and-white *Person to Person* (only NBC, which was affiliated with RCA and several other manufacturers of color televisions, was then broadcasting prime-time shows in color) is vintage 1950s. The effortlessly iconic Ed Murrow, sitting in a comfortable armchair in a New York studio, clutching one of the unfiltered Camels that would kill him at age fifty-seven between the second and the third knuckles of his left hand, intones his trademark opener: "Good evening, I'm Ed Murrow. The name of the program is 'Person to Person.' It's all live—there's no film."

In the days before celebrity interviews went viral, *Person to Person* was a national institution, and its host, who earned more than William S. Paley, the head of CBS, had unparalleled influence. Murrow was larger than life, a nonfiction, non-Jewish Rod Serling before Rod Serling, heavy eyebrowed, deep-voiced, almost absurdly authoritative. Every line he spoke sounded as though it were coming straight from the London Blitz (from which Murrow had reported as the bombs were falling) or his famous 1954 takedown of Senator Joseph McCarthy on the CBS news show *See It Now*.

Of course Sinatra too was larger than life, but he seems strangely diminished on Murrow's show. Television was not his medium. After the host's orotund introduction ("Frank Sinatra is—well, Frank Sinatra. In twenty years, he's traveled from Hoboken to Hollywood, with stops in between"), the remote camera (transmitting by microwave to New York) picks up Frank, jauntily knotting his tie in front of his bedroom mirror and tossing off a couple of bars of "The Tender Trap," like some average Joe preparing for a date. He's playing a role here, and his demeanor is eager and lightweight. "How are ya, Ed? Nice to see you," he pipes up.

"Good," Murrow says in his funereal baritone. "Good luck in your new home, by the way."

"Thank you very much, and welcome." Frank finishes tying his tie and leans on the bureau, facing the camera expectantly.

"Tell me—have you been home long enough to make sure there's a place for everything, and everything in its place?" Murrow asks, all folksy bonhomie.

Frank smiles and channels Nathan Detroit: "I have just been home long enough to change clothes and say hello to you and your wonderful audience, and get in the car and drive to the airport and go right back up to the Sands in Vegas," he says.

And so the house tour begins. The camera moves with Sinatra from his bedroom to the living room, where a large autographed portrait of Franklin

D. Roosevelt hangs prominently. (Murrow: "You must prize that very highly." Frank: "I really do, Ed.") Nearby hang three framed photographs of his children; the camera closes in on each in succession. After Murrow asks Frank about the two Oscars sitting side by side on a bookshelf (one is for *From Here to Eternity;* the other is a special award for Sinatra's 1945 short on tolerance, *The House I Live In*), he says, "Well, Frank, I gather the night you won the Oscar for *Eternity* was the high spot in your professional career, wasn't it?"

It's an interesting moment. The *Person to Person* shows, all set in celebrities' homes with Murrow looking in from his New York studio, were carefully choreographed ahead of time, from the cameras and lighting to the topics to be covered, but even if the programs were scripted—there has been some controversy on the subject—Frank seems to have been caught off guard here. Plainly uncomfortable, he tries to settle himself on the edge of a sofa and blinks several times. He's flustered and, beneath his carefully composed face, probably annoyed. He might have smacked anyone else for bringing this up. For as great as winning his Best Supporting Actor Oscar was, the wound from being passed over for *The Man with the Golden Arm* is still fresh.

"Well, it's one of the high spots," he says. "Uh, Ed, there've been several others, too. For instance, *Golden Arm*—when I did *The Man with the Golden Arm,* I think was one of the true high spots." He blinks rapidly again, trying to gather himself. "And, uh, one of the—it was one of the difficult things to do, by the way, the *From Here to Eternity* role, because it was the first time I had ever done anything like that. And the other difficult thing I'd ever do was to sing the National Anthem in the Polo Grounds . . ."

Momentarily unhorsed, he's lost the thread, then steers the conversation back into safe territory with a lighthearted anecdote. Murrow plays along for a moment, then lowers those thick brows and drills in with almost sadistic pleasure: "Well, so, from *Golden Arm,* you had a great deal of satisfaction but not the big award, is that right?"

And Frank parries! "That's quite true," he says, smiling. "No, we didn't get the award for that, but you just reminded me—I got something to show you, speaking of awards."

He leads the way into the foyer, where a big beribboned gift box sits on a table. The box is a prop, as it turns out; Frank lifts it to reveal a huge, hideous trophy, two feet high if it's an inch, all bronze terraces decked with figurines. It's an award from the Al Jolson Chapter of the Los Angeles B'nai B'rith, and Frank is to receive it the next night in a ceremony at the Cocoanut Grove in Hollywood. Mysteriously, though, the thing has found its way to 2666 Bowmont Drive so that he can display it on national TV. Murrow asks him to read the inscription.

Frank is all self-deprecation as he picks the monstrous trophy up. "Well, it says—let's see if I can lift this thing—it says, 'The first Al Jolson Memorial Award, the Entertainer of the Era, Frank Sinatra, who by his deeds and talents most exemplifies the tradition of the great Al Jolson.' I really shouldn't have read that," he says quietly. "Somebody else should be doing that."

Yet he has thus had the chance to give himself a testimonial before millions, as balm for the wound of the lost Oscar.

––––––

That Sunday, Frank threw Betty Bacall her birthday party at the Sands. Not only were Kim Novak, the Durochers, the Riddles, the Goetzes, and Van Heusen present, but so were Cole Porter, the Nivens, the Romanoffs, Swifty Lazar, and many others. A photograph taken at the time shows some of the above at ringside in the Copa Room (the casino's main showroom, named after the New York nightclub), along with Mr. and Mrs. Jack Benny, George Burns and Gracie Allen, Louella Parsons, and a certain youngish, sunglasses-wearing gentleman—not Sam Giancana, not Joe Fischetti, but, judging from his proximity to the stage and his clear wish, unlike the stars surrounding him, to conceal rather than display his identity, of their ilk. Unlike virtually everybody else in the room, the man is not looking at Sinatra but staring straight at the photographer, with what might be construed as an interested expression.

Sinatra had had a two-tiered cake made for Bacall, inscribed "Happy Birthday Den Mother." He gave her a large stuffed horse for her and her children, introduced her, and sang "Happy Birthday" from the stage.

Humphrey Bogart, however, was not present. He had, in Bacall's loaded phrase, "decided to withdraw," opting instead to spend the weekend aboard his beloved sailboat the *Santana* with his seven-year-old son, Stephen. According to Bacall and one of Bogart's biographers, the actor had rallied somewhat and felt well enough to go to the party; at the same time, he must have realized how distracting his presence would be. He had lost thirty pounds from an already slight frame: "His neck," a waiter at Romanoff's recalled, "had gotten so thin that the skin was just hanging over the bones." Instead, he phoned his wife at the Sands to wish her happy birthday. "I hadn't expected it and screamed with excitement and pleasure," she wrote. "Should I have gone with him? I kept wondering. I was escaping from reality until that call—I must have needed the noise, the extravagance and general insanity of Las Vegas, the feeling of no responsibility, the feeling that life was being lived."

She returned home to find her husband "a bit edgy and resentful," as she carefully put it—understandably furious seems more likely. "Finally he calmed down enough to hear who'd been there and what we'd all done. He was somewhat jealous of Frank," she recalled, treading delicately.

Partly because he knew I loved being with him, partly because he thought Frank was in love with me, and partly because our physical life together, which had always ranked high, had less than flourished with his illness. Yet he was also crazy about Frank—loved having him feel that our home was his home. Knowing Bogie, I suspected he was beginning not to feel quite so well as he had been.

Bogart, who had had few illusions about anything, might have sensed how little time he had left. He also knew well that no matter how crazy he and Frank were about each other, his wife was thirty-two years old, in the prime of her life, and Frank Sinatra lived by his own set of rules.

"Frank loved Bogart," Peggy Connelly said, "but his woman was . . . just something else."

The playwright and screenwriter Ketti Frings, a close friend of the Bogarts', put a finer point on it. "Everybody knew about Betty and Frank," she said. "We

Lauren Bacall's thirty-second birthday, at the Sands. She and her husband, Humphrey Bogart, had been the center of the original Rat Pack, and Bacall had given the group its name.

just hoped Bogie wouldn't find out. That would have been more killing than the cancer."

—————

Back from the Sands in early October, Frank pulled down a cool $40,000 for doing *The Dinah Shore Chevy Show* on NBC. Though he had barely rehearsed, he gave good value, performing a dozen songs, half of them duets with the charming and easygoing host, the first woman to have her own TV variety show (theme song: "See the U.S.A. in Your Chevrolet"). Critics praised Frank and Dinah's unforced rapport, which certainly had something to do with the fact that Shore, though married to the actor George Montgomery, had long been an on-again, off-again paramour of Sinatra's.

Ten days later, he went to work on *The Joker Is Wild*. Joe E. Lewis, a long-time drinking buddy of Sinatra's, had been a popular comic and singer in Chicago in the 1920s when he ran afoul of a lieutenant of Al Capone's, Machine Gun Jack McGurn (born Vincenzo Antonio Gibaldi). McGurn had ordered Lewis killed, but though the entertainer's attackers fractured his skull and slit his throat, Lewis survived and, with damaged vocal cords, became a singing comedian rather than a singer who told jokes. He was a lifelong boozer and inveterate horseplayer whose shtick was carrying a highball onstage and toasting audiences with his catchphrase, "It is now post time!" The drunk act—if it was an act—inspired the likes of Dean Martin, Phil Harris, and Foster Brooks.

With Sinatra's new power in Hollywood—all his recent films except *Johnny Concho* had been box-office hits—he was able to strike a sweet deal for *The Joker Is Wild*: he optioned the Lewis biography while it was still in galleys, hired a director (Charles Vidor), and sold the package, with himself in the starring role, to Paramount for $400,000. Frank's end of the deal was $125,000, plus 25 percent of the film's profits. (He also had the power to give the studio's publicity chief a list of banned reporters. "I don't want any of these crumbs on the set when I'm around," Frank said.)

Vidor was a smart choice on Sinatra's part. The director had recently helmed *Love Me or Leave Me,* another musical biopic set in 1920s Chicago, starring Doris Day as the singer Ruth Etting and James Cagney as the gangster who loved her. The picture had won an Oscar (for Best Motion Picture Story) and had been nominated for five others; Vidor knew what he was doing.

He and Sinatra click perfectly in the black-and-white movie's superbly assured first half. Frank is effortlessly convincing as a lovable, cheeky nightclub singer, and his singing is terrific, as are Nelson Riddle's 1920s-style arrangements of "At Sundown," "I Cried for You," and "If I Could Be with You." The film's theme is a great new Cahn–Van Heusen number, their best (and least ambivalent) love song: "All the Way."

Sinatra's performance is equally fine after Lewis is horribly wounded and sinks to working as a mute burlesque clown and hitting the bottle. The problems crop up in the second hour, when Lewis finds a new career as a stand-up comic, loves and loses a society dame (Jeanne Crain), then marries and loses a chorus girl, played by Mitzi Gaynor. Both relationships fail for the same reason—Joe drinks too much and can't connect—and neither relationship is very interesting.

Nor, unfortunately, is Sinatra very interesting as Lewis the comedian. For one thing, as a stand-up comic he isn't just not funny; he's deadly. Over the years, Frank tried to do jokes in his nightclub acts, and they fell flat because they were just that: jokes. Humor, as anyone who's ever watched a nervous young comedian debut on a late-night talk show will know, is based not just on material but on timing, which is an innate gift, and, every bit as important, the quick establishment of a character that the audience likes and wants to laugh *to*. Sinatra lacked the natural comic timing that his friend Dean Martin possessed in such abundance (and that Frank so envied); as for character, audiences felt they already knew him well: he was a hot-tempered singing genius, with barely a laid-back bone in his body. The jokes he made on a nightclub stage usually carried an undertone (or an overtone) of anger.

This is somewhat true of the material he does as Joe E. Lewis in *The Joker Is Wild*, but the main problem with the portrayal is one of reverence. It's not an interpretation so much as a bad imitation. Frank loved the older man—for his earthy, self-deprecating humor, for his deep flaws, for his wounds themselves. Talking to the Hollywood reporter Bob Thomas just before production on the film began, Sinatra said excitedly, "I'll do some of Joe's parody songs, and I'll have a gravelly effect on the high notes, the way Joe does when he can't reach them. I'll also do some standup comedy routines, and I've done a pile of research on those. I watched Joe work several times at the Copacabana when I was in New York and picked up some routines from his writers that are real gassers. And I've been studying a film that was made of his act at the El Rancho Vegas."

Lewis was a homely man and a drunk, and his persona onstage was that of a poor schnook who just couldn't help himself. (The persona was very close to reality: a compulsive and reckless gambler, he was deeply in debt to the owners of El Rancho, and his employment arrangement at the casino was a kind of indentured servitude.) Lewis had a rascally twinkle in his eye; you rooted for him even when the jokes fell flat. Frank could play drunk pretty well, but he couldn't or wouldn't efface his considerable sexual charge: watching him try to be Lewis, you feel all too strongly that he just isn't. He's far more convincing (and funny) at the beginning of the movie when he's playing a nicer version of himself.

On the first of November, Sinatra returned to Capitol, at long last, to finish his album with the Hollywood String Quartet, *Close to You*.

The title track was the last tune recorded that night. The 1943 number by Jerry Livingston, Carl Lampl, and Al Hoffman was particularly dear to Frank: it was the first song he'd ever recorded for Columbia Records (backed up by the Bobby Tucker Singers instead of instrumentalists, because of the American Federation of Musicians strike of 1942 to 1944). The 1943 "Close to You" had been vintage wartime Sinatra, soft and youthful and ardent, music to send bobby-soxers into moist ecstasies—and to remind troops far from home of all they were missing.

The 1956 "Close to You" was no less ardent, but of course, with the almost forty-one-year-old Frank singing it, it took on different colors and depths. Against the sparse instrumental background, with its hints of Debussy and Ravel and led by Felix Slatkin's ravishing violin, the song sounded simple but wasn't. Rather than the young and yearning Sinatra, this was the middle-aged man, with his middle-aged voice, reaching out, not to the girl on the other side of the phonograph speaker, but to the magical lover—perhaps Ava, perhaps not—he seemed to keep trying to find:

You'll always be near, as though you were here by my side.

Unlike *In the Wee Small Hours*, the album of fresh heartbreak, *Close to You* was gentle, even hopeful. It was astonishingly intimate singing, created in the one place where Frank Sinatra was capable of creating intimacy.

———

A week later—in the interim, Dwight Eisenhower and Richard Nixon waltzed back into office—Frank was back at Capitol and in a very different mood, laying down the first tracks for a new album meant to take advantage of the resounding success of *Songs for Swingin' Lovers!* Sinatra himself came up with the new LP's reverberant title, *A Swingin' Affair!*, and he'd moved on with whiplash speed from the quiet world of *Close to You*. Saxophonist Don Raffell described the first full recording session for the album, on November 15, 1956:

We had rehearsed the music and we're sitting there. The double doors at Capitol open up and there's Sinatra. He's got a black hat on with a white band, black suit, black shirt, black shoes, white necktie— gangster. He doesn't say anything to anybody, walks into the recording booth, and says, "You've had plenty of time to get the balance on this thing. I don't want any fooling around or it'll be your ass!"

We did one take on each thing that we did. One! That's it. That's all he wanted to do. No slips, no nothing. He was an evil mother!

Could he even help himself?

A Swingin' Affair! was an even more upbeat affair than *Swingin' Lovers,* and once again Nelson Riddle's arrangements were magnificent. "Where *Lovers* included several slower pieces, such as 'We'll Be Together Again,' *Affair* is practically all variations on ['I've Got You Under My Skin']; crescendos and bolero patterns abound," Will Friedwald writes. "Almost every track is directly or indirectly patterned after that chart, starting slow and gradually mounting in dynamics, speed, and intensity."

Once again, sex was on Riddle's mind. "I usually try to avoid scoring a song with a climax at the end," he said. "Better to build about two-thirds of the way through, and then fade to a surprise ending. More subtle. I don't really like to finish by blowing and beating in top gear."

Affair's opening number, "Night and Day," was, perhaps, the exception that proved the rule. The great Cole Porter ballad was a keystone for Sinatra: he had sung it as a waiter at the Rustic Cabin and included it in his first recording session as a solo vocalist in 1942. As Friedwald notes, Frank treated the song "in nearly all tempos and moods and in every era of his seven decades of performing."

This exuberant version is done at the same loping tempo as *Swingin' Lovers'* "I've Got You Under My Skin," and the arrangement pays direct homage to that classic track: the first chorus has a similar repeating bass figure in the background; there's even another trombone buildup to the bridge (this time by Juan Tizol). But unlike "Skin," which hews to Riddle's rule and closes tenderly, like a lover murmuring postcoital endearments, *Affair's* "Night and Day" really does finish blowing and beating in top gear. Geniuses contradict themselves.

Between *A Swingin' Affair!* and soundtrack sessions for *The Joker Is Wild,* Sinatra spent much of November in the recording studio, logging an amazing eight dates in the month. The session of November 26 might have been the most remarkable of all: besides "Night and Day" and two other numbers ("Lonesome Road" and "If I Had You"), Frank recorded a tune that would become a classic for him, Rodgers and Hart's "The Lady Is a Tramp," for the first time. (The song, which was to play a pivotal role in Frank's next movie, *Pal Joey,* would wind up on the film's soundtrack album rather than on *Affair.*)

"Tramp" spoke to him in some deep way. Frank "seemed to take a particular delight in that song," Nelson Riddle said. "He always sang it with a certain amount of salaciousness. He savored it. He had some cute tricks with the lyric, which made it especially his." (There was actually only one trick, and how cute it seemed depended on your taste for the drolleries of Sammy

Cahn—increasingly Sinatra's go-to guy for special lyrics—who was probably responsible for the three changed lines: "She'll have no crap games with sharpies and frauds/And she won't go to Harlem in Lincolns or Fords/And she won't dish the dirt with the rest of the broads." It might reasonably be argued that Lorenz Hart didn't need another artist painting on his canvas.)

Might Frank's affinity for the song have had anything to do with Ava, whom the lyric seemed to fit like a glove? Another inspiration could have been Betty Bacall, who also tended to speak her mind and brook no nonsense. But in truth, the lady of the song, that free-living beauty who took no guff from anyone and did precisely as she pleased, didn't exist in real life. She was an ideal—someone, if the truth be told, who was a lot like Frank's ideal image of himself.

Dreaming of this paragon, Sinatra gave the tune a loving, lilting reading at a medium-swing tempo,* launched by Bill Miller's deliciously inventive piano intro (improvised and not written, and showing the great keyboardist, as in many other instances, to be his boss's musical equal). Then, opening like a great jewel box, comes Riddle's terrific chart, with its sequential reveals of strings, woodwinds, and brass (including Harry "Sweets" Edison's dulcet, minimal trumpet fills).

On the evening of November 26, Sinatra was magnificently in voice and relaxed, a fact that is especially striking in light of the news he'd heard that morning: Tommy Dorsey, who had been depressed over his health, his finances, an impending divorce, and the decline of the big-band business, and who'd been taking barbiturates in order to sleep, had choked on his own vomit and died in his bed the previous night in Greenwich, Connecticut.

———

It is hard to know Frank's true feelings about the death of his old boss, his musical mentor, the man he'd once tried to imitate in every possible way, from his astounding breath control to his spectacular wardrobe to the powder he used to clean his teeth.

In his biography of Dorsey, Peter Levinson claims Sinatra was so upset when he heard the news that he had to leave the *Joker Is Wild* set and go home for the day.† Yet Frank also failed to attend Tommy's funeral in New York on the twenty-ninth (though Sinatra had a lifelong aversion to funerals, which spooked him) and begged off from appearing on a televised memorial tribute put together by Jackie Gleason that Sunday, officially claiming he had back and neck pains but reportedly saying in private, "I didn't like him. It would be

---

* Soon to be disparaged by jazz purists as "the businessman's bounce."
† Levinson misidentifies the movie as *Pal Joey*.

inappropriate for me to appear on a memorial show." (Bill Miller later speculated that Frank had refused to appear because he wanted to produce the
show.)

"I didn't like him." But Frank had also idolized Dorsey. The brilliant, cold,
and domineering bandleader had generated ambivalence in almost everyone
who ever came in contact with him, his own brother included. But there was
also this: on the very day of Tommy Dorsey's funeral, Frank signed an extraordinarily lucrative television deal with ABC for a new series, to begin in 1957
and extend for three seasons. The contract called for thirty-six half-hour episodes: a blend of variety shows and mini-dramas, some of which Sinatra would
appear in and some of which he would only host. In return, he would receive
$3 million up front and 60 percent of the residuals. The network also bought
stock in Frank's movie-production company, Kent Productions. And Jackie
Gleason's tribute to Dorsey, which appeared on December 2 in place of his
regular variety show, was on CBS.

On the night of December 13, the day after his forty-first birthday, Frank
attended the Hollywood premiere of Ingrid Bergman's comeback film, *Anastasia*. In 1949, Bergman had created an international scandal when she left
her husband after conceiving a child with the Italian movie director Roberto
Rossellini. Bergman's frequent co-tenant in the lurid headlines that year had
been Frank Sinatra, whose affair with Ava Gardner was just becoming public.

Never one to risk boring the press, Frank attended the *Anastasia* premiere
with a gorgeous eighteen-year-old actress named Joan Blackman (she would
later co-star with Elvis in *Blue Hawaii*). When Kendis Rochlen of the Los
Angeles *Mirror News* asked him who his date was, he said, "Ezzard Charles."
The next day Rochlen wrote, "Ezzard was an eyeful in shocking-pink gown,
shoes, coat and lipstick."

On the fourteenth, Blackman accompanied Sinatra to Las Vegas, where he
was scheduled to perform at a gala show in honor of the fourth anniversary of
the Sands, in which Frank owned a 4 percent share. His other guest for the
evening was Joe Fischetti, the youngest (and least bright) of the three Fischetti
brothers of Chicago, first cousins to Al Capone and toilers in the same field.
"When no rooms were immediately available for [his guests]," Bill Davidson
wrote, Frank "threw a tantrum in the lobby of the hotel, almost engaging in a
fist fight with his old friend Jack Entratter."

Jerry Lewis, who had broken up with Dean Martin in July, was then headlining in the Copa Room. Two special shows were planned for the evening,
featuring Lewis, Sinatra, and Danny Thomas. Twelve hundred gamblers

waited in line to get in. Liberace, Lucille Ball, Esther Williams, Mitzi Gaynor, Jayne Mansfield, and Marlene Dietrich were there. But during the first show, at 1:00 a.m., Frank's voice cracked, apparently once more with laryngitis, and he sat out the second, 4:15 a.m., show at the bar. He then failed to show up for the anniversary cake-cutting ceremony at the pool. Jerry Lewis, who did appear, amused all present by jumping into the water fully clothed, though the trick had been done more than once by then.

Dorsey had died; Bogart was dying. And Ava was driving Frank crazy. She was announcing to all who would listen that she might marry the handsome Italian comedian Walter Chiari, the so-called Danny Kaye of Italy, whom she'd been stringing along for a couple of years but whose attractiveness the recent mess with Sinatra in Spain seemed to have sharply increased.

Gardner had also just sat for a two-part profile in *Look* (the two install-ments were picturesquely titled "The Private Hell of Ava Gardner" and "Ava Gardner: In Search of Love"). Hedda Hopper later alleged that the writer, Joe Hyams, hid a microphone in Ava's car and rode around the desert near Palm Springs with her, secretly recording her incendiary comments about Sinatra. Speaking in confidence (she thought), she complained, "Frank double-crossed me . . . made me the heavy . . . I paid many of the bills."

Hopper, who interviewed Sinatra in his dressing room on the set of *The Joker Is Wild,* claimed that with the *Look* piece, "the Ava era finally ended for him . . . Frank sat with a copy of the resulting magazine story in his hand, cringing like a whipped dog . . . Even the ashes were cold after that."

Sinatra had spent the entire month of November shuttling back and forth between a movie set and the recording studio. And then there was the fact that he was forty-one now—not just forty but *in* his forties, officially middle-aged. Is it any wonder that over the winter of 1956–57, he began to fear that he was losing his voice?

7

||||||||||

What do you think I'm made of? Don't you know I got a low
boiling point?

—SINATRA'S CHARACTER JOEY EVANS IN *PAL JOEY*

After the vocal glitch at the Sands anniversary show, Frank played the rest of his stand without incident, finishing out his eventful 1956 by entertaining a gala New Year's Eve party in the Copa Room: every woman present was given twenty-five newly minted silver dollars in a velvet bag. (One of which, considering Sinatra's ownership stake in the casino, could have been said to be coming from him.) He rested for a few days in Palm Springs, then headed east for his January 10 opening at the Copacabana. Though she had a bad cold, Peggy Connelly postponed a doctor's appointment to meet him at the airport. A questionable favor.

The week was bitterly cold in New York, but that couldn't keep the crowds away from the hottest act in show business. Among the hundreds jamming the basement nightclub for Sinatra's premiere were Joe DiMaggio, Judy Garland, Pat Boone, Yul Brynner, Sammy Davis Jr., Johnnie Ray, Edith Piaf, Sugar Ray Robinson, Judy Holliday, Dinah Shore, Errol Flynn, and the ever-present Marlene Dietrich. Joey Bishop, opening for Frank, looked out at the glittering assemblage and said, "Are all these people out of work?"

Davis, sitting ringside with a party of ten (he would sit ringside not just at the opening but at Sinatra's every midnight show), ran backstage to wish his idol luck. "When I got to the dressing room Hank Sanicola told me that Frank had gone out for a walk, by himself," he recalled.

> If ever there was a time for a performer to be alone, this was it. The strength to face that fantastic audience could only come from the same place that he'd drawn the power to attract them. I went back downstairs, not envying him this hour. It's great to know that the world is out there waiting for you, but who could know better than Frank how easily you can close your eyes to bask in the flattery and the admiration of millions of people and then when you open your eyes they can be gone. It's great to be the absolute hottest thing in the business but how do you live up to being a legend?

Davis contrasted the new Sinatra with the one he'd spotted in Times Square during the down period just a couple of years earlier:

> I vividly remembered that night on Broadway in '53 or '54: the same man, walking by himself, hands in his pockets, coat collar turned up— nobody recognizing him. To see him come back from that, not only a better performer but bigger than ever, was a sight to behold. And he'd done it alone.

Now "the lights lowered and a single spot shone on the microphone in the center of the stage," Davis wrote.

> The music started, only the brass and the drums, like a signal, an announcement. I glanced toward the stairs. Frank was standing motion-less, looking straight ahead, waiting.
>   It was all there: the sound, the confidence, the distinctive hands, the shoulders, the cigarette cupped in his palm, the slight stretching of his neck—everything, and within three songs he'd more than lived up to the legend, he'd surpassed it.

"Frankie sang for approximately an hour," Earl Wilson wrote, "and also did several comedy hits in the manner of Joe E. Lewis whom he portrays in 'The Joker Is Wild.' Testing out his voice key, Frankie said, 'If I could find my key— I'd [go to] my room.' Lifting his glass in a toast he proclaimed, 'Here's to our greatest ally—Scotland.'"

Ba-da-boom—the jokes were not only corny but canned: it was Lewis's material. The audience didn't care; they were crazy for Frank. He could've read the phone book and gotten ovations. He saw it; he felt it. Excited, he threw in an ad-lib. "Dot Kilgallen isn't here tonight," he said, grinning. "She's out shopping for a new chin."

A momentary hush, nervous laughter. The patrons would have well known Kilgallen's less than classic features from her weekly appearances as a panel-ist on the quiz show *What's My Line?* The crowd had now tasted Sinatra's real sense of humor: this was payback for the columnist's snarky Sunday-supplement series on Frank the previous March. The next day, two usually friendly if not sycophantic journalists, Walter Winchell and Louis Sobol, both took Sinatra to task for the remark, Sobol calling it "in bad taste" and "inexcusable."

It all rolled off his back. He was flying, supercharged. "It was more than just his performance that was causing a sort of mass hysteria," Davis recalled.

The women were gazing at him with greater adoration than ever and now even the men were giving him a beyond-envy kind of respect, leaning in toward him, approving, nodding like *Yeah!* because Frank . . . was the guy with the guts to walk alone, the guy who'd fought the odds and won.

But the guy with the guts to walk alone was increasingly getting liquid help. We have the testimony of an average citizen, one Harry Agoratus of Staten Island, who was fortunate enough to attend one of Sinatra's Copacabana shows that January: "Mr. Sinatra was in excellent voice, very much at ease, establishing a marvelous rapport with the audience," he told Richard Havers.

After a few songs and a bit of chatter, he motioned with outstretched hand, thumb and forefinger a few inches apart, to a nearby table that had bottle and setup on it. Were they friends or strangers? I don't know. But someone poured a few fingers into a glass and handed it to him. I subsequently heard from others that he routinely did that and picked up the tab for the table. He was at the absolute top of his game. He had the audience, men as well as women, entranced. There were hundreds in the room, but he sang to each of us individually. While he sang there was total silence; when he finished, the room erupted. Those same women, who as teenagers jammed the Paramount Theater fifteen or so years earlier, now stood on the tables of the Copa to get a better view. When the show ended some tables did not want to leave. We left at close to midnight, and walked into a raging snowstorm.

———

Bogart died in the early-morning hours of January 14. Frank heard about it just before he was to go on at the Copa that night; he called Abe Lastfogel, his agent at William Morris, and canceled. "I can't go on," he said. "I'm afraid I wouldn't be coherent." Jerry Lewis stepped in for him at the dinner show, doing a Copacabana single for the first time; Sammy Davis Jr. did the midnight show.

The funeral was on January 18 at All Saints' Episcopal Church in Beverly Hills. Thousands gathered outside; inside, the two hundred mourners who filled the pews were a Who's Who of Hollywood: Jack Warner, Harry Cohn, David O. Selznick; Hepburn and Tracy, Gregory Peck, Gary Cooper, James Mason, Joan Fontaine, Danny Kaye, Ronald Reagan; William Wyler, Richard Brooks, Billy Wilder. Three members of the original Rat Pack, David Niven,

Mike Romanoff, and Swifty Lazar, served as ushers. John Huston gave the eulogy.

Sinatra was absent.

He had sent Peggy Connelly in his place. A terse item in Louella Parsons's column of January 17 read, "Frank Sinatra will be unable to make it for Bogey's funeral. His doctors won't let him fly."

Perhaps he had simply caught Connelly's cold. Then again, things were rarely simple with Frank.

———

Close to You was released the following Monday. Capitol ad copy—"A New High in Intimate Song Styling"—hopefully touted the album's strongest suit. And the reviews largely agreed. *Playboy* wrote, "Sinatra is still the chairman of the board at the handling of material like 'Everything Happens to Me,' 'With Every Breath I Take,' 'It Could Happen to You,' 'Blame It on My Youth,' 'The End of a Love Affair,' and the other seven quiet standards in the collection." But there were reservations. "The writing for the quartet is unobtrusive and caressing enough," the review continued, "but with a singer who pulsates as surely as Sinatra, his background must have a rhythmic swing, too, even in ballads; especially in ballads. The Hollywood String Quartet doesn't."

The album did not fly out of the record stores. It wound up charting respectably, rising as high as number 5 on *Billboard*'s album chart, but it didn't have staying power. After the blockbuster success of *Songs for Swingin' Lovers!*—whose sales would only be surpassed by Sinatra's 1993 *Duets*—*Close to You* had to be counted a commercial disappointment. Intimacy didn't seem to be what the record-buying public wanted from Frank.

———

Earl Wilson and Walter Winchell might have palled around with Sinatra, Hedda Hopper might have batted her eyelashes at him, but no columnist felt quite as possessive about Frank—and indeed the entire Sinatra family—as the redoubtable, relentlessly mother-hen-ish Louella Parsons. Parsons, who in the second decade of the twentieth century had become America's first gossip columnist, then the nation's first movie columnist, was preeminent in her field and enormously powerful, owing her international stature and her forty million readers to a rock-solid relationship with her boss, the politically and socially conservative William Randolph Hearst. However, unlike her archrival, Hopper, who was fiercely Republican and anti-Communist, Parsons wasn't inclined to be publicly political. Also unlike Hedda, Louella lacked a certain vindictiveness. She could scold her subjects, she could fall out with them, but she was keenly aware of the theatrical value of forgiving and forgetting. This came in especially handy with Frank Sinatra.

Parsons, more a social conservative than a political one, consistently pushed family values in her columns, despite or because of the fact that she was based in a company town that relentlessly undermined family values even as it touted them in public. Accordingly—and wisely, and humanely—she forged an early (and visible) bond with the wronged woman in the Sinatra-Gardner affair, Nancy Barbato Sinatra. Parsons was a regular visitor at the Carolwood house; she wrote regularly about Nancy's social doings and played up her "dates" (the divorcée apparently had no romantic interests besides her ex); she performed the real and valuable service of buttressing Big Nancy's dignity. And she doted on the three children in print, whether she was writing about little Tina's shyness or Nancy Sandra's teen romances or the more elusive charms of the remote and wistful little boy who had been given his father's name* but little of his time or attention.

But on February 1, Louella triumphantly told the world that she had at last found something of substance to say about Frank's son:

> I don't like to call a child a prodigy, but 13-year-old Frank Sinatra, Jr. comes close to qualifying in that class. He played the piano for us at a buffet dinner Nancy Sinatra gave in honor of Lorayne Brock Busse and Joseph Hall, who will be married Feb. 14.
>
> Young Frankie doesn't care for Rock 'N' Roll, and says he's never seen Elvis Presley. But he feels that Elvis came up too suddenly and that he should work as hard as Frank, Sr., Bing Crosby and Perry Como did for their success.
>
> We played Frank Sr.'s new record [*Close to You*], and Frank, Jr. congratulated Jimmy McHugh on "I Didn't Sleep a Wink Last Night," included in the album. Believe me, coming from Frankie that was a compliment.
>
> Joseph Schenck, Dorothy Manners, the William Perlbergs, the George Seatons, the Harry Brands and the Ed Leshins gathered around the piano to hear this talented boy play.

It was a strange occasion: the middle-aged to elderly group of Old Guard Hollywood types (Parsons herself was now seventy-five; Joe Schenck, at seventy-

---

* Little Frankie's name was officially Franklin Wayne Emanuel Sinatra, but he was saddled at an early age with the easier to remember—but far harder to bear—moniker of Frank Sinatra Jr.

eight, was about to retire from 20th Century Fox, the studio he'd co-founded a quarter century earlier), standing around the piano while the slick-haired boy played standards. The assemblage listening reverently to the absent master's Voice. The precociously opinionated but oddly unemotional thirteen-year-old holding forth about the weakness of the new music and the strength of the standards. In a way, everything Frank Sinatra Jr. was to become was contained in that evening.

February was a strange blur. In Honolulu on the sixth, Frank's long-planned tour of Australia, the Philippines, Hong Kong, and Japan ended before it began over an absurd airport misunderstanding. Traveling with Sanicola, Van Heusen, and five musicians, Sinatra claimed to have reserved sleeping berths for Hank, Jimmy, and himself aboard the fifteen-hour flight to Sydney; Qantas had only two berths for them. Frank turned on his heel and took his whole party back to Los Angeles. He wound up paying $75,000 for lost bookings and compensating his musicians for the loss of earnings. Fans Down Under were understandably furious. "CRANKY FRANKIE" GIVES US THE BIG BRUSH-OFF, read the headline in the Sydney *Daily Mirror*.

Something was gnawing at him. Was he still worried about his voice—worried enough, perhaps, to have canceled the Far East tour on a pretext? He had always been an enthusiastic consumer of alcohol; suddenly his drinking seemed to have turned more serious. On Valentine's Day, at a big Friars birthday benefit for Jack Benny at the Beverly Hilton, Frank sat on the dais and polished off most of a bottle of Scotch in front of eight hundred eyewitnesses, including, besides the saintly Benny, Bob Hope, George Burns, George Jessel, Dean Martin, Tony Martin, Deborah Kerr, and Ronald Reagan.

In the early hours of February 16, he was asleep in his Palm Springs bedroom when he was awakened by what sounded like an inebriated woman outside. "Daddy, darling!" she was calling. "Lover boy! Frankie, Frankie!" Before Frank knew what was happening, he heard a key in the lock, and the woman, along with two men, had entered the house, walked into his bedroom, and shone a flashlight into his face. One of them shoved a piece of paper into his hand. The three were Los Angeles police detectives, there to serve Sinatra with a subpoena to testify before a California state senate committee about his role in the Wrong-Door Raid of November 1954.

Until September 1955, when the Hollywood scandal sheet *Confidential* published an exposé about the raid ("The Real Reason for Marilyn Monroe's Divorce"), the LAPD had treated the incident as a burglary. But the magazine had pointed out inconsistencies in Sinatra's account of the evening—he claimed that he'd stayed in the car while a group of his buddies smashed down the door they thought Monroe was behind; eyewitnesses claimed otherwise—and now there was talk that while the state senate investigated the methods and ethics of private investigators and scandal magazines, Frank could come up on perjury charges.

It was all a huge headache. After talking with his lawyer Mickey Rudin, Sinatra said he was contemplating filing a damage suit against the LAPD. He got a court order requiring the police detectives to attend a deposition and explain themselves. Though their methods had been unorthodox, to say the least, their story held up in court. After the policewoman's love calls had failed to roust Frank from his bed, they had gained access to the house, they testified, with a set of keys provided by "an informant." "It's a good thing I was asleep, or you could have gotten a bullet in you," Frank told them. (He had had a pistol permit since 1947.) "If *I* had had a gun, *you* might have gotten shot," one of the officers volleyed back. The Los Angeles police chief, William Parker, gave Frank a fishy look. "It seems to me," Parker said drily, "that somebody is attempting to take the spotlight away from the real issue in the matter."

The newspapers made comic hay of the hearing, reporting that Frank had called the lady cop "a loud-mouthed blonde." "I am not now nor have I ever been a blonde," the policewoman, Gloria Dawson, retorted. But it was all a distraction; the subpoena stood. On February 28, Frank, "snappily clad in a charcoal gray suit with black knit tie and dapper black hat," according to the *Los Angeles Times,* walked into the State Building in downtown L.A. to testify before a committee headed by the state senator Fred H. Kraft about his activities on the tragicomic night of November 5, 1954.

The black hat might have been an unfortunate choice.

On his way through "the forest of newsreel and TV cameras," Sinatra was handed *another* summons, by a lieutenant from the LAPD's bunko squad, to appear in March before the county grand jury's separate probe into the Wrong-Door Raid. The whole mess would distract him until well into July.

With Martin Gang, the sober-faced senior partner of his law firm, sitting behind him, Frank raised his right hand—pinkie ring prominently displayed—and the hearing began. The main point of contention was whether Sinatra had, as the *Confidential* article reported, joined Joe DiMaggio and the others in breaking into the apartment where they expected to catch Marilyn Monroe in flagrante but instead found (and flash photographed) the startled and terrified thirty-seven-year-old legal secretary Florence Kotz. Under oath, Frank insisted he'd stood by his car smoking a cigarette throughout the whole misadventure.

"Throughout his questioning, Sinatra was alternately flippant and serious," the *Times* reported.

Asked at the outset which DiMaggio he had reference to, he retorted, "There's only one that I know."

When it was pointed out that Joe DiMaggio has several well-known brothers, the crooner amended his reply to:

"Well, Joe's probably the hottest one."

Asked if he once made a picture called "The Tender Trap," the singer-actor responded readily, "It was a smash. Of course I remember."

Also to testify before the Kraft Committee that day was Phil Irwin, the young operative who on the night in question had been assisting the private detective Barney Ruditsky. (Ruditsky, who was recuperating from a heart attack, did not appear at the hearing.) Frank denied knowing Irwin. He said someone he didn't recognize had come to the MGM set of *The Tender Trap* and told him that Ruditsky had sold the story to *Confidential*. "I don't know why he came to tell me that," Sinatra said. "I assume he, for some reason, was trying to play hero with me. I don't know why."

Taking the stand after Frank, the baby-faced twenty-four-year-old said, "Almost all of Mr. Sinatra's statements were false."

Irwin told the committee that in fact he was on a first-name basis with Frank; he had even been to his Wilshire Boulevard apartment. After the *Confidential* story on the Wrong-Door Raid came out, containing details only an insider would have known, the young investigator immediately realized that Ruditsky (whose employ he had left) had sold the story to the scandal sheet, but was fearful of the consequences if Sinatra suspected Irwin of the betrayal. Irwin testified that he went to see Frank on the MGM set of *The Tender Trap* and swore he wasn't to blame. Frank believed him, Irwin said, and agreed with his contention that Ruditsky was responsible. According to the young investigator, Sinatra then told him that if there were any further questions about the raid, Irwin should say that he, along with DiMaggio and everyone else involved, had all been at a party at Frank's house.

The state senator Edwin Regan, a member of the committee, looked back and forth between the two men and said, "There is perjury apparent here."

More than perjury was apparent. Young Irwin was terrified. After he'd reported his side of the story to the committee's investigator, he'd been beaten up by six thugs on a Highland Park street corner. When the committee asked him if he thought Sinatra was connected with the beating, Irwin said he had no evidence to that effect.

"Do you still fear him?" the committee's counsel John Arden asked.

"Still very much so."

"What do you fear?"

"I'm afraid of being beaten up again."

"Aside from being beaten up, have you no other fears?" Arden asked.

Irwin shrugged and thought for a moment. "Yes," he said. "I have other fears."

———

Around the time of the hearing, Louella spotted Frank sitting in a corner at Romanoff's with Jack Entratter. "Frankie looked as if he had the weight of the world on his shoulders," she wrote.

The Wrong-Door Raid might have been the least of it.

———

He got off. Not quite scot-free, but he got off nevertheless, in part through the expert ministrations of Gang and Rudin, and perhaps those of Sidney Korshak, the all-powerful Chicago lawyer (his clients at various times included Al Capone, Sam Giancana, and Jimmy Hoffa) famed for being able to untie the knottiest situations with a single phone call. During Frank's fifty-minute testimony before the grand jury in March, he displayed some of the same insouciance he had shown the state committee. When the district attorney asked how he could account for the stark discrepancies between his story and Phil Irwin's, Sinatra answered, "Who are you going to believe, me or a guy who makes his living kicking down bedroom doors?"

The DA elected not to pursue an indictment against Frank. "There is definitely a bald conflict in the testimony," he said. "But the transcript falls short in its present form of showing the complete elements of a perjury." The result was seen as an implied criticism of the LAPD for failing to act at the outset of the case.

Yet even without an indictment, the whole episode was a very public black eye for Sinatra and the end of his friendship with DiMaggio, who ducked the state committee hearing (he managed to be in New York at the time) and felt ever afterward that in underwriting and encouraging the Wrong-Door Raid, Frank had made him look bad in order to get into Marilyn Monroe's good graces, and her bed.

———

At the end of the 1955 *Time* cover story on Sinatra, Frank had been quoted as saying, "I'm going to do as I please. I don't need anybody in the world. I did it all myself."

The problem was, Frank Sinatra had never said these words: some enterprising editor at *Time* had simply made them up, to round out the story nicely and put a point on its thesis. Accordingly, Frank did not have a warm spot in his heart for *Time* magazine or for its Hollywood correspondent Ezra Goodman, who had nominally written the piece. Thus, when Goodman showed up one day on the set of *Pal Joey*—to interview Kim Novak for a *Time* cover story—Frank spotted him and walked away from the camera. "He informed director George Sidney that either Sinatra or Goodman was leaving the set, which was simply not big enough for the two of us," Goodman recalled.

> The fact that I was there to see Novak and not Sinatra was beside the point. Inevitably, I left the set.
> Studio boss Harry Cohn received me in his office. He was sympathetic. "But what can I do?" he said helplessly. "We're doing a big musical number with all the stars and if Sinatra walks we'll be out a day's shooting." So I saw Novak away from the set of *Pal Joey*. The next day I found out that, although I had left the set, Sinatra had walked out anyway, thereby fouling up production for the day and costing Columbia a small fortune.

Everybody survived. Goodman got his story, and Cohn got his movie, Frank having returned to the set and completed what Tom Santopietro calls "the last great musical of his career."

Pal Joey really was something like great, or two-thirds great. In playing a cocky heel of a nightclub singer, Sinatra was edging very close to reality. With his lined face, his shameless eye for the main chance, and his unapologetically unleashed libido, Joey Evans looks an awful lot like the Frank Sinatra of 1957, minus the millions and the overweening power of course. The fact that Joey is down-and-out at the beginning of the story is a necessary contrivance, a quick nod at dramatic necessity. He may be down-and-out, but from the word go he sure can sing the hell out of (and Nelson Riddle can arrange the hell out of) those great Rodgers and Hart tunes. And—until about two-thirds of the way through the film—the fact that the characters vocalize in show-business settings, rather than just breaking into song wherever and whenever, gives *Pal Joey* a smooth and powerful momentum. You believe what's happening on-screen, and details like the tough byplay between Joey and Mike (Hank Henry), the hard-to-charm nightclub manager, lend the movie real grit. As does the studio's wise decision to make extensive use of actual San Francisco exteriors (giving *Pal Joey* a big leg up, in this regard, over *Guys and Dolls* and *The Man with the Golden Arm*).

As does the picture's sheer sex. Frank's famous sandwich comment about taking second billing between Rita Hayworth and Kim Novak might have been playfully crude, but to watch the three of them at work in *Pal Joey* is to understand exactly what he was talking about. The auburn-haired thirty-eight-year-old Hayworth and the blond twenty-four-year-old Novak are glorious opposites, and the forty-one-year-old Sinatra plays perfectly against them, and vice versa. When Joey remarks to Linda (Novak) that she'd look better out of those silk pajamas (though she looks pretty terrific in them), you get an idea where the movie is going. When he pressures the stuffy Vera (Hayworth) to reveal her stripteaser past at a charity auction, and when she reluctantly—but quite beautifully—does so in the musical number "Zip" (choreographed by the great Hermes Pan), you're certain. In her immortal "Put the Blame on Mame" in 1946's *Gilda,* Hayworth memorably took off nothing but her gloves, but forever set masculine pulses racing. In "Zip," she takes off nothing at all, yet with a shrug of those exquisite shoulders and a flick of those hips she shows she's still got It.

The sex in *Pal Joey* is all suggestion, which of course is the sexiest kind. When Joey sings "The Lady Is a Tramp" to Vera, the acting is all in her eyes— she's first outraged, then intrigued, then hot and bothered—and it's perfect. When the two of them dance, and she takes his hand afterward and says, "Come now, beauty," the thermometer has officially hit the boiling point. The same is true whenever the camera simply lingers on Novak's killer cheekbones

Frank with his *Pal Joey* co-stars Kim Novak and Rita Hayworth. Sinatra happily yielded his top billing for the picture. "It's okay to make it Hayworth/Sinatra/Novak," he said. "I don't mind being in the middle of that sandwich."

and abandoned gaze. The movie's ludicrous ending—after a corny dream ballet, Vera blithely gives up Joey to Linda (who mouths "thank you"), and Joey
and Linda literally stroll off into a Technicolor sunset—says more about marketing than it does about the great work of all concerned.

Frank's previous close-to-real-life role, as the über-swinger Charlie Reader
in 1955's *Tender Trap,* was a hit with moviegoers because it was a kind of car-
toon: Charlie was the untrammeled character a fearful and restricted America
wanted and needed Sinatra to be. But *The Tender Trap* was pure artifice (and
pure saccharine), an MGM product through and through. Two years on, *Pal
Joey,* Frank's second outing as a producer (after *Johnny Concho*), was a tougher,
darker, sexier piece of work—a movie for grown-ups. And Sinatra is a grown-
up in it. (The new lines around his eyes, the hints of hooding in the lids, are a
harbinger of the fuller, older face to come.) Joey Evans almost entirely lacked
a central element in most of Frank's screen work to date: ingratiation. If Hollywood had made him play the self-effacing Nathan Detroit rather than the
smooth Sky Masterson in *Guys and Dolls,* he now had the wherewithal to
confer the latter role on himself. More than that. In his eyes, on-screen and in
life, there was a new look of command: he wasn't high-paid help anymore; he
was, as his friends and hangers-on called him, the Leader.

––––––

"Lauren Bacall, whom the whole town likes and respects for the way she made
Bogie's last days happier, is starting to get out in the less conspicuous places,"
the Behind the Scenes in Hollywood column noted, anonymously, on April 2.
"She was at the Peacock Lane with Adolph Green, Irving Lazar and Frank
Sinatra to hear pianist Errol Garner."

It wouldn't do, yet, for the two of them to go out alone; these things had to
be handled delicately.

––––––

Sinatra and Riddle had reached a curious juncture in their great collaboration.
After finishing the sublime *Close to You,* they'd closed out 1956 on an undistinguished note: in early December, Frank had recorded a heart-sinkingly pallid
"Young at Heart" imitation called "Your Love for Me" ("It's fabulous, it's fantasy,
it knocks me out tremendously/Your love for me") and a charming if superficial
bopper, "Can I Steal a Little Love?" Riddle arranged both, and not on one of
his best days. He and Sinatra then hadn't made it back to Capitol Studios
until mid-March, and they didn't do much better upon their return. The two
tracks Frank laid down on the fourteenth were a bright trifle called "So Long,
My Love" and the pleasant but unmemorable "Crazy Love." Sammy Cahn had
penned the lyrics for both; the composers, however, were neither Jule Styne

nor Jimmy Van Heusen but Lew Spence (who was capable of better) and Phil Tuminello, the writer of "Can I Steal a Little Love?"

All singer-arranger collaborations, even the great ones, have their highs and lows: it wasn't that Sinatra-Riddle had gone stale but rather that Frank, in his restless search for hit singles—in which he was aided by Hank Sanicola, Voyle Gilmore, Jimmy Van Heusen, and others—had made some dicey choices along the way. The great Riddle had had to arrange some not-so-great tunes. But Frank's eternal restlessness was of a piece with his great artistic imagination: even if his dazzling streak with Riddle had remained perfectly unbroken, it also makes perfect sense that he would begin looking for a new sound in the mid-1950s. And a new sound meant a new arranger.

"Without intending any slight to Riddle, [Sinatra] had at least two good reasons for turning to Billy May and Gordon Jenkins," Friedwald writes.

> First, he didn't want to be "married" to any one particular arranger's sound; he feared that ten years earlier he had relied too heavily on Stordahl and had been chained to one approach when his audiences tired of the Sinatra-Stordahl style. Like Nat King Cole, who wisely switched from a small combo to solo microphone when his trio was at the very height of its popularity, Sinatra knew that the time to switch to something new was before what he was currently doing had worn out its welcome. Second, as early as 1956, Sinatra had begun to think about not only controlling but also owning his recorded performances outright. Whether he could achieve that in conjunction with Capitol or if he needed to go elsewhere, he seems to have anticipated wanting a brand-new sound to distinguish the new venture.

Sinatra might not have intended to slight Riddle, but that was the way Riddle took it. His teaming with Frank had rocketed the singer back to the summit of the popular-music world, and Frank paid back Riddle in kind. "Sinatra took good care of Nelson," Alan Livingston said. "[He] would not work with anybody else. Riddle was his man. And Frank was very protective of him: he took Nelson on the road with him and did everything he could for him. And Nelson was delighted because he emerged far bigger than he had been before that . . . Sinatra took him with him, really."

Then—just for the moment—Frank let him go.

"Frank used Nelson for many albums until one day he decided on Gordon Jenkins," the music publisher and Sinatra friend Frank Military said. "I remember Nelson calling me and saying, 'What did I do? What's the matter?' I said, 'Frank just wants a different sound.' But Nelson was really upset about it."

Frank had known both May and Jenkins since the big-band days; he turned to Jenkins first for very specific reasons. In addition to being an arranger, the quirky, multitalented midwesterner was a pianist, a record producer, a recording-company executive, and an extremely successful songwriter. Soon after leaving Dorsey and making his big move to California, Frank had performed Jenkins's tune "San Fernando Valley" on the radio. It was a beautiful, upbeat song, and at twenty-seven Sinatra invested it with an irresistible optimism and sense of possibility:

> *I'll forget my sins*
> *I'll be makin' new friends*
> *Where the West begins,*
> *And the sunset ends.*

Direct emotion was key to Gordon Jenkins's artistic sensibility: old-fashioned sentimentality was no sin to him. He was a left-handed (literally) American original, a man of many parts, by turns warm and reserved, effusive and misanthropic. Born in Missouri in 1910, he had bounced all over the music business. In his twenties, he played piano and wrote charts for the bandleader-composer Isham Jones, orchestrated in Broadway and Hollywood, and then, after World War II, went to work as a producer-arranger-conductor for Decca Records. Throughout, he was also a highly prolific composer, writing such hits as "Goodbye" and "Blue Prelude" (used, respectively, as theme songs by the bandleaders Benny Goodman and Woody Herman), "Homesick, That's All," and "P.S. I Love You." In 1946, Decca released his suite *Manhattan Tower*, a groundbreaking composition—some have called it an early concept album—based on the life and loves of a fictional young man, a sort of twentieth-century young Werther, who comes to New York from the hinterlands seeking love and meaning. The highly expressive (and often excessive) work contained original songs, mood music, and spoken narration: it all seemed new and daring, and critics and record buyers alike loved it. Over the next decade, Jenkins rewrote and expanded the piece; when he moved from Decca to Capitol in 1956, his new label reissued it.

As an arranger, Jenkins also hewed to old-fashioned values: he loved strings—lots of strings—and he disliked dissonance and modern chords. No Ravel and Debussy for him; he was a Tchaikovsky man all the way. As a musical mind, he was far closer to Axel Stordahl than to Nelson Riddle.

And in truth, Jenkins the arranger had been on Frank Sinatra's mind since 1946, when Frank heard some of the string-heavy orchestrations he had done for Judy Garland; more recently, he had admired the work the arranger had done with Nat King Cole, especially Cole's recent number 1 album *Love Is the Thing*.

Sinatra had, as music aficionados say, big ears. His tastes in classical music ranged from the impressionist textures of Debussy and Ravel to the complex harmonies of Ralph Vaughan Williams to the Slavonic lyricism of Reinhold Glière to, even, the dissonances of Stravinsky. But he also felt a strong attachment to—and an ethnic identification with—the rich emotionality of Puccini, and he felt this same vibration in Gordon Jenkins's arranging. Frank loved Nelson Riddle's genius, but he also loved straightforward sentiment and simple chords and heavy layers of strings every bit as much as Jenkins did, and in the early spring of 1957—for at least one major reason, if not more—he needed musical swaddling. The writer Bruce Jenkins, Gordon Jenkins's son, contends that it was more than artistic restlessness that moved Frank to seek a new and more overtly emotional collaborator. "Why not have time in your life to really dwell on [sadness] in a dark and quiet room?" he writes in his book about his father. "There should be no fear of crying, no harm in appreciating a brand of despair so vividly captured in words and music. That's what happened when Sinatra and my father got together. That's the sole reason Frank ever sought him out."

What was the source of the despair? Sinatra was in strange emotional ter-

Sinatra with the arranger Gordon Jenkins. Deprecated by some, Jenkins wrote openly emotional arrangements that appealed to the sentimentalist in Frank.

ritory in early 1957: having gained the world, he was feeling its weight. He was also more worried about the faculty at the center of his existence than he let on to lovers, close friends, or collaborators. "He felt," Jonathan Schwartz says, "he was beginning to lose his voice, not trusting his own instrument."

Frank Military described to Schwartz a crucial April 1957 session on the album that Sinatra and Jenkins had just begun making together, *Where Are You?* One of the songs Frank was to record that night was a tune that meant a great deal to him: "Lonely Town," by Leonard Bernstein, with lyrics by Betty Comden and Adolph Green. In 1949, when he was singing and dancing in a sailor suit—and not feeling very good about himself—in the MGM musical *On the Town,* Sinatra had eagerly looked forward to performing Bernstein's complex hymn to urban solitude. But the studio had yanked the song (along with much of the rest of Bernstein's score) at the last minute, feeling it wasn't commercial enough. Frank had been furious.

This April night, then, was a chance at redemption—if not revenge. Unknown to everyone but Frank, it was also a vocal test. In some deep part of himself, he wasn't sure if his voice was what it had been. After he recorded the song, Schwartz says, "The room emptied, and he asked the booth to play it back. He stood by one of the walls, [leaning] on one of the railings, and just held on to the railing and listened, and he heard the truth. He was even better. He was so grateful to Jenkins."

———

Frank had huge admiration for Nelson Riddle, but Riddle, with his dour and professorial mien, was difficult to warm up to. He was like a great research chemist, going into his lab and coming back with complex formulas that worked brilliantly. Jenkins, on the other hand, gave Sinatra something visceral. "Frank sure loved Gordon," the drummer Nick Fatool said. Why? The pianist Bill Miller, himself the possessor of a highly subtle musical mind, once hazarded an educated guess. "There's a certain squareness about Frank; I say that affectionately," he said. "He has an old-fashioned side, and Gordon Jenkins represents that. As a singer he doesn't hear the harmonies the way we would. He hears those high singing strings—that was Gordon's gimmick."

To listen to *Where Are You?* is to hear those singing strings in abundance— and also to hear a new side to Sinatra's voice that at first had some of his deeper listeners concerned. "When I first heard it," Jonathan Schwartz recalled, "I said, 'What's the matter? Is there something wrong?' It just seemed there was something different. Not the guy we knew on *Wee Small Hours, Swing Easy, Songs for Swingin' Lovers, Swingin' Affair* and so on. This was a different sound. And it was even more adult."

The difference is palpable. Compare the superbly assured vocals on a couple of tracks from *A Swingin' Affair!* or *Close to You* with any song from *Where Are You?*—say the melancholy title number by Harold Adamson and Jimmy McHugh—and you can hear it in a second. Jenkins's strings are singing, all right; they're right up front (the fact that *Where Are You?* was the first Sinatra album in stereo might have emphasized the strings' frontality). The effect is a sheltering of Frank's voice, which has a roughness and a slight quaver that has never been present before. A new boundary has been crossed.

On "Lonely Town," the tune he was so concerned about, an ensemble of horns, rather than strings, leads in rather triumphantly, with echoes of Bernstein, Comden, and Green's "New York, New York" (not the Kander and Ebb "Theme from New York, New York," popularized by Sinatra in the 1980s), before Frank's vocal turns melancholy:

> *A town's a lonely town when you pass through,*
> *And there is no one waiting there for you.*

It's a brilliant vocal, and he had every right to be pleased with it. But this truly isn't any longer the Sinatra of 1955 and 1956. If Nelson Riddle had been glad to hear "the rather angular person" replace the romantic Voice of the 1940s, this was a more angular person than ever. *Where Are You?*'s cover painting shows a sweatered, pensive-looking Frank, his mouth and chin leaning on (and obscured by) his left hand, which holds a cigarette emitting a meditative-looking trail of smoke. It was one of many thousands he'd smoked to date: his voice had every reason to sound rougher.

That slight quaver was another matter. Surely it was intentional—perhaps, like the catch he'd once put in his voice to drive the bobby-soxers wild, a dramatic device, in this case to convey the album's sense of sadness? Or did it somehow reflect the vocal and emotional uncertainty that now and then overwhelmed him that spring?

Early in 1957, Charlie Morrison, the colorful, white-haired owner of the colorful Sunset Strip nightclub Mocambo, died. Mocambo, with its decor of exotic birds in glass cages and its dance floor full of movie stars eyeing each other until all hours, had been the site of Sinatra's Los Angeles solo debut in 1943. In late April, to benefit Morrison's widow and to try to help keep the place open (Vegas was killing the L.A. clubs), Frank did a ten-night stand there gratis. It was a generous gesture, but it was also a smart public-relations move in the wake of the Wrong-Door hearings. "Not only did it turn the tide of publicity in Frank's favor, it also afforded the movie colony a closeup look at the Sinatra magic," reported a non-bylined piece on April 23.

> As someone pointed out, the guy comes out on the night club floor and defies you not to like him. While his voice is past its prime, his style is better than it ever was. He sings each song as if he had just grasped the meaning of the words. His ballads are great and now he can handle faster tunes with rare skill, something he lacked in his earlier days.

The piece might have lacked a byline for a reason: fear. After all, there amid the praise was that "past its prime" comment, probably a reflection on Sinatra's recent bouts of real or contrived laryngitis. Before the start of the charity run, Frank had consulted his publicists on which journalists planned to attend, and he crossed off several names: "Four long-time viewers of the Movietown scene, three with national news syndicates and one with Variety, were blacked out for the opening by Frankie because, I'm told, of old feuds," wrote the columnist Erskine Johnson, who himself had been barred for having had the nerve, in 1946, to criticize Sinatra's temperamental behavior on the set of *It Happened in Brooklyn*.

Then he had been an MGM contract player and a singer with a fading reputation. Now all he had to do was check off names on a list.

Only Sinatra could so seamlessly have compounded charity with vendetta.

Power might have conferred coolness, but as Jimmy Van Heusen noted in a new *Look* magazine profile of Frank, "His boiling point is close to the surface." The first part of Bill Davidson's three-part piece appeared in the May 14 issue: Frank took one look at it and boiled. The piece was extensively reported, psychologically probing, and deeply personal, and—as would be the case with Gay Talese's great *Esquire* profile of Frank in 1966—the writer never met with the subject.

Not that actually sitting down and talking with Sinatra would have netted Davidson any deep insights. As long as an approved journalist—an Earl Wilson, say, or a Walter Winchell or a Bob Thomas—made happy talk about approved subjects (singing and movie acting), everything was fine. If not, not. And the approved list seemed to be shrinking all the time.

Davidson tried hard to meet with Frank, but there was a twist: in 1955, Sinatra had contracted with *Look* to collaborate with his friend the sportswriter Jimmy Cannon on his life story and had taken a sizable advance for the project. The story never came to fruition after Cannon sent Frank a list of questions in advance, and Frank, seeing that some of the questions were personal—as might be expected with a life story—changed his mind.

He hadn't returned *Look*'s money, though, and so in early 1957 Davidson drew the unenviable assignment of approaching Sinatra with the aim of reviving the project. "My mission was to try to persuade him to commit a few words to paper, with my help, if necessary," Davidson recalled. "This offended Sinatra's dignity and he issued an ukase to his subjects to the effect that I was to be treated as if I did not exist. I had incurred The Leader's disfavor and I was now a nonperson."

The writer finally tracked Frank down in the cocktail lounge of the Sands, surrounded by a bevy of beautiful women. At first, Sinatra refused even to look at Davidson, but eventually his curiosity got the better of him, and he sent over Jack Entratter, the hotel-casino's president and entertainment manager, to see what Davidson wanted. Entratter reported Davidson's answer to Frank, then relayed Frank's reply to Davidson, and so on. This process continued for almost an hour until Sinatra lost patience with it. But he could honestly say afterward that he had never spoken a word to *Look*'s writer.

———

Unlike the Kilgallen Sunday-supplement series on Frank, Davidson's profile had no nasty edge; it lacked the stylistic excesses and high-handedness of the *Time* cover story. What it mostly had was exhaustive documentation of Sinatra's power, success, and mercurial nature:

> There is Sinatra the devoted family man and Sinatra the libertine.
> There is the Sinatra who is a fine amateur painter and an expert on
> Puccini and Berlioz, and the Sinatra who likes to hang around with
> bums and gangsters. Even his friends are confused by his many faces.
> They [Sammy Cahn and Jimmy Van Heusen, respectively] call him
> "The Man With the Golden Charm," but they also call him "The Monster." He is completely unpredictable, but his predominant moods seem
> to be those of anger and self-doubt.

The profile interspersed descriptions of some of Frank's more spectacular good works, such as his extensive financial and moral support of Lee J. Cobb when Cobb suffered a heart attack and a severe depression, with accounts of his bad behavior and colorful love life. It contained many facts and figures about Sinatra's movie deals and record sales. It detailed his feuds with Jackie Gleason, Judy Garland, Phil Silvers, and Jule Styne. It quoted psychological experts on the sources of his emotional problems.

What it left out was, exactly or approximately, what it was that happened when Frank Sinatra opened his mouth to sing.

Nevertheless, Frank saw the trees instead of the forest. The part of himself that insisted on distracting himself from his art rose to the current distraction. Against the advice of his lawyers, he brought a $2.3 million libel lawsuit against Bill Davidson and *Look,* claiming that the profile had portrayed him as a "neurotic, depressed, and tormented person with suicidal tendencies and a libertine." He should have sued them, if such a thing were possible, for failing to portray him as a great artist.

Whatever dyspepsia Frank might have been feeling, though, the completion of *Where Are You?* and the release of *A Swingin' Affair!* seem to have dispelled it. On May 20—having wooed back Nelson Riddle, bruised feelings and all—he lavished two and a half hours of a singles session (three other songs were recorded that night; it scarcely matters which) on a new number by Cy Coleman and lyricist Carolyn Leigh. The song was the great "Witchcraft," and the time was well spent. From Riddle's shimmering, downward-spiraling string intro (we've definitely left Gordon Jenkins territory) to the sensual, glance-over-the-shoulder flute outro, the tune is a finger-snapping dream of a sound, the perfect marriage of music, lyric, arrangement, and vocal—and quite simply one of the sexiest numbers ever recorded. Sinatra could sing the hell out of a torch song; no one else could make you feel love's ache quite so piercingly. But "Witchcraft" was the perfect antidote to the melancholy of *Where Are You?* and to the tyranny of love songs in general.

Proceed with what you're leadin' me to.

It was pure abandon: rapturous, guiltless. It was everything the 1950s wanted but couldn't have—all the fun that everyone knew Frank was having all the time.

8

|||||||||||

After some libation, the transformation
From boy to beast.

—SAMMY CAHN LYRIC ON THE OCCASION OF FRANK SINATRA'S
FORTY-SECOND BIRTHDAY

However miffed Nelson Riddle might have felt about Frank's musical infidelity, that June the arranger accompanied Sinatra and twenty-six cream-of-the-crop studio musicians on a seven-city tour to El Paso, Albuquerque, Salt Lake City, Vancouver, Seattle, Portland, and San Francisco. Frank, of course, had been feeling his own deep insecurity. The successful completion of *Where Are You?* might have temporarily allayed his vocal worries, but if the June 9 concert at Seattle's old Civic Auditorium is any indication, he still had cause for concern.

A recording made of the second show of that Sunday night reveals a Sinatra in fine spirits and enjoying a splendid rapport with a very appreciative audience; it also shows a singer who's not only ambivalent about some of the material he's performing but nervous enough about his vocal abilities to copy his pal Joe E. Lewis and have a slug of booze onstage. During the intro to "When Your Lover Has Gone," Frank calls out for "Herman," and then, a moment later, thanks him for something (a glass, no doubt). Then he sings the verse of the song—

The dreams that you cherish so often may perish,
And leave you with castles

—and then suddenly breaks off. "I'm getting larger, aren't I?" he asks the audience impishly. The crowd laughs delightedly. "Those are large glasses you got," Sinatra says in a rascally voice. "I must be awful large at this point."

He then resumes singing, giving a smooth and feeling rendition of the song. Sinatra singing well *is* awful large. But "When Your Lover Has Gone" isn't a particularly rangy number, and two tunes later, on "My Funny Valentine," it becomes all too clear why Frank was trying to steady his nerves: he was feeling a breathtaking—literally—uncertainty about hitting the high notes.

His doubts were justified. To hear Frank's voice simply give out on the high D of "Stay, little Valentine, *stay*" is like watching a Wallenda fall off the wire: heartbreaking, unbelievable.

Then again, this must be taken in context. The vast majority of us know Sinatra best from his studio recordings, which he polished to perfection. Those fortunate enough to have seen him perform onstage would know that Frank could hit clams like any musician—except that when he did it, there was no one to fix him with an ice-blue stare and say, "Where you workin' next week?"

Remarkably, though, he was in high spirits throughout that Seattle show, his good humor seeming to help his voice gain in strength. After the glitch on "Valentine," he comes up with his familiar save—"I think I got a shot glass stuck in my throat"—and then, singing the verse of Rodgers and Hart's "Glad to Be Unhappy"—"And look at yourself, do you still believe the rumor that romance is simply . . ."—he simply whistles the high note, instead of singing the word "grand," then calmly tells the audience, "It's safer that way." He performs the rest of the song beautifully. In the second half of the line, "But for someone you adore, *it's a pleasure to be sad*" (italics mine), his voice drops to a supremely tender whisper, telling us more, in six words, about who he really is than any three-part magazine profile could.

But of course he was so many people, and in front of an audience he could be several of them. His stage patter ranges from the stilted to the vulgar to the awkwardly sincere, with stops in between. He sets up his great saloon song, Harold Arlen and Johnny Mercer's "One for My Baby," with a stiff little monologue that tries—but thankfully fails—to undercut the tune's deep emotion: "Now, you know that it's pretty difficult when you got this kind of problems. Now, let's face it—wars, you can win. But this is a different kind of thing. Oh, it's moider, doc, I tell ya. Shake hands with the vice president of the club."

He gives his pianist, Bill Miller, a zinger for coming in too early on the intro to "Tender Trap"—"You're pretty impatient, aren't you? Charlie?"—then proceeds to forget the lyric, substituting a bunch of da-da-duh-dums for one of the verses.

And, introducing his hit single "Hey! Jealous Lover," he declares, "I absolutely and unequivocally *detest* this song." He then detours into a weird Freudian ditty—"Trow your mudder off the train, but quick, but quick"—before complaining, "Oh, that pizza's murder."

Of course he detested "Jealous Lover." If his greatest strength as an artist was to plumb the truths of the great songs he sang, how could he not abhor a catchy but cheesy rhythm-and-blues knockoff with a lyric that included lines such as

I was much too busy, baby, bein' faithful to you.

Had he ever been faithful to a single one of his lovers? Acting a role in a movie was one thing; pretending to be somebody entirely different onstage was another matter. (It was the reason his corny, elaborate setup for "One for My Baby," with the business about the "young fellow" supposedly complaining to the bartender, fell so flat: what makes the song great, every time, is that we know in our heart of hearts that it's really Sinatra singing it.)

But by the time he gets to his second-to-last number, the great Dorsey-era swinger "Oh! Look at Me Now," he's found his voice and with it his ease onstage. He introduces the 1941 song—"I think you'll recognize this if you're over twenty years old," he says, then growls, "If you're not, you should be"—and then, as the band strikes up Riddle's thrilling arrangement, he blurts, in a moment of rare, gee-whiz honesty, "This thing brings back such wonderful memories for me."

Until the end of his life, Frank would wreathe his Dorsey days with a rosy nostalgia, whatever the realities. It wasn't just his youth that Frank romanticized; it was the time before he'd had to stand, alone, astride the world.

He gave an ecstatic, goose-bumps-raising performance that night in Seattle, and when he sang,

I'm not the guy who cared about love,
And I'm not the guy who cared about fortunes and such,

he sang with a fond smile at the dream of that poor but happy guy he used to be.

———

In early June, Ava was in Mexico City, wrapping *The Sun Also Rises,* in which she played the manslayer Lady Brett Ashley, alongside Errol Flynn, Tyrone Power, and a very young Robert Evans, in his first major movie role, as the bullfighter Pedro Romero. Accompanying her on location was Walter Chiari.

While she was in Mexico, she finally took the opportunity to file divorce papers against Frank, charging desertion and absence for more than six months. He did not contest the charges, and on July 5 the Mexican court issued a divorce decree. There was a strange air of anticlimax about the news, which failed to generate headlines in the American press.

Ava would never marry again.

———

The day before, on the Fourth of July, Sinatra and a group of friends had set sail on a chartered 102-foot yacht, the *Celeste,* for a cruise down the Baja California coast. The event was carefully kept out of the press. Among those aboard was Lauren Bacall, whom Frank had been quietly squiring to dinner parties and his recording sessions for the past few months. It was during this cruise, Bacall later recalled, that their relationship became romantic, even though, at one of the ports along the coast, Sinatra "became drunk and abusive with a waiter, which, Bacall shrugged, was par for the course."

In any case, he was now officially a single man and would remain so for nearly a decade.

In quieter moments out on the water, Frank, always on the lookout for potential movie properties, read the script of a comedy then running on Broadway. The play, *A Hole in the Head,* was about the financial and domestic difficulties of a widower raising a young son and trying to run a Miami hotel. As soon as Sinatra got back to Los Angeles, he had his agent at William Morris, Bert Allenberg, option the play for $200,000—big money that the $3 million from his recent ABC TV deal made a lot easier to spend.

In expansive spirits, Frank returned to Capitol Studio A in July to record a Christmas album. Feeling that Yuletide music required an old-fashioned, honestly sentimental touch, he once again tapped Gordon Jenkins to conduct and arrange. The results, with Sinatra backed by a twenty-two-piece orchestra and a twenty-five-member chorus (the Ralph Brewster Singers), were impeccable. As Friedwald points out, on "The Christmas Song," "Mistletoe and Holly," and "The First Noel," among others, Frank "seems to be reaching back to the innocent sound he used on his first Christmas concept set, done a decade earlier with Axel Stordahl." And on the sacred songs, such as "Hark! the Herald Angels Sing" and "Adeste Fidelis," there was a new authority, even a majesty, to his voice.

He had put his vocal difficulties behind him and created a holiday album for the ages, and when he wrapped up *A Jolly Christmas from Frank Sinatra* on July 17, he was in the mood to celebrate. "He threw a huge Christmas party for everyone," Frank Military recalled. "It was incredible—catered food, drinks, everything. It was really something to see—Christmas in July!"

It was also a rare occurrence. Despite Sinatra's great esteem for the musicians who worked with him, "he rarely socialized with them outside of the studio setting," as Charles Granata notes. "On the one hand, he respected and appreciated their talents and understood their importance to his career. On the other hand, there must have been some subconscious desire on his part to keep them at arm's length, perhaps to insure that they would remain in awe of him."

The trombonist Milt Bernhart recalled, "Once in a while he did invite the musicians over to the Villa Capri restaurant after a record date. Even there he almost never made the rounds of the room, staying at his table in the back. We would approach him and say, 'thanks,' and he'd beam, and that was that."

On the other hand, Bernhart also remembered a mid-1950s party at Frank's Coldwater Canyon house with about twenty musicians present, along with "three or four very important Hollywood people: Lauren Bacall, Adolph Green, Bill and Edie Goetz." Sinatra spent hours with the instrumentalists, completely ignoring his other guests, who left one by one. "But this was his day with us, and I got the feeling that he enjoyed it—that it gave him a kick, making them wait. Only Sinatra would do that!" Bernhart said.

Felix and Eleanor Slatkin, who'd become close friends with Frank in the mid-1940s, were a special case: Sinatra clearly saw them as equals—or possibly, because of their deep grounding in classical music, inhabitants of some higher cultural plateau. Their two young sons, Leonard and Fred, literally grew up around "Uncle Frank" in the Slatkin home and at Sinatra's residences. Leonard Slatkin has clear memories, from the age of five or six, of Frank singing him and his brother to sleep.

"We also were guests of his in Vegas quite often," Slatkin says. "I remember my brother and I would be sitting out at the pool, and these announcements would come over a PA system—'Such and such, please come to the office.' And every so often, 'Will Freddie and Lenny please come to see Mr. Sinatra?' We were little. We didn't know any different. It was all very sweet and very innocent. I think really that when you were a friend of his, you were a friend for life; if you were an enemy, you were an enemy for life."

Between Frank and his arrangers, on the other hand, there was purposeful distance. "During recording sessions with Sinatra, a magic takes place . . . between Frank and myself," Gordon Jenkins recalled.

> It's as close as you're gonna get without being opposite sexes! I like to have him right in front of me, and I just never take my eyes off him, so it's kind of a hard thing to describe. But there's a definite mental connection between the two of you when it's going down well . . . he lets loose—he's all over the place when he's going—he doesn't hold anything back. It's in his personal life that he holds back.

Jenkins tried to stay away from Sinatra when they weren't working together. "It's a temptation to hang around him, 'cause he has so much to offer," he said, "but I figure that we've gotten along fine by not being buddies, so when we get through at night, if he goes out the left door, I go out the right. I think it's worked out fine."

With Nelson Riddle, it wasn't even a matter of choice. Jenkins was capable of a certain midwestern bonhomie; he also possessed the confidence of a man of parts. He enjoyed a steady income from his songwriting royalties. Riddle, whose dry sense of humor was apparent to his friends but less so to outsiders, had no such luck. For all his brilliance, he was essentially an arranger for hire who now and then wrote a piece of music that sold (he had a couple of Top 40 hits in the mid-1950s with the lounge-y instrumentals "Lisbon Antigua" and "Port au Prince") but mostly had to grind out charts at about $100 a pop—with no royalties. Until the end of his life, he would suffer a deep envy of the composer, conductor, and arranger Henry Mancini, who, although considered by some music aficionados a far lesser artist than Riddle, had a Midas-like ability to crank out award-winning movie and television scores (the themes to *The Pink Panther* and *Peter Gunn*) and mega-selling singles ("Moon River"). "Nelson said to me once," Milt Bernhart recalled, "that he would have traded all those arrangements, for which he was paid a flat fee, for one song of Mancini's. Just one song!"

With his serious nature, a certain lack of self-assurance, and his fear of Sinatra, he projected a completely businesslike and self-protective demeanor in the recording studio that was a sharp contrast to Frank's overweening self-confidence and nervous energy, his need to play to all present.

"During their first several recording sessions Frank would make fun of Nelson without his realizing it, but the orchestra caught it," the French horn player Vince DeRosa recalled. "He took advantage of his seriousness. Nelson was so serious that Sinatra would just kind of give him a jab. The musicians felt, 'Jesus, this guy's really nailing him.' But Sinatra was that type, you know. However, obviously he had complete respect for him."

Riddle's daughter Rosemary remembers attending some of her father's recording sessions with Sinatra, Ella Fitzgerald, and Nat King Cole as a small girl in the mid-1950s. "Boy, would I see the entourage for Frank," she says. "And it wasn't like you were going to walk up to him. As generous as he was in many ways, this was serious business. Whereas if Ella saw me, it would be this warm, cozy feeling. And Dad and Nat were totally tight. Dad was more confident, I would imagine, at an Ella or a Nat date. He wasn't waiting to hear [their reaction to an arrangement]."

Sinatra's reaction could be abrupt. The bass trombonist George Roberts told Riddle's biographer Peter Levinson of several occasions "when Frank would walk in and ask Nelson to have the orchestra run down the arrangements they were about to record that night. 'I was on dates when Frank didn't like the charts [Roberts recalled] . . . . He would say, "The date's over. You'll get paid," and he walked out the door and that was the end. He wouldn't really say why he didn't like the charts, but you'd know why he was leaving.'"

Small wonder that Riddle felt intimidated by Sinatra, but then, on some basic level, he allowed himself to be intimidated. "I think he never really appreciated his own talents," Alan Livingston said.

———

Frank Sinatra and Dean Martin had first met when Frank introduced Dean and his partner, Jerry Lewis, to the audience at Martin and Lewis's Copacabana premiere in 1948. From 1946 to 1956, while Frank's career crashed and then miraculously rose again, Dean and Jerry were the biggest thing in show business—on TV, in the movies, and in live performance. Yet nobody predicted a comeback for Dean Martin after the 1956 breakup of Martin and Lewis: the smart money bet that the multitalented Jerry would flourish and Dean, who was widely viewed as merely Lewis's straight man, would more or less vanish.

It came close to happening. His records sold pretty well—he had hit singles in 1954 with "That's Amore" and "Sway" and in 1956 with "Memories Are Made of This"—but the thing that had made him world famous was no more. In February 1957, Martin's first movie after the breakup with Lewis, a romantic comedy unenticingly titled *Ten Thousand Bedrooms*—he co-starred with Anna Maria Alberghetti—was dead on arrival. The reviews were pallid. Martin was "an affable leading man," *Variety* said, with "an easy way with a song." Ticket buyers stayed away. Yet the next month, he opened in the Copa Room at the Sands, to far better notices. "If audience reaction is any criterion, Martin will be around long and strong as a single café entertainer and headliner," *Variety* opined.

In other words, he could keep playing Vegas indefinitely, but the greater world would be closed to him.

In the meantime, though, Frank Sinatra never stopped believing in him. The two men had hit it off from the beginning, for complex reasons. Though on the surface it would have seemed Sinatra and Martin had much in common—both were magnetic Italian-American singer/actors with swinging reputations—in fact, they were different in more ways than they were similar, and their differences interested each man.

Sinatra, a molten cauldron of oversensitivity and insecurity, had been an adored and abused only child and remained a conflicted mama's boy. The man born Dino Paul Crocetti was the younger of two sons, but from childhood he seems to have lived in a world of his own. He was detached and ironic, imbued with a quality known in Italian as *menefreghismo*—in translation, not giving a fuck. His biographer Nick Tosches also speaks of a certain cultural trait: "the taciturn harboring close to the heart of any thought or feeling that ran too deeply . . . that wall of *lontananza* [distance] between the self and the world."

It was an old-world quality, cultivated among the peasantry, and one that Dean took in naturally on the Italian-American streets of Steubenville, Ohio, in the 1920s and 1930s. He also learned it directly from his *abruzzese* parents. As Jerry Lewis, who knew Gaetano and Angela Crocetti, recalled, "Dean's mother and his father told him the following: One, 'You're going out into the real world; there is no one there that will care for you.' Two, 'Be sure that the money you have in your hand goes in your *pocket.*' Three, 'You cry, you're a fag. You show any kind of warmth, and *they* will get closer to you. If you show them that you have your own persona you're happy with, they *will* stay away.' He was brought up with these ground rules. From a mother and a father—nice people. But from Italy, and 'This is the first order of business—distance.'"

Though both Sinatra and Martin had dropped out of high school in the tenth grade, Frank possessed a restless, ravening intellectual curiosity; Dean loved watching Westerns on TV and reading comic books. While Sinatra was short, slight, and magnetic more than handsome, Martin was tall, strong, and devastatingly good-looking, with an athlete's easy grace. He had huge hands (he had briefly boxed professionally and had worked as a card dealer) and was a six-handicap golfer.

But perhaps most impressive of all Dean's gifts—and most enviable to Frank—was a natural flair for comedy. (What the audiences at the Sands were reacting to, besides Martin's affability and easy way with a song, was his new shtick, borrowed from Joe E. Lewis: carrying a glass of what looked like Scotch onstage—it was apple juice—and acting drunk. The drunk act also dovetailed nicely with Dean's natural emotional distance—as Jerry Lewis said, "If you make believe you've had a few . . . usually people will stay away.") And one of the things Frank Sinatra, who was almost incapable of ad-libbing a comic line onstage, desperately wanted to be was funny.

Frank envied and admired almost every one of Martin's innate qualities, almost to the point of idolatry. "Sinatra was enthralled by Dean," Tosches writes. "In his eyes, he saw the man he himself wanted to be. The racket guys sucked up to Dean, not the other way around. To Sinatra, who always seemed to be crying or killing himself over one broad or another, who always seemed to be dispatching others to do his dirty work, whose *mammismo* relationship with his mother was that of a little boy—to Sinatra, Dean was *la cosa vera*, the real thing, with *la stoffa giusta*, the right stuff."

As for Dean's feelings about Frank—well, who knew? He certainly admired him as a singer. Yet, Tosches contends, Martin felt Sinatra "took it all so fucking seriously. He thought he was a fucking artist, a fucking god." And while Frank's charisma, volatility, and huge success in the 1950s made him a natural leader, with a group of followers and hangers-on who jumped at his every wish—and often flinched when his temper flared—Dean Martin wasn't one of his followers. Martin followed nobody. He built his life around golf, and he liked to hit the links early, which meant going to bed early—far too early to be on Sinatra's clock. When he was in town, he also liked to have dinner with his family. He doted on his children—as Frank did with his daughters but on more of a drop-in basis. Though (at Frank's initiation) the two men's paths crossed with increasing frequency in the mid-1950s, and though they now and then drank or gambled together, their time together was more about work than play.

That spring, to the surprise of everyone (including himself), Dean landed a serious role alongside Marlon Brando and Montgomery Clift in the World War II movie *The Young Lions*. The movie would do great things for him when it was released the following year; throughout 1957, his star ascended. NBC wanted him to host a thirteen-show TV variety program starting in the fall (given his increasing commitments, he negotiated the network down to six shows). Then he went to Europe to shoot the movie.

Martin got along well with both Brando and Clift, who discovered that he was a natural actor. Monty Clift coached Dean through their dramatic scenes together, much as he'd done with Frank on *From Here to Eternity*. And unlike Frank, Dean enjoyed spending off-set time with Brando: in July, the two were sitting together in the café of a Paris hotel when Brando accidentally spilled a cup of scalding tea in his lap, burning his genitals so badly that he had to be briefly hospitalized.

The incident was commemorated at a surprise coming-home party Frank threw for Dean upon the latter's return to Los Angeles in August. For the occasion, a boisterous gathering at Villa Capri, Sammy Cahn, a close friend to both Sinatra and Martin, had written a handful of parody songs to be sung by Frank, including one, "Tea in Gay Paree" (to the tune of "Tea for Two"), based on Brando's mishap.

Martin and Brando might have gotten along fine, but Sinatra's dislike for "Mumbles" was well-known, and Sinatra was, after all, the Leader. Since someone had thought to bring a tape recorder to the party, we're able to hear the raucous laughter that greeted almost every word Frank said, as well as his raffish rendition of the song itself, which began,

When Marlon Brando said, "I'd like some tea,"
He startled all of gay Paree,
They hadn't served a cup of tea in years,

and continued,

So finally they brought the tea,
And poured it right above his knee—

Frank paused. "Course ya gotta figure out what's above your knee," he said. " 'Cause if you don't figure this out, you're in a lot of trouble—your *birdie* is there."

This got a big laugh. He concluded,

Don't ever ask for tea in gay Paree!

Amid much similar hilarity, the festivities finally broke up at 4:00 a.m.

———

Lauren Bacall popped up regularly in Frank's company that spring and summer. She was "an attentive member of the audience" when Sinatra's tour hit Salt Lake City in mid-June, and she wouldn't have traveled to Salt Lake City on her own. When the lowly local paper, the *Deseret News,* speculated about a romance between the two, Hollywood columnists huffily—territorially—denied it. Whether or not Bacall attended Dean's Villa Capri party, she was spotted there frequently with Frank; "intimates" at his headquarters restaurant—no doubt meaning well—told reporters that the two were "very much in love."

On August 23, she was Sinatra's date at the gala Las Vegas premiere of *The Joker Is Wild.* It was an eventful evening. As the newsreel cameras rolled, Frank, wearing a tuxedo and a jockey cap with the bill turned sideways, attempted to lead a horse ridden by Joe E. Lewis into the theater. The horse balked, then defecated. "Everybody's a critic these days," Lewis said.

"After the screening, there was a big, public party at El Rancho Vegas, where Lewis was then appearing," Arnold Shaw wrote.

Lewis introduced Frank to thunderous applause. Then, instead of continuing with his own comedy routine, the comic invited Frank to do a song. The audience liked the idea. Frank remained seated. Lewis waited, and repeated the invitation. Then, in plain view of the large audience, Frank rose from his chair, helped his date (Lauren Bacall) from hers, and walked rapidly out of the room.

It was a resounding rebuff to Lewis, even though, as became later apparent, Frank had reason to feel provoked. The audience could not have known that Frank had exacted a promise that Joe would not ask him to sing. Joe had agreed, knowing that it was Sinatra's policy not to perform in any Las Vegas hotel other than the Sands.

It wasn't just Frank's policy; it was part of his contract with the owners of the Sands—both the official owners and the actual ones, the latter being men whom it would have been unwise to cross. After leaving El Rancho, Frank took over the Sands cocktail lounge for an Italian breakfast that lasted until 6:15 a.m.; Betty sat at his right. The rumors about the two heated up.

Still, as Earl Wilson wrote in his memoir, "it was a jolt to all of us"—"all of us" being the cognoscenti of the New York–Hollywood gossip axis—"when *London Evening Standard* columnist Thomas Wiseman reported September 14 that Sinatra and Miss Bacall would marry within six months, 'barring an act of providence or Ava Gardner.'"

Where had this overseas upstart gotten his information? In fact, he hadn't: in the grand tradition of British journalism, he had simply made the whole thing up out of whole cloth, hoping to smoke out anything that might be developing between the couple. "I understand that Sinatra is anxious to keep his marriage plans secret," Wiseman wrote, with maddening certainty, "and that he will probably deny that he has any intention of marrying Miss Bacall. You can take his denials with a pinch of salt."

He then added a fillip: Bacall, he opined, would find Sinatra "an even tougher assignment" than the late Bogart.

He had that right.

"There was a circusy atmosphere to the journalistic follow-up that made Frank uncomfortable," Wilson recalled. "He was put on a spot."

Amazing that the relationship didn't come apart then and there.

Wire-service reporters contacting Frank in Palm Springs got only a brisk "no comment." Meanwhile, at the center of it all, things were considerably more complicated than any column could convey: Bacall was having to contend with her own hectic emotions and the mercurial quantity that was Sinatra.

She tried to put it into words at the time. "I'm not one of those emancipated women who likes to live alone," Bacall told Hedda Hopper. "I hate it. I certainly want to marry again."

"You have some mighty nice beaux," Hopper said.

"'Tell me,' Bacall replied. 'No. 1, Frank Sinatra; No. 2, Frank Sinatra; No. 3, Frank Sinatra.' At which she threw back her head and laughed. 'But who knows what Sinatra's going to do six months from now?'"

On September 23, the two of them attended a closed-circuit TV broadcast of the Sugar Ray Robinson–Carmen Basilio middleweight-title boxing match at a Hollywood theater. In a way, it was their official coming-out. "I had never thought much about celebrity after the insane exposure I'd had at the time of *To Have and Have Not* and my marriage to Bogie," Bacall said years later. "I gave no thought to being noticed on such a quiet evening, even with Frank, but when we emerged from the theater, there were photographers waiting and the resulting pictures ended up in newspapers around the world."

One of the images showed the two of them shoulder to shoulder, Bacall laughing delightedly, a fedora'd Sinatra caught—quite remarkably—smiling as if all were right in the universe. Just for the moment, perhaps just for the instant that the shutter opened, they were utterly happy together.

Reflecting back in her memoir, the actress was better able to understand that loaded period in her life, and Frank's. "The house had been so quiet for so long, then so noisy for the week after Bogie's death, then so quiet again," she wrote.

> The nights especially. I had never known that kind of quiet before. Or that kind of aloneness. I felt as though a large chunk of me were missing. I felt physically mutilated.
>
> I wanted it all to come back. I wanted to wake up smiling again—I wanted something to look forward to—I hated feeling that my life was over at thirty-two.
>
> If I was included by friends at any small dinner, it was natural for Frank to pick me up if he was going. He was alone too. And he always made me feel better—I was even able to laugh. He was a good friend. We enjoyed being together. He was helping me, looking after me.

Swifty Lazar was another attentive friend. "But Frank answered a more basic, unarticulated need," Bacall wrote.

> When I was in New York and he called all the time to see how I was, I loved those calls. Even began to feel rather girlish—giddy. There was a man somewhere—a man who was alive—who cared about me as a woman. I came to expect those calls—to wait for them . . .
>
> The fact of my being alone was crucial. Up to that time there had been either my mother or Bogie to lean on. Now there was no one. If I'd stopped to verbalize that, I'm sure I couldn't have functioned. Would have been paralyzed with fear. Now . . . I see how hopeless it was from the start. How there was no way for me to think straight, how there was no way to really feel anything positive—like loving; no way for there to be a solid, good future for me and Frank. I was silently asking more than anyone has a right to ask—burdening him with my terrors, my unspoken demands. Had he been sure of himself and his own life then, it might have worked. But he wasn't.

After Bogart's death, Sinatra answered Bacall's need to be cared about as a woman. In the end, though, he would disappoint her cruelly.

By blaming herself for the ultimate failure of their romance, Bacall, a dignified writer with a keen intelligence, was doing a noble thing and telling a partial truth. She had brought out what was best in Frank: his strong feelings for humans (and especially damsels) in distress, and that higher part of his nature that responded in kind to people of good upbringing and fine sensibility. And she had seen what was worst in him (alcohol usually played a part in it) and shrugged it off as par for the course. Yet so far he had only shown his worst to others, and the course was to be far bumpier than she knew at the time.

———

Billy May was Frank's kind of character. In any description of the trumpeter-arranger-conductor, the word "Falstaffian" inevitably appears: until he went on the wagon at age forty-seven in 1964 (he would live forty more years), May—somewhat like Jimmy Van Heusen, except for the sex addiction—was a true wild man, unapologetically potbellied, boisterous, and merrily alcoholic, given to holding his conductor's baton in one hand and a fifth of Scotch in the other during recording sessions.

There was something wild, too, about his musical gifts. He was a legend-arily fast orchestrator, renowned for doing on a regular basis what Nelson

Riddle had been forced to do with the arrangement for "I've Got You Under My Skin": arriving at recording sessions still in process. "If the session was at eight," Alan Livingston recalled, "a few minutes after eight, Billy would come in with copyist behind him, still copying, literally, at the session." But, as Eleanor Slatkin noted, "Billy May was the most *meticulous* of arrangers. When you looked at his manuscripts, it was as if they were *printed,* they were so gorgeous. He might have acted sort of, well, carefree, but when it came to the music, he was a perfectionist."

It wasn't Riddle's brand of perfectionism. "Recording with Billy May is like having a cold shower, or a cold bucket of water thrown in your face," Sinatra told the English journalist Robin Douglas-Home.

> Nelson will come to the session with all the arrangements carefully and neatly worked out beforehand. But with Billy, you sometimes don't get the copies of the next number until you've finished the one before— he'll have been scribbling away in some office in the studio right up until the start of the session! Billy works best under pressure. He also handles the band quite differently than Nelson or Gordon: with Billy, there he'll be in his old pants and a sweatshirt, and he'll stop them and he'll say, "Hey cats, this bar sixteen. You gotta oompah-de-da-da-ch-Ow. OK? Let's go then . . ." And the band will GO! Billy is *driving*.

May was also allergic to taking himself seriously: he was the only one of Sinatra's arrangers who was able to defuse Frank's famous intensity during recording sessions, with a joke, a wry look, a swig of Scotch on the podium. Musicians loved it. "I figured, 'What the hell?' " May told Charles Granata. "If you're going to go in and do it, what the hell is the use of doing anything unless you're having fun with it?"

Sinatra and May had first crossed paths in 1939, when May was playing trumpet and arranging (and Bill Miller was playing piano) for the wild and woolly Charlie Barnet big band. Subsequently, May moved over to Glenn Miller's outfit, then to Les Brown's, and then, in the post-swing era, bounced around much as Nelson Riddle and Gordon Jenkins did, working in radio, arranging children's records (like the Bozo the Clown series) for Capitol, and then, in the early 1950s, becoming a bandleader with a signature sound marked by sexy smears and glissandos among the reeds and brass—known as "slurping saxophones."

The first song that Frank Sinatra recorded for Capitol Records, in April 1953, was a Billy May composition, an infectiously jivey blues about a skinny girlfriend called "Lean Baby." And when Sinatra demanded his old Columbia arranger Axel Stordahl, and Alan Livingston felt Frank needed to move along artistically, Livingston pulled a fast shuffle by promising him Billy May—and then, when it turned out May was on the road with his band (as Livingston had known all along), substituting the new and untried Riddle in his stead.

All of which is to say that in the fall of 1957, when Sinatra wanted once again to move along artistically—or at least branch out—Billy May was very much on his mind. Frank had a new idea for an album: a record based on something he knew a good deal about: travel. The songs would alternate between the wry and the romantic, between straight-out swingers and lush ballads. And the LP would come as a nice piece of counterpoint after the sentimentality of the two Jenkins albums. He called Billy May to write the arrangements, and he commissioned Sammy Cahn and Jimmy Van Heusen to write a title song and a closer. The album and the opening number, Sinatra told the songwriters, were both to have the same name: *Come Fly with Me.*

As if to underline the project's distance from Riddle and Jenkins, the opening recording session, on October 1, was fiddle-free. The band, featuring brass (five trumpets, five trombones, and a tuba), reeds (five saxes), a rhythm section, and a harp, backed Frank on three numbers that night: "On the Road to Mandalay," "Let's Get Away from It All," and "Isle of Capri." ("Flying Down to Rio" was rehearsed but not recorded.)

Nelson Riddle, who liked and respected Billy May, was nevertheless further offended by being—in his eyes—passed over once more by Sinatra. But it was a different sound that Frank wanted, and a different sound was what

The arranger Billy May. Falstaffian in appearance, he liked to play the wild man, but his swinging and brassy orchestrations were meticulously written.

he got: you can hear it in the first notes on the first number laid down on that first session. "On the Road to Mandalay," with lyrics taken from the Rudyard Kipling poem "Mandalay" and a tune composed in 1907 by the Ohio songwriter Oley Speaks, had been a popular parlor ballad in the early twentieth century, then a dance-band fox-trot in the 1920s. In Billy May and Frank Sinatra's version, the number is jerked into a present that both swings like mad and is weird around the edges. Against the sounds of tam-tam cymbals, temple bells, wood blocks, a big gong, and all other manner of Eastern percussion (in the able hands of Frank Flynn), the tuba oompahs, the brass and reeds swing, and so does Sinatra. Sounding as though he hadn't a care in the world, he imparts some ring-a-ding-ding to Kipling:

> By the old Moulmein Pagoda, lookin' eastward to the sea,
> There's a Burma broad a-settin', and I know she thinks of me.

What on earth is going on here? Will Friedwald maintains that Frank felt a certain connection to the great English chronicler of fading empire. "After the success of the film *From Here to Eternity*, with its Kipling-inspired title," he writes, "Sinatra seems to have nurtured a spiritual kinship with Kipling's recurring hero, the warrior with a conscience." He goes on to cite Frank's dreadful 1962 film *Sergeants 3*, with its title echo of the Kipling story collection *Soldiers Three* and its vaguely "Gunga Din" plot, as well as Sinatra's truly bizarre 1966 spoken-word recording of the Kipling poem.

Okay, but . . . What really seems to be going on with "Mandalay," and much of the rest of *Come Fly with Me,* is that Frank and Billy May and the musicians are having fun, maybe the time of their lives. Listen to the glorious title song, the peak of Cahn and Van Heusen's art, and a high point for Sinatra, too. Sammy Cahn originally wrote the more family-friendly

> If you could use some exotic views
> There's a bar in far Bombay,

which Frank recorded. Then, at the end of the session, Sammy told Frank he'd also written a Vegas version:

> If you could use some exotic booze.

"Upon learning this," Friedwald writes, "Sinatra immediately recoralled [sic] the musicians, who were then heading for some exotic booze of their own, and rerecorded the song with this somewhat more colorful line."

Thank God! (No; thank Frank.)

This spirit of free-flowing fun and come-what-may adventure infuses all the album's up-tempo numbers, from the title tune to "Mandalay," to Matt Dennis and Tom Adair's great "Let's Get Away from It All," to Cahn and Van Heusen's bouncy lead-out, "It's Nice to Go Trav'ling," wherein the stay-at-home lyricist channels Chester Babcock's wanderlust:

The mam'selles and frauleins and the senoritas are sweet,

he writes, but they can't compete with the models on "Madison Ave."

And at the same time, the romantic numbers possess a lush fullness that is all Billy May's own: no comparisons with other arrangers are necessary. He might have had a natural affinity for horns, but he could write for strings as well as anybody: "Moonlight in Vermont" and "London by Night" shimmer lunarly, and the twelve violins, five violas, and four cellos soar heartrendingly on the classic Vernon Duke bookends "Autumn in New York" and "April in Paris." (The chart was May's, yet he wouldn't have had the benefit of a twenty-person string section with any other vocalist. "When you hired the band," the arranger recalled, "all the record companies used to say, 'Use as few men as possible,' because they didn't want you to spend too much money. But with Sinatra, you'd ask 'How many strings shall we get, Frank?' and he'd say, 'Fill up the outfield!' He knew, as we all knew, the more the better, especially with strings.")

———

For the third and final *Come Fly with Me* session, on the night of the eighth, there were two English visitors in Studio A: the composer and conductor-arranger Ron Goodwin and a thirty-one-year-old record producer named George Martin. The two worked for Capitol's parent company, the London-based European musical colossus EMI, which had bought 96 percent of the American label in 1955. In the years since, EMI's executives had been continually frustrated by their inability to sell English singles to Capitol—specifically to the producer Dave Dexter Jr., who ran the company's international department. Somewhere over the Atlantic, something was simply lost in translation, and the two Englishmen were on a tour of U.S. radio and television stations, not only to promote Goodwin's new instrumental single, but to try to better understand what made American popular music tick.

"Invited to look on, they were fascinated to watch The Voice at work and observe the equipment and technical processes," writes the English biographer Mark Lewisohn.

Sinatra liked to record at night, and he taped five tracks (including the album's title song) with some ease, surrounded by the professionalism of Billy May's orchestra . . . Feeling like "the country cousins from England," George and Ron also witnessed the evening's only sour note, when Sinatra kicked up a stink over the artwork designed for his album, which showed him in front of a TWA plane. Sinatra blew his top, alleging that surely someone somewhere at Capitol was getting some kind of rake-off from TWA for the free publicity he'd be giving them.

This aside, the session left the best of impressions on George Martin, and it was no coincidence that after returning home he immediately set about getting himself a British Frank Sinatra—and found one within twelve days. London-born singer and jazz pianist Jeremy Lubbock had a voice more like Sinatra than Sinatra; although other record companies said it was "uncommercial," George signed him to Parlophone and started to sift songs and discuss arrangements with Ron Goodwin suitable for a dynamic debut to be recorded in January.

The quest to find another Sinatra, like the search for the lost city of El Dorado, has gone on over the years; many are the Jeremy Lubbocks who have been discovered and then forgotten. (Lubbock himself went on to a successful career as an arranger of easy-listening albums.) George Martin would of course have far more success, seven years hence, with the discovery of four lads from Liverpool who sounded like nobody else.

And Dave Dexter would—at first—turn down the Beatles, too.

———

On October 13, Frank guest starred along with Rosemary Clooney, Louis Armstrong, the Norman Luboff Choir, and the Four Preps (Bob Hope also did a surprise walk-on) on a Bing Crosby CBS TV special, *The Edsel Show*. The telecast (it replaced *The Ed Sullivan Show* for that one Sunday evening) introduced Ford's racy and much-heralded new 1958 model, the car with which the auto company hoped to finally gain an edge on General Motors.

Ford had thrown huge resources into developing the Edsel, which featured a distinctive (if, in convenient retrospect, quite hideous) vertical grille and such technical innovations as a "rolling dome" speedometer, a push-button automatic transmission, and optional seat belts. "A new vista of motoring pleasure, unlike any other car you've ever seen," the ad copy read.

Of course the car would become a commercial disaster of historic proportions, losing Ford millions. "The only Edsel I ever saw was the one they gave me to drive while I was rehearsing," Rosemary Clooney recalled. When she first opened the car door, the handle came off.

During rehearsal, she noted another bad sign: all too predictably, Sinatra hadn't bothered to show up. Crosby was worried, Clooney wrote in her memoir: " 'Frank's gonna blow it,' Bing said to me. 'He's gonna blow it, and you and I are gonna have to bail him out . . .' There was a difficult chord change in a medley we were doing, and we knew that if he didn't rehearse with us, he wouldn't get it."

The show was broadcast live (on the East Coast; it was also the first telecast to employ the new technology of videotape, for later airing in the West)—no retakes, no margin for error. The medley began: Bing and Frank and Rosie, with Clooney standing in the middle. "When Frank started in with 'Blues in the Night' a capella, it sounded fine for about a bar, until the band came in with a chord in a totally different key," she recalled. "Bing had been right— Frank blew it. But it didn't matter, because Frank shrugged and laughed at himself—'The note's *somewhere* in there'—and the audience loved it. Bing and I just looked at one another. The Voice could get away with anything."

Almost anything. It was one thing to slough off someone else's broadcast (although *The Edsel Show* got great reviews and drew big ratings, unlike the Edsel). Frank's ambivalence about television was about to come back, very quickly, to nip him where it hurt.

Sinatra's first major excursion onto the small screen, the original *Frank Sinatra Show*, on CBS in 1950, had been catastrophic. Admittedly, it was in television's early days, but then some people—notably Sid Caesar, whose smash *Your Show of Shows* on NBC Frank had been up against on Saturday nights— were already exploiting the new medium's inventive possibilities. Sinatra, in the midst of an epic career meltdown in music and movies, treated TV like a poor second cousin, sometimes showing up hours late for rehearsal and sometimes refusing to rehearse at all. The series had trouble finding a sponsor, drew scathing reviews ("a drab mixture of radio, routine vaudeville and pallid pantomime," the *New York Times*'s Jack Gould wrote), and lost CBS a mint.

The plans for Sinatra's new series were grand, befitting the sum ABC had paid for it. The network secured a couple of big sponsors (Bulova watches and Chesterfield cigarettes); Frank himself would executive produce. "If I fall on my face, I want to be the cause," he told the *New York World-Telegram*. "All of the years when I was taking advice from others they told me wrong 50 percent of the time." The new *Frank Sinatra Show* would have a splashy premiere, kicking off on Friday, October 18, with a live, hour-long musical-variety episode guest-starring Bob Hope, Peggy Lee, and Kim Novak. Subsequently, the program would air on tape for half an hour every Friday evening, mostly in the musical-variety format, but now and then in thirty-minute dramas that Frank would either star in or produce. (He had one in the can already: he played a taxi driver who adopted a couple of war orphans.)

Sinatra, who had classy taste in collaborators, hired Kirk Browning, who'd helmed opera and dramatic series for NBC television, to direct the musical installments. Browning came up with a brilliant idea for the premiere's opening segment. It would start with a tight shot of Frank's hand, snapping out the tempo for "Lonesome Road," a gospel-tinged number from *A Swingin' Affair!* The camera would then pull back to reveal Sinatra standing at the top of a grand stairway; then the view would widen to show the staircase in the midst of a starry universe. Frank adored the idea.

All went well in the early stages. "We put all the numbers together with Bob Hope; then Kim Novak and Peggy Lee came in, and we started rehearsing and everything was totally harmonious," Browning recalled. "We got within about a week of the show and we'd go in to rehearse and change little things, but basically Frank would approve everything we were doing. He behaved wonderfully!"

Then, a little less wonderfully. One day, during run-throughs, Sinatra came in and said, "I don't like some things about this show." The director told him, "Well, Frank, we can change some things."

"And that's when he decided to change *everything*," Browning remembered.

He kept the opening, but other than that he changed the numbers, the set, the order and the attitude. I remember the last few days of rehearsals when everything was different every day. Bob Hope came over to me and said, "Kirk, what's going on here? What's Frank doing? Things were going perfectly well, and suddenly he's changing everything!" When you can throw Bob Hope, you know that things are getting painful.

Things settled down; camera rehearsals and the dress rehearsal went okay. Show night came: the broadcast was to air live at 9:00 p.m. Browning told his stage manager to keep track of Frank so he could be in place atop the big staircase in front of a crane camera that was ready for the opening shot.

Then, at five of nine, when the director was ready for Sinatra to take his place, "the stage manager says, 'Kirk, I can't find Frank,'" Browning recalled.

"What do you mean, you can't find him?" Browning asked the stage manager.

"Well, he said he was just going to go out for a second and I can't see him anywhere," the man replied.

THE WHIRLWIND | 173

"There was a total frenzy in the studio, everybody getting more and more hysterical," Browning remembered.

> There was no Sinatra anyplace. One minute to airtime, no Sinatra. 45 seconds, thirty seconds, no Sinatra. At 20 seconds before nine, a side door opens. Frank strolls in and slowly, slowly, slowly walks up those stairs. At 5, 4, 3, 2, 1 he hits the top stair, puts his hand in front of the camera and clicks his fingers.
>
> He wanted to have the tension, and he wanted to feel that he was the one person totally in control. Obviously we went on the air, and survived. He was very sweet at the end of the show, and gave us all a big party, and by then the memory of the opening had already begun to fade. I remember he turned to me and said, "Kirk, we've had a good time working on this show. You know, I have a couple scripts for films that I'm doing, and if you'd like, you could do either one of them." Well, I took a long breath and said, "Frank, that's so sweet of you, I think I'm just going to go back to TV."

"I'm a real stickler for perfection in my work, and in most other people's work, too," Sinatra had told Edward R. Murrow. "I find myself picking whatever I do apart. Which I do believe is quite healthy."

"Healthy" was an interesting form of self-applause. "Unavoidable" was more like it. Frank's perfectionism served him splendidly in the recording studio, where he was more or less in complete control. "A Sinatra album is a Sinatra album," Nelson Riddle once told Jonathan Schwartz. "The cover, the liner notes, the songs, the arrangements. Everything. There was no producer— Frank produced. It was Frank."

Riddle was exaggerating, of course, but not by much. The recording studio was Sinatra's domain. Movie sets and television studios were not, but that didn't mean he didn't try to take over there, too. In films, the question, always, was, whom was he up against? In television, he was up against the medium itself. The critics took notice, and soon the public would too.

The $3 million deal and the advance hype couldn't have helped, but all might have been forgiven if, somehow, Frank had been able to guest star on his own show. Instead, he took control—or rather dictated a process he didn't truly understand—and the result was a broadcast that lacked free flow (in between the singing, which everyone seemed to like) and brought out Sinatra's flaws as a 1950s TV personality: his unruly ethnicity and his uneasy humor, that always imminent threat of anger. His heat in a cool medium.

Some of the critics were kind. The *New York Herald Tribune*'s John Crosby wrote of the premiere, "Sinatra has bounced back to become the hottest thing in Show Business, and for very good reason. He is one hell of a performer and his first TV show was a triumph in almost all departments." What that slightly hedged sentence hinted at, and what others wrote explicitly, was that Frank did exactly one thing well on television; once he tried for more, trouble crept in. "When he was singing the program held our attention and he did some excellent numbers," Jack Gould of the *New York Times* wrote. "But an hour's show cannot be sustained by one man alone and Mr. Sinatra's writers let him down badly. His patter with Bob Hope was second rate, and their sketch with Kim Novak never came off."

Was it really the writers' fault? *Variety* compared Frank's premiere unfavorably with his guest shot on *The Edsel Show*: "There's no disputing that Sinatra's own show lacked much of the spark and free wheeling quality of the automaker's presentation." Yet what *Variety*'s critic couldn't have known was that much of that freewheeling quality flowed from careful rehearsal—on the part of Bing Crosby and Rosemary Clooney. Frank had treated *The Edsel Show* high-handedly, but he'd had Bing and Rosie there to bail him out. To make him look good. With his own program, his arrogance—always a mask for his deepest fears—undercut his collaborators and leached into his on-air manner. "We prefer the Sinatra of the Edsel show," the radio and television critic Jack O'Brian wrote, "rather than the Frankie boy of his own ABC-TV premiere Friday night—the night club hero, cock o' the walk, the self-confident ruler of all he surveys."

Despite the fears of the two rival networks that *The Frank Sinatra Show* would clobber them on Friday nights, the program's ratings began to slip almost immediately. (The first dramatic half hour, with Frank as the warmhearted cabbie, aired the week after the premiere.) A few weeks in, Charles Mercer of the Associated Press offered a trenchant analysis. "What is wrong with the Sinatra show?" he asked.

> Without knowing anything about his TV production schedule, I get the impression from watching his shows that they have been put together in great haste. A regular weekly TV variety show is almost a full-time job for any performer; care and diligence pay off when the show goes on the air.
>
> I also get the impression that Sinatra is doing something he never has done in the movies or in his outstanding guest appearances on Dinah Shore's TV show: He is condescending to his audience.

Mercer was right on the money. The demons were the same ones as always: Frank hated to rehearse and showed up late or not at all for rehearsals; he didn't take the medium seriously. "I couldn't escape the feeling," Paul Molloy of the *Chicago Sun-Times* wrote, "that Sinatra's thinking was something like: 'Let's give the peasants out there a few songs and jokes and get this nuisance over with.' There is effrontery about this attitude that has no place in show business."

———

At the end of October, Frank made front-page news by denouncing "the most brutal, ugly, degenerate, vicious form of expression it has been my displeasure to hear." He was referring to rock 'n' roll. According to the Associated Press, Sinatra had written the words in a piece for a Parisian magazine called *Western World*. The AP report quoted Frank further:

> It fosters almost totally negative and destructive reactions in young people. It smells phony and false. It is sung, played and written for the most part by cretinous goons and by means of its almost imbecilic reiterations and sly, lewd—in plain fact dirty—lyrics . . . manages to be the martial music of every sideburned delinquent on the face of the earth.
>
> This rancid smelling aphrodisiac I deplore. But, in spite of it, the contribution of American music to the world could be said to have one of the healthiest effects of all our contributions.

The story gained such instant worldwide currency that the Sideburned One, Elvis Presley himself, felt compelled to rebut Frank's characterization the very next day. "I admire that man, he has a right to say what he wants to say," Elvis told reporters. "He is a great success and a fine actor, but I don't think he should have said it. He is mistaken about this. This is a trend, just the same as he faced when he started years ago. I consider it the greatest in music."

Presley's words, filled with quiet dignity, contrast starkly against Sinatra's rant, which bristles with hostility and defensiveness—and conveniently leaves out the fact that black rhythm and blues, from which, early and late, rock begged, borrowed, and stole, was filled with "imbecilic reiterations" and dirty lyrics, that it was an important American art form, and that it was, in many cases, great music.

Comparing rock 'n' roll to the music that had made millions of bobby-soxers scream, faint, and wet their pants was a more complex proposition. In Sinatra's case, it was the artist, not the art form, that was transgressive and world changing: the sexuality of the rather tame ballads he sang was more romantic than carnal. The little things that drove the bobby-soxers wild—that little catch Frankie put in his voice in quiet passages, that spit curl that fell over his forehead—were more mild, on the face of it, than Elvis's swiveling hips, which Ed Sullivan famously ordered his cameramen to leave out of the shot.

But it has to be admitted that Presley had a point. A trend was a trend. How different, really, was the sexuality unleashed by the Sinatra phenomenon in the late 1930s and early 1940s from the carnality unleashed by rock 'n' roll fifteen years later? How hypocritical was it of Frank to claim chastity for himself or what he did onstage? Comparisons between the intrinsic quality of the songs Sinatra sang and the varied corpus of rock 'n' roll are another discussion. (Though, even putting aside "Mama Will Bark," Frank sang his share of fairly cretinous numbers himself: "Red Roses for a Blue Lady," anyone?) The most striking comparison between Sinatra's teen-idol phase and rock 'n' roll is the brevity of the former against the amazing durability of the latter. Frank couldn't have known this in 1957, but it seems clear that he feared it.

On November 1, seventeen-year-old Nancy Sandra Sinatra made her television singing debut on *The Frank Sinatra Show*, along with two high-school friends, Belinda Burrell and Jane Ross. The trio—they called themselves the Tri-Tones—performed two distinctly noncontemporary songs, 1930's "Exactly like You" and 1927's "Side by Side." Frank chimed in on the latter.

Grandmas somewhere might have been charmed, but TV audiences continued to edge away from the show, displeased with the host's forced patter and the general lack of flow and spontaneity. It didn't help that after the premiere, the musical installments were taped rather than live; also, inexplicably, Sinatra had vetoed the use of a studio audience. It all felt canned and slipshod.

Variety wondered why he was doing the show at all. What seemed to rankle the entertainment journal particularly were Frank's little endorsing lead-ins to the Bulova and Chesterfield commercials. In a piece headlined SINATRA: SINGER OR SALESMAN?, the magazine decried the star's "commercial prostitution": "Sinatra isn't the first and won't be the last of the entertainers to become a dollar happy commercial pitchman, though rarely has an actor or singer of his stature (and he's in the upstairs level in both depts.) gone so heavy in personalizing the pitch. Does he need the money? Does Rockefeller?"

Frank might have been accused of a mild lapse of taste, but really, wasn't shilling just the American way? All kinds of stars endorsed products, from cigarettes to automobiles; even Ernest Hemingway pitched Ballantine Ale, Pan Am Airways, and Parker pens.

And in truth, though Sinatra's income was substantial, he did need the money. He hadn't finished paying off the back taxes he'd owed since his down period. He maintained two residences, several automobiles, a private plane, and a helicopter. He was supporting one ex-wife (his divorce from Ava didn't include alimony) and three children. And he continued to spend as if there were no tomorrow, not just on himself, but, as always, on others in need.

More to the point was the time he was failing to spend on his TV show. As always, he was pillar to post: he was shooting a new movie at Paramount, *Kings Go Forth,* a World War II drama co-starring Tony Curtis and Natalie Wood; he found time to guest star on another TV show, a tribute to Ethel Barrymore on NBC's *Texaco Command Appearance;* and three days before Thanksgiving he returned to Capitol Studio A and recorded four singles, singing magnificently as an apparently unreproachful Nelson Riddle conducted his own arrangements, which were as beautiful as ever.

The first three songs were updates of Sammy Cahn–Jule Styne compositions that Frank had sung in his 1947 movie *It Happened in Brooklyn,* then recorded with Axel Stordahl for Columbia: the irresistibly perky "I Believe," the torchy "It's the Same Old Dream," and the great standard "Time After Time." Throughout his career, Sinatra would often come back, to great effect, to material he'd recorded before. These new versions showed his spectacular growth as an artist, his ease and maturity. They also demonstrated his wisdom in returning again and again to the great Riddle.

The fourth song, Sam Coslow, Ken Lane, and Irving Taylor's "Everybody Loves Somebody," was another that Frank had recorded in the mid-1940s. Dean Martin had sung it on the radio at around the same time. The agreeable if not especially impressive number hadn't done much for either Sinatra or Martin in the 1940s, and the slow and bluesy Riddle version would never come near the charts in 1957. That Dean Martin would score a number 1 hit with the song seven years later, knocking an English group called the Beatles off the top of the pops, would have been beyond the imagining of the wildest prognosticator.

Feeling his TV show needed freshening up, Frank did the November 29 broadcast live for the first time since the premiere and, for the first time, in front of a studio audience. His guest was Dean Martin. Wearing tuxes and sitting at a bar with drinks in front of them, the two sang a medley of song snippets and clowned around. To watch the sequence at a distance of decades is fascinating. Seated on Dean's right, Frank, though still the far bigger star and Martin's senior by a year and a half, comes across as a hyperactive, eager-to-please little brother. For one thing, Dean, with his leonine head, broad shoulders, and huge expressive hands, physically dwarfs him.

But for another thing, though Martin was ostensibly a man whose career was recently in danger, he simply galvanizes the television screen. (His own variety-show premiere, on NBC in October, had won critical raves.) That he will become a massive star within six months is no surprise. The camera loves him: he's in his physical prime, conveying an easy grace and charisma. His singing is smooth and utterly charming; his comedy is effortless. He not only dwarfs Frank physically; he outclasses him.

By contrast, the TV camera, working in close-up here, isn't doing Sinatra any favors. It doesn't love him; it doesn't even especially like him. His hair and face are thin, and so is his material. He trots out some corny *Amos 'n' Andy*–style humor ("Dis muss be da *place* heah"); he smiles delightedly as he makes lame jokes about fried rice and fortune cookies while Martin sings "Slow Boat to China." His figurative flop sweat is showing; he's thrilled his big friend is there to help out.

Dean looks delighted, too. (And drunk, though you can tell it's an act: when he picks up his glass and sniffs the contents, he makes a face and puts it back down—must be that apple juice.) He's glad to be there and glad to be with his pally: ingratiation, of Frank or the audience, has nothing to do with it. He just has plenty of charm to go around. The mutual affection of the two men is unapologetic and palpable. Martin even teasingly blows cigarette smoke in Sinatra's face while Frank sings Cahn and Styne's "Saturday Night (Is the Loneliest Night of the Week)"; Sinatra obligingly coughs. Frank then chimes in with an annoyingly loud "sweet sweet" backup as Dean croons his big hit "Memories Are Made of This."

But the best moment comes when Dean starts another hit, the lush, accordion-y "Innamorata," with the words

If my lips should meet
With Frank Sinatra's . . .

"It's a raid!" Frank yells, genuinely funny for once.

A moment later, the gay humor established, Frank sings "I've Got a Crush on You" in Dean's direction, and to his mock horror. "What I look like?" Martin cries, then proceeds to *hand his cigarette* over to Frank, who puffs on the smoked-down butt until the end of the medley. These two are best pallies, and they don't care who knows it.

Dean really did give the show a lift, though not quite in the way Frank had hoped. Jack O'Brian wrote a couple of days later, "The 'live' Frank Sinatra show

Friday night seemed to be more a Dean Martin show. Dean really took charge as he out-casualed the voice."

The skids were greased for *The Frank Sinatra Show;* the knives were sharpened. *Variety* primly declared the program "still wanting in smoothness and substance" and took Frank to task for "spouting a torrent of flip expressions that presumably are supposed to be sophisticated and hep but come across in a completely affected manner."

True enough. But the flip expressions, and the byplay between Frank and Dean, would carry both men a good ways over the next few years. *Variety*—and America, still logy from its Thanksgiving turkey—had no idea what they had just witnessed: the Holmby Hills Rat Pack might have died with Humphrey Bogart, but a new one had just been born.

———

"Frank Sinatra hasn't worked enough," Hedda Hopper wrote a few days later, "so he'll produce a picture he and Pete Lawford bought, titled 'Ocean's Eleven . . .' They want Dean Martin and Sammy Davis Jr. for the stars."

The concept had sprung from a chance meeting on the beach in Santa Monica between Lawford and an aspiring director named Gilbert Kay. Hollywood being Hollywood, Kay had shaken hands with Lawford, then pitched him a movie idea: a group of World War II veterans, former commandos, join forces to rob five Las Vegas casinos simultaneously. It sounded like a great notion, but Kay wanted to direct the picture. Hollywood projects happen when powerful people make them happen, and Lawford and Kay were near the bottom of the food chain. But with this idea in hand, Peter Lawford saw a way to get even further into the good graces of the man at the very top. When he told Sinatra about the idea, Frank smiled. He didn't just like it; he loved it.

———

On the night of December 12, an all-star group of friends—including Dean Martin, Bing Crosby, Jack Benny, Tony Curtis, Eddie Fisher, Debbie Reynolds, Vic Damone, Jack Entratter, Leo Durocher, Mike Romanoff, Jimmy Van Heusen, and Sammy Cahn—threw Frank a forty-second-birthday party at Villa Capri. Cahn, who wrote a dozen special-material songs for the evening, also served as an efficient, articulate, somewhat overbearing master of ceremonies. (In his defense, it could be said that working a roomful of personalities this large was like going into a cage full of big cats armed with just a chair and a whip. Also, Cahn was overbearing in general.) As at Dean's welcome-home bash in August, someone had thought to bring along a tape recorder, and so the clever songs, sung by various attendees as well as the birthday boy—

Bill Miller was the very able pianist—were preserved for posterity, along with much of the party's byplay.

It was a lively, hilarious, and no doubt highly bibulous occasion. There is something haunting about listening to these bell-clear recordings (which were only privately circulated at first, but eventually, like so many other private Sinatra tapes, managed to leak out to Frank-ophiles: the celebrants were all so vivid, so charming, so *necessary*. This assemblage represented a certain crème de la crème of American show business when such a quantity still existed and seemed to matter to the culture at large, and when such a starry group could still convene around a central figure for what felt like an important occasion.

Given Sammy Cahn's special-lyrical skills, the evening was cast as a kind of roast, but by today's standards—and also perhaps out of respect for, if not fear of, the roastee—it was a rather mild affair. No vulgarities or overt sexual references were caught on tape, in the songs or the remarks. The honoree was fond of liquor and the ladies, the lyrics claimed; he was less fond of reporters and rehearsing, he was quick to anger, and he could hold a grudge for a long time. None of it would have come as a shock to anybody, even Frank.

Dean Martin sang the first number, a parody of Cole Porter's "You're the Top":

> *He's the wop,*
> *Records sell like Nestlés . . .*

Except that Dean pronounced it "nestles." "Nestlés!" the stage-managing lyricist called out irritably. "You'll see why in a minute."

Martin resumed. Frank's records might be the top, the song continued, but they didn't top Presley's.

It got a light laugh, as did most of the other numbers. The true, table-pounding hilarity happened between the carefully prepared songs, triggered by you-had-to-be-there things: the infinitely perishable, non-fungible stuff of a life that was fleeting every second, even while Frank was seizing every moment as though his life depended on it.

———

In Spain in October, Ava Gardner, who lived exactly as she pleased and let the consequences be damned, did a profoundly stupid thing. Visiting the Andalusian ranch of a wealthy bull breeder she'd met through Hemingway, she let herself be persuaded, after drinking a great deal of absinthe and Spanish cognac, to ride a horse into a bullring.

It was all a drunken stunt: she was playacting at being a banderillero, carrying a pair of the barbed spears that are thrust into the bull's back before the matador takes over the final act of the pageant. The problems were twofold. "For starters," as her biographer Lee Server writes, "she had little experience on horseback. And then there was this: It was a good way to be killed."

As the bull charged, her horse reared. "She was thrown from the saddle and sent to the ground with the speed of a whiplash," Server writes, "landing with a great thump in the dirt, the ground hitting the right side of her face with the force of a wooden bat swung straight at the cheekbone." The result was a swollen purple bruise atop her right cheekbone. A London plastic surgeon advised her to wait and hope for the wound to heal rather than take any measures that might permanently affect her face. In time, the swelling went down, but a solid bump the size of a walnut remained.

Frank had called to console her as soon as he heard about the accident. Then, in December, Ava decided to fly to New York to consult with a plastic surgeon Sinatra had recommended. Not long after his birthday party at Villa Capri, and a few days after squiring his steady date Betty Bacall to Mocambo to dine with the David Nivens, Frank flew east to see his ex-wife. Bacall was not pleased.

Act Two

THE
CHAIRMAN

Here goes, baby, here goes,
Every worry, every fear goes,
Every dull day in the year goes,
I'm about to fall in love.

—"HERE GOES," SONGWRITER UNKNOWN

Six days into the New Year, on the same day *Come Fly with Me* was released, the *New York Times* ran a piece about the seismic changes occurring in the movie industry. The article recalled the benevolent despotism of the studio system, under which actors, directors, and writers had been signed to long-term—usually seven-year—contracts and in return had had to take whatever projects the studio assigned, and otherwise do the studio's bidding (there was the infamous MGM morals clause, for example) or risk suspension.

"Today," the *Times*'s Thomas M. Pryor wrote, "most stars and other movie creators no longer do business as individuals but as corporations." High personal income tax rates, Pryor wrote, were responsible for the change. In those less wealth-friendly days in America, an individual was subject to income taxes as high as 92 percent. Corporate taxes, on the other hand, could not exceed 52 percent. An individual who incorporated could pay him- or herself a nominal salary and take a far smaller tax hit. As examples, the piece listed such "incorporated stars" as Burt Lancaster, John Wayne, Kirk Douglas, Alan Ladd, Bing Crosby, Bob Hope, Jerry Lewis, Gregory Peck, and Frank Sinatra. (Women were notably absent from the roster.) These stars "are in many respects big business," Pryor said.

> They employ anywhere from a handful to several dozen persons, regularly or part-time, and their corporate gross earnings can run into several million dollars a year. It is estimated that Mr. Sinatra, as an artist–business man, currently has a gross annual income from movies, records and television of about $4,000,000.

Interestingly, the article failed to mention—perhaps because precise accounting figures would have been hard to track down—another income stream for Frank: the Sands Hotel and Casino.

Four years earlier, when Sinatra had been down on his luck, Joseph "Doc" Stacher, the lieutenant of the New Jersey crime boss Abner "Longy" Zwillman and one of the masterminds behind the national merger of the Mafia and the Jewish Mob, had fronted Frank $54,000 to buy two points in the Sands, then less than a year old. The idea of listing Frank as a shareholder was attractive for all kinds of reasons, chief among them his drawing power (an exclusive performance contract was part of the deal) and lack of a criminal record. That Mob figures were the true owners behind the Vegas casinos was still unproved at the time but strongly suspected by government and law enforcement. But the Nevada Tax Commission, smelling an eastern rat, had vigorously challenged Sinatra's fitness to be a part owner, citing the significant back taxes he then owed the IRS and wondering how he could afford the $54,000.

Then, for whatever reason, the commission suddenly caved, and Frank got his gaming license and his two points in the Sands.

In the years since, his stake had risen to 4 percent, and by the beginning of 1958, through the munificence of the owners—some say a gift from the mobster Vincent "Jimmy Blue Eyes" Alo—Sinatra owned nine points in the Sands Hotel and Casino.

What, exactly, did this mean?

Not a tremendous amount, according to Ed Walters, a pit boss at the Sands from 1959 to 1967 and a friend and confidant of Sinatra's. "Frank got paid—not as much as people think, but he got paid and he got all the money," Walters claimed. "He was not fronting for anybody. He got paid a check, every month—no cash, ever. He did not want to wind up in front of the FBI."

Walters said that Frank was paid separately—also by check—for performing in the Copa Room. "I know some guys we paid false checks to for entertaining—not Sinatra," the former pit boss recalled. "Frank was always worried about the Mob getting him in trouble. He used to tell me, 'These assholes are all gonna go to jail.' He was caught between wanting to be one of them and [his fear of legal entanglements]. So he cleverly had his lawyers do the speaking for him. Frank was a very astute businessman."

The myth has arisen that Frank Sinatra's unfortunate reverence for the Mafia—"I would rather be a don for the Mafia than president of the United States," he once told Eddie Fisher—meant that he was all but a made man. In fact, while his mother's north Jersey connections had helped get him a couple of singing jobs early in his career, and a few of his wiseguy friends steered some work his way during his down period (but only some; not enough to turn his fortunes around), Sinatra's Mob associations had far more to do with mutual admiration than affiliation. The gangsters liked his singing, his flash, and (at times) his unrepentant unruliness; he liked their power, their toughness, their swaggering style. Growing up in an era when power was largely in the hands of white Protestant men, a time when Italian-Americans were just a half step up the social ladder from African-Americans—and, like black people, were seen as simple, happy, and musical—Frank viewed the Mafia as a kind of unelected elect, an alternate aristocracy. He idolized them all his life, much as a small boy might idolize cowboys or soldiers.

"By the thirties and forties, when Dad was in the business, they were controlling the nightclubs," Tina Sinatra told Seymour Hersh.

They were controlling the entertainment world. They were a motivated bunch. The power of an entertainer and the power of a mobster—it's all very much a part of America. They were all from the same neighborhoods. My dad grew up with gangsters next door. He was living with them. They were his personal friends, and he's not going to cast away a friend. The great vein through Frank Sinatra is loyalty. There is an absolute commitment to friends and family. It's very Italian and probably gave him a little more in common with the mob types.

For their part, the Mob tolerated him, now and then found him useful, sometimes threw him a bone. His New Jersey godfather Willie Moretti—who was much more like a gabby, tubby, slightly hovering uncle than a criminal mastermind—might have intervened when Sinatra was arrested for adultery and seduction (when those statutes were still on the books) in 1938. He tut-tutted by telegram when Frank left his first wife, Nancy, for Ava Gardner. Then he got rubbed out in 1951, perhaps for being too forthcoming with the Kefauver Committee, probably also for welshing on sports bets. The etiology of Mob executions is rarely unmixed.

A couple of years later, Frank met Sam Giancana.

Giancana, born in 1908, began his criminal career in a Chicago street gang and soon graduated from small-time mayhem to getaway driving, extortion, and murder for the Chicago Outfit—a group whose bosses, after Al Capone was imprisoned in the early 1930s, were Frank "the Enforcer" Nitti, Paul "the Waiter" Ricca, and Tony "Joe Batters" Accardo. After the death of Nitti and the semiretirement of Accardo in the 1940s, Giancana, nicknamed Momo or Mooney, became a boss himself.

He was not a physically impressive man. He was small and big-nosed, with close-set eyes—weasel-featured. He wore large, dark-rimmed spectacles and a fedora to cover his bald pate. George Jacobs recalled that the mobster had "a high, almost girlish voice that mispronounced half of the few things he would say. He got everybody's name wrong, from President Eisenheimer to Clark

Grable." Though he was always elegantly turned out in silk suits and neck-ties, and his hands were beautifully manicured, Giancana's general aspect was "mousey," according to Jacobs. He "looked dazed, lost, a scared rabbit . . . He seemed totally paranoid." In his line of work, of course, paranoia amounted to a survival skill.

To some, Giancana seemed bland to the point of invisibility. Those he wanted to impress, however, could be impressed by him. "I thought he was a very nice man," the actor Robert Wagner recalled. "I had a very good time with him." Many women, too, found the Mob boss appealing. "He really was a sweet guy," remembered the nightclub singer Betsy Duncan Hammes. "Respectful and charming, with good manners."

But the veneer of politesse could give way very quickly to the sadistic thug beneath. "He could give you a look that was second to none," an associate remembered. "A killer look." "He had a look about him that scared me," said Sammy Cahn's first wife, Gloria Franks. "I didn't want to be around him." She recalled an incident at a party in Frank Sinatra's Sands suite in the late 1950s: as a prank, Giancana unscrewed a hot lightbulb and applied it to the chest of Jimmy Van Heusen, who was reclining drunkenly on a sofa. "I thought, 'My God, this man is a monster,'" Franks said. "He was a monster."

The unremarkable-looking Chicago Mob boss Sam Giancana was actually a cold-eyed killer. His friendship with Sinatra was a strange dance between two men, both determined to lead.

Sinatra would later claim, in sworn testimony to the Nevada Gaming Control Board, that he hadn't made Giancana's acquaintance until 1960 and that even then they had only had a superficial relationship. But in fact, the two men first met in the early 1950s through the New Jersey gangster Angelo "Gyp" DeCarlo, an avuncular executioner who had helped get Frank work in the early days. Frank sang at a charity event organized by Giancana's wife in 1953, and the following year, according to Giancana's daughter Antoinette, Sinatra and her father embraced affectionately when they met privately. At some point in the mid-1950s, Frank gave Giancana a star sapphire pinkie ring as a gesture of friendship. The mobster wore it proudly but, significantly, did not give Sinatra a ring in return.

Two years after that embrace, according to George Jacobs, Giancana paid an epochal visit to Frank at the singer's house in Palm Springs. Sinatra might as well have been welcoming a president. "He even hired a mariachi band to entertain," Jacobs wrote, remembering his boss's obsessive concern that everything in the house, from the linens to the soap to the Iranian beluga caviar, be perfect for the distinguished visitor.

According to the valet, Frank was all meek deference during Giancana's stay, following the mobster around the golf course as he—not Sinatra—played, hanging on his every word. The main topic of discussion was the casino business, Jacobs said, with Giancana the learned lecturer on all the crooked ins and outs and Frank, the upward-aspiring Sands shareholder, the eager student.

And yet, by Ed Walters's account, when it came to the casino business, Frank was more spectator than participant. Or rather more labor than management. He might have owned nine points in the Sands, but in an enterprise with a steady volume in the hundreds of thousands, if not the millions, Sinatra's allegedly nominal monthly check would have reflected a basic disparity that can only be accounted for by one of the terms Giancana dazzled him with: the skim.

The Mob's involvement in Vegas left the realm of rumor after the May 1957 assassination attempt against the crime chieftain Frank Costello in New York. When a dazed and bloody Costello arrived at a hospital emergency room (the .38 slug fired by the Genovese family hit man Vincent "the Chin" Gigante had creased the Mob boss's scalp but not entered his skull), detectives went through his pockets and found a wad of cash and a crumpled piece of paper. The paper read, "Gross Casino wins as of 4-26-57 $651,284. Casino wins less markers [Vegas-speak for IOUs] $435,695. Slot wins $62,855. Markers, $153,745. Mike $150 per week. Jake $100 per week. L. $30,000. H. $9,000."

That $651,284, as it turned out, was the exact amount the newly opened

Tropicana casino in Las Vegas had taken in during its first twenty-four days of operation.

Costello was sentenced to thirty days in jail for refusing to cooperate with a grand jury investigating his shooting. "At least part of the reason for his refusal, he indicated, was the Bureau of Internal Revenue, a number one bugaboo for gamblers," the United Press reported.

The Feds had long been trying to figure out how to accurately tax gamblers and gambling casinos, and gamblers and gambling casinos had worked assiduously, for just as long, to avoid paying taxes. As the brilliant opening sequence of Martin Scorsese's *Casino* shows, the economy of Las Vegas gambling establishments in the days before the corporations took over the town was cash based, rigorously controlled by management, and subject to regular— routinized—depredations by the casino's true owners, the bosses of organized crime. These periodic withdrawals were known as the skim. The existence of the skim was finally proven by that Rosetta stone, the crumpled note in Frank Costello's pocket.

But greed was always a problem where the Mob was concerned; it had been the tragic flaw of Bugsy Siegel's Flamingo, the defining hotel-casino of Vegas's post–World War II renaissance. Siegel had skimmed the Flamingo for all it was worth and then some; the result was his elimination. And so when it came to the Sands, the Mob decided to keep things on the square, in organized-crime terms. To share the wealth. The true ownership of the Sands was a purposefully complex affair—more complicated than the title to the Tropicana or, for that matter, any other casino in Vegas. "Pieces of the hotel were secretly held in New York, New Jersey, Chicago, Boston, Kansas City, Los Angeles, Texas, St. Louis—just about anyplace there was a group of gangsters worthy of the name," writes Rat Pack chronicler Shawn Levy. "If the other Strip hotels were like little mom-and-pops run by the various out-of-state mobs in competition with one another, the Sands was owned by a syndicate so egalitarian in its ownership as to be tantamount to an honest-to-pete corporation."

Never had organized crime been so organized. Vegas was a gold mine, and nobody in the Mob wanted to roil the river of revenue. Gambling had only been legal in Nevada since 1931: legislators were sensitive to public opinion; therefore gangsters had to be sensitive to the legislators. The sheriff of Clark County was an all-powerful figure. "If mob figures in Las Vegas behaved as they did in other cities, where bloody factional fighting was common, reform-minded Nevadans might once again have outlawed gambling," a labor history of the city asserts.

But men like Meyer Lansky [a part owner of the Sands] knew the importance of appeasing the local electorate and insisted on keeping the city a relatively pleasant place to live. Las Vegas was what one former police officer called an "open city," where warring factions from across the country shared in the gambling industry's profits. "This was not the mob that had terrorized the cities of the East," the officer explained. "This was the mob on its best behavior. This was a mob that was careful to offend no one among the townspeople, and in fact, made every effort to endear itself to the population." If mobsters wanted to kill someone, they normally waited until the person was away from Las Vegas, as the case of "Bugsy" Siegel [who was executed at home in Los Angeles] reveals.

From the day of its opening in December 1952, the Sands was state-of-the-art, commercially and aesthetically. The Los Angeles architect Wayne McAllister, a pioneer of the Googie style—a free-form, *Jetsons*-esque aesthetic that reflected the new space age—had designed the place to transcend his earlier creations, the more rustic El Rancho Vegas and the Desert Inn. The Sands' main building, a low, strikingly spare pueblo-modern structure in red sandstone, fronted the sixty-five-acre plot; in back, ten low-slung outbuildings containing guest apartments and named after racetracks (Arlington Park, Belmont Park, Santa Anita, Aqueduct, and so on) surrounded the huge Paradise Pool. In front of the main building, alongside Highway 91, the two-lane blacktop that continued, as the Strip, into what was then the center of town, stood the hotel's fifty-six-foot-high crowning glory, the Sands sign. All around was open desert.

The sign, the background for the iconic 1960 Rat Pack photograph (Frank, Dean, Sammy, Peter Lawford, and Joey Bishop standing and squinting raffishly into the late-afternoon light), was the tallest sign on the Strip when it was built, a five-story blare of self-importance. The hotel's name, in upward-angled, lightbulbed script, its giant initial S like a great wanton ribbon, was a declaration that the gambler looking for action need look no further: here was the place of places, the joint of joints. Beneath the hotel's name, in smaller caps, the clever slogan "A PLACE IN THE SUN" seemed to promise that the fates would be kind. Title and slogan rested above a great marquee that listed the showroom acts, and a lesser one, showing who was playing the lounge.

McAllister had devoted equally great care to the hotel's interior, whose elegant wood surfaces and muted lighting contrasted sharply with the glaring lighting and shiny surfaces inside other casinos. The 450-seat Copa Room, just off the casino, featured a dramatic Brazilian carnival motif and an open stage. The showroom, like its New York namesake, offered an extensive Chinese menu, and the food was said to be among the best on the Strip.

"But it wasn't the facilities that would make the Sands the 'in' spot for

Texas high rollers and New York and Hollywood sophisticates," writes the William Morris Agency historian Frank Rose. "It was Jack Entratter and the people he knew."

The Sands' way-behind-the-scenes owners had made a brilliant move by persuading the Copacabana's general manager to move west and run their hotel-casino. Jack Entratter, once the bouncer at the Stork Club, was a big, tough bear of a man with a bad foot (the result of a childhood case of osteomyelitis) and a disposition at once warm, formidable, and politically canny. He knew how to work with the Mob: Frank Costello was the Copa's real owner, and the club's on-site boss, Jules Podell, was said to be connected.

He certainly acted that way. Podell was a frog-voiced, stogie-chewing, pinkie-ring-wearing despot, a man so legendarily disagreeable that once, when Sammy Davis Jr.'s act went on too long, he banged his huge ring on his ringside table and yelled, "Get off my stage, nigger!"

But Podell was also a stickler, whose "unwavering demand for professionalism and perfection in every aspect of the club's operation was one of the key ingredients in the Copa's success," according to a history of the nightclub. As the Copa's general manager, Entratter learned attention to detail at Podell's feet and followed his lead, with a twist: he was the good cop to Podell's bad. Entratter was much beloved by performers, on whom he doted. He paid them well; he put them up in lush suites in the Hotel Fourteen, the hostelry in whose basement the Copa nestled. He listened to their problems. Taking the helm of the Sands, he replicated Podell's perfectionism, brooked no nonsense, but ruled benevolently. He never lost sight of who his bosses were, but he was given his head, and maintained a solid sense of self-respect.

And where Jack went, the stars followed. Top-billed talent played out their contracts at other casinos and migrated to the Sands: Martin and Lewis (together, then separately; Dean was ultimately offered one point in the casino), Danny Thomas, Lena Horne, Tony Bennett, Nat King Cole, Red Skelton, Milton Berle, Sammy Davis Jr., and, of course, Frank, who left the Desert Inn as soon as he could to join Entratter.

Sinatra was a friend, and a project. At the Villa Capri birthday party in December, Entratter had (a little grumpily) recited, not sung, a Sammy Cahn lyric that reflected Frank's constantly overstretched work life: "At the Sands he must play each year/In his contract it's very clear/But who can get the silly bastard to appear?"

The other piece of the puzzle was the casino manager Carl Cohen, hired away from El Rancho Vegas in 1955. Cohen was another big, tough Jew—like Entratter, six feet three and 250-plus pounds—but he was a blunter instrument, slow to anger but fast and skillful with his fists when provoked. He was, however, brilliant at his job, which involved managing many people, from dealers to pit bosses to cocktail waitresses, and keeping airtight control over a human activity that by its nature triggers highly volatile emotions and tempts the most straitlaced. "There wasn't nothing you could pull over on him," his brother once said.

―――――

At the end of December, the nineteen-year-old Natalie Wood and Robert Wagner, twenty-seven, had married, much to the chagrin of Wood's overbearing mother, Maria Gurdin—the infamous Mud. It had been a quintessentially Hollywood wedding, but in part due to Mud's disapproval the ceremony was small. The fact that Wood and Wagner were madly in love made the occasion all the more romantic. Among the few guests present were Sinatra and Tony Curtis, Wood's co-stars in *Kings Go Forth*. Frank's date was Betty Bacall, leading a non-bylined Hollywood Roundup column to speculate, "The affection these two show for each other inclines us to believe they might marry."

Two weeks later, marriage was again in the air; love, though, was a different matter. On January 10, Sammy Davis Jr. married a twenty-six-year-old singer named Loray White in the Emerald Room at the Sands. Frank did not attend. As late as the ninth, Davis had told the press that Sinatra was going to be his best man, but on the day of the ceremony Frank called from Los Angeles and said that he was unable to get away. Harry Belafonte stood for Davis instead.

Of course Frank was busy—but then, he was always busy, and he frequently shuttled from L.A. to Vegas, on necessary business or just on a whim: to him the one-hour flight was the equivalent of a car commute for most people. The musical episode of *The Frank Sinatra Show* broadcast that night (Robert Mitchum and his sixteen-year-old son, Jim, were the guests) had been pretaped. He wasn't in the recording studio that night.

But Sinatra would have known all too intimately the true story behind Sammy's marriage to the tall, handsome, and black Loray White: that it was a sham union between two people who barely knew each other, thrown together hastily when Davis's romance with Kim Novak threatened to come to light and—in an era when America at large still looked upon interracial sexual relations with horror—become a national scandal. It was a poorly kept secret that Sammy, who hated the color of his own skin, was obsessed with white women, and Novak was, after all, a kind of white goddess. But beyond her substantial surface appeal, the actress shared a deeper connection with Davis: as an undereducated brunette from Chicago who had been turned into a blonde and a movie star by Harry Cohn, and an actress of limited skills and confidence, she suffered from a shaky sense of identity to equal Sammy's; on a certain level, the two were soul mates.

But Novak was a rebellious Galatea. She enjoyed using the relationship to provoke Cohn, who felt the casting couch was his droit du seigneur. He was also a man easily provoked, not to mention a studio chief worried about how a scandal of such proportions might affect box office. Cohn fought back, warning Novak that she was jeopardizing her career. And according to the photographer William Read Woodfield, a frequent documenter of Sinatra's career and a friend of Davis's, the studio head called on his longtime Mob associations (Cohn and the Los Angeles gangster Johnny Rosselli wore matching friendship rings) to have Sammy threatened, in stark terms, by armed hoodlums. Sammy then went to Frank for help. Woodfield claimed that in his presence, Frank phoned his Chicago friend Joe Fischetti to ascertain the source and credibility of the threats; Sinatra then told Davis what he needed to do to make them go away.

By the time of Sammy's wedding to Loray White—the marriage would last nine months—Frank's nonattendance at the ceremony was overdetermined. For one thing, hadn't he done a substantial enough favor for his friend not to have to fly to Las Vegas and dignify a fraud with his presence? For another, Sammy, as a little brother surrogate, could be annoyingly unruly. A few years earlier, he had palled around rather publicly with Ava, and though both swore up and down that they weren't involved, where Ava was concerned, who ever knew? The thing with Kim, whether Frank was done with her or not, had been a little too close for comfort. Like all unequal friendships, Sinatra and Davis's would continue to be fraught with volatility.

In the meantime, an ancient friendship was nearing its end. Emanuel Sacks, Manie, the record executive who had believed in Frank from the beginning and had signed him with Columbia, who had nurtured Sinatra's recording career and extended him every possible indulgence even as Frank strained his heroic patience by demanding more and more, lay dying of leukemia in a Philadelphia hospital. He was fifty-six. It didn't matter that the two had had cross words; it didn't matter that—in part because of the mounting exasperation of working with Sinatra—Manie had moved on to RCA before Columbia dropped the singer, nor that Sinatra was now with Capitol. Sacks, along with Tommy Dorsey, had been one of the two true father figures in Frank's life, and though fathers are meant to be contended with, and rebuked, and transcended, they remain fathers still.

That January, Frank, doing location shooting in France for *Kings Go Forth*, took time off to fly to Philadelphia and sit by Manie's side. He paid for the lost production days. On February 9, Sacks died. Sinatra, now back in Los Angeles, flew east for the funeral.

———

On March 3, when Frank stepped into Capitol Studio A for the first time that year, it was Billy May and not Nelson Riddle who met him there.

Sinatra recorded four ebullient tunes that night, three of them Cahn and Van Heusen compositions, and two of those, "Nothing in Common" and "How Are Ya' Fixed for Love?," charming duets with Keely Smith, whose vocal expressiveness belied her visual shtick: the deadpan she wore in her Vegas lounge act with her husband, the wild-man vocalist and trumpeter Louis Prima.

Nelson Riddle had vast scope and depth as an arranger, but nobody could do ebullience like Billy May. Though not one of the tracks Frank laid down that night was close to a classic, the music was sparkling and thoroughly worthy of this high-water period in Sinatra's career. The last number of the evening, the undistinguished but winsome "Here Goes," a blaring, Vegas-style roof raiser that Frank performed at an uncharacteristically breakneck tempo, was supremely upbeat, and—especially after a February that saw the deaths not only of Manie Sacks and Nelson Riddle's baby daughter (of bronchial asthma) but also of Harry Cohn, who succumbed to a heart attack[*] on the twenty-seventh—he managed to imbue the lyric with what sounded like real optimism:

> *Here goes, baby, here goes,*
> *Every worry, every fear goes,*
> *Every dull day in the year goes,*
> *I'm about to fall in love.*

It was a hopefulness he almost certainly felt in that moment. As Bing Crosby said, any singer worthy of the name is acting when he sings a song. But as was not the case with Crosby, who managed to blend emotional believability and clinical coolness in his delivery, inspiring the sentiment more than enacting it, Sinatra's genius was to give you the emotion in the moment, to make you feel he was feeling it as you were. The transporting pleasure he felt

---

[*] Though Cohn gave Frank his big chance in *From Here to Eternity*, his tyrannical and ill-tempered style made him widely detested in Hollywood, and his well-attended funeral inspired a famous remark by Red Skelton: "It proves what Harry always said: give the public what they want and they'll come out for it."

while recording his best takes communicated itself clearly to everyone in the studio—as did its converse, his chagrin when, for whatever reason, he wasn't feeling the song.

"As a singer, there's no one like him," said the producer Voyle Gilmore, whom Sinatra would fire not long after this session. "As a guy, there was no one more difficult to handle. Each time you saw Frank, it was like meeting a different guy. How he treated you depended solely on how he felt at *that* moment and what was bugging him. And, believe me, he has a lot to bug him. Because he's gotta be on the move all the time, he keeps getting involved in more than any human being can handle."

———

"As a couple we were combustible," Lauren Bacall writes in her memoir. "Always when we entered the room the feeling was: Are they okay tonight? You could almost hear a sigh of relief when we were both smiling and relaxed."

Between Frank and Ava, combustibility had been an aphrodisiac; infidelity—the threat of it, the idea of it, the reality of it—had been the tinder. With Sinatra and Bacall, commitment itself seems to have been the unspoken but flammable subject. Frank liked to make dreamy marriage talk with his girlfriends, but Betty, beautiful, formidable, and thirty-three, was serious business—serious enough to make him clam up about how far things might go. He loved squiring her—she was his intellectual and charismatic match; she was wonderful to be seen with—but what would come next? She was too proud to pressure him.

But then as now, publicity conditioned the private lives of public figures. Throughout the fall and into the winter, the papers kept up an incessant drumbeat of speculation about whether the two would marry. The press of the day might have lacked the instantaneousness of the Internet, but not its power or tenacity. Bacall writes, "I recall a wire-service man on the Coast saying, 'When are you and Frank getting married?' and me pleading to be left alone, asking why they wouldn't stop. He said, 'We'll keep at it until you do or you don't.'"

Paying a visit to the *Kings Go Forth* set at Paramount in December, she had watched the shooting of a scene in which Sinatra, playing the battle-weary lieutenant Sam Loggins, advised the young radio technician in his platoon, played by Tony Curtis, about his relationship with the gorgeous young Monique (Natalie Wood). When "Sinatra counseled Tony Curtis to marry the girl," the biographer Arnold Shaw wrote, "Miss Bacall let out a huge horse-laugh."

In her memoir, Bacall is such a graceful and intelligent prose stylist, such a penetrating analyst of her own psyche and of the emotional states of her friends and intimates, that it's easy to overlook the little things she leaves out—things like her own sharp tongue and hot temper, not to mention Humphrey Bogart's affair with his makeup artist and wig maker Verita Peterson, not to mention her own jealousy about Sinatra's unending attachment to Ava Gardner. Bacall mentions Gardner just twice in the memoir, and Frank's unwelcome visit to Ava in December 1957 comes up not at all, though it certainly played a part in the blowup of the marriage that never was.

Ava or no Ava, Betty and Frank "had a lovely Christmas eve at his house," she insists. "We were planning New Year's Eve in Palm Springs. He told me what food to buy—more than fifty friends were coming to his house. I was excited. Playing house, going to the market as though I were Mrs. Him. What a babe in the woods!"

At Sinatra's request, she hosted a small pre-party at the new Romanoff's in the Springs, holding the fort until he arrived from Los Angeles. "I remember his arriving—my getting up to greet him—his saying to everyone, 'Doesn't she look radiant?'" she recalled. "The next day he wanted me to go home. No specific argument—that click again. Of course I was in tears, wanting to be there, thinking of everyone expecting me to be there. I made up my mind it would be better to stay and not to have to answer questions later."

On New Year's Eve, as the crowd arrived, she put on her best smile, but everyone sensed that something was wrong. She and Frank never interacted; their friends' eyes shifted uneasily from one of them to the other. "A nightmare," Bacall remembered.

> That was the first time Frank really dropped the curtain on me. A chilling experience. I still don't know how he did it, but he could behave as though you weren't there. He drank heavily, which led me to believe he wasn't very happy himself. I had to try to rationalize his behavior. I absolutely could not comprehend his ability to ignore me so totally.

This seems disingenuous. How could the redoubtable Bacall have failed to reproach Sinatra, by word or by gesture, for flying to his ex-wife's side? And if Betty had merely arched one of those famous eyebrows, let alone uttered a rebuke, Frank—who had once warned Ava, when she'd had the temerity to scold him for coming home late, "Don't cut the corners too close on me, baby"—knew just how to retaliate. Alcohol was his self-anesthetic; ice, rather than fire, his weapon of choice. Fire, he knew, would lead to combustion, which could only lead to bed. Which would lead back to the question he preferred not to answer.

By January, according to the ever-vigilant Louella Parsons, Frank and

Betty were "in the deep freeze romantically. They haven't seen each other in
10 days . . . Until just recently, neither dated anyone else and they were constantly together at Palm Springs, at his recordings and TV show. It's impossible
to predict about this unpredictable couple—so we'll just wait and see what
happens."

For all her grandiosity, the columnist could scarcely have imagined how big
a part she would play in what did happen.

Soon afterward, Bacall had to go to New York, reluctantly, to publicize a
not very good film she'd just made, a weeper called *The Gift of Love*. Out of
the blue, Frank, who'd come east for Manie Sacks's funeral, called, "almost
as though nothing had happened," Bacall recalled, and invited her to dinner
when he arrived in Manhattan. He came, they supped, they talked "like two
friends who had insane electric currents running between them all the time."
She felt stronger in New York, away from Hollywood and close to her family;
she even "felt in a position of strength with Frank," she remembered. "I told
myself that I expected nothing, but I knew I wanted everything. Though his
erratic behavior was very much a part of him, I flatly refused to face what it
might portend for our future together. I probably thought that if I didn't face
it, it might go away."

This is what she was thinking. But the way she behaved—acting from
strength, keeping a slight distance—egged him on. He was "wildly attentive"
in New York and, the night she returned to California, came right over to see
her. "He didn't know how to apologize, but he was fairly contrite, at least for
him," Bacall writes.

> He said he had felt somewhat trapped—was "chicken"—but now could
> face it. "Will you marry me?" He said those words and he meant them.
> Of course all my barriers fell. I must have hesitated for at least thirty
> seconds. Yes, I thought to myself, I was right all along—he couldn't deal
> with it, was afraid of himself, but finally realized that he loved me and
> that marriage was the only road to take. I was ecstatic—we both were.
> He said, "Let's go out and have a drink to celebrate—let's call Swifty,
> maybe he can join us." I questioned nothing. That was my trouble—
> one of my troubles.

It was a strange choice, so quickly diluting the fresh intimacy by adding an
outsider—and this outsider. The little literary agent had been Bogart's best
friend; he was also the ultimate pragmatist and Hollywood operator, the man
who had blithely counted Sinatra out when he was down, then welcomed him
back open-armed when he rose from the ashes. The man who embodied Oscar

Wilde's definition of a cynic: one who knows the price of everything and the value of nothing.

When the lovebirds told Lazar of their plan—they were sitting in a booth at the Imperial Gardens, a Japanese restaurant on Sunset—he didn't take them seriously at first. Chillingly, the agent "thought it a 'great idea,' but didn't believe it—until Frank started to plan the wedding," Bacall writes.

> "We'll get married at the house and instead of our going away, we'll have our friends go away." He knew the way he wanted it—he didn't ask what I might want. He wasn't dictatorial, he just had his plan and it never occurred to him I might not accept it. I didn't disappoint him. I was too happy, and I loved his taking over, that being one of my most acute needs.
>
> A young girl came over for autographs. Frank handed me the paper napkin and pen. As I started to write, he said, "Put down your new name." So "Lauren Bacall" was followed by "Betty Sinatra." It looked funny, but he asked for it and he got it. I often wondered what became of that paper napkin.

Then Frank headed to Miami, where he was to open on March 11 for a twelve-night stand at the architect Morris Lapidus's great Collins Avenue Xanadu, the Fontainebleau.

———

Ava Gardner hated and distrusted Frank's gangster friends, preferring to have as little to do with them as possible. Lauren Bacall mentions no mafiosi in her memoir, a fact that suggests one of the many firewalls Sinatra built, or attempted to build, between the classy and the less than classy parts of his life. But Frank's old friend Joe Fischetti, who had a no-show job as "entertainment director" of the Fontainebleau, based solely on his ability to persuade Sinatra to perform at the hotel, was there with Sam Giancana to greet Sinatra at his sold-out opening. And in March 1958, the crowd in the La Ronde Room, not to mention the nearly three thousand miles between Miami and Los Angeles, stood all too eloquently for the yawning gulf between Frank and his new fiancée.

"The Fontainebleau (where Frank Sinatra is the King of Miami Beach biz) turns away over 300 unhappy rich people at every show," Walter Winchell wrote in his March 19 column. "The star appears to be more at home before this kind of an audience. Sports and their ladies, gamblers and gonniffs and glamorous guys and girls. 'They are my kind of people,' says Frank."

In the meantime, Lauren Bacall was taking in Noël Coward's play *Nude with Violin* at the Huntington Hartford Theatre on Vine Street in Hollywood. Swifty Lazar was her date. During intermission, Louella Parsons loomed up before the pair, all five feet three of her, and asked Bacall, point-blank, if she and Frank were to be married. "Why don't you ask him?" Bacall said.

She went to the ladies' room, and when she emerged, she claims, she saw Lazar and Parsons still conversing. By the time Bacall made her way over to Swifty, the columnist had vanished into the crowd. Betty thought no more of the encounter. She and Lazar saw the rest of the show, then went out to dinner.

On the way home, the pair stopped at a newsstand to buy the early edition of the morning paper. "I saw enormous black letters jumping out at me from the *Examiner*: SINATRA TO MARRY BACALL," she writes.

> I gasped—oh my God, what a disaster—how the hell did that happen? How could Louella have printed that? "My God, Swifty. You told her— are you crazy? Frank will be furious!" Swifty just laughed: "Of course I told her—I didn't know she'd do this. I just said I happened to know that Frank had asked Betty to marry him. So what? He did! What's wrong with saying it?"

She marched Lazar back to her house, she says, and had him call Frank: "I don't want him to think I did it," she said.

Swifty made the call but didn't take responsibility. Instead, he treated the whole thing as a joke—"Ha ha, the cat's out of the bag now, old boy."

"I got on the phone briefly, saying I was ready to kill Swifty," Bacall writes. "As I recall, Frank was not overjoyed, but at least he was prepared for the coming onslaught of the press, and he didn't chastise me. I must have sounded contrite, though I had no reason to be. I was just frightened of making waves. Hopeless for any relationship, much less a marriage."

Her friends began to phone; her mother called from New York. Bacall told them all that she didn't know; there was no final decision.

From Miami, silence.

A few nights later, Frank phoned.

"Why did you do it?" he demanded.

"I didn't do anything," Bacall answered, her heart knocking.

"I haven't been able to leave my room for days—the press are everywhere," he told her. "We'll have to lay low for a while, not see each other for a while."

It was their last phone call.

A month later, Bill and Edie Goetz asked the two of them to a party. "We had one person between us at dinner," Bacall writes, "but Frank didn't acknowledge my existence. He did not speak one word to me—if he looked in my direction, he did not see me, he looked right past me, as though my chair were empty. I was so humiliated, so embarrassed. Nothing would bring my sense of humor back—it deserted me that night and for some time afterward. I would have preferred him to spit in my face, at least that would have been recognition."

The same thing happened in Palm Springs a few months later. After a concert at which Sinatra had sung, Bacall found herself accidentally standing face-to-face with him: "He looked right at me again as though I were not there—not a flicker of recognition—called his group—got into his car. The blood ran to my face, then away. I felt sick. My humiliation was indescribable."

What would possess a man to behave so savagely toward a former lover, a woman he had once treated with tenderness, courtesy, respect? He wielded humiliation like a weapon, as payment in kind. Her alleged sin having been not just to cut the corners on him but to do so in the most public way possible.

––––––––

In his column of April 2, Walter Winchell, traveling with Frank, reported that he had a nude statue of Ava—it had been used as a prop in *The Barefoot Contessa*—on the lawn of his Coldwater Canyon house.

––––––––

In early May, Sinatra and Riddle returned to Capitol Studios to begin the album that both of them would come to think of as Frank's finest: *Frank Sinatra Sings for Only the Lonely*. Ironically, Sinatra initially planned the project as a collaboration with Gordon Jenkins, a follow-up to *Where Are You?*, but Jenkins was busy working in Las Vegas, so Riddle got the job. If he ever found out he was second choice, he kept it to himself.

Frank always prepared his albums carefully, thinking about not only the character of the record itself but also each LP's place in the sequence of his work. Charles L. Granata considers *Only the Lonely* a kind of complement or bookend to the minimal classicism of *Close to You*. "While the orchestrations for *Close to You* express the intimacy of a chamber-music setting," he writes,

> for *Only the Lonely* the arranger chose to unfurl his musical canvas,
> painting aching portraits of loneliness on an expansive landscape
> sparingly dotted with musical colors and textures. Against a somber
> backdrop of understated strings speak judicious traces of instruments
> like French horn, oboe, flute, clarinet, bassoon, and trombone, and

the barest wisp of a rhythm section. Semi-classical in feel, each four-minute tune is a short story of gloom and despair transformed into a cry for sympathy.

There were a lot of instruments: thirty-eight in all. "We had so many instruments," the guitarist Al Viola recalled, "that when I got to the first date, I thought it was a union meeting!" As Riddle wrote the arrangements, he was delighted "to contemplate the luxury of a full woodwind section with all the misty, velvety sounds that issue from such a group if properly used." To some degree, he was using these sounds to express a deep personal sadness: that spring, while still in mourning for his infant daughter, the arranger was also watching his mother succumb to terminal cancer.

The already gloomy Riddle might have found himself totally paralyzed had it not been for a peculiar remedy. "I'd be painting the house during the daytime," he told Jonathan Schwartz in 1982. "I find it's good therapy for any arranger to paint his house because arrangers work in small jerky motions to write notes, and painting a house requires long, sweeping motions. For me, it was therapy."

Riddle had house painting to soothe his gloom, and arranging as catharsis. But what did *Only the Lonely* mean for Sinatra? Clearly the album, with its sequence of melancholy songs, beginning with the masterly Cahn–Van Heusen title tune and ending with Harold Arlen and Johnny Mercer's immortal "One for My Baby (and One More for the Road)," was meant as a statement, but a statement of what? "The Frank Sinatra that we know and have known (and hardly know)," Sammy Cahn wrote in the liner notes, "is an artist with as many forms and patterns as can be found in a child's kaleidoscopticon. *Come Fly with Me* is one Sinatra. *All the Way* is another Sinatra. A Sinatra singing a hymn of loneliness could very well be the real Sinatra."

He lived with loneliness: the solitude of the only child who grows up with inexpressible feelings of otherness, the self-inflicted isolation of the man who'd brutally pushed Lauren Bacall away, the aloneness of the great artist who mused on the sonorities of Ravel and Ralph Vaughan Williams while feeling compelled to pal around with hoodlums. The cover image of *Only the Lonely*, a painting of a pensive Sinatra, his face in clown makeup and half in shadow, fetishized his loneliness, made a fungible commodity of it. He was a kind of hunger artist, one who starved himself so the rest of us could feel better about our own hunger.

———

On the night of May 5, Frank, Nelson, and a thirty-eight-piece orchestra began the album by recording three numbers: Sammy Cahn and Jule Styne's "Guess

I'll Hang My Tears Out to Dry"; a Ravel-colored version of the pop hit "Ebb Tide"; and, for the first time, a song that would become a kind of theme, Matt Dennis and Earl K. Brent's great "Angel Eyes."

It was a false start. Something about the session—in particular the guitar accompaniment for the verse of "Guess I'll Hang My Tears Out to Dry"—struck Sinatra as off, and the recordings weren't used. (It turned out that Riddle, who arranged beautifully for strings but had little understanding of the guitar, had written chords that were extremely difficult for the instrumentalist, George Van Eps, to play; Riddle rewrote the verse.)

On May 29, Frank and the musicians reconvened in Capitol Studio A, although Nelson, who was in London with Nat King Cole, was absent. The first violinist, Felix Slatkin, conducted in his stead. Having lost time with the discarded May 5 session, Frank recorded an amazing seven songs on the night of the twenty-ninth—or rather six songs and part of a seventh. Thereby hangs a tale.

Besides "Monique," a tune written by Sammy Cahn and Elmer Bernstein for *Kings Go Forth,* Sinatra rerecorded the three numbers he'd done three weeks earlier and laid down three other tracks for *Only the Lonely:* the title number, Rodgers and Hart's "Spring Is Here," and Ann Ronell's Gershwin-esque classic "Willow Weep for Me." Before "Willow," however, Frank attempted Billy Strayhorn's majestic, fiercely difficult "Lush Life."

Born the same year as Sinatra, Strayhorn wrote much of the great song-poem at the astonishing age of eighteen, and its precociously world-weary lyric—"I used to visit all the very gay places/those come what may places/where one relaxes on the axis of the wheel of life/to get the feel of life"—is filled with subtexts: not only was Duke Ellington's future arranger and song-writing collaborator a genius; he was a homosexual, in an era and a culture when this was the love that dared not speak its name. The lyrics of "Lush Life" therefore have a coded quality, a slightly uneasy mélange of brilliance and pretentiousness, with a dash of awkwardness thrown in ("The girls I knew had sad and sullen gray faces/With *distingué* traces that used to be there"). And the number's rangy chromatic melody—written as though warning the listener not to understand the composition or composer too easily—has the complexity of an art song by Schubert or Fauré.

It was wrong for Frank.

He certainly had the musical chops for it, but we'll never know if he could have brought off "Lush Life" with his usual élan, because he never attempted it again. Granata contends that Sinatra might have left the song unfinished out of fatigue—it was the sixth song of the evening's seven—and weariness might have factored into it. But more to the point is that Frank's initial approach to a song was through the words: he studied a lyric like a literature professor analyzing an Elizabethan sonnet, bringing his formidable intelligence to bear on every nuance. By the time he sang a tune, he inhabited it, possessed it. And in some basic way, "Lush Life" didn't speak to him.

Nat King Cole had thrown down a formidable challenge with his great 1949 version of the song, but Cole was a very different singer from Sinatra—no less great, but like Tony Bennett and Ella Fitzgerald less deep. Cole's reading of "Lush Life" (based on Pete Rugolo's arrangement) is rather sprightly and so assured as to be almost facile. It's wonderful and highly listenable, but Frank meant to explore the canyons of solitude on *Only the Lonely*, and "Lush Life"—which in the end was an art song rather than a ballad—stopped him.

After two brief takes, he began a third, getting through the verse and beginning the chorus: "Life is lonely/again, and only last year/everything seemed . . ." And it's strange: he's beautifully in voice, but he's also singing without assurance and not entirely on key.

"Hol' it!" he suddenly barks, shifting abruptly from perfect song diction to Hobokenese. The musicians wind down as fast as they can. "It's not only tough enough with the way it is," Sinatra says, "but he's got some *clydes* in there!" Referring, presumably, to the ranginess of the melody. To cover his embarrassment—and not being able to master a complex song in a studio full of brilliant musicians, with Slatkin at the podium, would have caused him embarrassment—Frank shifts into his *Amos 'n' Andy* voice: "Ooohh, yeah! Well, ahhh . . ."

Slatkin suggests that he put the song aside for a minute.

"Put it aside for about a year!" Sinatra exclaims, and that is that.

Nelson Riddle wasn't the only one absent from Studio A that evening. The mild-mannered Voyle Gilmore was also gone—permanently in his case—the victim of a Sinatra tantrum. On his way home from Miami in March, Frank had stopped in Chicago to catch the rematch between Sugar Ray Robinson and Carmen Basilio; while there, he made the rounds of the local disc jockeys. To his horror, he found that none of the DJs had received a copy of his latest single, a duet with Keely Smith, "How Are Ya' Fixed for Love?"

Sinatra saw red, phoned Hank Sanicola, and ordered him to replace Gilmore. Sanicola told Frank that Gilmore wasn't responsible for shipping. Frank called his lawyer Mickey Rudin and had Rudin call Glenn Wallichs, the president of Capitol (Frank's rabbi Alan Livingston by now having left to become vice president of programming at NBC), to demand that the label assign Sinatra a new producer, one who would be answerable to Frank and no other artist. Wallichs refused but offered to substitute another producer, a former saxophonist named Dave Cavanaugh, for Gilmore. And so it was Cavanaugh who was sitting in the control booth on the eventful night of May 29.

When Wallichs told Gilmore he had been replaced, "I felt only relief," the producer recalled.

> No artist is easy to handle. But when they're as complex as Frank . . . Which is not like saying he's a bad guy.
>
> With musicians he was a prince . . . But he'd never take a suggestion [from the producer] in the presence of a musician—or anybody else, for that matter. You'd have to come out of the booth and go into the studio. If you tried talking to him over the speaker system, as you frequently did with other artists, you were dead.
>
> Once when he was really acting up, I went at him: "I'm trying pretty hard, Frank," I complained, "and all I get is abuse." He broke into a broad smile. "Don't let any artist get your goat," he said, "not even me." He was so appealing at times he could charm butterflies—and then again, so miserable he could bother a snake.

But Sinatra's replacement of his old producer was only a shot across Capitol's bow. As Frank's power grew—his last two albums, *A Jolly Christmas* and *Come Fly with Me,* had gone platinum and gold, respectively—so did his discontent with his record label. He wanted a bigger share of the profits he was generating, and, most important, he wanted a right no other major recording artist, anywhere, had: ownership of his own master recordings. Owning his masters would give Sinatra unprecedented control over his financial destiny, allowing him, once his contract with Capitol was up, to make a more favorable deal with any other record label.

Or even to start a record label of his own.

10

||||||||||||

*If you're his friend, that's IT. If you need him, DADDY, HE . . .
IS . . . THERE!*

—SAMMY DAVIS JR. ON SINATRA

He was forty-two now, still a demon of energy, but every now and then show-ing ever so slight signs of wear. With the world premiere of *Kings Go Forth* set for mid-June in Monte Carlo, Frank had planned to travel to Europe via the Far East, accompanied by Peter and Pat Lawford. But in early May, tired out by two weeks of doing two standing-room-only shows a night at the Sands, Sinatra canceled the Asia jaunt and let it be known that he was going to take a long rest in Palm Springs.

The cancellation sparked all sorts of rumors: that his marriage plans with Lauren Bacall were alive again; that there had been a rift with the Lawfords; that he had had a severe throat hemorrhage. The first two weren't true; the third might have been. While some stars grabbed publicity by insuring their legs or other body parts with Lloyd's of London, Frank had taken the opposite tack, holding all information about his golden pipes as closely as possible. His instrument could be a fluky one, and while he famously built it up by swim-ming laps underwater and doing vocal exercises, he did himself no favors by chain-smoking Camels, drinking to excess, and generally living a life of oper-atic emotionalism. None but the inner circle had known the full story of his vocal problems in 1956, nor of his terror, around the time of *Close to You,* that he was losing his voice altogether. Toward the end of his Fontainebleau run in March 1958, he'd had to cancel a couple of shows because of vocal difficulties, possibly a result of overuse, possibly also arising from general strain in the wake of the Bacall breakup. No one subbed for him; the customers got their money back.

But the Sands run in May might have triggered something more serious. An alarming June 1 wire-service report, which made the front pages in some papers, claimed that Frank had suffered a ruptured blood vessel in his throat and was seriously ill at home. A prominent New York specialist had been sum-moned, the item said.

Then, in a piece that ran two days later, Sinatra simultaneously shrugged off and confirmed what might have been a well-founded but erroneously time-stamped rumor. "He laughed when he heard about the report he was ill," a representative from Frank's agency told UPI. Jack Entratter, chiming in on Sinatra's behalf, said that the singer had "made six records last Thursday" and that "the incident involving the badly-strained vocal chords [*sic*] occurred about a month ago"—around the time of the Sands engagement—"and that Sinatra had been at Palm Springs, Cal., much of the time since then."

The to-do casts new light on the discarded May 5 recording session, which might have been scuttled not just by Nelson Riddle's awkward writing for guitar but also by Frank's insufficiently recuperated vocal cords. Sinatra really does seem to have spent much of May resting, even though resting never was his forte. Looked at from a distance, the month represents an interesting fermata in the ordinarily jam-packed score of Sinatra's life. For one thing, his frenetic moviemaking schedule of the past two years had abated considerably. Though Frank had two films on his immediate slate (*Some Came Running* was scheduled to start shooting in August, *A Hole in the Head* in November; *Ocean's 11* was still in the talking stages), in remarkable contrast to 1956 and 1957, 1958 actually contained a six-month period when he was on neither a soundstage nor a location.

Recording, too, was proceeding deliberately, while Frank rested and Riddle worked out the kinks in the arrangements for *Only the Lonely*. And *The Frank Sinatra Show* was officially kaput; the last musical installment, with the guests Natalie Wood and Pat Suzuki, aired on May 23, and the final dramatic episode ("The Seedling Doubt," co-starring Phyllis Thaxter and Macdonald Carey) was shown on June 6. Sinatra had delivered thirty-one of the thirty-six episodes stipulated in his $3 million contract with ABC; he would fulfill his obligation by doing four musical specials for the network in 1959 and 1960.

Even his love life seems to have slowed just a touch. No grand affairs were afoot. Whatever hopes Louella Parsons expressed in her column, Frank and Lauren Bacall had split definitively; the two wouldn't even run into each other for six years. Peggy Connelly had long since moved along, having married the comedian Dick Martin in 1957. Frank's always genteel relationship with Jill Corey appears to have become completely platonic. There was an actress named Sandra Giles; a model named Nan Whitney. (To the detriment of her column's credibility, Dorothy Kilgallen remained steadfastly convinced that the latter was the same unfortunate woman in whose New York apartment the actor John Garfield had died, at age thirty-nine, in 1952; but the far less interesting story is that that was another Whitney.) Rumor had it that Frank and the forty-two-year-old actress/Westinghouse spokeswoman Betty Furness had been affectionate seatmates on a TWA flight to Rome; someone who claimed to be in the know even asserted that Furness—rather than Swifty Lazar or Frank himself—had been responsible for breaking up the Sinatra-Bacall relationship.

———

In the meantime, he briefly slipped under the radar. In early June, Sinatra landed in London en route to Monaco, angrily fending off a reporter's shouted question about the status of his relationship with Bacall. Shortly afterward, he took the aforementioned TWA flight to Rome. On which it seems highly likely that Betty Furness was a chance encounter rather than Frank's traveling companion, for he was headed to see Ava.

She was about to start filming the last film in her MGM contract, *The Naked Maja,* a story of the painter Goya's steamy romance with the Duchess of Alba, the Spanish noblewoman said to have posed for his most famous nude. The movie had begun as a passion project of the writer-director and Gardner obsessive Albert Lewin, who'd created Ava's quirky 1951 vehicle *Pandora and the Flying Dutchman.* But an Italian production company took over *The Naked Maja* and bought Lewin out, rewriting the script, hiring the journeyman director Henry Koster, and turning the project into a piece of hackwork. Lewin alone might have been able to sweet-talk Ava into believing the movie was another great vehicle for her; instead, as she waited in Rome for filming to start, she was bored and alienated, and afraid.

She was thirty-five, a dangerous age for a female movie star, and though the facial welt raised by her bullfighting accident had subsided over the past months, it had not disappeared. A star was what she was: she'd never considered herself much of an actress or especially enjoyed making movies. Her stardom had bought her the freedom to live exactly as she wished, and now her stardom was in grave peril. Her intermittent flame, the ruggedly handsome Italian actor Walter Chiari, was in Spain making a movie. Frank, who wrote and called her regularly, who could never forget her, was increasingly on her mind—she had rescued him once; perhaps he could now rescue her. And so when he told her he was traveling to Europe, Ava asked him to come and see her in Rome.

Something went wrong. Gardner's biographer Lee Server contends that between Ava's invitation to Frank and his arrival in the Eternal City, she got wind of a new romance of his, with Lady Adelle Beatty, a divorced English socialite and former Oklahoma beauty queen. In Server's dramatic account, Sinatra arrives in Rome and promptly contacts Ava, who suddenly won't take his calls or return his messages. Unable to sleep one early morning, Ava takes her corgi, Rags, for a walk; she winds up at the Hotel Hassler, where Frank is staying, and has someone take her to his suite.

THE CHAIRMAN | 209

In a scene that might have come from a movie, Rags leaps into Frank's arms, but Ava doesn't. Instead,

> she took the dog back and she reached out to Frank and put in his hand the wedding ring he had given her long ago.
> "Give that to your English lady," she said and turned and went out the door . . .
> Sinatra, with the ring she had given him still gripped in his hand, . . . called for a car to take him to the airport; he was gone from Rome three hours later.

Though Server is usually dependable, this episode feels implausible. Ava's wedding ring from Frank had undergone quite an odyssey: the platinum band he slipped onto her finger in November 1951 had been lost and then replaced with a duplicate amid the couple's marital woes in 1953; Gardner then took the ring off and definitively put it aside when she and Sinatra separated. Still, what was she doing with it in Rome, and why would she have taken it along on a walk that impulsively turned into a visit to his hotel?

George Jacobs contends that the ring in question was a ten-karat "re-engagement" band Frank bought for Ava at Bulgari in Rome and that "when Ava found out about Lady Beatty, she left Sinatra's ring with the concierge at the Hassler Hotel, where he was staying, with instructions to give the ring to Lady Beatty. By then, however, the lady had chosen [movie director Stanley] Donen over Mr. S."

The problem with Jacobs's account being that the Beatty-Donen romance— quite certifiably—didn't begin until the spring of 1959.

Lady Beatty, née Adelle Dillingham, from the oil town of Ardmore, Oklahoma, would indeed swirl into Frank's life but, from all accounts, not until the fall of 1958. Perhaps Ava had gotten wind of Betty Furness. In any case, as Hedda Hopper wrote later in June, "To set those nosey minds at ease who are dying to know if Frank Sinatra saw Ava Gardner in Rome, I can say definitely he did. He spent one evening with her. But I doubt if the old flame was rekindled."

No, but it burned on low and steady, like a pilot light.

———

Quincy Jones was twenty-five in the spring of 1958, living in Paris and enjoying life as an expatriate jazz musician to the hilt. Between gigs with various bands, he was studying composition and music theory with Nadia Boulanger and the composer Olivier Messiaen; he also had a day job as music director, arranger, and conductor for Barclay Disques, the French distributor for

Mercury Records. One day a call came in to Barclay from the Sporting Club in Monte Carlo, requesting the services of the label's fifty-five-member house band—which included such great musicians as the jazz violinist Stéphane Grappelli, the drummer Kenny Clarke, and the saxophonists Don Byas and Lucky Thompson—at a benefit Prince Rainier and Princess Grace were holding on June 14. The band was to back Frank Sinatra, and Quincy Jones was to conduct.

"Even though I was only twenty-five years old, by then I'd learned that every great singer is different; each has different nuances, and you have to know what makes them comfortable so they can let loose," Jones writes in his memoir.

In a way a conductor and arranger has to put an emotional X ray on the singer, and to explore their creative psyche. You have to understand their ranges and registers, the place where they break between natural voice and falsetto . . . That's why Nelson Riddle and Sinatra enjoyed such a long and successful collaboration: Nelson knew Sinatra's soul. He gave him his space, never putting instruments in his register so that he felt crowded.

Jones admitted in an interview that he was intimidated by the prospect of meeting the great man. "I didn't know what to expect," he recalled. And in his memoir he writes,

I was curious to see how Frank liked his music cooked up. He was straight ahead about it. He walked into the rehearsal at the Monaco Sporting Club with his "Swinging Lovers" hat on, hit me with those steely blues, and said, "You've heard the records, you know what to do. You know where I'm coming from."

We rehearsed the show with that fifty-five-piece orchestra for four hours until it couldn't get any tighter. When we were done he said, "Koo-koo," shook my hand, and walked out. He didn't say more than ten sentences to me the whole time. He was all business.

Frank liked to create an air of drama and mystery about his entrances, often simply walking onstage unannounced, embodying the idea that he was one entertainer who needed no introduction. He made an exception for the European audience at the Sporting Club concert, allowing Noël Coward to introduce him (in English and French), but held on to his need for drama by failing to tell his conductor, who after all had to cue the music to Sinatra's entrance, exactly when, and from where, he would appear.

As the houselights dimmed and Coward made his introduction, "I was still mouthing the words 'Where is he?' to the stage manager, who kept looking around and shrugging," Jones writes.

> When I heard the words "Frank Sinatra!" and heard the audience applauding, I cued the orchestra into "The Man with the Golden Arm" theme and conducted while keeping an eye on both sides of the stage so that I could lead them into "Come Fly with Me" as soon as Frank hit the stage . . .
>   The applause grew louder. I still didn't see him.
>   Finally I glanced over my shoulder and said, "Oh, shit."
>   He was coming from the back of the room.

"It's a big oblong room in the Sporting Club," Jones recalled, many years later. "He's in the back of the room high-fivin' with Yul Brynner and Noël Coward and Cary Grant and Grace Kelly, and partying and kissing and everything. And I'm stupid enough to think that the applause is going to run out. And he's just hangin', man, and drinking and stuff like that, and we're playing the play-on for him, the beginning of the show. He kept stopping in the middle of the walk to the stage, and I was saying, 'What is he doing now, man? Hurry up!'"

"Then after a few more steps toward the stage, he stopped altogether, stood right in the middle of the floor, reached into his pocket, pulled out his gold cigarette case, opened it, took out a cigarette, tapped it on the case, and lit the cigarette," Jones writes.

> I was dying. Three minutes of clapping and that's long. Four minutes of clapping, five minutes . . . finally he reached the stage and they were *still* clapping. I steered the orchestra into "Come Fly with Me." He turned, faced the audience, and hit them with that signature voice, and I knew then why the applause had held up so long.
>   Some singers like to work in front of the beat. Some lag a little behind it. Frank did it all: in front, dead center, and slightly behind, as though it were inevitable. Just like Billie Holiday and Louis Armstrong, whom he adored, Frank had grown up singing with the big bands and learning how to sound like a horn, so he knew exactly where the beat was at all times. He swung so hard, you could've turned him upside down and shaken every piece of change out of his pocket, and he would have never missed a beat. He grooved through the first sixteen bars of "Come Fly with Me," then took a long drag on his cigarette just before the bridge. When he hit the bridge and sang, "When I get

you up there, where the air is rare . . . ," he turned his head so that a pinspot of blue light onstage would catch his profile, and finally blew a stream of smoke out of his mouth. It was incredible. He had every delicate nuance down. He wasted nothing—not words, not emotions, not notes. He was about pure economy, power, style, and skill.

Or, as Noël Coward later said, "Never once a breach of taste; never once a wrong note."

———

He moved on a bubble of agitation, always with a pack, searching for the next amusement. Boredom was the enemy; and sleep, death's counterfeit. And solitude. There had been an entourage since the beginning. In the 1940s and early 1950s, it was called the Varsity: Hank Sanicola and Toots Shor and Jackie Gleason, and Jimmy Van Heusen and Sammy Cahn were part of it, and now and then Manie Sacks; the music publisher Ben Barton; the latest prizefighter. Anyone who was willing to accept Frank as the alpha dog, to drink and stay up late and laugh at his jokes. And at the rest of the world: the squares, the losers. The composition of the pack morphed, of necessity, over the years. Van Heusen and Sanicola, of course, were still around, and Toots, when Frank was in New York; but Manie had died, and Gleason, with his huge television success, now had an ego to match Frank's and hangers-on of his own. Others stepped in eagerly to fill personnel gaps. Lawford. Art Buchwald, when Sinatra was in Europe. Winchell and Earl Wilson. Joe Fischetti and Sam Giancana— although when Momo was present, the question of who was the alpha dog grew more complex.

More and more, as Frank's fame and wealth and power increased, the pack became an activity in itself, rather than a mere diversion from his other activities.

Those who trailed in his wake were delighted to be there; at the same time, they watched his moods anxiously for the next change. It would always come, more quickly than anyone expected.

Like all clubs, his had its special codes and modes and passwords. There was a special language: it had started in the early 1950s, inspired by the inside talk of jazz musicians (the king of all of whom was Lester Young, who coined his own verbal world); now in the latter part of the decade, the journalists who infiltrated the outer edges of Sinatra's pack began to catch on and feel fascinated by what they could understand but not quite penetrate.

Art Buchwald devoted an entire column to the idiolect. "One of the reasons Frank Sinatra is misunderstood by so many people (i.e., Dorothy Kilgallen, Jack O'Brian, etc., etc., etc.) is that he speaks a language all his own," Buchwald wrote.

> No one has been able to get this language down on paper, and it was only in Monaco last week that he agreed to discuss it with anyone.
>
> "I notice you use the words gas and gasser quite frequently," we said. "Would you explain to our reading audience exactly what they mean?"
>
> "A gas is a good situation," he said. "An evening can be a wonderful gas. Or you can have a gas of a weekend."
>
> "I see. And a gasser?"
>
> "A gasser applies to a person. He's a big-leaguer, the best, he can hit the ball right out of the park. The opposite of a gasser is a nowhere, a bunter, he can never get to first base."

That category, of course, applied to virtually everyone outside Sinatra's in-group. As far as he was concerned, Frank explained to Buchwald, anyone he didn't know could be referred to as Sam or Charley. "Even a girl turns around if you say, 'Hey, Charley,'" Sinatra said. Real squares, on the other hand, were called Harvey, or Harv. And for those he really disliked, he favored the word "fink." "A fink is a loser," Frank told the columnist. "To me a fink is a guy who would kill his own friends."

There was also a kind of in-group infield chatter. " 'Hello' is not a greeting but a word that alerts everyone at Mr. Sinatra's table that a broad has come into the room," Buchwald wrote. "If it's a good-looking broad, 'Hello' will be followed by 'Say now,' or 'Something is coming in on the starboard.'"

And then there was the ineffable, all-purpose "clyde." "If I want someone to pass the salt I say: 'Pass the clyde,'" Frank explained. "'I don't like her clyde,' might mean I don't like her voice. 'I have to go to the clyde' could mean 'I have to go to the party.'"

But by the peculiar logic of Frank's posse, a clyde could also be a Harv. "A real clyde," said Sinatra, "is someone who stands by the crap table and doesn't play. He really doesn't belong in the crowd. He's a 'poor soul' who will stick both feet in the cement up to his neck."

Unlike Humphrey Bogart, who viewed the idea of leading a Rat Pack with supreme irony, Sinatra was an eager autocrat, and a real clyde was anyone who didn't play along.

The European excitement spent, he headed back to Los Angeles for Nancy junior's high-school graduation, with a quick stopover in New York, where he took in Ella Fitzgerald's set at the Copa. Frank adored Ella, who was his near contemporary and had also come up singing with the big bands. At the same time, he was intimidated by her sheer genius as a singer: her three-octave range, her flawless diction, her high-wire virtuosity at scatting; the gorgeous girlish tone that made every American Songbook rendition sound definitive. In a 1959 interview, Sinatra admitted as much. "Ella Fitzgerald is the only performer with whom I've ever worked who made me nervous," he said. "Because I try to work up to what she does. You know, try to pull myself up to that height, because I believe she is the greatest popular singer in the world. Barring none—male or female."

On one level, he had good reason to be intimidated. As a horn—which is what every singer who performs with instrumental accompaniment essentially is—Ella had no equal. Her ear (much like Mel Tormé's) was staggering, as her spot-on scat singing showed. She was always in command musically: so much so that it was easy to lose sight of her Achilles' heel, the emotional rendition of a song. She could do cool, she could do warm, every once in a while she could sing with abandon. But she never came close to *living* in the lyric the way Frank did—which, for many listeners, is even part of her appeal. Living Sinatra's songs with Sinatra is totally engaging, and constant emotional engagement can be exhausting. The sheer entertainment value of Fitzgerald's great musicianship can't be underestimated.

But the fact that she had the technical potential to sing rings around Frank put him on his mettle. That June night at the Copa, Ella had wowed a house full of prom-night celebrants, but their demands for encores were starting to wear her out when she called Sinatra up for a duet that would give her an easy bow off. The crowd went nuts when he strolled onto the floor to join her. It made sense that the number they chose to do together, "Moonlight in Vermont," was one they'd sung together recently; they'd duetted it on a May *Frank Sinatra Show,* probably the best musical episode of the series. At the same time, the song was an interesting choice. It's a pretty tune, evocative without being emotionally compelling, and the rhymeless lyric—the only one in the entire Sinatra canon—follows suit. The words ("Pennies in a stream/Falling leaves, a sycamore") are richly scenic, cinematic, yet completely impersonal. No one in the audience had to worry their heads about any hint of a love lyric between a white man and a black woman, and neither Frank nor Ella had to bother about emotional content. All they had to do was let those gorgeous instruments run free.

———

Depending on who's telling the story, Don Rickles insulted Frank Sinatra for the first time either at Murray Franklin's, a tiny nightclub in Miami, or at the

Slate Brothers, a small nightclub on La Cienega Boulevard in Los Angeles. By Rickles's account, his mother, Etta, met Frank's mother, Dolly, while Sinatra was playing the Fontainebleau in Miami and persuaded her to persuade Frank to catch her son's act. Sinatra walked into Murray Franklin's with an entourage, whereupon the young comedian spotted him and uttered the immortal words, "Make yourself comfortable, Frank—hit somebody." The entourage caught its collective breath and watched for Sinatra's reaction. He howled with laughter, and a career was born.

On the other hand, Rickles is known to have been insulting Frank at Slate Brothers before he ever played the Fontainebleau: a photograph in the February 3 *Life* literally caught the comedian in the act. And a June 22 wire-service report about the La Cienega club—where Rickles had been hired to replace the controversial stand-up comic Lenny Bruce, whose raw language had been offensive to some patrons, even by West Hollywood standards—noted that the comedian had recently asked Sinatra, "Remember the good old days, Frank, when you had a voice?"

It was a toothless barb: his voice was back, and he was singing better than ever. "Gone with the Wind" was one of six numbers Frank recorded when he returned to Capitol on the nights of June 24 and 25 to finish *Only the Lonely*, and any one of the songs—besides "Wind," there was "Blues in the Night," "What's New?," Gordon Jenkins's "Goodbye," "It's a Lonesome Old Town," and "One for My Baby"—can be read as a gloss on a relationship that refused to resolve itself, for either party. Any of the lyrics could have been spoken by Frank to Ava, or vice versa. ("What's New?," Johnny Burke and Bob Haggart's devastating dirge of ex-love, was said to be Gardner's favorite song.)

Sinatra had recorded the saloon number of saloon numbers, Johnny Mercer and Harold Arlen's "One for My Baby (and One More for the Road)" once before, for Columbia in 1947, which, in all fairness, was at least a year before the affair with Ava began. Sounding as though he had a head cold, and backed by a Dixieland-like small orchestra and rhythm guitar, Frank turned in an upbeat if slick rendition that owed a lot to the vocal stylings of Mercer himself—who was no mean vocalist but no Sinatra.

Yet eleven years later, Frank was a different man, one both hardened and softened by heartbreak, and a mature artist at the top of his game. On the night of the twenty-fourth, he recorded a rehearsal version of the song, accompanied only by Bill Miller; on the next night (the date is sometimes given as the twenty-sixth, because the session extended past midnight), he laid down the subtly orchestra-backed album track. But it was the hauntingly spare voice-and-piano-only version, the one most consonant with the saloon lyric, that stayed with Frank and over the years became a signature number.

In the middle of July, Sinatra hosted a large party—including the Lawfords, Harry James and Betty Grable, and Jimmy Van Heusen—at Louis Prima and Keely Smith's opening at the Cal-Neva Lodge in Lake Tahoe. As the resort's name indicated, Cal-Neva straddled the California-Nevada state line, which was painted on the bottom of the swimming pool and across the floor of the cavernous Indian Room in the main lodge. Gambling was allowed only on the Nevada side of the resort.

Cal-Neva was a glorious, secluded spot, set in pine forest over a mile above sea level, alongside the huge, pristine alpine lake. Besides the lodge, there were twenty guest cabins, known as chalets, scattered around the grounds. It was an ideal hideaway, reachable only by a single, curving mountain road. The air was cool—cold at night—and clear as a bell in the summer months. Frank had vacationed there for years, as had Pat Lawford's father, the investment banker, former movie executive, and former ambassador to the Court of St. James, Joseph P. Kennedy. In the summer of 1958, the elder Kennedy was deeply involved in his son John's campaign for reelection to the U.S. Senate and also laying the groundwork for his presidential run. But in June and July, Joe Kennedy took some time off from the stress of political machinations to relax at Cal-Neva, where he visited with his daughter and her husband and their friends, including Frank Sinatra. (Around this time, behind the cover of a front, Joe Kennedy also bought a share in the resort.) Frank and the Ambassador, as he was called, seem to have hit it off from the first moment they met, and they loved Cal-Neva for many of the same reasons. Kennedy's biographer David Nasaw writes,

> The principal owner of the lodge, at the time Kennedy stayed there, was "Wingy" . . . , the nickname cruelly given Bert Grober, the shriveled-arm gambler and owner of the Park Avenue Steak House in Miami. The Cal-Neva, or "Wingy's place," as Kennedy would refer to it, was a first-class resort that had everything Kennedy required. It was on the water . . . ; the rooms were large and the dining superb; there were trails for horseback riding, a bay and pools for swimming, a fine golf course, a casino, which Kennedy did not patronize, and attractive, available women in no short supply.

Wingy Grober was the front for Joe Kennedy's stake in Cal-Neva.

Also in abundant supply at the resort were the louche characters who frequented Nevada casinos—including, now and then in the pre–Black Book days of 1958, another fan of Cal-Neva, Sam Giancana. The Black Book was the popular name for the list, first published by the Nevada Gaming Control

Board in 1960, of individuals prohibited from setting foot in the state's gambling establishments.

But Nasaw, whose mission seems to be to rehabilitate Joseph Kennedy's considerably tarnished image, goes to preemptive lengths to distance the Ambassador from organized crime and criminals. "There was nothing very remarkable about Kennedy's summers at the Cal-Neva," he writes.

> Only in the middle 1970s, as journalists, historians, and conspiracy hunters looked high and low for clues to tie John F. Kennedy's assassination to organized crime, would attention be paid to his father's stays at Cal-Neva and the "gang" connections he supposedly made, renewed, and exploited there. Joe Kennedy did not go out of his way to avoid the presence of unsavory characters, nor did he stay away from the places they frequented: Cal-Neva, Hialeah [racetrack], and nightclubs and restaurants in New York, Chicago, Miami, and Palm Beach. But neither did he seek their company.

Perhaps. But what Joe Kennedy was adept at was having others seek their company on his behalf.

At around the same time as Joseph Kennedy was enjoying himself at Cal-Neva, his two older sons were beginning to investigate some of the very characters whose company his father ostensibly did not seek. Senator John F. Kennedy was one of four Democrats on the Select Committee on Improper Activities in the Labor or Management Field, popularly known as the Senate Rackets Committee, chaired by Senator John McClellan of Arkansas. Robert F. Kennedy was the chief counsel for the high-profile committee, whose investigations into labor racketeering put a particular focus on the activities of James R. Hoffa, head of the Teamsters.

Joe Kennedy, who feared losing union support for Jack's presidential run, was bitterly opposed to his sons' involvement with the Rackets Committee. He and Bobby Kennedy argued furiously about it; Bobby refused to back down.

In July, the committee opened hearings on alleged Mob control of Chicago's restaurant industry. Among the witnesses under subpoena were former Al Capone associates Tony "Joe Batters" Accardo and Paul "the Waiter" Ricca. "Committee counsel Robert F. Kennedy," reported a wire-service dispatch of July 7, "said agents of the investigating group have been trying to locate several men wanted as witnesses. Describing them as lower echelon hoodlums, Kennedy said they are Gus Alex, Joey Aiuppa, Sam Battaglia, and Sam Giancana. Giancana also goes by the name of Tom Mooney, Kennedy said."

It would have been too ironic if Giancana had been cooling his heels at that moment on the picturesque shores of Lake Tahoe. But Sam Giancana—a man of many aliases, honored early in his career with the nickname Mooney because even gangsters saw him as a crazed killer—would make an appearance soon enough.

———

Dean Martin, who much of the world thought would sink out of sight after the breakup with Jerry Lewis, was doing quite nicely, thank you. His records were selling, he was wowing the crowds in Vegas, his television specials for NBC were beginning to make the world think of him as a star in his own right. And by the spring of 1958, to everyone's surprise, he suddenly had a real movie career.

It didn't hurt a bit that he had some powerful friends. For one thing, he was represented by Hollywood's leading music-booking agency, MCA, whose boss, the legendary Lew Wasserman, had taken Martin on as a personal project. It was Wasserman who'd come up with the idea of putting Dean in his first post-Jerry movie, the romantic comedy *Ten Thousand Bedrooms;* when the picture tanked, the agent simply brushed off the failure and looked for an even bigger opportunity. He found it in *The Young Lions,* the World War II picture in which (after MCA muscled Tony Randall out of the project) Martin co-starred—and held his own—with Marlon Brando and Montgomery Clift.

When Frank Sinatra announced that May that his first film in a new three-picture deal with MGM would be an adaptation of the James Jones novel *Some Came Running,* it made perfect sense that Frank, who was co-producing, would stipulate Dean Martin as his co-star. Not only had Frank and Dean been running together for a while, in L.A. and Vegas, but Dino now had proven dramatic chops. It was just another reason for Frank to admire him extravagantly.

Some Came Running was yet another doorstop by Jones (the joke about *From Here to Eternity* had been that it took an eternity to read); this time, though, the reviews ranged from very bad to savage. The novel was once more World War II based and autobiographical, an attempt to take on Important Themes: the protagonist, Dave Hirsh, is a failed writer who comes back from the war to his small Indiana hometown (Jones was from a small town in Illinois) with a chip on his shoulder about his family and life in general and, through many turns of plot and subplot, finds his disillusionment confirmed. He befriends a fellow cynic, the gambler Bama Dillert, and falls in love with Gwen, a refined schoolteacher; in the meantime, though, a floozy Dave has picked up, Ginny Moorehead, falls in love with him. Trouble ensues. Dean was to play Bama, and for the plum role of Ginny, Frank selected the twenty-four-year-old Shirley MacLaine, whom he'd met in 1956 while doing a cameo in the film *Around the World in Eighty Days* and with whom, his makeup man Beans Ponedel later said, he'd had a fling.

Both turned out to be inspired choices. More problematic were *Some Came Running*'s director, Vincente Minnelli, and the film's shooting location, the tiny southern Indiana hamlet of Madison, where, in the stifling heat of August 1958, Frank Sinatra found himself stranded—desperately bored as always with the process of filmmaking but, dangerously, with nowhere to go to amuse himself.

The production began amid great excitement among the locals, many of whom were recruited as extras or hoped to be, and Indianans from all over who drove down to see what the Hollywood people were up to. "Nothing so exciting had happened to the green, hilly little Ohio River town," *Time* reported in typically florid style, "since P. T. Barnum brought Jenny Lind to sing in the Pork Palace in 1851."

Disenchantment set in at once. Frank was openly scornful of the townsfolk and the town. "This place is worse than skid row in Los Angeles," he proclaimed for all to hear. Shooting the first scene, in which Dave Hirsh arrives by bus in his hometown, Sinatra smiled through the window at the local extras, "but back of the sound-killing glass he was snarling out of his hangover: 'Hello, fat boy . . . Look at that ugly broad over there. Hello, you horrible bag.'" The magazine's 1955 cover story on Frank had been tough but grudgingly respectful; the latest dispatch was an out-and-out slam.

Frank didn't help his own case. He drank steadily on and off the set. Feeling that someone was listening in on his calls, he ripped a telephone out of the wall of the hotel he was staying in. He smashed the screen of a TV set with a beer bottle. And then there was the hamburger incident. Late one afternoon, the Sinatra group—Frank, Dean, and Dean's manager, Mack Gray—called the elderly clerk at the hotel desk and ordered three hamburgers. The order was then changed to four burgers, then to five. The clerk got flustered, and Sinatra and Gray came down to confront him. Gray called him an old bastard. Frank grabbed him by the shirt collar and started dragging him around. The clerk cried on the manager's shoulder and went home for the rest of the week. Word got around fast. (And Frank and Dean moved to a rented house.)

"The violent displays of temper," Sinatra film chronicler Tom Santopietro writes insightfully, "often seemed to start when Sinatra sensed weakness on the part of others, as if the sight of such weakness infuriated him, perhaps because it reminded him of weaknesses within himself."

Nor did things go easily with Minnelli. The acclaimed director of musicals (*An American in Paris, The Band Wagon, Kismet*) and emotionally pitched dramas (*The Bad and the Beautiful, Tea and Sympathy*) was fussy and painstaking, qualities guaranteed to drive Sinatra up a wall. When Minnelli's slow pace caused the shooting schedule to fall days behind, Frank—who after all was a co-producer—ripped twenty pages out of the script and refused to film any of the excised scenes (one of which was MacLaine's biggest in the picture: Sinatra compensated by suggesting her character instead of his die at the end, a change that garnered the actress an Oscar nomination).

And in a famous incident, after the director spent hours arranging the camera setup for the movie's climactic sequence—in which Ginny's old boyfriend, a Chicago gangster, pursues her and Dave through a carnival—Minnelli announced that the Ferris wheel had to be moved six feet (or three inches, depending on who's telling the story). Frank pulled a *Carousel,* walking off the set (taking Dean with him) and flying back to Los Angeles. "He did not return for several days," Santopietro writes, "until producer Sol Siegel reassured him that there would be no further instances of such directorial obsession."

Minnelli's wasn't the only obsession Sinatra had to deal with. "Outside Frank's door, there was constantly a crowd of eight hundred people, mostly women," the actress Martha Hyer recalled. "Some had songs they wanted him to listen to. Others had won a beauty contest and were waiting to be discovered."

Nor was Minnelli unsympathetic to Sinatra's claustrophobia. "We were virtual prisoners in Madison," the director said. "We couldn't go to a restaurant. It was a terrible way to live. And Frank was all cooped up in that little bungalow, along with Dean and a couple of characters from Chicago. You know, he attracts characters."

He certainly did. Among the visitors to the little bungalow were Jimmy Van Heusen, Leo Durocher, a couple of redheads imported from Los Angeles, and those characters from Chicago: Sam Giancana and several associates, who had apparently made the long drive to southern Indiana not just out of friendly feelings for Frank. Rather, as Momo and his friends explained to Shirley MacLaine, who at first had no idea who these dead-eyed, well-dressed men were, they were "on the lam"—presumably from the long arm of the Senate Rackets Committee.

Life in the bungalow was a strange combination of fun and games and tense machismo. Van Heusen played piano and served as all-around court jester, MacLaine recalled, while "the nightlife of poker, jokes, pasta, and booze went on until five a.m. Our calls were at six a.m."

It was like a frat house, except the fraternity brothers were movie stars, gangsters, and hulking hangers-on. The gamine MacLaine was accorded the ambivalent role of house mascot—the one woman allowed on the premises except for sexual purposes. As such, she saw and heard a lot. "One evening during a night shoot, as we sat around Frank's house waiting for director Vincente Minnelli and his camera crew to call us to the set, there was the sound of screaming and a door being crashed open," she recalled.

> One of the legion of women who surrounded the house twenty-four hours a day had broken through security and into the house. She barreled down the hallway and into the living room looking for Frank. "Frankie, I love you!" she wailed as she spotted him teaching me gin rummy. She pounced on him, began kissing him all over, and ripped off his shirt.

After a security guard pried the woman off, Frank threw the torn shirt under the coffee table and straightened his hair. "I feel dirty," he said. "I'm going to take a shower."

"There was something chauvinistic about the way he said he felt dirty . . . as though women soiled a man's existence," MacLaine wrote. "I remember wondering why he didn't at least crack a smile or feel a little flattered that someone was that crazed for him."

What she could have said—since quite a lot of this kind of thing had happened to Sinatra fifteen years earlier—was *still* that crazed for him.

And no less remarkable was the fact that the crazed intruder had run right past the tall, strong, and preternaturally handsome Dean Martin to throw herself on this small, thin, balding man.

MacLaine's keen intelligence and mascot status made her a uniquely valuable observer of Frank and Dean at high tide. She recalled accompanying the two of them on a side trip to "some gambling joints near Cincinnati":

> I'd sit in their hotel suite, fascinated at the spectacle of them primping for a night out. They didn't mind my watching them. They thought of me as a loyal pet. They splashed on their cologne, each dousing himself with his own favorite brand . . . Their white shirts were crisp and new, the ties well chosen, the suits expensive and impeccably tailored. But what got me were their hats. They wore wide-brimmed hats right out of the racetrack number from *Guys and Dolls* . . .
>
> They took me with them everywhere, trailed by these friends who looked like gangsters. The "friends" adored basking in Frank and Dean's fame, fame that was earned legitimately. Giancana was recognized in some places; in others he went unnoticed. But when he was recognized it was with fear.

The young actress didn't get it at first. Then it began to sink in. One day on location in Madison, she and Giancana were playing gin in the kitchen of the bungalow. Sitting by the window, "I wore sunglasses to cut down the sun's glare and to disguise my reactions to my cards," MacLaine writes.

> Unbeknownst to me, Sam was reading my cards from my *sunglasses.*
> I kept losing—I couldn't understand why. Just then the doorbell rang.
> Since I was the official butleress, I went to answer it. It was a delivery
> of cannolis from Chicago. I brought them back to the kitchen, opened
> the refrigerator door, placed them inside, and noticed that one of the
> boys had put a toy water pistol on the first shelf. I pulled the pistol out
> and trained it on Sam.
> "Don't I know you from somewhere?" I questioned, thinking of the
> wall of a post office.
> Sam leaped to his feet and pulled a .38 pistol, a real one, out of a
> holster inside his jacket. Just then, Frank and Dean walked in looking
> for something to eat. They saw Sam and me with guns trained on one
> another and fell down laughing.

It seemed they could afford to laugh. On the other hand, as FBI files would later reveal, both Frank and Dean had already established their fealty to Giancana and his associates. An entry in Sinatra's 1,275-page FBI dossier (released in December 1998, seven months after Frank's death) states that on August 10, 1958, the day before *Some Came Running* began shooting in southern Indiana, "Frank Sinatra was met at Midway Airport, Chicago, by Joe Fischetti, a former Chicago hoodlum,[*] then residing in Miami, and taken to the Ambassador Hotel. After lunch, Sinatra, Fischetti and Dean Martin, a well-known entertainer who was also in Chicago, were taken by [name redacted] of the Chicago PD to the River Forest residence of Anthony Accardo where they gave a 'command performance.'"

In his past life, Dean, who preferred not to be bothered by gangsters or anybody else, had usually found a way to resist the Mob's approaches. Now that he was spending more time around Frank, it was a little more difficult.

At first glance, the goings-on in Madison, Indiana, in the late summer of 1958 were nothing but good copy: yet another chance to cluck over Frank's misbehavior, not to mention a priceless opportunity to contrast Hollywood's presumptions with the pieties and verities of rural America. Reporters swarmed

---

[*] In its awkward way, the bureau was trying to say that Fischetti no longer lived in Chicago, not that he was no longer a hoodlum.

the little town along with the gawkers and autograph seekers. Sinatra was still the show. But Martin, in his quiet way, was quickly gathering heat, and the combination of the two stars suddenly felt intriguing. No sooner had *Time* run its broadside than *Life*—the big-format picture weekly was very much a national institution—sent a reporter and a photographer to Madison to sniff around.

The reporter's name was Paul O'Neil, and Frank brushed him off. Dean and Shirley followed suit. "We wouldn't talk to him," MacLaine said years later. "And because we were never apart he dubbed us The Clan."

The pieces of a new myth were falling into place. Some of its gods—but not all—would soon come to believe in it themselves. "If people wanted to call him part of Sinatra's Clan," Nick Tosches wrote of Martin, "so be it, fuck it; it made no difference."

––––––––––

At the end of August, Frank gratefully returned to Los Angeles, where the filming of *Some Came Running* continued on the soundstages of Metro-Goldwyn-Mayer. The studio lot was familiar territory—he'd been a contract player there from 1944 to 1951—but MGM was a very different place. The Old Man, Louis B. Mayer—Sinatra's champion and friend and then his nemesis—had died in late 1957. That year, for the first time, Metro ran in the red. As the television industry boomed, the studio system was fading away. Power in Hollywood had devolved from the studio chiefs and production heads to the independent producers and stars who headed their own production companies, of whom there was no greater power than Frank Sinatra. Accordingly, the new shooting schedule, by Frank's fiat, would be from noon to 8:00 p.m., with a break at four for lunch.

The shoot continued throughout September; early in the month, Sinatra went back into the recording studio. On the eleventh, he rejoined Nelson Riddle in the Capitol Records Tower and laid down three tracks: a lively but mediocre up-tempo number called "Mr. Success"; a tender and pretty ballad, "Sleep Warm" (the title was Frank's TV sign-off catchphrase), by the up-and-coming songwriting team of Alan Bergman, Marilyn Keith, and Lew Spence; and a meltingly lovely update of Rodgers and Hart's "Where or When," which Sinatra had last recorded in 1945.

Mr. Success could have been his nickname in the fall of 1958. He was writing his own rules, and the world was buying what he was selling. *Frank Sinatra Sings for Only the Lonely* was released in mid-September; the album hit number 1 two weeks later and stayed on the *Billboard* chart for 120 weeks.

In the meantime, Mr. Success pressed forward his alliance with Mr.

Menefreghismo. Over three nights in mid-October, Frank conducted the orchestra for Dean's new Capitol LP, *Sleep Warm*. (The composer Pete King did the arrangements.) The title and title number were a friendship gift from Sinatra to Martin—the equivalent of the star sapphire ring Frank had given Sam Giancana. The theme was bedtime. Besides the title song, the record's tracks, described in the liner notes as "a beguiling set of lullabies for moderns," included "Cuddle Up a Little Closer," "Good Night Sweetheart," and "Let's Put Out the Lights (and Go to Sleep)." The album cover would show an appropriately sleepy-eyed Martin gazing out over the image of a bare-shouldered beauty smiling between the sheets.

Dean had had a number of best-selling singles, but his albums, unlike Frank's, had never done much commercially. (It grated on him endlessly that his former partner, never short on presumption, had scored a big hit in 1957 with his LP *Jerry Lewis Just Sings*.) As an attempt to redress that shortcoming, *Sleep Warm* ("Dean Martin with Orchestra Conducted by Frank Sinatra," the cover copy read, the two names in type of equal size) fell short: it never charted. What was most remarkable about the LP was the size of Sinatra's footprint; he was all over the project.

It was typical Frank. Where friendship was concerned, he called the shots. "Of course, he's prone to tell friends how he'll help them rather than ask how he can help," Vincente Minnelli would observe, sagely. "But I suppose that's the prerogative of any leader of the clan."

The question is, did Dean accept friendship on Frank's terms? To a certain extent: witness his presence at Sinatra's Villa Capri birthday bash; his acceptance of the role in *Some Came Running*, and all that went with it, including the trip to Tony Accardo's house. Witness *Sleep Warm*. But in general, Martin was such a closed book that friends, lovers, and wives felt they barely understood him. "He *cannot* communicate," his wife Jeanne once said. "He's one of the rare human beings who's not comfortable with communicating. He's just not interested." His nature was deeply passive and guarded: he would go along with anything if it served his self-interest, without ever fully committing emotionally.

Martin seems to have been similarly distant with his wives. "Dean doesn't have an overwhelming desire to be loved," Jeanne said. "He doesn't give a damn. He doesn't get involved with people because he really isn't interested in them."

She was largely speaking for herself; she felt she bored Dean. Was he interested in Frank? "He never had a male friend," Jeanne asserted flatly. Nick Tosches punts on the issue. "He was close to Mack Gray, to Sammy Cahn, to Sinatra, to others," he writes. "But he did not need friendship. Men who did were probably looking to take it up the ass. 'Yeah,' he told a reporter who asked him about that other golden guinea. 'Frank is my dearest, closest friend. In fact, we slept together last night.' "

Jerry Lewis, like Frank an only child, once said that Dean was the big brother he never had. Sinatra looked up to Martin in similar ways—and looked to dominate him in similar ways. A song Cahn and Van Heusen would later write for Frank put it unapologetically: "I like to lead when I dance." With Martin and Lewis, the dance had ended badly. With Dean and Frank, the dance—a strange, close waltz between two men who had no use for intimacy— went on and on.

In September, Frank had renewed and accelerated his acquaintance with Lady Adelle Beatty, the woman who almost certainly had *not* been the cause of the trouble between him and Ava in Rome in June. Frank and the former Oklahoma beauty queen seem to have first crossed paths some years before, when she was still on her first marriage, to William O'Connor, a deputy attorney general of California. She divorced O'Connor in 1949 and two years later became the third American wife of David Beatty, a dashing, witty, very rich— and titled—English war hero. She made the shift from Beverly Hills housewife to London peeress with ease; she also led her husband on a merry chase. In March 1958, Lord Beatty sued her for divorce on the grounds of adultery. The suit went undefended. She was left with her title and a pile of money.

Adelle Dillingham O'Connor Beatty, of Ardmore, Oklahoma, was a type out of Edith Wharton or Henry James: not the heroine—who after all would have to possess some tragic dimension—but a figure in the middle foreground, one lacking depth and ever so slightly caricatured. Tall, cool, and elegant, she had a sharp eye for the main chance, excellent taste in clothes and furnishings, and, it seemed, not much of a sense of humor about herself or anything else. Frank would see her type again. Ava Gardner, whose dirt-road origins in Grabtown, North Carolina, trumped Ardmore, Oklahoma, any day but who had a temperament to match her beauty, dismissed Beatty as a mere social climber. Ava always did see things clearly.

Yet Frank had a fatal weakness for class, and Beatty had worked hard to acquire it. When he reencountered her at a Hollywood party as production of *Some Came Running* came to a close, it seemed like kismet. She was forty now, but with her good jawline and high cheekbones and Mayfair bearing, her pearls and dark flashing eyes, she was more stunning than ever. He was smitten.

On October 19, he flew to London, ostensibly to emcee a benefit premiere, for the British Empire Cancer Campaign, of Danny Kaye's new comedy, *Me and the Colonel*. He arrived a week early for the event. When a pesky wire-service reporter asked what other business he might have in town, Frank referred him back to the benefit. "That's the only reason for me being here," he growled.

"But within minutes of checking into the Dorchester Hotel Sinatra came bounding out again, jumped into a chauffeured limousine and called at Lady Beatty's house in upper-class South Kensington," the UPI reporter wrote. The pair had lunch there, then that night she took a taxi to his hotel, and "talked with him in his suite for 30 minutes," the dispatch continued, omnisciently. They emerged amid a mob of autograph hunters and newsmen, got into Sinatra's car, and drove a hundred yards down the street to a dinner party at a movie producer's house.

The circus continued for the next week, the London tabloids and public hungrily following the couple's every move. The *Daily Mail* proclaimed the two would wed, quoting anonymous friends of Beatty's as saying, "The only questions to be answered were when and where." The *Daily Express* ran a picture

Lady Adelle Beatty, a former Oklahoma beauty queen, was tall, cool, and elegant, without much of a sense of humor but with a sharp eye for the main chance. Frank would see her type again.

of the couple every day. The pair were spotted at the Satire Club, where Frank wooed her with a chorus of "How About You?"—and then, when his mood turned, stung her with a rebuke. She fled to Zurich, where a psychotherapist diagnosed nervous exhaustion. Sinatra sent a friend to cajole her back to London. She returned; the press swarmed afresh. Things got so bad that when the premiere finally came, Frank took the stage and announced, even before presenting Danny Kaye and the film's other stars, "I'm here in London solely for this film, the charity of tonight's showing, and to introduce the cast. I did not come here to get married."

What was there between them, besides sex and mutual titillation at the swath each cut through the world? They found out all too soon. Frank flew back to New York without Lady Beatty.

But where the press was concerned, Sinatra was a movable feast. One night as he left the Harwyn Club, on East Fifty-second Street, in the company of Joe E. Lewis, David Niven, and Nan Whitney, a reporter made so bold as to call out, "Frank, what are your plans?"

"When will you——stop calling me Frank?" he replied. (The newspaper account of the event omitted the offending word.) "I am Mr. Sinatra." Then he added, "I just stopped off in New York for a hamburger. That's all this town's good for."

Seeing a *Journal American* photographer named Mel Finkelstein aiming his camera at him, Frank said, "You want to try it, buddy? No pictures." As Lewis attempted to calm him down, Sinatra jumped into a waiting limousine shouting, "You newspapermen are all a bunch of——!" And then, as several photographers crowded in front of the car, he yelled to the chauffeur, "Run the——down! Step on the gas! Kill the no-good——!"

The driver stepped on it, knocking Finkelstein down as the limo sped away with an illegal siren blaring. The photographer was taken to the hospital for X-rays. When Frank arrived in Miami a week later to begin shooting *A Hole in the Head,* one of the reporters who met him at the airport was wearing a catcher's mask.

Rat Pack lore—we speak of the second, Sinatra-led incarnation of what was called at first the Clan—cites two possible origins for the group: the Frank-Dean-Shirley troika on the Indiana location of *Some Came Running,* and the night, in the fall of 1958, that Frank and Dean joined Judy Garland onstage during her act at the Sands.

The time was early October, just before Frank's trip to London; the stars were descending on Las Vegas to watch the greatest entertainer of the era fight for her professional life—and in many ways, for her life itself. At thirty-six, Judy Garland was grotesquely overweight, alcoholic, addicted to pills, and psychologically brittle. She had been struggling for the better part of a decade. In 1950, MGM, the studio she had virtually carried on her back since the late 1930s, had dropped her; in 1954, her comeback vehicle, the hugely expensive musical *A Star Is Born,* flopped at the box office. Garland and her husband, Sid Luft, who had produced the picture, lost a fortune, and the Best Actress Academy Award Garland seemed assured of went instead to the twenty-five-year-old Grace Kelly for *The Country Girl.* Over the next five years, Luft, who had extremely expensive tastes in clothing and racehorses but scant business sense, drove his wife on a relentless round of concertizing to try to recoup their losses. Las Vegas was a fabulous source of revenue—the New Frontier paid her $55,000 a week (over $470,000 in today's dollars) when she opened there in 1956; subsequent gigs at other casinos would yield similar paychecks—but between Luft's high living and the couple's mountain of debt the money vanished as soon as it came in.

Garland's extreme vulnerability had always been integral to her appeal as a performer, but more and more it was interfering with her act more than informing it. "It's a disheartening, somewhat nerve wracking, experience to watch Judy Garland perform in her current stint," a *Billboard* reviewer had written that March. In July, she clawed back her confidence and redeemed herself with a spectacular opening at Los Angeles's Cocoanut Grove (Sid Luft had to take out a loan to get her costumes out of hock). Garland's first engagement at the Sands was therefore especially important to her, a chance to solidify her gains: the Sands was the crème de la crème in Las Vegas, and it was Frank's place. She arrived ten days prior to her opening, with her music and props, to begin rehearsing.

Sinatra, her old lover, stayed away from her opening and the first few nights, perhaps to let her get her act on its feet. She pulled it off. *Variety's* critic wrote, "Judy Garland has no dancing boys with her in the Copa Room; her act is pure Judy Garland, and on opening night it was Judy Garland at her best. Her voice was clear at all times, it was on pitch, she had perfect intonation, she showed confidence, and there was no wavering. If the quality of that first performance is repeated for the two-week run, then Jack Entratter has for himself a gem of a package."

Hollywood came to watch, and Frank followed. On October 10, he took some seventy of his friends—including the Dean Martins, the David Nivens, Natalie Wood and Robert Wagner, Shirley MacLaine, the Sammy Cahns, and Jimmy Van Heusen—to Vegas in a private railroad car to, as Wagner recalled, "go up there and support Judy and help her get on her feet again. Everybody was very much for her to get going and get off the ground."

As Garland paused between numbers, Dean, in drunk persona, called a rude remark from his seat; the audience tittered. Frank chimed in. Finally, she summoned the two of them, like reprobate schoolboys, onto the stage. They bounded up, drinks in hand, and elbowed her out of the spotlight while she feigned outrage. She finally elbowed her way back in, and the three of them, as Louella Parsons wrote, "put on a comedy routine that was out of this world."

"Frank and Dean joked around and loosened up the show and made the whole night a lot easier," Robert Wagner recalled. "They had great camaraderie and wonderful material, and they loved Judy."

Was it material? Had it been sketched out beforehand? "I don't think so," Wagner said. "I wasn't aware that it was a setup; it was all very impromptu. The heckling bit—that was all very new then." As was Dean's drunk act. Shirley MacLaine writes that soon after Martin and Lewis broke up and Dean was singing in small clubs with little success, a comedy writer named Ed Simmons (who'd written for Dean and Jerry on *The Colgate Comedy Hour*) called and offered his services. Dean refused at first—"I'm just gonna sing," he said—but Simmons insisted: "You've gotta find a character out there on that stage, you know that."

Dean knew that. ("He was as sharp as a shit-house rat, and he understood every move he ever made," Jerry Lewis once said.) And so the character of "Dean the Drunkie" was born, with bits written by Simmons. This was the Dean Martin who swayed onto the stage, glass of amber liquid in hand, looked blearily out at the audience, and asked, "How long I been on?" The Dean Martin who told the nightclub patrons, "I don't drink anymore. I don't drink any less, either." The Dean Martin who could barely finish a song without turning it into a parody (for "It Happened in Monterey": "It happened in Martha Raye, a long time ago"). Joe E. Lewis had pioneered the shtick, but with Joe E. the chemistry was different. Lewis was a rascally old uncle with a face only a mother could love. Dean Martin was a supremely handsome and charismatic man's man whom men and women alike were ready to love unconditionally, especially if he avoided even the slightest hint of vanity.

In the fall of 1958, Dean's drunk act was still nightclub rather than television material, and Judy Garland might never have seen it before that evening at the Sands. But whether she was in on the joke or not, she was a wily enough trouper to understand instantly what worked, and this worked. Frank's playing along certified it.

Still, what was happening onstage in the Copa Room was complex. Was Garland annoyed, even momentarily, at being heckled? At being, even briefly, upstaged? Was she needy enough at this moment in her career to feel she had to play along, to yield to Sinatra on his home turf? The evening had all the hallmarks of the Rat Pack era to come: genial sadism and coerciveness, combined with boozily uncertain entertainment value that shimmered away the morning after, leaving only the dull ache of a you-had-to-be-there hangover. And Sinatra was always in charge.

––––––

At sixty-one, Frank Capra was a former great, the director who had defined American optimism from the mid-1930s to the early 1940s with movies like *It Happened One Night, Mr. Deeds Goes to Town, Mr. Smith Goes to Washington,* and *Meet John Doe,* the filmmaker who had buoyed the country's spirits during World War II with his "Why We Fight" propaganda series and then created a final masterpiece with 1946's *It's a Wonderful Life.*

Despite its eventual status as an American classic, *It's a Wonderful Life* was a commercial flop when it was released, and its failure took the wind out of Capra's sails. After turning in a couple of undistinguished follow-ups to that picture, he spent the mid-1950s making educational films for television—until Frank Sinatra decided, in the summer of 1957, that he wanted Capra, and only Capra, to direct *A Hole in the Head.* The project was a package deal, put together by Bert Allenberg of the William Morris Agency: Sinatra, Capra, and Arnold Schulman, the playwright who'd written the original material for Broadway, were all WMA clients. But what Capra had failed to fully realize in the years since he'd left Hollywood was the extent to which movie stars had come to dominate the business formerly controlled by the studios and a few major filmmakers, including, once upon a time, Frank Capra himself. Sinatra, of course, being the biggest star of all.

When it came time to put together the deal for *A Hole in the Head,* the great director, sitting with Allenberg, found himself being directed: the production company for the project was to be called SinCap, the beginnings of the star's and the director's names in that order; moreover, Sinatra's company would own two-thirds of the picture, and Capra's company, one-third. These were the take-them-or-leave-them terms.

"Does Sinatra know I make my own films, make all the decisions?" Capra asked Allenberg. It was a purely reflexive question. Sinatra knew that had once been the case. What he knew now was that Capra made unapologetically sentimental movies—Capra-corn, as they called them—and that the director might have some greatness left in him but that only one Frank would truly be in charge.

All that said, Capra seems to have gone into the project in an admirably flexible state of mind, with his sense of humor intact and with a keen eye for the strengths and foibles of the man who was his star and—in effect—his boss. "Sinatra is a great singer . . . and he knows it," the director wrote in his autobiography, poignantly called *The Name Above the Title.*

He has total command of his performances; selects his own songs, songwriters, orchestras, audiences. Sinatra is also a great actor, and he knows that, too.

But in films he is not Sinatra doing Sinatra's thing with song . . . He performs for a never-changing audience of busy, dispassionate cameramen, sound men, script girls, make-up people, dead-pan electricians who have "seen it all before," and other actors who don't bewitch easily—if at all.

Nor is Sinatra in total command of the shooting of a film. There are budgets and schedules to confine, and directors to heed. But Sinatra "heeds" very badly.

Still, Capra came up with some creative ways to preserve a certain degree of autonomy while managing to keep his star from storming off the set. In Miami early in the shoot, the director—who appears never to have gotten the memo about One-Take Charlie—noticed Frank getting into a funk as a scene (featuring Sinatra, Keenan Wynn, and Joi Lansing) at a dog-racing track was rehearsed and shot. "First rehearsal: Sinatra great, others need straightening out," Capra recalled. "Second rehearsal: Sinatra cools off, others improve. First photographic take: Sinatra cold, others fine."

In that moment, the director realized that Frank was "a performer first, actor second. He never repeats a song to the same audience." Capra took Wynn and Lansing aside and told them to change their cues, mix up their lines, interrupt Sinatra during his speeches. He even shuffled around the extras in the scene so Frank wouldn't have to look at the same faces. Taken aback at first, Frank lit up, ad-libbed along with Wynn and Lansing, and Capra got the fresh performance he wanted from all three actors.

A Hole in the Head, the director's second-to-last feature, has many charms, not the least of them Sinatra's graceful performance as Tony Manetta and his rapport with the terrific Eddie Hodges, as Tony's twelve-year-old son, Ally. As Tom Santopietro points out, "Frank always worked well with children on film, his gentle quality coming to the fore as their innocence relaxed him." "He really didn't treat me like a kid; he treated me like a friend," Eddie Hodges recalled. "Somebody on his level. If people would talk down to me, he'd dart his eyes at 'em and say, 'Hey. Watch it.'" Sinatra gave the young Hodges acting tips, spoke to him of the value of single takes in keeping a performance fresh. Their winning, slightly bumbling duet on Sammy Cahn and Jimmy Van Heusen's Oscar-winning "High Hopes"—they'd had only half an hour to learn the song from the songwriters themselves, who were sitting just off camera with a small upright piano—is practically worth the price of admission.

And Edward G. Robinson and Thelma Ritter as Tony's stuffy brother and fretful sister-in-law are perfect. But in essence the picture is *The Tender Trap* redux, except with Capra at the helm instead of Charles Walters. The comedy mostly flows, the sentiment is affecting, and you see remnants of Capra's former greatness, but much of the film feels merely stagy, and the whole thing is a poignant reminder that this was a directorial career that didn't survive the transition from black and white to color, from great themes to lesser ones. The 1950s themselves were inimical to Frank Capra's sensibility, that of a grateful Sicilian immigrant who had fallen in love with America. Television and the bomb had diminished the world.

————

Some Came Running premiered in mid-December. It was a big, soapy, Cinema-Scope and Technicolor mishmash with too many subplots: the critics hated it, but late-1950s audiences loved it. That was then; *Some Came Running* holds up poorly. Unlike *From Here to Eternity,* which brilliantly crystallizes a last moment of pre–World War II peace and innocence in Hawaii, James Jones's second novel strives too hard for great themes amid heartland America and loses itself in the cornfields. The adaptation founders amid the book's overreach.

Still, the movie has its pleasures. Sinatra and Martin click wonderfully in their first of nine pictures together, and the very young Shirley MacLaine is effective if over-the-top in her first major film part: her performance as the sexual doormat Ginny Moorehead is a kind of rough draft for her role, two years later, as the exploited elevator operator Fran Kubelik in Billy Wilder's *Apartment.*

Sinatra is effective, too, as the bitter ex-GI and failed writer Dave Hirsh, though it feels as if we've seen him do this before (see *Young at Heart*). The movie's real star is Martin, in perhaps the best performance of his career. Implausibly tan and photogenic, he somehow manages, in quick succession, to ooze charm, convey convincing vulnerability, and be mean as a snake (his reptile-skin luggage is a great character cue). Bama Dillert is a dark character—self-destructive, evasive, and cruel (especially when it comes to Ginny)—and Dean clearly found he had something to work with in creating him.

As did Frank in creating Dave Hirsh. In a harrowing sequence toward the end of the film, he viciously lays into the calflike Ginny, telling her she's too dumb to understand the story he's just published in the *Atlantic*—and, by the way, she's a tramp, too. When she protests weakly that he shouldn't say such things to her, he takes her in his arms and apologizes (by far the weakest piece of acting in the movie, by a man who in real life never apologized), then, by way of reparation, asks if she'd like to clean up the house he shares with Bama. She acts as if he'd just handed her a sack of gold.

But the torment isn't through. In the next scene, Dave reads Ginny his story, then quizzes her on it. Her enthusiasm strikes him as uncomprehending. "What'd you like about it, Ginny?" he asks coldly, and his pointed cruelty, so much more chilling than any he was able to project as the would-be presidential assassin in *Suddenly*, feels too close to the bone for comfort. As do Dave's whipsaw emotions. When Ginny bursts into tears, he asks her to marry him, even though he doesn't love her. Of course the poor, dumb girl is over the moon. Then Bama walks in.

When Dave tells his pal that he and Ginny are to be married, the gambler first thinks it's a joke, then he's horrified. "I got nothin' agin Ginny—nothin' at all," Bama drawls. "But even she knows she's a pig."

The wheel has turned too many times for postfeminist audiences to hear these lines with anything but revulsion. And there's an extratextual shudder, too, at the sight of these two middle-aged men verbally brutalizing this very young woman, who so longs to be with them. It smacks of Rat Pack abuses to come. When Shirley MacLaine writes in her memoir about being "Mascot to the Clan," it's with the wisdom—but also the self-protective veneer—of hindsight. It's clear how strongly she desired Frank and Dean's company. There's a certain discomfort in reading that on location in Indiana she

> was the only woman they allowed in the house, but that was because there had been a kind of communal decision made that I wasn't really a girl—I was a pal, maybe even one of the boys.
>
> It would come as a shock (but a predictable one) to me later when gently and separately both Dean and Frank visited my hotel room when no one else was looking. I wouldn't classify either of their approaches as a pass, nor was I offended in any way. As a matter of fact, their visits helped alter the sagging image I had of myself as a not very sensual woman.

This suggests, though it doesn't say directly, that she didn't feel free to turn either man away. The message is mixed: "visited" suggests entry; "approaches," rebuff. But if the visits/approaches weren't passes, what were they but tokens of entitlement on the part of the new kings of ring-a-ding-ding?

———

A few days before Christmas, *Life*'s U.S. Entertainment issue featured a picture-spread coronation of Dean—"the biggest new blue-chip star in entertainment"—titled "Make-a-Million Martin." The piece was packed with charming images of the infinitely photographable Dino at work and at play (really, for him the two seemed to be more or less the same thing) and at home with his charmingly huge family: his blond wife, Jeanne, and their three cute kids, plus the four handsome older children from his first marriage. On the face of it, Dean was perfect, straight-down-the-middle *Life* material: just an easygoing knockabout guy who could sing a little bit and act a little bit, who pretended to be drunk onstage and generally couldn't believe his good fortune. Significantly, the non-bylined piece lacked an interview with its subject.

But the article that followed, titled "The 'Clan' Is the Most" ("Led by Sinatra and Martin, it hoots at Hollywood's names and old traditions"), muddied the issue. Paul O'Neil's arch and labored sociological analysis of Sinatra and his crowd tried to be inside and outside at once, its breezy tone both hinting at familiarity with the players and smelling of jargony *Time-Life*-speak. "The uninitiated sometimes refer to the clan as the rat pack," O'Neil wrote. But, he continued,

> The rat pack is no more; it died with Bogie. Today there is no Frank but Frank, [who] . . . personifies [the Clan's] nonconformist attitude: a public and aggressive indifference, not only to what the customers expect of their movie stars but also to what Hollywood expects of its own citizens. He is known, variously, among the faithful as The Pope, The General or The Dago. Dean Martin, who is next in influence (and who also calls meetings), is known as The Admiral.

With the ham-handed certainty of an FBI report, the piece went on to identify the other key players. Besides Sinatra and Martin, O'Neil asserted, "the hard core of the clan . . . sometimes referred to as the cell" included Eddie Fisher, Peter Lawford, Tony Curtis, and Sammy Davis Jr. Positioned on the cell's immediate periphery, the writer claimed, were the actor-comedian Ernie Kovacs, David Niven, Milton Berle, Sammy Cahn, and Jimmy Van Heusen. Judy Garland, Debbie Reynolds, and "a new young actress," Shirley MacLaine, were "the females whose talent the clan admires most."

Uncomfortably, O'Neil tried to make a connection between the group's putative outsider status and the money it took to maintain it. "Most members of this group are at least 40 years old and either live or aspire to live in $250,000 houses," he wrote, adding, with thumping obviousness, "Their nonconformity must obviously be of an especially tailored type." Tailored, that is, by the Hollywood clothier Sy Devore, "who will produce a seersucker jacket for $125 (New Yorkers can buy a seersucker jacket, with pants, at high-style Brooks Brothers for $28.75)." To blend in with these nonconformists, O'Neil wrote, it also helped to drive a Dual-Ghia like Frank's ("a hot-looking automobile with an Italian body and a Dodge engine"); both Fisher (who could afford it) and Lawford (whose wife could) eagerly emulated him. Dean, on the other hand, was "perfectly content with a Thunderbird and a Cadillac."

The piece's breathless inanity wasn't helped by the substantial contribution of the man who appeared to be O'Neil's single inside source, Sammy Davis Jr. Davis—to the delight of comedians and imitators then and since—was a tap dancer of a talker, with a hip style all his own and a Sodium Pentothal disinclination to censor himself. "As soon as I go out the front door of my house in the morning, I'm on, Daddy, I'm on!" he crowed.

> But when I'm with the group I can relax. We trust each other. We admire each other's talent. People think we're troublemakers. But only two of us have escapades—Frank and I . . . You gotta know about Frank to know about us. Frank is the most generous man in the world. He's restless. He can't sleep. He says what he thinks. But he's pertinent! There's nobody, absolutely nobody, who won't like Frank if Frank wants them to. Frank has a lot of chicks, but nobody is more gentlemanly around women. And if you're his friend, that's IT. If you need him, DADDY, HE . . . IS . . . THERE!

The piece's first glaring flaw was positioning a group of wealthy, middle-aged entertainers as nonconformists. The word had a sociological sound to it; it smacked of rebellion, when what was essentially being talked about was the heedlessness of the spoiled and domineering genius who stood at the group's center, one for whom rules were made to be broken.

But the second problem was the definition of the group itself. Who really was in it? How did it cohere? Bogart's Rat Pack, with its tongue-in-cheek assignment of club offices, had really been an elaborate put-on, the ultimate jab at the Hollywood press and panting movie fans by its central figure, a man who arguably *was* a kind of nonconformist: one at ease in his craft but deeply uncomfortable in his profession and the polymorphous phoniness that surrounded it. Bogart's Rat Pack was a cult of personality that grew around a man who disdained cults and personalities. When Bogart died, the group faded like a dream.

Sinatra's Clan—soon the only Rat Pack that later generations would remember—was a cult that grew around a man who welcomed worship and demanded fealty. Its—his—gravity at any moment waxed and waned according to the enchantment or disenchantment of the worshippers. And woe betide the acolyte who, even momentarily, assumed the solidity of the ground he stood on. Or worst of all, questioned his own faith.

On New Year's Eve, Frank had dinner at Romanoff's with Peter and Pat Lawford and Robert Wagner and Natalie Wood. As the meal wound down, Sinatra proposed they all drive to Palm Springs to see in 1959. "He always had that kind of thing—hey, let's go down to the desert," Wagner recalled. "I'll get whoever's down there to fix it up, and we can have a nice weekend." Then Frank went to the men's room. While he was gone, "the girls said that it was too chilly to go that night," Peter Lawford recalled.

> They preferred driving in the morning, but then we said, "Who's going to tell him?" Knowing his temper, Pat out and out refused to say anything, and Natalie didn't even want to be in the same room when he was told. Finally, R. J. [Wagner] insisted that I be the one to do it, so when Frank got back to the table, I explained as gracefully as I could that we'd prefer joining him in the morning. Well, he went absolutely nuts. "If that's the way you want it, fine," he said, slamming his drink on the floor and storming out of the restaurant.

> Lawford phoned Frank the next morning, and George Jacobs answered, whispering that his boss was still asleep, not having turned in until 5:00 a.m. Then Jacobs said, "Oh, Mr. Lawford. What happened last night? I better tell you that he's pissed. Really pissed off. He went to your closet and took out all the clothes that you and your wife keep here and ripped them into shreds and then threw them into the swimming pool."

While Frank was having his tantrum in the desert, a world he had been part of was changing forever. As 1958 clicked over into 1959, the revolutionary forces of Fidel Castro—the *barbudos* (bearded ones), as they were known in Cuba—entered Havana, ending the Mob-friendly government of Fulgencio Batista and taking axes and sledgehammers to the syndicate-run casinos in the great hotels of the capital: the Capri, the Plaza, the Riviera.

"The greatest indignity of all was saved for the Riviera," writes T. J. English, a chronicler of the Mob's rise and fall in Cuba.

> In an act of revolutionary audacity, campesinos [peasants] brought into the city a truckload of pigs and set them loose in the lobby of the hotel and casino, squealing, tracking mud across the floors, shitting and peeing all over Lansky's pride and joy, one of the most famous mobster gambling emporiums in all the world.

In the great movie *The Godfather: Part II*, the character Hyman Roth (Lee Strasberg), based on the top gangster Meyer Lansky, is forced to flee Havana amid the highly dramatic events of New Year's Eve 1958–59. In real life, Lansky flew back to Miami a week after that fateful night, still hopeful that Castro would reopen the casinos, which, besides making millions for the Mob, had employed many Cubans and contributed substantially to the capital's economy. But in the end, Fidel closed the casinos, and the Mob's dream of a great gambling Xanadu in the Caribbean died in Castro's revolution.

Yet organized crime had wisely hedged its bets. Havana's loss would be Las Vegas's gain.

II

|||||||||||||

Let's just say that the Kennedys are interested in the lively arts,
and that Sinatra is the liveliest art of all.

—PETER LAWFORD

In the waning months of 1958, Frank had been developing a new movie project: an adaptation of *Never So Few,* a best-selling novel about OSS operatives in World War II Burma. The film, the next on his three-picture MGM contract, was to be a starring vehicle for himself and a co-production between his production company and the studio that had dropped him in 1950. With his power as star and co-producer, he pressured Metro to sign its other early-1950s reject, Peter Lawford—then starring in the tepidly successful TV series *The Thin Man*—to co-star at an extortionate salary. (Metro originally offered Lawford $1,500 a week for three weeks' work; thanks to Frank, he wound up getting ten times that amount.) Sinatra also prevailed upon the studio to put his pal Sammy Davis Jr. into the picture at a salary of $75,000. When an MGM producer objected, "Frank, there were no Negroes in the Burma theater [of operations]," Sinatra said, "There are now."

Frank was due to open at the Sands on January 14 but was once again worried about his voice. Before heading to Vegas, he wired Dean: "Dear Dago, stand by." Dean wired back: "Of course I'll stand by, but at least OPEN."

He opened. Yet—it had become all too predictable—a few days into his two-week run, his instrument gave out. As Mitch Miller once said, "Sinatra had a marvelous voice, but it was very fragile. There were certain guys like Gordon MacRae who could stay up all night and drink and sing the next day—he could sing underwater. But if Frank didn't get enough sleep or if he drank a lot the night before, it would show up."

And, of course, all he was doing these days was drinking a lot and not getting enough sleep. On Tuesday the twentieth, he put in a distress call to Dean, who was dining at his Sunset Strip restaurant, Dino's. Martin caught the 10:00 p.m. flight to Vegas, did a midnight show for Frank, returned to Los Angeles on the 4:00 a.m. plane, and reported to NBC Studios in Burbank at 9:00 a.m.

to rehearse for a guest spot on Phil Harris's upcoming TV show. Apparently, Dean, too, could sing underwater.

Martin himself opened at the Sands on the twenty-eighth. "Dean Martin, another in Jack Entratter's stable of surefire draws for the Copa Room, is in for a 16-night stand with his trademarked casual approach to songs and comedy," *Variety*'s reviewer wrote.

> Martin, a heavyweight who appeals to both distaffers and their gaming escorts, sparks casino activity even if he doesn't double as stage performer and blackjack dealer—which he usually does. First-nighters got an extra added attraction.

Did they ever. A waiter launched the show by walking into the Copa Room holding a sign that read, "Sorry, folks, Frank Sinatra will not appear tonight"—the very sign the Sands used on nights Sinatra's voice was shot. Frank then came out, wearing a Las Vegas Department of Sanitation jacket, and the place went nuts. Or, as *Variety* put it, "Frank Sinatra joined his Great & Good Friend onstage, and the pair put on one of the best shows ever seen at the Sands."

They were on TV together, they were in the movies together, and now they were tearing up Vegas together. They stood astride the world, and the sky seemed to be the limit.

———

From Las Vegas on January 30, Frank sent a brief note, handwritten in pencil on Sands stationery, to his old friend the composer Alec Wilder at the Algonquin Hotel in New York—surely one of the very few pieces of correspondence ever to travel between those two institutions. He was glad Wilder was well, Sinatra wrote; so was he—very much so. The note ended,

> Things are going well and I'm at peace with the universe.
>
> Take Care
> Frank

———

Ava was in Australia shooting *On the Beach,* an adaptation of Nevil Shute's novel about the aftermath of a nuclear war, and she wasn't having an easy time of it. Though she had freed herself from MGM servitude and managed to extract $400,000 for her role in the independent production from the producer-director Stanley Kramer—Frank's nemesis on *The Pride and the Passion*—she wasn't getting any younger, her facial injury had barely healed, she had always been ambivalent at best about making movies, and this location wasn't helping matters. It was midsummer Down Under, with temperatures above a hundred and biting flies swarming everywhere. The natives were also swarming. *On the Beach* was the first major motion picture to be shot in Australia and had created a ruckus around Melbourne. It didn't seem to matter that Gregory Peck and Fred Astaire, Gardner's co-stars, were also in town; the city had gone gaga for Ava. She couldn't go out without being mobbed—not that there were many places to go. Melbourne in the late 1950s was a buttoned-up town; the bars closed at 6:00 p.m. If Spain was heaven for her, this was hell.

Then came the Quote. "*On the Beach* is a story about the end of the world, and Melbourne sure is the right place to film it," Ava said in a piece in the *Sydney Morning Herald*. It was a great quote, and it got picked up all over the world. The problem was, Gardner never said it. The *Herald* had sent a reporter to interview her, and she had turned him down, so he simply put a choice bit of dialogue in her mouth. Melbourne didn't take it well. In short order, she went from idol to pariah.

Moreover, after seeing that her face looked puffy in early rushes, she had gone on the wagon. Ava without alcohol was a different person: shy, self-conscious, and even more easily bored than usual. What was there to do in Melbourne Fucking Australia if you couldn't drink? An on-set romance didn't seem to be in the cards: Peck was there with his wife; Astaire was Astaire. She made a play for her young co-star Anthony Perkins and quickly found she was barking up the wrong tree. And so she did her work during the day, and did it well. "She's avid to grasp every nuance of her next scene," Kramer would write later. "Her projection really is extraordinary. Swiftly she can go from softness to pathos to violence." And at night she went back to her hotel and picked up the phone.

Mike Wallace and his wife, Buff Cobb, were the original hosts of *The Chez Show*, a late-night radio-interview program broadcast from the Chez Paree, a popular nightclub on Chicago's Near North Side. But in 1951, Wallace and Cobb left for New York, and a New York radio personality named Jack Eigen came west to take over. By 1959, the sour-faced Eigen had become a Chicago institution. He was like a rougher version of Wallace: sometimes insulting to his show-business guests, sometimes kindly and paternal. The uncertainty kept interviewees off balance, occasionally making them say things they later regretted. Audiences loved Eigen or hated him, but people paid attention.

On a Friday night in mid-January, Sammy Davis Jr. opened at the Chez

Paree, whose regular customers included Sam Giancana and the Fischetti brothers. Not long afterward, Davis sat for an interview with Jack Eigen, who was all sweetness and light. The strategy worked. The discussion ranged widely, and Sammy, perhaps with a drink or two in him, spoke freely. It didn't take long for the subject of Frank Sinatra to come up. When Eigen mentioned that Sinatra could be a difficult person, Davis said, "I love Frank and he was the kindest man in the world to me when I lost my eye in an auto accident and wanted to kill myself. But there are many things he does that there are no excuses for. Talent is not an excuse for bad manners—I don't care if you are the most talented person in the world. It does not give you a right to step on people and treat them rotten. This is what he does occasionally."

"Why is it that most stars when they finally make the big time forget how to be humble?" Eigen asked, provocatively.

DAVIS: They stop being hungry . . . You don't care whether a guy asks for your autograph or not. I've been with the Sinatras, the [Dean] Martins, all the top stars. I always stop . . .

In the case of Sinatra, whom I idolize, he can do no wrong . . . I look at Frank and I think it's absolutely inexcusable . . . The whole thing of it is that Frank has a tremendous talent. I don't think anyone is allowed that particular privilege of abusing the position the public has put him in . . .

But you got to respect him for his honesty. Because on top of the things that I hear him do bad, I've seen him do ninety thousand things that are fantastic.

Davis then told of how Sinatra had gathered celebrities to help pay for the funeral of Tim Moore, the actor who played the Kingfish on TV's *Amos 'n' Andy Show* and who had recently died penniless. Sammy said that this was only one of a hundred such incidents he knew of that the newspapers had never written about.

EIGEN: I was wondering, Sammy—is this guy happy at all?
DAVIS: No! No! Frank is not a happy guy.
EIGEN: What is it, a wife missing there, you think?
DAVIS: I think most important, Jack—the one thing he misses dearly is his family. He loves his children dearly. The relationship that he has with his wife [Nancy] is one that is very pleasant.

It is fantastic that in the last year particularly . . . Frank has cooled down considerably with his—shall we say—his nonperforming activities. He sits at home and works constantly. The man works constantly for one reason. He doesn't want time enough to sit and think quietly.

This was not all. To put a maraschino cherry on the sundae, Eigen mischievously asked Davis who the number one singer in the country was, and Sammy, having worked up a full head of steam, replied that it was none other than he.

"Bigger than Frank?" Eigen asked.

"Oh, yeah," Sammy said.

———

Davis would later maintain ("Who's better than Sinatra? Nobody") that that last fillip had been a joke. Still, this was bad. Very bad. And Chicago being Chicago, it wasn't long before Frank got wind of Sammy's insubordination. Then he got hold of a tape of the interview. "That was it for Sammy," Peter Lawford recalled. "Frank called him 'a dirty nigger bastard' and wrote him out of *Never So Few*." Sinatra often descended to ethnic slurs when he was furious, as though recalling the worst slights of his youth. He cast the twenty-eight-year-old Steve McQueen in Davis's place.

"You wanna talk destroyed," recalled Lawford's manager, Milt Ebbins. "Sammy Davis cried from morning to night. He came to see us when Peter was at the Copacabana [where he did a double act with Jimmy Durante]. He said, 'I can't get Frank on the phone. Can't you guys do something?' Peter told him, 'I talked to Frank but he won't budge.' Sammy never did the picture, never got any money. He could have sued because he had a contract, but he didn't dare. You don't sue Frank Sinatra."

"For the next two months Sammy was on his knees begging for Frank's forgiveness, but Frank wouldn't speak to him," Lawford said.

———

Bored and lonely, Ava called Walter Chiari in Italy and demanded he come to Australia at once. He made the thirteen-thousand-mile journey by air and landed in Melbourne several days later. "But by the time he arrived," Gardner's biographer Lee Server writes, "it was too late. The lovelorn mood in which Ava had longed to resume their feisty romance had dissipated. Chiari, desiring a reason for flying halfway around the world other than to be yelled at or ignored, made contact with an Australian promoter who booked him for a performance at the local stadium."

Chiari, who could also sing a little bit as well as act and do comedy, performed "to a packed house, mostly Italian emigrants," Hedda Hopper wrote on February 18. "Ava came in dressed to the teeth accompanied by Gregory Peck, Fred Astaire, and Tony Perkins." Chiari's opening number was "Tenderly," and he chose to do as close an approximation of Frank Sinatra as he was capable of. "Ava gasped, then fled," Hopper wrote.

––––––––

In his *Variety* column of February 26, Army Archerd wrote, "Milton Berle tapes his March 11 show next week, wings to Florida to vacation and to be on hand for Frank Sinatra's Fontainebleau bow. Yes, Sammy Davis Jr. will be at the Eden Roc same time. Look for a reconciliation attempt between these two."

It didn't happen. "Even when they were in Florida together and Frank was appearing at the Fontainebleau and Sammy was next door at the Eden Roc, Frank still refused to speak to him," Peter Lawford recalled. "He wouldn't even go over to see his show, which was something we always did when one or the other of us was appearing someplace. He left word with the doorman that Sammy was not to come in. If he did, Frank said he'd walk out."

As was so often the case, Sinatra's wrath was stoked by humiliation. Sammy had spoken nothing but the truth (except for that final boast), but he had declared the emperor naked, and worse still, he had done so on the home turf of those Men of Respect, the Fischetti brothers, Sam Giancana, and Tony Accardo. "That was the unforgivable part—to embarrass Frank in front of the Big Boys," Lawford said. "Those Mafia guys meant more to him than anything. So Sammy was quite lucky that Frank let him grovel for a while and then allowed him to apologize in public a few months later."

On March 4, Army Archerd wrote, "Both Frank Sinatra and Sammy Davis Jr. were on hand for Judy Garland's jam-packed finale at the Fontainebleau in Florida. If the boys have made up, Metro hasn't heard that Davis is back in 'Never So Few.' Matter of fact, New Yorkers hear Sugar Ray Robinson was offered the Davis role in 'Ocean's 11.'"

Once Sammy was able to work his way back into Frank's good graces, he got his *Ocean's 11* role back. He would play a garbageman.

––––––––

Judy Garland's Fontainebleau finale might have been jam-packed, but the rest of her second week in the hotel's fabulous La Ronde Room was anything but. As *Variety* noted, her opening night had been "one with a 'we're with you' atmosphere that served to swing her into a big reaction wind. Her name held the crowd-pull strong for initial seven nights . . . But in second week, the talk about a vocal lack as compared to her heyday; the physical factor that dissipated the preconceived image of the Garland seen in tv film revivals, and her by-rote manner of delivery worked their b.o. havoc to the point where the biggery had its 'softest' week of the season.

"It took Frank Sinatra to bring the 750-plus seater back into sell-out status."

The piece went on to note that Sinatra's stand at the Fontainebleau, which immediately followed Garland's, left hers in the dust. Frank had attracted five thousand advance reservations, and his first week had broken all records at the hotel, even the ones he'd set the previous March. His shows pulled in over $22,000 a night, with more than sixteen hundred customers springing for the $17.50 prix fixe dinner plus the $5 beverage minimum. The second week was projected to be equally profitable.

Unlike Garland, who rode into town on fumes, evoking a combination of sympathy and horror from her audiences and unable—at just thirty-six—to escape her past, Sinatra was at his absolute pinnacle. Based on his drawing power, the Fontainebleau's owner, Ben Novack, had expanded the La Ronde's seating capacity from 450 to over 750; with Frank he filled every seat and then some. Amid the blue haze of cigarette smoke and the tinkle of clinking glasses, the shows in the great circular room were electric, their understated format bespeaking the singer's supreme confidence and concentrating the excitement.

"Sinatra has a revised act this trip," *Variety* observed. "He's discarded the theatrics of former entrances down middle aisle, hat shoved back, coat 'carelessly' slung over one shoulder." Frank was also trying out a new approach, using the Red Norvo Quintet as accompaniment instead of a twenty-piece orchestra. The effect was both quieter and more electric: the audience hung on every note.

———

The vibraphonist Norvo, born in 1908, was a superb and multifarious musician who had led his own big band in the 1930s, with his wife, Mildred Bailey, doing vocals (he'd come within an inch of hiring Sinatra before Frank joined Harry James in June 1939), and had played with Charlie Parker and Dizzy Gillespie in the mid-1940s. Sinatra admired Norvo extravagantly and in 1958 got the vibraphonist and his quintet a job playing in the lounge at the Sands. "While listening to Norvo's group in Las Vegas," Will Friedwald writes, "Sinatra hatched the idea of using the fivesome, with the addition of pianist Bill Miller (his regular accompanist since 1951) as both his permanent rhythm section and his opening act." The lightly swinging sound of the de facto sextet not only complemented Frank's voice beautifully but added an element of hipness that relaxed the singer, inspiring some of the most swinging vocals he'd done since working (all too briefly) with the Metronome All-Stars in 1946.

A few days after Miami, he was wallowing in gloom.

On the night of March 24, Sinatra joined Gordon Jenkins and a thirty-seven-piece orchestra in Capitol Studio A to begin recording the LP that would forever be known as the Suicide Album: *No One Cares*. That night he laid down four tracks: Victor Young, Ned Washington, and Bing Crosby's "I Don't Stand a Ghost of a Chance with You"; Cy Coleman and Joe McCarthy's "Why Try to Change Me Now?"; "None but the Lonely Heart," from a voice-and-piano romance by Tchaikovsky, with a lyric translated from Goethe (!); and Harold Arlen and Ted Koehler's "Stormy Weather."

To listen to these numbers, and the six recorded on the following two nights, is to taste mixed pleasures. Frank, despite having just completed two weeks of two shows a night at the Fontainebleau, displays no trace of the vocal problems that had sidelined him in January: he is in magnificent voice. The songs themselves verge on lugubriousness, and many would say they come closer than that. Listen to "I Don't Stand a Ghost of a Chance": it begins with a sad and stately woodwind passage that for a few bars sounds like the national anthem of a particularly gloomy Eastern European republic. Then the strings, merely sweetly sad, arrive by way of relief. Sinatra begins to sing,

> *I need your love so badly*
> *I love you, oh, so madly.*

The vocal is supremely tender, the tempo . . . like molasses. This is not material that would have thrilled ringside at the Sands or the Fontainebleau. But this is not the point—a fact that becomes all the clearer on Ira Gershwin and Vernon Duke's great "I Can't Get Started," customarily performed in chorus only (see Bunny Berigan; Billie Holiday), as a light to rousing torch song, a complaint so witty that the singer seems bound to succeed somehow, in spite of everything.

Here Sinatra and Jenkins are up to something entirely different. After a dignified French horn opening statement—the notes could practically be echoing across an Alpine valley—Frank begins with the tune's seldom-heard verse:

> *I'm a glum one, it's explainable, . . .*

Gershwin's breezy complaint about the unattainable love object is all but tossed off by most singers, but not in this version. Instead, Sinatra gives the lyric a soulful, earnest reading, with the strings and reeds rising heavenward behind him. Then, before the chorus can even begin, those Jenkins strings (in tight, foursquare harmony; no Riddle impressionism here) swirl through a couple of arabesques and then and only then Frank proceeds, at a tempo almost too slow for a fox-trot:

I've flown around the world in a plane.

It's not a dirge, it's not a blues, it's a Sinatra-Jenkins. The form is unique to the team, and some can take it and some can leave it. In those days, a lot could take it: their first outing, 1957's *Where Are You?*, had made it to number 3 on the *Billboard* album chart; *No One Cares* hit number 2.

Since 1955, Sinatra's album releases had followed a manic-depressive pattern, sad or contemplative LPs alternating with brisk and bouncy ones, as though Frank were trying to tell the world about itself, and himself. Thus that year's *In the Wee Small Hours* was followed in 1956 by *Songs for Swingin' Lovers!*, which segued into 1957's *Close to You, A Swingin' Affair!*, and the first Jenkins albums, *Where Are You?* and *A Jolly Christmas from Frank Sinatra*. Nineteen fifty-eight brought Sinatra's initial collaboration with Billy May, the exuberant *Come Fly with Me*, followed by the melancholy Nelson Riddle LP *Frank Sinatra Sings for Only the Lonely*. Both went to number 1 on the *Billboard* chart.

Soon after the September 1958 release of *Only the Lonely*, Frank recorded *Come Dance with Me!*, a high-spirited bookend to *Come Fly with Me*. Released in January 1959, *Dance* never broke number 2, but it stayed on the charts for 140 weeks, becoming Sinatra's most successful LP. Besides the irresistible Cahn–Van Heusen title tune, the album was filled with upbeat delights, the likes of Johnny Mercer's "Something's Gotta Give"; Styne, Comden, and Green's "Just in Time"; Rube Bloom and Johnny Mercer's "Day In, Day Out"; Irving Berlin's "Cheek to Cheek"; and a soaring version of Jerome Kern and Oscar Hammerstein's "Song Is You." Sinatra and May even managed to turn Howard Dietz and Arthur Schwartz's pensive and foreboding "Dancing in the Dark" into an out-and-out romp: dancin', rather than dancing, in the dark.

But then, that was Frank; he could make you want to die, and he could make you want to live.

It was in the latter spirit that he decided to go to Australia at the end of March: to help Ava. Since Walter Chiari's departure, she had been especially lonely, and without alcohol and the adventures it stimulated to keep her occupied, she was feeling especially pent-up and bored. Gardner's biographer Lee Server maintains that she spent many hours on crackling transoceanic phone calls with Frank, that "she had come to think of him as the one person in the world who understood her, who wanted nothing from her, who cared only for her friendship and her happiness." During one of their conversations, the biographer says, Frank was telling Ava "about a concert he had just done, and she said to him that she wished she had seen it and then that she wished she could see him."

What about if he came down there and sang to her? he asked.

She eagerly accepted.

Frank contacted Lee Gordon, an American promoter living in Australia, and set up two concerts, one in Sydney, the other in Melbourne. The Red Norvo Quintet and Bill Miller would back him. He and the musicians, along with manager/bodyguard Hank Sanicola, landed in Sydney on March 31. Frank's arrival in Australia was big news, in part because of the brouhaha that had followed his aborted trip Down Under in 1957 (that promoter had threatened to sue; Sinatra had settled for big bucks) but mostly, of course, because of Ava.

It was easy enough to imagine the real reason behind Sinatra's hastily arranged concert visit—*they must be thinking about getting back together*—and delightful to contemplate the sparks that would fly: between Frank and Ava, between Frank and Ava (together or separately) and the press. The tabloid frenzy that Ava had initially stirred up had died down; she'd simply failed to provide good copy. How nice it was of Frank to liven things up. And just in case he wasn't in the mood to do so, the wild and woolly Australian press was ready to help. As the saxophonist Jerry Dodgion told Will Friedwald, two photographers followed Sinatra's entourage everywhere, one continually provoking Frank to take a swing at him, the other with his camera at the ready. "After one particularly enervating evening, in which Sinatra vainly tried to escape by hopping from one restaurant to another," Friedwald writes, "he finally instructed manager and companion Hank Sanicola to slash their tires."

As always in Frank's life, less than sublime goings-on bracketed sublime music. On April 1, in West Melbourne Stadium, he gave one of the greatest—and strangest—concerts of his life. Ava was sitting in the front row. Something about her presence, and the unconstrained Aussie crowd, uninhibited him. At one point, as he began "I've Got You Under My Skin," a woman in the audience screamed with delight, and Frank called out, "Get your hand off that broad!" And the minimal but swinging backing of Miller and the Norvo Quintet brought out, for the evening, his abilities as a great jazz musician.

"I don't think he ever sang any better in his life," Red Norvo told Friedwald. "I loved the way he sang with the small band. It was very free, and he was right on top of everything we were doing. He just melted into it, I thought . . . And the band played great for him, they loved working with him. He gave us the feeling he was part of the group."

For all his life, Frank would nourish nostalgic memories of his big-band days with Harry James and Tommy Dorsey, when he wasn't yet a superstar burdened with the crippling demands of fame but merely one of the musicians, the boy singer. (It was easy to forget the overnight rides on unheated band buses in the dead of winter, the hunger and low pay, the feuds with Buddy Rich and Dorsey.) Working with a small combo helped him relive those feelings.

He seemed to sing every number that night with a smile on his face. When one listens to the concert, and to Sinatra's interplay with the audience and the musicians, it's hard to keep from smiling oneself. The up-tempo tempi were fast, and the mood was up, even on bluesy numbers like "Willow Weep for Me" and "Angel Eyes." On "The Lady Is a Tramp" and the *Come Dance with Me!*-style "Dancing in the Dark," Frank was so loose that he even threw in a bit of quite credible scatting. His closer, "Night and Day," was a tour de force jazz dialogue with Norvo, Sinatra singing gently but ardently, playing off the vibraphonist's brilliant improv with his own, skipping around the melody, toying with the words, even violating his own cardinal rule about never breaking a lyric in order to give the vibes space to dance in.

Frank was in the mood: it was intimate, ebullient singing. Seeing Ava's face before him made it a perfect night.

Then back to reality. "The scene afterward was chaos and invective," Lee Server writes.

> Sinatra bodyguards played rough with the local rubberneckers. The singer's imprecation to a photographer was widely reported: "Take another picture and I'll ram that camera down your throat. You stink!"
> She went with him in the limousine to his hotel, a dangerous chase as a fleet of reporters' cars followed them, everyone moving at high speed, and Sinatra screaming for his driver to run them off the road.

And then, the twin aphrodisiacs of sweet music and hot chaos having done their magic, "they went up to Frank's suite, and had some food sent up and drank champagne and talked and looked at each other and they went to bed."

They left Australia separately, within days of each other, not to see each other again for more than a year.

———

The first Grammy Awards were given on the night of May 4 at the Beverly Hilton hotel. Frank took as his date the young actress Sandra Giles, a busty bleached blonde who bore a more than passing resemblance to Joi Lansing, an actress who had worked on *A Hole in the Head* with Sinatra and whom he was also seeing. He was feeling upbeat and optimistic. He had been nominated six times in four categories—including Best Male Vocal for "Witchcraft" and "Come Fly with Me" and Best Album for *Come Fly with Me* and *Frank Sinatra Sings for Only the Lonely*—and fully expected to skip up to the podium and graciously accept a couple of awards.

Instead, he won just one, not even for his singing, but for allegedly being the art director of the Best Album Cover award winner, the very late-1950s, harlequin-themed sleeve of *Only the Lonely*, featuring Nicholas Volpe's bathetic painting of a sad-looking Sinatra in clown makeup and deep shadow. Bitterly disappointed, Frank started drinking as soon as the ceremony ended. Giles drank along with him but couldn't keep up. Back at Sinatra's Coldwater Canyon place, as she recalled many years later, she passed out and awoke to find herself naked in Frank's bed, with a naked Frank. He claimed they had had sex; she was sure they hadn't. She locked herself in the bathroom and told him she was going to call the police. He talked her out of it and had George Jacobs drive her home. She later found a $100 bill—roughly a week's income for a U.S. family in 1959—stuffed in her purse. When a shaken Giles called Sinatra to ask about the money, she remembered, "He said, 'Yeah, that's something for your daughter for a Christmas present.' It was his way of apologizing. He never actually said he was sorry."

That was Monday. On Friday, his sensitivity ascendant, he joined Riddle and a thirty-three-piece orchestra in Studio A to record two singles: the winsome theme from *A Hole in the Head*, Cahn and Van Heusen's "High Hopes," which Frank sang with a youthful choir billed as "A Bunch of Kids" (but not with his eleven-year-old co-star Eddie Hodges, whose ironclad contract with Decca prevented him from joining Frank on the date), and "Love Looks So Well on You," another tender ballad by Alan Bergman, Marilyn Keith, and Lew Spence. The ballad never charted, but "High Hopes" became a huge hit, the rallying cry for a generation that would, after all too brief a moment, be disabused of its optimism.

The following Thursday night, Frank recorded two Riddle-arranged numbers, "This Was My Love" (as grandly sentimental as the title) and the bluesy-seductive "Talk to Me," along with two songs orchestrated by Gordon Jenkins, the Cahn–Van Heusen "When No One Cares" and a reprise of Sinatra's great Dorsey theme "I'll Never Smile Again."

It was an odd night, and the last number was particularly strange. In May 1940, a twenty-four-year-old Frank, with the Pied Pipers' exquisite harmonies and a tinkling celesta behind him, had turned Ruth Lowe's musical elegy to her young husband into a thing of innocent beauty, an ode to youthful yearning in a world sinking into war. In May 1959, the forty-three-year-old Frank was singing the same song, but it sounded very different.

For the past year and more, he had been growing steadily more impatient with Capitol Records, with which his contract would expire in November 1962. Sinatra had been agitating for many things—a greater share of the profits, a producer of his own, control of his master recordings—but it's hard to escape the impression that what he wanted most of all was out. Power was central to his thinking in the late 1950s, and with power in mind he'd been hammering Capitol's president, Glenn Wallichs, with a big idea: he wanted to start his own record label. It would be part of his movie-production company, Essex, and would have the same name; Frank and Capitol would each own half. Sinatra would hold title to the masters of his recordings and lease them to Capitol for processing and distribution. Capitol would pay all costs and expenses; Essex and Capitol would share profits fifty-fifty.

Frank wouldn't let go of the idea, and Wallichs wouldn't budge. After all, the executive said, if he agreed to such an arrangement with Sinatra, Nat Cole, Peggy Lee, and others would expect the same, and where would Capitol be then?

Frank told Wallichs that he, the straw that stirred the drink, would record no more for Capitol until Wallichs changed his tune.

When one listens to the recordings Frank made on the night of May 14—and especially to his new "I'll Never Smile Again"—it's hard to escape the impression that, consciously or not, he already had one foot out the door. Singing over Jenkins's sad strings, Sinatra sounds tender and vulnerable and middle-aged; there's a slight quaver to his voice that's not at all unattractive. Yet as he sings the first chorus—

> *I'll never smile again, until I smile at you*
> *I'll never laugh again, what good would it do*

—something quite strange happens. His pitch is uncertain from the first syllable, and—after weirdly mispronouncing the word "laugh" as "luff"—he hits an unmistakable clam on the word "do." A Sinatra wrong note—understandable enough in the heat of a nightclub performance, but on a recording session? Frank's ear was exquisitely tuned: he was famous for bringing a take to a grinding halt if, say, the third violin was a half note off, fixing the offender with an ice-blue glare and saying, "Where you working next week?" He would do multiple takes of a song if anything about his vocal or the accompaniment displeased him: more than fifty years after attending a late-1958 session at Capitol, the former child actor Eddie Hodges vividly remembered Sinatra stopping a song mid-recording, furious at the string section. "He yelled, 'What is with you guys? You sound like a bunch of girls!'" Hodges recalled. "Then he said, 'Why don't you play it with some balls?' And they did another take, and he got exactly what he wanted. They sounded great."

Sinatra would sometimes listen to his playbacks in the recording studio; other times, he simply walked out when the session was done, secure that he'd nailed it. He was more keenly aware than anyone of his own strengths and weaknesses. Why did he not rerecord this "Smile"? Perhaps he had some important business to attend to on the night of the fourteenth; perhaps he just didn't care. In any case, he wouldn't set foot inside Capitol Studio A for almost another year.

———

George Jacobs maintains that his boss and Pat Lawford had eyes for each other from the moment they first met. Jacobs places that first meeting at a party at the Gary Coopers', the one that most writers set in the summer of 1958, but as we have seen, Sinatra and the Lawfords had been socializing since at least June 1955—which is around the same time Frank and Jack Kennedy met at a Democratic fund-raiser.

Nevertheless, Sinatra's relationship with the Lawfords and his friendship with Pat Lawford's politically ambitious older brother had accelerated in 1958. Frank was developing *Ocean's 11* with Peter Lawford and had a strong interest in the presidential prospects of Lawford's brother-in-law. And Frank's fascination with John Kennedy and his family was richly returned. "Let's just say that the Kennedys are interested in the lively arts, and that Sinatra is the liveliest art of all," Peter Lawford would tell a reporter in 1960. The man who would be called the first celebrity president had his own fascination with celebrities. For her part, Patricia Kennedy Lawford had long been enthralled by Hollywood, had had frustrated ambitions to be a movie producer (a career path not open to women at the time), and was well aware of her husband's incessant woman-izing. A relationship with Frank would have seemed to her like a kind of power play, not to mention a form of manifest destiny. And Frank would have felt much the same way.

There was an intense—and complex—chemistry between the two. Pat Lawford, according to Jacobs, "had had an admitted crush on Frank since his crooner days"; as for Frank, the former valet writes, "Mr. S smelled a potential seduction of one of the most high-profile 'super-broads' in America . . . The prospect of Pat Kennedy opened Mr. S's eyes to the even more exciting pros-pect of John Kennedy."

Thanks to an organized and energetic presidential campaign begun virtually the moment he lost the 1956 vice presidential nomination, Jack Kennedy's presidential prospects had been growing steadily more exciting through the late 1950s. In a field of gray-colored candidates—fiftyish politicians like Adlai Stevenson, Stuart Symington, Lyndon Johnson, and Robert Meyner—the impossibly glamorous senator from Massachusetts—a Harvard graduate, a reputed war hero, and a Pulitzer Prize winner for *Profiles in Courage,* the book about breakaway senators that bore his name on the cover—stood out like a bird of paradise.

Nevertheless, a look beyond Kennedy's sexy exterior into his political heart might have given Sinatra pause. Frank had grown up imbued with FDR liberalism; Jack Kennedy had not. As a junior senator in 1954, he had dragged his feet on censuring Joseph McCarthy (for whose Red-baiting Senate Permanent Subcommittee on Investigations his brother Bobby had worked as an assistant counsel and whom Pat Kennedy had briefly dated). He'd waffled on the Civil Rights Act of 1957. "I wish Mr. Kennedy had a little less profile and a little more courage," Eleanor Roosevelt famously remarked. Amid 1950s paranoia about Communism, John F. Kennedy and his whole family were eager to distance themselves from Stevenson, whom most of America considered pinkish and an egghead to boot (the candidate's bald dome and refined manner had originally inspired the term), and the Democratic Party's liberal wing.

Yet class and charisma, whatever the substance beneath, held a deep and unsalubrious attraction for Sinatra—witness Lady Beatty—and Jack Kennedy possessed both in spades. "For Sinatra," Ronald Brownstein writes,

> Kennedy seemed to represent more than just power; despite his own rakish behavior, JFK conveyed a weight and solidity suggestive of Harvard, summers on the Cape, lazy days surrounded and protected by a vivacious family. All that the bright, garish Rat Pack lifestyle—a blue-collar fantasy of what it meant to be rich—eminently lacked. Like his acceptance at the [Bill and Edie] Goetz table, Kennedy's favor gave Sinatra respectability—a reason to be admired, not just feared, by his peers.

And Kennedy, a longtime habitué of Hollywood who moved easily among movie stars, feeling himself their equal, if not their superior, was an ahead-of-his-time politician, one who understood the enormous political potential of show business and its players. He was also enthralled by the business and its players themselves, and no one was a bigger player than Frank Sinatra. As the two men rose to the peaks of power, they were destined to enter each other's orbit.

Joseph P. Kennedy, both explicitly and by example, had taught his son well. He had understood the financial possibilities of the movie business when he bought into RKO Studios in the 1920s; he had formed a longtime liaison with Gloria Swanson not just because of the charms of her person but because of her worldly power as a film star. He had consciously cultivated Sinatra at Cal-Neva for much the same reason, but for other reasons as well.

Joe Kennedy's chief aim in life, his reason for being, was to get his oldest living son elected president of the United States. After two decades of successful investment banking, he had the money to do it, and beginning with Jack Kennedy's congressional campaign in 1946, he'd set about converting money into power. "We're going to sell Jack like soap flakes," he famously said, and he was as good as his word, laying out enormous amounts for billboard space, newspaper ads, and radio spots.

Once the presidential campaign began, the elder Kennedy raised his game, spending ever more lavishly. The stakes were immeasurably higher, and so were the goals: magazine covers now instead of billboards. And men of national influence, not just local political bosses, had to be rallied to the cause. Some of these men occupied high positions in organized crime.

In his life of Joseph Kennedy, David Nasaw devotes just a single page to debunking the longtime allegations that Kennedy was involved in bootlegging during Prohibition, mentioning "unsubstantiated, usually off-the-cuff remarks [on the subject] made in the 1970s and 1980s by Meyer Lansky, Frank Costello, Joe Bonanno, and other Mob figures not particularly known for their truth telling." The implication is to dismiss any other connection Kennedy might have had, at any time, with any of these men.

Sheer practicality, Nasaw argues, kept Kennedy from having anything to do with the Mob. "He had disposed of his liquor import business and his stake in Hialeah because he did not want his children to be tarnished with the stereotypes he had so scrupulously avoided all his life," the biographer writes.

> He had lived his life and made and kept his millions by carefully evaluating risk/reward ratios and avoiding any and all unnecessary dangers, in business and politics. It would have been extraordinarily reckless— and he was not a reckless man—for him to do business with or consort with known mobsters, especially as they had nothing to offer him he could not obtain elsewhere.

The last sentence contains two ideas: The first, that it would have been supremely reckless for Joseph Kennedy to consort with mobsters, is clearly true. The second, the notion that the Mob had nothing to offer him, is problematic, to say the least. And the one sure way to deal with the problem of needing something without being able to ask for it directly is to proceed through intermediaries.

The Mob boss Joe Bonanno's son Bill Bonanno, whom Gay Talese considered trustworthy enough to collaborate with on Talese's massive history of the Bonannos and the Mob, *Honor Thy Father*, asserts that this is precisely what Joe Kennedy did. Kennedy wanted organized crime's help in rallying organized labor behind his son, and so in the winter of 1959, according to the younger Bonanno, he sent a representative to talk with a representative of Joe Bonanno's.

"I was instructed to go back . . . to New York and sound out other leaders about a concerted effort to back JFK," Bill Bonanno told Anthony Summers. "The divisions over Kennedy were deep. Joe Profaci [a New York Mob boss], for example, said he just didn't trust Kennedy. Midwestern leaders—in Cleveland and Michigan—had let it be known that we should get behind someone who was more rooted in the unions, where we had more influence."

"Giancana, on the other hand, appeared to be in favor," Summers writes, "and Joe Kennedy needed a way to reach out to him."

That Frank Sinatra and Sam Giancana were friends was a fact of which Joe Kennedy would have been well aware. And Giancana, feeling the heat of the Senate committee on which Kennedy's younger son served as counsel, needed something from the Ambassador, too.

———

The Joe Kennedy whom George Jacobs remembers was a very different person from the rough-edged but dignified power broker portrayed in David Nasaw's biography. A late-1950s weekend Kennedy spent at Sinatra's desert home made an indelible impression on Frank's valet, who at first assumed, not unreasonably, that the cold-faced Ambassador was another of Mr. S.'s gangster pals. For one thing, there was the resplendent welcome Sinatra laid on, including a quintet of hookers flown down from Vegas; for another, there was the guest of honor's dinnertime patter, a steady barrage of nasty cracks about blacks and Jews. Especially Jews. To the onetime studio owner, the former furriers and glove makers who had founded Hollywood were "Sheenie rag traders"; Kennedy called Louis B. Mayer a "kike junkman." Frank sat through it all with a forced smile.

Why? Because Joe Kennedy held the key to something that Frank wanted badly: political power. Sinatra's Democratic politics went back to Dolly's Hoboken and the early FDR days. But under the old, Waspocratic worldview, still tenacious in America through the 1950s, an Italian-American like Frank, no matter how much money he made from music and movies, was still just a minstrel. He could sit at the feet of power, he could contribute to the cause, but the grown-ups, the white men who went to Protestant churches, made the decisions. Now it looked as though there could be a real sea change—a young, Catholic, ethnic president—and Sinatra wanted in. And "in" meant access and influence: quantities that Joe Kennedy carried in his attaché case.

The royal road to the son passed through the father. "I think that in understanding Jack Kennedy, you have to go back to his father and [Jack's] growing up, and how his mother was treated as this side issue over here—the saintly mother, but not the person you really had any fun with," said Alan Livingston's widow, Nancy Olson Livingston, who knew JFK from the late 1940s on. Jack Kennedy, the soap flakes the old man was selling, appears to have paid his first visit to Frank's Palm Springs place in the eventful summer of 1958. But while JFK might have been a chip off the old block in some respects—his cool toughness, his sexual voracity—he lacked the old man's blunt force, his unapologetic gracelessness. Those were survival skills for Joe Kennedy, who'd had to fight his way into polite society, had had to slug it out with robber barons and just plain robbers. Jack had only had to fight Japs in the South Pacific. He was brave, but he was spoiled, an Irish-American prince supremely confident of his charm and good looks. (Nobody had ever accused Joe Kennedy of being handsome.) And his charm, which comprised a keen intelligence and a quick wit, was overwhelming. Frank fell for him—much as he had fallen for Dean—like a ton of bricks.

Few people, male or female, had the power to resist Jack Kennedy. George Jacobs was no exception, although the photo-realistic portrait he gives of the president-to-be is remarkable in its coarseness. Jacobs saw JFK with his hair (and sometimes his pants) down, and his picture of the man is very different from the iconic images of the young president with his thumbs hooked in the pockets of his suit jacket or reclining in sweater and sunglasses on his yacht the *Honey Fitz*. Like his father (and like Frank), Jack Kennedy lacked apology. He knew what he wanted, and he said so. But unlike the old man, he said so with a twinkle.

"As much as I disliked his father, that's how much I was crazy about John Fitzgerald Kennedy," Jacobs writes.

He was handsome and funny and naughty and as irreverent as Dean Martin. "What do colored people want, George?" he asked me the first time he visited Palm Springs, not long after Mr. S and Peter Lawford became bosom buddies.

"I don't know, Mr. Senator."

"Jack, George. Jack."

"What do *you* want? Jack?" I asked.

"I want to fuck every woman in Hollywood," he said with a big leering grin.

And that, in short, was why he was there. Kennedy's close friend and campaign aide, Dave Powers, tried to soften the focus. "His fondness for Frank was simply based on the fact that Sinatra told him a lot of inside gossip about celebrities and their romances in Hollywood," Powers told Kitty Kelley in 1982. George Jacobs certainly confirms JFK's love of celebrity dirt, which Kennedy loved to dig for while Jacobs, an expert masseur, kneaded his bad back. "I would work on his back for a good hour, all the while being peppered with prurient questions about his favorite topic, celebrity 'poon-tang,' as he liked to call it," the valet recalled. Whenever Jacobs tried to ask a political question, the senator firmly steered the conversation back to whether Janet Leigh was cheating on Tony Curtis or what was going on with Eddie Fisher and Debbie Reynolds. Kennedy apparently read every issue of *Confidential* magazine.

Sex, Jack Kennedy's obsession, was always the main topic. But he didn't want to just talk about it. He knew that no one in Hollywood—meaning no one in the world—had more sex than Frank Sinatra: it made Frank a hero in Kennedy's eyes, and, more important, it promised Kennedy the kind of access he was most interested in.

Each man knew what the other could do for him; each wooed the other in his own way. Frank came to Jack with an agenda, but also with a large degree of idealism and genuine affection. Jack came to Frank with a cool eye for what he could get—not just sex, but the political power of Hollywood—and the charm to convince Sinatra the affection he showed was real. By October 1958, Sinatra, who had told the press, "Senator Kennedy is a friend of mine," had endorsed JFK for the presidency. In November of that year, Walter Winchell speculated in his column that John F. Kennedy, if elected, might appoint Frank Sinatra ambassador to Italy.

One night in May 1959, Frank and Dean were the emcees at the SHARE Boomtown show, a star-studded charity event at the Hollywood Moulin Rouge. It was a wet and wild evening, all partygoers clad in outlandish western regalia and imbibing liberally. Dean made his entrance from the ceiling on a wire-suspended saddle slowly lowered sixty feet to the stage. When the saddle was hauled back up, Dean called, "So long, Jerry."

"Because it was an 'inside' soiree, the boys were really swinging," UPI's Hollywood correspondent Vernon Scott wrote. "The singers rarely were without a highball in their mitts . . . The longer the show went on the wilder it became. As leaders of Hollywood's 'clan,' Martin and Sinatra had the jam-packed Moulin Rouge crowd howling with glee."

A funny thing happened when Sammy Davis Jr. came on to perform "Birth of the Blues." While Frank and Dean ad-libbed a boozy introduction, Frank looked at Sammy and Sammy looked at Frank. Suddenly, with the all but undetectable nod of a true *padrone*, Frank was beckoning Sammy over, and before anyone knew what was happening, the two were embracing, to the crowd's loud delight. The feud was done.

After Frank and Dean had vocalized separately, they sang a pair of duets, "Come Fly with Me" and "I Can't Give You Anything but Love, Baby." As the applause for the second number died down, Sinatra and Martin went into a shambling Sammy Cahn parody, to the tune of "You Oughta Be in Pictures":

We're glad that we're Italian,
Authentic Abruzzi, . . .

Dean owned "that lodge called Dino's," he crooned; for his part, Frank put in that he had "a hunk of Puccini."

The well-oiled showbiz crowd ate up the inside humor: though Sinatra had wined and dined for years at Patsy D'Amore's Villa Capri, he'd recently opened his own Italian restaurant, Puccini (named after his favorite composer), on South Beverly Drive in Beverly Hills. His partners in the venture were Hank Sanicola, Mickey Rudin, and Peter Lawford, though apparently Lawford, a notorious tightwad, didn't put up a dime. He didn't have to: he was married to a Kennedy. And by May 1959, Patricia Kennedy Lawford's brother had become the presumptive Democratic candidate for the presidency.

12

Oh, you're a colorful gypsy.

—BING CROSBY TO FRANK, ON *THE FRANK SINATRA TIMEX SHOW*,
OCTOBER 1959

At the Desert Inn in March 1959, a process server walked up to a short, dapper, bespectacled man, spoke his name—his real name, not Sam Flood, the handle under which he'd checked into the DI—and handed him a subpoena. The surprised recipient was Frank Sinatra's friend Sam Giancana, making hay in Vegas during the slim interval between Fidel Castro's New Year's Day shutdown of Havana's casinos and the Nevada Gaming Commission's 1960 issuance of its first so-called Black Book, a list of "persons of notorious or unsavory reputation" who were to be banned for life from owning, managing, or even entering any of the state's gambling establishments. Giancana would be one of the eleven charter members of this exclusive fraternity.

The subpoena ordered the mobster to appear before John McClellan's Senate Rackets Committee, which had been hunting for him for over a year while he gadded around the country under various aliases, enjoying himself—on the *Some Came Running* location, among other places—but never failing to glance over his shoulder for whichever white or black hat might be in pursuit.

Giancana almost seemed to savor the subpoena. He certainly took full advantage of the drama of testifying before a U.S. Senate committee, perhaps considering his appearance a kind of redemption for missing out on the Kefauver Committee when he had been too small a fish to reel in. Now, however, Giancana was regarded as "either the number one or two man in the shifting hierarchy of the old Capone mob," and he arrived in Washington on June 9 fully prepared for his close-up. "A handsome-type hoodlum in dark glasses," UPI reported,

> he came equipped with a printed Fifth Amendment plea which began: "I respectfully decline . . ." but the word "respectfully" had been crossed out and Giancana never used it. Giancana gave a raucous laugh when committee investigator Pierre Salinger identified him as a top figure in the Chicago underworld. He continued to laugh derisively when

asked about a couple of Chicago gangland murders and about his role in a juke box racket.

Giancana also found amusing a Chicago newspaper interview in which he was quoted as telling his draft board that "he steals for a living." Committee counsel Robert F. Kennedy brought out that Giancana was rejected for military service because of a "constitutional psychopathic" condition and "strong anti-social trends."

"Are you happy at being a thief?" asked Chairman John L. McClellan (D-Ark.). "Is that what you're laughing about?"

Bizarrely, Giancana continued to laugh each time he took the Fifth while Kennedy asked him about several specific accusations. Exasperated, the committee counsel finally asked, "Would you tell us anything about any of your operations or will you just giggle every time I ask you a question?"

"I decline to answer because I honestly believe my answer might tend to incriminate me," Giancana replied.

"I thought only little girls giggled, Mr. Giancana," Kennedy said.

It was tough talk from the boyish, high-voiced committee counsel, all of thirty-three years old on that June day—and exceedingly strange talk too, given that both his father and his adored older brother shared at least one close connection to the man on the stand: a friendship with Frank Sinatra. Further connections were soon to come, and Frank would help facilitate them.

A certain part of him fell away when he wasn't making records. How to fill the void? That June and July, he commuted to the MGM back lot and played soldier from 11:00 a.m. to 6:00 p.m. each day, shooting *Never So Few* amid fake foliage simulating the steamy jungles of Burma. Boredom was the real enemy. To divert himself one day, Sinatra had the entire roster of the Milwaukee Braves, including the greats Hank Aaron and Warren Spahn, to lunch in the Metro commissary. During another lunch break, he brought Nelson Riddle and a full orchestra onto a soundstage to rehearse for a Capitol recording session. The actor Dean Jones recalled conspiring with Steve McQueen to rig Sinatra's trailer with cherry bombs. A highlight of the production, Jones remembered, was when Frank's toupee fell off during a fight scene. Utterly unfazed—he was after all the star, co-producer, and master of all he surveyed—he retired to his makeup chair to have the wig glued back on.

He was beginning to see himself as a key part of the Kennedy team. One night in late June, he threw a dinner party on Bowmont Drive for Governor Abraham Ribicoff of Connecticut, the man who had nominated Jack Kennedy for the vice presidency at the 1956 Democratic National Convention and one of the first public officials to support JFK's presidential run. Dean Martin and Shirley MacLaine were present, as were Tony Curtis and Janet Leigh and nineteen-year-old Nancy Sinatra, sans Tommy Sands, the young singer-actor she'd lately been dating.

Frank's own love life—as opposed to his sex life—was sparse. Lady Beatty, after dallying awhile with him in the States, returned to Europe, where she took up with Aly Khan, then married Stanley Donen. Frank was not heartbroken. Despite troublemaking news reports, mostly from Europe and entirely invented, he did not have an affair with his *Never So Few* co-star Gina Lollobrigida, who had been accompanied to Hollywood by her manager-husband. (Despite MGM's marketing strategy—the trailer for the film showed Frank and Gina kissing strenuously under titles reading, "SOONER OR LATER THIS HAD TO HAPPEN—SINATRA MEETS LOLLOBRIGIDA," as the screen burst into process-shot flames—the lack of on-screen heat between them was palpable.)

It was time for some therapy by geography.

When his work on the picture was done in early July, Frank and Dean flew to Miami to attend the wedding of Sam Giancana's nineteen-year-old younger daughter, Bonnie. "Giancana apparently chose Miami Beach for the wedding to avoid the publicity he received when his 24-year-old daughter [Antoinette] was married to a bartender in Chicago," UPI reported. Press coverage of the earlier affair, which had cost $20,000 and featured two bands, a four-foot wedding cake, eight hundred guests, and Joey Bishop as the main entertainment, "apparently resulted in embarrassment to Giancana when mobster names on the guest list were published widely," the account continued.

Determined not to be embarrassed again, Giancana did all he could to keep the press at bay. The wire-service reporter on the scene could only pick up tidbits:

> Giancana, who appeared last month before the Senate Rackets Committee investigating the prostitution and pinball rackets in Chicago, dabbed at his eyes with a handkerchief when he gave his daughter away.
>
> But little else could be learned about the affair. Guests slipped unobtrusively into town, attended the ceremony at St. Patrick's Roman Catholic Church and the reception at the luxurious Fontainebleau Hotel, then left as quietly.
>
> The hotel even denied that the reception took place. "There is no wedding reception or party of any kind today," a Fontainebleau spokesman insisted.

But observers noted burly men guarding the doors to the plush party rooms where bejeweled women and men in dark suits and dark glasses mingled while strolling musicians serenaded them.

———

From Miami, Frank headed to New York to see some shows and to be given a personal tour of the UN by the Nobel laureate Dr. Ralph Bunche himself, as the ever-anodyne Louella Parsons reported. But Bunche wasn't the only distinguished person of multiracial background Sinatra saw while in the city: according to George Jacobs, Frank spent a good deal of time and energy trying to succor the forty-four-year-old Billie Holiday in her final illness.

Holiday, just eight months older than Sinatra, had been a success long before he was, recording through the mid- and late 1930s with Benny Goodman, Duke Ellington, Teddy Wilson, Count Basie, and Artie Shaw while Frank, still wet behind those protruding ears, was scrounging for singing gigs in Hoboken. As a very young man, he had gone frequently to hear her perform at small West Fifty-second Street clubs like the Onyx, and he'd been in love with the ragged texture of her voice and her incomparable laid-back phrasing, and in love, too, with Billie herself: her sultry, wounded, distant presence, both regal and ravaged. He learned from her, as from no other singer, the intertwined arts of phrasing and storytelling. As Frank told *Ebony* magazine in 1958, "With few exceptions, every major pop singer in the U.S. during her generation has been touched in some way by her genius. It is Billie Holiday who was, and still remains, the greatest single musical influence on me. Lady Day is unquestionably the most important influence on American popular singing in the last twenty years."

In July 1959, Holiday, a longtime narcotics addict, lay dying of cirrhosis of the liver and multiple organ failure in Harlem's Metropolitan Hospital. She was also in heroin withdrawal. She was not only mortally ill but also under arrest; the police had recently found a glassine envelope of the drug in her purse. Picketers with signs reading "Let Lady Live" marched outside the hospital. William Dufty, who was Holiday's close friend as well as the author of her autobiography, *Lady Sings the Blues* (Holiday bragged that she had never read it), told the singer's biographer Donald Clarke, "This was a horrifying outrage, arresting somebody in their hospital bed. But how to impress it on people's consciousness?" Dufty began putting together a petition to be sent to the office of Mayor Robert Wagner of New York. He recalled,

There was the problem then between Mayor Wagner and the police as to whether [addicts] should be thrown in jail or treated in hospitals. Dorothy Ross [a press agent] and I were calling people like Frank

Sinatra, Steve Allen, Basie, Ellington, Ella, Sidney Poitier. And nobody responded. Sinatra said, "Wagner hates my ass."

Jacobs tells a somewhat different story. According to the valet's vivid account, he and Frank visited a gaunt and wasted Lady Day in her hospital room, where three cops were stationed at the door. "A beautician was doing her hair and nails, and she was smoking outside her oxygen tent and begging the nurse to get her a beer," Jacobs recalled. She was thrilled to see Sinatra, who made happy talk about how he'd loved her latest album and how much she'd influenced his phrasing when he was starting out with Harry James. "I may have showed you how to bend a note, Frankie, that's all," Holiday said. Then she leaned over to him and whispered, so the police couldn't hear, "Will you cut the shit, baby, and get me some dope?"

Apparently, Sinatra, despite his hate of drugs, tried to get heroin for Holiday through legitimate channels, as a medical necessity. When that didn't work, Frank bought it himself from a dealer. But with the police outside Holiday's door, there was no way to get the drugs through. The singer's liver failed, and she went into a coma. She died on July 17.

Sinatra was disconsolate, and guilty. He holed up in his apartment, drinking, weeping, and playing her records over and over. Then, four days later, he brushed himself off and headed for Atlantic City.

————

Frank Sinatra first met Skinny D'Amato in the summer of 1939, when the boy singer performed with Harry James and his orchestra at the Steel Pier, a thousand-foot-long pleasure palace jutting out from the Boardwalk over the Atlantic surf. Skinny—Paul was his given name—was running a small gambling joint on Pacific Avenue at the time, but his importance in that wide-open city by the sea was large. He was a fixer, a genial man-about-town who knew every somebody that passed through and knew exactly what kind of fun they liked, too. Harry James was a pal, and James's new singer would soon become one, too.

Frank and Skinny hit it off from the start. Both were Italian Jersey boys, both disdained the police and other authority figures (Skinny had recently served time for pimping), both loved nightclubs, and the night. Seven years older than Sinatra, almost to the day, D'Amato was good-looking in a street kind of way—long face, prominent nose, spit curl—and possessed a kind of hood-elegant flash. He wore beautiful suits, French cuffs, silk ties, and custom shoes—all this at a time when Frank was not only poor but still fresh out of Hoboken.

Skinny also palled around with the important types who came from Phila-delphia to play, men like Marco Reginelli, the reputed head of the Mob in the City of Brotherly Love. Rumors persist to this day that D'Amato himself was mobbed up, or at the very least in business with organized crime—some say he was fronting for Reginelli—but the truth seems to be that while he liked and respected these men, he had been in jail once and didn't want to go back. He worked hard at keeping his dealings legitimate, and mostly managed. The young Frank Sinatra watched and admired Skinny's easy style and his way with these *uomini di rispetto*. Tommy Dorsey, for whom Sinatra would leave Harry James that fall, might have been Frank's most important early mentor, but Skinny came first.

In 1943, D'Amato and a rough-edged partner named Irvin Wolf bought the 500 Café, a yellow-brick-fronted building with a theater-style marquee on South Missouri Avenue, just a couple of blocks up from the Boardwalk. The Five, as everyone called it, was a nightclub with an off-the-books gambling casino in the back room, and under Skinny and Wolfie's guidance it became an Atlantic City institution. In 1946, for various legal reasons, its name was changed to the 500 Club.

In July of that same year, D'Amato and Wolf were about to fire a strug-gling twenty-year-old nightclub comic named Jerry Lewis—his act consisted

Skinny and Skinnier, circa late 1950s. In Paul "Skinny" D'Amato, who ran the legendary 500 Club in Atlantic City, Sinatra found some of the same traits that drew him to Dean Martin—an easy style and a certain way with the *uomini di rispetto*.

of making faces while he lip-synched to Enrico Caruso and Carmen Miranda records—when Lewis came up with a desperate save: he told the club's owners he could do a double with a handsome nightclub singer he'd met when they were both working at the Glass Hat in New York. The singer was Dean Martin.

Martin and Lewis exploded out of Atlantic City to national fame and quickly discovered that unlike the Five, most major nightclubs were owned behind the scenes by the Mob. This was certainly true of New York's Copacabana, where Frank Costello called the shots and where, on April 8, 1948, they opened for the first time. Skinny D'Amato brought Frank Sinatra to the Copa that night to show off his good pal and his sensational discoveries to each other; it was the first time Frank met Dean and Jerry. "Frank's career was just beginning to take a nosedive, and he had performed for the first time at the 500 Club the summer before," writes D'Amato's biographer Jonathan Van Meter. "His acquaintance with Skinny had turned a corner into something more intimate."

———

Sinatra's career might have been slumping, but Atlantic City, which had a large Italian-American population, loved him, and he loved A.C. The ocean air revivified him, reminding him of past glories. After the bad spring and summer of 1951—in May, Frank, under the aegis of Columbia's Mitch Miller, recorded "Mama Will Bark"; in August, after an especially nasty quarrel with Ava at Lake Tahoe, he had made a halfhearted suicide attempt, taking just enough sleeping pills to make himself sick and get her attention—Skinny D'Amato gave Sinatra a huge shot in the arm, booking him over Labor Day at the 500 Club, now one of the hottest joints in the country, and paying him at his top rate. "When Frank got to town, Skinny took him around to all his favorite joints, showed him off, and boosted his ego," Van Meter writes. "A couple of days before his first performance at the 500, Skinny went to a local jewelry store and bought Frank a gold watch. When he gave it to him, he said, 'Don't ever think you're down-and-out, pal. This is to remind you that when you come back you're going to be bigger than ever.' "

Once again, he was a smash hit. Every show—even the 4:00 a.m.—was mobbed.

And, while Frank was playing the Five, Skinny put in a call to Moe Dalitz—the Cleveland Mob boss who in 1950 had taken over the building and ownership of the Desert Inn when the front man Wilbur Clark ran out of money—and persuaded him to book Sinatra for five weeks at Las Vegas's newest and most luxurious hotel-casino. The DI was Frank's first Vegas stand

and, as a bonus, the place where he first met Bill Miller, who was to become his nearly lifelong pianist and musical secretary.

Once his comeback was solidified, Sinatra's loyalty to Skinny and the 500 Club was absolute. In the summer of 1956, when Frank was unhappily shooting *The Pride and the Passion* in Spain, he thought longingly of Atlantic City, sending D'Amato a telegram that simply read, "How about August 24, 25, 26, 27?" He signed the wire "El Dago." That summer, and for years thereafter, Skinny announced Sinatra's presence with a billboard that read, simply, "He's Here!" Once the stand was over, the message changed to "He Was Here!"

In 1959, when Frank had become the biggest thing in show business, he told Skinny he would do his nine nights gratis. The result was a nine-day mob scene. Sinatra, who returned as a conquering hero, flying in Red Norvo's quintet, Bill Miller, and a dozen Hollywood friends on a chartered plane, had to travel the streets of Atlantic City by police car. "Skinny often said, 'Many entertainers can fill up a room, but Frank filled up the town,'" writes Sinatra archivist Richard Apt. One night, the crowd on Missouri Avenue grew so frenzied that a police cruiser—accounts fail to mention whether or not it was the one Frank was riding in—was almost turned over.

The crowds jamming the club, sometimes for six shows a night, were no less passionate. Apt recalled being taken by his parents to the 500 that July to celebrate his tenth birthday. "The smoke bothered my eyes," he writes.

> Ventilation was a rumor in 1959. I consistently dipped my cloth napkin into my water glass, dabbing my eyes over and over. More than six hundred people were packed into the little saloon. Next to us were two nightclub owners from Boston. I remember them saying that it was their sixth night in a row and that they were getting tired of eating bad steak . . .
>
> Then Red Norvo said, ". . . now our boy singer," and out from the wings came Frank Sinatra. Somewhere in between "High Hopes" and "All the Way" he noticed me and leaned over to our ringside seats and gave me a couple of exaggerated winks. My mother later told me that I blushed quite deeply.

He had this effect on people. At one performance, Earl Wilson reported, Frank stamped out a cigarette butt onstage. "'Kick that cigarette butt over to me and I'll give you $20,' a woman fan of supposedly mature years called over to the bandleader—who complied. She took it away as a souvenir."

In his dressing room backstage, Sinatra, like a lord of the manor, wore a smoking jacket with an emblem depicting a bottle of Jack Daniel's on the breast pocket and the initials JD embroidered underneath. And in his hotel, the Claridge, where he and his entourage were occupying the entire first floor— Frank's fear of heights getting the better of him and anyone who wanted an ocean view—he threw a notable, and notably protracted, party, during which, according to FBI files, Hollywood mixed with organized crime. In 1960, an agent filed a report, titled "Samuel M. Giancana," in which an informant "advised on September 16, 1959, that [Giancana] had recently been to the Claridge Hotel in Atlantic City, New Jersey, in order to see Frank Sinatra . . . The informant stated when they [*sic*] got off the elevator on the first floor they were approached by two 'tough looking men' and asked for identification and the purpose of their visit. The informant stated one individual in Sinatra's suite at this hotel was identified to him as Joseph Fischetti, described as the 'well known hoodlum from Miami.'"

In another report, from 1962, an FBI agent had interviewed a showgirl whose name was redacted from the file. "She stated that at the age of approximately eighteen she became employed as a professional dancer, appearing in chorus lines at various hotels, night clubs and casinos around the country," the report read.

> She became acquainted with Frank Sinatra during approximately 1958. During this period she traveled throughout the country and worked for some time at the Tropicana and Riviera Hotels in Las Vegas.
>
> In July 1959, she attended a party given by Frank Sinatra in Atlantic City, New Jersey, at the Claridge Hotel. Sinatra at that time was appearing at the 500 Club as the featured entertainer. The party referred to lasted approximately two weeks and normally started at about 8:00 P.M. and lasted until about 4:00 or 5:00 A.M. the following morning . . . She mentioned other persons in attendance at this affair, in addition to the ones mentioned above, as actress Natalie Wood, actor Robert Wagner, then the husband of Natalie Wood, Rocco Fischetti, his brother, Joseph Fischetti, John Foreman (true name John Formosa) and Paul "Skinny" D'Amato.

Another FBI report claimed that Joseph Bonanno was also present at the party, making it a Mafia mini-summit of sorts. Not to mention a party that might have challenged the imaginations of Visconti, Kubrick, and Scorsese.

In early August, Frank went to work on the film he had agreed to do for 20th Century Fox in return for having walked off *Carousel* in August 1955—except that after four years he had become so powerful that instead of repaying the studio for his dereliction (he'd taken a fee of $150,000 for the Rodgers and Hammerstein musical), he could now dictate far more lucrative terms: for the new picture, the musical *Can-Can,* he would receive a fee of $200,000 plus a huge 25 percent of the picture's gross profits (as opposed to the net, which Hollywood accountants could always make vanish). A neat trick, and one that only the Frank Sinatra of 1959 could pull off.

An adaptation of *Can-Can,* the hit Broadway musical with songs by Cole Porter and book by Abe Burrows, seemed like a good idea at the time. Though there was ample evidence by the late 1950s that movie musicals were a dying genre, 1958's *Gigi*—with an Alan Jay Lerner and Frederick Loewe score and direction by Vincente Minnelli, just before he made *Some Came Running*—had been a monster hit, winning Academy Awards in all nine categories for which it was nominated and generating huge box-office profits for MGM. The folks at 20th Century Fox had high hopes that another musical set in fin de siècle Paris, not to mention one starring Sinatra, with a score by the great Porter and arrangements by Nelson Riddle, could make lightning strike a second time. As insurance, the studio borrowed two of *Gigi*'s French stars, Maurice Chevalier and Louis Jourdan.

Unfortunately, Fox had the merely competent Walter Lang (*The King and I*) as director, rather than the great (with musicals) Minnelli. But what made matters even worse was the degree of control Frank exerted over the project. As we've seen, he was a far better movie actor when under the guidance of a strong director; when he had a strong director and something to prove, as was the case with *From Here to Eternity* and *The Man with the Golden Arm,* magic could occur.

Yet by 1959, he had gathered a degree of virtually unchecked power never seen before in show business. As *Can-Can*'s co-producer (under yet another pseudo-British company name, Suffolk), star, and eight-hundred-pound gorilla, he had a whip hand over the project, and one of his first demands was that Fox hire Shirley MacLaine as his co-star, even though she was under contract to Columbia to make another film, and an expensive buyout was required to dislodge her.

The buyout wasn't the bad part. The bad part was that MacLaine, with her wide-open American features, broad comedic acting, and disinclination to feign the slightest hint of a French accent, would wind up looking glaringly miscast as the proprietress of a racy Parisian dance hall. But Sinatra's portrayal of the Paris attorney François Durnais would go beyond miscasting. Feeling— not without justification—that what movie audiences really wanted in a Frank Sinatra musical was Frank Sinatra, he made not the slightest attempt to subsume himself into the role. Like MacLaine (and no doubt stung by the bad experience of *The Pride and the Passion,* in which his Spanish accent and his luxuriant wig had vied for awfulness), he spoke Americanese—except that more disconcertingly, in Frank's case, it was Hobokenese. His entire presentation was unapologetically Sinatra-esque. In a crucial court scene, "defense attorney François arrives in court sporting a rakishly tilted Cavanaugh [*sic*] hat," Tom Santopietro writes.

> It has absolutely nothing to do with the wardrobe of a Parisian lawyer in 1890, and the disconnect is made worse when a very French prison guard interacts with the very American Sinatra and MacLaine. Sinatra is not even trying; his performance is all thumbs in his waistcoat, as if he prepared for playing a lawyer by looking at political cartoons. The slipshod work is a very long way from the meticulous preparation found in *From Here to Eternity* and *The Man with the Golden Arm.*

Still more egregiously, Frank, who in asserting his artistic prerogative as a singer was wont to alter the lyrics of even the greats, slips a coy "ring-a-ding-ding-ding" into the coda of Cole Porter's "C'est Magnifique" and, with five short syllables, lays waste to the audience's willing suspension of disbelief. Porter wasn't present on the shoot—though one can imagine the smoke coming out of his ears when he heard the line—and the director, Lang, might have simply lacked the courage to correct Sinatra's supremely presumptuous ad-lib. "Alas, this one phrase instantly yanks the viewer out of Paris and back to Las Vegas," Santopietro writes.

> It may just be one ring-a-ding-ding, but it is a significant moment in Sinatra's film career, because after appearing in forty films, it's the first time Frank doesn't bother to try . . . He is, in effect, saying, "Hey, I'm Frank Sinatra—I'll coast along here on my charm . . ." Such an attitude can be charming in a nightclub, but on film it's disconcerting at best, and deadly at worst.

She looked like an optical illusion walking across the 20th Century Fox back lot: five feet eleven, voluptuous, and red-haired, with legs that went on forever—thirty-nine inches, to be exact. "Everywhere she goes on the lot, jaded studio personnel stop cold in their tracks to ogle the leggy newcomer," UPI's Hollywood correspondent Vernon Scott wrote in early July. "The brass is convinced 22-year-old Juliet Prowse will be the biggest star developed at the studio in many a year."

The choreographer Hermes Pan had discovered the South African dancer in Europe and persuaded Fox to sign her to a seven-year contract and a co-starring role in *Can-Can*. Frank took notice. Immediately.

Her face and body alone would have stopped him in his tracks. But she was a terrific dancer, she could act and sing, and with that odd accent—kind of British, kind of not—she had a presence about her. Though she was very young, she was thoughtful and a little serious. Kept her own counsel. "Naturally, I hope to become a star," she'd told Vernon Scott. "It's something I've always wanted. But I'm not counting on it. Too many people come to this town with high hopes only to see them dashed out. I am not going to build myself up to a letdown."

She was flattered—very flattered—at Sinatra's instant focus on her, the mesmerizing pinion of those blue, blue eyes. He was the biggest star in the world! She had a pile of his records back home in Johannesburg: she listened to them, but quietly. She didn't squeal like the silly teenagers she'd heard about.

He liked her reserve. So she didn't have round heels like every other starlet in town; he liked the challenge. Not to mention her height: she towered over him. And that accent—the whole package was classy.

Frank with Juliet Prowse at the SHARE Boomtown benefit. The South African actress-dancer was strong-minded and independent—a little too much so for Sinatra's liking.

He began to take her places, giving her his entire attention. Though unsurprisingly, their conversations always came back to him.

———

On August 27, Frank had recorded for the first time in over three months—but at 20th Century Fox, not the detested Capitol. This was a soundtrack session, with Nelson, for *Can-Can*, the resulting songs to be dubbed into the film afterward; on set, he would lip-synch to a playback—right down to that "ring-a-ding-ding-ding" on "C'est Magnifique." And while his heart wasn't quite in that song—the lyric was artificially gay; the thrown-in French words seemed to make him self-conscious—he gave an exquisitely tender reading of Porter's great "It's All Right with Me," which Frank's character François Durnais sings to Prowse's character, the dancer Claudine.

On the Fox soundstage, of course, Sinatra was just acting with sad eyes while moving his lips (and if the truth be told, not doing the greatest job at the latter; though perhaps the stage business of singing while taking a puff of the cigarette that Prowse lit for him in between syllables was too much even for him); in the recording studio, though, he was summoning something meaningful and doing it magnificently:

> *There's someone I'm trying so hard to forget,*
> *Don't you want to forget someone, too?*

Her memory was always right there, on tap whenever he needed it.

———

After completing *On the Beach,* Ava drifted through the summer of 1959. "No plan, no itinerary," Lee Server writes. "She would stay somewhere for days or weeks. One morning she would head for the airport again. She went to San Francisco, Palm Springs, Florida, and Haiti." And Cuba.

In Havana, she had an audience with the newly triumphant Fidel Castro, whom she found unexpectedly tall and very magnetic. She asked him if it was true he hated all Americans. Only Richard Nixon, Castro told her. Apparently, he said it with a smile, because the leader's beautiful nineteen-year-old translator-mistress, Ilona Marita Lorenz, quickly came to feel something was going on between the "middle-aged woman" and Fidel. "The two rivals at last came face to face in the lobby of the Hilton, and it was an ugly scene," Server writes.

> Ava was staggeringly drunk, said Marita, and called the girl "a little
> bitch" for hiding Fidel from her. Ava followed her into the elevator and

then, said Marita, slapped her hard in the face. A Castro bodyguard named Captain Pupo, also in the elevator, drew his pistol from its holster and told everybody to cool it.

From there, the Ava Show headed for points north. "Movie actress Ava Gardner made a brief stopover at Miami International Airport Wednesday night en route to New York," a wire-service item of September 17 noted.

> It required 45 minutes for custom agents to process the 36-year-old former wife of Frank Sinatra, a maid, secretary, two small caged dogs, 19 pieces of luggage, a hi-fi set and a hand-carved bongo drum.
>
> Miss Gardner told newsmen she was going to New York for talks about a new motion picture, "A Fair Bride."

The project, like a number of others Ava discussed during that period, came to naught.

While she was in Manhattan, Frank lent her his two-bedroom pied-à-terre in the Hampshire House on Central Park South. It was an astonishing time for jazz in New York—giants like John Coltrane, Miles Davis, and Thelonious Monk were not only making great albums but playing in clubs where you could go and see them up close—and Ava loved jazz. But as great as they were, Trane and Monk possessed no sexual charge; Miles, with his high cheekbones, satiny skin, and piercing malevolent eyes, was right up her street. And at that moment, Davis, who was the hottest thing around (his masterpiece LP *Kind of Blue* had just come out in August), was playing at Birdland, at Broadway and Fifty-Second. She went to see him. Often. "Pee Wee Marquette, the famous midget emcee, who was the mascot at Birdland, was introducing Ava Gardner from the bandstand every night, and she was throwing kisses and coming backstage and kissing me back there," Davis wrote in his autobiography. Ava, he wrote,

> was a stunningly beautiful woman, dark and sensuous with a beautiful full mouth that was soft as a motherfucker. Man, she was a hot number . . . We didn't get down or nothing like that. She was a nice person, though, real nice, and if I would have wanted to we could have had a thing. I just don't know why it didn't happen, but it didn't, even though a lot of people swear that it did.

Castro, Miles . . . She could keep up with Frank and his gangsters any day of the week.

On the third Saturday in September, an astonishing spectacle took place at 20th Century Fox's elegant commissary, the Café de Paris: Nikita Khrushchev, the premier of the Soviet Union and the face of world Communism, the man who had said of the capitalist West, "We will bury you," sat down to lunch with the cream of Hollywood: four hundred movie executives and stars, including Frank Sinatra, Cary Grant, Marilyn Monroe, Gary Cooper, Elizabeth Taylor, Kirk Douglas, Kim Novak, Gregory Peck, Dean Martin, Shirley MacLaine, Sammy Davis Jr., Eddie Fisher, Tony Curtis, Janet Leigh, Judy Garland, Nat King Cole, Edward G. Robinson, Shelley Winters, Rita Hayworth, and Zsa Zsa Gabor.

Terror of Communism had been woven into the fabric of Hollywood since 1947, when the House Committee on Un-American Activities began its investigation of the movie industry. The blacklist was still going strong in 1959. But one thing Hollywood respected was star power, and that fall Nikita Khrushchev was a star. His impromptu debate with Vice President Richard Nixon in a model kitchen at the American National Exhibition in Moscow that summer had led the Eisenhower administration to invite the Soviet premier to visit the United States; Los Angeles was the second stop on a thirteen-day tour that quickly became a media circus.

An invitation to the Fox luncheon had been the hottest ticket in Hollywood, which was infected with what the *New York Times* correspondent Murray Schumach called "Khrushchev fever." "The ownership of a mansion at Bel Air, of impressionist paintings, or of a Rolls Royce or membership in an exclusive club could not console a producer who did not receive a telegram permitting him to sit in the Fox commissary with the Soviet Premier to eat shrimp, squab chicken and cantaloupe," Schumach wrote. So select was the list of invitees that spouses of stars and talent agents were excluded.

Still, not everyone jumped at the chance to attend. Bing Crosby, Adolphe Menjou, Ronald Reagan, and Ward Bond all declined on political grounds. "I believe that to sit socially and break bread with someone denotes friendship," Reagan said, "and I certainly feel no friendship for Mr. Khrushchev."

Khrushchev sat at the head table, along with 20th Century Fox's president, Spyros Skouras, and the U.S. ambassador to the United Nations, Henry Cabot Lodge. At an adjacent table, the tiny, potato-faced Mrs. Khrushchev sat sandwiched between Bob Hope and Frank Sinatra, seeming overwhelmed by the entire experience—though not by Hope or Sinatra, whom she didn't appear to recognize.

The luncheon quickly turned into a kind of Kitchen Debate redux— perhaps an inevitability given the combative natures of the keynote speakers: the short, stocky sixty-six-year-old Skouras, who held forth in a thick Greek accent on his own up-by-the-bootstraps story and the virtues of capitalism, and the short, stocky sixty-five-year-old Khrushchev, who at first managed to charm and amuse the show-business crowd by throwing a few zingers at the Fox president but then gave a forty-five-minute speech, committing what the Associated Press called "the unpardonable sin to show business: staying on too long."

In the end, it turned out that the premier was furious at being denied the chance to see Disneyland.

"What do you have, rocket launching pads there?" Khrushchev said, as his personal interpreter, Viktor Sukhodrev, translated. "And just listen to what reason I was told, 'We cannot guarantee your security if you go there.' What is there, an epidemic of cholera there, or have gangsters taken hold of the place that can destroy me? Your policemen are so tough they can lift a bull by the horn. Surely they can restore order if there are any gangsters around."

The assembled luminaries cleared their throats. A star the premier might have been, but in Hollywood a star without charm might as well have been an extraterrestrial.

After the meal, on a Fox soundstage, the premier and his wife watched as Frank—who, it would have now been clear to them if it hadn't been before, was the star of stars on hand—emceed a live presentation of musical highlights from *Can-Can*. Sinatra grinned suavely as he announced that the first number would be a song done by Louis Jourdan and Maurice Chevalier. "It is called 'Live and Let Live,'" Frank said, "and I think it is a marvelous idea." The scene in which the song occurred, he told the Russians, was in "a movie about a lot of pretty girls and the fellows who like pretty girls."

As the translator spoke into his ear, Khrushchev's mood seemed to soften. The premier grinned and applauded.

After Sinatra sang "C'est Magnifique," he said he was turning the show over to the dancing girls, calling them "my nieces." Shirley MacLaine, Juliet Prowse, and a dozen cancan girls exploded onto the stage and, shrieking and whirling their voluminous skirts to reveal pantaletted haunches, performed the dance number that had titillated and scandalized the world at the turn of the century.

After it was over, Mr. Khrushchev affably posed for pictures with the cast. When a reporter asked him what he thought of the cancan, he replied, impenetrably, that this dance was obviously just for this picture and that he was not an expert on nightclubs.

By the time he formulated his official response, however, the grin had vanished from Khrushchev's face. The cancan number was "lascivious, disgusting and immoral," he declared. "The face of humanity is prettier than its backside."

The Soviet premier's critique would generate a huge advance ticket sale before *Can-Can* was released the following spring, with *Newsweek* commenting that "being condemned by Khrushchev may be an even bigger commercial asset than being banned in Boston." But the reviews would prove poor, and ticket sales would drop off quickly. Frank's impetuous "ring-a-ding-ding-ding," though, was soon to find its true home.

———

Without anything too demanding on his plate—by day he was traipsing through *Can-Can;* by night he was gazing into Juliet Prowse's eyes—Sinatra did a lot of TV that fall. At the end of September, he was a guest, along with Louis Armstrong and Peggy Lee, on Bing Crosby's Oldsmobile show on ABC: it was superbly assured, late-1950s, black-and-white musical television, with all four stars in fine voice and apparently high spirits. Frank did three numbers, including a beautiful "Willow Weep for Me," and duetted charmingly with Bing on Irving Berlin's "I Love a Piano," backed by the keyboardists Joe Bushkin, George Shearing, and Paul Smith.

At the end of the hour, Sinatra and Crosby, in dueling toupees, parked themselves on clear Lucite chairs ("Pull up a glass and sit down," Bing told Frank) for an odd, apparently impromptu conversation. The two then proceeded to have a winking tête-à-tête, mostly about their mutual weekend retreat, Palm Springs. The banter seemed to charm some viewers and annoy others. "Their colloquy may have relied too much on special, coterie humor," wrote the syndicated critic Harriet Van Horne.

> But it was racy, vivid, real talk. It does no harm to learn of some of
> the odd folkways in Palm Springs ("The house dick rides around on a
> burro," said Sinatra of a certain motel) but most of all, it was a joy to
> hear TV talk that did not sound "scripted" by six gag writers.

UPI's Fred Danzig was rubbed the wrong way. "Of course, a meeting of Bing and Frank also serves to advise us of the latest 'in' conversational devices," he wrote. "Unfortunately, their chit-chat Tuesday night produced no new fetishes, only a sordid plug for a chain of health clubs and poorly-timed Sinatra-isms about motel living. The lad does seem to be enjoying his bachelor status."

A couple of weeks later, *The Frank Sinatra Timex Show* aired, the first of the four hour-long musical specials Frank had vouchsafed ABC after the collapse of his weekly series the year before. The October 19, 1959, broadcast, co-starring Bing Crosby and Dean Martin and featuring an aggressively perky Mitzi Gaynor (Jimmy Durante also showed up for a surprise cameo at the end), was everything the series hadn't been—tight, energetic, funny, and exciting. It seemed to help greatly that the network had hired a dynamic thirty-six-year-old director-producer named Bill Colleran, who had proven himself on Crosby's ABC series. Frank also brought in talent of his own: not only was Nelson Riddle back to arrange and conduct, but Sammy Cahn and Jimmy Van Heusen executive produced—which meant, of necessity, a lot of sprightly special lyrics.

The reviews were ecstatic, if slightly hedged. "One of the brightest and most thoroughly enjoyable special programs television has produced this season," the Associated Press's Cynthia Lowry wrote. "The singing was handled effectively by the three eminent baritones, all of whom kept 'inside' jokes to a minimum and stuck to amusing, nonribald remarks." UPI's Danzig struck a similar note. "Fortunately, the trio managed to avoid embarrassing, or ultra-inside ad libs," he wrote. "Working in front of proper, dignified and sedate sets, [they] frolicked in a carefully carefree fashion and displayed huge quantities of personal magnetism. These three men can entertain just by snapping their fingers."

"Carefully carefree": an interesting concept. But then, carefulness was a quality much prized in 1950s America—and one that reviewers had missed on Sinatra's ABC series, where Frank often seemed underprepared and overfond of the kind of ring-a-ding-ding humor that grated on the sensibilities of Middle America. This time around, just for the moment, Sinatra seemed committed to behaving himself. It undoubtedly helped him to be working with his pals and personal hit makers Cahn and Van Heusen, two expert courtiers who knew how to twit but never defy him.

But first old demons had to be exorcised. The show began with Bing, Mitzi, and Dean singing a parody of "High Hopes" that referenced Frank's notorious unreliability when it came to television work and struck Sammy's familiar note of respectful weariness when it came to all matters Sinatra. (The old Spanish proverb "With the rich and mighty, always a little patience" could have been inscribed on the lyricist's coat of arms—along with an addendum: "and a lot of deference.")

When you're working with You Know Who,
You show up and so does the crew . . .

You Know Who finally showed up as the second chorus began, standing with his back to the camera, beckoning the trio with an imperious finger. Then he turned, looked at the audience, and barked, "Who are all these people, and what do they want here?"

Cut to a close-up of Frank's face as he sang,

I just dropped by to have a chat
Nothing more than that
Call me devil-may-care.

And with that, looking like the essence of devil-may-care—tanned, handsome, and endlessly, shamelessly pleased with himself—he gave a boyish fake laugh: hah-*hah*!

To which wise old Bing responded, "Oh, you're a colorful gypsy."

———

Two weeks later, the TV roundelay continued, as Frank and Mickey Rooney joined Dean on his NBC hour, *Ford Startime*—prompting UPI's Danzig to crack, "Gee. Dean is the only one on-stage who hasn't married Ava Gardner."

Sinatra and Martin had officially become a team. It was just an act—they weren't teaming up on the golf course or in after-hours high jinks—but the act took an instant and powerful hold on America, or at least that part of America that paid attention to star behavior, which was much of America. The Associated Press's Lowry dubbed the two the Rover Boys. "If the boys keep up their busy schedule of visiting around on musical specials we will await their appearances with the same keen anticipation we accord the fastest gun in the West," she wrote. (It was also an era in which television Westerns were enormously popular.) "The two singing stars acquitted themselves professionally when they were singing old songs, but the show sagged mournfully in the gay banter department. It was a ragged show."

She neglected to mention Dean's drunk act.

Danzig didn't. He observed that "some disciplinary problems were evident" on the show, which "wasn't one minute old before reference was made to Martin's tippling. Such things, strangely enough, didn't happen the last time Martin and Sinatra were seen on the TV tube together."

The disciplinary problems, the drunk act—the whole thing was a dress rehearsal for what was soon to come.

———

John F. Kennedy at least got to visit Disneyland. At the end of October, the front-runner for the Democratic presidential nomination traveled to California to gather support in a key state whose enormously popular governor, Edmund "Pat" Brown, stood squarely in his way. Brown, who seemed a shoo-in as a favorite-son candidate, had already served notice to the young upstart that he would get short shrift if he entered the state's winner-take-all primary in June.

Kennedy was out to prove Brown wrong. Over two days, he made a lightning-like north-to-south swing through Oakland, Fresno, Bakersfield, Santa Barbara, Santa Maria, San Diego, and Riverside, drawing big crowds that "grew visibly warmer as he spoke," according to Relman Morin, the Associated Press's Pulitzer Prize–winning reporter. Stopping by Walt Disney's four-year-old fantasy park, Kennedy smiled for photo ops next to Snow White and the Mad Hatter, then stepped into a helicopter that wafted him to Los Angeles. There he met with representatives of minority groups and labor leaders and gave talks at UCLA and USC, where his receptions "were little short of spectacular," Morin wrote.

> At UCLA, 1,900 people filled every seat of the auditorium. Hundreds milled around outside. When he emerged, a student called out, "Come back again and speak to the 1,000 who couldn't get in."
>
> Without advance publicity from the campus newspaper, and speaking in the afternoon well after classroom hours, Kennedy filled almost as big an auditorium at U.S.C. "I'm still a Republican," a pretty co-ed told him, "but I think you're marvelous."

On Monday, November 2, he spoke at the Jefferson Jackson Day dinner at the Beverly Hilton. Governor Brown, who attended the fund-raiser, was the event's honorary chairman.

Kennedy gave a tough, stirring speech that night, charging that the love of luxury was undermining America. "The harsh facts of the matter," he told the $100-a-plate audience, "are that as a nation we face a hard, tough course ahead for perhaps a generation or more but also, as a nation, the harsh facts of the matter are that we have gone soft—physically, mentally and spiritually soft."

He cited breakdowns in self-discipline among U.S. troops taken prisoner in the Korean War, as well as alarming rates of desertion among American forces. "What has happened to us as a nation?" Kennedy asked. "Profits are up, our standard of living is up, but so is our crime rate. So is the rate of divorce and juvenile delinquency and mental illness. So are the sales of tranquilizers and the number of children dropping out of school."

The words on the page don't do the man justice: Jack Kennedy was simply a spellbinding speaker, with an impact on listeners not dissimilar to Sinatra's when he sang. That star quality had been there since the beginning of his political career: in 1946, during Kennedy's first congressional campaign, girls at a Boston high-school appearance gathered around him chanting, "Sinatra! Sinatra!"

Relman Morin, who attended the UCLA and USC speeches and the Jefferson Jackson dinner, wrote afterward that he had discovered two things:

1. **Women get starry eyed** over the boyish-looking Bostonian. They either sat looking mesmerized as he spoke or murmured, "terrific . . . cute . . . wonderful."
2. **His youthful appearance** may be his greatest handicap. "He looks awfully young . . . is he really 42?" people commented.

Two nights before the youthful candidate decried America's loss of Pilgrim spirit and Spartan devotion, he attended a glittering party for Mr. and Mrs. Henry Ford II at the Bel Air home of Merle Oberon and her husband, the Italian industrialist Bruno Pagliai. Hedda Hopper was present. Among the other guests was Mrs. Alfred Bloomingdale, "in a divine Sophie gown highlighted by a new diamond necklace," Hopper wrote. "Joan Cohn in a Fontana gown, so was Merle . . . Frank Sinatra in a gay mood, everybody was. Sen. John Kennedy arrived at midnight, two of his sisters beat him there by three hours."

As he always did while in Los Angeles, Jack Kennedy stayed at the beachfront house of his sister and brother-in-law Pat and Peter Lawford in Santa Monica. And as always, he meant to enjoy himself while he was in town, in ways that had nothing to do with the Pilgrims or the Spartans. One night—by process of deduction, probably Sunday, November 1—Frank Sinatra, whom Kennedy had found to be a reliable guide to such pleasures, took the candidate to dinner at Puccini, the Beverly Hills restaurant that Frank co-owned with Peter Lawford.

We have an account of the evening from Nick Sevano, Frank's old Hoboken homeboy and former gofer, who claimed to have been present. We must parse Sevano's words with care. During the late 1940s, he served as a traveling pal and valet to Sinatra until Frank had one too many tantrums about overstarched shirts and misplaced cuff links. A few years later, Sinatra apparently hired Sevano back to work alongside Hank Sanicola in a semi-managerial position, but it's important to realize that Frank had many hangers-on, titled and untitled, at all times and that details grow vague in the case of people who were tangentially associated with him and subsequently traded on the association. What we do know is that in the late 1950s, Sevano worked as an agent, then manager, for Nelson Riddle. Eventually, he would fulfill some of the same functions for Glen Campbell. Having been around Frank Sinatra got Nick Sevano far in Hollywood.

Sevano claimed to Sinatra biographer Anthony Summers that he had accompanied Frank and Jack Kennedy to Puccini on that early-November night. He asserted "that Kennedy and Frank took a great interest in two women seated at another table—the actress Angie Dickinson and a dark-haired beauty named Judith Campbell. 'Frank sent a note to me saying "Bring the broads over,'" Sevano said."

Dickinson and Sinatra had first met six years earlier, when Frank was doing a guest spot on *The Colgate Comedy Hour*. During a commercial for the sponsor, Halo shampoo, he warbled the jingle "Halo Everybody Halo," while the gorgeous twenty-two-year-old beauty-pageant winner from North Dakota smiled and showed off her silky tresses for the camera. Later, she and Frank— and then she and Frank and Jimmy Van Heusen—struck up a conversation backstage. Angeline Brown Dickinson was very young and, as she remembered vividly many years later, "bursting with awe" at being in Sinatra's presence. She had a humorous, easygoing way about her that he liked a lot. She was witty but not caustic; she knew how to talk, but she knew how to listen, too. It turned out she was married in an informal sort of way, yet she was also an extremely practical girl, and her sights were set firmly on Hollywood. Chester asked her for her number—for Frank, of course—and of course she gave it to him.

Angie Dickinson could easily have gone the way of so many beautiful girls who made the hopeful journey from the provinces to Hollywood. Instead, she steadfastly built an acting career, mostly on television for the first few years, bootstrapping her way up from credits like Party Guest and Cigarette Girl to featured roles—often, because of her rawboned prairie features, cast in Westerns. She also built a unique, triangular relationship with Frank Sinatra and Jimmy Van Heusen. In an arrangement that remains striking to this day, both singer and songwriter seem to have been able to maintain their interest in Dickinson, and she hers in both of them, without anybody's getting hurt. "They both loved women; that was something very much in common," she said. "And yet, never in competition. I saw both of them alternately. I mean, I just adored them both. When Jimmy asked me out, it was a natural. You don't have to plan to marry somebody to go out. Sometimes I'd say, 'Yes, I'm free, Jimmy,' and then, 'No, I'm not.' Whatever. I was very, very happy with either one, whomever I was with."

Judith Campbell—born Judith Eileen Katherine Immoor in 1934, and later to become infamous as Judith Campbell Exner—is a massively controversial figure. The light of truth bends around her presence in any historical narrative, because of the gravity of her known associations—with Frank Sinatra, Sam Giancana, and John F. Kennedy. And also, it appears, with Joseph P. Kennedy. In his memoir, George Jacobs bluntly maintains that Campbell was "a major player"—a prostitute, in plain English—and claims that the elder Kennedy patronized her, gratis, courtesy of Sinatra, more than once in Palm Springs.

One would scarcely have picked her for whoredom. Judith Immoor grew up in a strict and well-to-do Catholic household in Pacific Palisades—her father was a successful architect—and she carried a quality of girl-next-door innocence into young womanhood, when she blossomed into a beauty. Remarkably, though she lived so close to Hollywood, she showed no interest in modeling or acting. Her older sister, Jacqueline, was the star of the family, a promising actress with a contract at Paramount.

In 1952, against her parents' wishes, Judith married an up-and-coming young movie actor named William Campbell. She was eighteen. As the wife of a contract player, she began to attend premieres and parties and to be noticed. "I'd say she was in the Elizabeth Taylor category," the reporter James Bacon, who covered Hollywood for the Associated Press, told Seymour Hersh. "She was a gorgeous, gorgeous girl." By the time she was twenty-four, her young marriage had soured, and she and Campbell had divorced.

"For the first time in my life," she wrote in her memoir, "I began dating the way most girls date when they're in high school." But she was also on her own in a tough company town. Could she have somehow wandered, through financial need or perverse interest, into prostitution? We are in the shadow world: precise map coordinates and passenger manifests are unavailable. Nick Sevano's Puccini story chimes precisely with Peggy Connelly's Villa Capri tale of a few years earlier: two attractive young women out on the town, one of them more than eager to meet Sinatra. A very interested Frank sends an intermediary to their table. It doubtless happened dozens of times. Many young

Judith Campbell. Her dark beauty and air of girl-next-door innocence beguiled Frank Sinatra, Sam Giancana, and John F. Kennedy and led to the split between Frank and JFK.

women were extremely eager to meet Frank Sinatra, and both Betsy Hammes and Gloria Franks, who spent considerable time in Campbell's presence in Los Angeles and Las Vegas in the late 1950s, observed that she seemed particularly determined to get close to him.

"I just was aware of her being around quite a bit," Franks recalled. "It was almost like somebody hanging around behind a pole, waiting around to be called to the table or go off with somebody."

Did Campbell seem like a prostitute to her?

"Growing up the way I grew up, as a young lady from a proper background, and being around Las Vegas with all those terribly weird people and all these people who seemed a little dangerous, [I thought] she seemed like somebody that was part of that ilk," Franks said.

On the other hand, it was a different era. Hammes, who earned a solid living as a nightclub singer, recalled, "I was working at the El Mirador Hotel in Palm Springs, and a friend of mine, a guy who owned a racehorse, said he wanted to give a party for around a hundred people. He asked me to arrange it, and I said, 'Great, I'll do it.' He gave me $5,000 and a gold watch! I never even kissed him on the cheek. Guys were throwing money around a lot in those days."

Especially Sinatra.

Who exactly was present on that November night at Puccini? Since Angie Dickinson has kept her counsel about most of the particulars of her relationship with Sinatra and has stayed entirely mum about her connection to JFK, we have only two unreliable narrators to attest to the particulars of this crucial evening. Sevano may be exaggerating his role; Judith Campbell Exner may be diminishing hers. In her highly selective and frequently ambiguous 1977 memoir, she leaves Kennedy entirely out of the anecdote, making it instead all about Frank. "The first indication I had that Frank Sinatra was interested in meeting me was when Nick Sevano approached me one night while I was having dinner with friends at Puccini's [*sic*]," she writes.

> Nick said, "I really would like you to meet Frank."
> I said, "Thanks, but I've met Frank at parties."
> Nick laughed. "You know what I mean. Would you like to go out with him?"
> "Yes," I said, without hesitation. "I'd like to go out with him."

Given Jacobs's testimony, "parties" can't help but have a loaded sound. And apparently Sevano's functions weren't just managerial. By his account, he then took Campbell and Dickinson to Sinatra's table. "I brought them over, and we wound up at Frank's house until three in the morning, watching movies. [The girls] didn't stay there—just watched the movies."

Come to think of it, "movies" has a loaded sound to it, too.

Between the night of Monday, November 2, and the night of Thursday, November 5, when he took his campaign to Oregon, John F. Kennedy—who had been stirring up crowds wherever he went in California, who had had reporters and fellow politicians hanging on his every dynamic word ("He had a big success," even Pat Brown had been forced to admit; "I admire him very much")—went off the radar screen. The press, even the gossip columnists, who saw him as a star among stars, seemed to lose track of him entirely. On November 3, the Associated Press reported, the Republican front-runner, Richard Nixon, took a "folksy stroll around Beverly Hills . . . and discussed sports with construction workers, visited a brokerage office, kibitzed with a lady supporter, joshed a waitress and ate a hamburger." Kennedy was nowhere in sight.

Frank Sinatra, too, seems to have gone missing. *Can-Can* had just wrapped, and he had a few weeks off before his late-November opening at the Sands. In the first week of the month, news tidbits and gossip items about him, usually abundant, dribbled down to next to nothing. His faithful shadows Louella and Hedda were mum. In New York, Dorothy Kilgallen could find nothing to tut-tut about. All Earl Wilson could manage was a paragraph about the nightclub act of a Sinatra look-alike named Duke Hazlett.

Frank was busy, but what he was busy with was nobody's business. His new best friend in show business might have been Dean Martin, but in real life—or what passed for real life in Frank Sinatra's strange orbit—he was head over heels for John Fitzgerald Kennedy, whom he hosted at his desert home for a lively, but thoroughly clandestine, couple of days that week.

JFK's pal and campaign aide Dave Powers gave Kitty Kelley a brief but rhapsodic account of the sojourn. "We stayed with Frank in Palm Springs one night in November 1959 after a big fund-raiser in Los Angeles," Powers said. "You could tell when Sinatra got up in the morning because suddenly music filled the house, even the bathrooms. Frank was a terrific host and we had a great time. When we left, he gave me, not Jack, a box of jewelry to give my wife to make amends for keeping us the two extra days."

The extra time away was probably not all Powers would have wanted to make amends for. An FBI memo of March 29, 1960, reads, in part,

The Los Angeles Office, by letter dated 3/22/60, advised that a criminal informant indicated that the editors of Confidential Magazine have had a reporter in the Los Angeles area during the past few days for the purpose of checking into a rumor regarding an alleged indiscreet party recently held at Palm Springs in which participants were said to be Senator John Kennedy, his brother-in-law Peter Lawford, the actor, and Frank Sinatra. The informant said that the last time Senator Kennedy was in California for a visit he stayed in Sinatra's home in Palm Springs.

The indiscreet party can only be imagined. And we will remember, in passing, that Jack Kennedy was an avid reader of *Confidential*.

More than a year later, Frank would have a gold plaque put on the door of the bedroom in which JFK stayed. The plaque read, "John F. Kennedy slept here November 6 and 7, 1960." The dates were wrong: on November 6 and 7, 1960, Kennedy was in Hyannis Port, Massachusetts, with his pregnant wife, the rest of his family, and his campaign staff, preparing for Election Day on November 8. Kennedy would return to the West Coast several times during his campaign, but there was only one November when he stayed in Palm Springs. In trying to tell one story, Frank was actually telling another one entirely.

————

No one alive can tell us whether Judy Campbell was part of that indiscreet party in Palm Springs, but it is striking, if she'd been on only one date with Frank—and if sitting around the Bowmont Drive house watching movies can even be considered a date—that he invited her, just days later, to accompany him to Hawaii.

By Judith Exner's own account, she hadn't even gone to watch the movies. In her memoir, Sevano approaches her at Puccini, asks if she'd like to go out with Sinatra, she says yes—and that's it. Frank then calls her a couple of days later and invites her to dinner, but she already has plans for the evening. "A few nights later, again at Puccini's, Frank himself approached our booth," she writes.

> He had been sitting at a large table with a group of friends and I could feel that he was watching me. He sat down and we talked briefly. He was extremely charming. Before going back to his table, he said he'd call me again, and I didn't discourage him . . .
>
> Frank called me the very next day and he didn't waste any time. He said he was going to Hawaii, and would I like to go with him. We had quite a discussion. I liked the prospect of going to Hawaii and of seeing Frank, getting to know him, but I wasn't giddy about it.

I refused to go on the same plane with him but I promised to meet him there.

It's a strange little verbal meringue: some substance but a lot of air, and a bit too sweet. Who was the hunted, and who the hunter? Exner is at great pains to stress her passivity and her propriety. She agrees to go to Hawaii with Frank but has to negotiate the terms. She is ultra-concerned about appearances. Still, who was going to pay for her plane ticket? Her hotel room?

Guys were throwing money around a lot in those days.

"I took the midnight flight on November 9, 1959, and I arrived at 6:45 the next morning," Exner writes. "I went directly to the Surfrider Hotel. They didn't have a reservation in my name, but they gave me room 1509. I just stretched out on the bed until Frank called me later in the morning and asked me to come up to his penthouse suite."

There she found quite a crew: Sinatra, Peter and Pat Lawford, the Beverly Hills obstetrician-gynecologist Dr. Leon "Red" Krohn and his wife, Esther, and a coarse, paunchy man named Al Hart. Both Krohn and Hart were longtime pals of Frank's and men of considerable power in Los Angeles. Red Krohn was the ob-gyn to the stars who'd tended to Ava after her 1952 miscarriage (and performed several abortions on Marilyn Monroe); Al Hart was the founder of the City National Bank of Beverly Hills, an institution that was famously resistant to IRS intrusion and allegedly did a large volume of business with organized crime. Frank Sinatra was a major depositor.

A round of hedonistic days and nights ensued, filled with little but sunbathing, swimming, shopping, dinner parties, and lots and lots of alcohol. "We sat in the sun—Frank worked hard on his tan—and drank Jack Daniel's," Exner recalled. "One day flowed into the other without any noticeable transition." Slack afternoons, Sinatra and his courtier Lawford bantering in Rat Pack–ese. "Their favorite words were gas and gasser, clyde, bunter, cool, crazy, Harvey, fink, mother, hacked, smashed, pissed, charley, and of course, ring-a-ding, or ring-a-ding-ding, depending on the enthusiasm of the moment," she remembered. "The meaning of many of these expressions seemed to change daily."

She and Frank became lovers then, she writes: "He was very gentle, romantic, expressive, sensual, and very active when we made love, and very loving afterward. He seemed genuinely concerned that I was happy and just kept his arms around me all night long. We made love again during the night and when we awakened in the morning."

Intimacy sharpened her perception of him. "I was not totally unaware of his reputation as a tough guy," she writes. "I had read about his bodyguards and his fights in public places. Without trying to analyze him [!], it's possible that much of it has to do with the fact that he's a tiny man with a big man complex. Frank gets considerably shorter when he takes his shoes off . . . [H]is bone structure is small. His wrists are delicate. In his mind he feels he's a big man, that he has power, and the way he proves it is to push people around."

Sinatra was tender when needy, callous when not, Exner recalled. Lawford was often his abettor and partner in crime. "One afternoon, while everybody was sitting around in the living room, two Japanese girls—pretty, delicate little things—were escorted into Frank's bedroom," she writes. "Frank and Pete stood up and Frank said something about it being time for their massage . . . Pat was furious."

————

An acute analyst of power, Campbell watched with fascination as the crowd swirling through the Surfrider penthouse danced attendance upon the mercurial Great Man. "Everybody around Frank walks on eggs all the time," she observed. "Everybody is smiling and happy when Frank is smiling and happy, but the minute Frank starts to frown, everybody is quiet and fearful. No one dares talk back to him. He berates everybody mercilessly and they take it and take it. It's a very distasteful atmosphere to be in . . . Frank knows what he's doing. He was always careful about what he said to Pat, since she was a Kennedy, but he just pulverized Pete at will."

The tropical idyll was full of strange crosscurrents. While Pat Lawford gazed adoringly at Frank, he flirted with her just enough to keep her hopeful (and keep himself in the Kennedy mix). Meanwhile, his attentions flickered in every direction. At a barbecue one evening, Exner writes, Sinatra was attentive and charming, humming along as his records played in the background. Then someone put on *No One Cares,* and Johnny Burke and Jimmy Van Heusen's great "Here's That Rainy Day" came on. "For some reason," she recalled, "I had the feeling that he associated it with Ava Gardner. He became quiet, very sad looking, as he listened to it. Later he said the song had a special meaning for him, but I didn't pursue it."

And yet—calculating that Campbell was of little real worth to Sinatra—Lawford pursued her one night after the Chairman retired unusually early, saying he wasn't feeling well. Campbell rebuffed him and soon came to feel that Lawford, by way of retaliation and self-protection, had sold her out to Frank as the sexual aggressor in their brief encounter.

With the expectable result. Sinatra's Mr. Hyde side emerged, he began to freeze her out as only he could, and she decided to go home. Absurdly, she was given a going-away party in Frank's suite. He was in a vile mood. "I didn't even want to sit next to him," she writes.

> It was a long evening. I just couldn't wait to get out of there, but finally it was time for my exit and I didn't even say goodbye to Frank . . .
> I don't have an ounce of respect for Pete Lawford. I think he's an ass. He makes the best flunky in the world because it's important to Pete to be with important people. He'll sacrifice himself, take a tremendous amount of punishment, just to be there with Frank. When Frank gets into one of his black moods and turns on him, Pete just sits there and takes it. And when Pat talked, he listened.

It's difficult to find good reviews for Peter Lawford as a human being, contempt and pity being the almost universal notes sounded. His louche parentage did him no favors. He allegedly pimped for both Sinatra and JFK, allegedly procured cocaine for (and used it with) Kennedy, was allegedly a sexual masochist and a serial customer of whores. He apparently never saw a check that he didn't allow someone else to pick up. "Cheap, weak, sneak, and freak" was Frank's summary judgment. Dean Jones, a kind man and one of Lawford's co-stars in *Never So Few,* said, "I felt kind of sad for Peter. He just seemed like he was lost—he was unsure of himself." But in the end, the harshest judgment on Lawford might have been his own. "I was a halfway decent-looking English boy," he once said, "who looked nice in a drawing room standing by a piano."

––––––––

After two weeks of sun and fun (the second week Judy Campbell–free), Frank returned in triumph to Vegas. "Frank Sinatra's big one week stand at the Sands is a hypo for business all over town," *Variety* reported on the thirtieth. "The Sinatra stint was sold out weeks in advance, and there are still local VIPs with juice who are trying in vain to get into the show before Tuesday's closing. Frank winged in from Honolulu for this one—he's rested and never was in better voice."

While he was playing the Sands, he got a telegram from the topical comedian Mort Sahl. "Schweitzer said because of nuclear tests he didn't know what was going to happen to the world's population," the wire read. "That's easy—they're all gonna be in 'Ocean's 11.'"

––––––––

Judy Campbell reentered the picture in early December—after, she says, Frank phoned and "sort of apologized" for his miserable behavior in Hawaii, then barraged her with calls until she agreed to meet him in Palm Springs on the seventh. "I wanted to see him," she writes, "but I didn't want to just go rushing in." The woman who claimed never to have been a game player in any relationship had apparently hit on exactly the right strategy for keeping Frank Sinatra interested.

In her memoir, Campbell alternates between elaborately defending her honor—she isn't a courtesan!—and raising tantalizing questions about the source of her income. On December 7, she checked in to the Racquet Club (where, she writes, she had become a regular weekend guest; she doesn't say of whom), had dinner with friends, then drove to Sinatra's house on Wonder Palms Road, alongside the seventeenth fairway of the Tamarisk Country Club, in Palm Desert. She'd never been there before, and the house surprised her. "It was nice and comfortable, but compared to the opulent homes I had lived in and the homes of others I knew, it was a modest, quite ordinary house. It certainly was not the home of a famous movie star," she writes, rather sniffily.

> Even the living room was small. There was a wall bar and a piano at one end. Two beige couches faced each other in front of the fireplace, with a large coffee table between them. There were sliding glass doors leading out to a patio and pool, and the motif was orange and black Oriental.
>
> The only impressive thing about Frank's bedroom, as I was to discover later that evening, were twin beds and a glass shower in the room itself. Luckily, there was another bathroom connecting with the bedroom which had a shower and tub. There was no way I would have used the bedroom shower.
>
> Frank's houseboy, George, opened the door and Frank was right behind him.

Relaxed and in fine spirits, Sinatra kissed her on the cheek and gave her a big wink. "I'm glad you could make it," he told her, taking her elbow and guiding her into the living room. There she saw Pat and Peter Lawford, Jack Entratter, Jimmy Van Heusen, and Johnny Formosa, "who, as best as I could make out, had some connection with the Chicago underworld," she writes, ingenuously. "Frank walked very carefully around him."

After introductions were made, Campbell says, Sinatra and Van Heusen went back to a song they'd been working on for the upcoming *Ocean's 11*. The process was also very much a performance: as Chester sat at the piano, Frank moved around the room singing, now and then stopping by the sofa and resting his hand on Campbell's shoulder, flirting with her as only he could, gently but with a twinkle.

Quite a scene: that kinky glass shower, that grab-bag cast of characters, that twinkling performance by Frank. It's hard to imagine what song he and Chester were working on, since the only two Cahn–Van Heusen numbers performed in *Ocean's 11* would be sung by Sammy ("Eee-O-Eleven") and Dean ("Ain't That a Kick in the Head").

And there in the same room were the sister of the president-to-be and a high-ranking Chicago gangster. For reasons that would become clear a couple of years later, Frank had good reason to walk carefully around Johnny Formosa, a henchman of Sam Giancana's and, as the newspapers referred to him, "alleged Lake County prostitution king"—the putative owner of a Gary, Indiana, brothel.

———

With her Racquet Club check-in shielding her respectability, Campbell stayed at Frank's that night. ("We made love and it was the same as it had been before. He was very gentle, very attentive, very loving, and very active. He did not expect to be made love to." Even in her sex descriptions, she's at pains to seem the lady.) The next evening, they went to dinner with the Lawfords at Romanoff's-on-the-Rocks. The table talk was all politics, and Pat Lawford, her father's daughter and her brother's sister, held the floor. "Frank was all ears as Pat analyzed Jack's chances in the coming primaries," Campbell recalled. "He seemed so subdued and respectful . . . After we made love that night Frank still had Jack Kennedy on his mind. 'You know,' he said, 'I'll bet even money Jack gets the nomination.'"

If Campbell's quotation is accurate, the usually immoderate Frank was being a cautious gambler. As of that day, December 8, 1959, the nation's newspapers were calling Kennedy the man to beat.

———

According to Tina Sinatra, Joe Kennedy summoned her father to the family compound in Hyannis Port late in 1959—possibly in mid-December, the one relatively empty spot in his busy schedule that season—with a delicate proposal. "Dad was more than willing to go," Sinatra told Seymour Hersh.

> He hadn't been to the house before. Over lunch, Joe said, "I think that you can help me in West Virginia and Illinois with our friends. You understand, Frank, I can't go. They're my friends, too, but I can't approach them. But you can." I know that it gave Dad pause. But it still wasn't anything he felt he shouldn't do. So off to Sam Giancana he went.

Sinatra said that her father met with Giancana on a golf course, away from the prying eyes and ears of the FBI, and told him, "I believe in this man and I think he's going to make us a good president. With your help, I think we can work this out."

Of course, Giancana and the men he represented would want something in return.

13

||||||||||||

What will probably be the wildest bill ever to hit a café floor is slated for the Sands Hotel, Las Vegas, starting Jan. 20 for four weeks. Frank Sinatra, Dean Martin and Sammy Davis Jr., charter members of Hollywood's "gas-house gang," will appear simultaneously at the Jack Entratter–operated inn.

—VARIETY, NOVEMBER 4, 1959

Never So Few premiered at Radio City Music Hall three weeks into the new decade. It was a load of tawdry nonsense, war as it had never existed on any planet, and the critics said as much. The public would mostly stay away.

Never So Few was sheer claptrap from the get-go—from the moment Sinatra, as the OSS commander Captain Tom Reynolds, first swaggers into his Burmese guerrilla camp wearing an absurd, all too goatlike goatee and a big, Aussie-style campaign hat that somewhat dwarfs the head he himself once described, painfully but rather accurately, as walnut shaped. Was there no one on the MGM back lot to tell him? *Frank, Frank, lose the chin whiskers and the big hat; they make you look like a little kid playing dress-up!*

There was no one to say such a thing, because he was the Chairman—the emperor, no matter how, or if, he chose to clothe himself.

Jesus, you look terrific, Frank!

Had the man who had once harbored aspirations of being a serious movie actor—and had brought it off in *From Here to Eternity* and *The Man with the Golden Arm*—simply given up? Or had he himself become bigger than the movies?

The best thing about the picture was Sammy Davis's replacement, Steve McQueen, who with his cat-ate-the-canary charisma more or less waltzed off with the show, making Frank look old and overheated.

It didn't matter. While *Never So Few* sputtered out, Frank was in Las Vegas, creating a show of shows that would echo down the decades, for better and worse.

———

"This is the West, sir. When the legend becomes fact, print the legend."

—*The Man Who Shot Liberty Valance* (1962)

The line is from an old movie about myth and reality in the Old West, but it might as well have been written about a legend that was born more than half a century ago in the town whose own myth has shimmered like a mirage on the high Nevada desert for as long as anyone alive can remember. The legend is the sometimes true, often highly imaginative story of the Rat Pack.

We will get to truth, but first, like the newspaperman in John Ford's *Man Who Shot Liberty Valance,* we must acknowledge the very real power of legends. They compel us, they stir us, they fill our dreams and guide our behavior. The idea of Frank Sinatra's Rat Pack was born at a hinge of time in the American consciousness, a moment between the conformism of the 1950s and the chaos of the 1960s, an eyeblink when the horrors and heroism of World War II were still in recent memory (and nuclear fear underlay every diversion), when compensatory excess, in the form of sex, alcohol, and cigarettes, was winked at and twentieth-century ideals of manhood hadn't yet been subverted by the androgynous aesthetic of rock 'n' roll.

"The Rat Pack embodied Hollywood's most elemental myth, its deepest unspoken appeal—that as its final reward, fame offered a life without rules, without the constraints of fidelity, monogamy, sobriety, and the dreary obligation to show up at a job every morning," writes the political journalist Ronald Brownstein.

> For Sinatra, for his cronies, life seemed a canvas with no borders . . .
> There was an electricity to it: to walk into the Sands Hotel with Sina-
> tra, a phalanx of guards leading the way, heads turning, whispers rolling
> through the casino like waves, men in tuxedos rushing to greet you,
> was mesmerizing, almost otherworldly. Just the sheer scent of celebrity
> at Sinatra's parties was intoxicating. "They charged off each other,"
> remembers [the playwright Leonard] Gershe. "The energy in the room
> was extraordinary."

The Rat Pack was an idea, even more than it was a reality. And though Frank, Dean, and Sammy were three real men, their respective myths tend, to this day, to jostle reality aside. Throw in Joey Bishop and Peter Lawford as window dressing, or ballast, and you've got a sharkskin-suited, skinny-tied, chain-smoking, chain-drinking, Dionysian parade float. Watch it trundle down

Main Street; cheer as it goes by. We won't see its likes again. Even if it wasn't quite there in the first place.

––––––––

Ocean's 11 had a plot that sounded great on paper: eleven former army buddies band together to rob five Vegas casinos—the Sands, the Flamingo, the Sahara, the Desert Inn, and the Riviera—simultaneously, at the stroke of midnight on New Year's Eve. Since Frank and Lawford had bought the idea (officially together, but as was the case with Puccini, almost certainly with Sinatra's money) from Gilbert Kay, the script had gone through half a dozen writers, turning into a hodgepodge of plot mechanics. But the film's plot was secondary in any case: it was ultimately a character-driven piece. And Frank Sinatra knew plenty of characters.

Frank would, of course, play the lead, Danny Ocean, the former sergeant

Frank, Dean, and Sammy (along with Peter Lawford and Joey Bishop) at the Sands, 1960. The naughtiness was real, the camaraderie more complex.

in the Eighty-Second Airborne Division who masterminded the heist and assembled the crew. Dean Martin would play Sam Harmon, a lounge singer who was ambivalent about taking part in the caper. Peter Lawford was to play Jimmy Foster, a playboy eager to get out from under the thumb of his rich mother. Sammy Davis Jr. was cast as Josh Howard, a former baseball player who'd lost an eye in the war and now drove a garbage truck in Las Vegas.

The movie had strands of reality woven in—some clear, some strange. It was no stretch for Sinatra to play the smooth kingpin of a group of men. Dean too was essentially playing himself: he'd begun his career singing in lounges and truly was reluctant about being part of any sort of group (the Rat Pack included). Lawford's part—that of a feckless, sponging playboy—was painfully close to the bone. And was Sammy made to play a garbageman as some kind of punishment for his sins against Frank in the Chicago radio interview?

The strangest casting of all was Joey Bishop's: his character, Mushy O'Connors, was supposed to be an ex-boxer, though it was difficult to imagine the slight, dyspeptic comic as any kind of fighter, ex or otherwise.

Ocean's 11 began shooting on location in Las Vegas in January 1960. And from the moment the cast showed up in town through the film's premiere that August, and ever after, none of the leading players, or Vegas itself for that matter, would be the same again.

———

Cmdr. and Mrs. Orville W. Dryer of Point Mugu just returned from a week's stay in that neon never-never land that is Vegas. They were on hand opening night to view a nightclub act to end them all—"modestly" referred to by its stars as the summit meeting, starring Frank Sinatra, Dean Martin, Sammy Davis Jr., Peter Lawford, plus a quiet, deadpan comic named Joey Bishop, all at the Sands Hotel.

—*Oxnard (Calif.) Press-Courier,* January 29, 1960

Three weeks, from January 20 to mid-February 1960, was really all the time it lasted. Everything afterward was an echo, a kind of parody—though parody was what it was kind of all about in the first place.

Wasn't it?

The point is, there *was* no Rat Pack in the first place. No plan, no script, no starting pistol. Nobody ever preconceived the idea of rolling out these five guys and their bar cart on the stage of the Sands' Copa Room that January, as shooting for *Ocean's 11* began. The Rat Pack wouldn't even be called that until much later, and Sinatra always hated the name anyway—the word "rat" having negative connotations where he came from. "The Clan" would be tried

Frank with the cast of *Ocean's 11*: A vision of unrepentant American masculinity that continues to reverberate.

out briefly, but Sammy Davis didn't like the sound of that too much. Finally, in tribute to the planned summit conference between President Eisenhower and Soviet premier Nikita Khrushchev, coming that May, someone—it might've been Sands manager and entertainment director Jack Entratter—decided to call the more or less spontaneous shows featuring Sinatra, Martin, Davis, Lawford, and Bishop on the Copa Room's stage the Summit. "You come to my summit meeting and I'll come to yours," Entratter wired the five entertainers late that January, signing the telegram "Khrushchev."

The Summit. A big, ponderous, vaguely hollow name for a couple hours' goofing around onstage. Goofing around that, surprisingly, was a fairly shocking thing in the small, tightly controlled, homogeneous town that was Las Vegas in 1960.

Anyone who's been to Vegas in the past decade or two, anyone who has been fascinated or repelled by the pulsating megacolossal electric ultra-corporate glass-tower light show that is Las Vegas today, will have to make a mental adjustment to imagine the Vegas of that distant and palmy time, a small place with a downtown consisting of a few honky-tonk, neon-lit blocks along Fremont Street and, out along the Strip, just those mere dozen or so casinos with lots of desert in between; a place where the tallest building was nine stories high and where, as Shecky Greene recalls, "everybody knew each other; everybody took care of each other." It was a time when the Mob controlled what went on in the casinos, and what went on outside was controlled by a kind of Old West justice; then as now, Vegas had an actual sheriff (in 1960, it was Butch Leypoldt; after him came the legendary Ralph Lamb), and the sheriffs have been famously tough and incorruptible. It was a time, older residents recall wistfully, when you could leave your doors unlocked.

It was also a time when gambling reigned supreme, and entertainers were the tail of the dog: entertainment was what drew the gamblers to town. Entertainers—even Frank Sinatra—were employees and, even in Sinatra's case, did what they were told. They came, and they sang or told jokes for two shows a night, sixty minutes each—not a minute more; the audience had to get back to gambling, or the house would lose money. The cover charge for Sinatra's shows in the Copa Room in that era was $6.50—the equivalent of about $50.00 today, but still a relative pittance. And the entertainers were richly paid for their efforts (and many of them gambled away their salaries before they left town). Then they cycled along to their jobs making records or movies or performing at clubs in other cities.

Ocean's 11 changed all that.

But things didn't change all at once. Though Sinatra, Martin, Davis, Lawford, and Bishop were all in town to act in the movie (and were all staying at the Sands), only Frank, Dean, and Sammy were scheduled to headline at the Copa Room—individually, on successive nights, not simultaneously, as *Variety* had breathlessly announced in November. As Ed Walters, who began working as a pit boss at the Sands in 1959, recalled, "Frank opened the first night, and all went well. Dean did the second night and did both shows." Then, on the third night, Sammy Davis Jr. was running long. A no-no.

"Frank came onstage, did some talking with Sammy, and ended the show," Walters says. "He said, 'He's got to go to bed; we're doing a movie all day. Sammy, say good night.' Sammy says good night. Frank takes him by the hand and tells the crowd, 'I've got to get him to bed.' They both walk off to a big round of applause."

One headliner breaking into another headliner's show was highly unusual. But the next night, something even more remarkable occurred. "Frank is doing his show," Ed Walters remembers, "and out walks Dean and tells everyone *Frank* has to go to bed. The audience is shocked at first. Remember, this is Sinatra in the Copa Room in full tux, doing his usual very professional job. Frank would start a song, and halfway through it Dean would cut in—'Frank, that's enough. Frank, that song's too long—sing something shorter.'

"The crowd doesn't know if Dean is serious or not, if Dean is drunk or not. Dean did drink a lot at the time. I know that this stuff would [later] become legend, but at the time it was a shocking thing to see."

What Martin was doing to Sinatra was the very thing Jerry Lewis had done to Dean Martin in 1946: interrupting a straight act with horseplay, to the discomfiture of the audience (and the performer) at first, but ultimately thrilling everybody. Everyone got to feel as if they were in on the joke; everyone could feel vicariously naughty. And Sinatra, by going along with the routine (and he seemed to have been truly startled by Martin at first), could feel vicariously funny. The laughs—the kinds he could never get with his own jokes or asides—were intoxicating to him.

"The audience just loved it and broke out in spontaneous applause," Walters says. "That show ended with the audience going out and raving about what they saw. Everyone in the casino talked about it: Dean and Frank were funny together! By the end of the first week, it was almost certain that at every show, no matter who was doing his show that night, Frank, Dean, and Sammy would [all] be onstage [together]. The fooling around became the talk of the Strip and then the city, and then it spread to L.A. and New York. People were flying in from all over. Frank's friends all wanted to be there. Kirk Douglas, Cary Grant, Roz Russell, Gregory Peck, and all his buddies came in and saw a show or two and went home raving about it."

The rumors were flying all over town, Ed Walters recalls: *Dean was drunk and stopped Frank from singing!*

Frank and Dean were so drunk they couldn't remember the words, so they yelled at each other!

You can't believe it, Sinatra was interrupted right in the middle of singing by Dean Martin and Sammy Davis, who told Sinatra to stand aside while they showed him how to do his act!

The word spread, and the stars, and the public, kept flocking to the Sands. Attention begat more attention. "Every night there was some important or well-known person at the shows," Walters says. "Marilyn Monroe, Cary Grant, Gregory Peck. If they were introduced during the show, and they all were, it made news. The press ate it up. They hadn't seen so many stars in one place in some time."

At one point in early February, the Sands had eighteen thousand reservation requests for its two hundred rooms.

Soon Peter Lawford and Joey Bishop were joining in, too. Lawford, who had sung and danced very creditably in MGM musicals, rolled out his old skills, and audiences were glad to see him. And Jack Entratter, who had learned to be an impresario under Jules Podell at the Copacabana and was behind the scenes at the Copa Room, stage-managing this new whatever-it-was, had a very special role in mind for Joey Bishop.

Entratter was delighted at the comedy chaos that was unfolding nightly and turning the Sands into the center of the entertainment universe, but he never forgot what the casino's main business was. Thus he assigned Bishop to perform the critical function of emcee. It was Joey's job to control the onstage bedlam by introducing the act and then, after not too much more than an hour, making sure it got off in time for the gamblers to get back to gambling. But gradually, with Dean's help and Frank's blessing, Bishop, the straightest of straight men, also became part of the act. In the midst of all the nonsense, one long-suffering stare could go a long way.

"Frank Sinatra, Dean Martin, Sammy Davis Jr., Joey Bishop, and Peter Lawford were supposed to take turns entertaining in the Copa room but save for one night when Dean was ill, they've all been on for two shows, and the performances get crazier each time," Hedda Hopper wrote in her column of February 11. "They had a cake throwing contest the night of Joey Bishop's birthday [February 3]. He saw it coming but Frank and Dean didn't and got it in the face and chest."

It was nonsense, mostly. What's usually said about the comedy that took place during those three weeks at the Sands is that you had to be there. What audio-taped and filmed records show students of the Rat Pack is that most of the humor was Neanderthal, if not antediluvian, at least by twenty-first-century standards. Lots of drinking jokes, mostly by Dean (after the initial ovation: "How long I been on?"). Lots of ethnic jokes, chiefly at Sammy's expense (Frank, from off stage: "Keep smiling so they can see you, Smokey"; and the famous—and frequently reused—bit where Dean picked Sammy up bodily and piped up, "I'd like to thank the NAACP for this award"), but even one or two at Sinatra's (Joey: "Stop singing and tell people about all the good work the Mafia's doing").

Not everyone was charmed. "I thought it was plain, unadulterated shit," said Shecky Greene, who knew all the participants well and attended some of the shows. He shook his head. "Calling [Sammy] Smokey and Blackie—I was offended."

But to the paying customers—say, the Orville Dryers of Point Mugu, California—it was all new and profoundly startling. It was startling to see grown men in tuxedos—*famous* grown men in tuxedos—behaving this way, and no doubt the Dryers told their friends about it (whispering the naughty bits), and the legend began to grow.

———

During the day, they made the movie. Sort of. "The earliest call was for 5:30 p.m., and no actor had to be on the set for more than three hours," writes Shawn Levy in *Rat Pack Confidential*. "On the first day of the Summit, January 20, there was no filming done at all. Thereafter, [the director Lewis] Milestone usually got one Rat Packer at a time, occasionally two, having the whole quintet at his disposal only once—to film the closing credits on a workday cut short by high winds."

How could, and why would, a movie be made under such circumstances? Because Frank Sinatra, the producer and star of *Ocean's 11,* was calling the shots, that's why. And as Tom Santopietro writes, "Frank looked upon the film, in essence, as a very well-paid vacation. He did not invest any of his artistry or passion in it, but rather viewed it as a means to make money and have fun with his friends."

The distinguished and distinctively named sixty-four-year-old Milestone (he'd been born Lev Milstein) had won an Oscar in 1930 for *All Quiet on the Western Front* but lately had mostly been working in television. A small, ironic man with a Slavic accent and an ever-present cigarette, he did the best he could under the circumstances but "certainly knew exactly who held the power on the set," Santopietro notes. "Sinatra . . . stood right next to him behind the camera whenever his presence was not required for the scene being shot."

"Milestone had a very loose grasp, shall we say," recalled the famed Hollywood photographer Sid Avery, who was working on the set of *Ocean's 11.* "He would always address Frank first, because that is who everybody else followed. He'd say, 'Frank. We need another take.' And [Sinatra would] say, 'Print that one twice.'"

Did Sinatra also hold the power over the other four principals? In a famous Vegas story, the actor Norman Fell, a co-star in *Ocean's 11,* is said to have awakened one morning—it must have been very late in the morning—and looked out his hotel window to see Dean and Sammy and Peter Lawford running past the pool. Fell stuck his head out and yelled, "Hey, where are you guys going?" And Sammy said, "Frank's up!"

It's a cute story; add it to the legend. The camaraderie onstage led the outside world to jump to conclusions. "Some eastern press, mainly one woman who had a column [Kilgallen], put it out as 'Frank Sinatra and his pack of regulars are up all night drinking and partying in Las Vegas,'" Ed Walters says. "That wasn't exactly the correct scene as I saw it."

The correct scene was considerably more nuanced. Was Sinatra the kingpin of the quintet? Without a doubt. "It's Frank's world, we just live in it," Dean Martin is famously supposed to have said; he might even have actually said it. All four of Sinatra's partners in the Summit were proud to call him a friend; they readily acknowledged him as the Leader. But the reality was thornier. Dean Martin had huge admiration for Frank as a singer and loved him as a friend. But Sinatra's version of friendship demanded fealty, and Martin kowtowed to no one. He went his own way, and if things ever became confrontational, his way was to vanish.

Though Sammy Davis Jr. had some talents that Frank Sinatra could only dream of, and was nearly his equal in stardom, his relationship with Sinatra was uneasily sycophantic. The sight of him onstage during the Summit performances, bent over and grimacing with seemingly uncontrollable laughter as Sinatra clumsily mocked him, is painful. But like Peter Lawford, Davis knew all too well what could happen when you got on Frank's bad side.

As for Lawford, he held a certain amount of reflected power in 1960 (Sinatra's nickname for him during that period: Brother-in-Lawford) but was widely seen as a toady and errand boy. "He was hanging around Frank all the time," Walters remembers. "It was Sinatra being the boss and Lawford being the employee. One of [Don] Rickles's great jokes was 'Peter, you can laugh. Frank says it's okay.' Because we all knew Lawford didn't do *anything* without Frank's okay. Frank didn't treat him like a friend."

And Joey Bishop was never going to be one of Sinatra's drinking buddies—the only kind of buddy Sinatra had—for one important reason: he didn't drink. "We've worked together many times, and I enjoy it, but we don't socialize afterwards," Bishop admitted.

The socializing afterward was one of the most important things in Frank Sinatra's life: he was a thoroughly nocturnal man who lived in desperate fear of being alone. Drinking buddies and hangers-on (they were usually one and the same) were required, at the pain of Frank's displeasure, to stay up with him until the sky over Vegas lightened to the shade of morning twilight that he loved so much—"Five O'Clock Vegas Blue," he called it. And woe betide the man who tried to sneak off to bed: Sinatra was known to roust the recalcitrant from their hotel rooms personally, sometimes with the aid of cherry bombs.

The single pass Frank issued to any of his drinking friends—and he issued it because there was no other choice—went to Martin. "All the guys would take a steam bath, they'd go out and gamble—[and] Dean Martin would say, 'I'm sorry, guys, I'm going to bed,'" recalled Sid Avery. "He'd get up early in the morning, go out and golf."

Sometimes Martin would soften the blow by telling Sinatra, "I've got a girl in my room," and sometimes there really was a girl in his room. But then, and throughout his life, Dean Martin preferred his solitude. "He was not like the rest of the Clan," Judith Campbell recalled. "He was the kind of person who wandered around by himself. He didn't need a retinue walking with him when he walked from one room to another . . . I don't think he could stand having a lot of people around him all the time the way Frank did." Despite his drunk act onstage, Martin wasn't really a convivial drinker. He liked to watch a Western on TV, get his beauty sleep, and hit the links well rested. Golf was his one great passion in life.

So the image of the Rat Pack as a kind of floating social club, merrily cavorting together when the cameras weren't rolling, doesn't quite jibe with reality. Sometimes they gambled together, but the five of them didn't even all go to the legendary Sands steam bath (in which Frank had had the management install a craps table) together: incredibly, Sammy was barred from entering.

Not that Sinatra was lacking for nighttime companionship. His usual entourage was always with him: Jimmy Van Heusen; bodyguard/drinking buddies like Jilly Rizzo, Hank Sanicola, and Al Silvani; and *Ocean's 11* cast members like Angie Dickinson, Richard Conte, Henry Silva, Buddy Lester, George Raft, and Shirley MacLaine (who played a bit part as a Tipsy Girl) orbited around him, as did such visiting luminaries as Kirk Douglas, Yul Brynner, and Steve Lawrence.

Frank's days, too, were populous. And bibulous. "There is no way anyone can ever spend a day alone with Frank Sinatra," Exner writes, recalling a weekend afternoon and evening, late that January, spent in his bungalow at the Sands.

> His quarters are a crossroads, with traffic moving in all directions, day and night. I think he would dry up and blow away if he were left totally alone.
>
> Everything considered, it was a peaceful, pleasant day. I brought a book and sat out in the sun on his patio and read while Frank talked on the phone, glanced through a pile of scripts, dictated a few letters, acknowledged the comings and goings of an endless string of visitors, growled at flunkies, drank martinis, ate lunch, drank Jack Daniels, ate hors d'oeuvres, drank Jack Daniels, ate dinner, and drank more Jack Daniels. Frank was not feeling well that day.

On January 28, 1960, in the midst of the shooting of *Ocean's 11*, Frank flew to Los Angeles to record a campaign song for the Democratic front-runner, who had formally announced his candidacy on the day after New Year's. The tune, Sammy Cahn's special-lyrics version of Cahn and Van Heusen's "High Hopes," was called "High Hopes with Jack Kennedy." It began,

> *Everyone is voting for Jack.*
> *'Cause he's got what all the rest lack.*

Everyone wants to back Jack,
Jack is on the right track.

'Cause he's got High Hopes!
He's got High Hopes!
1960's the year for his High Hopes!

The original "High Hopes," charmingly sung by Sinatra and Eddie Hodges in *A Hole in the Head* and a big hit as a single, deserved its popularity: though nothing like a great song, it was madly catchy, and its message, a clarion note of optimism in a nation that was materially comfortable but mired in a fog of conformity and nuclear fear, was irresistible.

The campaign version, released in advance of the all-important Wisconsin primary in March, raised the original song's gauzily abstract confidence to a specific, even an aggressive, level. With its explosive *k* end rhymes ("Jack," "lack," "back," "track"), it was the sonic equivalent of the pointing, sawing hand gestures Jack Kennedy deployed on the podium, challenging America to rise from its stupor and seize the future from the Soviet Union.

———

Frank Sinatra introduced Sen. Kennedy at the Las Vegas Sands Hotel a couple of nights ago—and there was wild cheering from the audience. Then Dean Martin stepped from the wings and said to Sinatra, "What was his name?"

—Earl Wilson's syndicated column of February 4, 1960

John F. Kennedy, the cultural historian Jonathan Gould writes, "was the first American president to be born in the twentieth century, the first to grow up in thrall to the movies, radio, and the glossy idealizations of magazine advertising—the first American president to have his sensibility molded in the crucible of modern mass culture." Kennedy recognized the power of show business, saw how it could help him in his campaign. He also recognized which show-business figure attracted more women than any other.

"Sinatra thought Kennedy was going to be a great president," says Ed Walters, who met the president-to-be on several occasions at the Sands. "Kennedy just wanted to get laid."

If the formulation is coarse, so was this side of John F. Kennedy. We are all divided souls; because Jack Kennedy was rich and brilliant, with movie-star looks and charisma, and because he became a world-historical figure, his contradictions stand out in especially stark contrast. "He was not a grown-up and he was a grown-up. He was both," Nancy Olson Livingston recalled. He could be deeply thoughtful or callous, sparklingly witty or boorish, empathetic or coldly calculating. Some found him warm and present; others didn't. "He was a little distant," Livingston added. "He was not that interested in what you thought and what you had to say." And where his personal life was concerned, he was a man who felt completely entitled to do precisely as he pleased, and pleasure was one of his highest values. All of which makes him a key part of the Rat Pack saga.

Crisscrossing the country on his campaign plane, the *Caroline,* in late January and early February 1960, Kennedy stumped in Illinois, Indiana, West Virginia, North Dakota, and New Mexico; strikingly, he also made it his business to visit Nevada twice within a one-week period: on January 31 and February 1,

Frank and the presidential candidate at the Sands, circa 1960. "There was no goddamn reason for stopping there except fun and games," a CBS reporter traveling with Kennedy recalled.

to powwow with the state's progressive Democratic governor, Grant Sawyer; and then on February 7 and 8, apparently for purely personal purposes. He took in the Summit's show at the Sands on both visits. On the second, he and his entourage (including his twenty-seven-year-old brother, Ted) stayed for two nights at the hotel-casino, as Sinatra's guests. "There was no goddamn reason for stopping there except fun and games," Blair Clark, a CBS reporter traveling with the candidate, recalled. On the other hand, "We all figured, 'How bad can it be to catch Sinatra at the Sands?'"

That was the whole thing in a nutshell. In an era when the (almost exclusively male) press corps covering politicians and candidates winked at sexual peccadilloes, Jack Kennedy had carte blanche. Sinatra would introduce him fulsomely at the Summit shows: "Ladies and gentlemen, Senator John F. Kennedy, from the great state of Massachusetts . . . The next president of the United States!" A blurry home movie taken on one of those nights shows the slim young senator grinning and standing to take a bow.

Judith Campbell Exner claimed in her book that she first met Jack Kennedy "at ten o'clock Sunday evening (February 7, 1960). He and Teddy were at Frank's table in the Sands lounge. He looked so handsome in his pin-striped suit. Those strong white teeth and smiling Irish eyes."

After a drink in the lounge, Exner maintained, someone mentioned dinner, and she found herself dining with Peter Lawford, Gloria Cahn, and Jack and Teddy Kennedy in the Garden Room.

Lawford's agent, Milt Ebbins—an apparently agenda-free witness—claimed that he had been at the table at the Sands when Campbell made her first appearance. "The lights were low," he told Anthony Summers, "but I sensed a lady come and sit down beside me—maybe it was her perfume. And she said, 'I'm Judith Campbell, I'm a guest of Mr. Sinatra's. He asked me to sit at this table.'"

Ebbins said that after the Summit show, Campbell left with Jack Kennedy. The agent told Summers that when he later asked Lawford who she was, Lawford said, "She's a hooker. Frank gave her two hundred dollars to stop at our table . . . to go to bed with Jack."

That is what Lawford said. On the other hand, as the singer Betsy Hammes recalled, guys were throwing money around a lot in those days. Campbell "was always kind of like a girl about town," Hammes said. "She was everywhere. In Beverly Hills nightclubs, you would run into her every night. She was always kind of out of it all the time—I don't know if she was a drinker or [it was] pills, or what."

Was she a pro?

"I don't think so—she just slept around."

After one of the Summit shows, on the night of February 7 or 8, there was a private party in Sinatra's suite; the candidate and some of his entourage were present, as were at least two young women. Two reporters who were there, Blair Clark and the *Washington Star* columnist Mary McGrory, excused themselves, Clark later recalled, "because we sensed that Jack and Frank and a couple of the girls were about to have a party." One of the women, Clark said, was Judy Campbell.

Campbell, who was "tremendously impressed by [Kennedy's] poise and wit and charm," formed a very different impression of him from Nancy Olson Livingston's. "When he listened, it was as if every nerve and muscle in his whole body was poised at attention," she recalled. "He had a habit when he listened of tilting his head slightly toward you, as if to facilitate the process, guarding against the possibility that a word might mischievously try to slip by him."

Of course the level of his interest might have varied directly with the degree to which he was on the make. Livingston claims that Kennedy tried to force himself on her in 1948, when she was a twenty-year-old junior at UCLA, and that she fended him off. He might have given her up as a lost cause afterward. Campbell, on the other hand, was to become his mistress.

And Frank had made the introduction.

He liked nicknaming people who meant a lot to him, and the handles were breezy but sharp edged: he was Dolly's son, after all. Dean was Dag, the *a* long, for "dago"; Sammy was Smokey, for his heavy smoking habit and the color of his skin. Brother-in-Lawford has been mentioned. But now there was a new pally, the brother-in-law's amorous brother-in-law, and so the candidate was dubbed: Chickie Baby.

Intent on establishing a decorous timeline for her relationship with John Kennedy, Judith Campbell Exner maintained that it was Teddy Kennedy who came after her—unsuccessfully—on the first night of the Sands layover and that her bond with the president-to-be was initially an intellectual and spiritual one, forged over a long, intense discussion about Catholicism and politics during a tête-à-tête lunch on the patio of Sinatra's bungalow. By her account, familiarity accelerated into heavy flirtation that afternoon at a reception for JFK ("I felt like a schoolgirl infatuated with the new boy from out of state that no one knows anything about . . . I thought that every time he came over and touched my hand, all eyes were focused on us"). That evening, she said, the two of them sat by themselves in Jack Entratter's booth in the back of the Copa Room and held hands in the dark while they took in the Summit show. And then Kennedy was off to Oregon to continue campaigning but not before telling her, "Don't worry, I plan to see a lot of you, campaign or no campaign, we can arrange it somehow if you're willing."

Exner writes that JFK telephoned her regularly, and even sent her roses, from the campaign trail. In the meantime, she followed his progress avidly in the newspapers and read *Why England Slept* and *Profiles in Courage*. The question of the time and the place of their next rendezvous, the meeting that would accelerate their relationship from the intellectual to the physical, hung in the air. Then Frank muddied the issue.

On the afternoon of February 24, Exner recalled (the *Ocean's 11* shoot had moved back to Los Angeles), she had lunch with her sister, the actress, at Warner Bros., then the two of them paid a visit to Sinatra on the set. "He was extremely solicitous and gallant, making sure that chairs were provided for us so that we could watch the shooting of a scene," she writes.

> Later, over drinks in his dressing room, I asked what he was going to do next. He said he had an engagement at the Fontainebleau in Miami and that the Clan was planning on joining him for some of the shows. Their show had been a huge success at the Sands and Frank thought it would be "a gas" to repeat it in Miami. "Hey, why don't you come down for the opening. Always great to have a pretty girl up front."
>
> I didn't accept, nor did I refuse. I said I would think about it. I wasn't about to make any plans that might later conflict with my seeing Jack. As luck would have it, we decided on the place and time for our next meeting that very evening when Jack called from Wisconsin.

The place was New York City, the Plaza hotel to be exact, on March 7—the night, according to Exner, that she and Kennedy first became lovers. Frank opened at the Fontainebleau the next night, and Judy Campbell found time in her schedule to fly down to Miami for a couple of weeks and catch his act, not once, but several times. It was at one of those shows, she maintains, that Sinatra introduced her for the first time to the charming and well-dressed middle-aged man whom he called Sam Flood.

On the night of February 15, the third *Frank Sinatra Timex Show* aired on ABC. "Here's to the Ladies" was the theme, and the guests were two of the grandest dames around, Eleanor Roosevelt and Lena Horne, along with Frank's new squeeze Juliet Prowse, the opera singer Mary Costa, and the impressionist Barbara Heller. The former First Lady came out in the slot of honor, second to last on the show, and the host introduced her with maximum deference: "a lady whose friendship I treasure very much . . . the most admired woman of our time, Mrs. Eleanor Roosevelt."

She was seated on a banquette, a vision in white silk, with room by her side for Frank. He sat, and she smiled with genuine pleasure. "Good evening, Mr. Sinatra," she said in her patented fluty, plummy tones.

"Mr. Sinatra? Why don't you call me Frank?" he replied.

She was a little old-fashioned, she told him; "Mr. Sinatra" seemed more natural to her. Her warm smile said otherwise. The two engaged in some scripted banter for a few moments. Mrs. R., charmingly obvious about reading the cue cards, wondered what she might be able to do after the other women had performed so beautifully. Mr. S. replied that just sitting and talking with him was enough.

"Now come, Frank," she said, thrillingly lapsing into informality, "there must be something I can contribute to the evening."

Frank with Eleanor Roosevelt. Sinatra admired the former First Lady and great humanitarian extravagantly; she returned his regard a little more coolly.

As it turned out, there was. As Nelson Riddle's strings struck up in the background and a choir began to hum, Mrs. Roosevelt proceeded to recite the lyrics to "High Hopes"—with humor, dignity, and a certain steel behind those long, slitted eyes (she was and would continue to be resistant to her host's chosen candidate, John F. Kennedy), not to mention a patrician lilt that Sammy Cahn hadn't quite had in mind:

Anyone knows an ahnt cahn't
Move a rubber-tree plahnt.

The message of hope was as powerful as its deliverer, and Frank's esteem for the great lady was palpable. As was his wish, signaled by her appearance on the show, to be involved in politics at the highest level. The man who could hold Eleanor Roosevelt in such high regard and also feel intense admiration for Sam Giancana and Johnny Formosa might have had a complex sense of self-esteem, but he also possessed a quite simple respect for power.

———

What's with Frank Sinatra?

Sinatra, who is the hottest thing in show business, has not made a record since last Aug. 1 when he recorded a single record called "Talk to Me." He has not made an album since July 20 when he recorded "No One Cares"—despite the fact that his albums sell more than those of any other entertainer . . .

As the situation stands, Sinatra can't make records for anyone but Capitol and he won't make them for Capitol. This deadlock could go on for years.

—John Crosby, syndicated column, March 2, 1960

Sometime in late 1959 or early 1960, Glenn Wallichs, the head of Capitol Records, called Alan Livingston and asked for his help in dealing with Sinatra. The previous May, after Wallichs had definitively nixed the singer's umpteenth demand that his Essex Productions become a sub-label under Capitol's aegis—with Capitol bearing all expenses and Essex and Capitol sharing profits fifty-fifty—Frank had walked out, refusing to make any more records until he got his way. Wallichs reasoned that Livingston (who was soon to quit NBC and return to Capitol as president) had a special relationship with Sinatra. After all, he was the man who'd signed Frank to Capitol in 1953 when no one else wanted him. But as Sinatra's Columbia Records rabbi and close friend, the late Manie Sacks, had learned to his sorrow, nothing—not friendship, not love, not loyalty—was more important to Frank than his career. Once he decided he wanted something, anyone who opposed it was the enemy.

"I called him up and said, 'Frank, I understand you've had a problem with Capitol . . . Can we sit down and talk about it?'" Livingston recalled. "He said, 'No way. I don't want to talk to you. I'm going to tear down that round building.' He was threatening to do this and that and using every four-letter word in the book. And I was shocked. I said, 'Frank, I'm sorry. I didn't know you felt that way.' And I hung up. That was it. From there on we dealt with lawyers."

Capitol's attorneys and Sinatra's lawyer Mickey Rudin worked out a deal: in return for giving Capitol the *Can-Can* soundtrack album, Frank would be released from the seven-year contract he'd signed in 1956. He would make five more albums for the label, under the current terms, and would then be free to leave. He began recording the first LP on the night of March 1, the first time he had set foot in Studio A since the previous May.

It was as though he'd never left. Nelson was at the podium, the Slatkins were in the string section, Dave Cavanaugh was in the control booth. Frank was relaxed and happy. The plan for the album (at first meant to be titled *The Nearness of You*)[*] was to update a dozen standard ballads Frank had recorded for Columbia a decade or more earlier: most of them, crucially, from the pre-Ava period—love songs, that is, rather than cries of desolation.

From the first track, he was right back in the pocket. He'd last laid down Fred Coots and Haven Gillespie's majestic "You Go to My Head" on July 30, 1945—a month before V-J Day, while he was still in his twenties. The Axel Stordahl–arranged version was beautiful, a wispy dream, like the curl of smoke from a wartime Lucky Strike. Frank's vocal was young, yearning, wistful: it was the sound that made the girls scream, that made the boys overseas long for home.

So much had changed in fifteen years. In Sinatra and Riddle's hands, the number turned from a thing of beauty to one of magnificence. It wasn't just the timbre of Frank's voice that had deepened; it was the song itself. Nelson's trademark swirling strings and flute in the intro, followed by Frank's deep, dark vocal, rendered "You Go" oceanic.

On the four tunes he recorded that night—he also sang "Fools Rush In," "That Old Feeling," and "Try a Little Tenderness"—Sinatra revealed a new

---

[*] According to Havers (p. 254); Friedwald (p. 256) says, "Nobody remembers what the original title for the project was, although it may well have been *The Nearness of You*."

side to his ballad singing. Once the ardent young lover, then, for so many years, the torch carrier, he was now the sadder but wiser swinger: an artist on the near edge of being an elder statesman.

On three consecutive nights, March 1, 2, and 3, Sinatra and Riddle made twelve gorgeous recordings, enough to fill the album Frank had in mind. But the restless perfectionist in him wasn't satisfied. He had Hank Sanicola call a number of songwriters, Cahn and Van Heusen among them, to ask for a brand-new number, a title tune for an album of "lightly swinging love songs"— that was the phrase. It was a tall order.

Among the songwriting teams Sanicola approached were the composer Lew Spence and the lyricists Alan and Marilyn Bergman, who'd already written a pair of singles for Sinatra: "Sleep Warm" and "Love Looks So Well on You." Spence had recently played a catchy song fragment for the Bergmans, wondering what to do with it; the piece's jaunty six-note core conjured a phrase for Alan Bergman: "Nice 'n' easy does it." The rest of the music and lyrics quickly followed.

Frank and the screenwriter Albert Maltz had been Hollywood liberals together in the 1940s, only Maltz—who wrote the script for the 1945 Oscar-winning short *The House I Live In,* starring Sinatra as himself in a paean to tolerance— was a little more liberal: in fact, he was a card-carrying member of the American Communist Party. Two years later, Maltz, along with nine other left-leaning writers and directors, was cited for contempt of Congress for refusing to testify to the House Un-American Activities Committee. The group, who became known as the Hollywood Ten, were all imprisoned and blacklisted. Upon his release, Maltz moved to Mexico, and it was there, in early 1960, that Sinatra called him about writing a new screenplay.

Frank intended to produce—and, for the first time, direct—the film, which was to be based on William Bradford Huie's book *The Execution of Private Slovik,* the story of a Detroit ne'er-do-well who became the only U.S. soldier executed for desertion during World War II. "It was a total downer," George Jacobs recalled, "but, as Mr. S put it, 'You don't win Oscars for comedies.' He still really wanted that Oscar."

Albert Maltz seemed the perfect choice to write the antiwar picture— except for one little detail: he was still blacklisted. The Writers Guild of America had dropped him; in theory, no studio could hire him or distribute a film he had worked on. (Many of the Ten, including Maltz, had skirted the blacklist by writing under pseudonyms.)

That January, though, Frank's *Man with the Golden Arm* director, Otto

Preminger, had struck the first major blow against the blacklist by telling the *New York Times* that he'd hired another member of the Hollywood Ten, Dalton Trumbo, to write his latest movie, *Exodus.** Sinatra, who admired Preminger greatly, was clearly making a political point in this supercharged year. "Frank said that he had been thinking of hiring me for a long time and that it was very important to him to do so and to make this film," Maltz recalled.

It was a typically headstrong decision, and cooler heads in Sinatra's circle questioned it at once. Frank's lawyer Martin Gang telephoned Maltz and asked if the announcement could be put off until after the first presidential primary, in New Hampshire (March 8), so as not to prejudice voters against John Kennedy, for whom Sinatra had been campaigning heavily.

Kennedy won handily in New Hampshire, and Albert Maltz phoned Frank. The longer the announcement was postponed, the screenwriter felt, the less impact it would have on the blacklist. "I asked him openly if he wanted to delay because he was raising money for Kennedy and was worried that being publicly involved with a blacklisted writer might dry up finances, but he said, 'No, I support Kennedy because I think he's the best man for the job, but I'm not doing anything special for him.' So I suggested we make the announcement right away, and he said fine."

As it turned out, it was not so fine. On March 20, speaking from Miami, where he'd gone to play a nineteen-night stand (along with Sammy Davis Jr., Peter Lawford, and his daughter Nancy) at the Fontainebleau, Frank let the world know he had hired Albert Maltz. (And that Steve McQueen was to play Eddie Slovik.) As the *New York Times*'s Murray Schumach noted, in a full-column story, it was a historic announcement. "This marks the first time that a top movie star has defied the rule laid down by the major studios," Schumach wrote. "Since stars have attained such power in Hollywood that they can now often choose their own writers, Mr. Sinatra's position may become a precedent in helping undermine the blacklist, the existence of which has often been denied."

Schumach asked Frank if he was fearful of the reaction in Hollywood. "We'll find that out later," Sinatra said. "We'll see what happens."

He didn't have to wait long. On March 23, under the headline STARS SCORN SINATRA'S HIRING OF "HOLLYWOOD 10" WRITER MALTZ, UPI noted that Frank's decision had "brought a salvo of criticism . . . from such stars as Ward Bond and Robert Taylor. Mr. Maltz's hiring is part of a trend

---

* In fact, Kirk Douglas had hired Trumbo to write the screenplay for *Spartacus* a year earlier but revealed the fact later. And Stanley Kramer had recently hired the blacklisted Nedrick Young to write the script for *Inherit the Wind*.

that 'might be called "hire the Commies" club,' said Mr. Bond." Bond's close friend, frequent co-star, and fellow right-winger John Wayne furiously asked reporters, "I wonder how Sinatra's crony, Senator John Kennedy, feels about him hiring such a man? I'd like to know his attitude because he's the one who is making plans to run the administrative government of our country."

Editorial pages around America laid into Sinatra. Predictably, the Hearst papers led the charge. "What kind of thinking motivates Frank Sinatra in hiring an unrepentant enemy of his country—not a liberal, not an underdog, not a free thinker, but a hard revolutionist who has never done anything to remove himself from the Communist camp or to disassociate himself with the Communist record?" asked the *New York Mirror*.

Hedda Hopper jumped on the bandwagon. "On returning from New York I found more than a hundred letters on my desk protesting Frank Sinatra's hiring of Commie Albert Maltz," the columnist, a fervent Republican and Nixon supporter, wrote.

I tried to reach Frank, but he was unavailable. He's given several reasons why he did this but none has met with approval of real Americans.

Personally, I don't believe the story should be filmed . . . But the people have the privilege of refusing to see his picture if it's ever made. They also have the privilege of not buying Sinatra's records and not looking at his TV shows. This is their right.

But what of the people of other nations—those who hate us? They will revel in an ugly story about our country. If Sinatra loves his country he won't do this. He'll write off the cost of the story and forget it. But will he? That's the question. He's stubborn, but not pigheaded. He has a fine family of which he's proud. Will he do this to them? There is also his friend Sen. John Kennedy for whom he intends to campaign. Has he thought of the harm this could do him? "Private Slovik" could be the end of a brilliant career. I ask you, Frank, can you afford to take the risk?

Frank wasn't worrying about his career. His records were selling better than ever; he had (as always) several movie projects lined up; and let the right wing tut-tut all it wished, his very large audience loved him. At the end of March, a front-page story in *Variety* reported that he had once more racked up a record gross at the Fontainebleau, $400,000 for the nineteen nights, the last three of which, a Summit reprise, were packed beyond capacity.

"Font's Ben Novack is shuttering club for week, feeling nothing can follow Sinatra," the *Variety* item noted.

But another, bigger story sat above this one, at the top of the front page, announcing that Frank was quitting the William Morris Agency to form his own management company. The Morris Agency had been "hard hit with the failure of Frank Sinatra to renew," the show-business daily said. "Sinatra's exit deprives the Morris office with [sic] its top earner in the personal appearance field and a major moneymaker in the film and television areas." *Variety* added that the new firm, to be headed by Hank Sanicola, with Milt Ebbins and Nick Sevano as associates, was "expected to represent some members of 'The Clan,' the show biz–socialite group that has been surrounding Sinatra for the past few years. Included in the new stable are likely to be Dean Martin, Sammy Davis Jr., Peter Lawford, Joey Bishop . . . as well as Tony Bennett, Shirley MacLaine, and others."

All of whom, of course, were represented by other agencies at the time. "Frank Sinatra's new talent agency's plans," Earl Wilson observed in his column, "are really raising hell in Show Biz." Frank had, in effect, staged a Hollywood coup.

Hedda Hopper's call for a commercial boycott of Sinatra sounded chilling, though in typical fashion Frank left the worrying to others. According to Nick Sevano, General Motors called him soon after the new management firm opened its doors and threatened to pull its ads from three upcoming Sinatra specials unless the singer disassociated himself from Maltz. Sevano recalled that he, Sanicola, and Rudin "flew to Palm Springs to try to talk Frank into firing Maltz, but he wouldn't budge. 'Fuck 'em,' he said. 'There will be other specials.'"

According to Peter Lawford, it took a greater force than General Motors—Joseph P. Kennedy—to finally change Sinatra's mind. Lawford said the old man got nervous after anti-JFK forces during the New Hampshire primary smeared the candidate as soft on Communism, and Cardinals Cushing of Boston and Spellman of New York warned the elder Kennedy about the Sinatra-Maltz connection.

"That's when old Joe called Frank and said, 'It's either Maltz or us. Make up your mind,'" Lawford told Kitty Kelley. "He felt that Jack was getting rapped for being a Catholic and that was going to be tough enough to put to rest. He didn't want him to get rapped for being pro-Communist as well, so Frank caved in, and dumped Maltz that day."

———

Tina Sinatra tells a different story: that the catalyst behind Maltz's firing was a force even greater than Joe Kennedy alone. "Both Joe and Bobby Kennedy told my dad flat out to fire Maltz," she writes.

I suppose they expected him to do the expedient thing without a second thought—which was, after all, how the Kennedys had made their
way in the world. They hadn't banked on my father's stubborn Sicilian
streak. He was willing to compromise, but not to compromise himself
in the process. And he resented being told what to do, even by the
father of the next president of the United States. He told the Kennedys
that he'd stick by Maltz, whether or not it jeopardized his role in the
campaign.

But what about the jeopardy to the campaign itself? Frank's first response
to Maltz—that he wasn't "doing anything special" for JFK—was both high-
handed and disingenuous: of course he was doing all kinds of special things
for JFK, some of them very far off the record. In his March 20 story, the *Times*'s
Schumach had noted, "It was reported, but without confirmation, that Mr.
Sinatra at first considered keeping news of his association with Mr. Maltz
secret until after the Democratic National Convention, for fear that the story
might hurt the chance of Senator John F. Kennedy for the Presidential nomination." The story reinforced the Sinatra-JFK connection in the newspaper of
record, remarking that Frank's recording of "High Hopes" was the senator's
campaign song and noting his close association with Brother-in-Lawford.

But Tina Sinatra writes that it was her father's consideration for her feelings, rather than for JFK's chances, that changed his mind. She was eleven
at the time, in the fifth grade at Marymount, a Catholic school for girls in
Brentwood, when a girl walked up to her and said, "My dad says your dad's a
communist. Does that mean you're a communist, too?"

"I went home in tears that afternoon," Sinatra writes.

> I ran off the bus and told my mother what had happened, and she
> got Dad on the phone right away . . . "I'm sorry that this happened,
> Pigeon," he told me. "This whole thing is very complicated, but I'm
> telling you that I'm not a communist, and neither are you. Don't cry,
> please. I'll take care of it" . . .
>
> Where Dad wouldn't bow to the mighty Kennedys, he buckled
> before his troubled child. After saying goodbye to me, he turned to Guy
> McElwaine, his publicist, and said, "Get Albert a check, and tell him
> I'm very sorry." He paid Maltz the full $75,000 for the job, which he
> didn't have to do. "It was my problem, not his," Dad said.

What makes most sense is that Frank bowed both to the mighty Kennedys
and to his young daughter. As George Jacobs remembered it, it "killed him to

have to eat Joe's humble pie and give up his own dream. He went on a three-day Jack Daniel's binge and totally destroyed his office at the Bowmont house. 'Who gives a shit? I'm outta this fucking business!' he screamed, ripping up books and scripts, hurling over bookcases. This time I felt his rage and frustration were understandable."

There was certainly tension in the air. A week later, Dorothy Kilgallen made a curious observation in her syndicated gossip column:

> It's mighty puzzling to members of Hollywood's famous Rat Pack, but intimates of Senator Jack Kennedy say the handsome Presidential candidate keeps disavowing any close friendship with Frank Sinatra and insists any publicity linking the singer with his campaign must have been "planted" by the Sinatra interests. They quote him as saying he's only met the singer "a few times" and protesting that Frank is brother-in-law Peter Lawford's pal, not his.

The item was doubly striking: for one thing, it marked the first use in print of the term "Rat Pack" as applied to the members of the Summit, as opposed to Humphrey Bogart's old coterie. For another, there was that strange and chilling, albeit anonymous, assertion of Kennedy's disaffection with Sinatra. And while it must be noted that there was no love lost between Frank and Kilgallen—she seemed to particularly enjoy needling him in print (and probably knew well how he would hate the Rat Pack label); he used to refer to her, onstage, as "that chinless broad"—it's doubtful that the columnist made her item up out of whole cloth. A number of people close to Jack Kennedy (especially his brother Bobby) were extremely uneasy about his palling around with a man who palled around with hookers and hoodlums. Not to mention Communists.

And yet Frank continued to campaign for Kennedy like a man possessed, singing at fund-raisers, leaning on the wealthy for contributions ("He'd get on the phone to somebody," Milt Ebbins recalled, "and before you knew it he'd be saying, 'Gotcha down for ten thousand'"), rallying his fellow celebrities to the cause. "If he asked people to go somewhere, they'd go," said Rosalind Wyman, a key West Coast campaign organizer. "Sammy Davis, Jr., Nat King Cole, Ella Fitzgerald, Milton Berle, Bobby Darin, Steve Allen and Jayne Meadows. Frank got them all to do events for us."

"We'd spread out," Sammy recalled. "I'd do rallies in L.A., San Diego, and up the coast to San Francisco, then we'd meet back at Frank's. 'How'd it go? What happened?' . . . There were always groups huddling, planning activities, and it was exciting to be there, everybody knew you and you knew everybody and you were all giving yourselves to something in which you deeply believed."

Frank, perhaps needling Kilgallen back, came up with a new label for his crew: the Jack Pack. Dean Martin, who was cynical about politicians in general and about Kennedy in particular, was conspicuously absent. "He'd met Jack Kennedy in Chicago about a decade earlier when he was still with Jerry, and the three of them scammed broads together," Shawn Levy writes. "He wasn't terribly impressed with the guy then, and he certainly wasn't willing to jump onto Frank's bandwagon, even if the Rat Pack *had* been renamed the Jack Pack."

Frank might have done well to cultivate a little more cynicism himself.

––––––––––

The Summit show at the Fontainebleau wasn't the only big news out of Miami that spring. The previous October, Frank had made a deal with Elvis Presley's manager, Colonel Tom Parker (born, in 1909 in the Netherlands, Andreas Cornelis van Kuijk), for the Pelvis to appear on Sinatra's final Timex special on ABC. The occasion was Presley's mustering out of the U.S. Army in March, a national event as far as his fans were concerned. Parker drove a legendarily hard bargain: the twenty-five-year-old superstar would be paid $125,000 for his appearance, more than Frank was earning for the entire show.

It was an epochal event in more ways than one. In appearing with Elvis, Sinatra would be not only acknowledging but in a way deferring to an artist whose records, to Frank's great chagrin, outsold his own and who was the chief exponent of a genre that only two years earlier Sinatra had called a "rancid smelling aphrodisiac" and a "brutal, ugly, degenerate, vicious form of expression . . . sung, played and written for the most part by cretinous goons."

As George Jacobs recalled, "Mr. S hated Elvis so much that he'd sit in the den all by himself at the music console and listen to every new track over and over, 'Don't Be Cruel,' 'All Shook Up,' 'Teddy Bear.' He was trying to figure out just what the hell this new stuff was, both artistically (though he'd never concede it was art) and culturally (though he'd never concede it was culture). Why was the public digging this stuff? What did it have? What was the hook? These questions got the better of Mr. S. I knew he was in trouble when he said he preferred Pat Boone."

But—Frank shrewdly calculated, putting his taste aside—Pat Boone didn't sell records like Elvis, and Pat Boone wouldn't draw television viewers the way Elvis would.

The show, titled "It's Nice to Go Traveling; or, Welcome Home Elvis," was taped at the Fontainebleau on March 26, in front of an audience liberally salted with adolescent girls, whose presence would quickly become apparent. First, though, Sinatra and company—Nancy junior (making her professional debut), Joey Bishop, Sammy Davis Jr., and the Tom Hansen Dancers—delivered a Vegas-style opening, coming out onstage one by one, each singing a couple of lines of a special-lyrics version of Cahn and Van Heusen's "It's Nice to Go Trav'ling."

Frank, looking lean, tanned, and handsome (and only lightly toupeed), led off with

> *It's very nice to go travelin', to join the Army and roam,*
> *It's very nice to go travelin', but it's so much nicer, yes, it's so much nicer to*
> *come home.*

Then the petite, nineteen-year-old Nancy, who'd recently announced her engagement to teen idol Tommy Sands, emerged, looking all grown up in a white décolleté gown and white gloves. She sounded a bit less than grown up, however, as she linked arms with her father and sang, in a pleasant but little-girlish voice, how nice it was to play hostess and help Daddy to welcome Elvis home.

And then, after the full ensemble gave a transcendently corny lead-in, complete with "drums . . . drummin'" and "guitars . . . strummin'," a prop door opened, and the girls in the audience screamed dutifully (but not uncontrollably) at the first sight of their idol, emerging in a dress uniform and hat and strolling downstage as the ensemble parted to form a worshipful aisle.

Towering over Frank, especially in that dress hat, Elvis faced the camera— the army had slimmed him, heightening his cheekbones and his long-lashed, Adonis-like good looks—and gamely but shyly sang, "It's very nice to go travelin', but it's so, so, nice to come home," before a bevy of young ladies, including Nancy, whisked him offstage.

And then he was gone for the next thirty-five minutes of the show, while Frank sang a few numbers and made corny chitchat with Joey Bishop ("I was just going to tell Elvis what happened to the record business while he was away: albums started selling again—my albums"), and Sammy Davis Jr. sang and danced, and the Tom Hansen Dancers danced, and Peter Lawford (who wasn't mentioned in the credits) came out and danced with Sammy and made more corny chitchat.

It was all pretty pallid fun—which Frank seemed to realize as he finally, rhetorically asked the audience, in quasi–*Amos 'n' Andy* accents, "Now, folks— what would you say if I was gonna sing another song now?"

"Nooo," the teenagers obediently groaned, segueing into a chant (was it all coached?)—"We want Elvis"—that didn't have to go on for long before their idol reappeared, dressed in a tux this time, his sideburns still cut military short ("It made a man of me," he'd said of the army, "and I don't intend to raise side-burns again") but the trademark pile of black hair, miraculously regenerated in the twenty-four days since he'd flown home from Germany, rising skyward with a life all its own. He gave the camera a knowing look—the dress uniform had seemed to inhibit him; now he was free—and then, with a slight smirk, went into his first number:

Fame and fortune,
How empty they can be.

It was a slow ballad, not much of a song, and the camera only showed him from the waist up. From the waist up, singing a ballad, he was just a handsome ballad singer. But when he started his next song, the rocker "Stuck on You," the angle lengthened to show him full body, and he began to snap the fingers of both hands (wrists close together), shake his hips, and rock that big heap of hair, which took on a life all its own. Now the screams were in earnest. As they had every right to be. Even through the grainy blur of a fifty-year-old kin-escope, his charisma pops from the screen. He radiates total authority.

As he finished, Frank and Joey emerged from stage right, two oldish, bald-ish guys in tuxes clapping dutifully, like members of the show-business Polit-buro. Frank shook Elvis's hand. "Elvis, that was great, and I'm glad to see the army hasn't changed you," he said. "Wasn't that great?" he asked Joey.

"That's the first time I ever heard a woman screaming at a male singer," the comedian deadpanned. Broadly.

Frank put his hands on his hips and gave him a look. Elvis laughed.

Then Joey teed up another one. "Excuse me, Mr. Presley," he said, "but would you think it presumptuous of Frank if he joined you in a duet?"

And so it happened: what the world wouldn't quite have been able to believe would ever happen. As Nelson Riddle swung the band into an upbeat tempo, the two of them traded fours, Frank singing a bar of a jazzed-up "Love Me Tender," Elvis singing a rockabilly bar of "Witchcraft." Endearingly, Pres-ley mocked himself with exaggerated head shakes and grimaces, and Frank grinned with what looked like real delight. Both seemed to be having the time of their lives.

Then Frank put an arm over Elvis's shoulder, Elvis put an arm over Frank's shoulder, and as the tempo slowed, they harmonized on the last line of "Tender":

For my darling, I love you—

Frank brightened. "Man, that's *pretty,*" he interjected.

And I always will.

Then, as the band went into the final chords, the two of them freed their arms, danced in place—Frank wriggling into a brief Elvis imitation—and it was done. They were equals onstage.

Elvis had been on, in aggregate from the start of the show, for a grand total of seven and a half minutes.

Clash of the titans: Frank and Elvis on Sinatra's final ABC television special, March 26, 1960. Sinatra swallowed his intense dislike of Presley to score a big ratings hit.

There's a tiny moment, three-quarters of the way through the duet, when Elvis goes cheekily off script, throwing in a word change: singing, instead of "there's no nicer witch than you,"

there's no nicer witch than—witchcraft.

And Frank takes it right in stride—more than takes it in stride: gives Elvis a foxy, appreciative laugh—*hah-ha!*—and, total pro that he is, goes on smoothly with the last bit of "Love Me Tender."

In that moment, Sinatra is welcoming Presley to the Great Showbiz Fraternity, and at this crucial hinge point in his career Elvis is headed straight to Hollywood and Vegas.

Cahn and Van Heusen, who contributed plentiful special material to the Frank and Elvis show, were also credited as the program's producers, and both were present in Miami Beach from rehearsals to broadcast. Sammy and Jimmy, as well as Sammy's wife, Gloria, were also present for Sinatra's final-weekend appearances with the Rat Pack at the Fontainebleau, as were Jack Entratter and Juliet Prowse and Judy Campbell and many others. It was a gala stand, every show packed to the gills.

Also present was Sinatra's good pal, the Fontainebleau's "entertainment director," Joe Fischetti. It's doubtful that Joe Fish, as Frank had introduced him, troubled himself much with booking singers and stand-up comics. Rather, the hotel was his Miami base of operations, as it was for his close associate Sam Giancana, and in March of that year Sinatra appears to have been eager to enlist their aid in the Kennedy campaign. In typically tortuous FBI syntax, a bureau report from March 1960 quoted an informant as saying that Frank was "being made available to assist Senator Kennedy's campaign whereby Joe Fischetti and other hoodlums will have an entrée to Senator Kennedy."

Being made available by whom? There's a hint in a recollection of Sammy Cahn's, portraying Sinatra as a matchmaker between two Joes, Fish and Kennedy: "Frank asked me, 'Sammy, take Papa Joe down the hall and introduce him to Mr. Fischetti.' So there I was, walking through the hotel, taking the father of the soon-to-be Democratic nominee down the hall to meet Mr. Fischetti. I mean, one of the best-known criminals in the United States!"

Cahn always was prone to bombast—in fact, Fischetti was more under the radar than a lot of other mobsters, and Joseph Kennedy wasn't exactly a

Sunday-school teacher when it came to consorting with criminals. Just possibly, Papa Joe had asked for the introduction. In any case, the point was clear: Sinatra, the senior Kennedy, and the Chicago mobsters were playing "a dangerous game," in Sammy Cahn's words, mixing the volatile elements of politics, organized crime, and show business.

Judy Campbell was now deep in the mix. For all the emotional candor of her memoir (the facts are a different matter: Judith Campbell Exner would later tell Seymour Hersh that she had "deliberately fudged" some of the details in her book "out of fear"), her recollections of Sam Giancana betray a surprising credulity. "I paid a terrible price for my association with Sam," she writes, "but I have never been one to judge people because of what others have said about them. I believe in finding out for myself."

What she failed to find out was that when Frank introduced her to the well-dressed Mr. Flood, Giancana was poised to pull her into an extraordinarily audacious and cynical scheme. "In March, when Mooney learned that Kennedy was bedding Judy Campbell on a regular basis, he was close to ecstatic," Sam Giancana and Chuck Giancana, Momo's godson and brother, write in *Double Cross*, their chronicle of the gangster's peak years. "He wanted Kennedy to have a 'regular,' someone he could eventually manipulate and use to his own advantage. With Judy Campbell, it appeared he'd struck gold."

The details of the setup, as recollected by Exner herself, are chilling. She was at a party in the French Room of the Fontainebleau with her date, the Texas oil heir and playboy Bob Neal. Suddenly, as if by chance, Neal spotted Joe Fischetti and Skinny D'Amato and steered her toward them. Behind D'Amato stood Sinatra, in conversation with a man she had never seen before. Frank smiled at her. "Come here, Judy," he said. "I want you to meet a good friend of mine, Sam Flood."

"I offered my hand, but instead of shaking it, Sam Flood held it in his two hands," Exner writes.

"It's a pleasure, Judy," he said, giving my hand a little squeeze but still holding on. He was middle-aged, of medium build and ruddy complexion, but with penetrating dark eyes. "Do you mind if I say something, Judy?"

"Not at all—I think."

He laughed, and it was a hearty laugh, the kind you hear from people who laugh a lot. "You're far too beautiful to be wearing junk— excuse me—I mean costume jewelry. A beautiful girl like you should be wearing real pearls and diamonds and rubies."

"A girl like me does sometimes."

She recounts the episode without a trace of irony, the lamb going blithely to the slaughter. Frank, on the other hand, knew all too well what he was doing when he made the handoff. Still, it must be asked: Did he fully understand the transaction's implications? Not to mention the extent to which he himself was being used?

———

The FBI's informant went on to claim that "Fischetti and other hoodlums"—for this, read Giancana and his minions—were "financially supporting and actively endeavoring to secure [Kennedy's] nomination." Yet organized crime continued to be deeply divided about JFK. There were many important figures—notably, top Chicago gangster Murray "the Camel" Humphreys and Teamsters chief Jimmy Hoffa—who hated the Democratic candidate for his tough stance on labor unions and for his and his brother's anti-Mob crusading on the McClellan Committee. (Hoffa would become a fervent Nixon supporter.) With this kind of opposition stacked against him and with key presidential primaries coming up, Kennedy needed all the help he could get. West Virginia—heavily Protestant, intensely anti-Catholic, and looking to be the key battleground between JFK and Hubert Humphrey—was going to be a special challenge.

———

As Lew Spence told the story, while he was in Las Vegas in early 1960, he played "Nice 'n' Easy," the song he'd written with Alan and Marilyn Bergman, for Hank Sanicola, and Sanicola loved it. Unfortunately, Frank didn't. Spence recalled to Will Friedwald that when he played the song for Sinatra during a break from the filming of *Ocean's 11,* "the singer's initial reaction was to pick up the music with the tips of his fingernails and let it fall to the ground like so much garbage."

Sanicola told him not to be discouraged and to play the tune whenever Frank came into the Sands lounge, where he often went after a show in the main room. "Sinatra finally asked, 'What is that cute little thing you keep playing?' And, as Spence recalled, 'Hank told him it was my song and that he was recording it in a couple of weeks. Frank said, 'Well, I better get Nelson and give him a key. I don't remember giving him a key on that one.' Frank not only recorded it but decided that he would make it the title of an album."

Sinatra recorded the number at Capitol on the night of April 13, and Alan and Marilyn Bergman were present, though it was a near thing. "Frank said, 'I don't like writers at sessions, but you guys can come,'" Marilyn Bergman recalled. "He told us where to sit, right in front of the glass in the [control booth]."

"He said, 'You kids can go there,'" Alan Bergman added. "And from then on, he called us 'the kids.'"

"When we were in our seventies he called us 'the kids,'" Marilyn said.

The Bergmans, who would go on to win three Oscars and pen the lyrics for numerous Barbra Streisand hits, were then in their twenties and virtual unknowns. They were surprised at Riddle and Sinatra's playful take on the song, which they had conceived as a sultry number about slow love-making. "I don't think we knew whether we liked [Frank's version] or not," Marilyn Bergman recalled. She was sitting in the booth with her husband, frowning with concentration as Frank sang, when he stopped a take and fixed them with a blue glare. "What is that, the Finch jury in there?" he asked. (Dr. Bernard Finch, a West Covina orthopedist, was then a defendant in a headline-making trial, accused of conspiring with his lover to murder his wife.)

As was usually the case at his Capitol sessions, Frank had an audience: some twenty friends, acquaintances, and ornamental females in folding chairs at the periphery of Studio A. The Bergmans were the only spectators in the booth but were clearly expected, like everyone else, to praise, rather than appraise, Frank's performance. The unspoken subtext was that he was learning a brand-new song at the same time he was trying to set it down for posterity: a high-wire act he was capable of but nervous about. As always, he covered his insecurity with bluster.

He did twelve takes of "Nice 'n' Easy" that night, and he was well aware of the song's sensual subtext—and well aware of his audience, both the appreciative ones on the floor and the judgmental ones in the booth. So he played with the number a little bit, toying with the melody and rhythm here and there (and going slightly flat here and there, too).

After take eight, producer Dave Cavanaugh spoke through the intercom. "Okay," he said. "Rolling right away. E 33650, take nine."

Frank pushed right back. "Ho! Ho! Wait!" he yelled in that big voice. "Ho! Time! What's the matter?"

"Oh, just a couple—" Cavanaugh began.

"Notes? Clams?" Sinatra said. "Whaddya expect? I don't know the song!"

It took him a while, but by take twelve he had it down cold, now interjecting the finger snaps in the second chorus that make the song so beautifully and finally deciding on the double entendre that seals the coda: "Like the man says, one more time."

To listen to the final take is to be unaware of the prickly Sinatra, the vain and insecure Sinatra, or the petty Sinatra: all one hears is hair-raising magnificence, the difference between art and life.

And that twelfth magnificent take changed the course of recording history: all at once, *The Nearness of You* was out as album title and concept (as was the song itself, not to be restored until the 1991 CD reissue of the LP), and suddenly an album of standard ballads was capped with one hell of a lightly swinging love song. It could have not worked, but instead *Nice 'n' Easy* simply *did* work, and superbly: after its issue in July, it spent nine weeks at number 1 on the *Billboard* chart and thirty-five weeks in the Top 40.

"Hollywood is talking about: The man of the week—ex-GI Elvis Presley back in Hollywood to start 'GI Blues' for Hal Wallis Monday morning, Elvis' first movie in over two years," Louella Parsons columnized on April 24.

> So you think his long stint in the army may have quelled the Presley craze? There's more press and TV attention centered on the return of the original rock 'n' roll kid than any local event since Vice President Nixon toured Disneyland.
> And—the girl of the week—pixie-faced French [sic] Dancer Juliet Prowse who picked off the lead with Elvis over the native talent which may make up to Juliet for the cooling of her romance with Frank Sinatra which started in "Can-Can."

"Welcome Home Elvis" aired on Thursday, May 12, and drew a gigantic audience: more than 40 percent of the American TV-watching public—a far greater rating than Frank had ever drawn by himself. It was event television, but it wasn't particularly good television. *Variety*'s reviewer pinned the blame equally on Sinatra and Presley: "Elvis Presley hasn't changed much in the two years since he went away, but the U.S.A. has," wrote "Tube."

> Officially returning to civilian service via "The Frank Sinatra Timex Show," the pomp-adored singer popped out of the picture tube like a pooped caricature of an outmoded image. It was the most significant facet of an hour-long exhibition of embarrassing self-idolatry mixed with occasional, but well-spaced, flashes of grace and talent.

Elvis might have been headed downhill, but Frank was at the top of the heap in every one of his enterprises. The wonder was that television kept throwing so much money at him when it so clearly wasn't his medium.

One year after Frank and Sammy Davis Jr. mended fences at the SHARE Boomtown benefit for retarded children at the Hollywood Moulin Rouge, Frank caused a melee at the same event. The benefit was once again a costume party with a western theme, and once again the evening was bibulous. Sinatra, never one for political correctness and apparently quite secure in his masculinity, came dressed as an Indian squaw, replete with a headband and a feather.

After the party broke up, in the early hours of Saturday, May 14, Frank, somewhat the worse for wear, headed out to the parking lot with Sammy Davis's bodyguard, the six-foot, 220-pound Big John Hopkins. There Frank spotted John Wayne, whose recent public critique of his hiring of Albert Maltz was still fresh in his mind. In the department of You Can't Make This Stuff Up, Frank, still in his squaw costume, stalked up to Wayne—who of course was dressed in full western regalia, complete with neckerchief and ten-gallon hat—and stood squarely in the much larger actor's path.

"You seem to disagree with me," Frank said.

The fact that Wayne had nine inches in height (more with the hat) and seventy pounds in weight on him meant nothing to Sinatra. It would probably have meant nothing even if he'd been cold sober. But John Wayne, to his credit, spoke conciliatorily. "Now, now, Frank, we can discuss this somewhere else," he said.

At this point, though both principals later denied it, a witness (a reporter for the *Los Angeles Herald-Express*) said that Frank shoved Wayne and that Wayne shoved him back. Friends separated them; Wayne walked away, and Sinatra turned to the newsman. "I suppose you'll write all this down," he said.

Still steaming, Frank stepped—whether intentionally or not isn't clear—into the path of a moving car being driven by a parking attendant named Clarence English. The car screeched to a stop. "Hey, Charley!" Sinatra yelled. "You almost hit me! You know what I'm insured for?"

English shook his head, and Frank raced around to his side of the car. "Can you fight? You'd better be able to," he said to the attendant. He reached for English through the driver's window, and another attendant, twenty-one-year-old Edward Moran, remonstrated with him: "Aw, Frank, he wasn't trying to hit you with the car. He's only trying to make a living."

"Who the fuck are you?" Frank said and pushed Moran, who then made the mistake of trying to defend himself, striking Frank.

Big John Hopkins stepped in and began raining blows on Moran, while Sinatra, the squaw costume dressing the scene, danced up and down, shouting, "Tell that guy not to sue me if he knows what's good for him! I'll break both his legs!"

Presently, Frank and Hopkins got into Sammy Davis's Rolls-Royce and drove away.

Moran, who was treated for facial cuts and bruises, disobeyed Frank's order, bringing a $100,000 suit against him for violent assault. Sinatra settled out of court.

14

||||||||||

He's no friend of mine, he's just a friend of Pat and Peter.

—JOHN F. KENNEDY, ABOUT SINATRA

The golf-course conversation between Frank and Sam Giancana seemed to have worked wonders.

On May 10, even though West Virginia was 95 percent Protestant and fervently anti-Catholic, John F. Kennedy somehow managed to defeat the Protestant Hubert Humphrey soundly in that state's key Democratic primary. Kennedy's victory finally crushed Humphrey's presidential hopes and proved that a Catholic was electable to the highest office in the land.

It was like the cautionary tale in *Guys and Dolls* about the jack of spades jumping out of a brand-new deck of cards and squirting cider in your ear: it couldn't have happened, it shouldn't have happened, but it did happen.

How? Start with a state whose politics even the relentlessly dignified Theodore H. White called "squalid, corrupt, and despicable." Having just squeaked past Humphrey in Wisconsin, the Kennedys did not want to leave anything to chance. In West Virginia, Seymour Hersh writes, the family "spent at least $2 million [comparable to nearly $16 million as of this writing] . . . and possibly twice that amount—much of it in direct payoffs to state and local officials."

A popular version of the story has it that this was Mob money, ordered up by Joe Kennedy in a chain of communication that went from Frank Sinatra to Sam Giancana to Skinny D'Amato. One writer asserts, "Giancana sent Skinny D'Amato to West Virginia to get votes for Jack Kennedy. He was to use his influence with the sheriffs who controlled the political machine of the state. Most of them had been customers at the 500 Club, and according to Skinny, love[d] him like a brother. Whether he helped turn the tide for Kennedy in that crucial primary state is not as important as the fact that Giancana sent him there on Kennedy's behalf."

And the fact that Frank got the ball rolling.

Even by his friends' estimation, Skinny was no political mastermind. Though folklore depicts him roaming West Virginia like a wiseguy Johnny Appleseed, "spreading money around like manure," he only owned up—in an FBI wiretap—to spending $50,000 in the state, "not for direct bribes, but to purchase desks, chairs, and other supplies needed by local politicians."

The bureau also overheard D'Amato talking about Las Vegas cash going to the Kennedys. Sammy Davis Jr. seemed to confirm the story. In a memoir, he wrote that while JFK amused himself in Sinatra's suite at the Sands in February 1960, Peter Lawford took Davis aside and whispered, "If you want to see what a million dollars in cash looks like, go into the next room. There's a brown leather satchel in the closet. Open it. It's a gift from the hotel owners for Jack's campaign."

But the Sands pit boss Ed Walters, who was privy to the dealings of the casino's real owners, vigorously disputes the idea that they would have backed Kennedy so heavily. "I'm positive it never happened," he insists. "Jack Entratter would have nothing to do with it"—primarily because the Teamsters, whose support was so important to the Sands and other casinos, were passionately anti-Kennedy. "We would have lost all our loans, all our power," Walters says.

As for that delectable vision of $1 million cash in a brown leather satchel, "It's a joke," says the former pit boss. "That's ten million today. We wouldn't give a million dollars to *anybody*."

And in any case, why would the Kennedys have needed money from the Mob? Joe Kennedy's fortune was vast, and he spared no expense in buying the presidency for his son. In late 1959 and early 1960, Teddy and Bobby Kennedy roamed West Virginia greasing the palms of committeemen, sheriffs, and clergymen—quite liberally. One estimate has the Kennedys' overall outlay in the state at between $3 million and $5 million. Wisconsin had depleted the war chest of Humphrey, a tough campaigner who was not averse to buying votes when it was necessary. The Kennedys simply outspent him.

Skinny D'Amato might have been more eyes and ears than pocketbook in West Virginia. And as crucial as that primary was, the true burden of Frank and Mooney's golf-course parlay was the election in Illinois.

Maybe the romance with Juliet Prowse had cooled; maybe it hadn't. The gossip columns were hinting something was going on between Prowse and Elvis on the *G.I. Blues* shoot, but then rumors like that were the stock-in-trade of the gossip columns, not to mention the Paramount publicity department. For his part, Frank, who could blow hot and cold from minute to minute, appeared less than obsessed with the leggy South African, never a good sign. As Judith Campbell Exner noted of Prowse's presence along with her own at the Fontainebleau in March, "Each girl in Frank's life has a certain amount of time allotted to her." Except for Ava, of course, who lingered like a haunting refrain.

At the end of May, with George Jacobs and Jimmy Van Heusen in tow, Sinatra flew off on a bachelor jaunt to the Far East. When a reporter for the

U.S. Army newspaper *Stars and Stripes* asked for his impressions of Japan, he seemed quite content to be away from home.

"I dig the sake and the kids," Frank said. And the women? "We had to travel around the world to learn that girls can be girls," he replied. "Japanese chicks don't have nicotine stains on their fingers. They don't wear trousers and you don't smell of Chanel Number Five after shaking hands with them. I'm not interested in defending individuals. If the boot fits—c'est la vie."

That last bit was strange and a little chilling. Whoever could he have been talking about?

He brought Prowse back a jade bracelet and a double string of matched pearls, but his main interest upon coming home was returning to the Kennedy campaign. This was where the action was—the grandest on earth that summer—and recording, filmmaking, and nightclub appearances would have to wait. Frank Sinatra (those distancing official statements of the campaign, no doubt generated by Bobby Kennedy, notwithstanding) had another key role to play, right in his hometown.

The Democratic National Convention was to be held in Los Angeles at the brand-new Memorial Sports Arena beginning on July 11, and the metropolis was at peak receptiveness as 45,000 visitors, including 4,509 delegates and alternates and 4,750 news representatives, streamed in to take part in and witness a pivotal moment in history. The weather was perfect that week, as Theodore H. White wrote, in *The Making of the President, 1960:* "Smogless and milk-blue, the skies stretched on day after day, as gentle and pure as they must have been a generation ago, before industry and the automobile fouled the air of the city with their wastes." The delegates were scattered in hostelries across the city, but the grand old Biltmore Hotel in downtown L.A., not far from Union Station and overlooking seedy Pershing Square, was the convention's nerve center.

Norman Mailer, on assignment for *Esquire,* observed,

> The Biltmore [was] where everybody gathered every day—the newsmen, the TV, radio, magazine, and foreign newspapermen, the delegates, the politicos, the tourists, the campaign managers, the runners, the flunkies, the cousins and aunts, the wives, the grandfathers, the eight-year-old girls, and the twenty-eight-year-old girls in the Kennedy costumes, red and white and blue, the Symingteeners, the Johnson Ladies, the Stevenson Ladies, everybody.

The severe, fifty-nine-year-old Stuart Symington was a very dark horse at this point; the fifty-one-year-old Lyndon Johnson had recently entered the race; and sixty-year-old Adlai Stevenson, who'd lost by landslides in 1952 and

1956, was the sentimental—if not the practical—favorite of the Democratic Party's liberal wing. But forty-three-year-old Jack Kennedy, who'd won seven primaries coming into the convention, was the man to beat. As of July 1, he had 550 delegates locked up, of the 761 necessary to capture the presidential nomination, and realistic—but by no means definite—hopes of capturing the remainder. (Predictably, if defensibly, Johnson was forecasting that Kennedy would lose on the second ballot.) JFK's young and dynamic campaign team, led by his relentless brother Bobby, would have to shift from its customary overdrive into an even higher gear to lock down the nomination for their man.

Theodore White wrote that he had discerned an emerging theme during those first days in July. "From the sounds and sights, from the hundreds of lost and milling faces in the Biltmore," he wrote, "the press distilled a swift truth that was a remarkably accurate historic assessment: that this was the convention where the young faced the old, this was the convention where one generation gave way to another, this was—in [the *New York Times* columnist] James Reston's felicitous phrase—the assembly that witnessed the Changing of the Guard."

Mailer was the sharpest of all witnesses. On Saturday, July 9, he trained his gimlet eye on Kennedy's arrival at the Biltmore. "He had the deep orange-brown suntan of a ski instructor," he wrote in his piece "Superman Comes to the Supermarket,"

> and when he smiled at the crowd his teeth were amazingly white and clearly visible at a distance of fifty yards . . . [A]nd then with a quick move he was out of his car and by choice headed into the crowd instead of the lane cleared for him into the hotel by the police, so that he made his way inside surrounded by a mob, and one expected at any moment to see him lifted to its shoulders like a matador being carried back to the city after a triumph in the plaza . . . And suddenly . . . I understood the mood of depression which had lain over the convention, because finally it was simple: the Democrats were going to nominate a man who, no matter how serious his political dedication might be, was indisputably and willy-nilly going to be seen as a great box-office actor, and the consequences of that were staggering and not at all easy to calculate.

This was the man with whom Frank Sinatra had thrown in his lot.

It is important to recognize the depth of Frank's discernment in this regard—a level of acumen not inferior to Norman Mailer's. The Jack Kennedy who dazzled Sinatra was the whole package: the radiantly charismatic super-star; the pussy-obsessed hound who showed George Jacobs his most merrily vulgar side; the man whom Theodore White observed quoting Churchill's history of Marlborough, citing Theodore Roosevelt's report on the funeral of Edward VII, and shifting

> from Marlborough and the writing of history to the personality of Adlai
> E. Stevenson and the quality of the American intellectuals. Then to
> a long, tender and perceptive disquisition on the Irish and the Jews
> in American life. From that to the American Negroes and what their
> problems were—and their search for leadership. Did so-and-so really
> control in Harlem? Was so-and-so really a reader of history, as reported,
> or was it just a story? Then to the Chinese again.

Kennedy's erudition was truly stunning (and try to imagine its like in any political candidate today). And Sinatra, an insecure autodidact, was stunned by it.

Leave the last word to Mailer. "Since the First World War," he writes,

> Americans have been leading a double life, and our history has moved
> on two rivers, one visible, the other underground; there has been the
> history of politics, which is concrete, factual, practical, and unbeliev-
> ably dull if not for the consequences of the actions of some of these
> men; and there is a subterranean river of untapped, ferocious, lonely
> and romantic desires, that concentration of ecstasy and violence which
> is the dream life of the nation.

Ever since his Hoboken boyhood, the son of the Democratic ward boss and all-around fixer Dolly Sinatra had understood acutely what politics was all about. "He was born into a family that was very politically motivated," Tina Sinatra said. "Dad says that he was carrying placards for candidates when he couldn't read what was on the signs." But from the first moment Frank encountered Jack Kennedy, he knew he had met a man whose political expertise far outweighed his—and the one other man in America whose connection with the nation's dream life was as deep and powerful as his own.

First the parties: a bash for Jack's sister Eunice Shriver on the night of the ninth at the Lawfords' Santa Monica beach house (Senator and Mrs. Kennedy were present, as was Frank); and then, the next evening, a $100-a-plate*

---

* By way of comparison, $100 in 1960 equates, as of this writing, to almost $800.

Democratic fund-raiser at the Beverly Hilton—twenty-eight hundred of Hollywood's elite were in attendance, including Tony Curtis, Janet Leigh, Sammy Davis Jr., Angie Dickinson, Milton Berle, Judy Garland, George Jessel, Joe E. Lewis, Shirley MacLaine, and Mort Sahl.

Santa Monica, Beverly Hills: the other side of the city from the Biltmore, the other side of America's political double life.

All the candidates were present at the glittering dinner. Symbolically, Jack Kennedy had been seated at the head table on the dais, next to Garland; Frank sat on the other side of the rostrum with Johnson, Stevenson, and Symington. It was a buoyant occasion, replete with proclamations of party solidarity. "For the candidates, the hour of unity is at hand," Jack Kennedy announced, and he could afford to be upbeat: California's governor, Pat Brown, had just endorsed him, though he had not yet released the state's eighty-one delegates. Just under the veneer of Democratic happy talk, though, was the customary political dissension and jostling. The former president Harry Truman, a Stevenson supporter, had elected not to attend the convention, because, the *Los Angeles Times* reported, it was dominated by Kennedy supporters. "I cannot lend myself to what is happening," Truman said.

When Eleanor Roosevelt made a surprise appearance, escorted to a head table seat between Senator Kennedy and Judy Garland, she "was wearing a lilac-flowered hat and print dress with a small Stevenson button," the *Times* noted. "She greeted her favorite candidate warmly and later moved to the other side of the rostrum to a seat between Sen. Symington and Gov. Brown"—and close to Sinatra, her friend, her television host, but not her political ally. He would have been less comfortable than she with the ambiguity.

Lyndon Johnson, the closing speaker, was making a final charge, "still trying hard to sink Kennedy without a trace," the *Times* said. "Speaking without any advance text, Johnson warned that 'Premier Khrushchev seeks to raise over the world a roof of rockets' and said the nation must choose new leadership which has 'the wisdom and soundness of the years.'"

That was Sunday night. Then came convention Monday.

———

Frank was among a star-spangled chorale scheduled to sing the national anthem at the televised opening session. The other performers included Ralph Bellamy, Nat King Cole, Tony Curtis, Sammy Davis Jr., George Jessel, Peter Lawford, Janet Leigh, Shirley MacLaine, Lee Marvin, Vincent Price, Edward G. Robinson, and Shelley Winters. Edward G. Robinson got a big hand when he was introduced from the rostrum, as did Janet Leigh, along with wolf whistles for her low-cut Don Loper gown. But when Davis was introduced from the rostrum, a deep sound welled up from one section of the vast convention floor: it was the sound of booing, coming from the Mississippi delegation.

Sammy had long been a lightning rod—among blacks and whites, in the press—for his relationships with white women. Columbia studio chief Harry Cohn had had a mobster friend threaten to put out his good eye if he didn't break off his relationship with Kim Novak, whom Cohn considered studio property. But then, after a short-lived sham marriage to a black woman, Sammy had found another white goddess, the blond, long-legged Swedish actress May Britt. The two announced their engagement in the spring of 1960, and in those racially benighted times much of the nation, not just the South, was scandalized and repelled.

But the Mississippi delegation was vociferous, and Davis was stunned at the eruption of raw racism at a forward-thinking political convention in sunny Los Angeles. As he blinked back tears, Frank whispered to him, "Those dirty sons of bitches! Don't let 'em get you, Charley. Hang on. Don't let it get you!"

It got to him, though afterward, as his fellow stars tried to console him, he did what he felt he had to: suck it up. "I don't know why they booed me," Sammy told a reporter. "But I can't blame anyone for the way they feel."

The booing returned on Tuesday night during the reading of the party's civil rights plank. Frank made his entrance around the same time, signing autographs in front of the California delegation. "Sinatra is for Sen. John F. Kennedy and wanders freely about the convention floor as the guest of Peter Lawford, the senator's brother-in-law," wrote United Press International's Merriman Smith. It wasn't just Frank. Although access to the floor was strictly limited to those with a pass, a certain core of celebrities—the Jack Pack—had carte blanche to roam the aisles, kibitzing and boosting their man. Sinatra, Peter Lawford, and Shirley MacLaine carried stopwatches, clocking the applause for each nominee. Adlai Stevenson, the sentimental favorite, drew the biggest ovations of all, but—especially after Kennedy held his own against Johnson in a televised debate—the only question now was on which ballot the charismatic young candidate would be chosen.

And as the torch passed to a new, camera-ready generation, technology came right along. Because it was 1960 and because it was Los Angeles, the capital of show business, this convention was more TV-friendly than any political gathering in history. Fifteen hundred correspondents, commentators, technicians, directors, and producers had descended on L.A. We take it for granted now; then it was all brand-new. "When the Democrats convene in the new blue and white Sports arena in Los Angeles . . . the searching eyes of 100 television cameras will be upon them," the *Milwaukee Journal*'s Don Dornbrook wrote.

This will put an estimated 92 million home viewers at the convention. It also will raise hob with the delegates' privacy.

Suppose, for example, that a delegate tries to remain inconspicuous on the floor of the 18,000 seat arena. He can be ferreted out by the creepy peepy portable TV camera. It has a pistol grip and can be aimed into the middle of a dramatic huddle on the convention floor to give the viewer at home a close-up of a key figure caught at a historic moment.

Portable TV cameras on the floor of the sports arena were a big step toward a future of omnipresent surveillance. But then, Sinatra was used to controlling his image. "Conscious of television," Kitty Kelley wrote, "Frank had painted the back of his head black so that the cameras would not pick up his shiny bald pate." In fact, there was no need for such a contortion: George Jacobs had been performing this service for his boss for quite some time. "Every morning after he shampooed," the former valet wrote, "I'd have to spray hair coloring on the ever-expanding bald spot on the back of his scalp." Jacobs also recalled another part of Sinatra's daily toilette, something Frank did himself: applying pancake makeup to the scarred left side of his face.

On the morning of Wednesday the thirteenth, Jack Kennedy addressed six caucuses, trying to nail down the votes he needed for a first-ballot victory, before returning to his rented hideaway, an apartment in the Hancock Park district. It was 3:30 p.m., half an hour before nominations were to begin. To his chagrin, he'd been discovered: the sidewalk in front of the place was packed with print and TV reporters. A few minutes later, Kennedy and his pal Dave Powers descended the fire escape in the rear of the apartment, climbed over the back fence, and drove to the Beverly Hills mansion that Joe Kennedy had rented from Marion Davies. (As a controversial figure, the elder Kennedy kept a low profile during the campaign.) JFK "spent the rest of the afternoon there at the swimming pool, dining on Irish stew with his father, his mother, Dave Powers and his cousin, Anne Gargan," Theodore White writes. Frank was also there—tending bar, to the surprise of another visitor, David McDonald, president of the steelworkers' union, who was handed a cold one by Sinatra himself.

As afternoon turned to evening, JFK stayed at the house to watch the nominating speeches on television while Frank returned to the sports arena. There he witnessed what White called "the high point of drama in the Los Angeles Convention . . . the placing in nomination of Adlai E. Stevenson by Senator Eugene McCarthy of Minnesota." Stevenson, who had decided not to run a third time, had nevertheless said that he would accept a draft. (He had also refused to support Kennedy, incurring the lasting enmity of the candidate and his family.) The erudite Illinoisan was a kind of prophet, and a kind of great man, heaped with honors—and heaped with scorn by much of the country as the original egghead. He was a great sentimental favorite among liberal Democrats, but at sixty he was a man of yesterday rather than a man of tomorrow. That man was Kennedy, whose nomination was now all but inevitable.

"This the delegates knew; but not the galleries," White wrote. As McCarthy concluded his speech, the floor erupted with a roaring chant: "WE WANT STEVENSON!" The tumult continued for five solid minutes. Conductor Johnny Green—the former musical director of MGM and the composer of "Body and Soul"—struck up the convention band to try to quell the tumult; someone even had the lights turned out. Frank sat backstage, watching the demonstration and shaking his head. He gave his friend Green the "cut" sign, drawing his hand across his throat; the band stopped playing, but the pandemonium continued.

When it finally died down, Minnesota governor Orville Freeman—scarcely as riveting a presence as Gene McCarthy—stood and placed Jack Kennedy's name in nomination, and then the chairman began to call the roll of states in alphabetical order. By the time Wisconsin cast its 23 votes, Kennedy's total of delegates stood at 748. Then came the last state, Wyoming.

" 'Wyoming,' chanted Tracy S. McCraken, Wyoming's national committeeman, 'casts all fifteen votes for the next President of the United States.' "

Now the pandemonium was Kennedy's. Across the floor, his supporters chanted, "All the way with JFK!" Backstage, Frank and the Jack Pack jumped up and down with excitement, pounding each other on the back. "We're on our way to the White House, buddy boy," Frank told Lawford. "We're on our way to the White House!"

Ambivalent about yielding his immense power as Senate majority leader, Lyndon Johnson had entered the presidential race late, and the Kennedy campaign machine simply mowed him down. At the convention, Johnson predicted that the power of his Stop Kennedy coalition—Stevenson, Symington, and Humphrey were all on board—would give him a second-ballot victory, but there was no second ballot: he received 409 votes to JFK's 806.

Then came the question of the vice presidency.

After losing the nomination, Johnson conferred with his close friend and mentor, Speaker of the House Sam Rayburn, and decided he wanted the office that former vice president John Nance Garner had once described as "not worth a bucket of warm piss." Once in office, LBJ reasoned, he could transfer his power as majority leader to his new position as president of the Senate. It would not work out that way.

The story of John Kennedy's surprise selection of LBJ as his running mate is a tangled thicket. A simple version is that despite JFK's apparently strong preference for Symington, and Bobby Kennedy's detestation of Johnson (who had all but called Joe Kennedy a Nazi during his sharp-elbowed campaign), Jack Kennedy's need to have LBJ's southern Democrats with him in what was anticipated to be a very tight race against Richard Nixon led him to make the practical, rather than the sentimental, choice.

A less simple version is that Johnson blackmailed his way into the vice presidency.

A senior campaign aide to JFK, Hyman Raskin, told Seymour Hersh that Kennedy had admitted as much to him soon after selecting LBJ. "You know we had never considered Lyndon, but I was left with no choice," the candidate said to Raskin. "He and Sam Rayburn made it damn clear to me that Lyndon had to be the candidate. Those bastards were trying to frame me. They threatened me with problems and I don't need more problems. I'm going to have enough problems with Nixon."

And in 1995, John F. Kennedy's personal secretary Evelyn Lincoln told Anthony Summers what problems had been threatened: J. Edgar Hoover, a friend and political ally of Lyndon Johnson's, had fed Johnson scandalous, FBI-sourced information about the Kennedys "during the campaign, even before the Convention. And Hoover was in on the pressure on Kennedy at the Convention . . . about womanizing, and things in Joe Kennedy's background, and anything he could dig up. Johnson was using that as clout. Kennedy was angry, because they had boxed him into a corner. He was absolutely boxed in."

If indeed he was boxed in, Frank Sinatra had helped put him there.

On the other hand, Lyndon Johnson's biographer Robert A. Caro devotes many thousands of words to the complex mystery of Kennedy's selection of Johnson without ever mentioning the extortion scenario. The decision was tortuous, Caro writes, and Bobby Kennedy bitterly opposed Johnson, but in the end it was John Kennedy's pragmatism that prevailed. It wouldn't be long before that same pragmatism would come back to bite Sinatra.

―――――

"It is my earnest conviction, as I depart" the convention, syndicated columnist Inez Robb wrote, "that the endorsement of the Democratic party by Frank Sinatra is not an unmixed blessing or any assurance of certain victory in November."

And the Washington columnist Drew Pearson wrote in his convention wrap-up, "Sen. Jack Kennedy passed the word through his brother-in-law, movie actor Peter Lawford, that he would rather singer Frank Sinatra didn't throw a party for him in Los Angeles . . . Kennedy is worried about Sinatra's association with notorious mobsters and connections with the Las Vegas gambling interests. Sinatra owns 4 per cent [*sic*] of the Sands at Vegas. Kennedy welcomes Sinatra's support but just doesn't want it advertised."

This was serious business. Not long after the convention ended, the Kennedy campaign sent an envoy to Las Vegas to pick up any photographs, and negatives, that showed the candidate socializing with Frank, Dean, Sammy, Peter, and friends.

On the very day that John F. Kennedy received the presidential nomination, a small wire-service dispatch, tucked back amid the entertainment items and gossip columns in many newspapers, reported that Frank and Dean Martin had applied to buy a majority stake in Cal-Neva.

"[Nevada Gaming Control] Board member Ned Turner said the singers and two associates—Henry W. Sanicola of North Hollywood and Paul E. D'Amato of Atlantic City, N.J.—seek 57 per cent of the plush Cal-Neva Lodge at Crystal Bay," the dispatch reported. "Sinatra already owns 6 [*sic*] per cent of the Las Vegas Sands. Now he is applying for 25 per cent in the Cal-Neva. Martin wants 3 per cent, Sanicola 16 and D'Amato 13."

However finely the numbers were parsed, they were largely window dressing. Frank—whose application was approved, along with Dean's and Hank's; Skinny's was held up—was fronting for Sam Giancana, who now effectively co-owned Cal-Neva with Joseph P. Kennedy, the father of the former chief counsel of the McClellan Committee, Robert Kennedy, soon to be the attorney general of the United States.

And Frank's friendship with Mooney had advanced: now they were also business partners.

"Frank Sinatra is extremely close to Paul D'Amato, who runs the 500 Club in Atlantic City," read a memo from Virgil Peterson, the operating director of the Chicago Crime Commission, to Charles LaFrance, chief investigator of the Nevada Gaming Control Board.

Sinatra is trying to get a joint in Nevada which he wants to have operated by D'Amato. D'Amato is associated with all the big hoodlums such as Jerry Catena, Longie [*sic*] Zwillman and Willie Moretti in New Jersey [*sic*: Moretti had been dead since 1951]. It is stated that Sinatra has been very close to D'Amato for a number of years. The 500 Club in Atlantic City has not been too successful, but D'Amato gets out of the hole each year when Sinatra appears as an entertainer for a couple of weeks gratuitously.

On July 20, Frank arrived, solo, in Atlantic City, two days early for his annual stand at the 500 Club. He and Skinny had business to discuss. Under too much heat from the Nevada Gaming Control Board, D'Amato had withdrawn his application for part ownership of Cal-Neva. But that didn't mean he wouldn't be intimately involved in the casino's workings: Skinny's years of running back-room cards and dice joints in Jersey made him the ideal candidate to supervise Cal-Neva's gambling operations. And as the man who had given Martin and Lewis their start, he was also perfectly qualified to oversee entertainment at the Lake Tahoe establishment. Whether or not he had an official piece of the action, Frank would see he was well taken care of.

From the twenty-second through the thirty-first, Sinatra worked his magic at the 500 Club, disrupting traffic on South Missouri Avenue and packing the Five to the rafters for four shows a night, the last at 5:30 a.m. The future New York City talk-show host Bill Boggs, then an eighteen-year-old college student, sneaked into the eleven o'clock show dressed as a busboy, and—never having been in a nightclub or seen Sinatra before—was mesmerized. "It wasn't a big room—maybe three, four hundred people," he recalled, "but the energy was unbelievable. Women with plunging necklines and blond hair, guys with giant cuff links, everybody smoking, drinking, screaming. I thought, How could a guy come out and sing with all this going on? And then he comes out, and everyone goes wild, then silent. He transports these people instantly. What really got me was the sense that he was really conveying real emotions—I could *feel* these emotions coming off him. The songs themselves were like a preview of adult life."

Over the nine nights, Sinatra grossed $400,000, taking home nothing but Skinny's undying gratitude.

Atlantic City loved him, but much of the world continued to give him a fishy eye. In his August 6 column, Leonard Lyons told of a recent high-powered dinner gathering he'd attended with, among others, the producer and screenwriter Charles Brackett, the impresario Billy Rose, the actress Ruth Gordon, and an unnamed TV bigwig. "A new arrival joined us, up from Atlantic City where he'd seen Frank Sinatra entertain at the 500 Club," Lyons wrote. "Sinatra, he said, plans to [continue to] campaign for Kennedy. 'No, he won't,' said the TV executive. 'He's too vulnerable. If they could make Joe Kennedy disappear, they could make Sinatra go 'way too.'"

––––––––

The world premiere of *Ocean's 11* took place—where else?—in Las Vegas at midnight on August 3, 1960. The cocktail party, dinner party, and Summit reunion leading up to the opening made for a Vegas blowout to top all Vegas blowouts, attended by the dozens of stars who'd descended on the gambling mecca for the premiere, which was televised on Jack Paar's *Tonight Show*. Frank, Peter, and Sammy joined Dean (who was already appearing at the Copa Room) and Joey (who'd flown in from a Chicago gig) for the show, which pulled out all the stops. "Their horsing around with race and religion has finally gotten out of hand," complained *Las Vegas Sun* columnist Ralph Pearl. "Mix an abundance of blue material with that and you have an inflammable situation."

The veteran Hollywood columnist Bob Thomas called the show "an experience difficult to describe," though he did a pretty good job of it. "The performers appear onstage as a group or singly, though seldom is one allowed to finish a number," he wrote.

> Many jokes are made about Sammy Davis Jr.'s race (Negro) and religion (Jewish) and the derivation of Dean Martin and Sinatra (Italian).
> Sad-faced Joey Bishop offers sardonic comments interlaced with references to Sinatra as "high lama," "potentate" and "our leader." Peter Lawford's brother-in-law Sen. John F. Kennedy comes in for mention, with speculation of an ambassadorship to Israel for Davis.
> A bar is wheeled out and Sinatra mixes Martin a drink in the ice bucket. Each sings solos in his husky baritone, highball in hand.
> During one number, Lawford, Bishop and comic Buddy Lester walk across the stage chatting, fully clothed except for pants over arms. All lapse into occasional Amos 'n' Andy "dialogue." They join at the end in a ragtag version of "Birth of the Blues."

And there you have it. You had to be there, and even for some who were there, it didn't quite suffice.

The movie itself was sedate by comparison. *Variety*'s review was clear-eyed and tough. " 'Ocean's Eleven' figures to be a moneymaker in spite of itself," wrote "Tube."

> Although basically a no-nonsense piece about the clan-destine efforts of 11 ex-war buddies to make off with a multi-million dollar loot from five Vegas hotels, it is frequently one resonant wisecrack away from turning into a musical comedy. Laboring under the handicaps of a contrived script, an uncertain approach and a cast weighted down with personalities in essence playing themselves, the Lewis Milestone production never quite makes its point, but romps along merrily unconcerned in the process.

To watch the picture today is a strange experience—especially in light of the George Clooney–Brad Pitt–Matt Damon remakes, two out of three of which are far more fun than the original. The 1960 film's story moves along breezily and stylishly as its multiple-casino-robbing plot proceeds, but the picture can't quite make up its mind whether it's a comedy or a drama: What else can you say about a caper starring Frank Sinatra in which Sinatra neither smiles nor sings? (The only Rat Packer who truly seems to be enjoying himself is Sammy Davis Jr. as that singing, dancing garbageman.) The movie's chief charms are visual: the opening credits by the great graphic designer Saul Bass are terrific (Bass had also created the opening sequences for *The Man with the Golden Arm,* as well as for two Sinatra movies in which the opening sequences were the best part: *Johnny Concho* and *The Pride and the Passion*). And the cinematographer William H. Daniels's vivid, dynamic rendering of the casinos and their denizens make you realize just how compelling, how *fun,* a place the small-town, gangster-run, pre-corporate Vegas could be.

What's far less compelling—to a present-day viewer, at any rate—is *Ocean's 11*'s vision of manhood, 1960-style. Why were the wartime buddies robbing the casinos? Not just for the money, but, as Santopietro notes, to "inject some sorely needed excitement into their postwar lives, which had been disappointing in their blandness and rigidity." The same might be said, Santopietro writes, for the audiences who flocked to see the Rat Pack in Vegas and the movie they made: "Onstage and onscreen, Frank Sinatra and friends were living out the fantasies of all middle-aged men who felt trapped in marriage, suburbia, and playing by the rules. They were men who wanted their freedom back."

Fair enough—in fantasy anyway—but what about the women who were the other side of the equation? The females in the film are mostly just ornaments or adjuncts, easily ordered around and put in their place, as when Sinatra's character Danny Ocean tells his estranged wife, played by Angie Dickinson, "Now just sit there and don't interrupt me." Or as when Danny walks into a room where Lawford's character is being massaged by a blonde in short shorts and tells the blonde and her similarly blond friend, "OK, girls—time for your nap. Beat it." Or, most startlingly, as when Dean Martin's character announces he's going to go into politics. His platform? "Repeal the Fourteenth [*sic*] and the Twentieth [*sic*] Amendment—take the vote away from the women, make slaves out of 'em."

In real life, of course, none of the Rat Packers enjoyed such commanding or tidy relations with the opposite sex. Both Joey and Dean had been married since the 1940s and had spent much of their lives on the road; infer what you will. Lawford, who had been fitfully employed and frequently unfaithful since his 1954 marriage to Pat Kennedy, had fallen in his wife's estimation as her family's political fortunes rose. And while Frank, in the midst of his most prolonged period of bachelorhood, was flying high—artistically, financially, sexually—he still carried a torch for the love of his life and battled constantly against the demons that always threatened. He was the Leader of the Clan—but he was also the one who needed the group most of all. The fun of his epic bachelorhood was long and loud and real, but there was also a desperate, million-miles-an-hour quality to it—a lunar loneliness just beneath the surface.

———

Writing about *Ocean's 11*, *Variety*'s reviewer had accused Frank, Dean, Sammy, and Peter of "acting under the stigma of their own flashy, breezy identities . . . [They] never quite submerge themselves in their roles, nor do they seem to be trying very hard to do so."

But why should they have submerged themselves in new roles when the flashy, breezy identities they had brought to the Copa Room seemed to be working just fine? The Summit's act wasn't demanding or sophisticated; it was just naughtiness, at a time (post-Havana) when Las Vegas was establishing itself as the nation's Capital of Naughty, in an era when the national bar for naughtiness wasn't very high (or low). It was a time when the lettuce was iceberg and the bread white, when there were three networks of television and one variety of sex (or you were in big trouble). When fellatio was a rumor rather than a commonplace; when Judy Campbell could be shocked, shocked, at Frank Sinatra and then Jack Kennedy for proposing she participate in a threesome.

This last was no coincidence. Frank and Jack were national pathfinders of sex, our proxy explorers, boldly going where few men had gone before. They recognized the inclination in each other at the start; they admired each other extravagantly for it. It was wise of the Kennedy campaign to seize those photographs and negatives of JFK with the Rat Pack in Vegas, the white-hot center, the national test lab, of naughtiness.

And yet there was a hollowness to all this misbehavior—and not just morally speaking. The Summit's act at the Sands was infantile, the grown-up equivalent of fart jokes. It was a reaction to the profound national torpor of the 1950s: the Rat Pack "depended for its vitality on what Gore Vidal has called 'the great national nap' of the 1950s—at times Frank and 'the Clan' seemed the only people awake after 10:00 p.m.," writes the professor and cultural critic T. H. Adamowski. The Summit was a declaration of superiority—except that the most superior one of all, the Leader, was himself a whirl of chaos, centerless. The emperor was not only naked but manic-depressive.

But he was still the emperor. No one could crack the whip at Frank in a TV studio, nor could Lewis Milestone rein him in on a movie set. No one was directing the Summit shows, and that was the trouble. The only place Sinatra could be controlled, could be artistically exacting, was where he could be his own boss—the recording studio.

And he didn't want to record in Capitol's studio anymore.

———————

Or did he? Over four nights, three at the end of August and one on the first of September, Frank went into that big round tower, the one he'd recently threatened to tear down, and laid down the very odd album that would be titled *Sinatra's Swingin' Session!!!*

The LP's core was a reprise of half a dozen standards that had appeared on Frank's first long-playing album, Columbia's *Sing and Dance with Frank Sinatra*. On the face of it, the idea of Nelson Riddle's ringing changes on Axel Stordahl's 1950 arrangements was unimpeachable: it had worked beautifully on *Nice 'n' Easy*. But for the new, up-tempo album, Sinatra wanted much shorter tracks, as Riddle recalled to Ed O'Brien. "He told me that Frank instructed him to do just one run-through on most of the songs," O'Brien said. "Frank didn't want to repeat a lot of choruses."

Fair enough. On a ballad, Sinatra might sing the song's verse (introduction), then its first and second choruses, then the bridge, then repeat one of the choruses—and then, after an instrumental, sing one of the choruses again. On up-tempo tunes, he usually eliminated the verse and extra choruses. Yet when Sinatra arrived at the first *Swingin' Session* recording date, he had a surprise for Riddle: he announced "that he wanted to do all the tunes at tempos twice as fast as he had previously planned," Will Friedwald writes. "Riddle hadn't given him any four- or five-minute epics to start with, so Sinatra's decision left them with a whole bunch of tracks that were short enough to fit on an answering machine message and a twenty-five-minute album—not much longer than the original ten-inch *Sing and Dance* disc."

Twenty-six minutes and nine seconds, to be exact, was the length of the album: this was an LP without the L. Every one of *Swingin' Session*'s twelve tracks was under three minutes, and three of the songs clocked in at close to a minute and a half.

What was going on?

"The whole album lasts six minutes because Sinatra sped everything up to fuck Capitol," Jonathan Schwartz says. In Nelson Riddle's opinion, *Swingin' Session* was "a disaster."

The argument has merits. Even as Frank sang in Studio A, his mind was on the new record label that (as we'll soon see) was already in the works. Listen to his update of the Walter Donaldson–George A. Whiting classic "My Blue Heaven," and you may find yourself shaking your head in disbelief: it sounds as though Sinatra were trying to set a land-speed record. The number has the drive of rock 'n' roll—Buddy Collette's honking, bopping tenor-sax solo seems to come straight from a juke joint—but it lacks the joy of rock 'n' roll. It's hard to imagine anyone dancing to this. To make sure you get the point—we're going *fast* here—Frank drops the first word of each phrase at the beginning of the lyric, so that

> *When whippoorwills call*
> *And evening is nigh*
> *I hurry to my blue heaven*

becomes

> *Whippoorwills call*
> *Evenin' is nigh*
> *Hurry to my blue heaven*

It's positively Hemingwayesque. Sinatra's hurry—to finish up with Capitol, to move on to the next thing—is so blatant that there's a kind of giddiness to it.

On its release early the next year, "the album reached Number Three on the *Billboard* chart and hung around for thirty-six weeks," Ed O'Brien says. "Disk jockeys loved it. They could lead into the news at one fifty-eight before the hour with a complete Sinatra song. The album got a great deal of airplay."

Norman Granz, the founder (in 1956) of Verve Records, worked with, and befriended, virtually every great jazz musician of the mid-twentieth century— the label's roster would grow to include Bill Evans, Stan Getz, Billie Holiday, Oscar Peterson, Ben Webster, and Lester Young, among many others—but Ella Fitzgerald was arguably the central figure in his career, as he was in hers, not only as the head of her record company, but as Fitzgerald's manager and concert impresario. Her first album at Verve was 1956's groundbreaking, Granz-produced *Ella Fitzgerald Sings the Cole Porter Song Book*, which became one of the best-selling jazz records of all time. Between 1956 and 1959, Ella and Granz followed that LP with four more songbook albums, devoted to the compositions of Rodgers and Hart, Duke Ellington, Irving Berlin, and George and Ira Gershwin. It was incomparable jazz singing, on what was quickly becoming the premier jazz label.

By the late 1950s, Norman Granz had begun to parlay his various jazz enterprises into great wealth. He was a connoisseur of fine food, wine, art, and automobiles and a lover of beautiful women. He was also handsome, athletic, magnetic, and blessed with an extremely good opinion of himself. And he was ferociously protective of his prime artist, Ella Fitzgerald. That stance, and his irrepressible personality, would soon put him on a collision course with Frank Sinatra.

Early on, Granz came to feel that Frank, who had enormous influence in Las Vegas, wasn't doing enough to promote tolerance in that historically racist town. During the 1950s, when Ella Fitzgerald or Sammy Davis Jr. or Lena Horne or Pearl Bailey performed at casinos on the Strip, they couldn't eat in the establishments' restaurants or stay in their hotels. After their shows were over, black entertainers had to go back to rooming houses on the run-down west side of Vegas. For a long time, Sammy wasn't permitted in the steam room at the Sands. Frank pushed for change, but Granz, a firebrand, felt he hadn't pushed early enough or hard enough.

This was his private opinion. But he would soon clash publicly with Sinatra, when Fitzgerald guest starred on Frank's ABC television show in May 1958 (or in another account, on the Timex show of December 1959). As Ella's manager, Granz naturally accompanied her to the taping. But the combination of two strong-willed and egocentric men in one place quickly turned volatile. When Granz began suggesting numbers Ella and Frank could sing together, Frank had him thrown out of the TV studio.

"Frank and Norman didn't see eye to eye," recalled Fitzgerald's pianist, Lou Levy. "Norman would always want to be on top, and no one is on top of Frank Sinatra. Oh yeah! That's Caesar, you don't mess with him!"

But Sinatra and Granz weren't through with each other by any means.

By 1960, Norman Granz had had it with the record business. He had made his real money as an impresario, and though Verve was now profitable—its roster had expanded to include comedy recordings (Shelley Berman, Mort Sahl, Jonathan Winters) and even, by 1958, big-selling pop discs by the likes of Ricky Nelson—Granz's true love was jazz, and trying to sell jazz records to a niche audience was a continual uphill battle. "The record business in jazz was very, very limited," recalled Verve's controller, Mo Ostin. "We sold twenty thousand albums, we sold fifty thousand singles; that was big numbers for us."

Nevertheless, Verve had a big fan in Frank Sinatra. "He loved the Verve roster," Ostin said. "He was a big jazz enthusiast, and we had the very, very best jazz artists at that time. Frank was in love with Billie Holiday, he loved Lester Young, Oscar, Ella—whoever it might have been. So he wanted to buy the company."

One thing did not necessarily follow the other. Yet for a long time, Frank had been itching to have his own record label, and to a man who craved class, Verve was a shining object of desire.

"Sinatra may have gotten wind of Granz's plan to sell Verve because they shared the same attorney, Mickey Rudin," writes Granz's biographer Tad Hershorn. A strange situation—and, as Granz admitted to Hershorn, a conflicted one: "Rudin represented me and Frank, which was one hundred percent against the law, or whatever they call it."

Conflict of interest is what they call it. But then, Milton Rudin knew how to play the angles. He'd been working for Sinatra since the early 1950s; as Frank's various enterprises prospered, Rudin, who had a keen eye for the main chance, became increasingly enmeshed in them—less an attorney for hire, more a consigliere. He was enmeshed in all kinds of ways. Oddly, or perhaps not so oddly, he was married to the classical cellist Elizabeth Greenschpoon, who played on a number of Sinatra albums and was the sister of the psychoanalyst Ralph Greenson (né Romeo Greenschpoon). Greenson had briefly treated Sinatra and also taken on the massive project that was Marilyn Monroe.

Mickey Rudin was a character: "a man born to twist arms . . . out of the *Harvard Law Review* mixed with a Brooklyn upbringing," as record executive Stan Cornyn recalled.

> He also had a cruel streak. When a negotiation was going bad, Mickey would write devastating letters about the guy opposite him at the table, letters doing everything from questioning his math competence to suggesting he enter his ass in the Kentucky Derby. Then Mickey would send this letter to the guy's boss, with a carbon copy to the guy himself. And just wait for the guy's insecurity and pain to turn the deal Mickey's way. Mickey once told me one of his power secrets: "I get a lot of questions about Frank's Mafia connection." Then he smiled the smile of a guy who knew how to turn fear into a business asset. "But, you know, whenever people asked me about it, I just would smile and look wise. It never hurt I wouldn't deny it." Even in the way Rudin confided in you, he made you realize there was a lot he knew that you didn't.

"He was as strong a lawyer as I ever knew," said Mo Ostin, who hired Rudin at Verve. "He had an incredible street sense. He could be very difficult. He was a wonderful negotiator. He could be a bully. He was very, very strong; he had that kind of strong personality which a guy like Frank would be attracted to."

Norman Granz had the other kind of strong personality, but Sinatra met with him anyway, and, according to Ostin, the meeting ended with a handshake. Also, apparently, with a degree of uncertainty. Frank wanted Granz to keep running Verve, but Granz wanted to get out of the business and move to Europe. As Hershorn writes, "The one thing Granz did not want to do was run a label and possibly take orders from Frank Sinatra."

The matter was left in Mickey Rudin's conflicted but adept hands.

———

Frank continued to campaign passionately for Kennedy, but his colorful activities continued to pose a problem. In mid-August, the conservative New York *Daily News* ran a two-page Sunday spread on the "gang of Hollywood fun and money seekers" soon to be widely known as the Rat Pack, which at this point most journalists were still calling the Clan. The piece's first sentence: "One question which will be answered once and for all by the 1960 Presidential campaign is: Can a man whose brother-in-law is a member of the Clan be elected President of the United States?"

Frank objected strongly enough to the term and the characterization that he was moved to issue a press release through his PR man, Warren Cowan. " 'The Clan' is a figment of someone's imagination," the release read, sounding a little like Sinatra but less so as it went along. "Naturally, people in Hollywood socialize with friends, as they do in any community. But we do not get together in childish fraternities, as some people would like to think."

On the one hand, he was protesting too much—enough to make people feel certain that the opposite must be true. On the other, he had a point. The Rat Pack was a myth, an act, a concoction. The cast of characters sitting around Frank's table every night—even sitting around him in the Sands steam room—varied widely, and some of them didn't like their names in the papers. The reality of his life was grittier and more complex than what the press prated about—but then, his reality was just what Frank wanted people to know less about, rather than more. What he really wanted was to be left alone.

Of course that was just a dream. Hanging around with Kennedys doubled the attention usually paid him. And the standard was double: politicians of the day were permitted to misbehave in private; show people, not so much. The mixture of the two groups was unstable—combustible—and the Kennedys were feeling the heat. Someone in the campaign, celebrity journalist Joe Hyams reported in the *New York Herald Tribune*, had warned Frank that he and his pals would be a liability to the cause unless they started acting like "serious citizens."

That warning sounded a lot as though it had come from the second (living) Kennedy son rather than the first. And Frank could have been forgiven for thinking (if not saying) that he would when Jack did.

Neither the first nor the second Kennedy son was present at the September 7 Key Women for Kennedy benefit at the Beverly Hills house of Tony Curtis and Janet Leigh. But the third was: young Ted Kennedy, the campaign's western states coordinator, who was there to certify the occasion, along with Peter and Pat Lawford and the controversial one himself, Frank Sinatra. Two thousand loyalists, mostly women, paid $5 a head to listen to a lot of speeches and hear Frank sing poolside, backed by the Red Norvo Quintet. A *Life* magazine photograph taken on that sunny afternoon shows Ted leaning over the back of the speaker's platform, in earnest conference with Frank, who stands behind and below. With his dark suit and furrowed brow, Sinatra looks the very model of a serious citizen—as does the menacing, crew-cut man standing next to him, puffing on a cigarette and glaring at the photographer.

This was clearly not a posed photo, and Frank and Teddy Kennedy were clearly not discussing monkey business. Whatever the papers (and the Kennedys themselves) were saying, Sinatra was still deeply enmeshed in this campaign.

As Dorothy Kilgallen—unfriendly but by no means unintelligent—would point out in her column of September 22,

> Only a few months ago Sen. Jack Kennedy had the crying towel out because "those columnists" were linking him with Frank Sinatra, and the Senator protested the association was unfair because he "had only met him a few times in California . . ." So last week the Democratic candidate for the presidency was guest of honor at a private little dinner given by Frank. No reason why he shouldn't of course—but why try to kid the press?

On Sunday, September 11—the day after that private little dinner—Frank gave his older daughter in marriage to Tommy Sands in a civil ceremony in the Emerald Room of the Sands. Nancy Sandra Sinatra was twenty; Sands was twenty-three. The bride wore a white veil and street-length gown designed by Don Loper; the groom, just coming to the end of a two-year hitch in the air force, wore his airman third class uniform. The father of the bride wept unashamedly. Just before he walked her down the aisle, Nancy recalled, he presented her with a pair of diamond star earrings, "to match the stars in your eyes."

" 'I love you, chicken,' he said.

"I said, 'I love you, too, Daddy.' And off we went down the aisle, both in tears."

Frank in earnest conference with the young Ted Kennedy at a Beverly Hills fund-raiser for JFK, September 1960.

The sight of a darkly handsome teen idol in a military uniform in the year 1960 inevitably evokes thoughts of the recently demobilized Private Presley, and indeed the faint air of Elvis hanging over the proceedings wasn't mere coincidence. Not only had Nancy briefly dated EP (and recently oohed and aahed over him when they both guested on Frank's Timex special), but the clean-cut and engaging Sands, a southern boy who'd dabbled in rockabilly (and was sometimes known as the Poor Man's Elvis), had been signed at age fifteen by Colonel Tom Parker—three years before Parker made his far greater discovery. In 1957, Sands played a Presley-esque heartthrob on an episode of *Kraft Television Theatre,* singing a song, "Teen-Age Crush," that was subsequently released as a single by Capitol and became a million seller. The wedding to show-business royalty was Tommy Sands's apogee: it would be all downhill from here.

Her father didn't lecture her on the dangers of marrying a singer, Nancy recalled. She and Frank both saw the blatant parallels, but Hollywood was Hollywood.

Big Nancy, who attended the wedding with Frankie junior and a weeping Tina in tow, also saw the parallels. "It's my own life happening twenty years later," she said.

Except, as would soon become achingly clear to all parties concerned, Tommy Sands was very far from being Frank Sinatra.

Frank spent the rest of September and all of October on Maui, shooting a potboiler for Columbia called *The Devil at 4 O'Clock*. Mervyn LeRoy, who'd directed Sinatra in *The House I Live In,* helmed the picture; the great Spencer Tracy, an old pal of Frank's from the Bogart Rat Pack, co-starred. The story, such as it was—a burned-out, alcoholic priest (Tracy) develops an unlikely friendship with a convicted criminal (Sinatra) on a soon-to-erupt volcanic island in the Pacific—was a psychological drama grafted uneasily onto a disaster movie. Tracy was the piece's center, and Frank, who idolized him, even ceded him first billing. But by 1960, the craggy actor, a tormented manic-depressive and alcoholic in a state of continual emotional and physical crisis, was "chronically tired, unhappy, ill, and uninterested in work," as his biographer James Curtis wrote. And the sixty-year-old Tracy, a former MGM mainstay, was keenly aware of Sinatra's status in the entertainment world. "Nobody had his power," he said. "*The Devil at 4 O'Clock* was a Sinatra picture. Sinatra was the star."

Remarkably, Frank found time in between shooting his scenes to keep campaigning for Kennedy, flying around the islands with Brother-in-Lawford for personal appearances. On October 12, he gave a benefit concert at the Waikiki Shell in Honolulu, drawing nine thousand JFK supporters—and the ire of one Frederick J. Titcomb, Hawaii's Republican candidate for the U.S. House of Representatives, who accused entertainers of making "a farce" out of serious politics.

Sinatra lashed back, a little illogically. "The Hearst newspapers throughout the nation are campaigning for Nixon and throwing a lot of propaganda in," he said. "If this organization of newspapers can do it, then why shouldn't I just by singing?"

Two weeks later, at an event in Newark, even singing proved a challenge. The occasion was New Jersey's annual Governor's Ball—a Democratic affair this year, with the former presidential candidate Robert Meyner in office, and therefore a de facto Kennedy rally. The place was the Essex Armory, where the rally turned into a near riot because of the presence of Sinatra and other luminaries. JFK wasn't even there. Perhaps Frederick J. Titcomb had a point.

"Dozens of policemen had their hands full controlling a surging mass of humanity estimated at between 25,000 and 40,000 persons," the Associated Press reported.

Fifteen women fainted. One man was carried out above the heads of the crowd. Cars crawled slowly along streets, looking for non-existent parking spaces.

The cause of the hubbub was not Adlai E. Stevenson, the featured speaker, but Frank Sinatra of Hoboken and Hollywood.

An ear-splitting shout came from the crowd as the singer and other celebrities were brought into the hall past girls trying to touch their idol.

Almost the entire crowd of 14,000 inside the armory—some in formal gowns and evening dress—stood on chairs to get a better glimpse of the Hollywood stars. Flash bulbs popped with machine-gun rapidity.

Sinatra tried to talk, but few could hear him . . . Sinatra made his way to the 14-piece orchestra stand. Introduced as "the next ambassador to Italy," he sang seven popular songs.

The affair was supposed to be the annual governor's ball. No one could dance in the mob.

The received wisdom is that the televised presidential debates effectively sold the tanned, handsome, coolly authoritative Democrat over the sweaty, nervous Republican with the five o'clock shadow and the widow's peak. (Nixon was a mere four years older than Kennedy, but it might as well have been twenty.) But the received wisdom focuses on the first debate, in which Nixon, who had recently been hospitalized with a staph infection, looked awful. (Many who listened in on the radio believed he'd won.) And the Republican candidate gained force and authority in the third and fourth debates.

Still, the genie was out of the bottle: the debates proved that the TV camera was no longer a mere recorder of events but an image maker. Jack Kennedy, the first show-business candidate, was a stylistic quantum leap past the previous president and vice president. And the youthful branch of show business (the John Waynes, the Ward Bonds, and their ilk were, after all, middle-aged or worse) that called itself the Hollywood Democrats, with Sinatra at the fore and Janet Leigh in her silver dress, chimed easily with the new brand. Poor Pat Nixon, in her good Republican cloth coat, was like one of the uncool kids in high school.

But not everyone was sold. Much of America distrusted the prospect of a young, Catholic, smoothly charming president. The country was deeply divided. The South feared the Democrats' high-minded talk about civil rights: the way was paved for the imminent defection by many southern Democrats to the Republican Party. Organized labor, too, had good reason to fear the Kennedys. Nixon promised to be the second coming of Eisenhower, and what had been wrong with Eisenhower? He had kept us out of war, built a highway system, and fended off the Soviets. He had tucked us in at night.

Jack Kennedy knew the election was going to be a near thing. And—as much as he loved show business—he and his camp continued to be uncertain whether his star supporter was an asset or a liability.

"It's not Sinatra's voice, it's his stamina. I wish I had Sinatra's stamina," Bobby Kennedy said in another context—grudgingly, one assumes. Remarkably, Frank flew back to Hawaii from the Newark rally, finished his couple of days of location work for *The Devil at 4 O'Clock,* then, on November 1, did a quick pivot and returned to Los Angeles to appear on *The Dean Martin Show,* where, as Nick Kenny wrote in the *New York Mirror,* "the chief disciple made obeisance to the Leader."

"We are dedicating our entire show to the one and only Frank Sinatra," a tuxedoed Dean announced, with high smarminess, at the top of the show. "Yes, tonight we're paying tribute to a man who has achieved fantastic success in every phase of show business—a man whose thinking is never narrow, but sees everything in terms of the broad."

It got the expected laugh, as did Don Knotts, who after the big buildup came out dressed as Frank—fedora on his head, trench coat slung over his shoulder—and mangled a "ring-a-ding-ding." The gimmick, whether true or not, was that Sinatra's flight had landed late and that Knotts would have to impersonate him for a while. And so he did. The joke (that Don Knotts was the opposite of Frank Sinatra in every way) ran along in rather pallid fashion until the next thing, which was the cute, blond, and perky Dorothy Provine—currently starring in the ABC series *The Roaring 20's*—doing a Roaring Twenties dance in a flapper costume. (As it turned out, Provine, along with Juliet Prowse and uncounted others, was also currently co-starring in Frank's life.)

After the half-hour break, the Leader himself appeared, also tuxedoed, and burnished by the Hawaiian sun. Frank looked fantastic. A month shy of forty-five, he was at his physical prime: no longer too skinny yet still a few years away from middle-aged plumpness, and lit from within with a self-confidence that periodically flared into preening arrogance. A *This Is Your Life* takeoff, with Dean in the Ralph Edwards role, was low-wattage fun, with some roast-style gibes at bad Sinatra movies (*The Kissing Bandit* and *Johnny Concho*). But Frank's *Amos 'n' Andy* ad-lib, and his general cock-of-the-walk air of having just stepped off the stage at the Copa Room, conveyed a smirky authority that much of the TV-watching public hadn't really bought before and wasn't really buying now; the *Hollywood Reporter's* critic would write that the show suffered from too many "inside buddy ribbings."

And then came a truly strange moment. "Yes, Frank, it hasn't always just been make-believe for you," Dean/Ralph Edwards intoned. "You've always wanted your pictures to say something. And in a movie called *Suddenly,* your deep interest in the national scene came to the fore. What a moment when you stood there and patriotically shouted—"

Suddenly a clip of a much younger and thinner Frank as the would-be assassin in *Suddenly* appeared on the screen: looking grim, he aimed a rifle with a telescopic sight at the camera and growled, "We got just three seconds to nail the president."

"How you gonna splain *that* to Peter Lawford?" Martin drawled, to uproarious laughter by Frank and the audience.

"Inside" was the word that critics of Sinatra's forays into television kept using, again and again. The *New York Journal American*'s Jack O'Brian wrote that he'd been put off by "a sick joke or two and an *inside* dirty reference" on the Martin show. Then he got really critical. "Such dedication to the morally shabby and the humorlessly disreputable," he huffed, "continues to infect the TV activities of the Rat Pack."

———

Debate will forever rage about whether John F. Kennedy stole the 1960 presidential election. It is widely agreed that there were substantial voting irregularities in Texas—laid by many at the feet of Lyndon Johnson—and even more substantially in Illinois, where Chicago's mayor, Richard Daley, in combination with Sam Giancana, almost certainly engineered an astounding 450,000-vote margin for Kennedy in Cook County. What is open to question is whether these irregularities are what put Kennedy over the top.

What is certain is that Giancana firmly believed he'd been instrumental in electing JFK. "Listen, honey," he liked to tell Judy Campbell, "if it wasn't for me, your boyfriend wouldn't even be in the White House."

"Controlling Chicago's powerful black wards and his own Mob wards—nine in all—Mooney had turned the screws with all the muscle he could muster," wrote Sam and Chuck Giancana, Mooney's godson and brother, in their exposé *Double Cross*.

> To assure the election's outcome, guys either trucked people from precinct to precinct and poll to poll so they could vote numerous times or stood menacingly alongside the voting booths, where they made it clear to prospective voters that all ballots were to be cast for Kennedy. Occasionally, some misguided citizen declared his independence from such tyranny and in so doing drew the wrath of Mooney's zealots; more than a few arms and legs were broken before the polls were closed that day.

Giancana was going to a lot of trouble because he expected a lot in return. Tina Sinatra's account of her father's golf-course speech to Mooney—*I believe in this man and I think he's going to make us a good president. With your help, I think we can work this out*—omitted what this meant. William F. Roemer Jr., a special agent in the FBI's Chicago office in the early 1960s, was privy to wiretaps that said exactly what it meant: "The agreement was that if Giancana used his influence in Chicago with the 'West Side Bloc' and other public officials on Kennedy's behalf, Sinatra felt he could get Kennedy to back off from the FBI investigation of Giancana."

It wasn't just personal. Giancana was part of a directorate of Chicago mobsters that also included Tony "Joe Batters" Accardo, Frank "Strongy" Ferraro, Murray "the Camel" Humphreys, and Paul "the Waiter" Ricca. The leaders of the Outfit had to vote on whether to support Kennedy, and Humphreys, the lone non-Italian in the group, dragged his feet. "Humphreys had himself done bootlegging business with Joe Kennedy during Prohibition and did not trust him," Seymour Hersh writes.

> "Murray called him a four-flusher and a double-crosser," [Humphreys's widow] Jeanne Humphreys told me. Kennedy was involved in smuggling liquor from Canada into the Detroit area, Humphreys told his wife, "and hijacked his own load that had already been paid for and took it and sold it somewhere else all over again. He [Humphreys] never stopped talking about what a jerk [Kennedy] was."

This was whom Frank was dealing with.

Humphreys finally, if reluctantly, went along with his fellow hoods. It was a crucial decision. The Camel was the brains of the Chicago Outfit, its chief fixer. Renowned for his diplomatic skills and a certain personal elegance—he never used profanity—he had enormous influence among political and labor leaders. Humphreys was instrumental in securing the massive loans from the Teamsters' Western States Pension Fund that allowed the Mob to bankroll the hotel-casinos of Las Vegas, including the Sands.

Of course the Teamsters also had something to gain from the deal: they too wanted in on Vegas. But their leader, Jimmy Hoffa, was severely conflicted, worrying aloud to Humphreys at one point that "my members' money is . . . going to get that son of a bitch elected."

Hoffa notwithstanding, Humphreys leaned on labor-union officials all around the country to get out the vote for Kennedy, confident of the result and glad to stay behind the scenes. "He didn't expect any accolades," his widow recalled, "and was content to see Mooney bask in the glory and praise."

All of it based on a promise from Joe Kennedy.

Frank spent Election Day, Tuesday, November 8, at his Essex Productions office at 9229 Sunset Boulevard, where his secretary, Gloria Lovell, had set up an open phone line to Chicago. On the other end was Jake Arvey, Democratic National Committee member and Giancana's political fixer, who gave Sinatra updates every half hour on the Illinois returns.

It went well for Kennedy all day. Early returns from Chicago—as well as from Boston, New York City, Philadelphia, Pittsburgh, and Detroit—showed the Democratic candidate opening up a large lead over Nixon in the popular and electoral vote. But as day turned to evening, and returns came in from suburban and rural areas, from the Midwest, the Rocky Mountain states, and the West Coast, the momentum began to turn toward the Republican ticket.

Frank had gone to Tony Curtis and Janet Leigh's Beverly Hills house, the site of the Key Women for Kennedy fiesta in September, and started to drink—first in celebration, then to blunt his mounting anxiety. He kept phoning Giancana for reassurance; Mooney told Frank he was doing his considerable best. "It's gonna turn, it's gonna turn," Frank told all who would listen.

It turned. Slowly, agonizingly. Sometime after midnight, John Kennedy, watching the returns in Hyannis Port, phoned Chicago's mayor, Daley, who, JFK told aides, assured him, "We're going to make it with the help of a few close friends."

At 3:10 a.m., Pacific time, Richard Nixon appeared before TV cameras at L.A.'s Ambassador Hotel and hinted that Kennedy might have won the election. Reporters on the scene were puzzled by the non-concession concession speech. Sinatra was furious. And by this time, as Janet Leigh recalled, drunk. "He yelled at the TV screen, 'Concede, you son-of-a-bitch! Concede!'"

Then he took matters into his own hands. He phoned the Ambassador and commanded the operator to put him through to Nixon's suite. The operator refused. Frank cranked up that big voice. "Do you know who this is?" he screamed. "This is Frank Sinatra, and I want to talk to Richard Nixon."

When the operator still wouldn't put him through, Frank yelled a message. *Tell the son of a bitch to concede!*

———

Around the same time, Richard Daley phoned Dave Powers in Hyannis Port. "We're trying to hold back our returns," the mayor said. "Every time we announce two hundred more votes for Kennedy in Chicago, they come up out of nowhere downstate with another three hundred votes for Nixon."

———

By morning, though, Illinois had finally come through. Despite Kennedy's 450,000-vote margin in Cook County, he captured the state by a razor-thin

8,858 votes. Nationwide, he captured the popular vote by a similarly slim majority: 112,881 votes out of 68,832,818 cast, about sixteen-hundredths of 1 percent of the whole. The electoral margin was more substantial: 303 for Kennedy to 219 for Nixon. But as Theodore H. White reminds us, "If only 4,500 voters in Illinois and 28,000 voters in Texas had changed their minds, the sum of their 32,500 votes would have moved both those states, with their combined fifty-one electoral votes, into the Nixon column"—and thus would have won the Republican the election.

Instead, Nixon finally conceded, and Kennedy claimed victory, on the afternoon of the ninth. It was a victory in which Frank could actually feel he had been instrumental. " 'Ye assholes of little faith' was all that Sinatra could say, with a weary victory smile," George Jacobs remembered.

Frank Sinatra and Norman Granz might have shaken hands, but they'd never liked each other and never would. Correspondingly—if not consequently—all was not well with the Verve sale. Strange things were going on: Will Friedwald cites a story that "someone in Sinatra's office loused up the deal—perhaps deliberately. He continually postponed appointments to sign the papers and kept asking to examine and reexamine the company's books."

That someone was Frank's lawyer Mickey Rudin.

Rudin, who as we've seen also worked for Norman Granz and Verve, had finally admitted he was fatally conflicted in this matter and recused himself. Verve hired another lawyer to handle the sale of the label.

But—recused or not recused—Rudin knew things. Was he urging caution on Sinatra's part because of inside knowledge about Verve's finances?

Or was it Frank's finances his lawyer was concerned about?

Frank was earning big in 1960, but he always spent it as fast as it came in, if not faster. Rudin knew that a realistic offer for Verve had to be at least $2 million. Was he worried about a hit of this size to his star client's bank account?

Then strange got even stranger. "Quite by accident," Mo Ostin recalled, "Granz ran into Arnold Maxin, who was then the president of MGM, in an airport. Maxin asked him, 'What's going on with your company?' And Granz said, 'Well, I'm in the process of selling it.' Maxin said, 'Look, I'll buy it from you.' Granz said, 'Well, I can't; I'm already in the midst of making a deal.' So Maxin said to him, 'I want you to promise me if it falls through that you'll come back to me and sell me the company.' "

Meanwhile—apparently without Sinatra's knowledge—Rudin dithered.

And then Norman Granz, impatient to cash out and move to Europe, went back to Arnold Maxin and made a deal to sell Verve to MGM—not for $2 million, but for $3.1 million. (Multiply by eight to ten to understand present-day values.)

And Frank hit the ceiling.

Sinatra felt that Granz had simply reneged on a handshake deal to get more money. Frank (who might not have known exactly how much cash he was capable of putting into play) felt that Granz could have, should have, simply come back to him with the MGM offer and he would have matched it.

"Frank was absolutely incensed," Ostin said. "I don't think he ever got the facts straight. I don't think he ever learned that in fact Granz went to Rudin first, to see if he could close the deal, and then, when he couldn't close, he went back to MGM."

With his fine Sicilian sense of vendetta, Sinatra made Norman Granz an enemy for life. And his powerful sense of loyalty clasped Mickey Rudin closer than ever. (With Frank, as we've seen, enmity tended to last longer than friendship.)

Did Rudin withhold critical information from Sinatra? "It's certainly possible," Ostin said. "And, I think to cool Frank out, Rudin then suggested to him that instead of spending all of this money on a record company, why don't we start one from scratch. He said, 'I have somebody who I think you can hire to run it,' and that, of course, was me."

Mo Ostin, who would go on to become the chief of Warner Music and a titan of the recording industry, has been cast, in his 1960 avatar, as a schnook—a mousy little bookkeeper manipulated by Mickey Rudin into running Frank Sinatra's new label, where he would be a mere rubber stamp for Rudin's schemes. Fredric Dannen's record-business exposé *Hit Men* describes Ostin as "short and slight, bald and bespectacled. His features were somewhat rodentlike . . . He had entered the music business as Frank Sinatra's accountant."

This is harsh, though not entirely off the mark. Ostin was small and unassuming, strictly a numbers guy, and at age thirty-three not imbued with self-confidence or a grand vision for his future. But as he recalled, Rudin saw potential in him. "I think he thought I was honest," Ostin said. "He thought I had learned a great deal in terms of my experience with Granz about the business itself. I was dealing with financial administration, contracts administration, distributors, international licensees. I had people who had worked for me, so I had good relationships with my employees. And he saw something in me that I certainly didn't see in myself. I didn't have that confidence. But having an opportunity to work for a guy who was perhaps the biggest artist in the world was something that I could never turn down. So when Rudin asked me if I'd be interested, I jumped at it."

First, though, Frank would have to approve him. And Ostin's initial encounter with Sinatra was inauspicious.

The shoot for *The Devil at 4 O'Clock* had moved from location work in Hawaii to a Columbia soundstage in Hollywood. "I went onto the soundstage with Mickey, and as we got there, Frank was having this incredible argument with Mervyn LeRoy," Ostin recalled. "I mean, he was enraged, in a tantrum—I mean, frightening. He was just screaming, and I'm about to go get his approval! This was the opportunity of a lifetime for me, and that's what I face.

"So Mickey said, 'Let's get out of here.' We went to Frank's dressing room. My heart was beating; it was a scary situation. I didn't know what his temper would be or what I would be confronted with. We waited until Frank finished whatever was going on on the set. He came into the dressing room, and it was like a 180-degree turnaround. He could not have been more enthusiastic. He could not have been more energetic. He could not have been more positive. He loved the idea of starting a record company."

It was the same old song with Sinatra and the movies: other people had control over him and the product, and it drove him crazy. The only way to get what he wanted was to throw a fit. But when it came to his new record label, the power was all his, and the slate was clean. He was excited, bursting with ideas. "He told me how important he felt it was to have a record company that reflected the artists' as well as the businessmen's point of view," Ostin said. "He wanted to encourage other artists to join him in what he felt would be a freer, more creative atmosphere. He wanted to build a better economic mousetrap for artists having ownership in a record company so that they'd have not only idealistic but business motivations as well."

It was all fresh and new and thrilling. Whether it could actually work was another question.

———

On Sunday, November 13, a safe five days after Kennedy was voted in, Frank stood as best man at Sammy Davis Jr.'s wedding to May Britt at Sammy's house in Beverly Hills. Invitations had been sent out for October 16, but Davis had postponed the ceremony after a characteristically blunt phone call from Joe Kennedy to Sinatra: Jack's chances could be hurt, the Ambassador said, if the wedding took place before Election Day. Frank put the directive to Sammy in the form of a request, and Sammy agreed—as "a huge favor" to Frank, according to George Jacobs, but according to Nancy Sinatra Jr., because Davis loved Jack Kennedy and "would do anything for him, no matter how hurt he was."

He had no idea how far he would have to go.

Sammy had seen, the moment he announced his engagement to Britt, how dangerous he was to the Kennedy campaign. "I combed the papers every day," he recalled. "The already stale news that Frank would be my best man continued making the front pages and too often by 'coincidence' right next to it were stories about Frank campaigning for Kennedy."

There had been hate mail ("Dear Nigger Bastard, I see Frank Sinatra is going to be best man at your abortion") and unsettling scenes of bigotry, along with the constant buzz that Sinatra's connection to the campaign implied, by association, that JFK approved of interracial marriage. "Right or wrong, fair or not, my wedding was giving the Nixon people the opportunity to ridicule Kennedy and possibly hurt him at the polls," Davis said later. "And every survey showed that [Kennedy] couldn't afford to lose a single vote. I could imagine the pressure Frank must be under. He must have eighty guys telling him, 'Don't be a fool. You've worked hard for Kennedy, now do you want to louse him up?'"

Sammy felt for Frank in all kinds of ways. The way he saw it, just appearing at the wedding was a risk for his idol: the press mobbed the event; seeing the coverage, a fickle public might take Sinatra's participation amiss and stop buying his records and tickets to his movies. Davis recalled that for Frank "to state, 'This is my friend, and in your ear if you don't like it,' means putting in jeopardy everything he'd worked for, lost and regained, and must fight to hold on to. It was not a minor thing for Frank to be my best man."

Nor was it a minor thing for Sammy to postpone his wedding: a good deed that would not go unpunished.

———

Among Frank's visitors on the set of *The Devil at 4 O'Clock* was the young composer and arranger Johnny Mandel, whom Bill Miller brought in for a special audience: Sinatra wanted to ask Mandel to orchestrate the first album for his new label, Reprise.

"I [arranged] a lot of club acts, and one of them was Vic Damone," Mandel recalled. "Vic used to come and play the Sands, and we had a real dynamite act at the time—I'd written a lot of hard swinging things. And Sinatra came in and heard it, and he came up to Vic and asked him, 'Who did those?'"

Hard and swinging was exactly the sound Frank wanted for the new LP—on which neither Nelson Riddle nor Billy May was allowed to work, both being under contract to Capitol. That business detail was fortuitous. Sinatra (much to Nelson's dismay) was always on the lookout for new sounds, and the thought of a fresh start filled him with excitement. He was bursting with ideas, "like a kid with a new toy," Mandel remembered. For one thing, the new label would press its records onto colored vinyl: "They were all going to be different colors, he said. And everybody's going to own their own masters, which was why he left Capitol . . . I remember just watching his eyes as he was talking about the company, you know, and they were sparkling. It was like he was very proud of this thing. He had the most striking kind of blue eyes. Man, they drilled right through you! When he was talking to you, he was talking to *you* and no one else. He meant what he said and said what he meant."

Frank decided to symbolize his break with the past by crowning the new album with a title song and a concept that were all about the present. The result was Cahn and Van Heusen's "Ring-a-Ding Ding."

The number was nearly identical in theme and structure to the team's 1955 composition "The Tender Trap." Musically, both tunes rise—hopefully, energetically, erotically—until the melody plateaus and the title is announced. Lyrically, both tunes were written in the second person, telling the story of a confirmed Every-bachelor who finds an enchanting young thing and is lured into wedded bliss. As crafted by the married Sammy (whose wedlock was growing less blissful by the month) for the relentlessly promiscuous Frank, the songs' stories expressed what was at once both a dream and a nightmare of Sinatra's: of finding true love, and of being ensnared in it after the thrill wore off.

The new number was also an act of sheer ego and defiance: "ring-a-ding-ding" was the signature catchphrase of Frank's own swinger's argot, his identifying code as America's bachelor in chief. It was an expression of exuberance born in the first flush of his early-1950s rise from the ashes, when after falling from the empyrean of 1940s superstardom, he'd once more found he could make the world dance to his tune. It was also, implicitly, an announcement that—at the moment he said it and felt it, at any rate—he was no longer in Ava's thrall.

"Ring-a-ding-ding" proclaimed he was at the summit. Where, as Frank had also admitted, he was quite alone.

———

And ring-a-ding-ding was the mood Frank was in on Monday night, December 19, 1960, at United Recording studios at 6050 Sunset Boulevard in Hollywood: the night he began recording the album of the same name.

He had just turned forty-five the week before, he had helped put his man in the White House, and he was starting his own record label, with a brand-new arranger, in a brand-new studio. He felt reborn.

Sinatra's previous recording home, Capitol Studio A, had had acoustical problems from the word go, and though various tinkers and baffles had improved matters, a nontechnical funk soon settled over the premises, at first

gradually and then precipitously, as Frank dueled for power with Glenn Wallichs and Alan Livingston.

United Recording was a new lease on life. The genius behind the facility was Bill Putnam, an inventor and independent recording engineer who'd
founded Chicago's Universal Recording studio, where he made historic discs
with Duke Ellington and Count Basie in the 1930s and 1940s before moving
west with the music business. Putnam had put all his considerable technical
ingenuity into building United's state-of-the-art Studios A and B; the larger
Studio A, in which Sinatra would make most of his Reprise recordings, had
concert-hall dimensions—it could accommodate seventy-five players—and
sound of an unparalleled richness. Frank felt immediately at ease there.

"Unedited tapes reveal a remarkably jovial tone for these sessions," Charles
Granata writes.

> In the studio, there is electricity in the air; the atmosphere is light and
> fun. The musicians are warming up, joking, and laughing . . . Happy
> sounds come from the piano, the horns, the percussion, as they find
> their pitches.
>
> Shuffling lead sheets at his music stand, Sinatra, anticipating one
> hell of a swingin' evening, addresses Mandel. "I'll tell you what we do,
> Johnny . . . let's do the title song, huh? That's the name of the album,
> so let's get in the mood!"

Frank, who of course couldn't read music, was about to take in Mandel's
arrangement of "Ring-a-Ding Ding" for the first time, the only way he could:
by hearing it played. And as the arranger recalled more than fifty years later, a
remarkable thing happened. "We played the song down once," Mandel said.

> And it's not a simple arrangement. I mean, any other singer—say it was
> Vic Damone or Perry Como or anybody else—would just not say any-
> thing. You'd play it through several times, and he'd start trying to learn
> it, and where he'd come in and where he didn't. Frank wasn't that way.
>
> We played this thing down once, and after that he said, "OK, this
> was a couple of ticks too slow, the tempo should be dah-DAHT-buh—"
> He put it right on the money, where the pocket should be. The pocket
> is when you've got the right tempo and it feels right to everyone—it's in
> the pocket. And in the third chorus, [he said] one of the trumpets had
> a wrong note, and he's right. He retained all of this. He could hear the
> finished record after he heard this once. He could see right where it
> was going to go.

Granata describes the scene as heard on the studio tapes: Frank snaps his fingers sharply, both to feel the right tempo and to demonstrate it to Mandel and the musicians. Once the beat is set,

> Sinatra continues to snap his fingers decisively, and Mandel, after tak-
> ing a moment to match the pacing Sinatra has delineated, counts off to
> cue the band. "One, two, three, four!" The rollicking sound of one great
> big band blares forth. After the test take, it is clear that Sinatra has a
> winner on his hands, and the rhythm section breaks into a celebratory
> jazz-club style improvisation of the song.

But that's only the beginning. It takes two more rehearsals and no fewer than twelve takes of the song, ranging from eleven seconds to full-length—this is, after all, a very important recording—before Frank is satisfied. And in the end, nothing could be more satisfying. This is Cahn and Van Heusen at the top of their game, and Frank at the top of his:

Life is dull, it's nothing but one big lull.

Until you find that you're reeling, your heart going, "Ring-a-ding ding!" The song and the feeling it engenders are one.

And amazingly, the next number, Harold Arlen and Ted Koehler's "Let's Fall in Love," was no less exultant. Frank had first sung the song on the radio in the early 1950s but had never recorded it before. Now he decided to do something with the tune that no one had ever done before: begin in the middle.

"Both casual listeners and serious fans generally like to hear songs they're already familiar with, and when an artist goes into a tune they know, they'll often start applauding," Friedwald writes.

> Realizing that this moment of recognition constitutes a dramatic epiph-
> any, Sinatra often delays it as long as possible. Sometimes he uses the
> verse, but if he doesn't feel the verse is strong enough, he often utilizes
> the bridge as an introductory verse.
>
> On "Let's Fall in Love," Sinatra does both: he starts with the bridge,
> which is well known enough that listeners will find it vaguely familiar,
> yet strange enough that it won't tip everybody off. He then moves on
> to the verse, which hadn't been sung at all since Harold Arlen [and
> Koehler] wrote it for the 1933 film of the same name. We then come
> to the one significant alteration of a chart made by Sinatra on the date
> itself: both singer and ensemble rest for an entire measure before leap-
> ing into the refrain.

Fifty years after the date, Johnny Mandel remembered that rest—a cavernous silence, falling between the last line of that gorgeous verse ("Why be shy?") and the sharply commanding first word of the chorus ("Let's")—as having lasted for two measures, rather than one. Maybe it just felt that way. It's an extraordinary, pulse-quickening pause, a lo-ong moment of absolutely erotic suspense, and just as extraordinary is the fact that Frank conceived of it on the spot, that night in the studio.

As Mandel recalled it, after the band ran through the tune once, "Sinatra said, 'You know, I've got an idea about this song.' He says, 'Right when we get to the end of the verse, right when I sing "Why be shy," I want everybody to lay out for two bars, and then I'll hit "LET'S-uh-fall-in-love . . . ," and nobody comes in until the second beat after "Let's." 'And we went back and just made the record like that. His instincts were that way. He just knew when he heard something how it should go and what would help it. I never have worked with anyone who had that kind of facility. I think he was the best musician I ever worked with."

As a young and unheralded arranger in the late 1940s and early 1950s, Nelson Riddle managed to eke out a living by ghostwriting charts for busier, more established colleagues. He was known inside the business for being able to turn out orchestrations in hours that would take others days; he was so adept at imitating the styles of others that as a ghost he was truly invisible.

Now he was, in effect, ghostwriting for himself. Though his contract with Capitol prohibited him from working for Frank Sinatra's new label, he did just that in December, writing anonymous charts for three songs Frank recorded four days before Christmas, all of them Cahn–Van Heusen numbers: "The Last Dance," "The Second Time Around," and "Tina." The first was a reorchestration of a tune Billy May had arranged for Sinatra's most successful album, *Come Dance with Me!*; oddly, Riddle's take on this good but not great song (with Reprise's newly appointed A&R man Felix Slatkin conducting) is less stately and square than the ordinarily ebullient May's version.

The other two numbers became the A- and B-sides of Reprise's first single. "The Second Time Around," a hymn to fresh starts in mature years—"Love is lovelier the second time around/Just as wonderful with both feet on the ground"—would become a perennial for Sinatra. (Though when, in immature or mature years, had he ever had both feet on the ground?) "Tina," the court songwriters' shamelessly obsequious tribute to Frank's twelve-year-old daughter ("Tina, Tina, nobody else but Tina/That's the little lady's name"), would take its place on the not-so-distinguished roster of tunes penned in honor of his womenfolk, joining "Nancy (with the Laughing Face)" and, years later,

"Barbara." (No one ever had the temerity to write "Ava"—but then, that was a song Frank sang dozens of times under various titles, always with torch in hand.)

All three of the arrangements are up to Riddle's high standards, but none of them is a knockout. Nelson's depression may be partly to blame. His marriage was falling apart, his affair with Rosemary Clooney was leading nowhere, he was drinking heavily, and he was grinding out too much work, at too fast a rate, in order to support his large family and his house in Malibu. Despite his brilliance, he persisted in not thinking well of himself. Though he was one of the busiest and most highly regarded arrangers in the business, though he was still working extensively for the movies and with Ella Fitzgerald and Nat King Cole, and though he'd written the gorgeous theme music for (and was also scoring) the hit TV series *Route 66,* the fact that he now couldn't receive credit for writing for Sinatra caused him intense unhappiness. "My association with Frank is what really got my career going," he told the writer Peter Levinson during this period. "And now I can't work with him."

It would change. But it would never be the same as it was before.

15

||||||||||||

I know we're all indebted to a great friend—Frank Sinatra.

—JOHN F. KENNEDY, AT THE INAUGURAL GALA, JANUARY 19, 1961

Sinatra's got it made—he's got his own President.

—JACK CARTER, COMEDIAN, MARCH 1961

The day after New Year's, UPI's Vernon Scott filed a report about the wardrobe Frank planned to wear to the presidential inauguration. The Hollywood couturier Don Loper, who'd created Janet Leigh's wolf-whistle-worthy silver sheath and Nancy Sinatra's wedding ensemble, had gone all out for his first male client. "Among the articles in the eight outfits designed by Loper for the singer," Scott wrote,

> were an Inverness cape, silk top hat, a double-breasted gray weskit, an ebony walking stick with a silver crook, a swallowtail coat and striped trousers.
>
> "Frank will be the most elegantly dressed man in Washington," predicted Loper . . . "Everything I've made for [him] is terribly small, elegantly tailored and terribly chic. To me he is one of the most elegant men in the world," Loper said.

The blowback was immediate. It was one thing for Gary Cooper or Fred Astaire to look debonair; inverness capes, silk top hats, and swallowtail coats were another matter entirely. Not to mention that silver-handled walking stick. Joe E. Lewis sent a telegram: "Have heard about your new Don Loper wardrobe. Save the first dance for me." Milton Berle quipped (at a testimonial for Gary Cooper, who was dying of cancer), "Sinatra would have been here tonight, but he was trying on his new Don Loper wardrobe and the zipper got caught in the sequins."

"This is the story of my life," Frank complained to the Hollywood reporter James Bacon. "I buy some new clothes and it becomes a big crisis. I never once opened my mouth to anyone. I like the clothes and I will wear them to whatever affair formal attire is called for."

Frank could be excused for being overexcited. In December, Joe Kennedy had asked him to produce (with Peter Lawford) and star in the biggest affair of all: the inaugural gala, a benefit to help defray the Democratic Party's $2 million campaign debt, to be held at the National Guard Armory on January 19, the night before the president-elect was sworn in. Twelve thousand people had been invited to the grand party, at $100 a pop; a box would set you back $10,000. Twelve thousand accepted. "This is the most exciting assignment of my life," Frank said. "It will be the biggest one-night gross in the history of show business." He had been working the phones for weeks, drumming up a crème de la crème cast of entertainers that only he could have assembled, a roster ranging from Joey Bishop, master of ceremonies, to Leonard Bernstein, who agreed to write a special composition for the occasion ("Fanfare for the Inauguration") and conduct "The Stars and Stripes Forever"; from Helen Traubel to Milton Berle, Mahalia Jackson to Jimmy Durante.

Frank used his considerable powers of persuasion to sweet-talk big names to fly in from around the globe: Ella Fitzgerald from Australia, Shirley MacLaine from Japan, Gene Kelly from Switzerland, Sidney Poitier from France. He persuaded the producers of two Broadway shows, *Gypsy* and *Becket,* to go dark for the night so Ethel Merman, Sir Laurence Olivier, and Anthony Quinn could come. Eleanor Roosevelt, letting bygones be bygones where Adlai Stevenson was concerned, happily agreed to do a reading. Nelson Riddle agreed to come with a full orchestra, which he would lead in the playing of "The Silver Bell Waltz" by A. A. Hopkins, an Abraham Lincoln favorite played at the sixteenth president's inaugural ball, and "Lisbon Antigua," a Portuguese popular song that Riddle had turned into a hit instrumental in 1956.

Dean and Sammy would of course be there. Fredric March agreed to participate, as did Louis Prima and Keely Smith, Juliet Prowse and the Tom Hansen Dancers, Pat Suzuki, Alan King, Janet Leigh and Tony Curtis, Nat King Cole, and Harry Belafonte and the Belafonte Singers. Sammy Cahn and Jimmy Van Heusen jumped at the chance to bring some *really* special material: a medley of song parodies called "Ode to the Inauguration."

Then the boat began to rock. Dean, who distrusted all politicians and had never had much use for Jack Kennedy, came up with an excuse: he was shooting a movie in Los Angeles—funnily enough, a political satire called *Ada;* Dino played a southern hick maneuvered by corrupt forces into becoming a puppet governor—and, he said, couldn't get away. Years later, the director of the film, Daniel Mann, said, "I never had a feeling that he was worried about the picture." He wasn't. But it didn't matter how hard Frank tried to persuade his friend: when Dean was out, he was out.

And then there was Sammy. After suspending his gig at the Latin Casino nightclub outside Philadelphia in favor of the inaugural gala, Davis ordered a new tuxedo from Sy Devore and had May, over her budgetary protestations, go to Bergdorf Goodman for a gown to wear to the show and a Chanel suit for the swearing in. He was thrilled. "It really can happen in America," he thought. "Despite all the obstacles, still in 1960 an uneducated kid from Harlem could work hard and be invited to the White House."

Then something strange happened. Kitty Kelley writes that Sammy suddenly and inexplicably begged off, "not want[ing] his interracial marriage to mar the gala in any way." But according to Davis himself, Jack Kennedy's personal secretary Evelyn Lincoln phoned him three days before the inauguration and said, "Mr. Davis . . . Sammy . . . the President has asked me to tell you that he does not want you present at his inauguration. There is a situation into which he is being forced and to fight it would be counterproductive to the goals he's set. He very much hopes you will understand."

He was devastated. "I lay on my back trying to understand it," he recalled.

> The election was over. The votes were in! We'd all worked so hard for Jack to be President . . . Obviously my presence would be bad for him. I knew that I was expected to understand that . . . My hurt and embarrassment turned to anger at my friends, at Frank and Peter: why didn't they stand up for me? But I knew they had, to the extent they could.

Yet Nancy Sinatra asserts that Davis was waved off not three days before the inauguration but weeks earlier, when the Kennedys sent word to Frank that because of Sammy's marriage to May Britt, he should not perform in, or even attend, the gala. Sinatra pled Davis's case in vain, he told his daughter; his inability to help his old friend pained him deeply. True, he could have withdrawn from the inaugural, "but Sammy would never have allowed that," Nancy writes.

As though Sammy ever had any control over what Frank did or didn't do.

Newspaper accounts bear out Nancy junior's chronology. Two weeks before the inauguration, an Associated Press dispatch about the gala reported, "Neither Dean Martin nor Sammy Davis Jr. will be in the show. Martin's working on a movie and, said Sinatra, 'Sammy's worried about his old lady.' He referred to the expectant May Britt, Davis' wife."

But whoever informed Sammy and whenever it happened, the one thing all accounts agree on is that Frank never picked up the phone himself.

Sinatra and Lawford arrived in Washington on January 6, aboard Jack Kennedy's private plane, the *Caroline*. A Lincoln limousine chauffeured by a GI whisked them from the airport to the National Guard Armory to continue preparations for the big show. Washington took notice of Frank's grand entrance, and Washington—one company town being invaded by another—was nervous. A Republican congressman rose on the floor of the House to decry the use of that car and driver. Editorial writers tut-tutted about the participation of "the Clan" in the inaugural festivities (even though two-thirds of the group's real talent was not participating). The keepers of decorum bemoaned the fact that Frank persisted in referring to the president-elect as "Jack."

D.C. was already on pins and needles about the installation of the glamorous young president. "Many Washingtonians are fleeing their homes to avoid the inauguration turmoil, but they are being replaced by hordes of visitors bent upon seeing the new administration take over," wrote the political columnists Walter T. Ridder, Robert E. Lee, and William Broom.

> Hotels are sold out for inauguration week, and many persons are being bunked in Baltimore. Every limousine rental agency in town was rented out by mid-November . . .
>
> Many residents of the Capital are renting their homes for the week to incoming visitors at fancy prices ranging from $75 to $200 per day. With those prices, they also must furnish full-time maid service. One dowager, who offered her mansion for rental, was worried lest a member of the "clan" or the Hollywood "rat pack" wind up in her house.
>
> She was about to withdraw it from the market when it was snapped up by Bob Kennedy. He lives about 25 minutes out of Washington and apparently decided that the festivities would leave him no time for such a long commute.

Frank continued to throw himself, unstintingly, into the role of producer. He paid Billy Ruser, the Beverly Hills jeweler, $90,000 to have silver cigarette cases inlaid with a silver replica of the invitation to the inaugural made for all the entertainers on the bill. He and Lawford attended closely to every detail of the program, brainstorming with the writers—who included Bob Hope's chief gagmen Melville Shavelson and Jack Rose, playwright Leonard Gershe, and famed humorist Goodman Ace, as well as Sammy Cahn—on scripted introductions and special lyrics. Frank even addressed himself to minutiae of transportation and accommodation, making sure that his performers were treated in a manner befitting the occasion. He hit up his old romantic rival Howard Hughes, a majority stockholder in TWA, for a chartered jet to transport Nelson Riddle and his orchestra, along with a Hollywood contingent that included Joey Bishop, Milton Berle, Nat King Cole, Jimmy Durante, Ella Fitzgerald,

Gene Kelly, Janet Leigh and Tony Curtis, Juliet Prowse, and Cahn and Van Heusen, from L.A. to D.C.

"It was a big plane," recalled the guitarist Bob Bain, part of the Riddle orchestra, "and they started serving as soon as you got on. The bar was open. I remember Felix Slatkin—he was a big, heavy guy, and he loved to drink—he got so inebriated that they had to carry him off the plane. All the comedians were telling these old vaudeville jokes. It was just a kick."

Frank had reserved an entire floor of the downtown Statler Hilton, where he was staying, for the performers—some of the performers. As Bain remembers, he and a number of the musicians—several of whom, including reedman Buddy Collette and bassist Joe Comfort, were black—were told when they arrived that "Frank had more guests than he realized, but we got you a nice motel in Maryland." The nice motel then refused to accommodate Collette and Comfort, who wound up staying at a private home in Washington.

On Tuesday night the seventeenth, Frank, dressed in Don Loper's finest, accompanied Nat King Cole and his wife to a party for the gala's entertainers thrown by Steve and Jean Kennedy Smith at their house in Georgetown. The evening was cold, and the 130 guests mingled in a heated tent in the back-yard. The starry contingent included Vice President elect and Mrs. Lyndon B. Johnson and "most of the Kennedy clan," the Associated Press reported. "These included Joseph P. Kennedy and his wife, the president-elect's parents." These did not include Jacqueline Bouvier Kennedy. The president-elect himself showed up solo and an hour late, tuxedoed, smiling, and tanned, having flown up earlier in the day from Palm Beach, where his wife remained with three-year-old Caroline and seven-and-a-half-week-old John junior, who had been delivered by cesarean section the day after Thanksgiving.

Jackie Kennedy, the biographer Barbara Leaming writes, was putting off her departure from Florida as long as possible. Her partly true cover story was that she was still exhausted from the birth and that her doctors had ordered rest. But there was more, much more. Though the inauguration "was an event the Kennedy family had been awaiting for much of their lives," the president-elect's wife dreaded it, and dreaded the public exposure that moving into the White House would bring. "It was a situation each new president and his family faced," Leaming writes, "but for someone like Jackie, fanatically obsessed with her privacy, the idea that she was under constant observation was particularly difficult . . . Jackie's husband of seven years cheated on her compulsively, a fact that was painful and humiliating to her. Now that he was president, she would have to live that nightmare in full view of a group of strangers."

Both the gala and the postinaugural festivities would also bring her into contact with Frank Sinatra, a man she "loathed," according to Leaming. "Aside from Jackie's personal dislike of someone she regarded as a crude, boorish thug who brought out the worst in her husband," the biographer writes, "there was a more serious aspect to her objections. During the campaign, she had tried . . . to make Jack understand that his association with Sinatra and the Rat Pack was utterly wrong for his image." Her stance was complicated by her fondness for Lawford, a man whose bad habits more than rivaled Frank's but who at least knew which forks to use.

Early in the afternoon of the nineteenth, snow began to fall on Washington, a city that was ill prepared for it. "The winds blew in icy, stinging gusts and whipped the snow down the frigid streets," wrote Arthur M. Schlesinger.

By six o'clock traffic had stopped all over town. People abandoned their cars in snowdrifts and marched grimly into the gale, heads down, newspapers wrapped around necks and stuffed under coats. And still the snow fell and the winds blew.

The show that Frank and Lawford had planned as carefully as a military operation (or the heist in *Ocean's 11*) was looking as if it might tank. "The stars who'd come to the armory to rehearse were unable to return to the hotel to change into their performance attire," writes Shawn Levy.

The gala was to begin at 9:00 p.m., but the auditorium was only half-full at that hour.

Frank would've been agitated even without the storm . . . But pacing backstage in his fancy duds, wondering if the president-elect would be able to make it through the snow-choked streets, he died a thousand deaths. As Bill Asher, who directed a taping of the gala, remembered, "Frank was really into the juice that night, and he got mad at Peter. We had a lineup of people in the show on a big bulletin board, and Frank kept coming into the room screaming, 'Fuck Lawford! I'm not gonna do this show. I'm out!' and then he'd pull his name down off the board."

Jackie had flown up from Palm Beach on Wednesday, nanny and babies in tow, and proceeded to her Georgetown town house, where her husband had been holding meetings amid boxes packed for 1600 Pennsylvania Avenue. Early on Thursday evening, "the young President-elect and his wife went to the Inaugural Concert at Constitution Hall," Schlesinger writes.

An hour later they left at the intermission to go on to the Inaugural Gala at the Armory. The limousine made its careful way through the blinding snow down the Mall. Bonfires had been lit along the path in a vain effort to keep the avenue clear. Great floodlights around the Washington Monument glittered through the white storm. It was a scene of eerie beauty. As stranded motorists cheered the presidential car, the President-elect told his friend William Walton, "Turn on the lights so they can see Jackie." With the light on inside the car, he settled back to read Jefferson's First Inaugural, which had been printed in the concert program. When he finished, he shook his head and said wryly, "Better than mine."

At 10:30 p.m., the radiant First Couple—he in a tuxedo, she in a white organza Oleg Cassini gown—arrived at the armory. Inside the cavernous building, where dozens of the nation's top entertainers had been wondering for an agonizing hour and a half whether or not the show would go on, just three thousand of twelve thousand seats were filled. But at the entrance, in the blowing snow, Frank Sinatra was smiling—suddenly all was right with the world—as he greeted his friend Jack, then took the arm of the woman who detested him and escorted her up the stairs.

———

After the big scare, the three-hour spectacular went as smoothly as its producers could have wished. All seats had been sold in advance, netting close to $1.5 million for the Democratic Party, and so the no-shows were of no practical consequence. The gala began grandly, with Bernstein's "Fanfare," Sousa's "Stars and Stripes Forever," and Mahalia Jackson's rendition of "The Star-Spangled Banner." Sir Laurence Olivier spoke stirringly but with an ominous prescience about the challenges facing the new president: "We see him entering these Olympian lists at a moment which must be as thickly crowded with hazards as any yet known to the history of civilization." Then Joey Bishop walked onstage, looked up at the presidential box, and said, "I told you I'd get you a good seat. And you were so worried."

The rest of the gala was a similar sandwich of high- and middlebrow. Frank, in the prime second-to-last spot before intermission, told the New Frontier what it wanted to hear with a rendition of "You Make Me Feel So Young," then, shifting gears, sang a hushed "The House I Live In" that had a surprised Jackie Kennedy dabbing tears from her cheeks. After the interval and Handel's "Hallelujah Chorus," Ethel Merman—who'd been a fervent Nixon supporter—looked straight up at the president-elect and belted out, "You'll be swell! You'll be great!/Gonna have the whole world on a plate!" from *Gypsy*.

Jack Kennedy was sitting at the front of the presidential box, next to his father, smoking a cigar and loving every minute. Nat Cole smiled through

"The Surrey with the Fringe on Top"; Jimmy Durante plucked the crowd's heartstrings with "September Song," Harry Belafonte and the Belafonte Singers did a stirring "John Henry"—and then, after a comedy bit by Milton Berle and Bill Dana, in character as the clueless José Jiménez, came the medley of popular songs Sammy Cahn had re-lyricized to make them apt to the moment. Frank, naturally, got to do the closer. To the tune of "That Old Black Magic," he sang,

> That ol' Jack magic had them in his spell
> That old Jack magic that he weaved so well
> The women swooned, and seems a lot of men did, too
> He worked a little like I used to do.

That pretty much hit it on the head. Or, as the cultural historian Mark White writes, "That deferential praise for Kennedy's sexual charisma from a man whose own star persona defined a brand of heightened machismo and sexual confidence served to authenticate JFK's allure."

JFK's effortless eloquence, of course, was a significant part of his spell. After the finale, he walked onstage to thank the cast. "I'm proud to be a Democrat, because since the time of Thomas Jefferson, the Democratic party has been identified with the pursuit of excellence, and we saw excellence tonight," he said.

> The happy relationship between the arts and politics which has characterized our long history I think reached culmination tonight.
> I know we're all indebted to a great friend—Frank Sinatra. Long before he could sing, he used to poll a Democratic precinct back in New Jersey. That precinct has grown to cover a country. But long after he has ceased to sing, he is going to be standing up and speaking for the Democratic party, and I thank him on behalf of all of you tonight.

Frank glowed as he listened to Kennedy's remarks and at the thought that he would get to listen to them again whenever he wanted. He had had the entire gala recorded, with an eye toward selling a commemorative double album on the Reprise label and donating the proceeds to the Democratic Party. It was a record that would have an interesting history.

Jackie Kennedy, emotionally and physically exhausted, had slipped out of the box during the intermission and gone back to Georgetown to try to get some sleep. Jack, on the other hand, was running on pure adrenaline (along with the cortisone injection he received daily for back pain). For Frank, of

STAIR-4

Sinatra escorting Jacqueline Kennedy to the inaugural gala, January 19, 1961. The First Lady deeply disapproved of Frank and his bad influence on her husband, yet here she seems caught up in the moment.

course, the night was still young. At 2:00 a.m., the president-elect and the stars got into limousines and buses and caravanned downtown to Paul Young's, an upscale steakhouse that the Ambassador had rented for a private party. Kennedy biographer Carl Sferrazza Anthony writes that when Jack Kennedy's close friend Paul "Red" Fay came in, escorting Angie Dickinson, "Joe Kennedy barked at him, 'Wait until I tell your wife how you are conducting yourself!' Joe then turned to Angie and snapped, 'Why are you wasting your time with a bum like this fellow?' They all laughed, and Joe waved them in as he greeted more of his arriving guests."

As the scent of brimstone hovered in the air.

Red Fay, who'd met JFK when they both served on PT boats in the South Pacific, had been drafted for the inaugural week to escort Dickinson to various functions—in short, to act as a beard for the president-elect, who had commenced a dalliance with the actress months before. A little later, Kennedy took him aside in the restaurant pantry and asked, excitedly, "Have you ever seen so many attractive people in one room? I'll tell you, Dad knows how to give a party."

Frank felt the same. When he told the Ambassador as much, the elder Kennedy said, "Wait until you see the party we throw four years from now!"

———

Hatless and coatless despite the bitter cold (his secret: thermal underwear), John Fitzgerald Kennedy, the thirty-fifth president of the United States, stood on the platform before the Capitol and began reading his inaugural address at 12:52 p.m. on Friday, January 20. The oration was a brilliant patchwork assembled by speechwriter Ted Sorensen and Kennedy himself: a lean, forceful, soul-stirring speech ("Let the word go forth from this time and place, to friend and foe alike, that the torch has been passed to a new generation of Americans"), delivered by the greatest performer ever to occupy the White House, and the entire occasion had a suitably august air. In a special section before the platform sat some 60 of the more than 150 prominent figures from the arts and sciences invited to the ceremony as a sign of the new administration's dedication to culture, among them W. H. Auden, Arthur Miller, Samuel Barber, Mark Rothko, Tennessee Williams, and John Steinbeck. Frank Sinatra sat in his suite at the Statler Hilton, watching the ceremony on TV.

Accounts differ as to the reason for his absence. The writer Leonard Gershe, who watched along with him, later said that Sinatra had stayed away because of the cold. But the New York *Daily News* reported that Frank—in his inverness cape with the red satin lining—had shown up drunk at the Capitol. Frank's friend Bob Neal recalled that—through an oversight or on purpose, if Jackie Kennedy had had anything to do with it—he had simply not been invited. "There was a stand that had assigned seats, and Frank was not on the list," Neal said. "He climbed up and said, 'I'm Frank Sinatra,' and a guy said, 'We don't care if you're the Pope. You're not on the list.' And the cops threw him out."

He had invested a huge amount in the gala; a postshow letdown was inevitable. That night, as President Kennedy circulated among five inaugural balls (without Mrs. Kennedy, who had returned to the White House, exhausted by being in public without letup for over twelve hours), Sinatra held his own party, at the Statler Hilton, for all the gala participants. The guests dined on caviar and champagne and received their silver cigarette cases. Frank had assured the partygoers "that Kennedy would stop by to deliver his personal thanks," Ronald Brownstein writes.

As the evening wore on and Kennedy made his way through the round of inaugural balls, Sinatra sat anxiously in the glittering company "very much on edge, waiting, watching, wondering when [Kennedy] was going to get here—because he had given his word that he would make this dinner . . . ," said Gloria Cahn Franks, who was there with her then-husband Sammy Cahn . . . Finally there was a rustle of activity at the door . . . Secret Service agents glided into the room, and then "in he came," Franks recalled . . . Kennedy graciously moved from table to table, greeting the stars, chatting, laughing, while Sinatra sat there "beaming, beaming . . . like the Cheshire cat."

But sometime between then and the next day, something happened to change Sinatra's spirits from ebullient to depressed and angry. Could it have been because the president had left Frank's party to head to a small gathering at the columnist Joseph Alsop's house? Frank had a keen antenna for slights, and being late-dated by the most powerful man in the world could have set him off. Whatever the reason, he abruptly changed his plan to join a group of stars whom Joe Kennedy had invited to come to Palm Beach. Expecting Sinatra to be ready to fly, Janet Leigh and Tony Curtis instead found him having breakfast in his hotel suite with Juliet Prowse.

"At the time I didn't know what happened," Leigh recalled. "But later we were told—I think by Peter Lawford—that something had been said after the ball, or that morning. Frank was not in a happy mood."

Something was eating at him. He and Prowse headed to New York, where he was scheduled to do a Carnegie Hall benefit for the Southern Christian Leadership Conference and the Reverend Martin Luther King on the twenty-seventh. Dean and Sammy were to join Frank. Early in the week, Sinatra told Earl Wilson that he'd skipped Palm Beach "because I had so much work to do, I'd have had a bad conscience." He claimed to Wilson that he needed to rehearse for his upcoming shows at the Sands and the Fontainebleau, but there is no record of his rehearsing or performing that week before Carnegie Hall. Gossip items had him out on the town in Manhattan, squiring Juliet Prowse to the Colony and an Upper East Side Italian joint called Tony and Tony's Wife, taking the Toots Shors to hear his old flame Peggy Lee at Basin Street East.

But another old flame—Ava Gardner—had popped into the city the week before to take in Peggy Lee's show at Basin Street, "with a guy nobody knew." That was nothing new for Ava: she was often with a guy nobody knew. Frank, who was in regular touch by telephone with her, would have been well aware of her proximity. Finding themselves on the same skinny island at the same time (whether coincidentally or not), could they possibly have avoided getting together? When the columnist Wilson asked Prowse about a rumor that she and Sinatra were going to marry, "she laughed for two minutes."

Sammy Davis Jr. emceed the King benefit; the bill also included Mahalia Jackson, Harry Belafonte, Count Basie and orchestra, and Tony Bennett. The great Sy Oliver was there to conduct for Frank. Early in the evening, Sammy announced from the stage that "the leader has arrived," accompanied by "his drunken Italian friend." Dean wasn't the only one imbibing. The writer Peter Levinson, then angling for a junior publicist's job with Sinatra, found himself in Frank's dressing room at Carnegie Hall, watching in amazement as he downed over a dozen bourbon and waters over the course of the evening, then went out and sang as though nothing had happened.

Frank didn't appear until after midnight, "rushing down the aisle to interrupt Davis doing an impersonation of Sinatra," the Associated Press reported.

> From then on it was the Rat Pack's show. They interrupted each other's
> songs with insults—sometimes slightly smutty—from mikes off stage;
> rolled in a cart loaded with liquor bottles and poured each other drinks;
> paraded on and off while one of the pack was trying to perform, and
> generally living up to Davis' introduction: "Now comes the tumult."

Nobody was even pretending the act was spontaneous anymore. It was what the people expected, and it was all more than a little predictable by now—putting aside the question of whether it was appropriate in this venue and for this cause.

On February 1, Frank opened a two-week stand at the Sands, his first in a year. The show had just one flaw, according to *Variety*'s adulatory review: "He did only 12 songs and the greedy audience seemed to want at least twice that many. Sinatra, the hottest star in Las Vegas, again displays his skill as a powerhouse performer, and it's certainly good to have him back."

Reprise employee number one, the newly hired Mo Ostin, was Frank's guest at the opening, ringside and starry-eyed with his young wife. "We were seated at a table with Marilyn Monroe, Elizabeth Taylor, Eddie Fisher, and two Kennedy sisters, Eunice Shriver and Jean Smith," Ostin recalled. "I hadn't been exposed to this kind of world, and here I am suddenly sitting with some of the biggest stars ever, at a show where Frank Sinatra was performing—I mean, we would have ordinarily probably asked for autographs."

Ostin smiled at the recollection. He would attend many Sinatra performances over the years but would never forget the first. "He very rarely gave a bad show," he said. "When he had friends in the audience, I think he really performed at his best. He exuded confidence. He knew he had power. And yet he could be charming, and he could endear himself to almost anybody."

Audiences felt the same. "Big doings in Las Vegas with Frank Sinatra crowding them in at The Sands," Louella Parsons wrote on February 8. "The whole Sinatra clan—Nancy, Frank Jr., 12-year-old Tina, and Mr. and Mrs. Tommy Sands caught Frankie's act and were his weekend guests."

He certainly was crowding them in. On the spur of the moment (and without the guy nobody knew), Ava had decided to fly out from New York to surprise Frank by showing up ringside at the Copa Room. The surprise, however, was on her: she arrived on the same weekend as Frank's family. The situation declined rapidly from there.

Ava could come on the spur of the moment because she had nothing else going on; at thirty-eight, she had declared herself retired from motion pictures. Though she'd been widely praised for her performance in *On the Beach,* "the commendations sometimes included a blurring of the line between the thirty-seven-year-old performer and the bruised, blowsy character she portrayed," writes Gardner's biographer Lee Server. "One critic declared that she had never acted better or looked worse."

The simple and brutal fact was that time and hard living had caught up with her. Not that they weren't also catching up with Frank. A recent newspaper piece noted that he'd begun wearing glasses for reading, TV watching, and driving. And Peter Levinson recalled, of seeing Sinatra in the Sands steam room in late January 1961, "I looked at his face; I couldn't believe it! Upper lip, all chewed up. Chin, all pockmarked. And then that scar . . . The booze, and sunken face . . . And of course, no hair. He had very little hair."

But a hairpiece and makeup could restore him to a visually acceptable state of ruggedness. Things were different for a woman in the movies, and standards for one of the greatest beauties of modern times were impossibly high. No one was more aware of this than Ava herself, but at the same time she couldn't help herself. "She lived now without plan or purpose, escaping the past, evading the future," Server writes.

> Happiness had proved elusive. Love didn't last. Beauty and fame and success were not all they were cracked up to be. She wanted to forget everything, said a friend, wanted only "to drink and dance and screw" . . .
>
> Impulse and indulgence became guiding principles. By day, like a beautiful vampire, she did little other than sleep; with nightfall came the drinking, and with the drinking came the taste for blood. These

years—the early 1960s—played out like a very long lost weekend. There
were scenes, reckless liaisons, unfortunate misadventures.

The spontaneous trip to Vegas was one such. "Apparently, she was much concerned about her looks as she traveled west," writes Sinatra biographer Arnold
Shaw, "for she monopolized the powder room of the plane to a degree that
created talk among passengers. Then, in her nervousness, she left her coat
aboard. Returning to find it, she missed Frank, who had come to the airport
to meet her."

Both Shaw and Lee Server claim that upon discovering that Big Nancy and
the kids were in Las Vegas, Ava turned right around: checked out of her hotel
and flew back to New York (and then home to Spain) without seeing Frank's
show—a sad enough story. But both *Variety* and the Associated Press assert
that she *did* take in Sinatra's show on Sunday the fifth, and, according to a
"spokesman" quoted by the AP, she and Frank "were together a short while
before she left Monday afternoon"—an even sadder story. To top it off, the
dispatch reported that Ava hadn't retrieved her coat at all: in fact, she'd "left
her full-length mink coat on the plane and it had to be shipped back from Los
Angeles."

It could almost be a Neil Simon comedy: the surprise arrival of the second
wife, a faded movie star, and the logistical contortions the hero must go
through to pay equal attention to the first and second wives (not to mention
his current lover), and keep Wife One and Wife Two from encountering each
other. Only it wasn't a comedy at all: it was serious, even tragic. The clash of
Ava and the mother of his children was the birthplace and the essence of his
bad conscience.

As soon as Ava and Nancy had left Las Vegas, Frank hosted Dorothy Provine.
After the show, Provine would have found that her boyfriend had a new way
of spending his off-hours. "We all had to sit around Frank's suite at the Sands
and listen to that record of Kennedy thanking him," a lady friend of Jimmy
Van Heusen's told Kitty Kelley. "Frank would stand by the mantel and play
it over and over, and we had to sit there for hours on end listening to every
word."

In the meantime, Mo Ostin was striving mightily to put together Reprise's
inaugural-gala LP. "Frank had me liaise with the White House on all things
involving the recording," Ostin recalled. His liaison was Joe Kennedy.

"I would talk to the Ambassador almost every day. He was courteous and formal. He always took my phone calls. And always had thoughts about what was going on in terms of the recording itself. Every time we'd finish one of the masterings of the record, he wanted to hear it, and also have the president hear it; he'd even apologize to me if the president didn't have a chance to listen to it. He said, 'You know, I'm sorry the president didn't listen to this yesterday, but he's been busy'—you know, dealing with Cuba or Lord knows what.

"Then he said to me, 'Who do you think should write the text material, the liner notes for this recording?' I said, 'I don't know. Who would you recommend?' He said to me, 'How about Carl Sandburg?' I said, 'Sure, that sounds fantastic. How do I get him?' He said, 'I'll give you [presidential press secretary] Pierre Salinger's number in the White House and he'll get you the number.'

"So I called Sandburg and told him what I was calling about. Sandburg said to me, 'Mr. Ostin'—he had this sort of gruff, curmudgeonly voice. He said, 'Before I respond, I want you to promise me that you will relate word for word what I am about to say.' I said, 'Of course I will.' And then he went off on a tirade about the Kennedys. They can't be trusted, they're disloyal, they're corrupt, the old man bought the election, they used all kinds of nefarious figures to help in getting votes; he must have gone on for several minutes! I was really taken aback, because he was so passionate.

"So I called the Ambassador back and merely said Sandburg had turned us down. Without batting an eyelash, the Ambassador says to me, 'You know what? Get ahold of Theodore White.'"

Securing clearances from the various performers was equally complex. "Harry Belafonte, for instance, refused," Ostin remembered. "He said, 'Look, this money is going to go to the Democratic Party. It could go to some bigot in the South that hates blacks, and I don't want to be party to that.' He just turned us down.

"So I called the Ambassador, and the Ambassador then told me to call Bobby Kennedy, who had strong relationships in New York and apparently knew Belafonte. Bobby Kennedy talked to Belafonte, and then Steve Smith called me back and told me they'd gotten Belafonte's approval. Then I went to Las Vegas with the documents for Belafonte to sign.

"This was Sinatra!" Ostin said. "His relationships ran the whole gamut. They could go from the lowest of the low to the highest of the high."

In the end, though, not even Frank's connections could untie the contractual conflicts that, according to Sinatra archivists Ed O'Brien and Scott P. Sayers Jr., "prevented many of the artists from signing release forms authorizing the use of their segments. A truncated seventy-five-minute version was mastered. It was never issued."

The reason, as we'll soon see, had nothing to do with release forms.

———

From the highest of the high to the lowest of the low. From the end of February to the middle of March, Frank played the Fontainebleau's La Ronde Room. "There would be long lines of fans in the lobby, desperate for tickets, and the only way to see the show was to discreetly tip the headwaiter $100," writes John Glatt, a chronicler of the Novack family, the owners of the Fontainebleau.

> "He'd make five thousand dollars a night when Sinatra was here," said hotel bellman Floyd "Mac" Swain, "and he had to split the cash with security and [Ben] Novack."
>
> Frank Sinatra was the engine driving the Fontainebleau, and whenever he was in residence, the money flowed. After the show, the action moved upstairs to the Sinatra penthouse suite, where anything could happen. The singer would party with his Mafia cronies Joe Fischetti and Sam Giancana, calling room service to send up the most beautiful girls from the Poodle Lounge, along with buckets of the best champagne.
>
> "God, did they spend money," Ben Jr. later recalled admiringly.
>
> The wild nights often finished with a drunken Frank Sinatra and his Mob pals in hysterics, throwing cherry bombs off the seventeenth-floor balcony.

Sinatra and Giancana both enjoyed scaring the bejesus out of friends and acquaintances with cherry bombs: Frank might even have picked up the habit from the gangster, according to Shawn Levy. With Mooney, though, those big bangs had an extra kick; the first thought of anyone who knew what he did for a living would have been that firearms, rather than fireworks, were the source. But Giancana had more on his mind than fun and games in Miami that spring.

———

While he was at the Fontainebleau, Frank allowed the celebrity journalist Joe Hyams to interview him for a new magazine, a G-rated (and short-lived) *Playboy* spin-off by Hugh Hefner called *Show Business Illustrated*. The breathless cover story, titled "Sinatra, Inc.," opened with a scene of Frank, wearing horn-rimmed glasses, driving the writer around and talking business. An attaché case on the car floor "bulged with books, fan mail, a Government brief on the Appalachin [*sic*] hearings,[*] movie scripts," as well as copies of the *Wall Street Journal* and *Publishers Weekly*. Wearily, Sinatra spoke of the pleasures and stresses of going it alone since the death of his William Morris agent, Bert Allenberg:

I haven't had an agent since Bert. That kind of business I do myself. We have a standard per-picture, per-TV-appearance contract. It's just a matter of going in and finding out what other points have to be settled. In the beginning I do my own representing, then turn it over to the lawyers.

But, I retain complete control of all final decisions in the end. I have to say the final yes or no. People have to get to me for that. I give the decision fast as I can. I don't like things to lay over long.

The piece went on to enumerate Frank's various businesses, which purportedly totaled "twenty-five million dollars' worth of investments":

Chairman of the board of a Beverly Hills savings and loan association, heavily invested in Reprise Records, four music publishing companies, a movie production company, the Sands Hotel, Las Vegas, in which he is a vice president and nine-percent stockholder, real-estate developments in San Rafael and Santa Barbara, California, Cal-Neva Lodge on Lake Tahoe, three radio stations in the Pacific Northwest, shares of the Atlantic City Racetrack, numerous and sundry other adjacent investments.

Then, in an expansive mood, the Chairman of the Board speculated about what his life would be like as he got older. "Four years from now I'll be 50 years old," he mused. "By then I'll have had it as an actor and singer. Not really had it, but . . . What the hell, when I get around that age there's not much I'll want to play or could play.

"When I think of myself five years hence," he said, "I see myself not so much an entertainer as a high-level executive, interested in business, perhaps in directing and producing films. My eventual goal is to broaden in the administrative sense.

---

[*] The Apalachin Meeting, held in the upstate New York hamlet of that name in November 1957, was a historic summit of the American Mafia. The conference came to an abrupt end with a raid by local and state police, causing dozens of gangsters to flee into the woods. The incident was memorably dramatized in the 1999 movie *Analyze This*.

"This past year and a half or so I've been getting fascinated with finances in general. I like it. I think it interesting as hell . . . The things I'm involved in personally—such as acting and recording—steadily earn less money while the things I have going for me earn most. And that's the way I want it to be."

At least that was the way he said he wanted it to be.

———

Frank closed at the Fontainebleau on March 13; the next night, in a suite upstairs, his friend Momo met with a representative of the Central Intelligence Agency and a couple of other men to discuss a plot to assassinate Fidel Castro. Some disparaging jokes about Sinatra were part of the small talk.

When it came to Giancana, Frank didn't entirely understand whom he was playing with. But then, in fairness, neither did the CIA.

Soon after Castro overthrew the Batista regime in early 1959, officials at the highest levels of the U.S. government began to fear, not unreasonably, that a Marxist-Leninist Cuba was going to help Russia extend its sphere of influence into the Western Hemisphere. Accordingly, in early 1960, President Eisenhower authorized the Central Intelligence Agency to bring down the Castro government. In August, with Eisenhower's tacit approval, the CIA began forming a plan to assassinate Castro himself. The plan became known as the Cuban Project, or Operation Mongoose.

Political assassination is a dirty business, and the CIA devised what seemed at the time a brilliant strategy for covering its tracks in the Castro matter: the agency would enlist the aid of organized crime, which had suffered a huge financial loss in the Cuban revolution, and thus had as much to gain as the U.S. government from the new leader's removal. If the Mob hit Castro (the thinking went), the government could plausibly deny any involvement, and everybody would be happy. To set the plan in motion, the agency called on a Washington private detective and former FBI agent named Robert Maheu.

In the summer of 1954, Howard Hughes, in a case of egregious overkill, had hired the high-level cloak-and-dagger man to surveil the Lake Tahoe cabin Ava Gardner was renting while establishing Nevada residence in order to divorce Sinatra. The madly jealous Hughes, whom Ava strung along because she liked the expensive gifts he bought her, was convinced a man was paying calls on her. He was right; it was Frank, hoping for a reconciliation. He didn't get one, nor did Hughes get anything for his troubles except a bill from Maheu.

Because of his FBI background, Maheu was a man whom certain case officers in the CIA trusted—and one who, these officers knew, had connections to organized crime. Maheu's main link to the Mob was the handsome and dapper Los Angeles gangster Johnny Rosselli, a mid-level hood whom Frank had met at the Havana Mafia summit in 1947. Rosselli had an affinity for the movie business; he and the late Columbia Pictures head Harry Cohn had frequented the racetracks together and worn matching gold-and-ruby friendship rings. It has also been alleged, but never proven, that Rosselli got Frank his career-saving role in *From Here to Eternity* by threatening Cohn on behalf of Frank Costello. Johnny Rosselli's chief use to Robert Maheu, and by extension to the CIA, was his close friendship with Sam Giancana.

And Giancana interested Maheu not only because of his high rank in the Chicago Outfit but also because of his connection with Santo Trafficante Jr., once the kingpin of organized crime in Havana and still in Florida. (Sinatra had also spent time with Trafficante at the Mob summit.)

Trafficante, Giancana, Rosselli, and Maheu were all present at the Fontainebleau meeting in March 1961.

Robert Maheu had an easy time enlisting Johnny Rosselli in the Cuban Project: having never bothered to obtain U.S. citizenship and under constant surveillance by the FBI, the gangster lived in perpetual fear of deportation. Doing his patriotic duty, he reasoned, would buy him a pass from being sent back to Italy. Sam Giancana, too, wanted the Feds off his back and was working all the angles: helping to put Jack Kennedy in the White House, he thought, would earn him a chit with the government, but participating in Mongoose would surely immunize him from prosecution altogether. Trafficante simply wanted to turn the cash valves back on in Havana. Eliminating Castro was the essential first step.

In the meantime, an absurdly spiraling chain of events would cause Operation Mongoose to explode in Sinatra's face.

While Giancana plotted in Miami, he began to fret about a woman he liked in Las Vegas. The woman was Phyllis McGuire, the star of the singing McGuire Sisters, and Mooney—ignoring the inconvenient fact that she was engaged to the handsome comedian Dan Rowan—had begun wooing her early in 1960, "in part by having the Desert Inn tear up nearly $100,000 in gambling markers she'd run up at the blackjack tables," according to Shawn Levy. This romantic gesture, Giancana felt, bound them together, Rowan or no Rowan.

The story will now begin to sound familiar. The jealous Giancana asked Robert Maheu if it might be possible to install electronic eavesdropping equipment in Rowan's room at the Riviera—where the comedian was then performing—to determine if McGuire was two-timing Mooney with the man she was engaged to. Wanting to keep the important mobster happy, Maheu used some of his fresh CIA money to hire a Miami operative, one Arthur J. Balletti, to fly to Vegas, where "Balletti and a cohort wired Rowan's room and telephone and took up a post in a room of their own," Levy writes.

On October 31, 1960, they took a break from their work for lunch, leaving their recording and monitoring equipment out in plain sight on their beds. They forgot to hang the Do Not Disturb sign: A maid came in to make up the room, got a look at all those sinister wires and machines, and called the cops. When Balletti came back from lunch, alone, he was arrested. Rosselli arranged for the $1,000 bail to be paid by a Las Vegas gambling buddy, and the bumbling wiretapper split town.

When Rosselli told Giancana how spectacularly his mission had failed, Giancana had a peculiar reaction. "He almost swallowed [his cigar] laughing about it," Rosselli recalled. To Rosselli, it was no laughing matter. "It was blowing everything, every kind of cover I had tried to arrange," he said.

That was the difference between the two: Johnny Rosselli felt the plot against Castro could actually succeed; Sam Giancana, a cynical nihilist, was happy just to take the government's money.

But now the cat was working its way out of the bag. And the absurd quickly turned serious. The famously tough Las Vegas sheriff Butch Leypoldt, proud of his control over the town, got annoyed at the incursion of this wild card from Miami, Balletti, and called the FBI. "The Bureau's interest increased when they came across Maheu's name in the case record," write Rosselli's biographers, Charles Rappleye and Ed Becker. When the bureau learned how Maheu was mainly spending his time these days, and whom he was working with, J. Edgar Hoover got personally involved.

The director was outraged. His agents had been working for years to develop cases against Giancana, Rosselli, and Trafficante; now it turned out they were working for the government. The turf war between the FBI and the CIA was aggravated, and once the new administration took office and Hoover found himself fighting for influence with the incoming attorney general, the director made it his business to let Bobby Kennedy know whom his brother was doing business with. The FBI stepped up its surveillance of the mafiosi; Frank Sinatra appeared in more than a few of the bureau's internal memos. A few months later Johnny Rosselli was spotted leaving Romanoff's in Beverly Hills with Judy Campbell, who had begun paying visits to Jack Kennedy in the White House while Jackie was out of town.

But we are getting ahead of our story.

The revels of early 1961 over, Frank headed back to the recording studio—or rather studios. He wanted to get moving on his second Reprise LP, a tribute to

Tommy Dorsey arranged by Sy Oliver, the man who, along with Sinatra, had transformed Dorsey's sound in 1939 and 1940. But because he still owed Capitol two more albums, he decided to begin the first, another swinger with Billy May, at the same time. Two albums at once—an amazing feat, if possible. As it turned out, it wasn't. The physical and emotional effort of commuting from United Recording to that big round tower on Hollywood and Vine on March 20 and 21 was too much even for Sinatra. He had always possessed nearly superhuman energy, but he was also every bit of forty-five years old, and on some of the outtakes from the Oliver sessions he sounds as though the proverbial shot glass was stuck in his throat.

On an aborted "In the Blue of Evening," for example, Frank's voice is ominously husky to begin with. Then, when he gets to

There in the dusk we'll share a dream—

he suddenly breaks off into a barrage of throat clearings, along with a strangely tame "excuse me." On Dorsey's great theme, "Getting Sentimental over You," he sounds magnificent—but also undeniably hoarse. You can see why he decided to pull the plug on the two sessions and regroup later. According to Will Friedwald, "Oliver later told Frank fan Ed O'Brien that they had come too close to the original Dorsey sound—a dance band with a small string section." But Friedwald also says that Frank was worried about more than an unoriginal arrangement: he "was afraid that his voice was thinning as fast as his hair and that he required the crutch of a lush violin section to cover up any technical shortcomings."

Come Swing with Me! is a different story. Working with the irrepressible, hard-drinking Billy May always invigorated Frank and was especially helpful during a time of ever-worsening tensions between the singer and the record label he was divorcing. (At one point, he reportedly walked into Studio A wearing a necktie embroidered FUCK YOU.) Yet "Sinatra was careful not to let his disdain for Capitol bring down either his relationship with May or the quality of the album," Friedwald writes. At the same time, "he just wanted to get the sides in," said May. "He didn't spend any extra time on them, but we just ran everything down and got them in as fast as we could. He sang everything at least twice, and there were no deliberate problems one way or the other. I mean, we were aware that he was pissed off at Capitol, and everybody in the studio was trying to be nice to him."

It was an up production, and Frank rose to the occasion. He had decided to base the album's sound on May's Capitol LP *Big Fat Brass*, which, as its title indicated, was a swinging, swaggering outing, built on a band without saxes or strings. Like *Big Fat Brass, Come Swing with Me!* was stereophonic, the band divided in the studio to give the new technology full emphasis and to underline its clever pleasures. From first track to last, *Come Swing with Me!* is a brassy, joyous affair, and Sinatra's voice is the greatest instrument in the band. If his singing understandably lacks the tenderness and passion of his work on *Ring-a-Ding Ding!*, a labor of love on a label of his own, it's never less than superlative. He was showing Capitol what it would be missing.

———

Exhausted by trying to make two albums at once and still suffering post-gala fatigue, Frank announced he'd be taking the entire month of April off. Leisure never sat well with him. As he told a reporter in 1957, "I've just got to be busy, that's all. I take a vacation for five days and I've had it. I get restless." His natural impatience quickly led to devilry of all sorts, and self-dislike always lurked in the shadows. Heavy drinking followed inevitably, and with drinking came the release of anger.

Allergic to solitude, he received a steady stream of guests in Palm Springs: Sammy Davis Jr. and May Britt, the Lawfords, Jimmy Van Heusen, Marilyn Monroe. Frank was always justifiably proud of his hospitality; at the same time, he was acting badly.

"Frank was awful during this time," an unnamed guest told Kitty Kelley. "He yelled at Marilyn, saying 'Shut up, Norma Jean. You're so stupid you don't know what you're talking about.' She was drinking out of a flask by that point and rather pathetic. He barked at George [Jacobs] constantly: 'George, get this; George, fill the drinks; George, clean my ashtrays; George, clear the table.' He never said 'please' or 'thank you' and was always yelling at that poor guy, but George never said a word. He just took it all with silent dignity."

He also took it all in. (He would serve his revenge quite cold and at book length but seasoned with remarkable amounts of empathy.) Like most men, Jacobs watched Marilyn Monroe with a particular fascination, yet as two of the world's downtrodden the valet and the tragic goddess seem to have enjoyed a close emotional bond. Monroe was in terrible shape in the spring of 1961, and George Jacobs felt for her. *The Misfits*—the film written by her then husband, Arthur Miller, directed by John Huston, and released to mixed reviews and indifferent box office—had been her latest Waterloo.

Newly divorced from Miller, Monroe had recently undergone a nightmarish confinement in New York's Payne Whitney Psychiatric Clinic and had returned to California in a delicate state, which made Frank's taunting about her stupidity all the crueler. And crueler still, because, according to the former valet, "she loved Frank Sinatra with all her heart," and, Jacobs said, the love was unreciprocated.

The situation seemed uncomfortably reminiscent of the floozy Ginny Moorehead's hopeless love for the aloof writer Dave Hirsh in *Some Came Running*. "Mr. S had a ton of misgivings about Marilyn," Jacobs writes, recalling that she was overweight, frequently drunk, and often unwashed, the last, of course, being the biggest turnoff for Frank. Sinatra claimed, according to the valet, that he didn't even want to sleep with her—but, ever chivalrous, now and then managed anyway.

With these two self-loathing icons, sex was the tail of the dog. Frank needed it for the sense of conquest and a flitting glimmer of intimacy; Marilyn needed it to validate the one thing the world respected her for. Because she almost entirely lacked self-respect, the fix could never be sufficient. Of course Frank, like Marilyn an autodidact, shared her deep fear of intellectual inadequacy, and of course he could never admit it, to her or anyone else. Far easier to enjoy the weak lift that mocking her afforded.

In an unsteady state to start with during that Palm Springs sojourn, Frank picked a fight with—of all people—Desi Arnaz.

In the decade since the Cuban-American former bandleader and his wife, Lucille Ball, had become America's favorite TV couple, Arnaz, an idiosyncratic but dynamic businessman, had built their production company, Desilu, into a television powerhouse. Desilu produced a long string of hit series during the 1950s, including *I Love Lucy, Our Miss Brooks, The Jack Benny Program,* and, starting in 1959, the ABC crime drama *The Untouchables*. Though Lucy and Desi divorced in 1960, their company, with its thirty-three soundstages in Culver City and in Hollywood, continued to thrive. In January 1961, Sinatra's production company, Essex, moved its offices into Desilu's Gower Street facility in Hollywood. Frank and Desi had been friendly acquaintances for years.

All was well until Sam Giancana decided he hated *The Untouchables*.

The heavy-handed hour-long show, narrated in hard-hitting tabloid style by the vinegar-voiced Walter Winchell, was based on the exploits of a group of real-life federal lawmen who tried to take down the Al Capone Mob in 1920s and 1930s Chicago. The Untouchables, so named because of their incorruptibility, were headed by the chief Prohibition agent, Eliot Ness (played on the show by Robert Stack), and not just Capone but many of the other gangsters on the series had Italian surnames.

In the spring of 1961, though *The Untouchables* had been on the air for over a year, certain groups began to get exercised about it. The Federation of Italian-American Democratic Organizations urged a boycott of Liggett & Myers Tobacco Company products—the show was sponsored by Chesterfield cigarettes—and a group of 250 members of the Brooklyn local of the International Longshoremen's Association picketed an ABC studio in New York, threatening to stop handling Liggett & Myers products on the docks in protest of the show's use of Italian names. In March, Liggett & Myers dropped its sponsorship of *The Untouchables.*

Though many perfectly respectable Italian-Americans were undoubtedly unhappy about the show, the moves against it that spring seem to have been initiated by men who felt the program cut a little too close to the bone. The head of the Brooklyn local of the International Longshoremen's Association was Anthony "Tough Tony" Anastasio, who controlled that borough's dockyards with an iron hand and, it was well-known, was a Gambino-family labor racketeer and the brother of the murdered mobster Albert Anastasia. (The brothers spelled their surnames differently.) And though the chief spokesman for the Federation of Italian-American Democratic Organizations was the distinguished New York congressman Alfred Santangelo, the federation's boycott of Liggett & Myers was apparently financed by Sam Giancana.

Giancana took *The Untouchables* personally, and not just because of his ethnicity: he had started his criminal career as a driver for Al Capone. Fidel Castro wasn't the only Cuban Sam Giancana wanted dead that spring; Desi Arnaz was now on his hit list too.

And though Frank Sinatra had never watched a single episode of *The Untouchables,* he suddenly decided that he felt Mooney's pain and—as his first vacation week in Palm Springs got under way—took it upon himself to give his old pal Desi a piece of his mind.

Late one night in the first week of April, well-oiled and accompanied by Dorothy Provine, Frank drove to the Indian Wells Country Club, whose restaurant Arnaz frequented. Jimmy Van Heusen and a lady friend followed close behind. When Arnaz appeared at the restaurant, accompanied by two bodyguards, there was a confrontation. Though *Variety* reported that "precise details of tiff are not known," a UPI dispatch described "a bitter argument that started between [Sinatra] and Desi Arnaz over portraying Italians as thugs in Desilu's television series."

According to Kitty Kelley, who interviewed Van Heusen's lady friend, Arnaz, who'd also been drinking, came over to Frank's table with his bodyguards. After introducing the producer to Provine, Van Heusen, and the other woman, "Frank turned to Desi and told him what he and some of his influential Italian friends thought about the show making the Italians gangsters. 'What do you want me to do—make them all Jews?' said Desi. He said that he wasn't afraid of Frank's friends, and the argument went on from there."

UPI reported, "Associates of the men said the discussion degenerated into an argument during which the Cuban is reported to have suggested Sinatra was a failure in the television industry."

Van Heusen's lady friend recalled Arnaz telling Frank, "I remember when you couldn't get a yob. Couldn't get a yob. So why don't you forget all this bullshit and just have your drinks and enjoy yourself. Stop getting your nose in where it doesn't belong, you and your so-called friends."

Very few people would have dared to talk this way to Frank Sinatra.

But the tactical fact was that Desi Arnaz had two bodyguards with him; Frank, a date and another couple. Arnaz and the two men went back to the bar, leaving Frank spluttering. "I just couldn't hit him. We've been pals for too long," he said.

"Yeah, what's the point," Van Heusen said.

According to the songwriter's lady friend, the two couples—along with two women Sinatra picked up from a nearby table—then headed to Van Heusen's Palm Desert house at 4:00 a.m. "for a party." What happened instead was an alcohol-fueled tantrum of epic proportions. Frank "walked into Jimmy's den, where a large Norman Rockwell portrait hung on the wall," Kelley writes.

> One of the composer's most treasured possessions, it portrayed Van
> Heusen sitting at the piano in his pajama top, and it was a special
> gift from the artist. Grabbing a carving knife from the kitchen, Frank
> lunged at the painting and slashed the canvas to shreds.
>
> "If you try to fix that or put it back, I will come and blow the fucking
> wall off," he said.
>
> Van Heusen did not say a word; the women exchanged frightened
> glances. Finally, one of the two women picked up at the country club
> said solicitously, "I love your records, Frank."
>
> Looking at her contemptuously, Sinatra said, "Why don't you go
> slash your wrists."

In fact he was brimming with self-contempt, and the whole incident was loaded with unconscious significance. In the fall of 1953, with the slow-motion car wreck of his marriage to Ava Gardner in a particularly dire phase (Ava was on her way to Rome to make a movie and to Spain to rendezvous with her bullfighter boyfriend), Frank had slashed his left wrist in Jimmy Van Heusen's New York apartment. Chester had found him just in time and got him to the hospital—yet in Sinatra-world Van Heusen had been not his rescuer but party to Frank's deepest humiliation. Now the songwriter had witnessed another humiliation, and he had been repaid.

"How could you stand there and let him do that?" Van Heusen's lady friend asked him later.

"Tomorrow he'll be so sorry that he'll send me some print worth five thousand dollars or something," the songwriter said.

"Why do you put up with his craziness?" she asked. "Pick up hookers for him? Go over there all the time and stay up with him until all hours of the morning and sit back and watch him treat people like dirt?"

"Because he sings my songs, that's why," Chester said. "I'm a whore for my music."

Several days later, just as Van Heusen had said he would, Frank sent him an expensive Japanese print. And three weeks later, with his leisure—and other things—eating at him, Sinatra flew Nelson Riddle and forty musicians to Mexico City, on his (considerable) dime, and played five concerts, gratis, for handicapped children. He would do several other benefits that spring and summer.

Promptly on the first of May, his sort-of vacation over, Frank got back to work on his Dorsey tribute at United Recording. This time around, Sy Oliver had a beefed-up string section for him: twelve fiddles, two violas, three cello. And those strings weren't a crutch but a velvety setting for that still-great voice. This time around, there was no shot glass in Sinatra's throat. He'd admitted to himself, if to nobody else, that one LP at a time was all he could handle.

And he did credit to the LP. At the same time, though, *I Remember Tommy* was an exercise in nostalgia rather than an important new statement: a good album, not a great one. To listen to the updated "Polka Dots and Moonbeams," for example, is to hear superb mid-career Sinatra—without either polka dots or moonbeams. Polka dots and moonbeams no longer existed. Frank's March 1940 recording of the great Burke–Van Heusen tune with the Dorsey orchestra may be a relic, an artifact of a romantic era (and a romantic twenty-four-year-old Frank, captured in amber) that the war and the nuclear era had all but effaced, but it tugs at the heartstrings in a way the new version simply can't. This isn't entirely Sinatra's fault. During the Dorsey era, Sy Oliver had arranged the band's up-tempo numbers and Axel Stordahl the ballads; during the Capitol era, Nelson Riddle had written Dorsey updates of both kinds ("Everything Happens to Me," "How About You?," "Oh! Look at Me Now," "Violets for Your Furs") and had improved on the originals. Oliver and Stordahl were great men, but their greatest days were behind them.

This was far from true of Sinatra, though nostalgia, especially about his Dorsey days, was a powerful force for him. While he would always be ambivalent about his crusty, domineering mentor, Tommy loomed larger in Frank's life than any other male figure, including his own father. Sinatra would continue to hold warm feelings about his days as a boy singer and would continue, throughout his career, to pay musical tribute to Dorsey.

Nostalgia was the last thing on Frank's mind when he recorded "The Curse of an Aching Heart" on the night of May 18, though the song was a very old chestnut indeed; it had been written in 1913, and twenty-two years later the Hoboken Four, including the nineteen-year-old Frank Sinatra, had sung it as their audition piece for Major Bowes's *Original Amateur Hour*. It got them on, and it got Frank started, and the rocket-fueled 1961 version was a sign of how far he'd traveled since.

The song, the first to be recorded for a new album of swingers, the first Sinatra–Billy May Reprise LP, jumped out of the gate like a racehorse. The hell-for-leather tempo and blaring Vegas-y brass bespoke lives lived late at night and without apology, the plaintive words strikingly out of sync with the music:

> *You dragged and dragged me down until*
> *The soul within me died.*

It was surely the most cheerful screw-you song ever sung. And Frank sang it without a hint of regret or reproach—whatever his feelings on the subject. Or subjects. For however often he'd carried Ava's torch into the recording studio, the lyric of "Curse" can also be read as a slap at Capitol Records.

Reprise had released its first group of albums in February: *Ring-a-Ding Ding!; The Warm Moods,* by the great tenor saxophonist Ben Webster; Sammy Davis Jr.'s *Wham of Sam; Mavis,* by the jazz singer Mavis Rivers; and a comedy LP by Joe E. Lewis, titled with his catchphrase, *It Is Now Post Time.* Sales and reviews were strong. And in conjunction with *Ring-a-Ding Ding!*'s release, the fledgling label ran an ad in *Billboard,* reading, "A new, happier, *emancipated* Sinatra . . . untrammeled, unfettered, unconfined." *

Capitol's Alan Livingston didn't appreciate the dig. With Frank's blister and bluster still ringing in his ears, he decided to take the battle straight back to him and kill Reprise in its infancy.

The strategy was simple and perfectly legal. "I put out so many Sinatra albums," Livingston said.

---

* The ad was written by Reprise's brilliant in-house publicity man, Mike Shore—who, forty-five years later, told me that he had come up with the label's name and denied the long-standing rumor that Sinatra had pronounced Reprise "re-prize"—as in "reprisal," against Capitol. Mo Ostin also said that he'd never heard Frank say the name that way.

I'd go into the catalog, find released masters and unreleased masters and put together combinations of records that were partly songs that had been released and some that hadn't been released. I'd do it by composer and say, "Frank Sings . . . Whoever" and put out a new album. I flooded the market with Sinatra albums, which [retailers] were willing to buy. And when Reprise came in, they said, "We don't need any more Sinatra records. We have more than we can handle." That hurt him. And I didn't care because I was angry with him. Frank was upset and threatened to sue me and everything else—which he had no basis to do. His contract was very clear. I could put out whatever I wanted. We had total control and we killed Reprise Records.

He was speaking only slightly hyperbolically. Reprise would survive, but it would be a near thing.

16

||||||||||||

Power tends to corrupt and absolute power corrupts absolutely.

—LORD ACTON

Frank had denied the Clan existed, but that didn't mean he couldn't make money from it.

The commercial success of *Ocean's 11* had inspired an ambitious plan: over the next four years, his company, Essex, would produce a series of four more Rat Pack movies. The first was to be an adaptation of "Gunga Din," Rudyard Kipling's great poem-tale of British colonialism, only set in the Old West instead of India, with U.S. Army cavalrymen rather than English soldiers. An okay idea, on paper.

Of course *Gunga Din,* the movie, had already been made: George Stevens's 1939 classic, starring Cary Grant, Douglas Fairbanks Jr., Victor McLaglen, and Joan Fontaine, with Sam Jaffe in burnt cork as the titular Hindu water bearer. It was hard to improve on Grant, Fairbanks, and McLaglen, though MGM put out a pallid remake in 1951 called *Soldiers Three,* starring Stewart Granger, Walter Pidgeon, and David Niven.

Frank Sinatra didn't care about classics or coattails. He dug Kipling (as he'd demonstrated on *Come Fly with Me*'s wacky "On the Road to Mandalay"), he had his four Summit pals on tap (plus a couple of *Ocean's 11* ancillaries, Henry Silva and Buddy Lester), and the public dug the act. What could possibly go wrong?

Plenty, as it turned out. In theory, Frank, with lots of money to spend and excellent taste in collaborators, had assembled a crack production team: the director, John Sturges, had a sure hand with Westerns and hard-hitting adventures (1955's *Bad Day at Black Rock,* 1957's *Gunfight at the O.K. Corral,* 1960's *Magnificent Seven*). The screenwriter was the prolific and distinguished W. R. Burnett (*High Sierra, The Asphalt Jungle*), and John Ford's poet of a cinematographer Winton Hoch (*She Wore a Yellow Ribbon, The Quiet Man, The Searchers*), an artist when it came to western vistas, would shoot the thing. Frank even hired Billy May to write a score.

But Sturges had also helmed Sinatra's recent *Never So Few,* an uneasy blend of crackling battle sequences and flatly unbelievable love scenes between Frank and Gina Lollobrigida. And that movie's shoot had been rife with cherry-bomb practical jokes, Frank initiating and Steve McQueen retaliating and all of it escalating, with close to anarchic results: not a sign of a director in control of his production.

The "Gunga Din" Western—its original title was *Badlands*; it then became *Soldiers Three* (until MGM threatened legal action), then, finally, *Sergeants 3*—was a co-production of Essex and Dean Martin's company, Claude Productions (United Artists would distribute), and therein lay the problem: the inmates had officially taken over the asylum. Warner Bros. had at least been able to give notes on *Ocean's 11*. Who would ride herd on *Sergeants 3*? Would the picture be a legitimate Western or a Rat Pack lark? The question was answered all too quickly.

Frank had sole producer credit—his first since that other Western of his, *Johnny Concho*—and he at least took his power seriously, as Essex executive producer Howard W. Koch discovered when, to his surprise, Sinatra flew in to the desolate Kanab, Utah, location a day after Koch and a skeleton crew had begun filming second-unit footage and demanded to see the rushes. When Koch told his boss he didn't have a suitable projector on hand (the film was being shot in Panavision and Technicolor), Frank told him to get one. Immediately. Koch remembered that Kirk Douglas was nearby in New Mexico, shooting his own Western, *Lonely Are the Brave*. He phoned Douglas, arranged to borrow a projector, and had it flown in so Frank could see the first day's dailies.

The movie shot from late May through June in Kanab, and the biggest challenge for the cast was the crushing boredom of the isolated high-desert location. "There was a Dairy Queen that was open until eleven o'clock," Bishop recalled. "My advice to everybody was to get two scoops, because after that there wasn't a goddamn thing to do."

A bored Sinatra was always dangerous. Out came the firecrackers: "Cherry bombs were quite normal all the time, in dressing rooms and whatnot," co-star Ruta Lee recalled. Between more staid diversions—poker games, screenings of Laurel and Hardy films—there were high jinks in the local hotel, where Frank had doors installed between adjoining rooms (the construction charged to the film's budget) so the cast could drop in on each other for impromptu visits and pranks.

Another line item was "a planeload of girls from Vegas," Lee remembered—a group of prostitutes flown in to play bar girls in the saloon scenes. A production supervisor, "an older gentleman, very moral and proper, who had to handle the arrangements was so upset," a secretary on the film recalled. "He had to pay them more than scale and he didn't know how to figure it all out, how to designate what they were *really* being paid for."

The film was Sinatra's plaything, and John Sturges had fallen into the unfortunate position of being Frank's puppet. "John *tried* to be in charge, but the jokes never stopped," Ruta Lee said, recalling that the director was "constantly, constantly" frustrated: "He was trying to make a decent film, but how do you tell the guy you're working for to shut up and do his thing?"

The *Los Angeles Times* movie critic Philip K. Scheuer, visiting the set, asked Sturges if he could get the Clan to take orders. "Once I get 'em in front of the camera, yes," the director replied.

"But," Scheuer noted, "Sturges didn't look so sure."

That uncertainty is all too clear in the finished film, whose tone constantly whiplashes between drama and wink-wink Rat Pack fun. The pattern is set in the first few scenes: the picture starts with Winton Hoch's beautifully photographed Monument Valley scenery, all red buttes and bluffs and electric-blue sky, and a deadly Indian attack on the peaceful town of Medicine Bend. When Sergeant Major Boswell (a glum, sideburned Joey Bishop, looking as if he'd rather be anywhere else) is sent to find the titular sergeants, the unfortunately named Mike Merry (Sinatra), Chip Deal (Martin), and Larry Barrett (a tubby-looking Lawford), he locates them in a saloon in the good-time town of Claymore—where Sammy Davis Jr., as the freed slave Jonah, the story's Gunga Din equivalent, is doing a cringe-worthy dance on the bar while mean mountain men shoot at his feet. The three sergeants emerge from the rooms where they've been shacking up with those bar girls, and a cartoonish brawl ensues, complete with bottles, picture frames, and chairs smashed over heads. All that's missing is tweeting cuckoo birds and spinning stars.

Soon we're back to another Indian attack, and somewhere in the midst of the nonsense a love interest for Lawford's character, the beauteous cipher Amelia (Lee), is introduced. Like Sinatra and Lollobrigida in *Never So Few*, the two have zero chemistry—which is easy, since Larry Barrett has zero personality. Frank and Dean's characters aren't much better, though Dean does look dashing in his cavalry uniform. The whole thing is difficult to believe and just as hard to like.

But everybody had fun; at least the stars did. "Oh my God, what laughter, what game playing, what gag playing—it was absolutely glorious. It was just such a good time," Ruta Lee recalled.

Like all Rat Pack merriment, it was great if you were on the inside, less so if you weren't.

It was a centrifugal production. "When we were shooting up there—this is how loose this ship was run—the arrangement was that Frank would play a week at the Sands, then Dean would play a week, and then Sammy would play a week, and Joey would play a week," Lee said. "And we all went down for each opening and for each closing. Frank had a fleet of planes, and that was it."

Marilyn Monroe's presence at Sinatra's Sands performance on the night of June 7 (it was also Dean Martin's forty-fourth birthday, the occasion for yet another riotous ringside party) was significant enough that he wanted it kept from the public—and especially from the eternally jealous Joe DiMaggio. A June 5 memo from Jack Entratter to his publicity and advertising directors read,

> Please be advised that under no circumstances is any backstage photographer permitted to photograph Mr. Sinatra and Miss Marilyn Monroe together at the cocktail reception to follow the performance on June 7. Any photographer who attempts to do so will be permanently barred from the hotel. Be advised that this is not only a Sands requirement, it is a requirement of Mr. Sinatra's and, as such, will be absolutely enforced. Thank you.

A follow-up memo the next day went to "All Concerned":

> Marilyn Monroe will be Mr. Sinatra's guest. It is Mr. Frank Sinatra's intention that Miss Monroe be accorded the utmost privacy during her brief stay here at the Sands. She will be registered in Mr. Sinatra's suite. Under no circumstances is she or Mr. Sinatra to be disturbed by telephone calls or visitors before two p.m.

Ruta Lee vividly recalled seeing Monroe walk in on Frank's arm. "She had a glow around her," she said. "A built-in klieg light that followed her everywhere. As beautiful as Elizabeth Taylor was, Marilyn stole the show."

But there was an eeriness about that klieg light: everything that happened in its hot beam seemed somehow askew. A reporter who, along with a photographer for World Wide, covered the cocktail reception after Frank's performance recalled, "She was beautiful, a vision with a great smile, lots of teased blond hair, and a dress that was so low cut you couldn't take your eyes off her bosom. However, she was quite inebriated.

"At the party, I remember Marilyn whining, 'Oh, Frankie, c'mon, let's make out for the photographers. I love you, Frankie. I want the whole world to know.' I remember that she was standing behind him and had her hands around his waist, almost as if she was leaning on him for support."

She was, in more ways than one. When Frank broke her hold to avoid being photographed, Marilyn nearly fell over. Worried, he told one of his bodyguards to keep an eye on her. But she sneaked back to Sinatra's side and beckoned to the photographer.

"Just as [he] was about to take the picture, Frank's bodyguard grabbed the camera," the reporter said.

He gave it to Frank and whispered something in his ear. Then Frank walked to where we were standing and hissed, "Next time you try that, I'll crack your skull open with this goddamn camera, the both of ya." I remember that he talked out of the corner of his mouth, like an uneducated hustler or gangster.

At that moment, Marilyn Monroe came over and said, "Frankie, I'm gonna throw up." He looked alarmed and said, "When?" and she said, "Now. Right now. I mean it, Frankie." He said, "Oh, Jesus Christ, Marilyn, not again." And he got her out of there quick.

Donald Spoto, one of Monroe's few credible biographers, calls Frank "apparently the more smitten" party in the relationship. He quotes Milt Ebbins, who knew both of them well, as saying, "There's no doubt that Frank was in love with Marilyn."

Ebbins, as we've seen, is a reliable witness. (Frank even bought Marilyn a dog around then, a miniature white poodle she named Maf—short for "Mafia." An odd thank-you.) What, then, to make of George Jacobs's firsthand observation that his boss was disgusted by Marilyn's slovenliness and disdainful of her intellect? What to make of the valet's claim that she was deeply and unrequitedly in love with Sinatra—versus Spoto's further assertion (widely supported by witnesses and correspondence) that DiMaggio was the only man the enigma known as Marilyn Monroe ever truly loved?

Simply that in the chaotic inner and outer lives of Frank Albert Sinatra and the former Norma Jeane Mortenson, all of the above was possible at more or less the same time.

In June, amid much drunken hilarity, the bored *Sergeants* 3 stars had made lightning heckling raids on the Vegas acts of Eddie Fisher, Vic Damone, and Danny Thomas. And on July 25, the Clan descended on Fisher again. It was a big occasion: Eddie was opening at the Cocoanut Grove in Los Angeles, and his wife, Elizabeth Taylor, who'd almost died of pneumonia earlier in the year, was out for the first time since having plastic surgery to hide a tracheotomy scar. Hollywood royalty was in attendance: John Wayne, Henry Fonda, Joan Fontaine, Lucille Ball, Kirk Douglas, Danny Thomas, Groucho Marx, Yul Brynner, Jerry Lewis, Shirley Jones, Merle Oberon, Edward G. Robinson, Shirley MacLaine.

And Sinatra, Martin, Sammy, Joey, and Lawford.

Fisher was nervous—for more than one reason, one suspects. He forgot the lyrics to several songs. After the third time, Dean called out, "Come on, Eddie!"

Fisher threw up his hands and surrendered to the inevitable. "Okay, you guys, what do you want to do?" he asked.

It was a rhetorical question. Frank, Dean, Sammy, and Joey "charged onstage, liquor glasses in hand," the Associated Press reported. (Perhaps tellingly, Lawford stayed seated.) "They took over, doing imitations, limericks, racial jokes and songs—while Fisher sat on the bandstand, somewhat forlornly."

The elegant Ambassador Hotel, the home of the Cocoanut Grove, was not the Desert Inn, and Wilshire Boulevard wasn't the Vegas Strip: Vegas was where Hollywood went to let its hair down. But at home, in grand assembly and celebrating the recuperating movie queen and her consort, Hollywood would have preferred decorum.

And the truth is that Hollywood now had an ax to grind. Sinatra and his set had accrued enormous power in the film capital—power that the inaugural gala had only enhanced—and were ripe for a takedown. The Fisher opening marked a turning point. "Frank and his henchmen took over and ruined Eddie's performance," Hedda Hopper sniffed. "This was a disgusting display of ego," Milton Berle harrumphed. And in a column in *Motion Picture* titled "Has the Clan Gone Too Far?," Sidney Skolsky wrote, "You sensed a feeling of audience resentment . . . This was the first time The Clan played to a hostile audience; the first time they received unfavorable comment in the press."

While the former might have been true, the latter certainly wasn't. And even though Eddie Fisher told Earl Wilson that he "felt honored, pleased and grateful . . . I like to be heckled by them and the audience was hysterical—it was marvelous," in truth, the Rat Pack's act was getting less marvelous by the minute.

———

That month, Reprise released its second album,[*] the one Frank had made with Billy May two months earlier. The LP was called *Swing Along with Me*. Alan Livingston, on the warpath against Sinatra, immediately cried foul.

The title, Livingston contended, was too similar to *Come Swing with Me!*, Frank's second-to-last Capitol album, which had also been arranged by May. Capitol's lawyers took the matter to court and won their case: Reprise was ordered to change its title at once. On subsequent pressings of the LP,

---

[*] *I Remember Tommy*, though recorded earlier, wouldn't be released until October.

Sinatra Swings, instead of the offending *Swing Along with Me,* was printed in white script over the image of a fedora-ed Frank opening a barroom's swinging door.

Despite any confusion the renaming might have caused, the Reprise album sold better than its Capitol predecessor, reaching number 6 on the *Billboard* charts despite Alan Livingston's market-flooding campaign. There was a good reason for this: as terrific as *Come Swing with Me!* had been, *Swing Along with Me/Sinatra Swings* was that much better. From the rip-roaring castanet camp of "Granada" (May actually has his sidemen chant "cha-cha-cha!" at the end) to Frank's magic-carpet-like vocal soaring over the twinkling, tinkling Arabian-bazaar melodrama of "Moonlight on the Ganges" to the thrill of the closer, "You're Nobody 'til Somebody Loves You," which starts as a caress and finishes as a powerhouse, a spirit of sheer fun infuses the Reprise LP, showing to what heights this artist was capable of ascending when he was artistically engaged.

A snapshot from George Jacobs's collection shows Frank Sinatra and Marilyn Monroe relaxing aboard Frank's yacht, photographed as Frank never wanted the public to see them. The picture can be dated exactly: Sinatra, wearing corduroys, a golf jacket, and a billed cap, lies on a couch, suntanned and smiling and reading the August 29, 1961, issue of *Look,* with a cover story about Clark Gable by his widow. Marilyn, dressed in a white blouse, white pants, and sunglasses, reclines close to him, her knee intimately touching his elbow. She looks overweight—her chin is double—and slightly pixilated: distinctly less than glamorous.

Dean Martin's wife, Jeanne, recalled that Frank had had to ask her help to get a disoriented Monroe dressed before the cruise. And a man identified by Sinatra biographer J. Randy Taraborrelli only as "a former associate" of Sinatra's said that Frank "couldn't wait to get her off that boat. She was giving him a hard time, pressuring him to marry her, taking a lot of drugs and drinking. Frank told me, 'I swear to Christ, I was ready to throw her right off that fucking boat.' Instead, he called one of his assistants at the end of the trip, when they were ashore, and had her taken away."

But that was at the end of the trip. At the moment the picture was taken, they looked very much like a couple.

Later in the month, Frank, Dean, Sammy, and Peter—minus Joey, who stayed in Hollywood to start shooting his new sitcom—flew blithely off to a Europe that was seething with tension. Berlin was the hot spot. The still-unwalled city, with its American, British, and French zones and relatively porous check-points, had long been the point of least resistance for East Germans wanting to escape to the West, and thousands were still doing so, proving a constant embarrassment to the Communist bloc. At the Vienna Summit in June, Khrushchev had threatened to make a separate peace with East Germany, restricting Western access to Berlin and effectively sealing off the city; having failed to challenge the Soviet leader on this crucial point, President Kennedy wound up looking weak and inexperienced. In the weeks afterward, he compensated by announcing a military buildup, doubling the draft, and ordering the construction of fallout shelters, ratcheting up anxieties around the world.

During a summer when American tourists stayed at home and European hotels were empty, Frank and Dean landed in London in an anxiety-proof zone all their own. They were there to shoot a cameo (as a pair of goofy astronauts) in Bob Hope and Bing Crosby's latest film, *The Road to Hong Kong*. "In their scene," UPI explained, "Crosby and Hope accidentally are rocketed to the moon. Instead of being the first humans on the moon, they find the clan—in the persons of Sinatra and Martin—singing a welcome." An Associated Press news photo showed Sinatra and Martin in space costume, looking tanned and plastered and holding cocktails, flanked by Crosby and Hope, who were dressed as coolies. An AP dispatch beneath the photo, under the headline "CLANSMEN" DELAY PLANE, described the next leg in Frank and Dean's excellent adventure:

> Frank Sinatra and Dean Martin lingered in a London Airport bar and firmly refused to board their Paris-bound airliner until downing their drinks.
>
> Red-faced air hostesses tried to hurry them into a waiting plane where 103 passengers were wondering what was holding up the flight.
>
> "Have a drink," Sinatra beamed at an embarrassed stewardess.
>
> A third member of the "clan," Peter Lawford, sat it out nearby.
>
> Finally the girls won. Strolling casually through customs, Sinatra and Martin clambered aboard the plane 3 minutes before take-off time. The plane got airborne 10 minutes late.

A background detail with foreground significance: once again, as in the breakup of Eddie Fisher's Cocoanut Grove show, Lawford was hanging back from the high jinks. Around the time of the inaugural gala, the Hearst columnist Suzy had predicted, "Peter Lawford is going to ease away from the Hollywood buddies as per request. No clean break, mind you, just an inch at a time."

Frank and Marilyn, aboard Sinatra's yacht, late summer of 1961. Her slovenliness and emotional chaos upset him, but the tenderness between them is evident here.

Wending their liquid way across Europe, Frank and Dean planned to head to Germany to pay a visit to Dean's son Craig, an army private stationed near Frankfurt. (A subsequent news photo showed the pair checking through German customs, looking like happy, snappy, sharkskin-suited visitors from the planet Vegas: if Dean was worried about world events, he disguised it well.) From there, they would head to the Riviera to drop in on Joseph Kennedy, who'd invited Sinatra, Martin, and the Lawfords to stay for ten days at his Cap d'Antibes villa. They would then spend a relaxing few weeks cruising the Mediterranean on a yacht chartered by the millionaire playboy Bob Neal.

Sammy was headed to Monte Carlo to star in Princess Grace's annual Red Cross benefit. Needless to say, Joe Kennedy hadn't invited him to stay at the villa.

But then, all at once, no one was invited. On August 3, under the headline JOE KENNEDY TELLS CLAN: NO BOARDERS, the *New York Post* ran a piece in which the Ambassador was quoted as saying, "I know they are coming to the Cote d'Azur. Certainly, they will come to visit me and I'll be happy to see them. But they will have to go to a hotel because I just don't have the room at my place to put them up."

Something was strange. While Frank and Dean visited Craig, UPI reported,

the 170-foot steam yacht *Hiniesta*, chartered from Britain's Sir John North, lay at anchor in Nice Harbor waiting to take part of the clan aboard.

August 1961: Frank and Dean do a cameo, as goofy astronauts, in the last (and worst) Bing Crosby–Bob Hope film comedy, *The Road to Hong Kong*. Fun was had by all.

"We don't know yet where we will cruise," Texas oil man J. Robert Neal said. "We are waiting for 'the leader.'"

But the leader would not come. Rather than proceeding from Germany to the Riviera, Frank and Dean flew back to London, where they crossed paths with Sammy—who on *his* arrival in Nice told the press that Sinatra and Martin had called off the cruise. "I saw them last night in London," Davis said, "and they told me that they had to get back to the States right away. I don't know why."

He didn't know, or he wouldn't say. But UPI would, in an August 17 dispatch headlined SINATRA CRUISE REPORTED CANCELED FOR D.C. REACTION:

> Texas oilman Robert Neal, who chartered the yacht for the Frank Sinatra "clan" cruise in the Mediterranean, was quoted as saying the jaunt was canceled because of "angry reaction in Washington groups."
>
> Neal, according to London columnist Paul Tanfield of the Daily Mail, said the reaction was stirred because [of] the timing of the cruise.

"It was being said that relatives and friends of the President were sunning themselves on the beaches of the Mediterranean while their fellow countrymen were being conscripted due to the crisis."

An August 18 editorial in Louisiana's *Monroe News-Star* expressed a widely felt outrage: "Certainly, it would have been better if Lawford, Sinatra, Martin and other members of the 'clan' hadn't chosen to visit the senior Kennedys on the Riviera at this particular time. As for the accompanying publicity stunts— including the delaying of a commercial airliner in England—they were in poor taste this time or any other."

But especially at this time. On the morning of August 13, thirty-two thousand combat and engineer troops of the East German army, with Soviet troops standing by to prevent interference, began building barbed-wire entanglements and fences around the twenty-seven-mile perimeter of Berlin's three Western sectors: the Wall. The president ordered fifteen hundred U.S. troops in armored vehicles into Berlin. For forty-eight hours, it seemed as though war might break out.

Joe Kennedy might have called off Frank, Dean, and the others at a direct suggestion from the White House. Or, as one who'd once before been burned by being on the wrong side of history, he might simply have been canny enough to realize what bad PR such a visit would create at this moment. But there was another thing: the attorney general and his family had decided to stay at the Ambassador's villa during the same week, and the attorney general and Frank Sinatra were not a mixture that worked well.

———

At its mid-August meeting, the Nevada Gaming Control Board approved Frank's application to buy a majority stake in the Cal-Neva Lodge. Earlier applicants for minority ownership had included Joe DiMaggio, Skinny D'Amato, and Dean Martin; all had now apparently dropped out. As of August 15, Nancy Sinatra writes, Park Lake Enterprises, Inc. (doing business as Cal-Neva Lodge), had an authorized capital of 1,000 no-par-value shares. Of these thousand shares, 540 were issued. Frank Sinatra owned 270; Hank Sanicola, 180; and Sanford Waterman, 90. The expectation, Nancy says, was that Frank would ultimately acquire all the shares and become the sole owner. Her father liked Cal-Neva, she writes, "because it was unpretentious yet glamorous, homey yet exciting."

Skinny D'Amato might have dropped out of the ownership sweepstakes, but he would still be intimately involved in casino operations at Cal-Neva. And while the Gaming Control Board's new Black Book now officially forbade

While the world frets about the Berlin crisis, Sinatra and Martin return from Europe in an anxiety-proof zone all their own.

Sam Giancana to set foot in any Nevada casino, he owned a substantial piece of the Lake Tahoe lodge, with Frank as his front. This was a matter of grave concern to Hank Sanicola, who stood to lose the $300,000 he'd invested in the place if Mooney showed up—which was a virtual certainty now that Sinatra was in charge.

Because Frank was capable of pure philanthropy—often anonymous—we may look for a certain altruism in his hiring Axel Stordahl, the great arranger of his Columbia years, to orchestrate Sinatra's final Capitol album: Stordahl, not yet fifty, was gravely ill with cancer. The guitarist Al Viola recalled the arranger's wife, the former Pied Pipers* singer June Hutton, going to Capitol producer Dave Cavanaugh to lobby for her husband. "She knew that Frank was leaving Capitol," Viola said, "and she also knew that Axel wanted to get in one last album with Frank because he might not be around much longer."

---

* The vocal group for the Tommy Dorsey Orchestra. Sinatra joined the band as a member of the ensemble and ultimately became its standout.

But there was more to the hire than charity: Stordahl had supervised Frank's first Capitol session in 1953, and even though the genius Riddle had quickly supplanted him, there was a nice symmetry to bringing Axel back for Sinatra's swan song with the label, the album that would be—pungently—titled *Point of No Return*.

There was symmetry, but there was also extreme ambivalence on Sinatra's part. Frank hated Capitol so vehemently by now that his initial impulse was to break his contract. "I'm sure his lawyers had to do a lot of talking to get him to do [the album]," said the trombonist Milt Bernhart. "I have a feeling he said, 'Let them sue me.'"

Sinatra also had mixed feelings about Axel Stordahl, the quiet, gentle Norwegian-American who smoked his pipe upside down sailor-style and rarely spoke more than a few words. In 1953, just as they'd started working together at Capitol, and before Frank's career slide had reversed course, Stordahl had taken a job as music director for Eddie Fisher's TV show. Eddie Fucking Fisher. That had been that for the decade-long Sinatra-Stordahl partnership, and eight years later the wound was still fresh as far as Frank was concerned. When it came to Frank and grudges, eight years was the blink of an eye.

And yet he decided to work with Axel. Because he had cancer, okay. But also because he could still arrange.

That didn't mean Frank had to be nice to him. Or to Capitol. There were two six-song sessions for *Point of No Return,* on the nights of September 11 and 12, and he showed up an hour and a half late for both of them, something he'd never done before.

The writer Robin Douglas-Home, young enough and British enough and affable enough that he had somehow persuaded Sinatra to give him an interview, was there to witness the scene. Just before Frank arrived, "the atmosphere was relaxed," he wrote.

The bass-player was smoking a cigarette through a long white holder. A trombone-player was surreptitiously following a ball-game on a transistor radio earplug. Buzz of talk, smoke rings, violin squeaks, drum thuds, horn blasts, trumpet trills, flute whistles.

Suddenly the cacophony died to a whisper and all heads turned to the door. In sauntered Sinatra. He wore a well-cut dark grey suit; a dark grey felt hat crowned him jauntily; a red and yellow silk handkerchief peeked perkily from his breast-pocket; the black bows on his patent leather pumps winked from under the knife-edge creases. His face was alert, purposeful, a shade nervous—the ice-blue eyes moved here and there . . . but a twinkle was either in them or a split-second away.

Milt Bernhart, in the orchestra, didn't see the twinkle. "When he did come in, Sinatra was all business," the trombonist recalled.

The usual audience was there and he walked in with his entourage and went right up to the microphone, and said, "What's up?" Didn't really even address Stordahl. On most of the tunes, he did only one, maybe two takes, with no run-throughs. At one point, Dave Cavanaugh asked him for another take on a song, because something had gone wrong in the booth. Sinatra refused. The lead sheet was already on the floor. He said, "Nope. Next tune." When Cavanaugh tried to cajole him into doing another take, Sinatra just glared at him, picked up the lead sheet, and tore it into about twenty pieces. "Didn't you hear me?" he asked. "Next number!"

"That Sinatra still harbored a grudge against Stordahl was obvious from the tension in the studio on these sessions," writes Charles Granata.

Listening to the album song by song, and understanding the stressful conditions under which it was recorded, one can easily distinguish between the "true" Sinatra and the lackadaisical, intractable singer that merely showed up because he had to. Albums are not usually sequenced in the order in which the songs were recorded, and the songs that Sinatra had invested real effort in are mixed with the ones he might as well [have] been phoning in.

The most egregious underachiever on the album, and one of the most notorious recordings in the Sinatra canon, is "These Foolish Things"—the great Harry Link–Holt Marvell–Jack Strachey ballad, which a young and ardent Frank had recorded to tremulous perfection (and a Stordahl arrangement) for Columbia in July 1945. Sixteen years later, pissy and distracted, he sleepwalks his way through the number, letting us know how much he doesn't care by singing the second word of the song, "cigarette" (as in "A cigarette that bears a lipstick's traces") defiantly flat. For the rest of the tune, he mostly sounds hoarse and listless, like the victim of too many hangovers, and only occasionally—as if he'd suddenly remembered who he was—rises to Sinatra-esque heights.

Then comes the capper. On the final line,

Oh, how the ghost of you clings
These foolish things remind me of you,

there's a painfully audible tape splice between "of" and "you," clearly revealing that on the last word Frank hadn't been able to hit the note and that
another take's "you" had been patched in. It's the kind of gross error Sinatra
would never have allowed onto an album he really cared about: with Capitol,
of course, he'd just stopped caring.

Yet just as Frank could create movie magic with one take, he couldn't help,
despite everything, despite himself, sprinkling stardust on some of *Point of
No Return*'s songs. The first two tunes on the album, "When the World Was
Young" and "I'll Remember April"—each the last number he recorded on the
successive nights—are the ballad-singing genius at his best: quiet, tender, and
incomparably expressive. Hearing him sing this way, you can forgive him anything; you forget that he is any man but this man. And Stordahl, as effulgent
as a lightbulb that shines more brightly just before it goes out, has done some
of his finest work here, showcasing his gift for lush and flowing string arrangements and showing a new flair for bright brass and pensive horns. Sinatra's
reading of "When the World Was Young," a French song with an English lyric
by Johnny Mercer, is a masterpiece: Frank brings all the weight and strength
of his years to the lilting reminiscences of an aging boulevardier. It's like "Lush
Life" without the self-conscious ennui.

And "I'll Remember April" is almost as great—a standard Sinatra makes his
own. Stordahl's beautiful orchestration, buoyed by tinkling percussion (Emil
Richards's jingling temple bells give the chart a Southeast Asian flavor), stands
squarely in the now, without a hint of musty nostalgia.

Frank tenderly sings the coda of "April":

I won't forget, but I won't be lonely,
I'll remember April, and I'll smile.

And then it's all over—the song, the album, and his days in Studio A. Robin
Douglas-Home described those final moments:

At 11:45, the last playback came to the final chord. There was a moment
of silence which, after the tremendous volume of noise, gave one the
strange feeling of being left suspended in mid-air. Then the orchestra
started clapping. Sinatra turned away pretending to be unaware of
the applause, and occupied himself by busily buttoning his shirt and
straightening his tie. He eventually raised an arm and said, "Thank you,

fellers," and walked toward the door. There was a disorderly shout of "Night, Frank," then the scores were folded, the instruments packed away, and in no time at all the studio was empty and quiet.

He wouldn't return to this room for more than thirty years.

———

It was strange but true: Brother-in-Lawford had suddenly acquired some heat in Hollywood, based not on nepotism ("I don't think anyone making a legitimate movie is going to put me in the cast just because of my brother-in-law," he said; "I know and they know that it wouldn't sell one extra ticket") but on the strength of his performance in *Exodus,* whose director, Otto Preminger, had recently signed him to play a U.S. senator in his new film, the political thriller *Advise and Consent.* That September, the movie was shooting in Washington, D.C., and Lawford asked Frank, as a favor, to do a cameo in which the real Frank Sinatra is spotted by a starstruck young couple at a Capital soiree.

Sinatra's high political profile over the past year and a half gave him a natural believability in a Washington story, lending real power to a fiction about power. And even if being the president's brother-in-law wasn't getting Peter Lawford any movie roles, another kind of nepotism was working in his favor: he would never have had the kind of visibility he was now enjoying if not for his association with Frank.

It was an association Lawford was eager to nourish. At the end of May, on location in Kanab, he'd phoned the White House to wish Jack a happy birthday—and then, as a special treat, patched the call through to Sinatra. "Happy birthday, Prez," Frank chirped. The favor had the desired effect: the Leader was in a good mood for the rest of the day.

But trying to satisfy his wish to actually spend time with that other leader, the leader of the free world, was an increasingly tricky task.

President Kennedy was eager enough to see Frank. Judith Exner writes that since the beginning of their relationship the president had never been able to leave her alone when it came to Sinatra ("Every time we talked on the phone . . . he invariably would ask, 'Have you seen Frank lately?'") and that now that she'd begun paying regular calls on Kennedy in the White House, he was still obsessed. She describes a lunch on her second visit, one Saturday in May:

> Almost immediately Jack started pumping me for gossip, most of it directed at Frank. What was Frank doing? Was it true that he was seeing Janet Leigh? We went through the same old routine. I denied I

knew any gossip and he insisted that I knew plenty. It went back and forth in a lighthearted way until Dave [Powers] said, "You're not going to get anything out of her, I can see it!" Jack said, "Come on, now, Judy, just a smidgen, nothing shocking or disgraceful, just something amusing."

"As I've said before, Jack, pick up a movie magazine."

"Thanks a lot," he said, turning to Dave with a helpless gesture. "Doesn't she remind you of a career diplomat?"

Mrs. Kennedy was of course not in Washington that weekend but at the family's weekend home, a horse farm in Middleburg, Virginia. And it quickly became apparent to Peter Lawford that Frank Sinatra was going to have to be smuggled in to see the president much as Judy Campbell was. "Jack was always so grateful to him for all the work he'd done in the campaign raising money," Lawford told Kitty Kelley.

He said, "I really should do something for Frank . . . maybe I'll ask him to the White House for dinner or lunch." I said that Frank would love that, but then Jack said, "There's only one problem. Jackie hates him and won't have him in the house. So I really don't know what to do." Here was the President of the United States in a quandary just like the rest of us who are afraid to upset our spouses. We joked for a few minutes about stuffing Frank into a body bag and dragging him around to the side door so the gardeners could bring him in like a bag of refuse and Jackie wouldn't see him. We also talked about sneaking him in in one of John-John's big diaper bundles.

But in the third week of September, the First Lady had to endure Sinatra's presence twice in the space of three days—and the first time was at the White House. The occasion was a luncheon for the cast and director of *Advise and Consent,* an event to which she had no intention of asking him. Yet when Mrs. Kennedy's chief of staff, Letitia Baldrige, phoned Peter Lawford at his hotel to make arrangements for the lunch, Sinatra was in the room, and there was no way to exclude him.

Jackie Kennedy was chagrined. She had worked hard to distance her husband from a man she felt would sully the president's image. "In her view, that was even more true after the Bay of Pigs disaster," writes her biographer Barbara Leaming. "The last thing Jack needed was to associate with a man linked in the public mind with the Mafia—certainly not in this of all weeks, as Jackie launched a full-scale rehabilitation effort."

By the end of the summer of 1961, the new administration had undergone a series of defeats and fiascoes, the abortive invasion of Cuba not least among them. The Bay of Pigs invasion in April, planned by the Eisenhower administration but carried out by Kennedy, had failed to liberate Cuba, leaving the new president with egg on his face and the Caribbean open to Soviet incursion. At the Vienna Summit on June 4, JFK had struck Nikita Khrushchev as a lightweight, while Berlin hung in the balance and Western and Soviet missiles faced each other across Europe. Accordingly, the First Lady had decided to remake her husband's image "as a mature, self-possessed leader who was already achieving great things" and, with her keen eye for appearances, to recast the image of the White House as "a symbol of national power and purpose."

The place, "which Jackie had once believed ought to be comfortable, cozy, and inviting, would be deliberately formal, finished, and above all intimidating," Leaming writes. "Rather than putting people at ease, those rooms would impress upon them the grandeur and power of the presidency—and of Jack. In her careful plans, she was doing everything possible to put Jack across as a statesman."

But Jack, who hated being told what to do, insisted the invitation stand, and with the prospect of Frank Sinatra's imminent arrival at the White House Jackie saw all her image-making efforts going down the drain. Hoping to keep the luncheon under wraps, Mrs. Kennedy sent orders that the occasion be strictly off the record. Meanwhile, the president couldn't disguise his glee at the prospect of an afternoon with his friend Frank.

"Ordinarily, the *Advise and Consent* luncheon would have been the sort of private event at which Jack and Jackie seized the opportunity to shine together," Leaming writes.

> On this occasion, Jackie had no interest in performing. Instead, she planned to keep her eye on Sinatra . . . and on the clock. The Kennedys were due at the Peruvian embassy at eight, and the President was scheduled to deliver a critically important address at the United Nations the following week. Jackie hoped the luncheon would end before anyone in the press room got wind of it.
>
> Things got off to a poor start when the Kennedys entered a quarter of an hour late and Sinatra called out, "Hey, Chickie baby!"

Three days later, she would have to see him again.

On September 24, at the invitation of the Lawfords (according to Peter Lawford) or Joe Kennedy (by other accounts), Frank headed to Hyannis Port aboard the president's private plane, the *Caroline*, accompanied by Pat Lawford, Ted Kennedy, and the Dominican playboy Porfirio Rubirosa and his fifth wife, Odile. With the Hyannis airport socked in by fog, the plane landed at New Bedford, fifty miles away, and the party, along with Frank's cargo—twelve pieces of luggage, a dozen bottles of champagne, a case of wine, three cartons of ice cream in dry ice, and two loaves of Italian bread for the Ambassador— proceeded to the Kennedy compound in a pair of taxicabs.

Peter Lawford awaited them at Joseph Kennedy's house, where the dinner table was set for twenty-six. The night was apparently eventful. In a tell-all memoir, Joe and Rose Kennedy's chauffeur Frank Saunders recalled that Sinatra arrived with not just Pat, Teddy, and the Rubirosas but "a crowd of jet-setters and Beautiful People," including some women who looked to Saunders like prostitutes. "The maids were buzzing," he wrote. "But the star was Frank Sinatra."

Intensely curious about the goings-on, the chauffeur took a pair of riding boots he'd polished for Joe Kennedy and, on the pretext of returning them, went over to the Ambassador's house and entered by the back stairs. There he happened upon the old man, in a dim hallway, fondling a buxom young woman:

> "I have your riding boots, Mr. Kennedy," I said. I said it loudly, as if to assert my excuse for being there.
>
> "My riding boots! Just in time!" The president's father laughed. The woman giggled.

The woman, Saunders later discovered, had been Porfirio Rubirosa's wife.

The next afternoon, a dozen members of the company, including Frank, went for a three-and-a-half-hour cruise aboard Joe Kennedy's yacht the *Marlin*. "The Marlin cruised about eight miles to Cotuit Bay, and anchored in a sheltered spot," an Associated Press dispatch reported.

> Most of the guests remained aboard, but Mrs. Kennedy, who took up the sport this summer, water skied for a while despite the chill.
>
> She wore a white petal bathing cap and the jacket half of a skin diver suit over her bathing suit, obviously as a protection against the chill.
>
> Mrs. Kennedy showed the result of her weeks of practice as she slalomed, on a single ski behind a speedboat.
>
> She smiled and waved as she sped past a nearby press boat.
>
> [The White House press secretary Pierre] Salinger said Sinatra is not staying at the President's house, but is visiting the Lawfords, who are at the home of the President's father, Joseph P. Kennedy.

Salinger's emphasis on Frank's accommodations in Hyannis Port represented an important distinction. A public barrier, however slender, had to be maintained between President Kennedy and Sinatra, who, according to Barbara Leaming, was "loud and obnoxious" (translation: drinking) that weekend. For her part, Mrs. Kennedy, showing off on water skis, seems to have been putting on her own remarkable show—but only up to a point. Leaming writes, "Sinatra's presence at the Cape [was] so disconcerting that, uncharacteristically, Jackie . . . failed to conceal her jealousy at Jack's interest in one of the women Sinatra had brought with him. Jackie's palpable upset had been so unusual that everyone noticed, representing a huge defeat for a woman who prided herself on her ability to disguise her emotions, particularly with regard to her husband's other women."

Which of "the women Sinatra had brought" so captivated Jack and so unhorsed Jackie? The simplest guess, based on documentation, is Odile, the beautiful wife of the playboy Rubirosa. The only other woman mentioned in press accounts is the president's sister Pat. But if Saunders the chauffeur is to be trusted, and Sinatra really did bring along beautiful prostitutes, anything is possible.

Frank had other matters to attend to in Hyannis besides amusing himself. One concerned a film project that had hit a snag, an adaptation of Richard Condon's political thriller *The Manchurian Candidate*. The best-selling novel, about the son of an important political family captured by the Chinese during the Korean War and brainwashed into becoming a presidential assassin, had attracted movie interest soon after its 1959 publication, but in the conservative climate of the final Eisenhower years the novel's bleak vision of human nature and American politics—one of the key characters, Senator Johnny Iselin, was patently based on Joseph McCarthy—made it too hot a potato to be picked up.

The book lay dormant until early 1961, when the dramatist George Axelrod and the director John Frankenheimer bought the screen rights. Axelrod, who'd written *The Seven Year Itch* for Broadway (and the script for Billy Wilder's film version), as well as the Oscar-nominated screenplay for *Breakfast at Tiffany's*, was one of the highest-paid writers in Hollywood and a pal of Sinatra's. Frankenheimer, a prolific and highly regarded young television director during the 1950s, was now successfully making his way into the movies: he'd made *The Young Savages* with Burt Lancaster in 1961 and was finishing production on two pictures that would have a great impact in 1962, *All Fall Down,* starring Warren Beatty, and Lancaster's *Birdman of Alcatraz*. Frank was a fan.

In spite of Axelrod and Frankenheimer's sterling track records, movie studios were still shying away from *The Manchurian Candidate*. It was a very dark book, and the subject of political assassinations was controversial in early 1961, when the causes of the recent killings of the Congolese prime minister Patrice Lumumba and the Dominican dictator Rafael Trujillo remained murky. But when the writer and the director approached Frank Sinatra with the project, he immediately wanted in, even though the screenplay wasn't yet complete.

Axelrod and Frankenheimer offered Frank the choice of playing the sleeper assassin Raymond Shaw or Shaw's former platoon mate, the army intelligence officer Bennett Marco, a fellow brainwashing victim and the discoverer of the assassination plot masterminded by Shaw's mother, Eleanor. Frank, who'd played a would-be presidential assassin once before in *Suddenly*, chose Marco, and Axelrod continued writing.

Sinatra, now a co-producer along with Frankenheimer and Axelrod, planned to have the film distributed, like his previous independent pictures, by United Artists. The only problem was that the president of UA, Arthur Krim, hated the project—hated it so much that he told Sinatra, Frankenheimer, and Axelrod that he "would try to dissuade any other studio they approached from backing it," Sinatra film historian Daniel O'Brien writes.

According to O'Brien, Krim, who was about to become national finance chairman of the Democratic Party, "felt that the political storyline—complete with corruption, communist infiltration and assassination—could be both embarrassing and harmful to Kennedy, especially given the ongoing American-Russian negotiations over limiting nuclear tests." To make matters still worse, Krim personally disliked Richard Condon, who had once worked for him as a publicity man (and had been unit publicist on *The Pride and the Passion*).

And so Frank took his case to the president of the United States.

When he wasn't falling for pap like the musical *Camelot*, Jack Kennedy was a tough, cool realist in life and politics. He'd loved *The Manchurian Candidate* when the book came out—loved it so much that he'd told Frank, who'd loved it too. When Sinatra filled Kennedy in on the film project that weekend in Hyannis, the president's first reaction was "That's great—who's playing the mother?"

And as to that little problem with Arthur Krim, Kennedy was glad to telephone the outgoing United Artists president and assure him that *The Manchurian Candidate* was a film eminently worth making. Unsurprisingly, Krim promptly changed his mind.

———

There was another problem to broach in Hyannis Port that weekend, one Frank had been avoiding because it wasn't his own. Back in March, in between throwing cherry bombs from the seventeenth floor of the Fontainebleau, Sam Giancana had asked Sinatra to intercede with the Kennedys on a matter increasingly important to the Mob boss: getting the FBI off his tail. Bobby Kennedy was his biggest problem. As one historian wrote, "Ever since Prohibition . . . Attorneys General have been 'declaring war' on organized crime, but Robert Kennedy was the first to fight one." Since Kennedy had taken office as attorney general, he had redoubled his efforts to bring Giancana in, and the pressure was beginning to get to Mooney, who felt that rather than persecuting him, the Kennedys should be thanking him for his financial help with the West Virginia primary and the election in Illinois. According to a December 1961 FBI wiretap of Giancana and an underling named Johnny—either Formosa or Rosselli—Frank had assured both men that there was nothing to it, he would talk to the Kennedys. But from the angry tenor of the hoodlums' conversation, two months after Sinatra's visit to the presidential compound, it appeared that Frank was full of empty promises.

JOHNNY: I said, "Frankie, can I ask one question?" He says, "Johnny, I took Sam's [Giancana's] name and wrote it down and told Bobby Kennedy, 'This is my buddy. This is my buddy. This is what I want you to know, Bob' " . . . Between you and I, Frank saw Joe Kennedy three different times. He called him three times, Joe Kennedy, the father.

GIANCANA: Well I don't know who the [expletive] he's [Sinatra's] talking to, but . . . after all, if I'm taking somebody's money, I'm gonna make sure that this money is going to do something. Like, "Do you want it or don't you want it?" If the money is accepted, maybe one of these days, the guy will do me a favor.

JOHNNY: That's right. He says he wrote your name down.

GIANCANA: Well, one minute he tells me this and then he tells me that. And then the last time I talked to him was at the hotel in Florida . . . and he said, "Don't worry about it, if I can't talk to the old man [Joe Kennedy], I'm going to talk to *the* man [President Kennedy]." One minute he says he talked to Robert, and the next minute he says he hasn't talked to him. So he never did talk to him. It's a lot of [expletive]. Either he did or he didn't. Forget about it. Why lie to me? I haven't got that coming.

JOHNNY: If he can't deliver, I want him to tell me, "John, the load's too heavy."

GIANCANA: When he says he's gonna do a guy a little favor, I don't give a [expletive] how long it takes, he's got to give you a little favor.

JOHNNY: He says he put your name, buddy, on—

GIANCANA: Aw, [expletive]. Out of a jillion names, he's gonna remember that name, huh?

JOHNNY: What's happened, Frank says to me, "Johnny, he ain't being bothered."

GIANCANA (pausing, taking a deep breath and then shouting): I got more [expletive] on my [expletive] than any other [expletive] in the country! Believe me when I tell you!

JOHNNY: I know it, Sam.

GIANCANA (still shouting): I was on the road with this broad, there must have been . . . twenty guys! They were next door, upstairs, downstairs, surrounded, all the way around! Get in a car, somebody picks you up. I lose that tail—boom!—I get picked up someplace else! Four or five cars . . . back and forth, back and forth!

JOHNNY: This was in Europe, right?

GIANCANA: Right here in Russia: Chicago, New York, Phoenix!

A little mobster black humor: How could such a thing happen in the U.S.A.? (And we see the inspiration for Uncle Junior's immortal remark on *The Sopranos*: "I've got the Feds so far up my ass, I can taste Brylcreem!")

Frank was playing a dangerous game. He knew Giancana was displeased with his failure to deliver (on the same wiretap, Johnny says, "He says he's got an idea that you're mad at him"; Giancana replies, "He must have a guilty conscience"), but he certainly hadn't tried very hard. Rather than approach the Kennedys directly, he'd asked Peter Lawford to talk to Bobby Kennedy about laying off the Mob boss. Bobby had told Lawford to mind his own business, and that had been that. As Dean Martin once noted, "Only Frank could get away with the shit he got away with. Only Frank. Anyone else would've been dead."

Giancana himself admitted as much. He once told a Chicago associate named Tommy DiBella that he'd considered putting out a contract on Sinatra until one night, when he was in bed with his lady friend Phyllis McGuire, a revelation came to him: "I'm fucking Phyllis, playing Sinatra songs in the background, and the whole time I'm thinking to myself, Christ, how can I silence that voice? It's the most beautiful sound in the world. Frank's lucky he's got it. It saved his life."

Frank knew it. And so he could continue to rub shoulders with Giancana and other hoodlums, doing small favors for them when it was convenient and doing nothing for them if he preferred. Sinatra's relationship with the Mob was a transaction, conducted in the counterfeit currency of the underworld: the gangsters got to bask in his aura, and he in theirs; each side pretended to do things for the other, and neither did much.

But in both worlds, show business and the crime business, illusion was powerful. If people were scared of Frank because they thought he was mobbed up, he didn't mind a bit. He got to take on his friends' power without paying for it.

So he thought, at least.

———————

Ava blew into New York again at the end of September. At almost thirty-nine, she was increasingly sensitive about her looks, if not appearances: one night she walked into the Chateau Madrid with a boy toy—a twenty-four-year-old named Guy Pastor, a son of the bandleader Tony Pastor—and promptly walked out when a flamenco dancer named Raul started taking snapshots in her general direction. She returned only after being persuaded that the dancer was photographing the floor show, not her. Frank was also in town, having bibulous fun with a posse that included Joe E. Lewis. Ava tried phoning him but missed him; he called back but missed her. Finally, they made contact and, a couple of nights later, went out—in a group that included the Porfirio Rubirosas, the George Axelrods, and Mrs. Mike Romanoff.

"About 1 a.m., Frank and Ava parted," Earl Wilson noted. "Frank took a taxi to El Morocco, and Ava went off somewhere by limousine.

"A photographer who earlier asked to take a picture of Frank and Ava was told: No, they were merely part of a group."

No doubt he was told more emphatically than that, but it was true.

———————

In a mid-October Voice of Broadway column, Dorothy Kilgallen wrote that she had received many letters like the following:

Dear Miss Kilgallen:

I would find my day lost if I missed your column in the Evening Journal, therefore I would like your opinion (according to the papers) why the President and his charming wife would entertain a person such as Frank Sinatra at their home, while the President's brother, Robert Kennedy, is supposed to be going to investigate Sinatra's friends the Fischettis. I can assure you that in my family there were more than 50 votes cast for the President, but from now on not one vote will be given to any of the Kennedys, and believe me there are more like my family who are disgusted with the President's choice of friends. May you and yours enjoy the best of health, and God bless you.

Sincerely,
Mary Ann Nolan

Kilgallen replied, in part:

Miss Nolan, you and all the others who wrote to me are an admirable but naïve minority. The majority of people in this country admire—openly or secretly—a successful tough guy who refers to women as "broads" and gets off airplanes with a drink of whisky in his hand. I suppose a parlor psychiatrist would deduce there are a great many conforming Milquetoasts in this land who would give anything to cut loose from the wife and kids and the mortgage and community mores and live in the Sinatra fashion, no rules and plenty of booze and a girl anywhere you look.

In any case, next to President Kennedy Frank Sinatra is the biggest man in America today. He is rich, powerful and adored by millions of fans. He is more famous than any writer, philosopher, clergyman or poet. If you don't believe me walk down your own street and ask the first 50 people you meet who is the author of the last Pulitzer Prize novel. Ask them who is Bertrand Russell. Ask them to name the present Archbishop of Canterbury. Ask them what Robert Frost does for a living. You'll be surprised at the blank looks.

But ask them who Frank Sinatra is and you'll get 50 right answers.

So why shouldn't President Kennedy entertain him, if he wants to? The election is over. He won it.

————

He returned to the Sands at the beginning of November for a two-week stand; as always, he was a smash. Among those attending his sold-out premiere were the ubiquitous Porfirio Rubirosas, along with the Sammy Davises, Mike and Gloria Romanoff, Vic Damone, Richard Conte, Leo Durocher, and Tommy Sands. Frank drew a big ovation when he introduced a surprise guest. "Here's the mother of my children," he said, indicating Big Nancy, who sat ringside.

Also present was a Reprise engineer: Sinatra was having the concerts (with Antonio Morelli conducting a twenty-four-piece orchestra, including Bill Miller on the piano) recorded, intending to make his first live album, a prospect that thrilled his most ardent fans, especially those who hadn't had a chance to see him in person. Frank's label taped nine of the shows from that Sands stand, and, according to Ed O'Brien, he considered "a lot of the songs from each show" good enough to be mastered. "Frank was very excited about a live set coming out on Reprise," O'Brien said. The tapes were stored at Reprise headquarters in Los Angeles, and then the relentless rush of Sinatra's life swept on.

The first item on the agenda was recording a new album—his sixth since the previous December.

He had been astoundingly productive during Reprise's first twelve months. As Friedwald writes, "The Chairman had made two full-length sets with Billy May, done two albums with collaborators so old that they were spanking new [Stordahl and Oliver], and done one uptempo set with a younger arranger with whom he'd never worked before [Johnny Mandel]. The only gap left to fill was to do the same with a ballad album. That would be *Sinatra and Strings,* his first of many projects with Don Costa, a fast-rising and extremely talented orchestrator and producer."

Costa, thirty-six, was a musical jack-of-all-trades: "a musician's musician; an arranger's arranger," the arranger-songwriter Mickey Leonard said. He was a superb guitarist who'd made hit instrumental recordings; a brilliant, lightning-fast (and self-taught) orchestrator who'd lately been writing successfully for Steve Lawrence and Eydie Gorme; and, recently as well, the A&R man, chief arranger, and producer for Steve and Eydie's label, ABC-Paramount Records. He was also a legendary character: charming, disorganized, perpetually over-committed, and always running late, in no small part thanks to his fondness for alcohol and late-night fun. The studio engineer Lee Herschberg remembered Costa, over many glasses of wine, thinking of a song idea, scribbling out the beginning of an arrangement on a restaurant tablecloth, then taking the tablecloth back to his hotel, staying up all night to complete a chart for full orchestra, and recording the tune the next day.

"Costa could write an intro that they could make a symphony out of," said the violinist Carmel Malin. "He'd write these chords that were quite intricate, and they'd say, 'That note isn't right.' He said, 'That note is right.' You'd play it again, and it *was* right. He said, 'Don't you ever listen to Ravel?'"

Of course there was another arranger who had listened to a good deal of Ravel, but Nelson Riddle, still at Capitol, remained contractually unavailable to Reprise—a fact that didn't prevent him from being "extremely upset" by Frank's decision to hire Costa, Peter Levinson writes. "As a result, he began to refer to Costa as 'Don Co-Star,' a term which indicated more than a touch of envy."

And also a grain of truth. As impressive as Costa's gifts were, commentators rarely assign him to the first rank of Sinatra's arrangers. "Don Costa was a great pinch hitter," Charles Granata writes. "He was the guy you called in when you needed someone else's sound, but that someone else wasn't available."

"Do you know who Don Costa really was all the time to Frank?" Sammy Cahn asked Will Friedwald. "Don Costa was Axel all over again, with those deeper, fuller strings."

Perhaps. And perhaps Costa's chameleonic qualities ever so slightly diminished him in Sinatra's eyes. As we've seen, every artistic relationship in Frank's life was also an intricate power struggle: he could run roughshod over any collaborator who betrayed the slightest weakness, and in years to come, he would dominate Costa, to their mutual detriment. Theirs was a partnership that began at its peak. "*Sinatra and Strings*," the arranger said in the 1970s, "was, and always will be, the hallmark of my existence."

There was another classical composer besides Ravel to whom Costa's beautiful work on this album has a kinship. A key lies in something else Mickey Leonard said: "Don Costa was among the most emotional writers, and his orchestrations are very theatrical. He wrote with a great sense of drama."

The words also describe Giacomo Puccini, a particular favorite of Frank's. The opera that was his life was now deep into its second act, and he wanted a means to express it.

"*Sinatra and Strings* opened up a whole new era," Frank Sinatra Jr. told Granata. "The orchestras were getting bigger, and Pop wanted that lush string sound."

They did it right. In the deep flow and shimmer of its arrangements and the magnificent ardor of Frank's vocals (just listen to his "Stardust" here—he only sings the verse!—or his "Night and Day"), *Sinatra & Strings* is unapologetically emotional and artistically superlative. Puccini would have approved.

At the end of November, Frank headed back to Australia for four nights of concerts in Sydney (to the tune of $100,000), to be followed by a jaunt to Hong Kong, Tokyo, and Thailand. An odd crew accompanied him: the pianist Bill Miller, the trumpet player Al Porcino, and the drummer Johnny Markham (they would work with local musicians in Sydney); Dorothy Provine; Leo Durocher; Mike and Gloria Romanoff; and a New York barkeep named Ermenegildo Rizzo—Jilly.

Jilly Rizzo was a character—Frank's kind of character: a knockabout New York guy who'd grown up in Greenwich Village, gone to war, then worked as a loading-dock laborer and bar bouncer before graduating to bar ownership himself, on West Forty-ninth Street in 1948. Though he'd never been a boxer, he had a detached retina (suffered as the result of horseplay with his brother and a paper clip, not in the ring) that gave him *that look,* and he was handy with his fists. (He also liked to carry a blackjack up his sleeve, for insurance.) He had never been a wiseguy, but he'd worked for them and palled around with them and could talk the talk. In 1954, he bought a new bar, in the north of the theater district at 256 West Fifty-second Street, and gave the place his own melodic first name.

Jilly's was a long, cozily dim space, a couple of steps down from street level, with a lengthy, beautiful oak bar on the right as you entered, a piano bar in the back, and a predominantly red decor. Nothing fancy; lots of smoke and laughs. It had, George Jacobs recalled, "one unusual distinction: it served Chinese food, perhaps the worst Chinese food in New York. New Jersey–style Chinese food, chicken chow mein, moo goo gai pan, sweet and sour pork, totally inauthentic and not even tasty as fake food. Mr. S thought it was magnificent, the franks and beans of the mysterious East."

Frank began gravitating there in the mid-1950s, after first gravitating to Jilly himself, in an incident that carries the nimbus of mythology.

As one of Rizzo's sons explained it,

> There was a beef in one of the clubs where my father used to be the bouncer, when he had his bouncing jobs all over town. There was a big argument, and they couldn't handle this guy who had come into the joint, so they called my father and said, "We need you over here."
>
> My father said, "I'll be right there," and Frank was in there that night. My father went in, gave the guy one, two, three—*gone*—and Frank said, "I gotta meet this guy." That's how it started.

The two of them became closer in Miami in November 1958, while Frank was shooting *A Hole in the Head.* Rizzo was there with his singular houseboat; let Earl Wilson describe it, in an item datelined Miami Beach:

> A remarkable Chinese houseboat—modern design, worth $140,000, which must be towed as it has no motors—is docked here, the property of Jilly Rizzo, owner of the NY pub, "Jilly's." The boat ("Jilly's Yen"), docked across from the Eden Roc, has a round bed and gold bathroom fixtures—and you have to take your shoes off when you enter.

Everything about Jilly was unabashedly just the way it was, from his speech, which was full of malapropisms and double negatives, to his wife, Sorrel "Honey" King, whose unusual hair tint inspired Frank to dub her "the blue

Jew." Rizzo was in some ways the kind of man Sinatra wished he had been: brave and tough and funny and apparently entirely without inner demons of any sort. And not impressed by much, including, at times, Frank himself, whom he called "the singer." Sycophants were easy to come by; Jilly was warm and loyal, but he went his own way. As a friend put it,

> Jilly was successful before he met Frank Sinatra. He had a very successful business, and he was just an attraction for people. A Who's Who of people went to Jilly's, before or after the theater. And when you went to Jilly's, you had nothing to worry about, because you were well protected.

"One night, somebody at the bar stole a woman's purse, and the word got back to him," recalled the pianist Monty Alexander, who began playing at Jilly's in the early 1960s. "Within no time, Jilly grabbed the guy, dragged him to the subway station and threw him down the stairs, [saying,] 'You don't come in my club doing this.' Jilly himself. He didn't have the bouncer do it."

Soon Sinatra and Rizzo began spending more time together. Jilly was someone he could talk to, someone he didn't have to watch his p's and q's with, and if need be, someone who could step in if trouble arose. (He also was not a drinker, which meant he was alert when trouble arose.)

And he was amusing company. As were Durocher and Mike Romanoff. The Sydney concerts went well, but the sightseeing afterward was shadowed by the gloom of the king. In spite of many amusements—in Thailand, the maharaja of Jaipur escorted Sinatra and company through his private zoo, racetrack, and golf course—Frank's "agonizing loneliness" on the tour "made up his mind to marry again," according to "a pal who made the trip to Australia with the star" (Durocher? Romanoff? certainly not Jilly) who spoke to Walter Winchell. Winchell wrote,

> Dorothy Provine, one of the cast, was written up in some columns as being his latest diversion, but the fact is that Sinatra spent most of his time alone in his hotel room brooding. He kept phoning Juliet Prowse, trying to persuade her to "take the first jet and please come see me. I miss you terribly." "Frank," she is said to have told him. "I don't want to be on your girl list. It can only be one way for us!"
>
> Relating this phone call to the pal, Sinatra pounded a fist on the table, exclaiming: "That's my kind of Doll!"

The Sinatra-Prowse relationship was a puzzlement to everyone, probably including Frank and Juliet themselves. She was determined, throughout their relationship, to maintain her independence and to keep working: this was problematic for Sinatra, who was captivated by independent women but didn't want them to stay that way. (And, naturally, got bored the moment a woman became dependent.)

They'd been on and off throughout 1961, mostly off. That fall, she told a reporter that their relationship was "serious inasmuch as I was very fond of him and still am. But how long can something go on without any ultimate goal?" When Frank failed to rise to the bait—if bait it was—she told another writer, "I go my way and he goes his. I have my life to lead and I'm not going to sit around. If I want to go out with someone else, I go out. No strings."

She meant it. She had a new manager, a handsome young fellow named Eddie Goldstone, and it soon became apparent to the world that he was more than her manager. The gossip columns eagerly charted the pair's appearances at restaurants and nightclubs on both coasts, breathlessly wondering if you-know-who was jealous. Sinatra's old nemesis Lee Mortimer claimed that Frank had had the pair tailed by a private detective, had had "friends" try "to induce [Goldstone] to lay off," and had threatened him personally. Though Mortimer was a pest and a scold, it was all too easy to believe.

In the meantime, Goldstone kept Prowse busy professionally as well. Though she'd turned down a second movie with Elvis, she played the lead or second lead in three movies released that year and did a lot of dancing on television. She also performed the title role in a Las Vegas production of *Irma la Douce* and then, in late December, traveled to New York to do a $10,000 guest spot on *The Perry Como Show*. Earl Wilson, whom Sinatra read religiously, wrote that he'd "got excited seeing attractive Juliet Prowse at the Copa with a young guy; turned out to be her mgr., Eddie Goldstone." Frank wouldn't have been pleased.

———

On December 19, Joseph P. Kennedy, seventy-three, suffered a stroke while playing golf in Palm Beach. He would survive for almost eight more years, outliving both his older sons. Confined to a wheelchair, apparently intact mentally—"soaking it all up with those cold blue eyes," as the chauffeur Frank Saunders recalled—Kennedy was able to utter only one word: no. "Only he did not speak it," Saunders wrote.

> He made a noise out of it. A long, loud no. NNNnnnooooo! Over and over again. Sometimes he could squeak a yes, and sometimes he'd use his good left hand and arm to make gestures and motion us. He tried to write with his left hand, to give us instructions and tell us what

he wanted, but it frustrated him. I would see this look of fear creep into his eyes, and at times there would be something more fleeting in his eyes too—the look you can get from a wild caged animal. He was trapped, and he knew it.

The description is pitiless, but then there were few people to pity Joe Kennedy. "I was surprised that a man who had been so powerful and was so rich did not have more close friends," Saunders said. On the short list of those who visited the Ambassador in the weeks and months after he was felled, Frank Sinatra's name does not appear.

———————

That same month, Frank and Peter Lawford dissolved their partnership in the Beverly Hills restaurant Puccini and sold the place to a Chicago syndicate.

*People who call me controversial are those who don't agree
with me.*

—FRANK SINATRA AT A PRESS CONFERENCE IN TOKYO,
APRIL 20, 1962

S*ergeants* 3 premiered on January 7, and the critical reception was predictably withering. "Somewhere east of Suez the ghost of Rudyard Kipling must
be whirling like a dervish in its grave," wrote Hazel Flynn in the Hollywood
Citizen-News. "It's more din than Gunga, believe me, starting with a barroom
brawl and ending with a howling massacre." *Time*'s reviewer said, "The Clansmen loaf kiddingly through their parts, acquiring suntans . . . Perceptive viewers will realize that Sinatra and his Cub Scout troupe are pioneering in a new
art form: the $4,000,000 home movie."

Not so surprisingly, despite—or possibly because of—the many public
decrials of the Rat Pack, the picture would be a moderate hit at the box office.

Performing at a New York nightclub, the group's most enthusiastic member
kept the flame burning bright. "Sammy Davis' idol worshiping of Frank Sinatra
increases—he now ad libs during songs, and drinks while performing," Earl
Wilson noted. "Opening at the Copa . . . he leaped atop a piano and began
dancing. Impersonating Dean Martin, he sang into a glass and took a drink out
of the microphone. 'I am a member of the Clan,' he shrugged. 'That's a little
group of ordinary guys that get together once a year to take over the entire
world.'"

Meanwhile, back in Los Angeles, the Leader found a way to distract the
world from the bad reviews. When Juliet Prowse returned from New York on
January 8, Frank was at the airport to meet her. And the next day, the world's
newspapers were blaring the tidings: Frank Sinatra, age forty-six, and Juliet
Prowse, twenty-five, were engaged to be married.

A strange dance ensued.

The news of the engagement came as a surprise to everyone, possibly
including the principals. "A great girl . . . a wonderful girl," Frank gushed to
the Hollywood writer James Bacon, who encountered him while he was finishing a round of golf at the Hillcrest Country Club in Beverly Hills.

"You really shook us up," Bacon told Sinatra.

"I'm a little shook up myself," Frank said. "I'm forty-six now. It's time I settled down."

Just then, George Burns ambled up. "Hey, Nat," Sinatra said. "I got engaged to Juliet Prowse today."

"Yeah," Burns said, uninterestedly, and changed the subject.

"He thinks I'm kidding him," Frank said after Burns left. "He doesn't believe me."

Neither did Prowse's mother, whom the Associated Press contacted in Johannesburg. "I don't believe there's any truth to it," she said.

> I don't believe it because I haven't heard a word from Juliet direct and
> we are a close family who keep in close communication. Furthermore,
> Juliet last told me she and Frankie were only good friends and there
> was no question of a big romance or marriage . . . Either this is untrue
> or it's something completely new and a sudden turn of events. Other-
> wise it just doesn't fit.

But she was clearly failing to understand her prospective son-in-law, for whom sudden turns of events were standard operating procedure. Apparently, Frank had taken Prowse to dinner at Romanoff's on the night she returned from New York and proposed marriage. One small condition: that she give up show business. He was expressing one of his deepest, most impossible wishes—that a woman of mettle subordinate herself entirely to him. (And, of course, remain a woman of mettle.)

Taken by surprise, Prowse said that she would have to think it over. Sinatra asked if she might do so while they drove out to Palm Springs. By the time the night was through, they seemed to have hit on a compromise: she would mostly give up the business, outside the odd motion picture and TV guest appearance; otherwise she would devote herself entirely to Frank. He produced a diamond engagement ring, and she accepted.

Sinatra's friends were shocked, shocked. Not long before the announcement, Van Heusen had said, "I don't think Frank will ever get noosed again." Lawford refused to believe the news until Sinatra wired a confirmation. Onstage at the Copa, Sammy asked the audience for "a few moments of silence for our Leader, Frank Sinatra, who is leaving us."

"Juliet Prowse will ascend to the loftiest heights of Hollywood and Frank will spend his nights at home, a tamed tiger," Earl Wilson teased. "We'll miss you around the joints, Frank. Maybe she'll let you out one night a week."

But not long after the announcement, shortly before leaving to visit her family in South Africa, Prowse suddenly told UPI, "I have no idea of retiring." Asked what had changed her mind, she said, "Just thinking about it. The idea of not performing any more. It's been a part of my life for many years, and I don't feel I can put my feet up on the desk and never dance again."

Not surprisingly, Frank was on his own page. At the same time Prowse was talking to UPI, he was enduring the unfailingly pleasant Bob Thomas, who visited him at Goldwyn Studios, where *The Manchurian Candidate* was starting production. "The word was out that he didn't want to speak publicly about his forthcoming marriage, but one has to take chances in this game," Thomas wrote.

> I hazarded that his choice of a bride was his smartest move since play-ing Maggio in "From Here to Eternity." Juliet is much admired in this sector of the press corps as bright, charming and talented.
>
> Sinatra failed to bridle, instead confirmed, "Yes, she's a wonderful girl."
>
> Encouraged, I pressed on: "And will it be a June wedding, as has been reported?"
>
> "I dunno," he replied. "She's going home to South Africa this week-end, and she'll work it out with her mother." Then lapsing into Sinatran [insert *Amos 'n' Andy* voice here]: "Those matters up to the broads."
>
> And what of reports that Juliet will give up her career after her mar-riage?
>
> "That's right: I think it will be better if she doesn't work."
>
> Show business' loss, I said.
>
> "Yeah, but my gain," he retorted.

But suddenly a juicy rumor began making the rounds: that in reality, the engagement was "merely a marvelous publicity stunt," as Dorothy Kilgallen wrote on January 17. "The camps are quite equally divided," she continued.

> To the loyalists who insist, "Frank's too big to pull a publicity stunt," the other experts explain wearily, "He'd do it to help the kid's career. He likes the kid. It would be kicks for him to help her." By a coincidence, the Sinatra publicity men were trying to book Juliet on at least one key television program on a date that would have followed the betrothal news immediately. They were turned down because the show's produc-ers didn't think Juliet was well known to the vast American viewing audience.

Even paranoids have enemies, and Kilgallen, no friend of Frank's, was lay-ing it on thick here. Prowse had been a steady TV presence throughout 1961, and she had just done the Como show for a big fee. Yet there was no denying that while her career had been doing fine, the betrothal had raised her profile considerably and been great for business—at exactly the moment when Frank wanted her to pull back.

"Irresponsible people are saying those things," he told Earl Wilson, about statements (Prowse's surely included) that she was going to stay in the business. He repeated, "She's not going to do any work. I'd rather not have it."

––––––––

He, of course, was working as hard as ever. In mid-January, he pulled Gordon Jenkins onto the Reprise roster (no doubt raising the blood pressure of Riddle, still stuck at Capitol) for, of all things, a new album based entirely on waltzes. It was a sweet idea, appealing to the old-fashioned side of Frank that Jenkins, with his singing strings and simple harmonies, represented. But it was also a business decision, and in a commercial climate where Reprise was struggling to get on its feet—and Capitol was swamping the market with Sinatra product—the move would prove problematic: on its release in October, the LP would rise no higher on the charts than number 26.

The new album was originally going to be called *Come Waltz with Me*, after the title tune Frank commissioned from Cahn and Van Heusen. The provocation would certainly not have been lost on Capitol Records, which after all had issued *Come Fly with Me*, *Come Dance with Me!*, and *Come Swing with Me!* and had recently won the *Swing Along with Me* legal battle. But Sinatra was saved the trouble of returning to court when he heard Sammy and Chester's song, which was a little sprightlier than most of the other numbers on the LP, five of which were decades-old work (none of it any later than 1927), in a bittersweet autumnal mode, by the great composer-lyricist Irving Berlin. Instead, Frank decided to name the album after the first track, Berlin's "All Alone."

Irving Berlin was one of the funniest writers on Tin Pan Alley, but his work also drew from a deep well of sadness—he became a widower at age twenty-four and lost an infant son early in his second marriage, to mention just two external events in his life—and his waltzes of the 1920s have a haunting quality unparalleled in American songwriting. But Berlin's sorrow and Sinatra's were not precisely the same, for Frank's musical melancholy came in one flavor only: torch.

For this reason, 1925's "Always," a sweetly sad hymn of devotion, wouldn't work on *All Alone*. But the title song was perfect for Sinatra's purposes, as was 1927's "Song Is Ended," which closed the album. In between came three other immortal numbers by the composer—"What'll I Do?," "When I Lost You" (from 1912, the year of his widowhood), and "Remember"—along with half a dozen other tunes by other writers, all in three-quarter time, but none possessing the quality of the Berlin compositions.

Those five alone are worth the price of admission. The conjunction of Frank's magnificent singing—he truly is at the zenith of his art in these years—with Berlin's deceptively simple, devastating songs and Gordon Jenkins's shamelessly sentimental arrangements is uniquely effective. In the case of lesser numbers like Hugh Martin and Ralph Blane's "Girl Next Door" (originally "The Boy Next Door," sung by Judy Garland in the 1944 MGM musical *Meet Me in St. Louis*) and the 1926 weeper "Are You Lonesome Tonight?" (which had been a campy hit in 1960 for the post-army Elvis), Sinatra manages to dignify the material into listenability. Even he, though, can't do much with a dog like Cahn and Van Heusen's by-the-numbers title song for the 1958 Cary Grant–Ingrid Bergman movie *Indiscreet*. With few exceptions ("All the Way" and "Only the Lonely," but not many others, come to mind), Sammy and Jimmy's best tunes together were ring-a-ding-dingers; for some reason, each wrote his best love songs with someone else.*

The late Peter Levinson attended the *All Alone* recording sessions on January 15, 16, and 17. "Those were really something to see," he recalled. "He really *performed* to the invited audience." On the other hand, Levinson said, as blissful as Frank apparently was about his engagement, he "looked like hell when he came in. It was as if he'd just been to nine orgies. Sweater; didn't have the rug on—nobody could believe that he sang as beautifully as he did on that album."

In fact, it might have been sorrow rather than dissipation that accounted for his haggardness at that first session: earlier in the day, he had been a pall-bearer at the funeral of a friend, the brilliant comedian Ernie Kovacs, who'd just died in a car wreck at the age of forty-two.

In the meantime, though, Frank was doing an astonishing thing: making a great movie. Coming on the heels of *Sergeants 3, The Manchurian Candidate,* another independent production in which he was intimately involved, might have been expected to suffer from the same problems: over-control by the star and under-control by the filmmakers. But every picture Sinatra had ever made had been a power game, and the very few good ones had all been directed by men who knew their own worth and understood the intricacies of working with a highly intuitive, infinitely impatient thoroughbred. And if Frank respected both his director and the artistic possibilities of the material, his

---

* Mostly Jule Styne, in Cahn's case; mostly Johnny Burke, in Van Heusen's.

investment of time and attention could be absolute, as Otto Preminger had discovered to his surprised pleasure on *The Man with the Golden Arm*.

With music and movies, the material was always what drew Frank in. He loved a great melody, but words also meant an enormous amount to him. For all his impatience, he was a close reader—of lyrics, fat historical biographies, potential movie properties, screenplays. He'd loved *The Manchurian Candidate* as a novel, and he was enthusiastic from the beginning about George Axelrod's script, which, with its nightmarish, hall-of-mirrors quality, was extraordinarily faithful to Condon's work.

And in John Frankenheimer, Sinatra knew from the start that he had a director worthy of his time and commitment: a filmmaker with a clear artistic vision, a strong personality, and the sensitivity not to butt heads with him.

Still just thirty when filming started, Frankenheimer was a big, handsome, athletic kid from Queens, with a presence not inferior to Sinatra's and a wunderkind reputation amassed in the mid- and late 1950s, when television was live and artistic. Between 1954 and 1960, he directed 152 live TV dramas, an average of one every two weeks, doing his most significant work for the acclaimed CBS anthology show *Playhouse 90* and only shifting to movies as the business changed. He'd directed adaptations of works by Hemingway, Faulkner, and Fitzgerald; he had an acute sense of his characters' psychology and a great visual flair, with a love of odd camera angles and movements. In a lengthy early 1960 appreciation in the *New York Herald Tribune*, the television critic John Crosby cited a number of fine directors produced by the still-new medium, among them Arthur Penn, George Roy Hill, Delbert Mann, Robert Mulligan, and Sidney Lumet. He called Frankenheimer, the youngest by far, "the most spectacular, most audacious, most colorful, most flamboyant."

By all accounts, John Frankenheimer was singularly obsessed with *The Manchurian Candidate,* a film that, according to Daniel O'Brien, the director regarded "as his first truly personal project, feeling that the story made an all too valid point regarding the political manipulation and conditioning of American society."

But then all three members of the production team seem to have been strikingly committed to the film and respectful of each other. Though Sinatra was clearly the straw that stirred the drink—"Without you, we wouldn't have had a movie," Frankenheimer told him in a conversation videotaped twenty-five years later—his dictatorial side was apparently not in evidence. "You let me do what I was able to do, you let George do what he was able to do," the director recalled. "There was none of this constant interference that you read about today."

The seventy-one-year-old Sinatra gently corrected him. "We three people *believed* what we were doing," he said. "We wouldn't have been together if we hadn't believed it. It's not that I let you do what you wanted to do—not at all."

Though nostalgia might have misted the three filmmakers' 1987 reminiscences, the proof is in the finished picture, which is Sinatra's (and Frankenheimer's) best, as well as in the fact that the shoot was completed in a lightning-like, and trauma-free, thirty-nine days. Much of the credit for this, Tom Santopietro writes, owed to Frankenheimer's decision to handle Sinatra as had George Sidney (*Pal Joey*) and Vincente Minnelli (*Some Came Running*): "rehears[ing] other cast members in advance, bringing in Sinatra for only one pre-shoot run-through before the actual filming of a scene. Keeping the need for retakes to a minimum, Frankenheimer thereby ensured Sinatra's continued goodwill."

Yet Sidney and Minnelli had made merely good, not great, movies with Frank: handling him wasn't the only part of the equation. *Pal Joey* and *Some Came Running* were both studio pictures, and Sinatra had been a cog—no matter how big a cog, still a cog—in a machine. *The Manchurian Candidate* was *his*. It was also, along with *Suddenly* and *The Man with the Golden Arm,* among the darkest material he had done—maybe the darkest. And with *Suddenly* and *Golden Arm,* he had still been in his thirties. In 1962, he was staring fifty in the face, and he looked it. "I thought it would be terrific to have that marvelous, beat-up Sinatra face giving forth long, incongruous speeches," said George Axelrod, who took those speeches straight from Condon's novel and put them in the screenplay.

Frank loved that screenplay. He carried it around and read it aloud at the drop of a hat. He told everyone who would listen (and when Sinatra was talking, everybody listened) that he was more excited about the part than any he'd ever played. He loved those long, incongruous speeches.

The words had entranced him, had drawn him in; he was fully engaged, and that was always the secret to his very best work. "Sinatra treated his fellow actors with courtesy and consideration, rehearsed with them when necessary, contributed his ideas for scenes and never questioned Frankenheimer's authority," O'Brien writes. "With Axelrod on set throughout the filming for consultation and dialogue changes, *Candidate* proved to be one of the smoothest productions of Sinatra's career."

Casting also had a lot to do with it. The first principal role after Sinatra's to be filled was that of the assassin Raymond Shaw: the thirty-two-year-old, Lithuanian-born British actor Laurence Harvey had signed on, for a fee of $270,000, in September. Harvey was a beautiful young man with a long, soulful face, a deep, resonant voice, and a slightly abstracted manner: he had had his first smash success in the 1959 English drama *Room at the Top,* as the social climber Joe Lampton. Hollywood had found him immediately and thrown him into a series of miscastings: as a southern colonel in *The Alamo,* as a romantic lead against Elizabeth Taylor (*Butterfield* 8) and Jane Fonda (*Walk on the Wild Side*). Harvey's problem, where Hollywood was concerned, was that he wasn't quite a lover or a fighter: he gave off an air of brittleness and confused sexuality. Fortunately, this was right on the money for the role of Raymond Shaw.

In December, Angela Lansbury had been signed to play Raymond's mother, the arch-villainess Eleanor Shaw Iselin. Apparently, Sinatra originally wanted Lucille Ball for the role, a fascinating casting notion, as Tom Santopietro points out: "As Ball aged, she grew into an increasingly hardened performer, losing all traces of the vulnerability that so informed her brilliant multiyear run on television's *I Love Lucy.* The resulting quality of toughness would have suited the role of [Eleanor] very well, although it is anyone's guess whether or not Ball would have felt comfortable delving into the dark recesses of [her] warped character."

Lansbury, a fearless actress, was comfortable delving into anything. John Frankenheimer had Frank watch her performance as the mother of the irresistible young stud played by Warren Beatty in Frankenheimer's about-to-be-released drama *All Fall Down.* In the Gothic piece, written for the screen by William Inge, there's a hint of incest between the creepily clinging mother and her wayward son, a note not dissimilar to the relationship between Raymond and Eleanor in *The Manchurian Candidate.* Sinatra was sold. At thirty-six, Angela Lansbury was all of three years older than Laurence Harvey, but her canny, lived-in face consigned her to a trilogy of maternal roles in the early 1960s, beginning with her turn as Elvis Presley's mom in 1961's *Blue Hawaii.*

The third big name to be cast was Janet Leigh, as Bennett Marco's girlfriend, Rosie, a small role with big significance. Leigh, who'd been separated from Tony Curtis for almost a year and devoting herself to raising their two young daughters, hadn't made a movie since Alfred Hitchcock's *Psycho* in 1960. For all the brevity of her screen time in *The Manchurian Candidate,* she and Sinatra (with whom she'd been rumored to have had an affair) would have one scene together that was equal or superior to anything either of them would ever do in the movies—and one of the greatest and strangest in modern cinema.

The *Herald Tribune's* celebrity interviewer Joe Hyams visited Frank at the Goldwyn Studios after hearing an intriguing rumor. "According to the gossip around town Frank Sinatra is a 'new man' since his engagement to Juliet Prowse," Hyams wrote.

Friends and gossips report he not only looks younger but he's become a lovable fellow. Over the years I've found Sinatra often affable but never, never lovable so I hastened to the set of "The Manchurian Candidate" to see the "new" man myself . . .

There sitting in the dressing room with the door open was the man himself. By George, there was a change. He did look younger with his hair in the short West Point style hair-cut, in keeping with his role in the film and the uniform he was wearing.

He was sitting quietly in a chair, Coke at hand instead of vodka, puffing leisurely on a pipe instead of dragging hastily on a cigarette. He was listening intently to a record album entitled "Relaxism," a gift from Dean Martin.

"What's new, Joe?" he asked me pleasantly.

"From what I hear, it's you that's new," I said.

It seemed to me that the calm blue of Sinatra's eyes was begin- ning to freeze rapidly into ice-blue. So since Sinatra's eyes have always been my barometer and I am a devout coward I changed the subject instantly.

A little later, an assistant director called Frank to the set, and Hyams fol- lowed. "The scene was a two-shot with Laurence Harvey, and the take, consist- ing of solid dialogue, ran seven minutes and 35 seconds without a fluff, which is remarkable enough for a single take to almost be a record," the reporter wrote. "Frank's sure changed," a member of Sinatra's coterie told Hyams. "He knows his lines letter-perfect and there's no clowning around."

How much of this was John Frankenheimer's influence and how much Juliet Prowse's was another question. (But the Coke, the pipe, and the relax- ation record might well have been props suggested by Frank's new press agent, Chuck Moses, who was also working as unit publicist for The Manchurian Candidate.)

In early February, the cast and crew traveled to New York City for a week of location shooting—at Madison Square Garden, in Central Park, even in Jilly's (Frank sent Rizzo a check—for $1—for the use of his joint). Another Herald Tribune reporter named Don Ross paid a call on Sinatra at the Garden, which was dressed as the scene of a political convention, with red, white, and blue bunting and several hundred male and female extras playing delegates, wearing summer clothing and carrying signs that said, "Benjamin K. Arthur for President" and "Big John Iselin."

Frank, once again in his army major's uniform, seemed determined to con- tinue the charm offensive. And when Sinatra was determined to charm, no human was immune. "Instead of putting a thumb in our eye, as he is said to do occasionally with newspapermen, he shook hands warmly," the reporter wrote, gratefully.

> We chatted with Sinatra off and on for an hour and a half. He left us
> for brief periods to play scenes before the camera. We discovered him
> to be a pleasant man with considerable charm and a nice smile . . .
> We kept looking around for a glimpse of the tough bodyguards who are
> reputed to hover around Sinatra but we didn't see anybody to fit that
> description. Neither were any of the madcap boy and girl clansmen
> around.

Ross had expected to find a hungover Vegas lounge lizard; instead, he witnessed a surprising demonstration of Frank at the peak of his powers.

> His role in the film requires him to run along one of the Garden
> corridors searching for [Laurence] Harvey who, he fears, is about to
> shoot somebody. Sinatra ran down the corridor—a distance of about
> 50 yards—at full speed. He ran fast. We went down the corridor to
> meet him walking back, expecting him to be blowing hard. He was just
> breathing a little fast. For a man of his age—it was remarkable.
> "You're in good shape," we said.
> "Oh sure," he replied, "golf, tennis, swimming and calisthenics three
> or four times a week."
> "Don't forget the blackjack games," somebody said. He grinned.

When the reporter asked Sinatra how he whiled away the long periods between takes, the answer befitted a man who always had a keen sense of his audience—and one who knew what the classy Republican readers of the *Herald Tribune* would appreciate hearing. "I like to read," Frank said.

> I'm working now on that "Agony and Ecstasy" book about Michelangelo, and I'm reading a law book. It's called "Musmanno Dissents . . ."
> I'm also reading Louis Nizer's "My Life in Court." I know him well.
> And, last, I'm working on "How to Train Your Dog." I just got a Saint
> Bernard. He refuses to learn anything but he's cute as hell.

Of course a guy's nose couldn't always be in a book. In the evenings, Frank batched it with his pal Mike Romanoff, who'd come along to keep him company: they hit El Morocco and, one memorable night, Toots Shor's, where the ubiquitous Earl Wilson witnessed an oddly portentous encounter. "Frank Sinatra and Richard Nixon—a couple of opposites if you can imagine a couple of opposites—were on opposite sides of Toots Shor's celebrity corner the other night," the columnist wrote.

> Mike Romanoff, dining with Sinatra, strolled over to Nixon and said a few Romanesque words . . .
>   Nixon came over and offered his hand to Sinatra.
>   Whereupon a barfly cried, "Attaboy, Frank, for making him come over to you!"
>   It was an expensive evening for Sinatra—probably cost him about $1,000 in Shor's. For Toots reached into Sinatra's pocket, extracted rolls of bills, passed out about $500 to waiters, captains, bus boys and bartenders.
>   Then, delighted at how easily he could do it, he followed Frank to his taxi, snatching out more $ . . . for everybody but the customers. Sinatra enjoyed it, evidently, immensely. Frank left because he had a 7 a.m. call for his picture, "Manchurian Candidate," at Madison Square Garden.
>   "I've often gone to bed at 7 o'clock in New York but this is the first time I've ever had to get up at 7 o'clock in New York," he explained.

His commitment to the movie was remarkable. His commitment to Prowse continued to wend its strange way. On February 4—twenty-three years to the day after Frank's wedding to Nancy Barbato at Our Lady of Sorrows Church in Jersey City—the columnist Hy Gardner aired a rumor couched in curiously unromantic language: "that, if Sinatra goes through with his plan to marry Juliet Prowse, they might jump the gun and elope in early March when Frank is booked to entertain at the Fontainebleau in Miami Beach."

If?

On Valentine's Day, Mike and Gloria Romanoff threw an engagement party, at Romanoff's, for Sinatra and Prowse. Louella Parsons opined, "All those who bet the marriage wouldn't take place are beginning to renege on their bets and now believe that Frank means it when he says he wants to settle down." Sammy Davis Jr. even announced that he'd secured the services of the great balladeer Joe Williams to sing at the wedding.

Then, on February 20, Louella, whose tentacles were everywhere, received the hottest of hot tips: Prowse had canceled her wedding gown and trousseau.

The next day, Essex Productions issued a terse announcement: "Juliet Prowse and Frank Sinatra today disclosed they have called off their wedding plans. A conflict in career interests led us to make this decision. We feel it is wiser to make this move now rather than later." A publicity spokesman added, "Neither will be available for comment. There will be no amplification."

No amplification was necessary. A couple of days earlier, Prowse had told a reporter, "I don't intend to give up my career. But naturally, I don't intend to go at it full blast."

The full blast would have come from Sinatra, who had made his feelings on the subject crystal clear. It seemed telling that Juliet Prowse was rehearsing for a Donald O'Connor TV special when the announcement came out. "No tears whatsoever," a spokesman for Prowse reported. "She's beautiful, she's fine." "You couldn't tell a thing," O'Connor added. "She worked just as hard as she did on other days." ("Why should she cry?" a friend of Prowse's said. "Her asking price at Las Vegas jumped from five hundred dollars a week to $17,500.")

Meanwhile, according to Sidney Skolsky, Frank had retreated to Palm Springs, devastated.

The barbs started flying at once. "Talk about short engagements!" a Broadway wag quipped. "Why, Frank has had longer engagements in Las Vegas!"

Dean Martin said that he knew the true story: "Juliet wanted Frank to give up *his* career."

And Dorothy Kilgallen couldn't help twisting the knife: "Frank Sinatra's pals say he's having a big laugh at the U.S. press, which he despises, for 'falling for' the story of his 'engagement' to Juliet Prowse."

It is highly doubtful that Frank was enjoying a big laugh about a love affair, even an inconstantly conducted love affair, that had gone bad. A few months later, Prowse would shed more light on the subject. "I would have married Frank," she said, "but I've always been a little too difficult for him." She also said that his flexibility about the subject of her working had diminished when he found out that his children opposed the marriage.

As Frank had learned before, two difficult people was just too difficult. And, as should have been clear to all parties, he liked to lead when he danced. The engagement had lasted forty-three days.

On Sunday night, February 25, Frank and Dean played supporting roles on Judy Garland's CBS musical special. Despite Garland's innumerable past woes, not all of them exorcised by any means (she and Sid Luft were about to separate yet again), her career was then on what Will Friedwald calls "an upward spiral," in the wake of her triumphant Carnegie Hall concert the previous April and a Best Supporting Actress nomination for her cameo role in *Judgment at Nuremburg*. At thirty-nine, she had—all too momentarily—risen from the ashes. She looked good—her weight was under control—and she sounded as extraordinary as only she could sound. Both Frank and Dean had had their ups and downs with TV (in Frank's case, mostly downs), but here they rose perfectly to the occasion, complementing Garland but never competing with her, in a charming format (a rising young Norman Jewison directed) that segued solo numbers and duets in a kind of dream logic, on stark sets and with minimal dialogue.

Martin was a well-behaved version of his usual twinkling self, not quite taking his singing seriously, largely getting by on his extraordinary looks alone. Frank, on the other hand, threw some real effort into his acting, gracefully playing the swain to Judy, holding both her hands and staring into her eyes, shifting smoothly from slight irony to wholeheartedness in a strange gloss on their real-life on-again, off-again relationship. God alone knows what they were thinking, but they're fascinating to watch. And Sinatra sang beautifully and feelingly, both in solo and in duet.

Not everyone was charmed. "The inclusion of Frank Sinatra and Dean Martin, neither in particularly good voice or well rehearsed, added little," opined the syndicated critic Cynthia Lowry. "They seemed much more interested in insulting each other and being cute than in backing up the star." And one William E. Sarmento, television critic for the Lowell, Massachusetts, *Sun,* singled out Frank for special censure. "Unfortunately the years have not been as kind to Sinatra's voice as Miss Garland's," he wrote. "He spoke instead of sang a good portion of his songs, striving to remain on key during most of them. Sinatra's real problem is that he is now stereotyped. He looks like someone doing an imitation of Frank Sinatra. He has been reading too much of his publicity."

This was circular: bad publicity about Sinatra's bad publicity. But then a dependable fact about Frank was that there was never any shortage of bad publicity where he was concerned: more and more of it all the time these days.

With the crises of the president's first year in office temporarily in abeyance, a nonpolitical trip to the Golden State could at last be scheduled. The visit was set for the weekend of March 23 through 25: Kennedy was to give a speech and receive an honorary doctorate at the University of California in Berkeley, view the missile facilities at Vandenberg Air Force Base, and possibly pay a call on former president Eisenhower, who was relaxing in Palm Desert. Kennedy too planned to relax, and—as arranged by Peter Lawford—the plan was for him to do it at Frank Sinatra's compound on Wonder Palms Road.

Since the First Lady was traveling in India and Pakistan, a jolly weekend was anticipated all around.

Jack Kennedy had stayed in Frank Sinatra's house in Palm Springs as a senator, but a presidential visit was something else entirely. "We worked for weeks getting everything perfect, planning parties, doing guest lists, trying to include everyone and not piss anybody off," George Jacobs recalled. Tina Sinatra writes, "The news fed Dad's fondest fantasy: that the Compound would become the western White House, Jack Kennedy's home away from home."

Upgrades to the property, some of which had been under way already, went into overdrive. Frank pushed the construction schedule to seven days a week on the Christmas Tree House, a bungalow designed for the Sinatra children but now necessary for housing the Secret Service. A concrete helipad was built, and a hotline installed—a blue-and-white telephone with a red handset and a blinking light. "Two days before the visit, workmen were still hammering round the clock," Tina writes.

And then the president withdrew.

———

Trouble had been in the air for a while. Jacobs asserts that Joe Kennedy's stroke had changed the family's relationship with Sinatra for good: "Bobby, the Puritan, and Jackie, the snot, took over and decreed that Mr. Sinatra was Not Our Kind. All of a sudden, the Irish eyes stopped smiling. And Mr. S went from being the First Friend to just another greaser from Hoboken."

February 1962: Frank and Dean help a revitalized Judy Garland out with her CBS musical special. Three fascinating creatures not wholly in sync but amazing to watch nonetheless.

In fact, as Ronald Brownstein writes, Frank had "simply misread his man" from the beginning.

> For Kennedy, the association with Sinatra was always more casual, its effect equivocal. Despite his infectious charm, Kennedy was a reserved man with very few close friends. "There was a barrier in Kennedy nobody got past; maybe Bobby didn't even get past," said [the Kennedy speechwriter Richard] Goodwin. "I don't think it was contrived; that was the man's nature." Kennedy enjoyed Sinatra's company, but those around him never sensed that the brassy singer penetrated the deeper fortifications that turned away so many others; to Arthur Schlesinger, the two men were "celebrity friends" whose relationship generated more sparks in public than private.

Senator Kennedy had been a celebrity friend, but in President Kennedy, Frank had encountered, for the first and last time, a man whose celebrity outweighed his.

> Sinatra had been at center stage for most of his adult life. But in the glow of Kennedy's glory he basked in the world's brightest spotlight. If Sinatra sought no tangible rewards, no honorary appointments, what he needed from Kennedy was, in fact, more demanding, more intimate; he needed the most personal gift of all, the benediction of his presence. It was, as Sinatra would learn, if not the easiest reward for Kennedy to dispense, the easiest for him to withdraw.

In fact, the wind had shifted early in the presidency: Frank was simply unwilling, or unable, to read the signs. Many news reports and gossip items throughout 1961 had spoken of displeasure in high places with Sinatra and the Clan. A couple of weeks before the Ambassador was felled, a UPI dispatch said, "Frank Sinatra has been asked officially to 'tone down' his public displays of affinity to President Kennedy and the administration. It is said that in conversation Sinatra calls Mr. Kennedy 'Prez.'"

According to Brownstein, Jack Kennedy had begun taking the final steps to dissolve his friendship with Sinatra soon after Frank's eventful visit to Hyannis Port in September. "The split came in two stages," Brownstein writes.

> That fall, Sinatra sent Kennedy several gifts; the return letters were brief and formal, no more expansive than "I am delighted by your very thoughtful gesture." By 1962, the Justice Department had launched a formal investigation of Sinatra's ties to organized crime.

The last act began in the fall of 1961, when FBI wiretaps of [Johnny Rosselli] discovered six calls to Judith Campbell Exner, the woman Sinatra had introduced to both Kennedy and Giancana.

The investigation began on February 27, 1962, when the FBI director, J. Edgar Hoover, "always the bureaucrat," as Seymour Hersh puts it, sent a memo to Attorney General Robert Kennedy officially notifying him of something both men had known about for quite a while: Judith Campbell had also been making telephone calls to the White House.

Hoover wasn't just following protocol; he was also using his findings as a weapon in his battle for power with the attorney general and the president. And while Jack Kennedy seemed regally unruffled by Hoover, Bobby was all too aware of his brother's exposure to "the extraordinary danger of blackmail."

In fact, the FBI had been conducting extensive surveillance of Campbell, Rosselli, and Giancana for years. A Mob informant had first brought Campbell to the bureau's attention in early 1960, soon after then senator John F. Kennedy "had been compromised" with her in Las Vegas—having been introduced to Campbell at the Sands by Frank Sinatra. Rosselli and Giancana had been on the FBI's radar since 1957's Apalachin Meeting but came even more prominently to the bureau's attention once they were recruited into Operation Mongoose, the plot to assassinate Fidel Castro, in March 1961. And by now, the FBI was well aware of Judith Campbell's friendships with Rosselli and Mooney Giancana—and with Sinatra. "A review of her telephone toll calls reveals four calls in December, 1961 to the Palm Springs, California residence of Frank Sinatra," reads an FBI internal memo of February 26, 1962. She had also made calls to Giancana.

"Now it was clear that President Kennedy was consorting with two people with mob affiliations—Sinatra and Campbell," write Tom and Phil Kuntz in *The Sinatra Files,* their book about Frank's FBI dossier. "The potential for a disastrous scandal must have been obvious to Hoover and the Kennedys, especially given what the FBI had been hearing about Giancana and Rosselli [and their involvement in Mongoose]."

Seymour Hersh claims that Bobby Kennedy was reluctant—perhaps afraid—to tell his revered older brother "that he had to stop seeing a woman who gave him pleasure." Instead, he asked one of his close associates, Assistant Attorney General Joseph Dolan, to order President Kennedy's secretary Evelyn Lincoln to stop taking Judith Campbell's phone calls. Hersh says that "it was left to Hoover to give the president the bad news" about the explosive situation, at a lunch with President Kennedy on March 22.

It was over two weeks earlier than that when Frank heard that the visit was off.

He heard it from the man who had arranged it in the first place—Peter Lawford, to whom the president had given the unpleasant task of calling Sinatra with the news. Lawford had a cover story ready, and it made some sense: the Secret Service said that because of the open setting of the Wonder Palms compound, in the middle of a golf course, the place would be too difficult to secure. But Frank quickly got the truth out of Lawford: Bobby Kennedy didn't want his brother staying at a house where Sam Giancana had also stayed.

Frank smashed the phone against the wall.

According to George Jacobs, he then went into another room and managed to reach the attorney general himself: " 'What *is* this shit?' I remember him repeating. Unfortunately, this shit was all coming down on Mr. S." Adamant, Bobby Kennedy hung up on Sinatra. "There went another phone, smashed to smithereens," Jacobs writes. Frank called Lawford back to try to figure out a resolution, telling him desperately that he couldn't afford to be humiliated this way.

Then the hammer fell. Lawford told Sinatra that the situation was past solving: new lodgings for the president had already been secured. Where? Frank asked. "There was an endless silence," Jacobs recalled. "Then Mr. S simply dropped the phone on the floor. He stood there staring out at the desert, as if someone had told him his folks had died. It took him about five minutes before he could tell me."

Jack Kennedy was going to stay at Bing Crosby's house, in Palm Desert. His Secret Service detail would be billeted in Jimmy Van Heusen's place right next door.

Jacobs writes that part of Frank's supreme humiliation was due to the fact that Crosby was a Republican, "an Eisenhower, Nixon guy." In fact, Bing had been a Kennedy supporter. But despite Sinatra's longtime veneration of Crosby and a veneer of friendship between the two men, the older man was no less aloof to Frank than he was to the rest of the world—and despite their brilliant work together in *High Society,* and on television and radio, the competition between Sinatra and Crosby ran deep. Now, in a very large and public sense, Bing had won and Frank had lost.

Sinatra went into a towering rage, smashing his precious collection of JFK photographs, kicking in the door of the presidential guest room, even trying to wrest the gold plaque from the door. Legend has it (though Tina Sinatra denies it) that he took a sledgehammer to the concrete helipad. But the primary target of his anger was Peter Lawford, whose double game—trying to be a member of America's royal family and the Clan at the same time—had finally come to an end.

"When Jack got out here for that weekend, he asked me how Frank had taken it," Lawford recalled.

I said, "Not very well," which was a mild understatement. The President said, "I'll call him and smooth it over." So he did. After the conversation Jack said, "He's pretty upset, but I told him not to blame you because you didn't have anything to do with it. It was simply a matter of security . . ." But Frank didn't buy that for a minute, and with a couple of exceptions he never spoke to me again. He cut me out of all the movies we were set to make together—*Robin and the 7 Hoods, 4 for Texas*—and turned Dean and Sammy and Joey against me as well.

Naturally, Frank hated himself for having hoped so high and been brought so low, but it was always easiest for him to direct his anger outward. Naturally, too, he was furious at Jack Kennedy, yet he seems never to have spoken a word against his idol. Peter Lawford, with his mild, self-deprecating manner, his indifferent career, and his bad habits, was the world's best whipping boy.

———

On the night of March 6, Frank went to United Recording to sing a song he had no wish to sing. The tune was Harold Arlen and Ted Koehler's "I Gotta Right to Sing the Blues," and Sinatra was laying down the track for his about-to-be-former label. Capitol, in the person of Alan Livingston, was "rubbing salt in a sore wound . . . [insisting] that Sinatra provide them with one additional single, as specified in their contract," Charles Granata writes. Frank had so had it with the company at this point that he refused to even set foot in its studios. But despite his temptation to deal a final screw-you to Livingston—and with due respect to Granata's assertion that Sinatra's rendering of "Blues" that night was "remote, affect-less"—Frank's performance sounds slightly under-energized, more ambivalent than distant: too angry to help Capitol in any way, but too proud to be recorded singing badly.

His emotions escape after Skip Martin's[*] orchestra blares the song's final bluesy notes: just audibly, Frank crows, "Awright, that's it!"

And that was it for Capitol Records.[†]

Yet "Sinatra's petulance was plain to everyone in the studio that night, and the cause not merely Capitol," Granata notes.

His anger over recording the song was actually mitigated by the presence of producer Dave Cavanaugh—one of the few people from his former label with whom he was still friendly.

---

[*] Martin, a veteran arranger-conductor, "occasionally pinch-hit for Sinatra around this time," according to Friedwald. *Sinatra!*, p. 384.

[†] Until 1993 and 1994, when Capitol would release Sinatra's *Duets* and *Duets II*.

But when the Capitol tune was dispensed with, Cavanaugh left, and Sinatra and [Billy] May set out to record two songs by Cahn and Van Heusen: "The Boys' Night Out" and "Cathy." When Jimmy Van Heusen showed up in the control room, the singer's already touchy mood darkened.

Frank "was in a snit," Billy May recalled. "We had done 'The Boys' Night Out,' and all during the recording, [he] just glared at Jimmy in the control room. Then, it came time to do the second song, 'Cathy,' which was a pretty song—a waltz. Frank . . . looked over at Van Heusen, and said, 'Tell you what, Chester. Why don't you get Jack Kennedy to record this fucking song, and then see how many records it sells?' "

The next day, Wednesday the seventh, Frank headed to Palm Springs, reportedly suffering from an attack of laryngitis, the malady he periodically came down with—or came up with—when other matters were troubling him. On Friday the ninth, UPI reported, he was still in the desert recovering, and therefore unfortunately unable to make a scheduled appearance at a dinner in Miami Beach given by President Kennedy to honor his good friend Senator George Smathers.

On March 22, the president had his fateful lunch with J. Edgar Hoover, who, Arthur Schlesinger writes, brought along a memo about Judith Campbell's phone calls. Schlesinger says that thenceforth "the Campbell calls ceased." Campbell herself later maintained, "I saw Jack in March and April and the calls did not stop until sometime in June. And they stopped, not because of any outside force, but because of natural attrition. The specter of the White House killed the romance. Not J. Edgar Hoover."

On the same day as the JFK-Hoover lunch, "Frank Sinatra flew out of Palm Springs for Bermuda the day before President Kennedy arrived," Louella Parsons noted in her syndicated column. "There is talk that Frank is very hurt, after he did so much to raise funds for the Democratic Party, that the President is not his houseguest." There was more than talk. The news about the president's change of plans had just begun to hit the papers, and the story was explosive. "Had the Kennedys sought deliberately to humiliate my father," Tina Sinatra writes, "they couldn't have done a better job."

The insult wasn't just personal. Rosalind Wyman, a prominent California Democrat who'd been a West Coast organizer for the Kennedy campaign, worried that the slight could permanently disaffect Frank from the party. "Sinatra was a great Democrat," she said. "He loved Harry Truman. He loved Roosevelt. Sinatra had performed for us before Kennedy, and we in the party were very grateful . . . We felt very strongly, and I did quite a few things to make our views known to the White House . . . Here was a man who had during the campaign done everything we asked him for and more."

The protests fell on deaf ears. The White House speechwriter Richard Goodwin recalled that the president didn't think twice about banishing Sinatra. "It meant nothing" to him, he said. "If Kennedy thought about it in any way, if he thought it would even in the slightest wound his presidency, of course he would cut it off; he would cut off people a lot closer than Sinatra if he had to."

Like a spurned lover, Frank was haunted by the rejection. "If he would only pick up the telephone and call me and say that it was politically difficult to have me around, I would understand," he told Angie Dickinson. "I don't want to hurt him. But he has never called me."

A couple of months later, Sinatra would send Kennedy a flower-decked rocking chair for his birthday. He would get another polite note in response.

———————

The presidential slight was not only a terrible loss of face for Frank but a public-relations disaster. Though the White House never commented explicitly on the reasons for Kennedy's change of plan, editorial writers and opinion makers felt they knew perfectly well what had caused it, and said so in print, repeatedly.

In early 1962, Sinatra's press agent, Chuck Moses, summed it up. "The breach with JFK was brutal for him," Moses said. "It gives the public a wrong impression. People think Frank and Dean and Sammy and a few others are inseparable. Sure, they're good friends, but Frank has many other friends, interests, and activities."

Sure, but Mr. and Mrs. America knew what they read in the papers. It was time for some serious image repair.

Sinatra's charitable instincts were real and his good works often private, but the idea of doing some major public kindness had been in the air for several years. His former publicists Henry Rogers and Warren Cowan first came up with the vague but impressive idea of an international tour to benefit underprivileged children, and then Sinatra fired them, after Rogers made an intemperate remark about Frank's being his own worst enemy. Chuck Moses took the ball and ran with it. The charity concerts for Mexican children the previous spring had been a kind of dry run, and a big hit, inspiring a tribute in the *Congressional Record* from California congressman James Roosevelt (son of FDR) that read, in part, "Sinatra's humane contribution entitles him to applause beyond that given a great entertainer."

Mickey Rudin, who was a partner at his law firm but had a lucrative subpractice as Sinatra's consigliere, paved the way for the grand tour, going out and booking concerts for Frank in places in Europe and Asia where his bad publicity might have preceded him. "We went all over the world—to Rome and Tokyo and London," recalled Rudin's then wife, the cellist Elizabeth Greenschpoon, "and I watched Mickey create an atmosphere of demand for Frank. Never mind the henchmen and goons. Mickey made them book Frank. Because of my husband's strong ties to Israel, he also managed to get a youth house named for Frank because supposedly this was a tour to benefit children and youth. I say 'supposedly' because the real purpose was to benefit Frank. He needed a good press at the time and Mickey saw to it that he got one."

This assessment contrasts sharply with Will Friedwald's contention that the tour was "the largest humanitarian gesture of Sinatra's career . . . distinguished by the remarkably high caliber of the music produced as well as the surprisingly low profile the tour itself and the documents of it . . . kept for the following thirty years."

> As one who fully comprehended the positive and negative power of the media, Sinatra had to decide whether or not to inform the American press about this undertaking, and he chose to exclude them. If it was ever construed that he was doing it for a tax write-off or for the publicity (neither of which would have been as valuable to him as two months of paid work), it would have undercut the whole purpose of the project.

The truth lies somewhere in between Greenschpoon's unsympathetic personal view (she was understandably embittered after her breakup with Rudin) and Friedwald's justifiably favorable musical take. In fact, a publicist and a photographer would accompany Sinatra on the trip, and Frank would receive respectful, if not awed, press coverage every step of the way: the kind of publicity that was worth far more than dollars. He would perform thirty concerts over two months, and every penny of the proceeds would go to children's charities. Sinatra would cover all travel and living expenses of his musicians and entourage.

But there was one other motive behind the trip: the newly single star was excitedly planning a reunion with his endlessly beguiling expatriate ex-wife in Spain.

With change in the air, and with a couple of days free in the week before he left, Sinatra went into the studio to make a new album with a new arranger, Neal Hefti.

The thirty-nine-year-old Hefti was a brilliant jazz songwriter and arranger whose compositions and charts had been key to the success of the Count Basie Orchestra in the 1950s. "If it weren't for Neal Hefti," Miles Davis said in a 1955 interview, "the Basie band wouldn't sound as good as it does." This was extraordinary praise, yet it was well deserved. As a young big-band trumpeter, Hefti had listened deeply to bebop, but the tunes he wrote for Basie—numbers like "Splanky," "Teddy the Toad," "Little Pony," and "Li'l Darlin'"—were as infectious as they were unpredictable, brilliantly bringing out the Count's minimalist piano playing and his great horn and reed sections. As a composer, Hefti would eventually become best known for his themes for *Batman,* the 1960s TV show, and the 1968 movie (and 1970s sitcom) *The Odd Couple,* the first showing off his gift for hard-driving horns, the second in the jazzy-wistful mood that also infused "Li'l Darlin'."

Frank had initially hired Hefti as a combination A&R man and producer, to replace Felix Slatkin, who'd recently gone to work at another label. But it was inevitable that Sinatra, an idolater of Basie, would turn to his new in-house talent as an arranger-conductor. It first happened with two singles recorded at the end of February 1962, though the work was less than distinguished all around: a regrettable throwaway called "Everybody's Twistin'," meant to capitalize on the current dance craze; and a pleasantly brassy but forgettable single called "Nothing but the Best" ("I like a new Lincoln, with all of its class/I like a martini, and bird under glass").

Things improved in April, when Frank and Hefti made the new album, *Sinatra and Swingin' Brass,* a Billy May concept with a whole new sound. Though, regrettably, Sinatra selected none of Hefti's own compositions for the LP (none had been lyricized to Frank's exacting standards), he and the arranger did manage to bring new, swinging life to a dozen numbers that were well on their way to becoming oldies, including the Gershwins' "They Can't Take That Away from Me" (1937), Cole Porter's "At Long Last Love" (1938) and "I Love You" (1944), and, perhaps most notably, Matty Malneck and Johnny Mercer's 1936 "Goody Goody," one of the best (and most rousing) kiss-off songs ever and one that would quickly become a staple of the Sinatra repertoire.

Frank's tantrum about JFK's snub and the snub itself were now weeks in the past, and making this cheerful album seemed restorative. Hefti later said that he found Sinatra "easy, very easy" to work with, and the evidence is audible, not just in the tracks themselves, but in the (always revealing) outtakes, where an artist who could be intensely perfectionistic in the studio sounds relaxed and happy to be doing what he's doing with the people he's doing it with.

A case in point is Jerome Kern and Dorothy Fields's great hymn to resilience, "Pick Yourself Up." It's a song that's particularly apt to Sinatra ("Will you remember the famous men/Who had to fall to rise again"), though he'd never recorded it before; it's also a song with a lot of words and a tricky, Kern-ian modulation in the bridge, and Hefti's chart moves at a very brisk tempo. Sinatra needed no fewer than seven takes to get it right, three of them quite short but four at full length, and—suddenly the lyric was all too appropriate—it was work.

On the sixth take, something remarkable happened. As Sinatra began the bridge for the second time, his "Will you remember the famous men" was just miles off key—as far off as it's possible to hear this greatest of singers sing any phrase on any recording, ever. He suddenly stopped, the orchestra stopped, and there was a deathly silence in United Recording Studio A. And with nowhere to hide, this man who famously never apologized quietly said, in front of dozens of people—musicians, technicians, onlookers—"Sorry. Sorry." No jokes, no excuses.

And then, after the engineer's "Ten-eighteen, take seven," he picked himself up, dusted himself off, and nailed it.

The oldest oldie on *Swingin' Brass* is Milton Ager and Jack Yellen's 1927 chestnut "Ain't She Sweet," another number Sinatra had never recorded before. He loped through it with charm and confidence, with no way to know and no reason to care that ten months earlier, in a Hamburg, Germany, studio, a black-leather-clad rock-'n'-roll group from northern England had recorded a growling, hard-driving version of the same tune. They called themselves, rather risibly to most ears, the Beatles.[*]

On April 15, with the album in the can, Frank headed out to wow the world.

He didn't like to be alone, and he made sure he wouldn't be. Besides George Jacobs, his entourage included Jimmy Van Heusen; the banker Al Hart; Mike Romanoff and his beautiful young wife, Gloria; Leo Durocher and his even more beautiful young girlfriend (a blonde who, to Durocher's chagrin, turned out to be a devout Jehovah's Witness and a virgin); Howard Koch, the

---

[*] June 23, 1961, in Friedrich-Ebert-Halle, Hamburg: John Lennon on lead vocal and rhythm guitar, Paul McCartney on bass, George Harrison on lead guitar, and Pete Best on drums. The Polydor single wouldn't be released until May 1964, after the Beatles, with a different drummer, had changed the world.

head of Frank's movie-production company; a publicist who spoke five languages; a still photographer; a three-man television crew; and Bill Miller and a jazz quintet.

No lady friend accompanied Frank on the trip, though, according to Jacobs, he had eyes for both Gloria Romanoff and Durocher's lady friend. And Van Heusen, of course, was expert in producing top-flight paid companionship at a moment's notice. And then there was the distant, shimmering prospect of Ava.

A combination of art and economics dictated Sinatra's choice of accompanists on the tour. As with his highly successful Australian swing of three years before, he decided to go with a small group, pianist Miller plus a vibraphone-based quintet. On the 1959 trip, the combination of Miller and Red Norvo's group had been all things to Sinatra, its tight, rhythmic backing on the fast numbers inspiring the jazz singer in him, its rich instrumental textures behind the slow numbers stirring the balladeer. Norvo wasn't available this time around, however, so Frank tapped the young vibraphonist/multi-percussionist Emil Richards, who'd been playing with him for a couple of years, along with three other old Sinatra hands: flutist and saxophone player Harry Klee, guitarist Al Viola, and drummer Irv Cottler. The only new face was a talented young Mexican-American jazz bassist named Ralph Peña. The group had rehearsed intensively with Frank at the Bowmont Drive house, with arrangements artfully written (by Hefti, Billy May, Johnny Mandel, and Bill Miller) to make six players sound—in combination with Sinatra—like five times as many.

The assemblage didn't exactly steal away in the dead of the night. Bob Hope came to see his pal Frank off at LAX, as did an appreciative corps of reporters, who scribbled away in their notepads as the new, nicer Sinatra told them he felt "not older, but a little more mellow." A UPI telephoto to the nation's papers transmitted a symbolic image: a fedora-ed Frank smiling at ten-year-old Lisa Ashworth and her puppy, boarding the same Pan Am plane on the tour's first leg.

There was just one problem with Frank's big trip: he hated traveling. He was superstitious about flying (he'd just missed accompanying Mike Todd on the flight that crashed and killed him) and, according to Jacobs, had a "total lack of curiosity about the outside world. For all his shelves of biographies, for all his hours in the dictionary, geography, history, and culture left him totally cold. He was a homebody, not an explorer." Where could he find his favorite snack, Campbell's franks and beans, while he was visiting exotic places? And the main advantage of the entourage, besides affording company, was "to insulate [him] from the local traditions."

This he seemed able to do all by himself. Upon arriving in Tokyo, he was reluctant to leave the New Japan hotel, even to see the Imperial Palace or the world-famous cherry blossoms. "The only cherries I want to see are the geisha girls," he said, but when Van Heusen brought some up to the suite, they refused to kiss him. "You eat sushi but you won't kiss my lips?" he yelled. Kissing was not popular in Japanese culture, a translator explained. "You call that culture?" Frank said.

He was more at ease giving a press conference (for which he didn't have to leave the hotel). Looking "tanned and dapper," according to a *Pacific Stars and Stripes* correspondent, Sinatra fielded reporters' questions patiently.

"You have position, wealth, everything—what more do you want in life?" one asked.

"I'm not seeking to achieve anything specific," Frank said. "I'd like to spend my time doing constructive work. I'm an overprivileged adult that would like to help underprivileged children."

It was a good line. He backed it up with equipoise. "Flashbulbs popped as photographers ignored their three-minute time limit, but at no time did the crooner show his famous impatience with newsmen," the *Stars and Stripes* man wrote.

> Asked whether he was trying to create a "new Sinatra image" of kind-
> ness and patience to replace his controversial publicity, Sinatra said:
> "I don't really think so. People who call me controversial are those
> who don't agree with me. I plan to remain controversial because we
> won't make progress unless we're controversial and rebellious from time
> to time."

He gave his first Tokyo concert the next night, April 20, at the Mikado theater-restaurant. Calling Sinatra "a living legend"—an epithet just then beginning to be hung on him—Al Ricketts, *Pacific Stars and Stripes'* entertainment columnist, enthused,

> Frank, a bright red handkerchief tucked in his breast pocket, kept the
> pace slow for the first 15 minutes, then moved into high gear for the
> rest of the show. He waltzed his way past tunes like "Moonlight in Ver-
> mont" and "My Funny Valentine," before capping his performance with
> a finger-popping version of "The Lady Is a Tramp . . ."
> He was in complete command throughout, undeniably retaining his
> right to the claim of being the most exciting performer in show busi-
> ness today.

After another show at the Mikado and one at Hibiya Park, Frank presented Tokyo's governor, Ryotaro Azuma, with a check for 9 million yen (about

$25,000) for children's charities, received a gold key to the city, and had an orphanage named after him. He then flew on to Korea and Okinawa, where he gave goodwill concerts at U.S. military bases and worried whether the young GIs, doubtless Elvis fans, would think him over the hill. But he'd underestimated his own appeal (and the hunger of soldiers far from home for American culture): Sinatra and his tight sextet wowed the kids, and their reaction gave Frank's own dented morale a big boost.

He began to feel better about the trip. The sheer magnificence of his accompaniment, the big sounds produced by that little combo, lifted him, and he drove the musicians hard in return. "Frank worked especially well with the small group," Al Viola recalled. "If you listen to those tapes, you'll hear that he was kickin' our ass! He would turn around to us as if to say, 'Hey, you guys, come on—this is a concert!' He didn't want us to sound like we were hanging out at some bar."

And then there were the children: in Hong Kong, crowds of kids waving flowers lined the streets to greet him. He played another four charity concerts there and, in between, amused himself by having custom clothing made—a dozen orange blazers, two dozen pairs of fine wool slacks, custom elevator shoes in alligator and snakeskin—and playing practical jokes.

It was in Hong Kong that he had his only major meltdown of the tour, over a failed lighting cue. The Chinese operator forgot to turn off the pin spot after the dramatic ending of "One for My Baby (and One More for the Road)," ruining the effect, and Sinatra went bananas, trashing his dressing room and his suite at the elegant Peninsula hotel. " 'Fucking slant-eye Chink bastards,' he'd shout and rip up a priceless antique screen or shatter a Ming vase," the valet noted. "The guy got off on breaking things, as if it were sex." On the other hand, only the performer understands the impossibility of discharging the energy built up by a performance. In any case, money made it all better afterward.

After handing a $17,000 check to the executive secretary of the Hong Kong Council of Social Service, Frank took his show back on the road, landing in Athens on May 1 and proceeding directly to Jerusalem.

———

He had never been to Israel before, and it was a revelation—the first place on the tour that really spoke to him. Israelis were not only soulful but tough—in their embattled little piece of land, they had to be—and both were qualities for which Sinatra had great respect. On May 9, for ceremonies marking the fourteenth anniversary of Israeli independence, he stood on the reviewing stand alongside Prime Minister David Ben-Gurion and General Moshe Dayan and watched male and female soldiers march by. The country's stark beauty and solemn history affected him deeply; he became a willing, even a passionate, tourist at last. He visited the Western Wall and the Via Dolorosa and the Yad Vashem Holocaust memorial, the Sea of Galilee and the Golan Heights. He played seven concerts in six cities over nine days and went to see every sight he could. In Nazareth, he laid the cornerstone of an Arab-Jewish youth center to which he said he would donate the entire proceeds of the Israeli leg of his tour. Afterward, he told George Jacobs that the country made him ashamed of not having fought in World War II. Israel, he said, was a land worth dying for.

While Frank was earnestly planting trees in Israel—one for his three children, another in memory of his late agent Bert Allenberg—the gossip columnist Dorothy Manners, filling in for the ill and aging Louella Parsons, ran an arrestingly strange flash: Ava Gardner and the sixty-six-year-old exiled Argentinean former dictator Juan Perón were the talk of Madrid, "seen everywhere together," Manners dished. And then, cattily: "Ava's preference for bullfighters is well-known. But this is the first time on record she's taken the bull by the horns, so to speak."

The reality was this: despite a rapidly diminishing bank account, Ava was still living like a star, in a duplex apartment in a sedate Madrid neighborhood of embassies and doctor's offices, with a revolving household staff, a driver, and a live-in (male) personal secretary. Perón, who'd been given political asylum by Francisco Franco, was—along with his beautiful young third wife, Isabel—her downstairs neighbor.

At thirty-nine, Ava was in the midst of a three-year hiatus from moviemaking, feeling she had lost her single amazing attribute, her astonishing looks. Her life had become shapeless and dissolute, a constant round of late nights, drunken scenes, and quickly forgotten amours. "My job was basically to keep her company," her personal secretary, an aspiring actor named Ben Tatar, recalled.

> Ava loved to dance, not only flamenco. We used to dance at home. It
> came over her: she *had* to dance. She'd put some music on and we'd
> dance a little bit in the foyer of the apartment, and into the living
> room . . . She played a lot of Frank Sinatra's records. She had every
> record he ever made. He called the apartment sometimes. I got the
> feeling they were still in love with each other. The first time I answered
> the phone when Sinatra called he said, *"Who the hell are you?"*

Juan Perón fully matched his upstairs neighbor's eccentricity. Like a character out of Gabriel García Márquez, the aged ex-dictator sometimes went out on the balcony to give speeches to imaginary supporters; he also kept a coffin containing the body of his second wife, Evita, in the apartment. He had apparently been a fan of Gardner's for years. "Ava did not think much of her new neighbor's politics," her biographer Lee Server writes, "but he was an old man now, and they were both occupying the same plot of land in Franco's Spain so she tried to be friendly." She went downstairs sometimes to eat Señora Perón's delicious empanadas while "Isabel would sit and chat, speaking without jealousy about how the late Evita remained the most important woman in her husband's life."

Then Ava's late-night flamenco parties—all that stamping on the ceiling—got on the Peróns' nerves, and the friendship ended. Such was the reliability of gossip columns.

Meanwhile, her truest admirer was approaching. In every one of the tour's shows, Sinatra had been singing one of his favorite standards, Cole Porter's "I Get a Kick out of You"—and every time he came to the line "Some like the perfume in Spain," he would add an emphatic "*Yeah!*" "because [he was] heading to go see Ava," the vibraphonist Emil Richards said.

Rubirosa the playboy arrived (by yacht, no less) to put an end point to all that Israeli solemnity—and not incidentally to ferry Frank's whole road show back to Athens. There, on the nights of May 18 and 19, Sinatra did two concerts at the Odeon of Herodes Atticus, an outdoor amphitheater in the shadow of the Acropolis. Bill Miller considered the first performance—unfortunately unrecorded—the best of all the world tour shows.

In Athens, Frank's incuriosity about tourism returned. Instead, according to his valet, he preferred sightseeing of the indoor variety, sticking to his suite at the Grande Bretagne and entertaining the hookers Van Heusen procured. Sinatra pronounced them "his favorite of all the international damsels he had sampled, not necessarily for their looks but for their warmth and hospitality." Two of them brought him a giant moussaka.

Then Frank surprised his musicians, suddenly announcing he was giving them ten days off. "He called all of us into his suite," Emil Richards recalled, "and—he was very embarrassed—he said, 'I'm leaving right now, but you guys, before you leave, go in the bedroom and just take everything that's on the bed; it's for you guys.' So he left. And we went into his bedroom, and the bed was full of drachmas, Greek money. We just stuffed our pockets with money to go have a good time for ten days."

Richards repaired to the island of Hydra, where he spent a hedonistic three days basking in the sun, drinking ouzo, and eating the fresh catch brought in by the local fishermen. Then, on the fourth day, he heard the deep whistle of a big boat and to his surprise saw Rubirosa's yacht in the harbor. "I look out, and there's Frank on the deck," Richards said. "And he says, 'Come on! Pack your stuff, we're going to Italy early.'"

The vibraphonist eventually pieced together what had happened: Frank had gone to Spain and dropped in on Ava—but not alone. "He brought Rubirosa, and he brought Romanoff, Howard Koch, and his valet George," Richards recalled. "And she was pissed. She fed everybody, and she left. So Frank said, 'Where the hell did she go?' And he went to some taverna way out in the country, and there she was with a bullfighter."

In Rome, something better awaited him: his personal airplane, flown over for him because it lacked the range for long transoceanic routes.* The *El Dago* was a Martin 4-0-4, a two-prop workhorse built to seat forty for commercial use but reconfigured to Frank's princely specifications with a hi-fi sound system, electric piano, movie projector, wet bar, and bedroom. The interior color scheme was (of course) primarily orange, with rich wood paneling, Asian touches (Balinese dancer prints), and deep pile carpet. Tiny twinkling electric stars dotted the ceiling.

The plane's name, proudly printed along a stripe on the custom livery, had caused a certain amount of controversy. In 1961, the Joint Civic Committee of Italian Americans, a Chicago organization dedicated to ethnic pride, had written to Sinatra urging him to change it, and now that the big new PR push was on, he finally had, rechristening it the *Christina*, after his younger daughter. "The switch is an improvement," Dorothy Manners noted drily.

From May 24 to 26, Frank played Rome and Milan, with middling success. For one thing, surprisingly, he didn't speak the language. (A planned album of Italian songs had been scrapped earlier that spring, reportedly because Sinatra had trouble pronouncing the words.) For another, perhaps because of his mixed heritage—his mother's people were from Genoa; his father had been born in Sicily—he had mixed feelings about the homeland itself. According to Jacobs, people in the street loved him, but those who could afford tickets to his shows in Rome acted rudely: there were shouts (especially unwelcome now) of "Ava, Ava."

---

* There is a minor mystery here. George Jacobs claims the *El Dago* was a DC-6, a four-engine prop with a range of approximately three thousand miles, but photographs clearly show a two-engine Martin 4-0-4, which had a range of only about a thousand miles. How, then, was the plane transported from Los Angeles to Rome? Most crucially, how did it get across the Atlantic (if not by boat)? The trip might just have been possible with hops from Gander, Newfoundland, to Nuuk, Greenland, to Reykjavík, Iceland, to Shannon, Ireland—a lot of work, but then, people were used to jumping through hoops for Frank.

At the May 26 concert in Milan, his entr'acte monologue, caught on a bootleg tape, sounds wooden, uncertain—a sure sign of disconnect with his audience. Trying for humor, he does an American imitation of an Italian accent as he picks up his teacup: "I'm-a have a little-a *tazza tè*." The laughter is scant.

The London shows, beginning four nights later, were far more successful. It was Frank's first appearance there since 1953, and anticipation was high. The English had long loved him—his had been the voice that had comforted them through the war, and they had stuck with him during his down period—and the feeling was mutual. Though Princess Margaret sponsored and attended the premiere at Royal Festival Hall, the atmosphere there was anything but restrained: the audience's welcome for Sinatra was rapturous. Still, on the first number, "Goody Goody," he's audibly nervous. And though he gains his composure—and, buoyed by the crowd's excitement, sings wonderfully—when the time comes for his tea break, he still sounds more than a little overawed by the occasion. "Thank you very much, Highness, lords and ladies, ladies and gentlemen," he starts out, a little breathlessly, the boy from Hoboken in some disbelief at his surroundings. He then trips through a minor minefield of Anglicisms before reverting to Hoboken: "We've been having a marvelous time with this trip we've been doing since about six weeks ago . . . Rather gratifying experience, really, in doing this kind of work—I'm enjoying it tremendously. We get back home, I plan to visit some of the depressed areas in New York, like Wall Street and a couple of other places, and see if I can help 'em out a little bit. And then check right into a hospital."

He was only half-kidding. In fact, his breathlessness during the tea break was probably about more than nerves: he'd been touring for a month and a half, singing night after night, meeting and greeting and patting kids on the head day after day, and that incomparable voice—always a delicate instrument—was showing the strain. Reviewing Frank's June 3 concert at West London's Hammersmith Odeon theater (his fourth in three days), Ray Coleman of *Melody Maker* commended him for showing "the height of professionalism" but added, "At times he sounded coarse, even nasal, and he certainly found it tough to sustain the note on certain occasions—notably on 'My Funny Valentine.'"

And the tour still had two weeks to go. In Paris on the fifth and seventh, he did two shows (his first ever in the City of Light, though he'd been singing Vernon Duke's and Cole Porter's odes to it for years): the first was at the Lido, a nightclub-theater on the Champs-Élysées, the second at the Olympia, a grand old music hall in the 9th arrondissement. The Olympia concert was the only performance on the world tour to be professionally recorded, with an eye toward an eventual release as a Reprise LP. Eventual almost became never: the record wouldn't come out for more than thirty years, and the 1994 CD—

only Sinatra's third commercially released live album—is a curious document. For one thing, it's mislabeled as having been recorded on June 5 at the Lido. But more important, and central to its long delay, is that despite the grandeur of the venue, the warmth of the audience, and the largesse of Charles Aznavour's introduction—"Frank Sinatra, Paris vous appartient!" (Frank Sinatra, Paris belongs to you!)—by the evening of the Olympia concert, Frank's voice was running on fumes.

At first it seems that, vocally, not much is there. There are some truly bad moments: at the beginning of the very first number, "Goody Goody," he jumps in ("So you met someone who set you back on your heels—goody, goody!") carelessly, almost defiantly flat. And on the fifth tune, "Moonlight in Vermont," he struggles, pitiably; his not-even-close-to-on-key "ski trails down a mountainside" is the sonic equivalent of a bloodied prizefighter staggering through the late rounds. Hunting for the pitch, barking instead of belting on some of the loud passages, he gives a strange foreshadowing of the performer he would become in old age.

At the same time, though—Sinatra is Sinatra—he rallies. He may not be 100 percent, but his pride and his love of singing are at stake, and he's got that terrific sextet to back him (and to prove something to). He finds his breath and his pitch and his confidence, and he gives the crowd a show. He delivers real performances on swingers and ballads: "Day In, Day Out," "I've Got You Under My Skin," "In the Still of the Night," and, importantly, "April in Paris."

Two of the best numbers in the show are duos, just Frank and an instrumentalist. Both are signature tunes. He does a beautiful "Night and Day" with guitarist Viola, and he gives "Ol' Man River," with Bill Miller on piano behind him, the majesty it deserves. He'd had long practice with both songs: he'd first performed "Night and Day," of course, as a singing waiter at the Rustic Cabin in 1939.

"Ol' Man River," too, was an essential part of his repertoire, as he had told his friend Alec Wilder. Amazingly, Sinatra had been singing the Jerome Kern–Oscar Hammerstein classic (written in 1927 for the musical *Show Boat*) for almost twenty years—since the age of twenty-seven, in 1943—and somehow, over those two decades, a skinny white Italian-American had managed to make a work song made famous by a great black baritone, Paul Robeson, authoritatively his own. "Sinatra needed 'Ol' Man River' to make a point about himself as a singer—a point no dreamy love song or, in later decades, swinging tune could drive home to listeners," the music historian Todd Decker writes. "With 'Ol' Man River,' Sinatra . . . declared in no uncertain terms that he could deliver a challenging melody and a serious lyric that dealt with life's biggest questions."

He gives the song a powerful performance and on the rousing finale ("He just keeps rollin' a-long!") finds the big volume, and a vocal flourish, that had eluded him at the concert's beginning. The crowd loves it. But Frank's deepest feelings are too tightly tied to his intense vulnerability: he can never stay serious for long. Once the applause dies down and the saucy intro to "The Lady Is a Tramp" begins, he cracks a smile. "That was a song about Sammy Davis's people," he announces. "And this is a song about *mah* people."

Well, the Rodgers and Hart song isn't about Italian-Americans, so one assumes he means female people. Lots and lots of them. Further driving home the point he made earlier in the show, when, on the number he'd been implicitly dedicating to Ava throughout the tour, he changed one key word: "Some like the perfume in Spain—yecchh!"

18

||||||||||||

I thought Italians were supposed to be liberals.

—SAMMY DAVIS JR. TO FRANK, ON THE STAGE OF THE 500 CLUB
ON AUGUST 25, 1962

The world tour limped to a close, just one concert to go: Princess Grace's annual Red Cross gala, on June 17 in Monte Carlo. Frank's voice had been in rough shape before the Paris concerts, but afterward, as Friedwald says, "he had next to nothing that he could sing with." The only problem was—sloth being the one cardinal sin Sinatra could never be accused of—he now planned to make an album.

After sampling richly of Paris's many pleasures ("We had our most fun in Paris," George Jacobs wrote with a wink, adding that he even managed to find the boss some Campbell's franks and beans at Fauchon, a luxury grocery store), Frank returned to London to complete a long-awaited project, an album of British songs with the Canadian-born arranger-conductor Robert Farnon. Like Billy May, the forty-four-year-old Farnon was lantern-jawed and ebullient; like May and Don Costa, he was also a gifted musician—the Englishman's instrument being the jazz trumpet, which he played so well that Dizzy Gillespie reportedly expressed relief that Farnon had turned from performing to composing, conducting, and orchestrating. At the latter, he had few peers. Quincy Jones cited him as a major influence, and André Previn called him "the greatest writer for strings in the world." It was Costa who'd commended him to Sinatra as the best arranger for the English album.

The LP—Frank's first, and ultimately only, album to be recorded overseas—had been in the making for years. The English music journal *Melody Maker* had reported in 1959 that Sinatra had "big disc plans" to record in London; he began putting together the repertory in December 1961. A producer for Reprise's British affiliate, Pye Records (whose head of A&R had recently turned down a certain Liverpool rock 'n' roll group seeking its first recording contract), compiled a list of almost seventy homegrown English tunes, which Frank then winnowed down to eleven. Farnon wrote the charts with carte blanche from Sinatra. They double-checked the keys and tempos on June 1, the day of the Royal Festival Hall concert, and "on the evening of June 12,

Sinatra arrived at the C.T.S. Studio in Bayswater in a Rolls-Royce lent to him by Douglas Fairbanks, Jr., and said to Farnon, 'Let's see how it fits, huh?' " Friedwald writes.

> Four trumpeters, four trombonists, eight saxophonists and woodwind players, five rhythm men (including both Bill Miller and a local pianist, as per union rules), twenty assorted strings, and an uncountable horde of well-wishers, several dozen in the control room alone, had already arrived. "There were so many people there who had nothing to do with the recording," said Farnon. "There were people all around us, sitting on my podium, under the piano, on the piano . . . The studio was absolutely crammed with people, and Frank loved it. He didn't mind at all."

And he didn't mind for a while, even though, in the outtake tapes, it's difficult to listen to him: his voice is a gorgeous ruin, deep and resonant, but hoarse and cracking periodically. His ability to sustain notes is severely compromised, the fabled breath control a distant memory. A remark he made during the tea break at Royal Festival Hall comes to mind. "This tea I drink during the performance is not a joke at all," he said. "It's not a prop; it's a necessity. It's very good for the throat, the tea and a little bit of honey mixed into it—I've been doing it for years. And then the cigarette ruins the whole thing after that."

He smoked. Immoderately, as he did so many other things: up to three packs of unfiltered Camels a day. How could he inhale this much tobacco smoke and still sing? How could he have any breath control at all? He was Sinatra. But the cumulative effects of the tour, and the smoking and the drinking and the late-night fun, had caught up with him.

Still, his good humor stayed with him over the rocky three-hour course of the first recording session. Toward the end of the evening, he prefaces a take of his pal Noël Coward's "I'll Follow My Secret Heart" with a minor coughing fit, which is then echoed by others in the studio. "Damn, we gotta sleep indoors," Frank says. And then, a little shamefacedly, he rolls out an ancient gag: "If I could find my key, I'd use it." As it turns out, the joke isn't so funny: that first take is not pretty to listen to.

But song by song over the course of three nights, with plenty of takes and great patience all around, *Sinatra Sings Great Songs from Great Britain* got recorded. Everybody involved, especially Frank, knew all too well that he wasn't really himself: at the end of the first night, after all the joking around, he disappeared without saying good-bye, a sure sign that he felt humiliated. "He was finding it difficult to sing," Farnon recalled. "His voice was tired, and it was breaking a lot. He was very angry with himself."

On the third and final evening, an unexpected guest dropped by. Nelson Riddle was in London to score *Lolita* for Stanley Kubrick, who had admired his artistry on *In the Wee Small Hours* and *Frank Sinatra Sings for Only the Lonely*. (While the arranger was in town, he was also working in a liaison with Rosemary Clooney.) Riddle had been part of Sinatra's rapturous audience at Royal Festival Hall: Frank's gravity was hard to resist anytime, and the fact that Nelson was prohibited from working with him then would have made the singer's tight work with that splendid sextet, and his power over a starry crowd, feel all the more poignant. To then see Sinatra working with another gifted arranger, and to hear him struggling vocally, would have stacked layers of envy, schadenfreude, and regret in Riddle's dark and complex spirit.

Sinatra Sings Great Songs from Great Britain is a curiosity, an asterisk, an honorable failure. Farnon's scoring for that big lovely orchestra is gorgeous, but both Frank and the players are heavily echoed to mask the vocal imperfections. Often the imperfections peek through anyway. He quavers, he cracks, and if you listen hard (and you don't really want to), you can hear him running out of breath. We don't expect Sinatra to run out of breath.

But the problem is ultimately with the material. Once the two great ballads—Jimmy Campbell, Reg Connelly, and Ted Shapiro's "If I Had You" and Ray Noble's "The Very Thought of You"—are out of the way, we have only the winsome but not immortal Noël Coward number, followed by a whole lot of flowers ("A Garden in the Rain," "Roses of Picardy," "We'll Gather Lilacs in the Spring"), some stiff upper lip ("We'll Meet Again"), and that poignant piece of wartime nostalgia, "A Nightingale Sang in Berkeley Square." The rest is pleasant but negligible. Even putting Frank's voice problems aside, it's a polite album, and politeness never was his strong suit.

After putting in at Monte Carlo, where he gave the final benefit concert, Sinatra returned home, elated: by the new vistas he'd seen, the good he'd done, and something else. When Earl Wilson checked in with his old friend at New York's Savoy Hilton, he found Frank and Mike Romanoff ensconced in the Presidential Suite, enjoying a welcome-home dinner ("salami, clam soup, veal, and VINO") sent over from Patsy's on West Fifty-sixth Street. "Frank was in a good mood," the columnist wrote. "He suddenly found himself popular in the world press."

It was true. Suddenly accounts of Sinatra's largesse—and a new note, his humility—were everywhere: he estimated that the tour had raised $1.2 million for children's charities but said, "I wish it was five million." The trip had changed him, he said. "I found out a lot of things I didn't know before," he told a reporter. "It was a revelation." One story that gained wide play concerned Frank's encounter with a blind six-year-old girl: "It was windy, and I brushed the hair out of her eyes and told her that the wind had been blowing up her hair. She stopped me cold when she said, 'What color is the wind?'"

He wafted back to Los Angeles, only to find his troubles right where he'd left them. Problem number one was Reprise Records. The label had gone into business in 1960 with high ideals and a capitalization of $300,000—borrowed from the ever-friendly City National Bank, which was run by Frank's pal (and world-tour travel companion) Al Hart. In its first year of operations, Reprise had turned a profit of $100,000, but in 1961 the company lost $400,000, bringing its cash balance down to zero. By the first quarter of 1962, the label was a further $250,000 in the red.

Reprise's problems were both external and self-inflicted. For one thing, it had a serious enemy in Capitol's president Alan Livingston. It wasn't enough for him that Capitol had won the suit over the title of the *Swing Along with Me/Sinatra Swings* album: now he decided to scorch earth. Frank's old label, record-industry veteran Stan Cornyn writes,

> offered its entire Sinatra catalogue to its distributors on a twofer plan, two albums for the price of one: an unprecedented 50 percent discount plan. Customers could snatch up complete Sinatra libraries at $1.99 per album. At $4.98—and able to offer only a one-fer—Reprise's newer product languished in bins. Soon Sinatra had thirteen albums on the charts. The bad news: twelve of the thirteen were on Capitol. Reprise's new album sold a humiliating 156,400 copies.

It was paradoxical: as a recording artist, Sinatra was doing better than ever; as a businessman, he was being blown out of the water by the competition. His bank account was thriving, but his pride was hurting badly. And his pride, which meant a great deal to him, had been getting shelled lately.

Things would have been bad enough if Frank had been the only artist on Reprise's roster. This was far from the case. He had started out by wooing Dean Martin away from Capitol—further angering Livingston—and built his stable from there, promising "that Reprise artists would have a latitude previously unknown in the business of record-contract rules," Cornyn writes.

> Reprise artists would keep the ownership of their masters. (Few did.)
> His artists would own shares in the company. (Never happened.)
> Reprise artists would have complete control over their record sessions.
> (Happened.) Reprise artists could record for other labels when they

wanted to. (Hardly.) "He divined that the thrust of this company should be its artists," [Mo] Ostin recalled. "It all seems logical today, but back then it was truly revolutionary."

Soon Reprise had signed the likes of Jo Stafford, Rosemary Clooney, Count Basie, Duke Ellington, Dennis Day, the Four Lads, the Hi-Lo's, Danny Kaye, the McGuire Sisters, Ethel Merman, Debbie Reynolds, Dinah Shore, Joey Bishop, Peter Lawford. (The same Earl Wilson column that welcomed Frank back from his world tour noted, as if it were a news flash, that Eddie Fisher had just been signed to Reprise.) "Cronies aside, the list read like Sinatra's master's thesis on Good Music," Cornyn continues.

In 1961, the year Columbia signed twenty-year-old Bob Dylan, Reprise's roster might have been drawn from the phone book of Palm Springs, a place that had become home to the Dinah Shore Set. Reprise's were singers who, on weekdays, spent little time in recording studios and lots more lunching at the Racquet Club.

"The only thing that was meaningful at Reprise was the kind of music Sinatra had been involved in all his life," Ostin said. Frank loved jazz, and Mo Ostin had worked at Verve, so he signed jazz acts: Ben Webster, Mavis Rivers, Jimmy Witherspoon, Calvin Jackson, Eddie Cano, Barney Kessel, Chico Hamilton, Dizzy Gillespie, Shorty Rogers, Marv Jenkins, a reissue of Django Reinhardt. Sales were almost nonexistent.

In fact, jazz, as a salable entity, had been dying for years. Rock 'n' roll, its ungrateful grandchild, was largely to blame. Billy Crystal, whose father co-ran a jazz record shop in Manhattan and an independent jazz record label, Commodore, recalled, "The bands that I loved, the music of Coleman Hawkins, Lester Young, Sidney Bechet, Ben Webster, Roy Eldridge . . . and all the others, were replaced now by the Duprees, the Earls, the Shirelles and the Beach Boys. These original American jazz giants, the men, and women, who gave birth to all the rest of our music, were now reduced to playing outside ballparks with garters on their sleeves, wearing straw hats."

But Sinatra could afford to make his own rules, and one kind of music was verboten at Reprise—no ifs, ands, or buts. "Frank actually forbade us from signing any rock 'n' roll artists," Ostin recalled. "He was very strong about that."

Mickey Rudin sued Capitol on Frank's behalf, alleging restraint of trade and violation of the Robinson-Patman Act. The lawsuit also demanded that the label be enjoined immediately from continuing the twofer campaign, which,

Arnold Shaw writes, had jeopardized the fledgling label's existence, bringing "dealer demands that Reprise adjust its prices to the level 'fixed by the defendant.'" Sinatra sought $1.05 million in damages.

———

Less than a year earlier, Frank and Marilyn Monroe had been lovers, lolling on his yacht and reading *Look* magazine; then they drifted apart. Her chaos had proved too much for him, and his engagement to Juliet Prowse hurt her badly, touching her deep insecurities about her age (Prowse was ten years younger) and her body (Marilyn feared that her legs, unlike Juliet's long stems, were too short and fat). After the engagement was called off, Frank and Marilyn saw each other a bit, but by then both had found other distractions: Frank, his world tour (and Ava); and Marilyn, the president of the United States.

By all evidence, the relationship between Marilyn Monroe and Jack Kennedy, such as it was, was more a mutual fantasy, icon for icon, than anything else and more her fantasy than his. "Well, it wasn't a big thing as far as he was concerned," Kennedy's close friend Senator George Smathers said of JFK's involvement with Marilyn. The reality—despite the insistences of supermarket tabloids and myriad Monroe and Kennedy biographies, and despite Marilyn's idolatrous musings about the president in a free-associative tape recording that came to light in 1997—appears to be that she and JFK met exactly four times: the first was in October 1961, at a party for Kennedy at Pat and Peter Lawford's Santa Monica beach house (to titillate his brother-in-law, Lawford also invited Kim Novak, Janet Leigh, and Angie Dickinson); the second, at a Manhattan dinner party for the president in February 1962. On neither occasion was she intimate with Jack Kennedy.

Their third meeting occurred during the infamous weekend of March 24 to 26: while JFK stayed at Bing Crosby's house in Palm Desert (and Frank sulked in Bermuda), Marilyn Monroe joined him—driven there by Peter Lawford—and for the first and only time she and Kennedy were together under intimate circumstances. "She spent the night in the President's quarters," according to Barbara Leaming. We can infer, but we do not know, that sex took place. The singularity of the occasion has been confirmed by several sources, including former Secret Service agents, Lawford, and Monroe's masseur and confidant Ralph Roberts.[*] The episode was, in a strange way, a kind of double betrayal of Sinatra: a triangle with an absent leg.

Their fourth meeting, while Frank was in Athens, was the briefest of all.

---

[*] Quite indiscreetly, Monroe phoned Roberts from Crosby's for advice on "a friend's" back problems; moments later, the startled masseur found himself talking with a man who sounded exactly like JFK.

On the night of May 19, 1962, before fifteen thousand people at a Democratic fund-raiser in Madison Square Garden, Marilyn stood at a podium in a sheer, rhinestone-spangled, skintight dress (with nothing on underneath) and sang "Happy Birthday, Mr. President" in her trademark breathy purr. The entire presentation was so combustible that everyone there (Jacqueline Kennedy was not present) assumed, as many have assumed ever since, that the two were having the hottest of hot affairs. (Taking the podium after the song, the president said, "Thank you. I can now retire from politics after having had Happy Birthday sung to me in such a sweet, wholesome way.") But they had had their fleshly moment; this was all show. After the gala, at a celebrity-packed party at the apartment of Arthur and Mathilde Krim (he was the United Artists chairman whom JFK had persuaded to release *The Manchurian Candidate;* she was a research scientist who would later do invaluable work on understanding AIDS), the Kennedy who paid the closest attention to her was Bobby.

According to Arthur Schlesinger, who was also at the Krims' that night, this was RFK's first meeting with Monroe. And according to Adlai Stevenson, also present, he and Bobby were both enthralled. In a letter to a friend, Stevenson described his own "perilous encounters" at the party with Marilyn, "dressed in what she calls 'skin and beads.' I didn't see the beads! My encounters, however, were only after breaking through the strong defenses established by Robert Kennedy, who was dodging around her like a moth around the flame."

"We were all moths around the flame that night," Schlesinger wrote.

> I do not think I have seen anyone so beautiful; I was enchanted by her
> manner and her wit, at once so masked, so ingenuous and so penetrat-
> ing. But one felt a terrible unreality about her—as if talking to someone
> under water. Bobby and I engaged in mock competition for her; she
> was most agreeable to him and pleasant to me—but then she receded
> into her own glittering mist.
>   There was something at once magical and desperate about her.

The strong pull that powerful and intelligent men felt toward her (include also Sinatra and Arthur Miller) went beyond the obvious but was always led by the obvious. The magic enticed, but the desperation appeared all too soon. And only Frank recognized something of himself in it, something he didn't like at all.

As for the president, after that night, he and Marilyn never saw each other again. Concerned that her over-the-top performance at Madison Square Garden could escalate the gossip about him and Monroe from talk to print, he assigned staff members to kill news stories and distanced himself permanently from her.

Sewn into her skintight dress, she was an illusion; that spring and summer, she fought a desperate battle to hold on to whoever she might actually be. She was sick, lonely, and afraid; she was addicted to a wide array of dangerously interactive drugs prescribed by two different doctors (one of them her—and formerly Frank's—psychiatrist, Mickey Rudin's brother-in-law Ralph Greenson). Bound by an ill-considered contract to star in a movie she didn't want to make for a studio that itself was falling apart, she grew increasingly unable to cope. The film—a remake of a 1940 Cary Grant–Irene Dunne screwball comedy, *My Favorite Wife*—was called, all too tellingly, *Something's Got to Give*. Dean Martin was to co-star. The script was a rambling mess. The director was the great but fussy George Cukor; the studio, 20th Century Fox, was hemorrhaging money on two fronts: in Rome, where amid a tabloid frenzy surrounding a train wreck of a romance between Richard Burton and a chronically ill Elizabeth Taylor, production costs of *Cleopatra* had hit a mind-boggling $30 million; and in Hollywood, where Marilyn Monroe's continual absences—she too was ill, with chronic sinusitis, with sleep deprivation and drug addiction and terror—had turned the production schedule into an expensive nightmare.

In the seven weeks since shooting had begun on *Something's Got to Give*, Marilyn had shown up for a total of five days' work. The picture was thirty-two days behind schedule and $2 million over budget. On June 9, the same day Frank was to perform at Princess Grace's Monte Carlo gala, Fox announced that it was firing her and replacing her with Lee Remick. In the battle between the sick superstars, on a much less expensive picture, Monroe was simply more expendable. "It's sad, but no studio these days can afford to have Liz Taylor and Marilyn Monroe working at the same time—especially at a studio that lost $25 million last year," a front-office executive (probably a Fox mouthpiece) told the Associated Press.

The same executive, who asked to be anonymous, predicted that Marilyn's firing could mean the end of a fabulous career.

"Marilyn claims she can't work because she was sick. I actually believe Marilyn thinks she is sick.

"It's all in her mind, of course, and maybe her mental condition makes her physically ill. I don't think she can control herself. She wants to work, wants to be a great actress, and is a great star.

"But whatever her ailment is, it just won't let her work."

It was not all in her mind. Ralph Greenson and other doctors had addicted her to uppers and downers and antianxiety drugs whose side effects and aftereffects left her scared out of her wits. What's more, Fox knew it had a dog on its hands with *Something's Got to Give*. The script was beyond repair, and Cukor's slow shooting was as much to blame for the delays as Marilyn's absences. She was, as one of the movie's producers later said, "a pawn—an interesting pawn, a sad pawn, it's tragic, it's funny—but a pawn. And that's the real Hollywood story."

Shortly after she was fired, Dean Martin, saying it was a waste of his time to make the picture with anyone but Marilyn, quit. The movie would never be completed.

———

Sinatra, who loved her in his own way and understood Hollywood as clearly as anybody, spoke out soon afterward. "Frankly, I don't know too much about it," he said in New York on June 18. "But, it is my contention from afar that there is a slight possibility that Marilyn and Dean might be whipping boys. Maybe the company wants to satisfy the stockholders. All in all, the public profited. It was a lousy script."

When he got back to Los Angeles, Frank did his best to help Marilyn out, putting his lawyers at her service and letting it be known that Essex Productions was prepared to make her next picture. "I think it would be good for Sinatra," he said. "It is good company. It is good chemistry. The public would find it exciting."

"In the meantime," wrote David Lewin of the London *Daily Express*, "Marilyn Monroe goes quietly about her own affairs, which at the moment consist mainly of decorating her new Mexican-style home near the Pacific Ocean and reading the scripts which are offered to her every day."

———

A third problem for Frank that summer—more like an irritant at this stage—was Sam Giancana, still chafing under the FBI's intense surveillance and furious that Sinatra's promises about intervening on his behalf with the Kennedys had been empty. "Lying [expletive]!" he exploded in a wiretapped conversation with an associate. He was referring to Frank. "If I ever listen to that [expletive] again . . . I figured with this guy, maybe we'll be all right. I might have known this guy would [expletive] me."

At one point, Giancana's underling (and Frank's occasional houseguest) Johnny Formosa suggested a remedy. "Let's show 'em," Formosa said. "Let's show those asshole Hollywood fruitcakes that they can't get away with it as if nothing's happened. Let's hit Sinatra. Or I could whack out a couple of those other guys. Lawford and that Martin, and I could take the nigger and put his other eye out."

"No," Sam said. "I've got other plans for them."

Mooney's restraint was remarkable: the Feds had severely hedged his power. The previous year, when he tried to borrow $3 million from the Teamsters' Central States Pension Fund for a major renovation of the Cal-Neva Lodge, Jimmy Hoffa turned him down personally. "Once I got $1,750,000 from him in two days," Giancana whined to a friend. "Now all this heat comes on and I can't even get a favor out of him now. I can't do nothing for myself. Ten years ago I can get all the fucking money I want from the guy and now they won't settle for anything."

A number of large figures had been bandied about for the renovation: $3 million, $4 million; a newspaper piece in the fall of 1961 quoted Hank Sanicola spinning the daydream of a $10 million transformation of Cal-Neva, including a new hotel. When construction and organized crime are intertwined, all bets are off as far as budgetary accuracy is concerned. But apparently Giancana did manage to get a $1.5 million loan from the Bank of Nevada (Skinny D'Amato was wiretapped discussing it)—enough to trick the lodge out with a rooftop helipad, a high-end beauty parlor, an I. Magnin clothing store, and "a completely new swank showroom," as a boosterish piece in the *Nevada State Journal* referred to the brand-new Celebrity Room.

> The new showroom, part of the club's current $3,000,000 expansion and remodeling project, will seat almost 500 for the first dinner show and more than 700 for the second no-food show. Seats in the room are on four levels, and the forward section of the stage is designed to be lowered to floor level for entertainers who like to work closer to the audience.

The piece did not mention the women who would be flown in from San Francisco to staff the prostitution business that would be run openly from the front desk.

Whether the remodel had cost $3 million or $1.5 million, a lot had gone into it, and Giancana was worried about what he was going to get out. "I am going to get my money out of there and I'm going to wind up with half of the joint with no money," he told Johnny Rosselli, a little cryptically. (Maybe he meant "or" rather than "and.") "Not going to make any difference . . . That joint ain't going to be no good because it's a very short season."

This much was true. Heavy Sierra snowfalls could begin in October and continue into May, and the roads to the resort were narrow. Frank, Nancy Sinatra writes, decided the only way to turn a profit was to "help improve local roads and develop winter activities," with an eye to turning Cal-Neva into a year-round business.

But Sam Giancana wasn't talking snowshoes and ski lifts, and he was very much a partner (if not, as some have asserted, the outright owner), despite the officially listed troika of Frank (said to own 50 percent of the resort), Sanford Waterman (16 percent), and Hank Sanicola (33 percent).

Sinatra had high hopes anyway. Whatever his precise arrangement with Giancana, he was, for the first time in his life, taking an active role in the management of a hotel-casino (his stake in the Sands was just that: Jack Entratter and Carl Cohen—and the boys back east—were the ones actually running the show). Frank was proud of his new baby, as the Associated Press's movie-television reporter James Bacon wrote.

> The dawn mists had barely lifted from Lake Tahoe, high in the California Sierras.
> And there, blueprint in hand, stood Frank Sinatra telling a carpenter where to build a partition.
> It was quite a sight but not quite as astounding as one later in the morning.
> There stood Sinatra in the midst of a group of busboys demonstrating the proper way to remove dishes noiselessly from a table.

Later, Frank walked Bacon around the grounds. "Next year we'll have our eight-story hotel built, and we'll stay open all year round," he boasted. When the reporter asked about the heavy snows, Sinatra shrugged off the issue, saying helicopter service between Cal-Neva and the Reno airport, some fifty miles away, was the easy fix.

"As I say," Frank told Bacon, "you gotta spend money to make money."

Yes, but whose money?

Naturally, the casino, not the showroom or the hotel, would be Cal-Neva's profit center. And where the casino was concerned, Giancana wasn't taking any chances. In 2003, Anthony Summers interviewed Dan Arney, who co-piloted the *Christina* in the 1960s, about what Arney called "the skim run." "They'd call up and tell us we were going to Truckee-Tahoe, and from there to the Sands and on to Burbank, which meant they were going on a money run," the pilot said. "I remember once there were three briefcases, and I got to go back during the flight and see inside one of them. The cash was in $10,000 stacks."

Another strategy for profitability.

Predictably, Frank's June 29 opening was, as *Variety* would put it, boffo. "Frank Sinatra's first business venture in northern Nevada is off to a swinging start," the show-business weekly opined, noting that the opening had "attracted a more than capacity crowd including many top business and film names from Hollywood." James Bacon noted in another AP dispatch that Juliet Prowse was present at ringside when Frank began to sing. "The shapely South African dancer arrived in Sinatra's private plane along with restaurateur Mike Romanoff, stylist Sy Devore, producers Bill Perlberg and Bill Goetz, actors David Janssen and Richard Conte and other Hollywoodites," Bacon wrote.

> While Sinatra was on a two-month world tour for the benefit of under-privileged children, Miss Prowse dated Eddie Fisher.
>
> When Sinatra returned, he and Miss Prowse resumed dating. That rekindled romantic speculations but both claim the dating is all on a friendly basis.
>
> At a post-midnight show Sunday, Sinatra barely opened his mouth before several tables of matrons started squealing like bobby soxers.
>
> It was reminiscent of World War II days—probably the same girls—when Sinatra was reigning king of the swooners.
>
> Once he yelled to the wings for a busboy to bring him some tea and honey.
>
> Out strolled deadpan comic Joey Bishop, complete with white coat, napkin on arm and a cup of tea.
>
> "Frank," said Bishop, "you asked me to work at Cal-Neva but you didn't say what I was to do. I gotta start reading these contracts better."

The headline? Frank's most passionate fans were now matrons. (The subhead: the Rat Pack wasn't quite what it used to be. Responding to rumors that his friendship with Sinatra had cooled, Sammy said, "Everything's wonderful. But I can't hang out all evening anymore or meet people at 5 a.m. I'm a married man.")

And the subtext was shifting alliances, with Cal-Neva the focus. No matter how scathing Giancana's personal feelings toward Sinatra, the gangster's weakness for Frank's singing kept him coming back for more. Sometimes, despite the Black Book's proscription, he came to Cal-Neva—sneaking in by helicopter, according to one source—not only to hear Sinatra, but to meet his girlfriend Phyllis McGuire and, of course, to check up on his investment.

All this made Hank Sanicola very nervous. The casino's gaming license was at stake, as was his own significant investment. Sanicola fretted more and more about the situation that summer, and he didn't like to keep his feelings to himself.

————

It was an eventful summer at Cal-Neva, though not all events made the papers.

The night after the opening, a local deputy sheriff named Richard Anderson came to the lodge to pick up his wife, Toni, an attractive cocktail waitress just finishing her shift. The two had been married for three months; prior to this, Toni had been involved with Frank Sinatra. Yet even though she was now a married woman, Frank—who was, after all, also her employer—continued to treat her in a proprietary way. Anderson had warned Sinatra to stay away from his wife.

On the night of June 30, as the deputy stood in the lodge's kitchen, talking to the dishwashers while he waited for his wife, Frank came in and asked Anderson what he was doing there. When Anderson said he was picking up his wife, Frank tried to throw him out. Anderson refused to leave; matters escalated. In the scuffle that ensued, Anderson punched Sinatra—so hard that Frank was unable to perform for the next couple of days. In retaliation, Sinatra had Anderson suspended from the police force.

Two weeks later, the deputy sheriff and his wife were driving to dinner when a car moving at high speed in the oncoming lane forced them off the road. The Andersons' car smashed into a tree, and Richard Anderson was killed instantly. His wife, thrown from the car, suffered multiple fractures. The other car—a maroon convertible with California plates, according to an eyewitness—never stopped, and the driver couldn't be traced.

————

Marilyn Monroe seems to have managed an almost miraculous turnaround after her firing from *Something's Got to Give*. Within a week of her dismissal, executives at 20th Century Fox, realizing what a valuable asset they were pushing away, had changed their minds and commenced discussions about rehiring her and revising the script. She emerged from the brouhaha looking like the innocent victim, and of course she was still a great star: scripts flowed in for her consideration; magazines lined up to interview and photograph her. At the end of June and the beginning of July, she posed for what would become a famous series of photographs by Bert Stern, who was on assignment for *Vogue*. Seen today, the pictures show her, at thirty-six, glowing with a new kind of serenity, a mature beauty.

But with Marilyn, serenity was always fleeting. That spring and summer, she also had a series of contacts, mainly by telephone but at least once in person, with Robert Kennedy, who, "with his curiosity, his sympathy, his absolute directness of response to distress, in some way got through the glittering mist as few did," Arthur Schlesinger writes. "He met her again at Patricia Lawford's house in Los Angeles. She called him thereafter in Washington, using an assumed name. She was very often distraught. [Kennedy's secretary] Angie Novello talked to her more often than the Attorney General did. One feels that Robert Kennedy came to inhabit the fantasies of her last summer."

Some have suggested that one of these fantasies was that Bobby Kennedy would marry her.

The younger Kennedy, by most accounts as uxorious as his older brother was promiscuous, seems to have had a shy crush on Monroe; she, on the other hand, appears to have been idealistically rather than physically drawn to him. Once, when Marilyn asked her masseur and confidant Ralph Roberts if he'd heard rumors that she and Bobby were having an affair, he said, "You can't not hear. It's the talk of Hollywood." She replied, "Well, it's not true. Anyway, he's too puny for me."

Did they sleep together? Did the Savonarola of Washington, Frank Sinatra's sworn enemy and Sam Giancana's nemesis, slip and fall with Marilyn Monroe? On the free-associative tape Marilyn made for her psychiatrist Ralph Greenson in the spring or summer of 1962, she went on at worshipful length about Jack Kennedy ("Marilyn Monroe is a soldier. Her Commander-in-Chief is the greatest and most powerful man in the world") and then remarked,

> I'm glad he has Bobby. It's like the Navy. The President is the captain and Bobby is his executive officer. Bobby will do absolutely anything for his brother and so would I. I'll never embarrass him. As long as I have memory I have John Fitzgerald Kennedy. But Bobby, Doctor, what shall I do about Bobby? As you see, there's no room in my life for him. I guess I don't have the moral courage to face up to it and hurt him. I want someone else to tell him it's over. I tried to get the President to do it, but I couldn't reach him. Now I'm glad I couldn't—he's too important to ask.

This is all very titillating—except that the words come not from the tape itself but from a "near-verbatim" transcript made shortly after Marilyn's death by John Miner, head of the medical legal section of the Los Angeles district attorney's office, and revealed by him, thirty-five years later, to the Kennedy muckraker Seymour Hersh. RFK might have slipped, MM might have let her fantasy carry her away, but there are just too many variables affecting the account—a transcript, after all, of a free-associative tape made for her hovering and possessive doctor by an actress of fluid ego and under the influence of many different drugs—to take it as a certainty.

What is certain is that that summer Monroe reconnected with the love of her life, Joe DiMaggio. Both had grown during the ten years since their divorce, and they spent some quiet days together in June and July, getting to know each other as they now were. Marilyn told DiMaggio of her concerns about Greenson. She might have said less about the psychiatrist's associate and pharmaceutical dispenser, an internist named Hyman Engelberg, who was constantly on call to give Marilyn "youth shots"—a combination of tranquilizers and speed—and other injections to help her get to sleep at night. Engelberg, too, had become proprietary about her and sometimes took it upon himself to dose Marilyn independently from Greenson's instructions.

Sometime toward the end of July, Monroe spent a weekend at Cal-Neva. Accounts of her stay there differ sharply.

Almost all assert that Marilyn spent the last weekend of the month, July 27 to 29, at the resort—an idea with a built-in poignancy, since this was also the last full weekend of her life. The assertion is almost certainly not true.

According to Donald Spoto, the Lawfords invited Marilyn to accompany them to Cal-Neva from the twenty-seventh to the twenty-ninth, and she happily accepted, telephoning DiMaggio and asking him to meet her there. Others say that it was Frank Sinatra who invited Monroe to Cal-Neva, because he was worried about her, and that DiMaggio wasn't there. "Frank is a very, very compassionate person," Mickey Rudin said later. "He brought Marilyn to Cal-Neva to give her a little fun, a little relief from her problems."

All accounts agree that Peter and Pat Lawford—despite Frank's ongoing feud with Lawford—accompanied Monroe to the resort. If this is so, then the weekend in question had to have been July 20–22 (*Variety* places the Lawfords there then), not July 27–29. And while Joe DiMaggio was verifiably in the Lake Tahoe area around that time, he was not there the following weekend: he was at Yankee Stadium, playing in the Old-Timers' Day game.

But even though DiMaggio did go to Lake Tahoe sometime over the weekend of July 20–22, he did not stay at Frank's pleasure dome.

Newspaper accounts confirm the Yankee Clipper's presence at Harrah's, on the south shore of Tahoe, over that weekend, and a former Cal-Neva bell captain named Ray Langford recalled that DiMaggio checked into the Silver Crest Motel, just down the road, rather than stay at Sinatra's resort.

Joe D. was the closest of friends with Skinny D'Amato, who was to Cal-Neva what Jack Entratter and Carl Cohen were to the Sands. But DiMaggio had come to hate his former drinking buddy Sinatra, whom he considered just another Hollywood phony and whom he knew to have been involved with Marilyn.

Knowing nothing of her reconnection with DiMaggio, Frank expressed annoyance when he discovered that Joe was in the vicinity. "If the guy don't want her, why doesn't he leave her the fuck alone?" he said. "He's just making things worse here." And why was DiMaggio at Lake Tahoe, if not to be with Marilyn? He appears to have gone to keep an eye on her rather than to spend time with her: he hovered around the edges of Cal-Neva that weekend, going fishing with Ray Langford, and was not spotted at the resort.

Sinatra, though, seems to have stayed close by Monroe's side. A former security man at Cal-Neva recalled,

> Mr. Sinatra wanted a special meal prepared for her—lots of food, a steak, potatoes, a cheesecake. He went to the kitchen and gave a menu for every day she was to be there. I know that the meal was sent to her chalet. Mr. Lawford answered the door in Marilyn's room. The waiter never saw her. Then the tray was back in the kitchen about two hours later. The only thing that had been eaten was the cheesecake, and someone said that Mr. Sinatra had eaten that.

The same employee reported that "when Frank saw Marilyn, he was alarmed at how depressed she seemed. He was on the phone to her psychiatrist, screaming at him, saying, 'What the hell kind of treatment are you giving her? She's a fucking mess. What the hell is she paying you for? Why isn't she in a sanitarium, or something?'"

Two persistent rumors cling around Marilyn Monroe's weekend at Cal-Neva: that she overdosed on barbiturates, and that she engaged in (possibly perverse) sexual relations with Sam Giancana, and possibly other mafiosi as well.

As to the first story: Spoto calls it "scurrilous and unfounded." Yet a former kitchen worker at the lodge reported receiving a frantic phone call from Peter Lawford: "'We need coffee in Chalet 52,' he screamed into the phone, then hung up . . . No less than two minutes passed and it was Mr. Sinatra on the phone screaming, 'Where's that goddamn coffee?' I learned later that they were in 52, walking Marilyn around, trying to get her to wake up."

Lawford also told Kitty Kelley, "I did see Frank briefly when we took Marilyn up to Cal-Neva, but he got so mad at her after she overdosed and had to have her stomach pumped that he just snarled at everyone."

As to the second rumor, Anthony Summers and Robbyn Swan assert that Giancana was present at Cal-Neva that weekend and that Frank supposedly shot, with his own camera, a series of shocking photos, showing (according to the photographer Billy Woodfield, who said he developed the film) "Marilyn, on all fours. She looked sick. Astride her, either riding her like a horse or trying to help her up—I couldn't make out which—was Sam Giancana."

Woodfield said that Sinatra took out his lighter and burned the pictures in his presence.

It's horrifying, but again direct evidence is missing—in this case, of the incident itself and even of Giancana's presence at Cal-Neva while Monroe was there. Betsy Duncan Hammes, a reliable witness who was close to both Giancana and Sinatra, claims that Mooney was absent. "I was in Lake Tahoe that weekend," she recalled, "and I saw Marilyn eating dinner. Giancana and his crowd weren't there, and I would have known if they were."

He had been there, though, and he would soon be back.

Why does it matter which weekend in July Marilyn Monroe spent at Cal-Neva?

Because she was in a fluctuating and delicate state of mind that summer; "she could have a crisis over what she was having for lunch, she was that emotional and high-strung," said Mickey Rudin, who was Marilyn's lawyer as well as Sinatra's.[*] In Peter Lawford's telling, Frank had thrown up his hands where she was concerned by the time she left Lake Tahoe.

In Donald Spoto's version, Monroe and DiMaggio spent a romantic and secluded last weekend in July at Cal-Neva, in the course of which he proposed that they remarry, and she accepted. "Marilyn and Joe planned a wedding date of Wednesday, August 8, in Los Angeles," Spoto writes, "and a radiant Marilyn returned home with Joe's pajamas."

It's pleasant to think it happened this way—pajamas and all—but by the last weekend in July, DiMaggio had flown east for Old Timers' Day. And his proposal is unlikely to have come before or during the previous weekend, when Marilyn Monroe, by most accounts, was not behaving like a blissful fiancée.

It's most likely that he proposed early in the week of July 23: by midweek, he was off to San Diego to celebrate the graduation of his son, Joe junior, from the U.S. Marine Corps Recruit Depot, and then he headed east, not scheduled to return to the West Coast until a charity baseball game in San Francisco on August 4. On July 25, Marilyn met at her home with the 20th Century Fox production chief, Peter Levathes, who brought welcome news: he was personally rehiring her for *Something's Got to Give,* at a higher salary. "She seemed to him very pleasant and reasonable," Spoto writes, "and before

---

[*] As well as the brother-in-law of Marilyn's psychiatrist, Ralph Greenson.

he departed she said something that stayed with him over the years: 'You know, Peter, in a way I'm a very unfortunate woman. All this nonsense about being a legend, all this glamour and publicity. Somehow I'm always a disappointment to people.'"

———————

Frank had considered marrying her himself, to save her. "He felt that if she were his wife, everyone else would back off, give her some space, and allow her to get herself together," a friend recalled. " 'No one will mess with her if she's Mrs. Frank Sinatra,' he said. 'No one would dare.'"

"Yeah, Frank wanted to marry the broad," Jilly said later. "He asked her and she said no."

She was saving herself for Joe.

———————

And then came August 5, and the terrible death that seemed, in an instant, to subtract a real measure of beauty and hope from the world. Marilyn's infinite vulnerability had stirred love and hate but seems to have left no one indifferent. Her sudden loss was an end of innocence and in its own strange way a herald of even worse things to come. Frank was "devastated," his valet recalled. Joe DiMaggio was devastated, too, and he was also furious: at Hollywood, which had chewed Marilyn up and spat her out, and at "the fucking Kennedys," as he called them that day. "She was a toy for them," he told a friend. "Bobby Kennedy was the one Joe talked about," the friend recalled. "He hated him. And Sinatra—Joe cursed Sinatra."

DiMaggio and Monroe's half sister, Berniece Miracle, agreed to make the funeral—at Westwood Village Memorial Park on August 8, the day Marilyn and Joe were to have been married—a strictly private affair. They invited some two dozen people: mostly, as DiMaggio biographer Richard Ben Cramer writes, "people who had served Marilyn—a maid, her housekeeper, her secretary, her driver, her masseur Ralph Roberts, her psychiatrist Ralph Greenson (and his family), her publicist, her lawyers, a couple of hairdressers, and her loyal makeup man, Allan 'Whitey' Snyder."

Patricia Lawford flew west for the funeral from the summer White House at Hyannis Port, only to find upon arriving that neither she nor her husband (who had been the last person to speak with Marilyn on the night of her death)* had been invited. "I'm shocked," Peter Lawford told the Associated

———

* Her last words to Lawford were "Say goodbye to Pat, say goodbye to the president, and say goodbye to yourself, because you're a nice guy." Strangely, she then whispered, "I'll see, I'll see," then was silent.

Press's James Bacon. "I don't know who's responsible but the whole thing was badly handled."

Joe DiMaggio was responsible. Not a single movie star had been invited. "Those in charge of the arrangements explained that if they invited one star, they would have to invite many, and to have a big crowd would mean a circus-like funeral," Bacon wrote. But he continued, doubtless expressing the feelings of many in Hollywood, "The absence of the big movie names may have given a dignified, almost quiet tone to the funeral, but it hardly seemed the type of final sendoff for a star of Miss Monroe's magnitude."

Marilyn's friend Inez Melson, who was present, later said that Frank arrived at the cemetery with bodyguards and tried to force, then bribe, his way in. He was turned away.

Mickey Rudin, who was invited, protested to DiMaggio that he was barring many important people in the movie industry, not just stars. What, Rudin asked Joe, was he supposed to tell them?

"Tell them," DiMaggio said, "if it wasn't for them, she'd still be here."

Frank returned to Cal-Neva. After all, the place now had his name on it (it was officially Frank Sinatra's Cal-Neva Lodge); there was business to be done. Joe E. Lewis, a strangely consoling presence with his tragic face and drunk jokes, was headlining in the Celebrity Room through the ninth, to be followed by Eddie Fisher.

Life went on in its often absurd way. The headlines were black with Marilyn's death, but the gossip sections lagged while the columnists assembled their tributes. And on August 6, oddly juxtaposed with the obligatory front-page story about the weekend's tragic events (CORONER AND POLICE PROBE MARILYN MONROE'S DEATH), many papers ran an assessment of the Kennedy presidency at midterm by the Associated Press's Relman Morin. Under the headline JFK SHOWS NO CRACKS IN HIS CALM, the piece began,

> President John F. Kennedy appears to be the best air-conditioned man in Washington these days.
>
> While the political sirocco blows hot from Capitol Hill, Kennedy looks cool.
>
> He sits in his rocking chair, crunching the ice from a soft drink, slowly smoking a thin cigar, examining the record as he approaches mid-passage in his first term in the White House. There are no visible cracks in his marble calm.

A year before, Morin wrote, America had been embroiled in foreign-policy problems, chiefly the Berlin crisis; now the president was plagued by relatively minor domestic matters: the Senate's killing of the Medicare bill; the shelving of the farm and school aid bills; the economy's slow rally after the previous year's recession. Yet though businessmen considered JFK antibusiness and conservatives called him "socialistic," the president's popularity, which had recently stood at an astounding 79 percent (and had slipped slightly), was still high.

Few outside Kennedy's inner circle knew of the turmoil behind the facade. Marilyn's death might have solved one potentially devastating problem for the president, but another was still boiling. "His liaison with Judith Campbell Exner was still a secret from the public," Seymour Hersh writes, "although J. Edgar Hoover and dozens of FBI agents now knew of Kennedy's involvement with her and that she met regularly with Sam Giancana and Johnny Rosselli. Hoover also knew that a senior employee of General Dynamics, one of two bidders for the $6.5 billion TFX [F-111 fighter] aircraft contract, had been part of a team that in August broke into Exner's apartment in Los Angeles." The burglars, Hersh contends, were seeking evidence with which to blackmail the president into giving General Dynamics the contract.

And despite Nikita Khrushchev's back-channel assurances that missiles were not being shipped to Cuba, Kennedy continued that summer to receive intelligence reports of a Soviet military buildup there. What's more, though any flare-up with Cuba would revive the subject of the Bay of Pigs and damage the Democrats in the midterm elections, not to say hurt JFK's chances for reelection in 1964, Operation Mongoose, the plot to assassinate Fidel Castro, was—whether with or without the direct approval of the president and the attorney general—still very much under way.

In the meantime, Frank had another dustup with a photographer.

He was on his way back to Los Angeles from Cal-Neva on the night of August 12, a week to the day after Marilyn's death. Stopping in San Francisco, he took a party of eight to a nightclub called New Facks. According to witnesses, the photographer began snapping pictures as "two unidentified girls" leaned over Sinatra's shoulders. Frank said something to the photographer, and a fracas ensued. At first, all concerned denied that Sinatra had grabbed the photographer, Jimmy Jaye Perrine, by the necktie and wrestled him to the ground. In Los Angeles, Chuck Moses said, "There was no bodily contact, no smashing of cameras." The club owner, George Andros, said that Sinatra merely demanded the photographer hand over his film. "He handed me the camera and I had the film taken out," Andros said. "Frank was the calmest I've ever seen him." Even the photographer—who said he'd been taking pictures of someone next to Sinatra, not Sinatra—denied that Frank had touched him. It had been a "guy" who had grabbed him, Perrine said; Frank even told him afterward that he was sorry it had happened.

Three days later, Perrine filed a suit against Sinatra for $275,390, alleging that Frank had choked him and smashed his camera.

What had really happened? Had Frank, all too predictably, simply lost his temper? Or was the photographer—who later settled out of court for $2,500—merely seizing an opportunity to make a few bucks off the fattest target in the business?

In a way, it didn't matter. No matter how many children's hospitals Frank visited, no matter how many anonymous good works he did, he would always stir things up. Numerous people have spoken of the electricity that could be felt across the floor of the Sands, even throughout Las Vegas itself, whenever Sinatra was there, even before anyone knew for a fact that he was there. Confined to a single room, a restaurant, or a small nightclub, that electricity could almost instantly escalate from the slightest spark to an explosion.

And then, a far bigger confrontation. According to Nancy Sinatra, her father and Hank Sanicola were driving from Palm Springs to Las Vegas when Sanicola worried aloud about Sam Giancana's visits to Phyllis McGuire at Cal-Neva in violation of Black Book rules. Frank tried to reassure him that Mooney kept to his cabin and the showroom, staying away from the casino, but Hank wasn't buying. Sinatra's old friend was in a fretful mood; Cal-Neva's losses were eating up the profits from Park Lake Enterprises, the corporation that also produced Frank's films and in which Hank held a large share.

Then and there, Nancy says, her father insisted on buying Sanicola out of the lodge and all other partnerships. The only problem was that Sinatra didn't have much cash to throw around. Accordingly, he gave Hank outright ownership of all five of his music-publishing companies: Sands, Saga, Marivale, Tamarisk, and Barton. Nancy claims that the firms' collective inventory was worth "well over $1 million." Sanicola told the driver to stop, she writes, then he took his bags out of the trunk and stood by the side of the road, watching Frank Sinatra drive out of his life for good.

In Sanicola's version, it was Frank who ordered him out of the car.

Just recently, Sinatra had reminisced to the British writer Robin Douglas-Home about his early, hungry years in the depths of the Depression: "I was seventeen then, and I went around New York singing with little groups in roadhouses. The word would get around that there was a kid in the neighborhood who could sing. Many's the time I worked all night for nothing. Or maybe I'd sing for a sandwich or cigarettes—all night for three packets [*sic*]. But I worked on one basic theory—stay active, get as much practice as you can. I got to know a song-plugger called Hank Sanicola . . . and he used to give me fifty cents or a dollar some weeks to buy some food. For some reason he always had terrific faith in me."

Sanicola had been Sinatra's right hand since the beginning: rehearsal pianist, musical adviser, music publisher, bodyguard, confidant, and friend. It was a relationship that had lasted longer than almost any other in Frank's life; he might have known Hank before meeting Nancy Barbato. But Hank had made demands. Suddenly stray gossip-column items took on new meaning: the antiques Frank had brought back for Jilly and Honey from the world tour; the Miami nightclub he was considering buying with Jilly. Jilly, who demanded nothing, now took over the latter three of Hank's old roles.

With Sinatra, only his children and his parents were forever, yet even they made uncomfortable demands on him.

———

And that he was strapped for cash, and that Cal-Neva was bleeding him— these were not good signs. Reprise was bleeding him too. Much was coming in in 1962 (and Frank continued to spend like a man with infinite resources), but more was going out.

———

A couple of weeks later, Frank flew east to do three nights at the 500 Club. He was joining Dean (who'd begun the week as a single) in an act of outright charity for their old pal Skinny D'Amato. Sammy would join them on the final night. The Five—and indeed the entire nightclub business—had been in steep decline for years, the victim of television, inflated salaries for headliners, and Las Vegas, where gambling was the dog and entertainment the tail. Without casinos attached, niteries (as *Variety* called them) were nothing but money pits. Atlantic City itself was also on its uppers. Skinny had expanded the 500 Club to a thousand seats in 1958, then watched many of those seats go empty for season after season. He'd been wise, it seemed, to branch out to Cal-Neva, where even if he couldn't share in profits on the books, there were still profits to share.

———

There was a kind of final-days-of-Rome decadence to those August days in Atlantic City. Not only was it the last time Frank, Dean, and Sammy would play the 500 Club together, but a number of top organized-crime figures were also in town, as a report from the Newark FBI office to J. Edgar Hoover noted:

> for two-fold purposes, that is to attend the wedding of [the Philadel-phia Mob boss] ANGELO BRUNO's daughter on August 26, 1962, and a performance of FRANK SINATRA–DEAN MARTIN–SAMMY DAVIS, JR., at the 500 Club.
>
> FRANK SINATRA arrived in Atlantic City . . . for the above sched-uled appearance with DEAN MARTIN and took over the first sleep-ing floor of the Claridge Hotel . . . which consists of approximately 40 rooms. SINATRA's representatives allowed no one on the hotel floor, including the hotel management, except by invitation . . .
>
> SINATRA and MARTIN were appearing at the 500 Club as a per-sonal favor to PAUL D'AMATO, also known as "SKINNY," for which they would receive no money but would have all of their expenses taken care of by D'AMATO . . .
>
> SINATRA's personal airplane landed at the Atlantic City Airport . . . and he departed from the Airport in an unmarked Atlantic City Police car.

The report went on to note that Sam Giancana was "observed . . . in a private dining room on Sinatra's floor of the Claridge Hotel."

A couple of days later, Hoover took the trouble to send a memo marked "PERSONAL" to Attorney General Robert F. Kennedy. It read,

> While conducting inquiry at the Claridge Hotel in Atlantic City, New Jersey, in connection with an investigation under our Criminal Intel-ligence Program, Agents of our Newark Office were confidentially advised by an official of this hotel that Frank Sinatra had received a personal telephone call from President John F. Kennedy on August 23, 1962.

It would have been months since they'd last talked. Was JFK trying to mend fences? Apparently, the hotel switchboard put the president through, but no one listened in. "The nature of [the call]," a later FBI summary noted, suc-cinctly, tantalizingly, "was not described."

On the final evening, August 25, Atlantic City police captain Mario Flori-ani personally drove the three entertainers to the 500 Club, where a scream-ing mob awaited them. Frank, Dean, and Sammy did five shows that night, the last one beginning as the sky was starting to lighten over the ocean. On a recording of one of the shows, a wildly appreciative audience eats up every line of Rat Pack repartee, some of it, by now, sounding merely stale:

FRANK [singing "The Lady Is a Tramp"]: She loves the free, fresh clyde in her bird, without a word . . .

And some of it both stale and offensive:

DEAN [to Sammy]: Don't touch me! You can sing with me and talk to me, but don't touch me!

And some, freshly offensive:

SAMMY [complaining that he alone hasn't been given a stool to sit on]: I don't think Martin Luther King is gonna like this.
FRANK: Listen, you want to buy a wrecked Freedom Bus? It's cheap.

To his everlasting credit, Sammy came back instantly: "I thought Italians were supposed to be liberals."

After the last show, "Frank and his entourage hit the town with Skinny and Sammy," Jonathan Van Meter writes. It was 8:15 a.m.

They stopped at Grace's Little Belmont across the street from Club Harlem on Kentucky Avenue to visit Sammy Davis Jr.'s mother, Baby Sanchez, who was now a barmaid at the famed jazz club, and then on to Timbuktu at Kentucky and Arctic Avenues, Frank handing out folded $100 bills to every bartender, porter, doorman, cook, waitress, and washroom attendant who crossed his path.

Strapped for cash, he was still the *padrone,* and the biggest thing in show business, bar none.

And the week—between Dean's five nights, Frank and Dean's three, and Frank, Dean, and Sammy's one—put $175,000 in the pocket of Skinny D'Amato, a friend with good friends.

———

"It is the belief of the Attorney General—and it is not exclusive with him—that the crime of gambling pays for other crime," read a late-August editorial in the Uniontown, Pennsylvania, *Morning Herald.* "Kennedy told the House subcommittee last year: 'Organized crime is nourished by a number of activities, but the primary source of its growth is illicit gambling.'

"This is the principal reason for a federal grand jury investigation of gambling at Las Vegas, Nev., where the pastime of course is legal. The Attorney General is checking on the possibility that bigtime racketeers have moved into secret ownership of some of the Las Vegas pleasure traps."

———

Frank got back on the *Christina* and flew west, continuing to follow Newton's first law of motion. The very night he returned, the twenty-sixth, he sang at a celebration of Sam Goldwyn's fifty years in the movie business; the next night it was back to United Recording to make an ill-advised single, "The Look of Love"—the perky and instantly forgettable Sammy Cahn and Jimmy Van Heusen number by that name, not Hal David and Burt Bacharach's classic— and a tune by two otherwise-unknown songwriters named George Cory and Douglass Cross, "I Left My Heart in San Francisco."

Yes, that "I Left My Heart in San Francisco." Tony Bennett had recorded it in January, as the B-side to a single whose A-side, his rendition of Lee Adams and Charles Strouse's Broadway classic "Once upon a Time," failed to grab anybody once radio stations started to play it in February. When DJs flipped the 45, though, Bennett's tribute to the City by the Bay quickly took off and went gold, soon becoming Tony's signature song. Why Frank chose to record it after it had been out for half a year and become a big hit is something of a mystery—except that Sinatra was Sinatra, and, though their relationship was fraught by Frank's domineering, he had been something of a mentor, and certainly an inspiration, to the younger singer (born in 1926). He might simply have felt it was his right to take a whack at it: again, the *padrone*.

He was wrong. Bennett's version has stardust sprinkled on it, and Sinatra's, though he is singing well, simply doesn't. Tony Bennett had (and continues to have as of this writing) the rare ability to bring joy to a song, and joy was an arrow Frank didn't quite have in his quiver. (Schadenfreude—literally, gloating joy—he possessed in full measure: witness "Goody Goody," the bouncy screw-you number with which he led off nearly every show on the world tour, seeming to dedicate it, more and more, to Ava.)

For whatever reason, very likely embarrassment, Sinatra withdrew the single after it had been out for just two weeks.

The August 27 session was also something of a waste of the talents of Nelson Riddle, who did the pleasant enough arrangements under the table (though his contract with Capitol was nearing its end, he was still bound by it), and the Reprise in-house jack-of-all-trades Neal Hefti, who conducted. Sinatra's failures were rarely less than interesting, but this one came close.

From L.A., it was a quick hop back up to Lake Tahoe, where he shuttered the Celebrity Room for the season after playing Labor Day weekend and three additional nights. It ran contrary to his grand plan to stay on until October, but he had many other fish to fry.

The casino stayed open, milking the suckers for all they were worth.

————

On September 18, *Variety* formalized the split between Frank and Hank, though in a slightly hedged fashion. "The 28-year-old association of Frank Sinatra and Hank Sanicola has struck a sour note," the show-business daily reported.

> In the wake of New York rumors of a rupture, Sanicola yesterday admitted, "We had one of our little beefs—about the operation of the Cal-Neva. We'll discuss it further . . ." He added, "It could be okay again by tomorrow. It's happened before. I guess I'm the only guy who will disagree with Frank once in a while."
> Sinatra, contacted on the set of his current film, "Come Blow Your Horn," gave more than his usual "no comment." He replied, "That's nobody's business!"

But Hank had disagreed once too often. It was over.

————

Early that fall, a box postmarked "London W1" landed on the desk of Capitol Records' head of international A&R, Dave Dexter Jr. The carton contained eighteen records sent by Capitol's British parent company, EMI, to be considered for U.S. distribution by the American label. Though Capitol didn't have an anti-rock policy—the Beach Boys were racking up big sales—Dexter didn't think twice about turning down one of the discs, a song called "Love Me Do," by the new British group the Beatles. The fact that the record was climbing the charts in the U.K. meant nothing to him. "I didn't care for it at all because of the harmonica sound," he recalled. "I didn't care for the harmonica because I had grown up listening to the old blues records and blues harmonica players, and I simply didn't . . . I nixed the record instantly."

————

Come Blow Your Horn was a big hit on Broadway when Frank signed on to do the movie version early in the year, and it was still playing at the Brooks Atkinson Theatre when production on the film began in mid-September. It was Neil Simon's first play, a semiautobiographical, bittersweet comedy about a playboy who teaches his worldly skills to his innocent and impressionable younger brother. Sinatra, of course, was a natural to portray the playboy—the part was an echo of his role in *The Tender Trap*—even though his character, Alan Baker, was meant to be somewhere in his thirties. The great Lee J. Cobb signed on to play Alan's father. Cobb, a serious Method actor (which Frank was most decidedly not), was four years older than Sinatra. A twenty-two-year-old newcomer named Tony Bill, who had never acted professionally, was cast as Alan's brother, Buddy. (Nancy Sinatra, wanting to give her husband's acting career a much-needed boost, had lobbied Frank hard to cast Tommy Sands in the role; Frank agreed, but after the screenwriter, Norman Lear, and the director, Bud Yorkin, argued strenuously against Sands, the unlucky son-in-law withdrew.)

In more than one way, the project was off-kilter before it began.

Paramount was to distribute the picture; Frank's company, Essex, co-produced along with Tandem, a new outfit run by Norman Lear and Bud Yorkin, both veterans of television comedy but relative newcomers to the movies. Lear and Yorkin (directing his first feature) had had to do some heavy persuasion to get Sinatra to play the role: there was the age issue for one thing, and the fact that in the play, Buddy, the younger brother (and Neil Simon surrogate), had the meatier role. Lear had to rewrite the play considerably, and Simon was not pleased.

Sinatra, never at his best in comedy, was entering new comic territory with *Come Blow Your Horn*. Neil Simon had made his bones as a writer for Sid Caesar's *Your Show of Shows,* and Norman Lear had written for Martin and Lewis, among others (his writing partner Ed Simmons had created Dean's drunk persona). Bud Yorkin had also worked with Dean and Jerry, as a producer and director, on *The Colgate Comedy Hour*. The thirty-six-year-old Yorkin was intimidated by the new assignment and especially cowed by the prospect of telling Frank Sinatra what to do. "I certainly didn't approach it with any great bravado," he recalled. But Frank would surprise him, beginning on the first day of shooting.

Sinatra had instructed the novice director how he wanted to proceed: Yorkin would stage beforehand each scene that had Frank in it; Frank would then come in and watch Yorkin act out the scene, playing the Sinatra role. Then Frank would do it for the cameras. Once.

On the first day of shooting, the first scene was a conversation between Sinatra and Lee J. Cobb. Yorkin staged it with Cobb before Frank came to work, blocking it out in the standard way: a medium two-shot of Sinatra and Cobb, then two close-ups, one over Cobb's shoulder, one over Frank's. "Frank came and sat down and watched it," Yorkin remembered, "and said, 'Yeah, I think it worked okay.' Then he said, 'I've got a couple of suggestions.'"

Sinatra proposed that the scene be shot in one continuous take, the camera gradually tracking in on the two men. "He said, 'What if I just came over and we talked like this,'" Yorkin said. "I knew right away that it takes two setups out. Because he likes to go fast." Yorkin's concern was that if the single take didn't go perfectly, "He's got me screwed." As a neophyte film director, he wanted coverage.

"I said, 'Gee, I think we could track that way, too, but I'd like to do my first this way.' We were all lit for him. Frank said, 'There's no reason to do it two ways. There's only one right way.' He said, 'The old-fashioned directors would do all that coverage stuff; you don't need all that.' Being naive as I was, I said, 'I kind of think I need this.' I started to explain." Frank cut him off. "Well, if you see it that way, then I guess everybody has their right," he said, then went off, Yorkin thought, to makeup.

After a while—the scene was lit; Cobb was ready—Yorkin said, "Well, guys, let's do it." But Sinatra was nowhere in sight. "I said, 'Guys, I'm sitting here. Let's bring him out here.' They said, 'He's gone.'

"I said, 'What do you mean, he's gone?' They said, 'He just drove off the lot.' I said, 'Oh my God, I can't believe it. My career is over before it started.' I didn't sleep all night.

"The next morning," Yorkin recalled, "I came in, and one of his guys came over and said, 'The boss wants to talk to you.'"

Yorkin went into Sinatra's dressing room, petrified. "Frank said, 'Sit down, Bud.' He said, 'Bud, let me ask you something. Did anyone ever tell you that I might be difficult to work with? Have you ever heard that?' I said, 'Yeah, I heard that.' He said, 'Did anybody ever tell you that I don't like to do a lot of takes and so forth? I don't think you need a lot. Did you ever hear that?' I said, 'Yeah, sure. I've heard it said.'

"Then Frank said, 'Have you ever heard that when five o'clock comes, it's martini time? We could be right in the middle of a scene, but it's over for me, because it's martini time. Did you ever hear that?' I said, 'Yeah, I heard that one.' And he said, 'Well, jeez, if you heard all that, why didn't you get Howard Keel to play the role?'"

Yorkin broke up. Sinatra did, too. "He [clapped his hands and] said, 'Come on, let's go!' He let me off the hook that way," Yorkin recalled. And they went back to work, doing it mostly Frank's way, but the resourceful young director came up with a surprising method for getting another take out of Sinatra when he really needed one.

"He was nobody's fool," Yorkin said. "He knew if a scene didn't work or if he forgot a line or something, he obviously had to shoot it again. But if there were other kinds of subtleties that I thought were missed, you couldn't say to him, 'I'd like to get another take.'

"So what I did one time—we did this scene, and I said, 'Gee, I think we can do it better.' And he said, 'Ah, I think it was pretty good.' I said, 'Hey, listen. I'll tell you what. Your mother and my mother couldn't care less as long as they spell our names right. My mother is going to love this scene, and I'm sure your mother would too. Billy Wilder will know we really fucked up.' From that point on he would go, 'All right, one for Billy Wilder; I'll do it one time for Billy Wilder.' We never had an argument after that point, literally."

––––––––

Maybe they should have. *Come Blow Your Horn* is fun to look at, especially Frank's character's splendiferous bachelor pad, whose onyx bathroom and plush walk-in closet alone are worth the price of admission—and appear realistically Sinatra-esque, as do Alan's many black-and-orange-accented outfits. But as a movie, it doesn't *move:* it feels like an extended sitcom, which is unsurprising given the pedigrees of the filmmakers. There are funny bits, and Frank is loose and charming—he even does a neat Bogart imitation—but with his picturesquely grooved and pitted face, ravaged-looking practically no matter how it's lit, he seems old for the character, and old to still be doing the bachelor bit. (Though age didn't stop him from having a fling with the twenty-two-year-old Jill St. John, a starlet claiming a near-genius IQ, who played his sexy, airheaded upstairs neighbor.)

The Feydeau mechanics of different girlfriends arriving at inconvenient moments, already creaky in *The Tender Trap,* were well worn by now. But one appearance is especially attention getting: Phyllis McGuire, in the minor role of Mrs. Eckman, the buyer from Dallas who's also a sometime squeeze of Alan's. When she shows up at his door, mad at him for standing her up, and grinds her high heel into his toes to try to get him to confess his sins, she's a scarily realistic dominatrix—an effect that's enhanced by her height (she towers over Frank in those heels), her cruel-looking, flattened features and feline eyes, her wasp-waisted all-black ensemble (complete with elbow-length black-leather gloves), and a leopard coat slung over her shoulder. She's a huntress, and Alan is a frightened rabbit in her clutches—it's all he can do to sweet-talk her out of the apartment.

In real life, of course, McGuire was the scary Sam Giancana's girlfriend, and Mooney proudly visited the set one day to watch her work, putting Frank into something of a tizzy, as Bud Yorkin recalled vividly: "He told me, 'Listen—when we're shooting, you've got to tell the crew, no jokes, let's just shoot this thing and get it over with.'"

Giancana stuck around the whole day, on his best behavior. "He seemed very nice," Yorkin said, remembering that Sinatra was as nervous as a schoolboy. "Frank was, 'Hey, get him a director's chair; let him sit right over here.' We took a leather chair, and there he was, sitting just out of the scene."

Maybe the fear on Sinatra's face in the scene with Phyllis McGuire wasn't a stretch. Shirley MacLaine, in her memoir, writes of a terrifying backstage encounter with Giancana at a Sammy Davis Jr. show: with no provocation, the mobster twisted her arm behind her back, and when Sammy asked him to let her go, Mooney punched Davis full force in the stomach, knocking the wind out of him. "I was confused," MacLaine writes.

> Sammy was in pain. My arm was wrenched. This man seemed to be a monster . . . Years later I saw Giancana with a woman he loved. I was startled to observe how she operated with such a man. "Dominatrix" would be a mild description. To his face she referred to him as a "cock-sucking sleazeball who's so chickenshit he loves to be whipped." He ate it up. For some reason that made inverted sense to me. Those who dominate must love to be dominated. I understood him a little better.

Did Frank love to be dominated? He was certainly eager to accommodate Sam Giancana, and all the more so that fall, when, as an October FBI memo implied, he put the *Christina*, a car, and his Palm Springs house at the disposal of Giancana and his lady love. "At 3:16 AM, September 26, 1962," the memo began, with Jack Webb portentousness, "PHYLLIS MCGUIRE was observed departing from a private plane at Palm Springs Airport and was met by three unknown males in a station wagon determined to be a 1962 Buick, bearing California License XDP318."

McGuire got in the wagon, which was registered to Sinatra's Essex Productions, and the car proceeded to the vicinity of the Tamarisk Country Club, where it was observed shortly afterward parked in the carport at Frank's compound. It was the opinion of the surveilling agents at the airport that one of the men who had met McGuire's plane was Sam Giancana.

———

While Sam and Phyllis were relaxing (or doing whatever they did) in the desert, Frank was doing what he liked best, with some of the people he liked best. On the nights of October 2 and 3, he assembled with Neal Hefti and Count Basie and His Orchestra—which included, besides the majestic William J. Basie of Red Bank, New Jersey, such greats as the trumpeter Thad Jones, trombonist Benny Powell, saxophonists Frank Wess and Frank Foster, guitarist Freddie Green, bassist Buddy Catlett, and drummer Sonny Payne—and recorded ten numbers for his latest Reprise album.

The LP would be called *Sinatra-Basie: An Historic Musical First,* and the grand-sounding title was not an exaggeration. Frank had idolized the incomparable jazz pianist and swing-era pioneer (born in 1904) since the Count and his band had burst into prominence in the late 1930s, and he had known Basie himself since the 1940s. "I've waited twenty years for this moment," Sinatra proclaimed at the beginning of the recording date.

Why had it taken so long? Sinatra archivist Ed O'Brien notes that some critics felt the collaboration "would be a bad musical marriage—the fear being that Sinatra's lighter sound and Basie's hard swing edge would be like oil and water." But the truth of the matter seems to be more banal: contractual conflicts had prevented the singer and the bandleader from recording together until this moment. As it turned out, the two were made for each other.

A case in point is the album's first tune, Johnny Burke and Arthur Johnston's 1936 "Pennies from Heaven." Frank had recorded the number six and a half years earlier, with a Nelson Riddle arrangement, for *Songs for Swingin' Lovers!*: to listen to the two versions is to hear how much Sinatra has changed in the interim, both musically and as a man. The earlier recording swings, but lightly—at a lope—and Frank's reading is full-voiced and wholehearted, capturing all the hopefulness of the Depression-era classic.

By contrast, the Sinatra-Basie "Pennies" (Bill Miller is at the piano)[*] is taut, clipped, tough: Sinatra is out to prove he can be a great jazz horn, and prove it he does. If the song's sentimental meaning is lost in the transition, a new meaning is found; any doubt about whether Frank Sinatra is a true jazz singer is hereby resolved. Though the cognoscenti had known it for years: none other than Lester Young, who played tenor in Basie's original band, told Nat Hentoff in 1956, "If I could put together exactly the kind of band I wanted, Frank Sinatra would be the singer. Really, my main man is Frank Sinatra."

No one was hipper than Prez, and no praise could be higher.

In late September, Earl Wilson reported, "Frank Sinatra, on a fast visit here with Mike Romanoff whom he shanghaied, dated model Joan Walker at Jilly's, and went to the Copa where he told singer Tina Robin she's the greatest." Wilson then noted, parenthetically, "FS may have surgery for a golf injury."

Golf had nothing to do with it. In fact, Frank had hurt his right hand badly early in the year, while filming a fight scene for *The Manchurian Candidate.* The martial arts sequence between Sinatra's character, Bennett Marco, and

---

[*] The Count could read music, but just adequately: on numbers he was less familiar with, he ceded the keyboard to Miller. See Ed O'Brien, *Sinatra 101,* p. 128.

Henry Silva's Soviet agent, Chunjin, is shockingly effective for its sheer unexpectedness: Marco knocks at an apartment door, expecting Raymond Shaw; instead, Chunjin answers, and the violence begins instantly. The scene is also jarring for its realism. Modern moviegoers have become so accustomed to choreographed martial arts in motion pictures that to see two men looking as if they're genuinely trying to kill each other is startling, upsetting, and, of course, thrilling.

"Using a double only for the shot where Marco is hurled across the room," Daniel O'Brien writes, "Sinatra suffered for his art while shooting the sequence. Karate-chopping a wooden table, he broke both the furniture and his little finger, though the injury went unnoticed until shooting on the sequence was completed, the star having shown no sign of discomfort."

But the injury triggered a condition called Dupuytren's contracture, a tissue disorder in which the little finger and the ring finger bend toward the palm and can't be fully extended. The ability to grip is compromised. Frank did many things with his right hand, including holding a microphone, and the condition would continue to plague him for years, despite several operations to try to correct it.

Sinatra's commitment to making the fight sequence realistic reflected his complete dedication to *The Manchurian Candidate*. "I thought this might be something extraordinary—and it was," recalled Angela Lansbury, herself extraordinary in the picture. Frank later said, "I remember a wonderful enthusiasm on the part of everyone involved in the film. It was a wonderful, wonderful experience—it only happens once in a performer's life." His work in the movie—coming more or less out of left field in between the heart-sinking inanity of *Sergeants 3* and the sitcom cuteness of *Come Blow Your Horn*—is nothing less than the pinnacle of his considerable acting art, in a film whose power remains undiminished by the decades.

"Following his own acting mantra to listen intently and react spontaneously, Sinatra is completely convincing in delineating all the different aspects of Marco's character," Tom Santopietro writes. "Sinatra's Bennett Marco stands as a perfectly wrought example of the disillusioned modern American male in post–World War II twentieth-century America."

The famous sequence in which Marco meets Janet Leigh's character, Rosie, begins as he sits in the lounge car of a train headed to New York, a twitching, sweaty wreck, struggling and failing to light a cigarette while Rosie looks on. She has no idea, of course, that he is on mental disability leave from the army: recurrent nightmares about his brainwashing in Korea have undone him. Finally exasperated, he bolts, knocking over a table as he goes, then pauses in the space between two cars, trying to gather himself. She follows him. In an act of stunning sexual directness, she lights a cigarette, takes it out of her mouth, and hands it to him. As he perspires and evades her eyes, the two proceed to have a surpassingly bizarre dialogue.

"Maryland's a beautiful state," she begins.

"This is Delaware," Marco answers.

"I know," she says. "I was one of the original Chinese workmen who laid the track on this stretch."

The talk proceeds in similarly surreal fashion—she just as bright-eyed and animated as if it all made perfect sense, he dull-eyed and disconnected—until she abruptly changes course. After asking if he's married, she volunteers, "I live at 53 West 54th Street. Apartment 3B. Can you remember that?"

"Yes," he answers, all but inaudibly.

"Eldorado 5-9970," she says. "Can you remember that?"

"Yes," he whispers, looking guilty, haunted, exhausted—a shell of a man, like the broken prisoner of war he once was. Even Frank's picturesque portrayal of a desperate drug addict in *The Man with the Golden Arm,* beautifully acted but Acted with a capital A, comes nowhere near the power of this emptiness. What could account for it? Who knew he had it in him?

The picture premiered on October 12 in Los Angeles, in New York on the twenty-fourth, and reviewers were appropriately awed. *Variety's* Anby wrote, "Every once in a rare while a film comes along that 'works' in all departments, with story, production and performance so well blended that the end effect is one of nearly complete satisfaction. Such is *The Manchurian Candidate.*" Many of the notices singled out Frank for praise. *The New Yorker* raved, "The acting is all of a high order, and Sinatra, in his usual uncanny fashion, is simply terrific."

Uncanny is appropriate. But there was nothing usual about this performance.

Nor about the movie itself. George Axelrod hewed closely to Richard Condon's off-kilter dialogue (the train sequence between Marco and Rosie comes virtually straight from the novel), and John Frankenheimer deployed all his considerable skills: his intense psychological sensitivity, his effective use of strange camera angles (in one scene, we're looking up from the point of view of a character lying on the floor), and an acute sense, brought straight from television, of how to mount scenes in a way that felt jarringly real and strange at the same time. (Shooting in black and white heightened the effect.) The press-conference sequence in which James Gregory's Senator Iselin announces he has a list of known Communists in Congress is groundbreaking in its verisimilitude—with its cameras and cables and smoky atmosphere, it could have been created by no one but a TV veteran—and haunting in its depiction of the rot at the heart of American politics. Is it paranoid? Or realistic?

With its brutal scenes of brainwashing, cold-blooded murder, and diabolical conspiracies and its climactic presidential assassination plot—carried out by a rifleman with a telescopic sight—*The Manchurian Candidate* was both powerful enough to attract moviegoers and upsetting enough that viewers needed to distance themselves from it. In his *Los Angeles Times* review, John L. Scott wrote, "The picture is really fascinating despite its rather far-fetched premise and wholesale slaughter during later passages, and if you're looking for a wild-and-woolly horror film fare—with psychological sidelights and political background—this is it."

At the moment he wrote the words, and for many months to come, political reality would trump any scenario even the most gifted filmmakers could create.

———

Two days after the Los Angeles premiere of *The Manchurian Candidate*, a U.S. Air Force U-2 spy plane obtained clear photographic evidence of what

Sinatra in his greatest movie role, as the brainwashed captain Bennett Marco in *The Manchurian Candidate*. His scenes with Janet Leigh are both profoundly moving and deliciously surrealistic.

military intelligence had been telling President Kennedy for months and what Premier Khrushchev had been assuring him was not the case: that the Soviets had installed medium-range and intermediate-range nuclear missiles in Cuba in direct defiance of the Monroe Doctrine. Demanding an immediate dismantling of the missile sites, Kennedy instituted a military blockade of the waters and airspace around the island. In the meantime, the Joint Chiefs of Staff urged an all-out invasion of Cuba and an overthrow of Castro.

For the next thirteen days, in the course of which Soviet ships attempted to run the blockade and a Russian missile shot down an American U-2, the world seemed to hover on the brink of nuclear annihilation. On Monday night, October 22, the president gave a nationally televised address announcing the discovery of the missiles, saying, "It shall be the policy of this nation to regard any nuclear missile launched from Cuba against any nation in the Western Hemisphere as an attack by the Soviet Union on the United States, requiring a full retaliatory response upon the Soviet Union."

On that same night, Frank Sinatra and Sammy Davis Jr., along with an orchestra conducted by Billy May, made a recording of their popular nightclub duet "Me and My Shadow." Despite the racist overtones, it's a jaunty and infectious rendition; Frank and Sammy are in great voice, May's arrangement kicks, and the harmonizing and clever (and updated) repartee are charming:

> *We're closer than smog when it clings to L.A.,*
> *We're closer than Bobby is to JFK.*

At the same time, Frank was preparing (as best he could) for nuclear war. Over the weekend, while he was in Palm Springs, White House press secretary Pierre Salinger had called to say there might be big trouble—a striking gesture from an administration that had officially distanced itself from Sinatra. Frank's daughter Nancy remembered that her father phoned her and her husband, Tommy Sands, in New York, telling them to pack a suitcase and watch the president's speech on television that night. They should be ready to leave, Sinatra said, the moment the broadcast was over.

What Frank knew was that President Kennedy was going to announce a military blockade of Cuba. Pierre Salinger had told Sinatra that if the Russians launched a retaliatory missile strike on Washington, missiles would hit New York, too. Frank told his daughter that he had a family survival plan in place: the Sinatras would fly from airstrip to airstrip aboard his jet, which he'd stocked with food and drink.

Tina Sinatra, then fourteen, remembered "fear and chaos [running] through the halls of Marymount," her private school. Irving "Sarge" Weiss, Sanicola's replacement as Frank's factotum, took her home, and Big Nancy drove with her younger daughter to Palm Springs. "Dad flew in and met us at the Compound," Tina recalled. "Nancy and Tommy were in from back east. We spent most of the weekend watching Huntley and Brinkley or Walter Cronkite, and I remember how somber Mom and Dad seemed for those few days. My father was calm but strictly business, as if gauging our next step."

Unable to fathom the gravity of the situation, Tina writes, she mainly had a good time, enjoying the temporary family togetherness. But she also remembered "stores of canned food and water that had been laid in" and the map her father had drawn "of the region's deserted airstrips, just in case we needed to use his plane."

Methodical Frank even took the time to track down Juliet Prowse in Manhattan. "I don't know how he found out where I was," she recalled, "but he called me at my hotel and said: 'I want you to get out of New York City because it's going to be blown apart.'" She told him she planned to take her chances.

Prowse, and everyone else in the world, lucked out. On October 27, after a two-week chess game involving many bluffs and much maneuvering all around to save face, Kennedy and Khrushchev agreed to a truce. The Soviets removed their missiles from Cuba in exchange for an American pledge not to invade; the United States also secretly removed its missiles from Turkey and southern Italy.

"On the set of 'Come Blow Your Horn,' Frank Sinatra is the most relaxed he's been in years," Louella Parsons wrote on October 29.

> One reason has to be the dialogue dreamed up by Norman Lear and Bud Yorkin, which included a scene that repeatedly broke up Sinatra and the whole company.
> Dan Blocker, who weighs in at 270 pounds and stands 6'4", suspects Frank of making a play for his screen wife, Phyllis McGuire. Dan drawls: "If ah evva catch you 'round my wife, ah'm gonna stomp a mud hole in you and wade you dry!"

The inside joke, of course, being that in real life six-four and 270 pounds were as nothing next to Sinatra's power.

Tony Bill, who would continue acting for a while after *Come Blow Your Horn*, then became a successful producer and director, has long remembered his first motion picture as one of the most pleasant shoots in his career. "It was low-key, it was fun, it was civil," he recalled. He attributed this directly to the ease of Sinatra and Bud Yorkin's collaboration.

"Bud was clearly not in control in the literal sense, because Sinatra had the power to overrule people," Bill said. "But I didn't notice him using that power very often."

He didn't have to. Yorkin amused him, the story amused him, and nobody had to kill themselves to make this picture. He could afford to treat the help well. A sensitive and bookish young man, Tony Bill was too naïve to be intimidated by Sinatra. "I came out of a Catholic men's college," he said. "I didn't relate to dressing nattily. I didn't relate to cool language, the Sinatra argot. I didn't relate to gangsters and dangerous women. I didn't relate to the trappings of that level of success."

With his sensitive antennae, Frank picked this up and respected it, taking the quarter-century-younger actor under his wing. He was "kind of avuncular," Bill recalled. "Thoroughly professional and courteous and often solicitous." Frank now and then included Bill and his then wife in dinner groups; he even flew the young couple, on the *Christina,* out to the Palm Springs compound one weekend.

"It was like visiting a very, very posh hotel, the owner of which was home but busy," Bill said. "I remember being enormously impressed by the fact that the bathroom was completely stocked with everything you could want. Not having been in any swell hotels in my life up to that point, it was a revelation that somebody could be that careful."

The young actor took careful note of the contours of Sinatra's superstardom. "He was the first movie star I met that had what I call the 'invisible protective shield,'" Bill said. "It is permanent, as far as I can tell. It's not something you turn on and turn off. It's a natural human response to stardom—as natural as responses to brainwashing are. I don't think that these people have become dehumanized altogether, but I think their ability to relate to other people on a totally non-star level becomes eroded to the point of nonexistence over a period of time—just like solitary confinement or torture. It's a reverse torture—the torture of privilege. To be fawned over, to have all your jokes laughed at, to never be criticized, never wait for anything, never want for anything—all of that stuff I found to be kind of an embarrassment. But there is almost no human way to resist it."

For all Frank's power, though, he had little control over those other plans Sam Giancana had made for him.

Villa Venice was a big, upscale Italian restaurant in the leafy village of

Wheeling, Illinois, a dozen miles north of Chicago. In the 1920s, it had been a major nightclub, hosting many of the jazz bands of the era; then the club closed, leaving a cavernous space perfect for catered affairs. It was the kind of place where a gangland wedding reception might be held, and where more than one had been held.

Giancana was a part owner of the Villa, though as usual other men fronted for him. In early 1962, he spent a great deal of money—some reports said as much as $250,000—to restore the place to its former glory as a nightclub, with actual canals, to be plied by actual gondoliers, out front, and a showroom capable of seating eight hundred. He planned to recoup his investment, and then some, and his idea was simple.

History had shown that nightclubs were a dying business—except in Vegas and Tahoe, where legal casinos could make up the revenue that the show-rooms lost to high-priced bookings. Mooney's scheme (hatched, astoundingly, under the nose of Bobby Kennedy) was to open a distinctly extralegal casino in a Quonset hut two blocks from the Villa Venice, for one month only—blink and you'd miss it—and to draw the high-rolling suckers with two of the big-gest acts in show business: first, Eddie Fisher, and then the Clan itself, Frank, Dean, and Sammy.

Giancana told Frank to take care of it; Frank took care of it.

"I was singing at the Latin Casino [near Philadelphia] when I got the call from Frank in August 1962," Fisher recalled. "It was the day Marilyn Monroe was found dead, and he was very upset. He said he wanted me to open for him at a club called the Villa Venice in Chicago. I said, 'Frank, I can't do it. I've been working too hard. I'm too tired to go to Chicago.' That wasn't good enough for Sinatra. He persisted until I said, 'All right. But I'm supposed to go back to the Desert Inn after I close at the [New York] Winter Garden. If you can get me out of that, I'll come to Chicago.' I thought I had the perfect excuse. Sinatra owned a piece of the Sands, one of the Desert Inn's chief com-petitors, and I was certain there was no way the Desert Inn would let me go. But somehow Frank arranged it."

Sinatra himself was not about to do Mooney's bidding without making a few demands in return. For one thing, he wanted Reprise to record the Sum-mit concerts: Frank figured the resulting LP would easily sell a million copies, netting him, at a profit of fifty cents per album, $500,000. In addition, he told the gangster, he and Dean would like a private train car to take them from Los Angeles to Chicago. In a wiretapped phone conversation, Giancana showed his frustration: "That Frank, he wants more money, he wants this, he wants that, he wants more girls, he wants . . . I don't need that or him . . . I broke my ass when I was talking to him in New York."

In the meantime, more than one newspaper declared that Sinatra was a partner in the Villa Venice, or even owned the place. ("Pretty soon, millionaire Frank will own everything," Sheilah Graham wrote.)

It has never been entirely clear whether Giancana paid the entertainers or demanded they work gratis. The gangster certainly had grounds to feel that Sinatra owed him, big-time, for helping Frank's buddy JFK win West Virginia and Illinois and for enduring the Kennedys' ingratitude afterward. And the attorney general was turning up the heat. After Eddie Fisher's October 31 opening at the Villa Venice, three FBI agents visited him in his hotel room, wanting to know what the singer could tell them about Giancana. The Feds were also curious about what Fisher was doing performing in Wheeling, Illinois. "Because a friend asked me to do him a favor," the singer told the agents. "I was paid next to nothing and even got stuck with a huge hotel bill at the Ambassador East. Doing favors for friends can be very expensive."

Sammy Davis (who himself owed Mooney $20,000, which the gangster had fronted him to buy jewelry) did a week at the Villa Venice after Fisher left, and then, on November 26, Frank and Dean joined him, filling out the Summit—and the showroom, in which, at least one article said, there had been empty seats during Sammy's stand.

For Frank, Dean, and Sammy—doing sixteen shows over seven nights—it was standing room only. "Lines snaked around the block from the unlikely nightclub's doors," Shawn Levy writes. "The Quonset hut casino was packed. The opening night crowd included a rogue's gallery of Chicago criminals: Marshall Caifano, Jimmy 'The Monk' Allegretti, Felix 'Milwaukee Phil' Alderisio, Willie 'Potatoes' Daddano, and, of course, Giancana, as well as Wisconsin gangster Jim DeGeorge and Joe Fischetti, Frank's guy from the Fontainebleau." The dapper crooks and their bouffanted dates sat in Italianate splendor in a showroom "sumptuously decorated with a thick burgundy carpet and discreetly tasteful wall furnishings."

For Sammy's week, the cover charge had been an already high $5 (the equivalent of about $40 today). For the Summit shows, the cover was doubled, and no smaller a party than ten could reserve a table; the Villa was making $100 a table per show before liquor and food were added. But Giancana made his real money at the Quonset hut, where the roulette wheels and craps and blackjack tables were all rigged.

Everything about the operation suggested an elegant sham; much of the show was done with a nudge and a wink. On opening night, Dean Martin ambled out onto the showroom floor, glass in hand, and, after delivering his usual line ("How long I been on?"), began to sing a parody of "When You're Smiling":

When you're drinking, when you're drinkin',
The show looks good to you.

He then segued into a takeoff (special lyrics by his pal Sammy Cahn) on "The Lady Is a Tramp":

I love Chicago, it's carefree and gay,
I'd even work here without any pay.

The audience ate it up. Then, after Dean had mellowed them down with only half-joking renditions of "Volaré" and "On an Evening in Roma," Frank came out and worked them up again, emerging to the bouncing beat of "Goody Goody"—Matty Malneck, the composer himself, was leading the band—as the men applauded fervently and the women screamed. As was so often the case when he performed this song, his pitch was all over the place, but it didn't matter: it was Sinatra.

Among the ringside couples were Sam Giancana and Judy Campbell. The two had become deeply involved that fall, despite his continuing relationship with Phyllis McGuire; according to Campbell, Mooney had even helped her get an abortion for the child she claimed she'd conceived with Jack Kennedy. Now, as Sam and Judy listened to Frank working his magic, the mobster was as entranced as anyone else in the room: in the end, he too was a fan.

————

The FBI also interviewed Frank while he was in town, but all he would tell them was that he was doing the shows as a favor for the nominal owner, Leo Olsen, who was an old Chicago friend. The agents tried to talk with Dean too, but he made himself scarce. Sammy, though, was just cowed enough by the pair of beefy white guys with suits and badges to let them into his suite at the Ambassador East one morning. When the agents asked him why he had turned aside lucrative nightclub gigs to work for free, he offered to fix them a drink—they declined—then took one himself.

"Baby, that's a very good question," Davis said. "But I have to say it's for my man Francis."

"Or friends of his?"

"By all means."

"Like Sam Giancana?"

"By all means."

The agents asked Davis to elaborate. "Baby, let me say this," the entertainer said. "I got one eye, and that one eye sees a lot of things that my brain tells me

I shouldn't talk about. Because my brain says that, if I do, my one eye might not be seeing anything after a while."

———

The last show was December 2; the trio left town. Dinah Shore had been scheduled to open next, but she mysteriously canceled at the last minute. On the third, just before it was to be raided by the Illinois State Police, the Quonset hut shut down, and the Villa Venice closed its restaurant and nightclub operations for good. From that day forth, it would operate solely as a catering hall. FBI wiretaps later discovered that Sam Giancana had cleared $3 million, tax-free, in the course of his lucrative November.

"Good thing Peter Lawford did not appear at the Villa Venice in Chicago with others of 'The Clan,'" Sheilah Graham wrote in her December 11 column. "Because of the current investigation of the nearby floating crap game, and the fact that the Villa Venice was reopened for only one month . . . Also I've been told that Sinatra picked up the hotel tab for his group, to the tune of $5,000 for one week. The whole business sounds somewhat odd."

19

||||||||||||

I don't know what other singers feel when they articulate lyrics,
but being an 18-karat manic-depressive and having lived a
life of violent emotional contradictions, I have an overacute
capacity for sadness as well as elation.

—MIKE SHORE, WRITING AS FRANK SINATRA IN THE FEBRUARY
1963 *PLAYBOY* INTERVIEW

Ava had turned forty on Christmas Eve: a difficult enough age for any woman in that prefeminist era, but a crushing passage for a screen goddess. Her self-esteem and her professional ambitions sinking, she continued to drift, scattering picturesque wreckage in her wake. In the latter half of the year, she'd made a rotten historical drama called 55 *Days at Peking*; in the course of the shoot, she had thoroughly alienated much of the cast and crew, especially her co-star Charlton Heston; possibly caused the director, Nicholas Ray, to have a heart attack; and suffered a kind of breakdown herself, suddenly finding it impossible to remember her lines.

She somehow finished the picture and even managed to get hired for a new one, Blake Edwards's *Pink Panther*, but her outrageous demands and impossible behavior got her dismissed as a bad bet before shooting began. One night in Paris around this time, she went to eat at the fabled restaurant Tour d'Argent, where the tall and dashing owner, Claude Terrail, greeted her personally.

"Do you remember me, Claude?" Ava asked. "I came here once long ago."

"I remember very well," Terrail said. "You came with Frank Sinatra."

They had a drink, a talk, and then they had an affair, for the next seven or eight months. "Claude Terrail was no naïf, no stranger to glamorous women or to the eccentric lives of show-business celebrities," writes Gardner's biographer Lee Server. He was an international playboy, he had seen and done many things, but he had never experienced anything like Ava's enduring fascination with Frank. "She would put one of his records on and have a private talk with him, as he was singing," Terrail recalled. "She would sit and listen and say, 'Yes, yes, I know . . .' or, 'No, don't say that . . . you must forget . . .' She would have a talk with the record itself. It was something almost mystical."

Theirs was a jet-set romance: in Paris, Madrid, America, the Pacific. "Always she liked to go," Terrail said, "to run, run, run. Keep on running." And even though she couldn't quite quit her old ways ("Ava Gardner and Yves Montand raising Basin Street eyebrows in a secluded corner," Walter Winchell wrote on January 16), the restaurateur managed to whisk her off for a charmed—and cursed—week in Hawaii. Ava shared one striking character-istic with her ex-husband: when she was sober, she could be sweetness itself, and when she wasn't, the anger and craziness came on fast. And now that she feared her looks were going, she was drinking more than ever.

"We stayed at a villa," Terrail recalled. "In Waikiki. A lovely house. A great time and also terrible. There is a wonderful drink in Hawaii—a mai tai. She loved mai tais. One is perfect. Two, okay. Three, four, too many. She would become unhappy, always fighting . . . In Hawaii every night Frank Sinatra called. It was difficult. He did not speak well of me. He would say to her, 'What are you doing there with that son-of-a-bitch? Do you know what I have heard about him?'"

———

By the twenty-first, the papers were reporting she was back in Los Angeles, where she underwent what was termed minor surgery at Cedars-Sinai Medi-cal Center. "The hospital didn't disclose the nature of the operation or where Miss Gardner is staying," the Associated Press reported. "She has a sister, Bea, who lives here."

She had an ex-husband who lived there, too. On February 3, Frank and Ava were sighted together in the gallery of a golf tournament on his home course, the Tamarisk Country Club in Palm Springs.

———

On January 1, the newspapers announced that Nelson Riddle, finally liberated from Capitol Records, had signed with Reprise. Three weeks later, he and Frank celebrated by getting together and recording two numbers, the Cahn–Van Heusen theme for *Come Blow Your Horn* and another new tune by Sammy and Chester, "Call Me Irresponsible."

Yet if Frank and Ava couldn't simply pick up where they'd left off, neither could Frank and Nelson. The infinitely sensitive arranger was still smarting from Sinatra's infidelities, especially the fling with Don Costa. Maybe Riddle could have evoked the spirits of Debussy and Ravel in his charts, had the songs commanded. But the songs were mid-level Cahn and Van Heusen: the first jauntily mediocre, and the second sweetly sentimental. A return to great-ness wasn't in the cards—not yet, at any rate.

Come Blow Your Horn was a cute title for a play and a movie, but what did it mean, anyway? Nobody involved with the picture seems to have seen it as anything but a light Hollywood entertainment. Sammy Cahn and Jimmy Van Heusen, on the other hand, took their position as house songwriters to the swinger in chief very seriously, hence a tune that aspires to the heights of "Come Fly with Me" but is instead thoroughly earthbound:

> *Make like a Mister Milquetoast and you'll get shut out,*
> *Make like a Mister Meek and you'll get cut out.*

The lyrics were Cahn at his arch and didactic worst; the tune was jaunty but indifferent, and Riddle, not having much to work with, couldn't do much with it.

"Call Me Irresponsible" was a more complicated matter. Cahn and Van Heusen wrote it, around this time, for Fred Astaire to sing in a movie called *Papa's Delicate Condition,* a schmaltzy comedy set in turn-of-the-century Texas about a ne'er-do-well father and his adoring young daughter. Cahn's lyric

> *Call me irresponsible, call me unreliable,*
> *Throw in undependable, too*

read like a personal confession of his own (considerable) shortcomings as a husband and father, and Van Heusen's melody is lovely, though second-rate. ("Here's That Rainy Day" is great; "Call Me Irresponsible" is pretty good.) Put together, words and music make a song with syrupy appeal—enough to win it an Oscar after the movie (which wound up starring Jackie Gleason rather than Astaire) came out.

Sinatra gives a beautiful reading of the song, and Riddle (who himself had deep-seated misgivings about his worth as a husband and father) has written a heartfelt arrangement, but the fit is off. For Frank, confession is akin to apology: an unnatural act. And Nelson's greatest ballad charts for Sinatra are love songs and torch songs—two sides of the same coin for Frank—into which the arranger could project his own tormented romantic yearnings. Frank wasn't really torching for Ava anymore, nor was she for him, not the same way. Each could still pique the other's jealousy, and they would always matter enormously to each other, but they were both middle-aged now: still filled with immortal longings, but looking square at mortality.

At the end of the first week of February, despite the torrid affair Frank was alleged to be having with the actress Rhonda Fleming, he flew to New York with his wounded Ava and then, at least temporarily, parted company with her.

He'd come east to celebrate his parents' golden wedding anniversary on the ninth by throwing them a lavish party; in the meantime, as many newspapers eagerly reported, he had bought Dolly and Marty a big house in a fancy section of Fort Lee—in prosperous Bergen County, a big move up in the world—and also had given his mother a $25,000 diamond bracelet from Tiffany, delivered in an armored truck.

They were a little old couple now, sixty-nine and sixty-seven—both had been teenagers when they'd married, much against Dolly's parents' wishes, in 1913—and they were living in quiet retirement, far from the battles of the past. Both were fiercely proud of their spectacularly successful only child, Dolly vociferously so (she had a disconcerting tendency, when speaking to others, to refer to her son as "Frank Sinatra," always the two names), Marty in his gruff and silent way.

Both were also intensely ambivalent about what they, and fortune, and Frank himself, had wrought.

When he was a boy, Dolly had both spoiled him and whacked him when he got out of line—sometimes with a nightstick kept behind the bar of the Hoboken saloon the couple had run for a while. "She was a pisser," he recollected to Shirley MacLaine. "She scared the shit outta me. Never knew what she'd hate that I'd do." Once he became Frank Sinatra, her physical control over him ended, but she continued to speak her mind and make demands. "I remember Dolly as a warm and fun-loving grandmother—and as a self-serving, rough-and-ready woman who perpetually had her hand out," Tina Sinatra wrote.

As for Marty, "Grandpa didn't believe in things that came easy, like Dad's singing," Tina continued. "He wanted his son to go to college and become an engineer; he couldn't endorse Dad's lofty dreams."

A human-interest reporter paying a visit to the redbrick house the couple still occupied in Weehawken found the place astonishingly modest ("For the [parents] of a millionaire singing-acting star, it would seem an incredibly tiny house, even to visit, but it is spotlessly clean and its five-by-10 foot 'front yard' immaculately planted") and Dolly uncharacteristically reserved. "I'm sorry, I haven't time to talk now," she said. "I'd like to, but I can't."

It was not the nature of convivial, rarely reticent Mrs. Sinatra, long known as "Lady Bountiful" in rundown New Jersey waterfront towns for her welfare and political activities, to be "too busy to talk."

But next Saturday there is to be a great celebration here, marking the 50th anniversary of her wedding to Martin Sinatra.

And it is understood that if the details are not kept in strict secrecy, fans of her only son may overrun the town and Frankie will cancel his plans to fete his parents.

Dolly's tongue must have hurt from biting it. Ordinarily, she had no problem speaking her mind. As George Jacobs recalled, "I've never heard a woman curse like Dolly. 'Fuck you, you fucking asshole son of a bitch fucking bastard motherfucker,' was a typical Dolly sentence. It probably came in handy when she needed to muscle up votes or favors." The old ward heeler in her was easily tapped. Frank had left the invitation list up to her, and she had asked three hundred Hobokenites, with two notable exceptions: her own sister, Frank's favorite aunt, Josie Monaco, who'd infuriated Dolly by telling a *Look* magazine reporter in 1957 that Dolly was an absentee mother to her lonely son; and Frank's godfather Frank Garrick, who'd fired the young Sinatra from a newspaper job in 1932. Neither Dolly nor Frank had ever forgiven him. "My son is like me," Dolly liked to say. "You cross him, he never forgets."

Another striking absence from the anniversary festivities was Ava's. Dolly and she adored each other. (Ava, too, swore like a sailor.) But she and Frank had plainly reached some sort of accommodation. Over the next week, they were spotted together and separately around town in Manhattan. "Everything happens to Frank Sinatra—including his ex-wife Ava Gardner," Earl Wilson wrote on Valentine's Day.

> Ava showed up while he was here celebrating his parents' 50th wedding anniversary—and Frank took her to dinner at La Scala with his dtr. Nancy Jr. and her husband Tommy Sands . . . Ava folded by 1:30 a.m. though—and Frank went on to his hangout, Jilly's, which had the biggest crowd in town . . . mostly people who wanted to have a look at the Thin Swinger.

A few days later, the columnist observed, "Ava Gardner has become almost Greta Garboish in her passion for privacy. After having supper here with ex-husband Frank Sinatra, she went back into her shell."

And a couple of days after that: "Ava Gardner, hair straight back, wearing little makeup, and very beautiful, emerged from seclusion to watch Lena Horne at the Waldorf and Peter Duchin at the St. Regis—with her sister and brother-in-law . . . and no beau of her own."

Five days later, not surprisingly, she had found company: "Ava Gardner and Peter Duchin visited the Colony, El Morocco and Lena Horne's packed house show at the Waldorf."

But Frank was long gone by then, back to Los Angeles and Nelson.

For his first Reprise album with Riddle, Frank decided to go big. *The Concert Sinatra* (so named for the size of the orchestra, not because it was a live album) was recorded over four nights, from February 18 to 21, on a soundstage at Goldwyn Studios, with the largest group of instrumentalists ever to back a popular singer, seventy-three pieces. (Frank junior says there were more than eighty.) Felix Slatkin, Sinatra's concertmaster and musical guiding light, was not among them. On February 8, the master violinist had died of a heart attack, at age forty-seven, the victim of a lifetime of bad habits. His loss tore a gaping rent in Frank's artistic life. Both for his own sake and for hers, "as a kind of work therapy to keep her from being overcome with grief," Will Friedwald writes, Sinatra insisted that Eleanor Slatkin participate in the making of the LP. "Unless she agrees to play," Frank said, "I won't do the album."

The album is gorgeous. Not to everybody's taste; perhaps too grandiose for those who like their Sinatra intimate or swinging. But Riddle, inspired by the great canvas afforded him, rose to the occasion, writing charts that contained both majestic vistas (listen to the cosmic, three-quarters-of-a-minute intro to Kurt Weill and Maxwell Anderson's "Lost in the Stars," from the Broadway musical of the same name) and unexpected intimacies (Rodgers and Hammerstein's "I Have Dreamed," from *The King and I*).

Besides the Weill-Anderson, the other seven tracks on the album were all in the Rodgers-Hart-Hammerstein domain and all also from Broadway: Rodgers and Hart's "My Heart Stood Still," from *A Connecticut Yankee;* Kern and Hammerstein's "Ol' Man River," from *Show Boat;* Rodgers and Hart's "Bewitched, Bothered, and Bewildered," from *Pal Joey;* and Rodgers and Hammerstein's "You'll Never Walk Alone" and "Soliloquy," from *Carousel*. They were theatrical pieces, because it was a theatrical album.

And no song was more theatrical than the great 1945 "Soliloquy." Sung by *Carousel's* antihero, the wastrel Billy Bigelow, the formidably lengthy aria to fatherhood demanded both vocal and dramatic skills of the highest order. Frank had recorded it for Columbia in 1946, taking two separate sessions to lay down the nearly eight-minute tune: it was released by the label's Masterworks (classical) division as two sides of a twelve-inch 78 rpm record. In 1955, he prerecorded the song, and three others in the score, for the movie version of *Carousel,* then walked off the picture, leaving the tapes in legal limbo. (Only one number, the Sinatra–Shirley Jones duet of "If I Loved You," has been heard since.)

Frank's tantrum on the set of *Carousel* was not only his loss but also the movies': he would have made a terrific Billy Bigelow. Yet even then, at age thirty-nine, he was getting a little old for the part. Now he was forty-seven, far too old to portray Billy on-screen, but the perfect age to sing him. A comparison of the 1946 and 1963 versions of "Soliloquy" tells the story in an instant: on the Columbia record (arranged by Axel Stordahl), Sinatra sings beautifully, but the youth in his voice detracts from the character's raffishness. On the Reprise track, the first sound of Frank's middle-aged baritone raises goose bumps: this is it. The years and the tears have given him the authority to sing this song.

And he brings it off with seeming effortlessness, even though the eight-minute-five-second-long number was taped (on 35-millimeter film) in sections, because, as Riddle later recalled, "it was such an incredibly taxing thing." The song is a triumph for both singer and arranger. Friedwald writes, "The Reprise version is about balances: Sinatra striking the right mix of aggressiveness and tenderness, Riddle finding the border between Broadway bravura and his own, less earthbound imagination." The same could be said about the entire album.

"Soliloquy" has been recorded by many other singers—by Sammy Davis Jr. and Mel Tormé in the 1960s; more recently by the Broadway stars Brian Stokes Mitchell and Mandy Patinkin and the bass-baritone Bryn Terfel. But Sinatra is Sinatra. No version besides his can reasonably be called definitive.

You can have fun with a son,
But you've got to be a father to a girl.

—Rodgers and Hammerstein, "Soliloquy"

Singing about fatherhood was one thing; being a father was something else. With his two daughters, Frank Sinatra appears to have found an equilibrium between doting and distance, making up with warmth what he couldn't provide in presence. Though he was absent most of the time, both Nancy and Tina seem to have lived with the expectation that he'd always be back, if only for a visit. (Their mother seems to have felt the same way.)

The same cannot be said about the unfortunate boy who both did and didn't bear his father's name. When Frank Sinatra left his young family for Ava Gardner in 1949, little Franklin Wayne Emanuel Sinatra[*] was five years old— "the worst possible time," his younger sister recalled. "My brother understood just enough to draw the loss inside. He felt bewildered and abandoned and quietly traumatized. I think that his world just fell apart."

As a little boy, Frankie was "cute, smart, and funny, the life of every party,"

---

[*] In the 2015 HBO documentary *Sinatra: All or Nothing at All,* Frank junior claimed— contrary to what had long been believed—that he was actually named Francis at birth.

Tina writes. "When he was ten or eleven, he'd perform for anyone who'd listen, and mimic Dad's TV appearance word for word."

By the time adolescence set in, though, so had a certain gravity. The thirteen-year-old who played the piano for Louella Parsons and others at a 1957 dinner party given by his mother pontificated about his distaste for rock 'n' roll and his love of the standards. He was still copying Frank senior, only less charmingly.

Aping his father was the one way Frankie could be close to him: any other intimacy wasn't in the cards. The awkward distance between Marty Sinatra and Frank had replicated itself in the relationship between Frank and his son. "They shared a certain shyness with each other," Tina writes. "That wasn't so unusual for fathers and sons of the time, but I think that Frankie needed something more."

With adolescence, he became isolated and troubled. He fell in with bad company, got arrested for shooting out streetlamps with a BB gun. His mother decided that there were only two options for him: to go live with his father or to be sent to boarding school. The first, of course, was not an option at all. He was packed off to a boarding school in the San Jacinto Mountains west of Palm Springs.

"Until September 1958, when I was put into a college preparatory school, my life with the family was very, very normal," Junior later said. "Once outside the inner circle, my position within was never re-established."

He would spend much of the rest of his life trying to reestablish his position within. The means were both simple and impossible: Frankie had spent enough time watching his father perform in recording studios, on movie sets, and in clubs to know that he wanted, somehow, to follow him into the business. He'd continued playing piano, and he had real talent: at first, he thought he might become a songwriter. Given the crushing burden he bore, it might have been wiser to go into almost any other field—to teach college, say (he was fascinated with military history)—but it was need, rather than wisdom, that propelled him: he wanted to be close to his father, even if his father had no idea how to be close to him.

By the fall of 1962, enrolled as a music student at the University of Southern California, Frankie found himself pulled in two directions. His parents were urging him to finish college. But that summer at Disneyland, he'd spontaneously asked to sing with the Elliott Brothers dance band, a group of clean-cut guys in matching red jackets, and he had been a hit—billing himself as Frank Sinatra Jr. When Jack Benny, an old family friend, heard about Frankie's performance, he called Frank and asked whether Junior might appear on his television show. "If my son is going into show business," Frank told Jack, "there's no one I'd rather he would start with than you." At the beginning of October, Frankie appeared on *The Jack Benny Program,* singing a song and acting in a comedy sketch. The reviews were decent.

By the end of the year, Frank junior was thinking less and less about finishing his studies and more and more about singing and acting. "He's more of an actor than a singer," Frank senior told a reporter. "His tonal quality's pretty good. But he needs more training. He's studying music and I want him to finish college."

But Frank claimed it was all right with him if Frankie went into show business. "If that's what he wants," he said. "Actually he wants to be an actor, arranger and singer in that order. That's okay, but I want him to learn to sing. Wherever he goes, they're going to ask him to sing."

In March, the serious nineteen-year-old formally decided that was what he wanted to do, signing a contract with Sam Donahue, the saxophonist, trumpeter, and arranger who'd taken over the leadership of the Tommy Dorsey–less Tommy Dorsey Orchestra (a ghost band, in jazz-band parlance). "I don't expect to create as much emotional excitement—with all the swooning—as my father did," Frankie said earnestly. "But I certainly hope to be an asset to the band."

Ten days later, the Beatles' debut album, *Please Please Me,* was released in Great Britain.

———

Mike Shore was a West Coast advertising genius whose signal achievement in the 1940s and 1950s was turning a Los Angeles used-car dealer named Earl Muntz into the sales sensation and media personality known as Madman Muntz. Shore's ad campaigns for Muntz made him nationally famous, deploying all manner of gonzo strategies to sell automobiles—wild costumes, bizarre billboards, and off-the-wall stunts: on one TV commercial, Muntz threatened to destroy a car with a sledgehammer if it didn't sell by the end of the day.

Shore first became involved with Reprise Records through his brother Merle, who had been Norman Granz's art director at Verve. After Mo Ostin hired Merle Shore to art direct for Frank Sinatra's new record label, Mike found himself spending time around the office; advertising and promotional ideas quickly followed. It was Mike Shore who had come up with the fledgling label's name, partly inspired by the lyric to "April in Paris" ("April in Paris, this is a feeling/That no one can ever reprise"), as well as the famous *Billboard* ad ("A new, happier, *emancipated* Sinatra . . . untrammeled, unfettered, unconfined") that so irked Capitol. "Mike was absolutely brilliant," Ostin said. "One of the smartest guys."

Mike Shore also wrote speeches for Frank now and then—little things the Chairman might have to say at sales meetings, for example—and in this capacity Shore, a thoughtful, intensely intuitive man, got to spend some time around his boss. The experience always unsettled him. "I used to go to have lunch with him," he recalled, "and I was very nervous—you're having lunch with a legend."

But Shore was also fascinated by Sinatra, admiring much about him, including his liberal politics. In writing for the superstar, the adman came to empathize deeply with him. "There was a fellow who used to write little things for Bing Crosby, which he did on his *Kraft Music Hall;* somehow he was in Crosby's head," Shore said. "I felt that way about Sinatra, at least when I would meet with him. I really understood him. I knew him pretty well."

In late 1962, *Playboy* decided to run a full-length Frank Sinatra interview, and the magazine's editor, Hugh Hefner, assigned the celebrity journalist Joe Hyams to the job. Hefner had sent Hyams to interview Frank two years earlier, for the *Show Business Illustrated* piece about Sinatra's diverse enterprises. The lengthy article had been highly positive, even starry-eyed—and, in places, somewhat imaginative—about Frank's business acumen. But sometime since, for reasons unknown, Frank Sinatra had taken an intense dislike to Joe Hyams. He canceled the *Playboy* interview.

The photographer Billy Woodfield, who was close to both Hyams and Sinatra (and to Mike Shore), went to Frank to try to broker a peace. "Sinatra said, 'I don't want Hyams on it,'" Shore recalled. Frank then suggested that Woodfield write the entire interview himself. "This was on a Friday," Shore said. "Sinatra said, 'Let me see it on Monday. As long as you make it interesting.' So Saturday morning, real early in the morning, Woodfield is sitting there, trying to do [the interview]. And he called me because he was stuck."

Billy Woodfield was a photographer, not a writer. Mike Shore wasn't just a writer; he was the writer who had created Madman Muntz. "I never dreamt it would ever be published," Shore said. "But I sat there for about four hours and did the whole interview. The questions and the answers."

Woodfield took the completed manuscript to Frank on Monday. "Billy called me on Monday afternoon," Shore recalled. "He had just had lunch with Sinatra. He said, 'Sinatra loved the interview!' I said, 'Oh, come on.'"

It was true. Frank loved the interview because somehow, in a singular Saturday-morning stroke of brilliance, Mike Shore had managed to create on the page a version of Sinatra that was both true to life and better than life, the embodiment of all that the intellectually striving and self-doubting star yearned to be. Hip, hyper-articulate, piercingly intelligent, but always self-effacing, Shore's Frank held forth so believably—not only on what made him tick, but on great world topics like organized religion, nuclear disarmament, and Communist expansion—that the interview continues to be quoted to this day, the idea that these golden words issued from the lips of the Man himself not even up for debate.

And, great adman that he was, Shore made Frank's remarks incessantly quotable, creating several formulations that have entered the culture:

PLAYBOY: Many explanations have been offered for your unique ability—apart from the subtleties of style and vocal equipment—to communicate the mood of a song to an audience. How would you define it?

SINATRA: I think it's because I get an audience involved, personally involved in a song—because I'm involved myself. It's not something I do deliberately; I can't help myself. If the song is a lament at the loss of love, I get an ache in my gut, I feel the loss myself and I cry out the loneliness, the hurt and the pain that I feel.

PLAYBOY: Doesn't any good vocalist "feel" a song? Is there such a difference . . .

SINATRA: I don't know what other singers feel when they articulate lyrics, but being an 18-karat manic-depressive and having lived a life of violent emotional contradictions, I have an overacute capacity for sadness as well as elation. I know what the cat who wrote the song is trying to say. I've been there—and back. I guess the audience feels it along with me. They can't help it. Sentimentality, after all, is an emotion common to all humanity.

("As far as the 18-karat manic-depressive, I was really talking about myself as well," Shore recalled.)

When *Playboy* asked if he believed in God, Sinatra waxed (if possible) even more eloquent. "First: I believe in you and me," he said.

I'm like Albert Schweitzer and Bertrand Russell and Albert Einstein in that I have a respect for life—in any form. I believe in nature, in the birds, the sea, the sky, in everything I can see or that there is real evidence for. If these things are what you mean by God, then I believe in God. But I don't believe in a personal God to whom I look for comfort or for a natural on the next roll of the dice. I'm not unmindful of man's seeming need for faith; I'm for anything that gets you through the night, be it prayer, tranquilizers or a bottle of Jack Daniel's.

In years to come, the songwriters Kris Kristofferson ("Help Me Make It Through the Night") and John Lennon ("Whatever Gets You Through the Night") would both take note of Shore/Sinatra's deathless words.

Though Shore's version of Frank often whiplashed between blatant Rat Pack–ese ("Look, pal, is this going to be an ocean cruise or a quick sail around the harbor?") and what might gently be called excessive articulateness ("Our civilization, such as it is, was shaped by religion, and the men who aspire to public office anyplace in the free world must make obeisance to God or risk immediate opprobrium"), the *Playboy* interview was no mere tour de force; Shore really *got* Sinatra, as a man and as a great artist. As Frank's interview avatar put it,

> SINATRA: Most of what has been written about me is one big blur, but I
> do remember being described in one simple word that I agree with.
> It was in a piece that tore me apart for my personal behavior, but the
> writer said that when the music began and I started to sing, I was
> "honest." That says it as I feel it. Whatever else has been said about
> me personally is unimportant. When I sing, I believe. I'm honest.
> If you want to get an audience with you, there's only one way. You
> have to reach out to them with total honesty and humility. This isn't
> a grandstand play on my part; I've discovered—and you can see it
> in other entertainers—when they don't reach out to the audience,
> nothing happens. You can be the most artistically perfect performer
> in the world, but an audience is like a broad—if you're indifferent,
> endsville. That goes for any kind of human contact: a politician on
> television, an actor in the movies, or a guy and a gal. That's as true in
> life as it is in art.

This was spookily effective ghostwriting: Frank on the money, and to the life.

On the night of April 8, Frank hosted the thirty-fifth Academy Awards. In a show that began with technical difficulties (ABC's cameras were out of focus, and the sound was fuzzy), Sinatra, too, hit some clams at the start. He looked handsome and elegant at the podium, his deep tan contrasting nicely with his white tie, but, either overawed or underawed by the occasion (perhaps a little of both), he failed at first to make contact with the industry crowd, many of whom had welcomed him back to stardom on Oscar night 1954.

He began unfortunately, giving "a little lecture in show biz slang on making better pictures in Hollywood, using the 'Mona Lisa' as an example," the syndicated TV writer Cynthia Lowry wrote. "At one point, he referred to La Giaconda as 'that chick,' but the laughs never came."

Yet the show soon found its feet, and so did Frank. Just before the presentation of the Best Picture award (it would go to *Lawrence of Arabia*), he looked evenly at the camera and spoke his mind. "Before we get on with the big one, I'd like to take this opportunity to level, you might say. To speak for just a second to us—we in the picture business. I, for one, am frankly a little tired of all of the talk about editorials, quote, 'What's wrong with Hollywood?,' unquote. I'm sick about hearing of runaway productions and costs. And the star system, and how we need government subsidies. I know it and you know it—what we need are good pictures." There was scattered applause. "And the way to get good pictures, as I rather obliquely hinted earlier in the evening, is to get back into the Mona Lisa business." He raised an instructive forefinger. "*Individual* pictures, handmade with love and passion and care by individual picture makers. Not by banks or committees or accountants or lawyers or office boys or boards of directors who are really in the real-estate business, but by picture makers."

It was a curious note to strike. On the one hand, Sinatra stood on firm ground, having just released *The Manchurian Candidate*. On the other hand, incredibly enough, he was about to replumb cinematic depths he had already explored in *Sergeants* 3.

On the sixteenth, Hedda Hopper ran a curious item. "Frank Sinatra sold his eagle's nest home to John W. Kluge, president of Metromedia, who bought KTTV from the L.A. Times and has latched onto another station here," she wrote. "[Kluge] has a beautiful home in New York, wants this one for weekends when he flies out on business. Kluge didn't haggle over the price—Frankie got what he asked for."

John Kluge didn't have to haggle: he was a real-life tycoon, a media multimillionaire who bought and sold television stations. But why did Frank sell his eagle's nest, the Japanese-themed ultimate bachelor pad with its breathtaking views of the Valley to the north and the city to the south? He loved the place.

Nevertheless, he moved into a new pied-à-terre, an apartment in a handsome white-brick 1950s-moderne mini-complex (five units) at 882 North Doheny Drive, just over the line that today separates Beverly Hills from West Hollywood. The apartment house still stands today in pristine condition.

It was built around a central courtyard that was hidden from the street and guarded by a metal gate with a life-size Chinese lion sculpture behind it. Around the corner on Cynthia Street, the building had a garage; tenants could pull in and enter the structure without having to use the front entrance.

Even in an era before relentless, ubiquitous media surveillance of the famous and near famous, 882 North Doheny afforded privacy and understated luxury, serving as a discreet, low-key hideout for a number of interesting characters: Marilyn Monroe lived there twice, once in the early 1950s, around the time of the Wrong-Door Raid, and again toward the end, just before she moved to the Brentwood house in which she died.

Besides Monroe, the building housed, at various times, the playboy millionaire Bob Neal, who sometimes ran with Frank; the tragic Hollywood costume designer Irene (who later jumped to her death from the Roosevelt Hotel); *Time*'s Hollywood correspondent Ezra Goodman (who might have hoped to rustle up some scoops close to home); Sinatra's secretary Gloria Lovell; and Frank himself.

It did not, however, house George Jacobs.

In Jacobs's winsome and creative memoir, the valet and his co-writer assert that at the height of Frank's romance with Marilyn Monroe in 1961, Sinatra had to decide whether or not to live with Marilyn and chose not to. Instead, *Mr. S* claims, Frank moved Jacobs into 882 North Doheny, both to watch over Monroe and as a kind of "consolation prize," because Jacobs had just gone through an acrimonious divorce.

There are two problems with this assertion: first, Jacobs was divorced in the fall of 1963, over a year after Marilyn Monroe's death. And second, Betsy Duncan Hammes, a consistently reliable witness who resided at 882 North Doheny from 1959 to 1967, firmly asserted that George Jacobs never lived there. His memoir gains a certain spiciness, and a narrative vantage, from placing him in the building, but loses something more important: veracity.

Betsy Hammes encountered her new neighbor soon after he moved in in the spring of 1963 and under the homeliest of circumstances: Frank asked to borrow a cup of sugar. "I had some sugar cubes in a demitasse, and I put it by his door," she recalled. "A little later, my doorbell rang, and I found a bunch of wadded-up dollar bills, like $15, in a cup by my door. He'd left the wrong cup."

They soon became friends. "He was like any neighbor you'd have next door," Hammes said. "Like, I'd come in, he'd carry the groceries in for me. One time I had a table I was bringing in, and he carried it in for me."

Frank seemed a little lonely to her. He liked to cook late at night—"He was very good at pizzas and spaghettis and things like that," she remembered; "he always had all the sauce and stuff all ready"—and he liked to talk into the wee hours. "He was interesting," she said. "Complicated. He loved to learn, loved

knowledge; he loved crossword puzzles. Sometime
ner. He said, 'After I broke up with her, thank God

As to the inevitable question—Hammes was an a
she says, "We dated a few times, but our careers w
liked each other. That was it, basically. There was no
each other. And if we were there, we were there. It was

Asked if she had any idea why Frank Sinatra, the mo
in the world, had suddenly decided to pull up stakes ar   ⌐ numbler
digs across town, Hammes said she had no clue. We cannot know much more.
Reprise was heavily in the red; Cal-Neva was a money pit. And though movie
money and record money and nightclub money were always coming in, along
with profits from his various real estate and corporate investments, his overhead was considerable. He now owned three aircraft: the *Christina;* a new toy,
a tiny (four-passenger) Morane-Saulnier jet; and a Hughes 269A helicopter
(frequently piloted by his pal Van Heusen). Then there was the Palm Springs
compound and its domestic staff; the Essex Productions office and its corporate staff; Reprise and its staff. He had also just bought a new aerie in Manhattan: a two-floor penthouse, with a rooftop "playpen" and a spectacular view of
the East River, in a recently completed tower at the far end of Seventy-second
Street. In the spring of 1963, he might very well have been feeling stretched
thin.

But there was also this: in January 1962, Frank had applied for a permit to
install a concrete helicopter pad on his half-acre Bowmont Drive property—
much like the one he'd had built at the Palm Springs compound in anticipation of JFK's visit. The rise in his power had magnified his impatience: when
he wanted to be somewhere, he wanted to be there *now*. His L.A. neighbors,
fearing they'd be subjected to loud and frequent landings and takeoffs, had
objected to the proposed heliport. Vigorously. "Every time Frankie spits you
can hear it down at our house," one said. "The acoustics in the canyon are
better than those of Hollywood Bowl," said another. "This would be a definite
noise problem."

Forty nearby residents signed a petition against the helipad. The president of the Mulholland Property Owners Association said that if Sinatra were
allowed to build his, others would surely follow: "If you approve one you will
have to approve all." There were a lot of rich folks in those hills.

At a planning-board hearing, Mickey Rudin argued (Frank was not present) that his client needed the heliport to beat rush-hour traffic to LAX when
he made out-of-town trips. The lawyer said the use of the landing area would
be infrequent: "not more than 35 or 40 times a year." Which didn't sound
very convincing. In addition, Rudin said, Sinatra had pledged to make landing

le to any public or private agency in case of fire or flood disaster.
se would be no more than that caused by trucks or autos," the lawyer
rted, not very credibly.

Frank's application was rejected. And that was it for Bowmont Drive.

The spring and summer found him often following in his own footsteps. At the end of April, Frank and Nelson made a new LP, *Sinatra's Sinatra*, rerecording ten songs that had already been hits for him, mostly on Capitol ("In the Wee Small Hours of the Morning," "Young at Heart," "All the Way," "Witchcraft," "How Little We Know," "I've Got You Under My Skin"), but a couple of them—"Oh! What It Seemed to Be" and the Phil Silvers–Jimmy Van Heusen "Nancy (with the Laughing Face)"—from his Columbia days. He also redid his old radio sign-off "Put Your Dreams Away," which had appeared on both of his former labels, and Cahn and Van Heusen's "Second Time Around," his first single for Reprise, in 1960.

To sweeten the deal, Sinatra added to the final LP the original recordings of two of Cahn and Van Heusen's sugariest movie themes, 1961's "Pocketful of Miracles," complete with children's chorus (from the dreadful Frank Capra picture of the same name), and "Call Me Irresponsible."

The purpose of the album was nakedly strategic: to try to wrest the Sinatra market back to Reprise. In this sense, it would be a success upon its release in August, rising to number 8 on the *Billboard* chart and scoring Frank's first gold record on the new label and the first since 1960's *Nice 'n' Easy*.

Artistic success was a knottier matter. Did you really need to buy this album if you already owned the original records? Sinatra had considerable artistic pride (though with Capitol in the end he'd been willing to cut off his nose to spite his face): he genuinely wanted to make these remakes fresh and new, and to a minor extent he succeeded. His singing is mostly great here, and Riddle's charts, largely the same as before, are unbeatable. As Friedwald points out, the instrumental backings sound amazing in stereo (many of the numbers were originally recorded in mono). The songs themselves are a mixed bag.

"All the Way" and "In the Wee Small Hours of the Morning" not only are beautifully sung but possess a mature wisdom not quite present in the original recordings. The difference is especially striking in the new "Wee Small"; the only difference is that the first, Ava-soaked version was devastating, and the update is not. The new "I've Got You Under My Skin," with Dick Nash playing the famous Milt Bernhart solo (Bernhart had a soundtrack-recording date and couldn't reappear), is a solid, hard-driving stand-in for the original. The second

"Second Time Around" is quietly lovely. And the 1963 "Young at Heart" should displease nobody—except those who re-listen to the 1954 version and find it sprinkled with stardust and needing no improvement.

The new rendering of Carolyn Leigh and Cy Coleman's "Witchcraft," on the other hand, is a good enough reading that goes south fast as Sinatra strains for novelty. There's nothing horribly wrong with changing "that wicked witch-craft" to "that coo-coo witchcraft"; all it does is cheapen the line and focus attention on the singer as a celebrity rather than on the song itself. But Frank goes for a jazzy melodic improv on "It is such an ancient pitch" (the kind of thing Ella Fitzgerald could nail without batting an eyelash) that, ironically enough, goes badly off pitch. By the time he throws a lame Reginald Van Gleason imitation into the outro—"Ew, you're a fine witch"—one is put in mind of Orson Welles's famous remark to the playwright Abe Burrows about the movie version of *Guys and Dolls:* "They put a tiny turd on every one of your lines."

As for "Nancy (with the Laughing Face)" and "Oh! What It Seemed to Be," the less said, the better. Sometime in his dewy past, Frank had brought a sweetness and feeling to these old-fashioned tunes that was no longer his to supply.

The lives of Sinatra and Giancana continued to intertwine. In January, the FBI had interviewed Frank and Mickey Rudin, in the Sunset Boulevard offices of Essex Productions, about the finances of Cal-Neva. Rudin told the agents that expansion plans for the hotel would necessitate a cash infusion of some $4 million and that Essex/Park Lake planned to apply for a loan from the Teamsters' pension fund. "Both RUDIN and SINATRA advised they wished to go on record that there were no under-the-table payments of any kind involved, that this was a simple straight forward business transaction with sufficient collateral involved," the bureau's report stated.

But after the FBI reviewed the minutes of a September 1962 Teamsters meeting at which Jimmy Hoffa had personally rejected Mickey Rudin's loan application (Hoffa turned down Giancana's request for a Cal-Neva loan at around the same time), the bureau smelled a rat. Just where was Sinatra planning to come up with this $4 million?

On April 24, 1963, five days before Frank began the *Sinatra's Sinatra* sessions, the FBI's special agent in charge for Los Angeles wrote an impassioned memo to J. Edgar Hoover, asking permission to plant a wiretap in the entertainer's Palm Springs house—which, the special agent noted, was now his primary residence. "The Los Angeles Division during recent weeks has been in receipt of information that would tend to indicate the above-captioned individual apparently intends to spend more of his time in the Palm Springs area, than in Los Angeles," the letter begins. (Apparently, he'd been reading Hedda Hopper.)

The memo continued at great length, reminding Hoover—no doubt redundantly—of Frank's past and present associations with "some of the more infamous individuals of modern times," their exotic names rendered, FBI-style, in attention-getting, all-capital letters: "BONANNO of Phoenix, FISCHETTI of Miami," "the late WILLIE MORETTI of New Jersey," "LUCKY LUCIANO,"* "SAM 'MOONEY' GIANCANA," and "JOHNNY FORMOSA," who, the special agent pointed out, had "during the past season at Cal-Neva [been] present at Cal-Neva Lodge with apparently a great deal to say about its operation."

But as the document gathered length, reminding the director of things he also already knew—Giancana's disappointment in Sinatra's efforts to get the Kennedy administration to tone down its antiracketeering efforts; Sinatra's stakes in the Sands ("SINATRA is an owner of considerable points") and Cal-Neva ("at present [he] is about a 100% owner")—it looked more and more like a request to conduct a fishing expedition. The memo concluded, hopefully,

The long continued association of SINATRA as a possible front for investments for hoodlums of both national and international stature has led to the belief by this division that a confidential source if established in Palm Springs concerning SINATRA would undoubtedly develop information of extremely valuable intelligence nature, and furnish a picture of top level criminal investments and operations.

Authority is requested to conduct a preliminary survey to determine the feasibility of a misur [microphone surveillance] installation at SINATRA's residence in Palm Springs, California.

In a memo written on the same day the *Sinatra's Sinatra* sessions began, the director gave the special agent a firm slap on the wrist:

TO: SAC [special agent in charge], Los Angeles
FROM: Director, FBI
SUBJECT: FRANK SINATRA

---

* The memo failed to note that Sinatra's old pal Luciano was also deceased, having lived in exile for the remainder of his days after his 1946 deportation and succumbed to a heart attack in Naples in January 1962. Among the personal effects found in his apartment was a gold cigarette case with an affectionate inscription from Frank. See Gosch and Hammer, *Last Testament of Lucky Luciano*, p. 444.

"Francis Albert Sinatra" (True Name)
ANTI-RACKETEERING
Re your airtel 4/24/63.

Bureau authority not granted at this time to conduct a survey to determine the feasibility of a misur installation in Frank Sinatra's Palm Springs, California, residence. In the event you develop information which would warrant such an installation, you may resubmit your recommendations. You are reminded that all misurs must be completely justified.

A May 1 Bob Thomas column spun Frank's change of residence as a sign he'd mellowed. "After going at top speed for most of his 45 [sic] years, Frank seems to have found the secret of slowing down," Thomas wrote.

> Whereas he once appeared to be an opponent of fresh air, he is now an ardent golfer.
>
> The change in the Sinatra way of life was signaled by his move from his mountaintop bachelor's place to his home in Palm Springs. He has followed the move of Red Skelton, Dinah Shore and other stars who now make the desert their permanent home. He maintains a flat here for use when he is working.
>
> "The life down there is wonderful," he remarked . . . "It's the only way I can get complete relaxation. Even if I try to stay home at night here [Los Angeles], something always comes up so I have to go out. Down on the desert nobody can get to me. It's surprising what a difference that much distance can make." He covers the 125 miles in 27 minutes by his private plane.

Eleven days later, Frank went to Hawaii to relax with a friend who might have been even more in need of a rest than he was. Under the heading "HOTELS AND RESTAURANTS FREQUENTED BY SAM GIANCANA," the mobster's FBI file lists the "Sheridan [sic] Surfrider Hotel, Waikiki Beach, Hawaii," and begins, "GIANCANA, under the name of J. J. BRACKETT, stayed in the Surfrider Hotel in the company of FRANK SINATRA from May 12, 1963 until May 16, 1963."

Three days after that, Frank was running hard again, flying to New York to do a benefit for the blind at Carnegie Hall, then making a quick turnaround to begin shooting a movie that would show his exquisite work in *The Manchurian Candidate* to have been a distinguished anomaly.

————

The name of the picture was *4 for Texas*: another craps-themed title in the Rat Pack series that had begun with *Ocean's 11* and continued with *Sergeants 3*. At this point, crap was more like it. The latest installment, a Western spoof, was to star just Frank and Dean, only one of whom knew how to do comedy. Anita Ekberg and Ursula Andress were on hand as eye candy. (Warner Bros. had offered Sophia Loren a cool million for just four weeks' work on the picture; she'd wisely declined.) Robert Aldrich was the director (and co-producer and co-screenwriter), and he was an accomplished pro. He had helmed the noir classics *Kiss Me Deadly, The Big Knife,* and *What Ever Happened to Baby Jane?*; he'd also made successful Westerns (*Apache, Vera Cruz*) and World War II adventures (*Attack, Ten Seconds to Hell*). He had handled big egos like Bette Davis and Joan Crawford and tough guys like Burt Lancaster, Jack Palance, and Lee Marvin. But the man who said that a director "needs the power not to be interfered with and the power to make the movie as he sees it" had never encountered Frank Sinatra before.

Aldrich had also never directed broad comedy before, and Western spoofs are tricky under the best of circumstances, and the circumstances on the shoot of *4 for Texas* were far from ideal. The newly relaxed and desert-dwelling Frank sounded an ominous note in mid-June. "Sinatra, tanned and rested, tells me he's taken up golf; is on the links every morning," Hedda Hopper wrote. "He doesn't dig these crazy people who go all over the world to make pictures. Even resents having to go to the Mojave desert for 'Four for Texas.'"

"Resents" was accurate. Unlike the untried Bud Yorkin, Robert Aldrich refused to jolly Frank along; what was worse, the director was uncomfortable making a comedy and refused to admit it. Sinatra, exquisitely intuitive, sensed Aldrich's unease and elected to torment him by putting minimal effort into his performance. "Out for a good time playing cowboys with Martin, the star had no intention of treating *Texas* as anything more significant than another Clan-style lark," writes Daniel O'Brien. "Frustrated at the latter's refusal to follow or even listen to his advice, Aldrich regularly argued with Sinatra, their fierce conflicts recalled by [the executive producer] Howard Koch at the director's memorial service over 20 years later. Aldrich got on much better with Martin, rating the actor as a true professional." Howard Hawks had felt much the same about Dean during the making of *Rio Bravo* four years earlier.

A couple of weeks into the shoot, Frank decided to take a break and fly to New York. This was his common modus operandi on a picture to which he felt minimal commitment: blow town for a while, let them film around him. Except that in this case, he had a far more compelling reason to beeline to Manhattan than mere escape.

———

They'd been talking on the phone again, in the deep watches of the night when talk verged on dream, and they'd forgotten all the impossible and remembered all the spectacular, and Ava had come back to New York. Not only come back: she had moved her suitcases into Frank's new penthouse, and all at once, implausibly enough, things between them seemed serious again. Frank, who knew little of the territory between agony and ecstasy, was over the moon. "She's back, and I'm the happiest man in the world," he told friends. "It's on. All the way."

The problem was that Sam Giancana was back too.

Frank's relationship with the Chicago gangster was not entirely dissimilar to his relationship with Ava: In each case, grand, incompletely understood passions were involved; in each case, togetherness and apartness were equally difficult. In each case, Frank gained by the association. Both Ava and Mooney dominated Sinatra and, to some extent, were also dominated by him. And apropos of dominance and subservience, the mobster was in town that week with Phyllis McGuire, who was appearing with her sisters on *The Ed Sullivan Show*.

Ava, who greatly regretted Frank's idolatrous fascination with the Mob, hated gangsters in general and Giancana in particular. Lee Server puts it well:

> Ava had met the fierce, gnomelike gangster on a number of occasions in her time with Frank, as she had met many others of his ilk . . . Often in the past she had found herself surrounded by them at her table in a club as she waited to watch Frank perform somewhere, or backstage where she'd see them swarm around their favorite singer kissing and grab-assing like—she'd tell him—so many gravel-voiced fags. It was one more thing for them to argue about. Frank thought the mobsters had style, guts, took no shit from anybody. Ava thought they were slobs and psychopaths who spent a lot of their adult years in jail.

"These creeps are going to bring you down," Ava once told him. "One of these fucking days, Francis, you are going to end up at the bottom of some river somewhere wearing cement shoes. And I'll be damned if I'm gonna end up down there with you, you stupid frigging wop."

But Sinatra and his weaselly friend were all but joined at the hip that June week. Ava seemed good-natured enough about it at first—even if in a hurry to anesthetize herself. On Saturday the eighth, Frank took her, and Mooney and Phyllis, to dinner at his parents' grand new house in Fort Lee. There, amid the brand-new furniture Frank had bought, just off the living room with its artificial Japanese cherry tree, plaster statues of the saints, small founts of holy water, an autographed chair from Sammy Davis Jr., and photographs of Popes John XXIII and Paul, Dean Martin, and Ava herself, "We had a great time," McGuire recalled. "We took Dolly and Marty a bottle of Crown Royal in a purple felt bag. Ava was so fascinated with it that she couldn't wait until we got there to have a shot, which she chased with beer. She was adorable, and Dolly loved her."

Dolly had always loved her. At one point during the evening, she grabbed Ava by the forearm and asked, "So when are you two gettin' married again?"

Yet Frank's domineering and narcissistic mother could only see her ex-daughter-in-law as a wish reflection of herself: foulmouthed, free-spirited, taking no prisoners. (And of course, wondrous to look at.) Her son's actual welfare concerned her no more than it had when she'd whacked young Frank with a stick or pushed him underwater at the Jersey shore.

The McGuire Sisters did their Sullivan stint (the twenty-one-year-old sensation Barbra Streisand also appeared on the show that night), then Giancana took Frank and Ava and Phyllis and her sisters, and a few others, out to celebrate. "We went to Trader Vic's, which was closed because it was Sunday," the McGuire Sisters' road manager, Victor Collins, recalled. "But Sam knocked on the door and another Dago opened it and said, 'We're closed.' Sam said, 'Yeah, well, you just opened,' and, by God, they opened."

Inside, the drinking began, and the demons were loosed. Frank and Ava "got into the worst fight you ever saw," Collins said.

> The names they called each other! She called him a bastard and said he was nothing but a stupid frigging Wop. Even though we were all feeling real good and half drunk by then, everyone looked at one another when she said this and then looked at her, but she just kept on like none of us were there . . . Frank kept telling her to shut up . . . Then they stormed out and the rest of us went to Phyllis's apartment on Park Avenue. A little while later Sinatra showed up with Sammy Cahn. It was raining to beat the devil, and so Sinatra started bending everyone's umbrella, thinking that was real funny. Or else he was still mad at Ava.

Of course he was. They were off to the races once more, back on their endless cycle of jealousy (Frank, being Frank, found time that week to slip in a visit with Jill St. John, which made the papers) and furious fighting and mad makeup sex. Frank strove to please Ava in other ways, too, enlisting Jilly Rizzo to fetch her special littleneck clams from Mulberry Street and to recommend out-of-the-way restaurants where the two of them could nestle unbothered.

Sinatra quite naturally wanted all his favorite people to like each other, and Jilly and Momo got along famously, but where Ava and Giancana were concerned, the hating was mutual. The gangster could charm many women, but these were women who were vulnerable or simply not that bright. Mooney "never liked women who were smart enough to ask intelligent questions," Giancana's brother Chuck once said. Ava didn't think much of her own intelligence, but she had a sharp intellect. And she had made up her mind about Sam Giancana, so he made up his mind back. "Sam didn't like her at all," Collins said. "He always said that she was a crazy bitch."

Let us keep in mind that this was a man nicknamed Mooney talking.

Push came to shove. One night that same week, Frank and Ava were sitting with a group at Jilly's when Giancana came over, and Frank eagerly asked him to join them. As a member of Sinatra's entourage recalled, after Momo had sat for a minute, Ava got up. "Excuse me, gentlemen," she said. "There's a fellow over there I simply must see."

"Who the hell's that?" Frank asked.

Ava ignored him. She crossed the room and sat next to a man who was at a table alone. She began to flirt outrageously with him, touching his arm, rubbing the back of his neck, and, finally, climbing onto his lap and giggling. She stared over at Frank to make sure he was taking it all in. "This was more than Frank could bear," writes J. Randy Taraborrelli.

Frank got up, and when he did, he pushed his chair back with such force it fell over, and he went over to the stranger's table. According to three witnesses, he pushed Ava off the interloper's lap. She nearly fell to the floor. Then he pulled the stranger up by his collar, looked him straight in the eye, and in a voice loud enough to be heard over the music said, "You're lucky I don't kill you with my bare hands, you idiot. Who the fuck do you think you are? Are you *crazy*? You want to *die*? Because I'm the guy to make that happen, you chump." When Frank finally released his grip, Ava's new friend fell to the floor.

Frank dragged Ava back to their table and pushed her into a chair. When she stood up, he pushed her back down. Giancana watched as if he were at a prizefight, goading Frank on. Then Ava grabbed Mooney's drink, threw it in Frank's face, and stalked out without looking back.

"Buddy boy," Momo said, "I ain't never seen anything like that. That was *classic*."

She had humiliated him often before, and they made up again. But the next day, as Frank, Jilly, and others were sitting and talking in Sinatra's penthouse, the doorbell rang. "Suddenly," a witness recalled, "Ava walked out of another room all dressed, carrying a suitcase, and headed straight for the door. She opened it, turned, and gave a little wave . . . Then she walked out. None of us knew what to do. We were so embarrassed for Frank. We were flabbergasted. Frank was stunned. Jilly told me later that the guy at the door was a Spanish airline pilot."

It was the close of another chapter, but by no means the last.

———

Frank went back to California to play cowboys; Mooney returned to Chicago to take on the Feds.

In June 1963, Bobby Kennedy, keenly aware of his brother's potentially explosive connection to Sam Giancana via Judy Campbell, ordered the Federal Bureau of Investigation to put its already tight surveillance of the gangster into overdrive. One side effect of this was that Frank Sinatra, who was spending a lot of time with Giancana that year, began making more guest appearances than ever in Momo's FBI file.

Agents observed the mobster in New York, where he'd accompanied his lady friend for the McGuire Sisters' *Ed Sullivan Show* appearance. His FBI dossier stated "that while GIANCANA will usually remain in the apartment residence of PHYLLIS MCGUIRE while in New York City, he has been known to stay at the Waldorf Astoria and Madison Hotels in that city. [Redacted] advised that GIANCANA dines constantly at the following New York restaurants: La Scala, The 21 Club, El Morocco, and the Chambord." Curiously, Jilly's was not mentioned.

That month, the bureau instituted what it called "lockstep surveillance": agents posted around Mooney's house in Chicago, questioning his neighbors and all visitors, playing one hole behind him on the golf course. Giancana's chief tormentors were Special Agents William Roemer, Marshall Rutland, and Ralph Hill. They drove the gangster to distraction. "Why don't you fucks investigate the Communists!" he screamed at them. "I'm not going to take this sitting down! I'm going to light a fire under you guys, and don't forget that!"

The oppressive scrutiny led to a highly unusual turn of events, described drily in a July 9 memo from J. Edgar Hoover to Robert Kennedy:

We have learned through our surveillance of Giancana that he has resumed holding meetings in the Armory Lounge in Forest Park, Illinois. Giancana's lieutenants have been shuttling carloads of individuals to and from this location where Giancana "holds court" at a large table just inside the entrance.

Last week one of Giancana's top lieutenants, Charles "Chuck" English [Charles Carmen Inglesia], contacted our Agents and requested an interview.

Toward the end of the interview, the memo continued, English, who was slightly intoxicated, tried to persuade Mooney to talk with the agents. Giancana declined, but as the agents got ready to drive away, English came out with a message for Special Agent Roemer: "If Bobby Kennedy wants to talk to Sam, he knows who to go through."

"Who?" Roemer asked. "Frank Sinatra?"

"You said it, I didn't," said English.

The implication was that the attorney general might have something to gain by talking with Giancana—or something to lose if he didn't. In some cracked gangster way, Mooney felt his role in Operation Mongoose meant that he was legitimately working for the U.S. government, even though he had taken the government's money and laughed all the way to the bank, contributing nothing to the project except his sinister name. But unknown to Giancana, Bobby Kennedy—officially, anyway—had no idea that he had ever been involved.

Momo, therefore, felt that the attorney general owed him a debt beyond the one the Kennedys theoretically owed him for their success in the election, while Bobby Kennedy felt that the mobster was merely a nuisance (or worse) to be quashed. But Sam Giancana had another card up his sleeve.

On the advice of his son-in-law Anthony Tisci, Giancana filed suit against the Justice Department in hopes of winning a court injunction against the FBI for harassment. The grounds: the agency was depriving him of his constitutional right to privacy.

The papers went nuts. The irony of it! SAD TALE, BUT FBI UNMOVED, read one July 1 headline, noting that the federal district court judge Richard B. Austin had turned down Momo's petition out of hand, despite an impassioned plea by Giancana's attorney, the famed civil-rights lawyer George N. Leighton, "that the G-men were ruining Giancana's social life, making his golf game go to pot and ridiculing him in front of friends and neighbors in suburban Oak Park," according to UPI's account. "How would you like it if you were on the 18th hole trying to sink a putt and there were six FBI agents watching you?" Leighton asked the judge, noting that agents had also followed Giancana to church and that Momo had had to hire photographers to take pictures of FBI photographers photographing him. Austin was unimpressed.

And the judge was unmoved once again when Leighton presented a second petition on the twelfth. But on July 15, Austin agreed to hear Mooney himself. Giancana was taking an enormous risk by taking the stand: he would have to undergo cross-examination by government attorneys who had thousands of pages of documents "detailing every aspect of his criminal history, enough ammunition to put him away for life," according to a memoir by Momo's brother Chuck Giancana and his namesake godson.

> But Mooney was enormously confident, telling Chuck he'd win his case for what he called "two very good reasons." First, he said, his civil rights were indeed being violated, and this he could prove in a court of law. And second, but more important, he'd win because by filing the suit he'd essentially called Bobby Kennedy's bluff: He was certain the attorney general would back down. As he saw it, Kennedy would have no choice: "I'll be sittin' on the stand holdin' a can of worms. And Bobby'll be scared to death I'll open it . . . because if I do, all their dirty little secrets will come out."

Bobby Kennedy blinked. On July 16, UPI reported, Judge Austin changed his tune utterly, ordering the FBI to stop its harassment of Giancana and also placing the FBI's chief agent in Chicago "in contempt of court for refusing on orders from Washington to answer questions in court." The orders had come from the attorney general.

From that moment forward, the court ordered, the FBI had to curtail its "rough shadowing." Agents tailing Mooney on the golf course would have to let another foursome intervene between them and the gangster. From then on, the bureau could post only one car, rather than a squad, on stakeout at Giancana's residence. And the FBI car would have to stay at least one block away from the gangster's house at all times.

Mooney smiled as the newly sympathetic judge issued his ruling. The next day, as a bureau memo reported, he took advantage of his new invisibility.

> [Redacted] furnished information in [redacted] which reflected that SAM GIANCANA immediately upon cessation of FBI surveillance eluded a surveillance placed by the Cook County Sheriff's Department and proceeded . . . to Lake Tahoe, California area where he met with PHYLLIS MCGUIRE, and reportedly stayed at the Cal-Neva Lodge, of which FRANK SINATRA is a part-owner.

Frank's next musical project, *Reprise Repertory Theatre*, seemed a highly worthy one on the face of it. The plan was to heighten brand identity by rerecording four great Broadway musicals (*Finian's Rainbow; Guys and Dolls; Kiss Me, Kate;* and *South Pacific*) with only Reprise artists—a limitation that was also a strength, given the roster Sinatra had to work with: besides himself, there was Dean Martin, Sammy Davis Jr., Jo Stafford, Rosemary Clooney, and Keely Smith; as the pièce de résistance, plans were in the works to sign the Old Groaner himself, Bing Crosby, to the label.

Frank also planned, for the first time, to produce the LPs himself. Looked at one way, this self-assignment was nothing new: no matter who was turning the dials in the control booth, Sinatra had always been the true producer of his records. But now he would have to make a number of artistic decisions, including whom to feature and when. He would be a generous impresario. Of the fifty-four numbers cut for the four LPs, Sinatra would sing on only fourteen of them; several of his appearances would be in duets or trios. He started the project with a bang on July 10 by teaming with Dean and Sammy to record Cole Porter's "We Open in Venice," from 1948's *Kiss Me, Kate.*

The track is a charming rendition of a sprightly but lesser Porter number: the Summit act now had the comfort and dependability of a well-worn baseball glove, and the trio clicks from start to finish, complete with Vegas-y asides and a dash of *Amos 'n' Andy.* Billy May's slightly cartoonish arrangement (Reprise's musical director, Morris Stoloff, conducted) moves things along at a brisk—almost manic—rate.

Yet something is wrong, and though hindsight is inevitable from a distance of fifty years or more, it's all too easy to ask: Just who was the audience for these albums? Each of the artists involved in the *Repertory Theatre* had his or her own following and sold (or failed to sell) albums based on airplay, advertising, and TV appearances. But while the concept of a Reprise-branded collection was meant to focus attention on the label, wouldn't combining artists—as selfless as this might have been on Frank's part where he was one of the singers—dilute their appeal?

And there was another important historical factor: by 1963, the golden age of the Broadway musical, which these four uplifting shows of the 1940s and 1950s richly represented, had passed. Broadway would continue to find hits, but the world was changing faster than anybody knew.

———

A *Repertory Theatre* recording session on the eighteenth, with arrangements by Riddle, was more successful. After Frank and Dean did a pleasant enough version of Frank Loesser's title song from *Guys and Dolls,* Frank recorded three solo numbers: Loesser's "I've Never Been in Love Before," from the same show, and Burton Lane and Yip Harburg's "Old Devil Moon" and "When I'm Not Near the Girl I Love," from *Finian.*

This version of "Moon," in stereo and with finger snaps, was a worthy successor to the 1956 mono version, also arranged by Nelson. But Frank had never recorded the other two songs before, and both were lovely, imbued with that indefinable something that Sinatra could lend to worthy material from any decade.

He recorded these beautiful songs on Thursday night; the next day, he headed to Lake Tahoe to meet Sam Giancana.

———

Despite the order to back off from Mooney, the Feds managed to keep the heat on, enlisting the aid of other law-enforcement agencies to tail the gangster— "much to the consternation of Giancana, [who] shouted a steady tirade of verbal abuse" whenever he saw he was being followed, according to an FBI memo.

On July 19, the McGuire Sisters opened in Cal-Neva's Celebrity Room for a one-week stand. Giancana, who had come to the casino in direct contravention of the Nevada Black Book's orders, was there to support his lady friend. He and Phyllis stayed in Chalet 50. "Most of the time," *Life* magazine subsequently reported, "Sam just stayed put on the front porch of Chalet 50, cultivating his suntan and contemplating the lake. Although he was an unofficial Cal-Neva visitor, he had only to whistle for room service, and a beige station wagon belonging to the lodge was at his beck and call." Kitty Kelley writes that the FBI photographed Momo and Frank playing golf together that week, even though the bureau's official position was that it hadn't followed Giancana to Nevada. (Soon, in any case, a federal court of appeals would reverse the decision, and the FBI would be back on Mooney's tail.)

But it wasn't golf that got Frank in trouble. As an FBI memo put it, tersely,

> [Redacted] advised that during GIANCANA's stay at the Cal-Neva
> Lodge, an incident occurred on one evening whereby GIANCANA
> became involved in a brawl with one VICTOR COLLINS, who was at
> that time the road manager of the MCGUIRE sisters.

Collins described the episode to Kelley, in rather more detail. While he was drinking in the chalet with the sisters and Giancana, he said, Phyllis McGuire kept playfully punching him on the arm, a little too hard, every time she passed his chair. Finally, the manager stood up, grabbed McGuire by both arms, and tried to sit her in the chair he had just risen from. Somehow— evidently much alcohol had been consumed by this point—she wound up on the floor, and Giancana became enraged.

"Sam came charging over from across the room and threw a punch at me wearing a huge big diamond ring that gouged me in the left eyebrow," Collins recalled.

> I just saw red then and grabbed him, lifted him clean off the floor, and was going to throw him through the plate glass door, but thought, "Why wreck the place?" So I decided to take him outside and break his back on the hard metal railing on the patio. I got as far as the door and then got hit on the back of the head. I don't know who hit me from behind, but the back of my head was split open. It didn't knock me out, but I went down and Sam was underneath me. He had on a pearl gray silk suit, and the blood from my eyebrow was running all over his suit. I had a hold of him by the testicles and the collar and he couldn't move. That's when Sinatra came in with his valet, George, the colored boy. They were coming down to join the party.
>
> The girls were screaming and running around like a bunch of chickens in every direction because nobody knew what was going to happen . . . George just stood there with the whites of his eyes rolling around and around in his black face, because he knew who Sam was, and nobody ever fought with Sam . . . Sinatra and George pulled me off Sam, who ran out the door. Then Sinatra called me a troublemaker, and said the gangsters were going to put a hit out on me because of this fight. I told him the only way they'd get me is from a long distance with a high-powered rifle because none of them had the guts to hit me face to face. "I'm not afraid of nothing, Wop," I said, and he started yelling that I was going to lose the place for him because of this fight. Because of the notoriety he was going to lose all his money. I said, "What do you mean, your money? You don't have a dime in the place. It's all Mafia money and you know it." He and George ran out then, and I left the next day for Nebraska.

George Jacobs's account of the incident more or less corroborates Collins's, except for the Stepin Fetchit eye rolling and a few interesting details. For one thing, "Phyllis was pounding on the manager's head with her high heel," the valet writes. Jacobs doesn't mention Frank's fears about losing Cal-Neva; instead, he says Sinatra had him drive Mooney to Palm Springs "in one of our low-profile station wagons," hoping the whole thing would blow over.

Instead, it blew up. Someone called the police about the fight, the police notified the FBI, and the FBI reported Giancana's presence at Cal-Neva to the Nevada Gaming Control Board, which promptly began an investigation.

While Frank was misbehaving in Tahoe, Dean was minding his business in Hollywood. Interviewing Martin on the *4 for Texas* set at Warner Bros., the *Los Angeles Times*'s Don Alpert found the star relaxed, funny, and—in sharp contrast to his good friend's frequent dyspepsia about making movies— philosophical about the profession. "I call it a wonderful job, working in pictures," Dean said. "When I finish here, I'll go to Tahoe with Frank, then I have a whole day off before I go to the Sands in Vegas. Then I do 'Robin and the Seven Hoods' with Frank."

Robin and the 7 Hoods was to be a gangster comedy, set in Chicago in the 1920s. The irony needn't be underlined.

Frank went back to work—grindingly, on *4 for Texas;* pleasurably, on new selections for the *Repertory Theatre* (including, on July 25, his first, magnificent recording of "Luck Be a Lady." He also cut a couple of new singles on the thirty-first: the charming "Here's to the Losers" and the less charming "Love Isn't Just for the Young."

Then came the black headline in the August 2 *Chicago Sun-Times:* MOE'S VISIT PERILS SINATRA LICENSE. The story, under the byline of Sandy Smith, detailed Sam Giancana's late-July sojourn at Cal-Neva and said that the chairman of the Nevada Gaming Control Board, Edward Olsen, had already begun an investigation. The altercation in Chalet 50 was related in detail: Smith had even determined that the person who hit Victor Collins from behind was Cal-Neva's maître d', Eddie King. The cat was out of the bag, but in those less interconnected days only in Chicago; the wire services didn't pick up the story. In the meantime, Frank made headlines of another sort.

Act Three

MIDAS

20

This is a way of life, and a man has to lead his own life.

—FRANK SINATRA, IN AUGUST 1963, TO EDWARD OLSEN,
CHAIRMAN OF THE NEVADA GAMING CONTROL BOARD

By early 1963, Reprise Records was losing so much money—a couple of million early-1960s dollars a year—that Frank Sinatra was rumored to be flying to Chicago on weekends to borrow cash from Sam Giancana, and other friends, just to make payroll. Things were so bad that Sinatra was finally forced to change his stance on the brand of music he detested. "I finally went to Frank and said to him, 'Look, we are going to go bankrupt unless we get into the rock 'n' roll business and become competitive,'" Mo Ostin recalled. "And Frank's business instincts overcame his emotions. He said, 'Well, if you feel that strongly about it, then okay, you can go ahead.'"

The hard truth was that Sinatra was no longer emotionally engaged with his own record label. Having signed all his friends and frittered away a pile of money, he had simply turned his attentions elsewhere. "Giving up on Reprise bothered Sinatra not for a moment," the former Warner-Reprise executive Stan Cornyn writes. "He'd had it. With his quick passions, Sinatra had craved his own label—the same as he'd other times craved that broad over there, or his own leather booth and bottle of Jack. Quick passion: You do it, you forget it."

Now he was forgetting about Reprise and leaving the mess for others to clean up. And it was a mess. The *Reprise Repertory Theatre* project had been enormously expensive: each album cost $100,000 to produce. "It was a gamble that defied the marketplace," Cornyn writes. "Only 17,900 real people ever showed interest in buying the series. It was Reprise's biggest gamble, its biggest disaster." And the label's roster was bloated—the likes of Sammy, Dean, Bing, and Rosemary Clooney counterbalanced by the likes of Soupy Sales, Arturo Romero & His Magic Violins, and Don Drysdale, the singing Dodgers pitcher. Hardly anybody on the list, high or low, was moving product. Even Sinatra was barely selling 100,000 units per album. Dean Martin was down to 20,000 to 25,000.

To try to generate some profits, Ostin had hired the acclaimed pop producer Jimmy Bowen, who led the label on its first baby steps into rock 'n' roll.

(At the same time, he also signed the distinguished former big-band leader Sonny Burke—the man who had first brought Nelson Riddle to Capitol's attention—as Reprise's head of A&R. Burke would also work as an in-house producer.)

One of Bowen's first moves was signing the cutting-edge producer-arranger-songwriter Jack Nitzsche. Nitzsche had a Top 10 single in the summer of 1963, a catchily grandiose instrumental (produced by Bowen) called "The Lonely Surfer." And then there was the twenty-six-year-old Mexican-American Trini Lopez, whose folky live debut album, *Trini Lopez at PJ's*, went gold. But one gold record and a hottish single alone couldn't reverse Reprise's losses. It took a feat of prestidigitation by Mickey Rudin to do that.

Jack Warner, the last Warner brother to stay in the movie business and the head of the studio that bore his name, had been wooing Frank Sinatra ever since *Ocean's 11* became a box-office smash. "It was a huge picture, and Jack was in love with Frank," Mo Ostin recalled. "So he wanted him for a film deal." The courtship grew hot and heavy throughout 1961 and 1962, and a two-picture agreement for *4 for Texas* and *Robin and the 7 Hoods* partly satisfied Warner, but he wanted more. In August 1963, he got it.

It all began innocently enough, if a meeting between Warner Bros.' dapper, dictatorial president (along with 20th Century Fox's Darryl F. Zanuck, one of the last of the Hollywood moguls) and Frank Sinatra's brilliant, pugnacious lawyer can be called innocent. Jack Warner wanted one thing badly—Frank Sinatra in his movie studio—and thought, when he first sat down with Mickey Rudin, that he was simply negotiating over Sinatra's acting and film-producing services. He quickly discovered otherwise.

That the deal came together just as the Cal-Neva affair was beginning to come to light was no coincidence. The casino was a money loser in any case; Frank's consigliere also knew there was trouble ahead in Tahoe. And Reprise was a problem that had to be solved quickly. Rudin's masterstroke was letting Jack Warner solve it for him.

Warner Bros., too, had a record label, one that had endured years of losses and only recently emerged into the black, with best-selling albums by the Everly Brothers, the folk trio Peter, Paul, and Mary, the jazz-pop singer Joanie Sommers, and the singing comedian Allan Sherman. Warner Bros. Records was profitable but by no means complacent, and when Mickey Rudin dangled the possibility of adding Frank Sinatra to its roster, Jack Warner jumped. All Warner needed to do, Rudin said, was buy Reprise and merge it with Warner.

"Because Mickey knew Jack Warner wanted Sinatra so badly, he went ahead and forced the record company on him," Mo Ostin said. "It wasn't something that [Warner Bros.] would have bought under ordinary circumstances."

And Jack Warner was willing to do almost anything to sign Frank Sinatra, and Rudin, a bulldog in negotiations and a no-holds-barred tactician, was ready to make demands that under any other circumstances would have seemed outlandish. What he had in mind was nothing less than unloading the two big money losers, Reprise and Cal-Neva, that Frank owned under the corporate umbrella of Essex Productions. And, of course, making a hefty profit in the bargain. Cornyn writes,

> Draft one of the deal got memoed by Warner attorney Peter Knecht, who synopsized the Reprise part in one sentence: "What they are asking is that in exchange for all of the outstanding Essex stock, Frank Sinatra receive approximately 350,000 shares of Warner Bros. stock . . ." That deal had a value of about $5.25 million.
>
> Warner balked. He didn't *want* the other stuff, like the Cal-Neva Lodge. He didn't want to co-own (with Danny Kaye) Essex's radio stations or residuals from old Sinatra pictures. As for Reprise Records, well, he didn't care one way or another.
>
> But closed-door talks sped along.

First and foremost, Rudin needed to establish a dollar value for the deep-in-the-red Reprise. This, Cornyn writes, took some serious creativity. "A startled Ostin was commanded to evaluate the label: Add up the worth of the record masters, the contracts, the tables, chairs, paper clips—anything you could sell."

Rudin, with a straight face, came up with a price of $2 million.

But, Ostin recalled, "Warner didn't want to pay more than one and a half million. Finally, Mickey, in order to reconcile the situation, compromised by saying, 'I'll tell you what. We'll make the price one and a half million. But for giving up on the other half-million, I want you to have Frank own all of his [Reprise] masters.' So that's how Frank got ownership of his masters." It was the prize Sinatra had always sought from Capitol and never won.

There was more, no less audacious.

"Mickey, it was known in town, had balls of brass," Cornyn writes. "To make the deal with Warner, Rudin threw in a curveball idea. What if Sinatra got 50 percent of the *combined* Warner-Reprise Records? Warner negotiated Rudin down to 33 percent." ("That turned out to be a windfall later on," Ostin said, putting it mildly: in 1969, Steve Ross's Kinney National Company would buy Warner-Reprise—by then called Warner Bros.–Seven Arts—for $400 million.)

The deal was sheer fiscal wizardry. "Selling his two-thirds interest in money-losing Reprise, Sinatra got cash, plus a one-third interest in moneymaking Warner Bros. Records," writes Cornyn. "Sinatra would own a third of Warner/Reprise but not have to underwrite it financially. Warner did all the funding."

On August 7, a headline on *Variety's* front page read SINATRA NAMED WB PROD'N CONSULTANT AS WAXERIES MERGE, 3D DEAL LOOMS. "Warner Bros. and Frank Sinatra shook hands yesterday on two far-reaching deals and renewed spade work on a third which, when and if finalized, would make their togetherness complete and involve over a period of years many millions of dollars," the article began.

> First link forged in extending chain is the merger, effective early next month, of Warner Bros. Records and Sinatra's Reprise Records under new corporate handle of Warner Bros. Records–Reprise Records Co. New company will become a major factor in disk business with total of 90 artists comprised of individuals and groups. The WB roster currently numbers 28, while Reprise has total of 62.
>
> Second phase of overall deal provides for Sinatra's employment by Warner Bros. Pictures to act as a consultant on theatrical and TV pix. He will be active in arranging package deals for the company . . . "under the guidance" of Jack L. Warner, prexy.
>
> Third and presumably last link hinges on outcome of continuing discussions which would see Sinatra Enterprises producing features to be financed and distributed by WB.

Frank didn't get any Warner Bros. stock out of the deal, but Jack Warner's company did issue Frank a nice down payment: a certified check for a million dollars. He carried it around for a week, showing it off to all who wanted to see. "This is what I call real pocket money," he said.

Yet money alone wasn't enough for him. As part of the agreement, Sinatra's production company—now called Artanis—would move to the Warner lot in Burbank, but Frank didn't want to be just another schmuck with a production deal. He told Mickey Rudin to tell Jack Warner he wanted a title. Say, assistant to the president. Warner agreed; the title was announced.

And press speculation began immediately: Jack Warner was over seventy. Was Sinatra planning to take over the studio upon Warner's retirement?

"Jack went crazy when he read the newspapers," Warner's mistress Jacqueline Park recalled.

> We were in New York at the Sherry Netherland having breakfast in Jack's suite. He was screaming mad and he showed me a newspaper

article. "You see, this is what I get for trying to be a nice guy to that son of a bitch," he yelled. He called Frank and said, "You better understand something, Frank, and understand it now. I'm the president of Warner Bros. Pictures and my brothers and I own the studio . . . I'll blow the whistle on you if you try anything funny. You tell your friends that I'm not afraid of them. I didn't get this far to have a gang of ruffians for partners."

Warner felt compelled to issue a press release the next day, elucidating the agreement between Sinatra and Warner Bros.:

> Since there has been considerable uninformed comment about this relationship, it is appropriate that these inquiries be answered. War-ner Bros. Records is owned two-thirds by Warner Bros. Pictures and one-third by Mr. Sinatra. That company is in the business of producing phonograph records which are distributed on the Warner Bros. and Reprise labels.
>
> As to motion pictures, there is an agreement between Warner Bros. Pictures and Artanis Productions, Inc., an independent producer, as the result of which Artanis produces features at Warner Bros. Studios, which are released by Warner Bros. Pictures. Mr. Sinatra owns sub-stantially all of the stock of Artanis Productions and is the president of that company. Mr. Sinatra does not own any stock of Warner Bros. Pictures, Inc.
>
> This association, plus the warm friendship that exists between Mr. Sinatra and myself, has led to a certain amount of speculation that I am considering Mr. Sinatra as my successor as president of Warner Bros. Pictures—or that Mr. Sinatra desires to be my successor. There is no evidence or reason for such speculation.

Frank wasn't a gangster, even if he sometimes liked to playact the part. And he wasn't trying to take over Warner Bros., but he had made out like a bandit, thanks to Mickey Rudin, who'd waved his magic wand and turned red ink into black. But all the lawyer's powers were of little use in the case of Frank's increasingly costly asset on the shores of Lake Tahoe.

———

On August 8, agents of the Nevada Gaming Control Board visited Cal-Neva, only to find the staff predictably mum. On the advice of his attorney, Skinny D'Amato declined to be interviewed. As Edward Olsen put it, "Everybody had a short memory and very limited knowledge of anything east of the Truckee River."

At 5:00 p.m. on the same day, Olsen himself spoke with Frank in his office at the Sands.

Ed Olsen was forty-four, a tough-minded, drily witty former Nevada journalist who knew the gambling industry from top to bottom. As a result of a childhood case of tuberculosis of the hip joints, he walked with difficulty on crutches and a built-up shoe. He seems to have taken his handicap with remarkable equanimity, and he brought this same composure to his meeting with Frank Sinatra. "We interviewed him at length, and he acknowledged that he had indeed seen Giancana," Olsen recalled. "He said he'd seen him rather briefly coming out of Phyllis's cabin and that they just exchanged greetings, and that was all. He said no, they didn't ask him to leave, they didn't inquire any further into it, he had no further knowledge of it or anything else."

On the subject of the alleged brouhaha in Chalet 50, Frank had a crafty answer. "If there was a rumble there while I was there, they must be keeping it awfully quiet," he said. When Olsen asked him if he would repeat this under oath, Sinatra said that he never talked under oath without consultation with his attorney.

Frank was polite but undeferential. "He explained his philosophy to us in a very reasonable manner," Olsen later recalled.

> He wasn't cantankerous or anything of that nature. He said that he saw Giancana perhaps six to ten times a year and occasionally played golf with him and said that Giancana had been a guest at his Palm Springs home. And he said that he would not associate with Giancana in Nevada, but he would continue his occasional association with him elsewhere whenever he felt like it. He said that he was acquainted with people in all walks of life and that Giancana was one of those that fit into that category. I asked him if he didn't feel that his association with Giancana and people of that notoriety, whether it be in Palm Springs or Chicago or New York . . . didn't reflect to his own discredit and also to the discredit of gambling in Nevada. Sinatra nodded at that, and he volunteered only a commitment that he would not see Giancana or people of that type in Nevada and he would continue to associate as he wished when he wasn't in Nevada. And as he said, "This is a way of life, and a man has to lead his own life."

His philosophy was quite clear: he would make some petty accommodations to the powers that be in order to stay in business, but the only rules he intended to follow were his own.

That night, a little after midnight, Frank Sinatra Jr. made his Las Vegas debut in the Driftwood Lounge of the Flamingo, singing with the orchestra that bore Tommy Dorsey's name. Frank sat ringside with the two Nancys, the underage Tina (fifteen) having been unhappily excluded. "I'm so nervous—this is killing me," the singer's father muttered to a companion. The place was packed: standing room only in the lounge; behind a cordon, casino customers stood six and seven persons deep and gawked as Frankie opened the show with "Night and Day" and continued with other Sinatra standards such as "Too Close for Comfort," "This Love of Mine," and "I'll Be Seeing You."

Variety was clear-eyed but impressed. "It's obviously good sentimental showmanship and great for the b.o. to have the 19-year-old Sinatra surrounded with a big show like his famed father started with, and since he revives some of the tunes identified with Sinatra, pere, there's bound to be unfair comparison," the weekly's reviewer began, continuing,

> Junior Sinatra has the potential for being highly successful on his own, and is young enough to develop his own style and sound. He may not now have the tonal texture of his father; he may not now generate the excitement; however, he has the stuff which can build into another Sinatra legend . . .
>
> Like his father did with the original Tommy Dorsey orch and the original Pied Pipers, he sings with the updated Pied Pipers "I'll Never Smile Again"—an amazing soundalike. With or without his present showcasing, Frank Sinatra Jr. is an extremely strong attraction for any showroom.

And Papa was pleased and relieved. "I'm very proud of him," said the man whom newspapers now had to call Frank senior. "He has done this all on his own, I've given him no coaching."

What he had given him: a new Pontiac convertible, courtesy of Pete Epsteen, the Chicago car dealer for whom Frank had done commercials (as a favor to Momo); all the money Frankie could spend; and, according to George Jacobs, "he had charge accounts so he could dress as well as dad, girls threw themselves at him, what more, Mr. S wondered, could the kid possibly need? Love? Love was for broads."

Frank would skip the 500 Club that summer for the first time in years. "That huge seashore resort nightclub in New Jersey, which almost didn't open for the season because of lack of money to cover theatrical and musicians' union bonds, is in serious trouble again," Dorothy Kilgallen had written in a July blind item that fooled nobody. "At the end of the first week of operation—and despite a healthy July 4 weekend crowd, they weren't able to pay off the stars of the show or the band, and the owners are frantically trying to borrow enough loot to keep going through the Summer."

Not only was the nightclub business in the toilet, but the nightclub's owner was in Nevada, facing considerable distractions of a legal nature.

———

On August 23, a color photograph of Frank and Frank junior graced the big cover of America's magazine, *Life*. Father and son stood side by side in tuxes, Frank beaming, Junior with his mouth open in song. The cover line read,

NEW

SINATRA

SOUND

Frank Jr.

Takes After Pop

"The new Sinatra sound is an eerie, incredibly exact echo of Frank Sr.'s singing," *Life*'s anonymous writer noted, somewhat inexactly. The brief piece sketched out the nineteen-year-old's astonishing if asterisked rise—the Disneyland gig, the Benny show, the Dorsey offer, the Vegas opening—and quoted him remarking, with unintentional poignancy, on his sole influence. "I've studied with Frank Sinatra, although he doesn't know I've studied with him," Junior said. "But I've been following him around all my life, and I've heard him everywhere—theaters, saloons, strip joints."

The pathos didn't end there. "He lugs a stereo tape recorder with him on tour and every night while he is getting dressed he warms up his voice for an hour by singing along with Sinatra recordings," the reporter wrote. "He can also quote whole scenes from his father's films verbatim."

"I think the kid has a future, but he needs experience," Frank senior told *Life*. Junior then quoted his father: "He added as only the boss can, 'by experience I mean he's got to learn to drink, carouse and stay up all night.'"

It was all so neat it could have been tied up with a bow. If you'd shaken the package, though, you would have heard a dry rattling sound.

———

That same Friday night, Frank had his own Vegas opening, with Dean and Sammy at the Sands. By night, they did their familiar thing in the Copa Room;

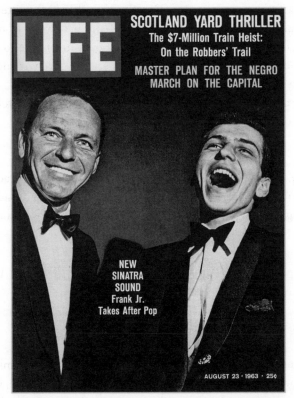

Frank and Frank junior, near the beginning of Junior's long and arduous career as a tuxedo singer. "I think the kid has a future," Frank senior said, "but he needs experience."

by day, Frank seethed at the newspapers, where the scoop that had broken in Chicago had begun to go nationwide. DID SINATRA HOST GANGSTER?, a typical headline read on the thirtieth, above the story that UPI was now running with: not only had Giancana been present at Cal-Neva, in direct contravention of Nevada law; he had been given "red-carpet treatment." In Los Angeles, the man Ed Olsen referred to as "Sinatra's attorney, a very charming gentleman by the name of Mickey Rudin of Hollywood," tried to stanch the flow with a stone wall. "There's no truth to the fact any underworld figure was at the lodge or got in a fight there," he told the *Herald Examiner,* in a curious turn of phrase. "Your information was wrong."

Olsen hit back, informing the papers that his investigation—he had issued subpoenas to the entire Cal-Neva staff, including Skinny D'Amato—was being "conducted very unhurriedly." It would not be concluded, he said, until "certain discrepancies in the information provided by various people at Cal-Neva could be resolved."

And Frank boiled over. He was like King Canute when it came to bad publicity, smiting the waves to no effect. In this case, the *Las Vegas Sun* had found out about the Cal-Neva subpoenas and started to run the story, which the wire services then picked up. But Sinatra suspected Olsen of grandstanding. From Cal-Neva, where he, Dean, and Sammy were appearing in the Celebrity Room for Labor Day weekend, Frank had his accountant, Newell Hancock, phone Ed Olsen. "Hancock opened the conversation with: 'Ed, what in the hell are you doing to us with all this publicity?'" Olsen wrote in a memo of September 4. "I explained to Hancock that the publicity did not originate with the Board . . . Hancock went on to say that 'Frank is irritated' and would like to meet with me."

In Frank's book, that meant that Ed Olsen was to come to him, at Cal-Neva. Grandly, Sinatra suggested, through Hancock, that he and the control board chairman meet informally over dinner; Olsen could then take in the show afterward.

Olsen declined. Such a meeting was inappropriate, he told the accountant, because he was in the process of investigating Cal-Neva. Half an hour later, his phone rang. It was Frank himself. "To describe him as 'irritated,'" Olsen wrote, "was a masterful understatement. He was infuriated."

Sinatra was enraged that the chairman wouldn't accept his dinner invitation. Patiently, Olsen explained why he couldn't come to Cal-Neva. To which Frank replied, "You're acting like a fucking cop . . . I just want to talk to you off the record."

Olsen explained that this was impossible. He could only meet with Sinatra in the Gaming Control Board's offices, he said, with others present and with his secretary making a record of the conversation.

"Listen, Ed, I haven't had to take this kind of shit from anybody in the country and I'm not going to take it from you people," Frank said. "I want you to come up here and have dinner with me . . . and bring that shit-heel friend, La France." Charles LaFrance, the board's chief investigator, was present in the office. At this point, Olsen motioned to him to pick up the extension.

"It's you and your goddamn subpoenas which have caused all this trouble," Sinatra continued.

Olsen said that only those who had been served knew about the subpoenas; the press knew nothing of them.

"You are a goddamn liar," Frank said. "It's all over the papers."

Olsen repeated his contention.

"I'll bet you fifty thousand dollars," Frank said.

"I haven't got fifty thousand dollars to bet," Olsen said.

"You're not in the same class with me," Sinatra said.

"I certainly hope not," Olsen said.

"All right, I'm never coming to see you again," Frank said. "I came to see you in Las Vegas and if you had conducted this investigation like a gentleman and come up here to see my people instead of sending those goddamn subpoenas, you would have gotten all the information you wanted."

Here Olsen pointed out that he had indeed sent three agents and a stenographer to Cal-Neva to interview witnesses on the same night as Frank's interview in the NGCB offices. He told Frank that both Skinny and Eddie King had declined to be interviewed and that King had lied about his involvement in the Chalet 50 brawl. Olsen added that he wasn't satisfied that Frank was telling the truth about his own role in the incident.

"I'm never coming to see you again," Sinatra repeated.

Olsen told him that if he wanted to see him, he would send a subpoena.

Already over the edge, Frank now lost it. "You just try and find me, and if you do, you can look for a big, fat surprise . . . a big, fat, fucking surprise," Frank said. "You remember that. Now, listen to me, Ed . . . don't fuck with me. Don't fuck with me. Just don't fuck with me."

"Are you threatening me?" Olsen asked.

"No," Frank said. "Just don't fuck with me. And you can tell that to your fucking board and that fucking commission, too."

Minutes after Sinatra slammed down the receiver, two agents from the gaming board's audit division walked into the Cal-Neva casino. Their visit was purely coincidental, having nothing to do with the investigation or the phone conversation: it had been the board's practice for several years to monitor the count of the gambling table drop boxes over Labor Day weekend. But their appearance threw Skinny D'Amato, already in a heightened state of alert, into a panic. He ran to confer with Frank, who yelled, "Throw the dirty sons of bitches out of the house!"

The situation was resolved without incident when Irving Pearlman, the casino manager, told the agents that the count had already begun. Concluding that there was no reason to enter the counting room at that point, the agents told Pearlman they would be back.

They returned at 6:30 a.m. on Labor Day and observed the count from start to finish in a completely routine fashion. Then things turned strange. As the casino employees concluded the count, Skinny walked in and touched one of the auditors on the arm. "Here's one for each of you," D'Amato said. When he left the room, the auditor found two $100 bills stuck in the crook of his arm. The auditors were horrified. D'Amato returned after a few minutes and explained that the money was for the inconvenience they'd suffered by having to come to the counting room twice.

As Skinny's biographer points out, the amiable D'Amato had no sinister purpose; he was just doing what came naturally. "Skinny tried to grease the wheels with money, as he had done hundreds of times before," Jonathan Van Meter writes. "He spent so much of his life in Atlantic City using cash as a salve that it must have been impossible for him to realize just how foolish a move this was."

The moment the two agents left the casino, they phoned Ed Olsen, waking him: it was 8:30 a.m., Labor Day. When they told their boss what had happened, "Well, that was just the straw that broke the camel's back, as far as I was concerned," Olsen recalled.

> I was just fed up with the whole organization. I couldn't get any straight answers to anything, and they were just nothing but headaches, the whole business up there. I felt that . . . continuation would be detrimental to the entire gambling industry in Nevada.
>
> So as quickly as I was able to get the lawyer to work and legal papers drawn up, we prepared a complaint, seeking the revocation of Mr. Sinatra's license at both Lake Tahoe and at the Sands in Las Vegas on the grounds of his having . . . conducted an unsuitable operation and having associated with people who were deleterious to the gaming industry.

Before filing the complaint, Ed Olsen took it to Governor Grant Sawyer for review. Sawyer, a progressive Democrat who'd entered office promising to clean up Nevada's gambling industry (and who'd appointed Olsen chairman of the Gaming Control Board), was not pleased. "This was the last thing in the world that he felt he needed at the moment!" Olsen said. Revoking the gaming licenses of the state's most prominent casino owner, the man who was Las Vegas personified, would be a black eye not just for Frank Sinatra but for gambling in Nevada, for the state itself, and, by extension, for Grant Sawyer.

The governor asked why Olsen intended to revoke Sinatra's licenses; Olsen showed Sawyer his voluminous files on the high jinks at Cal-Neva and Frank's obscene and threatening language during their phone conversation. Sawyer asked when Olsen intended to file. Just as soon as the legal details could be worked out, Olsen said.

"Well, you'd better be right," the governor told him.

On Thursday night, September 5, Frank performed for the last time at Cal-Neva, singing and clowning with Dean and Sammy and pulling Judy Garland onto the stage for a final quartet of "Birth of the Blues." The next day,

Sinatra, Martin, and Davis decamped for the Sands, where they sang and did their Summit act through the weekend as Reprise tape machines recorded the engagement for posterity. Twelve reels of tape comprising six shows were recorded; most of the material was never released.

On Sunday, September 8, Cal-Neva closed for the season. The next day, Frank flew to New York, ahead of gathering winds.

———

On Monday night, Junior had had his biggest opening to date, fronting Sam Donahue's Tommy Dorsey Orchestra at the Americana Hotel in New York City. Jackie Gleason was there, as were Joe E. Lewis, Toots Shor, Jack E. Leonard, and Alan King. Frank wasn't. In honor of the occasion, *Variety*'s editor, Abel Green (he'd been writing for the show-business weekly since 1919), sent himself to review the show, and he was impressed with what he heard.

Most impressive to Green was how well Frankie performed despite formidable obstacles: not just a snobby and slightly skeptical, $6-cover-charge crowd, but an under-amplifying microphone, turned down so as not to interfere with WNEW radio's live pickup. (No less a personage than William B. Williams, the coiner of the epithet Chairman of the Board, conducted the broadcast.)

And then there was the biggest obstacle of all, the man who stayed away that night, presumably to avoid stealing his son's thunder. "He is handicapped as much as helped by his heritage," the perceptive Green wrote of Frankie.

> None the less, despite all the travail of facing up to a $6 cover-charge trade, a meek mike, and a show-me turnout, he clicked. The show-me turnout, incidentally, were not-from-Missouri—they were Manhattanites who were rootin' for a tradition. Junior sustained it.

But to what extent was he sustaining a tradition, and to what extent was he an oldies act? (Not to mention a novelty act.) Abel Green called the show—which, besides the neo-Dorsey band, included the forty-six-year-old former girl singer Helen Forrest and the reconstituted Pied Pipers—"a nostalgic harkback for the adult set who were musically reliving the days of their younger years with a musical pot-pourri that sounded, played, and thrushed like the 'Variety Music Cavalcade' of a quarter century ago."

After the show, reporters quizzed Junior about Senior's absence. Frankie handled them with aplomb. "I spoke to Dad on the phone, and he was coughing," he said. "He was very tired. He'd been working all afternoon on his record business. He thought he'd stay home until he felt better."

Then, just to show Junior what the game was really about, one newspaperman winged a curveball at him: "Did your father stay away because of the Nevada situation?" At this point, the situation was still so contained that not everyone knew what he was talking about.

Frankie did, and he didn't bat an eye. "I've discussed it with my father," he replied, "and he said when he's ready, he'll make a statement."

———

That Wednesday, the Nevada Gaming Control Board filed its formal complaint against Frank's corporation, Park Lake Enterprises Inc. In the first count, the board charged that at various times between July 17 and July 28, Sam Giancana "sojourned to Chalet No. 50 at Cal Neva Lodge with the knowledge and consent of the licensee" and that "Giancana was served food and beverage by employees of the licensee with the right of transportation by said employees and representatives of the licensee in automobiles owned and/or controlled by the licensee . . . and was extended other courtesies and services by the employees and representatives of Park Lake Enterprises."

Count two alleged that Frank "had openly stated that he would continue his association with Mr. Giancana, and had thus defied the law of the state."

The third count alleged that Sinatra had engaged in a phone conversation "designed and intended to intimidate and coerce the chairman and members of the State Gaming Control Board to discontinue performance of their official duties, and to drop the investigation then pending regarding the visits of Sam Giancana at Cal Neva Lodge . . .

"In said telephone conversation, Frank Sinatra maligned and vilified the State Gaming Control Board, the Nevada Gaming Commission, and members of both said Board and Commission by the use of foul and repulsive language which was venomous in the extreme."

Count four alleged that Paul D'Amato, "the managing agent and representative of Park Lake Enterprises, Inc., listed on the payroll records as advisor of said corporate licensee in the operation of Cal Neva Lodge, attempted to force money upon" the two NGCB agents, which "was tantamount to an attempt to bribe them."

The next morning, the news hit front pages everywhere, and, as Edward Olsen put it, "all hell broke loose in the press and all over the country."

———

Throughout the 1950s, unfriendly columnists—in particular Hearst's Westbrook Pegler and Lee Mortimer—had now and then dredged up Frank's old underworld associations: his early sponsorship in New Jersey by Willie

Moretti; his attendance at the 1947 Mafia conference in Havana, where he'd hobnobbed with Lucky Luciano. But until now, no publicity had directly connected him with the Mafia, an organization whose existence the FBI had acknowledged for only half a dozen years and one whose reach and scope most Americans were just beginning to understand and become fascinated with.

As the Mob's public profile rose, Italian-Americans and other right-minded citizens quite properly pushed back. In a 1959 editorial titled "Italian-Americans Make Good Citizens," Hearst columnist George Sokolsky wrote, "To assume . . . that all Italians in the United States and their descendants are criminally organized in a body called 'The Mafia' is to accept not only guilt by association but damnation by birth and nationality . . . Do we have to balance Enrico Fermi against Vito Genovese? Do we have to balance Frank Sinatra against Lucky Luciano?" The uncoupling of Sinatra and Luciano by a columnist for the press syndicate that had been Frank's worst enemy just ten years earlier was striking. Even in the heat of the 1960 presidential campaign (and even as the unholy triangle of Jack Kennedy, Judy Campbell, and Sam Giancana was taking shape), the worst accusation the papers could come up with was that Frank was engaging in ring-a-ding-ding activities with his Rat Pack cronies: conduct unbecoming a friend of the Democratic candidate for the presidency of the United States, to be sure, but in itself kind of charming.

There was nothing charming about the fix he was in now. This wasn't another punch-up with a photographer; this was, as the caption under a photo of a grinning Sinatra on the front page of the September 12 *Arizona Republic* read, "Trouble, trouble." SINATRA MAY LOSE NEVADA GAMBLING PERMIT, blared the banner headline. The *Republic,* and many other papers, carried UPI's full account of the Nevada Gaming Control Board's complaint, Sam Giancana in the spotlight alongside Frank, the four counts laid out in gory detail. In its equally thorough account, the Associated Press called Giancana "one of the 12 overlords of American crime."

"Sinatra has 15 days to file a notice of defense before the [Nevada Gaming Commission] will act," the AP story continued. "He is entitled to a hearing by the five-man commission before his license could be revoked. If it is revoked, he can appeal to the Nevada courts."

Meanwhile, the court of public opinion set to work. "Sinatra being the national public figure that he was, I guess I should have realized that [the complaint] would attract a tremendous amount of attention, not only [in] the press but from individuals all over the country," Ed Olsen recalled.

There were literally hundreds of letters that came from every part of the nation. And the unfortunate thing that I found out was that so many people had a—apparently an ingrained resentment of Sinatra because he had been successful, or he came from a poor background and made money, or something like that. And so many of these things were racial overtones. People were just *bitter* about the man. So they were very complimentary to the state for trying to do something with him . . .

On the other hand, there were some delightful letters from people who were either Sinatra fans, or had known him—friends, something like that—which were in his support.

Hank Greenspun, the publisher of the *Las Vegas Sun,* a friend and big fan of Frank's, climbed onto a soapbox, writing a series of daily front-page columns that lauded Sinatra's philanthropy and generosity and raked the Gaming Control Board over the coals. "If I'm ever roasted again in my life I'll never be roasted like I was by Greenspun," said Olsen, who also noted that while the columns weren't completely accurate, "they're so well written that they're well worth reading."

This was generous of him; Greenspun's prose seems more emotional than finely wrought. "I cannot think of any individual who has possibly been more instrumental in spreading the name and fame of Nevada to the outside world than Frank Sinatra," one column read. "I think [revoking his license] is a rotten, horrible, mean, and cheap way to repay this man for all the good he has brought this state."

———

Frank, of course, was out of state—in Manhattan, to be exact. On the night of the twelfth, he finally made it to the Americana to catch Frankie's act, which he found wanting. "I'm going to kick you right in your Francis!" Senior yelled at Junior afterward. "Don't ever let me catch you singing like that again, without enthusiasm."

The boy tried to explain. "I'm upset over something," he said.

"Get lost!" Frank replied. "No matter what your name is, you're nothing if you aren't excited about what you're doing."

Unlike his father, Frankie hadn't learned to shut out the world, which is a lot easier to do if you feel you're at the center of it. After the show, reporters hit Frank with the inevitable questions about Cal-Neva. "There's nothing I can say," he told them. "I won't know anything until I get back to Los Angeles and talk to my lawyer." But, he said, "We'll fight this."

The next day, with his old friend Skitch Henderson as piano accompanist, he was the featured entertainment at United Nations Staff Day. Secretary-General U Thant himself introduced Sinatra, as "the great uplifter of spirits."

To prove the secretary-general's point, Frank looked around the great hall of the General Assembly and asked, rhetorically, "Do you mind if I smoke?" He lit a cigarette and looked around the big room. "It's essential to relax, with the hot spots around the world," he explained. "Vietnam . . . Congo . . ." He paused for an instant. "Lake Tahoe . . ."

As the audience tittered, he added, in a stage whisper, "Anybody want to buy a used casino? I didn't want it anyway." It got a big laugh.

———

"There are legal brains around," Earl Wilson noted on the eighteenth, "who think Frank Sinatra has a couple of legs to stand on in his battle with the Nevada Gaming commission." The equally Frank-friendly columnist Louis Sobol concurred. "What the local gambling fraternity can't understand," he wrote, "is all this fuss about Sam Giancana's stay at the Cal-Neva Lodge when it is no secret that he has financial interests in several casinos in Nevada and has occasionally lodged in Las Vegas hotels." And attorney Greg Bautzer—who, oddly enough, had represented Nancy Sinatra in her 1949 divorce from Frank—also stuck up for Sinatra. "I don't think it should be possible," he said, "that an individual can lose a property right by virtue of having a friend. I can even have a convicted individual as a friend if I desire and there's no law that says I cannot."

Nobody mentioned Frank's threat to Ed Olsen.

———

At the end of September, as the Nevada Gaming Control Board prepared its case against Frank Sinatra, President Kennedy stopped in Las Vegas to give a speech about preserving the nation's natural resources. As he rode to the Convention Center in an open car with Governor Grant Sawyer, Kennedy turned to him and said, "Aren't you people being a little hard on Frank out here?" The governor replied, "Well, Mr. President, I'll try to take care of things here in Nevada, and I wish you luck on the national level." Taking this for the "fuck you" that it was, JFK pushed back. "Is there anything you can do for Frank?" he asked. "No," Sawyer said.

Ed Olsen, who later heard about the exchange from Sawyer, was impressed. "Now, that's about the highest degree of political pressure that you could ever put into the thing!" he said. While there is no evidence that Sinatra asked for the president's intercession, or that any political pressure ever came to bear, Frank did go to considerable lengths to prepare his defense before the Gaming Control Board, retaining a well-known Las Vegas criminal attorney named Harry Claiborne. Mickey Rudin consulted. The lawyer later told Nancy Sinatra he'd been ready to prove that Frank hadn't invited Sam Giancana to Cal-Neva, that Giancana had not stayed at the resort in any case, and that Sinatra had had no idea Momo was in the area. Rudin said that even if he and Frank lost the disciplinary proceedings, he was fully prepared to make an appeal.

On October 3, Harry Claiborne cross-examined Ed Olsen for four hours. Rudin, a daunting presence, was also there. The Gaming Control Board chairman, creaking in on his crutches, was unintimidated. He had come well prepared: he had a briefcase full of papers attesting to his investigators' findings and his own recollections of the memorable phone conversation with Sinatra (which he'd transcribed after the fact, not recorded) and, just for insurance, a couple of reels of blank recording tape, which he placed conspicuously on the table.

It was a brilliant tactic, but it would have taken more than a bit of stagecraft to stop Frank's attack dogs. What it took, in the end, was the intercession of his new business partner. In the midst of the proceedings, Jack Warner phoned Mickey Rudin and said that if Sinatra were going to be associated with Warner Bros. as an executive, any publicity about Cal-Neva and Giancana was bad publicity. Unless Frank surrendered his casino license, the crusty studio chief commanded, the Warner deal was off. Rudin, who'd been itching to do battle with the Gaming Control Board, heeded his client and reluctantly threw in the towel.

In the end, though, Sinatra claimed that any worries about losing the Warner Bros. deal had been secondary. The chief reason her father failed to fight the Control Board, Nancy Sinatra writes, was "because the investigation was potentially embarrassing to his friend President Kennedy."

Few people besides Frank Sinatra knew just how embarrassing "potentially embarrassing" might be.

On October 7, Frank officially capitulated. Through Claiborne, he issued a statement saying that "not only as an entertainer, but as an investor and an executive," he had long been planning—anyway—to divest himself completely from the gaming industry in Nevada and that besides, he had better things to do. "I have recently become associated with a major company in the entertainment industry," he said, "and in forming that association, I have promised not only to devote my talent as an entertainer to certain of our joint investments, but I have agreed to devote my full time and efforts to that company's activities in the entertainment industry. Accordingly, I have instructed my attorney to notify the Nevada Gaming officials that I am withdrawing from the gambling industry in Nevada."

He could afford to walk away. Not only did he have his Warner money and his Warner respectability, but, as *Variety* pointed out, "Even this enforced unloading of his Cal-Neva Lodge in Lake Tahoe and his 'points' in The Sands, Las Vegas, will prove an economic windfall. He is certain to turn a capital gain profit on both. In the case of the 9% holdings in the Vegas hostelry, Sinatra envisions a $800,000 capital gain." In the case of his 50 percent share in Cal-Neva, valued at $3 million, he theoretically stood to take out far more, though the uncertain size of Sam Giancana's stake muddies the mathematics.

For all his high-sounding protestations, Frank was desolate about having to give up what his daughter Nancy called "his dream, Cal-Neva," and furious with Giancana. "That fucker shouldn't have been there in the first place," he said. "Look at the trouble he caused. This is *his* fault, not mine." For his part, Mooney was incensed with Frank for losing his temper at the chairman of the Nevada Gaming Control Board, a tirade that wound up costing the gangster some $465,000. Sinatra "called Ed Olsen a cripple," Phyllis McGuire said. "Sam couldn't get over the fact that Frank had done that. Sam said, 'If he'd only shut his damned mouth.' But Sam never could figure out why Frank would deliberately pick fights . . . He would always say to him, '*Piano, piano, piano*'—'take it easy, take it easy.' Sam could never get over the hotheaded way Frank acted."

That a psychopathic killer had to tell Sinatra to curb his temper is a remarkable statement in itself.

"That bastard and his big mouth," Giancana told another friend. "All he had to do was keep quiet, let the attorneys handle it, apologize, and get a thirty- to sixty-day suspension . . . but no, Frank has to get on the phone with that damn big mouth of his and now we've lost the whole damn place."

Conveniently forgetting that it was his own temper that had led to the Chalet 50 fracas and uncorked this whole bottle of woes in the first place.

The relationship ended the same way most of Frank's relationships ended: not with a confrontation, but angry silence. "Mr. S never met with or even called Mr. Sam to tell him he was going the Warner route," George Jacobs writes. "He just stopped talking to him. He was dumping Sam the same way he dumped his mistresses. Unlike with the girls, he *wanted* to talk, he *planned* to talk to Sam, but it didn't happen."

A few months later, Ed Olsen took in Sammy Davis Jr.'s late show at the Sands with friends of his, a couple from California. After the show—which Olsen enjoyed greatly—he went with his friends to the lobby gift shop to buy a newspaper. To the couple's delight, they spotted Sammy himself off in a corner, taking practice swings with a putter the store had on display. The man and woman took it into their heads to go introduce themselves to Davis, and before Olsen knew it, they were introducing him to the entertainer as well.

As Olsen recalled, "And Davis looks at me for a second, then he turns to the California people, and he said, 'I'd like to talk to this man alone.'

"Then I thought, 'Oh, God, here comes a brawl for sure.'

"So they go on their way. Davis gets me off in a corner, and . . . he undertakes to tell me in many of the same four-letter words that Sinatra used what a great thing I had done. He says, 'That little son of a bitch, he's needed this for years. I've been working with him for sixteen years, and nobody's ever had the guts to stand up to him!'"

By all accounts, Frank Sinatra's relationship with Jack Kennedy was now nearly nonexistent: no more visits in Palm Springs or Washington or Hyannis Port; no more thrilling phone calls from "the prez." Yet Frank's telling his daughter that he'd given up on his Cal-Neva defense to avoid embarrassing the president, though self-protective (and self-aggrandizing) on the face of it, made a certain kind of sense. Despite the White House's distancing—and Jackie Kennedy's intensive behind-the-scenes efforts—some part of the public still saw Sinatra and JFK as friends. And no matter how venial his sin as Cal-Neva's licensee, Frank (and the president, by association) had much to lose in the court of public relations if the full extent of his relationship with Giancana were brought to light.

And of course the president of the United States stood to lose far more than reputation if the full extent of his own connection to Sam Giancana were brought to light.

Mickey Rudin maintained that the newspapers had sentenced Frank Sinatra to a lifetime of disgrace on two false charges: that he had invited Giancana to Cal-Neva, and that his gaming license had been revoked as a result. And Rudin was right. His client was innocent on both counts: Giancana had in fact invited himself to Cal-Neva, and Frank had surrendered his license voluntarily.

But was Sinatra, as Cal-Neva's licensee, responsible for upholding the rules of the Nevada Gaming Commission—the Black Book? He was. Had he used vile and intemperate language and threatened the chairman of the Nevada Gaming Control Board? He had. Would he have lost his license if he had kept fighting? We can't know.

Nancy Sinatra maintains that her father was persecuted, despite his alleged innocence, because he was "the single most visible figure in Nevada in those days" and that he never recovered from the Cal-Neva episode. "The press, of course, had a field day," she writes. "Or a week or month."

Because of continual errors in newspaper accounts of the episode, she claims, Frank lost what remained of his naïve ideals and became more apt to carry grudges. He turned more vulnerable and pessimistic, even cynical. Mostly, though (Nancy says), her father was hurt.

The image of Frank Sinatra as a starry-eyed naïf blinking back tears because those mean newspapermen had turned him into a grudge holder may be absurd; certainly Lew Wasserman, Peter Lawford, and Hank Sanicola would have found it so. But even if Nancy Sinatra understandably saw her father in the most forgiving light, she also knew him the best, and the fact that she now saw a change in him has real meaning. Staring down the barrel of age fifty (he would turn forty-eight in December), Frank was richer than he had ever been and—in part because of it—more isolated and suspicious than ever as well. As had happened with the legendary king, everything he touched turned to gold: he had achieved vast power, but love and nourishment were ever harder to come by.

———

Gene Kelly had left MGM in 1957, gradually transitioning from acting to directing and producing, his greatest years behind him along with the greatest years of the Hollywood musical. But in 1963, as Frank Sinatra proposed to revive the genre with *Robin and the 7 Hoods* (it would be his last musical), he turned to his old Metro stablemate for help.

With his Warner Bros. deal newly in hand, Frank was feeling expansive. He not only wanted Kelly to co-produce *Robin* with him; he envisioned a three-picture deal: Sinatra would star in all three, of course; Kelly would co-star with him in the second and direct the third. Kelly, whose phone wasn't ringing as often as it used to, was happy to play second fiddle.

Robin and the 7 Hoods, starring Frank, Dean, Sammy, and Bing Crosby (to whom Frank apparently bore no ill will for lending his house to the prez), was to start shooting in mid-October, with Frank Sinatra and Gene Kelly listed as co-producers. But before the cameras began to roll, Kelly had, as *Variety* would put it, ankled the project.

"The reason isn't too hard to guess," Dorothy Kilgallen wrote on the twenty-first. "Gene discovered, in discussions with Frank Sinatra, that he wasn't exactly going to be given free rein as the producer. The star intends to get into that part of the act, too."

Kilgallen had guessed right. It was Frank's picture, Frank's money, and Frank's rules. Kelly had told Sinatra he thought there were too many musical numbers in the picture; Sinatra had disagreed. No contest. There was another equally important disagreement: Kelly, a past master of the movie musical, felt rehearsals were crucial. Sinatra had long ago made clear his position on rehearsals.

"I wasn't making any decisions," Kelly later said. "I was taking orders. Quietly, I like the boys, but friendship isn't always everything in this business." With Frank, it was far less than that. He took over as sole producer as well as star of *Robin and the 7 Hoods,* and the three-picture deal was quietly dropped.

He had long dreamed of being a Mob boss; now he was getting to play one in the movies.

Turning the story of Robin Hood and his Merry Men into a gangster musical set in Roaring Twenties Chicago wasn't a bad premise, as premises went— not much worse, say, than basing *Guys and Dolls* on Damon Runyon's Times Square tales—and if Sammy Cahn and Jimmy Van Heusen, whom Frank had tapped to create *Robin's* score, weren't quite Frank Loesser, they weren't far behind. Along with Sammy and Chester, the rest of the production team had also by now become Sinatra-movie regulars: Koch, the musical director Nelson Riddle, the director of photography and associate producer William H. Daniels. And back in the director's chair was Gordon Douglas, who'd shown such remarkable tolerance for Frank's unique style of moviemaking on 1954's *Young at Heart.*

Gene Kelly might have lifted the whole project to a different level, but Kelly had been insubordinate, and he was history. No one who was left was likely to repeat his mistake.

The wispy plot of *Robin and the 7 Hoods,* cooked up by a sitcom writer named David Schwartz—his most extensive prior experience consisted of writing the 1950s television version of Frank's boyhood radio favorite, *The Amos 'n' Andy Show*—spun off from a gangland rivalry between Robbo (Sinatra), the boss of the North Side, and his South Side counterpart, Guy Gisborne (Peter Falk). There was some misplaced reward money; there was a romantic competition between Robbo and Gisborne over Marian (Barbara Rush), the daughter of a dead gangster. On paper, it was amiable nonsense, but what musical plot isn't?

The songs and the cast were the best parts. Dean played Robbo's gambling sidekick Little John, Sammy was his machine-gun-happy aide-de-camp Will Scarlet, and Bing portrayed a charmingly corrupt orphanage administrator named Allen A. Dale—a role that had once, long before, been promised to Peter Lawford. Edward G. Robinson had a walk-on as Big Jim, the mobster who gets rubbed out, and veteran Hollywood tough guys like Victor Buono, Allen Jenkins, and Jack La Rue lent color.

Production began on Halloween with location shooting in Chicago, then shifted to the busy Warner Bros. lot, where *Sex and the Single Girl, My Fair Lady, Dear Heart,* and John Ford's *Cheyenne Autumn* were all under way. *Robin* clicked right along at first, the agreeable and technically proficient Douglas executing his setups smoothly and making no unreasonable demands on the boss. Morale was high. The sixty-year-old Crosby, always on the verge of retirement in those days, was delighted to be in his first musical since *High Society* and elated at the camaraderie with Sinatra, Martin, and Davis. The only hint of tension came from May Britt, who refused to visit the set because her husband's obsequiousness to the Leader—a posture Sammy had developed to a fine art—had begun to drive her to distraction.

On the night of November 13 at Warner Bros., Frank recorded *Robin*'s one certifiably great song, Cahn and Van Heusen's first-rate hymn to the Second City, "My Kind of Town." He was in great voice, full of confidence. By the third week of November, the shoot was a day ahead of schedule.

Then the unimaginable explosion.

The story goes that Frank was filming a scene in a Burbank cemetery when the news came from Dallas, but the story is a little too good—or bad, in this case—to be true. On his audio commentary for the DVD of *Robin and the 7 Hoods,* Frank Sinatra Jr. says that in fact the cemetery location was shot on November 21 and that Frank, wandering off for a smoke between setups, leaned against a tombstone, then noticed its inscription: JOHN F. KENNEDY, 1873–1940.

The truth appears to be that on November 22, Sinatra, the only star on the call sheet for the day, was filming a courtroom scene on a Warner soundstage (Mickey Rudin, his unlovely mug memorialized for all time, was playing a cameo as the judge) when word of the president's assassination reached the set. Her father was stunned into silence when he heard the news, Nancy Sinatra writes. Then Frank ordered an aide to get him the White House on the phone. When he returned to the crew, he said, "Let's shoot this thing, 'cause I don't want to come back here anymore."

Production had stopped for all of half an hour. When the cameras started to roll again, veteran tough guy Jack La Rue fainted—perhaps the one honest reaction on the set to the day's events—and had to be revived. Gordon Douglas shot nine more setups, nineteen takes, before Frank went home at 2:50 p.m.

In Las Vegas, *Variety* reported, a twenty-four-hour blackout of all entertainment went into effect after news of President Kennedy's death. "Casino execs reported gambling came almost to a complete halt early in the afternoon on the day of the assassination," the weekly noted.

Sinatra and George Jacobs retreated to Palm Springs, where even his daughter Nancy was unable to reach him by phone. For three days, "he holed up in his bedroom, watching the assassination circus, freaking out along with the rest of the world when Ruby shot Oswald, eating nothing but occasional fried-egg sandwiches, and drinking vast amounts of Jack Daniel's," the valet writes.

> He called Pat Lawford in Washington to express his regrets, though he still refused to speak to Peter. Nor did he telephone Jackie or Bobby, who, he said, "wouldn't return my calls." He sent an enormous floral display instead. For all his hatred of Bobby, for all the pain "TP" had inflicted upon him by cutting him dead, Mr. S would never say one unkind word about the man he once loved and continued to admire as a leader, if not as a man. "I really liked Jack," I told Mr. S. I'd been crying. I couldn't help it. "He liked you, too, George," Sinatra answered sadly. "Probably more than me."

"Frank was pretty broken up when he talked to Pat and would have given anything to come back to Washington for Jack's funeral, but it just wasn't possible to invite him," Peter Lawford recalled, with a certain amount of schadenfreude. "He'd already been too much of an embarrassment to the family."

When filming resumed on *Robin and the 7 Hoods* the next week, the set's sense of high-spirited efficiency had evaporated. Suddenly the subject of gangland shootings had lost its humor. After Frank overheard some of the cast and crew making dark comments about Dallas and its citizens, he got on the soundstage's PA system and gave an impassioned impromptu speech pleading for tolerance. There was a moment of stunned silence, then the group burst into spontaneous applause. The Hollywood trade papers picked up the story.

The nation had been through dark periods before, but nothing like this. Had the president been gunned down in the lobby of a building or at a private gathering, it would still have been awful, but it would have been different. Instead, it had been the most public and gruesome of murders. In a second, in the bright sunlight of an autumn midday in Dallas, the image of vigor and glamour that had inspired the whole world, whatever its true substance, had been replaced with one of pornographic violence: frame 313 of the Zapruder film, the pink flash. It was as though the jaws of hell had suddenly opened and

Satan had laughed at the folly of human vanity. It was impossible to have lived through that day and not taken on a heightened sense of one's own vulnerability and the transience and fragility of every human activity. Frank would have felt all this as he felt everything: in the keenest possible way.

And who had done it? He knew things; he had been told things. To live alone with what he thought might be true seemed truly awful.

But worst of all would have been the idea that all the power in the world ultimately meant nothing.

That was the Thanksgiving everyone sleepwalked through, and Sinatra was no exception. The assassination had shaken him badly; mortality was on his mind. He was going to be forty-eight in a couple of weeks, no longer on the green upslope of the decade, but headed toward a future of diminishing returns. The Camels and the Jack Daniel's stayed with him longer; the first sight of his face in the morning was not encouraging.

The holiday dinner, as always, was at the Palm Springs compound, Big Nancy and Frankie and Tina all in attendance. Nancy senior did the cooking: two tomasina (hen) turkeys, with yams, mashed potatoes, cranberry sauce, her special stuffing (with pecans, apricots, and celery, the top slightly burned), and pumpkin pie.

To Frank it tasted like ashes.

"Thanksgiving was a jovial holiday for our family, but that year my father was subdued," Tina Sinatra recalled. " 'This shouldn't be happening anywhere,' he kept saying, 'but certainly not *here*.' "

Did Frank have feelings for Dean, and did Dean feel for Frank? Surely; deeply. And either man would rather have had a molar extracted, sans anesthesia, than look the other in the eye and express *feelings*. The same, and then some, held true for the way both Sinatra and Martin felt about Bing Crosby. Both had long idolized him: Dean had stolen from him; and Frank had recently resented him. And Bing, the perfect idol, was even further—light-years away—from doing anything like expressing feelings like (as he thought of them) those warm-blooded Italian boys.

The whole farrago is what makes the trio's performance of Cahn and Van Heusen's superbly stylish "Style"—

A flower's not a flower if it's wilted,
A hat's not a hat till it's tilted

—so delicious. Wearing tuxes and boaters and wielding walking sticks, the three are the furthest thing from a crowd: each man is eye-catching in his own way, but nobody steals the show. And the feelings each had for the others are there too, only deep under the surface, which is, of course, pure style.

They recorded it on the night of December 3—five days after Thanksgiving, eleven days after the assassination. All feelings, except the joy of performance, buried deep beneath the surface, where all three men felt that feelings mostly belonged.

Barry Keenan was the kind of talented screwup everyone has encountered, a guy who peaked too early and burned out young. As a student at University High School in West Los Angeles in the late 1950s—Nancy Sinatra was a friend and fellow student, as were Jan Berry and Dean Torrence, soon to become the successful singing duo Jan and Dean—Keenan had a seemingly contradictory reputation: he was a charming, hard-drinking partier and also an extremely clever and ambitious kid, fascinated with the stock market and determined to become a millionaire before he turned thirty.

He almost made it. By age twenty-one, he was a successful real estate investor and the youngest member of the Pacific Coast Stock Exchange, earning in the neighborhood of $10,000 a month in early-1960s dollars. He married young and lived well. But then he was badly injured in a car wreck, and in short order he became addicted to painkillers and lost all his money. His marriage fell apart. There were some minor scrapes with the law.

In 1962, he began to hit up his old friend Dean Torrence for money—not much at first, just a couple of hundred here and there. Torrence could easily afford it. By now, he and Jan Berry had forged a successful rock 'n' roll career, and an atypical one: both were still living at home and completing their college studies, Berry in premed at UCLA, Torrence in architecture at USC. Dean Torrence had a substantial bank account, partly thanks to stock investments he'd made on Keenan's recommendation.

Keenan and Torrence had another bond: at Uni High, along with Jan Berry and another friend, a tough guy named Joe Amsler, they had been part of a social club called the Barons, many of whose members maintained a close fraternal tie in the years after high school. As a friend and a former Baron, Torrence felt obliged to help Keenan out; at the same time, he did his best to make himself scarce whenever Keenan came calling.

In the spring of 1963, Barry Keenan contacted Dean Torrence again, saying he wanted to talk to him. "I knew what that meant," Torrence recalled. He told Keenan he was on his way to class at USC. When Torrence came out of class, he found Keenan waiting for him. "I need to speak to you in kind of a quiet place," he said.

They sat on the quad. Keenan told Torrence that he was in desperate financial shape, that a job in door-to-door sales had led nowhere. He owed his family a lot of money. Now, he said, he had a venture in mind; he produced a three-ring notebook in which he had carefully outlined the business plan. He spelled it all out as Torrence sat in disbelief. Barry Keenan told Dean Torrence that he had carefully researched different sorts of crimes and had come up with the one that involved the least risk and would deliver the biggest payoff: kidnapping the son of a famous entertainer.

Snow was falling over Lake Tahoe on Sunday, December 8; cars with jingling snow chains on their tires crawled over icy Route 50, which skirted the southeast edge of the lake and ran by Harrah's hotel-casino, on the state line. Unlike Cal-Neva to the north, Bill Harrah's resort operated throughout the winter, drawing crowds for the gambling and the star attractions in the South Shore Room. The entertainment this weekend was Frank Sinatra Jr., singing with Sam Donahue and the Tommy Dorsey Orchestra.

Frankie, in boxer shorts and a white T-shirt, was relaxing in his suite before the first show, eating room-service chicken with a trumpeter in the band named John Foss. The phone rang, and Frankie picked it up. "Not here," he said after a moment. "Wrong number."

At about 9:30 p.m., there was a knock on the door. "Room service," the voice outside said loudly. "I've got a package for you."

Foss opened the door, and a man wearing a brown ski parka and carrying a wine carton entered. The man put the box on a table, then, fumbling, pulled a blue-steel .38 revolver—loaded—from his pocket and pointed it at John Foss and Frank Sinatra Jr. He told them to lie on the bed. Another man now entered the room. The two were Barry Keenan and Joe Amsler. Keenan had lured Amsler—who since high school had earned a marginal living as a prizefighter and a fisherman, as well as a minor criminal record—to Tahoe with the lie that a construction job awaited both of them; he'd put off telling him about the kidnap plot until the last minute. Both were almost incapacitatingly nervous. "Where's the money?" Keenan demanded, as though robbery were what they'd come for. (In fact, he was broke again, lacking enough cash to buy gas for the getaway car, a 1963 Chevrolet Impala.) Frankie and Foss gave him all they had in their wallets, $20 and change.

"We'd better take one of you guys with us," Keenan said. He pointed at Frankie. "You," he said.

"But I'm in my underwear," Frankie said.

"Then get dressed, because you're coming with us," Keenan said.

While Frankie put on a pair of gray slacks, brown loafers without socks, and a blue Windbreaker, Keenan bound Foss's wrists with surgical tape. Amsler tied Frankie's wrists behind his back and blindfolded him with a sleep mask, and then he and Barry Keenan hustled Junior out of the room, into the dark and snow. A moment later, Keenan returned to the room and tore the telephone wire from the wall. He left not realizing he had accidentally left his gun in the hotel room.

––––––––

In a few minutes, John Foss managed to free himself and run to the lobby, where he told the receptionist that Frank Sinatra Jr. had been kidnapped; he then gave the news to Frankie's manager, Tino Barzie. Within half an hour, the hotel was swarming with police. Faced with the unpleasant duty of phoning Frank senior with the terrible news (and perhaps remembering Lawford's fate), Barzie punted, calling Big Nancy instead. Nancy, who was having dinner in her Bel Air house with the Hollywood gossip columnist Rona Barrett,* put her hand over the telephone. "Good Lord, Rona," she said. "They've kidnapped Frank Junior!" She then phoned Frank in Palm Springs. "Oh my God, I can't believe it," Sinatra said. "Oh, no. Oh, no. Oh, no."

Frank quickly chartered a plane (the *Christina* was in Los Angeles) and flew through the blizzard to Reno: no small matter for him; he was always more frightened of flying than he let on. William Raggio, the district attorney of Washoe County and an old friend, met him at the airport, as did a crowd of reporters and photographers. "I got no comment to make," a shaken Frank told them brusquely. "Just get away from me, you bums." Together, he and Raggio got in the DA's car and headed toward Harrah's, sixty miles to the south, but by now blizzard conditions had made the roads impassable, and the two had to return to Reno. There, in a sixth-floor suite of the Mapes Hotel, a grand old Art Deco high-rise downtown, Frank—along with Mickey Rudin, Jack Entratter, Jim Mahoney (who had now replaced Chuck Moses as Sinatra's publicist), Jilly Rizzo, and five FBI agents—awaited a call from whoever it was that had taken his son.

Back at Harrah's, the FBI administered lie-detector tests to John Foss and Tino Barzie, asking them, among other things, if the kidnapping was a hoax. It

---

* Nancy senior had sold the Carolwood house in 1961 and downsized—but not down-classed—to 700 Nimes Road, Bel Air, "a sleek, contemporary three-bedroom with a pool and a cantilevered deck, but no grounds," according to *My Father's Daughter* (p. 87).

was a strange question, but one that, in the present strange conditions, had to be asked. Both men said that they knew of no hoax, and both passed the test.

————————

There was no word that night, though as Frank sat by the telephone, chain-smoking and beyond agitation, many other calls came in, some from unexpected quarters. Bobby Kennedy phoned, and within five minutes the man Sinatra had hated became his ally, as the attorney general promised the Justice Department would give the investigation top priority. Sam Giancana called, offering to conduct his own form of investigation, and Frank alienated his former friend even further by telling him to back off: "Please. Don't do a damn thing. Let the FBI handle this."

Pierre Salinger also phoned, as did Pat Brown, the governor of California. And then J. Edgar Hoover himself, ordering Sinatra not to speak to the press. It was not a moment for the savoring of irony.

On Monday morning, the newspapers were black with headlines, not just about the kidnapping, but about the horrific crash of a Pan Am 707, in a fireball, over Elkton, Maryland, killing all eighty-one people aboard. It was a bleak season. Snow blanketed much of the country. LIGHTNING TURNED PLANE TO FIREBALL?, read the eerie banner headline on the front page of Kansas's *Hutchinson News*. The kidnap story ran next to the jet-crash story, a soulful photo of Frankie in a tux cheek by jowl with a picture of the wreckage in Elkton. Underneath was a text block promoting *The Torch Is Passed*, the Associated Press's instant book about the Kennedy assassination. "The Hutchinson News has arranged to make it available to all its readers at the very reasonable rate of $2," the text ran. "It will not be sold through bookstores."

The AP story about the jet crash described, in detail, a scene of hellish carnage and destruction. There were a lot of plane crashes in those days. The piece about Frank junior said that the police were seeking two escaped convicts, bank robbers Joseph James Sorce, twenty-three, and Thomas Patrick Keating, twenty-one, in connection with the case. The pair were presumed to be armed and dangerous.

Frank continued to sit by the phone in the Mapes Hotel, leaving only to go to the bathroom and, for a few minutes, to get some fresh air on the roof. Jim Mahoney issued a statement to the press: "Sinatra is ready to make a deal with the kidnappers, and no questions asked." The day wore on, but no word came.

————————

It would have been easy for Frank and his family, in the midst of their unspeakable torment, to have imagined the worst: that violent and desperate career criminals with itchy trigger fingers and little to lose had taken Frank junior. (Many years later, Tina Sinatra recalled that her father had fretted the abduction might have been a message from the Mob to keep quiet about anything that might link organized crime to the Kennedy assassination.) Yet it is hard to imagine that the Sinatras would have derived much comfort from knowing the true story of the kidnapping and the ragtag trio who had pulled it off:

That Barry Keenan, who was a devout Catholic in addition to being addicted to Percodan and alcohol, had, months before, begun to hear the voice of God. "God talked to me, particularly when I would go to church and light a candle and be still and I would hear God talking to me and telling me what I had to do," Keenan recalled. "And He was very definite about nobody can be hurt, and I had to pay the money back." He also planned to tithe 10 percent of the ransom to the church.

That one section in Barry Keenan's divided three-ring binder outlined in detail his five-year investment plan for the ransom money, which he intended to put into real estate projects in West Los Angeles and Chrysler Corporation stock, then at an all-time low. Having made a list of the funds he needed for investments and to help his parents, he hit upon the precise amount he needed: $240,000. "Since I was going to have to pay it back," he recalled, "I didn't want to raise more money than I could easily pay back." At the end of five years, he fully intended to return Frank Sinatra's money to him, with interest. "And just imagining the reaction that he and the FBI would have when the ransom money starts coming back to him," he said. As it turned out, Keenan's investment plan, had he had the chance to carry it through, would have been highly successful: Chrysler stock soared, and the West Los Angeles tracts he intended to buy became Marina del Rey.

That another section in the notebook outlined the potential benefits of the kidnapping to the Sinatra family. "It would bring father and son closer together," Keenan said. Also, "At the time, Sinatra was being investigated for his connections with the mob and money laundering through the Cal-Neva Lodge and Sands casino in Las Vegas. And I thought, well, this might even help him there . . . I felt that, if the public would perceive him as a worried parent rather than a famous singer hanging out with the Mafia, that would cast him in a more favorable image."

That Keenan, having to press the dim and frightened Joe Amsler into participating in the abduction of Junior, quickly came to feel that he was kidnapping two people: Frankie and Amsler. To help his sidekick to feel calmer and more confident, Keenan gave him some of his Percodans.

That Frank junior, initially believing that he was only a robbery victim who had been taken hostage, cooperated fully at first with Keenan and Amsler, promising to help them in every way possible and even agreeing to down a couple of sleeping pills with whiskey in order to appear plausibly passed out, rather than kidnapped, if police stopped the getaway car.

That at one point during the getaway, when the Impala was approaching a police roadblock, Joe Amsler climbed out of the car into the heavily falling snow and knocked himself out by running into a tree branch.

That upon finally hearing that he had in fact been kidnapped, Frank junior flew into a rage, refusing to give Keenan his father's private telephone number for a ransom call. "No. Fuck you," Junior said. "I'm not cooperating anymore. Go ahead, shoot me. Go ahead. I fucking dare you. *Shoot me.*"

That, not trusting himself to be able to handle the job of telephoning Frank senior with the ransom demand, the twenty-three-year-old Barry Keenan had enlisted a second confederate named John Irwin, a gravel-voiced, forty-two-year-old housepainter who, like his accomplices, had a record of petty crimes.

———

On that same Monday morning, Dean Torrence's phone rang. It was Barry Keenan calling. "He asked me if I'd turned on the radio yet," Torrence recalled. "I said, 'No—why?' He said somebody had kidnapped Frank Sinatra Jr. from Lake Tahoe."

Torrence was thunderstruck. "I never thought he'd do it," he said. "I thought somebody else must've heard his plan."

A few moments later, the musician realized that his old friend really had pulled off his crazy scheme. "I was in shock," Torrence recalled. Keenan, he said, "sounded pretty calm. He was tired; he hadn't slept in a day or two. Then he got to the basics of it, which was that he needed more money."

Barry Keenan and Joe Amsler, who now had Frank junior padlocked in the back bedroom of a rented house in Canoga Park in the San Fernando Valley, had not yet made their ransom demand, because they themselves were too frightened to talk to Frank Sinatra on the telephone.

———

At 4:45 p.m. on Monday, the phone finally rang in the room at the Mapes Hotel.

"Is this Frank Sinatra?" the deep-voiced caller asked.

"Speaking," Frank said.

"It doesn't sound like Frank Sinatra."

"Well, it is," Frank said.

"Can you be available at nine a.m. tomorrow?"

"Yes, I can."

"OK. Your son is in good shape. Don't worry about him."

There was a click on the line, then silence.

———————

Not long afterward, police captured the bank robbers Sorce and Keating twenty miles from the kidnap scene. The pair were indeed heavily armed. When the FBI showed photographs of the two men to John Foss, however, he was unable to identify them. "The development apparently left police without a major clue to the kidnapping," UPI's account said.

———————

Frank endured another sleepless night in the suite at the Mapes, as did Big Nancy and fifteen-year-old Tina at 700 Nimes Road in Bel Air. Nancy junior was in New Orleans with Tommy Sands, where Sands was appearing at the Roosevelt hotel. FBI agents had been assigned to the whole family. Frank had also hired private guards to patrol the Nimes Road house.

On Tuesday morning at about nine, John Irwin, the deep-voiced kidnapper, phoned again; this time, he put Frank junior on the line.

"Hello, Dad," Frankie said.

"Frank junior?"

"Yeah."

"How are you, son?"

"All right."

"Are you warm enough?"

There was no response. "You on the other end of the phone there?" Frank asked. "You on the other end of the phone there?"

But it was Irwin who answered. "Yeah," he said.

"You want to talk to me about making a deal?" Frank asked. "You want to resolve this thing?"

"Yeah, I do," Irwin said. "But I can't do it now, Frank."

"Why not?"

"Gotta wait till around two o'clock."

"Well, do you have any idea what you want?"

"Oh, naturally we want money."

"Well, just tell me how much you want."

"Well, I can't tell you that now."

The FBI agents had already asked Frank how much cash he could get together on short notice: a million to a million and a half, he'd said. "I don't understand why you can't give me an idea so we can begin to get some stuff ready for you," he said.

"Well, that's what I'm afraid of. I don't want you to have too much time to get ready."

Subtly, Sinatra had shifted into command mode. "Well, hey, I gotta have some time," he said.

"I know. But you see—don't rile me. You're making me nervous. I'll call you back about two o'clock."

"Well, can you call before that?"

"I don't think so. I gotta hang up now."

"Hey, can I talk to Frankie again?"

The line went dead.

"Frank was shaken when he hung that phone up, let me tell you," former FBI agent John Parker recalled. "I was right there, in the room. I saw him break down. 'I just want my kid back,' he said . . . 'That's all I want. Give me back my kid.' I don't think anyone had ever seen Sinatra like this. Everybody just sort of looked at him, not knowing what to do. I mean, do you comfort him or leave him alone?

"When I saw all of this, that's when I started thinking, Man, this guy's got no mobster connections. This guy's got no underworld ties. 'Cause if he did, Jesus Christ, that would've been the time to use 'em, wouldn't it have been?"

———————

In the interim, the kidnappers told Frank to go to Ron's Service Station in Carson City, thirty miles south of Reno, where he would receive further instructions on the station's pay phone. "So, you know, Frank Sinatra, Senior and the FBI go racing down to Carson City, 30 minutes away," Keenan recalled.

And in about 15 minutes, John started calling for Frank Sinatra to the gas station. And the mechanic at the gas station—who was busy and by himself—kept answering the phone. And this caller was asking for Frank Sinatra, the most famous entertainer in the world at the time, and the guy got very angry when this caller was calling back time and again for Frank Sinatra.

He thinks it's a prank of some sort. And so, as soon as he hung up from the third time after letting John have it with four-letter words . . . in screeches two FBI cars and Frank Sinatra, Senior jumps out of the car and says, "My name is Frank Sinatra, have I had any calls?" And you can imagine the reaction that that poor mechanic had. So finally, one more time, John called back, and this time Frank answered the phone. And John told them what the next step was going to be.

The kidnappers wanted $240,000, Irwin told Sinatra. "That's exactly what I've decided we needed," he said.

Frank was mystified by the strange—and strangely low—number. "What are you talking about?" Frank asked. "I'll give you an even million, nice and clean and easy."

"We don't need that much," Irwin said. "We're not gonna take advantage of you, Mr. Sinatra. We need $240,000." He then told Frank to proceed to Nancy's house in Bel Air and await yet another call.

"By this time, Junior was calmed down," Barry Keenan recalled. "He and Joe Amsler were cracking up, telling each other dirty stories. He said to us, 'You know what? I hope you guys get away with this. You guys got guts.'"

———

In Mexico, where she had just finished shooting *The Night of the Iguana*, Ava found out about the kidnapping—perhaps Frank had sent her word—and sat up drinking with a local acquaintance named Nelly Barquette. "She was very upset, Nelly remembered, and she cried because of the boy who had been kidnapped," Lee Server writes.

> She cried out, "That boy—he could have been *my* son!" She had never had a child, she said, and for this she felt much regret. She could have had one with Frank Sinatra, she said. And she cried some more, and it seemed like she was no longer crying for the boy who had been kidnapped but for herself and the things in her life that she had done wrong. And she told Nelly Barquette that she was still in love with Frank Sinatra and it hurt so much to be in love with someone you could not have.

"Yes, she said this to me many times," Barquette recalled. "She was in love with him. She would always be in love. And it hurt so much."

———

Frank was now irritated as well as terrified. The kidnappers seemed to him to be making it up as they went along: the ransom amount was too small, too strange. The FBI agreed with his assessment. (The crooks also appeared to be deriving a certain amount of satisfaction from ordering the most powerful man in show business around the landscape.) If the kidnappers truly were bumbling amateurs, of course, the news was both good and bad: on the one hand, they might be easily outwitted; on the other, they might panic and harm Junior.

In the meantime, Sinatra had phoned his banker Al Hart and told him to withdraw $240,000 from his account, in bills of varying denominations, 12,400 bills in all: $70,000 in hundreds, $35,000 in fifties, and the rest in twenties, tens, and fives. Hart and his staff photographed every bill. It was a lengthy process. At the end of the afternoon, an FBI agent asked the bank president, "What are we going to put this money in, a paper bag?" The bills weighed twenty-three pounds. Hart said, "Go buy a valise." The agent went to the department store J. W. Robinson's but didn't have enough money for the $56 bag. He returned to the City National Bank, where Al Hart gave him $15 from the ransom money to cover the shortfall.

Hart took the money, $239,985 in thick stacks of bills bound with rubber bands, to Nancy's house in the new leather valise.

On Tuesday at 6:00 p.m., Frank, having been spirited out of the Mapes, flew back to Los Angeles with his retinue. The hilly neighborhood around 700 Nimes Road was jammed with reporters' and photographers' cars. Twenty-six FBI agents and more than a hundred members of the LAPD were on the case, the biggest kidnapping since the Lindbergh baby in 1932. The FBI had set up a command center in Frankie's old bedroom. When her father walked through the back door, Tina Sinatra saw in Frank's face "a mix of barely contained emotion, of grief and rage . . . and something else," she writes. "Dad felt helpless. It was a foreign sensation for him, and sheer torture."

Throughout Tuesday evening, Frank's fifteen-year-old daughter watched with alarm as her parents came close to falling apart. Her mother, she recalled, "had refused any sedatives and was just this side of hysterical." But, she said, it was her father who made her most nervous. "I'd seen him truly frightened just once before, on a very bad flight to New York. Now I saw the same chilly look in those blue eyes, and it chilled me in turn. My father did his best to conceal his emotions. He wanted to lead by example, not exacerbate the problem. But he couldn't fool his daughter, and it was tough on me to watch him wrestle with his fear."

"Why haven't they called?" Frank kept muttering. "Why haven't they *called*?" It helped her, Tina said, that he seemed to be getting angry.

At 9:26 p.m., the phone rang. Frank picked it up on the fourth ring, as the FBI had instructed him. This time, Irwin directed him to go to a phone booth at a gas station at Camden Drive and Santa Monica Boulevard in Beverly Hills. Sinatra carried with him a roll of dimes—$5 worth—to use for pay-phone calls, should he need to make any.

The coins came in handy: for the next hour or more, Frank would be making a tour of West and Southwest Los Angeles phone booths, placing and receiving calls to and from the kidnappers and others. At the Camden and

Santa Monica booth, John Irwin told Frank to have a courier bring the ransom to yet another telephone booth, at the Western Airlines terminal at LAX, and answer to the name Patrick Henry. Sinatra called J. Edgar Hoover and asked for a man who could stay cool and not endanger his son. Hoover tapped an agent named Jerome Crowe for the job.

With the valise full of cash and Crowe alongside him, Frank headed to the airport. The phone in the booth at the Western terminal rang, and Crowe picked it up.

"This is John Adams, to whom am I speaking?" the voice said.

"This is Patrick Henry," Crowe replied.

The kidnapper instructed the agent to go to still another service station and ask for a road map. From then on, the man said, Crowe would be observed. The kidnapper then told the agent to proceed to a gas station at Sepulveda and Olympic boulevards in West Los Angeles. Crowe would get a call three minutes after his arrival there, he was told.

At this next station, Crowe answered the phone and was told that Frankie would be released unharmed at the Mulholland Drive exit of the San Diego Freeway three to four hours after the agent dropped off the money.

Wanting to make sure the hostage was still alive, Crowe asked if he could speak to Frank junior. The caller said he could not, because Junior wasn't with him—perhaps a sign that Keenan was now speaking for the trio, since John Irwin was with Frankie at the Canoga Park hideout. The kidnapper then directed Crowe to proceed to a Texaco station near a cemetery on Sepulveda Boulevard. At this last gas station, Crowe was told, he would see two parked school buses. He was to leave the valise between the buses, then check into a hotel. As a squad of FBI agents hovered nearby in taxis and a Good Humor truck, Jerome Crowe put the satchel on the pavement between the buses, then he and Frank left.

––––––––

The kidnappers, sleepless for days and high on various drugs, were now in full disarray. Barry Keenan had picked up the ransom, but Joe Amsler, also detailed to the pickup, had panicked and fled after he saw what he thought was an FBI agent lurking at the Sepulveda gas station. When Keenan called John Irwin to say he had the money but that Amsler was missing, Irwin instantly suspected that Keenan had killed him to eliminate a witness. Meanwhile, Frankie, who through some combination of Stockholm syndrome and personal neediness had now grown close to Irwin, was causing problems. When Irwin told him that the kidnappers had received the ransom but that there was a problem—Amsler's panicked flight—Junior bridled. He told Irwin that if he didn't let him go, he, Frankie, would kill him—or Irwin would have to kill Frankie.

"Junior was now highly irate that we had caused his family all this trouble," Keenan recalled. "He was sick of us. He wanted to be set free. This was not the fun we thought it was going to be. John and Frank had bonded, and John wanted to set Frank free. He thought maybe I had gone crazy and killed Joe, and he didn't want to take any chances."

Frankie had also suggested another possibility to Irwin: that his accomplices had absconded with the ransom money and left him to take the rap.

Exhausted, guilty, and worn down by his captive, John Irwin had lost his taste for the whole enterprise. At 2:00 a.m., he phoned Frank Sinatra at Nimes Road and said, "Something has gone wrong."

Frank's heart stopped. "What do you mean, something has gone wrong?" he yelled into the phone. "We did every goddamn thing you said. Now where's my son?"

"No, not with you," Irwin said. "Something has gone wrong here. So I just dropped your son off at the San Diego Freeway and Mulholland. I wish to hell I hadn't gotten into it, but it's too late to get out. I'm sorry."

Sinatra took Tina's face in his hands. "I'm going to bring your brother home," he said.

———————

But he didn't. Driving alone as he'd been instructed, but with an FBI agent tailing him, Frank had circled and circled the Mulholland overpass area and come up empty. Half an hour later, he returned to Nimes Road without his son. "I cried the whole way back," he later told a friend. "I cried, man. I was losing it. I couldn't even drive the fucking car . . . I thought, Jesus Christ, they took the money, and they killed Frankie. They murdered my son."

At the same time as Frank was searching for Frankie, so was Barry Keenan. "When I got back to the hideout with the ransom and found that John and Junior were both gone and I had already lost Joe, I just burst into tears," he recalled.

> None of this had worked out. I had the money, but I had lost the kidnap victim and both of my partners. And it was very important to my plan that *I* have the opportunity to let Junior go. I didn't want to get caught and not have Junior. I wanted everyone to know I had good intentions. This had turned into a comedy of errors.
>
> I freaked out, got into my car, and started looking for Frank Junior. As I'm out there looking for him, who do I pass on the road? Frank

senior and an FBI agent, doing the same thing, *looking for Junior*. My
heart stopped as they just passed me by.

When Frank returned empty-handed, "the look on his face alarmed me,"
Tina recalled. "I had never seen a face like that: stunned, angry, wired, and
terminally tired, all at the same time. 'I'm sorry,' he told us. 'He wasn't there.'
It was the day before my father's forty-eighth birthday, but he suddenly looked
old to me."

"This isn't good," said one of the FBI agents, "but it's not necessarily the
end."

The kidnappers had failed to take into account that there was no Mulholland
Drive exit on the southbound San Diego Freeway. Heading south from Canoga
Park, John Irwin had exited on North Sepulveda Boulevard and dropped Frank
junior off a quarter mile past the Mulholland overpass, on the wrong side of
the highway. In his agitated state, Irwin had also neglected to tell Frankie that
his father was coming to pick him up. It was 2:30 in the morning. Well oriented
in spite of being freezing, hungry, and exhausted, Frankie walked back to the
overpass and crossed it, heading toward Bel Air. The sleep mask still dangled
from his neck. He turned right on Roscomare Road, proceeding by dead reck-
oning toward his mother's house, which lay two miles to the southeast, across
the twisty, hilly, densely foliaged roads of the world's wealthiest enclave. Every
time a car passed, he ducked into the bushes, fearful that the kidnappers
might have changed their minds and come after him.

Twenty minutes later, George C. Jones, a private policeman cruising in
his Bel-Air Patrol car, heard a voice call out, then saw a skinny young man
flagging him down. Then he saw the sleep mask. Everyone who had read a
newspaper or listened to the radio in the last two days knew about that sleep
mask.

Inside the house at 700 Nimes, Frank was falling apart, railing at what he
felt sure was a double cross, shouting orders at the FBI agents ("Call Bobby
Kennedy! Call Hoover! Jesus Christ, call the president, I don't care! Wake up
the fucking president! Somebody *do* something!"), and remonstrating with the
Almighty Himself, who, he was certain, was paying special attention. ("God,
look, don't take it out on Frankie, okay? I'm the one. I'm the jerk. Punish me.
Not Frankie. That's what you're doing, anyway—punishing me, ain't you? Taking it out on me?")

And if God, Washington, or fate didn't intervene in the next five minutes, he told the agents, he was going to call Sam Giancana.

———

George Jones knew about the hordes of reporters and photographers outside 700 Nimes Road, and so he told Frankie to get into the trunk of his car. It wasn't the first car trunk Junior had been in in the last couple of days. As Jones passed the crowds of journalists outside Nancy Sinatra's house, he leaned his head out the car window. "Any news yet, boys?" he asked. Then he headed up the driveway to the back door and rang the bell.

An FBI agent answered the door; Nancy Sinatra stood just behind him. "Mrs. Sinatra," Jones said, "I have your boy in the trunk of my car. And he's all right."

Jones opened the trunk, and Frank junior climbed out—skinny, very hungry, but otherwise none the worse for wear. He embraced his hysterical mother. "Hi, Ma," he said. "Don't cry—it's over." Then he turned to Frank. "Dad, I'm sorry," Frankie said.

"For what?" Frank asked. "Jesus Christ. For what?"

———

Smiling, Frank walked out to the waiting crowd of reporters—there were about 150 in all—and apologized for keeping them waiting in the cold. It was close to four in the morning of Wednesday, December 11. He turned to go back into Nancy's house, then turned back to the newsmen once more. "Tomorrow is my birthday," he said, "and it's the best present I could get."

———

"Frankie wolfed down an overdue meal and then was questioned by the FBI," Tina Sinatra recalled. "After they were done it was family time. We were exhilarated just to be safe and together again. At some point Mom opened a magnum of Dom Pérignon. She drank the entire bottle by herself and never got a headache.

"We'd all caught a second wind, and it was close to dawn before Dad left with Mickey Rudin. Mom called out after him, 'Frank, button your coat, it's drizzling.'"

———

All day Wednesday, like some manic secret Santa, Barry Keenan drove around Los Angeles, stowing paper bags of cash in the houses of various friends and relatives without their knowledge. The unwitting beneficiaries, soon to stumble upon their good fortune, were people to whom he owed debts; they included his parents and his ex-wife. Keenan's reasoning—if reasoning it was—seemed to be that if he didn't personally hand them the money, they might be able to keep it with impunity. Another recipient was his old friend Dean Torrence. "I left you something nice in the shower," Keenan told him.

"It was a big bag of cash," Torrence recalled. "I have no idea how much it was. I don't think Barry knew either; he was so delirious that he just threw a bunch of money in the bag. I didn't call the cops," he said—once a Baron, always a Baron. "I made arrangements to get it back to him the next day. Luckily for me, he got caught that night."

"My brother broke open the case," Nancy Sinatra writes. While Frankie was blindfolded, she says, his senses became sharper: he heard small planes over the hideout; he identified the make of a station wagon in which he'd been driven by the sound of the tailgate; he deduced John Irwin's probable profession from the roughness of his hands. But in the end, it wasn't Frank junior's acute observations or brilliant detective work by the FBI that brought the perpetrators in; it was Joe Amsler's brother, who phoned the FBI while Joe was sleeping in James Amsler's house in Imperial Beach. Fifteen agents arrested Barry Keenan as he walked into his girlfriend's parents' house in La Cañada. Keenan claimed they beat him to force him to tell where the ransom money was.

December 11, 1963: Frank junior speaks to the press after returning physically unharmed from his kidnapping ordeal. "Tomorrow is my birthday," Frank senior told reporters, "and it's the best present I could get."

"The next day, the police interviewed everybody," Dean Torrence said. "The FBI were a little curious that I was the only one that didn't get any money."

"Virtually everything I had outlined in my plan of operation in terms of how the Sinatras would be affected had worked," Barry Keenan told Randy Taraborrelli in 1997. "Father and son were hugging. Divorced parents were reunited in the moment. And the public now viewed Sinatra in a sympathetic light rather than as a hoodlum. They had a big celebration party that night. It couldn't have worked better if they had paid me to do it, which, by the way, they hadn't."

It is a remarkably detached and self-serving assessment. And the benefits to the Sinatras, such as they were, lasted no longer than the bags of cash Barry Keenan spread around Los Angeles. The repercussions, though, would last for decades.

"Thank God it's over," Frank had said when the ordeal was done. "I'm gonna sleep for a week."

That, of course, was unlikely to happen at any point in Sinatra's life, even this one. By the following weekend, he was onstage again.

The Sands had opened on Frank's thirty-seventh birthday, December 12, 1952; on the Saturday after the kidnapping, he took the *Christina* to Las Vegas with Jill St. John, Dean Martin, and Yul Brynner, among others, to celebrate his forty-eighth birthday, the eleventh anniversary of the casino in which he no longer held a stake, and the successful resolution of the kidnapping. As Sinatra and Martin rose unannounced to join Sammy Davis Jr. and Danny Thomas onstage, the audience gave Frank a standing ovation. He traded repartee with Sammy, Danny, and Dean, then sang three numbers, including "Luck Be a Lady."

In the wee hours, as Frank and his group took in Don Rickles's late show at the Sahara, the comedian looked down at Sinatra and grinned ominously. "Do you know why the kidnappers let Junior go?" he asked. "Because they heard him humming in the trunk."

Oh, I just got a little water on my bird—that's all.

—FRANK SINATRA, ON HIS NEAR DROWNING IN THE SURF
OFF KAUAI, MAY 1964

inatra, like most Americans, was in a somber mood at the beginning of the
New Year. The triple blows of the fall—Cal-Neva, the assassination, and
the kidnapping—had hammered a new sense of vulnerability into him, one
that wouldn't go away easily. "Our world felt turned inside out," Tina Sinatra
writes. "My father had been sick, off and on, since Kennedy was shot. Now
his immune system was in shreds . . . Mom wouldn't be herself for a long time.
She'd go out on a simple errand and turn the wrong way; she was discombobu-
lated."

So was Frank. Over the holidays, he'd retreated to Palm Springs, where he
laid low and tried to recuperate from whatever bug he'd caught. In a spirit of
solemn generosity, he sent Jacqueline Kennedy a brooch for Christmas, and,
forgetting how much she had detested him, she wrote him a heartfelt thank-
you note:

Dear Frank

I do want to thank you for the enchanting pin you sent me for Christmas. You have always been so thoughtful.

The only happy thing that seems to have happened at the end of this
year is the way your son was brought safely back to you.

Please know I am so deeply happy about that.

With my appreciation—the very deepest—for all you did for Jack—
and for believing in him from the beginning.

Jackie

It was hardly the time for ring-a-ding-ding. The day after New Year's, Frank
began a new album of patriotic songs dedicated to the slain president, a collaboration with Bing Crosby called *America, I Hear You Singing*. The bandleader
Fred Waring and his ensemble, the Pennsylvanians—an orchestra and a glee-

club-style chorus—would back them up. Each singer was to record three solo numbers, and Sinatra and Crosby would do two duets, a Cahn–Van Heusen rouser called "You Never Had It So Good" ("Miles of happy faces/Different styles and races") and a spiritual, "Let Us Break Bread Together." On the night of the second, Sinatra laid down his three tracks: "Early American," a vague paean to basic values by Johnny Burke and Jimmy Van Heusen; "The House I Live In," a remake of the hymn to tolerance from his Oscar-winning 1945 short; and "You're a Lucky Fellow, Mr. Smith," a flag-waver originally sung by the Andrews Sisters in the 1941 Abbott and Costello movie *Buck Privates*. The chorus backed Frank, fulsomely, on all three tunes.

It was all very earnest and a little strange. On the one hand, it was a time when patriotic music still had wide currency, when American schoolchildren could sing, unself-consciously,

This is my country, land of my birth
This is my country, grandest on earth.

Sinatra really did love his country, in his fashion, even if its love for him was conditional. Bing, as warm in the public's eyes as he was cold in real life, was widely adored, as were the publicly charming and inoffensive Italian-Americans Dean Martin, Perry Como, and Tony Bennett. Frank could be infinitely charming, but his Italianness was a chip on his shoulder, and inoffensiveness rarely concerned him: he mostly spoke his mind, frequently to his detriment. His popularity played on darker themes like seduction and envy. It was one thing for Bing Crosby to sing patriotic songs; for Frank, it felt off-kilter, as though he were protesting too much or wearing a suit that didn't fit.

The album was more than a little deadly: the musical equivalent, in this dark season, of banging pots and pans to chase the demons away. The old saying that military justice is to justice as military music is to music should have a corollary about patriotic music, and patriotic music with chorus is yet another circle of hell. Everyone involved was very talented—a recuperated Sinatra sang as only he could; the musicians and chorus were top-notch; Nelson Riddle even wrote handsome arrangements for the first two songs of the January 2 session—but none of it could rescue the enterprise. Frank had felt strongly about it, as he felt strongly about all his ideas, good and bad alike. He would live it down.

———

The season of reflection passed quickly. Two weeks later, Frank and Dean headed north to Pebble Beach to take in Bing's annual pro-am golf tournament, also known as the Crosby Clambake. The two arrived late on Friday the seventeenth and at about 1:00 a.m. walked into the dining room of the tony Del Monte Lodge, where Frank demanded something to eat. It would be unreasonable to assume he hadn't been drinking. On an empty stomach. When a clerk told Sinatra the kitchen was closed, he made his unhappiness known as only he could. The clerk called his boss, Richard Osborne, the president of Del Monte Properties. While he was placing the call, Frank grabbed the telephone and told Osborne to get his ass over there right away.

The large, athletic, and socially prominent club president—the kind of man the newspapers used to call a sportsman—thought it might be amusing to try to placate Frank and Dean with a bottle of champagne. Frank, to whom Richard Osborne would have suddenly personified all the accumulated evils of American Waspocracy, was unamused. As Osborne re-explained to him that the kitchen was closed, Sinatra coldcocked him, sending the champagne bottle flying. Frank then continued to rain blows on the club president as Osborne warded off the punches as best he could, then fled the room. "I guess I overestimated Sinatra's sense of humor," he said afterward. He wasn't the first to have done so, and he would be far from the last.

If Frank had brought his worst self to the dining room at the Del Monte Lodge, he brought his best to United Recording a week and a half later, laying down ten tracks (on two nights) for a new LP, the unmellifluously but descriptively titled *Frank Sinatra Sings "Days of Wine and Roses," "Moon River," and Other Academy Award Winners*. Riddle arranged and conducted, and it is an almost entirely beautiful album.

Almost, because with Sammy Fain and Paul Francis Webster's beyond-bombastic "Love Is a Many-Splendored Thing," from the 1955 William Holden–Jennifer Jones weeper of the same name, there is nothing that can be done, even by Frank Sinatra. But on the ten other numbers, Frank does a great deal indeed, and from three of them—Fain and Webster's "Secret Love" and Henry Mancini and Johnny Mercer's "Moon River" and "Days of Wine and Roses"—he and Nelson wrest redemptive surprises.

Doris Day had starred, charmingly, in *Calamity Jane*, Warner Bros.' 1953 petty theft of *Annie Get Your Gun* (Jack Warner had tried to buy the movie rights but was outbid by MGM), and had a number 1 hit with its theme, "Secret Love." But as wonderful a singer as Day was, everything that was sizzlingly tomboyish about her character in the movie evaporated in the number, which was—as the early 1950s demanded—wholehearted and, well, *clean*. The 1964 Sinatra, on the other hand, gave the tune a slight edge of world-weariness, his lived-in voice playing off gorgeously against Riddle's sublime strings, somehow managing to make you believe that in a relentlessly publicized life he'd actually managed to have a secret love.

Nelson Riddle might have been gritting his teeth while arranging Henry Mancini's megahits "Moon River" and "Days of Wine and Roses," but you wouldn't know it to hear the results: he did his musical archrival proud. In the case of the latter song, the theme from the tormented 1962 Jack Lemmon–Lee Remick drama about alcoholism, Riddle had the brilliant idea to go upbeat, with George Roberts's bouncing bass trombone anchoring a chugging horn section, and Frank—whose own prodigious intake of alcohol, and the behavior it unleashed, were steady problems—was somehow able to alchemize this lament into a compelling finger snapper.

By 1964, "Moon River," the theme from 1961's *Breakfast at Tiffany's,* had become a mammoth hit, so ubiquitous both in the Muzak-ized instrumental version and in Andy Williams's honeyed rendering (from his own best-selling movie-theme LP) that Johnny Mercer had come to detest it. "I hate that fucking song," he told a friend. It took Sinatra and Riddle to give it new life, by—not so simply—being Sinatra and Riddle. Frank, who was of course a passionate student of lyrics, adored Mercer's work and had done justice to many of his greatest creations: "Blues in the Night," "One for My Baby," "That Old Black Magic," "Day In, Day Out," "Laura," "Autumn Leaves," and on and on. "Moon River" was a late work by the great wordsmith, written after a long fallow period, and Sinatra managed to find its dignity and its melancholy, as did Riddle's elegantly spare chart, which began with Frank backed solely by Al Viola's lovely and plaintive Spanish-flavored guitar.

The album was, with the one exception, a treasure chest of pleasures, and no track was quite so pleasurable as Sinatra's first and only recording of Jerome Kern and Dorothy Fields's timeless "The Way You Look Tonight," first sung by Fred Astaire in the 1936 musical *Swing Time.* Astaire, not a great vocalist but a great singer—which is to say a matchless interpreter of the American popular song—had all but closed the books on the number with his ardent rendition, but Frank and Nelson opened the books again with an upbeat version that was cool and warm in precisely the right proportions. Singing just behind the beat (and giving the tune a frisson of sexual tension), Sinatra managed to convey an intimacy that he could never find in real life: his loss, our gain.

But then it was his gain too, since his primary relationships were never quite with people but rather with the words, the music, the microphone, the audience. Frank's "The Way You Look Tonight" may not be perfect, but it is majestic—a recording that could be beamed out into space to tell the universe endlessly what human love is about.

And so what, by comparison, could a seemingly simpleminded pop tune called "I Want to Hold Your Hand" be but—really—a kind of joke? A fad, a hula hoop or a Frisbee of a song, a trivial diversion for America's youth, still so saddened by the slaying of their youthful president?

Capitol's Dave Dexter had steadfastly rejected the Beatles throughout 1963, turning down their first three singles, "Love Me Do," "Please Please Me," and "From Me to You." But beginning in March of that year, with the release of their first LP, *Please Please Me,* the group had become a huge sensation in Great Britain—the singles "She Loves You" and then "I Want to Hold Your Hand" each sold a million copies, in a market one-tenth the size of the United States—and in December, through a strange concatenation of events, the Beatles skipped over the Atlantic and planted a toehold in America.

It had started on Halloween, when Frank's old friend and enemy Ed Sullivan happened to be in London's Heathrow Airport at the same time as the Beatles were returning from a five-day tour of Sweden. In a heavy rain, "several hundred screaming fans," according to Mark Lewisohn, greeted the group, as did several dozen journalists, photographers, and representatives of the BBC. Sullivan was impressed. He had virtually broken out Elvis Presley by putting him on his show in September 1956, and he felt the Beatles might be the next Elvis. On November 12, Sullivan met with the group's manager, Brian Epstein, and offered not one but two successive live appearances on his show—in terms of impact, the television equivalent of two feature stories in *Time* or *Life*—at $3,500 per appearance, considerably less than his top rate. Epstein, a shrewd bargainer, accepted the low fee but demanded top billing for the group. Though the Beatles were unknown in the United States, Sullivan agreed.

In the meantime, Beatlemania was overtaking the U.K., and America had begun to take a bemused and condescending interest. On NBC's *Huntley-Brinkley Report* on November 18, the reliably crusty Edwin Newman did a four-minute report on the group, scowling at the camera and saying, "It's anybody's guess why the Beatles emerged from [Liverpool's] cellar nightclubs to national prominence, but emerge they did." And four days later—on the morning of November 22, the day of the assassination—on *CBS Morning News with Mike Wallace,* the London correspondent Alexander Kendrick did an equally sardonic five-minute piece on the group ("musicologists say it is no different from any other form of rock 'n' roll, except maybe louder") that began with footage of the Beatles performing "She Loves You" in concert.

In Maryland, a fourteen-year-old named Marsha Albert—twenty years earlier, she would have been a bobby-soxer—was watching, enthralled.

Much like the first-person narrator of Chuck Berry's "Roll over Beethoven" (a tune the Beatles had been covering from the beginning), Albert wrote a letter to her local DJ—Carroll James, of Washington's WWDC—telling him that he really ought to try to get one of the Beatles' records and play it on the air.

Meanwhile, on December 14, "I Want to Hold Your Hand" knocked "She Loves You" off the top spot in the British charts—the first time in British history that an artist or group had replaced themselves at number 1. Taking notice, Carroll James ordered a copy of the new hit single, which the Beatles' label, EMI, shipped over posthaste aboard a BOAC jet. On December 21, James had Marsha Albert introduce "I Want to Hold Your Hand" on his WWDC show, the first time the single was played on American radio. Over the next weeks, the song turned into a huge hit as WWDC played it nearly incessantly, and as a result EMI and Brian Epstein were finally able to convince Capitol to release a Beatles record. It was "I Want to Hold Your Hand," with "I Saw Her Standing There" on the B-side, and—to take advantage of the sensation building on WWDC and, soon, on other radio stations—Capitol put it out the day after Christmas, December 26, 1963.

All this during Frank's sad sojourn in Palm Springs.

———

The movie *4 for Texas* premiered during the same week as "I Want to Hold Your Hand" and did considerably less well. The critics flayed it. "*4 for Texas* . . . is one of those pictures that are known in Hollywood as Clanbakes," *Time* wrote.

> They are made by Frankie and his friends . . . and if showbiz-buzz can be believed really are a lot of fun to film. Unfortunately, they are not much fun to see . . . It isn't really funny to see two overage destroyers (Martin and Sinatra) wallowing in floods of booze. It isn't really funny to see two top-heavy tootsies (Anita Ekberg and Ursula Andress) involved in a tasteless chest contest. And it isn't really funny to hear line after line that develops a double meaning from a single idea.
>
> What's mainly wrong with *Texas,* though, is what's wrong with all Clan pictures: the attitude of the people on the screen. They constitute an ingroup, and they seem bored with the outside world. Sometimes, perish the thought, they even seem bored with each other.

The press had been laying for the Clan for years, even if the Clan, insofar as it still existed, had essentially become an oldies act. But Frank had opened himself to fresh opprobrium by failing the most basic test of all: he wasn't selling tickets. You could displease the critics as long as the people showed up, yet after the success of *Ocean's 11* the Rat Pack pictures—which were essentially Frank's baby—interested ticket buyers less and less. In *4 for Texas,* the *New York Times's* Bosley Crowther wrote, Sinatra's character Zack Thomas "behaves like a pasha, flanked by adoring handmaidens and servile flunkeys." It was a little too close to real life, a little too unironic, and moviegoers picked up on it. Frank had violated his own rule, as expressed by Mike Shore: an audience is like a broad; if you're indifferent, endsville. Sinatra had taken Jack Warner's money and lost much of it (to gild the lily, the kidnapping had cost $1 million in production costs on *Robin and the 7 Hoods*), and by Hollywood logic Warner was determined to keep throwing money at him.

———

Jack Kennedy and Hank Sanicola weren't the only friends Frank had lost by the end of 1963. Sam Giancana had phoned soon after the kidnapping with a mixed message: he was pleased and relieved that Frankie had come home safely but disappointed that Frank hadn't accepted the help he'd offered. "Disappointed" was a grave word in Mooney's lexicon. But he had a further proposal: there were ways of dealing with these three mopes who had done the job, even if they were in police custody. Frank politely declined. "He knew that if anything ever happened to those kidnappers, the finger of guilt would be pointed straight at him, and he was already in enough trouble because of Cal-Neva," Giancana's friend Tommy DiBella said. "Plus, I know that Frank Sinatra would never have wanted to be so indebted to Sam Giancana."

There might have been other reasons, at that moment, to distance himself from the Mob.

In any case, Frank and Mooney were officially over. Sinatra, who once had been able to engender fear by association, had lost the association, just like that. "He missed Sam Giancana and all the tough guys, all the unspoken, never-bragged-about danger and swagger and confidence that having the mob in his corner gave him," George Jacobs writes. Now Frank bought a pistol, a .38 Smith & Wesson, and never left home without the gun in its holster.

And there was still Jilly.

With Sanicola and Giancana out of the picture, the Broadway barkeep loomed ever larger in Sinatra's life. The previous June, Earl Wilson had run a tiny item in his column: "Café owner Jilly Rizzo will open a H'wood branch of his Jilly's, with Frank Sinatra as a partner." (It never happened, though Rizzo would open a Palm Springs Jilly's in 1968.) Three days later, Walter Winchell's column featured a little dithyramb about the friendship under the heading "Novelet":

You may have seen the name Jilly's over a night spot in a Frank Sinatra film [*The Manchurian Candidate*] . . . Or in a syndicated column . . . Sinatra often takes Jilly along on those distant tours—mainly for laughs—he's a Fun Guy . . . In one remote place several years ago Frank decided to stroll alone near his hotel for the fresh air . . . In the shadows, two hoodlums sized up the scene, and seeing that Frank was solo, decided to mug him . . . But Jilly sixth-sensed it . . . He waited until the punks were directly under the 2nd floor mezz of the hotel and he leaped right on top of them—just like in the movies . . . That's why Frank Sinatra and Jilly of West 52nd Street are buddies . . . Forever.

Just like the movies—or a boy's adventure story. Like Hank and Mooney, Jilly conveyed the kind of power Frank lacked himself. Unlike them, Rizzo asked nothing in return. And he wore his toughness lightly, which Sinatra found both amusing and admirable. "His speech was right out of *Guys and Dolls*, but much dirtier, all 'dese fuckers' and 'dose cocksuckers,' and Mr. S liked to imitate him," Jacobs writes. " 'I smashed the rat bastard in the mouth and the cocksucking motherfucker went down.' That was how Jilly talked." Frank also laughed at all of Rizzo's (invariably bad) jokes, just like a teenager with a crush.

"Frank was a lonely guy," said the jazz pianist Monty Alexander, the house pianist at Jilly's in the 1960s. "Jilly filled that empty space, and they became like brothers. Frank confided in him; he gave Frank advice, feedback—not telling him what to do, just good advice. He also had a way to play the role that he was capable of playing—tough guy—and sending out that signal if he needed to, because he knew certain people. I knew that if anybody ever messed with me, the feeling I had with Jilly was like he was my uncle or godfather looking out for me. He'd say, 'Kid, stay out of trouble.' I always thought I could, as they say, make a phone call. Just get that dime if anything ever happened—'I've got a problem, Jilly.'

"One time I had a girlfriend, and we had a lovers' tiff, and she scratched my face. Jilly said, 'What happened to you?' I said, 'This broad scratched my face because of—' He said, 'I'm going to break her neck!' I said, 'No, no, really, boss . . .' I called him boss. I said, 'Boss, everything's cool, don't worry about it.' 'I'll break her neck!' That was his vibe."

It was a decidedly prefeminist vibe: Betsy Hammes remembered Jilly, for a laugh, throwing her and another young woman, who couldn't swim, into the Sands swimming pool. But it was the perfect vibe for Frank, now that Momo was gone. "I liked Jilly; I had nothing against him," Hammes said. "He could be very sweet, but he wasn't the brightest on the boardwalk. Frank would have

Frank with Jilly Rizzo and Sands president Jack Entratter. Sinatra considered the rough-hewn Rizzo—friend, bodyguard, factotum—the brother he'd never had.

these characters around him—troublemakers. He loved to be around the bad boys. And whenever he was around them, he'd change into a totally different person. Trouble—Jilly would drum it up."

———

On Sunday night, January 12, Frank junior—now traveling with "unusual protection" (namely his father's bodyguards Al Silvani and Ed Pucci, man stoppers both of them)—made his first television appearance since the kidnapping, on *The Ed Sullivan Show,* along with Sam Donahue and the Dorsey ghost band, Helen Forrest, and the Pied Pipers. Fellow guests included Connie Francis, the comedy team of Jerry Stiller and Anne Meara, and ragtime pianist Big Tiny Little. It was good early-1960s fun, but the tsunami was on the horizon.

———

Even before "I Want to Hold Your Hand" was officially released, radio stations all around the country were playing it: at first Capitol tried to enjoin them legally from doing so, then simply gave up, realizing the publicity could only help. In the first three days after its December 26 release, the record sold a quarter-million units: ten thousand copies an hour in New York City alone. By January 18, the single had begun its fifteen-week run on the American charts;

on February 1, it hit number 1. It would stay there for seven weeks, finally relinquishing the top spot to "She Loves You."

And this is how a television-viewing audience of seventy-three million people—twenty-three million households; 34 percent of the American population; the largest TV-watching audience of all time, including that for the Kennedy assassination and aftermath—happens. Was Frank one of the seventy-three million watching the Sullivan show on the night of February 9? History doesn't tell us, though it's more likely he'd caught Frankie on the broadcast in January, singing Sinatra songs with Helen Forrest and the Pied Pipers, than tuned in to watch some British rock 'n' roll band with a funny name. He was in Palm Springs that night—he could fly there on his Morane-Saulnier jet in seventeen minutes—trying to relax while he waited to see if he'd be subpoenaed to testify in the kidnapping trial of Barry Keenan, Joe Amsler, and John Irwin, which was to start the next day, February 10. And relaxing didn't mean sitting around watching meaningless junk on television.

———

"In the opening day of the trial Monday a jury of nine men and three women was selected with unexpected speed under the guidance of federal district Judge William G. East," UPI reported on February 11. The story also noted that the kidnappers' defense attorneys were about to make their opening statements and were expected to offer the theory that Frank junior had been abducted "with his own consent."

It was not a good sign.

The perverse idea that the kidnapping might have been some sort of hoax, perhaps even a publicity stunt to aid Frankie's budding singing career, had been in the air since the kidnapping itself, when the FBI had taken the trouble to give lie-detector tests to John Foss and Tino Barzie. Whatever had been behind the crime, some felt that young Sinatra had benefited from it, professionally if not psychologically. "The attendant publicity has unquestionably added to the marquee value of the singer's name," *Variety*'s Art Stone had written on January 15. "In the case of Harrahs at Tahoe, Sinatra Jr. was listed on the bottom of the marquee when the TD band first opened. But after the kidnapping his name was moved to the top, just under the Tommy Dorsey Orch listing."

True enough—Harrah's had even posted an outsize welcoming message, "FRANKIE JR. IS BACK"—but that wasn't the whole story. After Frank senior had heard about the marquee, he'd phoned Harrah's and complained, heatedly. The message was removed, and Frankie's name moved back to the bottom in small letters.

The idea of a hoax was in the air, and a clever lawyer plucked it out of the air. "I was in jail, lonely and desperate," Barry Keenan recalled.

> And one of the attorneys—not my own—came in one night and said to me, "Look, if this was a publicity stunt and you are able to tell us that it was a publicity stunt, then that would be a very strong defense." Since I was the ringleader, I was the one who had to make the statement.
>
> By that time I had sobered up, and I realized we were all in a heap of trouble. I slept on it. The next morning, I came out with this lie about the kidnapping being a publicity stunt, and that's all my attorneys needed to hear. It became our defense. I'm not proud of it. It was a lousy thing to do to the Sinatras. But I did it, I'm sorry to say.

Keenan was represented by Charles L. Crouch; Joe Amsler by George A. Forde and Morris Lavine; and John Irwin by Gladys Towles Root. Root, fifty-eight, was a flamboyant character, a woman in what was then a man's business, given to wearing large and dramatic hats to court and conducting withering cross-examinations, and it was she who had suggested the publicity-stunt angle to Barry Keenan and then asserted it to the jury on February 11. "This was a planned contractual agreement between Frank Sinatra Junior and others connected with him," she said.

"An apple doesn't fall far from its tree, and Frankie Junior just wanted to make the girls swoon as his papa once did," she continued, adding that Junior had told John Irwin, "The ladies used to swoon over my father. Then some wise publicity agent took that on and made my father into an international star. The press hasn't found me as exciting as my father."

And then Amsler's lawyer, George Forde, after pointing out that Junior's career had been on an upswing since the kidnapping, introduced a mysterious, anonymous "fourth defendant."

"There is a vacant seat here for that fourth defendant," Forde said. "A financier who financed this whole thing . . . He paid for the liquor that two of the defendants and Sinatra Junior shared together. He financed the rise of young Sinatra from a hundred-dollar-a-week band singer to an international star." The mystery financier, he continued, was an unnamed singer who had "cut two million records."

Despite the sensational implication that Forde was talking about Frank Sinatra, it would soon turn out that he was referring to Dean Torrence.

The international stardom of Frank junior consisted of a tour he was currently making with the Dorsey band in England and on American military bases in Europe. "There are a lot of kids who sing better than I do but don't have the opportunity to be singing with the Tommy Dorsey Orchestra. I am very grateful for my position," he'd told *Variety* with poignant truthfulness. "If I left the band now—I'm not strong enough to be on my own. I'd be dead without the people I'm working with. I'm a novice in this business. I'm just another guy in the band, not the star of the show."

He left the tour and returned to Los Angeles. On February 13, news of his first court appearance ("It's Showtime for Sinatra, Jr.") shared front pages with reports about the Beatles' performance at Carnegie Hall the previous night. "The Beatles looked like an amusing parody of the worst elements of American rock 'n' roll music," the Associated Press reported. "The word 'looked' is used advisedly, for no one, especially the screaming little girls, actually heard the Beatles." Frank senior's shows at the Paramount two decades earlier had been similarly inaudible and similarly amusing to the press. And like Sinatra in 1943, the Beatles were in the process of taking the country like wildfire. By early April, they would hold all five top spots on *Billboard*'s Hot 100 and fourteen positions in all on the chart.

On Friday the fourteenth, Frankie underwent a cross-examination by Mrs. Root, who had earlier posed for a news photographer in her courtroom outfit, a champagne-beige wool sheath dress with scoop neckline outlined in beige fox fur, a cape of purple wolf fur, and a champagne-beige wool trooper hat. As Frank junior sat on the witness stand, she demanded to know why he had said nothing when Nevada police stopped the kidnappers' car at a roadblock.

"Because, Mrs. Root, the number one man stated before we came to the roadblock that there was going to be some shooting," he told her. "I did not want a sudden and idiotic move to cause this man who was stupid enough to kidnap me to voluntarily blow the brains out of this officer."

"Indeed," Mrs. Root said. She turned to the jury. "The truth is you would have wrecked your little kidnap plot, which you arranged, and it would not have been successful," she said.

"That is not true," Frankie said emphatically.

But on Monday, the defense began to unravel with the publication of a Sunday *Los Angeles Times* story headlined SINATRA JR. DESPERATELY FIGHTS CHARGE OF HOAX. The subhead read "Looks Grim and Pale as He Tries to Refute Claim He Sought Publicity for Career." "I was outraged," Judge East told the court, "when I read that headline and doubly outraged when I read the contents of the story." In the piece, Amsler's attorney, George Forde, said Barry Keenan had admitted to him that the kidnapping had been a planned publicity stunt, financed by a mysterious man named Wes. Keenan's lawyer, Crouch, asked for a mistrial. When the judge wouldn't grant it, Crouch said, "From now on, I'm working alone."

Judge East allowed Frank junior to return to his European tour, with the proviso that he be on call to come back and testify again. Frankie flew to London. The proceedings were thrown into further disarray when Dean Torrence took the stand, testified he'd known nothing ahead of time about the kidnap plot, then, later the same day, asked to return to the stand. "I'm afraid I made up some stories," he said. Now Judge East had to decide whether to indict Torrence for perjury. "I'm desperately disturbed about it," he said. Later that week, the defense won a motion to recall Frank junior to the stand and to call Frank senior to testify for the first time.

———

Frank, who had stayed clear of the trial, anxiously waiting to see if he'd be subpoenaed, had Mickey Rudin fend off the motion while he flew to Tokyo to finalize arrangements for the first movie in his Warner Bros. deal (and his first without Dean or Sammy in over a year), an antiwar World War II drama called *None but the Brave*. The picture would also feature a couple of other firsts: it was to be an American-Japanese co-production, and for the first time in his career Sinatra would direct. In the meantime, Frankie returned from Europe once more in an understandably testy mood. He spent all of twenty minutes on the witness stand on Friday the twenty-eighth, once again fending off questions about why he had cooperated with the kidnappers. "I didn't want to get killed," he said simply.

After he was excused—this time for good—and the jury dismissed for the day, an exasperated Judge East rebuked the defense. "You have abused the processes of the court in bringing this witness here," he said.

Frank junior was also exasperated. The trial and the attendant publicity, he claimed, had caused a singing engagement in Paris to be canceled. "Those people over there apparently didn't believe the kidnapping story," he said during an impromptu news conference outside the courtroom. "The seeds of doubt have been sown on my integrity and guts and will stay with me for the rest of my life."

It was agonizingly well put and heartbreakingly prescient.

———

The jury heard six hours of closing arguments on Friday, March 6, the twentieth day of the trial. "This is the strangest kidnapping case I ever heard of," defense lawyer Lavine said.

The nine men and three women were then sequestered for the night, and on Saturday they returned their verdict, finding Barry Keenan and Joe Amsler guilty on all charges and John Irwin guilty of all charges save the actual kidnapping. Judge East handed both Keenan and Amsler the maximum sentence:

life in prison plus seventy-five years. Irwin would eventually be sentenced to sixteen years and eight months for conspiracy.

All three were remanded to the federal medical facility in Springfield, Missouri, for psychiatric evaluation.

"The report that came back was that I was legally insane and that I had duped Joe into the kidnapping," Keenan recalled. "They said we had not intended to harm Junior. For a probation report, they interviewed family and friends and determined that we were nice kids. They kept trying to make John the fall guy because he was older and should have known better. After all of that, our life sentences were reduced to twenty-five years, a fairly light sentence for that crime. All the rules were different in those days. John and Joe kept their appeals going, and that's really how we got out."

In fact, after Judge East discovered that the prosecution had tampered with a psychiatric report, he reduced Keenan's sentence to twelve years. In the end, Amsler and Irwin spent three and a half years in prison; Barry Keenan got out in 1968, after four and a half years, and went on to become a millionaire real estate developer.

———

It was Frank junior who really received the life sentence. According to a former servant of Bill and Edie Goetz, Frank's Hollywood-royalty friends, even the Goetzes secretly believed Junior had staged his own kidnapping. As did much of the rest of the world. "Frankie was utterly blameless, but he couldn't unring the bell," Tina writes.

> He'd get heckled at his shows, and it hurt him deeply; he'd be dogged by public stigma for years. Nancy will tell you that this incident soured his life and ultimately hurt his career. I'm not so sure, because my brother was also swimming upstream in the music world. By the mid-1960s, tuxedo singers with big bands were an endangered species. Frankie might have been a victim of bad timing and his own stubbornness as much as anything.
>
> As for the two men in my family, and their choked and halting relationship . . . Our family crisis didn't forge a breakthrough, as it might have in the Hollywood version. Dad and Frankie went on as they had in the past, not quite connecting. They loved each other and knew it, but it had taken a near-death experience to bring them close and together. When the trauma was over, the connection was broken.
>
> They were two men who shared a name and a history and a pure passion for music, and all of that wasn't quite enough.

In July, after legal maneuvering by Frank Sinatra and Mickey Rudin, a federal grand jury would indict Gladys Root and George Forde for conspiracy and subornation of perjury. "I feel sorry for anyone that vindictive," Mrs. Root said of Sinatra. "I have always believed in the power of truth, and truth will be the winner in this case."

All charges against the pair would be dropped the following year.

At the end of April, Frank went to the island of Kauai, at the western end of the Hawaiian archipelago, to begin shooting *None but the Brave*. Jilly and Honey Rizzo accompanied him, as did a song-plugger pal named Murray Wolf (also an old friend of Van Heusen's) and George Jacobs. The relationship with Jill St. John having run its course for the time being, Sinatra was traveling stag.

He was not only directing the movie but starring in it as the whiskey-swigging chief pharmacist's mate Francis Maloney, leading a cast that included the hulking TV actor Clint Walker; Nancy's husband, Tommy Sands; Frank's second cousin Richard Sinatra (son of the bandleader Ray Sinatra, who'd been a modest success in the swing era before the other Sinatra came up); the tough guy Brad Dexter; and Frank's *Come Blow Your Horn* co-star Tony Bill. In keeping with the spirit of the binational co-production, however, the film's Japanese actors, all of them unknown in the United States, would be listed first in the credits.

Still trying to give voice to his liberal and idealistic sentiments, Frank was serious about the story he was making: a small group of American soldiers crash-land on a remote Pacific isle during World War II, only to find an abandoned Japanese platoon already occupying the island. Both sides have to decide whether to coexist and even help each other or to carry on the broader conflict, which in the context is meaningless.

And he was relatively serious about directing his first movie, although given his deep natural impatience with the process of filmmaking, he was wise to surround himself with solid support: his trusty producer Howard Koch was once again on hand ("He really knew the movies inside and out," Tony Bill said; "he was a real stalwart as a filmmaker"), as were William Daniels, now producing instead of directing photography, and, in an uncredited co-directing role, the reliable Gordon Douglas.

For the duration of location shooting, Sinatra rented a $2,000-per-month beachfront house on Wailua Bay, redecorated in orange by the owner for Frank's benefit. In front of the house, a little too symbolically, a Jack Daniel's flag fluttered at the top of a tall pole.

On Sunday, May 10, a sparkling Hawaiian afternoon, Sinatra had a houseful of guests, including Howard Koch and his wife, Ruth, Brad Dexter, another tough-guy actor in the film named Dick Bakalyan, Murray Wolf, and Jilly and Honey Rizzo. George Jacobs stood by to mix drinks and prepare food.

The movie had been shooting for two weeks, and though it was going well, Howard Koch recalled, "Frank was getting itchy" to finish, though almost ten days of work remained. Koch sensed Sinatra's restlessness as soon as he entered the house, and while everyone else headed out to the beach, the ever-accommodating producer sat down at a desk with the production schedule to see if he could find a way to tighten it.

In the meantime, despite warnings of a strong undertow, Ruth Koch decided to go swimming in the surf in front of the house. What happened next is the subject of a *Rashomon*-like array of recollections.

"The water was quite shallow very far out, so there wasn't really much risk of drowning," George Jacobs remembered.

However, the undertow tripped Ruth up and Sinatra, who swam over to help her, got tripped up as well. Immediately a young Hawaiian surfer

"They were two men who shared a name and a history and a pure passion for music, and all of that wasn't quite enough," Tina Sinatra wrote.

paddled over to help them both out. As he was helping them back to the beach, [Brad] Dexter, who saw from the house that something was going on, dove in and assisted him.

They may have swallowed a lot of salt water, but neither Ruth nor Frank was in mortal danger. However, it seems as if *everyone* near the incident made it appear far worse than it was and took credit for helping save Mr. S's life.

Brad Dexter, who played the hard-assed Sergeant Bleeker in *None but the Brave,* was a big, cheerful-but-dangerous-looking tough guy of Serbian extraction (his birth name was either Veljko Soso or, according to other sources, Boris Milanovich)—"kind of a beer-drinkin', world-weary, worldly-wise guy," Tony Bill recalled—who'd made a solid but unremarkable career as a character actor in the movies and on television. Before that fateful afternoon, Dexter had been best known for two things: his tempestuous ten-month marriage to Peggy Lee in 1953, and the fact that he'd co-starred with Steve McQueen, James Coburn, Yul Brynner, Charles Bronson, Robert Vaughn, and Horst Buchholz in John Sturges's 1960 cult classic *The Magnificent Seven*—the one man of the seven, he and others joked, whom no one could ever remember.

Speaking to Kitty Kelley some twenty years after the incident—in the course of which he became first central and then a nonperson in Frank Sinatra's life—Dexter spun a richly detailed tale of that afternoon's events, featuring himself as the heroic rescuer and Sinatra as the contemptibly weak and helpless victim. "It was a sun-drenched afternoon and we were all on the beach enjoying the ocean and that great tropical sun," Dexter recalled.

The waves were billowing higher, though, and I noticed a treacherous riptide developing with a very strong undertow. I warned everyone to be careful in the water. Frank asked me to go to the house to bring him some wine and soda, so I went on up. While I was collecting everything in the kitchen, I heard Murray screaming hysterically from the living room that Frank was drowning.

According to Dexter, he dropped the wine and soda, tore out of the house, and ran down to the beach, where, between the big waves, he could just make out Sinatra and Ruth Koch's heads bobbing in the water. As everyone else stood immobile with fear, Dexter dived into the surf and fought through the waves to Ruth Koch, who was gasping for air. "Save Frank," she said. "I can't go on."

"Nobody's going to die," Dexter said he told her. "We're all going to come out of this alive. C'mon, fight. C'mon. You're going to be okay."

Sinatra with Clint Walker, Tommy Sands (l.), and a cigar-chewing Brad Dexter on the set of *None but the Brave*. Tough guy Dexter saved Frank's life in the Hawaiian surf, a good deed that did not go unpunished.

Holding Ruth Koch under one arm, he then swam out to Frank, who was suffering from hypoxia: his face was bluish, and his vision was impaired. "I can hear you, but I can't see you," Dexter remembered Sinatra saying.

Did he think of Dolly, pushing him under the surf at the Jersey shore? "Frank was pathetic, helpless like a baby," the actor told Kelley.

> He kept sputtering to me, "I'm going to die. I'm finished. It's all over, over. Please take care of my kids. I'm going to die . . ." I tried desperately to instill in him the will to fight for his life. I kept slapping him repeatedly on the face and back with stinging blows. I pulled him up and out of the water, over and over again, but he was as limp and lifeless as a rag doll . . . I tried to get him angry enough to start fighting back by calling him a fucking lily-livered coward. A spineless, gutless shit. But he didn't react. He seemed like he wanted to die, like he had no will to live. He just caved in.

Frank had lost consciousness, as had Ruth Koch. As the waves crashed over them, Dexter cradled one of them in each arm as he treaded water, knowing that time was running out. Finally, he said, he saw "four heads in the ocean coming toward us. I don't remember how long it took for them to reach us, but the time seemed endless. Someone later said that it was forty-five minutes."

In Dexter's telling, the (anonymous) men on surfboards lashed Sinatra and Ruth Koch to their boards with ropes, then turned around and paddled back toward shore, leaving the exhausted actor to fend for himself. Dexter nearly slipped under the waves, but then, he said, he became inflamed by a single thought: if he gave up, "I'd be finished forever, and for what? For two people who wanted to die? Who had given up trying to save their own lives and could[n't] have cared less about mine? . . . I swam like a crazy man with an extravagant passion to live, defying the waves to take me under. By some miracle that I don't understand to this day, I reached the beach before the life-saving party."

Miraculous indeed. Dexter said he then ran to the rescuers, who were just reaching the shore with Sinatra and Mrs. Koch, both still unconscious.

"I stretched Frank out on the sand and gave him artificial respiration," Dexter recalled. "Once he started vomiting the water out of his lungs, I turned him over to the lifeguards. Jilly Rizzo ran up to me and shouted, 'You're a hero, Brad. You're a hero. Without you, Frank would be dead.'"

Nancy Sinatra's non-eyewitness version of the episode (she was on the island with Tommy Sands but arrived at her father's house afterward) introduces a cast of characters involved in the rescue and omits Brad Dexter entirely. After a wave swept Ruth Koch out to sea, she writes, her father tried to swim to her; but then a second wave brought Mrs. Koch back to shore, and the undertow carried Frank even farther out. Though a strong swimmer, he struggled against the surf for long minutes, unable to get back to the beach.

As Jilly raced in vain to find a boat, Nancy claims, a neighbor named Alfred Giles jumped into the waves with his surfboard, and County Supervisor Louis Gonsalves and hotel manager Harold Jim swam out to Sinatra. Giles, Gonsalves, and Jim flailed in the heavy surf until a fire lieutenant named George Keawe managed to toss a rope to the rescuers and pull them and Frank to the beach. Sinatra's face was turning blue—a sign, Keawe felt, that he wouldn't have lasted much longer in the water.

Frank was then taken back to the house on a stretcher, Nancy writes. When she arrived, Frank was in bed, pale but hungry. They ate pepper-and-egg sandwiches and watched television together until he dozed off.

After the rescue, Dexter told Kelley, he went back to his hotel room and collapsed. A couple of hours later, he went over to Sinatra's place to find the house filled with "newspaper reporters, photographers, island officials, friends, members of the cast and crew, and representatives of the Red Cross." And

Frank's older daughter. Frank, in bathrobe and slippers, was sitting in an easy chair, trying to comfort her.

"He looked up at me when I entered the room and I observed that he was still in a state of shock," Dexter recalled. "His eyes were bloodshot and he had the expression of a felled ox. When our eyes locked, it seemed that he didn't know what to say. He was embarrassed. He hung up the telephone and said, 'My family thanks you.'"

Tony Bill remembered that not much was made of the incident on the set the next day. "It was like, 'Hey, Frank was having trouble getting back to shore; he went out for a swim, so Brad went out and brought him back in,'" he said.

But in the meantime, the press, spoon-fed the story by unit publicist Harry Friedman and hungry for fresh Sinatra sensation—it had been almost six months since the kidnapping—milked the thing for all it was worth. SINATRA NEARLY DROWNS, the headlines read; SINATRA HAS CLOSE BRUSH WITH DEATH. The reports were all similar but didn't quite dovetail. The wave had been huge, UPI reported. (The agency's first bulletin about the incident also contained the interesting statement Sinatra "was rescued in a matter of minutes.") Two other people had also been swept out to sea, UPI said, but had managed to fight their way back through the surf and shout for help. "Brad Dexter, an actor, swam out to Sinatra but could not bring him in," the Associated Press wrote.

This last actually jibes with Dexter's own description: it was the anonymous surfboard paddlers who brought Frank and Ruth Koch in. Why, then, in Brad Dexter's telling, did Jilly greet him as a hero? And why, in Nancy's telling, did Dexter disappear entirely?

My family thanks you. "It was such a strange remark, almost as if I had put him in the uncomfortable position of having to thank me for saving his life," Dexter said. "He never thanked me then or later, and I realize now that my rescue efforts probably severed the friendship right then and there by depriving him of the big-benefactor role which is the one he liked to play with his friends."

It was more complicated than that. The next night, Dexter recalled, Jilly phoned to invite him to dinner at Frank's house. It was clearly a special occasion: George was making spaghetti pomodoro—Frank's favorite—and Patsy D'Amore of the Villa Capri had had fresh Italian bread and prosciutto flown over.

Yet "Frank appeared uptight and depressed when I arrived," Dexter said. "I didn't realize how angry he was until we sat down to dinner and George started serving the spaghetti." According to the actor, Sinatra began yelling that the pasta wasn't prepared properly, then threw the platterful in Jacobs's face, screaming, "You eat this crap! I won't!"

The valet simply peeled the spaghetti from his face and went back to the kitchen. "That was unkind, Frank," the stunned actor finally said. "A very unkind thing to do."

"Goddamn it!" Sinatra yelled. "That bastard doesn't know how to cook al dente and that's the only way I'll eat it!"

Dexter's first thought was that "maybe Frank was suffering from the aftershock of almost drowning and just wasn't quite himself." But then, he said, he realized Sinatra "was unconsciously lashing out at me for putting him in the awful position of having to be grateful for his own life. He couldn't deal with his feelings toward me, so he took it out on poor George, a black man who would never fight back and who Frank treated like chattel."

It makes sense, except that George Jacobs tells a rather different story. In the valet's version, it was spaghetti marinara, not pomodoro, and the dinner guests were none other than Spencer Tracy and Katharine Hepburn. Like Nancy Sinatra, Jacobs omits Brad Dexter entirely. According to the valet, Frank had, much to his surprise, conceived a powerful lust for the fifty-six-year-old actress after happening upon her in a formfitting tank suit as she took her dawn swim in the ocean. (As Tracy's character said of Hepburn's in *Pat and Mike*, "Not much meat on her, but what's there is cherce.")

Yet Hepburn and Tracy were such a tight couple—for all kinds of complex reasons of their own—that Sinatra had no chance with the Great Kate. "It could be that Mr. S was feeling particularly horny and frustrated, because he was extra edgy" the night of the dinner, Jacobs writes. He served the spaghetti, which, he says, he had made "a million times" for his boss. Then, as in the Dexter story, Frank tasted the pasta, started raving that it wasn't al dente, picked up the serving bowl, and threw the contents all over Jacobs and his white jacket. "This was the only time he had ever abused me, but once was enough," the valet recalled. "Tracy and Hepburn were so appalled that they left immediately, while Sinatra cleared the table by smashing all the dishes."

Jacobs says he walked out too and bought $2,000 worth of new clothes in Honolulu, having the bill sent to Sinatra. When the valet returned the next day, Frank "tried to treat the incident as a big joke. 'You're not pissed at me, are you, Spook?' he asked, trying to make me feel like a square for not playing his party game . . . Mr. S never apologized, but he never complained about the bill, either. Being Frank Sinatra meant never having to say you're sorry, but it didn't mean he was without remorse. You just had to know how to read his 'Remorse Code.' Whenever he tried to treat a slight as a big chuckle, you knew he was trying to apologize to you."

Though Jacobs's version is plausible, Dexter's is more believable. Frank's fury about his impotence in the waves and his displaced terrors about aging and mortality (how could the world go on without him?) seem more likely triggers for a spaghetti-throwing tantrum than thwarted lust. Dexter said Sinatra admitted to having terrible nightmares about the near drowning yet, when asked about the episode by outsiders, would only say, "Oh, I just got a little water on my bird—that's all."

Forced into a profoundly uncomfortable position of gratitude toward a man who had just been fetching him wine ("Frank would go get a cup of coffee for you," Dick Bakalyan recalled. "You didn't want to go get the cup of coffee for him, though; people would start to treat you like a gofer"), Sinatra went, for a couple of years, into a fury of payback. He granted Brad Dexter access to the inner circle. He cast him in his next movie; he even gave him a producer credit for a later picture. And then, once he felt the obligation was discharged, he cut him off without thinking twice.

Quincy Jones had last worked with Sinatra as a brilliant but intimidated twenty-five-year-old arranger-bandleader, conducting the stellar Barclay Disques house band at Princess Grace's 1958 Monaco benefit. Jones was all but unknown to the outside world then, but Frank had found him the way he found all his important musical collaborators: he listened. His great ears told him all he needed to know. Though young, Jones had already written impressive charts for Count Basie, Dinah Washington, and others; he happened to be working at Barclay in Paris, and Sinatra happened to be doing the benefit in Monte Carlo: Frank picked up the phone, and a great collaboration began.

By 1964, Jones was in New York, with a day job as musical director for Mercury Records and on the side a thriving arranging career. He'd written charts for a number of singles for Basie and, in 1963, for two albums: *Li'l Ol' Groovemaker . . . Basie!* and *This Time by Basie!* Sinatra, who loved everything the Count did, listened. The latter LP contained a 1954 song by Bart Howard that had originally been titled "In Other Words." Like the rest of the album, the track—now called "Fly Me to the Moon"—was an instrumental, but Frank, who'd known Howard since he'd played piano for Mabel Mercer, Eartha Kitt, and other cabaret singers at New York's Blue Angel in the early 1950s, knew the lyric well. The song had been written as a waltz, and it had gained tremendous popularity as such: "Fly Me to the Moon" had been sung and recorded (over a hundred times), often by female vocalists, wistfully, dreamily. Frank had a different idea. And that May in Kauai, not long after the near drowning, he picked up the phone and called Quincy Jones again.

Nearly fifty years later, Jones remembered the call vividly. "He said, 'Hey, Q—this is Francis. I'm in Hawaii doing *None but the Brave,* and I just heard that record you did with Basie, and you did Bart Howard's ["Fly Me to the Moon"] on there.' It's a waltz; we did it four-four with Basie, naturally. Frank said, 'That's the way I want to do it. Would you consider doing an album with me and Basie? Can you get over here next week?'"

Jones hadn't spoken with Sinatra since Monaco in 1958. "I nearly fell out of my chair," he recalled. "Can I get over there next week? Shit, I was in Kauai two days later."

He arrived on the island, proceeded to Wailua Bay, and sat down with Frank in his office. "In the middle of our conversation, he says, 'Excuse me a minute, Q,' and he calls the Pentagon. He says, 'Jim'—or whatever the hell the guy's first name was—'do you think you could get the Pacific Fleet over here tomorrow at eleven-thirty? I'm shooting a scene.' The next morning, here comes destroyers, aircraft carriers—they were all there."

Location shooting for *None but the Brave* concluded while Jones was in Hawaii, and he and Sinatra headed back to Los Angeles together. On the way, they laid over in Honolulu, where Frank celebrated by organizing a bacchanal of epic proportions for Quincy and a few other pals. "It started out with seven of us, plus Francis, but after a call to some local ladies and starlets, within forty-five minutes there were nineteen," Jones recalled. "Partied our brains out, man, for three days, man. I woke up one morning in a closet with Frank. I said, 'How the hell did we get in here?' We were all fucked-up!"

Death had been exorcised, and power thoroughly reasserted.

———

And a new friendship forged. Frank quickly formed a closer bond with Quincy Jones than he'd had, or would have, with any of his other arrangers. When the two of them landed in Los Angeles, they went straight to the Warner Bros. lot, where Frank installed Jones in Dean Martin's bungalow, next to his own offices. Quincy quickly got to work, against a tight deadline, on the Basie album.

On the first night, Jones became so involved in writing that he lost track of time and got locked in Martin's suite, where he fell asleep at 4:00 a.m. "At around 6:30 a.m. I heard a knock on the door," he recalled.

> I opened it. Frank was standing there wearing fatigues, his costume for the war film he was directing. He looked me dead in the eye and said, "How do you like your eggs, Q?"
> I mumbled, "Scrambled."

He scrambled them up, we ate breakfast, and from that day on, we were tight.

Tightness with Sinatra almost invariably came about at his initiative, on his terms, and as a result of his needs. In this case, the intimacy indisputably had to do not only with Jones's formidable skills and genuine personality but with the color of his skin. Ever since Sinatra was an unknown young singer prowling the jazz clubs of Fifty-second Street, he had been crazy about the style and the genius of the great black musicians he'd seen and heard there: Basie. Billie. Art Tatum. Fats Waller. Lester Young. "He was a brother in disguise," Jones wrote of Frank. "He was crazy about the big-band culture, his roots. One late night in Palm Springs, he told me about a crush he'd had on Billie Holiday when he was young, but you couldn't follow it through because of the times. 'Q, you couldn't get away with that back in those days, no matter who you were,' he said."

Now he was in the same league with his idols, but some part of Sinatra would always remain both an aspirant to blackness and an outsider. He was, after all, a man of the mid-twentieth century, a product of the insufficiently melted melting pot. The *Amos 'n' Andy* jokes ("I'm not crazy about that sort of stuff," Quincy Jones would admit late in his life; "I couldn't get used to it") reflected Frank's mixed feelings: idolatry and otherness. For his part, Jones, who in his young life had already played with and arranged for many if not most of jazz's greats, was thrilled to add Sinatra to his life list. "Frank was my style," he recalled.

He was hip, straight up and straight ahead, and, above all, a monster musician. I loved him, man, I admit it, I loved him as much as anyone else I ever worked with, because there was no gray to the man. It was either black or white: If he loved you, there was nothing in the world he wouldn't do for you. If he didn't like you, shame on your ass. I know he loved me too. In all the years of working together, we never once had a contract—just a handshake. The Sinatras always made me feel like part of their family, children, grandchildren, and all.

All the arrangers who had loomed large in Frank's career to date—Stordahl, Riddle, May, Jenkins—had purposely kept their distance from him (as he had from them). Sinatra was not only an overwhelming personality; he was the boss. Letting friendship into the equation could conceivably affect the work, and not for the better. Moreover, the time would inevitably come when an orchestrator would collaborate with other singers, and the incomparable intensity of working with Frank would pass. Best, most thought, to be able to move on easily, to keep things professional and clinical. (Riddle, who had little gift for friendship but took his professional relationship with Sinatra deeply personally, was a special case.) Because of Sinatra's fascination with black culture and jazz, and because of Quincy Jones's gift for agreeableness without sycophancy, the arranger was able to work with Frank on a nearly even footing and to be a friend as well: an unprecedented situation, and one never to be duplicated.

On the night of June 9, Sinatra, Jones, and the Basie band began recording *It Might as Well Be Swing*. They started with a bang, laying down one of Frank's masterpieces, "The Best Is Yet to Come," by Cy Coleman and Carolyn Leigh, the composers of "Witchcraft."

Coleman and Leigh had originally written "Best" for Frank in 1959: it was a finger-snapping, deceptively simple vamp, with a tricky modulation from A-flat to C between the first and second choruses and a sexy, syncopated lyric. He liked the number but then—possibly because his disaffection with Capitol was coming to a head and Reprise wasn't yet begun—sat on it for a year without recording it. The publishers then passed the tune along to Tony Bennett, who released it as a Columbia single in early 1961. "Frank was lazy," Quincy Jones said. "He'd let Tony Bennett do it first, and then he'd do it. Tony always took pride in that; he kind of led Frank into the music, the songs."

Frank quickly formed a closer bond with Quincy Jones than he had with any of his other arrangers. But tightness with Sinatra, like almost everything else in his life, was on his terms.

Bennett had good reason to be proud. His version is so brilliant, so infectious, that it was an act of sheer hubris for Sinatra to follow him—but then, what was Frank if not the embodiment of hubris? The fact that he had failed with "I Left My Heart in San Francisco" seems never to have entered his mind. He loved Bennett's singing, even if he didn't always love Bennett (as recently as December, the two had been rumored not to be speaking), but he yielded to no one in his field. If the two men's relationship was fraught, it had largely to do with the fact that Bennett had had to make his own way in Sinatra's exceedingly large shadow.

And he had made his way. He had his own big career, his own following, his own demons. Offstage, he was a recessive personality; onstage, he possessed the theatrical gift of coming alive when he opened his mouth to sing. Joy was his special gift, and joy was what he brought to "The Best Is Yet to Come"—he even laughed as he sang the outro. In Bennett's hands, the great love song, with its tap-dance rhythm and message of soaring optimism—

Out of the tree of life I just picked me a plum . . .
Still, it's a real good bet the best is yet to come

—seemed to have found its truest interpreter.

Once again, Sinatra had a new approach. As he'd often done before, he gave the number a sexual charge that no other male singer could come close to. He reveled in Jones's swinging arrangement, heavy on the brass and brought to glorious life by Basie's incomparable ensemble. Frank's version evoked sheer mastery, not only of the music itself, but of the "you" of the song, the woman he was telling that if she thought what the two of them had together was great, she hadn't seen nothin' yet. His unapologetically macho rendition had a whiff of Mephistopheles about it: he was a sorcerer, and some of his tricks promised to be on the dirty side. But it also contained Sinatra's signature quality: defiance. Even if fifty was rapidly approaching, even if death could lay its cold fingers on his shoulders—and even if the great love of his life was behind him—his power was such that he could surely make the world dance to his tune.

"The Best Is Yet to Come" wasn't his only challenge to Tony Bennett. The second number of the evening, "I Wanna Be Around," had been a hit single for Bennett in 1963, and the tune had a singular origin: in 1957, a Youngstown, Ohio, grandmother named Sadie Vimmerstedt had written a letter to Johnny Mercer, on the sheets of an old desk-pad calendar, saying she'd come up with a song idea. She had been outraged, she explained, when Frank Sinatra left his first wife for Ava Gardner and delighted when Ava gave "Frankie boy" his just deserts by leaving him. She had a title in mind—"When Somebody Breaks

Your Heart"—and one line of a lyric: "I want to be around to pick up the pieces when somebody breaks your heart." Mrs. Vimmerstedt addressed the letter to "Johnny Mercer, Songwriter, New York, NY," and dropped it in the mailbox. The Manhattan Post Office forwarded the envelope to ASCAP, which sent it on to Mercer.

The songwriter, a depressive alcoholic, was then in a fallow period, but with the success of "Moon River" and "Days of Wine and Roses" in the early 1960s his confidence picked up, and he wrote the music and lyrics for "I Wanna Be Around," which began, almost verbatim, with Sadie Vimmerstedt's line. Mercer wrote back to her, saying he would give her co-composer credit and split the royalties with her but that he didn't want the tune recorded until he found the right singer for it. A couple of years went by before Mercer told Mrs. Vimmerstedt that he finally had the perfect voice. "When he told me that Tony Bennett was going to record it," she said, "I really got excited." She was equally excited when she got a royalty check for $50,000 a few months after Bennett's single charted.

Here, though, Tony Bennett is the winner. His version, kiss-off though it may be, is ecstatic—his voice has the quality of a great jazz horn—while Sinatra's competent interpretation of "I Wanna Be Around" is emotionally muted: almost as though he realized Ava had already received in excessive measure whatever comeuppance he might ever have wished on her.

———

There was nothing muted about the last song of the evening, "Fly Me to the Moon"—Sinatra nailed it in one take. Quincy Jones had taken the loping, flute-driven 4/4 of the Basie instrumental—which felt a lot like easy listening, albeit great easy listening—and turned it into a barn burner: still 4/4, but at a faster tempo and with propulsive brass. And Frank, driving the Rolls-Royce that Q and the Count had provided, kicked this modern standard into a new high gear. From here on, only revisionists would sing it in waltz time. Sinatra's rendition was a superbly masculine invitation to levitation, one to stand along-side, even above, "Come Fly with Me." Frank and Quincy and Bill Basie had taken a song that had been recorded a hundred times and made the definitive version.

There were lesser pleasures to be found on the subsequent nights. At the second session, on June 10, Sinatra recorded yet another Bennett hit, "The Good Life." The song had originally been a French tune called "La belle vie"—a perfectly Gallic title, conjuring images of bread, wine, and *l'amour*. And even though the English lyric (by Jack Reardon) contained darkness and ambiguity—

Yes, the good life lets you hide all the sadness you feel

—Bennett's soaring rendition of the title phrase *conveyed* the pleasure of life. Sinatra's version is upbeat but strangely superficial: as though on this one occasion, he couldn't find the meaning in the lyric. The song also contains one line—"You won't really fall in love 'cause you can't take the chance"—that cut a little too close to the bone where Frank was concerned. He wasn't majoring in torch anymore; his disengagement showed.

This made three times on one album that Sinatra had gone up against Bennett: Frank scored one draw and two losses on points. Although he wasn't purposely setting out to record tunes that other male singers had made hits—he and Jones had come up with the song list together—it happened to work out that way in seven of the LP's ten numbers: besides Bennett's three, there were Ray Charles's "I Can't Stop Loving You," Jack Jones's "Wives and Lovers," Steve Lawrence's "More," and—of all things—Louis Armstrong's "Hello, Dolly!"

In a way, Sinatra had sung this not very interesting song before: when his career was in decline in 1948, Mitch Miller had persuaded him to record a bouncy, pedal-steel-backed trifle called "Sunflower," whose refrain would be echoed, almost note for note, in Jerry Herman's razzle-dazzle 1964 show tune.*

Armstrong's version of the number had just come out in January and quickly became the biggest record of his career, reaching number 1 on the U.S. *Billboard* Hot 100 and ending the Beatles' run of three number 1 hits in a row over fourteen consecutive weeks. Maybe Frank was grateful. He certainly had vast respect for Armstrong as a colossus of jazz and popular music, and so he did a brilliant thing: he couched his version of "Hello, Dolly!" as a straightout tribute to Pops and, with Basie's band kicking Vegas-style behind him, a rollicking, stomping hoot, complete with apostrophes to the Great Man—

Hello, Satch! This is Francis, Louis—
It's so nice to see you back where you belong

—and even a growling, Satchmo-esque "Oh, yeahh!" at the coda.

Imitation was less than flattering in the ill-conceived Ray Charles knockoff "I Can't Stop Loving You." Frank's version begins promisingly enough as he channels Charles's hoarse shout on the title phrase, then quickly sinks like a stone with a faux-twangy, badly off-key melisma on "I've made up my *mi-*

---

* The composer of "Sunflower," Mack David, sued Herman and won an out-of-court settlement.

ind." No one—not the sweet-tempered producer Sonny Burke in the sound booth, not Quincy Jones or Bill Miller—had the nerve to tell Frank he had hit a serious clam. No one had the nerve to tell him he was off his turf and out of his wheelhouse in attempting Charles's unique blend of C&W and R&B, but such was Sinatra's omnipotence, and his pride in his honorary blackness, that he felt he could do anything—even when he couldn't. And as always, he was looking for hits. And he had the last laugh, as he so often did, when his "I Can't Stop Loving You" became, along with "Fly Me to the Moon" and "The Best Is Yet to Come," one of the most popular numbers from the album, clam and all.

He would keep looking for hits, but as popular music changed, swiftly, irrevocably, and beyond recognition, he would find them ever harder to come by.

On Saturday, June 13, the Rolling Stones, on the western leg of their first U.S. tour, appeared on ABC-TV's weekly variety show *The Hollywood Palace*. Dean Martin was the guest host, and he took the opportunity to go after the Stones, and the nascent British Invasion, with a vengeance.

Ruggedly handsome in his tux, Dino clapped earnestly ("Beautiful. Beautiful") as the old-style stand-up comic Joey Forman left the stage, then suddenly turned mock fearful. "Now!" he announced, to knowing laughter from the audience. "Something for the youngsters. Five singing boys from England who sold a lot of al-byumes. Albums. They're called the Rolling Stones. I've been rolled while I was stoned myself, so I know what they're singin' about. But here they are at."

The Stones did two numbers, both covers: Buddy Holly's "Not Fade Away" and Willie Dixon's "I Just Want to Make Love to You." (Like the pre-1963 Beatles, the group had little original material at the beginning.) They performed well and charismatically; a couple of modest screams broke out, though a quick camera cutaway to the audience showed a lot of neckties and gray hair. If Mick Jagger seemed mildly cowed by the alien circumstances, he had a demonstrably greater command of the black musical idiom than Frank Sinatra.

Then Dino returned to the stage, clapping vigorously, though his broad deadpan told a different story. "Rolling Stones—aren't they great?" he said, then rolled his eyes heavenward. "They're going to leave right after the show for London. They're challenging the Beatles to a hair-pulling contest. I could swear Jackie Coogan and Skippy were in that group," he said, apparently making a fractured reference to *Skippy,* a 1931 film starring the nine-year-old Jackie Cooper. The Stones, in other words, were young.

Dean was on a roll. "Well, I'm going to let you in on something," he said puckishly. "You know these singing groups today—you're under the impression they have long hair. Not true at all. It's an optical illusion—they just have low foreheads and high eyebrows." It made no sense, it wasn't very funny, but it got a laugh.

It was all relatively toothless—the old Dino treatment—until the next artist, Larry Griswold, a comedy trampolinist, finished his act. Martin perked up: "Larry Griswold—isn't he wonderful? He's the father of the Rolling Stones. And ever since he heard them sing, he's been trying to kill himself."

On the one hand, this was just ancient, roast-style comedy, but it was also a chink in the facade of fond condescension: in some inner recess of his cool and inaccessible soul, Dino was nervous. As was Frank. It was all well and good for him to insist to George Jacobs that the Beatles "were a stupid fad like hula hoops and Davy Crockett coonskin caps . . . He didn't give them long." But fourteen positions on the Hot 100—to Sinatra and Martin's zero, in June—wasn't quite a laughing matter. The barbarians were at the gates, and Dean and Frank and the rest of their ilk were seeing the gates rattle.

Stephen King, then sixteen, was watching the show in Durham, Maine. As Martin winked and rolled his eyes at the audience, he recalled, "I thought, 'Fuck you, you old lounge lizard. You're the past, I've just seen the future.'"

———

Frank made his own *Ed Sullivan* appearance on June 28, forgetting past feuds with the combative host in the interests of pushing *Robin and the 7 Hoods,* which had just premiered. He made nice with Sullivan and sang "My Kind of Town," the best song from the movie—and the best part about the movie. The critics were united in their indifference to the picture. Calling it "an artless and obvious film," the *New York Times*'s Bosley Crowther said, "The brightest thing about it is its color photography . . . [A]t least, one can say this for it: The usual Sinatra arrogance is subdued."

The picture did a little better than *4 for Texas,* which isn't saying much. The elusive El Dorado of *Ocean's 11*—the pot of gold that had inspired Jack Warner to open his checkbook, expecting more riches to rain down—remained elusive.

———

As did hit records, though Frank kept trying, even as the rock revolution threatened to overwhelm popular music. As the storm blew outside, Reprise's "youth A&R man," Jimmy Bowen, a good ol' boy from Texas, assumed an ever-greater importance at the label. "Bowen drawled and shucked and jived and was your pal," Stan Cornyn writes.

He wore clothes that were too tight, or else he'd overeaten inside of them. He wore aviator glasses with a beige tint and heard musical arrangements (not just tunes) in his head. He stayed up all night, drank Jack, and got hot girls. He never wore a pocket handkerchief. His drive: just make hit singles.

And his new chief mandate was to make hit singles for the boss. "Jimmy never cared about an album," the engineer Lee Herschberg said. "He never would have an album concept. If you have enough hit singles together, you had an album. It didn't have to have a continuity or a theme behind it or anything like that." During their first meeting, Bowen recalled, Frank said, " 'Listen, if you're going to produce some music for me, what would you do?' I said, 'Well, I wouldn't bastardize you. I'd change the music around you but keep you who you are.' "

To that end, Bowen hired a new arranger, a former jazz and R&B pianist and organist named Ernie Freeman, who had gone into the profitable business of making white teen idols like Bobby Vee and Paul Anka sound like credible rock 'n' rollers.

It was a new world, and on July 17, Frank's first recording session with Freeman, Sinatra saw it up close. Gone were the studio musicians he was used to, the stalwarts and giants of classical and jazz, replaced by "Nashville rock-style players, such as drummer Hal Blaine and keyboardist Leon Russell, along with concertmaster Sid Sharp, who knew how to get fiddlers 'who didn't mind busting a string,' " Will Friedwald writes.

Oh, and a full choir, too.

When Frank walked into the studio that night, he "heard two flutists playing triplets (*tweet*-tweet-tweet)," Cornyn writes.

> From the control booth, Bowen, sweaty-palmed, watched Sinatra, who stared down at the flute players, then turned to Jimmy.
> "What's that?" Sinatra asked.
> "Them's triplets," Bowen answered.
> "Oh."

Frank made three recordings that night: "Softly, as I Leave You," an Italian love song translated into English and, earlier in the year, a hit for "the British Sinatra," Matt Monro; "Then Suddenly Love," by Roy Alfred, the writer of "The Huckle-Buck," Sinatra's misguided 1949 attempt at R&B, and 1953's similarly jazzy "Lean Baby"; and a Sammy Cahn, Ned Wynn, and L. B. Marks tune called "Available." All at once Sinatra had a new sound, marked by insistent, metronomic rhythm and grandiose string and choral backgrounds. Sinatra sang wonderfully, but the music, more than slightly Muzak-y, called attention to itself, and not in a good way. It was as if the Voice were wearing a polyester suit and standing in front of a cheesy backdrop.

"When we finished cutting 'Softly,' we were listening to the playbacks and Frank said, 'Well, James, what do you think?' " Bowen recalled.

> And I said, "I think it's [only] about a number thirty record, but it'll get us back on radio." He looked at me like that didn't please him too much, and he left. And I think the record went to twenty-seven or twenty-eight. But with Sinatra that would be important because your word is very important to him, and that's what I felt. We had a challenge to get Sinatra on top-forty radio when the Beatles were happening.

"Softly, as I Leave You," with "Then Suddenly Love" on the B-side, would hit number 27 on September 5: mission accomplished. But at what cost?

This was the year Frank Sinatra got fat. Not fat fat, but thicker, more middle-aged. Until now, he'd always been defined as thin: in a thousand newspaper columns, in Bob Hope monologues, even in Warner Bros. cartoons. From the early 1940s to the late 1950s, the Homeric epithet "skinny crooner" could apply to no one else. The image had held fast until the thick hair thinned and the crooner became a swinger.

This was the middle period, say 1957 through 1963, when he was still slim but had lost the starved appearance that had defined him as a young man, the looks that had made women want to feed and protect him. Now, with his toup and his gaunt, scarred face, he was cigarette-smoker-skinny rather than endearingly thin. That look stayed with him through the Hawaii shoot of *None but the Brave,* where numerous on-set photographs showed him histrionically directing the actors, lean in his army suntans.

But sometime over the summer of 1964—maybe the near drowning triggered it, maybe the Honolulu saturnalia got the ball rolling, maybe it was just the onset of middle-age spread—Frank began to put on weight: five pounds, ten, fifteen. And with the weight, the sharp contours of his face, the physiognomy that had reminded the sculptor Jo Davidson (who did a bust of him in 1946) of Lincoln, disappeared forever. Sinatra's head became more spherical and bull-necked and bald; the hairpieces perched ever more obviously.

This was the look he brought to his latest film, *Von Ryan's Express.*

The picture was for 20th Century Fox (Frank's movie deal with Warner Bros. was nonexclusive), where Sinatra hadn't covered himself in glory: his misfires there included his walkout on *Carousel; Pink Tights,* his aborted musical with Marilyn Monroe; and *Can-Can,* a major flop. But Fox, having almost been brought down by the colossal fiasco of *Cleopatra,* was now in a new phase, back under the guidance of Darryl F. Zanuck, and Zanuck, like Jack Warner, wanted Sinatra.

Von Ryan's Express was another World War II story, but a very different one from *None but the Brave.* Adapted from the successful novel of the same name, it fit squarely in the boy's-adventure take on the war that flourished in the early 1960s: much like 1963's smash hit *The Great Escape, Von Ryan* told the tale of a group of Allied prisoners who stage a daring mass escape, in this case by hijacking a freight train. Frank played the ringleader, Colonel Joseph Ryan. (The promotion from the chief pharmacist's mate he played in *None but the Brave* reflected his fuller, prosperous-looking face.)

Sinatra had misgivings about the project from the beginning, primarily because it required several weeks of location shooting in Italy and Spain: he disliked leaving his home base, and he had bad associations with both countries. In the former, he was expected as an Italian-American to speak the language but did not, and audiences at the concerts he'd given there in 1953 and 1962 had been indifferent or rude.

Spain was not only the land of that memorable disaster *The Pride and the Passion;* more damningly, it was the land where Ava had declared her full independence, conducting two internationally publicized love affairs with bullfighters while the world reveled in Frank's humiliation. And Rome was where his marriage to her had finally fallen apart.

Despite all the negative baggage, though, his intuition told him that *Von Ryan's Express* could be a hit, and he hadn't had a big movie since *Ocean's 11.* Zanuck was dangling gross-profit participation, an almost unheard-of deal. When an old pal of Frank's, the acerbic screenwriter Harry Kurnitz, told truth to power—the world had had it with those Rat Pack home movies—he listened.

It was also time for a shift of scenery. Los Angeles, like much of the rest of the country, was undergoing earthshaking change in the late summer of 1964. It was Freedom Summer in the South; it was the summer the Republicans nominated Barry Goldwater ("Extremism in the defense of liberty is no vice") as their presidential candidate. There were race riots in Harlem; protests against the Vietnam War began to swell into a nationwide movement. Hollywood was no longer the Tinseltown Frank had ruled, on and off but mostly on, for two decades. The movie business was a mess (*Cleopatra* had been both a cause and a symptom). The grand old nightspots of the Sunset Strip, Mocambo and the Trocadero, were long shuttered—Ciro's, under new management, had been repurposed as a rock club—and the elegant, red-banquette restaurants where Hollywood's Old Guard gathered to hoist giant menus and look at each other were fewer and farther between. Discotheques like Whisky a Go Go and the Daisy were starting to sprout like toadstools after a rainstorm. Long hair began to appear on the Strip. The Beatles, and other alien sounds, were coming out of every radio, though in August Dino got his (and Frank's) revenge on the Fab Four, the Stones, and all the rest of them when his Reprise single "Everybody Loves Somebody" (a 1947 number—Sinatra had sung it then—turbocharged by Jimmy Bowen) knocked "A Hard Day's Night" off *Billboard*'s number 1 spot. It was a moral victory, but a temporary one. The young, emboldened by rebellion and the ecstasy of new possibilities, knew they were taking over. Sinatra didn't like any of it a bit.

In early August, he packed up and headed for Rome, stopping in New York to pick up Jilly, who, Earl Wilson wrote, would "be in charge of 'the Sinatra security,' protecting Frank from the Italian photogs, the paparazzi . . . It could be a bloody war with Frank cherry-bombing the photogs."

Frank took along the rest of his posse—Brad Dexter and Dick Bakalyan and Mike Romanoff all had roles in the movie—and a suitcase full of his favorite fireworks. He was in a fuck-all mood, ready to play whenever he felt like it and work on his terms. And he took an instant dislike to the director and producer of *Von Ryan's Express,* the methodical, Canadian-born Mark Robson. "Priding himself on being a painstaking craftsman, Robson would probably have clashed with Sinatra on the easiest of shoots, the latter ever-eager to work through his scenes at top speed," Daniel O'Brien writes. "Out on difficult, isolated locations, a clash was inevitable, the star failing to show Robson the kind of respect he'd afforded to Otto Preminger or John Frankenheimer. Deaf to all explanations of production logistics, Sinatra demanded that his scenes be filmed consecutively, with minimum waiting time between set-ups."

Robson said this method of shooting was possible but would involve considerable extra effort and expense. Frank cut him off. "I know all that," he said. "I didn't tell you how to schedule the picture. I just told you what I wanted, and you told me, in front of witnesses, that you could do it. That was the deal. So now *do* it! You hear?"

The witnesses to the face-off were other members of the cast and crew, including Frank's posse, who cheered on the Leader, openly flouting Robson. When the director failed to jump at Sinatra's order, Frank walked off the set.

To try to appease the star, Fox made a yacht available for a cruise down the

Sinatra in *Von Ryan's Express*, 1965. This was the moment Frank's face and body began to grow thicker: the sharp contours of his youthful physiognomy were gone forever.

coast. Sinatra took his posse and basked in the sun at Portofino, Santa Margherita, and Rapallo while Robson stewed.

He had the director by the purse strings. Not only was the studio on the star's side, but production costs were $25,000 a day (roughly $200,000 in 2015), and Robson's deal, unlike Frank's, gave him a percentage of the movie's net, not its gross. Sinatra could afford to delay indefinitely; Robson couldn't.

Fox bowed to Frank's every whim. When he refused to put up in Rome with the rest of the cast—screw Rome!—the studio rented him an eighteen-room villa outside the city, surrounded by a ten-foot wall and complete with indoor and outdoor swimming pools and a helipad. Each day a chartered helicopter whisked him to the location in Cortina d'Ampezzo, in the Dolomite Alps, while the rest of the cast and crew made the long drive by car. "Between takes," George Jacobs writes, "he would listen to Puccini and old Neapolitan folk songs and throw cherry bombs at the elegant but pompous ski crowd of Cortina d'Ampezzo." He also deployed the powerful firecrackers to destroy Dexter and Bakalyan's hotel toilets.

He was in full midlife frenzy (midlife if he lived to a hundred, which he had every intention of doing), a second adolescence. Romantically speaking, he was footloose and fancy-free: he'd seen—as the expression goes—Angie

Dickinson in L.A. earlier in the summer, but with his power at its height and his capacity for intimacy at its lowest ebb he was flying solo these days. He conceived a crush on a beautiful Italian production secretary, but she had recently married and had no interest in a fling, even with Sinatra.

According to Jacobs, his boss simply couldn't fathom this. "One weekend," the valet recalled, "when the husband came up to Cortina to visit, Sinatra ran into the couple in the lobby of the Miramonti Majestic Hotel. The secretary proudly introduced her husband to Mr. S," who responded by taking a fountain pen and signing his autograph in big letters on the back of the white cashmere sweater she was wearing, a gift from her husband. The secretary broke down in tears. "The next Monday," Jacobs writes, "when the stores opened, he had me go and buy three identical cashmere sweaters, in red, white, and blue, and deliver them, without any note of explanation or apology, to the secretary's hotel."

He exerted such power as he could. When Frank was a lonely, spoiled boy in Hoboken, Dolly had bought flashy orange-and-black jackets for the members of his after-school club, the Turk's Palace, to ensure that his circle stayed close. Now he used a similar strategy to keep his crew (including a visiting Jack Entratter) happy. One weekend, Brad Dexter recalled, Sinatra had several of Rome's upscale haberdashers bring a selection of their finest goods to the villa—silk shirts, neckties, cashmere sweaters, gold cuff links, alligator belts— and invited Jilly, Entratter, Bakalyan, Dexter, and the publicist Jim Mahoney to help themselves. According to Dexter, everyone but him grabbed eagerly at the swag. "What are you being so generous for?" he asked Frank. "You don't need to lay it on like this."

"It means nothing to me, Brad. Take something. Help yourself."

Dexter said he shook his head and walked out of the room.

Ava was also in Italy, shooting *The Bible,* again under John Huston's direction, and in the midst of an abusive relationship with her co-star and fellow alcoholic George C. Scott. She played Sarah; he played Abraham. Scott, an ex-marine, was a great actor and a powerful, glowering presence, subject to drinking binges, blackouts, and towering rages. Of course Ava was no stranger to rage herself. Scott had abstained from liquor for several years until he met Ava; he fell madly in love and off the wagon. The fact that he was married to a pregnant Colleen Dewhurst failed to discourage him. One night, in the village of Avezzano, he and Ava had both been drinking, and she happened to mention Frank's name. Scott beat Gardner up, dropping her to the floor and punching her repeatedly in the head. The next day he apologized abjectly. The makeup artist covered her bruises, and she continued her work on the movie and continued her relationship with George C. Scott.

As always, she had been in touch with Frank by phone. He had planned to come see her but then called it off: the Italian papers had a bounty out for a photo of the two of them together. Ava never told him about the beating—she was afraid Sinatra would have Scott killed—but somehow he found out. When *The Bible*'s shoot moved to Sicily, Gardner began to notice three burly men appearing on the set every day. She writes in her memoirs that she assumed Huston had hired them to protect her, but a friend of Jilly's insisted to Randy Taraborrelli that Frank had sent the three. One night in Taormina, Ava and Scott got to drinking and began to argue loudly. As Scott raised a hand to strike her, the three men appeared out of nowhere, grabbed the actor by both arms, and dragged him to a car. He showed up for work the next morning uninjured but considerably subdued.

Whether out of gratitude or nostalgia, Ava flew to Rome one long weekend to see Frank. Dexter and Bakalyan met her at the airport and drove her to the villa. "Frank was affectionate, sentimental," Lee Server writes. "There was some of the old talk about them getting back together. But there was a sense of strain in the air. There was no sex that weekend."

There was a good reason for this, as Brad Dexter recalled. One night when he had dinner with the two of them, Ava, looking haggard and drawn, drank herself into a near stupor and simply staggered upstairs to bed. Frank turned to Dexter. "She's the only woman I've ever been in love with in my whole life, and look at her," he said. "She's turned into a falling-down drunk."

It was painful for him to see, but he might have been equally pained if he'd been able to take stock of himself.

In early September, the shoot moved on to Spain, where a ridiculous incident occurred: in Torremolinos, on the night before the completion of filming, Sinatra, Dexter, the manager of their hotel, and a few others were having a drink when Frank felt a tap on the shoulder. When he turned around, a young woman embraced him and flashbulbs popped.

She was an aspiring actress, and it was a cheap trick to get a publicity shot with Sinatra, probably with a tabloid story thrown in. Properly furious, Frank threw her off, screaming that nobody was allowed to take his picture without permission. The manager told the photographers to leave.

Meanwhile, the young woman went to the bar and ordered a drink—then threw it in Sinatra's face, covering him in whiskey and cutting his cheek. The manager had her ejected; when she showed up in the hotel lobby afterward, he called the police. Frank made a report but declined to press charges.

The next morning, the lobby was swarming with police; jeeps with machine guns mounted on them were parked outside. Everyone from the movie company was detained, and two crew members were arrested. Frank and Dexter managed to avoid the police and go to work for the final day of filming.

The following morning, as the two were about to leave Madrid, plain-clothesmen from the Guardia Civil stopped them in the hotel lobby and told them they would have to go to the police station for questioning. The young woman had accused them of assault, and under Spanish law they could be detained for questioning for three days before being officially charged. While Dexter phoned the U.S. ambassador, Frank screamed at the cops, calling Spain's fascist leader, Generalissimo Franco, a "spic faggot." It did not go down well. The police locked Sinatra and Dexter in separate cells and interrogated them at length. The film's producer, Saul David, finally came and paid 25,000 pesetas ($416 in 1964 dollars; a substantial portion of a Guardia Civil's annual salary) to bail them out. The police hustled Frank straight to the airport without allowing him to pack his bags; he got on a plane and flew to Paris, where he stewed in luxury in the Hotel George V.

"I'll never go back to that fucking country again," he said. "I hate those dirty Fascist bastards."

Even Ava was beginning to tire of Spain. But unfortunately not, for the moment, of George C. Scott.

———

In October, the filming of *Von Ryan's Express* moved to a soundstage at 20th Century Fox. Zanuck had tightened the studio's belt, firing staff and selling off the back lot, and he was keeping the machine running with lower-budget pictures and increased television production, a strategy that would help Fox get back on its feet. (Both *Von Ryan* and *The Sound of Music,* budgeted at $5.7 million and $8.2 million, respectively, were relatively big movies, but nowhere near *Cleopatra*'s bank-busting $44 million.) Among the TV series being made that fall in the studio complex between West Pico and Olympic boulevards were the science-fiction adventure *Voyage to the Bottom of the Sea,* the World War II drama *Twelve O'Clock High,* and ABC's new prime-time soap opera, *Peyton Place.*

The last series was based on Grace Metalious's steamy 1956 novel about the sordid secrets of a small New England town, and though the TV show toned down the novel's squalor, its insistent, racy-for-the-early-1960s sexuality made it both controversial and instantly popular. Tough blonde Dorothy Malone starred as Constance MacKenzie, the woman with a dark past who owned Peyton Place's bookstore; the nineteen-year-old newcomer Mia Farrow played her alienated, virginal, but sexually curious (and secretly illegitimate) daughter, Allison.

Slim, ethereal, and faintly androgynous, Farrow had high cheekbones, huge blue eyes, and a slightly tarnished Hollywood pedigree. Her Irish-born mother, Maureen O'Sullivan, had been a true star in the 1930s and 1940s, most famous for playing Jane to Johnny Weissmuller's Tarzan in half a dozen pictures but able to branch out to more substantial roles in films like *The Thin Man, Anna Karenina,* and *Pride and Prejudice.* O'Sullivan's movie career declined throughout the 1950s, as did that of her husband, the Australian-born, B-level director John Farrow (*A Bill of Divorcement, The Big Clock*), a devout Catholic—he wrote a well-regarded biography of Sir Thomas More—and a cold-eyed drunk who cheated on O'Sullivan persistently as he fathered their seven children. "He was an intelligent, talented, unhappy, bedeviled, frequently frustrated, insecure and arrogant man who should have become an actor—only he disliked actors intensely," the columnist Lloyd Shearer wrote. In 1953, Farrow directed the forgettable Western *Ride, Vaquero!,* starring a reluctant Ava Gardner, who had a fling with him out of sheer boredom. She remembered him as "a mean and lecherous character, cruel in equal measure to the horses and to the whores he flew in from Los Angeles." In early 1963, Farrow dropped dead of a heart attack at age fifty-eight, mourned by few.

María de Lourdes Villiers Farrow, nicknamed Mia, idolized her frequently absent father and her beautiful mother, who was present but absent at the same time. In the Hollywood style of the era, Mia and her siblings (she was the third child, and the eldest of the four girls) were raised by nannies, but the Farrows went even further: the children lived in a nursery separate from the main house, with its own kitchen. Her childhood was riven: by a case of polio when she was nine; by her glamorous parents' eroding marriage (they slept in separate bedrooms after O'Sullivan learned of the affair with Gardner); by the death of her adored oldest brother in a plane crash in 1958. She attended a convent boarding school in England and hated it; she developed an active fantasy life, a certain detachment from the everyday. "I was the loner of the family," she told columnist Bob Thomas. "I was able to shut out the household noises by living with my own dreams."

Late at night in her childhood home, she writes in her memoir, she used to wander around and watch her family while they were fast asleep: "every once in a while, with my thumb, I'd very carefully open up somebody's eye, just for a second, to look at the eyeball in there."

In a way, it was a foregone conclusion that this strange, dreamy, exotically beautiful girl, whose godparents were Louella Parsons and George Cukor, would become an actress.

Spending time with her mother in New York one Christmas—O'Sullivan was starring in a Broadway comedy—the seventeen-year-old Farrow begged for acting lessons and took instantly to the craft. "I discovered that only in drama class could I manipulate people, amuse them, even make them notice me through this marvelous game of pretending, where I didn't have to be me," she recalled. Things moved fast from there. When an actress dropped out of a role in a Broadway revival of *The Importance of Being Earnest*—the cast was all-English—she read for the part, got it, and drew rave reviews. Fox signed her to a contract. With the exception of a bit part in one of her father's films as a girl, the pilot of *Peyton Place* was her first time before the cameras.

Her first movie role came just as rapidly: when Britt Ekland, playing the ingenue in a Richard Attenborough adventure called *Guns at Batasi,* had to drop out because her husband, Peter Sellers, had had a heart attack, Fox flew Farrow to London to fill in. She did a couple of weeks' work, then returned to the States, where the *Peyton Place* pilot had already aired, to find herself being proclaimed a new star.

She greeted her instant success with open arms. "I want a big career, a big man and a big life!" she told Hedda Hopper, soon after production began on the series. "You have to think big—that's the only way to get what you want."

Mia Farrow on *Peyton Place*, 1965. Slim, ethereal, and faintly androgynous, she had high cheekbones, huge blue eyes, and a slightly tarnished Hollywood pedigree. Here she bears a striking resemblance both to her late father, the director John Farrow, and to her future son Ronan.

In a way, it was also a foregone conclusion that she would find the biggest man of all.

The plausible pretext for Farrow's visit to the set of *Von Ryan's Express* was that the young English actor John Leyton, with whom she had had a love scene in *Guns at Batasi,* was working in the picture.

Restless during a long break between takes on *Peyton Place,* she wandered over to the *Von Ryan's Express* set and watched Frank Sinatra filming a scene on a fake train with the beautiful Italian actress Raffaella Carra. Farrow had first met Sinatra eight years earlier at Romanoff's restaurant, where she was having dinner with her father. She was eleven. "Pretty girl," Frank had joked. "You stay away from her," John Farrow had replied, perhaps only half jokingly. Now as she stood on the dark soundstage watching Sinatra act, she thought how beautiful his face seemed, "full of pain and somehow familiar."

She neglects to mention that her late (high-foreheaded, blue-eyed) father bore a more than passing resemblance to Frank Sinatra. And—strange detail— that the two men wore the same cologne. "I can say it now," she later wrote. "They had the same identical smell."

She also fails to note that she had dressed for the set visit in a sheer night-gown from the *Peyton Place* wardrobe department, and nothing else, and that though she had made much in the press of her sticklike body (she told *Life* that her measurements were 20-20-20), she had protested too much. Frank looked, and then he looked again.

———

And she visited the set again, and again. Brad Dexter recalled that Farrow was there every day, making "googly eyes" at Sinatra, and that at the end of the first week, as Frank, Dexter, and the cinematographer William Daniels were pre-paring to leave for Palm Springs in Frank's jet, she said, "How come you never invite me to come along?"

"Frank did a double take," Dexter said. " 'Huh? Are you kidding? Would you like to come?' Mia beamed and said, 'Sure.' "

Farrow's version is considerably more chaste. As she was watching the film-ing, she writes, she became aware of Sinatra, seated some distance behind her amid a boisterous group of men. All at once, one of Frank's entourage, a big man with a pleasant face (probably Brad Dexter), came up and said that the group had been wondering how old she was. Mia pulled herself up to her full height—with her long braids and girlish features she looked considerably younger than her age—and proudly told him: nineteen. A short time later, the man came back and asked her to join Sinatra's group. She came along at once, so nervous that she dropped the contents of her straw bag at Frank's feet—her retainer, keys, coins, glasses, tampons, bubble gum. She apologized profusely as he helped her pick everything up.

It's a scene straight out of a movie. The music rises. Their eyes meet. She felt "a column of light" rising inside her, she recalled. Dazed, she finally left to go back to work. Sinatra walked her to the stage door and asked if she'd like to join him at a private Friday-night screening of *None But the Brave*. She told him she would love to.

Friday night arrived; they met at the Warner Bros. screening room. The lights went down, and she watched the war movie in a fog, dimly aware of American soldiers and Japanese soldiers and skirmishes—but then came the momentous part: Frank Sinatra held her hand.

When the lights came up, he invited her to accompany him to Palm Springs, that very night: There'd be other guests, he told her; it would be fun.

She mumbled something about her cat. He had to be fed, and he ate only baby food. And she didn't have her clothes, her pajamas, her toothbrush. None of it made sense. She thanked him for the invitation, and apologized.

But meanwhile, a parallel apology to Frank was forming in her mind. She shouldn't have held his hand, she thought; she'd given the wrong impression. She couldn't go to Palm Springs with him, or anywhere else. She had no idea what she was doing; she would only disappoint him. She had no birth control, no experience at all along those lines, in fact.

Then he asked her if she could come tomorrow. He would send his plane for her; she could even bring her cat.

His *plane*? she thought. For her cat and her? "Reality tiptoed out of the room," she writes.

In truth, both of them have entered exceedingly strange territory. She is a virgin! (We will take her word for it. Had Frank known, would he have been so quick to send his plane?) She has never listened to a Sinatra record or seen one of his movies—except for *None but the Brave*; even her parents never owned a Sinatra album: they listened to Gregorian chants.

She listens to the Beatles. She smokes marijuana and has taken LSD. She does yoga. She has palled around with Salvador Dalí. This is the girl who examined the eyeballs of her sleeping family with her thumb (shades of *Un chien andalou*). Who has said, "Sometimes I think I'd like to put my soul somewhere where nobody could get it. I'd have a castle with a moat and a drawbridge and people could never stomp on me and take chunks out of my soul until there's nothing left." This is the girl who has floated loose in the world for a long time yet also harbors a fiery ambition. Who has a sense of direction so bad that she needs to be driven by others if she wants to get anywhere, but at the same time knows precisely where she's going. Who has let others take care of her—and has never been taken care of enough—yet also seems strangely capable of taking care of herself. She has a three-room apartment on the second floor of a little house in the flats of Beverly Hills, like a thousand other young actresses, and she's decorated it with furniture from Sears and wall-to-wall carpet and a fake rock pond with a little waterfall and fake moss all around it for her deaf Angora cat, Malcolm. But unlike the thousand other young actresses, she has the lineage and a will of iron. The big life awaits.

Sinatra is Sinatra, and he will soon be forty-nine, and he has seen this slim girl with the surprising body shake her long blond hair and stare at him with those great blue eyes and stammer charmingly awkward sentences in her soft, trembling voice, and he has conceived a powerful desire to take her, and to take care of her. He saw death in those waves off Kauai, and here is life, in its freshest form.

And so he stares into her eyes with those irresistible electric-blues, giving her the attention that every woman in the world craves, only now it is hers alone, the complete attention that John Farrow never quite gave her. And, with honest audacity, she stares back, unflinchingly, stunned into silence by the power of "all this eyeing"—and struck by a new idea, full of music and light: that she would love to be in Palm Springs, or anywhere else, with Frank Sinatra.

Thus she finds herself, the next day, sitting with her cat aboard his jet as it taxis along the desert runway toward a remote corner of the Palm Springs Airport, where she spots Frank Sinatra leaning against his car, arms folded, looking handsome in an orange short-sleeved shirt. She walks down the plane's steps holding her cat and her straw hat; he walks up to them and laughs.

And both of them have now walked through the looking glass.

They began to explore the strange new territory of each other.

Almost in solitude at first, in Palm Springs on the weekends, with a puzzled George Jacobs looking on: "It wasn't that Mia was a Beatles girl or a Stones girl, as opposed to a Frank girl. She was a *nothing* girl, a total space cadet . . . a clueless nineteen-year-old whose main passion was her deaf cat." Almost always, because Frank needed company, there was a little company—his pals Yul Brynner and Jack Entratter, and Entratter's girlfriend, later to be his wife, Corinne Cole.

Years later, in a letter to Farrow, Cole reminisced about those autumn weekends when she and Mia sat in the living room trying to learn backgammon while Entratter did casino business on the phone and Frank swam in the pool. At one point Sinatra bobbed to the surface and exclaimed to Farrow, in that biggest of big voices, "I love you!"

"I love you too, Charlie," Mia called back, softly.

It is weird to realize that she was five years younger than his older daughter. Yet Mia's calm revealed a deep assurance that Nancy did not own. Her spaciness was real, but it was also a mask, a shield, covering a closely observing ego and that iron will. Despite the braids and the soft voice and the carefully contrived dither, she knew just what she was about and where she was going. Jack Warner's mistress Jacqueline Park marveled at Farrow's equanimity in a house filled with photographs of Ava: "There was one of Ava in the bathroom, in the bedroom over his bed, in the living room, and even one in the kitchen, but Mia never said a word about them . . . I asked her if she was happy with Frank and she said, 'Yes, we're going to get married. I just know we are. This is my destiny and there is nothing I can do about it.'"

Even though she was doing everything she could about it.

She called him Charlie or Charlie Brown, his ever-rounder head (which she got to see sans toupee) putting her in mind of the *Peanuts* character. He called her Angel Face or Baby Face. He tried his best to bring her into his world. He put Ralph Vaughan Williams symphonies on the stereo—she loved them; he tried to interest her in golf—she hated it. He bought her a set of clubs in a white leather bag with her name embossed on it in pale blue: it didn't help. Even worse than trying to play the game, she recalled, was having to watch endless televised golf tournaments along with Frank.

And then there were firearms, a crucial part of the Sinatra courtship ritual ever since Frank and Ava had drunkenly shot up the desert hamlet of Indio in 1949. The update was more sober and practical and, as befitted the mid-1960s, justifiably paranoid: driving home from Frank's L.A. apartment one night, Mia had found herself being tailed by a car with a couple of men in it. She pulled into a brightly lit gas station and called Sinatra, who appeared within minutes packing heat. The men departed. Frank promptly bought Farrow a pearl-handled revolver and took her out into the desert to target-shoot tin cans. She was an unwilling pupil, she writes, and a terrible shot, even with her glasses on. Finally Frank had to admit it would be safer for her to stay away from firearms altogether.

The desert was also a place for meditation, and education: as they walked the narrow roads near Tamarisk, Frank tried his best to fill in this child of another era on what had made Sinatra Sinatra, spinning the story as might any swain trying to impress his girl. Thus, he had not been a cosseted (and bullied) Fauntleroy in his Hoboken past, but a street-smart kid navigating his way through one of the toughest neighborhoods anywhere. He covered his first marriage in greeting-card shorthand: Nancy, his boyhood sweetheart, was an exceptional woman; they both adored their three children—two of whom were older than Mia. Farrow wondered what Sinatra's son and daughters might think of her.

As for Ava, she who (while married to Frank) had triggered the destruction of Mia's parents' marriage, she of whom "there were many lovely photographs . . . around the house," such a pained look came into Frank's eyes at the mention of his ex-wife that Farrow felt relieved when he switched the topic.

He changed the subject to the subject he always got around to eventually: his Rosebud, his touchstone. But when Sinatra told her how he'd learned the art of phrasing and the science of sneaking breaths from Tommy, Farrow looked blank. "Who's Tommy?" she asked—not, to her credit, without embarrassment. Patiently he told her about the great Dorsey and his own experience as a boy singer with the band.

Maybe it was he who should have been embarrassed that his conversational arsenal was so threadbare. (As late as 1988, as Jonathan Schwartz recalled, Sinatra was still trying to interest young women—in this case Schwartz's girlfriend—in his reminiscences about Dorsey.) But now and always, what he had to say was less interesting than what he had to be.

The gulf between the two of them was deeper and wider than either of them knew (though Frank may have had a clue). Yet in the way of all new lovers, they—or at least she—imagined their physical bliss mirrored a spiritual merging. Sometimes, as they strolled silently under the desert stars, Mia felt closer to him than she'd ever felt to anyone. But then, inevitably, came the times when she realized his silence only indicated remoteness. At these moments she would feel adrift and uncertain. Yet, she insists, these early, quiet days, before the world found out about them, were their happiest.

Then, slowly in the beginning, in came the world.

First came the Hollywood Old Guard, Frank's new set now that he was middle-aged and upward aspiring: "that stuffy, older crowd that he cultivated to be more respectable," Brad Dexter said. "I called them 'the late show.'"

They were Bill and Edie Goetz; Rosalind Russell and her husband, the Broadway producer Freddie Brisson; the film producer Armand Deutsch and his wife, Harriet; Claudette Colbert and her husband, the Beverly Hills ear, nose, and throat surgeon Dr. Joel Pressman. Frank brought Mia to Thanksgiving dinner at the Goetzes' (where he ordered her to clean her plate), and though at first, as George Jacobs noted, "no one, absolutely no one, took this romance seriously," Edie Goetz observed that "Mia was a very clever young lady and she knew exactly what she was about and what she wanted. She was crazy about Frank and she intended to marry him."

And soon, his Late Show friends, the Goetzes and the Brissons and the Pressmans, began to nudge him in that direction, too.

In early November, an inconceivable horror: a heavy Los Angeles rainstorm triggered a mudslide in the hills above Burbank that swept through the house of Sinatra's pianist Bill Miller, seriously injuring him and killing his forty-seven-year-old wife, Aimee. Miller, who had desperately tried to save his wife when she was washed away, was discovered by rescuers three-quarters of a mile away, clinging to an automobile. Frank would find the pianist a new house, pay the part of his hospital bills that weren't covered by insurance, and personally supervise and pay for the furnishing of the new home, down to the silverware, linen, and clothing. Doing all he could do short of comforting his musical right hand face-to-face.

The great man and the brilliant, gaunt pianist Sinatra teased as Suntan Charlie had always had—and always would have—a complex relationship; now it was more complicated than ever. "Bill didn't really care for Frank," Sinatra's former flame Peggy Connelly insisted. "It was like a valet never seeing the boss as a hero. He said once, 'What do you see in him? He repeats his stories all the time.' Bill could've had a huge career outside of Frank, but he just wasn't that sort of person."

"Bill always took a lot of flak from Frank, but he had a way of getting back at him," Emil Richards recalled. "If Frank said, 'Bill, give me a tone,' then Bill would just hit one note. One little-bitty 'boop,' and that would be it . . . It's as if Bill were saying, 'Come on, bitch, find it! You've had it over me all this time, now I got you!' "

He didn't take her to Vegas with him—not yet. It could've been awkward: on the night after Thanksgiving, he opened at the Sands with Count Basie and His Orchestra; after introducing some friends at ringside, he turned to a nearby table and said, "And now, the mother of my three children, Mrs. Nancy Sinatra." Two of the three, Nancy Sandra and Frank junior, sat with her. Quincy Jones, who conducted the two-week stand, recalled a Sinatra who was focused and completely on his game, the master of the Honolulu revels nowhere in evidence.

"Jack Entratter said, 'What do you guys do to Frank? When he's with the Rat Pack, those guys are in the steam room till 5:30 a.m., drinking Jack Daniel's, they're just fuckin' around all night. But when you guys work with him, he's here forty-five minutes early with his sheet music and a manila folder, and [vocal exercises].' You know he was ready to kill. Because after everything else, movies and TV and all that other stuff, he first was a big-band singer, and that's where his roots are."

He seemed to have moved on from the Rat Pack. He was in love. Attending the filming of a *Peyton Place* episode, Sheilah Graham noticed Farrow receiving what seemed a significant phone call. "I can still hear Mia telling me breathlessly in the Twentieth Century Fox commissary, 'I've just had a call from the man I love,'" Graham recalled. "I had heard some rumors and queried, 'Frank Sinatra?' 'Yes.' It was a clear, confident affirmative."

On November 30, Graham gleefully broke the news in her column, calling Frank and Mia "the maddest, merriest romance of the year." She added that the couple "have not yet discussed marriage, but it could be very much on the agenda." For the next twenty-four hours, Farrow's phone rang off the hook with calls from New York, London, Paris—and Maureen O'Sullivan. "I have been meeting Mr. Sinatra, but only to discuss a film we might do together" was Mia's response to all and sundry. The ever mother-hen-ish but increasingly out-of-touch Louella Parsons noted the romance rumors but echoed her goddaughter's denial. "I don't believe it," she wrote. "I think Frank's been talking to Mia about a movie role." The movie in question was a farce unpromisingly titled *Community Property*. Farrow was to play Frank's daughter.

Variety went gaga for Sinatra and Basie's Sands act, calling it "an obvious blockbuster even before the curtain went up . . . the kind of dream hip musical which Entratter of course would like to hold beyond its skedded two weeks. There is no chorus line—it's pure Sinatra and pure Basie. The combination of personalities and talent is overwhelming."

The review went on to note that Frank, "in good voice [and] good humor," sang "In Other Words" ("Fly Me to the Moon"), "My Kind of Town," and a new addition to his repertoire, "Get Me to the Church on Time."

Old habits died hard. Besides Nancy, Nancy junior, and Frank junior, Frank had another special ringside guest in the Copa Room on opening night, as Sinatra's *Von Ryan's Express* co-star John Leyton, who was present with his girlfriend, recalled: Frank "took us over to the table and introduced us to some people, one of whom was Sam Giancana—I called him Sir! Frank said to me to ask him what he did for a living. I wasn't sure . . . but Frank insisted with a smile . . . Well, I asked him . . . and sure enough he stood up and shouted it out: 'I own Chicago, that's what I do for a living!' He realized that Frank had put me up to it, so it was said with a smile on his face!"

The FBI and the Nevada Gaming Control Board, presumably, having been napping for the evening.

22

||||||||||||

I am a symmetrical man, almost to a fault.

—SINATRA IN *LIFE*, APRIL 23, 1965

The calendar page had turned with a crash. "America in 1964 was straining to break out of black and white and into color," the critic Dwight Garner has written. He was speaking of far more than just television—though between 1964 and 1966 color-TV ownership in the United States more than tripled.

The assassination's deep shadow had begun to lighten. In 1964, while the British Invasion stormed ashore, American boys picked up guitars and started growing their hair. (Even Dean Martin's son Dean Paul got into the act, forming a rock trio, Dino, Desi & Billy, with his friends Desi Arnaz Jr. and Billy Hinsche.) In 1965, American boys, and a couple of girls, got record deals. Nineteen sixty-five brought the Association, the Blues Project, Canned Heat, the Doors, the Electric Prunes, the Grateful Dead, Jefferson Airplane, the Lovin' Spoonful, the Mamas & the Papas, the Sir Douglas Quintet, and the Stone Poneys, with Linda Ronstadt. *Hullabaloo,* NBC's new musical-variety show for the youngsters ("in living color"), brought the new acts to millions in prime time, complete with the titillating sight of seventeen-year-old Lada Edmund Jr. go-go dancing in a cage.

Warner-Reprise Records was soaring, lifted not just by Dino (*Dream with Dean,* including "Everybody Loves Somebody") but also by Mo Ostin's new signees the Kinks, whose witty, irresistibly sexy "You Really Got Me," with its insistent power-chord obbligato—duh-*da*-da-da-*dah*—rattled woofers and grown-ups' nerves, and rang cash registers, across America.

Sinatra wasn't fulminating anymore about cretinous goons, imbecilic reiterations, and lewd lyrics these days: the Kinks were putting big bucks in the till. "It [rock 'n' roll] belongs to the younger generation and I'm not going to try to knock it," he'd told *Variety,* with diplomatic restraint, in November. But he sensed which way the wind was blowing, and he wasn't thrilled. In February, he and his boon companion Joe E. Lewis—the sad-eyed old comic who was as close as anyone on earth to an opposite species of human from Mia Farrow—did two weeks at Miami's Eden Roc, then went straight to the Sands. Scanning the full house in the Copa Room, Sinatra turned to Jimmy Van Heusen and said, "Look at that—why don't they buy my records?" But Vegas audiences weren't his problem: it was the rest of the country. He hadn't cracked the Top 20 of *Billboard*'s Hot 100 since 1958.

They were hiding in plain sight.

"Mia Farrow and Frank Sinatra were letting the world know all about their swinging new thing at The Daisy," Hollywood columnist Mike Connolly snarked on January 22, "and I do mean they were NOT discussing a Partisan Review thesis on whether Hollywood's western movies are mass myth or mass rite." The Daisy was *the* new discotheque in Beverly Hills, even hotter than Whisky a Go Go, for one reason: it was private and exclusive. A $250 one-time membership fee (later raised to $1,000) kept out the riffraff—and sometimes, to the delight of the movie colony, luminaries like Peter O'Toole and Jason Robards Jr., both of whom were turned away that spring for not being members or members' guests. The club's owner was Jack Hanson, the inventor of Jax slacks, the slim-lined, derriere-flattering pants made popular by such delectable young things as Jane Fonda and Jill St. John (who was said to own $2,000 worth) and instantly de rigueur on Madison and Worth Avenues and Rodeo Drive. Fonda and St. John, no surprise, were also habitués of the Daisy, which, as *Time* salivated in an early 1965 piece, "has some of the most eye-filling females in the U.S. frugging and swimming their little hearts out in poorboy sweaters and nothing underwear."

Hollywood had always paired rich old goats with nubile beauties and always managed to come up with a latest variation on the theme. "One night last week," the *Time* piece continued, "Carol Lynley, Jane Fonda, Jill St. John and Jill Haworth shimmered and bobbed beautifully on the tight little dance floor, while Anthony Quinn, Dean Martin, George Hamilton and Eddie Fisher gave the girls something to stare at." Of course the staring went both ways— "nothing underwear"—and of the four men only Hamilton was under thirty (Quinn and Martin were fifty and forty-seven) and Fonda, at twenty-seven, was the oldest of the young women. Nuzzling on the Daisy's dance floor, Frank and Mia fit the club's template perfectly.

Which didn't mean they fit together perfectly. If his default mode was listening to Ralph Vaughan Williams and watching golf on TV and drinking until dawn in the Sands lounge, hers was most assuredly not. His new lover wanted to go out and dance to her music, and the Daisy wasn't playing Tony Bennett or Ella Fitzgerald records.

In early 1965, Larry King was a brash young Miami broadcaster fortunate enough to have acquired Jackie Gleason as a mentor after the Great One—like King, a transplanted Brooklynite—appeared on his local television show. One night, King was at a party at Gleason's house when his host, who had a philosophical bent, asked the men in the room, "What in your profession is impossible? What will never happen?"

"We had a doctor there," King recalled, "and he said, 'They will never make blood in a laboratory. They will never manufacture blood that you can transfuse into someone. That will never happen.' Then he went to another guy, and then he came to me. I said, 'I do my television show and I write my column, but I do a three-hour radio show every night, from nine to twelve, a very popular local radio show. Sinatra is opening at the Eden Roc. Frank Sinatra to do my radio show for three hours.'

"Now, this is 1965," King continued, "and there's no bigger person in the world than Frank Sinatra in 1965. Capitol, Reprise, the whole thing; he's opening at the Eden Roc with Joe E. Lewis. Jackie asked, 'What night is he dark?' I said, 'Monday.' And Jackie said, 'You got him next Monday.'

"So I said, 'Jackie, can I go on the air tonight and say that next Monday I'll be having Frank Sinatra on my show?' 'Go ahead.' So I go back on the air, I say, 'Frank Sinatra next Monday night.' Now the station calls me in. They asked, 'Are you sure?' I said, 'Jackie says so.' I told the story. Now it's Friday, and they're taking full-page ads in the *Miami Herald* announcing this, but they're also saying they've left messages at the Eden Roc, and nobody's returning their calls.

"Anyway, it's now Monday night. Nobody went home. The secretaries all stayed. It was on at nine o'clock. At about two minutes to nine, this limo pulls up, and out comes Sinatra. We had little stairs to walk on. It was a very beautiful radio station. He walks up the stairs, and everybody's standing there, and he goes, 'Who's Larry King?' I go, 'Me.' He says, 'Okay, let's go.'

"I never was nervous on the air except my first day and that day," King said. "We sit down, and—my truism in life was, 'Never lie to your audience, and it ain't brain surgery, so go to the moment.' So all I said was, 'Why are you here?' I didn't go through 'my friend Frank Sinatra' and a lot of baloney. He said, 'Five or six years ago, I was singing at Ben Maksik's Town and Country in Brooklyn, and I had laryngitis, it was closing night, and I called Jackie. I said, 'Jackie, could you come over and do a show?' And Jackie came over and did an hour. I walked him out to his car, and I leaned in, and I said, 'I owe you one.'

"Now in Miami, I get a message to call Jackie, and I call Jackie, and all he says is, 'This is the one.'

"A lot about Gleason was ego," King recalled. "It was an enormous thing that he was able to do this. So from Jackie's standpoint, it was a favor and a great thing to do, but it also extolled Jackie."

It was the first of several Sinatra interviews King would conduct over the next quarter century. "It turned into a wonderful interview," he said. "There was a PR guy who came along with him, who said, 'I don't know how you got this, but do not mention the kidnapping, because he doesn't want to talk about that, and he'll walk off.' But what happened was, the interview went so well that in the course of it, all I said was, 'The thing between you and the press—have you been bum-rapped or is it overblown?' And he said, 'It's probably overblown, but I've been bum-rapped, too. Take the kidnapping.' And he went through the whole thing. He hated the press, and he hated tabloids. He gave me a great quote. He said, 'These people live off the real or imagined fortunes or misfortunes of those with much greater talent than them.'"

Thanks in large part to an active campaign of disinformation and squelching by Frank's publicist, Jim Mahoney, and 20th Century Fox—where, in the days when it was still possible to do such a thing, studio executives ordered a "kill" on all photographs taken of Sinatra and Farrow together—America was slow to react to the Frank-Mia story. Newspapers from early 1965 show a surprising paucity of dish about the pair. A February column by the syndicated television writer Alex Freeman leads with an item about Sinatra and Natalie Wood being turned away from "New York's swinging Ondine Club." (The place was filled to its legal limit; the doorman apologized.) Later in the column, Freeman hammers home the point: "Indicative of the unimportance of Frank Sinatra's much-publicized romance with teen-ager Mia Farrow, they bumped into each other at a party at New York's El Morocco restaurant, Mia with a date and Frank escorting Jean Kennedy Smith, sister of RFK and wife of Steven [sic] Smith, and barely exchanged hellos."

Sinatra wasn't quite ready to spring Farrow on his new New York crowd, the East Coast equivalent of the Late Show. It wasn't all Jilly and Toots Shor when Frank was in Manhattan; sometimes it was the Leland Haywards and the Bill Paleys and the Bennett Cerfs. Sinatra and Cerf, the gregarious publisher, columnist, and television personality (*What's My Line?*), had met at a Manhattan party in the 1950s, and it had been love at first sight for both of them. Frank, the class-aholic and autodidact, was instantly drawn to the witty and glittering milieu through which the co-founder of Random House moved with effortless command: a cross section of literature (Sinclair Lewis and William Faulkner were both regular visitors at the Cerfs'), the theater, and assimilated New York Jewish society. For his part, Cerf, who was unashamedly fascinated by Hollywood and celebrity, could hardly resist the allure of the biggest star in show business.

"I think they had a mutual excitement in being from different worlds," Bennett Cerf's son Christopher said. "My dad loved to be part of everything. He was endlessly curious, and he thought Sinatra was really glamorous and exciting. I think Sinatra liked the idea that he had a connection with the literary world and publishing. But beyond that, they really genuinely had a great time together. Frank kidded my dad a lot, which my dad loved. He called him Bennett the Bookie."

Cerf and his wife, the former movie actress Phyllis Fraser (a cousin of Ginger Rogers's), had a grand estate in Mount Kisco, the Columns, and entertained lavishly there and in their Upper East Side town house. Sinatra would often visit the Cerfs when he was in town and mingle with the likes of Moss Hart and his wife, Kitty Carlisle Hart (after Hart's untimely death in 1961, Frank attended the playwright's funeral, a big gesture for him); Bennett Cerf's fellow *What's My Line?* panelist Arlene Francis and her husband, the actor Martin Gabel; the movie producer Arthur Hornblow and his wife, Leonora, nicknamed Bubbles; the industrialist William Green and his wife, Judy, a dazzling, sharp-witted brunette with blue-green eyes who now and then wrote novels and whom men universally found enchanting. The women in the Cerfs' set were smart and dynamic (Frank's nickname for the formidable Phyllis Cerf, who tended to take command of social occasions and her friends' lives, was the General) and attractive, and Sinatra, in more than one case, followed his time-honored custom of befriending the man and sleeping with the wife.

The Cerfs' world was the East Coast equivalent of Bill and Edie Goetz's world in Hollywood: rich and intelligent and exclusive and delighted to lay claim to Frank. There was (and would continue to be) a certain amount of interlock between the two milieus: both Bennett Cerf and Bill Goetz were also at Moss Hart's funeral, as was Zeppo Marx, whose wife would one day marry Frank Sinatra, and the Broadway lyricist Alan Jay Lerner, formerly married to the actress Nancy Olson, who was soon to marry Capitol Records' Alan Livingston.

Frank navigated both worlds with a combination of ease and unease, some hidden part of him always feeling like the high-school dropout from Hoboken, the tension expressing itself in his dominating and unavoidable charisma. Christopher Cerf's main memory about Sinatra's presence in his family's household (besides the incomparable thrill of Frank's now and then standing by the family piano and singing a few tunes) was the room-filling sound of that big speaking voice. "He was *loud*," Cerf recalled. "Not obnoxiously so. But he projected. He would get excited; suddenly it would be, 'GET DOWN HERE!'

"He was never offstage. He would ask really meaningful questions and listen to the answers, but he didn't just go sit by himself while other people talked. He was certainly the central presence in any room that I can remember his being in."

Being friends with Sinatra was never boring. Once, in the summer of 1964, Cerf remembered, he and a date, along with his parents and Frank, attended a party at the Westchester house of the newlyweds Bill and Judy Green. After the party, the five of them drove back to Mount Kisco, with Bennett Cerf at the wheel. "I'm sure we'd all had a bit to drink, it having been a long night," Christopher Cerf said. "Just before we passed Arlene Francis and Martin Gabel's house, which was a quarter of a mile before our house on the same road, Frank suddenly said, 'Stop the car, Bennett. I want to go up and see Marty.' My dad said, 'No, they're not home.' Sinatra said, 'How do you know that?' My father said, 'I know. They're not even in Mount Kisco.'

"Frank got angry," Cerf said. "My dad kept saying he wouldn't stop, and Frank kept saying, 'Goddamn it, I'm going to get out. You stop the car and I'll *walk* up there if you won't drive me up the driveway.' My dad said, 'This is really stupid. It's a long, dark driveway; I'm not going to stop.' And he didn't. He drove all the way to our house. By the time we got there, Frank was fuming. As I recall, he walked back and went up to Arlene and Martin's house and found out they weren't there. But he was still furious when he came back, because my dad wouldn't do what he wanted.

"He started screaming, and my dad held his ground, and my mom, who would I think in many cases have defended Sinatra, said, 'Don't yell at my husband!' I remember her shaking her fist at him. My friend Helene was just sitting there saying, 'I can't believe that this is my weekend with you.' It was like the most exciting thing she had ever seen. Frank actually called for a helicopter to come and land on our lawn. He spent the night, but the next morning, very early, maybe eight o'clock or so, a helicopter lands on the back lawn of our house, and Sinatra got in and left. Everybody was very worried that this would be the end of the friendship, but it wasn't at all. I think within a week or so, it was all forgotten—or, if not forgotten, laughed at."

But this had been before Mia, with the salt spray of Kauai still in his nostrils and no young girl by his side to guarantee him eternal life.

———

Sinatra and Basie in Vegas were one thing; Sinatra directing a movie was something else. *None but the Brave* premiered in February, and while some reviews were respectful ("Provocative and engrossing," the *Los Angeles Times*'s Kevin Thomas wrote; though he also dismissed Tommy Sands's performance as "hopelessly hammy"), some were rough. Bosley Crowther, in his now familiar fashion, was particularly harsh. "If the threat of Frank Sinatra as a film director is judged by his first try on 'None But the Brave,' it is clear that there need be no apprehension among the members of the Screen Directors Guild," he began, going on to cite "a minimum show of creative invention and a maximum use of cinema clichés."

> In putting it all together in a joint production with two Japanese companies, Mr. Sinatra, as producer and director, as well as actor of the secondary role of the booze-guzzling medical corpsman, displays distinction only in the latter job. Being his own director, he has no trouble stealing scenes, especially the one in which he burbles boozy wisecracks while preparing to saw off [a] shivering Japanese's leg. Mr. Sinatra is crashingly casual when it comes to keeping the Japanese in their place.
>
> He has a good deal more trouble with the American fellows. Clint Walker as the captain of the plane, Tommy Sands as the cocky lieutenant, Brad Dexter as a sergeant and Tony Bill as the radioman make over-acting—phony acting—the trademark of the film. What with incredible color and the incredible screenplay of Katsuya Susaki and John Twist, this adds up to quite a fake concoction.
>
> They used to make better war films at Monogram.

It has to be said in retrospect that Crowther had a point. The core concept of *None but the Brave* might have been provocative and engrossing at a time when triumphalism about World War II was still gospel, but seen today, the movie looks merely comic-bookish: as cinema, it's pretty thin stuff. Nor did it excite a mass audience. Box office—$2.5 million, about half of *Ocean's 11*'s receipts—was pretty good, but nothing to make Jack Warner kick his heels.

Yet far worse was to come. In early March, Frank began his thirty-eighth film, a comedy for Warner Bros. ominously titled *Marriage on the Rocks*.

———

The title was a not-so-clever pun, but at least it was better than the deadly original, *Community Property*. This was the project in which Mia was supposedly to have played Sinatra's daughter. It would have made a lot more interesting casting than the real one, which unfortunately put Frank's real daughter Nancy, a very nervous fledgling actress, into the role.

Misbegotten from the get-go, the movie cast Sinatra as a proto–Don Draper named Dan Edwards, an overworked ad executive with a bored wife and a couple of kids at home. Frank could play many things—a soldier, a heroin addict, a swinging bachelor—but he was always best, or at least most interesting to watch, when he portrayed a rebellious outsider, a role that fit his perpetually uneasy personality. Portraying a Serious Executive in horn-rimmed glasses and a three-piece suit, no matter how successful, was very far from his wheelhouse. Moreover, he lobbied hard to get Deborah Kerr, his *From Here to Eternity* co-star and an actress of great skill and dignity (and a smoldering, repressed sexuality)—but with absolutely no visible gift for comedy—to play Dan's wife, Valerie. Dean Martin, less interested than ever in being an Actor and preparing to take his smoothly polished, wisecracking image to his own NBC variety show, didn't need a lot of persuading to sign on as Dan's associate and best friend, Ernie, this film's happy-go-lucky bachelor (and proto–Roger Sterling), the man Valerie had passed over for Dan eighteen years earlier.

The gag writer Cy Howard, a veteran of Martin and Lewis (*My Friend Irma; The Colgate Comedy Hour*), was responsible for the sub-sitcom plot: Dan and Valerie are accidentally divorced, Val marries Ernie to make Dan jealous, daughter Tracy rebels. Frank (Sinatra Enterprises was co-producing with Warner Bros.) tapped Jack Donohue, a former choreographer (he'd worked with Sinatra on 1946's *It Happened in Brooklyn*) turned TV director (*The Frank Sinatra Show, The Lucy Show*), to helm the picture.

"I'm well aware of the shortcomings of some of my recent pictures," Frank told the *New York Times*'s Peter Bart in April. "I guess the trouble has been that at the time I did these pictures nothing better seemed to be available. It all boils down to material."

But in his fiftieth year, with a changing face and physique and ever-accumulating power, Sinatra was shifting into a different gear as a movie actor: he seemed more interested in product than material. He was still a commanding screen presence—no matter how bad the material—but he could no longer disappear, or even partially disappear, into a role: he might be playing Chief Pharmacist's Mate Maloney or Colonel Ryan or Dan Evans, but who he really was was Frank Sinatra, ruler of worlds. The Chairman. It happened, it happens, to a lot of stars; rather than disappear into a role, they disappear into themselves. It can work for a while, until it doesn't.

He ruled worlds. He might have been out of the casino business, but he was into the movie production and commercial real estate businesses; he ran a private airline with half a dozen planes; he had an interest in a metal parts company and even owned a share in a corporation that manufactured missile parts.

He had called it, more or less on the nose, in the 1961 *Show Business Illus-*

trated interview. "Four years from now I'll be 50 years old," he'd said. "By then I'll have had it as an actor and singer. Not really had it, but . . . What the hell, when I get around that age there's not much I'll want to play or could play.

"When I think of myself five years hence," he continued, "I see myself not so much an entertainer as a high-level executive, interested in business, perhaps in directing and producing films. My eventual goal is to broaden in the administrative sense."

It was not incidental that he had also broadened in the physical sense.

But he was wrong in predicting his time as a singer would be up. Even as he commuted to Burbank to shoot this dreadful farce (he livened up the proceedings by trying to break up Dino on set: one of his favorite tricks was a fake mustache made of black electrical tape, stuck onto his upper lip just before the camera rolled), he returned to United Recording to start a new album with Gordon Jenkins, and it would be not only beautiful but mature in the finest sense.

With fifty looming up fast, Mia was making him feel young and old at the same time. Early in the year, Frank had put out the word that he was looking for September songs for an autumn-of-his-years-themed new LP, and inventory began to accumulate at once. Three of the songs he chose were numbers he'd recorded previously: Rodgers and Hammerstein's "Hello, Young Lovers," Harold Arlen and Yip Harburg's "Last Night When We Were Young," and, naturally, Kurt Weill and Maxwell Anderson's "September Song."

The rest of the tunes were a mixed bag, including two new ones by Cahn and Van Heusen, "It Gets Lonely Early" and the heartfelt if plodding number that would give the album its title, "The September of My Years":

> As a man who has always had the wandering ways,
> Now I'm reaching back for yesterdays.

It was Sammy at his most didactic, Chester at his most grandiose.

But there was another, much better song, by the writer of "Good Morning Heartache," Ervin Drake.

The tune, which used the metaphor of wine vintages to chart the progress of a middle-aged man's life, had originally been recorded by the Kingston Trio at the height of the folk-music craze in 1961. Backed by soulful Spanish-flavored guitar and sincerely sung by the trio's Bob Shane (then in his mid-twenties), "It Was a Very Good Year" had an earnest, low-grade charisma, and the album it appeared on, *Goin' Places,* peaked at number 3 on the charts.

Then Frank heard it on his car radio one day and decided he could show the kids a thing or two.

———

Over the Easter holiday, Nancy Sinatra's husband, the world's unluckiest son-in-law, walked out on her. She writes that she was blindsided: she'd thought that her marriage to Tommy Sands was happy. But suddenly, she says, he told her that his fear of commitment, and with it his disinclination to be a family man, would never go away. Telling her she should get a divorce, he left and never returned.

Fear of family mainly meant fear of Frank. Having failed to get Sands into *Come Blow Your Horn,* Nancy had pushed her father to cast her husband in *None but the Brave,* and this Sinatra did, to almost everybody's immediate regret. Cast as the militantly by-the-book lieutenant Blair, the small, tragically unmagnetic Sands proceeded to stick out his chin and growl every line at the top of his lungs, turning in a performance that would've been embarrassing in a high-school production. "He chewed up scenery that hadn't even been built," his co-star Tony Bill said. "It was a career ender for him."

But the real career ender was disrespecting Frank Sinatra's daughter. According to Quincy Jones, Sands had begun living the Hollywood nightlife and being not so discreet about it. "PJ's and all those clubs were opening up then, and Tommy got to playing around a little," Jones recalled. "I said, 'Tommy, you're playing with fire, man. I'm telling you. Wrong family.' He said, 'Oh, Quincy, it'll be okay. Francis will understand.' I said, 'Okay, I'm glad you think so.' And he goes and tells Frank that he and Nancy had been going through [some troubles]. He said, 'Francis, we're going to try a light separation for a while. I know you'll understand.'"

Sinatra understood all too well. He was enraged, all Hollywood knew it, and—whether Frank had anything to do with it or not—Sands's show-business career ended at roughly the same time as his marriage.

———

Tommy and Nancy had a little house in the Hollywood Hills; now she left it and went to her mother's place in Bel Air. "I remember coming home from school on a Monday and finding Nancy in Frankie's old room, with Dad sitting at her bedside and holding her," Tina Sinatra writes. "They were shooting a movie together . . . and Dad came by after work each day for the next week or so, until Nancy felt strong enough to rejoin him on the set. He was there as much as she needed him; he was a rock whenever one of us felt forlorn. No one understood emotional breaching better than Dad."

No one.

In the evenings, he made the album. He had chosen Gordon Jenkins to arrange it, rather than Nelson Riddle, for a compelling reason: he was feeling pensive about mortality, and Jenkins was able to create string passages of such wholehearted and unapologetic sentimentality that listeners caught unawares might find themselves reaching for a tissue before they knew what was happening. Riddle got to your heart through your head, via the medium of high art; Jenkins took those high, singing strings and went right for the emotional jugular.

His detractors are vociferous, if not legion. "He's awful," Jonathan Schwartz says, simply. The genius Riddle, of course, being the shining exemplar. And Riddle was a genius. But comparing the two is unfair to both. Musicians understand Jenkins's lack of subtlety but appreciate his effectiveness. "Gordon had his identity and his sound," said the pianist Lou Levy, an occasional substitute for Bill Miller on Sinatra dates. "Everything was sort of a wail and a moan. He had a way of getting that kind of sound. I could take only so much of it, but with Sinatra, it worked. And I know Frank liked it. How can you knock an arrangement like 'Very Good Year'? That's really sort of a masterpiece."

It is. The song is the peak of Sinatra and Jenkins's collaboration. Thanks to the presence of a CBS camera crew—Frank had just agreed to an interview with Walter Cronkite, to be aired in the fall—we can watch it being recorded: the studio clock reading 8:35; the solemn spectators, men and women alike dressed as if for the theater; the white-shirted, steel-haired Jenkins conducting the musicians in his unique left-handed style, sweeping his arms back and forth, up and down, as though he were scrubbing floors, washing windows. Frank, dressed to the nines in a dark suit and light vest, tie carefully loosened, toup perfectly groomed, performing the song—it is a performance, to this audience—in a voice like the ocean. And then, between takes, listening thoughtfully while he smokes, his endlessly expressive face registering the scintillas of emotion in every bar.

And if the rest of the album doesn't quite meet the quality of this one great number, it provides a similarly autumnal, and similarly moving, experience. "Jenkins relied on the most uniform textures of any Sinatra arranger," Friedwald writes, "and as with *All Alone,* not only do all the orchestrations seem to be cut from the same cloth but so do the songs themselves. And despite the eventual predictability of the recurring images—the falling leaves, graying hairs, Technicolor breezes, a preoccupation with gazing forlornly at children . . . the concept itself almost never seems forced."

What elevates it all, even as it skirts kitsch and at times veers straight into it, is the majestic voice singing it: meaning it, believing it. A poet, Stan Cornyn called Sinatra in the liner notes he eventually wrote for the album. But a poet of a very specific kind: an alchemist, one who could turn what other artists might leave as dross into gold.

Cornyn, who began in the record business churning out liner notes by the dozen for Capitol, then Warner, could have proceeded similarly mechanically with *September*. "I could have stayed back in my office and written, 'The ages of man are measured in months, and September . . .' That kind of stuff," he recalled. Instead, he attended the sessions—mainly because it was Sinatra, and he just wanted to. He took along some scratch paper, a pencil, and a pen and jotted down what he saw. The resulting notes give a crystalline picture of the occasion and have a wry poetry of their own:

Tonight will not swing. Tonight is for serious.

Inside, the musicians, led by coatless, posture-free Gordon Jenkins, rehearse their voice-empty arrangements. Waiting for his arrival.

Outside, in the hall, the uniformed guards wait and wonder what to do with their hands . . .

He arrives. Tie loosened, collar loosened. The guards at the studio door edge out of the way.

"Good morning, sir," he says. "Who's got the ball game on."

Thirty orchestra wives wish they had the late scores memorized. Four men look around for a transistor radio.

"Hello, Sidney, how are ya. What's happening in the music business?"

He strolls up behind Gordon Jenkins, who is rehearsing his strings. Sinatra listens for 32 bars, then turns to Mike Romanoff. "The way this guy writes strings, if he were Jewish, he'd be unbearable."

The Prince wakes up a bit.

"You ready, Gordie?"

"I'm ready," replies Jenkins. "I'm always ready. I was ready in 1939."

"I was ready when I was nine."

He walks to his music stand, clearing his throat. "Think I swallowed a shot glass."

Jenkins starts a song, conducting with arms waist high, sweeping them side to side. Not leading his orchestra: *being* the orchestra.

Sinatra begins to sing his September's reflections. Jenkins, on the podium two feet above, turns from his orchestra to face his singer. He beams down attentively, his face that of a father after his son's first no-hitter.

The wives in their black beaded sweaters muffle their charm bracelets.

As the CBS camera crew got it all on film. Many years later, the producer Don Hewitt recalled how he'd persuaded Sinatra to sit for the Cronkite interview: Frank would, Hewitt said, be occupying "the same seat Dwight Eisenhower, Jack Kennedy and Lyndon Johnson sat in." And then the masterstroke: the producer told Sinatra to pass on doing the show if he didn't feel up to it. The cameras were in the recording studio the next night.

The drumbeat began. The April 23 issue of *Life* carried a big cover story on Sinatra—in the world of 1965, a major cultural event. In the world of 1965, *Life* magazine was as important as television: it went to Park Avenue and Chicago's Gold Coast and San Francisco's Nob Hill; it went to Kansas farms and Wyoming ranches and Arkansas shotgun shacks; it sat in every doctor's and dentist's waiting room in the country. The color photograph on the front of the magazine showed Frank looking snappy in a houndstooth fedora, white turtleneck, and orange cardigan; his expression was vaguely amused, his mouth was opened in song. "SINATRA OPENS UP," the headline read. The eighteen-page feature, which *Life* called "an intimate picture essay–interview" ("The Private World and Thoughts of Frank Sinatra"), comprised a lengthy piece by associate editor Tommy Thompson, a series of posed and candid shots by staff photographer John Dominis, and an essay ("Me and My Music") by Frank himself.

Thompson was a former stage actor, a tall, handsome, quietly charming Texan; "Tommy was the kind of person that everyone was drawn to," the former *Life* publicity director Fifi Booth recalled. He'd first approached Sinatra about doing a story the previous November, over drinks in New York, only to find him typically distractible: "He kept hopping up to talk to Jackie Gleason in Miami or Dean Martin in Hollywood and finally just muttered, 'Come see me on the coast.'" Thompson did so, buttonholing Frank on the set of *Von Ryan's Express* and proving his charm by getting him to agree to sit for an interview.

But when Thompson and Dominis caught up with Sinatra during the February Eden Roc stand, they found all they had gained was a foot in the door. Over the next two weeks, they shadowed Frank as he worked and played, gradually accustoming him to their presence. Dominis, who had photographed lions at close range in Africa, found working around Sinatra a similar experience: no sudden moves; many hours of quiet waiting to get the perfect shot, only when the flow of the moment allowed it.

The moment was invariably in the wee small hours, as Dominis wearily recalled, more than forty years later. Thompson remembered pleading exhaustion and turning in at 2:00 a.m. one night, only to be awakened at 5:00 by a phone call from Frank's suite. "He was having an all-night party with Joe E. Lewis," the writer said, "and they couldn't stand my being asleep."

In all, Thompson and Dominis spent seven weeks on the Sinatra beat, in Miami, Vegas, Hollywood, and Palm Springs. "I became fascinated with the depth of the man," Thompson wrote. "You could see that people watching us thought we were talking about girls and such. But he is a whiz at the stock market and can go on for hours about finance. He has a love for opera, and thinks Callas sings off key. He really wants to try conducting a symphony some day, if he can do it without it being a stunt. And he knows every boxing statistic there is in the file."

All this was no doubt true, but it also failed to take into account actual depth, not to mention the Heisenbergian principle of the observer's effect on the observed. If Tommy Thompson was a charming man, Frank Sinatra, never one to be outdone, was going to go him one better. Aggressively. (Though in all likelihood, it was probably minutes rather than hours that he could go on about finance.) Like all of us, Sinatra was a chameleon to a degree, but if the company was impressive—or seemed to require impressing—he could take mutability to extremes. And he was never above putting on a show.

Thompson took note of Frank's contradictions. "He is a man who will angrily throw an over-cooked hamburger at his valet or an ashtray at an inept assistant—and yet never fires anyone from his huge staff of aides and hangers-on," he wrote. (True; he let others do the dirty work for him.)

> He will spend 10 minutes of his nightclub act attacking a woman columnist [Kilgallen] so venomously that the audience gasps—and will send $100,000 to a Los Angeles college with the strict instruction that the gift not be made public. He sneers "Charley brown shoes" at people he thinks are squares and always says "thank you" when someone asks for his autograph. He is the legendary ladies' man—and he says he has flunked out with women.

All true, but true on the surface only. His ugly fury and his grand (and atoning) acts of generosity; his arrogant disdain and his exquisite manners; his ravening sexuality and his inability to maintain an intimate relationship—all these came from what were the real depths of the man, depths unplumbed by Tommy Thompson and legions to follow, all mesmerized by what was, for nearly sixty years, the real greatest show on earth.

A preface to the piece mentioned the upcoming big birthday, though the subject was then dropped, its possible effects on Frank's psyche left unexamined. Instead, Thompson began with a topic guaranteed to fascinate Americans: Frank's wealth. "Sinatra is rich and has weight to throw around—and he

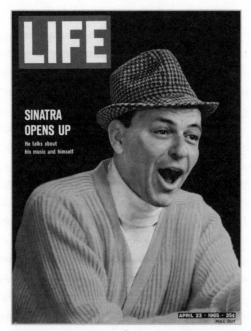

Life begins the countdown to the great event: at the end of the year, Sinatra will turn fifty. Frank's portion of the eighteen-page feature, an essay called "Me and My Music" (note billing), is extraordinarily authoritative and smart.

throws it," he wrote, enticingly. One photograph showed the Chairman sitting in one of his two helicopters, about to take off for Palm Springs ("He owns three other planes, including a new eight-seat Lear jet"). Another showed him lunching (on "prosciutto and melon, fruit salad, cheese and chilled red wine") with Jack Warner. "I guess I'm now financially secure," he coyly told Thompson.

Less than accurately, the writer called Sinatra "a hard-eyed businessman," rather than the impatient and mercurial artist, given to delegating responsibility instead of grappling with it, that he really was. Yes, he nominally ran Sinatra Enterprises and Artanis Productions; true, he was an executive at Warner Bros. and a director of Warner-Reprise. But the personal staff of seventy-five admiringly mentioned in the piece, "ranging from girls who answer his fan mail to pilots and bodyguards," also included men like Howard Koch and Mickey Rudin and Mo Ostin, who did most of the heavy lifting where business matters were concerned. The real Frank Sinatra was the man pictured in the cockpit of his helicopter, always on his way to someplace else.

But the pictures in the piece told the story more acutely than Thompson. This was *Life*'s great strength. For decades, the magazine, a great American institution, existed in a meta-realm of popular culture, between the visual world of newsreels and television and the still-respected sphere of print.

Life was first and foremost a picture magazine; the text was commentary. The big Sinatra piece was most notable for its many impressive black-and-white images: Frank standing moodily in smoke-wreathed chiaroscuro as he rehearsed a band; looking authoritative in a three-piece suit and eyeglasses on the set of *Marriage on the Rocks;* reading a script in an Eames chair in Palm Springs amid Oriental sculptures and state-of-the-art audio equipment, a loyal Australian sheep dog (named Ringo!) by his side and a bowlful of cigarette packs on the table by his feet. There were touching shots of his immediate family: Marty and Dolly, looking old, outside the Sands; sixteen-year-old Tina getting a kiss on the cheek from her doting father. And then there was a more ambiguous image: twenty-four-year-old Nancy Sandra, décolleté and in pearls, leaning against Daddy on a restaurant banquette, her arms encircling him with slightly discomfiting amorousness, her cheek resting in his hair. Frank, his hands holding hers, looks well pleased. Poor Tommy never had a chance.

Symbolically, the one photo of Frank junior showed him not with his father but watching in awe from backstage while he performed.

But some of the most arresting pictures within were a series of late-night shots taken by Dominis in Frank's Eden Roc suite: in one sequence, Sinatra, crisply tuxed and amid riotous company, performs (semi-successfully) his old trick of snapping a tablecloth from a table without breaking the crockery; in another, he lies on the floor, helpless with laughter, after Joe E. Lewis has apparently told a howler. In still another photograph, he and the baggy-faced old comic, "at dawn after an all-night party," as the caption tells us, stand in a closet looking pie-eyed and swapping old jokes. Dominis even captured Frank in the steam room the morning after, a half-naked pasha, pudgy and looking distinctly the worse for wear with a towel wrapped around his head.

The text, reflecting the boozy pictures, described a night after the second show at the Eden Roc: beginning at around 1:30 a.m., Sinatra had a drink in the hotel lounge, signed autographs, then decamped to another nightclub, where he drank Jack Daniel's (he would down half a bottle in all: "But he didn't seem to be drunk—he never does," Thompson wrote) and reminisced with Lewis. His entourage, which had begun with just three or four, increased to eight to ten, then more. Inevitably, Frank grew restless again. As his motorcade headed back to the hotel, he spotted a hot dog stand, still open at 5:30 a.m. "Let's get some franks," he said, and everybody piled out.

> It was 6 a.m. before the party got to Frank's hotel suite. But the evening was not over because Frank hadn't said it was over. "Everybody have a little more gasoline," he ordered. Everybody did. They threw darts at a target set up on the wall.

And then the king of this court, the man who had murdered sleep, finally decided to call it quits.

> The sun was up at 7 a.m. when Frank announced he was going to bed. The room cleared suddenly. Frank put on orange pajamas, turned on some music and read a while. It took him a long time to drop off to sleep.

The women in these hotel-suite photographs are, to put it diplomatically, not lookers. One wonders whether they were friends, friends of friends, or perhaps ad hoc company. "Women are constantly around Sinatra," Thompson wrote. "When he is in a hotel they send notes to him, call him up, try to sneak past the guard at his door. Although he is often seen with famous women, Sinatra also takes out cigaret girls or chorus girls."

By way of illustration, the piece includes a photograph of Frank, backstage at a Broadway show, lighting a cigarette for a fur-coated and seductive-looking Natalie Wood (her deep cleavage, visible in a similar shot in Nancy Sinatra's book, is airbrushed), and another shot of him holding a cup with a straw for what the caption identifies as "a date in Miami, a cigaret girl named Yumi Akutsu, who works in the hotel where he was singing."

Mia Farrow is mentioned nowhere in the piece.

"Women often find him a puzzling escort," Thompson wrote.

> "Frank is a very attentive man," says an actress, "but I don't understand him. He takes me out, then seems to spend most of the evening talking to the guys."
>
> "I'm supposed to have a Ph.D. on the subject of women," Frank says ruefully, "but the truth is I've flunked more often than not. I'm very fond of women; I admire them. But, like all men, I don't understand them . . .
>
> "I like a woman's clothes to be tasteful and subtle. I don't like excessive make-up. I know that a woman must have a little, but I think that women—generally—have enough beauty without doing the circus tent type make-up. And women who smoke from the moment they open their eyes until they put out the light at night—that drives me batty. It's unfeminine and dangerous—burn up the whole damn house, you know."

He was a man ahead of his time.

On the subject of marriage he was equally specific:

"I don't say that marriage is impossible," he says. "But if I did marry, it would have to be somebody out of show business, or somebody who will get out of the business. I feel I'm a fairly good provider. All I ask is that my wife looks after me, and I'll see that she is looked after.

"I don't feel that I've ever been a demanding man, but in some respects I'm a hard man to live with. I live my life certain ways that I could never change for a woman. I am a symmetrical man, almost to a fault. I demand everything in its place. My clothing must hang just so. There are some things I can't stand in women. Strong colognes, for example, drive me out of the room. First of all I've got an allergy to them. I begin to sneeze, which is not very romantic—and this certainly might annoy a woman."

What mainly seemed to concern him, however, was how a woman might annoy him.

———

In an eerie way, his remarks looked ahead, not to his next marriage but to the one after that, his fourth and final one, to Barbara Blakeley Marx: *If I did marry, it would have to be somebody out of show business, or somebody who will get out of the business. I feel I'm a fairly good provider. All I ask is that my wife looks after me, and I'll see that she is looked after.*

As for Mia Farrow, though, his comments boded ill.

———

Frank's own part of the package, the long essay titled "Me and My Music," is an extraordinary work. Whoever did the actual writing crafted it expertly: the piece sounds very much like Sinatra and—as was not the case with his Mike Shore–crafted *Playboy* interview—*feels* precisely like him, the voice conversational and never overarticulate, yet expert, reflecting technical knowledge and musical opinions that could only come from the greatest popular singer of all time.

He speaks from the chair of authority, a place he had richly earned. He had battled a hundred other boy singers during the big-band years and outlasted them all, the Jack Leonards and the Bob Eberlys and the Dick Haymeses. He had gone out on his own when to do so was highly unusual and professionally perilous and succeeded beyond all expectations. He had narrowly skirted career extinction, overcoming his own self-destructiveness and America's vindictiveness, to mount the greatest second act in show-business history. He had made dozens of records that would last as long as music itself. He was an immortal, and he knew it.

The essay is masterly. Sinatra is trenchant and at times prophetic ("The era of *cool* jazz is gone"). He tells only one outright lie: "I never had a vocal lesson—a real one—except to work with a coach a few times on vocal calisthenics." (In fact, in the 1930s and 1940s, a former Metropolitan Opera tenor named John Quinlan had worked extensively with Frank to take the Hoboken out of his diction and put more power into his voice, which was thin and high at the time.) But his occasional arrogance never feels undeserved, and his revelations about the art and science of singing, if sometimes a little too technical, are sensationally enlightening for all who cared to pay attention.

He begins by describing how his early idolatry of the inimitable but all too widely imitated Bing Crosby evolved into a determination to be different. "What I finally hit on," he wrote, "was more the *bel canto* Italian school of singing, without making a point of it." He doesn't make a point of it, because it's a hard point to make: the bel canto style first evolved in the eighteenth-century operas and oratorios of Handel, reached its full flower in the early-nineteenth-century operas of Rossini, Bellini, and Donizetti, and had a broad range of hallmarks, some of them, but not all, strictly applicable to Frank Sinatra. But some of the style's chief characteristics—a flawless legato, perfect diction, and graceful phrasing based on a total mastery of breath control—fit him like a glove, and he went on to describe how he had arrived at them.

He had said these things before but never at such length and so clearly. "How in the hell did he do it?" he wrote of Tommy Dorsey.

> I used to sit behind him on the bandstand and watch, trying to see
> him sneak a breath. But I never saw the bellows move in his back. His
> jacket didn't even move. I used to edge my chair to the side a little,
> and peek around to watch him. Finally, after a while, I discovered that
> he had a "sneak" pinhole in the corner of his mouth—not an actual
> pinhole, but a tiny place where he was breathing.

Dorsey was able to hide the opening at the corner of his lips with the trombone's mouthpiece; Sinatra, by contrast, was out in the middle of the stage with just a smile and a shoe shine. How the hell could *he* do it? In the piece, he told the familiar stories about how he'd built up his lung capacity—swimming laps underwater at public pools, running laps around the track at Hoboken's Stevens Institute—but, strikingly, avoided giving away his own trade secret. Whereas Dorsey sneaked breaths through the hidden pinhole, Sinatra did it by widening his mouth at key moments in a song—it looked as though he were smiling—and taking in air through both corners of his lips. Watch him singing on film or video: you can see him doing it, and he makes it look (and sound) good.*

He was more forthcoming about his unparalleled microphone technique. The mike is a singer's instrument, he wrote—a lesson, he scolded, that many vocalists never learn. He described how to use the device subtly—"like a geisha girl uses her fan," he wrote: when to move close, when to lean back, how to avoid popping *p*'s and taking audible breaths.

"When I'm using a microphone I usually try to have a black one so that it will melt into my dinner jacket and the audience isn't aware of it," he continued. "Many years ago I found that I could take the mike off the stand and move around with it. That's a boon, and so many singers don't take advantage of it. Ella Fitzgerald, poor girl, still doesn't. They set up a mike for her and she never touches it. You can't even see her face."

Poor girl. (Fitzgerald was all of sixteen months younger than Sinatra.) It was the first dig at another singer in the piece, and more were to follow. The comments weren't gratuitous: in each case, Frank had a point. Fitzgerald, for all her greatness, was an odd, uncomfortable personality, uncertain about her looks and sometimes apt to be recessive onstage or on record. She was capable of retreating, even disappearing, behind her blistering proficiency: her genius didn't sit easily with her. Her greatest performances happened when she forgot herself and let fly. But her brilliance also didn't sit easily with Sinatra: as he'd confessed in a 1959 interview, it intimidated him. Maybe, now that he had the power and the forum, he was taking a certain measure of revenge.

The one colleague he praised without reservation was Tony Bennett, whom he called "the best singer in the business, the best exponent of a song . . . He's the singer who gets across what the composer has in mind, and probably a little more. There's a feeling in back of it."

With others there were reservations. Vic Damone ("has better pipes than anybody, but . . . lacks the know-how or whatever you want to call it") and Lena Horne ("a beautiful lady but really a mechanical singer. She gimmicks up a song, makes it too pat") came in for particularly stinging lashes. Was he settling scores? In the case of Horne, certainly.[†] But why did he take out after (his former lover) Judy Garland and, once again, Ella? "Technically two of the

---

* The great singer Jo Stafford, one of Dorsey's Pied Pipers along with Frank, told me she felt Sinatra, like her, also had an innate anatomical advantage when it came to breath control: a congenitally broad rib cage.

† Frank went way back with Lena's husband, the (white) conductor and former MGM music director Lennie Hayton, and had heard Horne put Hayton down in front of audiences.

worst singers in the business," he wrote, castigating both for perpetuating his bugbear, the taking of an audible breath in the middle of a phrase. Yet Garland was a nonpareil interpreter of song, an emotional force of nature: when she took the stage, her technique (she also had the proverbial vibrato you could drive a truck through) was the last thing audiences cared about. And Fitzgerald's voice was such a powerhouse that sometimes the notes took precedence over the sense: both her strength and her weakness. (Frank also took a slap at poor Ella for recording uncommercial material like Cole Porter's "Down in the Depths on the 90th Floor"—which was really a slap at his old enemy, her producer Norman Granz.)

After faulting Sarah Vaughan for taking so long to arrive at a musical identity, he favored her with a strange encomium: "Sassy is so good now that when I listen to her I want to cut my wrists with a dull razor." Surprisingly, he gave a passing compliment to Barbra Streisand ("an artist"), though George Jacobs claimed he despised her. Peggy Lee, though—or because—a former lover, received condescending praise ("pretty good with the lyrics. She sustains a little more than the other girls do"); he complimented Jo Stafford for technique only and vouchsafed Rosemary Clooney just two words: "sings well."

He liked Jack Jones best of the male newcomers. "He has a distinction, an all-around quality that puts him *potentially* about three lengths in front of the other guys," Frank wrote. "He sings jazz pretty good, too. But he's got to be handled very carefully from here on out. The next year is going to tell. One thing—he should stop singing those gasoline commercials that they play on the Dodger baseball broadcasts."

Tough words, but as it turned out, Sinatra was right on the money: Jack Jones, a wonderful singer, suffered from a mismanaged career (by himself as well as others) and never reached his true commercial potential. Frank knew all too well what he was talking about.

And he was almost as tough on himself, even if his narcissism was impenetrable. "I smoke too much and drink too much," he admitted, yet couldn't help adding, "But I've learned that the vocal cords aren't bothered too much by that—they're in a protected part of the body." He failed to mention his lungs, which apparently were in a part of his body protected by good luck, as had not been the case with Nat King Cole, another lifetime smoker, who'd died in February, at age forty-five, of lung cancer.

As for the future, he sensed a certain narrowing. "At this stage of my career," he wrote, "I don't have any mountains left to climb." He had never done a Broadway show and had absolutely no desire to start now, he said. The repetition would bore him to death, and besides the money was lousy. About poor Sammy Davis, then lighting up the Great White Way in *Golden Boy,* Frank said, "I don't think he's going to come out financially too well, and he's tied up for two years." Another piercingly accurate forecast.

He then delivered a self-prophecy that would become perfectly self-fulfilling. "One thing I would like to do," he said, foretelling the years from the 1970s into the mid-1990s, when he would thrive as a concert artist, "is a long series of one-nighters . . . all over the country. I'd take an orchestra, like Basie or some big band, and a few other performers, comics, what have you, and hire a train. I'd like to go into a town and just sing for an hour or so, concert-style . . . I'd also like to do a few weeks in New York if I can find the time. I haven't worked the big town in many years."

But what about age and decline, those annoying conditions that affected the rest of humanity? Here he whistled in the dark. "Since I'm almost 50 years old, I've given a lot of thought to how long can the voice hold out," he wrote.

> I don't think age has as much to do with it as does physical condition. In other words, as long as I stay in shape, I should be able to keep singing. My voice is as good now as it ever was. But I'll be the first to know when it starts to go—when the vibrato starts to widen and the breath starts to give out. When that happens, I'll say goodbye. I wouldn't want to make a recording and have to listen to it 20 years from now with those symptoms turning up. I can't kid myself into thinking my voice will be as strong or my enthusiasm as buoyant a few years from now.
>
> I don't believe in self-indulgence, anyway. In all my years as a performer, I've believed in taking only the nucleus of an act, that part which is so good, then getting off quick. I don't do a long time on stage. That goes for my life, too.

He was good at getting off quick. Saying good-bye, though, would be far more difficult than even he could predict.

———

There was another thing. Now, while his voice was still strong but popular music was changing so rapidly—even more quickly than it had changed after the war, when his public had turned from him—what would he sing? In the November *Variety* interview, Frank had complained that the old warhorses Harold Arlen and Harry Warren and Hoagy Carmichael weren't turning out product anymore; Cahn and Van Heusen, and Cy Coleman and Carolyn Leigh, he said, were the only proven songwriting teams still producing consistently.

But even they were bucking the rising tide, and Sinatra admitted he was at sea. "Even though I've been singing for a quarter of a century, and I'm the president of a major record company, I still don't have a good idea as to what the public will buy and what they won't," he wrote.

Music is so fragile—from day to day—that you never know.

I get about 500 new songs a year sent to me, and chances are 497 of them will be lousy. But I look at them all, anyway. There's always the chance one good one will come in over the transom . . .

I don't read a note of music. I learn songs by having them played for me a couple of times while I read the lyrics. I can pick up the melody very quickly. I learn the lyrics by writing them out in longhand.

When I get a new song, I look for continuity of melody that in itself will tell a musical story. It must go somewhere. I don't like it to ramble. And then, by the same token, I like almost the same thing—more, as a matter of fact—in the lyrics. They must tell you a complete story, from "once upon a time" to "the end" . . .

When a song doesn't follow in continuity, it doesn't continue to hold the interest of an artist. And the only time that songs hold the interest of the public is when an artist . . . understands the song and sings it properly. Throughout my career, if I have done anything, I have paid attention to every note and every word I sing—if I respect the song. If I cannot project this to a listener, I fail.

Yet the question lingered: What songs would he sing now?

———

May was the month Frank and Mia first came out as a couple, at the SHARE Boomtown charity show, which always received wide press coverage. She was shocked when he told her they'd be attending—at that point they were even staying away from restaurants. They put on Western garb, Mia got to meet Sammy Davis and Shirley MacLaine, and Dean Martin toasted her from the stage: "Hey, I got a bottle of scotch that's older than you."

Everybody laughed, the photographers snapped away, and the frenetic press scrum began. The world was puzzled, horrified, and endlessly titillated by the spectacle of the forty-nine-year-old professional swinger stepping out with the virginal, baby-faced nineteen-year-old—who played a shy, dreamy sixteen-year-old on one of America's most popular television series. It was unseemly; it was delicious.

Proudly, defiantly, he began to take her out to parties and restaurants, to introduce her to more of his friends in L.A., Vegas, and New York. She discovered that Frank could finish off a fifth of Jack Daniel's in a night, that the nights he liked best were filled with loud jokes and stories and a perpetually whirling cast of characters: friends, hangers-on, stayers-over. Her hours alone with him, she soon found, were growing rarer all the time.

———

In June, Frank, Dean, and Sammy did a benefit in St. Louis's Kiel Opera House for Dismas House, a halfway facility for ex-cons and a favorite charity of Sinatra's friends in the Teamsters. The show, broadcast via closed-circuit TV to movie theaters in New York and Los Angeles, was emceed by Johnny Carson, who had taken over *The Tonight Show* from Jack Paar in 1962 and become a star in his own right. He was young (thirty-nine) and cheeky, at once provocative and inoffensive: his button-eyed, pointy-nosed midwestern face was flawlessly all-American, yet his wit was lightning fast, and he carried a subliminal hint of anger. Physically, he looked bland alongside the show's other three stars, but his ego was such that he didn't wilt in their presence: instead, he got into the spirit of the proceedings and roasted them. When it came time to introduce Sinatra, who (of course) followed Dean and Sammy, Carson stared at the camera and intoned solemnly, "Ladies and gentlemen, on behalf of Dismas House, I present our hoodlum singer."[*]

Frank loved it. He came out beaming; he and Carson bowed to each other. Then, after some obligatory offstage heckling by Dean, he sang eight numbers, topped off by a "Happy Birthday" for the now seventeen-year-old Tina Sinatra, who came out onstage to give him a kiss.

Her father's cheeks and neck were growing beefy; his hair, even with a piece, looked thinner than ever. But his smile was real and incandescent, and with the Count Basie Orchestra behind him (Quincy Jones conducting) he sang with incomparable style and power. Basie simply charged him up; in the opinion of longtime Sinatra observer Rob Fentress, who attended many recording sessions and shows at the Sands, Frank's time with the Count had made him a much more dynamic performer. Onstage at the Kiel, Dean, as usual, mostly made fun of his own singing (though he didn't need to); Sammy sounded as only he could sound. But only Frank was Frank: he was alone at the summit, and he knew it, as did everyone else.

As for *the* Summit, whose final performance this was, it was clear that its moment had passed. The presence of Carson and television cameras flattened the act, made it presentational rather than unpredictable. The button-eyed

---

[*] The founder of Dismas House, Father Charles Dismas Clark, was known as the Hoodlum Priest.

host, with his smooth patter, was like a lion tamer working with three big cats, and he effectively tamed them. (Though in fact Dean, about to begin what would become an enormously successful variety series on NBC that fall, had done the job on himself, distilling his drunkie routine into camera-ready perfection.) Even though all three men ad-libbed delightfully at times, with Johnny now and then chiming in, the set pieces—Dean's by now hoary stunt of carrying Sammy onstage, chirping, "I'd like to thank the N-double-A-C-P for this wonderful trophy"—and obligatory ethnic humor, most of it directed at Davis and uncomfortable in this era of intense civil rights turmoil, were feeling shopworn. The fact that the benefit was broadcast in black-and-white seemed all too symbolic.

Three days later, Frank was in New York City, celebrating the premiere of *Von Ryan's Express* at Toots Shor's with Dean, Joey Bishop, and Count Basie. (Critics and audiences alike would enjoy the movie, which would become Sinatra's highest-grossing picture of the decade.) He'd come east in his new Lear Jet, the *Christina II*. The plane, he told Earl Wilson, allowed him to make lightning publicity runs "to Detroit or Chicago or Washington any evening, and be back here at Jilly's by 2 a.m."

In the meantime, Mia was in Los Angeles, working hard on *Peyton Place*, which had become such a runaway hit that ABC planned to hike its schedule from two shows a week to three in the fall. The pressure was relentless: as the key character Allison MacKenzie, Farrow was in every episode, and production would continue through the summer.

She didn't seem to mind. Sounding like the seasoned pro she had quickly become, she told Bob Thomas in a spring interview, "We now have two companies shooting simultaneously, instead of one. And we're not even into the summer's product yet."

The spring and summer also brought another product: a steady drumbeat of rumors about Farrow's relationship with Sinatra. "I've read that Mia Farrow of Peyton Place is married to Frank Sinatra. What are their ages?" Mrs. M. Jones, of Portsmouth, Virginia, wrote to the syndicated TV Scout column in April. (The answer incorrectly gave Frank's age as forty-seven and Mia's as nineteen: he was forty-nine and counting, of course; she had just turned twenty.) In May, the usually gimlet-eyed Dorothy Kilgallen signaled her belief in the tales, managing to get in a dig anyway:

When Mia Farrow first confided her love for Frank Sinatra, it was regarded by most of the show business wiseacres as a "phony romance" or a publicity ploy he permitted "to help the kid"—as he helped Juliet

Prowse make the front pages by giving her a big diamond that was never followed by a wedding ring. But now some of the toughest cynics are beginning to believe Frank adores Mia, chiefly because someone very very close to him thinks they're going to be married—and is embarrassed by the possibility, because Mia is younger than Frank's daughter Nancy.

Kilgallen might well have been referring to the reliably outspoken Dolly Sinatra. "My son is just helping this girl become a star," Frank's mother proclaimed.

How many times has Frank helped somebody to the top? This is what he is doing now . . . This Mia, she's a nice little girl, but that's all. Remember, Frank's children are older than this girl. I'm going to spend the next two days in New York City with my son in his apartment. I'm sure I have some influence left with him. If there is any truth to these rumors—which I personally know there is not—I will use my influence to discourage any marriage.

But Dolly had no idea whom she was up against. "She is not as fragile as she looks," Bob Thomas noted. "In some matters she can be iron-willed."

He was referring to her new policy of not speaking about her personal life, a sensible stance that nevertheless communicated much by omission. As for Frank, "The La Rue crowd, [the West Hollywood restaurant] where Frank Sinatra and Mia Farrow dine often, say they never saw him so smitten," Walter Winchell wrote in early June.

"Never" was going a long way. But it had certainly been a few years.

———

Frank put a lot of miles on the *Christina II* that summer, hopping over to Israel in late June to do a three-day cameo on a Kirk Douglas movie, *Cast a Giant Shadow,* then jumping back to the States to make a dramatic Fourth of July appearance at the Newport Jazz Festival.

The festival, started in 1954 by jazz promoter George Wein, had generated a certain amount of social and artistic controversy over the years, stirring up the wealthy locals who were disturbed by the traffic jams the event produced, not to mention the annual influx of African-American musicians and scruffy young fans. In 1960, the National Guard actually had to be called in to quell a riot that began when a large crowd of boisterous fans who hadn't been able to gain admission stormed the venue. That same year, Charles Mingus and Max Roach staged a rival jazz festival across town, in protest against Wein's payment policies, which favored mainstream (mostly white) artists. The promoter had first run the event on a not-for-profit basis, but by 1965 it had been a business for several years, and as jazz's record sales dropped, so had attendance at Newport. (The hullabaloos of the past hadn't helped either.) Asking Count Basie to ask Frank Sinatra to play there on the event's final night was a canny commercial move on Wein's part, and deciding to take the impresario up on his offer was a smart choice by Frank.

Loving Basie's band and cherishing the charts, conducting, and friendship of Quincy Jones, Sinatra had decided to take the whole aggregation out on a six-city tour—the first time he'd gone on the road with a big band since his 1957 western swing with Riddle. The Dismas House benefit was, in effect, the dress rehearsal for the new tour. And though it had come off beautifully, Newport in 1965 was "the only time I've ever seen Frank nervous," as Jones recalled. His performance would be climaxing four days of concerts by some of the greatest names in jazz: Dizzy Gillespie, Joe Williams, the Modern Jazz Quartet, Thelonious Monk, John Coltrane, Art Blakey, Lee Morgan, Carmen McRae, Duke Ellington, Herbie Mann, Dave Brubeck, Earl Hines, and Frank's old Dorsey-days roommate, nemesis, and friend Buddy Rich.

Could he have felt intimidated? He tended to keep his fears to himself; it is a mark of his intimacy with Jones that he let down his guard. What might have been nibbling at Frank's nerves was the tiresome old question of whether or not he really was a jazz singer. The silly subject wouldn't go away, despite what should have been the final word, Lester Young's wholehearted 1956 validation. Certain carpers and purists would forever deride Sinatra as white and square, the chief exponent of the so-called businessman's bounce: a great pop singer, to be sure, but just that. Even Frank declined the mantle of jazz vocalist— probably, in all truth, because he found it limiting. With a combination of sly machismo and slightly spurious modesty, he preferred to call himself a saloon singer.

In his July 17 piece on the Newport Festival, *The New Yorker*'s imperiously tradition-minded and blazingly articulate jazz writer Whitney Balliett could hardly contain his scorn for the event in general ("bland, banal, occasionally professional, occasionally original, never exciting") and for Sinatra in particular, whom he dubbed "the celebrated New Jersey Meadows jazz singer"—this at a time when the area's sole associations were with industrial pollution and marshy stink.

"Sunday evening was a circus," Balliett wrote.

Sinatra's stint was carried out with Commando precision. Late Sunday afternoon, during a Stan Getz bossa-nova number, a couple of helicopters scouting the area . . . touched down briefly just behind the bandstand. At exactly seven-forty-five, they returned, carrying Sinatra and his entourage, and at nine, after half a dozen desultory Count Basie numbers, Sinatra paraded onstage with his own drummer [Sonny Payne], his own trumpet player—Harry (One-Note) Edison— and his own arrangements. Basie put on a pair of businessman's glasses and started reading his part, and Sinatra sang "Get Me to the Church on Time." Seven or eight vocals later, Sinatra paused, got himself a cup of tea from the piano, and, sipping it stage center, delivered a mono- logue made up of Bob Hope gags larded with plugs for a Las Vegas hotel that Sinatra has an interest in . . . Then he replaced his teacup, sang ten more songs, and waved goodbye. He was airborne before the Basie band, struggling to regain its soul, had finished a concluding "One O'Clock Jump." The tab was reportedly thirty-five thousand dollars.

It was the Eustace Tilley treatment. All the fleering code words were there: *New Jersey Meadows; businessman; "Get Me to the Church on Time"* (distinctly middlebrow material); *Bob Hope; Las Vegas;* and the capper, *thirty-five thou- sand dollars.* A very large sum in 1965, enough to buy a substantial subur- ban house in Short Hills or Shaker Heights. In fact, $35,000 was only Frank's guarantee: including his percentage of the gate, his total fee was closer to $40,000.

Yet Balliett somehow failed to mention the quality of Sinatra's singing, or the other songs he sang, or the considerable commercial value he lent to the festival: whereas in past years the Sunday-night concert had always been the worst attended, Frank's show was a sellout, helping to raise Newport's overall attendance to forty thousand, an increase of six thousand over the previous year. In his memoirs, George Wein described the unforgettable scene as two helicopters bearing Frank, his retinue, and Quincy Jones arrived. "When the dual aircraft landed at 7:45 p.m. there was a mild ruckus," he wrote.

No one was performing at the time, since the concert was scheduled for 8 o'clock. The hatch opened, and Sinatra emerged. There could be no better way to describe it than this: He became, for that moment, the festival's deus ex machina. A god stepping out of the machine. Frank walked from the landing pad to his trailer by way of a lane that had been fashioned out of double rows of snow fencing flanked by bodyguards.

As for the set itself, Wein called it "a glorious performance," expressing the minor regret that "his program was heavy on swing and short on ballads."

Among the numbers Frank sang that night, besides "Get Me to the Church on Time," were "Fly Me to the Moon," "Street of Dreams," "I've Got You Under My Skin," "You Make Me Feel So Young," and "Where or When," all either Quincy Jones arrangements or reorchestrations by Jones to capture the spirit of the Riddle originals. As the jazz critic Arnold Jay Smith wrote, "Many believe [Jones's] were the heartiest, most satisfyingly comfortable charts Sinatra had ever worked with. Even when he revisited the Riddle, May, and Don Costa arrangements, there was now a looser suave, bravura feeling that suited the elder statesman Sinatra. Thanks to the Jones arrangements, Sinatra could play around more with the lyrics, punctuate with vocal rhythmic interpolations, and elongate musical phrases crossing bar lines."

Sinatra biographer Arnold Shaw, who had attended every Newport Jazz Festival since the beginning, wrote, "There have been many memorable moments, like the 'discovery' of trumpeter Miles Davis in 1955 and the first appearance of Dave Brubeck in 1958. No one individual so electrified and literally possessed the Festival as did Sinatra in 1965."

Variety agreed, calling Newport 1965 "Sinatra's festival" and his set an "overpowering, hour-long vocal assault." He "added a new dimension to the festival," the show-business weekly's David B. Bittan wrote, supplying "glamour showmanship—his own brand of casual hipness. The jazz purists may have been unhappy about his appearance, since Sinatra is technically not a 'jazz singer.' But he brought something to Newport that no other artist could have." Frank's $40,000 fee, Bittan wrote, "was worth every penny to Wein and the festival."

At 10:25 p.m., Sinatra waved good night, to the biggest ovation of the four-day event. "As he left the stage, he said: 'Thank you, Father O'Connor [the Paulist priest and jazz fan who had emceed the festival], and thank you, George,' and walked straight toward one of the helicopters," Wein recalled.

> Two minutes later, he was airborne. Both choppers lifted out of the park as suddenly as they had arrived; their landing lights blinked a wistful farewell. Sinatra was off to New York where he wanted to be in Jilly's restaurant by midnight and tell everyone what had happened at Newport. It was the most dramatic exit he could possibly have made. Even as the birds disappeared into the night, thousands of people just stood silently and watched, transfixed. Frank had literally come down from the heavens to bestow his gift, and now he was making his ascension.

The religious imagery would be embarrassing were it not so apt. In the middle of his fiftieth year, he had become a kind of demigod, not just by virtue of his presence—any movie star had presence—but through his incomparable ability to manipulate human emotion with the sheer power of his voice.

Four days later, Frank fulfilled his *Life* magazine promise to return to the big town, playing three sellout nights at the West Side Tennis Club stadium in Forest Hills, Queens. "The audience was made up mostly of middle-aged matrons, whose reactions were almost as voluble as their teen-age daughters' at a Beatles concert," Arnold Shaw wrote. "The three performances hit a record gross of $271,886."

In his *Life* essay, Sinatra had discussed the Fab Four, who had played their own sold-out show at Forest Hills the previous August and had now become undismissable. "I get a kick out of reading what the kids today are doing to the Beatles," he wrote. "They seem a little more aggressive than they were a hundred years ago at the Paramount Theater when the kids liked me. I'll never forget the first time I heard that strange sound in the audience—the old swooning business. I didn't know what was happening. This moaning just started, then it began to build."

If Frank's characterization was mildly condescending, he could hardly be blamed. The Liverpool quartet weren't just upending the music business; they were dividing the world of pop godhood with him and taking the lion's share. Queens, New York, was the site of another memorable musical event a month after Sinatra's Forest Hills stand: the Beatles' Shea Stadium concert on August 15. More than fifty-five thousand fans attended the unprecedented show, screaming so loud from beginning until end that the music was inaudible to everyone present, the musicians included. Gross ticket sales for the evening were $304,000, more than Frank had made over three nights at the West Side Tennis Club.

But more important to the British group than the money was this vivid demonstration, at the start of their third American visit, that touring was quickly becoming irrelevant for them. Inaudibility was a strong deterrent to playing live, and the exhausting grind of the road militated against composing the new material they needed to feel vital as artists. Having begun smoking marijuana (to which Bob Dylan had introduced them the previous year) and experimenting with LSD, they were turning inward and would soon abandon the road altogether to become purely studio musicians.

In the meantime, Dylan, their model and idol, was also transforming, and transforming the world as he did so. At the Newport Folk Festival, just twenty-one days after Sinatra's Newport theophany, the groundbreaking singer-songwriter born Robert Allen Zimmerman had been roundly booed for playing an electrified version of his soon-to-be-released anthem "Like a Rolling

Stone." Logging in at an unparalleled six minutes and thirteen seconds, the single quickly came to dominate American airwaves that summer, despite the initial reluctance of Dylan's record label, Columbia, to release it and the early unwillingness of DJs to play such a long track. It was a new kind of popular music: you couldn't dance to it; you certainly wouldn't make love to it or listen to it raptly in a coffeehouse. It was pure rebellion, jagged poetry for a jagged time, and for ears young enough to hear it, it was purely thrilling.

———

But if you couldn't dance to it or make love to it, and if other singers wouldn't cover it—not many, anyway; it was such a personal statement—what was it? Would it be sung and cherished decades hence, like "I've Got You Under My Skin" or "Where or When," both of them already almost three decades old in 1965? Was what many called the Great American Songbook closing for good? Was a new book opening? It was impossible to tell, easier simply to note that a great schism had split the landscape, with youth and tradition fulminating at each other across the divide.

———

They were a strange hybrid, this May-September pair, holding hands over a chasm, trying to stay together in spite of everything.

In her memoir, Farrow wrote of the three distinct worlds into which Sinatra's life was divided. The first was the private time they shared, an increasingly imperiled quantity now that they had gone public. The second was the social world of the Beverly Hills/Manhattan establishment, on the West Coast the Goetzes and the Deutsches and the Billy Wilders and the Jack Bennys and the Kirk Douglases and Ruth Gordon and Garson Kanin and Roz Russell and her husband, Freddie Brisson; on the East, the Cerfs and the Paleys and the Haywards and the Arthur Hornblows and Claudette Colbert and her husband, Joel Pressman. The A-group, as Farrow called them, adored Frank, and he behaved around them—though, as we have seen, not always.

At the Goetzes' in Beverly Hills, she recalled, the walls were lined with Renoirs, Cézannes, Gauguins, Bonnards, and Picassos. The Friday-night dinners were cooked by a French chef. After dinner, as if by magic, paintings rose, a movie screen descended, and the invitees were treated to an advance showing of one of Hollywood's latest films. The guests, Farrow writes, were mostly friends of her parents; they'd known her since she was a little girl, "which was strange in one way and nice in another." When they came to visit Frank in Palm Springs, they sometimes brought their adult children, who at meals would sit together at "the kids' table" while Mia sat with the grownups.

It was all more than a little surreal.

Equally strange was Frank's third world, in late-night Las Vegas or Miami or Palm Springs, or in what Farrow calls "that *other* New York": the hard-drinking, tough-talking milieu of Jilly Rizzo and Toots Shor. The moment Sinatra arrived at a Las Vegas or Miami hotel or a New York restaurant, Mia remembered, men—and women—she didn't know would appear out of nowhere. She had no idea, she writes, how it was all pulled together.

But he didn't really care to pull it together: compartmentalization was the name of the game. Often, Farrow found herself inside a compartment all by herself.

In August, the triumphant Basie tour was over, and Frank was between albums and movies, so he decided to take her on a cruise: "a boat trip," as Farrow called it. The boat in question was a 168-foot motor yacht, the *Southern Breeze,* chartered for $2,000 a day. Frank had carefully planned an itinerary stopping at ports along the New England coast. Her television series seemed an obstacle at first, Farrow wrote, but such obstacles were child's play when Sinatra had made up his mind: thanks to his influence at 20th Century Fox (and every-where else), the writers on *Peyton Place* conveniently had Allison MacKenzie get into an auto accident that left her in a coma. "If Mia decided to marry," the Associated Press noted, "the script may call for Allison to die."

It was a not-so-subtle shot across Farrow's bow showing how Sinatra val-ued her work.

It was also a strange boatload. Apart from the crew, Mia was by decades the youngest person aboard, and even Frank was basically in a different generation from Claudette Colbert (born 1903), Rosalind Russell (born 1907), and Bill and Edie Goetz (born 1903 and 1905, respectively). There was something both respectable and slightly unseemly, a premonitory whiff of *Rosemary's Baby,* about "the coven of golden oldies" hovering about the unregenerate middle-aged swinger and his apple-cheeked honey.

The press felt the same way.

As Farrow had noted, the world had been unable to get a handle on Frank-and-Mia from the beginning, and feeling puzzled, outraged, and titillated, the world had been unable to leave the couple alone. This cruise was far more than a photo op at a premiere or a nightclub: for the press it was four weeks of solid copy during the month that, in the palmy days before the twenty-four-hour news cycle, used to be known as the silly season. Here was America's Fun Couple on a half shell, sitting ducks at sea.

Not even Frank, a battle-scarred veteran of the paparazzi wars, had antici-pated the mania the cruise would set off, Farrow recalled. It was an act of imperious blindness on Sinatra's part. Did he really expect that he could shield them?

Almost at once, Mia writes, boatloads of photographers were bobbing along beside them, helicopters were whirring deafeningly overhead, and it was impossible to turn on the television without seeing endless reports about how old Frank was, how young she was, how they soon would marry, how many beautiful women Sinatra had been with, how many fistfights he'd had, how many gangsters he'd befriended, how big the *Southern Breeze* was . . .

But the oddest thing, she remembered, was that she and Frank never spoke a word to each other about the press frenzy. She had no idea if he was angry or embarrassed; all she knew was that as a stubbornly good host, he was "absolutely determined" that everybody would have fun. He never thought for a moment about cutting the cruise short, and so they sailed on, and the press sailed with them.

Rather pathetically, the contingent paid a call on Rose and Joe Kennedy in Hyannis Port; the Goetzes, who knew Mrs. Kennedy, seem to have initiated the visit rather than Frank, who hadn't been in touch with the family since Bobby had thrown his weight into the kidnapping investigation. The Ambassador was still in a wheelchair, unable to speak. A measure of relief was attained all around when the sisters Kennedy—Jean Smith, Eunice Shriver, and Pat Lawford—came aboard the *Southern Breeze* with their husbands for an evening. The curtains were drawn; charades was played and alcohol consumed copiously as Mia marveled at the youth and exuberance of the Kennedy crowd—especially in contrast to the elderly voyagers.

It is a mark of how deadly things had become that Frank temporarily relaxed his fatwa against Peter Lawford.

Mia Farrow saw deeply into Frank Sinatra. His image as a swinger and a brawler, she thought, was all wrong. He was filled, she knew, with a "wounding tenderness," a vulnerability he couldn't bear to admit to, except when he sang. Perhaps, she felt, if people looked at pictures of the young Frank, the skinny boy singer with the bow tie and the beautiful, angular face, they would see who he really was and what he was trying to shield with his tough exterior.

At the same time, this was the man she'd seen—often—polishing off a bottle of Jack Daniel's in an evening. Liquor was an essential part of his armor, and on the *Southern Breeze* he girded and isolated himself. Amid the constant press barrage, Farrow recalled, the hardest thing for her, besides the hubbub and the confinement, was Frank's emotional distance.

She also writes, tellingly, that the moment he entered a room, no matter who else was present, he became the center of attention. And that nobody was ever truly comfortable with him, even when he was at his most charming. She

The boat trip from hell, August 1965. What began as a pleasure cruise for the forty-nine-year-old Sinatra and his twenty-year-old sweetheart quickly turned into a media feeding frenzy, then a tragedy.

goes on to say—as if it were an explanation—that in a world of phonies, he utterly lacked artifice. That—as if they were virtues—he possessed "a child's sense of outrage at any perceived unfairness and an inability to compromise." That he was equally judgmental with others and himself.

And this too was true. Yet there is a disconnect in Farrow's sensitive appraisal between the something about Frank that made people uncomfortable and what it was. He did lack artifice, and on a boatload of theatrical socialites playing charades and backgammon and kissing up to him and pretending everything was hunky-dory, he would have retreated ever further into himself. But he also possessed deep wells of self-dislike and anger and entitlement and grandiosity, he was irretrievably Frank Sinatra and no one else, and the gulf between himself and anyone, no matter how intimate, would always be as deep as the ocean.

———

The *Southern Breeze* docked at Martha's Vineyard, where Claudette Colbert and Rosalind Russell met with reporters to try to defuse the media hysteria. They were friends of Mia's mother and watchful chaperones, the two grandes dames insisted; no wedding was planned. The denial only fanned the flames: when the group visited James Cagney at his Chilmark house, fresh rumors leaped up that Frank and Mia were to be married there. A heavy fog rolled in. On August 10, a group of crew members on their night off went ashore for some fun; at the end of the evening, their launch returned to the yacht, minus the steward, James Grimes, and the third mate, Robert Goldfarb, who'd managed to miss the boat. Grimes and Goldfarb got two waitresses to row them back in a dinghy, but when they encountered heavy chop in the harbor, the craft was swamped and the twenty-three-year-old Goldfarb went missing. While the coast guard dragged the harbor (the young crewman's body would wash ashore weeks later), Frank pulled the plug on the boat trip from hell. What *Time* had called "the most closely watched [voyage] since Cleopatra floated down the Nile to meet Mark Antony" had lasted all of one week.

He took her to Joey Bishop's opening at the Sands; Vegas bewildered her. Sitting at a table in the Garden Room with Frank, Frank junior (who was appearing with the Dorsey orchestra at the Flamingo Lounge), Joey and his wife, Jack Entratter, and, as UPI reported, "10 other persons—including a 250-pound man who hovered over Sinatra and Miss Farrow protectively," Mia got up to go to the bathroom, and Frank handed her a $5 bill. Did he want her to buy something? she asked. As the whole table laughed, he explained the money was for the attendant in the ladies' room.

Typical nights in Vegas, she recalled, were full of booze and betting and "sitting around cocktail lounges telling stories until dawn." The atmosphere was uproarious: Once Frank offered a waiter a hundred-dollar bill—surely as much as the poor man made in a week—if he would drop a tray filled with glasses. (The waiter declined; Sinatra gave him the C-note anyway.) The "broads" all sat up straight, their legs crossed demurely, sipping white wine, smoking cigarettes, and laughing at the men's jokes. They made girl talk among themselves, carefully watching and listening to the men all the while. One by one they faded as the men partied on. Often, Farrow writes, she nodded off herself, her head drooping onto her folded arms.

At 3:00 a.m., after attending Bishop's second show (Frank got onstage and clowned around with Joey—"Anybody want to buy a ship?" he ad-libbed), the two of them got on Frank's little jet and flew back to California. It was time for Allison MacKenzie to come out of her coma and for Frank to go back to work.

In early September, Sinatra taped his guest appearance on the premiere episode of *The Dean Martin Show*. Like Frank, Dean hated rehearsing: the program took a lightning-like two hours to make, and the resulting broadcast looked it. The skits felt undercooked, the cameras occasionally seemed uncertain about just where to point, and Martin appeared to be fine with whatever happened. He was in high drunkie mode, tuxed and deeply tanned; his great rectangular head looked like a teak sculpture. His eyes gleamed naughtily at the whole silly shambles, which turned out to be nothing less than a formula for staying on the air forever.

Frank, his toupeed pate trimmed Caesar-close, was loose if not very funny and, as always, just a bit too hot-blooded for television. Dean addressed him as the Chairman of the Board; Frank liked that. A sketch where Sinatra brought six statuesque young women ("If you'll pardon the expression, this is my sextet") into Dean's den started out lame and deteriorated as the parade of other guest stars—Danny Thomas, Bob Newhart, Jack Jones, Steve Allen, Eddie Fisher—entered the room one by one, each to obligatory applause. As the set filled, like the stateroom scene in *A Night at the Opera,* Sinatra, not knowing what to do with himself, kept sitting down and standing up and yelling out ad-libs, intent on remaining the center of attention. It was hard work on a crowded set. The best moment occurred when Fisher made a remark about his new album, and Frank shot him a hard stare of what looked like real dislike. "If it's not Reprise, shut your big mouth!" he barked. Then he grinned, having made his point.

No record exists of whether he encountered two of Martin's other musical guests, Jan and Dean, singing (*something for the youngsters!*) their hit "The Little Old Lady from Pasadena." Dean Torrence having been, of course, indicted but never tried as a co-conspirator in the kidnapping of Frank Sinatra Jr.

———

Warner Bros. essentially dumped *Marriage on the Rocks,* releasing it in the third week of September, well after the summer peak and well before the holiday rush. An added bonus for the studio was a newspaper strike in New York City, which meant that only two reviewers for unaffected papers covered the picture: the *Post's* Archer Winsten ("well below the best Sinatra-Martin movie levels and almost out of sight of Deborah Kerr's best") and the *Herald Tribune's* Judith Crist ("flat, insipid and watery"). Frank and Dean's film partnership, which had begun so promisingly with *Some Came Running,* hereby ended with a thud—although they would briefly reunite, as old men who ought to have known better, in 1984's *Cannonball Run II.*

They weren't old in the fall of '65, but both were well into middle age, and the movies had simply run out of ideas for the two of them. Drama was out as far as Dean was concerned. He had played his last straight role in 1963's *Toys in the Attic,* had taken stock of the box office (the film lost $1.2 million), and had made a simple calculation: screw drama. But comedy wasn't working for them either: *Sergeants 3* and *4 for Texas* had taken Sinatra and Martin farther and farther out onto that limb, and with *Marriage on the Rocks* the limb had snapped. Frank had gone it alone in the movies before, and now he would do it again.

In October, he would begin another picture, this one for Paramount: it was called *Assault on a Queen*.

———

It was a caper picture, "a lackluster nautical variation on *Ocean's 11*," in the words of Daniel O'Brien, a story about a crew of misfits who attempt to rob the passenger liner *Queen Mary* using a salvaged U-boat and a dummy torpedo. The Italian bombshell Virna Lisi co-starred with Frank, who played the head of the gang, a tough former submarine lieutenant named Mark Brittain. It was a role that fit him like a glove in a property that creaked like an old shoe. Tellingly, Sinatra's pal the Hollywood grandee Bill Goetz produced the film. The barbarians might have been at the cultural gates in the mid-1960s, but in the movie industry the power structure was still firmly in place, and creative exhaustion prevailed. New voices were starting to be heard, however. In the words of the recently hired, eager-to-rock-the-boat Paramount executive Robert Evans, "*Assault on a Queen* was a B-picture inflated to A status only because it had Sinatra." It was a "dinosaur," he told his bosses. "If the product stinks, you can't sell it."

But Frank had to keep moving, so he made it.

———

Bob Thomas visited him on the set at Paramount and found him trying to get it all over with as quickly as possible. "It's a good story and a forerunner in the field of far-out plots," Sinatra told the columnist, sounding none too convinced himself.

> "But listen, you can get away with these stories—if you hook the audi-
> ence in the first eight to twelve minutes. And if you keep moving fast.
> And we move fast in this one, believe me."
>
> I believed him. You need only to watch Sinatra at work to under-
> stand the swiftness of his operation.
>
> "What are we waiting for?" he asks when there is a lull in shooting.
> "Let's get moving."
>
> A lull gave me a chance to inquire about current and future plans of
> the phenomenon known as Sinatra.
>
> "On Thanksgiving Eve I'll have a special on [NBC] television," he
> reported. "A week before that, CBS is putting on *The World of Frank
> Sinatra*. [The title would be changed to *Sinatra: An American Original*.]

They've been following me around for six months, shooting everything I do, almost.

"Then a couple of weeks ago Walter Cronkite came down to Palm Springs and taped a long interview. That guy is great, you know. I think he's the best of the newscasters, a real reporter who can dig in an interview and come up with interesting questions. A real gentleman, too."

A couple of weeks later, Frank had changed his tune about Walter Cronkite. A *New York Times* story of November 6 said that CBS had received a letter from Mickey Rudin expressing Sinatra's grave reservations about the documentary and asking to preview the show. CBS declined. Rudin also charged the network with a "breach of understanding" and suggested that the Cronkite interview be re-filmed.

The crux of Frank's objections was "CBS insisting on the right to cover matters in the program not related to his activities as an entertainer," the *Times*'s Val Adams wrote.

He had consented originally to cooperate in filming the show, he added, because he was led to believe it would be a commentary on his professional career in the same manner CBS news had done shows on the careers of Pablo Casals, Isaac Stern and Marian Anderson.

The statement by the singer, issued through his press representative, Jim Mahoney, in Hollywood, did not define the matters outside his entertainment activities that CBS insisted on covering. However, the show contains an interview by Walter Cronkite in which the CBS correspondent poses questions about the singer's private life . . . Authoritative sources have said Cronkite asked tough questions that irritated the entertainer.

Some questions were about Sinatra's romances, his relations with the press and certain business activities. He declined to answer some questions. All this is in the show that CBS plans to televise.

The reality of the veteran newsman's sit-down with Frank was a good deal juicier than the *Times*'s dry portrayal, especially when it came to those certain business activities. "We were getting along famously," Cronkite remembered,

when Don [Hewitt] leaned over and whispered to me not to forget to ask him about the Mafia. My question was simply how he responded to charges that he had Mafia connections. Sinatra's lips tightened to a tiny line. He gave me a piercing look through narrowing eyes.

"That's it," he said, practically leaping up from his chair and waving his sidekick, Jilly Rizzo, and Hewitt back to his bedroom. I wasn't invited to the private conference, which featured the great voice raised to a level seldom used in the concert hall. The only coherent phrase I picked up was a charge that Hewitt had promised him that the Mafia question would not be raised.

They worked out a compromise that I never would have thought possible, and Sinatra came back to answer the question.

In his own memoir, Don Hewitt leaves Jilly out of the bedroom conference but makes the menace of the situation clear. According to the producer, Frank reproached him, alluding to Mickey Rudin's advance visit to Hewitt to discuss the interview: "You broke all of Mickey's rules."

"No, Frank," the producer told him. "We never agreed to those rules."

"I ought to kill you," Sinatra said.

"With anyone else, that's a figure of speech," Hewitt claims he said. "But you probably mean it."

"I mean it," Frank said.

Hewitt writes that he then "scurried out of [Sinatra's] house and back to my hotel." But in truth, something was worked out, for Cronkite got to ask the question—albeit off camera—and Frank answered it, after his fashion.

————

An unwitting victim of Hewitt and Cronkite's indelicacy was the journalist Gay Talese, who had recently left the *New York Times* and signed a contract with *Esquire,* where his new editor, Harold Hayes, assigned him in the fall of 1965 to go to Los Angeles and write a profile of Frank Sinatra.

Talese had accepted the assignment somewhat reluctantly. A writer of style and dignity, he didn't want to be pigeonholed as a celebrity journalist, and then of course Sinatra was known to eat journalists for breakfast. But it was the big year, the year of the great chronicles (*Billboard* would also publish an eighty-nine-page piece on Frank in late November; *Look* would run a cover story a couple of weeks later), and Jim Mahoney assured Harold Hayes that Sinatra would be agreeable to an interview, and so Talese swallowed his misgivings and flew to the Coast.

He arrived in Los Angeles on Sunday, October 31, rented a car from Avis, and checked into the Beverly Wilshire (*Esquire,* large in format in those days and flush with success, did things in style), where he ogled the pretty chambermaids, had a room-service feast and a bottle of wine, and prepared, not without pleasurable anticipation, to meet with Sinatra, perhaps the next day.

On Monday morning, Mahoney told Talese that Frank Sinatra had a cold and would not be meeting with him soon, or perhaps at all.

It was more than just the cold, the publicist explained. "Cronkite's doing this thing—this fucking Don Hewitt," Mahoney sputtered. "This exposé that CBS is doing has got Sinatra very upset."

"I said, 'I'm not talking about organized crime,' " Talese recalled. " 'I'm not interested in the Mafia. I'm out here, and I'd love to do this piece.' "

Mahoney then told Talese that Sinatra would only consent to an interview if Frank or Mickey Rudin could see the piece when it was done. Sinatra and his lawyer wouldn't change anything, the publicist assured Talese; they just needed to see it before it was published.

Talese told Jim Mahoney that this was impossible, and Mahoney told Talese that in that case Sinatra would not be available.

The rest, of course, is history. God, the common cold, and CBS News had given Gay Talese the greatest gift a journalist could possibly receive: a central but surmountable obstacle. On *Esquire*'s considerable dime (Talese would remain at the Beverly Wilshire, on and off but mostly on, for six weeks; his expenses would run to some $5,000, twice as much as his contract paid him per article), he proceeded to construct the greatest write-around in the history of magazine journalism, "Frank Sinatra Has a Cold." Deprived of access

Dressed as conservatively as a banker, Frank sits for an interview with Walter Cronkite in late 1965. On camera, butter wouldn't have melted in Sinatra's mouth; off, he exploded after an inconvenient question was raised.

to his subject (although, according to a source who wished to remain anony-mous, the journalist did eventually interview Sinatra briefly), Talese doggedly sought out anyone and everyone in Frank's ambit who would speak to him—including Mahoney—and, in much the same manner as the *Life* photographer John Dominis stalking lions in Africa, placed himself in proximity to the big cat whenever possible. The journalist also benefited from the kind of good luck that results from hard work: because he had previously written about Jack Hanson, the owner of the private Rodeo Drive discotheque the Daisy, Talese was able to gain admission to the club; because he started spending time there, he happened to be present on a night when Frank, out of sorts and in his cups, had a memorable run-in with the young novelist and screenwriter Harlan Ellison. He turned the encounter into his piece's most vivid and dis-turbing scene.

"Watching him at recording sessions, on a movie set, at the gambling tables in Las Vegas," Talese later wrote,

I was able to perceive his changing moods, his irritation and suspicion when he thought that I was getting too close, his pleasure and courtesy and charm when he was able to relax among those whom he trusted. I gained more by watching him, overhearing him, and watching the reac-tions of those around him than if I had actually been able to sit down and talk to him.

It is a self-serving argument, of course, but—especially in Sinatra's case—it is also a cogent one. Frank was not an un-self-knowing man: in fact, he knew too much about his inner chaos for comfort. Accordingly, he feared solitude, reflection, and probing inquiries by would-be intimates or others. Cornered into an actual interview, he was likely to recite banalities or give clues that might or might not be metaphorical ("I am a symmetrical man, almost to a fault") or merely dazzle an interlocutor, as he had dazzled Tommy Thompson, with a wide but shallow show of knowledge. In any case, dazzling was always easy: few, if any, could resist him when he turned it on. Like death and the sun in La Rochefoucauld's famous maxim, Sinatra was best observed not head-on but from a perspective slightly to the side.

———

On Monday, November 8, Frank showed up at NBC Studios in Burbank to begin taping *A Man and His Music,* a celebration in song of his career as a vocalist. (This year also officially marked the twenty-fifth anniversary of his start in show business, though in reality he had begun singing with Harry

James in April 1939.) Nelson Riddle and forty-three musicians were waiting eagerly, along with production staff, "security guards, Budweiser ad men . . . [and] a dozen or so ladies who worked as secretaries in other parts of the building but had sneaked away so they could watch this," Talese wrote. "[Sinatra's] face was pale, his blue eyes seemed a bit watery," he continued.

> He had been unable to rid himself of the cold, but he was going to try to sing anyway because the schedule was tight and thousands of dollars were involved at this moment in the assembling of the orchestra and crews and the rental of the studio. But when Sinatra, on his way to his small rehearsal room to warm up his voice, looked into the studio and saw that the stage and orchestra's platform were not close together, as he had specifically requested, his lips tightened and he was obviously very upset. A few moments later, from his rehearsal room, could be heard the pounding of his fist against the top of the piano and the voice of his accompanist, Bill Miller, saying, softly, "Try not to upset yourself, Frank."

The next day would be the one-year anniversary of the death of Miller's wife in the Burbank mudslide, and he was the one comforting Frank.

Jim Mahoney arrived a while later, and he and Sinatra discussed the death of Frank's old nemesis Dorothy Kilgallen. The body of the fifty-two-year-old columnist had been found that morning in her New York apartment, her demise apparently due to a fatal combination of alcohol and barbiturates.* "Dorothy Kilgallen's dead," Sinatra said as he walked into the studio. "Well, guess I got to change my whole act."

The dreaded CBS documentary aired on November 16, and it proved to be an utter anticlimax. To the sound of Walter Cronkite's sonorous voice-over, footage of Sinatra's past and present life and career flickered across the screen, now and then cutting away to a one-shot of Frank sitting in his Palm Springs living room, dressed like an investment banker or corporate lawyer (or the ad agency head in *Marriage on the Rocks*) in a dark three-piece suit with French cuffs and a collar pin. He wrinkled his forehead thoughtfully and more or less

---

* Because Kilgallen had been an outspoken critic of the Warren Commission's findings on the assassination of John F. Kennedy and had reportedly told friends that she was "about to blow the JFK case sky high," rumors later arose that she had been murdered.

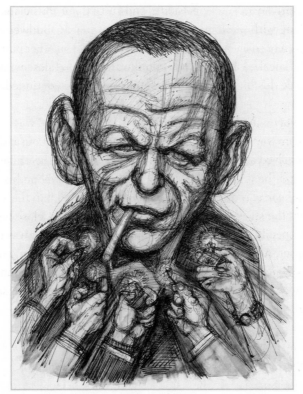

Edward Sorel's cover illustration for the issue of *Esquire* containing Gay Talese's great profile, "Frank Sinatra Has a Cold." Sinatra wouldn't sit for a photograph or an interview; Talese turned Frank's evasiveness into journalistic gold.

answered Cronkite's questions—the screaming tantrum having of course gone unrecorded—and generally appeared as sober as a judge.

This was the problem with questioning Sinatra directly. What you got were vague, well-chewed-over formulations: "What I do with my life is of my own doing. I live it the best way I can. I've been criticized on many, many occasions, because of—acquaintances, and what have you. But I don't do these things to have anybody follow me in doing that same thing, is what I mean."

Or, in the case of the casus belli, the time-honored question (people still ask it today, long after his death; people will never stop asking) about his associations with those . . . acquaintances, elaborate nonanswers:

The fact that I used to be involved was a legitimate business reason. We built a hotel in Las Vegas and finally, I just—there was so much work to be done of my own natural—vocation—pictures, singing, recording—that I just dropped all of the fringes of business.
But I do meet all kinds of people in the world because of the natural

habitat from day to day in theatrical work and night club work, in concerts, wherever I might be, in restaurants, you meet all kinds of people. So that there's really not much to be said about that, and I think the less said the better, because it's—there is no—there's no answer. When I say no, it's no; but for some reason it keeps persisting, you see. And consequently, I just said I just refuse to discuss it, because you can't make a dent anywhere.

Or, if you were probing into his psychology, wishful happy talk.

CRONKITE: Do you think your boiling point is low?
SINATRA: Not anymore. It used to be. I think that comes with a normal growing up, and the—way of living, friends, people with whom you become acquainted. I've always admired people who are gentle, and who have great patience, and apparently, what I've done is, without knowing it, is I've aped these people, and begun to follow that kind of line. When I say I had a low boiling point, it doesn't mean I went around kicking dogs and old ladies, and people.

"This is the great age of candor," Paul Newman told *Playboy* in 1983. "*Fuck* candor." Frank Sinatra felt the same way, but still they kept coming, these reporters demanding he *explain* himself. Voicing the same sentiment as Newman, only in 1965, prime-time television terms, he said to Cronkite, "Bogart, when he was alive, once told me . . . the only thing you owe the public is a good performance."

This he gave, playing himself (his greatest role, after all) in several of the special's contemporary film clips. Viewers saw him as the anxious perfectionist in magnificent voice, recording "A Very Good Year"; as the man of good works, entertaining convicts at a prison outside Washington, D.C., with a loose, easy "Fly Me to the Moon"; as *il padrone,* jovially holding court in the back room of Jilly's. To the apparent delight of everyone at the long table—among others, Big and Little Nancy, Tina, Sammy Davis, and Alan King—Frank recalled Sammy being blindsided by a pie in the face when the two of them guested on *The Soupy Sales Show* in September. It wasn't really a very funny story: Davis was, after all, blind on one side. It was sadistic humor, Dolly Sinatra humor. Frank looked transported with joy.

At the end of this last clip came a strikingly plaintive sound bite from a baby-voiced Nancy junior: "When you have a daddy, you kind of want him to be a daddy all the time. And sometimes, when he's with his friends, they carry on like a bunch of kids. And it's great they're having a marvelous time, but that bothers me a little."

The critics were united in their disdain for what the Associated Press's Cynthia Lowry called "a nice little pussycat of a show." "CBS and the public [have] been had," wrote the *Herald Tribune*'s John Horn. "Tough it wasn't. Searching it certainly wasn't either," the *New York Post*'s Bob Williams said. *Variety* called the broadcast "an unmitigated rave for Frankie Goodfellow, star performer, tycoon with heart of gold, family man (yet), and all-around ball-haver."

The *Daily News*'s Kay Gardella felt that Cronkite's tough questions "were edited down to appease the temperamental star," and the *Journal American*'s Jack O'Brian (New York had a lot of papers in those days) opined that the newsman's queries "seemed gentlemanly and restrained in areas from romance (not a question about Mia Farrow) to hoodlums . . . CBS didn't pinpoint the names of gangsters and others whose personalities, characters or lack of same have touched the life of this gifted, superb-singing sorehead."

The *New York Times*'s Jack Gould summarized: "*Sinatra* wasn't authorized but it could have been."

Perhaps their pique stemmed from the vague feeling that they'd been had. "Although it seemed at first that Sinatra was genuinely concerned about the [show's] contents," biographer Arnold Shaw wrote, "it later appeared that he had once again given the country's publicists a lesson in how to build audience through controversy."

Nearly all the reviewers mentioned Nancy junior's wistful quotation. "His daughter Nancy's low-keyed whimper seemed somewhat embarrassing, plaintive, even poignant," Jack O'Brian said.

Frank's grand year had been a rough one for his devoted older daughter: Tommy Sands's walkout, her breakdown and meek performance in *Marriage on the Rocks,* and now this. But then Little Nancy turned around and showed them all.

She had originally been signed to Reprise on the condition that she not record any rock 'n' roll. Obediently, she cut a few novelty songs with the former Mouseketeer Annette Funicello's producer, a man named Tutti Camarata. Nancy Sinatra "struck marinara," in her words, with her second single, a heavily echoed, bubblegummy thing called "Like I Do," which went to number 1 in Italy and Japan but got zero play in the United States. The record brought a few dollars in to the failing label: enough to make her papa proud, not enough to make a difference to the company or her singing career.

By the end of 1965, though, Warner-Reprise was a hit-making machine, Nancy hadn't panned out, and Reprise president Mo Ostin, who was beginning to acquire enough clout in the record industry that he could contemplate such a move, was about to cut her loose. Enter Duane Eddy's producer Lee Hazlewood, a friend of Jimmy Bowen's and a man convinced he could make a hit single with Nancy Sinatra.

He wrote the song, a pounding rockabilly strut, and had an instrumental track made. On Friday, November 19, three nights after her little-girlish plaint was heard in the CBS documentary, Nancy went to United Recording Studio B and laid down the vocal.

When she asked Hazlewood how she should sing the number, he said, "Like a fourteen-year-old girl in love with a forty-year-old man." She didn't know what he was talking about. After a polite first take, Sinatra recalled, the producer hit the talk-back button in the control booth and gave her both barrels. She'd been a married woman, he told her; she wasn't a virgin anymore. According to some sources, he then ordered her to sing the tune as if she were "a sixteen-year-old girl who fucks truck drivers."

She complied. Three weeks later, "These Boots Are Made for Walkin'" was a number 1 song. And very soon, though in real life she was still Daddy's Little Girl, a publicity makeover had turned her into an international sex symbol, complete with blond bouffant, frosted lipstick, low-cut blouses, miniskirts, and, of course, those high white boots. Soon she would travel to Vietnam to entertain American troops, who listened to "Boots" over and over in places like Da Nang and Pleiku, counting the days and dreaming of raunchy fun with Nancy Sinatra.

———

Frank Sinatra: A Man and His Music—no guest stars; minimal script; just Frank, head cold and all, singing through a chronological roster of some of his greatest hits before a live audience—aired on NBC the night before Thanksgiving. The critics loved it ("An hour of consummate artistry," wrote UPI's Rick DuBrow) and the ratings were sky-high. All he had to do was that in which he had no equal, and nothing stood in his way.

———

At the end of November, Frank was back in the studio to record a new album, an LP full of songs about the moon: it would be called, obviously but affectingly, *Moonlight Sinatra*. Riddle wrote the charts and stood at the podium in United Recording Studio A. Frank's cold was now just a bad memory, and Talese—who had now gotten closer than ever to his quarry—recorded his high spirits on the eve of the big birthday. "When Frank Sinatra drives to the studio, he seems to dance out of the car across the sidewalk into the front door," the journalist wrote.

Then, snapping his fingers, he is standing in front of the orchestra in an intimate, airtight room, and soon he is dominating every man, every instrument, every sound wave . . .

When his voice is on, as it was tonight, Sinatra is in ecstasy, the room becomes electric, there is an excitement that spreads through the orchestra and is felt in the control booth where a dozen men, Sinatra's friends, wave at him from behind the glass . . .

After he is finished, the record is played back on tape, and Nancy Sinatra, who has just walked in, joins her father near the front of the orchestra to hear the playback. They listen silently, all eyes on them, the king, the princess; and when the music ends there is applause from the control booth, Nancy smiles, and her father snaps his fingers and says, kicking a foot, "Ooba-deeba-boobe-do!"

At the end of the recording session, as the musicians filed by Sinatra to say good night, Frank—who knew them all by name and seemed to have a phenomenal recall of every detail of their personal lives—stopped the French horn player, Vince DeRosa. DeRosa had accompanied him since the Lucky Strike *Your Hit Parade* days on the radio.

"Vicenzo," Sinatra said, "how's your little girl?"

"She's fine, Frank."

"Oh, she's not a little girl anymore," Sinatra corrected himself, "she's a big girl now."

"Yes, she goes to college now. U.S.C."

"That's great."

"She's also got a little talent, I think, Frank, as a singer."

Sinatra was silent for a moment, then said, "Yes, but it's very good for her to get her education first, Vicenzo."

Vincent DeRosa nodded.

"Yes, Frank," he said, and then he said, "Well, good-night, Frank."

"Good-night, Vicenzo."

When the musicians had left, Frank met Don Drysdale, the golfer Bo Wininger, and some others in the hallway to head out for a night of drinking. First, though, he walked to the other end of the hall to say good night to Nancy, who was about to drive home in her own car.

"After Sinatra had kissed her on the cheek, he hurried to join his friends at the door," Talese wrote.

Daddy's little girl, all grown up: Lee Hazlewood, the writer of "These Boots Are Made for Walkin'," reportedly told Nancy Sinatra to sing the tune as if she were "a sixteen-year-old girl who fucks truck drivers."

But before Nancy could leave the studio, one of Sinatra's men, Al Silvani, a former prizefight manager, joined her.

"Are you ready to leave yet, Nancy?"

"Oh, thanks, Al," she said, "but I'll be all right."

"Pope's orders," Silvani said, holding his hands up, palms out.

Only after Nancy had pointed to two of her friends who would escort her home, and only after Silvani recognized them as friends, would he leave.

———

Moonlight Sinatra was a fitting bookend to Frank's golden year, a luminescent counterpoint to the earlier, darker albums of romantic songs. Riddle, who hadn't arranged a full Sinatra LP since *Academy Award Winners,* was back in full fettle, showing that while Gordon Jenkins could tug at the heart with strings, only Nelson could make them sound like Debussy. On the edge of a new age, Sinatra was singing in a different key, walking in a different light. *Clair de lune.*

———

This is the Month of Sinatra . . . a sledgehammer trade and consumer promotional effort of unprecedented intensity to highlight—and sell— the most memorable anniversary in music history.

—Warner-Reprise ad in *Billboard,* December 1965

This is what it was like for a man whose private and public lives were as one to turn fifty.

His record label had every reason to crow: Sinatra and Jenkins had each earned a Grammy for "It Was a Very Good Year," as had *September of My Years.* Two compilation albums—*Sinatra '65,* consisting of singles and other sessions and released in July, and *My Kind of Broadway,* an LP of show tunes released in November—jumped quickly onto the charts, as did *A Man and His Music,* a two-LP career retrospective.

In honor of the grand birthday, the mother of his children, along with his two daughters, made an extraordinary gesture: on Sunday night, December 12, fifty years to the day after Frank Sinatra had made his perilous entrance into the world in the cold-water flat on Monroe Street in Hoboken, the two Nancys and Tina threw him a black-tie party in the Beverly Wilshire hotel's palatial Trianon ballroom. "All of Hollywood show biz was there—and most of New York," Nancy junior recalled. Milton Berle emceed; Jack Benny and George Burns performed. Tony Bennett sang with a full orchestra—as did Sammy Davis, who flew in from New York for the occasion and popped out of a six-foot-tall cardboard birthday cake, belting out a Sammy Cahn parody, "My Kind of Man, Sinatra Is."

Little Nancy sang another Cahn takeoff, to the tune of Gilbert and Sullivan's "Tit-Willow":

Who in the forties was knocking them dead?
My daddy, my daddy, my daddy.
The rug he once cut he now wears on his head.
My daddy, my daddy, my daddy.

"If Frank Sinatra had been five instead of 50 he couldn't have been more excited," wrote Dorothy Manners, who had now taken over Louella Parsons's column.

Frank got a kick out of every little detail, including the way his dinner table was marked with a photograph of him in a little Lord Fauntleroy suit superimposed on a sheet of music, "Oh, Look at Me Now!" . . .

Hilarious highlight of the evening was a screened Walter Cronkite–type interview with [the *Screen World* editor] John Willis doing the questioning to "answers" clipped from Frank's old movies. It's funny enough for a TV fling on its own.

But here I would like to say that the star of the evening was Nancy Sinatra Sr., beautiful, glowing and gracious, who worked for weeks to make this an unforgettable night for Frank.

The only person missing was Mia.

A certain amount of chaos underlay the smiles and stage scenery in the Trianon ballroom. According to George Jacobs, Big Nancy had put her foot down when it came to the question of inviting Frank's new girl. "Mia threw a fit, Big Nancy threw a fit, Mr. S threw a fit," the valet recalled. "That the party ever came off at all is a miracle . . . At one point, however, Little Nancy prevailed on Big. Let's make Dad happy, was her plea, and Big Nancy, ever the good sport and blessed peacemaker, relented."

After thanking his first wife, Frank told Mia she could accompany him to his party. Overjoyed, she bought a blue chiffon gown for the occasion at a pricey Beverly Hills shop.

Then Frank junior weighed in.

Earlier in the week, Frankie had had his own big moment, opening at New York's Basin Street East as the star of the newly christened Frank Sinatra Jr. Show, Sam Donahue having turned Tommy Dorsey's name back to the estate. On opening night, he informed Earl Wilson he'd be flying west on Sunday, his night off, to attend his dad's big celebration.

But having heard that Frank had relented and invited Mia, Frankie called his father in a fury, asking how he could embarrass his mother that way. Father slammed down the phone on son, Frankie stayed in New York, and Frank told Mia she'd better not come after all. Dorothy Manners's happy talk notwithstanding, Jacobs remembered that Sammy's popping out of the fake birthday cake gave Frank his only real smile of the evening.

———

Mia made Frank's birthday unforgettable in her own way: when he went to her apartment after the party, he found, amid the reek of marijuana, that she had cut her flowing, waist-long ash-blond hair to less than an inch in length. In her memoir, Farrow claims she did the deed one morning before work, out of a "horror of vanity," in her dressing room on the *Peyton Place* set. Putting the shorn locks in a Glad bag, she said, she turned to her dressing-room mirror. She liked the way she looked, but the hairdresser was horrified, as were the show's producers. Mia was fitted with a wig and lectured sternly; she apologized profusely but didn't mean any of it.

The story hit the news and blew up. Speculation was rife: Had she done it to spite Frank? Salvador Dali, from New York, called it "mythical suicide." Farrow insists that there was no drama with Sinatra, that he loved her new look immediately.

Yet Ryan O'Neal, her co-star on the show, later insisted, "She didn't cut it at the studio. She came in with it already cut." And according to George Jacobs, there was drama aplenty when Frank saw Mia's shorn scalp. "Now I really will look like a fag," he moaned.

That would show *him* to disinvite her.

And who was the real center of attention.

Act Four

FURIES

23

||||||||||||

*Here's a song that I cannot stand. I just cannot stand this song.
But what the hell.*

—FRANK SINATRA, INTRODUCING "STRANGERS IN THE NIGHT,"
AT A NOVEMBER 1975 CONCERT IN JERUSALEM

Time had shifted by a halftone: a difficult modulation.

The New Year began auspiciously enough. On the seventh, Sinatra
returned to the Sands with the Basie Orchestra, the Count and Bill Miller
on twin pianos, Quincy Jones conducting. *Variety* waxed ecstatic about the
star-studded first night. "The showmanship vibrations of Frank Sinatra seem
to mesmerize Sands by at least 99%," its reviewer wrote, giddily if incoherently,
"and it's possible that figure was passed at his celeb-heavy preem. Even a luke-
warm fan would have to admit that at his current outing he hits a new peak of
personal magnetism which is superb entertainment."

The Basie band continued to thrill Frank and audiences alike. Lacking a
string section for the Riddle and Jenkins charts of such numbers as "I've Got
You Under My Skin" and "It Was a Very Good Year," Jones came up with a
brilliant fake, bucket muting the brass section and doubling the lead trumpet
melody with three flutes playing in unison. Frank smiled. There were also several new arrangements by Quincy's old associate the trombonist and orchestrator Billy Byers: a quiet and lovely version of Johnny Mandel's new ballad
"The Shadow of Your Smile," a polyrhythmic "Get Me to the Church on Time,"
and a swinging but intimate "Where or When" that became Sinatra's default
version. The glorious show would stay on throughout January, and it was all
the more glorious because Reprise was recording the concerts for Sinatra's first
live album.

Mia was with him in Vegas, in body if not quite in spirit. On their first
Christmas together, the previous year, he had disappointed her with a gift of
a diamond koala bear pin instead of the puppy she'd been hinting about—a
cold, expensive, artificial thing instead of a warm, real one. This year his present to her was a solid-gold cigarette case, inscribed "Mia, Mia, With Love,
From Francis." She kept marijuana joints in it.

An item in Hedda Hopper's column (one of her last; she would die in February) mentioned a Sands sighting: "At 5 a.m. you could see Mia Farrow in the dining room with her sister[-in-law] and brother eating ham and eggs. With her haircut nobody recognized her." Frank was presumably with more riotous company. Mia wrote of her alienation at seeing her proto-hippie brother and sister-in-law, in Vegas as Sinatra's guests, their pure faces in stark contrast to the tawdry surroundings of the casino, as Frank blew twenty thousand dollars at the roulette table.

He was excess personified: What did she expect? Their sexual bond persisted; their spiritual connection had begun to fray. The age difference was mammoth enough, but there was also a sociological gulf between them. A pampered child of Hollywood artistes, she could afford to look down on the shiny things that meant so much to a parvenu Italian-American from blue-collar Hoboken.

And he continued to counter intimacy with society. Frank's love of hosting was such, she writes, that he soon added a two-bedroom bungalow and a four-bedroom, New England-style cottage to the two octagonal outbuildings already existing on his Palm Springs property, raising the compound's capacity to 22 guests at a time. Sinatra's friends called him the Innkeeper.

And he ran the place like a four-star inn, with meticulously stocked bathrooms, cars on call for those who wished to go shopping, evening movie screenings. All the minute attention to detail gave her a migraine, she recalled.

That wasn't the only thing that alienated her. In the first week of February, she obligingly played hostess at several parties Frank threw for his Palm Springs friends and pro golfers during the Bob Hope Desert Classic golf tournament: it was a nonpareil culture clash, white shoes and plaid pants versus granny glasses and love beads. Dorothy Manners (who'd now officially taken over for the eighty-four-year-old Louella Parsons) was present at one of the parties, where she observed Farrow sitting in a corner, working on her needlepoint rather than mingling. "Now and then she looks up and smiles at one of the regulars," the columnist wrote.

> She's a quiet girl who suddenly looks like a young boy with her sheared haircut and her slacks.
>
> It's time for dinner, and the group follows Frank into the dining room.
>
> Mia decides to finish the row she's working on before putting down her hoops.
>
> Everyone must be seated by now. And suddenly, there's Frank.
>
> There's no anger in his face. Just sort of blank patience, as if he had played this scene many times.

"Are you going to join us?" he asks, "or are you going to eat that stool?"

By way of reciprocating, Frank threw her a twenty-first-birthday party at Chasen's on the eleventh—which was really just a culture clash in a different location.

The thirty-year-old West Hollywood restaurant, with its dark-wood walls and red-leather banquettes, was old-line Hollywood at its fustiest. Sinatra hired two bands for the occasion and was the only partygoer who never danced: the first sign that something was off.

Ten days later, the couple appeared to be a couple no longer. "Don't get a headache trying to figure out what broke up Frank Sinatra and Mia Farrow," Dorothy Manners wrote on the twenty-first.

They never were headed for marriage, at least, he wasn't. The worlds of a 21-year-old girl and a 50-year-old man are far apart.

There was no big blow-up or argument. In fact, the whole thing was over and done with before Frank hosted the party for Mia's 21st birthday at Chasen's. They both carried the evening off so well, none of the guests suspected.

There were just a few things in the wind: Mia did not sit at Frank's table. She left with Roddy McDowall. And the gift Frank gave her was a "friendship" ring that never could have been mistaken for an engagement sparkler.

In fact, there had been a blowup. At her apartment shortly before the party, Mia had suggested to Frank that they live together before they marry. He dismissed the idea out of hand, saying he could never embarrass his family that way. She had had it with his family, she told him. According to a friend of Farrow's, she then threw a lamp at Sinatra, narrowly missing his head, and he grabbed her by the throat, raising a hand as if to strike her. She told Frank to leave, and he walked out.

In her memoir she writes that the particulars of their first breakup "were absurdly insignificant, even then"—a statement more revealing about her wish not to discuss the particulars than about the event itself. She attributes the split to a mutual "chasm of insecurities" and an inability to talk about their differences. There was no animosity, she insists, just a familiar numbness and resignation.

And a flying lamp, and a grabbed throat.

She began to see another man, she writes. He was "delightful" and "not at all frightening." And young and brilliant and funny, just like the rest of his set. She was particularly struck by how little everybody drank. On her Easter break from *Peyton Place*, Mia and her new friend went to Rome and Venice.

Her new friend was Mike Nichols. At thirty-four, Nichols had recently put aside a thriving stand-up comedy career with Elaine May to become the hottest young director around, first on Broadway (*Barefoot in the Park*, *The Odd Couple*) and now in the movies, with the recently completed *Who's Afraid of Virginia Woolf?*, starring Elizabeth Taylor and Richard Burton. With his quiet, dry wit and courtly ironic manner, the Berlin-born Nichols could not have been more different from Frank Sinatra, except in one respect: he was a powerful show-business star to whom the twenty-one-year-old Farrow deemed it worthy to hitch her wagon, even if temporarily.

"With a week's vacation from 'Peyton Place,' where do you think Mia Farrow went?" Harrison Carroll wrote in mid-April.

> To Rome, where she saw a lot of Elizabeth Taylor and Richard Burton. I hear she was their house guest, but am not positive of that.
> Furthermore, and this is even more intriguing, Mia did the town with famed director Mike Nichols, whom she met several weeks ago in Hollywood . . .
> Important days are coming up in Mia's life. It hasn't been confirmed yet, but I am assured she is quitting 'Peyton Place' in June, and will substitute a deal where she does one picture a year for 20th Century–Fox.

Frank had had her hanging out with Bob Hope and Dinah Shore in Palm Springs; with Nichols, she got to spend time around Liz and even more thrillingly, Dick, who could spout Shakespeare or Dylan Thomas (and match Sinatra drink for drink). She was heading for a movie contract, moving up in the world, Frank or no Frank.

While she was away (and as Talese's *Esquire* piece came out), he recorded a monster hit.

The German orchestra leader, songwriter, and record producer Bert Kaempfert is credited with composing the lilting, demonically catchy tune, for the score of a James Garner spy movie called *A Man Could Get Killed*. Kaempfert was a supreme operator in the European music business, a giant of easy listening with a sure ear for an infectious melody: he was not only the first man to record the Beatles (backing the singer Tony Sheridan on a rockin' cover of the old chestnut "My Bonnie") but the composer of Nat King Cole's lamentable but chart-topping final hit, "L-O-V-E."

When Reprise's Jimmy Bowen first heard Kaempfert's new tune, he sat up and took notice. "I said, 'Man, get me the lyric on that, and I'll do it with Sinatra.' I'd never said that to anybody because, obviously, nobody knows what Frank is going to do till he says what he's going to do. [But] I knew that melody [would be a hit]. So they sent me a couple of lyrics I didn't like, but then finally they got me one that I thought was right. And we went in and did that song."

The song was "Strangers in the Night," and Sinatra hated it the minute he heard it.

"I don't want to sing this," he told Sarge Weiss, who first brought him the sheet music. "It's a piece of shit."

But he was conflicted. Throughout the 1950s and 1960s, Frank had been a more reliable seller of albums than of singles: where the latter were concerned, he hadn't even scratched the stratosphere since 1956, with "Hey! Jealous Lover," a number 6. (His last number 1 single had been "Five Minutes More" in 1946.) He wanted back.

And Jimmy Bowen knew how to make hit singles; Bowen and the arranger Ernie Freeman had put Frank back on the *Billboard* singles charts, in a modest way, with "Softly, as I Leave You," then Bowen and Freeman had given Dean a number 1 with "Everybody Loves Somebody." And as much as Frank loved Dean (and as much as he loved Nancy junior, who was kicking ass worldwide with "These Boots Are Made for Walkin'"), Frank badly wanted to be back atop the pops.

He decided to record the thing.

Freeman wrote an arrangement, and the date was set at United Recording for April 11. Between the month with Basie at the Sands and a subsequent gig at the Fontainebleau, Sinatra hadn't set foot in the studios for four months.

On Sunday night, April 10, Jimmy Bowen went to dinner at Martoni's, a Hollywood pasta restaurant popular in the music industry, and ran into the singer Jack Jones—the guy Frank had touted, in his *Life* piece, as having real breakout potential. Jones told Bowen how excited he was about a single he'd just recorded: "Strangers in the Night." Copies had already been mailed out to all the leading radio stations. "I must have turned white," Bowen recalled. "My heart started pounding. I mumbled something like, 'Yeah, well, great. Good luck with it.'"

He phoned Sinatra.

"I don't give a damn if *God* recorded it, we're gonna do it!" Frank said.

He did it. With one hitch: two-thirds of the way through, there was a difficult modulation—a halftone-up key change that Frank couldn't quite (or didn't really want to) get the hang of. Bowen suggested an ingenious solution: "Frank, sing it right up to the key change and cut. Then we'll give you a bell tone and we'll go from there in the new key to the end."

It worked. Bowen then "set up an all-night mastering session to follow Sinatra's recording," Stan Cornyn writes. The producer then made a couple dozen quick dubs—acetates—of the single. In the meantime,

> Sinatra called Ostin to describe plainly about how he'd broken his back to make the record and wanted it out. Now. Eight hundred dollars in twenties set aside for spiffs ("gratuities" to make sure things got done). Runners heading down to LAX, setting up "need a favor" courier duties with stewardesses heading off across America. For a twenty, they'd take a package with the Sinatra acetate in it to, say, O'Hare, where they'd be met with Reprise's Chicago promotion man. Another twenty and thanks and a cab to Chicago's Top Forty program director and hand over the package with "For you. From Frank." Jack Jones got leveled, flatter than the Death Valley Freeway.

It was good to be king, even better to know how to work the angles.

———

He could make almost anything work, especially when he was in great voice. As the strings swooped and swirled and the rhythm guitar (Glen Campbell played on the session) chink-a-chink-a-chinked insistently behind him, Sinatra sang the goopy lyric with the conviction of a man who wanted a big hit with his whole heart, and somehow—by now, after thirty years onstage, he had mastered the sorcery—he made the dumb thing work.

After the insult of the final couplet—

> *It turned out so right*
> *For strangers in the night*

—he finally began to have a little fun with it, scatting,

> *Dooby dooby doo*
> *Doo doo doo-bee ya*
> *Da da da da da ya ya ya.*

Sinatra would hate "Strangers in the Night" ever after. "He thought it was about two fags in a bar!" said Warner-Reprise's Joe Smith. (Singing it for audiences, he sometimes changed the lyric "Love was just a glance away/a warm embracing dance away" to "a lonesome pair of pants away.") In 1975, in a concert in Jerusalem, Frank would introduce it thus: "Here's a song that I cannot stand. I just cannot stand this song. But what the hell."

What the hell indeed. The song hit the *Billboard* charts on May 7, joining fellow new entries "I Am a Rock" by Simon & Garfunkel, "Did You Ever Have to Make Up Your Mind?" by the Lovin' Spoonful, and "Come Running Back" by Dean Martin. Two months later, it reached number 1, overthrowing the Beatles' "Paperback Writer," which had unseated the Rolling Stones' "Paint It Black." In the U.K., it sat atop the singles charts for three weeks that summer.

He had shown Dean and Nancy who was boss. Dooby dooby doo was the new ring-a-ding-ding.

Meanwhile, Mia continued to have a merry time without him. "Just as predicted, director Mike Nichols and Mia Farrow got together as soon as he returned from Europe," columnist Jack O'Brian wrote in early May. "They were at the Cocoanut Grove with the Tony Newleys and the Rex Harrisons . . . and naturally, they showed up later at the Daisy Club."

Frank, always an assiduous reader of the gossip columns, paid attention. "That's not so good," he told a friend at Jilly's. "I think I'm gonna have to be the one to straighten this out with Mia. Can you believe that? Sinatra on his knees?"

She was playing Ava's game, enjoying herself publicly, flaunting other lovers in his face. He couldn't dominate her, and it excited him unspeakably.

The night she came back to Los Angeles, a phone call from Frank in Las Vegas woke her from a sound sleep, Farrow recalled. As she slowly gained consciousness, she found herself agreeing to get on his plane and fly to him the next night. They began to plan a future together, against formidable obstacles. Both of them were needy and complicated people, she writes; neither of them was especially self-aware. What they did know about themselves, they had trouble saying: "Blindly we sought completion in each other."

Hardly a recipe for a lasting union. But for the moment, she had his complete attention.

Another union, a far more important one, was coming to an end, though neither Sinatra nor Riddle knew it at the time. In May, they recorded what was to be their last full album together, a project originally slated for a later date but now rushed into production to capitalize on the huge success of the new single. Naturally, the album would be called *Strangers in the Night.*

Nelson hadn't arranged the title song, but the rest of the material, with the exception of Frank's ill-conceived and halfhearted cover of the Petula Clark hit "Downtown," would be as sublime as "Strangers" was ridiculous.

The LP was subtitled *Frank Sinatra Sings for Moderns,* and even though only half the songs were of 1960s vintage, the feeling throughout was light, upbeat, free—Riddle in a new key, as symbolized by his use of a hip, Basie-esque organ (the Count often doubled on the instrument) on several numbers, most notably the sublime "Summer Wind" and an equally gorgeous remake of Sinatra's first big hit, 1939's "All or Nothing at All."

"Summer Wind" was a 1965 German pop song by Heinz Meier, translated into pure poetry by Johnny Mercer:

Like painted kites, those days and nights
Went flying by

The androgynous-voiced Wayne Newton had had a breezy minor hit with the tune, but in Frank and Nelson's hands it became something altogether different, and magnificent. With Riddle's shimmering strings and Artie Kane's Hammond organ portraying a warm, lazy wind, and Frank's deep, wise baritone hanging as far behind the beat as a leisurely walk along the beach, the song distilled the pure, fleeting essence of summer romance.

As for the updated "All or Nothing at All": a quarter century earlier, it had been pure prewar opera; in the 1966 version, a quick lope with devil-may-care muted horns and raffish organ fills, a wised-up Sinatra gave bittersweet testimony about love's mutability.

The album was a knockout.

It would hit number 1 and stay on the charts for seventy-three weeks, Frank's biggest LP success since *Only the Lonely* in 1958. Yet when it was all said and done, Sinatra decided the Riddle era, as great as it had been, was history.

"There is no particular story, and if there is one, I don't know it," Riddle told the NPR interviewer Robert Windeler not long before the arranger's death in 1985.

[Sinatra] is not inhibited by any particular loyalty . . . He had to think of Frank. I was hurt by it, I felt bad, but I think I was dimly aware that nothing is forever. A different wave of music had come in, and I was closely associated with him in a certain [other] type of music . . . So he moved into other areas. It's almost like one changes one's clothes. I saw him do it with Axel Stordahl, my favorite; I should have realized that it would be my turn. He just moved on.

His restlessness—in his art, in his personal relations, in everything—was his genius and his illness, and a permanent condition.

———

No more Mike Nichols. By the beginning of June, Frank and Mia were seen around Hollywood, "looking madly devoted and happy," according to Earl Wilson, and the marriage rumors began all over again. And on the fifth and sixth, that other devoted couple, Frank and Nancy junior, taped a new TV special, *A Man and His Music Part II*, at NBC Studios in Burbank. The shy and mousy Little Nancy had now transformed into a vamp in pink fringed minidress and pink go-go boots, her hair big and blond and her eyes slitted knowingly.

But still the Daddy's Girl act (which of course was not entirely an act) persisted. Striding out onto the op art set and throwing those boots apart boldly, she sang an oddly creepy intro—

My pa can light my room at night
With just his being near
And make a fearful dream all right
By grinning ear to ear

—before a smash cut revealed a tuxed Frank, belting out "Yes Sir, That's My Baby," which then turned into an oddly incestuous duet.

Nevertheless, it was a smooth and entertaining television hour, and Frank seemed to be having a grand time, with both Nelson Riddle and Gordon Jenkins on hand to conduct their respective segments.

June's blissful beginning made the events of the night of the seventh and eighth all the more strange.

Dean Martin turned forty-nine on the seventh, and late that night Frank took his pal and eight other people, including Jilly Rizzo, Richard Conte, and three women (Mia not among them), to celebrate at the Polo Lounge of the Beverly Hills Hotel. In an adjacent banquette sat fifty-four-year-old Frederick Weisman, the president of Hunt's Foods (and brother-in-law of the philanthropist and art collector Norton Simon), and Franklin Fox, a Boston businessman. The men had come to the Polo Lounge for a drink in honor of their two children, who were about to be married, but soon the commotion from the next booth made conversation impossible. Weisman leaned over and asked the group if they could keep it down and also asked them to tone down their language.

Frank gave Weisman a withering look. "You're out of line, buddy," he said. "I don't think you ought to be sitting there with your glasses on talking to me like that."

As Fox later recalled, Sinatra then made an anti-Semitic remark.

Weisman stood and took exception, but by now Frank and Dean and their party were starting to leave. A moment later, though, Frank turned and came back to Weisman's table.

"He came back to vent his anger and Fred stood up," Fox remembered. "My efforts were simply to keep Sinatra away from him and I did that by sidearming him. I was standing in front of Fred when Sinatra threw the telephone . . . Dean Martin was trying to get him out of there, and the next thing I knew Fred was lying on the ground, and Sinatra and his party had walked out. I was trying to help Fred on the floor . . . When we weren't able to revive him, we called an ambulance and he was carried out of the room on a stretcher."

George Jacobs tells a different story, saying that the telephone in question— "one of the phones the Polo Lounge was famous for parvenus wanting to be paged on"—was not thrown by Sinatra but used as a weapon by Jilly, who bashed Weisman's head repeatedly. Still another account had the attack occurring in the valet parking area outside. And years later, Dean Martin's ex-wife Jeanne insisted that it was Frank who had struck Weisman.

In any case, Sinatra and Martin were long gone by the time the police arrived, Frank to Palm Springs, Dean to Lake Tahoe. And Frederick Weisman, his skull fractured, lay unconscious in the intensive-care unit of Cedars-Sinai Medical Center, not expected to live.

In the immediate aftermath of the incident, Beverly Hills police chief Clinton Anderson publicly embarrassed Frank, telling reporters, "Sinatra has been in hiding, but we'll get him. We want to find out the cause of the fight and the physical condition of Weisman at the time."

Frank called Anderson and told him the fight had been Weisman's fault. The businessman had cursed at him, then hit him, then fallen to the floor, Frank said; "I at no time saw anyone hit him and I certainly did not."

Frank was terrified. "Now I've gone and done it," he said to a friend. "I really fucked up. If this guy croaks, I'm fucking finished."

Mia had flown to Palm Springs to keep him company, as had Jack Entratter and his wife, Corinne. "That's the only time I think I ever saw that man scared," Corinne Entratter recalled. "For two weeks we all sat there staring at each other. Mia and I tried to learn how to play backgammon. Nobody went anywhere. We were like prisoners . . . Nobody knew how it would come out."

Weisman regained consciousness seventy-two hours later, but his condition remained serious, and Frank remained guilty and scared. According to a friend of Farrow's, she and Sinatra argued when she told him that what had happened in the Polo Lounge had probably not been his fault. The adverb disturbed him.

By the twenty-seventh, Weisman was able to talk to the police about the incident, but he remembered nothing after the moment he was struck. This of course implies that he would have remembered who struck him. But due to the conflicting stories and lack of evidence—and, according to one source, threatening phone calls—his family decided not to pursue criminal charges against Sinatra. George Jacobs claimed that Frank paid Weisman "millions" in hush money, although Weisman's brother said at the time, "There's nothing to settle. We just want to forget it ever happened." On June 30, the Los Angeles district attorney closed the investigation.

Sinatra was enormously relieved, and with relief came a kind of euphoria. Farrow was not surprised, she recalled, when, one morning in Palm Springs, Frank led her outside, clasped her hands, and asked her to marry him. "In the closing space between us," she writes, "I placed all the hope of my lifetime."

He went to Billy Ruser's in Beverly Hills—the same store where he'd bought Ava emerald earrings he couldn't afford in 1953—and paid $85,000 for a nine-carat diamond ring. He was headed to Europe to start making a new movie for Warner's (as it turned out, it would be his last film for the studio), a spy picture called *The Naked Runner*. Sinatra was to play an ex-assassin for the OSS who is forced back into action when his son is kidnapped—a plot twist that might have given Frank pause but didn't. He asked Mia to come with him to New York before he left.

As they flew east in his Learjet, Farrow recalled, Frank was, as was his wont, pushing her to eat. He urged her to try the dessert. Under the cake was a little box, and in the box was an engagement ring with a huge pear-shaped diamond. He had to tell her which finger to put it on. This, Mia thought, was a ring she'd better not swallow.

They spent the Fourth of July weekend at the Cerfs' in Mount Kisco—"I don't have a recollection of burning passion," Christopher Cerf recalled, "but he was very, very attentive to her"—and then Sinatra flew on to London with George Jacobs, Jimmy Van Heusen, and Brad Dexter (now a vice president of Artanis Productions as well as *The Naked Runner*'s producer) for company, but without Mia.

It was the greatest culture clash London had ever seen. While the Beatles and the Stones, just then shifting into psychedelic mode, strode the streets of the British capital in tinted granny glasses and feather boas and great bird's nests of hair, the toupeed little American who'd kicked them off the top of the charts jetted in and took over the town.

Sinatra rented a big apartment in Grosvenor Square, across from the American embassy, and, between commuting to Shepperton Studios to make the movie, spent his evenings at the Playboy Club and befriending the locals: "countless Mia-like waifs in their Biba miniskirts and Mary Quant tights strutting their great stuff on the King's Road. This was heaven on earth for leg men," George Jacobs wrote. Chester, in his time-honored fashion, made sure Frank didn't lack for female companionship.

Back in New York, in the middle of a heat wave, Farrow was letting the world know what a hot commodity she'd become. On July 7, she finally announced she was leaving *Peyton Place* and signing with 20th Century Fox. Her asking price for a starring movie role was $200,000. On Sunday night, July 10, she hobbled into P. J. Clarke's, the celebrity watering hole, on crutches—she'd cut her leg badly when she accidentally sat on a pair of scissors in her mother's apartment—but beaming as she flashed her new rock. "It's a friendship ring from Frank," she said, her smile suggesting that no one should mistake the enormous piece of ice on her finger for anything but exactly what it really was.

Her mother was concerned—first, that Mia was rushing into this ill-considered union ("If Mr. Sinatra is going to marry anyone," the fifty-four-year-old Maureen O'Sullivan had said the previous year, "he ought to marry me!"), and second, that she was going to embarrass herself. Lauren Bacall had famously scuttled her chances of marriage to Frank, and wound up publicly humiliated, by mentioning their engagement before he'd officially sanctioned it. O'Sullivan phoned Sinatra in London and put it to him straight: What could be said publicly about the nine-carat diamond on her daughter's finger?

Frank thought for a moment before answering. Mia could announce the engagement, he said, but not a definite date for the wedding. O'Sullivan summoned up her dignity as a grande dame and a mother. Couldn't he do any better than that?

All right, Sinatra said. Sometime between Thanksgiving and Christmas.

Maureen O'Sullivan let the world know on July 14. "I couldn't be more delighted," she told the Associated Press. "Frank is a wonderful person and I know they'll be very happy together." The age difference didn't matter, she insisted. "I know people who are antiques at 35 and others who can watusi at 70. Frank has always been absolutely sweet when I've seen him," she said, not very convincingly.

Back in Los Angeles, Farrow found herself the biggest story around. Photographers were camped out around her house; she had to crawl on the floor to avoid being seen. She phoned Frank and asked him what to do. "Let's get married right away," he told her. They would meet in Vegas.

Brad Dexter told a different story. The night of the announcement, he recalled, after having dinner and playing blackjack at the Colony, a London gambling club managed by Sinatra's old pal George Raft, Frank asked Dexter what he thought of the engagement.

Dexter didn't hold back. "It's too big an age difference, Frank," he said. "You're talking about thirty years in age. It doesn't make sense. When she's forty you'll be seventy, but if that's what you want, go ahead and marry the girl."

"The age business doesn't mean a thing," Sinatra contended. "Besides, she's a good kid and I'm lonely. I need somebody."

"I know you're lonely, but I think you're confusing the love you have for your son with what you feel about Mia. Junior won't respond to you, but Mia does." Dexter then told Frank that he ought to consult a psychiatrist.

"He went crazy," Dexter recalled. "Went ape, began to tear up the apartment on Grosvenor Square, busted lamps, turned the table over."

Still furious, Frank picked up the phone and called Jack Entratter in Las Vegas. "Make all the arrangements," he told him, "because I'm leaving London tomorrow and Mia and I are getting married."

———

Don Digilio, the managing editor of the *Las Vegas Review-Journal,* had been covering the town for a long time. He knew Jack Entratter as he knew all the casino managers, and somehow he got wind from an unidentified source that the wedding would not take place between Thanksgiving and Christmas as Frank had vaguely said, but at 5:30 p.m. on Tuesday, July 19, at the Sands Hotel. The source told Digilio, strangely, that "the ceremony would definitely take place unless an emergency occurred or news stories brought newsmen and photographers to the hotel." The source further said that Sinatra wanted the wedding kept secret until after the ceremony. The news appeared on the front pages of many papers on the morning of the nineteenth, and the world's press quickly descended on Las Vegas.

———

The next day, Farrow writes, she put on a white suit, and Bill and Edie Goetz picked her up and they flew to Vegas on Frank's plane. She was to tell no one about the wedding, he'd commanded; even Nancy and Tina didn't know. Mia worried about how hurt her mother was going to be—and wondered how the news had leaked to the press. She found Frank in his suite at the Sands, look-ing handsome in his dark suit. Supercharged with emotion, they burst into laughter—and then were unable to look at each other.

Sinatra's primary feeling on the flight from New York to Vegas seems to have been dread. He didn't drink much aboard the Lear Jet, his valet recalled, but he chain-smoked and "looked grim, as if he were on his way to major surgery, or his own execution." He hadn't told his family about the wedding, dreading their finding out before he had a chance to let them know himself but not realizing the news had already leaked.

He had informed Ava, however. A number of sources, including Gardner's biographer Lee Server, say that Frank had George Jacobs phone her with the news in London, shortly before the ceremony. Strikingly, though, Jacobs's memoir, which makes much of the valet's friendly relationship with the love of his boss's life, makes no reference to such a call. And equally strikingly, Randy Taraborrelli adduces "a close friend" of Ava's, one Lucille Wellman—unmentioned in Server's book—who claimed Gardner had told her that Frank phoned himself, right from the Sands, just before the ceremony, "upset and nervous" and hoping, aloud, that he wasn't making a big mistake. According to Wellman, Ava advised Sinatra to rethink his decision, and he told her, "It's too late, baby. The judge is standing right there." He is then said to have said, "No matter how I feel about this young chick . . . I will always love you."

But on one fact accounts agree: when Ava heard the news, she cried and couldn't stop crying.

––––––––

The civil ceremony, Judge William Compton presiding, took place precisely at 5:30 p.m. in the living room of Jack Entratter's suite and took all of four minutes. Frank wore his three-piece suit, an unfortunate visual echo from *Marriage on the Rocks;* Mia wore a short, sheer white dress with caftan sleeves. It was a toss-up whose hair was shorter. Bill and Edie Goetz were best man and matron of honor; Entratter gave the bride away. Adding to the bizarreness of the occasion was the presence of Red Skelton, who was performing at the Sands and who, as Farrow noted without further comment, "had just shot his wife." (The newspapers reported that early that morning, a .38 pistol in the Skeltons' suite had "accidentally discharged," the bullet hitting Georgia Skel-ton in the left breast. No criminal charge was ever filed.)

As for the bride and groom, "I've never seen such anxiety before," Edie Goetz remembered. "They were both so nervous you couldn't believe it. Frank's face was flushed and he twitched nervously as they repeated their vows."

"Mr. S looked nervous and shell-shocked," George Jacobs concurred.

"Mia looked radiant, as if she had won the Irish Sweepstakes. The girl had gotten her man, at last. Now the even harder part was figuring out how to keep him."

"This is the happiest day of my life," Farrow said as she hugged Edie Goetz.

There were champagne toasts—Mia said "thank you"—and Frank finally broke into a smile. He took his new wife by the hand and led her from the air-conditioned room to the patio of Entratter's Japanese garden, where—after an aide announced, "Still photographers and reporters only," barring television crews lest Sinatra's family find out about the wedding on TV before he had a chance to tell them about it—a crowd of newsmen had gathered in the 107-degree heat. Someone noticed that Mia hadn't given Frank a ring.

"How are you, baby," he asked Farrow. "My bride!" he announced.

As dozens of shutters clicked and the journalists began to blurt out questions, he held up a hand. "This is a big day, fellas," he said. "I can't think of what to say. We just decided to get married last week. We were both out west, it seemed right, and we're in love, and it was logical."

As logical as Lewis Carroll. A reporter piped up. "Will Mia accompany you to London?"

"Oh, yes, by all means, yes," Sinatra replied.

———

Frank had evidently made another call before the ceremony. At 5:30 p.m. on the nineteenth, Tina Sinatra recalled, she was dropping her friends Deana and Dino Martin off in their driveway when "Uncle Dean beckoned me inside,"

Frank and Mia, the Sands, July 19, 1966. "My bride!" Sinatra announced, as dozens of shutters clicked.

she writes. "He took me into his little den, where he'd retreat to watch his golf on TV. He sat me down on his sofa with an Indian blanket, and said, 'I want you to know that your dad is marrying Mia as we speak.'"

She was understandably shocked and hurt at having been kept in the dark. Dean told Tina she'd better go home and tell her mother: the news was going to break any second. But by the time Frank's younger daughter got home, Big Nancy had already received a call from her friend Dorothy Manners.

"My mother was stunned, and insulted that Dad had failed to confide in us," Tina remembered.

> It was the first time we'd been excluded from something important in his life.
>
> An hour or so later, Dad left his reception and called us at Nimes Road . . . I happened to pick up the phone, and he could hear how angry I was.
>
> He said, "I want you to be happy for me—I want you to wish me well."
>
> I said, "I'm too busy resenting you for not telling me." I wouldn't give him my blessing; it was not a pretty conversation. (I'd apologize to him and Mia later.)
>
> Looking back, I can't blame Dad for keeping his secret. He couldn't trust his family because he didn't want to hear what he already knew: that he was nuts. He could go through with the marriage only by living in denial. "I just didn't want anyone ruining it for me," he'd confess to me long afterward.

He sounds like a sulky child. And he was acting like a child: furtive, impulsive, self-involved. But his child bride, wise beyond her years, was just as complicit as he in this strange liaison, and it was surpassingly strange. A Venn diagram of the marriage would have shown a small shaded intersection representing sex and affection; two large areas outside would have remained blank. And antithetical.

———

They cleverly threw the press off their trail, announcing they were flying to New York and going to Los Angeles instead, only not to Frank's house (he was now renting a big place in his old Holmby Hills stomping grounds, just off Sunset Boulevard), but to the Goetzes', where their matron of honor and best man threw them a glittering party. "My brother Patrick and his wife came," Farrow recalled, "and Prudence, Maria [her close friend Maria Roach], and

Lenny Gershe, and my godfather, George Cukor, brought Katharine Hepburn; Spencer Tracy arrived separately. Edward G. Robinson was there, and Dean Martin, Ruth and Garson Kanin, Richard Attenborough, and the Billy Wilders. There was a huge wedding cake."

There were, however, no Sinatras. And no Maureen O'Sullivan.

The newlyweds spent their first night as husband and wife at the Goetzes', then headed to London.

————

Stopping in New York on the way to London, the honeymooners were feted by the Cerfs and Leland Hayward at "21" on the night of July 25. As Frank and Mia emerged from the restaurant, a diminutive *New York Post* photographer named Jerry Engel moved in to get a shot. Wrong move. Sinatra slugged him, knocking his glasses off.

The next night Frank took his bride to dinner at Marty and Dolly's house in Fort Lee, an event also left unrecorded in Farrow's memoir. Dolly had cooked for two days in preparation for the big event: among the blue-collar bric-a-brac, the pictures of the popes and statues of the saints and the artificial cherry tree, the big dinner tables groaned with ravioli, scaloppine, scungilli, lasagna, fettuccine, calamari, osso buco, mortadella, and mounds of cold cuts and sugary desserts. Toots Shor and Joe E. Lewis and Jilly were there, and Roz Russell and Freddie Brisson, and Mia's girlhood friend Liza Minnelli, who smoked little cigars. Farrow ate only salad and, seemingly intimidated by the boisterous company, said as little as Marty Sinatra. Dolly, who had always been crazy about Ava and still was, was underwhelmed. "This one don't talk," she told a friend. "She don't eat. What's she do?"

And, taking George Jacobs aside: "She's a little nothing. Is that the best he can do?"

————

She had underestimated her, of course: Mia was formidably intelligent, graceful, and willful—and ambitious. "She was a voracious reader with a sprightly intelligence and an active imagination," wrote Tina, who was drawn to her as Nancy junior (who felt threatened and competitive, at least at first) was not.

> She was interesting and interested in what was going on around her. If anything, Mia brought something extra to the table: a firm set of [liberal] politics.
>
> Mia could also be silly, and Dad loved silly. She possessed an intriguing physical dexterity; rather than simply walk through a room, she'd

dance through it. And she had a flair for being part of a group—she was both entertaining and easy to entertain. Mia could make you feel like you were the only one in the vicinity worth listening to.

It wasn't hard to see how Dad could have fallen in love with her.

Naturally, Tina Sinatra was speaking not objectively but from the point of view of a young woman three years Mia Farrow's junior. (And as a middle-aged woman writing a memoir, she was also spinning a political line against her father's fourth wife, Barbara Marx, who had become her bitter enemy.) And Farrow was not just being wisely political in cultivating Tina but naturally drawn to people her own age.

———

Which proved to be an immediate problem when they got back to London. "Mia knew far more people in England than Frank, including half the rock stars on the radio, and she wanted to see all of them," Jacobs recalled. "Mr. S wanted to see all of them dead, so that was a big conflict."

Sinatra now refused to go out, fearing they'd run into Farrow's hip young friends. While London was swinging like mad, she was under a kind of house arrest. Frank's Grosvenor Square apartment was a domain of "shiny green silks with lots of tassels, little glass-top tables, and jade ashtrays," she wrote, with a prisoner's keen eye for her fuddy-duddy surroundings. The company was just as deadly. When he was on the set, his London friends' wives would pop by unannounced to look in on her or to try to take her shopping—Mia would hide in the bedroom while her secretary fended them off.

The couple spent a lot of time in the bedroom, Jacobs recalled, but outside it weren't as overtly affectionate as blissful newlyweds should be. His boss seemed testy and unfocused, he said. On weekends, to keep Mia from bad influences, Frank jetted her away from London to visit more rich and elderly friends, like Jack Warner (aged seventy-four), business magnate Loel Guinness (sixty), and *My Fair Lady* composer Fritz Loewe (sixty-five). Aboard Loewe's yacht, she ate flower-petal sandwiches.

Mia wasn't the only one who was bored. Sinatra had gone into *The Naked Runner* with a reasonable degree of commitment—God knew he needed a movie hit after the consecutive disasters of *Marriage on the Rocks* and *Assault on a Queen* (which had been released in mid-June to yawns from audiences and critics alike)—but he had lost interest. He was still furious at Brad Dexter for calling him out on his ill-considered marriage and had grown sick of England. After a helicopter transporting him to a location outside London became lost in a fog, making him forty-five minutes late to the set, Frank went into a rage and demanded the entire production be moved to Palm Springs—a strange idea for a spy film largely set in gray East Germany. When Sinatra stalked off, sulking and refusing to work, director Sidney Furie went him one better, bursting into tears, jumping into his jeep, and speeding away. Dexter had to use all his diplomatic skills to get star and director to finish the U.K. shoot.

————

At the end of August, filming of *The Naked Runner* moved to Copenhagen. Equilibrium had been more or less restored, and shooting was on schedule. After a couple of days' work, Sinatra told Dexter he wanted to take the weekend off to fly to Los Angeles and host a fund-raiser for California's governor, Pat Brown, who was running for a third term against the Republican challenger, Ronald Reagan. Frank had known Reagan since the 1940s and had no use for him, or his wife, the former actress Nancy Davis. "He hated the guy, just hated him," said a former girlfriend of Jimmy Van Heusen's. "We'd be at some party, and if the Reagans arrived, Frank would snap his fingers and say, 'C'mon, Chester. We're leaving. I can't stand that fucking Ronnie. He's such a bore. Every time you get near the bastard he makes a speech and he never knows what he's talking about.'"

Beginning in the late 1930s, Reagan had had a middling career as a movie actor (*Knute Rockne All American, Kings Row, Bedtime for Bonzo*); like many other movie careers, it faded in the 1950s with the rise of television. Bowing to the tide, he took a job as host of the drama series *General Electric Theater* in 1954. The sponsors were intensely politically conservative, and soon Reagan, who had been a lifelong Democrat (though in the late 1940s he'd secretly informed to the FBI on Communist sympathizers in Hollywood), took a sharp turn to the right. He was a conservative president of the Screen Actors Guild and a fervent and powerful supporter of Barry Goldwater in the 1964 presidential election.

All this was, of course, anathema to the FDR Democrat Sinatra; he also hated Reagan's genial, folksy manner ("I couldn't stand listening to his gee whiz, golly shucks crap"). Frank "swore he'd move out of California if Reagan ever got elected to public office," Peter Lawford recalled.

Brad Dexter, who felt similarly about Reagan, freely assented to Sinatra's rhetorical request for a weekend off. Thus began the bizarre endgame of *The Naked Runner*.

Sidney Furie comfortably shot around Frank for several days. Dexter "then received a communication from Mickey Rudin, the star's lawyer, to the effect that Sinatra would not be returning to Copenhagen," writes Sinatra film historian Daniel O'Brien.

His outstanding scenes could be filmed on a Los Angeles soundstage, much as he'd finished off the otherwise Spanish-shot *Pride
and the Passion* a decade earlier. [But] instead of dispatching the
existing *Runner* footage to Warner, as requested by Rudin, Dexter
refused to follow Sinatra's orders. Citing the existing post-production
contracts back in England, he and Furie chose to complete the film
without its star. Reworking the script to minimize the number of
essential Sinatra scenes left unshot, producer and director filmed the
required material with a double, subsequently editing in close-ups
of the star taken from existing footage. When Rudin showed up in
person to reiterate Sinatra's ultimatum, Dexter declined to comply,
opting instead to deliver the finished film to Jack Warner in person
two months later.

When Dexter walked into the Sinatra offices on the Warner Bros. lot, Milt
Krasny, the vice president of Sinatra Enterprises, said that Mickey Rudin had
instructed him to inform Dexter that he was fired from the picture. He was to
pack his things and leave the lot immediately. Saying he would allow only one
man to fire him, Dexter phoned Frank in Palm Springs.

It was 9:00 a.m., and George Jacobs answered, saying Sinatra was asleep.
Dexter told Jacobs to wake him. A couple of minutes later, Frank came on the
line and in a sleepy voice said, "How are you? How was the flight? You sure
took your time in getting back here."

Dexter told Sinatra the movie was ready for him to view but that he'd just
been told he was fired. "I'm not taking orders from any of your lackeys," he
said. "If you want to fire me, fire me, but I want to get it straight from you—no
one else. Do you understand, Frank?" There was a long silence, then a click.
Sinatra had hung up.

Dexter refused to accept his firing, fine-tuning the release print and
demanding the $15,000 remaining of his $50,000 producer's fee. He never got
the money. "Questioned about the incident, Sinatra publicist Jim Mahoney
argued that Dexter had brought his dismissal upon himself," O'Brien writes.
"Not only had the novice producer hijacked the film, he wouldn't even let
Sinatra look at the rough cut. Whatever the truth of these various allegations,
the net result was a film almost unreleasable."

"He was the producer, of course, but he seemed to have forgotten it was
Frank who gave him the job," Mahoney said of Dexter. "Anyway, that was the
end of it."

And that was the end of Brad Dexter, as far as Frank was concerned. The
greatest good deed of all could not go unpunished. "Brad didn't really save my

life," Sinatra later said of his near drowning in Hawaii. "It was an old guy on a surfboard."

———

On September 7, Frank hosted a fund-raiser for Pat Brown at San Francisco's Civic Auditorium. Joey Bishop emceed; Dean Martin, Connie Francis, Rowan and Martin, the Step Brothers, Trini Lopez, and Ella Fitzgerald were also on the bill. Outside the building, "a straggly line of creepy looking, bare foot anti-war marchers schlepped around . . . making a pathetic attempt at singing some song they didn't know the words or tune to," wrote *San Mateo Times* columnist Barbara Bladen. No such unseemliness troubled the proceedings inside, which were Vegas slick. "Mia Farrow Sinatra, whose close cropped coiffure shone in the spotlight like a bald spot . . . got a big round of applause, probably for having snagged The Leader," Bladen wrote.

The newlyweds house-hunted that September, a process that drove Mia to despair. The realtor was showing them Beverly Hills mansions, she writes, and she couldn't picture herself in any of them. Frank's patience was wearing thin, and she was unable to say why she was so upset. After a while they saw an English Tudor–style house, not too aggressively posh, that appealed to both of them. Frank bought it.

It was a five-bedroom, five-and-a-half-bath fake English country home cozily nestled in a wooded bend of Copa de Oro Road, just north of Sunset in Bel Air. Copa de Oro—Spanish for "cup of gold." Dick Powell and June Allyson had lived in the house in the late 1940s and early 1950s, while Allyson had an affair with Dean Martin. Such was Hollywood domesticity. But Powell and Allyson managed to stay married for eighteen years anyway, until his death in 1963. Frank wasn't thinking on such grand terms. "If I could have one or two good years, that's all I can expect," he'd told Dean just before marrying Mia. He said the same to both his daughters after the wedding.

Still, Frank had never bought a house with Ava. Edie Goetz found the newlyweds a decorator, and they moved in, though settling down wasn't quite on the program. As September turned to October, Frank tended to his busy slate of record and film projects, while Mia, too, actively sought movie work, somewhat to her husband's chagrin.

———

Ava came to New York at the end of September for the world premiere of *The Bible*. The *Daily News* film critic Rex Reed, profiling Gardner for *Esquire*, caught her in a candid mood. Young, prettily handsome, and provocative, Reed was carving out a reputation as a bad boy, shouldering into the ranks of the

New Journalists, and he made sure to take note of the drinking Ava. As the world had long known, Ava plus alcohol equaled great copy, and Reed waited until she'd had plenty of it to ask her about her three famous ex-husbands, Mickey Rooney, Artie Shaw, and Frank Sinatra. Ticking down the list, he finally came to Frank:

> Sinatra? "No comment," she says to her glass.
> A slow count to ten, while she sips her drink. Then, "And Mia Farrow?" The Ava eyes brighten to a soft clubhouse green. The answer comes like so many cats lapping so many saucers of cream. Unprintable.

Interestingly, though, Reed bowdlerized the passage when it was reprinted later in his anthology *Do You Sleep in the Nude?*:

> A slow count to ten, while she sips her drink. Then, "And Mia Farrow?" The Ava eyes brighten to a soft clubhouse green. The answer comes like so many cats lapping so many saucers of cream. "Hah! I always knew Frank would end up in bed with a boy."

According to another source, what Gardner really said was, "I always knew Frank always wanted a boy with a cunt."

And according to two sources, Sinatra was in New York that same weekend, and Farrow was conspicuous by her absence.

The previous spring, a record by the soul singer O. C. Smith had grabbed Frank's attention. The song, a chorus-backed blues taken at a meditative tempo, was called "That's Life." Sinatra liked the number enough that he called Jimmy Bowen into his office and played him Smith's single. "I think we ought to make a record of this, James," he said. "What do you think?"

Bowen, who had now gained Frank's trust by being unafraid to tell him the truth, happened to agree with him. "Absolutely," he said.

In June, Sinatra taped the tune, with a Nelson Riddle arrangement, for his second *Man and His Music* special with Nancy. To the accompaniment of an orchestra and a jumpy blues organ, Frank transformed the soul singer's mellow reading into something tough and canny, rendered in the rascally rasp he had now polished to perfection.

Still, Bowen knew well that a hit single would require something more. He had Ernie Freeman modify Riddle's arrangement considerably, speeding up the tempo and adding a gospel choir backing, à la Ray Charles.

The session for Sinatra's "That's Life" single was set for the night of October 18, in Western Recorders' new state-of-the-art eight-track facility, next door to United Recording on Sunset Boulevard. Neither Jimmy Bowen nor his engineer, Eddie Brackett, had ever cut anything in eight tracks, so they booked the musicians an hour earlier than Sinatra to make sure everything would go smoothly.

But there were technical problems from the beginning, and in the midst of them Frank walked in half an hour early, accompanied by Mia, Mo Ostin, and a contingent of cronies. Even before Sinatra started, he was impatient to leave. "James," he said, "I gotta get this thing done. I got a dinner date I've gotta go to."

"When he was in a hurry, he wasn't thinking chart position," Jimmy Bowen recalled. Sinatra sang the song twice with the orchestra, then came into the booth to listen to the playback. Something bothered Bowen about the takes: the rhythm section was obediently reacting to the beauty of Sinatra's vocal and calming down with him. It wasn't the big, macho sound the producer wanted. Frank looked at Ostin and asked what he thought. "It's great, Frank," Mo said. "Frank shot me a look of impatience," Bowen remembered, "and put me on the spot. 'Well, okay?'"

> I knew this wasn't going to go over real well, but I had to stick to my instincts. That was my job. "Well, not if we really want a killer hit, it isn't. We've got to cut it one more time and make it stronger on the bottom."
>
> Dead silence for what seemed like a minute—but was probably fifteen seconds. Sinatra fixed those cold, steely-blue eyes on me during that silence. The cronies were cringing, thinking I'd lost my marbles. "Let's do it," he mumbled, and headed back out into the studio.

With his back against the wall, Bowen read the riot act to his rhythm section. "Now look, I want you to *stand* on this son of a bitch," he said.

> They went back out and nailed it, just drove the song and gave Sinatra a huge energetic push. Frank was pissed, and you could hear him channeling it when he snarled, "That's life, that's what all the people say." He came off wonderfully intense, and when it ended, he signed off, "Ohh, yeahhh."
>
> Frank turned and walked out the back door. Never said "Thanks," "Good night," "Good job," nothing. His people were still staring at me like, *You have fucked up big-time.* My feeling was, *Screw it, I got what I wanted, which is what he wanted.*

The producer spent the rest of the night mixing the record, finally leaving the studio with an acetate at 4:00 a.m. Bowen also left an acetate to be delivered by hand to Sinatra's house later that day. He went home and fell into an exhausted sleep, only to be awakened some time later by a call from Sinatra. "James," Frank said, "it's just brilliant. Thanks." Then he hung up.

A month later, the song would enter a *Billboard* chart crowded with the likes of the Supremes' "You Keep Me Hangin' On," the Beach Boys' "Good Vibrations," and the Monkees' "Last Train to Clarksville" and muscle its way up to number 4. Seldom had Frank's anger been put to such constructive use.

On November 3, he began a two-week stand at the Sands, accompanied by Antonio Morelli's orchestra, Gordon Jenkins conducting. It was Sinatra's twenty-eighth opening in the Copa Room and his first since marrying Mia Farrow. The standing-room crowd craned their necks as Joe E. Lewis escorted Farrow, who'd let her buzz cut grow out to Peter Pan length, to her ringside seat. Then Lefty delivered the downbeat, and Frank began his act with "The Shadow of Your Smile." He looked straight at his bride as he sang; she gazed back lovingly. She knew the lyrics word for word, she recalled; she breathed along with him. She felt his emotions flow out into the showroom. She was part of his voice, part of him. It was an indescribable thrill to be the one woman, amid a roomful of women each of whom felt he was singing to her, to whom Frank Sinatra really was singing.

The room exploded with applause after every number. (As he performed "Strangers in the Night," he consulted a cheat sheet, because, as he said, "Believe it or not, I never learned the lyrics.") Half a dozen songs later, Sinatra paused, sipped from his glass, stared out at the silently worshipful audience, and introduced a few celebrities: Don Drysdale, Willie Mays, and Leo Durocher; Richard Conte, Andy Williams, and Tina Sinatra—who, having turned eighteen in June, was finally old enough to get in. "Smokey the Bear was supposed to be here tonight," Frank began.

> You all know Smokey. That's Sammy Davis. But he couldn't make it. He has an opening of his own—down in Watts. It's a gas station. He calls it Whitey's. He sells three kinds of gas—regular, ethyl, and burn, baby, burn.

He was referring (in Las Vegas, which was still prehistoric in its racial attitudes) to the summertime 1965 riots in the Watts district of South Los Angeles, disturbances triggered by the African-American residents' unhappiness at their treatment by the Los Angeles Police Department. Though the riots had calmed and not recurred in the summer of 1966, racial unrest, and sporadic violent incidents, continued throughout the city.

"But Sammy's okay," Frank continued.

> He had a wedding anniversary recently, and I sent him a gift—yeah, I sent him and Mai [*sic*] a love seat covered in zebra skin, so when they sit together they won't be so conspicuous . . . Well, let's see. What else is new? Oh, yeah. I got married—she's here.

Mia stood, to an ovation from the audience. "Yeah, I sure got married," Sinatra said. "Well, you see, I had to—I finally found a broad I can cheat on."

It was as though he had slapped her face in front of five hundred people. There was a collective intake of breath: Farrow hung her head and reddened.

Frank tried for a save. "Ain't she pretty?" he said. And then, "I guess I'd better sing. I'm in a lot of trouble."

After his show—it was only midnight; the evening was just getting started—he took Durocher and a few other buddies to the Aladdin to see Joe E. Lewis's set. First, though, Earl Wilson wrote, "he stopped at a blackjack table, got a fistful of $100 chips and won about $3,000, stuffing several big chips in the pocket of a chum who had previously lost." He spent nearly two hours gambling while Mia sat and watched, though her alienation from Las Vegas was now complete. One night around that time, Sheilah Graham looked on as Sinatra gambled heavily in the Sands casino while Farrow waited patiently on the sidelines. Finally, the columnist recalled, "she touched his craps-swinging arm and said, 'Let's go.' He flung her hand off angrily and shouted, 'Look, don't tell me what to do. Don't try to change me.'"

On November 8, Ronald Reagan was elected governor of California, defeating Pat Brown by almost one million votes.

Despite the greatness that *Strangers in the Night* had contained, Jimmy Bowen considered the album retrograde; the last thing he wanted was to build another old-fashioned-feeling (read: Riddle-influenced) Sinatra LP around a hit song he, Bowen, had proudly produced. "We can't do just one thing that's modern and innovative and then go back and do 'Wee Small Hours' for the other nine tunes," he told Frank.

Accordingly, *That's Life,* the album, recorded over two nights in mid-November, contained eight tunes that jibed completely with the title song in composition and production, only they were less interesting. The result was an LP that was, in a formal sense, the mirror image of *Strangers in the Night*: strong title number, weak backup. Even though only some of *That's Life*'s material—the beyond-cheesy "Winchester Cathedral," for example—was completely bad, none of the rest was especially good, or even especially catchy. And outside hit-single territory, the thinness of Ernie Freeman's arranging became all too conspicuous. It was, and is, dispiriting to hear Frank sing "The Impossible Dream" ("That was Mia's request," said Rob Fentress, who attended the session, "and he didn't like the song") against a background of swelling chorus and screechy strings: it was the sonic equivalent of *Assault on a Queen* or *The Naked Runner,* and a listener could be forgiven for wondering whether Sinatra was past it as a singer as well as a movie star.

———

He and Mia went to New York together at Thanksgiving, to see Dolly and Marty, to do some Christmas shopping, and to attend the social event of the year, Truman Capote's Black and White Ball. The air was crisp; Sinatra bought Farrow an early present, a long gray mink coat, as an unspoken apology.

The ball took place on November 28, at the Plaza hotel. Four hundred eighty attended, carefully chosen from the elite of two continents by the pixie-ish author, who was newly rich from the huge success of *In Cold Blood,* his "nonfiction novel" about the 1959 murder of the Clutter family of Holcomb, Kansas.

It was heaven for Capote, his apotheosis in society and the media. He'd invited everyone who was anyone, from the honoree, Katharine Graham, to Alice Roosevelt Longworth and Margaret Truman Daniel and Lynda Bird Johnson, to Henry Ford II and Tallulah Bankhead and Rose Kennedy and Gloria Vanderbilt Cooper and Marianne Moore and the maharani of Jaipur. And, of course, the Cerfs. Christopher Cerf, who remembered the evening as "a black-and-white blur," danced with Mia Farrow, on whom he had a shy crush. "That's one of the highlights—at least from other people's point of view—of my life," he said. Naturally, Frank had sanctioned it.

Farrow's eye mask was a white butterfly; Sinatra's, also appropriate, represented a black cat. Peter Lawford was another invitee. The masks, and the crowd, and the blur, and Capote's painstaking seating arrangement, made it easy for Frank to ignore him completely.

The ball was a real arrival for Truman Capote and another form of arrival—in New York and in glittering political-social-literary society—for Frank Sina-

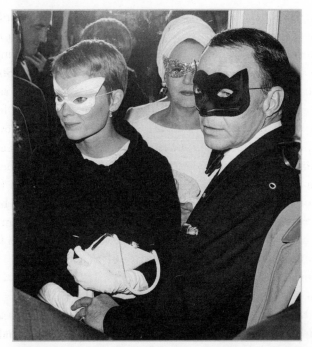

The newlyweds at Truman Capote's Black and White Ball, November 1966. Frank's fifty-first year was a time of short-lived joy and devouring furies.

tra. Even if he had well and truly arrived many years earlier, and again and again in the years since, there was never anything wrong with arriving one more time.

———

Then, two weeks later, another birthday, with the strange and unmagical number fifty-one.

24

||||||||||||

Never fight a Jew in the desert.

—FRANK SINATRA

In December 1966, the Brazilian songwriter Antonio Carlos Jobim was having a few beers with friends in his favorite Rio de Janeiro bar when a waiter brought him a telephone and told him he had a call from the United States and that the caller was Frank Sinatra.

Jobim was shaken but not stunned: Sinatra, the idol of his generation, had first expressed interest in recording his compositions in 1964, the year Stan Getz and João Gilberto's recording of the songwriter's most famous tune, "The Girl from Ipanema" ("Garota de Ipanema"), became an international hit, propelling Brazilian bossa nova—literally, "charming new trend"—to worldwide popularity. The following year, Sinatra's home label, Warner Records, had released an album called *The Wonderful World of Antonio Carlos Jobim,* on which Jobim played (and sang, in a rudimentary but soulful voice) his own songs and Nelson Riddle wrote the arrangements.

When Jobim took the telephone that day in December, Frank told the composer that he would like to make an album with him. The songwriter didn't have to think twice. "It's an honor, I'd love to," he said.

At thirty-nine, Jobim was already a colossus: a unique composer whose influences included Heitor Villa-Lobos, Debussy, and Ravel. His songs, many with lyrics in Brazilian Portuguese by the poet Vinicius de Moraes, were like nobody else's: deceptively simple, faintly melancholy, and iridescently lovely. They hummed with eros and nostalgia and lingered in the ear, comparing favorably with the greatest works in the American Songbook. (The lyrics to a number of his compositions had been translated into English by less-than-stellar writers—Norman Gimbel's all-too-easy-to-parody text to "Girl from Ipanema" was a case in point[*]—but the tunes themselves were strong enough to weather the transformation.[†])

---

[*] See Stephen Sondheim's wicked takeoff, "The Boy From . . . ," from the 1966 Off-Broadway revue *The Mad Show*.

[†] Strikingly, both the Portuguese and the English lyrics to Jobim's greatest song, "Águas de Março" (Waters of March), were written by the composer himself.

Unknown to Jobim, Sinatra was calling at a critical moment in his own career. Maybe Frank had a bad taste in his mouth after "Winchester Cathedral" and "The Impossible Dream"; certainly, as always, he was restlessly seeking fresh inspiration. He had complained that the old giants, the Harry Warrens and the Harold Arlens, weren't turning out songs anymore; he couldn't lean on Cahn and Van Heusen, and Cy Coleman and Carolyn Leigh, forever. He couldn't record standards forever. With rock shaking the foundations of popular music, Sinatra needed something new. What better than the delectable fusion of samba and jazz whose very name spoke of newness?

To underline his wish for change, Frank told Jobim that he wanted Claus Ogerman—the German composer-conductor who had written the charts for the Brazilian's first American LP, 1963's all-instrumental *The Composer of Desafinado, Plays*—to arrange their album. Sinatra asked Jobim if he could get to Los Angeles right away to start working on the arrangements. It was a more or less rhetorical question.

"On the night of Thursday, January 12, 1967, Frank gave a sixty-fifth birthday party for Joe E. Lewis at Jilly's South in Miami Beach," Earl Wilson recalled, omitting to mention that the comic had recently suffered a mild stroke. "It was the wettest party I ever attended."

> The little bride, Mia Farrow, was the hostess. At times she sat on Frank's knee. Frank and Mia made a tour of the room, greeting personally each of the 150 guests, talking with them for a few minutes, making them feel welcome.
>
> "Have you met my girl?" Frank asked the guests, tweaking her on the cheek. He said he would be back in New York in midsummer to film *The Detective*.
>
> What would Mia be doing? No films in Europe! "I don't want to leave my fella," she said, holding his hand.
>
> The happy Sinatras went island-hopping in their private jet, but came back in a week, with Mia denying rumors that she was pregnant and letting it be known that she would make her first major movie with a starring role, *A Dandy in Aspic*.

The couple's Caribbean sojourn might have been happy—they stayed at Claudette Colbert's place on Barbados—but their return was less so: soon after Frank landed in Miami, he was handed a subpoena to testify before a federal grand jury investigating profit skimming at Nevada gambling casinos.

And Mia's film would be shot in Europe.

While Frank and Mia sunned on Barbados, Jobim flew to Los Angeles and went to work with Claus Ogerman, who had been installed by Sinatra's people in a suite with a piano at the Beverly Hills Hotel. There were to be seven Jobim songs on the album: "The Girl from Ipanema," "Dindi," "Quiet Nights of Quiet Stars (Corcovado)," "Meditation (Meditação)," "If You Never Come to Me (Inútil Paisagem)," "How Insensitive (Insensatez)," and "Once I Loved (O Amor em Paz)."

Frank had also decided to include three American tunes, updated with a bossa nova beat: Irving Berlin's "Change Partners," Cole Porter's "I Concentrate on You," and "Baubles, Bangles, and Beads," adapted from a theme by Alexander Borodin by Bob Wright and George Forrest for the 1953 Broadway musical *Kismet*. (Sinatra had recorded the last once before, at a brassy gallop, on 1959's *Come Dance with Me!*) Ogerman would arrange these three without Jobim's input.

The work was pleasant and quick. The composer and the arranger knew each other well, got along famously, and were not averse to mixing business with pleasure. There were many late dinners with champagne at Chasen's—on Frank's tab, of course—and Ogerman wrote the orchestrations afterward, starting at midnight and working into the wee small hours, producing arrangements that startled Sinatra's longtime copyist Vern Yocum.

"When he picked up the charts at the Beverly Hills Hotel, he looked at them and he looked at me and he said, 'Claus, do you think this is going to work?'" Ogerman recalled. "The pages looked so empty to him. He was used to having full scores, movie scores or whatever, and my scores were really light. But that is also a plus, because if you write too much, you get in the way of the performer."

It was a lesson Frank had taught Nelson Riddle at the beginning of their relationship; Ogerman knew it intuitively, and he had worked with Jobim before. What he had in mind was nothing less than a revolutionary album, one that would use the Brazilian's quiet genius to bring out Sinatra's sublime artistry, an LP that would achieve great power with as little ornamentation as possible.

In the meantime, Frank had returned to Los Angeles and thoroughly rehearsed the new material with Bill Miller. He also went into training, cutting back on his drinking and smoking, getting as much rest as possible, and deploying his old voice-conditioning trick, swimming laps underwater, to build his lung capacity.

(On January 26, he took a side trip to Las Vegas to testify in a closed-door hearing before the federal grand jury, appearing relaxed and confident as he stepped from a limousine with his attorney Rudin, the Associated Press reported. Sinatra's remarks to the grand jury—which handed down no indictments—remained sealed.)

Frank was no less relaxed and confident when he walked into Western Recorders on the night of the thirtieth. "He really knew every word and every nuance and every tone, every melody, perfectly," Ogerman remembered. "I think he said it once—'I have to be as good as or maybe better than every musician in the studio.' That was his goal. So he prepared himself."

On the other hand, the composer, referred to poetically by Stan Cornyn in the album's liner notes as "this slight and tousled boy-man, speaking softly while about him rushes a world too fast," was unprepared for meeting his idol. "This man is Mount Everest for a songwriter," Jobim had admitted to the lyricist Gene Lees. "He was in awe of Frank," Lee Herschberg, the recording engineer who worked on the date, said of the shy Brazilian. "Maybe too much, *ja,*" Claus Ogerman agreed.

But Jobim quickly relaxed, along with everyone else in the studio, including Frank. "Sinatra, I think, understood that he had to be, how do you say, joyful, to make life easier for all of us," Ogerman said. "It was a very pleasant atmosphere."

And a very quiet one. Like the charts, the instrumentation was sparse: ten violins, four cello, one trombone, three flutes. A piano (Miller), a double bass,

Sinatra and Antonio Carlos Jobim, 1967. In the songs and the personality of the shy Brazilian genius, Frank found a serenity that eluded him elsewhere. The two made sublime art together.

drums (played by a Brazilian named Dom Um Romão), and Jobim on guitar. The sessions began "like the World Soft Championships," Cornyn wrote in his liner notes. "And Sinatra makes a joke about all this. 'I haven't sung so soft since I had the laryngitis.'"

"Very gentle with this piece, fellas," Frank told the string players, just before recording "How Insensitive."

He was serious. He had a way of rising to the occasion among those he respected, and the presence of the shy and quiet Brazilian poet and the serious German arranger-conductor calmed him. As did the music itself. "The arrangements were just spectacular," Lee Herschberg said. "It was a simple album to make, actually; it went very quickly." The musicians, some of the cream of L.A. studio talent, "were running like a Rolls-Royce, with very little repeats," Ogerman remembered. "One or two takes, and this was it."

Behind the double glass of the control booth, a small crowd—Sonny Burke, Lee Herschberg, Stan Cornyn, Warner Records executive Mike Maitland, Mia Farrow, Nancy Sinatra, and Keely Smith, among others; "gold cuff-links, Revlon red fake nails, Countess Mara ties," in Cornyn's words—looked on in wonderment as Sinatra sang with an exquisite tenderness he hadn't tapped since *Wee Small Hours,* twelve years before.

After the final session, the beautiful album in the can, Sinatra took a small group of the guys—Jobim and Ogerman and Dom Um Romão, Mo Ostin and Mike Maitland and Sonny Burke—out for a late dinner at Stefanino's on Sunset. "What was nice there, Sinatra was very loose," Ogerman recalled. "It was like a two-hour monologue. He talked about the old days with the Tommy Dorsey Orchestra, and who was his roommate and all. And he knew all the names still of every musician in the Tommy Dorsey band. It was amazing. Very pleasant. It was all very pleasant."

And it was always the same.

On that last night, after Jobim and Ogerman's work was done and the musicians had gone home, Nancy Sinatra brought in her own players to record a novelty number called "Somethin' Stupid."

The love duet was a trifle from the pen of former folkie C. Carson Parks, whose brother the multi-instrumentalist, songwriter, and musical eccentric Van Dyke Parks might have first brought it to Frank's attention. Another account says that Carson Parks's manager got a version that Parks had recorded with his partner Gaile Foote to Mo Ostin, whereupon it found its way to one of the Sinatras, Frank or Nancy.

Whatever the case, Frank, having just descended from the Parnassian heights, hardly took this throwaway single seriously. While Billy Strange, the arranger of "These Boots Are Made for Walkin'," conducted the orchestra, he began the vocal, in tight harmony with his daughter:

I know I stand in line
Until you think you have the time
To spend an evening with me.

Except that he was pronouncing his s's like Daffy Duck. After the laughter subsided, they completed the opus on the second take. Mo Ostin bet Frank the song would bomb. It didn't.

Released on March 18, "Somethin' Stupid"—which, with its chorus of "And then I go and spoil it all/By saying somethin' stupid/Like 'I love you,'" quickly became known as the Incest Song—would soon climb to the top of the *Bill-board* singles chart. *Francis Albert Sinatra & Antonio Carlos Jobim*, by contrast, only went to number 19 on the Top 40 and stayed there just six weeks. *That's Life,* which had been released on the last day of 1966 and risen to number 6, would be the last Sinatra album to hit a single-figure position on the charts until *Duets* and *Duets II* in 1993 and 1994. Frank was still on top of the world, but his recording career had officially begun its commercial decline.

———

"They were model, adoring newlyweds," Tina Sinatra wrote of her father and Mia.

> There wasn't anything Mia wouldn't do for Dad, or he for her. She
> brought out my father's gentlest, most caring side: the fireside
> Frank . . .
>   I didn't feel threatened by Mia. I felt grateful to her, because she
> made my father happier than I'd ever seen him. When I spent time
> with them in the desert, Dad's old restlessness was missing in action.
> As we passed the time playing word games, he seemed quiet and
> relaxed. Mia was so proud of how she'd converted the guest room into
> her dressing area, and Dad glowed along with her. She'd had it done all
> in pink, which didn't quite blend with the earth tones in the rest of the
> house, but neither of them cared. They were making up the rules as
> they went along.

But then she went away.

In the middle of February, as Frank prepared to go to Miami to open a two-week stand at the Fontainebleau, Mia flew to London to begin shooting the spy thriller *A Dandy in Aspic*. Her co-stars were Tom Courtenay and Frank's old friend and *Manchurian Candidate* opposite number Laurence Harvey. "It'll be the first real separation since their marriage," Earl Wilson wrote in his column. "But Frank'll join her in England when able to do so. All is happiness."

"Frank didn't seem to mind, although he wouldn't come back to London with me," Farrow wrote in her memoir.

Frank minded. *I think it will be better if she doesn't work,* as he had once said of Juliet Prowse.

———

Jackie Mason, born Yacov Moshe Maza, was a former rabbi turned fast-talking borscht belt comedian: he had a Yiddish accent and a sense of humor even more lacerating, if possible, than Don Rickles's. Rickles, after all, had taken on the role of court jester: he could say whatever he wanted to the king (or the Chairman, in this case) as long as the king laughed. Mason didn't care whom he offended; his was a high-wire act without a net. He had been mocking Frank's hair transplants (the surgeries, which began not long after Sinatra's fiftieth birthday, were an open secret) and elevator shoes for a while and had begun mining rich material from the Sinatra-Farrow marriage at the beginning: "Frank soaks his dentures and Mia brushes her braces . . . then she takes off her roller skates and puts them next to his cane . . . he peels off his toupee and she unbraids her hair."

Frank didn't like it. Taking in Joe E. Lewis's late show at the Aladdin (where Mason was also playing) the previous November, he'd heckled his old pal from the audience. "I really came in to see Jackie Mason," he said.

"Aw, shut up," Lewis shot back. "Why don't you go to a brewery and let them put a head on you?"

"Nah, I'm just kidding," Sinatra said. "If that bum came out here on the stage now, I'd bite him on the neck. He's a creep."

Before too long, Frank, or someone acting on his behalf, put a real bite on Mason: the comic got a phone call threatening his life if he didn't stop making jokes about Sinatra. Mason hired a bodyguard and kept making the jokes. A few days later, three shots were fired through the glass patio door of his hotel room at the Aladdin. The bullets lodged in Mason's bed, on which he had been sitting minutes before. The Clark County sheriff's office investigated the shooting but eventually closed the case due to uncertainty about whether the attack had been motivated by the comedian's Sinatra jokes or Mason's complicated love life.

Insisting it was the former, Mason cleaned up his act, removing Mia jokes and trimming back the Sinatra humor to bland gibes about Frank's womanizing. But then, appearing in early February at the Saxony Hotel in Miami, he said, "I have no idea who it was who tried to shoot me . . . After the shots were fired, all I heard was someone singing: 'Doobie, doobie, doo.'

"I was warned by anonymous threats all week, on the telephone and by people I don't know in the hotel lobby, to shut up about Sinatra," Mason recalled, "but I didn't think much about it."

Then, at 5:00 a.m. on February 13, while Mason sat in his car with a lady friend, a few blocks from the Saxony, "all of a sudden," he remembered, "the door opens and a fist comes in, right into my nose and busted me—a fist with some kind of a ring on it that's supposed to cut your face open." He sustained multiple face lacerations and a broken nose—he was hospitalized—and told reporters he was convinced his remarks about Sinatra had led to the attack.

Mason later told his lady friend, who'd jumped out of the car and fled during the incident, that the assailant said, "This is not the worst that can happen if you don't keep your mouth shut about Frank Sinatra."

Frank arrived in Miami two days later.

———

Laurence Harvey had assured Mia Farrow that the *Dandy in Aspic* shoot would require her to be in London for only ten days, followed by three days in Berlin. The work in London went fine, Farrow recalled, but then in Berlin the film fell behind schedule, and the three days turned into a week, then more. Frank seethed with impatience on the transatlantic phone line.

Impatience was putting it mildly. Many years before, as Dolly roamed Hoboken, busy with her Democratic Party work and her midwife and abortion work, she had had little time for her only child. She had dominated him with her distance, making him feel small. It was the last way he wanted to feel, then and now.

———

Shecky Greene had been drawing his customary big crowds at the Riviera in Vegas when Jilly Rizzo called him with an unusual request: Would he consider opening for Frank at the Fontainebleau in February?

Ordinarily, Greene didn't open for anyone: he was a star in his own right, a "topliner," as *Variety* would put it, earning $25,000 a week at the Riviera. But this was Sinatra, and Rizzo told Shecky he'd be paid his Vegas rate in Miami, so he said yes.

Frank Sinatra was fascinated with Greene for several reasons: for one thing, he was a brilliant, original comedian who didn't do material as such; "I never had an act," he said. Instead, the compact, beefy comic, a Jew from Chicago with the build of a football lineman, a square athletic jaw, and sad, basset-like eyes, simply came out onstage and did mostly improvised bits, frequently breaking into Yiddish, which he knew, or other dialects that he didn't (like Sid Caesar, Greene had a genius for making faux French, German, or

Chinese sound like the real thing), or bursting into song, in a rich and tuneful baritone.

By the mid-1960s, Greene had become a Las Vegas institution and, as he freely admitted, frequently lost most of his big salary at the racetrack. He had a serious gambling addiction, a drinking problem, and anger issues, all compounded by a disintegrating marriage and a deep ambivalence about show business. "Fear," he said. "I had terrible fear." He sometimes suffered crippling anxiety attacks, occasionally onstage. And these things, too, fascinated Sinatra, because to some extent they reminded him of himself.

But there was also a third quality about Shecky Greene that intrigued Frank endlessly: Greene was not afraid of him.

"I watched guys, successful guys, Italians and Jews, fall on their knees to this guy," Greene recalled. "I watched Jews that I had respect for in Miami; they'd kiss his ass. One day we were on what's-his-name's boat that owned the Fontainebleau—Novack—and the food came, and Sinatra threw the food over the side of the boat. I said, 'Why the fuck did you do that?' He said, 'It's none of your business.' So I took my shoes off and I threw them over. He said, 'What did you do that for?' I said, 'I've got to go down now and get the food.' Every time he did something, I did something. And there was this strange thing, that the people that he couldn't control, he gained a respect for.

"I didn't kiss his ass," Greene said. "And he loved that. His mother once said to me, 'He likes you because you're me.'"

For his part, Greene was impressed by Sinatra—to a point. "The man was a great singer, and I appreciated his talent. But his talent didn't have anything to do with who he was." Who was he? "When I wasn't drinking, I really studied him," the comic said. "He wanted me around all the time; he always wanted to go for fuckin' Italian food. So I studied him, I watched him do fuckin' things, and I said, 'Is this show business, or is it life? I don't know.' I couldn't figure it out."

Being part of the entourage meant being available at all hours, especially the hours before dawn. "He couldn't go to sleep, so he'd love to tell stories," the comic recalled. "The more he drank, the more stories he would tell. After a while, they were very boring. He'd talk about the Tommy Dorsey days—he did this, and then he did that. Very boring."

Greene was then in a pitched battle with his own demons. He, too, was drinking massive amounts, and alcohol unleashed furies in him. He was alleged to have pushed a piano out a penthouse window at the Fontainebleau; whether this was or was not the case, he did admit to having torn a hotel room apart in Frank's presence. "Every piece of furniture was that big when I finished," Greene said, holding his thumb and forefinger a few inches apart. "I was insane. But my match was him, because he was completely insane."

The comedian recalled a time when he and Sinatra were alone in Frank's suite at the Fontainebleau. "He grabbed me and says, 'Come here.' He puts me in front of the mirror and he says, 'You're the sickest son of a bitch I have ever met in my life.' Well, I was doing some very weird things at the time. But I said, 'No, you come here.' And I grabbed him under his arm and put *him* in front of the mirror. I said, 'No, *there's* the sickest son of a bitch.' I said, 'I may be second, but believe me, you're first, and I'm a long way from you.'"

———

Like Greene, Sinatra had mastered his performing fears by creating an assertive stage presence; unlike Shecky, Frank carried this aggression—which often magnified into brutality—to his offstage life. "It was a cross between megalomania and fear," Greene said. "But it was a silent fear; he thought nobody else knew about it." The effect was compounded by fame and power. And alcohol. "After two drinks, I saw a change," the comic remembered.

Also unlike Greene, Sinatra usually vented his furies on people rather than objects. "I watched him throw food on the floor," Greene recalled. "I saw him have Jilly kick people. Once we went downstairs to the Fontainebleau coffee shop. It was four or five o'clock in the morning. Sinatra liked these hot brown rolls they had, so we went down there to see if they were done yet, and they weren't done. And Frank got mad, and he said something to Jilly, and Jilly kicked the baker and broke his ankle.

"I said, 'Are you guys fuckin' sick? What are you doing?' I used to see these things, and I didn't want to be with him. I wanted to quit every two minutes."

But he stayed.

———

Farrow flew to Miami to spend a few days with Sinatra; he behaved. Then she returned to Germany, and the misbehavior resumed. Joe Fischetti, still nominally connected with the Fontainebleau, found women for Frank. And he drank steadily.

"We're sitting in the Gigi Room at the Fontainebleau," Shecky Greene recalled, "and he says to me, 'He's using my name.' I said, 'I beg your pardon?'

" 'That son-of-a-bitch is using my name,' Sinatra says. So I said, 'Who are you talking about?'

" 'My kid,' he says.

"I said, 'Well, you named him Frank Sinatra, Junior. Isn't that his name?'

" 'Whattaya mean?' he says. 'He's out there using my name.'

" 'Well, Jesus Christ, what name is he gonna use? Charles Bronson? That's his name.'

" 'Shut up,' he said."

On March 13, *Rosemary's Baby,* Ira Levin's horror novel about witchcraft and devil worship in modern-day New York City, was published. The book immediately jumped onto the best-seller lists, and by the end of the month Paramount had bought the film rights for the producer William Castle (*House on Haunted Hill, I Saw What You Did*) and hired the young Polish director Roman Polanski (*Knife in the Water, Repulsion*) to helm the movie. The project quickly became one of Hollywood's hottest, the title role eagerly sought after by every young actress in town.

"No better evidence of the marital status of the Frank Sinatras than that Mia Farrow jets back from England to see Frank on every possible occasion," Harrison Carroll wrote in his Hollywood column on March 14. "With two weeks off from 'Dandy in Aspic,' she flew straight here. Frank was to fly here from his Florida singing engagement. His movie, 'Shamus,' probably won't start down there until around April 1. Meanwhile, crews are working on the double to complete the redecorating of the pair's new Bel Air home."

But why was evidence of the Sinatras' marital status needed at all?

On March 2, Frank had had his best night ever at the Grammys, winning both Record of the Year and Best Male Vocal Performance for "Strangers in the Night" and Album of the Year for *A Man and His Music.* On the other hand, moviemaking had come to bore him—a fact to which the three flops in a row he'd made (*The Naked Runner* would be released in July to the box-office fate it deserved) attested. With *Marriage on the Rocks* and *Assault on a Queen,* the material, as he'd told Peter Bart, had been the problem. *Runner* had had more to build on, but then the mad marriage to Mia exploded in the middle of it, and Frank simply checked out.

Before his partnership with Brad Dexter went down in flames, Dexter had attempted to revive Sinatra's flagging interest in films with a William Goldman script called *Harper,* a detective story based on the Ross Macdonald novel *The Moving Target.* But then negotiations with the owners of the property, producers Elliott Kastner and Jerry Gershwin, fell through, and the movie ended up getting made with Paul Newman instead of Frank Sinatra.

With its dark, witty screenplay and its superb cast (Lauren Bacall, Julie Harris, Arthur Hill, and Janet Leigh co-starred), *Harper* was an artistic and box-office success in 1966: a tough, cool, cynical story revolving around a flawed hero—Newman at his most winningly roguish—and some not-so-admirable characters. The winning formula harked back to Humphrey Bogart's detective movies *The Maltese Falcon* and *The Big Sleep*—sex, danger, humor, and a sardonic central character. Following the lead of his old idol Bogie, Sinatra now realized, could revive his film career.

That career would last just thirteen more years; in five out of six of his starring roles between 1967 and 1980, he would play a detective. As Tom Santopietro points out, "The persona of a private investigator fit Frank Sinatra perfectly . . . Audiences expect detectives to resemble their idealized version of Frank Sinatra: the man in question has been around the block more than once, is bruised, tough, cynical yet still possesses a small private reservoir of hope. Tough with men, wary with women, the chivalrous knight who has seen it all but still fights the daily fight—it all fit Frank Sinatra like one of his custom-made suits."

Still, he was fifty-one and looked it: plumper, balder, puffier about the face, though still rugged. If he couldn't pull off the Cary Grant trick of playing the swain to much younger women, he could still portray their protector, a father figure with a sexual charge. And a solitary righter of wrongs. Solitude was the key. In his greatest movie roles and in his recording career, the overriding image was of a man alone. And if the man himself was less tough and certain than the image, less wise and witty, the solitude was real.

———

Early in the morning of November 27, 1966, the same day that Mia and Frank would appear on *What's My Line?*, another legendary loner, Howard Hughes, moved into the ninth-floor penthouse of the Desert Inn. He would remain there for the next four years, secluded in a room with blacked-out windows, as he took over Las Vegas.

Having just been forced by a U.S. federal court to sell his majority stake in Trans World Airlines, Hughes was now the richest man in America, with cash and holdings worth $1.5 billion. "He had not come to Las Vegas with a master plan," Hughes's biographer Michael Drosnin writes.

> He had come only because he didn't know where else to go and
> because he had been there before and liked it. He liked the all-night
> ambiance, he liked the showgirls, he liked the whole tone and feel of
> the place. In the early 1950s, before he went into seclusion, he used
> to fly in regularly for a night or a few days or a few weeks, catch the
> shows, perhaps pick up a showgirl, dispatching one of his lackeys
> to arrange the assignation, always ordering him to first get a signed
> release. He rarely gambled, just occasionally dropped a nickel in a slot

machine, but he cruised the casinos and was a familiar figure at ringside in the showrooms, and he kept coming back.

But as the 1950s became the 1960s, the inventor, aviator, and company
builder once thought of as a dashing eccentric had descended into madness,
his obsessive-compulsive disorder blooming unchecked. He lay naked in his
bed in the Desert Inn penthouse in unspeakably filthy conditions, urinating
into bottles, cleaning himself with paper towels, which he then wadded and
threw aside. He let his hair and fingernails grow grotesquely long. Yet there
was a certain cracked logic to all his obsessions, a logic that pivoted on the
idea of control.

Hughes had a vision: he would rescue a town that reveled in its crassness
and vulgarity from itself. He would purify Sin City. He would, he wrote in a
memo to his right-hand man Robert Maheu, "make Las Vegas as trustworthy
and respectable as the New York Stock Exchange—so that Nevada gambling
will have the kind of a reputation that Lloyd's of London has, so that Nevada
on a note will be like Sterling on silver."

And it didn't stop there. "We can make a really super environmental 'city of
the future' here," Hughes wrote. "No smog, no contamination, efficient local
government, where the tax-payers pay as little as possible, and get something
for their money."

"There it was," Drosnin writes. "Hughes Heaven—no contamination, no
taxes, and lots of class. There was, of course, one other requirement: he had
to own it all."

And he would have to buy it from the men who currently owned it—the
overlords of organized crime.

Hughes's tenancy in the penthouse of the Desert Inn was a thorn in the side
of its owner, tuber-nosed Cleveland Mob boss Moe Dalitz. Dalitz wanted to
rent his ninth-floor suites to high rollers, and he wanted Hughes out. Hughes
came back with a counteroffer: he would buy the Desert Inn.

In truth, Dalitz, who like other Mob bosses around the country was under
intense scrutiny by the Justice Department, was eager to sell. But he wasn't
about to tip his mitt to Hughes. Three months of haggling ensued, the negotiations carried on by the principals' seconds, Maheu and the Mob's ambassador
to Vegas and Hollywood, Johnny Rosselli. The two, of course, were old friends
and partners in the failed CIA plot to assassinate Fidel Castro. In true cloak-
and-dagger fashion, however, neither man scrupled to pull a fast one on the
other.

Finally, after byzantine negotiations, sale terms agreeable to both sides
were reached. And on the last day of March 1967, Howard Hughes received

permission from the Nevada Gaming Commission to purchase the Desert Inn's operations for $13 million. The Clark County Gaming License Board also approved a casino license for Hughes. Frank Sinatra's old rival for the affections of Lana Turner and Ava Gardner had now bested him in the one arena where Sinatra couldn't compete and taken the first step toward permanently altering the character of the town that Frank Sinatra had lifted to greatness on his narrow shoulders.

––––––

Tony Rome, the first of what would be three Sinatra detective films for 20th Century Fox, began shooting in Miami on April 3. Frank played the title character, a wisecracking, down-on-his-luck private detective who lives on a cabin cruiser; Richard Conte played a police lieutenant; Jill St. John, a sexy divorcée; Gena Rowlands, Tony's ex-wife; and Sue Lyon, late of Stanley Kubrick's *Lolita,* co-starred as a dissolute rich girl. Frank enlisted Billy May to write the score, and the ever-reliable (and ever-amenable) Gordon Douglas directed.

During the day, Sinatra made the movie; each night, he did one show at the Fontainebleau, once more with Shecky Greene as his opening act. Frank had also given Shecky a small role in the movie (so that 20th Century Fox, rather than Sinatra, could pay the comic's Vegas-size salary), as a limping crook named Catleg. He cast some other pals in bit parts, too: Jilly; Mike Romanoff; Rocky Graziano; and, returning to the screen in a surprisingly effective turn as a fat, menacing pawnbroker, Mickey Rudin.

The movie shoot was brisk and efficient, Douglas displaying a craftsman's skill at moving the story along (the screenplay, based on Marvin Albert's novel *Miami Mayhem,* was by Richard Breen) and an old Sinatra hand's flair for ensuring, each day, that the set was lit and ready for Frank to do as few takes as possible.

Sinatra responded in kind, hitting his marks and delivering the most effortless performance of his movie career. Tony Rome was a man who appeared closer to the real Frank Sinatra than any character Frank had ever played. He seemed liberated in every word and gesture—even in his accent; Tony might well have come straight out of Hoboken. The man who portrayed him had almost always been a riveting presence on the big screen, in a sailor suit or a military uniform, sticking a needle in his arm or sweating out a remembered brainwashing. Yet even watching Sinatra's finest performances, you did a mental calculation: the man emoting so effectively on-screen, the amazingly natural actor, was the same man who grinned as he wore a tux and sang "Fly Me to the Moon." Of course that was acting, too. There were a dozen (or more) real Sinatras, many of which you never saw in the movies. But Tony

Rome—a man alone, a man who chased women or let them chase him; who drank and smoked and loosened his tie; who joked wryly and acted tough but now and then went down for the count—felt real, because Frank clearly felt so comfortable playing him.

And his comfort with the material and the process ensured the comfort of the rest of the cast and crew. "It was really enjoyable; it was fun," Gena Rowlands recalled of the shoot. "Everything went just easily and smoothly. Frank came in very prepared; he had no temper towards anyone that I saw."

Rowlands, who had never met Sinatra before but had heard the stories, was pleasantly surprised. "I found him to be a wonderful actor; he could do a whole complicated scene in one take, and I never saw him do more than one take," she said. "He was funny, too. He had a good sense of humor, and he was generous in his behavior with all the actors. There was nothing pretentious about him; he was just awfully nice.

"He was kind of that old-fashioned sort of Italian who always helped you," the actress remembered. "We shot a lot on the boat, so we'd have to get from the pier to the boat. He was always right there, giving you a hand, making sure you didn't knock yourself out on some of those lights that were in peculiar places because of the water and all. Just a very polite guy."

Frank as Tony Rome, early 1967. In the most effortless performance of his movie career, Sinatra played a character who seemed closer to his real self than any he had ever portrayed.

Nighttimes were different. Mia was back in Berlin, and though she and Frank spoke on the phone several times a day, there was a six-hour time difference, and the moment always came when she had to get some sleep, and that was when his night was just beginning. He began drinking when the shoot ended each afternoon, and those who were around him after that saw a very different Sinatra than Gena Rowlands saw during the day. "The air was volatile and violent around him all the time," Shecky Greene remembered. "We played the same audience every night, and when I was onstage, there was nothing but laughter. Yet when Frank came out, that same audience erupted and people started fighting."

In a newspaper story about Sinatra, the syndicated entertainment reporter Dan Lewis portrayed the fourteenth floor of the Fontainebleau, where Frank was staying, as a virtual armed camp, thick with an air of menace, swarming with security men and the bodyguards he called his Dago Secret Service. "Everybody wants to see Frank," the hotel's head of security told Lewis. "Everybody wants to talk to him. The toughest time I have is when Frank's staying at the hotel here."

"Frank had so many people sucking around him then, it was sickening," Greene said. "And those bodyguards would attack on command, so naturally people were frightened. Even if he doesn't order the beatings, he allows the violence to happen by having those guys around."

Sinatra's mood worsened when, one night as he was coming offstage, one of the bodyguards handed him a newspaper with a publicity photo of Mia dancing with Laurence Harvey. The two were closely entwined, Farrow's long thin arms wrapped around Harvey's neck. This was the final straw in a charade that had been going on for a couple of months: in *A Dandy in Aspic*, Farrow played a photographer who has an affair with Harvey's character, a KGB assassin, and both the celebrity press and, to a certain extent, Harvey had been making much of their on- and off-screen chemistry. "I have some hot love scenes with Mia," he'd boasted to Leonard Lyons in mid-April, and at least one newspaper account described one of those scenes in detail as graphic as the journalistic standards of 1967 would allow.

Frank had become close to Laurence Harvey during the making of *The Manchurian Candidate* and knew well that he was a closeted homosexual: Sinatra's nickname for him was Ladyboy. At first he'd been tolerant. "Frank Sinatra has given his approval for Laurence Harvey to escort Mia Farrow around London," Sheilah Graham had written in March. But then, already detecting chinks in the marriage, the columnist couldn't help adding kittenishly, "Mia will positively not date anyone unless."

Yet this photograph wasn't a question of reality; it was a matter of reputation. ("His anger was not that she was dancing with Larry," Graham recalled; "it was the too-friendly picture that he thought would cause gossip. It did.") Laurence Harvey was thirty-eight years old and, in the eyes of the world, a handsome, heterosexual leading man. And Sinatra had endured enough gibes about his advanced age and the youth of his wife to enrage any man, even one with a far longer fuse than his. He got on the phone, waking Mia in the middle of the night in Berlin, and screamed at her for the better part of an hour. She got on the next plane and flew to Miami to try to placate him. He was implacable. She turned around and flew back to work.

On April 15, "Somethin' Stupid" hit number 1 on the *Billboard* Hot 100 chart. That made two number 1's in two years, with two songs he didn't think much of.

He wasn't thinking too much of himself at this point, either.

Two nights later, Frank, frequently refilled glass in hand, sat in the television room of Harry Mufson's house in Miami Beach. Mufson, the owner of the Eden Roc, had originally been Ben Novack's partner in building the Fontainebleau, but had parted with him on bitter terms, and was now his main—and next-door—competitor. Sinatra bounced back and forth between the two establishments. That night, Frank, Mufson, Mufson's wife, Shecky Greene, Jilly Rizzo, Joe Fischetti, and several others had gathered to watch the premiere of Joey Bishop's new late-night talk show on ABC.

The band played Bishop's theme song—Frank Loesser's "Joey, Joey, Joey," from *The Most Happy Fella*—and the host came out and did his monologue. Bishop went to commercial. When he returned, he bantered with his sidekick, Regis Philbin, for a moment, then introduced his distinguished first guest: "Ladies and gentlemen, the governor of our state, Ronald Reagan."

As Reagan strolled out, grinning, from the parted curtain, Frank Sinatra stood, walked to the television, and kicked the screen with all his might, shattering the picture tube.

There was Daytime Frank, and there was Nighttime Frank.

During the days, he made the picture, a model of equipoise and friendly—if brisk—collegiality. During the nights, he made Miami mayhem. He drank; he was rumored to be picking up where he had left off with Jill St. John, even though she was nominally involved with Jack Jones. Meanwhile, Fischetti continued to bring him pretty women, and what happened afterward wasn't always pretty.

One Saturday night, Shecky Greene recalled, "he got completely crazy." A girl, he hazily remembered, had been beaten up. And the burly comedian, who had been matching Frank drink for drink, then did a crazy thing: he picked the very drunk Sinatra up, "threw him over my shoulder, and got in the elevator, and brought him all the way up to his suite, and put him down."

Greene shook his head at the memory. "I threw him over my shoulder, and he's kicking like a little kid," he said. "Richard Conte is with us. It's Frank, myself, and Richard Conte, and Conte goes, 'Put him down, Shecky! We're gonna get killed! Don't you understand?' This tough guy in movies. I said, 'What the fuck is the matter with you? The man's insane.'"

As drunk as Sinatra had been, though, he remembered something of the incident, and it did not go down well with him. "He kept on saying to me, 'You're gonna get it,'" Greene remembered. "I said, 'Get what? What the fuck are you gonna give me, Frank? You want to fight? Well, let's fight.'

"'Oh, you're gonna get it,' he kept saying. 'When am I gonna get it?' I asked him."

Tiffany Bolling was twenty-one and blond and gorgeous, a free-spirited California girl from an interesting background: her biological father was the jazz pianist and singer Roy Kral; her mother, who broke up with Kral soon after Tiffany was born, had also worked as a singer and a comedian. Performing came naturally to Bolling, and finding herself in Miami in the spring of 1967, she auditioned for Gordon Douglas and landed a small speaking part in *Tony Rome*. She played a sexy nightclub photographer, in a Playboy-bunny-style outfit, who takes a picture that Sinatra's character winds up needing as evidence.

Frank met Bolling one night a few weeks into the shoot in the Gigi Room at the Fontainebleau, where he was giving a small dinner for a few cast and crew members, serving pasta with his special marinara sauce; he had cooked the meal himself in the restaurant's kitchen. In time-honored fashion, he had a friend go over to the young actress and ask if she would like to sit at his table. She would, and she did.

Bolling had done some coffeehouse singing herself, and though her tastes leaned toward Janis Joplin and Linda Ronstadt, she thought Sinatra "had one hell of a great voice," she recalled. "I told him that—I said, 'You know, I gotta tell you, man—you got a great voice.' He cracked up laughing. He said, 'Who *are* you?'"

They began an affair. Bolling was one year younger than Mia Farrow and a very different person: a beautiful but unformed girl, feisty yet undemanding. Mia never came up, Bolling remembered; the young actress seems to have been under the impression that Sinatra and his wife were no longer together.

"I didn't ask questions; I didn't really care," she said. "I knew he had separated from her, or I wouldn't have gotten involved with him. I wasn't that kind of a person."

Bolling, who had an apartment in Fort Lauderdale, soon moved into the penthouse at the Fontainebleau. (She also found Jill St. John staring daggers at her. "I don't think she liked me very much, and she made it plain," Bolling recalled.) She sat at Sinatra's table as he performed in the La Ronde Room; during the day, having completed her two short scenes in the movie early on, she read or walked on the beach. One day, a salesperson from the women's-wear store in the hotel lobby came up to the suite with a large selection of clothing. "What do you want?" the salesperson said. "Mr. Sinatra would like to dress you."

"I think Francis was going through a major transformation in his life," Bolling said. "I think middle age was hitting him very hard. He was having hair transplants put in, and I'm sure they were very painful. I know he was conscious of his looks—Mia was very young; I was very young—and he was trying to hold on to his youth. Didn't you ever notice that twinkle in his eye? He couldn't go there. I felt bad for him, 'cause he could never go *any*where. Yet there was this child in him, screaming to get out, to jump up and down and play and be silly.

"I really did love that man," she said. "He was a king of men, and he treated me like a princess and a queen all the time. Never, ever, was there any kind of abuse or any kind of weird stuff—except one time, he hired some hooker, and he wanted me to participate, and I said, 'Eff you, man, I'm leaving'—and I did."

One night soon after, as Shecky Greene was about to go onstage in the La Ronde Room, Sinatra said, "Shecky, stick with me and I'll make you the biggest star in the business."

"I looked at him and said, 'If being a big star means being like you, then I don't want it,' " Greene recalled.

At four o'clock that morning, as the comedian walked through the lobby, he was attacked by three men: Joe Fischetti and Sinatra's two bodyguards, Ed Pucci and Andy Celentano. Fischetti hit Greene with a blackjack. Greene, who was literally and figuratively feeling no pain, fought back ferociously. "Fischetti, that fuckin' moron—I split his whole face open," he recalled. "I didn't even know what I was doing. I didn't even feel anything because I was so drunk that morning."

Like Jackie Mason before him, Greene wound up in the hospital, with a concussion and a large gash on his temple. At first, he was furious. "I said, 'I'm gonna kill him. I'm gonna kill that dago son of a bitch,' " he recalled.

But as word filtered out about the attack, both Sinatra and Fischetti begged Greene not to tell the one man they both feared: a fan of Greene's and an old acquaintance from Chicago, Sam Giancana. Mooney was now living in Mexico, having fled the country to try to elude the FBI's intense surveillance. And within a couple of days, the old Mob boss phoned Shecky Greene.

"He said, 'What happened? Tell me what happened with that asshole,'" Greene recalled. "I said, 'Nothing, I fell down the stairs.' He says, 'You didn't fall down the stairs.' He said, 'Shecky, Milwaukee Phil is downstairs.' He was in Mexico talking to me. I know the FBI is listening. He says, 'Milwaukee Phil is downstairs; go down and tell him what you want.' So all I had to say to him was 'I want this asshole beat up.' They would have done it. I said, 'Sam, I'm telling you, I fell down the stairs.'"

The famous joke came later: "Sinatra saved my life in 1967. Five guys were beating me up, and I heard Frank say, 'That's enough.'"

"That joke got around the world," Shecky Greene said, an old man recalling a bad time.

———

Nighttime Frank was alienating those who were closest to him, one by one. "Jilly came to me," Greene recalled, "and said, 'Shecky, I'm running away from it; I can't take any more—so I'm going away for three days. I'll call you; you'll be the only one who knows where I'm at. I don't want him to know where I'm at.'

"So he did have that part of him that wanted to get away from Sinatra. Yet he loved Sinatra. I don't know why; I don't know how. That I can't take away from him."

Tiffany Bolling, too, fled. "I flew to New York; I didn't know where to go," she remembered. "I just went to Jilly's, and Jilly was in New York! It freaked me out! I thought, What are you doin' here, man? You're supposed to be with Francis in Miami! And he said, 'What are you doing here, Tiffy?'"

She went back. Jilly went back. Even Shecky Greene went back to *Tony Rome* once he got out of the hospital. The gash on his temple was written right into the movie.

The pull of Sinatra was just too strong. And Daytime Frank had a way of patching things over.

"Francis called me and said, 'Please come up to my room,'" Bolling recalled. "And he opened the door and said, 'I'm so sorry. I'm really sorry.' Not only did he say those words to me, but that night he invited me to the show that he was still doing at the Fontainebleau, and before we went down, he honored me with the most beautiful pair of opera-length pearls that I have ever seen."

But when Sinatra asked Shecky Greene to do a concert tour with him over the summer, the comedian drew the line. "I said to him, 'I'm not going on the tour.' So he stayed up all night to call all of the papers, telling them he canceled me out of the tour. I was never in the tour. I wasn't going to go with him. Just to see the kind of life he led—I hated myself for staying as long as I did. It was frightening. And I am not absolved from all of the stuff that happened. I mean, I wasn't exactly sane at the time."

This was Miami in the spring of 1967.

In early May, the American-Italian Anti-Defamation League named Frank national chairman of a campaign to discourage the identification of Americans of Italian descent with the Mafia and Cosa Nostra. It was a curious, almost provocative, move on the league's part, given how recently, and why, Sinatra had been forced to give up his Nevada gaming license. "The Frank Sinatra–Italian Anti-Defamation League headlines were valid news but how could they have passed up a Joe DiMaggio or a Perry Como?" entertainment columnist Jack O'Brian asked on the ninth.

Three days later, a nationally recognized authority on the Mafia, former NYPD Central Investigation Bureau detective Ralph Salerno, asked roughly the same question, this time in the pages of the *New York Times*. Sinatra's friendship and association with identified members of the Mafia "hardly matches the image the league is seeking to project as representative of the 20 million Americans of Italian birth or ancestry," Salerno told the *Times*. "Over a period of years Frank Sinatra has done things which make it a matter of public knowledge whom he chooses to be friendly with in Nevada, New Jersey, Brooklyn, Miami and Havana," he said.

"There may be some basic need for the Italo-American community to enhance its image," Salerno continued, "but I feel the best way to do this is to find some spokesmen who have the stature and can command the respect of a Roy Wilkins [executive director of the NAACP]."

The league's president, the civil court judge Ross J. Di Lorenzo, thundered back. "It is this kind of defamatory attack that made it necessary for us to create our organization," he said. "Mr. Sinatra has associated with many of the world's great leaders—presidents, governors, heads of state and other notables [and] has done as much, if not more, than any other human being for the causes of minority groups of every ethnic, racial and religious background."

It was perfectly circular: an Italian-American defaming another Italian-American for defaming still another Italian-American. And in a further nod to illogic, some saw Frank's ability to avoid trial as prima facie evidence of his innocence. "It was obvious that Mr. Salerno had not done his homework, since my father had never been indicted for anything," Nancy Sinatra wrote.

————

Mia finished her work in *A Dandy in Aspic*—the director, Anthony Mann, had unfortunately dropped dead of a heart attack at the end of April; Laurence Harvey completed the picture—and returned to New York, and Frank, and discord.

She and Sinatra had agreed that she would make one movie a year, yet as Farrow knew well, film parts, especially starring roles, the kind she wanted, didn't just drop into your lap at the appointed moment; a young actor or actress had to campaign vigorously for work well ahead of time or risk losing out and becoming yesterday's news. And *Dandy* had placed her on the map—she appeared on the cover of *Life* on May 5—but she still needed a breakthrough role to succeed in her own right.

She knew she could always be news as Mrs. Sinatra, but that wasn't quite what she had in mind. "There would be no point in having a wife who stayed home and cooked his spaghetti for him," she told a reporter. "Any number of women could have done that."

Nor did co-starring with her husband appear to be in the cards. "I don't think a man and his wife should act together—at least that goes for us," Frank said. Mia seemed to agree. "I've got to do things on my own," she said. "If I were his leading lady, too many people would think he just handed me the role."

Conflict appeared early. She very much wanted to have children (Frank very much wanted not to) and yet somehow keep working: signals were mixed. "There's talk that Mia Farrow will retire now that she's had her taste of stardom in 'Dandy in Aspic,' that she'll settle down to the full-time chore of being Frank Sinatra's wife," columnist Marilyn Beck wrote on May 19. "She's already turned down several attractive offers for films." Two days later, Leonard Lyons announced at the top of his column that Farrow's next movie would be *The Severed Head*, with Richard Burton and Elizabeth Taylor.

She might have turned down some jobs, but she was lobbying, hard, for others. The producer David Susskind was casting a TV-movie remake of *Johnny Belinda*, the 1948 film that had won Jane Wyman an Oscar for her performance as a deaf-mute rape victim. Farrow badly wanted the title role, and Susskind didn't want to go anywhere near her.

Susskind, a prickly egotist, had history with Sinatra: he and Frank had once had a well-publicized telegram battle after Susskind tried and failed to get him on his talk show. "I don't want any trouble on this production," he told

Farrow's agent. "And with the wife of Frank Sinatra, you've automatically got trouble."

Mia then called Susskind herself to beg for the part. "Please, please, please reconsider me," she said. "I'd give anything in the world to play that part."

Susskind told her that he couldn't chance it. He knew Frank didn't want her to work, he said. "And he's not all that keen on me anyway," he told Farrow.

"Mr. Susskind, my career is very important to me," she said. "I need a role like this. Please listen to me. I'm an actress first and a wife second. Please."

She was apparently making the same speech to more than one producer. "Frank Sinatra may have to stamp his foot down," Sheilah Graham wrote on June 4.

His young wife, Mia Farrow, was all poised to sign for "Rosemarie's Baby" [*sic*], the Roman Polanski–William Castle production at Paramount, when George Cukor requested her for his "Nine Tiger Man" for 20th Century–Fox, which owns her contract. "Rosemarie's Baby" will be made in New York. "Nine Tiger Man" starts in London, then travels to India with Robert Shaw co-starred. Frankie, who hated it when Mia was in London for "Dandy in Aspic," might insist on keeping his bride in Hollywood, where the Sinatras have a big beautiful home, or in New York, where they have a big beautiful penthouse, air-conditioned and overlooking the East River.

Then, on June 8, newspapers reported that Mia Farrow would play the starring role in the ABC TV movie of *Johnny Belinda*.

Mia Farrow doesn't mention *Johnny Belinda* in her memoir, which strangely juggles the timeline in this critical period of her marriage to Sinatra. She writes of how stressful her long absences for *A Dandy in Aspic* were to both of them. Now that that picture was done, she recalled, she and Frank were looking forward to some free time at home before beginning to shoot *The Detective* together at Fox. Farrow wondered how it would be to be in scenes with Sinatra; she fretted that she would disappoint him.

It was just then, she writes, that Paramount offered her *Rosemary's Baby*. Not only would it be her first chance to star in a film but, even more important to her, a chance to make her mark as an actress. If the movie did well, she thought, she would have her choice of plum parts in worthwhile pictures; she'd be able to achieve what she says was then her life ambition: to make one worthy film a year and thus be able to devote herself to being a wife and sometime, perhaps, a mother.

But contrary to what she has written, in fact there was no solid plan in

place that June for Mia to co-star in *The Detective,* and Paramount hadn't yet
offered her *Rosemary's Baby,* though it looked as though both were about to
happen. Which was a problem, because *Rosemary* was set to start shooting in
New York in late August, and that would make three movies in a year, not one.

––––––

The telephone operators at the Sands—these were the days when outside calls
still had to be routed through a hotel switchboard—routinely listened in on
guests' conversations, not out of a wish to eavesdrop, but as a matter of management policy. In the days when the Mob owned the casinos (Meyer Lansky
oversaw the Sands' operations from his Miami condo), "We needed to protect
ourselves," the Sands pit boss Ed Walters recalled. With ever-greater pressure
on organized crime from the Justice Department, who knew when the skim
itself might be imperiled?

But there were also other considerations. In Vegas's Mob era, some of the
casinos' biggest customers were men who, for all kinds of reasons, didn't want
it known they were there. Often—identity was a hazier quantity in the pre-
computer age—they traveled under assumed names. Sometimes these men
lost substantial sums of money at the tables: What was to prevent any one of
them from falsely claiming he was unable to pay up or from vanishing altogether? In Sin City, all kinds of mischief were possible. For casino management, listening in on calls was an essential means of control.

Early in 1967, one of the Sands' telephone operators came to Walters with a
dilemma: Mrs. Sinatra, Mia Farrow, had been making numerous early-morning
calls to a man in New York who seemed to be her agent and discussing work,
all kinds of work. And Mrs. Sinatra kept telling the man in New York, over and
over, that Mr. Sinatra must not, under any circumstances, know about any of
this. Should she, the operator asked Walters, tell Mr. Entratter about these
calls?

If Entratter found out, he never told Frank: stirring him up was just too
risky.

––––––

"I'm not sure when I got the first inkling that Dad and Mia might be in trouble," Tina wrote.

> Maybe it was the afternoon I dropped by their new place on Copa
> d'Oro, the English Tudor-style house they would barely have time to
> decorate before parting company. Dad was out, no doubt working, and
> I found Mia in the loft over her dressing area. It was a bright, beauti-

ful day, but she was content to stay inside reading a book, cuddling her puppies at her side.

Here, I thought to myself, was a woman who could live very quietly.

When she wasn't on the phone with her agent. Or listening to the just-released—"groundbreaking, earthshaking," Mia called it—*Sgt. Pepper's Lonely Hearts Club Band,* which would quickly change the whole world, thrusting Frank Sinatra and his musical generation to an even farther shore.

Rehearsals for *Johnny Belinda* began in the first week of June. On the fifteenth, Reuters reported that Mia Farrow was under observation at Cedars-Sinai Medical Center. "She is just run down," Jim Mahoney, now also working as Farrow's press agent, told reporters. "She is in the hospital for an examination and a rest," Mahoney said, adding, "She has just completed a strenuous film role in England."

Worried that he might have to replace his star, David Susskind flew to the Coast. What he said he saw when he met with Farrow upset him deeply. "She was bruised from head to foot, with mean red gashes and marks all over her arms and shoulders and throat as if she'd been badly beaten," he told Kitty Kelley. "I sat down with her and said, 'Mia dear, I don't think someone wants you to do this role.' She lowered her eyes and said that she still wanted to do it. She begged and pleaded with me and said she would be fine. She pointed out that most of the damage was done below her face, so we could cover her up with makeup, which we did, but in certain lights you could still see those awful welts. I felt so sorry for that poor kid."

Though rumors of Sinatra's physically abusing women have long circulated, Susskind's is the only implication that Frank ever struck Mia Farrow, and both the source—Susskind harbored no affection for Frank Sinatra—and its uniqueness should be taken into consideration before judgment is passed. In 1986, Farrow herself said that "the references [in Kelley's *His Way*] as to how Frank Sinatra treated me . . . are absolutely untrue."

Yet Frank could be a mean drunk at the best of times, and the spring and summer of 1967 were not the best of times. His wife was frequently absent and, when present, was both passively and—sometimes—actively defiant. Not only was she constantly seeking the work he didn't want her to take; she was also, George Jacobs wrote, "a creative genius at starting fights that got Mr. S crazy. She'd push all his hot buttons, long hair, drugs, mysticism, rock, Vietnam, making him feel like the Ancient Mariner for being so out of it to disagree with her. 'How can you *say* that?' was her favorite expression, delivered in a tone of insulting intolerance."

Her usual modus operandi, the valet said, was to then redirect the heat of their arguments to the bedroom. Physical passion had been the keystone of their relationship, but they were now nearing the three-year mark, and an inevitable cooling had begun. Other aspects of the relationship needed to take on more importance if it were to continue. She passionately wanted to have a baby with him; he passionately wanted no such thing.

More and more, it seemed as though their differences overshadowed their similarities. "Maybe it bothered him not being young," she said years later. "He felt things getting away from him. My friends from India would come into the house barefoot and hand him a flower. That made him feel square for the first time in his life."

He tried. Tina remembered joining Frank and Mia at the Daisy, "Dad wearing a Nehru jacket and love beads, or silver-studded denim—he got downright funky, as cute as he could be. He'd sit and smoke and drink with us, and he loved to get up and dance to the latest tune from Motown." But his former girlfriend Sandra Giles, who also saw the pair at the Daisy, took a different view. "Mia Farrow was dancing with all the men," she recalled. Frank "looked very lonely. And he came up to my table and said, 'Sandra, would you mind if I sit with you guys?'"

He was growing old in a time that worshipped youth; for all his money and power, the world seemed to be getting away from him. He had just helped carry Spencer Tracy's coffin, and the young were celebrating their immortality. And the music, always the new music, coming out of radios everywhere, incessantly. That was the summer the Doors' "Light My Fire" seemed to be on a tape loop; according to Jacobs, Frank kicked a car radio in with his heel when the song turned up on three stations in a row.

A television; a radio. If he was unleashing his fury on things, could people be far behind?

———

Work, as always, was the balm. He began making a new album: the first recording session was in New York at the end of June, Frank's first date in the Big Apple in almost fifteen years. The LP, *The World We Knew* (alternately, *Frank Sinatra*), was a hodgepodge, more a singles collection than a unified concept: no fewer than five arrangers were involved, including Gordon Jenkins, Claus Ogerman, and the now inevitable Ernie Freeman. Nelson Riddle was nowhere in sight.

The album was another chapter in Jimmy Bowen's continuing quest to keep Sinatra relevant; as always, Frank went along with reservations. He had—so recently—*been* the times; why should he now have to keep up with them? The tone of the LP was set by the Freeman-arranged, Bowen-produced title track, a poundingly catchy weeper from the pen of "Strangers in the Night" composer Bert Kaempfert, who knew how to write a hook that really got its hooks into you. Backed by a portentous fuzz-bass figure, a chink-a-chink rhythm section, and a soaring choir, a heavily echoed Frank goes into the grabby, empty lyric:

> *Over and over, I keep going over the wor-lld we knew,*
> *Once when you-u walked beside me.*

It's like the theme to an imaginary mid-1960s movie, some unholy mélange of spaghetti Western and achingly triste Continental romance—a short way from "Strangers" and a long way from great Sinatra. (And consciously or unconsciously, the song's message harked back to a time that had been kinder to him.) But Kaempfert, Bowen, and Freeman knew what they were doing, as far as it went: when the song was released as a single later that year, it would spend five weeks atop *Billboard*'s easy-listening chart.

Virtually the entire album had an easy-listening quality: highly produced, determinedly contemporary, edging on (and into) vacuity. Besides the unavoidable "Somethin' Stupid," there were two actual movie themes, "Born Free" and "This Is My Song" (written by Charlie Chaplin for *A Countess from Hong Kong*); the lesser Petula Clark hit "Don't Sleep in the Subway"; and, for whatever reason—some say Frank's pique at Richard Rodgers for a scolding reminder to sing his songs "as written"—a screechily swingin' update of Rodgers and Hammerstein's "Some Enchanted Evening."

But the enterprise was somewhat redeemed by the weirdly wonderful "This Town"—the closest thing to a straight-up blues Sinatra ever recorded, complete with wailing harmonica—and the LP's one truly fine track, Claus Ogerman's gently lovely arrangement of the Johnny Mercer and Doris Tauber lament "Drinking Again."

Significantly, Frank performed none of this material when he toured in July, hitting the heartland—Pittsburgh, Cleveland, Madison, Detroit, Chicago, Philadelphia, and Baltimore—to meet his true audience. They came out in droves—the tour would be an unprecedented success—to see Sinatra and his opening act, the Buddy Rich Orchestra; also on the bill were comedian Pat Henry (filling the Shecky Greene slot) and Jobim's protégé Sergio Mendes. Knowing where his bread was buttered, Frank mostly stuck to the classics—songs like "Day In, Day Out," "Moonlight in Vermont," "Fly Me to the Moon," the inevitable showpiece "Ol' Man River"—and mixed in some of the best new material, like "Summer Wind" and "Quiet Nights of Quiet Stars." Naturally, he had to acknowledge the big new hits, "Strangers" and "That's Life."

He sang the latter twice in Philadelphia's Convention Hall on July 13, reprising his defiant new anthem at concert's end, to the delight of an audience that included Mia Farrow. "I remember how he played to her throughout the show, blowing her an occasional kiss, playfully sticking his tongue out and making faces at her," recalled the Sinatra archivist Richard Apt, who was also present. "I also recall Ed McMahon sitting with her in a special section set up against stage left. After every song Mia stood up and cheered. She was really quite cute."

The two of them were working hard to put the best possible face on the marriage. What went on behind closed doors was another matter. When Paramount officially offered her the role in *Rosemary's Baby* at the beginning of July, "the timing . . . was terrible, and I was in a quandary," she recalled. She was in the midst of rehearsing for *Johnny Belinda;* she had recently been hospitalized for exhaustion, or worse.

She and Frank discussed the pros and cons, she writes, perhaps euphemistically. The shoot for *Rosemary* was scheduled to last twelve weeks; Farrow asked Sinatra if he could deal with her working for a few more months. And it wasn't just work, she maintained: it was her big chance at last. Furthermore, she reminded him, she'd be on set at Paramount for almost the whole three months; she could come home every night. There'd be only ten days of location work in New York, a week at the beginning of the shoot and three days at the end.

Frank tried hard to see it her way, she writes, but still had doubts about the project. In bed one night in Palm Springs, he finally read the script. His verdict: he couldn't see Mia in the role. So strong was his influence on her, she recalled, that all at once she couldn't imagine herself in the role, either. Part of her hoped he would simply forbid her to do it. He didn't.

Filled with misgivings, she accepted the part.

What rings truest in the account is his coolly trying to deceive her out of taking the role of a lifetime.

Throughout July, Howard Hughes negotiated with the eighteen official owners of the Sands—including Jack Entratter, Carl Cohen, and Dean Martin, but not, any longer, Frank Sinatra—to purchase the hotel-casino that had been Sinatra's Vegas headquarters for fifteen years. As the talks proceeded, Frank got an idea: Since Hughes seemed bent on buying up the state, perhaps he would like to pick up Cal-Neva, too?

In the wake of the Giancana imbroglio, Sinatra had been forbidden to operate the Tahoe hotel-casino but had maintained his majority stake, leasing the place to a pair of gamblers from San Francisco. An outright sale would take the white elephant off his hands and put a lot of money in the bank.

But the billionaire refused to bite. He wouldn't even take Frank's calls. Then, on July 22, it was announced that Howard Hughes had purchased the Sands—property and operations—for an estimated $15 million (the figure was later revealed to be $23 million). A spokesman for Hughes issued a statement: "We are buying a very successful operation which has been built by a success- ful management, executive and employee team which we welcome into the Hughes family. We plan no changes in operation of the Sands."

Nobody had ever talked this way about a casino before: it wasn't the way the men who had built Las Vegas talked. But it was exactly the way corporate spokesmen talked.

———

Despite Frank and Mia's longtime contention that they wouldn't, couldn't, shouldn't work together, it appeared, at the end of July, that that was exactly what they were about to do—and not once but twice. "We were half-kidding a few months ago," Earl Wilson wrote on the thirty-first, "when we suggested that Frank Sinatra & Mia Farrow should make movies together and become another Richard Burton–Liz Taylor item—but it looks like that's precisely the plan 20th Century–Fox has for them in 'The Detective' and 'The Chairman' (a spy story about Red China). And if 20th doesn't manage to get them in a love scene, the whole world will be disappointed."

Talk of *The Chairman,* which would wind up as a lesser Gregory Peck vehi- cle, was just that: movie talk. But *The Detective* had been in the works since the previous fall—just not with Mia in it—and was now set to start shooting in mid-October in New York City. Because she was to play a pivotal yet support- ing role, her work was set to begin on November 17. The timetable dovetailed tightly with the shooting schedule of *Rosemary's Baby,* which was due to have wrapped by November 14.

———

For all her ambivalence, self-doubt, and anxiety, Mia was the eager focus of a Paramount publicity stunt on August 16, smiling and making faces in front of dozens of reporters and photographers gathered on a cavernous soundstage as Vidal Sassoon trimmed her already short hair by exactly one inch, ceremonially kicking off the production of *Rosemary's Baby*.

After two weeks of rehearsal, she went to New York to shoot exteriors, and as the Labor Day weekend began, Frank opened at the Sands for the twenty- ninth time.

He was socko, as always. "Frank Sinatra, still the strongest attraction on the Strip, is back," *Variety* wrote. "At one point he kids Howard Hughes' Sands takeover by singing 'Fairy tales can come true, it can happen to you—if you're Howard Hughes.' As usual, Bill Miller at the 88 conducts the festivities."

The festivities quickly grew testy. "You're wondering why I don't have a drink in my hand," Frank told the Copa Room audience one night. "Howard Hughes bought it." He would repeat the joke at several subsequent shows.

The Sands had changed, abruptly and dramatically. "The Sands' owners got their money and Hughes brought in his own people," Ed Walters recalled. "It was done at midnight to start a new day. The Hughes people, a combination of accountants and lawyers, came in heavy and strong. Stopped all casino transactions and did accounting on everything. These guys had never been in the casino business before and looked on us as mobsters and gamblers. They immediately put in a long list of new casino rules, especially concerning the taking in and giving out of casino credit."

The Hughes foot soldiers were also, to a man, Mormons: teetotalers and non-gamblers, humorless bean counters taking over a world that only yesterday had been full of freewheeling, naughty fun. Overseeing the operation was the casino's new manager, a retired air force general named Edward Nigro.

And Sinatra was pissed off, in plain English: at Hughes, for neutering the Sands, for not taking his phone calls, for challenging his supremacy in Las Vegas—and everywhere else. Who was the most powerful man in the world? A billion dollars went a long way toward settling the question. ("I'm here to buy Howard Hughes out," Frank joked at another show. "Who else would be able to do it? I got it on me!") And he was furious at Jack Entratter, secure in his new five-year contract as the Sands' president—and rolling in the nearly $3 million he'd pocketed in the sale—for not persuading Hughes to buy Sinatra's share in Cal-Neva.

And, of course, at Mia, for being in New York. And for advertising his inability to rein her in.

How could he be so big and feel so small?

On Labor Day, the biggest night of the year at the casino, he abruptly canceled both shows, claiming he had strep throat. He flew back to Palm Springs. Over the next three days, while Sammy filled in for him, Frank met secretly with the owners of Caesars Palace, the brand-new (and still Mob-run[*]) hotel-casino across the Strip from the Sands, about jumping ship. One of his conditions was that Caesars buy out his stake in Cal-Neva. It looked as though he was going to be able to get everything he wanted.

Yet he was still in a rage. Eventually—Thursday—he had to go back to

---

[*] Ed Walters maintained that Caesars stayed under organized crime's dominion longer than any other Las Vegas casino.

work, and working for Howard Hughes was innately demeaning. He stomped around the casino in an especially ugly mood, announcing to all within earshot that there was no reason that Hughes, with all his money, shouldn't share it with him, because he had made the Sands what it was. And he gambled as if there were no tomorrow.

"Like somebody deranged, he was flinging away his chips, losing thousands," recalled Earl Wilson, who was there that week. "He was soon into the Sands for $200,000 in markers."

In the pre-Hughes Sands, Frank Sinatra had operated under a unique set of rules: he never paid off his markers when he lost; when he won, he kept his winnings. Nobody else did this, but nobody else was Sinatra.

But this wasn't the old Sands. On Thursday, September 7, casino manager Carl Cohen went into Jack Entratter's office and told him that General Nigro (though he had retired, the honorific stayed with him) had decided to cut off Frank's credit in the casino because he hadn't settled his debt. Entratter's assistant, Eleanor Roth, later wondered why the Sands would cut off Sinatra's credit when he hadn't yet been paid for the engagement: the markers could have been deducted from his salary without embarrassing him, she felt. In any case, Roth asserted, "Jack Entratter didn't have the balls to tell Frank about the situation."

For the second time.

Early the next morning—Friday, September 8—Frank went to a blackjack table in the casino and asked for $200 in chips. Walters, the pit boss on duty, regretfully told him the new rules. "He just shook his head and walked away," Walters recalled. "He seemed annoyed, but not that mad."

He was keeping it in for the time being. But Mia had returned from New York to find him deeply roiled. As was his custom, he went to sleep at an hour when most Americans would eat breakfast and didn't awaken until late afternoon.

On Friday night, six of the *Apollo* astronauts—Jack Swigert, Gene Cernan, Tom Stafford, Walt Cunningham, Wally Schirra, and Ron Evans—came to see Sinatra's midnight show in the Copa Room. When the show was over, Eleanor Roth recalled, Frank took the astronauts to the baccarat table and asked for credit. He no longer had credit at the Sands casino, he was told—not just a humiliation, but a humiliation in front of American heroes. Sinatra was predictably enraged.

Mia Farrow's account of the first scene in this memorably mad weekend—the time is sometime after dawn on Saturday—begins placidly, if bizarrely. After yet another endless Vegas night, she writes, she and Frank were in a golf cart, headed back to their suite and bed at last: "He was wearing a shoe box on his head to keep the sunlight out of his eyes."

A memorable image, and not a good sign. Sinatra had been upset in the casino, she writes, but everything had been ironed out. Now, all at once, he jerked the golf cart into a U-turn and floored it, heading straight for the lobby's plate-glass window. Farrow knew her husband too well to try to protest. Her life flashed before her eyes: How, she wondered, had she wound up in a Vegas casino, riding in a golf cart driven by a man wearing a shoe box on his head, heading toward what appeared to be certain disaster?

At the last second, Frank jerked the steering wheel: Instead of hitting the window head-on, the cart sideswiped it. Miraculously, the two of them were uninjured. Filled with a demonic energy, Sinatra jumped out of the golf cart and strode purposefully into the casino, as Farrow "trotted after him, clutching my little beaded evening purse." He picked up some chairs and threw them into a pile; he tried to set them ablaze with his gold cigarette lighter. Casino guards were hurrying over. But, Mia writes, when the chairs refused to ignite, Frank grabbed her hand and led her out of the building.

Yet oddly, Farrow's memoir has once again juggled events, situating the episode not in September 1967 but before their marriage, over a year earlier than it actually happened, thus pulling it out of context and rendering it both stranger and less significant than it really was.

Why would she have done this?

Memory is the flukiest of faculties, yet the golf cart incident was extensively documented in the press soon after it happened; there can be no mistaking it for any other Sinatra escapade. But by decontextualizing it, Farrow has removed its meaning, presumably because the meaning is too painful to bear: Frank was in a fury, not just at Hughes and the Sands, but at her. The gambling humiliation was only part of it. She had humiliated him again and again.

Ed Walters, who was on the casino floor that night, found her revisionism entirely understandable. "The cocktail waitresses at the Sands knew Frank well and wouldn't put up with any of his bullshit," Walters said. "If Mia hadn't been there, they would've told him, in no uncertain terms, to go back to his room. And he would have listened. But when Mia was with Frank, nobody went near him."

Far simpler, in retrospect, not to have been there at all.

There are large holes in all accounts of Frank Sinatra's memorable last weekend at the Sands: though the crazy events have been written about many times, a precise sequence has never been fixed—first, well, because things were just too crazy; second, because the highlights (or lowlights) seem sufficient to satisfy morbid curiosity.

But a timeline might lend some clarity to the chaos.

In a memo to Hughes later that day—Saturday, September 9—Robert Maheu broad-brushed the drama. "For two successive nights into the wee hours of the morning Sinatra has made a damn fool of himself in the casino at the Sands," he wrote. "He moved around insulting people with vile language. Last night he drove a golf cart through a plate glass window and was disgustingly drunk. In an effort to protect him from himself Carl Cohen stopped his credit after he had obtained $30,000 plus in cash and had lost approximately $50,000.* Sinatra blew his top and late this afternoon called me to tell me that he was walking away from the Sands and would not finish his engagement."

News accounts corroborate this. "A spokesman for the Sands Hotel Sunday said he had no idea why Frank Sinatra broke off his engagement there 'without explanation,'" UPI reported on Monday the eleventh.

> "I don't think Sinatra knows why either. He just left," the spokesman said.
>
> The singer opened a three-week run on Aug. 30. He was to have appeared in the strip hotel's Copa Room through Sept. 20. Singer Frankie Avalon was booked to complete the engagement.
>
> "This is the first time anything like this has happened," the Sands representative said.
>
> Sinatra, who was making his 29th appearance in the hotel since 1952, left for his Hollywood home Saturday night before the first show.

Mia Farrow writes that that night—there is no fudging the timeline here, because of the events that followed—she and Frank went out to dinner with Nancy junior and her new beau, Jimmy Bowen, at Trader Vic's in Beverly Hills.

They all chatted agreeably and everything was fine, she writes, until the evening took a turn. Well lubricated, Frank suddenly decided he was going to Vegas, that instant, and Mia was going with him.

She was all too used to his quick mood swings, his abrupt need to go somewhere else—wherever the action was. And once there, she knew, he would be caught up in the spirit of the nighttime world, a place where her existence barely registered.

But that night Mia had an excuse: She had an early call at the studio. And so, she writes, Frank drove her home, gave her a sweet goodnight kiss, and headed to the airport. He phoned later to tell her he'd arrived safely.

The next morning, she recalled, he phoned her on the set at Paramount, his speech indistinct, to tell her there'd been a fight, and the caps had been knocked off his front teeth: It would soon be all over the papers, and his dentist was bringing new teeth.

---

* *Jilly! Sinatra's Right-Hand Man,* an oral history of Rizzo, maintains that Mia lost $20,000 at the tables, and Frank lost the $50,000 trying to win it back.

All of the latter was true, except that the fight, such as it was, had been very brief.

Sometime before sunrise on Sunday the tenth, Frank had returned to the Sands, smashed his hand onto the desk of a startled bell captain, and demanded to see Carl Cohen. "He threatened to kill anyone who got in his way, used vile language, and said he would beat up the telephone operators if they did not connect him with Cohen," Maheu reported to Hughes later that day. "In an effort to calm the situation, Carl agreed to meet him."

"I built this hotel from a sand pile and I can tear the fucking place down, and before I'm through that is what it will be again!" Sinatra announced, in that big voice, to one and all.

It was 5:45 on a Sunday morning, the casino otherwise relatively quiet, and Sands employees were shaken. Cohen got dressed, came downstairs, and went to the Garden Room to get something to eat before dealing with Sinatra. "When Carl is mad," his brother once said, "he eats with both hands and he don't give a shit about nothing."

Cohen wasn't mad now, merely annoyed. He was a tough Jew, a Cleveland protégé of Moe Dalitz's who had risen to the top of the gambling business through a combination of cunning and implied physical menace. The implication was strong. Cohen stood six-three and weighed 250 pounds; his smile— when he smiled—was somehow warm and chilling at the same time. Very few men had ever been foolish enough to cross him. "You didn't fight Carl Cohen," Ed Walters said. "There were a couple guys that got on the wrong side of him who were never seen again." He had absolutely no fear of Frank Sinatra, whom he knew to be a hothead and nothing like a fighter.

Cohen was sitting at his table in the Garden Room when Frank stalked in, accompanied by Jilly Rizzo and a wealthy Miami friend named Stanley Parker. Sinatra demanded to know why his credit had been curtailed, and Cohen, who didn't know Parker, asked him to leave. The conversation was private, he said.

"You son of a bitch, he can hear anything I have to say to you," Frank told Cohen.

"What did you call me?" Cohen asked.

"You heard me, you son of a bitch," Sinatra said. "What are you so nervous about?"

"You just got me out of bed," Cohen said.

Frank stared at him. The Jack Daniel's talking, he repeated himself. "What are you so nervous about?" he said.

That did it for Carl Cohen. He stood up, said he was tired of the one-sided conversation, and began to leave.

From this moment, things got very crazy very fast. Accounts accordingly vary. "Sinatra called Cohen every dirty name in the book," Maheu reported to Hughes. Among the names, according to law-enforcement officials, were "motherfucker," "rat fink," and "cocksucker." (Dolly herself could have done no better.) One source says that Sinatra overturned Cohen's breakfast table, spilling a pot of hot coffee in Cohen's lap and scalding his abdomen and groin. Another says that Cohen himself knocked over the coffeepot when his substantial belly caught the table's edge as he rose to leave. Some sources say that Frank flung a handful of casino chips into Cohen's face; others disagree. But most concur that after Sinatra threatened to have Cohen killed ("I'll get a guy to bury you, motherfucker"), Frank pulled the one weapon from his verbal arsenal that finally drove the big man over the edge.

"You kike!" he screamed.

A dirty secret about Frank Sinatra, the FDR Democrat and champion of tolerance, a man who had himself often been the victim of ethnic prejudice, was that if he was drunk enough and in the wrong kind of mood, he was apt to revert to the language of the Hoboken streets—to "get racial," as a longtime employee of the Sands recalled. As a rule, the victims of his demeaning epithets tended to be bewildered menials, waiters and busboys and parking attendants, who had somehow gotten on his bad side—perhaps brought him a hamburger done the wrong way—or merely walked into his peripheral vision at the wrong moment. They were the easiest to pick on; their very existence also tapped that part of Frank that felt weak and contemptible.

But now he had picked on the wrong guy. Carl Cohen, slow to anger, instantly drove his big fist into Sinatra's mouth, smashing the caps off his two front teeth and knocking him straight to the floor.

Bleeding and furious ("You broke my teeth! I'll kill you, you motherfucker son of a bitch!"), Frank got up, threw a chair at Cohen (it missed and hit a security guard in the head), then barked a command to Rizzo: "Get him, Jilly! Get him!"

Jilly Rizzo might not have been a rocket scientist, but he had an advanced degree in the mathematics of the streets, and an instant calculation told him to stand quietly with his hands visible at his sides. "Jilly ain't going to go up against Carl," Ed Walters noted. "In this town, there were some people no entertainer better fuck with. There's no entertainer bigger than the whole town. Entertainers have bosses. They work for us. And we have bosses."

But as of this moment, Frank Sinatra no longer worked for the Sands.

Frank's people tried to soft-pedal the incident for a couple of days, but it finally blared onto the world's front pages on Wednesday the thirteenth, along with the news of his defection to Caesars—and Caesars' purchase of Cal-Neva for

$2.5 million. UPI's story quoted a Sinatra spokesman as admitting, "We can't deny any of what happened in Las Vegas. There were too many witnesses. I have to assume it is all true. We can't even deny his teeth were knocked out."

The story also noted that "Dr. Abe B. Weinstein, who has been the singer's dentist since 1943, flew Monday [from Connecticut] to Sinatra's home in Beverly Hills, Calif., to repair the damage . . . The dentist said on his arrival back in New York Tuesday that the incident had been 'quite a shock' for Sinatra. He said after the dental operation, 'he put his arms around me and was very emotional.'"

The news cycle moved on, and, as Frank's friend Kirk Douglas remembered, most people around Sinatra studiously avoided referring to the humiliating episode. Douglas couldn't resist. When he asked if the one-punch fight had really occurred, Frank admitted it had. Then he looked at his old friend with a twinkle in his eyes and added, "Kirk, I learned one thing. Never fight a Jew in the desert."

At the Sands in the aftermath of the episode, Kitty Kelley writes, "Cohen was . . . treated like a conquering hero, especially by employees who had suffered Frank's wrath over the years. Some even considered giving him a testimonial dinner."

Ed Walters disagreed vehemently. "Carl was not a hero and we weren't glad Frank got hit," the former pit boss recalled. "Hell, we had just witnessed a fight between two of the most talented and loved people in the town. I personally looked up to and respected them both. They were the best at what they did. Together with Jack [Entratter], they made the Sands into what it had become. And we all knew from that day forward, we would never be the same."

"Sinatra's fight at the Sands destroyed Jilly's reputation as a tough guy," Leonard Lyons noted in an early-October column. "Jilly stood by and watched his idol flattened without raising a finger."

————

Variety's long page-one account of the Vegas fracas ended with Frank's carefully yet oddly worded official statement: "I regret the termination of my long association with the Sands hotel. I have admired and respected Howard Hughes for many years and regret that my decision to accept the Caesars Palace offer comes so soon after his acquisition of the Sands. In addition to performing, I have agreed to assist management in getting talent, both for Caesars Palace and the Cal-Neva."

As to the last, the entertainment weekly wondered whether "Sinatra will influence Dean Martin, [Sammy] Davis, possibly Joey Bishop and other intimates to shift bookings to Caesars Palace."

It didn't happen. Sammy would remain at the Sands; Dean would play out the last year of his contract there, then move to the Riviera; Joey would stay on TV until his show tanked, then, in 1970, return to the Sands.

At the end of the *Variety* piece, another Sinatra item was tagged on, on a very different subject. "Out of friendship for Vice President Hubert H. Humphrey, a Minnesotan," it read, "Frank Sinatra is donating his services Oct. 8 for a one performance Sunday night 'Evening of Stars' benefit show in St. Paul Auditorium to raise campaign funds for Citizens for Johnson-Humphrey Committee of the Minnesota Farmer Labor Party." Frank, the story continued, had lined up his daughter Nancy, Dean Martin, Milton Berle, Pat Henry, the Step Brothers, the Fifth Dimension, "and possibly Buddy Rich and Trini Lopez" for the show.

Frank had first met Humphrey in New York in November 1966: not long after Pat Brown lost the California governorship to Ronald Reagan, Sinatra and his young wife paid a courtesy call on the vice president and his wife, Muriel, who were staying at the Waldorf Towers. "Frank stopped by on a Sunday afternoon with Mia, who was quite kittenish and curled up on the couch beside him, but didn't say a word," Norman Sherman, Humphrey's press secretary, recalled.

> She just listened as Sinatra and Humphrey reminisced about the big
> bands in the 1930s in South Dakota. Hubert was a nut on boxing and
> knew all sorts of trivia about who weighed what and which contender
> won what crown, so they shared that as well. There was an instan-
> taneous bonding between them, an immediate good feeling that led
> to a nice friendship. Humphrey thought highly of Frank, but then he
> thought highly of everyone. And let's face it, friends were not that easy
> to come by then, especially in the entertainment industry, which was so
> violently opposed to President Johnson's Vietnam policies.

A strange scene: the two public figures in intimate yet utterly impersonal converse; Mia, who had already begun differing vehemently with Frank about the war, biting her tongue and being subjected to yet another geriatric chat.

Sinatra had no love for Lyndon Johnson (the feeling was mutual: Frank not only was rumored to have disrespected LBJ's revered mentor Sam Rayburn at the 1956 convention, but had thrown in his lot with the Kennedys in 1960, when Johnson hated them). But he badly missed the grand game of political kingmaking, and now, in the run-up to the 1968 presidential election, Humphrey was as close as Frank could get. So, with his new front teeth in place, he would once again lend his time and his voice to the Democrats: life went on, showbiz and politics went on, despite disasters elsewhere.

Now and then showbiz went on sublimely. At the beginning of October, Frank taped the third *Man and His Music* special, with guest stars Ella Fitzgerald and Antonio Carlos Jobim and with Nelson Riddle conducting the orchestra. Televised popular music simply didn't get any better. A kind of magic happened when Sinatra and Fitzgerald sang together: they duetted on "They Can't Take That Away from Me" and "It Don't Mean a Thing if It Ain't Got That Swing"; then they did a "Lady Is a Tramp," with special lyrics, that was such a barn burner that when they were done, Frank said, "I think I hurt myself."

The feeling was naturally very different on his four-song medley with Jobim. The two tuxedoed men sat side by side against a dark background, Sinatra with a cigarette and the Brazilian with his guitar, and segued from "Quiet Nights of Quiet Stars" to "Change Partners" to "I Concentrate on You" to "The Girl from Ipanema," without a wrong note or a false step. Frank's singing was so quietly gorgeous (Jobim now and then vocalized soft harmonies in the background, with the effect of cello notes) that it called to mind what Ava had once said about his voice: that it had "a quality that makes me want to cry for happiness, like a beautiful sunset or a boys' choir singing Christmas carols."

A quality that only made the madness at the Sands seem that much more surreal.

Mia Farrow recalled that Roman Polanski preferred to film long scenes in one extended take, which called for great precision in the moving of actors and the camera. For this reason, and because of the Polish director's perfectionism, he often shot up to forty takes of a scene—a method, she writes, that drove the hot-tempered John Cassavetes to distraction.

Cassavetes, Farrow's co-star in *Rosemary's Baby,* was himself a writer and director who made personal, highly improvisatory films that had a raw, almost documentary quality; his artistic vision was diametrically opposed to Roman Polanski's, and the two men quickly came to loggerheads. The conflict, combined with Polanski's painstaking methods, put *Rosemary* seriously behind schedule almost at once, and Mia, who was in almost every scene, would not be able to get away before the shooting of the picture was completely finished.

The Detective was in every way a more substantial picture than *Tony Rome,* a complex crime drama with a gritty New York City setting, dark themes (police corruption, homosexuality, social hypocrisy), and a no-nonsense main character in Sinatra's Sergeant Joe Leland, an NYPD detective forced to grapple with a very nasty crime and the failure of his own marriage. Even the supporting cast made Frank's previous film look lightweight by comparison: Lee Remick, Ralph Meeker, Jack Klugman, Al Freeman Jr., Robert Duvall, Horace McMahon. The thirty-one-year-old Remick, who played Leland's estranged, promiscuous wife, Karen, was an accomplished actress who'd starred in distinguished movies such as *The Long, Hot Summer, Anatomy of a Murder,* and *Days of Wine and Roses.* She was a striking screen presence, with extraordinarily wide and haunted-looking china-blue eyes. Mia Farrow was to play Norma MacIver, the widow of a closeted gay man who, in a key plot point, commits suicide. The role was small but important, yet Farrow's nervousness at having to pit her still-minor luminosity against the star power of the woman playing Joe Leland's wife was not entirely misplaced.

The Detective brought together virtually the same production team as *Tony Rome's*—producer Aaron Rosenberg, director Gordon Douglas, director of photography Joseph Biroc—and the new movie's shoot proceeded no less smoothly, on location in Manhattan and then back on the studio lot at 20th Century Fox. But while Frank's movie clicked along under the direction of Douglas, a capable craftsman working at the height of his powers, Mia's picture fell ever further behind schedule as the meticulous artist in charge battled his male lead and shot take after take.

A curious item appeared in Earl Wilson's column on October 11, under the headline SINATRA APPROVES MIA TRIP TO INDIA:

> Maureen O'Sullivan tells me she and her son-in-law Frank Sinatra both approve Mia and Prudence Farrow going to India to study and meditate with a famous mystic.
>
> "I'd like to go myself. We're all interested in religion and philosophy," Maureen says. "Whether I'd go would depend on whether I get a show to do. And I'm sure Mia wouldn't go without Frank's approval."
>
> Maureen adds cheerfully: "Oh, everything's just fine in that department." Meaning marital relations.

The famous mystic was Maharishi Mahesh Yogi, India and the Beatles are in the wings, and a riddle hereby arises, involving—once again—the timeline of Mia Farrow's relationship with Frank Sinatra, as related in her memoir.

In the book, she speaks in agonized detail of the collapse, at the beginning of 1968, of her strangely filial marriage, comparing it to an adoption that she had managed to spoil. She felt as if she'd been "returned to the void," she writes. Her life had fallen away; she could no longer imagine a satisfying future. Her work, she feared, had by its very nature doomed her to triviality: Acting in general and movie stardom in particular fostered her natural selfishness and arrogance. Once she had cherished idealistic dreams of becoming a nun or a pediatrician ministering to impoverished children overseas; now she was just "a lightweight," just another Hollywood starlet about to divorce.

In her recollection, she desperately pondered how she might transform her life: change her name; dye her hair brown; get fat; move to Peru. In the midst of her psychic disarray, she writes, a phone call came in the night from her sister Prudence, in Boston, "unmoored in some nightmare of her own : . . talking about transcendental meditation."

In Farrow's book, all this happens after the turn of the year, when any hope for a reconciliation between her and Frank has withered. But in real life, here are Mia and Prudence planning their getaway in the early fall of 1967, and Frank (between whom and Mia, we have it on Maureen O'Sullivan's breezy authority, everything's just fine) surely approves.

Frank was puzzled and infuriated by the slowness of the *Rosemary's Baby* shoot, Farrow recalled. He went to New York to do a few weeks of location work for *The Detective*; she flew out to see him on weekends, hoping to keep their relationship intact. The date for her joining Sinatra's film was looming; Frank made it clear that he expected her to satisfy her commitment, even if she had to quit *Rosemary's Baby* before it was finished. Mia saw that her marriage itself was at stake. But so, she felt, was her honor: If she abandoned *Rosemary*, she thought, eventually even Frank would come to respect her less.

She imagined herself back in Vegas again, desperately bored and sleepy at 4:00 a.m. while the men yelled their jokes and the women, in their best dresses, chatted about cats.

He gave her his ultimatum, and she explained how impossible it was. He called Robert Evans at Paramount and demanded Mia be released from *Rosemary*; Evans said that Polanski needed her for another month. "While she's working for us, she's Mia Farrow, not Mrs. Sinatra," he told Frank.

In her absence, he began a halfhearted affair with Lee Remick: just another on-set romance, compounded of loneliness and boredom. Word got back to Mia. She gritted her teeth and went on working.

The picture was grueling: sometimes in the evenings she went dancing, to let off steam—at the Whisky, at the Daisy, at the Factory. With unimpeachable escorts, Lenny Gershe or Larry Harvey or Roddy McDowall.

Then came the night of November 13.

The occasion was a benefit at the Factory for a project to bring theater to inner-city schools. The entertainment was a fashion show by the wildly popular French fashion designer André Courrèges, "a gay, fast-paced romp of models dancing to African jazz music," according to the Associated Press. Much of Hollywood was there: the Gregory Pecks and the Kirk Douglases; Barbra Streisand and Omar Sharif and Lucille Ball and Shirley MacLaine and newlyweds Jack Jones and Jill St. John. Even Ava, in town to begin work on the historical drama *Mayerling,* was there, looking radiant in white organdy and green satin. And Robert F. Kennedy and his wife, Ethel, who were visiting the Douglases in Palm Springs, were also present. As was Mia.

And sometime during the evening, Mia, who loved to dance, danced with Bobby Kennedy in front of hundreds of people, including many of Frank's Hollywood friends. They danced again and again.

Word got back. Fast.

––––––

All this time, she had tried to tell him how important her work was to her; she had believed that their special bond, the thing they shared on the rare, quiet occasions they were alone together, would make him understand. And he did love her in his way (though the rare, quiet occasions also made him uncomfortable), as she loved him in hers, but she didn't understand: she had humiliated him again and again. Intentionally, unintentionally—it didn't matter.

November 17 came and went. The world knew she hadn't shown up for *The Detective*—then production shut down on the movie, its star too upset to work. On the twenty-second, the day before Thanksgiving, Mickey Rudin appeared on the *Rosemary's Baby* set at Paramount, went to Farrow's dressing room, and, with all the charm of the pawnbroker he'd played in *Tony Rome,* handed her a sheaf of papers.

Made out in her name, it was an application for a divorce from Frank Sinatra. She saw an "unprofessional look of surprise" pass over Rudin's face as he realized how blindsided she was by this. Holding herself together as best she could, she quickly signed the papers, reading nothing. She told Rudin she would do whatever he and Frank wished; she would not hire a lawyer herself.

When it was time to resume shooting, Roman Polanski found Farrow in her dressing room, "sobbing her heart out," he recalled. "What hurt her most was that Sinatra hadn't deigned to tell her himself, simply sending one of his flunkies. Sending Rudin was like firing a servant. She simply couldn't understand her husband's contemptuous, calculated act of cruelty, and it shattered her."

"I had nothing I wanted to live for," she said many years later. "Nothing. My life was over."

"Frank Sinatra and Mia Farrow spent Thanksgiving day apart by mutual agreement, the first day of a trial separation that ended 16 months of marriage," UPI reported on November 24.

The singer and his willowy young wife were in seclusion, Sinatra at his swank desert retreat in Palm Springs and Miss Farrow at her fashionable Bel Air mansion where an armed guard patrolled the entrance gate.

Sinatra, 52 [*sic*], made the announcement of the trial separation through his public relations representative, who said after reading the statement that there would "be no further comment from either party."

The actress refused to accept telephone calls but a maid gave an indication of her emotional state by saying she was eating very little and keeping to herself.

On the twenty-ninth, 20th Century Fox's production chief Richard Zanuck announced that the twenty-three-year-old British newcomer Jacqueline Bisset would replace Mia Farrow in *The Detective*. (The role of Norma MacIver would be cut down considerably.) Meanwhile, the movie was still shut down. "Zanuck said he hoped production on 'The Detective' would resume next week when Sinatra returns from his home in Palm Springs," UPI noted.

In the desert, Frank too was desolate, feeling, as his valet vividly remembered, that he had "no one, nothing." Now and then he consoled himself by playing with his vast set of electric trains, housed in its own cottage on the Wonder Palms compound: a boyhood dream fulfilled. Electric trains had also been a passion of Sinatra's great and severe mentor, Tommy Dorsey—another man who had often found human relations an insuperable challenge.

———

Sinatra had signed Duke Ellington to Reprise in the first flush of excitement with his new record label, at a time when he still believed that his passion for jazz would be shared by the record-buying public. It hadn't happened. Soon after the Warner-Reprise merger, Ellington, along with a number of other jazz artists, including Count Basie, was cut from the roster.

Though Frank had lost interest in being a record executive, he still loved jazz and had long harbored a desire to make an album with Duke; he'd first considered the idea in 1947, back in the Columbia days. Twenty years later, the album finally happened, though just barely.

Duke Ellington was a great artist in decline at the end of 1967. His longtime collaborator, arranger, and muse, Billy Strayhorn, had died in May; the sixty-eight-year-old Ellington, who as a bandleader had always depended on Strayhorn and the musicians to inspire and piece out his great compositions, was now finding, as his biographer Terry Teachout writes, "that his music was no longer in vogue." (Much to Duke's annoyance, Sinatra had tried hard to steal Strayhorn away from him in Reprise's early days.) After leaving the label,

Ellington had to stoop to recording albums of contemporary pop tunes, including Beatles music; he also continued to tour with his band, which included many of the musicians he'd worked with for years—legendary players such as Johnny Hodges, Paul Gonsalves, and Cootie Williams. But it was ever harder to find an audience, and though the players were still great, they were no longer as great, or as committed, as they had once been.

Sinatra had tapped Billy May to write the arrangements, and the two of them came up with the song selections, a slightly melancholic mixture of unexpected jazz numbers (including only one Ellington original, "I Like the Sunrise"), Broadway tunes, and one contemporary hit (Bobby Hebb's "Sunny"). The album would have just eight tracks in all, in order to give the great soloists time to show what they could do. Yet when May and Bill Miller flew to Seattle, where Duke and the band were playing an extended stand, and rehearsed the charts, May's heart sank. "Jesus, the rehearsal was *terrible,*" he recalled. "That band, you know . . . they're terrible sight-readers. So we got it to where they ran them down, and they sounded okay." With two weeks to go to the session, Ellington promised May that the band would continue to rehearse the charts in concert, with Duke playing Frank's vocal parts on piano.

But the moment Ellington and his men straggled into Western Recorders (forty-five minutes late for the session), Billy May realized "they [had] never touched the charts again; they never even looked at 'em after that day." As Will Friedwald writes, "The Ellington organization was not only the greatest amalgamation of soloing and composing talent the jazz world has known, it was also a band of prima donnas who could only be held together by the biggest ego of them all . . . The band just didn't care to put any effort into the work of outside arrangers."

"May's solution," Friedwald continues, "was to add a couple of 'ringers' to the band, [music-]reading studio men who could follow the charts and play in the Ellington style." These included the trumpeter Al Porcino, a veteran of many Sinatra dates, and the keyboardists Jimmy Jones and Milt Raskin, to reinforce the aged maestro's fading pianistic skills.

It was a strange meeting that took place on the night of December 11: Ellington the old genius, a regal, feline, elusive presence ("He was very quiet," engineer Lee Herschberg remembered; "he didn't have much to say at all"), had an ego every bit as grand as Frank's and might still have held a grudge against him over Strayhorn. And understandably, Sinatra, the grieving soon-to-be ex-husband, was not in good voice that week; between his own condition and the band's poor preparedness, he'd briefly considered scuttling the project. But the chance to record with Ellington, he realized, might not come again.

And somehow, between Sinatra's determination, May's brilliance, the skill of the ringers, and the residual greatness (and sheer pride) of Duke and his men, it all came together. The great alto saxophonist Johnny Hodges played gorgeous solos on "Yellow Days" and the exquisite "Indian Summer"—a track Nelson Riddle later described as his favorite Sinatra chart and the only arrangement he wished he'd written. And tenor-sax legend Paul Gonsalves blew beautifully on the last song of the evening, the album's one up-tempo number: the blistering, brassy, bravura "Come Back to Me."

That song (by Alan Jay Lerner and Burton Lane, from the Broadway musical *On a Clear Day You Can See Forever*), with its plangent lyric—

Have you gone to the moon,
or the corner saloon and to rack and to ruin—

—was all too appropriate that week (as was the session's first number, Stephen Sondheim and Jule Styne's "All I Need Is the Girl," from *Gypsy*). And all too appropriately, Frank's long final note, the *me* of "come back to me," was one of the flattest he had ever hit.

The next night was his fifty-second birthday, and he couldn't have felt less festive. He wasn't in the mood for a party, he had told friends. "He wasn't really thrilled," recalled Milt Bernhart, who was visiting from the next studio. "At that point somebody wheeled in his birthday cake."

But, Lee Herschberg remembered, Frank's mood soon picked up: "Somebody, Jilly or one of his guys, came in with two really nice-looking ladies on his arm, and said, 'Frank, here's your birthday present.' We were out of there in an hour and a half that night!"

———

"Mia Farrow Sinatra slipped quietly into town to finish filming 'Rosemary's Baby,'" Earl Wilson noted on December 12.

In her memoir, Farrow recalled filming her last scene, in front of Tiffany on Fifth Avenue. In a perfectly poignant moment, she stands on the sidewalk as the crew members, her family for the last three months, stow away the gear and head home to their lives. It's Christmastime; she's alone. She goes back to Frank's penthouse and packs her things; all at once she sits down next to her bags, uncertain where to go next. Just then, Pamela Hayward—the wife of Leland Hayward and part of Sinatra's A-list set—breezes in. She tells Mia she's been worrying about her. She's headed to Palm Springs, right away, to stay at Frank's for Christmas. She phones Frank and chides him good-naturedly: This girl needs some sunshine and a good meal. The next thing she knows, Farrow writes, they're landing in the desert.

That's the written version. Back in 1968, she'd told *Photoplay,* "I begged him to take me back, at least for the holidays. For just another try. He told me that he had invited a lot of people to spend the holidays with him and that if I didn't mind a crowd, he would be happy to have me there."

It was always safer in a crowd.

It wasn't much of an invitation, but then she was desperate. "I would have taken him up on the offer if the crowd had been big enough to fill the Colosseum," she said.

It almost was. Frank had invited no fewer than twenty-seven people to Palm Springs to salve his birthday/holiday/marital blues: the Deutsches, the Goetzes, the Brissons, the Cerfs, the Hornblows, Harry Kurnitz, the Haywards, the Brynners, Garson Kanin and Ruth Gordon; a dozen more. All of them old and staid and rich, except Mia. "It was a fun crowd; two weeks of fun and games," she insisted to *Photoplay* just after the holiday, her desperate smile readable between the lines. "I never had such a marvelous time. Frank was surrounded by the people he likes best, me included. And he was so relaxed and happy. I have never seen him so happy. Maybe the happiness of those two weeks had a good effect on our marriage. I hope so."

It's eerily like the brittle Daisy Buchanan—a character Farrow would play six years hence—sobbing about how beautiful Jay Gatsby's shirts are.

In fact, Mia found Frank "withdrawn and stern" when she arrived in Palm Springs. At the same time, she writes, she felt thankful to be there and anxious not to make any mistakes. They discussed nothing of substance—not *Rosemary's Baby,* or *The Detective,* or Lee Remick, or the papers she had signed. Most of all, she recalled, they avoided discussing the future.

As in the past, Sinatra asked her to arrange the seating for each night's dinner, specifically instructing her never to seat him next to a certain woman, because she was so boring. He tolerated the couple, established A-listers in Frank's life, because the husband was so amusing.

And so every night Farrow dutifully shuffled the two dozen guests around the three dinner tables, taking care never to place the offending woman next to her host—until, one night, the woman's husband caught Mia alone in the living room. She smiled, but he was screaming at her, she remembered. They had been there for four days, the man yelled, and Farrow hadn't seated his wife next to Frank once. The woman was unhappy and humiliated, he told her. " 'You are a stupid, rude little girl—you will *never* be a hostess!' "

Farrow was so unnerved by the assault, she writes, that she said nothing, to the man or to Sinatra. She was convinced that the man would never have lit into her this way if he hadn't felt certain she would soon be out of Frank's life. As a final slap she adds that the couple were friends of Ronald Reagan and would eventually play a key role in winning Sinatra's support for Reagan and the Republican Party.

Her Christmas present to him was a genuine London taxi, bought while she was filming *A Dandy in Aspic*. She had gone to considerable trouble to have the vehicle converted to U.S. specifications, and Yul Brynner, she recalled, had planned an elaborate ceremony, complete with rented livery uniforms for himself and George Jacobs. That afternoon, as cocktail hour began, Brynner would honk the horn and Farrow would roust Frank and the rest of the company outdoors, where Brynner and Jacobs, with much ado, would present the taxi.

Five o'clock came, the horn tooted, and the guests, all of them in on the big surprise, trooped out the door, followed by Frank and Mia, tugging his arm. But Frank was grumpy—he didn't like being told what to do—and so he told *her* what to do: it was cold out, she should go back inside and put on a sweater. She tried to jolly him along, but he was getting mad; he wouldn't budge until she put on that sweater.

The guests had gone silent; all eyes were on Sinatra and Farrow. She blushed hotly; her smile stuck to her teeth. She ran back indoors, fetched a sweater from her dresser, threw it around her shoulders, and ran back out. Frank was still annoyed, and still in command mode. He told her to put the sweater *on*. She obeyed, buttoning every button. Only then could they proceed down the path to the taxicab. The guests stood aside. Brynner, in livery, bowed and handed Sinatra a scroll while Jacobs beamed and saluted. The company applauded as Frank and Mia stood there, staring at the shiny automobile.

It was an Austin, black and square and hopelessly duddy. He hated it. Yes, he was fifty-two; yes, he hung out with rich Republicans. But he was *Frank Sinatra,* for Christ's sake—he drove a Dual-Ghia! How could she have ever thought he would like such a thing?

Of course it didn't help that they weren't talking about much of anything these days.

Another thing they had failed to talk about was just what was going to happen with the two of them after this holiday idyll. On New Year's Eve, Frank transported the whole contingent, "dressed to the nines and already tanked up," as Farrow remembered, to L.A. for a party. The lyricist Alan Jay Lerner and the director Joshua Logan were there; they told Mia they'd already seen some dailies of *Rosemary's Baby* and that she was fantastic—would she consider starring in the film they were preparing, an adaptation of the Lerner-Loewe musical *Paint Your Wagon?*

She was transported by the respect they were showing her. Sinatra was silent. A couple of hours later, Frank told her he was leaving. Could she come too? she asked, running along after him. He drove her to their house in Bel Air and said he was going to Acapulco.

He was going to visit Merle Oberon and her husband, and his plans did not include his wife.

He's the king, isn't he?

—HUBERT H. HUMPHREY, WATCHING SINATRA
IN CONCERT ON MAY 3, 1968

While Frank stewed in Mexico, Mia languished in the big house on Copa de Oro Road, lying exhausted on the new king-size bed. The house was cold, but she couldn't bring herself to ask the housekeeper or the Japanese cook how to turn on the heat. At night, she would creep down to the refrigerator for comfort food (Sara Lee chocolate cake), passing Frank's favorite room, with its bar and big TV and orange furniture. " 'Evening, Mrs. S.,' said the guard, no matter what," she recalled. "He had a gun."

She writes that in her fog of despair, she unwrapped a Wilkinson razor blade that lay by the bathroom sink, then carefully rewrapped it. She couldn't concentrate, even on suicide. She had no idea where to go, what to do.

Then Frank himself arrived in a dark suit and shiny shoes, redolent of the aftershave John Farrow had also worn, bringing her a present, the nicest thing he had ever given her: a beautiful antique music box. He showed her how to crank it; they listened to it play seven songs, she writes.

Reality, or a dream?

Or perhaps just another juggling of the timeline. Unmerciful reality brought another visitor to her front door, the ever-charming Mickey Rudin. Sinatra had phoned him from Acapulco, the lawyer told her, and said that Farrow could stay anywhere she wanted—he would pay for it—but she couldn't be in the house when he returned. Rudin said he was sorry, but she would have to leave.

She threw a few things in a small suitcase, got into the yellow Thunderbird he'd bought her, and drove, sobbing, to a hotel.

———

"The New Year's reconciliation of Frank Sinatra and Mia Farrow seems to have taken," the syndicated columnist Florabel Muir chirped in her Hollywood column of January 12.

They're back from Palm Springs and everything is hunky-dory.

Mia has agreed to give up her acting career and concentrate on being Mrs. Frank Sinatra, housewife. And that's a full-time career for any gal!

She has also given up her proposed pilgrimage to India to meet with the Beatles' guru. The next thing you know, she'll let her hair grow, put on some weight and stay out of the spotlight.

It was, of course, the sheerest fiction. Muir—a former crime reporter whose claim to fame was once having been shot in the behind while covering the gangster Mickey Cohen—was nearly eighty, close to the end of a long career; God knows who had fed her the story. A few days later, Frank phoned Mia and said that he couldn't get her off his mind, but it was over between them. He would give her all the money she wanted, he told her; she wanted nothing, she said, except him. It was the one thing he was powerless to give. The next day, Farrow flew to New York to join her sister Prudence to travel to the foothills of the Himalayas to meditate with Maharishi Mahesh Yogi.

"I want to be a better person," a shy and nervous Mia Farrow told the Associated Press as she prepared to board a plane to India. With the fur-trimmed hood of her winter coat pulled close around her face, she resembled an eager space traveler or a child in a snowsuit.

The blonde actress, estranged wife of singer Frank Sinatra, made the brief statement at Kennedy Airport while seated next to the smiling, bearded Indian guru.

Miss Farrow's departure for India apparently was a last-minute decision.

The guru said she spoke to him Monday night about "higher spiritual experience which is common to the youngsters today" and indicated she wanted to go to India with him.

"She will make a good disciple," the guru said, adding, "she is a good person—good human material. I will guide her to higher spiritual experience . . ."

He . . . was asked if Miss Farrow mentioned her husband during her brief talk with him.

"She didn't speak of him," he answered. "Maybe hearing of her experience, he will come along."

In the meantime, though, Frank was headed back to the Fontainebleau. He was booked for an unprecedented six weeks in the La Ronde Room, two shows a night, six days a week. Once again, he planned to shoot a movie during the daylight hours: a *Tony Rome* sequel called *Lady in Cement,* like its predecessor heavy on sex, violence, and tough-guy jokes and light on deep meaning. The same production team—producer Aaron Rosenberg, director Gordon Douglas, director of photography Joseph Biroc—was in place. The reliable Richard Conte returned as Miami police lieutenant Dave Santini; *Bonanza*'s Dan Blocker played a giant heavy named Waldo Gronsky, and the eye-candy quota was filled by the twenty-seven-year-old Raquel Welch, who on the strength of her breakout role in 1966's *One Million Years B.C.* (in an animal-pelt bikini she looked ready to break out of any second) had become an instant international sex symbol. Welch, so intimidated by the prospect of acting with Sinatra that Gordon Douglas had to rehearse her separately for their first big scene together, had been given second billing.

This was a last-minute development. Sammy Davis was to have played Tony's sidekick, a Miami cop named Rubin, but then, practically as soon as he was in, he was out—"forced to bow out," in the dire words of a *Variety* item. Frank's warm-up comic Pat Henry, who had done a deft job with a small part in *The Detective,* replaced Sammy, at a considerably lower salary.

Davis's ejection from *Lady in Cement* was part of a chain of events that began in early February, when Sinatra postponed his Fontainebleau opening—which he'd originally set for Friday the ninth, in honor of his parents' anniversary—and then postponed it again. Something volcanic was bubbling in Frank.

Whatever chaos rumbled through Sinatra's life that February had its roots in the previous summer, when Mia had first gone to work on *Rosemary's Baby* and his marriage had begun to fall apart. As furious as he might have been at her, he was also reeling. He was always far more sensitive than he liked to let on, her running off to India had thrown him for a loop, and as had happened often before when relationships blew up, he took ill.

His world was out of balance. Not only had his wife flown the coop, not only had he fallen out with Sammy for the umpteenth time, but he was, Earl Wilson reported, "causing talk in Miami Beach. There was a rumor he'd rapped Eddie Fisher in the mouth. Also other people. And that he'd been refusing calls from Mia Farrow. Probably all untrue. Who'd want to rap a nice guy like Eddie Fisher and who'd want to turn down calls from Mia? Frank's opening at the Fontainebleau postponed from today (Feb. 9) to next Friday because Frank has been in bed . . . with a 102 degree flu."

Sinatra's displeasure radiated out from the penthouse suite. Earl Wilson rapidly found himself in retraction mode—for himself and others. "It wasn't true at all that Frank Sinatra rapped Eddie Fisher in the teeth in Miami Beach, as was rumored down there," he wrote, awkwardly, on February 14.

Fact is, when Eddie had to drop out of his Fontainebleau show one night, sick, Frank, who was also sick, got Pat Henry to go on for him. And then Frank lent Eddie & Connie Stevens his jet so they could go off for a few days' rest. Eddie said he never had had such great respect for Frank before.

The broadcast rumor that Frank Sinatra divorced Mia Farrow in Mexico was denied instantly by Sinatra's publicist, Jim Mahoney.

A front-page *Variety* story on the same day also cited other rumors, including one claiming "Sinatra wasn't ill, just mad at one thing or another. His physician, Fontainebleau medic Dr. Ralph Robbins, says no, the singer has pneumonia."

In truth, the singer was both ill and mad. At Sammy, for unspecified reasons (though his running off to London a few months earlier to make some crappy movie called *Salt and Pepper*, with Lawford, didn't help); at the comedian Jack E. Leonard—with whom he almost came to blows in the Fontainebleau's Club Gigi—for continuing to do Mia jokes. And at Earl Wilson, his oldest and most steadfast friend among the columnists, who'd betrayed him twice within the space of a week.

───────

Finishing *Mayerling*, Ava got a call from Florida. Frank had pneumonia, the caller said; he was very sick. He was asking for her, saying her name over and over. She flew to Miami, arriving with her maid, Reenie Jordan, a secretary, and twenty-nine pieces of luggage. "She was taken by private elevator to his inner sanctum at the top of the Fontainebleau, behind sprawled layers of hangers-on, yes-men and three-hundred-pound gorillas—Frank's mouth-breathing *cuadrilla* he now took with him wherever he went," Gardner's biographer Lee Server writes.

"You glad to see me, baby?" Frank said.

"They told me you were dying, Francis," she said. "I've been traveling for 24 hours to get here."

He'd had a virus in the lungs, it was bad, not quite bad enough to go to the hospital and lose his penthouse view. But when Frank got sick he needed a lot of people at his bedside, praying. She remembered that time in Lake Tahoe when the stooge, with tears, told her Frank was at death's door and she had to turn around and rush back from Los Angeles at dawn. In Miami, stressed from worry and jet-lagged, she screamed at him for being a selfish prick.

A witness recalled, "She walked right into Frank's room, took one look at him, and said, 'Jesus Christ, you're not dying, are you? Here we fucking go again. What the hell is really wrong with you? You got a cold or what? What am I doing here, anyway? Do you know what I had to go through to get here?'"

She left the next day.

Yet he truly was sick—too sick to open on February 16 or 23; ill enough, George Jacobs maintained, that he had to be briefly hospitalized. "I was very worried about his health," the valet recalled. "I assumed he was indestructible, and here he was, at the mercy of the place he hated above all others, a hospital. His skin was sallow, greenish. He was too weak to insist on wearing a hairpiece. He seemed to have given up. He looked frail and old and helpless, as well as furious at himself, and the heavens, for letting him get this way."

"Frank Sinatra remains weak—and unusually quiet—from his pneumonia," Earl Wilson noted on the twenty-eighth, "and the boss of the Miami Beach Fontainebleau, Ben Novack, is unable to say whether he'll open there Friday as announced."

Then he was better. "The Jet Set rush to Miami Beach'll be on this weekend with Frank Sinatra definitely opening at the Fontainebleau Friday," Wilson wrote, breathlessly, on March 1.

The columnist and his wife, Rosemary—whom he'd immortalized in print as his BW, or Beautiful Wife—packed their bags "for a fast weekend trip to Miami Beach to catch the long-delayed opening of our friend, Frank," Wilson wrote in his memoir.

But when he arrived, he was told that Sinatra wouldn't go on if Wilson was in the audience.

"It was like being hit in the stomach," the columnist recalled. "In my whole life, I had never suffered such shock."

And it was true. "Frank Sinatra refused to open engagement at Fontainebleau here Fri. (1) if columnist Earl Wilson was in audience, according to spokesman for singer," *Variety* noted on March 4.

> Same source reports Sinatra learned there was a reservation for Wilson and notified captain he would not entertain if scribe was permitted in. Wilson wasn't, and show went on.
>
> According to Sinatra's spokesman, performer has taken exception to two recent items in Wilson's pillar anent the singer.

"Pillar": *Variety*-ese for "column." But it wasn't just the two recent items that had gotten under Sinatra's skin; once again, his simmer had come to a boil. Months earlier, Jim Mahoney had told Wilson, "Frank didn't like the way you handled the story of the fight." Meaning the Carl Cohen fight.

The columnist was amazed. " 'Did he like the way *anybody* handled it?' I asked Mahoney. Could he have been pleased at anything written about such a display? Should I have defended his outrageous conduct?"

In Frank's mind, he should have. Earl Wilson had been covering Sinatra since the Tommy Dorsey days, and though he stopped short of fawning, over the years he had been so reliably friendly in print that a friendship had formed, and in truth a journalistic line had been crossed. Every gossip columnist had to work out the uneasy equation for him- or herself: agreeableness, however disingenuous, was the price of access. If it went too far, though, credibility was lost. Some writers, like Kilgallen, played it tough, but then they often had to make do with secondhand reports and blind items. Earl Wilson had tried to have his credibility and his friendship too and in the end—buffeted by the force of Frank's raging—had found it impossible.

He was devastated. "I surrendered to Sinatra's decree in what was one of the saddest moments of my career," he recalled.

> I cannot describe the shame I felt, the dejection and the hurt of the rejection. After trying to be an honorable newspaperman with a reputation for getting along with big personalities, to get this slap in the face made me crumble spiritually.
>
> The word *barred* is a degrading one in my business, and it had never been used against me before. A thicker-skinned columnist might have taken it as a compliment, but I could not be flippant about it; I was hurt.
>
> "It's finally happened to me," I said, "the thing that's always happened to his other friends, and I never believed it did."

What had made him think he was any different?

A little pale, a little thin, Frank bounded back from his sickbed and gave 'em hell. When he took the stage in the La Ronde Room—with a new, kind of hippie-inspired look, a white turtleneck sweater and a pendant, instead of a tux—he made the crowd forget there was anyone else.

Under the headline SINATRA COMES ON WITH THE OLD GUSTO, George Bourke wrote in the *Miami Herald:*

> Fourteen pounds and several shades of suntan lighter than normally, Sinatra belted out an hour and ten minutes of song, most of which was as good as he ever did it, albeit with a throatiness not too distracting to the ear with decades-long tuning to his style.

Sinatra didn't stack the deck with easy numbers either. There were some songs that stood for no faking, and it seemed Sinatra undertook them defiantly, aware that a guy who'd had pneumonia shouldn't be expected to handle them and that there were some people who'd be making bets he couldn't.

All the while, his waif of a wife was in India, seeking purity and truth.

The mountainside ashram was cold and hard and austere in the dead of winter. She lived in a small room with a hard bed, a chest of drawers, and a dim lamp; ordered to meditate twelve hours a day, she did her best, she recalled, but rarely came close (unlike her sister, who rarely emerged from her room). Instead, she read and thought her thoughts and walked by the rushing Ganges. Nearly every afternoon, the maharishi summoned her to his bungalow for a private talk; he gave her mangoes. She responded, she said, with wary resentment: Why was he singling her out?

Up till now, Farrow recalled, the ashram had been a cold, hushed, monotonous place, with practically every waking hour devoted to meditation. Then one afternoon, the Beatles arrived.

The group had turned to transcendental meditation—and said they'd given up drugs—the previous August; they had planned to travel to Rishikesh in October, before the death of their manager, Brian Epstein, threw them into disarray. Led by George Harrison, the one of them who truly believed in the maharishi's discipline ("Whenever I meditate," John Lennon complained, "there's a big brass band in me head"), they finally made it to India in February and arrived at the ashram like a traveling circus, disrupting the solemn atmosphere with their music and jokes.

Mia Farrow was transformed by their presence. They sat by the river, playing their guitars and singing; as she talked with them, she recalled, the heaviness that had descended on her lifted. "They seemed beautiful and fearless," she writes. And young. Amazingly, she hadn't spent time with people her own age since high school.

All at once, Farrow recalled, the ashram changed from a gray place into a colorful one. The Beatles and their music seemed omnipresent—even at meals, to which they brought their guitars, improvising ditties for the amusement of the other pilgrims, Farrow recalled. Many of these tunes—including "Dear Prudence," imploring Mia's sister to leave her cloistered meditating and come out to play—would wind up on *The White Album*.

Then, one day, the maharishi invited Mia to a personal meditation session in his cave. After twenty minutes, as they rose to their feet, he was suddenly embracing her with surprisingly hairy arms.

She fled—the cave, the ashram, the country. A movie, *Secret Ceremony*,

Mia Farrow with three Beatles, Donovan, and Maharishi Mahesh Yogi, Rishikesh, India, March 1968. On the run from her disintegrating marriage, Farrow found momentary peace at the ashram; soon she would be running again.

was waiting for her in London if she wanted it. Joseph Losey directing, Elizabeth Taylor and Robert Mitchum co-starring. She decided to take it.

And Frank had finally decided to take her calls. From Miami, he invited her to stay in the vacant flat in Grosvenor Square, an idea that appealed to her, Farrow recalled, because she imagined it would make her feel somehow close to him. Instead, though, staying in the place where they'd lived as newlyweds only made her miss him more sharply.

The previous months' events, in her case with the chaotic overlay of the ashram and India, had undone her no less than they had him. With two weeks to kill before filming began, she slowly unraveled. Unable to sleep at night, she spent her days in bed, afraid to go outside. Then, one day, her doctor found her incoherent and checked her into a clinic. After spending three days there, heavily medicated, she enlisted her secretary's help to escape, climbing out a window and down a fire escape. "If you kill yourself," the secretary told her, "I'll never forgive you."

She flew to Miami.

Her taxi pulled up to the Fontainebleau on a hot, humid night; the big marquee read FRANK SINATRA. From the driveway she could hear the band playing "My Kind of Town (Chicago Is)." Walking into the showroom, she saw Sinatra as she had seen him so often before: standing in the smoky spotlight in his tuxedo, microphone in hand.

"Near the end, when the lights went up, the audience suddenly turned,"

Hollywood reporter Hal Bates wrote. "There was a low murmur. Someone spotted Mia Farrow standing in the La Ronde Room, near the entrance. Frank hadn't seen her."

According to the Associated Press, Farrow had slipped into the Fontaine-bleau at 1:30 on the morning of Saturday, March 9, sneaking in by way of the hotel tennis courts and basement, much as she had sneaked out of the London clinic. She watched the rest of his show, then went up to the penthouse with him.

A couple of days later, she returned to London. They'd agreed they would finish their respective movies. Then they would see.

―――――

His energy was back, but not his equilibrium. "He was sad. He was hurting," said Nancy junior, who'd traveled to Miami to comfort her father. He was determined to wrap up the silly movie—in three weeks, he said.

His haste showed: the good feelings of the *Tony Rome* shoot faded into memory as the irritable star intimidated much of *Lady in Cement*'s cast and crew. "He was real upset," an extra named Al Algiro recalled. "I remember Pat Henry messed up his lines real bad, and after three takes Frank got so mad he went over and slapped Pat in the face a few times and told him to shape up."

Kitty Kelley charged the star with "refusing to do more than one take and ripping out handfuls of the script to save time" and treating Gordon Douglas "like a lackey who was on the film simply to accommodate him. At Frank's insistence, Douglas scheduled his scenes so that he never had to come to work before noon; the sets were pre-lit, and his double plotted every move so that by the time Frank arrived, he could complete action on one set and proceed to the next without delay."

But Sinatra had been One-Take Charlie since the start of his film career; ripping out script pages and starting work at noon were nothing new, either. Frank well knew the difference between an entertainment and a work of cinema, and he was no longer in the cinema business: Zinnemann and Preminger and Frankenheimer were figures of his past. He had hired Gordon Douglas—and had kept on hiring him—not because he was a lackey, but because he was a skillful journeyman who could be depended on to get the best possible work out of Sinatra in the shortest possible time.

―――――

Screw the movies; singing was the only thing that really mattered. Raquel Welch remembered attending one of Sinatra's shows that March, accompanied by a reluctant Elia Kazan, who wanted to talk to her about a possible movie role. "Gadge said, 'Where can we meet?'" Welch recalled. "I said, 'Every night, I go to see Frank at the Fontainebleau. Would you like to have dinner with me there?' He said, 'Oh, I hate that son of a bitch.'" She persuaded Kazan to go anyway.

"So we're sitting there," the actress said, "and Gadge is saying, 'This son of a bitch, he only does one take—who the fuck does he think he is, telling some director that that's it, he's done?' I said, 'Okay. But I've been with him on the set, and actually Frank's first take is a pretty remarkable first take; he actually does seem to get it. It's kind of annoying if you have to wait for everybody else to catch up with you.'"

She kept trying to soften Kazan's stance, but the director "kept going on and on about what a son of a bitch Sinatra was, how he thought he was such a big shot and a tough guy and all the rest. Finally, the overture starts and they're playing all these amazing arrangements, and Frank comes out from the wings, grabs hold of the microphone, hits center stage with the spotlight, and just starts singing. He gets halfway through the first song, and Gadge turns to me and says, 'My God! This fuckin' guy is the best actor I've ever seen in my life. He's completely naked up there; I take back everything I said. He's a genius.'"

―――――

Early in that presidential election year, Communist forces in Vietnam launched the surprise Tet Offensive, killing thousands of American and South Vietnamese soldiers and significantly eroding U.S. confidence that the war could be won. In early March, as domestic resistance to the conflict intensified, the antiwar Democratic candidate Eugene McCarthy made a surprisingly strong showing against President Johnson in the New Hampshire primary; four days later, Robert F. Kennedy, also an opponent of the war, declared his candidacy. On the Republican side, Richard Nixon held a strong lead in the polls against Ronald Reagan and Nelson Rockefeller.

On the night of March 31, as Frank Sinatra and his older daughter watched the television in Frank's penthouse suite at the Fontainebleau, the president— who privately worried about his health and felt he had lost control of the Democratic Party over Vietnam—stunned the nation by announcing he would not seek reelection.

After the broadcast, Nancy Sinatra remembered, she and her father talked about the war and the upcoming presidential election. Frank told Nancy he felt strongly that Hubert Humphrey should run. Nancy, a Bobby Kennedy supporter, said she believed Humphrey would have to weigh in on Vietnam. Her father agreed, but said that as Lyndon Johnson's vice president, Humphrey couldn't embarrass LBJ by denouncing the war. Nancy, who had seen the hostilities at close range, bridled at this: the war had to stop, she believed passionately. Frank told her he felt the same way, and knew Humphrey did too.

This was the sober and contemplative Frank. The less sober, vindictive Frank immediately began salting his onstage patter with nasty cracks about Bobby Kennedy. And soon, he had something more immediate to be irked about: the *Miami Herald,* the very paper that had just given him such a glowing review, was threatening to subpoena him in the Fontainebleau's $10 million libel suit against the newspaper, which had run a story two years earlier charging the hotel with being run by the Mob.

Sinatra had briefly testified in the suit while he was in Miami the previous spring. But the *Herald's* attorney, William Steel, now said, "Sinatra played fast and loose with us on his deposition. There were misleading answers. We want to explore the curious relationship of Sinatra to the Fontainebleau and whether he is an owner or not."

Frank's curious relationship to the great and tawdry Miami hotel went back a decade and was tightly entwined with his longtime friendship with Joe Fischetti. And as the libel trial now proceeded, an odd piece of information emerged: "Hotel executive v.p. Frank Margulies testified that Sinatra has not been paid anything by the Fontainebleau for his six-week engagement this year, nor for a double date in La Ronde Room a year ago," *Variety* reported on April 10.

Margulies said Fontainebleau prexy Ben Novack handled Sinatra arrangements and that Joe Fischetti was instrumental in them.

Hotel records show that Fischetti, a cousin of the late Al Capone, was paid $1,080 a month by the hotel on and off between 1959 and 1962. Fischetti's two dead brothers, Rocco and Charles, were leaders in the Chicago Mafia organization before their deaths.

When Joe Fischetti was called for pre-trial deposition, he took the Fifth Amendment to all Herald questions. Several Fontainebleau employees have testified that Fischetti is Sinatra's constant companion when at the Fontainebleau.

In a fury about the *Herald's* subpoena, Frank almost canceled his last four nights at the Fontainebleau, but then, having suddenly and strangely calmed down, he decided to take the summons and finish his engagement. "We're having a wonderful time in Miami Beach," he told his audience on the night of April 3. "Get a subpoena every day." He was served the next day and ordered by a circuit-court judge to show up or risk going to jail.

On April 4, while Sinatra contemplated his legal woes, Martin Luther King

Jr. was assassinated in Memphis. Rioting broke out in Washington, D.C., Baltimore, Kansas City, and Chicago.

But not in Miami, where Frank wrapped *Lady in Cement* on the fifth, having completed the picture as speedily as he'd wished. He finished his Fontainebleau engagement the next night.

Then he skipped town.

"The Miami Herald reported today that Frank Sinatra abruptly left Florida Tuesday to avoid testifying under oath about his relationship with the owners and operators of the Fontainebleau Hotel here," the Associated Press reported on April 10.

But the Miami–Dade County circuit court was saved the trouble of trying to extradite Frank: on the twenty-first, the *Herald* suddenly retracted its accusations, and Ben Novack just as suddenly dropped his lawsuit against the paper. If it all smelled slightly fishy—had the *Herald* buckled to financial pressure? Had Joe Fischetti simply covered his tracks too well?—Novack got exactly what he wanted: a front-page statement in the *Miami Herald* saying, "We are of the opinion that the Fontainebleau is not owned or controlled by any gangsters or any underworld characters."

A curiously backhanded retraction.

Mickey Rudin wasn't so easily placated. The *Herald*'s subpoena of Frank Sinatra, he sniffed, had been "simply an attempt to harass and an unsuccessful effort to embarrass" his client about his relationship with the Fontainebleau and Ben Novack.

Once again, the newspapers had impeached Sinatra's reputation; once again, he had emerged tarnished but unindicted. But the papers weren't done with him yet.

––––––

Hubert Humphrey announced his candidacy in Washington, D.C., on April 27. Three days later, Frank Sinatra returned to the nation's capital for the first time since the Kennedy inaugural gala, ostensibly to give a benefit concert for the Big Brothers of America at the Shoreham Hotel on May 3, but actually to get back into the kingmaking business.

The syndicated political columnist Drew Pearson, who was president of the Big Brothers, had invited Frank to do the show; the payback was good publicity. At seventy, the distinguished-looking, white-mustached Pearson was the best-known columnist in America, famous for his liberal stances and muckraking investigative pieces. He'd battled Joseph McCarthy in the 1950s and more recently had gone after Governor Ronald Reagan. But in the May 1 column, he welcomed Sinatra to town, giving a glowing nod to the singer's participation in the benefit and adding as a lagniappe a refutation of the old rumor that Frank had dodged the draft in World War II. Pearson failed to mention his own connection to the Big Brothers, plus the fact that the vice president would be speaking at the event.

President Johnson, hearing that Sinatra would be starring at the Shoreham affair, had declined to attend.

Both Frank and Hubert Humphrey were guests at a cocktail party at the columnist's Georgetown house on the night of May 1. Tantalizingly, the invitations read "To meet Frank Sinatra and his candidate," but Sinatra's choice of candidate surprised nobody in Washington: he struck no one as a Eugene McCarthy man and had already said, for the record, "I don't think Bobby Kennedy is qualified to be president of the United States."

In a town of massive egos, Frank could more than hold his own. "I'm really going to make this town jump for the next two days," he told Mayor Walter Washington, as the cocktail music tinkled in Drew Pearson's colonial garden. Among the other guests that evening were two friends of Sinatra's, Teamsters vice president Harold Gibbons and a gray-haired, rugged-looking Chicago businessman named Allen Dorfman. Gibbons, the head of St. Louis Local 688, had organized the 1965 benefit for Dismas House at which Frank had entertained; he was also the heir apparent to the Teamsters' president, Jimmy Hoffa, then residing in the federal penitentiary in Lewisburg, Pennsylvania.

Allen Dorfman, officially in the insurance business but in reality a close associate of Hoffa's, had been acquitted of the same charges on which Hoffa had been convicted: bribing a juror and defrauding the Teamsters' Central States Pension Fund by making large loans to organized-crime figures. Hoffa was in prison largely due to the efforts of Bobby Kennedy, who before resigning as attorney general to run for a U.S. Senate seat in New York had made convicting the Teamsters leader a personal crusade.

Frank had flown into Washington with Allen Dorfman.

Maxine Cheshire, the *Washington Post*'s gossip columnist, was also at Pearson's party. She found herself intrigued by the sight of a man widely reputed to be mobbed up socializing with not only Frank Sinatra but also the vice president of the United States. "While Sinatra and several Teamsters had Humphrey back against a brick wall at one end of the terrace, I cornered Dorfman," Cheshire recalled. "I put my question bluntly: 'I understand you're here to make a deal with Humphrey; he'll pardon Hoffa in exchange for your help in getting him elected.'"

"Yeah, honey, we're here to buy everybody in town who's for sale," Dorfman said, adding charmingly, "What's your price?"

When Sinatra left, Cheshire followed him to one of Georgetown's most expensive restaurants, the Rive Gauche. Frank's dinner companions were

Harold Gibbons, Allen Dorfman, and Mrs. Jimmy Hoffa. The columnist approached their table and asked, quietly but firmly, whether Humphrey had promised to pardon Hoffa. No one answered.

Mrs. Hoffa "was tight-lipped and non-committal when asked if she had come to talk politics with a group that obviously was going to have unkind things to say about the man who put her husband in the penitentiary," Cheshire wrote in the *Post*.

> She stared grimly at her plate and the only time she opened her mouth was to nibble the minced clams in front of her.
>
> Sinatra disappointed other diners at the posh Georgetown restaurant. Many who have read of his public displays of pugilistic prowess expected him at least to take a swing at the Washington Post photographer.
>
> But Sinatra controlled his temper, despite the fact that he had asked the management to protect his party from publicity . . .
>
> The group also included dapper, sun-tanned Allen Dorfman of Chicago, whose green-suited sartorial splendor had been attracting attention at the Pearson party. He was one of Jimmy Hoffa's co-defendants in the latter's jury bribery trial.

It was not the kind of publicity Frank had been looking to get in Washington.

He did better with the *Star*'s society columnist Betty Beale, who went gaga for his concert. "Sinatra, wearing the gold Russian cross of St. Anne on a chain with his white Cossack-type shirt and tuxedo, wowed the 1,600 people who subscribed to the Big Brothers benefit dinner honoring its president, Drew Pearson," Beale wrote.

> All 1,600 listened spellbound to the performance that helped raise the dinner's profits of $50,000.
>
> "He's the king, isn't he?" exclaimed Vice-president Humphrey.
>
> Washington also saw a different Sinatra than the one generally portrayed in print . . . At the dinner here, Frank told Mayor Walter Washington that during the poor people's march in the Capital he will need to keep people occupied to keep the situation under control.
>
> "At any time if you need me to come back and help," he said, "just give me a few days' notice and I will do it."

Sinatra told Beale that he planned to do fund-raising shows for Humphrey in six to ten cities starting at the end of May; he said he also intended to organize a committee of a hundred entertainers for the candidate, including his daughter Nancy. (He had pulled this number out of the air; because of Humphrey's continued support for the war in Vietnam, Hollywood Democrats, including Nancy junior, were staying away from the candidate in droves.) When the matronly columnist asked him about the diamond-studded cross he was wearing, Frank, turning on the charm, told her it had been a gift from Mrs. Leland Hayward. "It was the first really valuable one your correspondent has seen on a man, though pendants are the new rage, and I must say it was very handsome," Betty Beale fluttered.

At the same dinner, Maxine Cheshire saw Frank come through the receiving line, again with Mrs. Hoffa, and heard Drew Pearson apologize to them both for Cheshire's unfortunate story in the *Washington Post*—which, he'd said on his radio show earlier in the day, had been completely fabricated.

Though President Johnson had skipped the concert, he'd suggested to Hubert Humphrey that he "bring Drew around to the White House after the party." Little did Johnson suspect that Pearson would himself bring a guest: the man the president had been trying to avoid in the first place.

The vice president, the columnist, and Frank Sinatra arrived in the Lincoln Bedroom of the White House after midnight to find a mildly surreal scene. "Lady Bird Johnson was already under the covers in the big four-poster Lincoln bed with its overhanging canopy," writes Pearson's biographer Oliver Pilat.

> The President, bare above pajama bottoms, was lying on a table being pounded by a masseur.
>
> After a quick glance, Johnson turned his head away from his visitors without saying anything. Humphrey's light conversation with Lady Bird gradually evaporated. The President finally threw a few words of greeting at Humphrey and Pearson, ignoring Sinatra, who had gone over to the famous mantelpiece, on which, Pearson had reported in the column, Jacqueline Kennedy had carved a strange record of her husband's tenancy.*

The president hopped off the massage table, picked up a souvenir booklet about the White House, and thrust it at Frank. "I don't suppose you read," Johnson said, "but this has lots of pictures."

---

* Reportedly, the inscription Mrs. Kennedy had placed on the mantelpiece read, "In this room lived John Fitzgerald Kennedy and his wife, Jacqueline, during the two years, 10 months and two days he was President of the United States." *Chicago Tribune*, May 22, 1994.

Frank and Hubert Humphrey, August 1968: a very temporary friendship. Sinatra's lifelong identification as an FDR Democrat would come to an end in this annus horribilis of assassinations, riots, and an escalating conflict in Vietnam.

Towering over his uninvited guest, the six-foot-four-inch president also handed Sinatra something else: a presidential trinket for women visitors, a lipstick with the White House seal on it. "It's a conversation piece," Johnson said. "It'll make a big man of you with your women."

Frank turned and left the room without saying a word.

—————

He hit the campaign trail hard, and alone. The Democrats were deeply divided that spring, and Sinatra's celebrity friends were either Republicans or—like Shirley MacLaine, Sammy Davis Jr., Gene Kelly, Gregory Peck, and Sammy Cahn—Kennedy supporters. A splinter group of stars (among them Paul Newman, Robert Vaughn, Dick Van Dyke, Carl Reiner) supported Eugene McCarthy. The California primary was set for June 4, and the state leaned heavily toward RFK.

But politics was almost beside the point when Frank gave a concert for Humphrey in Oakland on May 22. "The King of the World—that would be Frank Sinatra, not Charles de Gaulle—came to Oakland the other night," wrote local columnist Al Martinez, "to give a benefit performance in behalf of the presidential candidacy of . . . of . . . oh yes, Hubert Humphrey, and it was a highly successful event. Sinatra ought to take the nomination on the first ballot easily."

It was funny, but it was pointed: Hubert Humphrey had energy and convictions—he'd been an outspoken liberal on civil rights since the late

1940s—yet unlike Frank's hero Jack Kennedy he barely moved the charisma meter. He wanted (a little too much) to be liked, and he was likable: certainly more likable than Dick Nixon. But Nixon had announced a "secret plan" to end the war, the country was sick of seeing the bodies come home week after week, and Humphrey kept waffling about the issue.

Bobby Kennedy, on the other hand, was an inspirational candidate, lacking his late brother's lustrous charm and dangerous sexuality but exuding an idealistic intensity which many found stirring in that tumultuous year. He wasn't just against the war; he spoke passionately for racial and economic justice; he visited and wooed the inner cities; he challenged America's young people to create a better future. Kennedy burned bright and pure, as though exorcising his Joe McCarthy past.

His backers felt that if Kennedy won the California primary, he could knock Eugene McCarthy out of the race and set up a face-off against Humphrey at the Democratic convention in August. This was the way it was heading. Kennedy won the June 4 primary (and on the same day beat Humphrey in Humphrey's birth state, South Dakota), but then shortly after midnight, after he addressed his supporters at the Ambassador Hotel in Los Angeles, the all-too-thinkable happened as he left the ballroom and walked through the hotel kitchen.

That night Sinatra was in Manhattan, drinking at Jilly's with a few friends, including the concert promoter Ken Roberts. "We were in the back, in Frank's booth," Roberts recalled.

> The hat-check girl, Fran, came in, and said, "Someone just shot Bobby Kennedy," and Sinatra made the comment, "I hope they shot him in the fuckin' head." That's exactly what he said, because we all thought she was kidding.
>
> A couple minutes later, she came back and said, "Yes, he was shot in the head." Sinatra turned white and became so frightened and panicked . . . He was panicked because he thought that, while he was singing, someone might shoot *him*.

According to George Jacobs, the assassination of Bobby Kennedy by Sirhan Sirhan brought Frank "no sense of satisfaction or retribution." This is hard to believe. Though Kennedy had come to Sinatra's aid during the kidnapping of Frank junior, deploying massive Justice Department muscle, it only underlined for Frank what he really was: a cop. And it never absolved him in Sinatra's mind of the primal sin of cleaving him from his friend Jack and bringing him massive public shame in the bargain.

More likely was that Frank felt a keen sense of retribution, mingled with guilt, horror, and, in this year of fire and upheaval, new vulnerability.

Her father was quiet for a while after the assassination, remembered Nancy Sinatra, who now, sadly, joined Frank in supporting Hubert Humphrey. Frank told his daughter he thought Humphrey was a decent man who seemed to care about people that others didn't care about. Frank believed him and believed in him, he said.

It was all very reasonable; all it lacked was passion. But then maybe passion was a thing of the past.

———

At the beginning of August, a strange item appeared at the top of Walter Winchell's column:

> Ava Gardner, who is mending rapidly from major surgery in St. Joseph's Hosp. where she was jetted in ex-husband F. Sinatra's private plane. It also flew her to his Palm Springs home to convalesce. The buzz adds that he also paid her hosp. bill ($8,000) etc.

In fact, Winchell's intelligence was almost two months out of date: Ava's surgery had taken place at the beginning of June. "An examination at the Chelsea Hospital for Women in London had detected the likely presence of a fibroid tumor in her uterus," her biographer writes. "Her mother's early death from uterine cancer had haunted Ava for more than twenty years. Any gynecological problem she ever experienced had provoked anxiety, and she would imagine a harbinger of that killing disease. Now, with little consideration, she elected to undergo a hysterectomy."

She had the operation at St. Joseph's Hospital in Burbank, and at first she recuperated at her sister Bappie's house nearby. The early-June date can be fixed through Ava's vivid memory of the surgery's aftermath. "I was lying in bed at my sister's house in California, recovering from my hysterectomy, which does jumble up a woman's mind, and I saw the assassination of Robert Kennedy on television," she recalled. "That night I had a terrible sort of vertigo, and by morning I was in a black depression. The deepest, blackest cloud descended on me; it completely engulfed me."

She was forty-five. The operation had definitely changed her as a woman; her career, too—such as it was—showed her age. In *Mayerling*, Omar Sharif and Catherine Deneuve had played the leads, the tragic lovers Crown Prince Rudolf and Baroness Vetsera; Gardner, though just ten years older than Sharif, had portrayed his mother, the empress Elisabeth, opposite James Mason's emperor Franz Josef. To crown the indignity, the dashing, certifiably hetero-sexual Sharif had insisted that their close friendship during the three-month shoot remain platonic.

On the other hand, some part of her was grateful not to be a star any-more, to no longer have to be the most beautiful woman in the world. She had stepped off that treadmill forever.

Still, she was adrift again, feeling low; she would eventually be put on the mood-altering medication Elavil. She convalesced from the operation at Frank's place in the desert, the tables turned oddly: just three months earlier, she had treated his illness with scorn; now he met her distress with a kindness as intense as the Palm Springs sun.

But then, he was the one who kept the torch glowing, even when all hope for rekindling it was gone.

The Detective opened nationwide on June 3 to mixed notices. "Critics praised the movie for its pungent, realistic dialogue," Nancy Sinatra said, which wasn't saying much. In fact, reviewers found much to fault about the picture: Vincent Canby of the *New York Times* called it "a film that haphazardly, even arrogantly, mixes the real and the fake," flaying Gordon Douglas's direction as "weak [and] unimaginative" and saying of Frank's performance, "Mr. Sinatra, whose toupee must be the best money can buy, has the waxy, blank look of a movie star as he moves through grimly authentic big city settings."

This was about right. In a time when the movies were going through big changes—Canby was writing in the stead of Frank's old nemesis Bosley Crowther, who'd been drummed out of the *Times* for his insistent and scath-ing attacks on Arthur Penn's groundbreaking, bloody 1967 feature, *Bonnie and Clyde*—*The Detective* had a dated look about it. As did its star. In *Tony Rome*, you thought less about Sinatra's age because he was having fun with the role; the movie never took itself seriously, nor did its star. *The Detective* was Seri-ous. And Frank, forced to be tough and grim, looked mostly old and puffy, as though the troubles with Mia were visibly weighing on him. His attempts to leaven the performance with humor didn't quite come off. (And the wig—though doubtless very expensive—wasn't that good.) Movie audiences were no longer sure why they wanted to see him. *The Detective* did so-so business.

On the other hand, *Rosemary's Baby*, which opened ten days later, quickly became the number one picture in the country, making an instant star of Mia Farrow in her own right and no longer as Frank's child bride. And that was the last straw for the marriage. The two of them had been talking on the phone, even writing to each other, but Mia's definitive box-office victory over him was the final humiliation.

She took no pleasure in the win. The movie's success, and her own, felt like abstractions to her, she recalled. She finished *Secret Ceremony*, reconnected with old friends, and prepared to move on. After a few months, she writes, though she still loved Frank, she stopped dreaming of a future with him. She had a summer fling with Peter Sellers; it made the gossip columns. Frank read the gossip columns.

———

He took Bill Miller and an orchestra back out on the road, singing for Humphrey in Cleveland, Minneapolis, Detroit. Then, on July 24 in New York City, he stepped into a recording studio for the first time in seven months to record a single that would take him in a new direction.

The A-side, arranged by Don Costa, was business as usual: another Bert Kaempfert song, with the strangely Germanic title "My Way of Life." The tune, complete with soaring chorus and rat-a-tatting drums, was imbued with the same kind of swelling Euro-drama as "The World We Knew" and was every bit as florid and vapid:

You are my way of life,
I'll never let you go.

It sounded as much like a threat as a promise.

But the B-side was a different matter altogether: a determined effort by Sinatra to come to terms with the musical times, his first foray into the new genre awkwardly known as folk rock. The number was titled, with breathy, earthy, late-'60s import, "Cycles."

Written by Gayle Caldwell, a former singer for the clean-cut ersatz-folk group the New Christy Minstrels, it was a lilting, bittersweet ode to the circularity of life: the being up and the being down, the passage of the seasons, that kind of thing. The songwriter Teddy Randazzo ("Goin' Out of My Head") had done a spare and gentle arrangement—a strumming guitar, a country-and-western-flavored piano, a small choir, some strings—and the song was, in its own pretty way, as vapid as the Kaempfert:

I've been told, and I believe,
that life is meant for livin'

It was thematic territory that Frank had covered before, far more powerfully, in "A Very Good Year" and "That's Life." But "Cycles" was here, and it was now; it matched the tenor of the times—or one kind of tenor, at any rate: a reaction against the harshness of the exploding world and corporatization; a retreat to natural things and youthful idealism.

It was just kind of ironic that Frank Sinatra was singing it.

In a certain way, he was bowing to the inevitable: youth was taking over the world, and youth had to be served. But he had had his fling with youth, and he'd been hurt: Was this pseudo-folk number his attempt at recovery or merely an attempt to sell records?

A song's meaning, residing in the words and music alike, meant almost everything to Sinatra. Among popular singers, he possessed a unique ability to penetrate to the core of a song's sense and convey it to a listener in ways that went beyond words. But selling records had always been equally important to him, even in the bad old Mitch Miller days. The sweet spot was when he could make great records that sold, and that had stopped happening. Now one out of two would have to do.

———

Mia, back in California, was living alone in the Bel Air house, waiting for the legal end of her marriage but managing to console herself in spite of it all. "Peter Sellers is in town seeing Mia Farrow," Dorothy Manners wrote from Hollywood on July 27.

> Mia's also seeing Sammy Hess, young realtor. Sometimes the dates overlap, and the three "losers" are spotted, a jolly threesome, at the fun-and-games spots.
>
> Losers? Well, Mia has lost Frank Sinatra; Peter has lost teeny-bopper wife Britt Ekland; and Sammy lost fiancée Tina Sinatra, the about-to-be ex-stepdaughter of Mia.
>
> The other night the trio went to Warner Bros.–7 Arts studio to see a special showing of "I Love You, Alice B. Toklas," Peter's starring picture. They thought it was pretty hilarious. And I hear it really is.

According to his valet, Frank was holed up in Palm Springs, too depressed about the divorce to do much besides watch *The Mod Squad* on TV—too down to "even want to dial up Jimmy Van Heusen's endless parade of call girls." Even so, he managed to make it to Los Angeles on Monday, August 12, to join his two daughters in recording a Sinatra-family Christmas album (Frank junior, touring county fairs in the Midwest, would dub in his vocals later). Though Nelson Riddle had done nice enough arrangements (Don Costa also contrib-uted) and obligingly stood at the podium, *The Sinatra Family Wish You a Merry Christmas* was a rather insipid affair. Still, the album has curiosity value, marking Frank's third recording of Sammy Cahn and Jule Styne's wonderful "The Christmas Waltz," and Tina Sinatra's only recorded vocals (she was "in a coma" with fear, she recalled). On a Cahn-reworded update of "The Twelve Days of Christmas," the youngest Sinatra even has a brief solo, pealing out,

On the third day of Christmas I gave my loving dad
Three golf clubs,

surprisingly on key and with girlish charm.

The divorce was planned for Friday, August 16. Mia was going to fly to El Paso with Mickey Rudin, who would bring the papers; they would drive across the bridge to Juárez and meet with a Mexican judge. It could all be done in an hour.

The night before, she badly needed to forget her troubles. Frank had Jack Daniel's and television; she had her own remedies. She would dance and dance, dance until her mind was empty.

That night, Thursday, August 15, George Jacobs had an evening to kill, a dead summer night in Beverly Hills. Not many nightspots were open: first he hit the Luau, a Trader Vic's–style restaurant on Rodeo Drive, with big banana trees and koi ponds and hurricane lamps and giant clamshell urinals in the men's room. But the Luau was dead, and so he ended up at the Daisy.[*] "I was just hanging out at the bar, when who should come in but Mia, with her dear friend John Phillips," Jacobs recalled.

> If the world thought Mia was in seclusion mourning her upcoming divorce from the Chairman, they would have been surprised by the gay party mood she was in that night. And if anyone symbolized the drug-rock culture, or lack thereof, that Frank Sinatra detested and feared, it was the long, greasy-haired, always stoned John Phillips, Mr. California Dreaming himself. Despite the drugs, Frank did covet Phillips's gorgeous blond wife, Mama Michelle, which probably made him hate Phillips even more. "Georgie Porgie, pudding 'n' pie, kiss this girl and make her sigh," Mia greeted me in a playful singsong voice, as if she

---

[*] In his 2003 memoir, co-written with William Stadiem, Jacobs asserts that it was the Candy Store where he wound up, after first stopping by the Luau and the Daisy. But because Jacobs spoke to Kitty Kelley in the early 1980s, when his memory was fresher, I've stuck with his first story.

hadn't seen me for years, though I had just been with her at the Bel Air house that afternoon. I thought she was high, high as a kite. "Dance with me, Georgie Porgie," she insisted, dragging me out to the floor while John Phillips went into the men's room to smoke a joint, or do something stronger.

They danced for what seemed to Jacobs like an eternity. He kept looking in vain for Phillips to emerge from the men's room while the music played: "Sunshine of Your Love"; "This Guy's in Love with You"; "Love Child." Jacobs felt uncomfortable, especially when the music was slow and he held his boss's soon-to-be ex, stoned and a little too affectionate, in his arms. When the DJ put on "Somethin' Stupid" and the voices of Frank and Nancy junior filled the club, the valet had had all he could take. Finally, he handed Mia back to Phillips and left.

———

She and Mickey Rudin were the only passengers aboard the Lear Jet, she recalled; she sat as far away from him as possible in the aircraft's small cabin. From the Juárez airport, they were driven at top speed to the courthouse, where a crowd of paparazzi waited. Once in the building, she went to the bathroom and threw up.

At a well-lit desk in the center of a courtroom filled with reporters and photographers—it reminded her, illogically, of a boxing ring—she was handed a pen. As flashbulbs exploded, she signed the divorce papers. The floor itself seemed to be shaking, she remembered.

Farrow's account more or less jibes with the wire-service stories. "Dressed in slacks, Miss Farrow appeared tired and nervous during the 30-minute proceeding in the civil court of Judge Lorenzo Holguin Seniceros," UPI's Vernon Scott wrote. "She told the jurist her life with Sinatra had been unbearable, and said she had not lived with him as man-and-wife since December, 1967." The Associated Press reported that Mia looked "lean and sleepless" and that "she appeared so nervous she could hardly hold the pen. Her hands trembled as she signed the papers."

Back in Los Angeles, Frank was on a soundstage at CBS Television City, wearing a white corduroy Nehru jacket and love beads as he taped a TV special with Don Costa, Diahann Carroll, and the Fifth Dimension. Nancy Sinatra recalled going to the studio to watch the dress rehearsal, which went smoothly—and which, as was the custom, was taped, in case any slipups in the final performance had to be covered. When Frank came off the set, Nancy remembered, Jilly took him aside and told him that Mickey Rudin had called to say the divorce proceedings had been completed. Sinatra asked Don Costa if the dress rehearsal had gone satisfactorily for the orchestra. It had. Frank was silent for a moment, then he said, "Let's go with the dress. I can't do it again now." "It was as if someone had turned out the lights in his eyes," Nancy recalled.

The wire services reported that Frank flew to the East Coast, and Mia went directly back to the Bel Air house, where her mother awaited her. Farrow writes that after she and Rudin returned to Los Angeles, they got stuck in traffic on the freeway, and as the lawyer chatted a blue streak to the driver, she simply stepped out of the car and hitched a ride to the house that was no longer hers, where Frank awaited her.

When she arrived, she writes, she found Frank furious about her hitchhiking escapade. Finally she reminded him that they weren't married anymore, so she could do as she pleased. This seemed to calm him; still, she recalled, she was careful not to stay too long.

The stories don't exactly line up, but the ending is the same.

She refused any financial settlement, leaving the Bel Air house with just the jewelry he had given her, their forty-eight-place set of silverware, and her stuffed animals.

That was the weekend. The following week got worse. On Monday morning, August 19, the *Wall Street Journal* ran a front-page story about Sinatra by the investigative reporter Nicholas Gage. "Frank Sinatra is rather sensitive about his baldness," it began, unpromisingly.

Only his closest friends are permitted to remain in his presence when he changes hairpieces. Among those select few is Joseph Fischetti, a cousin of the late Al Capone, and, enforcement officials say, a veteran Mafia man.

It comes as no surprise to those who know the mellifluous actor-singer well. For nearly 30 years, some of Mr. Sinatra's best friends have been—to put it bluntly—gangsters. Not just two-bit hoods, either: Mr. Sinatra hobnobs with the Mafia's elite.

Mr. Sinatra is nothing if not loyal to those he considers his friends. His associations at several times have threatened his business interests. They cost him his amiable relationship with the late President John F. Kennedy. Still Mr. Sinatra has stuck by his pals. He refuses even to talk about them with a reporter.

Ordinarily a man's friendships are nobody's business but his own. But Mr. Sinatra once again is back in public affairs—in politics, and Presidential politics at that.

Frank, in Nehru jacket, taping the CBS special *Francis Albert Sinatra Does His Thing*, August 1968. With the ink on his divorce papers with Mia Farrow barely dry, Sinatra was so distraught he could barely make it through the dress rehearsal.

Frank's indiscreet associations had been in the news before, but as his daughter Nancy writes (often), he had never been indicted for anything, and the court of public opinion usually let him off with a wink and a warning: his talent and charm seemed to redeem him at every turn, as did popular envy of his large living and authority-flouting exploits.

But he'd hankered to get back into the kingmaking business, and back in it he was, and he had somehow imagined he could broker power as he did nearly everything else—on his own terms. The *Journal* piece, a transparent attempt by the paper to undermine Humphrey, dictated new terms.

After allowing Jim Mahoney a brief rebuttal—"These reports are rumors and vicious, unnecessary attacks. Mr. Sinatra has associated with Presidents, heads of state and hundreds of personalities much more interesting and copyworthy"—Gage went into considerable detail about Frank's friendships with the copy-worthy personalities Willie Moretti, Lucky Luciano, the Fischetti brothers, and Sam Giancana. He recapped Sinatra's adventures with the Nevada Gaming Control Board and his forced departure from the casino business, unearthing a new tidbit, Frank's involuntary exit from the racetrack business.

"Before Mr. Sinatra sold his interest in the Cal-Neva, he was forced also to sell an interest in Berkshire Downs race track in Massachusetts," Gage wrote.

He and singer Dean Martin had become directors of the track in 1963. Their interest ran afoul of a Nevada regulation forbidding casino owners in the state [Martin held shares in the Sands] to hold gaming interests elsewhere.

Other, though secret owners of Berkshire Downs at the time were Raymond Patriarca, the New England Mafia boss, and Gaetano (Three Finger Brown) Lucchese, the late head of one of New York's five Mafia "families," or organizations.

As a final fillip, the reporter noted that while Frank had seemingly kept clear of gangsters in recent months, he'd consorted with them privately: "Last October, Mr. Sinatra came to New York to make a speech [a benefit for the American-Italian Anti-Defamation League at Madison Square Garden]. According to police reports, he also drove up to Turnbull, Conn., to visit the home of Dave Iacovetti, a member of the Mafia's Carlo Gambino family in New York."

Nancy junior called it slander. Gage had managed to link her father's name to every mafioso and every Mafia incident in America, from the early 1940s to the present, she harrumphed, hyperbolically. But writing much later, after her father's death, Tina Sinatra spoke more temperately—and realistically—about Frank's persistent attraction to highly placed hoodlums whose names ended with a vowel. "My father had known people like Willie Moretti and Johnny Formosa all his life," she admitted. "He'd come of age at a time when politics, show business, and the underworld formed an overlapping triumvirate. The people in them had a lot in common; they were all looking for money and power."

And now the times had changed, suddenly and radically. The JFK assassination was the line of demarcation, separating the old days from the new. The flowering of the counterculture, in no small part a reaction to the war in Vietnam, quickly generated a reaction from the Right. And in 1968, Richard Nixon, for all his talk of a secret plan to end the war, was running as a law-and-order candidate. In a season of assassinations and fury over Vietnam, tension was rising between the Right and the Left, and Hubert Humphrey, now the presumptive Democratic candidate for president, was caught somewhere in the middle. The Republicans were prepared to take him down by any means necessary, and Nicholas Gage's *Wall Street Journal* piece gave them ammunition.

Reaction to the piece was swift and widespread. "There is a good chance we will all be 'law and ordered' to death in the campaign about to get under-way," Miles McMillin, a columnist for the Madison, Wisconsin, *Capital Times,* wrote on August 21. "The way Nixon is talking you'd think he was Matt Dillon running against Billy the Kid. And now the groundwork is being laid to fry Humphrey about the part played by Frank Sinatra in his campaign."

In 1951, a young attorney named Joseph Nellis, a counsel to Senator Estes Kefauver's Special Committee to Investigate Organized Crime in Interstate Commerce, had taken a secret deposition from Frank on his ties to the Mob. Now Nellis wrote a private memo to Humphrey, warning the candidate that little had changed with Sinatra. He cited Frank's visit to Washington with Allen Dorfman in May and his involvement with the American-Italian Anti-Defamation League, whose leadership included at least one man with Mafia ties. When Humphrey's special counsel Martin McNamara discovered that Sinatra was part of a new investigation by the Justice Department into connec-tions between the entertainment industry and the Cosa Nostra, McNamara, too, wrote a memo. Soon Humphrey stopped returning Frank's calls.

——————

Sinatra was furious, and not just at the *Wall Street Journal.* The night of the divorce, the syndicated gossip columnist Rona Barrett, who also did a segment on KABC-TV's eleven o'clock news, made a brief, insinuating on-air mention of Mia Farrow's dance at the Daisy with George Jacobs. When Jacobs went back to the Palm Springs compound, Frank wouldn't speak to him.

"The maid came to me and said, 'Mr. Sinatra wants you to get out of the house,'" the valet recalled. "Frank had locked himself in his room and wouldn't come out. I banged on the door and said, 'What's wrong? What's going on?' He wouldn't open the door. 'Mickey will tell you. Mickey will tell you,' he said. 'Call Mickey.'"

Mickey Rudin told Jacobs that the Barrett item had upset Sinatra and that Jacobs had better move his belongings out of the house until things cooled off. Things didn't cool off. "Everyone around the old man—Jilly and all of them—poisoned his mind until he actually believed that his valet was sleeping with his wife," Jacobs said. It was a kind of coup on the part of Jilly, who had long felt competitive with Jacobs for Frank's attention. And it was a firing offense.

"After fourteen years together he dropped the net on me just like that and he couldn't even look me in the face to do it," the valet said incredulously.

> I had been so close to that man. I even signed his name better than
> he did. In fact, I did all the autographs. "Just give it to George," Frank
> would say whenever someone wanted a signed Sinatra picture. I went

everywhere with him. I nursed him through his suicide attempt in Lake Tahoe. I helped him get through Ava, who was the only woman he ever loved. I was even the nurse after his hair transplants . . . I drove all the girls to Red Krohn for their abortions, and I treated each one of those dames like a queen because that's what he wanted me to do. The women that man had over the years! I still remember Lee Radzi-will sneaking into his bedroom. How do I know? I heard her. I always had a room next to Frank so he could slap the wall for me if he needed anything.

In the wake of his dismissal, Jacobs was so angry at Sinatra that he threw away everything his boss had ever given him: expensive watches, clothing, shoes, cameras. "I didn't want anything from the bastard around," he recalled. "I got twelve thousand dollars in severance pay and blew it, and then I sold all my shares in Reprise Records."

But toward the end of his own life, years after Frank's death, Jacobs forgave his former boss. "Oh, man, I had a life with that poor man," he said. "I miss him so fuckin' much." The ex-valet, elderly and almost blind, was sitting and reminiscing in his little house on the wrong side of Palm Springs, the fierce desert sun blazing outside the windows.

"Oh, God—I think every day about him," Jacobs said. "He was like a father to me. The motherfucker, every time he left the house, it was, 'You got any money in your pocket?' Didn't matter what I said. 'Here's two more hundred,' he'd say.

"I can see him standing there—'Well, it's about time you got here.' I'd say, 'Mister S, I have a lot of things to do; you know that, sir.' He'd say, 'How much do you have to do for somebody else that you don't do for me?' I'd say, 'Well, there's a lot of things.' Because I had families. I had to support families. But he gave me the money, so I had to do the work. And I worked my ass off."

Did he seem lonely? I asked.

"Many times I thought so," Jacobs said. "He didn't have to feel alone. Everybody in Hollywood tried to fuck him. Pat Lawford—anybody. Oh, man. This guy, all he had to do was snap his fingers, and the room would be full. I'd go to wake him up for breakfast, and five chicks come out of the room.

"But he and I used to sit talking all the time. He was on his couch in the living room, foot up on the table. We'd sit and chat. And then, when he'd sit out in the sun, I'd bring him a drink or something and put oil on his back or his legs. He had attention, because I was right there with him all the time."

What did they talk about?

"He always wanted to know what was going on in the town before he went in there," he said. "I had to go make a circulation. It's so funny how he trusted me, with anything. And when Sam and those guys came out there from Chicago, them motherfuckers thought I was the leader. I knew about everybody in town. I knew everything. So they figured, 'Ask George, he knows. Shit, if he don't, he'll find out.'"

I asked Jacobs if he ever dreamed about Sinatra.

"Quite often," he said. "I've had some midnight fuckin' dreams. I wake up and I can't go back to sleep. It's always about something, and me and him. 'Hey, Spook.' That was my nickname. I'd take his fuckin' Dual-Ghia, go in town, and get laid every fuckin' night. 'Hey, Spook. Do you ever leave the car for me to drive?' I'd say, 'I didn't know you wanted to use it, sir. I'll let you have your car.' He'd laugh! Oh, could he laugh."

And had Jacobs forgiven the woman who was the cause of his firing?

The old man shook his head. "Oh, God, she was a child," he said. "I couldn't stand that little bitch. Mia put me in the middle of things. If she did something wrong, she'd say, 'George must have done that.' It was like minding somebody's child.

"She was a make-believe," Jacobs said. "She always had these little stories and things that she would bring up, and Frank would look at me and say, 'Boy, she should write movies instead of be in them.' She had a great imaginary mind."

Sinatra was scheduled to emcee and sing at a luncheon for Muriel Humphrey and two thousand female delegates at the Democratic National Convention in Chicago and to appear at a gala for Mayor Richard Daley—but then, suddenly, he wasn't. On the Sunday before the convention, he announced that a "pressing recording commitment" would keep him in California for the entire week.

There was no recording commitment, pressing or otherwise. In truth, he had nothing more pressing going on that week than halfheartedly romancing the twenty-six-year-old Carol Lynley, who was shooting a picture at Warner Bros. by day and dancing at the Daisy by night.

As it turned out, though, he missed a hell of a convention. Amid violent clashes between antiwar protesters and the Chicago Police Department—abetted by Mayor Daley, who had intended the convention to showcase his status as a Democratic power broker and felt personally affronted by the disorder—the Democrats nominated Hubert Humphrey as their candidate for president. Sinatra would continue to campaign for him, less out of love for Humphrey than hate for Richard Nixon, the man with the secret plan to end the war.

Between mid-August, the time of his divorce, and early November, Frank was very little in evidence. He did not record, and though he was scheduled to start shooting a 20th Century Fox movie called *The Only Game in Town*, with Elizabeth Taylor and the director George Stevens, in Paris in early September, he abruptly dropped out of the project after Taylor, who'd had another of her innumerable health crises in August, announced she needed to postpone the start of shooting.

He doesn't seem to have agonized over the decision, despite the rich income stream that moviemaking brought him. "Frank Sinatra, who receives a million dollars and a percentage for each of his movies, also gets to own the negative after seven years," Sheilah Graham wrote in her column. "The only other actor I know who receives this bonus is Cary Grant." She then added a perceptive postscript: "I doubt whether Frankie is rich. He splashes his money all over the place."

Sinatra's excuse for quitting the movie was scheduling conflicts—the conflicts in question being a benefit concert for the Teamsters in St. Louis on October 30 and his November 22 opening at Caesars Palace in Las Vegas. One would think a determined man could have worked around these two events, but even at $1 million per picture Frank was not especially eager to have his schedule dictated by Liz Taylor, nor to work in Paris—nor, on balance, to work with George Stevens, a stickler famed for demanding many takes of his actors. The role went to Warren Beatty; the movie was a flop.

What Sinatra seems to have been most determined about that fall was erasing the memory of Mia. He was dating again: along with Carol Lynley, there were—on the radar screen, anyway—such exotic (and young) actresses as the Shanghai-born twenty-three-year-old Irene Tsu (*Flower Drum Song*) and the Edinburgh-born twenty-seven-year-old Quinn O'Hara (*The Ghost in the Invisible Bikini*). And then there was the most exotic-sounding and youngest of them all. "Frank Sinatra's name is being linked overseas with that of a Swedish blonde, 20-year-old Ingalill Klippinger, whom he met in a London gambling joint," *Chicago Tribune* columnist Robert Wiedrich wrote on September 27.

Ingalill Klippinger?

The name sounds phony because it was, as fake as everything else about her. In reality, Ingalill Klippinger was Diane McCue, a lost girl who'd run away from her dysfunctional family in Pittsburgh and become a stripper in the notorious tenderloin of Baltimore known as the Block. In the summer of 1968, a Baltimore club owner named Sammy Goldstein, a friend of Jilly Rizzo's, sent McCue to New York City as a gift for Frank Sinatra. A man named Nick the Pig met her and a friend, a present for Rizzo, at Kennedy airport and drove her to Jilly's, where introductions were made. On the day Diane McCue met Frank, she appears to have been just about, but not quite, fifteen.

Like a number of other women who claimed to have been lovers of Sinatra's, McCue wrote a memoir years later, and it is a seamy tale indeed, revolving around mobsters, drugs, and the brutal murder of Sammy Goldstein, who was a friend of Frank's as well as Jilly's. Much of her story checks out. There is evidence that she and Sinatra were actually involved: there are press accounts linking them and photographs of the two of them together. There is also evidence that she actually was about fifteen when they met, making her his youngest lover since Natalie Wood in 1954.

Like Wood, McCue was sexually precocious, but the fact that the relationships were consensual makes them no less disturbing. Still, a kind of amoral sense can be made of them: in both cases, Frank was reeling from the end of a marriage and seeking a kind of reset with a fantasy virgin. It was a brand of consolation that his power could afford him. He was also a romantic: he spoke of Ravel's ethereal ballet of young lovers, *Daphnis et Chloé,* as one of his favorite pieces.

Diane McCue came from a very different place—the 3:00 a.m., comewhat-may world of the Block and West Fifty-Second Street, a milieu in which Jilly was both Frank's accomplice and his facilitator. But that fall, she accompanied Sinatra to an event in a different kind of world, one that was increasingly becoming his center, the Old Guard, golf- and tennis-playing, celebrity-and-society scene in Palm Springs. "On October 15, 1968, Frank and I arrived at the grand opening of Jilly's West in a large stretch limo," she recalled.

> There was a big gathering of movie stars and celebrities in front of the bistro. One of the female stars looked at me and leaned over to another male star. She asked him, "Who is that girl with Frank?"
>
> "I don't know; she looks a little like Mia," he said.

The two stars, she later writes, turned out to be Lucille Ball and David Janssen.

The *Oakland Tribune*'s society columnist, Robin Orr, took note of the event, chiefly because Jilly's backer (and Frank's friend) Danny Schwartz had made his pile in the Bay Area before relocating to the desert. "[Schwartz] and his wife, Natalie, for whom his Lear jet *Natilus* is named, were co-hosts at the swinging affair that opened the new night club," Orr wrote.

> Four hundred members of the glittering worlds of society and Klieg lights attended, among them the Schwartzes' good friends, Frank

Sinatra, Lucille Ball and her husband Gary Morton, and Jilly Rizzo, the official proprietor of the new club.

Jilly is also an old friend of Sinatra's and his piano bar on West 52nd Street in New York City has been the setting for many a Sinatra film. Scenes from "Come Blow Your Horn" and "Manchurian Candidate" were shot there.

In any event both Jilly and Frank were on tap for the Tuesday night party and for the going-away party at the airport that sent Frank on his political campaigning way.

The columnist failed to make mention of the blond fifteen-year-old stripper on Sinatra's arm at the glittering party.

———

Diane McCue did not ride Frank's Lear Jet to his next two stops, the Teamsters' benefit in St. Louis and a rally for Hubert Humphrey at the Houston Astrodome on November 3, two days before the election. On Tuesday the fifth, the Democrat lost the presidency to Richard Nixon by just half a million popular votes, his campaign having been irremediably damaged by the chaos in Chicago, the continuing trauma of the war, and the former Alabama governor George Wallace's independent candidacy, if not by the stain of Frank Sinatra's Mob connections.

It was a depressing outcome: in 1960, Frank had been able to use his influence to keep Nixon—a man, Shirley MacLaine recalled, Sinatra "hated with a deep vitriol"—out of office; now his influence had clearly waned. But he would soon find a way to adjust to the times.

———

The following week, he went to Western Recorders to make two singles with Nelson Riddle; neither man knew, on the night of November 11, that it would be the last time they would work together for eight years.

The calls to Nelson came far less often now; Don Costa had become Frank's go-to guy in his vain quest to produce Top 40 hits ("My Way of Life" and "Cycles" had both charted briefly, but the former only hit number 60, and the latter—close but no cigar—just number 41). And though Riddle's livelihood no longer depended on Sinatra—he was making a good living writing scores for the movies and television—he resented his inconstancy. "Toward the end, Nelson didn't particularly like Frank," Bill Miller recalled. "He felt as if he was being fluffed off."

The two songs recorded that night were a so-so ballad called "Blue Lace" (music by Riziero Ortolani, lyrics by Patty Jacob and Bill Jacob) and Cahn and Van Heusen's boppy title theme for the Julie Andrews movie *Star!* Neither added much luster to the Sinatra-Riddle oeuvre. The familiarly flickering flute figures in "Blue Lace," though lovely in themselves, only harked back tantalizingly to the truly great work Frank and Nelson had done together: a dim reflection of a distant fire.

The next night it was back to Costa. Because of the (relative) success of "Cycles," Frank had decided to build an album around the song, an LP that was folk rock at its core, country and western around the edges—all except for the pounding "My Way of Life," which was neither. *Cycles* was recorded over three nights, November 12 through 14, with Bill Miller conducting Don Costa's arrangements.

The spectators had changed. Gone were the Countess Mara ties and dangling charm bracelets, replaced by turtlenecks and chains with medallions and miniskirts. A new brand of celebrity onlooker had also appeared: among those attending the *Cycles* sessions were the falsetto phenomenon Tiny Tim and George Harrison and his wife, Pattie. A photograph from the session shows Sinatra in earnest conference with the Beatle, who looks delighted to be in Frank's presence. It's a touching image, also a stark contrast of musical present and past. Harrison, who was especially impressed by Sinatra's efficiency, might well have just asked the main question on his mind: "How do you do it? It takes us months just to do one album."

The Beatles, whose performing days were over, were now exclusively a studio band, making musical magic with their brilliant producer George Martin and their audio engineer Geoff Emerick. Sinatra was still doing it the old-fashioned way, but the harsh truth was that trying to adapt to the present at the same time ill suited him.

The terrible paradox was that the great and gentle voice singing the saccharine "Cycles," and now the truly awful "Pretty Colors" and "Moody River," was the same great and gentle voice that had sung "Dindi" and "Everything Happens to Me" and "What Is This Thing Called Love?" It was genius misused—or at best misplaced. There was worthy material on *Cycles*; both Joni Mitchell and Judy Collins had made a beautiful thing of Mitchell's "Both Sides Now" (which Frank, for some reason, insisted on calling "From Both Sides, Now"), and Glen Campbell (who'd played guitar on several Sinatra sessions) had made brilliant singles of Jimmy Webb's "By the Time I Get to Phoenix" and John Hartford's "Gentle on My Mind."

But while Frank could sing these tunes magnificently—or, more correctly, could lend the magnificence of his voice to these tunes—his heart wasn't in them, and it showed. They were songs of another generation, and for Frank Sinatra to sing them was much the same as for Frank Sinatra to put on stud-

ded denim and medallions and turtlenecks and Nehru jackets: he could bring
the thing off, just barely, by force of personality; but the note was ajar, and the
risk of risibility was real.

Lady in Cement was released on November 20 to not entirely terrible reviews.
Flexing his new chief-film-critic muscle (and showing off a bit), the *New
York Times*'s Vincent Canby gave the candy-colored, Miami-based picture an
energetically ambivalent, so-bad-it's-good-but-it's-really-bad kiss-off, calling it
"such a perfect blending of material with milieu that the movie's extraordinary
vulgarity and sloppiness can almost be cherished for themselves, like wide-
screen graffiti." But Charles Champlin of the *Los Angeles Times* echoed the
feelings of many by focusing on Frank: "He projects the ex-cop turned private
shamus with a time tested fictional blend of insouciance, cynicism, battered
but surviving idealism, wisecrackery, courage, libido, thirst and all the more
interesting hungers. He clearly enjoys the role and it is this evident pleasure
which carbonates the thin material with lively amusement."

All true. *Lady in Cement* made *The Detective* look leaden by comparison, and Sinatra, as he had not in his previous picture, looked terrific in it.
Deeply tanned and rail thin in his tan summer suit (all the troubles with Mia
seemed to have shaved pounds off him), he bounced through the cartoonish
proceedings with surprising humor and energy, given his purported testiness
during the filming. Frank's scenes with Dan Blocker, who was wonderful as

George Harrison visiting Frank in the recording studio, 1968. Sinatra called Harrison's
"Something" "one of the best love songs to be written in fifty or a hundred years," but he was
never really comfortable singing it.

the mountainous, menacing Gronsky, were a delight, even if his repartee with Raquel Welch, who stepped neatly into Jill St. John's high-heeled footprints, was very far from Bogie and Bacall. If you turned off your critical faculties, a lot of the movie was pretty good fun, and enough people did so to make *Lady in Cement* pretty profitable.

"As he has proved in the past, Mr. Sinatra has a very fine and rare talent," Vincent Canby wrote at the end of his review, "but he needs good people to bring it out, like John Frankenheimer in 'The Manchurian Candidate' or Ella Fitzgerald and Antonio Carlos Jobim in last year's television special."

This was both perceptive and prescient. It was unclear in November 1968 just where his film career might go next. "Frank Sinatra has had it playing detective roles," Dorothy Manners wrote; "producers needn't bother offering him one." But what did that leave? Whether he liked it or not, he had aged out of the romantic-lead business. As it turned out, *Lady in Cement* was a kind of anticlimactic swan song. In the movies as in the rest of his career, Sinatra was stuck in a strange spot, a gigantic figure with narrowing possibilities.

As if to signal his retrenchment, he announced he was leaving Los Angeles, his hometown of twenty-five years. In early November, after professors and scientists at the UCLA School of Medicine issued a statement warning of the dangers of the city's persistent blanket of smog and urging all who were able to leave the city to do so, Frank took them at their word. "The air isn't fit to breathe, so I'm moving out," he announced. "The smog is so bad I had to visit my doctor three days a week because my nose and throat are affected by it."

"The most surprising thing about Frank's latest statement," the columnist Joyce Haber wrote, "is that, as his intimates know, the singer hasn't got a nose and throat doctor. (He hasn't got any doctor at all, unless you count his friend, the obstetrician Leon Krohn.)"

(Actually, the most surprising thing about Frank's latest statement was that it failed to mention the effects on his nose and throat of his on-again, off-again, but mostly on-again, habit of smoking two packs of unfiltered Camels a day.)

"Sinatra said he was selling his house (or houses?) in L.A., which leaves him with his desert retreat, a brand new, stylish townhouse in Manhattan, and a brand new, stylish apartment in San Francisco, which he calls 'a grownup, swinging city,'" Haber continued.

> But insiders, and me, are betting on Manhattan. Manhattan has Jilly's, that tavern on West 52nd Street whose walls are covered with photos of Frank, including one monstrous blow-up with his friend, Larry Harvey. Not to mention a sign, near the men's room, which flashes, on and off, "Home of the King."

But it wasn't as though Manhattan's air was a vast improvement on L.A.'s. And those insiders, and Joyce Haber, were failing to take into account Sinatra's deep and abiding love for the desert. Palm Springs would remain his home and center of operations for the rest of his life.

———

"The Nehru jacket seems 'in' but the end's beginning," Jack O'Brian had written in an April column, adding the coup de grâce, "Half a dozen unchic restaurants ordered them onto waiters and they've become uniforms in beauty salons everywhere."

Frank seemed not to have gotten the memo: here he was in that white corduroy Nehru jacket (and love beads) in late November, in the fourth television special in his rebooted TV career, the coyly titled *Francis Albert Sinatra Does His Thing*. He still looked great—lean and with the same deep suntan he had worn in *Lady in Cement*. The toupee, though, was different: for his mod-themed TV show, he wore an aggressively modern, Caesar-fringed rug.

Yet the note he struck at the top of the show was conciliatory. "Nobody would explain to me what my thing is supposed to be," he said, grinning, "but it can't be very bad since they're letting me do it on television."

What he did was good enough. He sang "Hello, Young Lovers" and "Baubles, Bangles, and Beads" and—of course—"Cycles"; he did a medley of spirituals with Diahann Carroll; and then, wearing an outrageous psychedelic ice-blue Nehru jacket (it seemed to be ruffled with Lucite), he danced gamely but a bit clunkily while he sang Laura Nyro's "Sweet Blindness" with the Fifth Dimension. "Thank you, group," he said, when the number was over. "And don't look now, Francis Albert, but your generation gap is showing."

It was. As was the fact—as evidenced by some awkward staging, extraneous sounds, and stiff byplay between Frank and a pair of ornamental female extras—that he'd allowed the dress rehearsal to go to air. But the reviews were respectful: out of touch or not, he skated by on being Sinatra.

———

Two days before Thanksgiving, he opened at Caesars, backed by—shades of 1939—the Harry James Orchestra. José Feliciano, the Fifth Dimension, and Pat Henry were also on the bill. The Sands fiasco was more than a year behind him, and Vegas was much changed. After purchasing the Desert Inn and the Sands, Hughes had continued his buying spree, snatching up the Castaways, the Frontier, and the Silver Slipper. His teams of Mormon bean counters were in place, making sure the count was correct and funny business kept to a minimum. Sin City was well on its way to being Disney in the Desert. "Vegas in the old days, when it was really owned and run by the Mob, was one of the great cities of all time," Polly Bergen said. "It only got boring when the corps [corporations] took over. It's sad to say that, but it's really true."

Nor was Caesars Palace's Circus Maximus anything like the Copa Room. "When Frank went to Caesars, it was like four of the Copa Rooms together," recalled the longtime Sinatra observer Rob Fentress, who attended many of Frank's shows at both casinos. He was exaggerating, but only slightly: the Sands' showroom seated about 350; Caesars', 1,100 or more. Sinatra could command an audience of any size—in Rio de Janeiro in 1980, he would sing for 175,000 people in a soccer stadium—but the thrilling intimacy of the Copa Room was now a thing of his past. For all *Variety's* enthusiasm ("Frank Sinatra's return to the Strip was, as someone might term it, a gasser," wrote the entertainment journal's longtime reviewer "Duke"), his most passionate fans could tell the difference. The stress of the past year, and the size of the big new room, combined to diminish him, slightly but noticeably. "The electricity of the Sands days was not there," Fentress said. "And his voice was not the same."

Paul Anka first met Frank in 1959 or 1960, when the young Canadian pop phenom was playing Vegas for the first time. "I was like eighteen or nineteen—they wouldn't even let me in the casino," he recalled.

I meet Sinatra and the guys, and they hang out. The greatest times I ever had were in that steam room. Everything went on in there that you could imagine . . . The women who were around all the time! Not only were they good-looking but they knew what they were doing . . . If you wanted to get laid—and really get laid—that's where you could get laid.

"The little Arab," as Frank called him—Anka was of Lebanese and Syrian ancestry—was a very talented young man, a skillful songwriter as well as a singer, and at the same time the perfect Sinatra acolyte: fun-loving, undemanding, and starry-eyed. "Frank Sinatra, Dean Martin, Sammy Davis Jr.—they were little gods in black tie and patent leather shoes," he wrote in his memoir.

They didn't talk like other people, they didn't behave like other people, they didn't have to play by the rules the way other people had to, the normal day-to-day regulations didn't apply to them . . .

Eventually Frank and the rest of the Rat Pack adopted me. I got little jewels of wisdom about performing and behavior from them. From watching the rehearsals in the Copa Room in the Sands Hotel I learned about style, and an insider's insights about how to present yourself on stage. It was like going to the college of cool.

Over the years, Anka became an adjunct member of Sinatra's circle, hanging out with him, when their schedules coincided, at the Sands, the Copa, Jilly's, the Fontainebleau. Sometime in the late 1960s, he recalled, he had a dinner in Florida with Frank "and a couple of mob guys" at which Sinatra suddenly announced, "I'm quitting the business. I'm sick of it, I'm getting the hell out."

The words triggered a memory. A couple of years earlier, on vacation in the South of France, Anka had heard a French pop song called "Comme d'habitude" (As usual). "I thought it was a bad record, but there was something in it," he recalled. He'd acquired the publishing rights. Now he thought he could turn the melody into a Sinatra song.

"At one o'clock in the morning, I sat down at an old IBM electric typewriter and said, 'If Frank were writing this, what would he say?'" Anka remembered.

And I started, metaphorically, "And now the end is near." I read a lot of periodicals, and I noticed everything was "my this" and "my that." We were in the "me generation," and Frank became the guy for me to use to say that. I used words I would never use: "I ate it up and spit it out." But that's the way he talked.

At least it was the way he talked when he was trying to sound tough. The words of the songs he sang, so carefully studied and taken to heart, were where he expressed his higher self. But Anka, thinking the new lyric was "all him," phoned Frank at Caesars and said, "I've got something really special for you."

Sinatra had misgivings. The song "really had nothing to do with my life whatsoever," he would later say. "I know it's a very big hit—and I love having big hits—but every time I get up to sing that song I grit my teeth, because no matter what the image may seem to be, I hate boastfulness in others. I hate immodesty, and that's how I feel every time I sing the song."

Still, his inner circle convinced him it could make a good single, and in a rare afternoon session on the second-to-last day of the year, with Bill Miller conducting a forty-piece orchestra, Frank recorded "My Way" in one take.

Ending a year that had begun in pain and sorrow with a cry from someone else's heart.

Act Five

THE
LATE SHOW

26

|||||||||||

Out in the garden munching on the green green grass was
Frank's adorable Christmas present, twin Sicilian donkeys,
which he named Cosa and Nostra.

—SUZY KNICKERBOCKER, IN HER COLUMN OF JANUARY 10, 1969

The desert was his home now; life had changed. If Frank Sinatra's life was a continual process of shedding intimates, a periodic molting, the company he gathered around him that Christmas spoke volumes about who he was becoming and who he wished to be.

For their part, Frank's glittering coterie of society friends, all of them wealthy and well along in years, were thrilled to be with him—he was *Sinatra*, for God's sake. The raffish charge he carried was also an important part of his aura. The society columnist Suzy Knickerbocker chronicled the meeting of the two worlds. "Just before Christmas when the snow flies in the East and the smog smogs in the West," she wrote, archly, in early January, "a brilliant, tightly interlaced little group from both coasts, carrying baskets filled with goodies, beats its way through the woods to Grandmother Frank Sinatra's Palm Springs house to spend the jolly holiday season."

Suzy, a.k.a. Aileen Mehle, was a petite, attractive blonde of a certain age—forty-four, to be exact—who affected a plummy, sardonic tone in her chronicles of the wealthy and celebrated but softened her pitch considerably when the subject was Frank Sinatra, whom she had now and then dated. This closeness to the subject gave her a big leg up over Earl Wilson, whose fortunes with Frank had faded fast after his unfortunate attack of candor in the Fontainebleau episode. In return for Mehle's kindnesses, Frank not only afforded her most-favored-columnist status but brought her right into the fold. It was a standing that allowed her to be both observer and participant during that season's festivities on Wonder Palms Road—a fatally conflicted perspective on the face of it, but then the papers weren't paying her for journalistic objectivity.

It was an era when society still seemed to matter, before mere coarse celebrity had become the coin of the realm. Mehle described the sparkling company, and Sinatra's five-house desert pleasure dome, and his hospitality, in lavish, loving detail, and the effect was (and is) not just envy inducing but queasy making, like being force-fed foie gras or caviar. You see and feel Frank's environment but search in vain for the messy humanity in it. "Sinatra is much much more than a superlative, totally charming host; he is an incredible innkeeper who never misses a trick," the columnist gushed.

The Sinatra compound radiates around the main house, where the master lives, tends bar, and presides at the cocktail hour and where the group lunches and dines in the beautiful new dining room lined with paintings . . .

To the left of the main house, which faces a backdrop of mountains looking as though they were placed there especially for the occasion, is the great hall, an enormous room with a roaring fireplace, a roaring bar and a tinkling piano. Here you can see a movie every night or listen to records on the Discomatic that Mrs. Loel Guinness gave to Frank last year.

Hooked onto the great hall and marked with a bronze nameplate is the Yul Brynner room.

Yul couldn't make it this year, Suzy wrote, nor could the Guinnesses, who were entertaining their grandchildren in Palm Beach, nor the Leland Haywards, who were producing a play in New York. Truman Capote had been expected but had motored across the country instead of flying and arrived "just in time to miss everything."

Fortunately, Mehle wrote, everyone else turned up: the Bennett Cerfs, who shared Cerf Cottage, their home away from home, with the Armand Deutsches "of Beverly Hills and the Sears, Roebuck fortune. Mr. and Mrs. Freddie Brisson (Rosalind Russell) were tucked away in Christmas Tree House, as were Mr. and Mrs. William Goetz, the czar and czarina of Beverly Hills society."

And the Joe Mankiewiczes and the Mike Romanoffs, in Christmas Tree House; and Claudette Colbert, in Hayward House; and Arthur and Bubbles Hornblow, in solitary splendor, in the house that bore their name.

Had Capote made it, he would have had a lot to write about. He also would have been the only guest besides Mehle under fifty.

"Out in the garden munching on the green green grass," the columnist concluded, "was Frank's adorable Christmas present"—she didn't say from whom—"twin Sicilian donkeys, which he named Cosa and Nostra. They are so identical, northbound or southbound, that sometimes they can't tell each other apart."

And they beat the hell out of a London taxicab.

Back in the East, the Old World intruded wrenchingly. In New York a few days after New Year's, Nancy Sinatra was taping a *Kraft Music Hall* special when Frank and Jilly showed up at NBC's Studio 8H. Pleasantly surprised to see her father, she hugged and kissed him—then suddenly saw that Frank wasn't smiling; his eyes looked bloodshot and tired. "Please call your grandfather," he told her.

Marty Sinatra, seventy-six, had been hospitalized with heart trouble—an aneurysm of the aorta. When his condition worsened, Frank had his father rushed to Methodist Hospital in Houston, home to the famed heart-transplant surgeon Dr. Michael DeBakey. But the elder Sinatra, a lifelong asthmatic, soon developed emphysema, and there was little DeBakey could do for him. Frank could do little, either, but sit by the old man's bed, powerless for all his power, holding his father's hand as he gasped for air.

Anthony Martin Sinatra, born Saverio Antonino Martino Sinatra in Lercara Friddi, Sicily, in 1894,[*] died on January 26. Small (three or four inches shorter than Frank), gruff, taciturn, and illiterate, his arms covered in tattoos from his days as a bantamweight prizefighter, the former Hoboken fire captain had been a model of masculinity, but Frank Sinatra was in almost every way his mother's son: impatient, irascible to the point of explosiveness, brilliantly verbal. In his sixties, he would recall listening to his parents through the bedroom wall as a child. "Sometimes I'd be lying awake in the dark and I'd hear them talking," he said. "Or rather, I'd hear her talking and him listening. Mostly it was politics or some worthless neighbor. I remember her ranting about how Sacco and Vanzetti were framed. Because they were Italians. Which was probably true. All I'd hear from my father was like a grunt . . . He'd just say, Eh. Eh."

Marty Sinatra, who had once kicked the teenage Frank out of the house for being a layabout, had taken a long time to approve of the strange profession his son had chosen. He kept himself to himself. But he had come to be proud of his only child; and a father was a father, and one more hedge against mortality was gone.

Her grandfather's funeral was nightmarish, Nancy remembered; a large crowd descended upon Holy Name Cemetery in Jersey City, where the scene was "pure bedlam." The chaos was Dolly's doing, a boyhood friend of Frank's felt. "Frank was pissed at his ma," Joey D'Orazio said. "She had told too many

---

[*] In their book *Sinatra: The Life,* Summers and Swan speculate that Frank's father was born two years after another son by the same name who died soon after birth—hence the birth date of 1892 sometimes assigned to Marty. To compound the confusion, his gravestone lists his birth date as 1893.

people too many things about the details of the funeral, made too many announcements, and so the scene was madness. There were cops and firemen everywhere, and it was a circus, something I know Frank would never have wanted."

There were celebrities, of course. Sammy Davis, in a Nehru jacket and fur coat. Twenty-five limousines, ten of them just carrying the floral arrangements sent from Vegas and L.A. Bodyguards with walkie-talkies, TV cameras and reporters with microphones. At the center of it all was Dolly, grieving without restraint. Frank and Jilly had to hold her back when she tried to throw herself on the casket; Frank grew visibly annoyed as she screamed, "Marty, Marty, please don't leave me!"

"Hurry up, Bob. *Hurry up,*" he told the priest, Father Robert Perrella. The priest rushed through what was left of the service; the family managed to hustle Dolly into a car.

Back at her grandmother's house, Nancy Sinatra recalled, the man she knew as Uncle Vincent[*] served food to around sixty mourners in Marty's beloved basement bar, amid many framed family photographs. Her father had been quietly strong through many crises, Nancy writes; "But when his father died, something snapped."

Frank began to lobby Dolly to move to Palm Springs. He would build her a house next to his, he told her. She resisted. It was too hot there in the summertime, she said. He told her he would also buy her a condo in La Jolla or Del Mar, near the racetrack. Still she balked. She didn't like Frank's friends, she told an acquaintance. "I don't want to move out there with all those big shots," she said. And what about her friends? How could she leave them behind? Frank told her he would fly any of them out, anytime she wanted.

Then the most serious objection of all: How could she leave Marty's grave untended? Who would take him flowers? Frank said he would have his father's remains moved to Desert Memorial Park Cemetery in Cathedral City, just down the road from Wonder Palms Road, if she would reconsider.

It would take more than a year, but in the end she would give in.

In the wake of his father's death, Sinatra felt intensely vulnerable. "He became a little more quiet, a little less ebullient," Tina remembered. "It was as though a piece of him had been chipped away." "In his down periods," Earl Wilson

---

[*] Martin Sinatra's cousin from the Old Country Vincent Mazzola, a shell-shocked World War I veteran mysteriously nicknamed Chit-U, had moved in with Dolly and Marty in around 1926.

wrote, "he feared that he'd 'had it' professionally and physically, as well as politically . . . He confided to one friend that his voice now got tired after three straight nights of singing. Were the pipes going? The pain in his right hand—the hand that held the microphone—actually scared him."

The pain stemmed from the tissue disorder Dupuytren's contracture, a memento from karate chopping a table in *The Manchurian Candidate*, and just one more thing that would keep him from making movies for the next two years.

But to counteract the gloom that followed his father's death—and perhaps the gloom of the new Nixonian era—Sinatra consoled himself with his favorite occupation. Between early February and late March, he recorded as though his life depended on it, laying down thirty-four new tracks in the course of ten studio sessions. And he began on a high note, bringing back his beloved friend and fellow genius Antonio Carlos Jobim.

Claus Ogerman had moved on to composing and conducting symphonic music; in his stead, Jobim brought in the twenty-six-year-old Brazilian composer and arranger Eumir Deodato. Morris Stoloff, a veteran of many movie-soundtrack sessions, conducted. The change from *Francis Albert Sinatra & Antonio Carlos Jobim* was small but discernible: the ten songs Frank recorded on the nights of February 11, 12, and 13 (all of them, this time, Jobim compositions) were slightly more propulsive than the tunes on the earlier album but no less rapturously beautiful. From "One Note Samba," with accompanying guitar and vocal (and a clever English lyric) by the composer; to the gorgeous "Wave," on which Sinatra several times hits a spectacularly low E-flat, a full octave below the tonic; to "Drinking Water (Aqua de Beber)," in which Frank sings a couple of lines in Brazilian Portuguese; to the haunting and brilliantly strange "Song of the Sabiá," the three sessions produced a bouquet of small masterpieces, a collection to stand proudly beside *Francis Albert Sinatra & Antonio Carlos Jobim*.

Except that Reprise—whose suits went as far as having an album cover made—never released the LP, which was to have been titled *Sinatra-Jobim*.

No one can say just why. As Will Friedwald points out, the earlier Sinatra-Jobim set "had charted quite respectably at number 19—and this in the face of formidable competition" from rock LPs on the pop-music charts. What was wrong with this beautiful new album? "Perhaps Sinatra wasn't happy with the cover," Friedwald writes, "which depicted him leaning against a Greyhound bus (what were they thinking?), or perhaps he wanted to remake 'Desafinado.'"

"Desafinado"—"Out of Tune" in English; English lyric by Gene Lees—was a duet, with Frank and Tom (Jobim's nickname) singing successive lines, addressed to a disapproving, elusive lover:

If you say my singing is off-key, my love,
You will hurt my feelings, don't you see, my love.

It's a thoroughly charming take, with Sinatra at his vocal best and Jobim—whose singing was imbued with a composer's passion for his own music, yet could never be described as polished—winsomely illustrating the concept of out-of-tune-ness. Yet once the recording was in the can, the idea of two men singing love lyrics in the same song alarmed someone: quite conceivably Frank, though no one knows. "Somebody didn't like the implication that there was some homosexuality or something, because of the way they were singing the lyrics to each other," recalled the engineer Lee Herschberg, who worked on the session. "It was a wonderful take, too."

Two years later, in 1971, Reprise would put seven of the sessions' ten numbers—all except for "Desafinado," "Bonita," and "The Song of the Sabia"—on the A-side of an album called *Sinatra & Company*. The B-side, unfortunately, consisted of seven of Sinatra and Don Costa's lowlights: the kind of soft-pop tunes that would give 1970s music the bad name it mostly deserved.

––––––––

Five days after bidding farewell to his friend Tom, Frank reconvened with Don Costa to start building an album around "My Way," which was now getting airplay as a single. Thanks in no small part to the arranger's pliability, the LP would be a decidedly mixed bag. On the plus side, Sinatra's tender reading of the Brazilian composer Luiz Bonfá's "Day in the Life of a Fool" (given an English lyric by Carl Sigman but best known as "Manhã de Carnaval," the theme to the movie *Black Orpheus*) was as fine as anything he'd done with Jobim. Cahn and Van Heusen's pretty ballad "All My Tomorrows" was a number Frank had recorded for the 1959 film *A Hole in the Head*: while he'd sung it more beautifully then, the 1969 version was deeper and darker, sadder but wiser. And his version of Paul McCartney's "Yesterday" was a feeling and respectful cover of the historic song, if not historic itself.

It was when the album moved up-tempo that things got problematic. Sinatra took Michel Legrand's "Watch What Happens," in most hands a hushed and sensitive ballad, at a lope—the dreaded businessman's bounce—and, on top of Costa's undistinguished chart, managed to drain all the meaning from the song. (In the bargain, he was persistently flat.) His "For Once in My Life," which made you long for Stevie Wonder, had exactly the same problem. And his bluesy-growly "Hallelujah, I Love Her So" was better, but nothing to make Ray Charles quake in his shoes.

His cover of Paul Simon's "Mrs. Robinson," though, was something else altogether. Frank took the number, which an uncredited someone, doubtless Sammy Cahn, had lightly special lyricized, and made a surreal lark of it, from beginning ("And here's to you, Mrs. Robinson, Jilly loves you more than you will know") to middle ("How's your bird, Mrs. Robinson? Mine's as fine as wine, and I should know") to fade-out ("Keep those cards and letters coming," Frank yelled: Dino's tagline). Costa's arrangement was as fast and brassy as anything Billy May might have written, and Sinatra's vocal was tough, even brutal, and assured. In the hands of Simon & Garfunkel, the song expressed a middle-aged woman's sorrowing remembrance of more understandable times; in the hands of Frank Sinatra, it expressed a screw-you to Simon, Garfunkel, and all the rest of the pukes—as Frank sometimes referred to the younger generation—who had cratered the once-familiar landscape of popular music. It was cruelly effective satire.

(And Paul Simon didn't, at first, appreciate the joke. "Paul told me many years later that he was quite upset that Sinatra had changed his lyrics," the producer Phil Ramone recalled, "and that he had every intention of suing him over it. And when he told me the story, he was kind of saying, 'Boy, was that naïve, or what?'")

———

"Putnam will publish 'The Godfather,' by Mario Puzo, 'The story of a Cosa Nostra "Family"'" with an internationally known male singer as a prominent fictionalized character," the columnist Jack O'Brian had written the previous September. "The last novel to drag The Voice even deeper through the muck, 'The King,' was a fictional bore and a disgrace."

The Godfather, of course, was neither, and Frank Sinatra was sufficiently concerned about the novel's portrayal of a Mafia-linked singer named Johnny Fontane that in the fall of 1968, soon after Paramount optioned the movie rights to the book—still in manuscript at the time—he had Mickey Rudin demand to see pages. Putnam refused.

Amid much fanfare, the book was published on March 10. It went straight to number 1 on the best-seller lists and stayed there a long time, jousting with Philip Roth's *Portnoy's Complaint* for the top spot. From the beginning, despite the colorful inventiveness of Puzo's novel, few people had any doubt that he had based the character of Fontane on Sinatra. "*The Godfather* is a work of fiction, though there is one character so accurately modeled on the life and times of Frank Sinatra that he, Frank, is bound to do some exceedingly vocal Italian-American roaring about it," wrote the Winona, Minnesota, *Daily News*'s book columnist, Jean Hurd, in a typical evaluation.

For the time being, Frank could do little but build up a head of steam.

Rod McKuen was an outsize western character—a big, rawboned guy, rugged but sensitive, who'd run away from home at eleven and worked as a ranch hand, lumberjack, and rodeo cowboy before he started writing poetry and songs. He found his way to the San Francisco Beat scene; he drifted over to Paris, where he met his mentor, the Belgian singer-songwriter Jacques Brel, and began translating Brel's songs into English. McKuen's early poetry, published by small presses, caught on by word of mouth; by 1968, Random House was his publisher and his three books of poems had sold a million copies. The public had also bought two million LPs of his spoken verse and songs.

Bennett Cerf, Random's co-founder and editor in chief, loved McKuen, not so much for the quality of his poems, which were shamelessly lowbrow, literal, and romantic—greeting-card sentiments for a hippy-dippy age—as for the quantity of his sales. When *Time* ran a piece calling the poet "Edgar Guest with lemon juice," Cerf retorted, "Nevertheless, he sells five or six thousand copies a week. This is poetry, mind you! If you sell two thousand copies of the average book of poetry in all sometimes, you're quite satisfied. I'd like to find a few more Rod McKuens!"

Early in 1968, Cerf gave a dinner for McKuen at "21": the guest list included Ed Sullivan, Walter Cronkite, Gloria Vanderbilt, Richard Rodgers, Arlene Francis, Mr. and Mrs. John Steinbeck, Mr. and Mrs. George Plimpton, and Osborn Elliott, the editor of *Newsweek,* and his wife. But "the most important guest, as far as Rod McKuen was concerned," Cerf recalled, "was Frank Sinatra. And before the evening was over, Sinatra had agreed to listen to some of Rod's music."

The venue and the company and the fact that Bennett Cerf published McKuen automatically conferred class on the poet-songwriter in Frank's eyes. For his part, McKuen was pre-impressed with Sinatra. "I had tried for years to reach Frank; wrote songs with him in mind, but could never get to him," he recalled. "When we finally met, instead of just offering to do just one or two [of my songs], he promised me an entire album, which he'd never done before for any other composer. It was incredible."

Or all too understandable. Rod McKuen sold like crazy; Frank Sinatra's sales were flagging.

Frank had recorded a McKuen-translated Jacques Brel song, "If You Go Away" (Ne me quitte pas), for *My Way;* the slow, brokenhearted, Frenchy melody and the poet's tear-soaked lyric were a queasy fit for Sinatra: it was as though he'd plopped a beret on his head. Nevertheless, three weeks after that LP was complete, he returned to the studio to make good on his promise to McKuen. The resulting album, based on a familiar theme and once more orchestrated by Don Costa, was called *A Man Alone*. But as starkly distinguished from 1962's *All Alone*, which in title and content was heavily influenced by Irving Berlin, *A Man Alone* was thoroughly saturated with Rod McKuen, about whom the most that could be said was that he sold a lot of books and records.

The record contained six songs, all with words and music by McKuen, and five spoken pieces. The title number set the tone:

> *In me you see a man alone . . .*
> *A man who listens to the trembling of the trees.*

The music was pretty and simple and heavy on the strings; the lyrics were— well, Johnny Mercer they weren't. As for the spoken pieces, "Empty Is" was typical:

> *Empty—the faces of women mourning, when everything has been taken*
> *from them.*

Sinatra recited the thing in hushed, reverent tones and in full Hoboken accent. The effect was vaguely menacing, as if he were murmuring threats late at night on the telephone: surely not what anyone had had in mind. Maybe Frank's one previous adventure in spoken-word recording should have alerted everyone to the dangers.

In June 1966, three days after the horrific Polo Lounge beating of Frederick Weisman, Sinatra, though technically in hiding from the law in Palm Springs, had, quite astonishingly, made a comedy record based on Rudyard Kipling's poem "Gunga Din." (One source says the recording was done at Frank's home in the desert.) The result was the most surrealistic product of his recording career. It began with a spoken preamble: "Let us re-create that moment. With the enemy waiting in ambush, the humble water boy sees his beloved comrades rapidly approaching the deadly trap. He realizes fully well that sounding the bugle to warn them might mean certain death."

Two solid minutes of sound effects follow: the warning bugle call, a gunshot, a distressed-sounding bugle call; hoofbeats, more shots, a more distressed bugle call; a lot more shots and a barely functioning bugle. It all goes on for what feels like forever, until the final shots silence the bugle for good, and Frank returns, intoning Kipling's words:

> *Though I've belted you and flayed you,*
> *By the living Gawd that made you,*
> *You're a better man than I am, Gunga Din.*

It must be heard to be believed.

Mo Ostin recalled the story behind the record: "Sinatra had watched this comic, Jimmy Komack, on television, doing a reading of Kipling's 'Gunga Din.' It was a joke; there was a trumpet blowing at the end and all that kind of stuff. Frank thought it was really funny. He said to me, 'Let's make that as our next record!' I said, 'What? You're going to follow up "Strangers in the Night" with that? We can't do that.' He said, 'I want to make that record, and I want it to go out.'

"So he recorded it, and then we went ahead and pressed up the record and [prepared to send] it out for distribution. Before we sent it out, I said to the head of production at that time, a guy by the name of Matt King, 'Matt, sit on this; don't put it out. Maybe he'll rethink this and recognize that he shouldn't be doing this.' But Frank didn't change his mind.

"One day, I was out playing golf with a guy by the name of Bob Cavallo, a very important manager, and a couple of other guys. We're on the eighth hole, and some caddie runs out, saying, 'Mr. Ostin, Mr. Ostin, there's an urgent phone call from Frank Sinatra!' The guy was so excited that Frank Sinatra was calling.

"I go over, pick up the phone. Frank says, 'I heard you held up the release of "Gunga Din."' He says, 'How dare you do that? You countermanded my instructions. I own this fucking company!' He went nuts on me. Shook me up. I said, 'You know what, Frank? I'll deal with it. I'll make sure it gets out.' That was that. Then I went back to the course. I didn't want those guys to know how shook up I was by the phone call! I took a nine on a par three."

In the end, Frank came to his senses. The 45 rpm single, with "Gunga Din" on both sides—what, after all, could one back it with?—was distributed only privately, to friends.

By 1969, Ostin, soon to become president of Warner/Reprise, wasn't quite as subservient to Sinatra as he'd once been. Having discovered rock and the softer quantity known as folk rock, he'd been instrumental in signing artists such as Jimi Hendrix, Joni Mitchell, and the Grateful Dead; he was in the process of acquiring the likes of Jethro Tull, Van Morrison, James Taylor, and Fleetwood Mac. The man who had once been a meek accountant, Mickey Rudin's whipping boy, was well on the way to becoming one of the most powerful men in the record business. And his company was raking in money by the bushel basket—but mostly not from Frank Sinatra. "When he started chasing pop records, he was not making great records, and a lot of them were not successful," Ostin recalled. "That Rod McKuen record was not good."

My Way, the album, wasn't especially good either, but it had "My Way," the song, which hit the *Billboard* charts at the end of March and would eventually rise to number 27. The LP, released around the same time, would hit number 11. Both the single and the album did far better in England, where the thrumming anthem whose message Frank found so distasteful somehow struck a popular chord.

———

By 1969, there was another regular visitor to the compound on Wonder Palms Road, one who was more dazzled by the place and its owner than she might have been willing to let on. Barbara Marx was a beautiful blonde at a dangerous age, just north of forty, and in a dangerous frame of mind: ready to dump an elderly husband—Zeppo Marx, the youngest and, once, the best looking of the Marx Brothers—and trade up.

Barbara Blakeley, the daughter of a Bosworth, Missouri, butcher, was never brilliant, but she was beautiful and tough and reasonably clever about capitalizing on her dazzling good looks. In 1948, after her family moved to Long Beach, California, she entered her first beauty contest and won it. She was twenty. "I met Barbara when I was fourteen years old, in Long Beach, and she was Miss Fiesta of Belmont Shore," Betsy Duncan Hammes—runner-up in the pageant—recalled. "She was really tall and absolutely gorgeous. But you know what? I've always said Barbara could have had a great career, but she always married the wrong men. They took advantage of her."

On the other hand, maybe she was just a late bloomer. Blakeley married her first husband, an aspiring band singer named Bob Oliver, when they were both twenty; two years later, they had a son, Bobby. Capitalizing on Barbara's looks, the couple started a modeling school—she did the actual work—and got in on the ground floor of a new beauty pageant called Miss Universe. But the marriage broke up after Oliver began fooling around with contestants, and Barbara bounced into the arms of another singer named Joe Graydon. The two, along with little Bobby, moved to Las Vegas (accounts differ on whether they ever married), where Graydon worked as a DJ and Barbara got a job at the Riviera as "a $150-a-week showgirl, gliding across a stage in towering headdresses that featured anything from the Statue of Liberty to the Eiffel Tower," she remembered.

The pit boss Ed Walters remembered seeing Barbara in the Sands often around this time—"she was stunningly beautiful," he recalled—walking through the casino with a friend, another statuesque blonde, the actress Dani Crayne, who later married the actor David Janssen. "They cruised the Sands like barracudas, looking for wealthy older men who wanted to remember what it was like to be young," he said. "It wasn't about money, and it wasn't about sex; it was about improving their place in the world."

Some time after Graydon lost his job and money troubles began, Barbara recalled, "a well-tailored, middle-aged man started appearing every night to watch me rehearse. At 56, Zeppo Marx had taken early retirement from show business to do the things he enjoyed—gambling, women and golf."

Zeppo—Herbert on his birth certificate—had appeared in the first five Marx Brothers movies, then bowed out after 1933's *Duck Soup* to join the Hollywood talent-management agency founded by the other retired Marx, Gummo, a.k.a. Milton. Zeppo was also a gifted mechanic: during World War II, he founded a company that developed the clamps that held the Fat Man atomic bomb in the B-29 that dropped the device onto Nagasaki; he also invented a wristwatch that sounded an alarm when the wearer's heartbeat became irregular.

Despite Zeppo's ingenuity, his engineering work failed to make him a wealthy man; according to one source, he lived off a family trust fund and eventually had to be supported in his old age by his brother Groucho. Whatever the case, he was a significant improvement over Joe Graydon, and when Barbara Blakeley wanted a thing, she went after it. "She was like a racehorse, you know, with blinkers on," Betsy Hammes said.

Zeppo "was an inveterate card player, but he was the most famous and important man she had met up to that point and so she set her sights for him," said the fashion designer and critic Richard Blackwell, for whom Blakeley modeled in the mid-1950s.

> I helped by borrowing jewels and mink coats for her to wear when she went out with him so that she would look good—like she didn't have to marry for money . . . She desperately wanted to marry Zeppo because of the good life he could give her and her young son.
>
> After three years Zeppo finally proposed and they were married in 1959. That got her into the Palm Springs Racquet Club and the Tamarisk Country Club, which was very important to her. She became good friends with Dinah Shore. Zeppo brought her·into a new world of money and social prominence that she had never known before. He wasn't the classiest man in the world, I'll grant you that, but he was the best that Barbara could do for herself at the time.

After a decade, though, she had had it. She'd never loved him in the first place, he wasn't as rich as she'd thought, and all he ever wanted to do was play cards. Not only that, but *he* had had the nerve to be unfaithful to *her*. She returned the favor. She and a friend "were always sharing some guy," Hammes recalled. "She always had guys around. Zeppo—that didn't stop her."

What's more, he was an old man, closing in on seventy, and she was in the prime of life. She loved to dance; she was a good athlete, an avid golfer and tennis player. The Racquet Club and Tamarisk were her second homes; her house with Zeppo was next to the seventeenth fairway, right across from Sinatra's compound. At first, she and Frank would "nod a hello each time our carts passed on the golf course, but I don't think he registered who I was unless he saw me with Zeppo," she remembered.

> Then, one day, he called me out of the blue. His ex-wife Ava Gardner was due in town, and he'd had a tennis court built specially for her—even though she was only staying a few days. Could I organize a doubles match for her?
>
> When I arrived at his court with two friends, I found Ava's maid mixing Moscow Mules at the side of the court. I think Ava was half-looped before we even started. Frank tried to make her jealous by flirting with me—even cornering me up against the chain-link fence—but I'd figured out his game.
>
> By the late Sixties, Zeppo and I were going out twice a week with Frank and his friends, or having dinner at The Compound.

This is verifiable. "On Saturday evening, saw Frank Sinatra at the Beachcomber with a party that included Barbara and Zeppo Marx (of the famous Marx brothers) and Jilly, who has Palm Springs' newest and foremost night spot," reads a December 1968 social-column item. At the compound, "those who drank and stayed up till the early hours—Bill Holden, Robert Mitchum, John Wayne, Glenn Ford and Orson Welles—were part of his in-crowd," Barbara recalled, still starry-eyed decades later. Her old man, who liked to turn in early, would have paled by contrast.

Then, one late night, there was a memorable game of charades. "I was on the opposing team to his, which included his drinking buddies the comedian Pat Henry, the golf pro Kenny Venturi, the songwriter Jimmy Van Heusen, and Leo Durocher, the baseball manager," she wrote in her memoir.

> Having placed a large brass clock on my lap, I called time before Frank's team guessed his charade—the government health warning on a pack of cigarettes.
>
> "Three minutes are up," I cried gleefully. "You didn't get it!"
>
> They began to howl their protests, but the look on Frank's face as he rose to his feet silenced them all. "Who made you timekeeper anyway?" he barked, his eyes like blue laser beams.

"Why, you did!" I replied.

Frank snatched the clock from my lap and gripped it tightly in his hands. For a moment I thought he might hit me with it. Refusing to be intimidated, I stared him out until he turned and hurled the clock against the door, shattering it into a hundred pieces. Springs, coils, and shards of glass flew across the room. The clock face lay upturned on the floor, its hands forever fixed at a few minutes after 4:00 a.m. . . .

I'll never forget the fire in Frank's eyes and the way he looked at me. His expression was full of anger and frustration, but there was some-thing else—desire. I think I knew then that something would happen between us someday. I just didn't know when.

Maybe that fire in his eyes was just irritation. "He hated her at first," George Jacobs recalled. "Wouldn't date her, and everywhere we'd go she'd show up. He said, 'Who keeps inviting her around?'"

Soon enough, though, the valet remembered, she was inviting herself. "Zeppo was in his sixties and sick all the time, and often at night when he had gone to sleep, Barbara would sneak out and visit Mr. S. I asked him what he saw in her. 'Grace Kelly with my eyes closed,' he answered."

Then Jacobs was gone, but Barbara kept coming around.

In May, Frank returned to Caesars, once more at a Circus Maximus–size salary of $100,000 a week, wearing a thin Mephistophelian beard to accent his turtleneck and medallion. He seemed mellower, according to *Variety*: "no lon-ger lean or rapacious with a desire to swing every second. By his own admis-sion, he speculates about this nitery aspect of his multifaceted career, saying at one intermission point of his songathon, 'It's for the kids.'"

Was he really growing weary or just trying on weariness? (He had lost his father: How could he explain to anyone?) But after singing "My Way" and "Cycles" for introspective effect, he revved up the beat on "The Lady Is a Tramp" and "I've Got You Under My Skin" and was as socko as he'd ever been.

"Epitome of his generation's affluential attainment via showbiz," *Variety*'s scribe wrote, "Sinatra cannot be compared to anyone else on today's polyglot scene. In every move and gesture, Sinatra reveals he's rather in a class by himself."

He knew it; he had always known it. Sad and tired as he might have felt sometimes, he was certain in his heart of hearts that he was indispensable.

———

That summer, Gay Talese and his wife went to a party for Rod McKuen at Phyllis and Bennett Cerf's country house in Mount Kisco. Nan Talese was

McKuen's editor at Random House and Bennett Cerf was her boss, and the occasion was celebratory. "McKuen was a star, because he was making a lot of money for Random House," Gay Talese recalled. "I was invited because of Nan. It was just a little summertime party—dinner was under a tent, near the pool house. I don't think there were more than eight people there."

To the writer's complete surprise, Frank Sinatra was one of the guests.

"He never said hello to me, never looked at me," Talese said. "It was the middle of the afternoon, he had a radio, and he was listening to a baseball game, turned up very loud."

Talese believed that Sinatra's rudeness had less to do with any annoyance about the *Esquire* piece than something else. "He probably felt awkward, because he was in the home of a person whose friendship he courted," he said. "Sinatra and I had a lot in common. We're the sons of immigrants, and Sinatra was a bit of a social climber. And the people he didn't need to climb, he paid no attention to."

———

It was a spooky summer, the last of the age of Aquarius, dense with event: the moon landing, Woodstock, Chappaquiddick, *Abbey Road,* the Manson murders. Frank's barber, Jay Sebring, would be one of the four people butchered along with Sharon Tate over the terrible midnight of August 8–9.

From June through mid-August, Frank took one of his longest breaks, cruising up and down the East Coast on his new eighty-five-foot yacht, the *Roma,* this time with a mystery blonde instead of Mia. He watched the *Apollo 11* takeoff at Cape Kennedy; he took the Cerfs along to drop in on the William Styrons in Martha's Vineyard; he sailed back down to Vero Beach, Florida, with entourage and the comedian Phil Harris. While relaxing off Atlantic Highlands, New Jersey, he was served with yet another subpoena, this time to appear before a committee investigating organized crime in the Garden State. He had Mickey Rudin put the pests off.

On August 16, he jetted to Houston to emcee a giant tribute to the *Apollo 11* astronauts at the Astrodome. (To Frank's delight, Neil Armstrong, Buzz Aldrin, and Michael Collins had listened to the Basie-Sinatra "Fly Me to the Moon" on a live feed from space while the whole world tuned in.) Two days later, he was back at Western Recorders for the first time since March, laying down a couple of Teddy Randazzo songs, the forgettable "Forget to Remember" and the catchy "Goin' Out of My Head," a big hit for Little Anthony and the Imperials in 1964 and soon to be a moneymaker, albeit of the bottom-of-the-chart variety (number 79 on *Billboard*), for Sinatra.

His rendition, with a pleasant enough Don Costa arrangement, was competent but bland. "Goin' Out of My Head" was a sound more than a song: meaning was not part of its essence. He had sought meaning his whole life—in fame, in love, in the words of the songs he sang. Of the three, the third had been the most reliable; no longer.

He was drifting, seeking. "For the second time in his life, his career had reached a crossroads," Tina wrote. "The Beatles were outselling him in the record stores. The nightclub era—*his* era—stood in eclipse, and he'd yet to plot his next move."

And the next week, he was back in New York to begin an album that would show how far he was willing to reach for something new.

———

The first meeting between Frank Sinatra and Frankie Valli, the pint-size, helium-voiced lead singer of the Four Seasons, occurred at Jilly's in the mid-1960s, when, according to one source, Valli simply had the temerity to go up and introduce himself. Dinner, drinks, and friendship ensued. When Frank expressed curiosity about the group's monumental success, Valli attributed much of it to the skills of the Seasons' co-founder Bob Gaudio. "He told Sinatra they had all these hit records because Bob Gaudio wrote and produced all their songs," recalled the producer-arranger Charles Calello, who had done most of the charts on the group's hits. "And Sinatra said, 'Well, could he write some songs for me?'"

Frank would have done well to inquire more closely. Bob Gaudio had co-written some of the Four Seasons' biggest hits—songs like "Walk like a Man," "Big Girls Don't Cry," and the million-seller "Can't Take My Eyes off You"—with the prolific songwriter Bob Crewe. In the late '60s, though, Gaudio began working with a talented but quirky lyricist named Jake Holmes. Together, Gaudio and Holmes created the Four Seasons' 1969 concept album, *The Genuine Imitation Life Gazette,* which eschewed love songs to take on heavy subjects like war and racial tensions in tracks that ran as long as six minutes plus. The LP was a resounding flop.

Gaudio and Holmes got to work writing some of their new songs for Sinatra. When Frank heard four of them, he was pleased. "And then," Calello said, "Gaudio laid on him the concept of doing it as the *Watertown* album."

Another concept album, that is, a song cycle revolving around a fictional character with a problem (the singer) and set in a fictional small town (and not, as has often been written, in Watertown, New York). "Jake and I discussed what would be an interesting thing to do for Sinatra," Bob Gaudio recalled. "What we could do that he hadn't done before. We just hit on putting him in a small town. Having a small-town approach and taking it down as much as we could to basic life in middle America. We tried to strip all of the gloss and sheen off of it."

It was a radical departure for Frank. "In a series of soliloquies, the name-less narrator tells us his heartbreaking story of personal loss and unrealized redemption," the Sinatra archivist Ed O'Brien wrote in the album's liner notes.

His wife has left him and their two boys for the lure of the big city, and her absence hangs palpably in the air. While it is altogether under-standable why someone would flee the stark and dreary landscape of Watertown, our empathy rests with the eloquent everyman left behind. He is a desperate man, the personification of all that is pedestrian in a small town, a solitary figure who suffers unbearable torment and despair. But, in expressing timeless sentiments to a love that is hope-lessly lost, he finds salvation in the written word and an extraordinary transformation takes place. In his grief, he achieves a deeper under-standing of himself, and a transcendent awareness of what he has lost and why. There is a terrible beauty in all of this.

But there were a number of problems. The first was that Sinatra was ini-tially not aware that it was a concept album; he thought that Gaudio and Holmes had just written him ten new—downbeat and literary—songs. "I don't think he was expecting it to be what it was, which was a story," Gaudio said. "He fell in love with something. We never really discussed it in detail, Frank and I. I don't know what turned him on to wanting to do it; I don't think he looked at it as being contemporary commercial. It was pretty obvious that it wasn't one hit song after another. I think he fell in love with the concept, the love story."

It was an admirable concept on the face of it. The problem was that Gau-dio and Holmes were skillful tunesmiths, but that was it. (Gaudio's zenith had been the terrific pop tunes he'd written with Bob Crewe; going deep was a wrong turn.) In the hands of great songwriters like Rodgers and Hammer-stein, a musical soliloquy could become a transcendent work of art. And in the late 1960s, important contemporary writers such as Lennon and McCartney ("She's Leaving Home"), Jimmy Webb ("Wichita Lineman"), and Joni Mitchell (anything in her oeuvre) were turning biographical or autobiographical narra-tives into great popular music.

But the overarching problem was Sinatra's failure to identify completely with the material. He was looking for something new, but his artistic sensibil-ity probably told him, deep down, that he was barking up the wrong tree.

Problems cropped up early. Calello and an arranger named Joe Scott wrote the charts for the album, and Frank did three New York sessions at the end of August, but they didn't sit well with him. "He felt he could do better in terms of his singing," Friedwald writes, "and not wanting to hang around the East Coast (Calello remembers somebody was trying to serve him with some papers at the time), he decided to overdub new vocal tracks in Los Angeles."

In fact, he had already been served with the New Jersey subpoena, and Rudin had had his appearance postponed until August 19. But that day had come and gone, and the East was suddenly beginning to feel hot. Frank was annoyed and distracted, whether it was the fault of the organized-crime investigation or *Watertown* itself. Still, overdubbing was an extreme measure, one he'd resorted to very seldom in his career, and with good reason. Standing in the midst of his fellow musicians while he recorded was one of his greatest pleasures in life; standing alone in a studio and singing with headphones on ran a very distant second.

"The only album we ever did that he overdubbed altogether was *Watertown,* because those parts were done in New York and they shipped the tapes over here," said Lee Herschberg, who engineered the LP. "He did not enjoy having to do that. I don't think he liked that project anyway. Those were not the best songs in the world for him to sing. They were difficult songs to sing. It felt like he never really connected with that project."

"He didn't know the songs well enough," Calello insisted. "One of the things I found out about working with him is that it took him a long time to learn a song. But I had spoken to Sammy Cahn about that. I asked him, 'How long does it take you to teach a song to Sinatra?' He said, 'Well, Frank doesn't like to speed-learn a song. He takes his time so he can really get it, to appreciate the value of the song. Sometimes it takes him a good week before he gets it under his belt.' So for him to learn all originals for a new album was a major task."

But learning the songs wasn't the problem; feeling them was. In the end, the first-person singer, the I, of *Watertown*—unlike the I of "Soliloquy" or even "Ol' Man River"—wasn't Frank Sinatra or anyone like him. The LP was a worthy try, and an interesting anomaly in his career, but, as Reprise neared its tenth anniversary, hardly an ornament to the label: Sinatra's latest album sold far worse than any he'd ever made—thirty-five thousand units. "That was unheard-of," Mo Ostin said. But there was a reason for it.

From mid-September through early October he played Caesars, then headed back out to sea—the Caribbean—aboard the *Roma*. It was an interesting time to be taking an ocean voyage, because there was a warrant out for his arrest in New Jersey.

Lawmakers in Frank's native state were annoyed at him. After they'd ordered him to appear at a private hearing of the State Commission of Investigation on August 19, Mickey Rudin had obtained a month's delay. But on September 19, instead of gracing the hushed halls of Trenton with his presence, Sinatra was opening at Caesars' Circus Maximus. The superior court judge Frank J. Kingfield issued the warrant—enforceable only in New Jersey—on October 14, charging him with contempt. It was a cut-and-dried legal term, but in Frank's case it had real meaning.

That same day, in Beverly Hills, Jim Mahoney said, "Mr. Sinatra left New York City this morning for the Caribbean and at present is unaware of the situation. We are trying to locate him now and I am certain that when he is advised of the matter he will have some comment."

Amid a collective throat clearing, the Associated Press managed to locate him in Freeport, Bahamas, where Frank and his retinue had taken up residence in an eight-room suite at the Lucayan Beach Hotel. "He went yachting Wednesday aboard a chartered boat, then gambled at several casinos," the AP reported. "Newsmen who tried to talk with Sinatra about the New Jersey subpoena were brushed aside. A bodyguard warned a photographer for the Nassau Tribune not to take any pictures."

While Frank relaxed in Freeport, his lawyers went into overdrive, filing suit in federal court to have the New Jersey State Commission of Investigation itself declared unconstitutional and asking for a temporary restraining order to keep the commission from taking any action. They also requested a permanent injunction to block any appearance by Sinatra before the body in the future.

The commission rattled its saber back, threatening to have Frank indicted for contempt and extradited to New Jersey.

A week later, back in Los Angeles, Sinatra issued a statement that was by turns passionate, sympathetic, and disingenuous. "For many years every time some Italian names are involved in any inquiry I get a subpoena," he said. "I appear. I am asked questions about scores of persons unknown to me. I am asked questions based on rumors and events which have never happened. I am subjected to the type of publicity I do not desire and do not seek."

He was willing, he said, to answer "any and all appropriate questions" by deposition or personal interview. But, he continued, "I am not willing to become part of any three-ring circus which will necessarily take place if I appear before the state commission of investigation in New Jersey, whether the hearings be public or private.

"Notwithstanding the fact that I am of Italian descent, I do not have any knowledge of the extent or the manner in which 'organized crime' functions in the State of New Jersey or whether there is such a thing as 'organized crime.'"

The wrangling would go on for the next four months; the case would eventually go to the U.S. Supreme Court, where Frank would lose on appeal.

There was much Sinatra-family togetherness that season. In Vegas, August 29 had been designated, with grand hyperbole, "The Night of the Thousand Sinatras." Actually it was only three, though that was plenty: Frank was booked at Caesars Palace; Frank Jr., at the Frontier; and Nancy was making her first nightclub appearance, at the newly opened International. The largest hotel in the world, it was the brainchild of Howard Hughes's fellow mogul and arch-rival Kirk Kerkorian; the corporatization of Las Vegas was accelerating.

On October 19, as Frank's legal war with the State of New Jersey raged, he appeared with Frankie on a CBS television special, *Frank Sinatra Jr. with Family and Friends*. (Around the same time, newspapers carried the story that Mia Farrow was expecting a child with André Previn; the two would marry the following September.) On December 12, Nancy junior threw her father a fifty-fourth-birthday party, and over the Christmas holidays the entire family— Frank, Frankie, Nancy senior and Nancy junior, Tina, and Dolly—went to Hawaii together. "But don't get your hopes up," wrote Hollywood columnist Norma Lee Browning. "It's just a family affair and not a rekindling of the old flame—between Frank and Nancy Sr."

Nevertheless, it was the first time in a long time that he hadn't spent the holiday with a wife or steady girl. One might almost think that he was growing staid.

HE'S HERE

— MARQUEE AT CAESARS PALACE, 1970

Metro-Goldwyn-Mayer had fallen a long way since Frank Sinatra had sung and danced in its movie musicals of the 1940s. After the studio dropped him as damaged goods, it bumped through the television age, battling the encroachments of the small screen by producing big-budget epics, some of which, like *Ben-Hur* and *Doctor Zhivago,* succeeded, while others, like *Mutiny on the Bounty* and *King of Kings,* did not. Then came the corporate raiders. In 1966, Seagram's Edgar M. Bronfman bought a controlling interest in MGM, and in late 1968 he appointed a thirty-eight-year-old studio chief named Louis Polk, a Harvard MBA and a former top executive at General Mills.

Louis Polk knew a lot more about the cereal business than he did about the motion-picture business, a fact evidenced by the laudable but clearly misguided high-mindedness he displayed on his brief watch. In 1969, the studio commissioned adaptations of Saul Bellow's novel *The Adventures of Augie March,* Tom Stoppard's play *Rosencrantz and Guildenstern Are Dead,* André Malraux's *Man's Fate,* and the experimental novelist David Markson's "anti-Western," *The Ballad of Dingus Magee.* Not long afterward—around the same time the tycoon Kirk Kerkorian purchased a 40 percent stake in MGM and began jockeying for power with Bronfman—MGM's accountants realized the studio was about to record a loss of $19 million. In the midst of this corporate ferment, the studio cut loose a number of projects, but *The Ballad of Dingus Magee* was not one of them.

Markson's novel, subtitled *Being the Immortal True Saga of the Most Notorious and Desperate Bad Man of the Olden Days, His Blood-Shedding, His Ruination of Poor Helpless Females, & Cetera,* was a postmodern picaresque, with a scabrous, surrealistic comic sensibility—a tone appropriate to the Vietnam era, the age of antiheroism and psychedelia. A screen adaptation would, of necessity, focus on the novel's broad comedy rather than the pleasures of the text. Toward that end, in late 1969, MGM signed the director Burt Kennedy—a specialist in Westerns who'd recently helmed a comedic entry in the genre, the James Garner vehicle *Support Your Local Sheriff*—and a writing team consisting of the brothers Tom and Frank Waldman, who had penned the screenplay for the 1968 Blake Edwards farce *The Party,* as well as episodes of *I Dream of Jeannie, Gilligan's Island,* and *McHale's Navy.* Joining the Waldmans was the novelist Joseph Heller, who'd written *Catch-22* and should have known better.

Frank Sinatra, too, should have known better. Instead, a few days before his fifty-fourth birthday, he signed on to play Dingus Magee (who in the novel was nineteen) and in a rare lapse of business judgment forewent his usual $1 million fee in exchange for a larger percentage of the box-office gross.

As the daughter of MGM's founder and the closest thing to a crown princess the movie capital had, Edith Mayer Goetz was imbued with a hauteur that could only accrue to one who had grown up, along with the movies, as motion-picture royalty. After her husband, Bill, had broken free from Louis B. Mayer's gravity and established himself as one of Hollywood's biggest producers, the Goetzes had become immensely wealthy: they owned racehorses and a legendary art collection; they gave the most glittering parties in the movie capital. They had been friends with Frank Sinatra for almost fifteen years when Bill Goetz died of cancer in August 1969. And after a discreet interval, Frank had begun courting Edie Goetz.

She was sixty-four, a full decade older than he, and handsome rather than beautiful, but the combination of her wealth, her loftiness, and her vulnerability was catnip to Sinatra. And she found the attentions of the most famous and charismatic man in Hollywood, a man with his own wealth and jet planes at his command, intoxicating.

"Frank took such good care of me, and was so good for me after Billy died," she recalled years later. "We traveled everywhere together. He took me to Palm Springs and to New York for Arthur and Bubbles Hornblow's twenty-fifth anniversary party. And, oh, the presents . . . one Christmas he gave me an embroidered bag—you couldn't see the embroidery under a magnifying glass it was so fine, and inside there was a solid gold box which was engraved: 'To Edie, With Much Love—Noel. Francis' . . .

"We had such a friendly love affair," she said. "He called me 'sexy'—it was gay and fun."

Then, one night, in the library of the Goetzes' mansion on Delfern Drive, just north of Sunset in Holmby Hills, Frank proposed to her.

It was something he did from time to time, with various women along a broad spectrum of age and accomplishment. He always meant it, just as he meant the words of the songs he sang . . . He was filled with the feeling of the moment and expected the object of his affections to feel the same.

Instead, however, Edith Mayer Goetz was taken aback. "Why, Frank, I couldn't marry you," she sputtered. "Why . . . why . . . you're nothing but a hoodlum."

He got up and walked out, never to speak to her again.

Throughout the latter part of 1969, Sinatra's team of lawyers had jousted with the New Jersey State Commission of Investigation on their client's behalf, boldly declaring the body unconstitutional, on the grounds that its proceedings were "accusatorial," and asking that a special three-judge panel be formed to hear Frank's argument. In January 1970, after the U.S. Court of Appeals for the Third Circuit turned down the request, Sinatra's case went to the U.S. Supreme Court, where his attorneys argued that an indictment against Frank would do him and his career irreparable harm.

But on February 3, the highest court in the land ruled against him, with the liberal justices Hugo L. Black, William O. Douglas, and Thurgood Marshall dissenting. Justice William J. Brennan recused himself—probably because his son was a New Jersey state investigator who had recently made the attention-getting declaration that, according to the *New York Times,* "organized crime had infiltrated nearly every facet of life in the state, including the Legislature."

On Tuesday evening, February 17, "shortly after he flew into nearby Mercer County Airport from New York City aboard his private jet airliner, a Grumman-4," the *Times* reported in a front-page story the next day, Frank went to Trenton and "testified for more than an hour . . . before a hastily summoned, extraordinary closed session of the State Commission of Investigation, which asked him what he knew about organized crime and official corruption in New Jersey."

Though the hearing was closed—and therefore by definition secret—it did not, as Nancy Sinatra wrote dramatically, take place at midnight. Prosaically enough, the proceedings began just before 7:00 p.m. after Frank, hatless and wearing a dark overcoat against the February chill, walked into the commission's executive offices a few blocks west of the statehouse with an entourage of six, including two lawyers. By previous agreement, he then entered the closed session alone and spent the next hour and a quarter being questioned by two members of the commission, Glen B. Miller Jr. and James T. Dowd. "Under questioning, Mr. Sinatra reportedly abandoned his customary breezy demeanor and appeared apprehensive," the *Times*'s Ronald Sullivan wrote (having apparently interviewed one of the participants afterward).

Though nothing of what Frank said in the hearing was divulged at the time, a dozen or so years later Kitty Kelley managed to obtain a transcript of the meeting. It appeared that Frank told the commissioners next to nothing.

Q: Do you know Willie Moretti?

SINATRA: No.

Q: Ever meet him?

FS: I'm not sure whether I ever have, because it seems so long ago that I had a house in Hasbrouck Heights, New Jersey, my wife and I. We bought a house, and the man from whom we bought the house, I think, brought him to the house one day to meet me.

Q: Do you know Meyer Lansky?

FS: I've met him.

Q: Who is he?

FS: I just read in the papers that he was an undesirable.

Q: You have never heard that "Skinny" D'Amato is a member of Cosa Nostra?

FS: Never.

Q: Are you familiar with Sam Giancana's reputation as a member of Cosa Nostra?

FS: No.

Q: Are you familiar with Joseph Fischetti's reputation as a member of Cosa Nostra?

FS: No.

Q: Are you familiar with Lucky Luciano's reputation as a member of Cosa Nostra?

FS: No, sir.

Q: Are you familiar with Willie Moretti's reputation as a member of Cosa Nostra?

FS: No, sir.

Q: Are you familiar with Joe Adonis's reputation as a member of Cosa Nostra?

FS: No, sir.

Q: I have been using the word "Cosa Nostra." If I were using the word "Mafia" with respect to any of those people named above, would your answers be different?

FS: No, sir.

Q: Do you know anybody who's a member of Cosa Nostra?

FS: No, sir.

Q: Do you know anybody who's a member of the mob?

FS: No, sir.

Q: Do you know anybody who's a member of any organization that would come under that category of organized crime?

FS: No, sir.

It was—in advance and in secret—like the Senate subcommittee's inter-rogation of Al Pacino's Michael Corleone in *The Godfather, Part II*: the strange and dangerous Italian names tripping, not lightly, from the tongues of the earnest, square white bureaucrats; the tense, grim Italian-American witness denying everything in monosyllables.

Nancy Sinatra wrote that the hearing was a mere publicity exercise on behalf of the State Committee of Investigation, not to mention a needless humiliation to her father. The questions the commissioners posed to Frank had been answered before, she contended—and once they ran out of ques-tions, they turned into starry-eyed fans, one commissioner asking if it had really been Sinatra, or a stunt double, running for the train at the end of *Von Ryan's Express*.

She had a point. The next morning, after the New Jersey State Commis-sion of Investigation announced it was satisfied with Frank's testimony and was dropping its contempt charges against him, "a high [commission] official who asked not to be identified revealed that the primary purpose in interro-gating Mr. Sinatra was not to learn more about underworld activities in New Jersey," according to the *Times*. "The official said the commission was bent on showing it had the power to elicit testimony from virtually anyone and that a primary factor in forcing Mr. Sinatra to appear here was the publicity his appearance would generate."

By then, however, Frank was long gone, having jetted back to California to trade one circus for another. A week later he would be in Arizona, wearing long johns and shooting *Dirty Dingus Magee*.

————

In early February, Sinatra had been scheduled to emcee a gala tribute to Harry Truman thrown by the Democratic National Committee in Miami Beach. He canceled, Don Rickles cracked onstage, because "he had an engagement in Newark"—"Newark" being a funnier-sounding word than "Trenton," the actual site of the New Jersey engagement that had unfortunately detained Frank.

At the end of the month, though, he was able to find a night off from his movie shoot and fly to Washington to entertain at another gala, a White House fund-raiser for a congressional research center in memory of the late senator Everett Dirksen. Although the black-tie dinner was "bipartisan, short on speeches and long on entertainment," the Associated Press reported— Danny Thomas, Dinah Shore, and Wayne Newton were also on the program— Dirksen had been a Republican, and President and Mrs. Nixon were listed as honorary co-chairmen of the event. It was the first time Frank had set foot in the White House since his Lincoln Bedroom encounter with Lyndon Johnson two years earlier and, nonpartisan though it might have been, a considerably more pleasant occasion.

————

The following day, back on the *Dingus Magee* set on two hours' sleep, Sinatra gave a long interview to *Cue* magazine's film critic, William Wolf. Jim Mahoney had reminded Wolf beforehand that his client's time was precious and inappropriate questions might cause the conversation to come to a sudden close. The warning was unnecessary. The ground rules had long been understood: Sinatra trusted that his eminence and overpowering personality would prevent most journalists from disrespecting him to his face, and most journalists, thrilled just to be in his presence, gladly toed the line. To Wolf, Frank seemed in the giving vein that day—or what, in him, passed for it: expansive and thoughtful, if not precisely candid. "He appeared tired, though relaxed and friendly," the critic wrote. "It seemed almost as if, for a rare change, he was anxious to talk to a reporter."

Maybe he really was. For whatever reason, Sinatra was in a philosophical mood. "Enough has happened to me," he said, squinting into the desert sun. "More than I deserve—all I'd ever want to use the rest of my life. Now I would just like peace of mind."

A tall order for him. But an odd new tune was playing in the background that year, wherever he went and whatever he did: he hurt, and he was tired. He denied it vigorously sometimes—sometimes a little too vigorously. "I never think about it," he said, when Wolf asked if he was concerned about growing old. "I feel in great shape. I keep fit." He also claimed that he was down to ten cigarettes a day, though drinking was a different story. ("He smiled and said, 'I'll handle several jars a night. I do it for pleasure and I enjoy it.'")

What to ask the man who has done everything? Wolf wondered what held Frank's interest these days, what kept him from getting bored with it all. "Every time a new song comes along, you have a whole new excitement again," Sinatra told him.

That's what makes entertaining an interesting business. No day is the same. Generally, what performers look for most is variance. If not, they should. It keeps you and the audience interested.

I loved pictures like "Man With the Golden Arm" because I played an interesting character. And I enjoy musicals. I don't think musicals ever will come back in the sense of the way they were. Now I prefer a story with songs. If it were possible, I'd like to do "Born Yesterday" as a film with songs, with Barbra Streisand.

There was a poignancy to all of this. It had been many years since he had made *The Man with the Golden Arm,* and he was right about musicals: they weren't coming back. Still, it was perceptive of him to say that a story with songs could work, given the right story: *Born Yesterday* really could have been a great vehicle for him and Streisand.

Frank had pride and intelligence enough to know that *Dirty Dingus Magee* fell into a different category altogether. "It's a funny part" was the best he could muster. "I've been looking for a comedy for some time."

Did he still get a thrill, the critic asked, at the prospect of making even more money? Frank shook his head. "Money never really interested me, and doesn't now," he insisted. "I made a lot of money working, but I never worked hard just to make money. I like to spend money. That's what it's for—move it around!"

With the mood up, Wolf decided to hazard a couple of delicate questions. Would Frank ever marry again?

The mood shifted instantly. "I have no thoughts about it," he said softly. "I wouldn't want to delve into that."

Properly warned, the writer let it go. But then he picked up another hot potato: Sinatra's recent adventures with the New Jersey State Commission of Investigation. Did he have any message for fellow Italian-Americans who were unhappy about perpetually being associated with the Mafia?

Frank was dismissive. "I don't think they are very upset about it," he said. "Most Italian-Americans are . . . pretty secure in their lives—the second and third generations. I don't believe they are too concerned about the Mafia thing." Much more serious, he went on, was a "general problem that affects everybody." He then revealed what concerned him most about American life today. "It's amorality!" Sinatra said.

> And so much restlessness. I guess we just got used to a way of life
> in my age bracket. Things are confusing a lot of Americans. Take the
> protestations, called for or uncalled for. I'm not against protestations,
> if they're for a cause. But I don't like rebellion without a cause. It's
> frightening.

Going on fifty-five, the man to whom enough had happened was sounding less like a swinger than a careful old bourgeois.

The New Jersey State Commission of Investigation's goal of generating publicity appears to have been successful, as shown by an unusual cable the FBI director, J. Edgar Hoover, received on March 10. The communiqué, marked "URGENT," came from a legal attaché to the U.S. embassy in London; "FRANK SINATRA, FOREIGN POLICE COOPERATION" was the subject line.

ON MARCH NINE LAST JOHN WALDRON, COMMISSIONER, METRO-POLITAN POLICE, NEW SCOTLAND YARD, ADVISED SINATRA AND COUNT BASIE ORCHESTRA ARE APPEARING AT ROYAL FESTIVAL HALL, LONDON, ON MAY SEVEN AND EIGHT NEXT IN A CHARITY PERFORMANCE FOR BENEFIT OF SOCIETY FOR PREVENTION OF CRUELTY TO CHILDREN. SOCIETY HOLDS ANNUAL PERFORMANCE, IS ONE OF ROYAL FAMILY'S FAVORITE CHARITIES, THEY ARE USUALLY INVITED AND USUALLY ATTEND.

THE COMMISSIONER IS EXTREMELY CONCERNED OVER RECENT PUBLICITY AFFORDED SINATRA OVER TESTIFYING RE MAFIA CONNEC-TIONS IN NEW JERSEY. COMMISSIONER MUST MAKE RECOMMENDA-TION FOR OR AGAINST APPEARANCE OF QUEEN AND OTHER MEMBERS OF ROYAL FAMILY. IF QUEEN ATTENDS SINATRA WILL BE PRESENTED TO HER AND HE FEARS UNFAVORABLE PRESS MAY RESULT.

COMMISSIONER WOULD BE MOST APPRECIATIVE FOR SUMMARY OF PERTINENT AVAILABLE INFO RE SINATRA TO INCLUDE IDENT RECORD, WHY HE HAD TO DISPOSE OF LAS VEGAS INTERESTS, RECENT NEW JERSEY MATTER, ETC. HE ASSURES ANY INFO WILL BE TREATED AS CONFIDENTIAL AND BUREAU POSITIVELY NOT IDENTIFIED AS SOURCE. HE NEEDS INFO AS SOON AS POSSIBLE AS ROYAL FAMILY HAS RECEIVED INVITATION.

The FBI willingly supplied the info: a memorandum from the bureau's A. Rosen stated, "Sinatra's affiliation over the years with such well-known hoodlums and members of the La Cosa Nostra as the late Willie Moretti, Paul Emelio D'Amato, and Salvatore 'Sam' Giancana." For good measure, Rosen added "the results of a security-type investigation conducted regarding Sinatra in 1955, which disclosed that his name had been associated with or lent to approximately 16 organizations in the early and middle 1940s which were either communist fronts or communist infiltrated."

A little regretfully, the FBI's Rosen then admitted, "This investigation did not uncover any actual Communist Party or front membership on Sinatra's part."

In other news from Great Britain, on April 10, Paul McCartney formally announced his departure from the Beatles, making the group's breakup—John Lennon had told his three bandmates months earlier that he was leaving—a fait accompli. Much of the world mourned, but few tears were shed in Las Vegas.

———

Another week, another hundred grand. At the end of April, after wrapping *Dirty Dingus Magee,* Frank did six nights at Caesars; attending the premiere on the night of the twenty-second, *Variety*'s Duke was predictably wowed:

> As a cabaret blockbuster, Frank Sinatra continues his ascent, and from the looks and sounds of his fifth surge into the Circus Maximus— populated at preem by a new high in bulk of blue chip celeb ringsiders—the coasting is nowhere in sight.
>
> Tossing his songs and hard-boiled but charming patter better than ever, Sinatra is well worth—and more—what they are paying him.

On April 24, Hank Greenspun, the publisher of the *Las Vegas Sun* and Sinatra's ever-reliable booster, wrote an "editorial," which read, "Frank Sinatra at Caesars Palace is equivalent to booking a 25,000-delegate convention. He is the king and his appearances here are marked by Strip and airplane traffic jams and crowded showrooms. Entry to a Sinatra performance is becoming a Las Vegas status symbol."

It was all true, and a powerful enough statement that Caesars ran the quotation as a full-page ad in *Variety,* Greenspun's words in white type floating dramatically on a stark black background. It was smooth synergy in the new, corporatized Vegas—except that secretly, the main gear in the grand machine was broken. Frank was tired, and his right hand, the one that held the mike as he tossed his songs and hard-boiled but charming patter, hurt like hell. More and more he wondered how much longer he could keep the whole circus going.

———

The trip to England, though, restored his spirits. The Brits always lifted him. His voice had carried them through the dark days of the war, while the Jerries bombed the daylights out of them, and they had never forgotten: they greeted him as a hero each time he returned. Lacking the Yanks' Puritan streak, the English saw his bad-boy side as lovable rather than reprehensible: our Frank. He'd thought of all this in the wake of the New Jersey hearing as the bad publicity mounted. How great would it be to play the Royal Festival Hall, in front of royalty and for a noble cause? He would take Basie and his great band and would pay all expenses himself. He would, of course, accept no fee. It would be the kind of public relations money couldn't buy—except, of course, he was buying it.

It went even better than expected. "They applauded and applauded," the *New York Times*'s Alvin Shuster wrote.

> They jumped from their chairs. They stayed up until the early hours of the morning. Frank Sinatra was in town giving his first of two charity concerts and about the only calm one in the Royal Festival Hall was the crooner himself.
>
> It was Sinatra's first London performance in more than seven years, and, as one exuberant critic said in the Evening News Friday, "dinner-jacketed socialites offered the loudest welcome since Winston Churchill took his V-Day tribute . . ."
>
> Princess Margaret and Lord Snowdon were among the guests who waited until 1 a.m. for Sinatra to appear and begin with "I've Got the World on a String." It was 22 songs later, many interrupted by applause at the opening phrases, before Sinatra and band leader Count Basie were finished.

The concert, geared to a tradition-minded audience, consisted almost entirely of chestnuts—besides "String," numbers like "April in Paris," "Pennies from Heaven," and "Moonlight in Vermont." Two exceptions were McCartney's "Yesterday"—a surefire crowd-pleaser in London—and, oddly, a composition called "Lady Day," originally written for *Watertown* but left off the album.

The background of "Lady Day" is that Bob Gaudio and Jake Holmes, who had little knowledge of jazz and barely knew who Billie Holiday was, had written a tune not about the great singer but about *Watertown*'s fugitive wife, Elizabeth. It contained lines such as

> *Poor Lady Day could use some love, some sunshine,*
> *Lady Day has too much rain.*

But after recording the song the previous August, Frank had turned to Gaudio and Holmes and announced, to their bafflement, that it was a perfect tribute to Holiday. It should be rerecorded at another time, he said, and for a different album. It wasn't much of a song (as a tribute to a lost jazz great, it was many levels beneath such sublime elegies as "I Remember Clifford" and "Goodbye Pork Pie Hat"), and Frank's affection for it reflected far more sentimentality than artistic acumen. But Sinatra was singing it, center stage in Royal Festival Hall, and the London audience listened reverently.

The two nights were, in the opinion of many—not least Frank himself— great concerts. "I have a funny feeling that those two nights could have been my finest hour, really," he said shortly afterward, unconsciously echoing Winston Churchill. One of the British musicians on the dates, bassist Daryl Runswick, recalled, "There are few occasions when a bunch of world-weary London musicians are provoked into awe by a performance. It happened [then]. The thing that I remember is how hard Sinatra appeared to work. I was a few feet away from him and I recall how much he was concentrating. He was flawless . . . He quipped to one of the musicians earlier in the day that this could be his last performance in London. That certainly surprised us."

At the end of April, President Nixon announced the expansion of the Vietnam War to Cambodia, a campaign that had been going on covertly for months. Massive protests erupted on college campuses across America: flags were burned; revolutionary rhetoric heated up. On May 4, the Ohio National Guard opened fire on protesters at Kent State University, killing four students.

Sinatra was no fan of Nixon's, but the flag burnings and the speeches about bringing down the government—"the protestations"—stuck in his craw.

On July 8, he made his own startling announcement: he was joining the campaign to reelect Ronald Reagan as governor of California. More than that—he was accepting the co-chairmanship of Reagan's campaign committee.

"It is my duty as a citizen to put aside partisan considerations when I think the other party's candidate is clearly the outstanding man for the office," Frank said.

Only eighteen months earlier, the columnist Vernon Scott had written, "Hollywood's glitter people are Democrats. The Republicans among them are few and silent." Sinatra, once the movie capital's Democrat in chief, now appeared to be edging rightward.

"He made it clear he has no intention of abandoning his Democratic party affiliation, but said he joined Reagan at the governor's personal invitation after they conversed about the state's problems," the *Oakland Tribune* reported.

> "Those who do not know Governor Reagan and me as we have known each other for more than 20 years may be surprised by the announcement," Sinatra said. "However our mutual friends always have been aware that we share the same desires for the welfare of the people of the state of California and the nation."

He made no mention of Jess Unruh, the Democratic party nominee, but Reagan campaign officials said they regard it as a "smarting rejection" of the former Assembly majority leader.

At the very least. Unruh, a former disciple of Bobby Kennedy's (bad enough, in Frank's eyes), had thrown his support to Eugene McCarthy after Kennedy's assassination, effectively torpedoing Hubert Humphrey's presidential chances. *The friend of my enemy* . . . But for Frank to join the campaign of a man he had only recently regarded as a bozo and a bore spoke volumes about Sinatra's fears for the country and his disaffection with the party that had slighted him during yet another presidential campaign.

The *Los Angeles Times* columnist Joyce Haber interviewed Frank by telephone a few days after the announcement. She broke the ice by telling him she'd polled a couple of secretaries in her office about his political bombshell, finding them nonplussed. Sinatra was all sweetness and light. "The divine Francis Albert simply chuckled, that sexy-soft chuckle, when I told him he'd set our town's prettiest heads on their ears," she wrote.

Haber asked him if, in coming out against Unruh, he was indulging his time-tested fondness for Sicilian vendetta. "The personal aspect, that's secondary," Frank insisted. "But now that you mention it, it's a damn good reason. Because [Unruh] hurt my man badly in Chicago. In fact, he hurt the whole Democratic party. Humphrey didn't lose. His people lost for him."

But Humphrey had also dumped Sinatra—a fact too humiliating to admit, but one that had influenced Frank's turn to Reagan just as strongly as had Jess Unruh's perfidy.

With admirable bluntness, Haber asked Frank how he could reconcile his own humanitarian, philanthropic philosophy with Governor Reagan's withdrawal, announced that very day, of $10 million in aid for California's aged, blind, and disabled.

Frank was silent for several seconds, apparently stunned. "Did he do that?" he finally asked. "Well, I suppose you don't withdraw your support for a candidate over one issue, but—I'll look into that. And you can bet I'll speak to him about it."

The record doesn't show whether he did. In fact, he was more tired than he let on and in pain. Two weeks earlier, he had had surgery to alleviate the Dupuytren's contracture in his right hand. "It looks like I held a cherry bomb in my hand," he told Haber. At the end of July, there was an embarrassment when NBC's publicity department impulsively announced that Sinatra would be the first guest on his pal (and sometime lover) Dinah Shore's new daytime talk show in early August. He didn't much feel like going on camera with a puffy and bandaged hand. He didn't feel like doing much of anything.

"Dad's convalescence was slow and painful," Tina wrote. "It was the first time I would see my father suffer, a helpless feeling that I would come to know too well."

In the past, Frank had always been a dynamo when it came to political campaigning, but he did little for Reagan at first besides lend his name to the cause. He did little over that summer in general besides giving a couple of charity concerts, clutching the microphone painfully as the one thing that continued to give him unalloyed pleasure kept him going.

He rose to a big occasion, though, on August 7, which marked both the fourth anniversary of Caesars Palace and Nancy junior's premiere in the Circus Maximus. After Caesars celebrated with a ribbon cutting for its new fourteen-story, 220-suite addition, Frank did the hotel-casino one better, throwing two extravagant galas for his older daughter: a cocktail party for Hollywood's finest on Friday night and, as *Variety* noted, "the topper on Saturday, a black-tie cotillion for Nancy's 'coming out' in Caesars' society to be attended by carefully selected couples and singles."

The paper was less starry-eyed about her lavish premiere, which was produced and choreographed by her fiancé, Hugh Lambert, and included five costume changes, plus the Osmonds (including seven-year-old Jimmy Osmond, who belted out a showstopping version of "My Way"), a black female vocal trio called the Blossoms, and a corps of ten male dancers. "Miss Sinatra is an uneven performer vocalistically," the paper's critic wrote, though he added, kindly, "To override the lack of warbling supremacy, a pleasant warmth issues, especially in regard to sharing the total show . . . Give a few performances and it will shake down to a good, tight 75 minutes."

A terse paragraph at the end of the review noted the next act due in the big room: "Frank Sinatra follows Sept. 3–16, with David Frye and The Four Seasons."

———

In early September, the multitalented talk-show host, entertainer, and liberal Steve Allen, a onetime ally of Sinatra's in John F. Kennedy's presidential campaign, wrote him an open letter. "Dear Frank: A great many uncomplimentary things are presently being said about you by Democrats around the country," it began.

> They can't understand how a lifelong liberal could suddenly switch to the support of one of the leading exponents of conservatism, Ronald Reagan.
>
> The more knowledgeable among your former political allies, Frank, are saying that the really surprising thing about your endorsement of Reagan is that you haven't substantially modified your views at all. They

say your hatred of Senator Bob Kennedy was so great—because he kept you away from the confidence of his brother, the president—that you have waited a long time to get revenge and would not even be denied by the Senator's assassination. The word is, Frank, that all you can do now that Bobby is gone is "get even" with his man, Jess Unruh and the Kennedy-McCarthy types who work for him.

I'd like to hear you do a chorus of Irving Berlin's "Say It Isn't So," Frank. Sincerely, I'd like to know that all the current rumors about "Sicilian vengeance" are untrue. No doubt you will tell us that they are. But if so, then consider a few of the social problems that make this moment of our history the most dangerous and perplexing the U.S. has ever known, because we know where Reagan stands on these issues. We thought we knew where you stood, too.

Allen went on to list Reagan's conservative, if not reactionary, positions on race relations, welfare, health care for the elderly, prison reform, campus demonstrations, abortion rights, capital punishment, and other issues. "Only a few thousand people may read this letter, Frank. I offer you access to a few million if you'd like to visit my TV show and explain your position."

Frank failed to take him up on his offer.

———

Wherever Frank is, there is a certain electricity permeating the air. It's like Mack the Knife is in town, and the action is starting.

—Billy Wilder

"When he arrived in Vegas, that was what people talked about," the producer George Schlatter recalled. " 'You see Frank? Frank's in town.' The cabdrivers, the bellhops, the hookers, everybody said, 'Frank's here.' "

"GUESS WHO," the marquee at Caesars Palace had read when Frank first played the Circus Maximus. By the time he opened there for the sixth time, for a three-week stand beginning September 3, 1970, the legend had evolved to a simple "HE'S HERE." Every paying guest was given a gold-toned medallion engraved with the legend:

HAIL
SINATRA
THE
NOBLEST ROMAN

IS AT
CAESARS PALACE

He was the show in Vegas, the main event, and the knowledge allowed him to assume certain privileges befitting emperors, including the small liberty of treating the cashier's cage at the casino as his personal drawing account. At the Caesars casino, Sinatra continued the habit he had long maintained at the Sands: he pocketed his winnings and took his losses in the form of markers, sums that were, in his case and his alone, imaginary—until the moment came when they no longer were. The moment had come at the Sands, and it now came at Caesars.

Las Vegas was growing, and as the new towers soared along the Strip, so did hotel and entertainment prices. While the corporations pushed to make Sin City family-friendly, the Mob continued to profit mightily from the casinos. The Justice Department and the Internal Revenue Service were paying careful attention.

In the summer of 1970, the FBI and the IRS were paying particular attention to Caesars Palace, which in late 1969 had been purchased for $60 million by the Miami fast-food chain Lum's—whose executives had retained the previous casino manager (and former Caesars part owner), Jerome Zarowitz, a protégé of Meyer Lansky's. But in the tighter regulatory climate of the new Las Vegas, Zarowitz soon had to be dismissed: because of his criminal record, Nevada refused to license him. The Feds also had their eye on a mysterious drop of $3 million in the casino gross under Zarowitz's tenure. When Zarowitz left the job, he was replaced by a man he had recommended, Sanford Waterman. In case the name rings a bell, Waterman—a former New York film distributor and Florida gambler, according to news accounts—had once been one of Frank Sinatra's partners in Cal-Neva.

According to Sands (and then Riviera) pit boss Ed Walters, Waterman was in fact a front man for "a major guy in New York." He had worked at the Sands throughout the 1960s, nominally as a casino host but actually to look after his eastern boss's interests. Nobody there, including Sinatra, liked him, Walters said: "He was a penny-pinching asshole." According to the former pit boss, after Sinatra left the Sands, Waterman's sponsor sent him to Caesars to keep an eye on Frank.

As part of a continuing investigation, the IRS was also watching Frank—and Waterman—through an undercover agent in the cashier's cage at the Caesars casino. And in the wee small hours of Sunday, September 6, in an episode eerily similar to the incident of almost precisely three years earlier at the Sands, the shit once again hit the fan.

Sinatra was sitting at the baccarat table, a glass of Jack Daniel's by his side, indulging in one of the few activities that took his mind off the pain in his hand. According to the undercover agent, a member of Frank's entourage came to the cashier's window during the graveyard shift and cashed in $7,500 in black chips. An hour later, the same man returned with another pile of black chips. "That's when we knew that Sinatra was using us for petty cash," the agent recalled. "Whatever he was winning off the marker, he was putting into his pocket, and whenever he ran out of money to bet, he just signed another marker for ten grand. It was a way for him to get some easy money.

"We were concerned about his paying his back markers. Sinatra told people that he didn't have to pay his markers. He said that when he performed at Caesars and then sat down to gamble, he attracted enough big money around him so that the casino made out and profited enough so that they didn't need to collect from him."

At around 5:00 a.m., the casino pit boss phoned the IRS agent to say that Frank had just signed another marker, for another $10,000, at the baccarat table. Witnesses later said that he was playing for $8,000 a hand at a table where the usual limit was $2,000. They said Sinatra was losing and wanted to raise the limit to $16,000 a hand.

In 1970, the U.S. median household income was in the vicinity of $7,500. To Frank Sinatra, $10,000 was somewhere past pocket change: just enough to be interesting, but run-of-the-mill money for the baccarat table at Caesars. In this case, of course, the sum would be purely imaginary unless Frank won. The agent phoned Sanford Waterman.

Much like Carl Cohen three years earlier, Sandy Waterman was unhappy at being awakened. He was sixty-six, a sad-faced old Jewish man with a checkered background: not quite a *shtarker*—a tough guy—himself, but one who had been close to quite a few of them, including Jerry Zarowitz. He also had enemies within Caesars, including Frank Sinatra. And so, when he got dressed to come downstairs and talk to Frank, Waterman—remembering Carl Cohen and knowing well that he himself was not physically equipped to take a punch at Sinatra, or whoever was protecting him—put a .38-caliber pistol into the waistband of his trousers.

He then went to the baccarat table and told Frank he needed $10,000 cash from him immediately.

"What's the matter? My money isn't good here?" Frank asked.

"Yeah, your money is good as long as you've got money," Waterman said. "You don't get chips until I see your cash."

In much the same way as in the Sands incident, things became heated immediately, and later accounts of exactly what happened varied widely. According to the IRS agent, "Frank called Waterman a kike and Sandy called him a son of a bitch guinea. They went back and forth like that in front of a big crowd of people, including three security guards, until Sandy whipped out his pistol and popped it between Sinatra's eyeballs."

The agent neglected to mention whether Frank had first put his fingers around Waterman's throat, a detail that doesn't quite square with the pain he was still suffering in his right hand but an accusation that would come up afterward.

According to Nancy Sinatra, her father reacted coolly to having a pistol pointed at his face, reaching for the weapon and telling Waterman that he hoped he liked his gun, because he might have to eat it. She also claimed that Jilly Rizzo, promptly redeeming himself for his failure to defend Frank in the Sands fracas, jumped over a desk and grabbed the pistol from Waterman's hand.

Frank flew straight home to Palm Springs, abruptly breaking off his Circus Maximus engagement after three days. The showroom was dark that night. The next day, Sanford Waterman was arrested for assault with a deadly weapon and released without bail. He declined to comment on the incident, but Las Vegas's sheriff, the redoubtable Ralph Lamb, had plenty to offer. "If Sinatra comes back to town," Lamb said, "he's coming downtown to get a work card. And if he gives me any trouble, he's going to jail." (Vegas entertainers were legally required to be fingerprinted and photographed and to be issued work cards before accepting jobs in Clark County. Like most headliners, though, Frank had benefited from a gentleman's-agreement exemption.)

"I'm tired of him intimidating waiters, waitresses, starting fires and throwing pies," Lamb continued, colorfully. "He gets away with too much. He's through picking on little people in this town." The sheriff, Vegas denizens knew, was not one to make hollow threats.

The Clark County district attorney, George Franklin, was also interested in seeing Sinatra. "One remark he supposedly made to Waterman as he was going out the door," Franklin said, "was, 'The mob will take care of you.' Now I'd like to have a little talk with Mr. Sinatra. I'd like to get together with him on the subject of his friendships with members of the underworld. And I'd like to know who owned the night clubs where he sang in the early days, who started him on his way and things like that." It all had a terribly tired sound by now.

Though in early accounts Waterman said nothing about Frank's grabbing him by the throat—"He was coming right at me," he told deputies when he was arrested, claiming self-defense—three days later his story, and the district attorney's, had evolved. On September 9, Franklin announced he would not charge the casino manager with assault with a deadly weapon, because Waterman still had Sinatra's finger marks on his throat when questioned by deputies.

Through Jim Mahoney, Frank said he had never touched Waterman. Sinatra had witnesses, he claimed, who would testify that bystanders had jumped the manager and wrestled him to the floor. This left open the intriguing possibility that the finger marks on Sanford Waterman's throat were Jilly Rizzo's.

Frank kept his own counsel for two weeks. Finally, in an interview with United Press International, he said, "As for the remarks attributed to me relative to the mob, they're strictly out of a comic strip. I don't make threats and I'm not running for re-election."

This was a pointed reference to the fact that both Sheriff Lamb and District Attorney Franklin were running for reelection.

"I wasn't in the baccarat game," Sinatra said. "There was no such argument about credit or how much I was going to play. As a matter of fact I just sat down at a blackjack table and hadn't even placed a bet since the dealer was shuffling the cards.

"At that point, Waterman came over and said to the dealer, 'Don't deal to this man.' I just got up and said, 'Put your name on the marquee and I'll come to see what kind of business you do,' and I walked away. That was all that was said."

"Sinatra did not say whether he planned to return to Caesars Palace to fulfill his contract," Vernon Scott wrote. "His friends seriously doubt it."

According to Joyce Haber, what Frank told his friends was that he would never go back to Nevada. Never was a long time, but he was almost as good as his word: he wouldn't play the Strip again for over three years.

He wasn't performing in Vegas; he wasn't making movies or records. What *was* he doing? The thought would have occurred to him often that summer, and it wouldn't have improved his mood.

———

Paramount, which had optioned *The Godfather* while the manuscript was still in progress, had initially shelved the book when *The Brotherhood,* a Mafia movie the studio produced, bombed. But now, in the late summer of 1970, with Puzo's novel selling like crazy in the United States and overseas, a film adaptation was imperative. With the whole movie industry in the creative and financial doldrums, Paramount was hoping the picture could turn its fortunes around. As the studio considered casting and searched for a director, Mario Puzo, who had been hired to write the screenplay, sat in a rental house in Malibu, making final polishes to his script. It was around this time, one night that September, that he crossed paths with Frank Sinatra.

Sinatra, the author wrote in a memoir, had been an idol of his from afar, but he had never wanted to meet him. "I just believed he was a great artist (singing, not acting) and that he had lived a life of great courage," Puzo said. "I admired his sense of family responsibility, especially since he was a Northern Italian [*sic*], which to a Southern Italian is as alien as being an Englishman."

Millions of book readers now knew that the character of Johnny Fontane had been based on Frank Sinatra and that Frank was upset about it. The issue had initially been shunted aside before the novel was published, when Puzo's publisher, Putnam, refused to let Mickey Rudin see the manuscript. "However, the movie was another story," Puzo recalled.

> In the initial conferences with Paramount's legal staff they showed concern about this until I reassured them the part was very minor in the film. Which it turned out to be.
>
> Now the thing was, in my book, that I had written the Fontane character with complete sympathy for the man and his life-style and his hang-ups. I thought I had caught the innocence of great show biz people, their despair at the corruption their kind of life forces on them and the people around them. I thought I had caught the inner innocence of the character. But I could also see that if Sinatra thought the character was himself, he might not like it—the book—or me.
>
> But of course some people wanted to bring us together. At Elaine's in New York one night Sinatra was at the bar and I was at a table. Elaine asked if I would object to meeting Sinatra. I said it was OK with me if it was OK with him. It was not OK with Sinatra. And that was perfectly OK with me. I didn't give it another thought.

But one night that September in Hollywood, Puzo—who normally preferred to stay at home at night with a good book—went to a birthday party for a producer friend of his, at Chasen's, and Sinatra was there, too, having dinner at another table.

A man Puzo called "a famous millionaire" was throwing the party for Puzo's friend; affably, the millionaire asked the author if he would like to meet Frank. Puzo said no. The millionaire had a right-hand man who tried to insist. Puzo said no again.

"During the dinner there was a tableau of John Wayne and Frank Sinatra meeting in the space equidistant between their two tables to salute each other," Puzo remembered. "They both looked absolutely great, better than on the screen, twenty years younger than they really were. And both beautifully dressed, Sinatra especially." But then the millionaire took Puzo by the hand. "You gotta meet Frank," he said. "He's a good friend of mine."

Puzo considered wrenching loose and walking away but didn't want to disrespect his host. As the millionaire made the introductions, Sinatra never looked up from his plate.

"I'd like you to meet my good friend, Mario Puzo," the millionaire said.

"I don't think so," Frank said.

Puzo was ready to leave immediately, but the millionaire somehow failed to get the message. He began to introduce Puzo again.

"I don't want to meet him," Sinatra said.

Now the scene had grown truly awkward. Puzo was trying to flee, and the millionaire, in tears, was stammering apologies—to Sinatra. "Frank, I'm sorry, God, Frank, I didn't know, Frank, I'm sorry—"

Sinatra cut him short. "His voice was now the voice I had heard while making love as a kid, soft and velvety," Puzo recalled.

He was consoling the shattered millionaire. "It's *not* your *fault*," Sinatra said.

I always run away from an argument and I have rarely in my life been disgusted by anything human beings do, but after that I said to Sinatra, "Listen, it wasn't my idea."

And the most astounding thing happened. He completely misunderstood. He thought I was apologizing for the character of Johnny Fontane in my book.

He said, and his voice was almost kind, "Who told you to put that in the book, your publisher?"

I was completely dumbfounded. I don't let publishers put commas in my books. That's the only thing I have character about. Finally I said, "I mean about being introduced to you."

Time has mercifully dimmed the humiliation of what followed. Sinatra started to shout abuse. I remember that, contrary to his reputation, he did not use foul language at all. The worst thing he called me was a pimp . . .

Sinatra kept up his abuse and I kept staring at him. He kept staring down at his plate. Yelling. He never looked up. Finally I walked away and out of the restaurant. My humiliation must have showed on my face because he yelled after me, "Choke. Go ahead and choke." His voice frenzied, high-pitched.

In the aftermath, Puzo wrote, he was depressed, feeling that Frank hated the book and believed the author had attacked him personally in the character of Johnny Fontane. But one night a few weeks later, after Paramount had named Francis Ford Coppola as director of the film, Coppola ran into Sinatra in a club, and Frank warmly put his arms around Coppola's shoulders. "Francis, I'd play the Godfather for you," he told the startled director. "I wouldn't do it for those guys at Paramount, but I'd do it for you."

———

Feeling better in October, Frank did three benefits for Reagan, in Los Angeles, San Francisco, and San Diego. He even managed to corral the usually apolitical Dean Martin—footloose and fancy-free, having recently separated from his long-suffering wife, Jeanne—into appearing with him. In L.A., Sinatra and Dino were joined by Bob Hope and John Wayne. "The audience at the Cocoanut Grove ballroom of the Ambassador Hotel chuckled through one-line jokes from Wayne and Hope and warmly applauded Martin's rendition of 'Everybody Loves Somebody,'" the Associated Press's reporter wrote. But "the loudest applause was for Sinatra, who sang such classics as 'Angel Eyes,' 'That's Life' and 'My Way.'"

After the performances, the actor turned governor took the stage with a fellow former actor, his wife, Nancy, standing by his side. "These wonderful entertainers," he said. "How do you find the words to thank them for all this?"

Reagan then shifted smoothly from vacuity to pointedness. "Many things have been said and written about people in show business," he said. "I have never ceased being proud of the people of the profession I belonged to or ceased being a fan."

What, exactly, was he talking about? Democrats? Hollywood's glitter people? In any case, the man who until recently had been the glitteriest of them all now waxed conspiratorial with a ballroom full of Republicans. "A lot of eyebrows have been raised," Frank quipped, about his defection. "We shook them up a little bit."

We.

———

He himself still seemed shaken up a couple of weeks later, when Norma Lee Browning grabbed him on the run ("he won't stand still for a sitdown interview," she wrote) at the Palm Springs Tennis Club. "To end all the speculation, I got it straight from the horse's mouth," the columnist wrote on October 24. "Frank Sinatra will never ever play Las Vegas again."

"Absolutely never," he told me when I asked him point-blank if the rumors were true.

What about all those fans out there who flock to Vegas to see him?

"I'm sorry," he said, "but I've suffered enough indignities there. No more."

Will Nancy be going back? (Her contract calls for two more appearances at Caesars Palace.)

"That's up to Nancy," said her father. "But I can tell you one thing, I wouldn't go back even for Nancy's opening."

Those are strong words from a man who idolizes his daughter, as Sinatra does. And vice-versa.

The loss of the Sinatra name on the Vegas scene signals the end of an era.

Sinatra also revealed he's going back into the hospital for more hand surgery, which may mean he'll have to cancel his upcoming movie with Otto Preminger. Which may mean "Dirty Dingus Magee" will be his last?

I didn't ask (one thing at a time), but I have a gnawing premonition that the entertainment world's Number One Star entertainer is getting ready to dump showbiz.

———

The movie with Preminger was to have been a thriller, adapted from a mystery novel with the strangely Sendak-ian title *Where the Dark Streets Go*. Frank was to play a priest who investigates a murder. But he developed cold feet early, telling the columnist Marilyn Beck in July that he wasn't looking forward to shooting in New York City in the wintertime. At that point, too, his hand still hurt like hell. And then there was the fact that the only other picture in which he'd played a priest, 1948's *Miracle of the Bells,* hadn't turned out too well. A month after Frank talked to Norma Lee Browning, he and Preminger would pull the plug on *Where the Dark Streets Go*. Preminger would blame intractable story problems—one problem undoubtedly being the difficulty of coming up with a plausible love story (he had offered the female lead to Jane Fonda). "I still want to make a movie with Frank," the director insisted.

But Frank's interest in making movies seemed to have dwindled to a reflex by late 1970. Over the past two years, his name had come up in connection with a number of film projects: a story in which Sinatra would play a deaf-mute and not say a word in the entire picture; a Sinatra and Goldie Hawn movie, *There's a Girl in My Soup;* even a picture co-starring Sinatra and Mia Farrow (one studio reportedly offered the exes $1 million apiece—for what property, it didn't say). None of them went anywhere.

In September, he'd signed with Warner Bros. to make a police thriller called *Dirty Harry,* but he would soon drop out of this project too, allegedly for medical reasons. The forty-year-old Clint Eastwood would take the role instead, and build a career on it.

Frank now seemed to be at the other end of his career. *Dirty Dingus Magee* wouldn't be his last film, but it would be his last for a good long time.

———

He wasn't ready to pack it all in; not quite yet. On October 26, he was back at Western Recorders for the first time in nearly a year, laying down the tracks for the second side of *Sinatra & Company* as well as a couple of singles.

He wasn't ready to pack it in, but he had somehow fallen out of sync with himself. Was it that he had left the torch behind? That he had left Riddle behind? Once he had recorded great songs; now he was mostly recording pap—or failing to make true contact with the few estimable contemporary tunes he did attempt.

For one reason and another (in good part because he was only one man and couldn't get to *everything*), he had left dozens of important songs unrecorded: from the Gershwins' "How Long Has This Been Going On?" to Rodgers and Hart's "Isn't It Romantic?" to Arlen and Koehler's "Between the Devil and the Deep Blue Sea"; the list goes on and on. Perhaps, in his terror of growing older, he felt the need to leave the American Songbook behind; perhaps he felt that to be associated with vanished or inactive greats like Porter and Gershwin and Berlin was tantamount to pigeonholing himself as a historical figure, no longer Young.

What else can explain the second side of *Sinatra & Company*? What else can account for Frank's decision to record the thumpingly banal "I Will Drink the Wine" and the abysmally titled "Sunrise in the Morning," by the twenty-two-year-old English songwriter Paul Ryan? Or the equally awfully titled "My Sweet Lady" and the vaporous "Leaving on a Jet Plane," by John Denver? Or one of Burt Bacharach and Hal David's most saccharine compositions, "(They Long to Be) Close to You," a tune whose most successful version was recorded by the Carpenters?

Yes, he wanted to sell records. He always wanted to sell records. And perhaps he could square the circle, could reach some mythic young audience that would be pleased to hear Frank Sinatra singing the songs of a new generation. The most poignant number on the B-side of *Sinatra & Company* is "Bein' Green"—a tune composed by the extravagantly talented Joe Raposo to be sung by *Sesame Street*'s Kermit the Frog.

Bennett Cerf and his son Chris had recently introduced Frank to the thirty-three-year-old Raposo, a genius pianist, brilliant composer, and overpowering personality who would die tragically young, of cancer, eighteen years later. Sinatra fell a little in love with Raposo, in a paternal way, mistakenly believing him to be an Italian-American (he was of Portuguese descent); the younger man would play an important part in 1973's *Ol' Blue Eyes Is Back,* the first album Sinatra would make after his short-lived retirement.

"Bein' Green" is a sweet song seemingly without much meaning beyond the pathos of Kermit, a lonely, slightly schnooky character who worries aloud about being overlooked:

> *It's not that easy bein' green,*
> *Having to spend each day the color of the leaves.*

Frank sings it in the gentlest of voices—his Jobim voice—and the effect is unexpectedly lovely and surprisingly moving. The song is, after all, about being different—something Sinatra had known a lot about since his earliest youth, and something he clearly still felt strongly about, despite all his wealth and fame. Coming from him, the tune is a strange cri de coeur, one that has nothing to do with lost love, and is unique in his vast repertoire.

It also could have occupied pride of place on a lost album called *Sinatra Sings Children's Songs*—another good idea Frank passed up.

On the night of October 28, he took a break to record two singles, both arranged by his old pal Lena Horne's on-again, off-again husband, Lennie Hayton: "I'm Not Afraid," a pretty Jacques Brel waltz with an okay English lyric by Rod McKuen, and George Harrison's "Something." Harrison had attended at least one of the *Cycles* recording sessions and had visited Frank in Palm Springs; the two men had formed an odd and temporary, but touching, bond. Sinatra would praise "Something" lavishly in concert, calling it "one of the best love songs to be written in fifty or a hundred years."

This was nice of him to say: it is a lovely song, and John Lennon and Paul McCartney were right to feel that it finally brought Harrison into their league as a writer. Yet many of the works of the great singer-songwriters of the 1960s and 1970s, including the Beatles' ballads, are so strongly stamped with the personalities, and life stories, of their individual composers that they can be tricky to cover. They tend to lose in translation.

This is very much true of George Harrison's *Abbey Road* recording of "Something." An argument might be made that the quality of the song universalizes it, but it's very hard to find good cover versions. Harrison himself said his favorite was James Brown's very James Brown–ian rendition, but he might have had his tongue at least partially in cheek when he said it. He did not single out Sinatra's covers of "Something." (Frank would rerecord the number, with a Nelson Riddle arrangement, for his 1980 album *Trilogy.*)

In a way, Sinatra's problems with "Something" crystallize his sometimes noble but almost always misguided attempts to record the work of modern songwriters: they just weren't his thing. The 1970 "Something," replete with groovy harpsichord and swingin' flute, puts one in mind of Samuel Johnson's notorious comparison of a woman's preaching and a dog's walking on his hind legs: it is not done well, but you're surprised to find it done at all. And by the time Frank recorded the number for the second time, he had compounded the error, adding Vegas finger snaps and the infamous interpolation:

> You're asking me, will my love grow . . .
> You stick around, Jack, it might show.

With that single syllable, he repelled sensitivity and completely undercut the essence of the song: he had made it his own, but not in a good way.

He finished the album on Thursday the twenty-ninth, laying down "Leaving on a Jet Plane" and "Close to You"; he took the weekend off and returned to the studio on Monday night to record three singles. The first two, duets with Nancy called "Feelin' Kinda Sunday" and "Life's a Trippy Thing," were a naked attempt to recapture the lightning in a bottle of "Somethin' Stupid."

They did not. Father and daughter's vocals and harmonies were sweet, but the songs themselves were bouncy and idiotic, and a peppy chorus doing the background vocals did not help matters. Nor did the lyrics:

> Hey, Mr. Sunlight, gonna outshine your bright,
> I'm talkin' outta my head, I'm so high on life.

The singles died the commercial deaths they richly deserved, though they conceivably found a warmer welcome in Italy, where Nancy had a big following.

The last tune Frank recorded that night, another John Denver opus all too fittingly titled "The Game Is Over," would not be released for a quarter century, when it finally came out on the 1995 Reprise box set. Sinatra wouldn't make another record for two and a half years.

Dirty Dingus Magee premiered on November 18, a week before Thanksgiving, the timing set hopefully by MGM for a successful run through the Christmas season. "It's kind of a western," the movie's coy tagline read. "He's sort of a cowboy." The poster showed Frank in a duster with a Stetson perched atop an outlandish wig, a hint of the kind of hilarity ticket buyers could expect.

Roger Ebert in the *Chicago Tribune* was very rough on the movie, and particularly tough on Sinatra. " 'Dirty Dingus Magee' is as shabby a piece of goods as has masqueraded as a Western since, oh, 'A Stranger Returns,' " he wrote, referring to *The Stranger Returns,* a notorious 1968 spaghetti Western starring the cult favorite Tony Anthony.

> It's supposed to be a comedy, and it was directed by Burt Kennedy, who is supposed to be a director of Western comedies ("Support Your Local Sheriff" wasn't bad), but its failure is just about complete.
>
> I lean toward blaming Frank Sinatra, who in recent years has become notorious for not really caring about his movies . . .
>
> This time, as usual, the supporting cast is good. We get George Kennedy as a cigar-chewing sheriff; Anne Jackson as a madam of sorts; Lois Nettleton as a sympathetic nymphomaniac and Jack Elam, naturally, as the villain. They're fun to watch, but where's Sinatra? In Vegas?

Unfortunately, Sinatra was in much of the movie, usually wearing pink long johns and a silly derby atop that big hairpiece (the *New York Times* called it a "youth wig") and looking unaccountably pleased with himself. The love interest, in a manner of speaking, was the leggy Michele Carey, who played Anna Hot Water, a sexy Indian girl in a miniskirt and deerskin go-go boots. Anna spoke pidgin English in a baby voice and, from a crouch in some bushes, got to utter the immortal line "What we do now? Make bim-bam?"

"Bim now, bam later," Dingus replied. The exchange, sadly, bore Joseph Heller's writerly fingerprints.*

"He needed this silliness after Grandpa died," Nancy Sinatra wrote in his defense. He might have, but the world didn't. The holiday turkey came and went with merciful quickness.

Though a Democrat, the ever-charming Dinah Shore found herself strongly drawn to the new presidential administration. Not only had Shore attended Richard Nixon's inauguration, but she soon became fast friends with Vice President Spiro Agnew, with whom she often played tennis at her house in Beverly Hills. And in September 1970, Dinah Shore told an Agnew aide named Peter Malatesta that, as Malatesta recalled in a memoir, "Frank Sinatra also admired the Vice President and respected him for being so forthright in his views."

---

* In *Catch-22,* Heller wrote, "I make you big Hollywood star, Yossarian. Multi *dinero.* Multi divorces. Multi ficky-fick all day long. *Sì, sì, sì!*"

"He needed this silliness after Grandpa died," Nancy junior wrote of Frank and 1970's *Dirty Dingus Magee*. He might have, but the world didn't.

Forthright was putting it mildly. Though while governor of Maryland Agnew had been a moderate on environmental and racial issues, as Nixon's number two he quickly became the president's hatchet man: a bellicose standard-bearer for the so-called silent majority, the disaffected Middle Americans who felt that opposition to the Vietnam War was unpatriotic, even immoral. The genial vice president, a decorated combat veteran of World War II, gleefully took on the protesters in colorful diatribes scripted by his speechwriters Pat Buchanan and William Safire, referring to the war's opponents as "pusillanimous pussyfooters," "nattering nabobs of negativism," and "an effete corps of impudent snobs who characterize themselves as intellectuals."

Frank, who liked words and feared the protestations, warmed to such talk. When he expressed an interest in meeting Agnew, the vice president was "surprised and somewhat flattered," Malatesta remembered, but also cautious enough to ask Malatesta to talk it over with Agnew's chief of staff Arthur Sohmer and his senior political adviser, Roy Goodearle. "These two gentlemen had mixed feelings about such an alliance, but they voiced only minor concern and left the bottom line to Agnew and myself," Malatesta wrote.

It made sense to me. Sinatra was one of the most charismatic and exciting performers in decades. I knew him to be a great host and a most generous person, and, though he had always been politically identified with the Democrats, particularly during the Kennedy years, I thought, why not? Let's introduce him to our man. Who knows where it might lead?

That November, Agnew traveled to California with his wife, Judy, to spend Thanksgiving in Palm Springs, which he had visited for the first time the year before and quickly come to love. Malatesta suggested to the vice president that he meet Sinatra while in the desert, and Agnew agreed. The aide then called Frank—whom he knew slightly—and proposed he join a golf foursome with him, the vice president, and Bob Hope. "He said he would like to meet Vice President Agnew but that recent hand surgery prevented him from playing golf at this time," Malatesta recalled; Frank said he'd grab a cart and join them on the second nine to kibbitz.

The spark of friendship between Agnew and Sinatra ignited on the first take . . . Over postgame cocktails, Frank invited the Vice President to visit his compound the next day. He explained that he had to return to Los Angeles but assured us that Nancy Sinatra, Sr., would be delighted to show us around. Agnew accepted with pleasure. As scheduled, he, Judy, and I made our first visit to the desert world of Frank Sinatra.

That Frank's desert world now and then included the mother of his children as guest, hostess, and perhaps more is a fascinating sidelight of Malatesta's account. "Although long ago divorced, Frank and Nancy were still very good friends, and even though we were newcomers it wasn't difficult to observe that a lot of love lingered between them," he wrote.

Nancy was to be, on several occasions, hostess and party planner at the compound. She totally complemented Frank's sense of style and understood the kind of ambiance he wanted his home to exude.

Judy and Nancy's rapport was as instant as Frank and Spiro's. We had a lush afternoon. I knew we'd be back!

Just before Thanksgiving, a full-length Norma Lee Browning column about Frank appeared in the nation's papers under an alarming headline: "DIRTY DINGUS" MAY BE LAST FOR RETIREMENT-BENT SINATRA.

"It's beginning to look as though an M-G-M Thanksgiving turkey, 'Dirty Dingus Magee,' will make history . . . as Frank Sinatra's swan song," Browning wrote.

> With those who know Sinatra best, it's retirement Two to One. But not retirement just to loaf in the Palm Springs sun. Among the handful of his most intimate associates, the word is that he's only quitting show business to go into some other kind—nobody's saying what. Some say he's retiring from ACTIVE performing to ACTIVE mogul-ing.

With the proceeds of the sale of Reprise Records to Warner Bros., Browning wrote, Frank had formed a holding company with Danny Schwartz and Mickey Rudin; the three now held a major stake in National General Corporation, which owned a movie-theater chain and produced and distributed films. "Schwartz is now executive vice president of that company and though it is sheer conjecture, I personally predict that Frank Sinatra may soon be joining it in an executive nonperforming capacity."

But she was grasping at straws; mogul-ing sounded like pretty dry stuff. Danny Schwartz's comment about his restless partner seemed closer to the truth: "He may become more involved as we get going but again he may not. He can change his mind every week, you know."

Frank himself vouchsafed no comment about future plans except "I like to keep busy. Solitude is very depressing. I need activity."

It was the truest thing he'd said in a long time.

On Saturday, December 12, Frank's fifty-fifth birthday, Nancy junior married for the second time, to Hugh Lambert. Ever filial, she said she'd decided on this date because, "since Daddy likes to give things away on his birthday he ought to give me away."

Like Nancy, Lambert had been married before: he had a young daughter and a teenage son. In a wedding photo, the forty-year-old groom—genial and boyish looking, with big spectacles and a mop of sandy hair—seems an apt, sunny consort; it is Nancy, with her raccoon eye makeup and unreadable smile, who appears to harbor depths. The ceremony took place at St. Louis Catholic Church in Cathedral City, two miles from Frank's compound; sixty friends and relatives attended, though two hundred others showed up unexpectedly.

The area's Mexican-American families usually attended Mass in the church on Saturday afternoons, Nancy later recalled. This Saturday, however, they found the church unexpectedly closed. All dressed up with nowhere to go, they were milling around in puzzlement when Frank Sinatra, Frank Sinatra junior, and Jilly Rizzo drove up.

When Frank learned St. Louis Church had been closed to its congregation, wedding party or no wedding party, the color came up in his face. He commanded the priest to open the doors, and the doors were opened. The townsfolk streamed in and filled the empty pews. "What they saw was like something out of a fairy tale," Joyce Haber reported. The decor included hurricane lamps bound in white, green, and blue garlands; the gowns of the ladies in the wedding party had been created by the Oscar-nominated costume designer Donfeld. The bride wore a floor-length, $2,500 dress of off-white silk georgette chiffon trimmed with fifty varieties of imported laces; sister Tina, the maid of honor, wore lavender chiffon.

"Tina, who's marrying Robert Wagner when his divorce comes through, later caught Nancy's bouquet, to everyone's delight," Haber wrote. (But Wagner—who had brought his old flame the sixty-three-year-old Barbara Stanwyck to the wedding—would throw over Tina Sinatra and remarry Natalie Wood when his divorce from the actress Marion Marshall did come through.)

"There were four buffet tables and an enormous multi-tiered wedding cake," the columnist continued.

> When the strains of the Latin combo (bongos, guitars) died away, Frank offered a toast to the newlyweds with Taittinger champagne: "May these two young people always have good health and happiness and may we have lots and lots of grandchildren!"

No word on whether Frank granted favors to postulants on his daughter's wedding day.

On the same day, at the same time, in a juxtaposition worthy of *The Godfather*, FBI and IRS agents were staging simultaneous raids of illegal sports-betting operations in twenty-six cities across the country, including New York, Detroit, Miami Beach, Los Angeles, Houston, and Las Vegas, "where agents arrested two executives of plush Caesars Palace, a gambling casino, on charges of using telephones to aid racketeering," according to the Associated Press. One of the two was Sanford Waterman. Upon opening his personal lockbox, agents discovered $400,000 in cash.

———

Fifty-five: there was a certain weight to it. Friends, musicians, and hangers-on had begun to call him the Old Man—the same nickname a young Frank and his bandmates had once used for Tommy Dorsey.

Peter Malatesta knew he and the Agnews would return to Sinatra-world—"a private world so full of excitement, luxury, and warmth that it is utterly mind-boggling"—and they did, dining with Frank at the compound on the second-to-last night of 1970 before helicoptering up to Bob Hope's new Hollywood estate for a big New Year's Eve bash.

Frank's own plans for the holidays were apparently more intimate. While rumors flew that (a) Ava had been sighted in the desert (in a chauffeured limousine cruising down Palm Canyon Drive) and (b) he was about to marry Aileen Mehle ("Says Suzy, not so, but we hear she wishes it were," Norma Lee Browning wrote), Sinatra was spotted "strolling into a Palm Springs eatery with Hope Lange on his arm, smiling good-naturedly when the restaurant owner greeted Hope as Mrs. Sinatra," Marilyn Beck noted in late December.

And though Frank, Lange, and the restaurant owner later assured the columnist that the episode had all been a joke, when the blond actress—who around the same time was also involved with John Cheever—divorced her husband, the director Alan Pakula, the following year, the proceedings revealed that she had been seeing a lot of Frank Sinatra.

Will somebody please get me the hell off the road?

—FRANK SINATRA

If there were any lingering doubts about Sinatra's political about-face, he dispelled them by flying to Sacramento three days after New Year's for Ronald Reagan's second inauguration as governor of California. On the afternoon of January 4, as demonstrators waved Vietcong flags, shouted obscenities, and chanted "Free Angela"—a reference to the radical UCLA philosophy professor Angela Davis, recently arrested for conspiracy in connection with the armed takeover of a Marin County courtroom—Reagan told a crowd on the capitol steps that his top priority was revising the state's welfare system, which he described as "a Leviathan of unsupportable dimensions."

That night, Frank dined at the Republican hour of 6:00 p.m. with the governor and his wife and a large, irreproachable contingent, including the governor's brother and sister-in-law, Mr. and Mrs. Neil Reagan; Nancy Reagan's parents, Dr. and Mrs. Loyal Davis; two of the Reagan children, eighteen-year-old Patti and twelve-year-old Skipper (the nickname of Ron junior); the Reverend Donn Moomaw, a former UCLA football star turned Presbyterian minister, and his wife; and a group from Hollywood that included Jack Benny; James Stewart and his wife, Gloria; Vikki Carr and her husband; Robert Cummings; Mr. and Mrs. Buddy Ebsen; Audrey Meadows and her husband; and Mr. and Mrs. John Wayne.

Jilly was nowhere in sight.

Afterward, Frank performed before five thousand people at a $500-a-couple inaugural gala at the War Memorial Auditorium: though Wayne, Benny, Carr, Ebsen, and Dean Martin also appeared, Sinatra was the shining star and the prize catch—as well as the producer of the show. He was the closing act, of course. After Jimmy Stewart introduced him, Frank sang a program of surefire hits, beginning with "You Make Me Feel So Young," "Pennies from Heaven," and "I've Got You Under My Skin," and concluding, naturally, with "My Way." Along the way, he threw in a tribute to the governor's wife, a woman he had once derided as a failed actress and failed Sinatra groupie, with a twinkling rendition of Jimmy Van Heusen and Phil Silvers's "Nancy":

Believe me, I've got a case
On Nancy, with the laughin' face.

She beamed with pleasure: she had always been obsessed with him and would remain so into her old age, a close friend recalled.

———

Ten days later, Ronald Reagan did Frank a solid in return, appearing at the January 15 dedication of the Martin Anthony Sinatra Medical Education Center at Palm Springs Desert Hospital. Vice President Agnew was also present. Frank had underwritten the entire $805,000 cost of the center in memory of his late father. "He's here," Frank said at the ribbon cutting, pointing to his head. "And here," he added, pointing to his heart.

It was a day of high purpose and emotional speeches: Frank Sinatra Day in Palm Springs, as officially declared by Mayor Howard Wiefels—although wasn't every day really Frank Sinatra Day in Palm Springs? Dolly was present, naturally, along with Nancy senior, Nancy junior, Frankie, and Tina. Frank's mother was in an uncustomarily sentimental mood. "It's been a wonderful day—but sad, too," she told Norma Lee Browning. "Frank is my only child and a wonderful son. And I love my grandchildren. But I just love Nancy Senior, too."

"Tears welled in her eyes," Browning wrote, "leaving no doubt where she stands on this touchy subject."

At a private luncheon later, Frank was named Honorary Doctor of Medicine and an honorary member of the Desert Hospital medical staff by Dr. Daniel Kaplan, who presented him with a black doctor's bag. "Does that mean he can operate?" someone called out.

"Frank's been operating for years," Kaplan said.

———

And two weeks after *that,* Frank was confounding his political critics by headlining at a Beverly Hills fund-raiser for John Tunney, the young (thirty-six) and Kennedyesque Democrat whom Californians had recently elected to the Senate. Not only did Sinatra sing for a Democrat; he had turned down a personal invitation from Alan Shepard to watch the launch of *Apollo 14* in order to do so. "Frank is married to the Democrats; it's just an affair with the Republicans," an unnamed pal told Dorothy Manners.

Yet just two months earlier, Dwight Chapin, special assistant to President Nixon, had taken the time to send a memo about Sinatra to Mrs. Nixon's chief of staff, Connie Stuart. "As you will recall, Frank Sinatra endorsed Ronald Reagan when he ran for the Gubernatorial election this year," Chapin wrote.

> The President and Mrs. Nixon invited Sinatra to attend the [president of Mexico] Diaz Ordaz dinner in San Diego. Sinatra did not attend the dinner but he did fly in for the reception, although he opened the same night in Las Vegas. Last weekend Sinatra played golf with the Vice President in Palm Springs.
>
> I talked with [*Laugh-In* producer and Nixon friend] Paul Keyes today and he offered the suggestion that perhaps Sinatra might be available to do an Evening at the White House. There are obviously strong arguments pro and con in giving Sinatra the White House forum. I am sure that many of our friends in the entertainment field would think it wrong to have a former anti-Nixon person entertain at the White House. I am fairly well convinced that the publicity value alone—not to mention the development of a relationship between Sinatra and the President—would far outweigh the negatives.

The wheels were in motion: he was being welcomed into the fold.

––––––

Nancy wrote that she felt closer than ever to her father after her marriage, recalling that Frank seemed more introspective yet also more relaxed. He and Big Nancy spent a good deal of time together, Nancy junior remembered; with Dolly living nearby, the family felt like a family again. But Frank's tours felt disruptive to one and all—including him. "Will somebody please get me the hell off the road?" he kept saying.

He wasn't making records; he wasn't making movies; besides the odd political event and benefit, he wasn't doing concerts. In his time-honored fashion, he was managing to juggle three relationships (or four, if you counted Big Nancy): with Hope Lange, with his *Dingus Magee* co-star Lois Nettleton, and, more and more in 1971, surreptitiously, with Barbara Marx. He was attentive, he was romantic, and then, always and quickly, he was on to the next thing.

No less important were the boys' nights out with Jilly and other pals, including Jimmy Van Heusen and Irwin "Ruby" Rubenstein, the proprietor of Ruby's Dunes. On Monday evenings, they met to watch the ABC football broadcast at Dominick's restaurant in Palm Springs; Frank even had special hats and jackets designed with the initials DOM—it stood for Dirty Old Men—superimposed on a football graphic for the guys to wear while they took in the game.

Just like those Turk's Palace jackets of forty years before.

He was a distinguished gentleman; his luster gleamed ever brighter. In mid-February, a Norma Lee Browning column chronicled just a couple of his good deeds—he was planning to send his personal jet to Monaco to bring Princess Grace and party to the June gala for the Motion Picture and Television Relief Fund; he was having a recreational center for teens built in Palm Desert—and a major feather in his cap: he had just won a Golden Globe, the Cecil B. DeMille Award for outstanding contributions to the entertainment industry.

In early March, he was on the other side of the camera for a change, photographing the first Muhammad Ali–Joe Frazier bout, the Fight of the Century, at Madison Square Garden for *Life*. Though he'd wangled the assignment mainly because—unaccountably—he'd been unable to get a ringside seat, his pictures were good enough that the weekly put one of them, an image of Frazier bashing Ali in the face, on the cover of the March 19 issue and an eight-page spread of Frank's surprisingly excellent fight snapshots inside, surrounding a four-thousand-word piece by none other than Norman Mailer.

Mailer titled his surging, bulging, coruscating essay "Ego," in honor of Ali, whom he dubbed America's Greatest in that department—and with whose ego he unsurprisingly managed to conflate his own. "Everything we have done in this century, from monumental feats to nightmares of human destruction," he wrote, "has been a function of that extraordinary state of the psyche which gives us authority to declare we are sure of ourselves when we are not."

He digressed and expanded upon Alan Shepard (who, despite Frank's not having been at Cape Kennedy to see him off, had successfully flown to the moon, landed on the surface, and whacked two golf balls) and Picasso and Hemingway and Tolstoy and Proust; he expatiated brilliantly about boxers white and black in general and Frazier and Ali in particular; and yet, sitting ringside at the Garden, he had somehow neglected to take in the little man nearby in the dark suit and graying toupee, one of the foremost avatars of the quantity he was writing about in the century he was writing about and, notwithstanding the big Nikon in his hands, the third-most-photographed person in the building that night.

I wish to announce, effective immediately, my retirement from the entertainment world and public life. For over three decades I have had the great and good fortune to enjoy a rich, rewarding and deeply satisfying career as an entertainer and public figure. Through the years people have been wonderfully warm and generous in their acceptance of my efforts. My work has taken me to almost every corner of the world and privileged me to learn by direct experience how alike all people really are—the common bonds that tie all men and women of whatever color, creed, religion, age or social status to one another; the things mankind has in common that the language of music, perhaps more than any other, communicates and evokes.

It has been a fruitful, busy, uptight, loose, sometimes boisterous, occasionally sad, but always exciting three decades. There has been little time for reflection, reading, self-explanation, and that need every man has for a fallow period, a long phase in which to seek better understanding of the vast transforming changes now taking place everywhere in the world. This seems a proper time to take that breather.

—Frank Sinatra, March 23, 1971

Receiving the Jean Hersholt Humanitarian Award for 1971. "No one within range of him who has needed his support has ever been refused it," Gregory Peck said. "Ladies and gentlemen, a man who pays his dues—Frank Sinatra."

Jim Mahoney had massaged the statement adroitly; the family knew about it all ahead of time, of course. "It didn't surprise me," Nancy junior wrote of her father's decision to retire. In truth, nobody was very surprised. "His record history was really falling; he also was not making good films," Mo Ostin recalled—facts not lost on many others in show business as well. The buzz had been circulating for quite a while. "You read it here first," Norma Lee Browning, one of the earliest buzzers, reminded her readers, stung by the fact that Frank had released the statement first to his now and then paramour Suzy Knickerbocker, as an exclusive for her New York *Daily News* column.

"I look forward to enjoying more time with my family and dear friends, to writing a bit—perhaps even to teaching," he added, taking the highest of high roads.

"His fade-out from the world of entertainment—movies, TV, night clubs, records, Hollywood, Las Vegas, New York, London, wherever—is a blow to an industry already deep in the doldrums," Browning wrote mournfully. "It marks the end of an era, and a rather marvelous one that will long be remembered, especially in this era of our so-called 'new' Hollywood's so-easily forgettables. The Sinatra name is magic on a marquee."

It sounded like nostalgia, but it was simple truth.

———

Hollywood, which Frank had steadily dishonored over the past decade, seemed to have grown instantly wistful at the thought of his departure. On Academy Awards night, April 15, at the Los Angeles Music Center's Dorothy Chandler Pavilion, Gregory Peck presented Sinatra with his third Oscar, this time for his charitable works but also as a kind of unofficial farewell.

It was a schizophrenic Oscars night: *Patton* won Best Picture; *Woodstock*, Best Documentary Feature. Starlets wore hot pants; grandes dames like Merle Oberon and Jennifer Jones drifted by in flowing gowns. The town's Old Guard cocked a skeptical eyebrow at the New but in time-honored fashion tried to adapt: youth was always magic in Tinseltown. Even the fifty-five-year-old Peck wore his graying hair on the shaggy side. But when he opened his mouth to speak, it was as though the Old Testament had come to life.

"Sinatra, Frank—baritone, as he is listed in the *Who's Who*, will be the recipient of the Jean Hersholt Humanitarian Award for 1971," he rumbled majestically under majestic eyebrows. Peck went on to speak of Frank's innumerable unpublicized charitable acts, then ticked off just a few of the more public ones: the children's institutions that had resulted from the 1962 world tour; the hospitals and colleges in America that had benefited from his largesse; the many benefit concerts. Then, in a neat trope, Peck springboarded

Sinatra's single acting Oscar into the present: "In 1953, this man was voted the Academy Award for his moving performance in a supporting role in *From Here to Eternity*. Never were the members of the Academy more prescient. Supporting actor—oh, yes indeed. No one within range of him who has needed his support has ever been refused it. Ladies and gentlemen, a man who pays his dues—Frank Sinatra."

As the orchestra struck up the title song from *The House I Live In,* the 1945 short for which Frank had won his first, special, Oscar, he took the statuette from his friend, looking pleased as Punch, and faced the camera. The toup was fringed, the face roundish: it was the Noblest Roman contour he would carry into the coming decades. The thickish sideburns were gray; the ears were beginning to sag ever so slightly with age. He rested his hands on the statuette. "This is truly an all-c—consuming thrill for me tonight," he said, stammering a bit.

Over the years, I've been part of the Awards wearing many different hats. Performer, emcee, presenter, recipient. But this is the top of the

Frank on assignment for *Life*, covering the Muhammad Ali–Joe Frazier heavyweight-championship bout, Madison Square Garden, March 8, 1971. Sinatra himself was the third-most-photographed person in the building that night.

moment of my—little walk-on in life, you might say. And I've been doing a little more thinking and contemplating these days than I did twenty-five years ago. That's because—

And suddenly, amazingly but not quite surprisingly, he was shifting with complete aplomb into his favorite impression, the always slightly offensive, never truly amusing, deep Kingfish voice from *Amos 'n' Andy*: "I'm what is known in the vernacular as a *re*-tired man now."

There was light, uncomfortable laughter from the audience—Coretta Scott King was in the house! It didn't matter to Frank; as always, he wrote his own rules. As a boy alone in his Hoboken bedroom, he had listened to *Amos 'n' Andy* on his big Atwater Kent, and the voices of Freeman Gosden and Charles Correll, white men imitating absurdly self-important black men, had enchanted and amused him, as they had much of America. He would remain amused by *Amos 'n' Andy* for the rest of his life, and so, it seemed to him, would his audiences; it simply stood to reason.

"One of the things I've been thinking about is why you have to get famous to get an award for helping other people," he continued sincerely.

I'm not being facetious about it . . . If your name is John Doe, and you work night and day doing things for your helpless neighbors, what you get for your effort is tired. So Mr. and Mrs. Doe and all of you who give of yourselves to those who carry too big a burden to make it on your own—

He picked up the Oscar and held it toward the camera. "I want you to take your share of this Jean Hersholt Humanitarian Award," he said. It was pure show business, and the audience ate it up. A camera picked up Roz Russell and George Cukor, applauding furiously.

But Frank wasn't quite done. "Because if I have earned it, so, too, have you," he went on. "In fact, your way of earning it was harder than my way. This has made it easier for me to spread a dab of sunshine here and there. I mean, in show business, they pay quite well. And being the quiet, conservative man that I am—"

He paused for the laugh.

"I have invested a chunk of three percent. And put the dividends to work in that noblest of all causes, charity toward your fellow men."

The camera cut to Nancy junior in the audience, sitting next to her beaming husband and dabbing a tear.

"It's the only investment in the world that pays a hundred percent," Frank said. "Anyway, it's put a great big bundle in here for me"—he pointed to his heart—"and I'd like to thank my dear brothers and sisters of the Academy for this joyous moment. Thank you."

He shook hands with Gregory Peck, and the camera pulled back to show the audience applauding—Tina, Nancy, Hugh Lambert, and next to him a tuxedoed Jilly, clapping wildly. And next to Jilly, Liv Ullmann.

What a strange and wonderful thing show business was.

There were rumors: there were always rumors. Some said he was quitting show business because of his bum right hand; others, that he was secretly Gravely Ill, a two-word euphemism for a one-word disease.

And then there were those who simply refused to believe it. "There are people taking odds in Las Vegas and in gin rummy games in Beverly Hills who doubt his retirement will last," one newspaper writer opined. "He is still in demand, and the enticement of a profession which has been his whole life may be too much to reject."

To a great degree, it was wishful thinking; it was also truer than anyone knew at the time.

He was back at the Los Angeles Music Center on Sunday night, June 13, officially to raise money for the Motion Picture and Television Relief Fund, but also, as all who attended knew, to perform his last two concerts ever.

The first was in the thirty-two-hundred-seat Dorothy Chandler Pavilion; the second, the one his family and friends would attend, in the more intimate Ahmanson Theatre. Gregory Peck produced the show. Jack Benny, Bob Hope, Sammy Davis Jr., Pearl Bailey, Don Rickles, Mitzi Gaynor, and Barbra Streisand were also performing, but Sinatra, fittingly, would close. Sinatra always closed.

He had finished the first show, and he was sitting in the dressing room, waiting out his high-powered opening acts. Tommy Thompson of *Life* was there to observe for what would become a cover story. "He was nervous," Thompson wrote.

> He had carefully orchestrated this finale and, being the most meticulous of men, he wanted it played with style and grace. He took the typewritten list of the 14 songs he would sing and he looked at it over and over again. He threw it down on the table and began doodling. His felt pen created a house, then he filled it in with black strokes, covering the windows and doors as if no one lived there any more.

The house he lived in. It was a picture of his unconscious, but the drawing of it was also a performance. He was so rarely alone that almost his whole life was a performance: the frightened, chaotic, relentlessly mercurial man inside playing Frank Sinatra, the role of a lifetime. He gave very good value in the role.

Various people visited the dressing room. Frank's guitarist, Al Viola, came in to rehearse the duet they were going to play, "Try a Little Tenderness." Cary Grant stopped by, another man who knew what it was to play a part the world expected. "Everybody wants to be Cary Grant," he had once said. "Even *I* want to be Cary Grant." Grant himself had retired five years earlier, without so much as a statement to the press, to take care of his young daughter.

Don Rickles burst in, dragging Sammy Davis under his arm in a bear hug. "We warmed 'em up for you, Frank," he called out. "You're gonna be great out there, Frank. People love pity, Frank."

They left, and the seventy-seven-year-old Jack Benny entered, complete with violin, and did three minutes. "This man," he said, waving a hand at Sinatra, "this man endorses Ronald Reagan for governor of California. Now *I* would have endorsed Reagan quietly, but Frank did it first. So I come out second with a little endorsement, and what do I get from Frank Sinatra the next day but a one-word telegram. It says 'COPYCAT.'"

Frank looked ready to fall off the couch. Benny started again. "Now, *I* would like to retire, only . . . ," Benny sputtered, "only, I *can't*."

Frank held his sides, shaking with laughter.

The old comedian left, and the room grew relatively quiet. "Are you *really* quitting?" Thompson asked Sinatra.

Frank didn't hesitate. "I'm absolutely serious about retirement," he said. "You can't make an idle statement like the one I made. At least *I* can't. I'm not built that way."

"He drank some more vodka, but it did not seem to be relaxing him," Thompson wrote.

The evening had too many ghosts in it. He was as tense as a fighter waiting for the bell. "I've had a handful," he said. "I've had enough. Maybe the public's had enough, too."

I shook my head.

"I've got things to do," he went on. "Like the first thing is not to do anything at all for eight months, maybe a year." He would roam around the desert taking pictures of cactus, he said. He would hang them on the brick walls of the hospital wing he has endowed in Palm Springs. He would "read Plato and grow petunias." He would paint a little, maybe try once again with watercolors. "I've never been able to control them," he said.

"Will you write that book?"

He shook his head, doubtfully. "I'm not that much of a talkative guy," he said. "I probably won't do a book."

Five years earlier, Thompson wrote, Frank had told him he would quit when he felt his voice was going, "when the vibrato starts to widen, when the breath starts to give out." Had that time come? Sinatra denied it vigorously.

"Physically, the voice is a long way from going," he said. "Hell, I just quit, that's all. I don't want to put any more makeup on. I don't want to perform anymore. I'm not going to stop living. Maybe I'm going to start living."

———

It was after midnight when Barbra Streisand finished her set: Sinatra time. Frank picked up his tuxedo jacket. Rickles, who had reappeared in the dressing room, perked up. "Somebody help the old man on with his coat!" the comic yelled. "Make way! Make way for the old-timer. Help him go out in a blaze of glory. Remember, Frank. Pity!"

Rosalind Russell stood center stage, struggling with her emotions. "This assignment is not a happy one for me," she began. "Our friend has made a decision," she said, then she had to stop. After a moment she started again. "A decision we don't particularly like, but one which we must honor. He's worked long and hard for thirty years with his head and his voice and especially his heart—"

Her voice broke, and she paused once more.

"But it's time to put back the Kleenex and stifle the sob," she finally said, "for we still have the man, we still have the blue eyes, those wonderful blue eyes, that smile—for one last time we have the man, the greatest entertainer of the Twentieth Century—"

Frank came out to relieve poor Roz of her misery, and the audience—which, besides his family and the cream of Hollywood included Princess Grace, Governor and Nancy Reagan, the Agnews, and Sinatra's new friend Henry Kissinger—leaped to its feet, clapping, stomping, yelling, refusing to stop. Frank embraced Russell, then quieted the crowd down. He looked around the auditorium and smiled a little. When he'd first started out, he said, he had worked some jobs for nothing but a pack of cigarettes. "So I figure if that's the way to begin, tonight's the way to end," he said.

He looked toward the orchestra podium and smiled: Nelson Riddle had returned for the final curtain. The dour, professorial, supremely brilliant arranger, Sinatra's greatest muse besides Ava, stood holding his baton expectantly.

"Might as well begin at the beginning," Frank said, and Riddle gave the downbeat: the song was "All or Nothing at All."

He sang for just half an hour, cycling through some of the high points, decade by decade: "I'll Never Smile Again," "I've Got You Under My Skin," "Ol' Man River," "The Lady Is a Tramp," "Try a Little Tenderness," "Nancy," "Fly Me to the Moon." The audience jumped to its feet again and again. He sang with seemingly effortless grace and power and deep emotion, closing his eyes during the ballads and, for the up-tempo numbers, snapping the fingers of his left hand and commanding the orchestra, "Jump on it—strings too!"

Finally, he came to the closer that was customary these days, the song he didn't like but the people always demanded. The silly words made a terrible kind of sense now:

And now the end is near.

But of course no one wanted any of it to end. The applause was deafening, as were the calls for an encore. Frank gave a signal to Nelson, and the band went into Riddle's hard-hitting rearrangement of "That's Life," which ended on the same kind of valedictory note:

But if there's nothing shakin' come this here July,
I'm gonna roll myself up in a big ball and die—my, my!

It was a game now: shouting and stamping, the audience refused to let him go. But he held the upper hand; he always did. He waved for silence and spoke softly into the microphone. He had built his career on saloon songs, he said; it made sense for him to end on one. And as the stage went dramatically dark, a pin spot picking out Frank's head, the band began to play "Angel Eyes."

Matt Dennis and Earl Brent had written the song in 1946; the great Duke Ellington vocalist Herb Jeffries made the first recording the following year. Ella Fitzgerald and Nat King Cole recorded it in 1952 and 1953, respectively, and their versions were as beautiful as could be expected. Sinatra didn't get around to it until *Only the Lonely* in 1958, but it was worth the wait: as he'd done and would continue to do, he wrested a song away from the greats and made it even greater, lifting the number beyond sheer beauty into sheer, gorgeously aching autobiography. The lyric wound up with the singer striking out to find his ever-elusive love—

I gotta find who's now the number one,
And why my angel eyes ain't here

—and ended with the haunting sign-off: "'Scuse me while I disappear."

Frank had been singing "Angel Eyes" in concert for years and had devised a dependable bit of business to close it: with the stage dark and the pin spot on his face, he lit a cigarette halfway through the song and then, on the last phrase—"'scuse me while I disappear"—gave a final puff of smoke as the spotlight irised down to darkness and disappeared himself. It was a killer; audiences loved it.

And it was a brilliant idea to close with "Angel Eyes" tonight—not just once, as myth would have it, but twice, first in the big early show at the Dorothy Chandler Pavilion, and now at the second, late one in the Ahmanson. Disappearance was the theme, but disappearance on Frank's terms, the power still in his hands even as he left the stage. The audience would be—was—

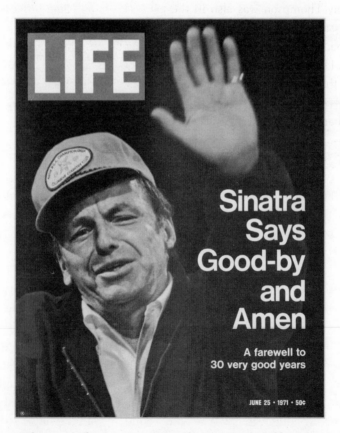

The retirement that wasn't: disappearing was one thing; staying invisible, quite another.

predictably floored, struck dumb by one of the greatest vanishing acts in stage history.

But disappearing was one thing; staying invisible, quite another.

———

The limousine sped through the dark streets of Beverly Hills, the same streets he had walked alone as a young man, holding his Oscar, seventeen years earlier. Now he was no longer young, and he wasn't alone; he was with his good friends Roz Russell and Freddie Brisson and a couple of others on his way to Russell and Brisson's house for an after-party.

"I'm tired," Frank said. "It's been a hell of a thirty-five years. I always sang a tough book, you know. Not a lot of phony talk. It used to wring me out."

He grew nostalgic. "I used to do five full shows a night at the Jersey shore," he said. "From eight-fifteen p.m. to four a.m. I'd see the sun come out as I'd walk home. And then, at the Paramount in New York, we did ten shows a day—eleven on Saturdays."

Tommy Thompson was also in the car. "The radio came on, a Spanish-language station sending out a south-of-the-border lament," he later wrote. "Frank made up some quick lyrics about a cowboy and his horse. He sang a few bars. He stopped."

"And that, ladies and gentlemen," Frank said, sinking back in his seat and closing his eyes, "is the last time Frank Sinatra will open his mouth."

Fat chance.

CODA

||||||||||||

Well, it seemed like a good idea . . . to loaf and play golf. After several years, I have a 17 handicap. And the other day, I made an overseas call and the operator asked me how to spell my name. I told her . . . and she asked my first name. Then she said, "Junior or Senior?"

—FRANK SINATRA, AT THE TAPING OF HIS NBC COMEBACK SPECIAL, *OL' BLUE EYES IS BACK,* SEPTEMBER 1973

He couldn't stand it. He had lived with that adulation, that spontaneous reaction from people that was almost like food to him. He couldn't live without it.

—SINATRA'S LONGTIME MUSIC COPYIST VERN YOCUM

Frank Sinatra's abortive 1971 retirement was by no means the end of his story, but his life after he returned to the spotlight—and of course he returned to the spotlight—was a very different story.

In the period between March 26, 1954, the day after he won the Oscar for *From Here to Eternity,* and June 13, 1971, the date of his retirement concert in Los Angeles, Sinatra made forty-six albums, many of them great. In the period between his second comeback, in 1973, and the end of his career—he performed his final concert in 1995—he made seven albums, a couple of them very good.

Between 1954 and 1971, he starred in thirty-two movies; after 1973, he starred in two, one of them made for television.

Between 1954 and 1971, he played innumerable engagements in nightclubs—rooms seating, at a maximum, three or four hundred people, and at a minimum many fewer than that—in Los Angeles, Las Vegas, Chicago, Miami, Atlantic City, and New York, among other places, thus justifying his claim to have been, first, last, and always, a saloon singer. After 1973, he became almost exclusively a concert artist, playing to crowds of a thousand or more—sometimes many more. These were, by and large, aging audiences that wanted *Sinatra,* and wanted his trademark numbers, a few of them new but most from the American Songbook. He had fought an ambivalent battle against the new music, sometimes trying to make it his own, almost always with heart-sinking results. Now, at last, he could be—exclusively and profitably—himself.

And between 1954 and 1971, despite brief marriages to Ava Gardner and Mia Farrow, he conducted an incomparably prolific love life, one that would have humbled Casanova himself, all the while, as his daughter Tina wrote, failing to make a truly intimate connection with any of the hundreds, if not thousands, of women he bedded. After 1973, due to the inevitable depredations of age, not to mention the effects of four decades of heavy smoking and drinking, his love life slowly, then suddenly, ground to a halt. After his 1976 marriage to Barbara Marx, he became, for all intents and purposes, and for the first time in his life, monogamous.

A far different story.

In the immediate aftermath of the retirement concert, he behaved—to a certain extent—like a good retiree: painting, taking pictures, playing golf. On the other hand, he *was* still Frank Sinatra. And so the relationships with Hope Lange and Lois Nettleton continued for the time being; the twenty-one-year-old actress Victoria Principal also came on the scene around that time, as did the fifty-two-year-old Eva Gabor. Frank even proposed to the beautiful, flirtatious, and much-traveled Pamela Churchill Hayward after the death of Leland Hayward in 1971; she opted instead for W. Averell Harriman.

And then there was the forty-three-year-old Barbara Marx, ever less married to Zeppo and increasingly present in his life. Tina Sinatra, visiting the Riviera with Robert Wagner soon after Frank's farewell performance at the Ahmanson Theatre, saw her father and Marx together in Monte Carlo, looking a lot like a couple.

It was the youngest Sinatra's first extended encounter with the woman Marx's friends had dubbed, for her unrelenting cheeriness, "Sunshine Girl." Through the dark lens of hindsight—Tina and Barbara would become bitter enemies over money and other matters—Frank's younger daughter claimed to have been both charmed and underwhelmed at first. On the one hand, she wrote, "Barbara had a fetching energy about her, an ability to enjoy herself that is invaluable when you're with someone in close quarters." When Jilly messed up the rental of a yacht for a harbor cruise—instead of a Sinatra-worthy vessel, he got a measly, fishy-smelling cabin cruiser—Barbara encouraged everyone to just roll with it and enjoy the boat ride.

On the other hand, "I sensed no real affection between them," Tina recalled. "Though constantly smiling and eager to please, Barbara was also quite demure. She and Dad stayed at arm's length from each other. They behaved like casual companions; they just didn't seem smitten to me. On instinct, I didn't trust the type."

Frank's younger daughter soon came to see Marx, with a certain grudging admiration, as a "relentless strategist, a professional survivor." Frank's mother took a more jaundiced view. As the relationship turned serious, Dolly, much to her son's chagrin, began proclaiming her disaffection in the only way she knew: loudly and without varnish. "I don't want no whore coming into this family!" she declared, giving the key word—*whoo-er*—a Hudson County punch.

She might as well have been spitting into the wind.

It wasn't a smooth courtship; in many ways, it wasn't a courtship at all. "From Jilly came a story that worried me," Tina Sinatra wrote.

> Late one night in 1973, Dad and Barbara joined a bunch of his pals at Jilly's after-hours spot in New York. Barbara could drink with the best of them; she'd keep right up with my father, shot for shot. The men began talking politics, and then Barbara jumped in to voice her opinion. In slow motion, the whole table turned and gaped at her, as if she'd said the dumbest thing they'd heard that night.
>
> My father laid into her: "What the hell do you know about anything? When I want to hear something from you, I'll ask you a question. Until then, you just *sit* there." And Barbara sat there. Perhaps her tenure in Las Vegas had hardened her to men's contempt.
>
> *Why was Dad acting out like that?* I wondered. *And why would she tolerate it?*

But the answers were simple. He was acting out like that because she had had the nerve to act as though she were an equal, in effect questioning his authority. With his posse looking on, it was an implicit humiliation, and humiliation was his hottest hot button.

And as for why she would tolerate his abuse: she would hold on tight for as long as it took, no matter how rough the ride, until the prize was hers.

———

The idea of his own mortality began to impinge on Sinatra's consciousness; losing old friends didn't help. Mike Romanoff and Bennett Cerf died within days of each other in the late summer of 1971, and Frank looked so stricken at Cerf's funeral that an FBI memo noted that he "appeared to be in extremely poor health," going on to speculate wildly "that FRANK SINATRA has been diagnosed as having terminal cancer, and estimates of life expectancy vary to as little as two months."

It was just wishful thinking on the FBI's part. However, another bureau communiqué shortly afterward noted more accurately that Sinatra had recently given Martha Mitchell, the wife of Richard Nixon's attorney general,

John Mitchell, a ride from San Francisco to Los Angeles on one of his jets. "It is apparent," the memo concluded, "that Frank Sinatra is becoming quite active in politics on behalf of the campaign to reelect President Nixon."

If he could accept Reagan and Agnew, why not Nixon too? By 1972, Frank was writing mash notes to the politician he had once detested most of all. When the president returned from a summit in Moscow, Sinatra sent him a letter saying "Bravo" for a job "well done." Nixon replied in kind:

Dear Frank:

After any long journey, the best part is always coming home, and your warm words of greeting made this occasion especially happy.

That same year, Sinatra rented an opulent house on Embassy Row in Washington, D.C., the better to be close to the political action he'd been missing since the Kennedy years. He got a little more action than he wanted, though, when he was served with a summons to appear before the House Select Committee on Organized Crime, which was investigating the Mob's influence on professional sports and wanted to talk to Frank about his investment in the mobbed-up Massachusetts racetrack Berkshire Downs. Loftily, Frank informed the congressional committee that he would testify "by invitation, not demand," and that he preferred to testify in closed session. The committee accommodated him on the former but not the latter, and Sinatra sailed into the hearing with a full head of steam. "I am not a second-class citizen," he told the committee counsel for starters. "Let's get that straightened out."

He gave a masterful performance, denying, stonewalling, and challenging. By the end of the hearing, Frank had a roomful of congressmen eating out of his hand. "You're still the chairman of the board," Representative Charles Rangel of New York told him as he left the chamber.

Delighted at the (largely Democratic) committee's public humiliation, Nixon personally phoned Sinatra to congratulate him on his performance. Touched, Frank decided to throw his official support behind the president's reelection. Many of his friends were appalled; Tina Sinatra was ballistic. "My hair was on fire," she recalled. "I called him at the Compound and vented my spleen: 'Damn it, Dad, I've been killing myself for McGovern, and now you come out for *Nixon*?'"

"That's the way it goes, kid—it's a free country," he told her.

In the end, "I decided to forgive him his appalling lapse in judgment, and we agreed to disagree," she wrote.

There were further appalling lapses to come. In January 1973, Frank—along with the freshly divorced Barbara Marx—attended Richard Nixon's second inauguration. Sinatra was scheduled to emcee the American Music Concert at the Kennedy Center, but when the Secret Service was unable to clear the comedian Pat Henry in time, Frank was left without an opening act. Furious, he bailed on the concert. And still furious, and with several drinks under his belt, he walked into the lobby of the Fairfax hotel a couple of hours later, Marx by his side, only to spot the *Washington Post* gossip columnist Maxine Cheshire, who had embarrassed him in person and in print with references to his Mafia associations.

He gave it to her as only Sinatra could. "You know Miss Cheshire, don't you?" he asked passersby. "That stench you smell is from her." Then he turned to Cheshire. "You're nothing but a two-dollar broad, you know that? You're a cunt! That's spelled C-U-N-T!" He took two dollar bills out of his pocket and stuffed them in the empty glass Cheshire was holding. "Here's two dollars, baby," he said. "That's what you're used to."

The incident, of course, made the papers: that was it for Sinatra and the inauguration.

But now the Nixon White House was in a bind; the president had already invited Frank to sing at a state dinner for the Italian prime minister, Giulio Andreotti, in April. Nixon's chief of staff, H. R. Haldeman, lobbied his boss hard to rescind the invitation, yet in the end Nixon was too thrilled at the prospect of having Sinatra in the fold to cancel.

With Nelson Riddle conducting the U.S. Marine Band, Frank performed ten numbers, beginning with "You Make Me Feel So Young" and ending with "The House I Live In." Outside Agnew rallies, it was the most he'd sung in public in almost two years. The voice was not what it had been, but the president, who dabbled at the piano himself, liked what he heard. At the end of the night, Nancy Sinatra wrote, Nixon took Frank aside and told him that he must get out of retirement. "Mr. President," Sinatra replied, "after tonight, I'll have to think about it."

In truth, he'd had to think about it for quite a while. The previous Fourth of July, aboard a chartered yacht off the Riviera, Spiro Agnew's aide Peter Malatesta had found Frank beset with a hacking cough and in a rotten mood. Sinatra "hinted that he might be coming out of retirement, but it wasn't spoken with excitement or anticipation," Malatesta recalled.

The year before . . . Frank was estimated to have spent approximately $10,000 a day, a figure which his attorney, Mickey Rudin, mentioned to

Sinatra and Nixon, August 1972. The world's upheavals, and Frank's everlasting attraction to power, made it easier to embrace a politician he'd once detested.

me during the course of a conversation. I was told Sinatra had an allowance of $2 million a year. Thanks to his savings and investments, Frank could have spent more, but $3.6 million was pushing things. As Mickey told me, "If he's going to spend that kind of money, he's going to have to go to work again."

Quintuple the amount to get a rough approximation of today's dollars. The spending rate is quite staggering by any measure—it is heroic, really; or, more properly, Sinatra-esque. The chartered yachts, the five-star hotel suites, the four-star restaurant meals for a crowd, the high-stakes gambling in Monte Carlo, the pricey baubles for the ladies; the jets and the jet fuel; the exquisitely outfitted compound in Palm Springs; the paintings by Monet, Pissarro, Utrillo, Hopper; the staff of dozens. It added up. If he didn't want to start eating into principal, he would have to sing for his supper again.

Three days after the White House concert, Frank announced that he would come out of retirement by taping a TV special for NBC to be aired in the fall. Ten days later—the very day Nixon's chief aides, including Haldeman, resigned in the mushrooming Watergate scandal—Frank walked into a recording studio (Samuel Goldwyn) for the first time in almost two and a half years and began making a new album.

It was a rough start. On that first day, he tried laying down a couple of tunes—Don Costa arrangements of Kris Kristofferson's "Nobody Wins" and Joe Raposo's "Noah"—and was so unhappy with what he heard that he had the masters destroyed. But a month later, he was back, for two nights in a row, with Gordon Jenkins this time, and by the end of August he had an LP. Reprise's art director, Ed Thrasher, who'd done album covers for Jimi Hendrix, Joni Mitchell, and the Grateful Dead, as well as for Sinatra's *My Way*, came up with the cover image—a simple, sepia-toned black-and-white image of Frank behind a music stand, smiling in an open-collared white shirt—and the title: *Ol' Blue Eyes Is Back*.

Sinatra loved it. His daughter Nancy hated it. "I said, 'You're kidding. That's awful,'" she remembered. "His choice prevailed."

Unsurprisingly. No one had ever called him Ol' Blue Eyes before; it didn't matter. It was the purest self-mythology, but he was sufficiently in sync with his own myth to know it would stick. It stuck.

He rousted Gene Kelly out of his own retirement to co-star in the TV special; he even got some voice coaching from the fifty-six-year-old opera singer Robert Merrill, who knew a thing or two about coaxing dramatic effect from aging lungs. The show was taped in mid-September; three weeks later, Spiro Agnew resigned in disgrace, having been charged with committing extortion, tax fraud, bribery, and conspiracy during his terms as Baltimore County executive, governor of Maryland, and vice president of the United States. He was allowed to plead no contest to a single count of tax evasion; he was never convicted.

In some ways, it was a bummer of a fall. Along with Watergate and the Agnew scandal, there were the so-so ratings for *Ol' Blue Eyes Is Back*, the TV special, which lost in its time slot to *The Hospital*, a 1971 movie starring Ava's old boyfriend George C. Scott, on ABC. On the other hand, *Ol' Blue Eyes Is Back*, the album, was released two weeks later amid a lavish publicity campaign and—in a landscape of fresh offerings by Pink Floyd, Led Zeppelin, Elton John, Paul McCartney, and others—charted at a respectable number 13. An optimistic Reprise press release accompanying the new LP said that

Sinatra would "record an album every six months and make a few personal appearances," yet subsequent albums of the 1970s would do nowhere near as well. The record-buying public, largely young, was sending Sinatra a clear message. Now and for the rest of his career, Frank would have to earn his real money—the money he needed to live in the style to which he'd long since become accustomed—playing concerts in the largest venues possible.

In his first official public appearance since the retirement, he returned in triumph to the state he'd said he would never set foot in again: in January 1974, with Caesars Palace under new management and Sanford Waterman under indictment, Sinatra opened in the Circus Maximus. The minimum was a hefty $30; each guest received a medallion engraved with "Hail Sinatra: The Noblest Roman Has Returned." The Noblest Roman looked a little jowly: he'd put on a few pounds during his off time. Along with "Come Fly with Me," "I Get a Kick out of You," and "You Make Me Feel So Young," Frank sang a track from the new LP, Stephen Sondheim's "Send in the Clowns," a theatrical master-piece he didn't truly connect with, and—displaying a pronounced new ability to whipsaw between the sublime and the far less than sublime—a song from his upcoming album, *Some Nice Things I've Missed,* the infinitely regrettable "Bad, Bad Leroy Brown."

And so out on the road, like a restless spirit condemned to wandering the big showrooms and stadiums of America: San Jose. The Fontainebleau. Carnegie Hall. Nassau Coliseum. Atlanta. Providence. Detroit. Philadelphia. Washington. Chicago. Back to Vegas. And that was just the first half of 1974. During the midpoint of each concert, he paused to sip some tea, or something stronger, and make a few remarks, often unfavorable remarks about journalists, especially female journalists. He directed special contempt toward Rona Barrett, who'd recently published a memoir in which she claimed that Frank junior had staged his own kidnapping to get Frank's attention. "Congress should give Rona Barrett's husband a medal just for waking up beside her and having to look at her," Frank told audiences. "She's so ugly that her mother had to tie a pork chop around her neck just to get the dog to play with her." Other report-ers, many of them writers Sinatra might have wanted to keep on his side, like Charles Champlin of the *Los Angeles Times,* took notice.

In October 1974, he did a series of concerts, billed as the Main Event, beginning in Boston and proceeding to Buffalo, Philadelphia, and Pittsburgh, then pausing at Madison Square Garden for a big live broadcast on ABC-TV before continuing on to the heartland for five more stops. The New York show was staged in the round with prizefight trappings: the brash young promoter Jerry Weintraub had come up with the concept. "You're the heavyweight champion of the world, Frank," he'd told Sinatra. "The number-one singer in the world. No challengers, no one even close. So let's do it in a ring, and make it like a heavyweight title fight, and invite all the people who go to heavyweight title fights, because they're your fans. And let's get Howard Cosell to be the announcer." The cover of the live album would depict Frank in a black trench coat, white scarf, tux, and leather gloves, looking like the round-faced middle-aged pugilist he had become. The audience loved him.

"We will now do the national anthem, but you needn't rise," Sinatra announced before beginning "My Way."

"Ah, Frankie everlovin'," Martha Weinman Lear, who'd been a bobby-soxer at the Paramount thirty years earlier, wrote in the *New York Times,* "here we are at the Garden dancing cheek to cheek, and the lights are low and it's oh so sweet . . . It's Ol' Blue Eyes now, with the paunch and the jowl and the wig, and the hell with them. The blue eyes still burn, the cuffs are still incomparably shot, the style, the *style,* is still all there, and what's left of the voice still gets to me like no other voice, and it always will."

But the influential jazz and pop critic Ralph J. Gleason, covering the Event for *Rolling Stone,* begged to differ. "That style he set was big enough and broad enough to carry the careers of half a dozen others, but Ol' Blue Eyes is a drag that Frankie never was," he wrote.

The Main Event, Madison Square Garden, October 13, 1974. "We will now do the national anthem, but you needn't rise," Sinatra announced before beginning "My Way."

It is simply weird now to see him all glossed up like a wax dummy, with that rug on his head looking silly, and the onstage movement, which used to be panther-tense, now a self-conscious hoodlum bustle.

His possible appearance is the occasion for bodyguards and hush-hush phone calls and big security plans and a blanket of secrecy . . . I don't think anyone but those clowns on his payroll really think any of this panoply of power is necessary . . . For Frank Sinatra, whose voice made him the friend of millions of Americans, to carry on like a Caribbean dictator holding back history with bodyguards and a secret police is simply obscene . . . I think he went somewhere that makes him alien now to me in a way he never was before.

This was the postretirement Frank in a nutshell: embattled, secure and insecure behind a guarded gate. Tougher than ever on the outside, still a molten puddle within.

———————

As Sinatra turned sixty, he grew less interested than ever in the chase. "There's nothing worse than being an old swinger," he once told a writer. At the same time, the realities of monogamy and marriage bored and terrified him. He had done it three times (the marriage part, anyway), and it hadn't worked out. And he had proposed to any number of women, always meaning it in the moment—as he meant the songs he sang—but quickly going on to the next thing once the moment had passed.

Moreover, two of the women he'd married, and any number of the ones he'd proposed to, had insisted, annoyingly, on having other jobs than taking care of him. He needed someone who would happily take him on as a full-time occupation. He was a major project, and as more and more women fell away or were pared away from his life, there were fewer and fewer who looked able to do it. One stuck around, though.

Even by Barbara Marx's own account, reeling in Frank Sinatra was no mean trick. Her idealized account, in the memoir titled, unfortunately and unforgettably, *Lady Blue Eyes,* lists many breakups and makeups and even a prolonged separation after the Madison Square Garden concert during which they both saw other people: remarkably, Frank dated Jacqueline Onassis, who while Jack Kennedy was alive had regarded Sinatra as a lowlife. Now he had gained stature in her eyes, but less romantically than literarily: apparently—she'd started working as a book editor—she just wanted him to write his memoirs.

In the spring of 1976, Tina Sinatra writes, her father surprised his children by conducting an extended liaison with their mother. It was at precisely the same time that Barbara Marx gave Frank an ultimatum: "Marry me or lose me."

"My dad's inner life was a maze with no exit," Tina wrote. "What could you tell a man in such turmoil that he hadn't told himself a thousand times over?" In the end, he listened to his own fears, which told him that he was getting old, and so was Big Nancy. Barbara, on the other hand, somehow seemed to be aging in reverse. In June, she showed up with Frank at the christening of Nancy junior's daughter Amanda with "a brand-new profile and look[ing] ten years younger," according to Tina. She was also wearing a diamond the size of a quail's egg on the fourth finger of her left hand.

Barbara writes that after her ultimatum Frank invited her to Chicago, where he was spending time with an old pal, and presented her with "an enormous pear-shaped diamond that I later learned was twenty-two carats" and an even larger stone, a perfect green emerald. "You can have them set any way you want," he told her.

"Praying that I was doing the right thing," she writes, "I asked [a jeweler] to set the diamond in an engagement ring setting. Once the enormous solitaire was ready, I had the jeweler return it to Frank, not me, so that he could present it to me whichever way he wanted."

It was determinism masquerading as free will.

At dinner a couple of nights later, she found the ring in her champagne glass. "Is this for me?" she asked.

"Yes, beautiful," Frank said. "Why don't you put it on?"

"Those were still not the words I wanted to hear," she recalled. So she handed him the ring and said, "Here, Frank, you put it on. Put it anyplace you want." She held out both her hands.

Shaking his head in defeat, he put the ring on the fourth finger of her left hand, and that was that.

They married on July 11, 1976, at Sunnylands, the three-thousand-acre Walter Annenberg estate in Rancho Mirage. Ronnie and Nancy Reagan, Sammy and Altovise Davis, the Gregory Pecks and the Kirk Douglases and the Ted Agnews were all in attendance. There had been a brief hiccup earlier in the day when Barbara balked at the prenuptial agreement Mickey Rudin handed her—it stipulated that none of his premarriage assets or future earnings would be hers—but in the end, over a barrel for the time being, she signed.

"When the judge asked Barbara, 'Do you take this man for richer or poorer?' my father interjected, 'Richer, richer,'" Tina recalled. "Everyone laughed, but Dad's face stayed straight. As he completed his vows, he sounded to me like a man who knew the terms of a deal and was determined to see it through. He would try like hell to make this marriage work."

His new wife, too, understood the terms of the deal, but that didn't mean the deal couldn't be sweetened somewhere down the line.

Barbara Marx and Frank in early June 1976, a month before their wedding. Reeling Sinatra in was difficult, but Barbara was tough, determined, and resourceful.

————

Frank's previous two wives had harbored lofty cultural aspirations, reflecting a side of him that hankered in the same direction. Barbara Sinatra was interested in glittering things and people, jewels and celebrities rather than ideas. With his marriage to Barbara, Frank shifted definitively westward and rightward, toward the sunstruck and unreflective life of Palm Springs. His contacts with the larger world now narrowed, in keeping with his fourth wife's overwhelming fascination with the shiny international rich who moved in elegant herds from one luxurious port of call to the next. A door in him closed, what he had thought and felt most deeply shut firmly behind it, and the person who shared his bed seemed to betray no interest in what was really inside.

————

In the year of his fourth marriage, he often opened shows with a number that Barry Manilow had recently made popular, "I Write the Songs." Sinatra added his own fillip to the tune by changing the key phrase:

I sing the songs that make the whole world sing,
I sing the songs of love and special things.

It didn't help much. The number was still irretrievably saccharine, as was much of the new material that now marbled his repertoire, special things like

Neil Diamond's "Stargazer," John Denver's "Like a Sad Song," and Eric Carmen's "Never Gonna Fall in Love Again." Frank was straining for relevance,
trying to gather in younger audiences, hoping to sell records. The records
didn't sell much, but the concertgoers kept coming anyway: he was the event.

Sam Giancana was gone now, rubbed out in his Chicago basement while he
cooked sausages, capped seven times in the head by someone the old man
had been foolish enough to trust. The following year, 1976, Frank had his last
close dance with the friends of the friends, at the Westchester Premier Theater, in Tarrytown, New York, a $7 million, thirty-six-hundred-seat Potemkin
venue, erected by the Mob with the sole purpose of milking it dry. Diana
Ross performed there, and Dean Martin and Tom Jones and Liza Minnelli
and Steve Lawrence and Eydie Gorme, and the Band and Harry Chapin,
but Sinatra was the beacon, the lead attraction: he played the Westchester
twenty-seven times in 1976 and 1977, making sure to be paid under the table
and in cash and seeing to it that Jilly and Mickey Rudin were also able to wet
their beaks.

On the night of April 11, 1976, Frank received a group of distinguished
visitors in his dressing room and posed, grinning, for a photograph with eight
of them. They were, as it turned out, a virtual Mafia directorate, including
Carlo Gambino himself and his anointed successor, Paul Castellano, as well
as Gambino capo Gregory DePalma, Los Angeles organized-crime chief (and
later FBI informant) Jimmy "the Weasel" Fratianno, and a couple of ancillaries
named Salvatore Spatola and Richard "Nerves" Fusco.

In 1981, when Sinatra reapplied for his Nevada gaming license, the Nevada
Gaming Control Board took a keen interest in the photograph. Frank claimed
that while he had met a couple of men in the picture in passing, he was meeting most of them for the first time, including Gambino, and had no idea what
they did for a living. The members of the board also asked Sinatra whether he,
Dean Martin, and Sammy Davis Jr. had done the 1962 Villa Venice concerts
for free as payback to Sam Giancana for the mobster's help in getting John F.
Kennedy elected: Frank denied it. "He lied," Tina Sinatra told the *60 Minutes*
correspondent Steve Kroft in a 2000 interview. Sinatra got his license.

The Westchester Premier Theater, having gone bankrupt in the late 1970s,
was razed in 1982.

On January 6, 1977, Dolly was to fly with Frank and Barbara on one of Frank's
jets to Las Vegas, where Frank was set to open at Caesars Palace. At the last
minute, for reasons she never explained, she changed her mind and chose to

go—along with a friend visiting from New Jersey, Anna Carbone—later in the day. Though Barbara Sinatra wrote in her memoir that she and Dolly had made their peace and even become friends, it has been suggested that Dolly didn't want to travel on the same plane with her daughter-in-law.

Late that afternoon, the chartered Lear Jet on which Frank's mother and Mrs. Carbone flew took off from Palm Springs, entered a snow squall, and vanished from air-traffic controllers' radar screens. Frank was quickly notified and assumed the worst: he somehow did the first show, then canceled the second and flew back to Palm Springs, where, Barbara writes, he "barely said a word for two days. He sat on a couch in a corner by the bar and stared into space." On the third day, the wreckage of the plane was found near the summit of nearby San Gorgonio Mountain. There were no survivors.

Barbara Sinatra and Tina Sinatra both write of the aftermath of the crash, each in character. "Life went on after Dolly's death, just as it always had," Barbara says. "Frank canceled two weeks of performances and we flew to Barbados to spend some time at the place we loved, but performing was Frank's therapy and he needed to get back on the stage. It was also what his mother would have expected, for there had surely never been a woman more proud of her son."

It was also what his wife needed him to do.

Frank's younger daughter tells of her and her sister's outrage at discovering that their stepmother had stripped their grandmother's house of china, silver, crystal, and jewelry. "It turned out that Barbara, who'd been in the family for ten minutes, had appointed herself custodian of Dolly's valuables," she writes. Eventually, Barbara returned most of the valuables, minus a number of things: "furs and jewelry, and several of Grandma's finer handbags."

Sinatra's last dance with the friends of the friends: On April 11, 1976, Frank posed backstage at the Westchester Premier Theater with a virtual Mafia directorate, including Carlo Gambino himself, second from right, and his capo Gregory DePalma, on Sinatra's right. The singer's lifelong attraction to the Mob was deep, genuine, and unfortunate.

Strikingly, neither Barbara nor Tina speaks of Frank's state after this sudden and unimaginable subtraction. His father's death had been a tragedy; his mother's death was a calamity. They had been a pair, Frankie and Dolly, for over sixty years: she had been his tormentor and his champion, but mainly she had been his mirror. Now he was that strangest of all things, a mirror reflecting nobody.

———

In March 1978, Frank was to present an award to Nelson Riddle at a testimonial dinner in the arranger's honor in Los Angeles. Sinatra was performing at a theater in Fort Lauderdale but had agreed to fly west for the event. At the last minute, though, he came down with a bad cold and flew home from Florida. The testimonial was postponed to Sunday, April 16.

On Thursday, April 13, Frank returned to the Sunrise Musical Theatre in Fort Lauderdale to make up the engagements he had missed. On the sixteenth, the night of the Riddle dinner, he performed his full closing show in Florida. Someone in his office—possibly Mickey Rudin—sent Gregory Peck to present Riddle with the award in Frank's stead. It has never been determined whose decision this was (though ultimately the buck stopped with Sinatra) or why he failed to attend the testimonial.

The following year, Frank's longtime producer Sonny Burke came up with a concept for a new album, a three-disc LP that would examine Sinatra's musical past, present, and future. The album would be called *Trilogy*. The plan was for its three parts to be arranged, respectively, by Nelson Riddle, Billy May, and Gordon Jenkins.

One night during the album's early planning stages, "Sinatra and I were in the dressing room in the suite at Caesars, and we were talking about Nelson, and I was shouting his praises," recalled Vincent Falcone, who started as Frank's pianist in the late 1970s, then later became his conductor.

> Frank turned to me, and said, "Call him on the phone, and ask him if he'll write a chart for me." And I said, "Wow, man—this is like *history!*" So I picked up the phone and called Nelson. I said, "Nelson, Mr. Sinatra asked me to call you. He would like to know if you would write an arrangement on . . ." And there was just dead silence on the other end of the phone for a good ten or fifteen seconds, and then Nelson said, "Tell him I'm busy," and hung up.

Frank's response, according to Falcone, was "Fuck him." Billy May wound up arranging the Past section of *Trilogy*, and Don Costa the Present.

On the night of September 19, 1979, the longtime Sinatra observer Rob Fentress—he had attended many of Frank's recording sessions and was a close friend of Sonny Burke's—was at Western Recorders in Hollywood when Frank laid down two tracks for *Trilogy*. The first, a new version of Irving Berlin's "Let's Face the Music and Dance," was arranged and conducted by May. The second, a recent composition by the Broadway songwriters John Kander and Fred Ebb, was the theme from a 1977 Martin Scorsese movie, *New York, New York*. Don Costa had written the chart; Vincent Falcone conducted. Barbara Sinatra writes that at first her husband hadn't wanted to record the song, feeling it was the property of Liza Minnelli, who'd sung it in the film; he changed his mind after performing it at Radio City Music Hall in October 1978 and bringing down the house.

After the final take that night, Fentress stood in the control room amid a crowd of people, including Jilly Rizzo, as Sinatra listened to the playback of the session. The atmosphere was boisterous. "They were playing back 'New York, New York,' and Frank was sitting in the engineer's chair, and he was just oblivious to all the noise," Fentress remembered. "He was just focusing on the song. And you could see how pleased he was. He wasn't laughing; he was just smiling slightly. I'd seen that focused look before."

It was a good sign.

———

By 1979, after Barbara failed in an attempt to have Frank adopt her twenty-six-year-old son, Bobby—Sinatra's children resisted her furiously—a chill had settled on the marriage. "They were averaging one nasty fight a week and sleeping in separate bedrooms, a development that owed to more than Dad's chronic sleep disorder," Tina wrote.

> I know that my father was a handful to live with. I doubt that he could have been happy with anyone at that point in his life. But if he showed unkindness, I am sure that it was in kind. Barbara could extract the deep, dark anger out of Dad. She had a street fighter's résumé, and Dad was a withering counterpuncher. They hit each other below the belt and didn't stop when the bell rang.

Frank was quick to forgive, his younger daughter remembered; Barbara, less so. She knew the most effective weapon against her husband and wielded it expertly: the silent treatment. She could hold out for days, while Frank grew more miserable by the hour.

Yet the ultimate punishment for Frank was something worse than silence: it was solitude. And now his wife began to pare away his friends.

Not the Late Show, the glittering Old Hollywood crowd who suited her social ambitions; not the Kirk Douglases or the Gregory Pecks or the Jimmy Stewarts or Cary Grant. She fixed on the closer, rougher-hewn ones, the ones who would never move in the circles to which she'd risen. She began with Jilly.

They had never liked each other much; by his own choice or Barbara's, Rizzo fell out of Frank's life for a couple of years at the beginning of the 1980s. Nancy junior often toured with her father then and witnessed the further decline of his marriage. Always a sensitive observer of his moods, she saw him acting like his old self, drinking and laughing through the night when Charlie Callas or other pals dropped by after the show, then losing his smile when Barbara showed up to cut the fun short.

By mid-1983, Sinatra and his wife were spending more and more time apart. As distinctly different from the past, infidelity on Frank's part does not seem to have been an issue: those days appeared to be more or less over for him. He had been complaining, seriously and humorously, of impotence for a long time; at some point, he was reportedly fitted with a penile implant. According to talk in urological circles, the device failed because Frank tried to use it too soon.

Not long after Sinatra produced Ronald Reagan's inaugural gala, rumors about him and Nancy Reagan sprang up: in her biography of the First Lady, Kitty Kelley writes insinuatingly of three-hour White House "lunches" between Nancy and Frank while the president was out of town. But no one who knew Sinatra well felt anything besides lunch was really going on. Tina Sinatra writes of an emotional bond between her father and Mrs. Reagan, saying that the two spoke on the phone every night at an appointed hour and that he poured his heart out to her about his marital problems. Barbara Sinatra writes that it was the First Lady who did the pouring: "During long-distance telephone calls and their lunches together whenever they were in the same town, I think he became Nancy's therapist more than her friend." Though there appeared to be little love lost between the two women, Barbara, perhaps armed with intimate knowledge, seems not to have considered the First Lady a sexual threat.

Still, according to Tina, it was Nancy Reagan, during one of her long phone conversations with Frank, who advised him to leave his marriage. "Francis, this woman is not for you," she allegedly said. "She's not going to make you happy. You've got one foot out the door—keep going!"

Ironically, Rizzo was the one who talked Sinatra into reconciling with Barbara. "If I would have left it alone the way it was," Frank's longtime shadow told a friend, "*I* would have ended up being Mrs. Frank Sinatra, and I wasn't ready for that."

Mr. and Mrs. Sinatra got back together—not for love, his daughters believed, but because Frank had nowhere else to go.

The road was his home. Vegas and Denver and L.A. Pittsburgh and Providence and Buffalo. Atlantic City and San Francisco; Portland, Maine, and Clarkston, Michigan. In Egypt, he sang before the Pyramids of Giza; in Rio de Janeiro, in front of 275,000 people; at Carnegie Hall and the Metropolitan Opera. Wherever he went, "New York, New York" became his closer; he liked it so much better than "My Way." In Monte Carlo and London; in Devon, Pennsylvania, and Boston; in Sun City, Bophuthatswana.

He did more than a thousand concerts between 1976 and 1990, and his wife accompanied him to almost all of them. (Except in Atlantic City. Vegas had formed her; A.C., a cut-rate Vegas with salt air, didn't appeal to her.) "I travel with him, that's really our life," Barbara said soon after their separation ended.

> We're really on the road most of the time, and a plane is almost our home, or a hotel or whatever. He starts out each year with a small schedule and somehow it just seems to get filled up.
>
> I think he's really happier working. I think it keeps his juices going and he likes it. I think he'd be very unhappy if he really retired totally.
>
> So in order to make some kind of normalcy out of it, out of that crazy kind of life, I travel with him and try to make it as comfortable as possible.

She made sure it was comfortable for herself as well. One musician who toured in Europe with Sinatra in this period remembered Barbara making a beeline for the hotel jewelry store at every stop along the way.

"I vocalize an hour a day whether we're working or not," Frank said in a 1979 interview. "Sometimes two hours a day if I feel I haven't had enough. So if I'm called upon, it's there. The muscles are all there and everything is fine, except if you go on a long hiatus, then it's murder to come back. Oh, it's murder to get there. It's like lifting weights. You can't get up there right away."

He had always worked hard on his singing, harder than anyone knew. But in his sixties, through the combined effects of age and unfiltered Camels and Jack Daniel's and late nights and guilt germs, the great voice began to alter and deteriorate. The cave-of-winds depths were still there, but the phenomenal breath control, the nearly freakish ability to sustain long notes, was not. The intonation, so glorious for so much of his career, now wavered.

What he retained, what would stay with him almost until the very end, was his unparalleled feeling for lyrics, his way around a song's story. Like that of his idol Mabel Mercer, who in the twilight of her career sat in an armchair onstage and recited the lyrics rather than really sang them, his sense of a song's essence was absolute. He proved it on his last album for Reprise, 1981's *She Shot Me Down.*

Doubtless inspired by the troubles in his marriage, and (as always) still thinking about Ava, he gave torch songs one last try and scored an artistic—if not a commercial—triumph. He was deservedly proud of this minor but affecting LP. "I was with him in Palm Springs when he played that album for friends the first time," Peter Bogdanovich remembered. "It was very touching how excited he still was—like a kid."

From an emotional standpoint, the album's first number, Stephen Sondheim's "Good Thing Going," from the musical *Merrily We Roll Along,* is one of the finest things Sinatra ever did. It's the unabashedly raw story of a shipwrecked relationship—

We had a good thing going—
Going, gone

—and he tells it masterfully, quite simply as no one else on earth could tell it, the ruined cathedral of his voice an objective correlative for the infinite sadness of a couple's sundering. He might not have known how to hold an intimate relationship together, but he understood deeply what it felt like when it fell apart.

———

Ava turned sixty in December 1982. Frank sent her an enormous bouquet, as he did every year on her birthday: she would let the flowers sit in their vase until they died and then keep them there, long dead, for the rest of the year until the next bouquet arrived. She didn't mind sixty so much, she said: fifty had been much harder. Nor did she particularly care any longer if people knew how old she was. "I'm one hell of an old broad," she'd say. "It's undignified to lie about it."

She wasn't making movies anymore, but in the mid-1980s, for the first time, she elected to work in the medium she had long disdained. In 1985, she did a seven-episode turn as a scheming widow in a Southern California spin-off of *Dallas* called *Knots Landing.* That February, while Gardner was in New York doing press for the show, Peter W. Kaplan, then a TV reporter for the *New York Times,* interviewed her in her suite at the Waldorf Towers. She wore a cherry-colored sweatshirt with a sequined letter *A* over one breast, tight watermelon-pink toreador pants, and rubber thongs. "With her green eyes and shaken-out auburn coif," he wrote, "Miss Gardner did not look so very different from the way she looked in 'The Barefoot Contessa,' 'On the Beach' and 'Mogambo.'"

As she swigged from a bottle of spring water and chain-smoked, Ava talked of many things, including her third husband, Frank Sinatra. She called him "a great artist" but denied that their doomed love affair had led to the anguished resonance of his classic albums of the 1950s. "Oh, no, no," she said. "He had just done a film he was proud of—'From Here to Eternity'—he had his strength back and all of his talent."

Forgetting that the one thing he didn't have was her.

Gardner's monumental sex appeal was still very much in place that afternoon, Kaplan later remembered. Yet a year later, her health began to decline rapidly. She was run down and losing weight; she had developed a hacking cough that wouldn't go away. Despite the cough, she continued to smoke heavily. In October 1986, her London doctor, fearing the worst, ordered her tested for lung cancer. She flew to California and checked into St. John's Hospital in Santa Monica, where tests showed no cancer. Instead, she was diagnosed with pneumonia.

She rallied briefly, but on her eleventh day in the hospital, she suffered a stroke. The left side of her body was partially paralyzed; her face was twisted, her mouth contorted. Though her cognitive faculties appeared undamaged, she had great difficulty speaking understandably.

"Frank would call, and the nurses would hold the phone to her ear," Ava's biographer Lee Server writes. "She tried to speak, but it was hard to make herself understood, and so she just listened to his voice.

"'I love you, baby,' he told her. 'It stinks getting old.'"

Days later, as Ava still lay in her hospital bed, Frank himself collapsed while performing in Atlantic City and was rushed to the Eisenhower Medical Center in Rancho Mirage with acute diverticulitis, an excruciating intestinal inflammation. His upset about Kitty Kelley's recently released biography *His Way* might have aggravated the condition. In an emergency surgery that lasted two hours, doctors removed a length of intestine and attached a colostomy bag, which he had to wear for months afterward. He unhappily showed the bag to Paul Anka backstage at Caesars. "He was utterly humiliated by this," Anka recalled.

He was threescore and ten, and he hated it.

In spite of it, though, he went to Hawaii to do a guest shot on a TV show he loved, Tom Selleck's *Magnum P.I.* In what turned out to be his final major acting job, Sinatra played a role that fit him like an old glove, a retired New York cop on the trail of his granddaughter's murderer. He did almost all his own stunts, Barbara notes admiringly: "Frank refused to let that darn bag beat him."

Uncomfortable and unhappy nonetheless, he spent the first three months of 1987 in Hawaii and Palm Springs. Sometime in March, Mia Farrow, then living in New York and in the midst of her thirteen-year relationship with Woody Allen, conceived a child; on December 19, she gave birth to a son, whom she and Allen named Satchel Ronan O'Sullivan Farrow. Years later, long after her acrimonious breakup with Woody Allen (whose legs Frank sweetly offered to have broken), Mia Farrow claimed that this son, now known as Ronan Farrow—who with his penetrating, deep-set, hooded blue eyes and bee-stung lips bears a strong resemblance to both her and her father, the director John Farrow—might "possibly" have been sired by Frank Sinatra.

Who was in Hawaii and Palm Springs all the while, wearing a colostomy bag and close by his ever-watchful wife.*

———

At the 1980 concert in Rio de Janeiro, Sinatra suffered a memory lapse. He was in the middle of singing "Strangers in the Night," a song he knew "as well as my hand," he recalled, when the rest of the lyric suddenly escaped him. The entire stadium began to sing it for him—in English. Frank was moved.

The lapses, onstage and off, became more frequent. "I saw his memory start to go," Vincent Falcone recalled. "He lost his ability to remember the lyrics. I remember when we did Mr. Reagan's inaugural, he had me write out some things that he could refer to when he needed them. Then he had a little lectern built, and if he had a new song that he didn't remember, he'd have the lyric."

Falcone worked elsewhere for a couple of years, then returned as Sinatra's conductor in 1985. "That year, he turned seventy," Falcone said. "You figure, 'Well, what the hell.'" But he had gotten markedly worse. Now there were teleprompters onstage for the lyrics, big twenty-one-inch monitors, the print so large—Frank had had cataract surgery—that sometimes there were just four or five words on the screen. "The audience was looking at the words," the conductor recalled. "They could see the lyrics. It got to be embarrassing.

"The family tried to hide that, telling everybody he was fine," Falcone said. "He wasn't fine. He could hardly read. He lost his hearing in one ear. He couldn't see the freaking monitor. Then it really got bad. It got to the point where he didn't know anything. Can you imagine what that must have been

---

* In 2015, Tina Sinatra also maintained that her father had had a vasectomy several years prior to 1987.

like for him? Tony Bennett told me, 'I went up to him and put my hand on his shoulder and said, "Hi, Frank," and he turned around and said, "Get your fuckin' hand off my shoulder." ' I said, 'Tony, don't you know that he didn't know who you were?' "

———

He was on a cocktail of medications: diuretics, sleeping pills, barbiturates for his migraines, and Elavil, an antidepressant. And he was continuing to self-medicate with Jack Daniel's, as he had for his whole adult life. Much of the time, especially to his daughters, he seemed flat, subdued. His feistiness was missing; *he* was somehow missing.

This is when he began to die.

———

In March 1987, Dino's adored son Dean Paul, a captain in the California Air National Guard, crashed his F-4 Phantom into San Gorgonio Mountain in a snowstorm. Neither he nor his navigator survived. It was almost exactly ten years after Dolly's Lear Jet crashed into the same mountain.

"Dean was half alive after that," Paul Anka recalled. "Whenever I would run into him at a little Italian restaurant in Beverly Hills called La Famiglia on Canon Drive, I would ask him, 'How are you doing, Dino?' He would be sitting there with his false teeth in a glass of water, look up at me and say, 'Just waiting to die, pally, just waiting to die.' "

That December, amid grand excitement, Frank, Dean, and Sammy held a press conference at Chasen's to announce a twenty-nine-city tour, named Together Again. It was the first time they'd worked together in twenty years. The tour began in March 1988 but quickly began to unravel: Dean was grieving, in his own fog of painkillers and booze; Sammy was suffering from liver problems and would soon undergo hip surgery. At the first concert, in Oakland, Martin flicked a lit cigarette into the audience. In Chicago, Frank told him he wasn't holding up his end of the tour: Dino chartered a plane and flew home. Furious, Frank replaced him with Liza Minnelli and didn't speak to his old friend for years.

———

For all the deficiencies of his voice and hearing and vision and memory, he was still capable of a good concert; on a good night, he could provide some of the same thrills he had always given. Writing in the *New York Times*, Stephen Holden praised "the spontaneity of phrasing and intonation he brings to almost everything he sings, no matter how many hundreds of times he has sung the songs. Even while reading lyrics from a prompter at the front of the stage, Mr. Sinatra still seemed compelled to experiment, trying out little tricks of phrasing, indulging in impromptu scoops and dives and interpolations that worked."

And after Daniel Okrent wrote an intelligent and graceful *Esquire* piece, "St. Francis of Hoboken," analyzing and praising Sinatra's late-age durability (and mentioning that his young son shared a birthday with Frank), he was delighted to receive, quite out of the blue, a lucid, graceful, and astonishingly mellow response from the Chairman himself, dated January 28, 1988.

"Dear Daniel," it began, and continued warmly, asking forgiveness for the letter's lateness (when had Frank ever asked forgiveness, even for a letter's lateness?) and adding the homey detail that it had been the Christmas season in the Sinatra household that had delayed him: "we are the bell-ringers and carol-singers and the tree-trimmers who lead the parade of peace to all of goodwill."

Okrent had clearly impressed Frank as one of the possessors of goodwill. Calling the *Esquire* essay "generous and insightful," Sinatra thanked the writer for "explain[ing] me to me with a rose in your prose" and applying his "X-ray word-processor to see so deeply into the heart and soul of this very lucky son of Hoboken who remains eternally overcome at God's plan for his life." In closing, Frank sent love to little John Okrent, with whom, he said, he was honored to share December 12th.

"God bless you always," the sentimental old man wrote above his signature.

———

The first half of his seventy-fifth year, 1990, was a kind of nightmare. On January 25, a month after her sixty-seventh birthday, Ava died. Unsurprisingly, Barbara Sinatra writes nothing about her husband's reaction to the loss of the greatest love of his life. Tina writes that she awoke to the news on the twenty-sixth and immediately phoned her father, only to be told that he hadn't stirred from his room since hearing the news the night before. When she called him again that evening, "he was distraught, barely audible," she recalled. "My heart broke for him. I wondered how long he'd stay in his room—and how he'd be received when he emerged."

Eleven days later, the last in a years-long series of strokes finally killed Jimmy Van Heusen. And in May, Sammy Davis died of throat cancer. Bowed by sorrow, Frank anesthetized himself as best he could.

And he kept on, at a dizzying rate: he played sixty-five dates that year; seventy-three concerts in thirteen countries, from Ireland and Sweden to Australia and Japan, in 1991. He did eighty-four shows in 1992. His manager, Eliot

Weisman, rationalized to Tina Sinatra that it was important to keep her father's income stream going so that Barbara wouldn't draw from the family trust—in which Sinatra's children shared.

In Rancho Mirage, early in the morning of May 6, 1992, his seventy-fifth birthday, Jilly died when his borrowed Jaguar was broadsided by a drunk driver. Rizzo's car exploded into flames; unfamiliar with the car's tricky interior door handles, he was unable to escape. Tony Oppedisano, a close friend of Jilly and Frank's and Frank's road manager, heard the news first, from the police. "I truly didn't know how Frank would react when I told him that his best friend in the whole world—the brother he never had—had been killed," he recalled.

Oppedisano went to Sinatra's house to tell him in person. "Frank collapsed," he said. "He literally just dropped to his knees and started sobbing."

After the funeral, Sinatra took Jilly's son Joey aside. "This is the worst day of my life," he told him. "That's it. My life is over."

Three days later, he did three nights at the Circle Star Theatre in San Carlos, California. He wasn't heartless; he was numb.

On March 1, 1994, the Irish rock singer Paul Hewson, in the persona of Bono, the front man of the band U2, stood at the podium at Radio City Music Hall and introduced Frank Sinatra at the thirty-sixth presentation of the Grammys. Thirty-five years earlier, in May 1959, Frank had attended the first Grammy ceremony; this night he was to receive a special honor, the Grammy Legend Award. But he wasn't just old news: in 1993, he had released *Duets,* an album on which, through the ambivalent magic of overdubbing, he was able to sing a baker's dozen of hits and standards with other great or celebrated vocalists such as Tony Bennett ("New York, New York"), Aretha Franklin ("What Now, My Love?"), Barbra Streisand ("I've Got a Crush on You"), Natalie Cole ("They Can't Take That Away from Me"), and Bono ("I've Got You Under My Skin"). Though the album was widely criticized for the sterility of its production—at no time was Sinatra actually ever in the recording studio with any of his duet partners; each sang his or her accompaniment to his recorded track—it was a huge international seller, going triple platinum in the United States alone. Frank was thrilled: he had always loved selling records.

Bono spoke reverently of the honoree, who was also a new friend, in a show-business way. "Rock 'n' roll people love Frank Sinatra because Frank Sinatra has got what we want—swagger and attitude," he said. "Rock 'n' roll plays at being tough, but this guy, well, he's the boss. The boss of bosses. The man. The big bang of pop. I'm not gonna mess with him—are you?"

The encomium continued for four long minutes, and then Frank emerged, looking pleased but bemused, in a tuxedo and a luxuriant, defiantly unnatural silver toupee. The audience leaped up, applauding and shouting, and Bono handed Sinatra the crystal gewgaw. "That's the best welcome—I ever had," Frank said, sounding a little choked up. There was a long pause. "This is like being in baseball, the bases are loaded, and you're at bat, you don't know what you're gonna do," he finally said, his voice rising emotionally to Lou Costello range.

Over the next couple of minutes, he seemed alternately with it and frail and disoriented. Just as in the old days, he made a mean, unfunny joke ("This is more applause than Dean heard in his whole career") and a crack about hitting the girl who threatened to water his drink backstage. The crowd tittered. Then, at sea, he held up his award. "I'm lookin' for my girl, where's my girl?" he said. "There she is. That's my girl. Say hello to Barbara, everybody, please." She stood, blond and gorgeous at sixty-six, and blew him a kiss. Frank blew her one back. "I love you," he said. "Do you love me?"

For just a second, he sounded genuinely uncertain. There was uncomfortable laughter.

He continued. "I don't quite know what to say to you," he told the audience. "You know, there was no discussions about singing a couple of songs; otherwise if we *had*, there would be an orchestra here with me, but apparently that's not what they wanted tonight, and I'm angry." He shrugged self-deprecatingly. More laughter. "I'm *hurt*." He said *hoit*. More laughter. "I'm just happy to be here in the Apple," he said. "I love coming back all the time; it's the best city in the whole world."

The remark produced the obligatory big applause, and Frank went on—only nobody heard him, because someone in the control booth had signaled the orchestra to strike up and, at the same time, cut off Sinatra's microphone. *Someone in the control booth had cut off Frank Sinatra's microphone.* A Grammys graphic came on the screen, and an anonymous announcer continued in voice-over: "In ceremonies tonight, Grammys were presented in the following categories . . ."

Someone in the control booth had cut off Frank Sinatra's microphone. Control had effectively been passed long before, but that night formalized it.

Five nights later, on a warm night at the Mosque in Richmond, Virginia—the air-conditioning in the theater was on the fritz; for some reason, the heat was running full blast—he collapsed while singing "My Way." Rising from the stool he'd been sitting on, Frank suddenly pitched forward, his head hitting the teleprompter screen and then striking the stage. "There was one giant gasp in the crowd; everybody stood up," saxophonist Jim Snidero recalled. The band stopped playing, despite Bill Miller's frantic signals to continue. Tony Oppedisano rushed to Sinatra's side and found him soaked through with sweat. As Oppedisano loosened his tie and opened his shirt, Frank's eyes blinked open. "What happened? Can the audience still see me?" he asked. He was lifted into a wheelchair—the audience applauded as he waved weakly—and taken to a local hospital, where tests revealed he had been dehydrated due to the heat in the auditorium and a diuretic he was taking, one of his many medications. A waiter in the restaurant at his hotel also said he had consumed six double Jack Daniel's with his steak dinner before the show.

Less than three weeks later, he was back in action at the Mabee Center in Tulsa, beginning with "Come Fly with Me" and closing with "New York, New York." Then on to Moline, Omaha, Wilmington, North Carolina, and Rochester, where he told the audience, "May you all live to be 750 years old, and may the last voice you hear be mine."

In August, at the Atlantic City Sands, he collapsed again onstage. After his medication was adjusted (he also started traveling with a doctor), his memory and energy were better, but his family and his manager concluded that after forty-eight concerts in 1994, he should tour no more.

He wound up the year with two disastrously jet-lagged shows at the Fukuoka Dome in Japan, concluding the last complete set of his career with the song he hated, "My Way." Natalie Cole, who had opened for Frank, recalled that he drank heavily on the flight home, then became disoriented and belligerent: "We had been in the air about an hour or so when Frank suddenly looked around at all of us in the cabin and bellowed, 'Who the hell are all these people?'" He stood and began confronting each person there—some of whom he had known for years—with the question, "Who the hell are *you*?" She avoided him as best she could, she remembered, by going to sleep.

There was still one final performance, at the end of the Frank Sinatra Desert Classic golf tournament, in Palm Desert, California, on February 25, 1995. A full complement of musicians Frank had worked with over the years was brought out from L.A., and on the stage of the ballroom of the Marriott in Palm Desert he sang six tunes, beginning with "I've Got the World on a String" and concluding with "The Best Is Yet to Come."

Sinatra sang as well as he was capable of singing that night, according to Tony Oppedisano. "High notes, fine," recalled the writer and radio personality Jonathan Schwartz, who was also there. "Shaky. No vibrato. No sustaining. But swing."

After Frank finished, his wife took his hand and guided him out to the front of the hotel, where a limousine waited. She went back inside to socialize, and for a few moments her husband stood there alone. Then Sinatra, being Sinatra, began to bang agitatedly on the top of the car. Schwartz was watching. "Finally," he remembered, "some Italian gentleman came and put his hand on Frank's head, Sinatra was gently pushed into the limousine, and the door closed on him forever."

———

That May, Frank left his beloved desert for good and moved to the pied-à-terre he and Barbara had bought in 1986, a nine-thousand-square-foot, California-modern mansion at 915 Foothill Road, Beverly Hills. It was a huge, somewhat sterile place—the Sinatras had purchased it furnished, right down to the con-temporary paintings on the walls—and, disoriented as he often was, he found it difficult to get used to. "When are we going home?" he kept asking his wife.

"We *are* home, darling," she told him.

"No," Frank said, "this is your home. When are we going to *my* home?"

There were times, Tina recalled, when he'd get confused by the house's open floor plan, which reminded him of a hotel lobby: "Sitting at the bar one day, he said to Tony, 'I never see any people here—they must be doing lousy business in this joint.'"

———

He had stopped painting and doing crossword puzzles, and reading was dif-ficult for him, even with magnifier glasses: the daily papers, which he'd once devoured, piled up. With little to occupy his mind, he grew steadily more bewildered and depressed. He stared at the TV, the volume turned up high. When an old friend, the television producer George Schlatter, put together an eightieth-birthday ABC special in Frank's honor—he would only have to sit and be sung to by an all-star cast, including Tony Bennett, Peggy Lee, Ray Charles, Bob Dylan, and Bruce Springsteen—Sinatra tried to beg off, but Schlatter, a persuasive man, prevailed. The night before the taping, to break the ice, Barbara invited Dylan and Springsteen over for dinner. Frank and his two fellow music legends sang together around the piano and generally "got on like a house on fire," she recalled. As for the show itself, Tina writes, Sinatra hated almost every minute of it.

The next month, after Schlatter and his wife threw him an eightieth birth-day party to which his children were not invited, Frank's younger daughter, the family's chief grudge collector, would not see or speak to her father for almost a year.

———

Thirteen days after Frank's eightieth, on Christmas morning 1995, Dean Martin finally met the fate he'd been waiting for for eight long years. The two men had reconciled after their breach, though neither had had much to give the other. Now Frank himself had little to do but wait.

———

On November 1, 1996, he suffered a serious myocardial infarction. He was admitted to Cedars-Sinai, where a hospital spokesman told reporters that Sinatra had a pinched nerve. His doctors were able to stabilize his heart, but he developed a critical case of pneumonia, and when he finally went home, he required round-the-clock nursing care. Though he was a candidate for open-heart surgery, his physicians declared it too risky. If Frank were kept as comfortable, calm, well fed, and mobile as possible, they said, he might be expected to live for another two or three years. "His geography was limited to his room, the adjoining den, the dining room beyond, and the garden, for a little afternoon sun," wrote Tina, who had now come back into his life—and, to a certain extent, mended fences with Barbara.

"That Thanksgiving would be the most thankful of feasts we'd ever had," Frank's younger daughter recalled. "We kept dinnertime loose, geared to whenever Dad woke up. He walked to the table unassisted, clean shaven and clearheaded—and obviously moved to have his children and grandchildren around him. It had been a long time since we'd come together as a family."

———

Two days earlier, the Sands—the site of so many revels and outrages, the essence of Las Vegas's golden age, the birthplace and playground of the Rat Pack—had been reduced, in a controlled implosion, to a thirty-foot pile of rubble. "It's sad to see it gone, but life goes on," the hotel's owner, Sheldon Adelson, declared briskly. "We're anxious to get on to the next level."

The next level, due in 1999, was the thirty-six-story, $1.8 billion, six-thousand-room Venetian resort-hotel-casino, the new pride of the Strip and the slick, towering embodiment of the town's faceless corporate era.

———

The bad days became more frequent. More and more, when he wasn't being rushed back to the hospital—the pneumonia lingered, and he had another heart attack—he was staying in his room. Tony Oppedisano was Frank's frequent companion during these long days. One night, Sinatra called him into his room and whispered, "I don't know how you are going to do this, but could you get my mother out of here?"

"I don't see her, Mr. S.," Oppedisano said.

"She's right over there in the chair," Frank said. "I'm trying to get some rest, but she keeps hanging around."

―――――

Not surprisingly, Tina Sinatra and Barbara Sinatra offer differing versions of the events of May 14, 1998. Tina had had a good visit with her father the previous Saturday—he'd been rested and lucid and had told her he planned to live until the turn of the century—and so she kept regular hours at work over the week of the eleventh, calling Foothill daily for updates and being told Frank was eating well, sleeping well, doing fine. She planned to return for the weekend on Friday the fifteenth, when Barbara was to begin a spa retreat at the Malibu beach house she and Frank owned.

Tony Oppedisano later told Tina that he'd visited her father every day from Monday through Thursday. On Monday night, he said, Frank asked him to order a pizza; they drank a couple of O'Doul's nonalcoholic beers and had a good time. But on Tuesday, Frank's spirits sagged. "I don't want to live like this anymore," he told Tony. "This is not a life."

Sinatra awoke agitated on Wednesday morning; when Oppedisano arrived later in the day, he found him withdrawn and unresponsive. "He perked up only when Barbara came down, on her way out to dinner," Tina writes. "He took one look at her and said, 'Oh, you still live here?'"

It was a line he used when she'd been out more than usual.

"On Thursday afternoon, feeling negligent, I rang Foothill," Tina continues.

> Vine [his longtime maid and majordomo, Elvina Joubert] said that
> Dad was tired and unsettled. She was trying to get him to calm down
> and rest; it wasn't a good time to visit. I meant to call back again,
> but I let the day get away from me. I was banking on our weekend to
> come . . .
>   And no one called to tell me that Barbara would be dining out for
> the fourth consecutive night.

Barbara Sinatra, on the other hand, portrays herself as attentive and consistently present for her husband. On Thursday the fourteenth, though, her friends Armand and Harriet Deutsch "insisted I take a break from Frank's constant care" and join them and some friends for dinner at Morton's in Beverly Hills. That afternoon, Barbara recalled, she and Frank had lunch in the sun by the pool. "He was in his wheelchair, and he didn't finish his favorite food, a grilled cheese sandwich," she writes, "but he was in good spirits and seemed fine."

On her way out for dinner, though, she stopped by his bedroom and found him sleepy and a little breathless. She made a mental note to call his doctors in the morning to see if the dosage of his heart medication could be altered. She turned down his blaring TV and kissed him on the forehead. Squeezing his shoulder, she said, "Good night, darling. Sleep warm." And then, leaving her husband in the care of Vine and the nurse on duty, she went out to dinner.

As Armand Deutsch drove his wife and Barbara Sinatra down Sunset toward the restaurant, Barbara writes, she "couldn't help but notice the moon . . . low and huge in the western sky like a peeled orange."

But they were driving east, not west, and the moon wouldn't rise until after eleven that night.

———————

Tina came home late from the office, put her dinner on a tray, and got in bed to watch television. It was the night of the *Seinfeld* finale. A while later, she had one arm in her nightgown when the phone rang, at exactly 11:10 p.m. It was Frank's doctor, Rex Kennamer. "I have bad news," he said. "We lost him."

———————

Vine Joubert had called Barbara Sinatra at Morton's—it was around 9:30 p.m.—and said, "You'd better come right away. The paramedics are here. They're going to take Mr. S. to the hospital."

"What happened?" Barbara asked her.

Vine hesitated a moment, then said, "They can't find a pulse."

Armand Deutsch drove her at an old man's snail's pace back to Foothill, where she discovered Frank had already been taken to Cedars-Sinai. A member of the household staff drove her to the hospital at top speed, she ran through the door of the emergency room, and here accounts diverge again.

In Barbara Sinatra's writing, she sat by her husband's side alone, gripping his hand, as three doctors worked on him. "You have to fight, Frank!" she said she told him.

"He really tried to," she writes.

He did. He must have clung to life for twenty minutes or more, although it seemed like considerably longer. I didn't leave him for a second, his hand like a bag of bones in mine. Briefly, his eyes flickered open. They were watery but still the same dazzling blue as when he'd first pulled me into his arms and kissed me all those years earlier, stealing my heart. He looked at me for just a moment and opened his mouth to speak. Leaning closer, turning my head to hear, I heard him whisper the words "I can't."

Then his eyes closed forever, and that was it.

Yet according to another source, Barbara was not alone with Frank; Tony Oppedisano was also present in the ER, and Barbara's publicist, Susan Reynolds, stood outside the room manning the phones in preparation for the massive media event that was about to occur. According to this source, Frank's wife grew dizzy and nauseated and had to leave the room for an extended period as the doctors did what they could for her husband.

We attach inordinate importance to the last words of great men and women. Nancy Sinatra wrote on her Web site that her father's final words were not "I can't" but "I'm losing." This phrase, so much more eloquent than a simple plea of inability, seemed to sum up the grand battle that was Frank Sinatra's whole life. It would take hold in the popular imagination.

Yet Nancy wasn't present when her father died, and it's possible that Barbara Sinatra was not in the room either. Every human being has last words, but they are not always uttered just before death and are not always eloquent or memorable. Frank Sinatra's vast legacy spoke for itself.

———

Tina had thrown her clothes back on and rushed out of the house to pick up her sister and go to the hospital. If it was too late to see her father while he was still alive—and this idea hadn't entirely sunk in—she had to see him before his body was taken away. As she sped down the street, she saw the moon, huge and waning gibbous, low in the east. It was orange, Frank's favorite color.

———

It was late, Sinatra's time of night just dawning, but too late for much of the world to hear the news. Yet he made the headlines black for one last time the next morning, and the world, stunned but not surprised, did what it could. Radio stations around the world played his records, the ones he'd loved and the ones he'd hated. Marquees along the Vegas Strip—the new Strip, the hedge of faceless glass towers—went dark; lights inside the casinos were dimmed for a minute. At Yankee Stadium, there was a moment of silence in his memory before Friday night's game.

And in honor of the eyes that had transfixed the world for sixty years, the Empire State Building was bathed in blue lights that night and the next. The great phallic tower of limestone and steel, symbol of America's resilience in the face of the Great Depression, had originally topped out in early 1931, when fifteen-year-old Frankie No-Name, soon to drop out of A. J. Demarest High and cast his fate to the wind, could stand on the Hoboken waterfront and stare at the end of construction, looking long and hard across the wide gray river as he dreamed his incomprehensible dreams and listened to the music of the spheres.

———

Ramon Road runs west to east from downtown Palm Springs toward Cathedral City and Thousand Palms, crossing Gene Autry Trail and Bob Hope Drive along the way: a long, straight shot lined with strip malls and gas stations and fast food—little tan and white buildings, bleached and insignificant under the enormous sky. Drive east, and there isn't much ahead but flat emptiness and shimmering heat. As the roadside commerce begins to peter out at the edge of Cathedral City, you might be excused for feeling a twinge of fear at the rim of the void, a fear that the sight of one more stray tire outlet or medical center does nothing to allay. This is the desert, and the desert wants to kill you.

Then comes the left turn, at Da Vall Drive, and another quick left, between gates, into the green expanse of Desert Memorial Park. The soothing sight of grass, trees, and shade is deceptive: the air is oven hot. A quick stop in the office, a low white structure, refreshingly air-conditioned, gets you a three-page pamphlet, stapled at the corner, whose cover sheet reads,

PALM SPRINGS CEMETERY DISTRICT

INFORMATION

Sonny Bono
Frank Sinatra
And
Other Interments of Interest

We respectfully present to you, information regarding interments in our cemeteries. If you need additional information or further assistance, we ask you make your inquiries at the office. For your **SAFETY**, we ask you, **PLEASE** do not approach the grounds employees while they are at work.

Kathleen Jurasky
Manager

After puzzling over that last sentence—are they armed?—not to mention the backward interments-of-interest billing, you look at the second page, a map of the cemetery. Desert Memorial Park is a hundred-acre rectangle perhaps a third of a mile wide on Ramon Drive and half a mile deep on Da Vall, a verdant tract divided into eighty-seven sections, with a gracefully looping, French-curve-shaped drive at the center. Besides the office and a maintenance shed, the map shows two artificial waterfalls and a chapel on the grounds. The locations of several notable grave sites are also marked. Toward the top of the map, which is the rear of the cemetery, near the Fountain Court Waterfall, is the simple notation, in bold type and emphasized with chartreuse highlighter, **Bono B-35**. Only one other location is highlighted, at the bottom of the map, very near the front of the grounds: **Sinatra B-8**. No first name needed.

And so it's back out into the unbelievable heat. You can proceed on foot from here—section B-8 is surprisingly close to the administration building, just a few yards away. The grass, thick and spongy, exudes a pleasant, loamy, golf-course smell. Then come the stones.

For aesthetic reasons, one guesses, the grave markers in Desert Memorial Park are not upright headstones but black or gray slabs set flush with the turf. This way, one guesses, the tract looks, at a glance, more like a park than a necropolis, a City of the Dead. And because the stones face the sky and the merciless sun, and because almost none of them are shaded—the cemetery is sparsely planted with piñon oaks—the stones are fading, some of them into near illegibility. In ten or twenty or fifty years, the sun will have done its work, and the grave markers here today will be, effectively, blank.

Which would seem to be a problem. The purpose of a memorial park, after all, is memorialization. Who wants to look at a blank stone? Who's going to come visit a blank stone?

The stone you're here to see today, though, is surely another matter. After wading through dozens of volumes about Frank Sinatra; after negotiating dozens of Web sites dedicated to him; after getting a taste of the widespread, quasi-religious dedication to the man and his music that lives on almost a decade after his death; after experiencing the vast seas of Sinatra expertise and encountering the myriad authoritative gatekeepers and ultra-possessive guardians of the flame—after all this, one half expects to find a traffic jam at the gates of Desert Memorial Park: a slowly moving procession of rental cars and sedans with out-of-state plates, of RVs and SUVs, all filled with solemn, wispy-haired, chubby-faced fans wearing nostalgic expressions. Surely there will be parking problems, frayed tempers, marshals, officious attendants, long lines. Take a number.

Instead, there is nothing, and nobody. The park, all hundred acres of it, looks utterly deserted ... not even any sign of those dangerous grounds employees. You tiptoe as delicately as possible over the spongy sod, with that strange heightened guilty awareness of walking *over people,* heading, with a tightening heart, toward B-8. That you're alone feels both incredibly fortunate and wrong somehow; it's reminiscent (if the over-fraught parallel can be forgiven) of that dark and strange moment in *The Godfather* when Michael Corleone discovers that his gravely wounded father, Don Vito, is lying comatose and unprotected in his hospital bed, his police cordon having mysteriously taken a powder.

Then here it is.

Near a little stand of trees, a mini-neighborhood of flat, fading grave slabs, four in a row:

BELOVED HUSBAND AND FATHER
ANTHONY MARTIN SINATRA
1893 † 1969

then,

NATALIE SINATRA
BELOVED WIFE MOTHER
GRANDMOTHER AND GREAT GRANDMOTHER
1894 † 1977

and then,

VINCENT MAZZOLA
1894 † 1973

It's Cousin Vincent, the shell-shocked World War I vet who lived with Dolly and Marty, and then just Dolly, for fifty years.

And then and only then,

THE BEST IS YET TO COME
FRANCIS ALBERT SINATRA
1915 † 1998
BELOVED HUSBAND & FATHER

And quite unanticipatedly, the little hairs rise on the back of your neck.

The only decorations around the interment of greatest interest are a little

American flag stuck in the ground in back of the grave, a couple of small vases of flowers in front. Period. No giant bouquets, teddy bears, CDs, panties, shot glasses. No scrawled verse or sorrowful mash notes. Just the flag, the flowers, the sun. And the stone, with its faded inscription.

And there you are, all alone with *him* . . . in a sense. Standing on the spongy turf six feet above the casket containing not just the blue-suited remains, the thing that's always too terrible to think about, but also—legend has it—several items of iconic (and personal, the boundary between the two always having been porous where Sinatra was concerned) significance: A roll of dimes, like the one he carried for pay phones when Junior was kidnapped. A bottle of Jack Daniel's. A pack of Camels. Items meant to commemorate but also, unavoidably, meant for a metaphorical and—human hope being what it is—perhaps actual trip to the afterlife. *The best is yet to come.* The ancient Egyptians did this too, sent along useful objects and food for the next world. In the case of the pharaohs, human retainers were (and were presumably honored to be) sacrificed, mummified, and placed in the royal vault so that they might help out in the heavenly household. It could be making too much of not enough to point out that Frank Sinatra's two best friends, songwriter Jimmy Van Heusen and restaurateur Jilly Rizzo—who predeceased him by eight and six years, respectively—are buried just yards away. Then again, there they are. If there is an afterlife, and if there are great-looking ladies and ambrosial beverages there—and gate-crashers, nuisances, and phonies, too—then surely Chester and Jilly are standing close by the man whose soul they loved.

And feared.

The gravestone, Desert Memorial Park, Cathedral City, California. "The Best Is Yet to Come," the inscription promises; the fierce sun that Frank loved has faded the letters.

ACKNOWLEDGMENTS

Back amid the swirling mists of time—September 2004, to be exact—I had a lovely, boozy, fateful dinner at a Santa Monica restaurant called Guido's with a lively, accomplished, and well-seasoned bunch of professional musicians. These half dozen men of a certain age were all working for Jerry Lewis on the Muscular Dystrophy Association Labor Day telethon; I was working with Jerry, finishing my work on his memoir *Dean & Me: A Love Story*. Sometime late in the evening, the subject of Frank Sinatra came up. Both surprisingly and unsurprisingly, it turned out that all these musicians had worked with Sinatra at one point or another.

I began to listen carefully. Tongues had been loosened throughout the evening; I was surely about to hear some choice dirt about the Mob, the women, the fistfights. But instead, to a man, these musicians spoke, their voices lowered by awe, about what an absolute musical genius Frank Sinatra had been.

I have told this story before. I repeat it now to remind the reader (and myself) how and why I set out on what would become a ten-year odyssey, a first-time biographer's quixotic—read laughably presumptuous—quest to chronicle in full measure the life and work of a man who was not only a genius—the greatest interpretive musician of all time, in the opinion of many, including myself—but also a man whose life touched almost every aspect of American life in the twentieth century.

My editor, the great Phyllis Grann—herself a historic figure in book publishing— took to my project at once, encouraged me at every timorous step of the journey, and, quite astonishingly, failed to blink when after five years (this was early 2010) I handed her an 800-page manuscript that covered Sinatra's life to not quite the halfway point—the night in March 1954 when he won the Oscar for *From Here to Eternity*, marking the start of the greatest comeback in entertainment history—and told her, "This is the book."

And that, by the way, I planned to write another.

To my relief, Phyllis was fine with it, Doubleday was fine with it, and almost all the readers of that first volume, *Frank: The Voice*, were fine with it too. There were some disgruntled Amazonians. (*Where's the rest of this?*) Yet to my happy surprise, though also my discomfiture, there were many e-mails from readers who'd liked volume 1 and were on board with my scheme but who were ready for Volume 2—right away.

Of course, to a word squeezer like this writer, "right away" is a foreign concept. And I also knew that for the second book I had set myself, if possible, a far tougher task. The mid-1950s and early to mid-1960s covered the greatest period in Frank Sinatra's career—the Capitol and the early Reprise years and also the years in which Sinatra was a major movie star, sometimes making as many as five pictures a year. He recorded groundbreaking albums and singles; he worked with Nelson Riddle and other great arrangers. This period also comprised some of the most complex times in America's history, times in which Frank was intricately involved. There was his friendship with John F. Kennedy, his troubled and abiding attraction to the Mob, and, not irrelevantly, his troubled and abiding and formative (for both Sinatra and the town) relationship with Las Vegas. There was the fabled Rat Pack (there were two Rat Packs, actually) and, of course, there were the women—the many, many women. And, finally, there was Frank Sinatra's impact on the world at large, his global profile. He was a great artist in these years, a world-changing artist; he was also a world-historical individual.

Writing volume 2, I knew at the outset, would be a very tall order.

I had help. Plenty of it. While I admit that to an alarming degree this was a solo project (I was unable—and, to be truthful, unwilling—to send out researchers and interviewers other than myself to cover the very many bases that needed to be covered), no biographer is an island, and I had crucial support for every day of the five years I worked on this volume.

First, I must extend profound thanks to my family, Karen, Jacob, Aaron, and Avery, for their endless and unquestioning support and for putting up with a husband and father who while mostly present, in the sense that he was on the premises, was also usually locked away in his attic office—the Man in the Ceiling—for entire days, especially during the final two years of writing. Particular thanks go to Aaron O. Kaplan for the major feats of compiling the book's endnotes and bibliography.

To my agent, Joy Harris, who has been by my side for twenty years, putting up with me through thick and thin (and helping to make the thick thicker and the thin easier to bear), goes a gratitude that only she will properly understand.

A thousand thanks to my indispensable first reader, Peter Bogdanovich: a lifelong friend, a unique American filmmaker and writer on film, a friend of Frank Sinatra's, and my crucial support on this project from day one of volume 1. Peter loves Sinatra and wanted to make sure I did right by him. To my humbled amazement he seemed to feel that I did. He read every word, loved almost every word, told me gently when I had wavered or omitted something, and—quite simply—kept me going every step of the way.

I miss my other indispensable first reader, my indispensable brother Peter W. Kaplan, more than I can say.

I want to give a deep bow to my editor, Gerald Howard. In Gerry, along with Phyllis Grann, I had the incomparable good fortune of having not one but two publishing legends concentrating on my work. "Concentration" is the key word. Gerry brought a fierce attention to every word of this huge volume, along with nonpareil qualities of intelligence, cultural reference, and wit. A formidable writer himself, he was a keen appreciator of what I did right; he also rescued me more than a few times from my easily tappable worst instincts.

I would like to extend particular gratitude to the John Simon Guggenheim Memorial Foundation, which graced me with a fellowship that not only provided essential financial support but, just as important, gave me a rocket-like spiritual and professional lift at precisely the midpoint of the project, a time when I needed it badly.

I will repeat what I said in volume 1 about my brain trust, and mean it even more emphatically: That Will Friedwald and Michael Kraus, who both know as much about Sinatra as anyone has a right to know, gave freely of their time and steadily approved of what I was doing continues to amaze me. I will always remember their generosity and treasure their friendship. I was wildly fortunate to have these two frighteningly learned, gimlet-eyed men parsing every sentence of the book. I am also indebted, for their vast Sinatra knowledge and easy generosity, to Chuck Granata, Rob Waldman, and Rob Fentress.

The Sinatra completist Ed O'Brien knows everything Frank-related and told me as much as I was able to take in. His regular bulletins from upstate New York kept me informed and kept me honest.

The legendary Jonathan Schwartz, whom I am honored to call a friend, lent a special insight and—of course—a vast body of knowledge of Sinatra and the American Songbook to this project.

I would also like to thank Rosemary Riddle Acerra, Monty Alexander, Rick Apt, Brook Babcock, Bob Bain, Alan Bergman, Marilyn Bergman, Tony Bill, Bill Boggs, Tiffany Bolling, Fifi Booth, Howard Bragman, Chris Brochon, Dr. Richard Burg, Anita Busch, Laurie Cahn, Christopher Cerf, Dr. Stanley Coen, Kenny Colman, Jill Corey, Steve Crosby, Paulajane D'Amato, Vic Damone, Angie Dickinson, Frank DiGiacomo, Gary Ebbins, Jack Eglash, Vincent Falcone, John Farr, Michael Feinstein, Gloria Delson Franks, Mike Franks, Gary Giddins, Steve Glauber, Bob Gottlieb, Mary Edna Grantham, Peter Greenberg, Shecky Greene, Colin Hall, Betsy Duncan Hammes, Bruce Handy, Bill Harbach, Richard Havers, Lee Herschberg, Eddie Hodges, Anne Hollister, Bill Hooper, Christopher Irving, Ann Jactel, Snake Jagger, Brandon James, Bruce Jenkins, Reuben F. Johnson, Dean Jones, Jack Jones, Quincy Jones, Shirley Jones, Robert E. Kaplan, Steve Khan, Larry King, Steve Koepp, Andrew Lack, Claudia Gridley Stabile Lano, Joe Lano, Angela Lansbury, Scott Latta, Ruta Lee, Dan Levy, Jerry Lewis, Nancy Olson Livingston, Jim Mahoney, Jim Mahoney Jr., Carmel Malin, Johnny Mandel, Sid Mark, Bill Marx, Jane McCormick, Sonny Mehta, Karen Meltzer, David Michaelis, Dale Monaco, Pat Mulcahy, Phyllis Newman, Liz Nickles, Eunice Norton, Kim Novak, Marianne O'Connell, Claus Ogerman, Dan Okrent, Tony Oppedisano, Mo Ostin, Ted Panken, Anna Pearce, Pat Politis, Adam Reed, Emil Richards, Jenny Romero, Jeff Rosen, Andrew Rosenblum, Ric Ross, Gena Rowlands, Tom Santopietro, George Schlatter, Paul Shaffer, Gary Shapiro, David Simoné, Winston Simoné, Leonard Slatkin, Liz Smith, Jim Snidero, Ted Sommer, William Stadiem, Jean Stein, Robert Sullivan, Gay Talese, Jordan Taylor, Angela Thornton, Linda Thorson, Dean Torrence, Gloria Vanderbilt, Jonathan Van Meter, Robert J. Wagner, Dr. William Walsh, Ed Walters, Artie Wayne, Steven Weissman, Esq., Raquel Welch, Dr. Preston Winters, and Fred Zlotkin.

And the following, who have left us but with whom I was fortunate to spend time: Jean Bach, Polly Bergen, Jeanne Carmen, Peggy Connelly, Stan Cornyn, John Dominis, Bob Eckel, Don Hewitt, George Jacobs, Mearene Jordan, Peter Levinson, Abbey Lincoln, Mort Lindsey, Bill Miller, Mitch Miller, Mario Puzo, Frankie Randall, Mickey Rooney, Jane Russell, Mike Shore, Jo Stafford, Jerry Weintraub, Roberta Wennik-Kaplan, Bud Yorkin, and Sidney Zion.

And last (but only as a mark of distinction), an extravagant thank-you to the great team at Doubleday, from copy to design to marketing to production, and to the truly heroic Bette Alexander, Todd Doughty, John Fontana, Jeremy Medina, and Ingrid Sterner.

If I have unwittingly omitted anybody, first blushes are mine. You reside deep in my heart, safe from the uncertain clutches of my short-term memory.

PHOTO CREDITS

Grateful acknowledgment is given to the following for permission to reprint:

NOTES

CHAPTER I

2　"He's a dead man": Jacobs and Stadiem, *Mr. S*, p. 21.
2　"The whole world": Louella Parsons, International News Service, syndicated column, April 19, 1954.
4　"One night we went to Frank's": Server, *Ava Gardner*, p. 295.
4　"Wondering if there": Ibid.
6　Any hint of romance: Ibid., pp. 295–96.
6　She had asked him to: Ibid., p. 298.
6　Frank not only won: Havers, *Sinatra*, p. 197.
7　"Mud was scheming": Finstad, *Natasha*, p. 141.
7　"consumed quantities": Ibid.
9　"Dad had a sadness": Rosemary Riddle Acerra, in discussion with the author, Oct. 2012.
10　"After all, what else": Friedwald, *Sinatra!*, p. 233.
10　"Most of our best": Shaw, *Sinatra*, p. 27.
10　"I loved how Nelson": Friedwald, *Sinatra!*, p. 224.
11　"the conservatory-trained": Ibid.
11　That idea went out: Cramer, *Joe DiMaggio*, p. 346.
13　"You knew this was": Nancy Sinatra, *Frank Sinatra: My Father*, p. 99.
13　"marked the start": Santopietro, *Sinatra in Hollywood*, p. 147.

CHAPTER 2

14　"The Cocoanut Grove": Hotchner, *Doris Day*, p. 166.
15　The production was overseen: Ibid., p. 167; Santopietro, *Sinatra in Hollywood*, p. 161.
16　"Of course Frank": Hotchner, *Doris Day*, p. 167.
16　"People think that": Wagner, *Pieces of My Heart*, p. 123.
18　"peonage": Hotchner, *Doris Day*, p. 175.
18　"She was very touched": Ibid., pp. 169–70.
19　"I have never seen": Louella Parsons, syndicated column, July 9, 1954.
19　"Nancy Sinatra insists": Erskine Johnson, In Hollywood, syndicated column, Aug. 4, 1954.
21　"Kramer had unwittingly": Server, *Robert Mitchum*, p. 276.
21　"The tippling would": Ibid., pp. 276–77.
21　"Why did Frank Sinatra": Santopietro, *Sinatra in Hollywood*, p. 164.
22　"Busy, busy, busy": Kelley, *His Way*, p. 223.
23　"A lot of drinks": Server, *Robert Mitchum*, p. 279.
23　"he was balling": Ibid.
23　"had a man keeping": Cramer, *Joe DiMaggio*, pp. 372–73.
24　"was supposedly having": Kelley, *His Way*, p. 241.
24　"in the arms of another man": Bruce Weber, "Hal Schaefer, Jazz Pianist and Marilyn Monroe Friend, Dies at 87," *New York Times*, Dec. 13, 2012, www.nytimes.com/2012/12/13/arts/music/hal-schaefer-jazz-pianist-and-marilyn-monroes-vocal-coach-dies.html.
25　"We all went back": Server, *Robert Mitchum*, pp. 279–80.
25　"was fast asleep": *New York Times*, ibid.
26　"For years": Haygood, *In Black and White*, p. 167.
27　"He helped me": Davidson, *The Real and the Unreal*, p. 22.
27　"On Fremont Street": Jerry Lewis, in discussion with the author, June 1999.
28　"Sammy Davis was one": Shecky Greene, in discussion with the author, Nov. 2012.
28　"I said, 'You don't'": Haygood, *In Black and White*, p. 169.
28　"My father was": Tina Sinatra, *My Father's Daughter*, p. 160.
29　"Sinatra said, 'What business'": Aline Mosby, United Press, Dec. 9, 1954.
30　"Get out of there": Kelley, *His Way*, p. 223.
30　"I am not": Mosby, United Press, Dec. 9, 1954; Kelley, *His Way*, pp. 223–24.
30　"The guy comes over": Michael Bitterman, http://www.midmod.com/newSite/bio.htm.
30　"I went back to Byron": Kelley, *His Way*, p. 224.
31　"may be the only": Friedwald, *Sinatra!*, p. 237.

CHAPTER 3

32 "Gloria Vanderbilt Stokowski": Dorothy Kilgallen, syndicated column, Nov. 3, 1954.
33 "a star in the making": Wendy Goodman, *World of Gloria Vanderbilt*, p. 126; *New York Daily News,* Dec. 28, 1954.
33 "You be nice": Gloria Vanderbilt, in discussion with the author, April 2011.
33 "The phone can ring": Vanderbilt, *Black Knight, White Knight,* pp. 308–9.
34 "She looks": Wendy Goodman, *World of Gloria Vanderbilt,* p. 127.
34 "I'm seeing him again": Ibid., pp. 310, 312.
35 "turned to me and said": Ibid., p. 311.
36 "He was very open": Vanderbilt, discussion.
36 "The list of celebrities": Dorothy Kilgallen, syndicated column, Jan. 8, 1955.
37 "Here's a song": Recording: *Frank Sinatra—New York 1: Manhattan Center, 1955 (Tommy Dorsey).*
39 "his musical confidant": Havers, *Sinatra,* p. 199.
39 "some intimate ladies' apparel": Nancy Sinatra, *My Father,* p. 129.
39 "I was devastated": Ibid., p. 75.
41 "inaugurated [Frank's] tradition": Friedwald, *Sinatra!,* p. 238.
41 "both singer and pianist": Ibid.
41 "Sinatra, a man who lived": Jonathan Schwartz, "Swingin' on a Century," *Vanity Fair,* July 1998.
43 "Nelson, you're a gas": Levinson, *September in the Rain,* p. 120.
43 *On the Waterfront*'s producer: Jacobs and Stadiem, *Mr. S,* pp. 52–53.
43 "Frank Sinatra would": Bosworth, *Marlon Brando,* p. 153.
44 "half destroyed": Jacobs and Stadiem, *Mr. S,* p. 51.
44 Betty Grable, Jane Russell: Berg, *Goldwyn,* p. 471; *Albert Lea (Minn.) Daily Tribune,* Jan. 17, 1954; Herald Tribune News Service, Aug. 17, 1954; Harold Heffernan, syndicated column, Oct. 3, 1954.
44 A Hedda Hopper column: *Altoona (Pa.) Mirror,* May 12, 1954.
44 But soon afterward: Berg, *Goldwyn,* p. 471.
44 By June, Earl Wilson: Earl Wilson, syndicated column, June 4, 1954.
44 "[My] agent said to me": First Libby Zion Memorial Lecture at Yale Law School, April 15, 1986.
45 "In the midst of negotiations": Berg, *Goldwyn,* p. 471.
45 "Brando's desire to continually": Santopietro, *Sinatra in Hollywood,* p. 171.
46 "Sinatra apparently felt": Loesser, *Most Remarkable Fella,* pp. 118–19.
46 "Frank Sinatra . . . never": Sheed, *House That George Built,* p. 275.
47 "It's a stalemate": Bob Thomas, syndicated column, April 7, 1955.
47 "I did everything": Peggy Connelly, in discussion with the author, May 2006.
48 "I had been in Hollywood": Ibid.
48 "And after ten minutes": Summers and Swan, *Sinatra,* p. 211.
49 "When I wrote 'But Beautiful' ": James Kaplan, "The King of Ring-a-Ding-Ding," *Movies Rock,* supplement, *Vanity Fair,* Fall 2007.

CHAPTER 4

52 "Every time Jack Benny": Cahn, *I Should Care,* p. 152.
53 "This comical dissertation": Bosley Crowther review, *New York Times,* Nov. 11, 1955.
53 "I had a date": Jill Corey, in discussion with the author, Nov. 2012.
54 "just a pal": *Dunkirk (N.Y.) Evening Observer,* April 22, 1955.
54 "the foreign beauty": Erskine Johnson, syndicated column, Dec. 1, 1953.
55 "to catch Rosemary Clooney's": Dorothy Manners, writing in Louella Parsons's syndicated column, June 9, 1955.
55 According to Manners: Ibid.
55 Nancy Sinatra writes: Nancy Sinatra, *My Father,* p. 132.
55 If it came to a choice: Summers and Swan, *Sinatra,* p. 256.
55 Among his many West Coast: Server, *Ava Gardner,* p. 151.
56 FBI files state: Parker and Rashke, *Capitol Hill in Black and White,* p. 85; Klein, *All Too Human,* p. 182; Summers and Swan, *Sinatra,* p. 256.
56 Even as he started: Santopietro, *Sinatra in Hollywood,* p. 182.
57 "For years people had": Cahn, *I Should Care,* p. 153.
58 "When you write lyrics": Ibid., pp. 154–55.
58 "wanted you to think": Will Friedwald, "They Went Together Like a Horse and Carriage," *Wall Street Journal,* Jan. 7, 2013.

58   "We began by rambling": Cahn, *I Should Care,* p. 152.

59   "didn't much care": Havers, *Sinatra,* p. 204.

59   "The first time we sat": Cahn, *I Should Care,* pp. 155–56.

59   "Frank Sinatra is more excited": Louella Parsons, syndicated column, July 4, 1955.

60   "When they told me": Shirley Jones, in discussion with the author, Feb. 2010.

61   "We had the two cameras": Ibid.

61   And 20th Century Fox sued: Santopietro, *Sinatra in Hollywood,* p. 183.

61   "How can I play": Davidson, *The Real and the Unreal,* p. 25.

61   "Through the years, some": Santopietro, *Sinatra in Hollywood,* pp. 182–83.

62   "Sinatra beat it": Friedwald, *Sinatra!,* p. 327.

62   "I think he did": Jones, discussion.

63   "jagged chunk": *Time,* Aug. 29, 1955.

65   "makes me want to cry": Peter W. Kaplan, "Gable to J.R. with Ava Gardner," *New York Times,* Feb. 25, 1985.

65   "one of his best friends": *Time,* Aug. 29, 1955.

65   "When I got up to Maine": Bob Thomas, syndicated column, Sept. 13, 1955.

66   "Everybody reads it": *Time,* July 11, 1955.

67   "magnificent entertainment": *New York Times,* Sept. 20, 1955.

68   "I got a call the next": Bogdanovich, *Who the Devil Made It,* pp. 627–28.

69   "Although Preminger publicly": Santopietro, *Sinatra in Hollywood,* p. 193.

70   "Sinatra arrived for work": Daniel O'Brien, *Frank Sinatra Film Guide,* p. 86.

70   "was surprised to discover": Preminger, *Preminger,* p. 112.

70   "She was terrified": Ibid., pp. 112–13.

70   Frank sent her: *Conversations with Robert Osborne* (TCM Originals, 2014), DVD.

70   "legs were too heavy": Jacobs and Stadiem, *Mr. S,* p. 68.

70   "What in the world": Levinson, *September in the Rain,* p. 135.

71   "Frank Sinatra reports": Harrison Carroll, Behind the Scenes in Hollywood, syndicated column, Oct. 18, 1955.

72   First, Frank failed: Gloria Vanderbilt, in discussion with the author, April 2011.

72   "Heiress Gloria Vanderbilt": Associated Press, Nov. 21, 1955.

73   "He bowed and thanked": Jim Mahoney, syndicated column, Dec. 19, 1955.

73   "Nothing has seemed impossible": Associated Press, Dec. 12, 1955.

73   "No matter what you": Erskine Johnson, syndicated column, March 11, 1955.

74   "Being in Hollywood": Shaw, *Sinatra,* pp. 200–201.

74   "Considering that there": Louella Parsons, syndicated column, Nov. 21, 1955.

74   "for all the delicacy": *New York Times,* Dec. 16, 1955.

75   "thin, unhandsome": Santopietro, *Sinatra in Hollywood,* p. 196.

75   "I think the whole world": Bogdanovich, *Who the Hell's in It,* p. 50.

76   "craved class": Jacobs and Stadiem, *Mr. S,* p. 113.

76   "I see the rat pack": Shaw, *Sinatra,* p. 210.

76   "In order to qualify": Bacall, *By Myself,* p. 296.

76   "Remember, it was": Shaw, *Sinatra,* p. 210.

76   "platform of iconoclasm": Bacall, *By Myself,* p. 296.

77   But he did stop by: Summers and Swan, *Sinatra,* p. 223.

77   "It is enjoyable": Payn and Morley, *Noël Coward Diaries,* p. 301.

77   Bogart had also been unwell: Sperber and Lax, *Bogart,* p. 509.

78   "as dinner came to a close": Bacall, *By Myself,* p. 254.

CHAPTER 5

79   "There was always a crowd": Granata, *Sessions with Sinatra,* p. 109.

79   "At a Sinatra session": Riddle, *Arranged by Nelson Riddle,* p. 171.

80   "I didn't care": Levinson, *September in the Rain,* p. 118.

80   "Everything I learned": Walter Winchell, syndicated column, Sept. 22, 1955.

80   "I've always believed": Granata, *Sessions with Sinatra,* p. 98.

81   "During the Capitol period": Ibid.

81   "Imagine that you're delivering": Leonard Slatkin, in discussion with the author, May 2013.

81   "Syncopation in music": Granata, *Sessions with Sinatra,* p. 98.

81   "In planning *Songs*": Riddle, *Arranged by Nelson Riddle,* p. 169.

82   "All the preparation": Levinson, *September in the Rain,* p. 127.

82   "Sinatra gave him three songs": Ibid., pp. 128–29.

83   Rosemary Riddle Acerra notes: Rosemary Riddle Acerra, in discussion with the author, Oct. 2012.

83 Sinatra recorded the first: Levinson, *September in the Rain*, pp. 128–29.
83 "make it sound like Puccini": Riddle Acerra, discussion.
83 "Why don't you steal": Friedwald, *Sinatra!*, pp. 233–34.
84 Sinatra was listening: Ibid., pp. 32–33.
84 "There's only one person": Granata, *Sessions with Sinatra*, p. 102.
84 "probably because somebody": Ibid., p. 101.
84 "This is awfully good": Levinson, *September in the Rain*, p. 130.
84 "it was unusual": Granata, *Sessions with Sinatra*, p. 100.
84 "I left the best stuff": Ibid., p. 101.
85 "Milt perspired a lot": Bob Bain, in discussion with the author, June 2013.
85 "After the session": Granata, *Sessions with Sinatra*, p. 102.
86 "I've always said": Bob Thomas, syndicated column, March 8, 1954.
88 "Frankie now looks": Earl Wilson, syndicated column, May 28, 1956.
89 "Sinatra got a kick": Jacobs and Stadiem, *Mr. S*, p. 73.
89 A friend of Kelly's: Taraborrelli, *Sinatra*, pp. 191–92.
89 Crosby and Armstrong had sung: Louella Parsons, syndicated column, Jan. 5, 1956.
90 "sing, dance, hit": Basinger, *Star Machine*, pp. 5–6.
90 "You know, I never": Jacobs and Stadiem, *Mr. S*, pp. 173–74; Zoglin, *Hope*, p. 243.
91 "So long as I keep": Shaw, *Sinatra*, p. 215.
91 In 1955, Capitol Records: *Variety*, Jan. 13, 1955.
92 Atop the Capitol Records Tower: Granata, *Sessions with Sinatra*, pp. 114–18.
92 Naturally, everything: Granata, *Sessions with Sinatra*, pp. 114–18.
92 "When we took him on": Friedwald, *Sinatra!*, p. 366.
92 RCA Victor: Ibid.
92 an annual guarantee of $200,000: Havers, *Sinatra*, p. 205.
92 virtual carte blanche: Ed O'Brien, in discussion with the author, May 2013.
93 Sinatra assigned each writer: Friedwald, *Sinatra!*, p. 329.
93 "Frank asked me": Ibid.
93 "My dad and Frank": Slatkin, discussion.
94 "conducting with the index finger": Shaw, *Sinatra*, pp. 248–49.
94 "Conducting is primarily": Slatkin, discussion.
94 "was damn near": Friedwald, *Sinatra!*, p. 329.
95 "purely a paper deal": Ibid., p. 367.
96 "Success hasn't changed": Havers, *Sinatra*, p. 214.
96 "a Jekyll and Hyde": Summers and Swan, *Sinatra*, p. 223.
96 "A few of the women": Kelley, *His Way*, p. 230.
96 "If I had as many": Kaplan, *Frank*, p. 282.
97 "always on his way": Summers and Swan, *Sinatra*, p. 213.
97 "I suppose I can": Jill Corey, in discussion with the author, Nov. 2012.
97 "I said, 'Certainly not' ": Peggy Connelly, in discussion with the author, Dec. 2006.
98 In Dorothy Kilgallen's case: Kelley, *His Way*, p. 230.
98 Frank was devastated: Nancy Sinatra, *American Legend*, p. 125.
98 "We became very close": Granata, *Sessions with Sinatra*, pp. 120–21.
99 "might not be enough": Friedwald, *Sinatra!*, p. 242.
99 "It was something that": Slatkin, discussion.
99 "It's the most stunning": Granata, *Sessions with Sinatra*, p. 121.
100 Frank was bothered: Friedwald, *Sinatra!*, p. 242.
100 "I had wanted to go": Summers and Swan, *Sinatra*, pp. 217–18; Peggy Connelly, in discussion with the author, May 2006.
101 "a joke on the Capitol executives": Nancy Sinatra, *My Father*, p. 350.
101 "obviously viewed [the song]": Ed O'Brien, in discussion with the author, Nov. 2006.
102 The attackers had apparently: Associated Press, April 11, 1956.
102 then phoned the singer's wife: Epstein, pp. 256–57.
102 Sinatra tended to spend: Goldstein, *Frank Sinatra*, p. 23.
104 Columbia had never been: Santopietro, *Sinatra in Hollywood*, p. 230.
104 "We talked things out": Shaw, *Sinatra*, p. 217.
104 "there was something 'special event' ": Jacobs and Stadiem, *Mr. S*, pp. 49–50.
105 The interior color scheme: Jacobs and Stadiem, *Mr. S*, p. 48.
105 "didn't seem ex": Ibid.
105 "I married one man": Tina Sinatra, *My Father's Daughter*, p. 108.
105 "actually *was* coming home": Ibid., pp. 108–9.
106 "If I do meet Ava": Server, *Ava Gardner*, p. 334.
106 They could discuss it: Sheilah Graham, syndicated column, April 14, 1956.

CHAPTER 6

107 "no other artist": Kelley, *His Way*, p. 231.
108 "I want to play this role": Shaw, *Sinatra*, p. 217.
108 "Only Frank Sinatra's most intimate": Louella Parsons, syndicated column, April 22, 1956.
108 They talked on the phone every week: Jordan, *Living with Miss G*, p. 227.
108 "all its from-the-blood passion": Server, *Ava Gardner*, pp. 270–71.
108 "It was so unspoiled": Gardner, *Ava*, pp. 246–47.
109 She had bought a house: Server, *Ava Gardner*, p. 341.
109 "We had just awakened": Peggy Connelly, in discussion with the author, May 2006.
109 "had not lived in such": Server, *Ava Gardner*, p. 334.
110 "You goddamned jerk": Kelley, *His Way*, p. 232.
110 "with two seats down front": Dorothy Kilgallen, syndicated column, May 30, 1956.
110 "professor": Alec Wilder correspondence, New York Public Library.
111 "Sixteen weeks!": Shaw, *Sinatra*, p. 218.
111 "Let's get this circus": Kelley, *His Way*, p. 233.
111 "He was always yelling": Ibid.
111 "When Sinatra walks into a room": Ibid., p. 232; Shaw, *Sinatra*, p. 218.
112 "It's no accident": Santopietro, *Sinatra in Hollywood*, p. 215.
112 "Throughout dinner": Kelley, *His Way*, p. 234.
113 "After dinner they parted": Server, *Ava Gardner*, pp. 334–35.
113 "The first thing": Connelly, discussion; Summers and Swan, *Sinatra*, p. 220.
114 "Hot or cold": Santopietro, *Sinatra in Hollywood*, p. 217.
114 "with potted palms": Ibid.
114 "When I first heard 'Heartbreak Hotel'": Lewisohn, *Tune In*, p. 257; Lennon, interview by Howard Smith, WPLJ-FM, New York, Sept. 10, 1971.
115 Both the thirteen-year-old: *Guardian*, Nov. 30, 2001; Richards, *Life*, p. 58.
115 "Frank Sinatra has been booked": *Terre Haute Tribune*, Aug. 4, 1956.
115 to the tune of: United Press Convention Preview, Aug. 6, 1956.
115 "Sinatra . . . has a police": Westbrook Pegler, syndicated column, Aug. 14, 1956.
116 "berating [the southerners]": Ibid.
117 "Aren't you going to": *Look*, May 14, 1957.
117 and brought a libel suit: Kelley, *His Way*, pp. 243–44.
117 What may be true: Summers and Swan, *Sinatra*, p. 466.
117 "In bars or nightclubs": Ibid., p. 216.
117 "When the lights": Nasaw, *Patriarch*, p. 706.
117 "Senator John F. Kennedy": *New York Times*, Aug. 14, 1956.
118 "Okay. That's it": Nancy Sinatra, *My Father*, pp. 132–33.
118 "were still a hard-working": Havers, *Sinatra*, pp. 219–20.
118 "that often when [he was]": Levinson, *September in the Rain*, pp. 132–33.
119 "We looked up at Tommy's": Ibid., pp. 133–34.
119 "If Tommy Dorsey was late": Cahn, *I Should Care*, p. 131.
119 "Mr. Sinatra, the actor": *New York Times*, Aug. 16, 1956.
120 three nights: Havers, *Sinatra*, p. 220.
120 Sinatra's opening act: Shaw, *Sinatra*, p. 220.
120 "Emotional tension": Ibid., p. 100.
120 An alternate theory: Sperber and Lax, *Bogart*, pp. 510–11.
121 That same week: Earl Wilson, syndicated column, Sept. 12, 1956; Louella Parsons, syndicated column, Sept. 14, 1956.
121 Less satisfyingly, Ava: Louella Parsons, syndicated column, Sept. 14, 1956.
121 "Hollywood people called": Jacobs and Stadiem, *Mr. S*, p. 81.
121 "When its owner": Hal Humphrey, syndicated column, Sept. 14, 1956.
122 Peggy Lee, too: Jacobs and Stadiem, *Mr. S*, p. 75.
122 who earned more than: Louella Parsons, syndicated column, April 22, 1956.
122 "How are ya, Ed?": All quotations from the Sept. 14, 1956, *Person to Person* are transcribed from a kinescope of the show on a private DVD.
123 there has been some controversy: "'Person to Person,' 1953–1961," *The Pop History Dig*, www .pophistorydig.com/topics/person-to-person1953-1961/.
124 Unlike virtually everybody: Havers, *Sinatra*, pp. 222–23.
124 He gave her a large stuffed horse: Bacall, *By Myself*, pp. 321–22.
124 "decided to withdraw": Ibid., p. 321.
124 "His neck": Sperber and Lax, *Bogart*, p. 511.
124 "I hadn't expected it": Bacall, *By Myself*, p. 322.

124 "a bit edgy and resentful": Ibid.
125 "Frank loved Bogart": Summers and Swan, *Sinatra*, p. 230.
125 "Everybody knew about": Kelley, *His Way*, p. 240.
126 Critics praised Frank: Jacobs and Stadiem, *Mr. S*, p. 68.
126 Frank's end of the deal: "The Joker Is Wild," AFI Catalog of Feature Films, www.afi.com
/members/catalog/DetailView.aspx?s=&Movie=52247.
126 "I don't want any of these": Shaw, *Sinatra*, p. 223.
127 "I'll do some of Joe's": Bob Thomas, syndicated column, Oct. 23, 1956.
127 The persona was very close: Fischer, *When the Mob Ran Vegas*, p. 72.
128 "We had rehearsed": Levinson, *September in the Rain*, pp. 136–37.
129 "Where *Lovers* included": Friedwald, *Sinatra!*, p. 235.
129 "I usually try to avoid": Granata, *Sessions with Sinatra*, p. 94.
129 "in nearly all tempos": Friedwald, *Sinatra!*, p. 43.
129 "seemed to take a particular": Levinson, *September in the Rain*, p. 132.
130 In his biography of Dorsey: Levinson, *Tommy Dorsey*, p. 302.
130 officially claiming: Associated Press, Dec. 3, 1956.
131 Bill Miller later speculated: Levinson, *Tommy Dorsey*, pp. 303–4.
131 The network also bought stock: Santopietro, *Sinatra in Hollywood*, p. 228.
131 "Ezzard Charles": Davidson, *The Real and the Unreal*, p. 48.
131 "When no rooms": Ibid., p. 18.
131 Jerry Lewis, who had broken up: United Press, Dec. 16, 1956.
132 the two installments: Server, *Ava Gardner*, p. 519.
132 "the Ava era finally ended": Shaw, *Sinatra*, p. 224.

CHAPTER 7

133 After the vocal glitch: Wire-service report, Jan. 1, 1957.
133 Though she had a bad: Dorothy Kilgallen, syndicated column, Jan. 15, 1957.
133 "When I got to the dressing room": Davis, Boyar, and Boyar, *Sammy*, pp. 250–51.
134 "Frankie sang for": Earl Wilson, syndicated column, Jan. 16, 1957.
134 "Dot Kilgallen isn't here": Shaw, *Sinatra*, p. 226.
134 "in bad taste": Nancy Sinatra, *American Legend*, p. 129.
134 "It was more than just": Davis, Boyar, and Boyar, *Sammy*, p. 251.
135 "Mr. Sinatra was in excellent": Havers, *Sinatra*, p. 225.
135 "I can't go on": Shaw, *Sinatra*, p. 225.
136 John Huston gave: Sperber and Lax, *Bogart*, pp. 517–18.
136 "Frank Sinatra will be unable": Louella Parsons, syndicated column, Jan. 17, 1957.
136 Then again, things: Wilson, *Sinatra*, p. 131.
136 "A New High": *Nevada State Journal*, Jan. 24, 1957, p. 7.
136 "Sinatra is still the chairman": Havers, *Sinatra*, p. 226.
136 rising as high as number 5: Ibid.
137 "I don't like to call": Louella Parsons, syndicated column, Feb. 1, 1957.
138 He wound up paying: Havers, *Sinatra*, p. 225.
138 "'CRANKY FRANKIE'": Wire-service report, Feb. 7, 1957.
138 On Valentine's Day: Davidson, *The Real and the Unreal*, p. 25.
139 "an informant": Wire-service report, March 8, 1957; Havers, *Sinatra*, p. 225.
139 "It seems to me": Wire-service report, March 8, 1957; Kelley, *His Way*, p. 242.
139 "a loud-mouthed blonde": Wire-service report, March 8, 1957.
139 "snappily clad": *Los Angeles Times*, Feb. 28, 1957.
139 "Throughout his questioning": Ibid.
140 "There is perjury apparent": Ibid.
140 "Do you still fear": Ibid.
141 "Frankie looked as if": Louella Parsons, syndicated column, Feb. 28, 1957.
141 "There is definitely a bald": Kelley, *His Way*, p. 243.
141 The result was seen: Wire-service report, March 27, 1957.
141 Yet even without: Cramer, *Joe DiMaggio*, p. 389.
141 "I'm going to do as": Ezra Goodman, *Fifty-Year Decline and Fall of Hollywood*, p. 245.
142 "He informed director": Ibid., p. 246.
142 "the last great musical": Santopietro, *Sinatra in Hollywood*, p. 229.
145 "Without intending any slight": Friedwald, *Sinatra!*, pp. 251–52.
145 "Sinatra took good care": Ibid., p. 251.
145 "Frank used Nelson": Ibid., p. 252.
146 The highly expressive: *San Marino (Calif.) Tribune*, Sept. 19, 1946; *Portsmouth (Ohio) Times*,
Dec. 13, 1946; etc.

147 "Why not have time": Jenkins, *Goodbye,* p. 206.

148 "He felt": Ibid., p. 210.

148 Frank had been furious: Friedwald, *Sinatra!,* p. 341.

148 "The room emptied": Jonathan Schwartz, in discussion with author, Dec. 7, 2011.

148 "There's a certain squareness": Friedwald, *Sinatra!,* p. 336.

148 "When I first heard it": Jonathan Schwartz, in discussion with author, Dec. 7, 2011.

149 "Not only did it turn the tide": *Lima (Ohio) News,* April 23, 1957.

150 "Four long-time viewers": Erskine Johnson, syndicated column, May 6, 1957.

151 "My mission was to try": Davidson, *The Real and the Unreal,* pp. 12–13.

151 "There is Sinatra": *Look,* May 14, 1957.

152 Against the advice: Kelley, *His Way,* p. 245.

152 "neurotic, depressed": Ibid., pp. 243–44.

152 he lavished two and a half hours: Friedwald, *Sinatra!,* p. 250.

CHAPTER 8

155 The day before: Shaw, *Sinatra,* p. 231.

156 "became drunk and abusive": Bogdanovich, *Who the Hell's in It,* p. 418.

156 "seems to be reaching back": Friedwald, *Sinatra!,* pp. 337–38.

156 "He threw a huge Christmas party": Granata, *Sessions with Sinatra,* p. 106.

156 "he rarely socialized": Ibid.

156 "Once in a while he did invite": Ibid., pp. 106–7.

157 "We also were guests": Leonard Slatkin, in discussion with the author, May 2013.

157 "During recording sessions": Granata, *Sessions with Sinatra,* pp. 133–34.

157 "It's a temptation": Ibid., p. 134.

158 For all his brilliance: Friedwald, *Sinatra!,* p. 252.

158 "Nelson said to me once": Ibid.

158 "During their first several": Levinson, *September in the Rain,* p. 135.

158 "Boy, would I see": Rosemary Riddle Acerra, in discussion with the author, Oct. 2012.

158 "when Frank would walk": Levinson, *September in the Rain,* p. 135.

159 "I think he never": Friedwald, *Sinatra!,* ibid.

159 "an affable leading man": *Variety,* Feb. 18, 1957.

159 "the taciturn harboring": Ibid., p. 54.

160 "Dean's mother and his father": Jerry Lewis, in discussion with the author, June 1999.

160 "If you make believe": Lewis and Kaplan, *Dean and Me,* pp. 33–34.

160 "Sinatra was enthralled": Tosches, *Dino,* p. 267.

160 "took it all so fucking seriously": Ibid., p. 322.

161 his increasing commitments: Bob Thomas, syndicated column, Oct. 1, 1957.

161 And unlike Frank, Dean: Tosches, *Dino,* p. 311.

161 "When Marlon Brando said": Transcribed from a private recording.

162 Amid much similar hilarity: Harrison Carroll, syndicated column, Aug. 16, 1957.

162 When the lowly local paper: *Deseret News,* Sept. 16, 1957.

162 "intimates": Wire-service report, Sept. 16, 1957.

162 "Everybody's a critic": Shaw, *Sinatra,* p. 231.

162 "After the screening": Ibid., p. 235.

163 After leaving El Rancho: James Bacon, syndicated column, Dec. 10, 1957.

163 "it was a jolt": Wilson, *Sinatra,* p. 132.

163 In fact, he hadn't: Shaw, *Sinatra,* p. 238.

163 "I understand that Sinatra": United Press, Sept. 15, 1957.

163 "There was a circusy atmosphere": Wilson, *Sinatra,* p. 133.

163 "no comment": Wire-service report, Sept. 16, 1957.

163 "I'm not one of those": Hedda Hopper, syndicated column, Sept. 19, 1957.

163 "I had never thought much": Bacall, *By Myself,* p. 304.

164 "The house had been so quiet": Ibid., pp. 372–73.

166 "If the session was": Friedwald, *Sinatra!,* p. 289.

166 "Billy May was the most": Ibid., p. 290.

166 "Recording with Billy May": Granata, *Sessions with Sinatra,* pp. 134–35.

166 "I figured": Ibid., p. 136.

168 "After the success": Friedwald, *Sinatra!,* p. 287.

168 "Upon learning this": Ibid., p. 286.

169 "When you hired the band": Granata, *Sessions with Sinatra,* p. 136.

169 In the years since: Lewisohn, *Tune In,* p. 396.

169 "Invited to look on": Ibid., pp. 396–97.

170 "The only Edsel": Clooney, *Girl Singer,* pp. 161–62.

171   "When Frank started in": Ibid., p. 161.

171   "a drab mixture": Shaw, *Sinatra*, p. 144.

171   "If I fall on my face": Havers, *Sinatra*, p. 230.

172   Frank adored the idea: Ibid., pp. 231–32.

172   "And that's when": Ibid., pp. 232–33.

173   "There was a total frenzy": Ibid., p. 233.

173   "A Sinatra album": Jonathan Schwartz interview, July 11, 2013.

174   "Sinatra has bounced back": "The Frank Sinatra Show, Season 1, Episode 1," TV.com, www
.tv.com/shows/the-frank-sinatra-show/bob-hope-kim-novak-and-peggy-lee-56545.

174   "When he was singing": Ibid.

174   "There's no disputing": Havers, *Sinatra*, p. 233.

174   "We prefer the Sinatra": Jack O'Brian, syndicated column, Oct. 19, 1957.

174   "What is wrong": Charles Mercer, syndicated column, Dec. 6, 1957.

175   "I couldn't escape": Kelley, *His Way*, p. 252.

175   "It fosters almost totally": Associated Press, Oct. 28, 1957.

175   "I admire that man": Havers, *Sinatra*, p. 233; Associated Press, Oct. 29, 1957.

176   In a piece headlined: *Variety*, Nov. 6, 1957.

176   All kinds of stars: "The Short Happy Ad Career of Ernest Hemingway," *Knopf Notes*, www
.knopfnotes.com/articles/the-short-happy-ad-career-of-ernest-hemingway.

178   "The 'live' Frank Sinatra": Jack O'Brian, syndicated column, Dec. 2, 1957.

179   *Variety* primly declared: *Variety*, Dec. 4, 1957.

179   "Frank Sinatra hasn't worked": Hedda Hopper, syndicated column, Dec. 15, 1957.

181   "For starters": Server, *Ava Gardner*, p. 348.

181   "She was thrown": Ibid., p. 349.

CHAPTER 9

185   "Today": *New York Times*, Jan. 6, 1958.

186   "Frank got paid": Ed Walters, in conversation with the author, Sept. 2013.

186   "I would rather be a don": Summers and Swan, *Sinatra*, p. 183.

187   "By the thirties and forties": Seymour M. Hersh, *Dark Side of Camelot*, p. 138.

187   "a high, almost girlish voice": Jacobs and Stadiem, *Mr. S*, p. 101.

188   "I thought he was": Robert Wagner, in discussion with the author, Nov. 2013.

188   "He really was": Betsy Duncan Hammes, in discussion with the author, June 2011.

188   "He could give you": Summers and Swan, *Sinatra*, p. 253.

188   "He had a look": Gloria Franks, in discussion with the author, June 2011.

189   Frank sang at a charity event: Giancana and Renner, *Mafia Princess*, p. 86.

189   At some point in the mid-1950s: Levy, *Rat Pack Confidential*, p. 136.

189   "He even hired": Jacobs and Stadiem, *Mr. S*, p. 100.

189   The main topic of discussion: Ibid., pp. 104–5.

189   "Gross Casino wins": United Press, May 8, 1957.

189   That $651,284, as it turned out: Levy, *Rat Pack Confidential*, p. 93.

190   "At least part of the reason": United Press, May 8, 1957.

190   "Pieces of the hotel": Levy, *Rat Pack Confidential*, p. 86.

190   "If mob figures": Kraft, *Vegas at Odds*, pp. 17–18.

191   "But it wasn't the facilities": Rose, *Agency*, p. 181.

192   "Get off my stage": Lewis and Kaplan, *Dean and Me*, p. 60.

192   "unwavering demand": Baggelaar, *Images of America*, p. 88.

192   Top-billed talent: Levy, *Rat Pack Confidential*, p. 84.

193   "There wasn't nothing": Ibid., p. 88.

193   At the end of December: Finstad, *Natasha*, p. 244.

193   "The affection": Hollywood Roundup, syndicated column, Jan. 5, 1958.

193   As late as the ninth: Wire-service report, Jan. 9, 1958.

194   Woodfield claimed: Summers and Swan, *Sinatra*, pp. 239–40.

195   He paid for the lost: Havers, *Sinatra*, p. 239.

196   "As a singer, there's no one": Shaw, *Sinatra*, p. 246.

196   "As a couple we were": Bacall, *By Myself*, p. 377.

196   "I recall a wire-service man": Ibid., p. 379.

196   "Sinatra counseled Tony Curtis": Shaw, *Sinatra*, p. 238.

197   "had a lovely Christmas eve": Bacall, *By Myself*, pp. 377–78.

197   "Don't cut the corners": Kaplan, *Frank*, p. 643.

198   "in the deep freeze": Louella Parsons, syndicated column, Jan. 23, 1958.

198   "almost as though nothing": Bacall, *By Myself*, p. 379.

198 "wildly attentive": Ibid., p. 380.

199 "thought it a 'great idea'": Ibid., pp. 380–81.

199 based solely on his ability: Kuntz and Kuntz, *Sinatra Files*, p. 113.

199 "The Fontainebleau": Walter Winchell, syndicated column, March 19, 1958.

200 In the meantime: Bob Thomas, syndicated column, March 12, 1958.

200 "Why don't you ask him": Bacall, *By Myself*, p. 381.

200 "I saw enormous black letters": Ibid., pp. 381–82.

201 "We had one person": Ibid., p. 383.

201 "He looked right at me": Ibid., p. 384.

201 In early May: Levinson, *September in the Rain*, p. 140.

201 Ironically, Sinatra initially planned: Friedwald, *Sinatra!*, p. 246.

201 "While the orchestrations": Granata, *Sessions with Sinatra*, p. 139.

202 "We had so many": Friedwald, *Sinatra!*, p. 245.

202 "to contemplate the luxury": Riddle, *Arranged by Nelson Riddle*, p. 48.

202 "I'd be painting": Nelson Riddle, interview by Jonathan Schwartz, 1982.

202 "The Frank Sinatra that": *Only the Lonely* liner notes.

204 Nat King Cole had thrown down: Ashley Kahn, "'Lush Life,' a Self-Portrait in Song," www.npr.org/templates/story/story.php?storyId=7200812.

204 "Put it aside": Private recording of "Lush Life" outtakes.

205 "I felt only relief": Shaw, *Sinatra*, p. 246.

CHAPTER 10

206 that his marriage plans: Vernon Scott, syndicated column, May 3, 1958.

206 that there had been a rift: Harrison Carroll, syndicated column, May 7, 1958.

206 that he had had a severe: Shaw, *Sinatra*, p. 247.

206 No one subbed: Wire-service report, March 27, 1958.

206 A prominent New York specialist: Wire-service report, June 1, 1958.

207 "He laughed when": Wire-service report, June 3, 1958.

207 Whatever hopes: Louella Parsons, syndicated column, April 17, 1958.

207 Frank and Lauren Bacall had split: Bacall, *By Myself*, p. 384.

207 To the detriment: See Kilgallen, syndicated column, Sept. 30, 1964.

207 but the far less interesting: *Reading Eagle*, May 22, 1952.

207 Rumor had it that: Erskine Johnson, syndicated column, July 11, 1958.

208 In early June: Earl Wilson, syndicated column, June 16, 1958.

209 "she took the dog back": Server, *Ava Gardner*, pp. 354–55.

209 "re-engagement": Jacobs and Stadiem, *Mr. S*, p. 198.

209 "To set those nosey minds": Hedda Hopper, syndicated column, June 30, 1958.

210 "Even though I was only": Jones, *Q*, p. 130.

210 "I didn't know what": Quincy Jones, in discussion with the author, Feb. 2013.

210 "I was curious to see": Jones, *Q*, p. 131.

211 "I was still mouthing": Ibid.

211 "It's a big oblong room": Jones, discussion.

212 "Never once a breach of taste": Britt, *Frank Sinatra: A Celebration*, p. 121.

212 "One of the reasons": Art Buchwald, syndicated column, July 1, 1958.

214 "Ella Fitzgerald is the only": Private 1959 interview, courtesy of Ed O'Brien.

214 The crowd went nuts: Shaw, *Sinatra*, p. 248.

215 "Make yourself comfortable": Rickles, *Rickles' Book*, p. 64.

215 On the other hand: *Life*, Feb. 3, 1958.

215 "Remember the good old days": Wire-service report, June 22, 1958.

215 "What's New?": Levinson, *September in the Rain*, p. 140.

216 In the middle of July: *Redlands Daily Facts*, July 16, 1958.

216 As the resort's name indicated: Van Meter, *Last Good Time*, p. 175.

216 It was an ideal hideaway: Ibid.

216 Around this time: Denton and Morris, *The Money and the Power*, p. 184.

216 "The principal owner": Nasaw, *Patriarch*, p. 719.

216 Wingy Grober was the front: Denton and Morris, *The Money and the Power*, p. 184.

217 "There was nothing very remarkable": Nasaw, *Patriarch*, pp. 719–20.

217 Robert F. Kennedy was the chief counsel: Seymour M. Hersh, *Dark Side of Camelot*, p. 135.

217 He and Bobby Kennedy argued: Ibid.

217 "Committee counsel Robert F. Kennedy": Wire-service report, July 7, 1958.

218 after MCA muscled Tony Randall: McDougal, *Last Mogul*, p. 236.

218 Dean was to play Bama: Kelley, *His Way*, p. 226.

219 "Nothing so exciting": *Time*, Aug. 25, 1958.

219 "This place is worse": Ibid.

219 "but back of the sound-killing glass": Ibid.

219 The clerk cried: Ibid.

219 "The violent displays": Santopietro, *Sinatra in Hollywood*, p. 254.

220 "He did not return": Ibid.

220 "Outside Frank's door": Shaw, *Sinatra*, p. 250.

220 "We were virtual prisoners": Ibid.

220 "on the lam": MacLaine, *My Lucky Stars*, pp. 64–65.

221 "One evening during a night shoot": Ibid.

221 "some gambling joints": Ibid., pp. 65–66.

222 "I wore sunglasses": Ibid., pp. 68–69.

222 "Frank Sinatra was met": Kuntz and Kuntz, *Sinatra Files*, p. 113.

223 "We wouldn't talk": Summers and Swan, *Sinatra*, p. 244.

223 "If people wanted": Tosches, *Dino*, p. 322.

223 Accordingly, the new: Shaw, *Sinatra*, p. 251.

223 the album hit number 1: O'Brien and Sayers, *Sinatra*, p. 260.

224 "Of course, he's prone": Minnelli, *I Remember It Well*, p. 339.

224 "He *cannot* communicate": Tosches, *Dino*, p. 263.

224 "Dean doesn't have": Ibid., pp. 263–64.

225 Jerry Lewis, like Frank: Lewis and Kaplan, *Dean and Me*, p. 20.

225 In September, Frank: *American Weekly*, May 31, 1959.

226 "But within minutes": United Press, Oct. 19, 1958.

226 The *Daily Express* ran: Wire-service report, Oct. 20, 1958.

227 Sinatra sent a friend: *American Weekly*, May 31, 1959.

227 "I'm here in London": Shaw, *Sinatra*, p. 252.

227 The photographer was taken: Associated Press, Nov. 5, 1958.

227 When Frank arrived in Miami: Shaw, *Sinatra*, p. 254.

228 the New Frontier paid her: Clarke, *Get Happy*, p. 329.

228 "It's a disheartening": *Billboard*, March 31, 1958.

228 In July, she clawed back: Frank, *Judy*, p. 444.

228 She arrived ten days: Louella Parsons, syndicated column, Oct. 1, 1958.

228 "Judy Garland has no": *Variety*, Oct. 7, 1958.

228 "go up there": Robert Wagner, in discussion with the author, Nov. 2013.

229 "put on a comedy routine": Louella Parsons, syndicated column, Oct. 11, 1958.

229 "Frank and Dean joked": Wagner, discussion.

229 "I'm just gonna sing": MacLaine, *My Lucky Stars*, pp. 57–58.

229 "He was as sharp": Lewis and Kaplan, *Dean and Me*, p. 33.

230 "Does Sinatra know": Capra, *Name Above the Title*, p. 449.

230 "Sinatra is a great singer": Ibid., p. 455.

231 "a performer first": Ibid., p. 458.

231 "Frank always worked well": Santopietro, *Sinatra in Hollywood*, p. 264.

231 "He really didn't treat": Eddie Hodges, in discussion with the author, Oct. 2013.

233 "was the only woman": MacLaine, *My Lucky Stars*, pp. 62–63.

233 "the biggest new blue-chip": *Life*, Dec. 22, 1958.

235 "As soon as I go out": Ibid.

236 "He's always had that": Wagner, discussion.

236 "the girls said that": Kelley, *His Way*, p. 257.

236 "The greatest indignity": English, *Havana Nocturne*, p. 305.

CHAPTER 11

238 Metro originally offered: Spada, *Peter Lawford*, p. 212.

238 "Frank, there were": Levy, *Rat Pack Confidential*, p. 73.

238 "Dear Dago": *Variety*, Jan. 16, 1959.

238 "Sinatra had a marvelous": Server, *Ava Gardner*, p. 187.

238 Martin caught the 10:00 p.m.: *Variety*, Jan. 22, 1959.

239 "Dean Martin, another": *Variety*, Jan. 30 and Feb. 4, 1959.

239 "Things are going": Alec Wilder correspondence, New York Public Library.

240 The *Herald* had sent a reporter: Server, *Ava Gardner*, p. 369.

240 "She's avid to grasp": Stanley Kramer, "The Many Moods of Ava," *American Weekly*, Jan. 24, 1960.

240 He was like a rougher: Jack Eigen obituary, *Milwaukee Journal*, Jan. 26, 1983.

241 "I love Frank": Kelley, *His Way,* pp. 255–56.
241 "Why is it that most stars": "Sammy and Frankie Feuding over Chicago Radio Interview," *Jet,* March 12, 1959.
242 "Bigger than Frank?": Levy, *Rat Pack Confidential,* p. 73; Taraborrelli, *Sinatra,* p. 482.
242 "Who's better than Sinatra": Taraborrelli, *Sinatra,* p. 482.
242 "That was it for Sammy": Kelley, *His Way,* p. 256.
242 "But by the time": Server, *Ava Gardner,* p. 372.
243 "to a packed house": Hedda Hopper, syndicated column, Feb. 18, 1959.
243 "Even when they were": Server, *Ava Gardner,* p. 372.
243 "That was the unforgivable part": Ibid.
243 "Both Frank Sinatra": Army Archerd, syndicated column, *Variety,* March 4, 1959.
243 "one with a 'we're with you' atmosphere": *Variety,* March 11, 1959.
244 The second week was projected: Ibid.
244 "Sinatra has a revised act": Ibid.
244 "While listening to Norvo's group": Will Friedwald, liner notes, *Frank Sinatra with the Red Norvo Quintet, Live in Australia, 1959.*
246 "she had come to think": Server, *Ava Gardner,* p. 374.
247 "After one particularly": Friedwald, liner notes, *Frank Sinatra with the Red Norvo Quintet, Live in Australia, 1959.*
247 "I don't think he ever": Ibid.
248 "The scene afterward": Server, *Ava Gardner,* p. 375.
249 "He said, 'Yeah, that's' ": Summers and Swan, *Sinatra,* p. 206.
249 but not with his eleven-year-old: Eddie Hodges, in discussion with the author, Oct. 2013.
251 "He yelled": Ibid.
251 George Jacobs maintains: Jacobs and Stadiem, *Mr. S,* p. 129.
251 "Let's just say": Ingham, *Rough Guide to Frank Sinatra,* p. 64.
251 "had had an admitted": Jacobs and Stadiem, *Mr. S,* p. 129.
252 "I wish Mr. Kennedy": Margaria Fichtner, "A National Treasure," *Chicago Tribune,* March 15, 1989.
252 "For Sinatra": Brownstein, *The Power and the Glitter,* p. 159.
253 "We're going to sell Jack": Thomas, *Robert Kennedy,* p. 48.
253 "unsubstantiated, usually": Nasaw, *Patriarch,* p. 80.
253 "He had disposed of": Ibid., pp. 719–20.
254 "I was instructed to go": Summers and Swan, *Sinatra,* p. 258.
254 "Sheenie rag traders": Jacobs and Stadiem, *Mr. S,* pp. 117–18.
255 "I think that in understanding": Nancy Olson Livingston, in discussion with the author, Jan. 2013.
255 Jack Kennedy, the soap flakes: Summers and Swan, *Sinatra,* p. 257.
255 "As much as I disliked": Jacobs and Stadiem, *Mr. S,* p. 135.
256 "His fondness for Frank": Kelley, *His Way,* p. 267.
256 "Senator Kennedy is a friend": Pietrusza, *1960,* p. 234.
256 In November of that year: Walter Winchell, syndicated column, Nov. 16, 1958.
257 "Because it was an 'inside' ": Vernon Scott, dispatch, May 14, 1959.
257 And by May 1959: *Lowell Sun,* May 1, 1959.

CHAPTER 12

258 At the Desert Inn in March: Giancana and Giancana, *Double Cross,* p. 274.
258 "persons of notorious": Christopher Turner, "Nevada's Most Unwanted," *Cabinet,* Fall 2005, www.cabinetmagazine.org/issues/19/turner2.php.
258 "either the number one": United Press, June 7, 1959.
258 "A handsome-type hoodlum": United Press, June 10, 1959.
259 During another lunch break: Dean Jones, in discussion with the author, Nov. 2013.
259 Utterly unfazed: Ibid.
260 Dean Martin and Shirley MacLaine: Hedda Hopper, syndicated column, June 30, 1959.
260 Lady Beatty, after: Dorothy Kilgallen, syndicated column, May 19, 1959.
260 When his work: Kuntz and Kuntz, *Sinatra Files,* p. 148.
260 "Giancana, who appeared": United Press, July 6, 1959.
261 From Miami, Frank: Louella Parsons, syndicated column, June 23, 1959.
261 "With few exceptions": Clarke, *Billie Holiday,* p. 96.
261 Holiday bragged: Ibid., p. 12.
261 "This was a horrifying": Ibid., p. 438.
262 "A beautician was doing": Jacobs and Stadiem, *Mr. S,* pp. 150–51.

262 But with the police: Ibid.
263 In 1946, for various: Van Meter, *Last Good Time,* pp. 69–77.
264 "Frank's career was just": Ibid., pp. 97–98.
264 "When Frank got to town": Ibid., p. 106.
264 And, while Frank was playing: Ibid.
265 "How about August 24": Richard Apt, "Sinatra and the Atlantic City Connection," in Mustazza, *Frank Sinatra and Popular Culture,* p. 224.
265 In 1959, when Frank: Hedda Hopper, syndicated column, July 19, 1959.
265 Sinatra, who returned as: Leonard Lyons, syndicated column, Aug. 3, 1959.
265 "Skinny often said": Apt, "Sinatra and the Atlantic City Connection," p. 224.
265 One night, the crowd: Earl Wilson, syndicated column, July 30, 1959.
265 "The smoke bothered": Apt, "Sinatra and the Atlantic City Connection," p. 223.
265 "Kick that cigarette": Earl Wilson, syndicated column, Aug. 10, 1959.
265 In his dressing room: Earl Wilson, syndicated column, Aug. 3, 1959.
266 "advised on September 16, 1959": Kuntz and Kuntz, *Sinatra Files,* pp. 195–96.
266 "She stated that at the age": Van Meter, *Last Good Time,* pp. 145–46.
266 Another FBI report claimed: Summers and Swan, *Sinatra,* p. 254.
268 "defense attorney François": Santopietro, *Sinatra in Hollywood,* p. 277.
268 "Alas, this one phrase": Ibid., p. 276.
268 "Everywhere she goes": United Press, July 8, 1959.
269 "Naturally, I hope": Ibid.
270 "No plan, no itinerary": Server, *Ava Gardner,* p. 376.
270 "middle-aged woman": Ibid., p. 378.
271 "Movie actress Ava": Wire-service dispatch, Sept. 17, 1959.
271 "Pee Wee Marquette": Davis, *Miles,* p. 237.
272 "Khrushchev fever": *New York Times,* Sept. 20, 1959.
272 "I believe that to sit": Carlson, *K Blows Top,* p. 150.
273 "the unpardonable sin": Associated Press, Sept. 24, 1959.
273 "What do you have, rocket": *Van Nuys News,* Sept. 20, 1959.
273 When a reporter asked: *New York Times,* Sept. 20, 1959.
273 "lascivious, disgusting": Daniel O'Brien, *Frank Sinatra Film Guide,* p. 126.
274 "being condemned by Khrushchev": Ibid.
274 "Their colloquy may": Harriet Van Horne, syndicated column, Sept. 30, 1959.
274 "Of course, a meeting": Fred Danzig, syndicated column, Sept. 30, 1959.
275 "One of the brightest": Cynthia Lowry, syndicated column, Oct. 20, 1959.
275 "Fortunately, the trio": Fred Danzig, syndicated column, Oct. 20, 1959.
276 "Oh, you're a colorful": http://www.youtube.com/watch?v=YDHX4Bw1pHs.
276 "Gee. Dean is the only": Fred Danzig, syndicated column, Nov. 4, 1959.
276 "If the boys keep up": Cynthia Lowry, syndicated column, Nov. 4, 1959.
276 "some disciplinary problems": Fred Danzig, syndicated column, Nov. 4, 1959.
276 Brown, who seemed a shoo-in: *Los Angeles Times,* Oct. 30, 1959.
277 "grew visibly warmer": Relman Morin, dispatch, Nov. 6, 1959.
277 Governor Brown, who attended: *Los Angeles Times,* Oct. 30, 1959.
277 "The harsh facts": *Los Angeles Times,* Nov. 3, 1959.
277 "Sinatra! Sinatra!": Michael O'Brien, *John F. Kennedy,* p. 198.
278 "1. Women get starry eyed": Morin, dispatch, Nov. 6, 1959.
278 "in a divine Sophie": Hedda Hopper, *Los Angeles Times,* Nov. 4, 1959.
278 "that Kennedy and Frank took": Summers and Swan, *Sinatra,* p. 260.
279 "bursting with awe": Angie Dickinson, in discussion with the author, July 2006.
279 "They both loved women": Ibid.
280 "I'd say she was": Seymour M. Hersh, *Dark Side of Camelot,* pp. 296–97.
280 "For the first time": Exner, *My Story,* p. 61.
281 "I just was aware": Gloria Franks, in discussion with the author, June 2011.
281 "I was working at the El Mirador": Betsy Duncan Hammes, in discussion with the author, June 2011.
281 "The first indication": Exner, *My Story,* p. 49.
281 "I brought them over": Summers and Swan, *Sinatra: The Life,* p. 260.
282 "He had a big success": Morin, dispatch, Nov. 6, 1959.
282 "folksy stroll": Associated Press, Nov. 4, 1959.
282 All Earl Wilson: Earl Wilson, syndicated column, Nov. 5, 1959.
282 "We stayed with Frank": Kelley, *His Way,* p. 267.
282 "The Los Angeles Office": Kuntz and Kuntz, *Sinatra Files,* p. 125.
283 "John F. Kennedy slept here": Kelley, *His Way,* p. 286.

283 "A few nights later": Exner, *My Story*, pp. 49–50.
284 "I took the midnight": Ibid., p. 50.
284 Frank Sinatra was a major depositor: Russo, *Supermob*, pp. 141–42.
284 "We sat in the sun": Exner, *My Story*, p. 54.
284 "Their favorite words": Ibid., pp. 57–58.
285 "Everybody around Frank walks": Ibid., p. 58.
285 "For some reason": Ibid., p. 54.
286 "I didn't even want": Ibid., p. 59.
286 "Cheap, weak": Jacobs and Stadiem, *Mr. S*, p. 126.
286 "I felt kind of sad": Jones, discussion.
286 "I was a halfway": Quirk, *Kennedys in Hollywood*, p. 175.
286 "Frank Sinatra's big": *Variety*, Nov. 30, 1959.
286 "Schweitzer said because": Ibid.
287 "I wanted to see him": Exner, *My Story*, pp. 60–61.
287 "It was nice and comfortable": Ibid., pp. 61–62.
288 "alleged Lake County": Associated Press, Aug. 25, 1960.
288 "We made love": Exner, *My Story*, pp. 63–64.
288 As of that day: *Salt Lake City Tribune*, Dec. 8, 1959.
288 "Dad was more than": Seymour M. Hersh, *Dark Side of Camelot*, p. 138.

CHAPTER 13

291 "The Rat Pack embodied": Brownstein, *The Power and the Glitter*, p. 155.
294 "You come to my summit": Wilson, *Show Business Nobody Knows*, p. 14.
294 "everybody knew each other": Shecky Greene, in discussion with the author, Nov. 2012.
295 "Frank opened the first": Ed Walters, in discussion with the author, Nov. 2012.
296 "The audience just loved it": Ibid.
296 At one point in early: Levy, *Rat Pack Confidential*, p. 108.
297 "Frank Sinatra, Dean Martin, Sammy Davis Jr.": Hedda Hopper, syndicated column, Feb. 11, 1960.
297 "I thought it was plain": Greene, discussion.
297 "The earliest call": Levy, *Rat Pack Confidential*, p. 108.
298 "Frank looked upon": Santopietro, *Sinatra in Hollywood*, p. 285.
298 "certainly knew exactly": Ibid.
298 "Milestone had a very loose": "The Rat Pack Photographer," *Los Angeles Times*, Dec. 12, 2001.
298 "Hey, where are you": Zehme, *Way You Wear Your Hat*, p. 44.
298 "Some eastern press": Walters, discussion.
299 "He was hanging around Frank": Ibid.
299 "We've worked together": Levy, *Rat Pack Confidential*, p. 76.
299 Drinking buddies and hangers-on: Zehme, *Way You Wear Your Hat*, p. 4.
299 "All the guys would": *Los Angeles Times*, Dec. 12, 2001.
299 "He was not like the rest": Exner, *My Story*, p. 82.
300 "There is no way anyone": Ibid., p. 83.
301 "was the first American president": Gould, *Can't Buy Me Love*, pp. 205–6.
301 "Sinatra thought Kennedy": Walters, discussion.
302 "He was not a grown-up": Nancy Olson Livingston, in discussion with the author, Jan. 2013.
303 "There was no goddamn": Martin, *Hero for Our Time*, p. 199.
303 "Ladies and gentlemen, Senator":" 'The Jack Pack,' 1958–1960," *The Pop History Dig*, www.pophistorydig.com/?p=9361.
303 "at ten o'clock Sunday": Exner, *My Story*, p. 86.
303 "The lights were low": Summers and Swan, *Sinatra*, p. 264.
303 "She's a hooker": Ibid.
303 "was always kind of like": Betsy Duncan Hammes, in discussion with the author, Dec. 2013.
304 "because we sensed": Martin, *Hero for Our Time*, p. 199.
304 "tremendously impressed by": Exner, *My Story*, p. 87.
304 Livingston claims that: Livingston, discussion.
305 "Don't worry, I plan": Exner, *My Story*, p. 94.
305 "He was extremely solicitous": Ibid., p. 99.
308 "I called him up": Havers, *Sinatra*, p. 252.
308 in return for giving Capitol: Cornyn, *Exploding*, p. 47.
309 "lightly swinging love": Alan and Marilyn Bergman, in discussion with the author, Nov. 2012.
309 The rest of the music: Friedwald, *Sinatra!*, p. 256.

309 Frank and the screenwriter: Kelley, *His Way*, p. 110.
309 "It was a total downer": Jacobs and Stadiem, *Mr. S*, p. 144.
309 That January, though: *New York Times*, Jan. 20, 1960.
310 "Frank said that he had been": Kelley, *His Way*, p. 272.
310 "I asked him openly": Ibid.
310 And that Steve McQueen: Associated Press, March 22, 1960.
310 "This marks the first time": *New York Times*, March 20, 1960.
310 "STARS SCORN": United Press, March 23, 1960.
311 "I wonder how Sinatra's crony": Munn, *John Wayne*, pp. 216–17; Kelley, *His Way*, p. 273.
311 "What kind of thinking": Kelley, *His Way*, pp. 272–73.
311 "On returning from New York": Hedda Hopper, syndicated column, April 8, 1960.
311 "Font's Ben Novack": *Variety*, March 30, 1960.
312 "hard hit with the failure": Ibid.
312 "Frank Sinatra's new talent": Earl Wilson, syndicated column, March 28, 1960.
312 "flew to Palm Springs to try": Kelley, *His Way*, p. 274.
312 "That's when old Joe": Ibid.
312 "Both Joe and Bobby": Tina Sinatra, *My Father's Daughter*, p. 78.
313 "It was reported, but without": *New York Times*, March 20, 1960.
313 "I went home in tears": Tina Sinatra, *My Father's Daughter*, p. 79.
313 "killed him to have to eat": Jacobs and Stadiem, *Mr. S*, p. 145.
314 "It's mighty puzzling": Dorothy Kilgallen, syndicated column, April 18, 1960.
314 "He'd get on the phone": Spada, *Peter Lawford*, p. 226.
314 "If he asked people": *Los Angeles Times*, Aug. 13, 2000.
315 "We'd spread out": Davis, Boyar, and Boyar, *Why Me?*, p. 111.
315 "He'd met Jack Kennedy": Levy, *Rat Pack Confidential*, p. 155.
315 Parker drove a legendarily: Guralnick and Jorgensen, *Elvis Day by Day*, pp. 146–47.
315 "Mr. S hated Elvis": Jacobs and Stadiem, *Mr. S*, p. 125.
316 First, though, Sinatra: https://www.youtube.com/watch?v=ngQbGj8aSWs.
317 "It made a man of me": *Redlands (Calif.) Daily Facts*, March 9, 1960.
319 "Frank asked me": Summers and Swan, *Sinatra*, p. 269.
320 "a dangerous game": Ibid.
320 "deliberately fudged": Seymour M. Hersh, *Dark Side of Camelot*, p. 299.
320 "I paid a terrible price": Exner, *My Story*, p. 122.
320 "In March, when Mooney": Giancana and Giancana, *Double Cross*, p. 282.
320 "Come here, Judy": Exner, *My Story*, p. 116.
321 "Fischetti and other hoodlums": Summers and Swan, *Sinatra*, pp. 268–69.
321 "the singer's initial reaction": Friedwald, *Sinatra!*, p. 256.
321 "Sinatra finally asked": Ibid.
321 "Frank said, 'I don't like' ": Alan and Marilyn Bergman, in discussion with the author, Nov. 2012.
323 "Hollywood is talking": Louella Parsons, syndicated column, April 24, 1960.
323 "Welcome Home Elvis": Havers, *Sinatra*, p. 255.
323 "Elvis Presley hasn't changed": *Variety*, May 16, 1960.
324 "You seem to disagree": Kelley, *His Way*, pp. 275–76; Associated Press, May 15, 1960.

CHAPTER 14

326 "squalid, corrupt": Theodore H. White, *Making of the President, 1960*, p. 97.
326 "spent at least $2 million": Seymour M. Hersh, *Dark Side of Camelot*, p. 90.
326 "Giancana sent Skinny": Van Meter, *Last Good Time*, p. 172.
326 Even by his friends' estimation: Ibid., p. 173.
326 "spreading money around": Summers and Swan, *Sinatra*, p. 271.
326 "not for direct bribes": Seymour M. Hersh, *Dark Side of Camelot*, p. 100.
327 The bureau also overheard: Ibid., p. 101.
327 "If you want to see": Davis, Boyar, and Boyar, *Why Me?*, p. 108.
327 "I'm positive it never": Ed Walters, in discussion with the author, Jan. 2014.
327 One estimate has: Seymour M. Hersh, *Dark Side of Camelot*, p. 98.
327 "Each girl in Frank's life": Exner, *My Story*, p. 113.
328 "I dig the sake": Associated Press, May 30, 1960.
328 The Democratic National Convention was: Theodore H. White, *Making of the President, 1960*, p. 151.
328 "Smogless and milk-blue": Ibid., p. 150.
328 "The Biltmore [was]": Mailer, *Mind of an Outlaw*, p. 117.

329 Predictably, if defensibly: *Los Angeles Times,* July 11, 1960.
329 "From the sounds and sights": Theodore H. White, *Making of the President, 1960,* p. 154.
329 "He had the deep orange-brown": Mailer, *Mind of an Outlaw,* pp. 120–21.
330 "from Marlborough and": Theodore H. White, *Making of the President, 1960,* p. 148.
330 "Since the First World War": Mailer, *Mind of an Outlaw,* p. 121.
330 "He was born into": Seymour M. Hersh, *Dark Side of Camelot,* p. 139.
330 a bash for Jack's sister: *Los Angeles Times,* July 8, 1960.
331 "For the candidates, the hour": *Los Angeles Times,* July 11, 1960.
331 "still trying hard to sink": Ibid.
331 The other performers included: Associated Press, July 11, 1960.
331 Edward G. Robinson got: Earl Wilson, syndicated column, July 15, 1960.
332 "Those dirty sons": Kelley, *His Way,* pp. 276–77.
332 "I don't know why they": United Press, July 12, 1960.
332 "Sinatra is for Sen. John F. Kennedy": Ibid.
332 Sinatra, Peter Lawford: Shaw, *Sinatra,* p. 273.
332 "When the Democrats convene": *Milwaukee Journal,* July 11, 1960.
333 "Conscious of television": Kelley, *His Way,* p. 277.
333 "Every morning after": Jacobs and Stadiem, *Mr. S,* p. 56.
333 "spent the rest of the afternoon": Theodore H. White, *Making of the President, 1960,* pp. 168–69.
333 Frank was also there: Kelley, *His Way,* p. 277.
333 "the high point of drama": Theodore H. White, *Making of the President, 1960,* p. 165.
334 He gave his friend Green: Kelley, *His Way,* p. 278.
334 " 'Wyoming,' chanted Tracy S. McCraken": Theodore H. White, *Making of the President, 1960,* p. 169.
334 "We're on our way": Kelley, *His Way,* p. 278.
334 At the convention, Johnson: *Los Angeles Times,* July 11, 1960.
335 who had all but called: Seymour M. Hersh, *Dark Side of Camelot,* p. 123.
335 "You know we had never": Ibid., pp. 125–26.
335 "during the campaign, even": Ibid., p. 129.
335 The decision was tortuous: Caro, *Passage of Power,* pp. 117–40.
335 "It is my earnest": Inez Robb, syndicated column, July 18, 1960.
335 "Sen. Jack Kennedy passed": Drew Pearson, syndicated column, July 15, 1960.
336 Not long after the convention: Shaw, *Sinatra,* p. 274.
336 "[Nevada Gaming Control] Board": United Press, July 13, 1960.
336 Frank—whose application: Kelley, *His Way,* p. 279; Summers and Swan, *Sinatra,* p. 289.
336 "Frank Sinatra is extremely": Van Meter, *Last Good Time,* p. 182.
337 On July 20, Frank arrived: Earl Wilson, syndicated column, July 26, 1960.
337 From the twenty-second: Earl Wilson, syndicated column, Aug. 3, 1960.
337 "It wasn't a big room": Bill Boggs, in discussion with the author, Nov. 2006.
337 Over the nine nights: Earl Wilson, syndicated column, Aug. 5, 1960.
337 "A new arrival joined us": Leonard Lyons, syndicated column, Aug. 6, 1960.
338 "Their horsing around": Levy, *Rat Pack Confidential,* pp. 118–19.
338 "an experience difficult": Bob Thomas, syndicated column, Aug. 5, 1960.
338 "'Ocean's Eleven' figures": *Variety,* Aug. 5, 1960.
339 "inject some sorely needed": Santopietro, *Sinatra in Hollywood,* p. 285.
340 "depended for its vitality": T. H. Adamowski, "Love in the Western World: Sinatra and the Conflict of Generations," in Mustazza, *Frank Sinatra and Popular Culture,* p. 36.
340 "what Gore Vidal has called": I could find no such quotation by Vidal; see, however, Eric Spitznagel, "Harold Ramis," *Believer,* March 2006.
341 "He told me that Frank instructed": Nelson Riddle, interview by Ed O'Brien; O'Brien, e-mail to author, Jan. 27, 2014.
341 "that he wanted to do": Friedwald, *Sinatra!,* pp. 257–58.
341 "The whole album lasts six": Jonathan Schwartz, in discussion with the author, Sept. 2011.
342 "the album reached Number Three": Ed O'Brien, e-mail to author, Jan. 27, 2014.
342 Norman Granz, the founder: Friedwald, *Sinatra!,* p. 224.
342 Her first album at Verve: Ibid., p. 221.
343 Early on, Granz came: Mo Ostin, in discussion with the author, Aug. 2012.
343 "Frank and Norman didn't see": Hershorn, *Norman Granz,* p. 361.
343 its roster had expanded: *Variety,* Nov. 21, 1960.
343 "The record business in jazz": Ostin, discussion.
344 "Sinatra may have gotten": Hershorn, *Norman Granz,* p. 293.
344 "a man born to": Cornyn, *Exploding,* p. 47.

344 "He was as strong": Ostin, discussion.

345 "The one thing Granz": Hershorn, *Norman Granz*, p. 293.

345 " 'The Clan' is a figment": Nancy Sinatra, *American Legend*, p. 148; Shaw, *Sinatra*, p. 274.

345 "serious citizens": Shaw, *Sinatra*, p. 274.

346 Two thousand loyalists: Mike Connolly, syndicated column, Sept. 15, 1960; *Delaware County Daily Times*, Sept. 17, 1960; " 'The Jack Pack,' 1958–1960," *The Pop History Dig*.

346 "Only a few months": Dorothy Kilgallen, syndicated column, Sept. 22, 1960.

346 the day after that private little dinner: United Press, Sept. 12, 1960.

346 The bride wore a white: Kelley, *His Way*, p. 280; Associated Press, Sept. 12, 1960.

346 "to match the stars": Nancy Sinatra, *My Father*, p. 131.

346 " 'I love you, chicken' ": Kelley, *His Way*, p. 280.

347 and was sometimes known as: Jacobs and Stadiem, *Mr. S*, p. 207.

347 had been signed at age fifteen: Kibbey, *Pat Boone*, p. 128.

347 Her father didn't lecture her: Nancy Sinatra, *My Father*, p. 131.

347 "It's my own life happening": Kelley, *His Way*, p. 280.

348 Tracy was the piece's center: Santopietro, *Sinatra in Hollywood*, p. 402.

348 "chronically tired, unhappy": Curtis, *Spencer Tracy*, p. 745.

348 "Nobody had his power": Ibid., p. 302.

348 "The Hearst newspapers": United Press International, Oct. 14, 1960.

348 "Dozens of policemen": Associated Press, Oct. 27, 1960.

349 who had recently been hospitalized: "Did JFK Steal the 1960 Election?," *The Stone Zone*, www.stonezone.com/article.php?id=391.

349 Many who listened in: http://www.museum.tv/eotv/kennedy-nixon.htm.

350 "It's not Sinatra's voice": Braden, *Just Enough Rope*, p. 148.

350 "the chief disciple": Shaw, *Sinatra*, p. 276.

350 "We are dedicating": https://www.youtube.com/watch?v=1Hb3R3S1_7k.

350 "inside buddy ribbings": Shaw, *Sinatra*, p. 277.

351 "a sick joke or two": Ibid.

351 "Listen, honey": Kelley, *His Way*, p. 281.

351 "Controlling Chicago's powerful": Giancana and Giancana, *Double Cross*, p. 290.

352 "The agreement was that": Roemer, *Man Against the Mob*, p. 158.

352 "Humphreys had himself": Seymour M. Hersh, *Dark Side of Camelot*, p. 143.

352 "my members' money": Ibid., p. 146.

352 "He didn't expect": Ibid., p. 145.

353 Frank spent Election Day: vault.fbi.gov/Frank%20Sinatra/Frank%20Sinatra%20Part%20 24%200f%2029.

353 On the other end: Kelley, *His Way*, p. 281; Giancana and Giancana, *Double Cross*, p. 289.

353 But as day turned to evening: Theodore H. White, *Making of the President, 1960*, p. 346.

353 "We're going to make it": Summers and Swan, *Sinatra*, p. 275.

353 "He yelled at the TV": Ibid.

353 "We're trying to hold back": Kelley, *His Way*, p. 281.

354 "If only 4,500": Theodore H. White, *Making of the President, 1960*, p. 350.

354 "Ye assholes of little faith' ": Jacobs and Stadiem, *Mr. S*, p. 167.

354 "someone in Sinatra's office": Friedwald, *Sinatra!*, p. 368.

354 That someone was Frank's lawyer: Will Friedwald, e-mail to author, Feb. 4, 2014.

354 "Quite by accident": Ostin, discussion.

355 "short and slight, bald": Dannen, *Hit Men*, p. 121.

356 "So Mickey said": Ostin, discussion.

356 "He told me how important": Havers, *Sinatra*, p. 259.

356 Invitations had been sent out: Levy, *Rat Pack Confidential*, p. 167.

356 Jack's chances could be hurt: Nancy Sinatra, *American Legend*, p. 150.

356 "a huge favor": Jacobs and Stadiem, *Mr. S*, p. 146.

356 "would do anything for him": Nancy Sinatra, *American Legend*, p. 150.

357 "I combed the papers": Davis, Boyar, and Boyar, *Sammy*, p. 377.

357 "Dear Nigger Bastard": Ibid.

357 "Right or wrong": Kelley, *His Way*, p. 284.

357 "to state, 'This is my friend' ": Davis, *Why Me?*, p. 121.

357 "I [arranged] a lot of club acts": Granata, *Sessions with Sinatra*, p. 156.

357 "like a kid": Johnny Mandel, in discussion with the author, Aug. 2011.

357 "They were all going": Granata, *Sessions with Sinatra*, p. 156.

358 "When he was talking to you": Mandel, discussion.

359 Putnam had put all: Granata, *Sessions with Sinatra*, pp. 155–56.

359 "Unedited tapes reveal": Ibid., p. 157.

360 "Sinatra continues to snap": Ibid.
360 "Both casual listeners": Friedwald, *Sinatra!*, p. 368.
361 "Sinatra said, 'You know' ": Mandel, discussion.
362 "My association with Frank": Levinson, *September in the Rain*, pp. 149–50.

CHAPTER 15

363 "Among the articles": Vernon Scott, dispatch, Jan. 2, 1961.
363 "Have heard about": James Bacon, dispatch, Jan. 13, 1961.
363 "Sinatra would have been here": Ibid.
363 "This is the story": Ibid.
364 "This is the most exciting": Kelley, *His Way*, pp. 283–84.
364 He persuaded the producers: Ibid., p. 284.
364 Nelson Riddle agreed: Inaugural Gala program.
364 "I never had a feeling": Levy, *Rat Pack Confidential*, p. 174.
365 "It really can happen": Ibid., pp. 174–75.
365 "not want[ing] his": Kelley, *His Way*, p. 284.
365 "I lay on my back": Davis, Boyar, and Boyar, *Sammy*, p. 388.
365 Yet Nancy Sinatra asserts: Nancy Sinatra, *American Legend*, pp. 150–51.
365 "but Sammy would never have allowed": Ibid.
365 "Neither Dean Martin": Associated Press, Jan. 6, 1961.
365 A Lincoln limousine chauffeured: Kelley, *His Way*, p. 283.
366 The keepers of decorum: Shaw, *Sinatra*, p. 279.
366 "Many Washingtonians are fleeing": Walter T. Ridder, Robert E. Lee, and William Broom, syndicated column, Jan. 8, 1961.
366 who included Bob Hope's chief: Inaugural Gala program.
366 He hit up his old romantic: Levinson, *September in the Rain*, p. 144.
366 a majority stockholder: Barlett and Steele, *Howard Hughes*, p. 254.
367 "It was a big plane": Bob Bain, in discussion with the author, Feb. 2013.
367 "Frank had more guests": Ibid.
367 "most of the Kennedy clan": Associated Press, Jan. 18, 1961.
367 "was an event the Kennedy": Leaming, *Mrs. Kennedy*, pp. 1–3.
368 Her stance was complicated: Ibid., pp. 149–50.
368 "The winds blew in icy": Schlesinger, *Thousand Days*, p. 1.
368 "The stars who'd come": Levy, *Rat Pack Confidential*, pp. 176–77.
368 Jackie had flown up: Anthony, *Kennedy White House*, p. 15.
368 "the young President-elect": Schlesinger, *Thousand Days*, p. 1.
369 Inside the cavernous: Summers and Swan, *Sinatra*, p. 279.
369 All seats had been sold: Shaw, *Sinatra*, p. 280.
369 The gala began grandly: Inaugural Gala program.
369 "We see him entering": www.dailymotion.com/video/x9gvl2_john-kennedy-inaugural-gala-20-01-1_music.
369 "I told you I'd get you": Levy, *Rat Pack Confidential*, p. 177.
369 Nat Cole smiled through: Belafonte, *My Song*, p. 222.
370 "That deferential praise": Mark White, *Kennedy*, p. 34.
370 "I'm proud to be a Democrat": Ibid., pp. 35–36; Kelley, *His Way*, p. 285.
371 "Joe Kennedy barked at him": Anthony, *Kennedy White House*, p. 17.
371 Red Fay, who'd met JFK: Reeves, *President Kennedy*, p. 35; Andersen, *These Few Precious Days*, p. 110.
371 "Have you ever seen": Reeves, *President Kennedy*, p. 35; Anthony, *Kennedy White House*, p. 17.
372 "Wait until you see": Kelley, *His Way*, p. 285.
372 Hatless and coatless: Smith, *Grace and Power*, p. 62.
372 In a special section: Mark White, *Kennedy*, p. 35.
372 "There was a stand that had": Summers and Swan, *Sinatra*, p. 280.
372 "that Kennedy would stop by": Brownstein, *The Power and the Glitter*, p. 159.
373 Could it have been because: Smith, *Grace and Power*, pp. 71–72.
373 "At the time I didn't know": Summers and Swan, *Sinatra*, p. 280.
373 "because I had so much work": Earl Wilson, syndicated column, Jan. 27, 1961.
373 squiring Juliet Prowse: Earl Wilson, syndicated column, Jan. 26, 1961.
373 taking the Toots Shors: Earl Wilson, syndicated column, Jan. 30, 1961.
373 "with a guy nobody knew": Earl Wilson, syndicated column, Jan. 20, 1961.
373 "she laughed for two": Earl Wilson, syndicated column, Jan. 25, 1961.
374 "the leader has arrived": Associated Press, Jan. 28, 1961.

374 The writer Peter Levinson: Peter Levinson, in discussion with the author, Feb. 2006; Levinson, *September in the Rain*, p. 146.
374 "rushing down the aisle": Associated Press, Jan. 28, 1961.
374 "He did only 12 songs": *Variety*, Feb. 3, 1961.
374 "We were seated": Ostin, discussion.
375 "the commendations sometimes": Server, *Ava Gardner*, p. 382.
375 A recent newspaper piece: Earl Wilson, syndicated column, Jan. 26, 1961.
375 "I looked at his face": Levinson, discussion.
375 "She lived now without plan": Server, *Ava Gardner*, pp. 383–84.
376 "Apparently, she was much": Shaw, *Sinatra*, p. 282.
376 "were together a short while": Associated Press, Feb. 8, 1961.
376 As soon as Ava and Nancy: *Variety*, Feb. 14, 1961.
376 "We all had to sit around": Kelley, *His Way*, p. 286.
376 "Frank had me liaise": Mo Ostin, in discussion with the author, Aug. 2012.
377 "prevented many of the artists": O'Brien and Sayers, *Sinatra*, p. 94.
378 "There would be long lines": Glatt, *Prince of Paradise*, p. 46.
378 Sinatra and Giancana both enjoyed: Levy, *Rat Pack Confidential*, p. 141.
379 "bulged with books, fan mail": *Show Business Illustrated*, Sept. 5, 1961.
380 Some disparaging jokes: Rappleye and Becker, *All American Mafioso*, p. 191.
380 Maheu's main link: Summers and Swan, *Sinatra*, p. 134.
381 It has also been alleged: Ibid., p. 181.
381 And Giancana interested Maheu: Schlesinger, *Robert Kennedy and His Times*, p. 483.
381 Sinatra had also spent: Summers and Swan, *Sinatra*, p. 134.
381 "in part by having the Desert Inn": Levy, *Rat Pack Confidential*, p. 218.
381 "Balletti and a cohort wired": Ibid., p. 219.
382 "He almost swallowed": Rappleye and Becker, *All American Mafioso*, p. 212.
382 "The Bureau's interest increased": Ibid.
383 "Oliver later told Frank fan": Friedwald, *Sinatra!*, p. 116.
383 At one point, he reportedly: Cornyn, *Exploding*, p. 49.
383 "Sinatra was careful not": Friedwald, *Sinatra!*, p. 294.
384 "I've just got to be busy": Havers, *Sinatra*, p. 223.
384 "Frank was awful": Kelley, *His Way*, p. 287.
384 "she loved Frank Sinatra": Jacobs and Stadiem, *Mr. S*, p. 152.
385 "Mr. S had a ton": Ibid., p. 153.
385 In January 1961: *Variety*, April 5, 1961.
385 The Federation of Italian-American: Associated Press, March 15, 1961.
386 And though the chief: *New York Times*, Sept. 25, 1960.
386 the federation's boycott: Kelley, *His Way*, p. 287.
386 Fidel Castro wasn't the only: Ibid.
386 And though Frank Sinatra had: Ibid., p. 288.
386 "precise details of tiff": *Variety*, April 5, 1961.
386 "a bitter argument": United Press, April 8, 1961.
386 "Frank turned to Desi": Kelley, *His Way*, pp. 287–88.
386 "Associates of the men": United Press, April 8, 1961.
387 "I remember when you": Kelley, *His Way*, p. 288.
387 "I just couldn't hit": Ibid.
387 "How could you stand there": Ibid.
388 And three weeks later: Associated Press, April 14, 1961.
388 He would do several other benefits: Havers, *Sinatra*, p. 263.
389 Sales and reviews were strong: Friedwald, *Sinatra!*, p. 377.
389 "A new, happier": *Billboard*, Nov. 20, 1965.
389 "I put out so many": Havers, *Sinatra*, p. 265.

CHAPTER 16

392 He phoned Douglas: Daniel O'Brien, *Frank Sinatra Film Guide*, p. 140.
392 "There was a Dairy Queen": Levy, *Rat Pack Confidential*, p. 180.
392 "Cherry bombs were quite normal": Ruta Lee, in discussion with the author, March 2014.
392 "a planeload of girls": Ibid.
392 "an older gentleman": Levy, *Rat Pack Confidential*, p. 180.
393 "Once I get 'em": Erskine Johnson, syndicated column, Aug. 3, 1961.
393 "When we were shooting": Lee, discussion.
394 "Please be advised": Taraborrelli, *Sinatra*, p. 252.

394 "All Concerned": Ibid.

394 "She had a glow": Lee, discussion.

394 "She was beautiful, a vision": Taraborrelli, *Sinatra*, pp. 252–53.

395 "There's no doubt that Frank": Spoto, *Marilyn Monroe*, p. 466.

396 "charged onstage": Shaw, *Sinatra*, p. 293.

396 "They took over, doing": Associated Press, July 26, 1961.

396 "Frank and his henchmen": Shaw, *Sinatra*, p. 293.

396 "You sensed a feeling": Ibid.

396 "felt honored, pleased": Ibid.

397 The picture can be dated: Jacobs and Stadiem, photo insert; and see image of Aug. 29, 1961, *Look* cover.

397 "a former associate": Taraborrelli, *Sinatra*, p. 253.

397 minus Joey: Louella Parsons, syndicated column, July 6, 1961.

398 At the Vienna Summit: Ritter, *Dangerous Ground*, p. 89.

398 During a summer when: Editorial, *Monroe (La.) News Star*, Aug. 18, 1961.

398 "In their scene": United Press, Aug. 4, 1961.

398 " 'CLANSMEN' DELAY PLANE": Associated Press, Aug. 11, 1961.

398 "Peter Lawford is going to ease": Shaw, *Sinatra*, p. 308.

399 A subsequent news photo: United Press, Aug. 9, 1961.

399 From there they would head: Associated Press, Aug. 1, 1961.

399 They would then spend: United Press, Aug. 9, 1961.

399 "I know they are coming": Shaw, *Sinatra*, pp. 294–95.

399 "the 170-foot steam yacht": United Press, Aug. 9, 1961.

400 "SINATRA CRUISE": United Press, Aug. 17, 1961.

401 For forty-eight hours, it seemed: Leaming, *Mrs. Kennedy*, p. 143.

401 But there was another: United Press, Aug. 4, 1961.

401 At its mid-August meeting: *Nevada State Journal*, July 13, 1961.

401 "because it was unpretentious": Nancy Sinatra, *American Legend*, p. 158.

402 "She knew that Frank was leaving": Friedwald, *Sinatra!*, p. 378.

403 "I'm sure his lawyers": Ibid.

403 "the atmosphere was relaxed": Douglas-Home, *Sinatra*, p. 15.

404 "When he did come in": Granata, *Sessions with Sinatra*, p. 149.

404 "That Sinatra still harbored": Ibid., pp. 149–50.

405 "At 11:45, the last playback": Douglas-Home, *Sinatra*, p. 19.

406 He wouldn't return: Granata, *Sessions with Sinatra*, p. 149.

406 "I don't think anyone": Vernon Scott, syndicated column, Aug. 28, 1961.

406 Otto Preminger, had recently: Earl Wilson, syndicated column, Jan. 25, 1961.

406 "Happy birthday, Prez": *Show Business Illustrated*, Sept. 5, 1961.

406 "Almost immediately Jack": Exner, *My Story*, p. 220.

407 "Jack was always so": Kelley, *His Way*, pp. 290–91.

407 "In her view, that was": Leaming, *Mrs. Kennedy*, p. 150.

408 "as a mature, self-possessed": Ibid., p. 146.

408 "which Jackie had once": Ibid., p. 145.

408 "Ordinarily, the *Advise*": Ibid., p. 150.

409 Peter Lawford awaited them: Kelley, *His Way*, p. 292.

409 " 'I have your riding boots' ": Saunders, *Torn Lace Curtain*, pp. 83–84.

409 "The Marlin cruised about": Associated Press, Sept. 24, 1961.

410 "loud and obnoxious": Leaming, *Mrs. Kennedy*, p. 151.

410 "Sinatra's presence at the Cape": Ibid., pp. 149–50.

411 Frank, who'd played: See special-features interview of Axelrod, Frankenheimer, and Sinatra on *The Manchurian Candidate* DVD.

411 "felt that the political": Daniel O'Brien, *Frank Sinatra Film Guide*, p. 143.

411 He'd loved *The Manchurian Candidate*: Capua, *Janet Leigh*, p. 110.

411 "That's great": Daniel O'Brien, *Frank Sinatra Film Guide*, p. 143.

412 "Ever since Prohibition": Navasky, *Kennedy Justice*, p. 46.

412 "JOHNNY: I said": Kuntz and Kuntz, *Sinatra Files*, pp. 152–54.

413 "He says he's got": Ibid., p. 153.

413 "Only Frank could get": Taraborrelli, *Sinatra*, p. 246.

413 "I'm fucking Phyllis": Russo, *Outfit*, p. 423.

414 Guy Pastor: www.imdb.com/name/nm1261248/bio?ref_=nm_ov_bio_sm.

414 She returned only after: Earl Wilson, syndicated column, Sept. 25, 1961.

414 Ava tried phoning: Ibid.

414 "About 1 a.m.": Earl Wilson, syndicated column, Sept. 29, 1961.

414 "Dear Miss Kilgallen": Dorothy Kilgallen, syndicated column, Oct. 14, 1961.
415 "Here's the mother": Earl Wilson, syndicated column, Nov. 8, 1961.
416 "a lot of the songs": Ed O'Brien, e-mail to author, March 24, 2014.
416 "The Chairman had made": Friedwald, *Sinatra!*, p. 381.
416 "a musician's musician": Granata, *Sessions with Sinatra*, p. 162.
416 He was also a legendary: Carmel Malin, in discussion with the author, Jan. 2006; Lee Herschberg, in discussion with the author, May 2006.
416 The studio engineer Lee: Herschberg, discussion.
416 "Costa could write": Malin, discussion.
416 "extremely upset": Levinson, *September in the Rain*, p. 156.
417 "Don Costa was a great": Granata, *Sessions with Sinatra*, p. 162.
417 "Do you know who Don": Friedwald, *Sinatra!*, p. 381.
417 "*Sinatra and Strings*," the arranger: Granata, *Sessions with Sinatra*, p. 162.
417 "Don Costa was among": Ibid.
417 to the tune of $100,000: Erskine Johnson, syndicated column, Dec. 12, 1961.
418 He also liked to carry: Anka, *My Way*, p. 193.
418 "one unusual distinction": Jacobs and Stadiem, *Mr. S*, p. 209.
418 "There was a beef": Nollen, *Jilly!*, p. 30.
418 "A remarkable Chinese": Earl Wilson, syndicated column, March 13, 1961.
418 "the blue Jew": Gay Talese, "Frank Sinatra Has a Cold," *Esquire*, April 1966.
419 And not impressed: Author's interview with confidential source.
419 "Jilly was successful": Nollen, *Jilly!*, p. 33.
419 "One night, somebody": Monty Alexander, in discussion with the author, Jan. 2006.
419 He also was not a drinker: Ibid.
419 in Thailand, the maharaja: Hedda Hopper, syndicated column, Dec. 27, 1961.
419 "agonizing loneliness": Walter Winchell, *Spartanburg (S.C.) Herald-Journal*, Jan. 24, 1962.
420 "serious inasmuch as I was": Shaw, *Sinatra*, p. 301.
420 Sinatra's old nemesis: Lee Mortimer, syndicated column, Jan. 20, 1961.
420 "to induce [Goldstone]": Lee Mortimer, syndicated column, Dec. 30, 1960, and March 6, 1961.
420 "got excited seeing attractive": Earl Wilson, syndicated column, Jan. 4, 1962.
420 "soaking it all up": Saunders, *Torn Lace Curtain*, p. 134.
421 "I was surprised": Ibid.
421 That same month: Shaw, *Sinatra*, p. 308.

CHAPTER 17

422 "Somewhere east of Suez": Santopietro, *Sinatra in Hollywood*, p. 310.
422 "The Clansmen loaf": Knight, *Sinatra*, p. 227.
422 "Sammy Davis' idol worshiping": Earl Wilson, syndicated column, Jan. 4, 1962.
422 When Juliet Prowse returned: Shaw, *Sinatra*, p. 308.
422 "A great girl": James Bacon, syndicated column, Jan. 10, 1962.
423 "I don't believe there's any": Associated Press, Jan. 10, 1962.
423 He produced a diamond: Shaw, *Sinatra*, pp. 301–2.
423 "I don't think Frank will ever": Ibid., p. 302.
423 "a few moments": Earl Wilson, syndicated column, Jan. 18, 1962.
423 "Juliet Prowse will ascend": Earl Wilson, syndicated column, Jan. 15, 1962.
423 "I have no idea": United Press, Jan. 29, 1962.
424 "The word was out": Bob Thomas, syndicated column, Jan. 26, 1962.
424 "merely a marvelous": Dorothy Kilgallen, syndicated column, Jan. 17, 1962.
425 "Irresponsible people": Shaw, *Sinatra*, p. 302.
426 "Those were really something": Friedwald, *Sinatra!*, p. 345; Peter Levinson, in discussion with the author, Feb. 2006.
427 He'd directed adaptations: Roberts, *Great American Playwrights*, p. 403.
427 "the most spectacular": John Crosby, syndicated column, Feb. 13, 1960.
427 "as his first truly personal": Daniel O'Brien, *Frank Sinatra Film Guide*, p. 142.
427 "Without you, we wouldn't": See special-features interview on *Manchurian Candidate* DVD.
428 "rehears[ing] other cast": Santopietro, *Sinatra in Hollywood*, p. 317.
428 "I thought it would be": Nancy Sinatra, *American Legend*, p. 161.
428 He carried it around: Daniel O'Brien, *Frank Sinatra Film Guide*, p. 142.
428 He told everyone who would listen: Nancy Sinatra, *American Legend*, p. 161.
428 "Sinatra treated his fellow": Daniel O'Brien, *Frank Sinatra Film Guide*, p. 145.
428 for a fee of $270,000: Ibid., p. 143.

429 "As Ball aged": Santopietro, *Sinatra in Hollywood*, p. 316.
429 "According to the gossip": Joe Hyams, syndicated column, Herald Tribune News Service, Feb. 10, 1962.
430 "The scene was a two-shot": Ibid.
430 Frank sent Rizzo: Earl Wilson, syndicated column, Feb. 1, 1962.
431 "Instead of putting a thumb": *New York Herald Tribune*, Feb. 21, 1962.
432 "Frank Sinatra and Richard Nixon": Earl Wilson, syndicated column, Feb. 9, 1962.
432 "that, if Sinatra goes through": Hy Gardner, syndicated column, Feb. 4, 1962.
432 "All those who bet": Shaw, *Sinatra*, p. 303.
432 Sammy Davis Jr. even: Ibid.
432 Then, on February 20: *Miami News*, Feb. 22, 1962; Shaw, *Sinatra*, p. 304.
432 "Juliet Prowse and Frank Sinatra today": United Press, Feb. 23, 1962.
433 "Neither will be available": *Miami News*, Feb. 22, 1962.
433 "I don't intend to give up": Ibid.
433 "No tears whatsoever": United Press, Feb. 23, 1962.
433 "Why should she": Shaw, *Sinatra*, p. 304.
433 Meanwhile, according to: Ibid.
433 "Talk about short": *Lakeland (Fla.) Ledger*, Feb. 27, 1962.
433 "Juliet wanted Frank to give up": Shaw, *Sinatra*, p. 304.
433 "Frank Sinatra's pals": Dorothy Kilgallen, syndicated column, March 4, 1962.
433 "I would have married Frank": Shaw, *Sinatra*, pp. 304–5.
433 "an upward spiral": Friedwald, *Biographical Guide to the Great Jazz and Pop Singers*, p. 195.
434 "The inclusion of Frank": Cynthia Lowry, syndicated column, Feb. 26, 1962.
434 "Unfortunately the years": William E. Sarmento, *Lowell (Mass.) Sun*, Feb. 26, 1962.
434 The visit was set: Associated Press, March 23, 1962.
434 as arranged by Peter: Tina Sinatra, *My Father's Daughter*, p. 78.
435 "We worked for weeks": Jacobs and Stadiem, *Mr. S*, p. 163.
435 "The news fed Dad's": Tina Sinatra, *My Father's Daughter*, p. 78.
435 "Bobby, the Puritan": Jacobs and Stadiem, *Mr. S*, p. 163.
436 "simply misread": Brownstein, *The Power and the Glitter*, p. 167.
436 "For Kennedy, the association": Ibid., p. 160.
436 "Sinatra had been at center": Ibid., p. 159.
436 "Frank Sinatra has been asked": United Press, Dec. 1, 1961.
436 "The split came in two": Brownstein, *The Power and the Glitter*, p. 164.
437 "always the bureaucrat": Seymour M. Hersh, *Dark Side of Camelot*, p. 312.
437 "the extraordinary danger": Ibid.
437 "A review of her telephone": Kuntz and Kuntz, *Sinatra Files*, pp. 158–60.
437 She had also made: Kelley, *His Way*, p. 300.
437 "that he had to stop": Seymour M. Hersh, *Dark Side of Camelot*, pp. 312–13.
438 "'What *is* this shit'": Jacobs and Stadiem, *Mr. S*, p. 163.
438 "There was an endless": Ibid.
438 though Tina Sinatra: Tina Sinatra, *My Father's Daughter*, p. 79.
438 "When Jack got out here": Kelley, *His Way*, p. 302.
439 "rubbing salt in a sore": Granata, *Sessions with Sinatra*, p. 150.
439 "remote, affect-less": Ibid.
439 "Sinatra's petulance": Ibid.
440 "was in a snit": Ibid., pp. 150–51.
440 "the Campbell calls": Schlesinger, *Robert Kennedy and His Times*, pp. 494–95.
440 "I saw Jack in March": Exner, *My Story*, p. 252.
440 "Frank Sinatra flew out": Louella Parsons, syndicated column, March 28, 1962.
440 "Had the Kennedys sought": Tina Sinatra, *My Father's Daughter*, p. 79.
441 "Sinatra was a great Democrat": Brownstein, *The Power and the Glitter*, p. 166.
441 "It meant nothing": Ibid.
441 "If he would only pick up the telephone": Schlesinger, *Robert Kennedy and His Times*, p. 496.
411 A couple of months: Peter Edson, syndicated column, June 15, 1962.
411 He would get another: Brownstein, *The Power and the Glitter*, p. 166.
411 "The breach with JFK": Kelley, *His Way*, p. 305.
411 His former publicists: Ibid., p. 304.
442 "Sinatra's humane contribution": Shaw, *Sinatra*, p. 309.
442 "We went all over": Kelley, *His Way*, p. 304.
442 "the largest humanitarian": Friedwald, *Sinatra!*, pp. 384–85.
443 "If it weren't for Neal": *Down Beat*, Nov. 2, 1955.

443 "easy, very easy": Friedwald, *Sinatra!*, p. 403.
444 Besides George Jacobs: Hedda Hopper, syndicated column, April 25, 1962; Kelley, *His Way*, p. 305; Jacobs and Stadiem, *Mr. S*, p. 180.
445 The assemblage didn't: Earl Wilson, syndicated column, April 26, 1962.
445 A UPI telephoto: United Press Telephoto, April 23, 1962.
445 "total lack of curiosity": Jacobs and Stadiem, *Mr. S*, p. 179.
446 "The only cherries": Ibid., p. 183.
446 "tanned and dapper": *Pacific Stars and Stripes*, April 21, 1962.
446 "a living legend": Al Ricketts column, ibid.
447 received a gold key: United Press, April 24, 1962.
447 and had an orphanage: Kelley, *His Way*, p. 304.
447 But he'd underestimated: Jacobs and Stadiem, *Mr. S*, p. 185.
447 "Frank worked especially": Friedwald, *Sinatra!*, p. 391.
447 "'Fucking slant-eye'": Jacobs and Stadiem, *Mr. S*, p. 185.
447 After handing a $17,000: United Press, May 2, 1961.
448 In Nazareth, he laid: United Press, May 7, 1961.
448 Israel, he said: Jacobs and Stadiem, *Mr. S*, pp. 188–89.
448 "seen everywhere": Dorothy Manners, syndicated column, May 17, 1962.
448 "My job was basically": Server, *Ava Gardner*, p. 389.
449 "Ava did not think": Ibid.
449 "Some like the perfume": Emil Richards, in discussion with the author, June 2011.
449 Bill Miller considered the first: Giuseppe Marcucci, interactive biodiscography, *Where or When: The Definitive Sinatra Database*.
449 "his favorite of all": Jacobs and Stadiem, *Mr. S*, p. 189.
449 "He called all of us": Richards, discussion.
450 "I look out, and there's Frank": Ibid.
450 In 1961, the Joint Civic: http://onlinelibrary.wiley.com/store/10.1111/j.2050-411X.1996.tb00141.x/asset/j.2050-411X.1996.tb00141.x.pdf?v=1&t=i9ack6gq&s=f113c9669853a566eb36e52a4a4c43aaa402bd78.
450 "The switch is": Dorothy Manners, syndicated column, June 19, 1962.
450 A planned album: Marcucci, *Where or When*.
450 "Ava, Ava": Jacobs and Stadiem, *Mr. S*, p. 191.
451 "I'm-a have a little": Recording of May 26, 1962, Milan concert.
451 "Thank you very much": Recording of May 30, 1962, London concert.
451 "the height of professionalism": Friedwald, *Sinatra!*, p. 390.
452 "Ol' Man River," too: Wilder, *American Popular Song*, p. 56.
452 "Sinatra needed 'Ol' Man River'": Decker, *Who Should Sing "Ol' Man River"?*, p. 188.

CHAPTER 18

454 "he had next to nothing": Friedwald, *Sinatra!*, p. 390.
454 "We had our most fun": Jacobs and Stadiem, *Mr. S*, pp. 192–93.
454 Like Billy May: Clarke, *Penguin Encyclopedia of Popular Music*, p. 409.
454 "the greatest writer": Ibid.
454 "big disc plans": Friedwald, *Sinatra!*, p. 392.
454 whose head of A&R: Lewisohn, *Tune In*, p. 589.
454 "on the evening of June 12": Friedwald, *Sinatra!*, pp. 395–96.
455 "This tea I drink": Private recording of June 1, 1962, Royal Festival Hall concert.
455 "Damn, we gotta sleep": Private recording of *Sinatra Sings Great Songs from Great Britain* outtakes.
455 "He was finding it": Friedwald, *Sinatra!*, pp. 396–97.
456 While the arranger was: Levinson, *September in the Rain*, p. 206.
456 Riddle had been part: United Press, June 2, 1962.
456 "Frank was in a good": Earl Wilson, syndicated column, June 21, 1962.
456 "I wish it was five": Kelley, *His Way*, p. 306.
457 "I found out a lot": Associated Press, June 20, 1962.
457 "It was windy": Associated Press, June 18, 1962.
457 By the first quarter: Cornyn, *Exploding*, p. 51.
457 "offered its entire Sinatra": Ibid.
457 "that Reprise artists": Ibid., p. 49.
458 "Cronies aside": Ibid., p. 50.
458 "The only thing that was meaningful": Ibid.
458 "The bands that I loved": Crystal, *700 Sundays*, pp. 112–13.

458 "Frank actually forbade": Mo Ostin, in discussion with the author, Aug. 2012.

459 "dealer demands that Reprise": Shaw, *Sinatra*, p. 311.

459 Her chaos had proved: Jacobs and Stadiem, *Mr. S*, p. 171.

459 "Well, it wasn't a big thing": Leaming, *Marilyn Monroe*, p. 403.

459 despite the insistences: Seymour M. Hersh, *Dark Side of Camelot*, p. 104.

459 Their third meeting: Spoto, *Marilyn Monroe*, pp. 486–87.

459 "She spent the night": Leaming, *Marilyn Monroe*, p. 403.

459 The singularity of the occasion: Ibid.; Michael O'Brien, *John F. Kennedy*, p. 697.

460 "Thank you. I can now retire": Reeves, *President Kennedy*, p. 315.

460 "We were all moths": Schlesinger, *Robert Kennedy and His Times*, pp. 590–91.

460 Concerned that her over-the-top: Leaming, *Marilyn Monroe*, p. 411.

461 On June 9, the same day: Associated Press, June 9, 1962.

461 "It's sad, but no studio": Ibid.

462 "a pawn—an interesting": Spoto, *Marilyn Monroe*, p. 535.

462 Shortly after she was fired: United Press, June 11, 1962.

462 "Frankly, I don't know": United Press, June 18, 1962.

462 "In the meantime": David Lewin, dispatch, July 18, 1962.

462 "Lying [expletive]!": Kuntz and Kuntz, *Sinatra Files*, p. 156.

462 "Let's show 'em": Kelley, *His Way*, p. 329.

463 "Once I got $1,750,000": Ibid., p. 313.

463 But apparently Giancana: Van Meter, *Last Good Time*, p. 186.

463 Skinny D'Amato was wiretapped: Kelley, *His Way*, p. 312.

463 an I. Magnin clothing: Van Meter, *Last Good Time*, p. 183.

463 "a completely new swank": *Nevada State Journal*, June 23, 1962.

463 The piece did not mention: Van Meter, *Last Good Time*, p. 184.

463 "I am going to get": Kelley, *His Way*, p. 313.

464 "help improve local roads": Nancy Sinatra, *American Legend*, p. 158.

464 if not, as some have asserted: Jacobs and Stadiem, *Mr. S*, p. 176.

464 "The dawn mists": Associated Press, July 15, 1962.

464 "They'd call up and tell": Summers and Swan, *Sinatra*, p. 289.

465 "Frank Sinatra's first business venture": *Variety*, July 11, 1962.

465 "The shapely South African": James Bacon, dispatch, July 2, 1962.

465 "Everything's wonderful": Hedda Hopper, syndicated column, June 14, 1962.

465 sneaking in by helicopter: Summers and Swan, *Sinatra*, p. 290.

466 In retaliation, Sinatra: Kelley, *His Way*, pp. 314–15; Van Meter, *Last Good Time*, p. 186.

466 a maroon convertible: *Nevada State Journal*, July 19, 1962.

467 "with his curiosity": Schlesinger, *Robert Kennedy and His Times*, p. 591.

467 "You can't not hear": Cramer, *Joe DiMaggio*, p. 404.

467 "Marilyn Monroe is a soldier": Ibid., pp. 404–5.

467 "near-verbatim" transcript: Hersh, *The Dark Side of Camelot*, pp. 103–4.

468 a combination of tranquilizers: Cramer, *Joe DiMaggio*, p. 402.

468 Engelberg, too, had: Spoto, *Marilyn Monroe*, pp. 537–46.

468 "Frank is a very, very": Taraborrelli, *Sinatra*, p. 272.

468 *Variety* places the Lawfords: *Variety*, July 24, 1962.

468 And while Joe DiMaggio: Associated Press, July 29, 1962.

468 Newspaper accounts confirm: Dorothy Kilgallen, syndicated column, July 27, 1962.

468 a former Cal-Neva bell captain: Van Meter, *Last Good Time*, p. 190.

469 "If the guy don't want": Taraborrelli, *Sinatra*, p. 273.

469 "Mr. Sinatra wanted a special": Ibid., p. 272.

469 "when Frank saw Marilyn": Ibid.

469 "scurrilous and unfounded": Spoto, *Marilyn Monroe*, p. 548.

469 "We need coffee": Taraborrelli, *Sinatra*, p. 272.

469 "I did see Frank briefly": Kelley, *His Way*, p. 329.

470 Woodfield said that Sinatra: Summers and Swan, *Sinatra*, p. 290.

470 "I was in Lake Tahoe": Spoto, *Marilyn Monroe*, p. 549.

470 "she could have a crisis": Taraborrelli, *Sinatra*, p. 272.

470 "Marilyn and Joe planned": Spoto, *Marilyn Monroe*, p. 549.

470 It's most likely that he proposed: Wire photograph, July 26, 1962.

470 "She seemed to him": Spoto, *Marilyn Monroe*, p. 547.

471 "He felt that if she were": Taraborrelli, *Sinatra*, p. 275.

471 "Yeah, Frank wanted to": Ibid.

471 "She was a toy": Cramer, *Joe DiMaggio*, p. 405.

471 "Bobby Kennedy was the one": Ibid., p. 415.

471 "people who had served": Ibid., p. 417.

471 who had been the last: Spoto, *Marilyn Monroe*, p. 571.

471 "I'm shocked": James Bacon, dispatch, Aug. 9, 1962.

472 Marilyn's friend Inez Melson: Cramer, *Joe DiMaggio*, p. 418; Summers and Swan, *Sinatra*, p. 311.

472 "Tell them," DiMaggio said: Cramer, *Joe DiMaggio*, p. 418.

472 Joe E. Lewis, a strangely: *Nevada State Journal*, June 23, 1962.

473 Yet though businessmen: *Petersburg (Va.) Progress Index*, Aug. 6, 1962.

473 "His liaison with Judith Campbell": Seymour M. Hersh, *Dark Side of Camelot*, p. 344.

473 What's more, though any: Kuntz and Kuntz, *Sinatra Files*, p. 166.

473 "He handed me the camera": United Press, Aug. 14, 1962.

474 It had been a "guy": United Press, Aug. 15, 1962.

474 Three days later: Associated Press, Aug. 18, 1962.

474 who later settled: Associated Press, March 13, 1964.

474 "well over $1 million": Nancy Sinatra, *American Legend*, p. 166.

474 In Sanicola's version: Freedland, *All the Way*, p. 299.

474 "I was seventeen then": Douglas-Home, *Sinatra*, p. 22.

475 Suddenly stray: Dorothy Kilgallen, syndicated column, April 26, 1962.

476 "for two-fold purposes": Kuntz and Kuntz, *Sinatra Files*, pp. 169–70.

476 "While conducting inquiry": Ibid., p. 167.

476 "The nature of [the call]": Ibid.

476 On the final evening: Van Meter, *Last Good Time*, p. 193.

476 On a recording: Private recording of Aug. 25, 1962, 500 Club show.

477 "Frank and his entourage": Van Meter, *Last Good Time*, p. 194.

477 And the week—between: *Variety*, Aug. 29, 1962.

477 "It is the belief of": *Uniontown Morning Herald*, Aug. 29, 1962.

479 "The 28-year-old association": *Variety*, Sept. 18, 1962.

479 "I didn't care for it": Lewisohn, *Tune In*, p. 731.

480 Nancy Sinatra, wanting to give: Daniel O'Brien, *Frank Sinatra Film Guide*, p. 150; Kelley, *His Way*, p. 333.

480 "I certainly didn't approach": Bud Yorkin, in discussion with the author, Feb. 2006.

480 "Frank came and sat down": Ibid.

483 "I was confused": MacLaine, *My Lucky Stars*, p. 68.

483 "At 3:16 AM": Kuntz and Kuntz, *Sinatra Files*, pp. 170–71.

484 "I've waited twenty years": Friedwald, *Sinatra!*, p. 404.

484 "would be a bad musical marriage": Ed O'Brien, *Sinatra 101*, p. 128.

484 But the truth of the matter: Will Friedwald, in discussion with the author, Feb. 2015.

484 "If I could put together": Friedwald, *Sinatra!*, p. 405.

484 "Frank Sinatra, on a fast visit": Earl Wilson, syndicated column, Sept. 20, 1962.

485 "Using a double only": Daniel O'Brien, *Frank Sinatra Film Guide*, p. 145.

485 The ability to grip: Winspur and Parry, *The Musician's Hand*, pp. 77–80.

485 "I thought this might": Santopietro, *Sinatra in Hollywood*, p. 327.

485 "Following his own acting": Ibid.

486 "Every once in a rare": Ibid.

487 "The picture is really fascinating": Ringgold and McCarty, *Films of Frank Sinatra*, p. 187.

488 Frank's daughter Nancy remembered: Nancy Sinatra, *My Father*, p. 185.

489 "Dad flew in and met": Tina Sinatra, *My Father's Daughter*, pp. 95–96.

489 "I don't know how": Freedland, *All the Way*, p. 285.

489 "On the set": Louella Parsons, syndicated column, Oct. 29, 1962.

489 "It was low-key": Tony Bill, in discussion with the author, May 2006.

491 In the 1920s, it had been: Sengstock, *That Toddlin' Town*, p. 144.

491 It was the kind of place: United Press, Feb. 12, 1961.

491 Giancana was a part owner: Levy, *Rat Pack Confidential*, p. 227.

491 some reports said as much: Taraborrelli, *Sinatra*, p. 277.

491 "I was singing": Ibid., p. 278.

491 "That Frank, he wants more": Kuntz and Kuntz, *Sinatra Files*, p. 168.

492 In the meantime, more: Sheilah Graham, syndicated column, Nov. 2, 1962; Ed Sullivan, syndicated column, Dec. 5, 1962.

492 "Because a friend asked me": Taraborrelli, *Sinatra*, p. 278.

492 "who himself owed Mooney": Ibid.

492 and the showroom, in which: Don MacLean, syndicated column, Dec. 8, 1962.

492 "Lines snaked around": Levy, *Rat Pack Confidential*, pp. 228–29.

492 But Giancana made his real money: Kelley, *His Way*, p. 296.

493 Matty Malneck, the composer: Marcucci, *Where or When*.
493 The two had become deeply: Seymour M. Hersh, *Dark Side of Camelot*, p. 323.
493 "Baby, that's a very good": Kelley, *His Way*, p. 297.
494 On the third, just before: Shaw, *Sinatra*, p. 314.
494 FBI wiretaps later: Ibid., p. 298; Levy, *Rat Pack Confidential*, p. 230.
494 "Good thing Peter": Sheilah Graham, syndicated column, Dec. 11, 1962.

CHAPTER 19

495 "Do you remember me": Server, *Ava Gardner*, pp. 404–5.
496 "Ava Gardner and Yves Montand": Walter Winchell, syndicated column, Jan. 16, 1963.
496 "We stayed at a villa": Server, *Ava Gardner*, p. 406.
496 "The hospital didn't disclose": Associated Press, Jan. 21, 1963.
496 On February 3: *Long Beach (Calif.) Independent Press-Telegram*, Feb. 3, 1963.
496 On January 1: *San Mateo (Calif.) Times*, Jan. 1, 1963.
497 At the end of the first week: *Parade*, Dec. 9, 1962.
498 He'd come east: United Press, Feb. 11, 1963; Kelley, *His Way*, p. 309.
498 she had a disconcerting: Author interview with confidential source.
498 "She was a pisser": MacLaine, *My Lucky Stars*, p. 85.
498 "I remember Dolly": Tina Sinatra, *My Father's Daughter*, p. 73.
498 "For the [parents]": *New Castle (Del.) News*, Feb. 11, 1963.
499 "I've never heard": Jacobs and Stadiem, *Mr. S*, pp. 120–21.
499 Frank had left the invitation: Kelley, *His Way*, pp. 309–10; also see Kaplan, *Frank*, pp. 23–24.
499 "My son is like me": Kelley, *His Way*, p. 310.
499 "Everything happens to Frank": Earl Wilson, syndicated column, Feb. 14, 1963.
499 "Ava Gardner has become": Earl Wilson, syndicated column, Feb. 18, 1963.
499 "Ava Gardner, hair straight": Earl Wilson, syndicated column, Feb. 20, 1963.
499 "Ava Gardner and Peter Duchin": Earl Wilson, syndicated column, Feb. 25, 1963.
500 Frank junior says there were: Nancy Sinatra, *American Legend*, p. 170.
500 "as a kind of work therapy": Friedwald, *Sinatra!*, p. 261.
501 "on 35-millimeter": Will Friedwald, in discussion with the author, July 2014.
501 "it was such an incredibly": Levinson, *September in the Rain*, p. 154.
501 "The Reprise version": Friedwald, *Sinatra!*, p. 328.
501 "the worst possible time": Tina Sinatra, *My Father's Daughter*, p. 70.
501 "cute, smart, and funny": Ibid., pp. 71–72.
502 "They shared a certain": Ibid., pp. 73–74.
502 He was packed off: Ibid., p. 81.
502 "Until September 1958": Shaw, *Sinatra*, p. 322.
502 But that summer: Associated Press, July 30, 1962.
502 "If my son is going": Louella Parsons, syndicated column, Oct. 9, 1962.
503 "He's more of an actor": Associated Press, Dec. 23, 1962.
503 a ghost band: Levinson, *Dorsey*, p. 309.
503 "Mike was absolutely": Mo Ostin, in discussion with the author, Aug. 2012.
504 "I used to go to have": Mike Shore, in discussion with the author, Jan. 2007.
504 "Sinatra said, 'I don't want'": Ibid.
505 "PLAYBOY: Many explanations": *Playboy*, Feb. 1963.
506 ABC's cameras were: Cynthia Lowry, syndicated column, April 9, 1963.
506 "a little lecture in show biz": Ibid.
507 "Before we get on": https://www.youtube.com/watch?v=T8vnDMyQcfo.
507 "Frank Sinatra sold": Hedda Hopper, syndicated column, April 16, 1963.
508 "consolation prize": Jacobs and Stadiem, *Mr. S*, p. 157.
508 And second, Betsy: Betsy Duncan Hammes, in discussion with the author, June 2011.
508 "I had some sugar cubes": Ibid.
509 a new toy: Sun Lakes Aero Club, "Frank Sinatra and His Lear Jet N175FS," www
     .sunlakesaeroclub.org/updates_web_data/081231/Sinatra.htm.
509 and a Hughes 269A: Jimmy Van Heusen, private memoir.
509 He had also just bought: Earl Wilson, syndicated column, Dec. 11, 1962.
509 "Every time Frankie spits": Associated Press, Jan. 10, 1962.
509 "If you approve one": Ibid.
509 "not more than 35": Ibid.
510 As Friedwald points out: Friedwald, *Sinatra!*, p. 260.
510 Bernhart had a soundtrack-recording: Ibid.
511 "They put a tiny turd": Berg, *Goldwyn*, p. 473.

511 "Both RUDIN": Kuntz and Kuntz, *Sinatra Files*, p. 181.
511 But after the FBI reviewed: Ibid., pp. 182–83.
511 "The Los Angeles Division": Ibid., pp. 184–85.
512 "TO: SAC": Ibid., p. 186.
513 "After going at top": Bob Thomas, syndicated column, May 1, 1963.
513 "HOTELS AND RESTAURANTS": FBI file on Giancana.
514 Warner Bros. had offered: Leonard Lyons, syndicated column, April 19, 1963.
514 "needs the power not": http://www.imdb.com/name/nm0000736/bio.
514 "Sinatra, tanned and rested": Hedda Hopper, syndicated column, June 14, 1963.
514 "Out for a good time": Daniel O'Brien, *Frank Sinatra Film Guide*, p. 154.
515 "She's back, and I'm": Taraborrelli, *Sinatra*, p. 282.
515 "It's on. All the way": Server, *Ava Gardner*, p. 408.
515 "Ava had met the fierce": Ibid., pp. 408–9.
515 "These creeps are going": Taraborrelli, *Sinatra*, p. 282.
516 "We had a great time": Kelley, *His Way*, p. 317.
516 "So when are you two": Server, *Ava Gardner*, p. 409.
516 the twenty-one-year-old sensation: *Lowell (Mass.) Sun*, June 9, 1963.
516 "got into the worst fight": Kelley, *His Way*, p. 317.
516 Frank, being Frank: Earl Wilson, syndicated column, June 14, 1963.
517 Frank strove to please: Ibid.
517 "never liked women": Taraborrelli, *Sinatra*, p. 226.
517 "Sam didn't like her": Kelley, *His Way*, p. 318.
517 "This was more than Frank": Taraborrelli, *Sinatra*, p. 283.
518 "Buddy boy": Server, *Ava Gardner*, p. 410.
518 "Suddenly," a witness recalled: Kelley, *His Way*, p. 318.
518 "that while GIANCANA": FBI file on Giancana, CG 92-349.
518 "Why don't you fucks": Kelley, *His Way*, p. 316.
518 "We have learned": Kuntz and Kuntz, *Sinatra Files*, pp. 186–87.
519 "If Bobby Kennedy wants": Kelley, *His Way*, p. 316.
519 But unknown to Giancana: Schlesinger, *Robert Kennedy and His Times*, pp. 496–97.
519 The grounds: the agency: Giancana and Giancana, *Double Cross*, pp. 321–22.
519 "SAD TALE": Van Meter, *Last Good Time*, p. 195.
519 "that the G-men were": United Press, July 1, 1963.
520 "detailing every aspect": Giancana and Giancana, *Double Cross*, p. 322.
520 And the FBI car: United Press, July 16, 1963.
520 "[Redacted] furnished": Kuntz and Kuntz, *Sinatra Files*, p. 187.
522 "much to the consternation": Ibid.
522 On July 19: *Oakland Tribune*, July 19 and 21, 1963.
522 "Most of the time": *Life*, Sept. 27, 1963.
522 Kitty Kelley writes: Kelley, *His Way*, p. 319.
522 Soon, in any case: Giancana and Giancana, *Double Cross*, p. 322.
522 "[Redacted] advised": Kuntz and Kuntz, *Sinatra Files*, pp. 187–88.
523 "Sam came charging": Kelley, *His Way*, pp. 319–20.
523 "Phyllis was pounding": Jacobs and Stadiem, *Mr. S*, pp. 202–3.
523 Someone called the police: Kuntz and Kuntz, *Sinatra Files*, p. 188; Kelley, *His Way*, p. 320.
524 "I call it a wonderful": Don Alpert, syndicated column, July 22, 1963.
524 The altercation in Chalet 50: "Edward A. Olsen," University of Nevada Oral History Archive, http://contentdm.library.unr.edu/cdm/ref/collection/unohp/id/2517, p. 159.

CHAPTER 20

527 By early 1963: Bowen, *Rough Mix*, p. 86.
527 "I finally went to Frank": Mo Ostin, in discussion with the author, Aug. 2012.
527 "Giving up on Reprise": Cornyn, *Exploding*, p. 52.
527 "It was a gamble": Ibid., p. 51.
527 And the label's roster: Ibid.
527 Dean Martin was down: Bowen, *Rough Mix*, p. 86.
528 the man who had first brought: Friedwald, *Sinatra!*, p. 214.
528 Burke would also work: Cornyn, *Exploding*, p. 51.
528 Nitzsche had a Top 10: *Van Nuys (Calif.) News*, Aug. 16, 1963.
528 And then there was: http://www.allmusic.com/album/trini-lopez-at-pjs-mw0000591232.
528 "It was a huge picture": Ostin, discussion.
528 "Because Mickey knew": Ibid.

529 "Draft one of the deal": Cornyn, *Exploding*, p. 52.

529 "A startled Ostin": Ibid., p. 53.

529 "Mickey, it was known": Ibid.

529 "That turned out to be": Ibid., p. 132.

529 "Selling his two-thirds": Ibid., pp. 53–54.

530 "SINATRA NAMED WB": *Variety*, Aug. 7, 1963.

530 He carried it around: Jacobs and Stadiem, *Mr. S*, p. 204.

530 "This is what I call": Kelley, *His Way*, p. 324.

530 "Jack went crazy": Ibid., pp. 324–25.

531 "Since there has been": Ibid., p. 325.

531 On the advice: Van Meter, *Last Good Time*, p. 196.

531 "Everybody had a short": Olsen oral history.

532 As a result of a childhood: Ibid.

532 "We interviewed him": Ibid.

533 Frank sat ringside: Walter Winchell, syndicated column, Aug. 16, 1963.

533 "I'm so nervous": *Life*, Aug. 23, 1963.

533 The place was packed: United Press, Aug. 9, 1963; *Variety*, Aug. 14, 1963.

533 "It's obviously good": *Variety*, Aug. 14, 1963.

533 "I'm very proud": United Press, Aug. 9, 1963.

533 "he had charge accounts": Jacobs and Stadiem, *Mr. S*, p. 207.

533 "That huge seashore": Dorothy Kilgallen, syndicated column, July 14, 1963.

534 "The new Sinatra sound": *Life*, Aug. 23, 1963.

535 "red-carpet treatment": United Press, Aug. 30, 1963.

535 "Sinatra's attorney, a very charming": Olsen oral history.

535 "There's no truth": Kelley, *His Way*, p. 321.

535 "conducted very": United Press, Aug. 30, 1963.

536 "Hancock opened the conversation": Olsen oral history.

536 Grandly, Sinatra suggested: Ibid.

536 "To describe him": Ibid.

537 "Throw the dirty": Ibid.

537 "Here's one for each": Ibid.

538 "Skinny tried to grease": Van Meter, *Last Good Time*, p. 199.

538 "Well, that was just": Olsen oral history.

538 "This was the last thing": Ibid.

538 On Thursday night: Marcucci, *Where or When*.

539 Twelve reels of tape: O'Brien and Sayers, *Sinatra*, p. 113.

539 Jackie Gleason was there: Earl Wilson, syndicated column, Sept. 13, 1963; Jacobs and Stadiem, *Mr. S*, p. 207.

539 "He is handicapped": *Variety*, Sept. 11, 1963.

539 "I spoke to Dad": Shaw, *Sinatra*, p. 321.

540 "sojourned to Chalet No. 50": Ibid.

540 "all hell broke loose": Olsen oral history.

541 "Italian-Americans Make": George E. Sokolsky, syndicated column, July 22, 1959.

541 "Trouble, trouble": *Arizona Republic*, Sept. 12, 1963.

541 "Sinatra has 15 days": Associated Press, Sept. 12, 1963.

541 "Sinatra being the national": Olsen oral history.

542 "If I'm ever roasted": Ibid.

542 "I cannot think of any": Kelley, *His Way*, p. 322.

542 "I'm going to kick": Shaw, *Sinatra*, p. 322.

542 "the great uplifter": Ibid., pp. 322–23.

543 "Anybody want to buy": Kelley, *His Way*, p. 323.

543 "There are legal brains": Earl Wilson, syndicated column, Sept. 18, 1963.

543 "What the local gambling": Shaw, *Sinatra*, p. 323.

543 "I don't think it should": Wilson, syndicated column, Sept. 18, 1963.

543 At the end of September: Associated Press, Sept. 30, 1963.

543 "Aren't you people being": Olsen oral history.

543 "Now, that's about the highest": Ibid.

543 The lawyer later told Nancy: Nancy Sinatra, *My Father*, p. 168.

544 He had come well prepared: Olsen oral history.

544 In the midst of the proceedings: Nancy Sinatra, *My Father*, p. 168.

544 "because the investigation was": Ibid.

544 "not only as an entertainer": Ibid.

544 "Even this enforced": *Variety*, Oct. 9, 1963.

545 In the case of his 50 percent: Ibid.
545 "his dream, Cal-Neva": Nancy Sinatra, *American Legend,* p. 176.
545 "That fucker shouldn't": Van Meter, *Last Good Time,* p. 201.
545 "called Ed Olsen a cripple": Kelley, *His Way,* p. 323.
545 "That bastard": Ibid., p. 327.
545 "Mr. S never met": Jacobs and Stadiem, *Mr. S,* p. 204.
546 "And Davis looks at me": Olsen oral history.
547 "The press, of course, had": Nancy Sinatra, *My Father,* p. 168.
547 Kelly, whose phone wasn't: Ibid., p. 156.
547 "The reason isn't too hard": Dorothy Kilgallen, syndicated column, Oct. 21, 1963.
548 "I wasn't making any decisions": Shaw, *Sinatra,* p. 329.
548 the three-picture deal: Louis Sobol, syndicated column, Nov. 24, 1963.
548 Dean played Robbo's: Daniel O'Brien, *Frank Sinatra Film Guide,* p. 157.
549 Production began on Halloween: Ibid., p. 158.
549 then shifted to the busy: *Colorado Springs Gazette Telegraph,* Nov. 16, 1963.
549 The only hint of tension: Daniel O'Brien, *Frank Sinatra Film Guide,* p. 158.
549 On his audio commentary: Santopietro, *Sinatra in Hollywood,* p. 347.
549 Her father was stunned: Nancy Sinatra, *American Legend,* p. 178.
549 "Let's shoot this thing": Nancy Sinatra, *My Father,* p. 171.
549 Gordon Douglas shot nine: Levy, *Rat Pack Confidential,* p. 259.
550 "Casino execs reported": *Variety,* Nov. 27, 1963.
550 Sinatra and George Jacobs retreated: Nancy Sinatra, *American Legend,* p. 178.
550 "he holed up": Jacobs and Stadiem, *Mr. S,* p. 205.
550 "Frank was pretty broken up": Kelley, *His Way,* p. 328.
550 The Hollywood trade papers: Daniel O'Brien, *Frank Sinatra Film Guide,* p. 158.
551 Nancy senior did: Tina Sinatra, *My Father's Daughter,* p. 97.
551 "Thanksgiving was a jovial": Ibid.
552 As a student: Dean Torrence, in discussion with the author, July 2013.
552 By age twenty-one: "205: Plan B," *This American Life,* www.thisamericanlife.org/radio
    -archives/episode/205/transcript.
553 "Not here": Wilson, *Sinatra,* pp. 200–201; Taraborrelli, *Sinatra,* pp. 297–98.
554 He left not realizing: "205: Plan B."
554 "Good Lord, Rona": Taraborrelli, *Sinatra,* p. 299.
554 "I got no comment": Ibid., pp. 299–300.
554 along with Mickey Rudin: Ibid., p. 300.
555 Both men said: United Press, Dec. 11, 1963.
555 "Please. Don't do": Ibid.
555 The pair were presumed: Associated Press, Dec. 9, 1963.
555 "Sinatra is ready": *Nevada State Journal,* Dec. 11, 1963.
556 Many years later: Summers and Swan, *Sinatra,* p. 293.
556 "God talked to me": "205: Plan B."
556 He also planned to tithe: Torrence, discussion.
556 "Since I was going to have": "205: Plan B."
556 "And just imagining": Ibid.
556 "It would bring father": Ibid.
557 "No. Fuck you": Taraborrelli, *Sinatra,* pp. 303–4.
557 "He asked me if I'd turned": Torrence, discussion.
557 Barry Keenan and Joe Amsler: Ibid.
557 "Is this Frank Sinatra": Taraborrelli, *Sinatra,* p. 304.
558 "The development apparently": United Press, Dec. 10, 1963.
558 "Hello, Dad": Taraborrelli, *Sinatra,* p. 304.
558 The FBI agents had already: Torrence, discussion.
558 "I don't understand why you": Taraborrelli, *Sinatra,* p. 305.
559 "Frank was shaken": Ibid.
559 In the interim: Nancy Sinatra, *My Father,* p. 175.
559 "So, you know, Frank": "205: Plan B."
560 "That's exactly what": Ibid.; Taraborrelli, *Sinatra,* p. 311.
560 "She was very upset": Server, *Ava Gardner,* pp. 429–30.
560 The FBI agreed: Tina Sinatra, *My Father's Daughter,* p. 105.
561 In the meantime, Sinatra: Wilson, *Sinatra,* p. 204.
561 Hart and his staff: Taraborrelli, *Sinatra,* p. 311.
561 Hart took the money: Nancy Sinatra, *My Father,* p. 176; Tina Sinatra, *My Father's Daughter,*
    p. 106.

561 "a mix of barely contained": Tina Sinatra, *My Father's Daughter*, p. 100.
561 "had refused any sedatives": Ibid., p. 103.
561 At 9:26 p.m.: Nancy Sinatra, *My Father*, p. 176.
561 This time, Irwin directed: Tina Sinatra, *My Father's Daughter*, p. 106.
562 "This is John Adams": Associated Press, Feb. 21, 1964.
562 Junior wasn't with him: Nancy Sinatra, *American Legend*, p. 181.
562 The kidnapper then directed: Wilson, *Sinatra*, p. 205.
562 Texaco station: Associated Press, Feb. 21, 1969.
562 As a squad of FBI: Nancy Sinatra, *American Legend*, p. 181.
562 When Keenan called John Irwin: Taraborrelli, *Sinatra*, p. 306.
562 When Irwin told him: Nancy Sinatra, *My Father*, p. 176.
563 "Junior was now highly": Taraborrelli, *Sinatra*, p. 306.
563 "Something has gone wrong": Ibid.
563 "I'm going to bring": Tina Sinatra, *My Father's Daughter*, p. 106.
563 "I cried the whole way": Taraborrelli, *Sinatra*, p. 307.
563 "When I got back": Ibid.
564 "the look on his face": Tina Sinatra, *My Father's Daughter*, p. 107.
564 Heading south from Canoga: Ibid.
564 In his agitated state: Taraborrelli, *Sinatra*, p. 308.
564 Every time a car: Ibid.
564 Everyone who had read: Wilson, *Sinatra*, p. 205; United Press, Dec. 11, 1963.
564 "Call Bobby Kennedy!": Taraborrelli, *Sinatra*, p. 308.
565 "Any news yet": United Press, Dec. 11, 1963.
565 "Mrs. Sinatra": Taraborrelli, *Sinatra*, p. 308.
565 "Hi, Ma": Ibid.
565 "Tomorrow is my birthday": United Press, Dec. 11, 1963.
565 "Frankie wolfed down": Tina Sinatra, *My Father's Daughter*, p. 108.
566 "It was a big bag": Torrence, discussion.
566 "My brother broke open": Nancy Sinatra, *My Father*, p. 179.
566 Keenan claimed they beat: Taraborrelli, *Sinatra*, p. 310.
567 "The next day, the police": Torrence, discussion.
567 "Virtually everything I had": Taraborrelli, *Sinatra*, pp. 308–9.
567 "Thank God it's over": Wilson, *Sinatra*, p. 208.
567 He traded repartee: Associated Press, Dec. 16, 1963.
567 "Do you know why": Kelley, *His Way*, p. 331.

CHAPTER 21

568 "Our world felt": Tina Sinatra, *My Father's Daughter*, pp. 108–9.
568 "Dear Frank": Nancy Sinatra, *American Legend*, p. 183.
570 While he was placing: Associated Press, Jan. 20, 1964.
570 As Osborne re-explained: Associated Press, Jan. 20, 1964; Associated Press wirephoto, Jan. 21, 1964.
570 "I guess I overestimated": United Press, Jan. 20, 1964.
570 Jack Warner had tried: Roger Fristoe, "Calamity Jane," www.tcm.com/this-month/article .html?isPreview=&id=966029%7C628438&name=Calamity-Jane.
571 "I hate that fucking song": Furia, *Skylark*, p. 220.
571 "Moon River" was a late: Ibid.
572 "several hundred screaming": Lewisohn, *Complete Beatles Chronicle*, pp. 92–93.
572 "It's anybody's guess": https://www.youtube.com/watch?v=SY9P0R7-XGA.
573 "It was 'I Want to Hold Your Hand'": *Billboard*, May 4, 1974.
573 "4 for Texas . . . is one": *Time*, Jan. 10, 1964.
574 "behaves like a pasha": *New York Times*, Dec. 26, 1963.
574 to gild the lily: Louella Parsons, syndicated column, Jan. 14, 1964.
574 "He knew that if anything": Taraborrelli, *Sinatra*, pp. 309–10.
574 "He missed Sam Giancana": Jacobs and Stadiem, *Mr. S*, p. 209.
574 "Café owner Jilly": Earl Wilson, syndicated column, June 20, 1963.
575 "You may have seen": Walter Winchell, syndicated column, June 23, 1963.
575 "His speech was right out of": Jacobs and Stadiem, *Mr. S*, pp. 209–10.
575 "Frank was a lonely guy": Monty Alexander, in discussion with the author, Jan. 2006.
575 "I liked Jilly": Betsy Hammes, in discussion with the author, June 2011.
576 namely his father's: Earl Wilson, syndicated column, Jan. 11, 1964; Louis Sobol, syndicated column, Jan. 21, 1964.

577 It would stay there: Bronson, *Billboard Book of Number One Hits*, p. 143.
577 he could fly there: Hedda Hopper, syndicated column, Feb. 12, 1964.
577 "The attendant publicity": *Variety*, Jan. 15, 1964.
577 "FRANKIE JR.": Associated Press, Dec. 22, 1963.
578 "I was in jail": Taraborrelli, *Sinatra*, p. 311.
578 Keenan was represented: United Press, Feb. 12, 1964.
578 "This was a planned contractual": Ibid.
578 "An apple doesn't fall far": Ibid.
578 "There is a vacant seat": Associated Press, Feb. 12, 1964.
578 "cut two million": United Press, Feb. 12, 1964.
578 "There are a lot of kids": *Variety*, Jan. 15, 1964.
579 "The Beatles looked like": Associated Press, Feb. 13, 1964.
579 On Friday the fourteenth: *Titusville (Md.) Herald*, Feb. 15, 1964.
579 "Because, Mrs. Root": Associated Press, Feb. 15, 1964.
579 "Indeed," Mrs. Root said: United Press, Feb. 15, 1964.
579 "SINATRA JR. DESPERATELY": *Los Angeles Times*, Feb. 16, 1964.
579 "From now on, I'm working": Associated Press, Feb. 18, 1964.
580 "I'm afraid I made up": United Press, Feb. 25, 1964.
580 "I didn't want to get killed": Associated Press, Feb. 29, 1964.
580 "This is the strangest": United Press, March 7, 1964.
580 Judge East handed: Ibid.; Associated Press, March 9, 1964.
581 Irwin would eventually: Taraborrelli, *Sinatra*, p. 313.
581 All three were remanded: Associated Press, March 9, 1964.
581 "The report that came back": Taraborrelli, *Sinatra*, p. 313.
581 According to a former servant: Ibid., pp. 315–16.
581 "Frankie was utterly blameless": Tina Sinatra, *My Father's Daughter*, p. 111.
582 In July, after legal: Associated Press, July 30, 1964.
582 "I feel sorry for anyone": Taraborrelli, *Sinatra*, p. 315.
582 All charges against: Associated Press, June 30, 1965.
582 And he was relatively: Daniel O'Brien, *Frank Sinatra Film Guide*, p. 161.
582 "He really knew": Tony Bill, in discussion with the author, May 2006.
582 For the duration: Daniel O'Brien, *Frank Sinatra Film Guide*, p. 162.
582 In front of the house: Jones, *Q*, p. 179.
583 "Frank was getting itchy": Kelley, *His Way*, p. 333.
583 "The water was quite shallow": Jacobs and Stadiem, *Mr. S*, pp. 210–11.
584 "kind of a beer-drinkin' ": Bill, discussion.
584 Before that fateful: Richmond, *Fever*, p. 269.
584 "It was a sun-drenched": Kelley, *His Way*, pp. 334–35.
586 After a wave swept: Nancy Sinatra, *American Legend*, p. 189.
586 As Jilly raced: Ibid.
586 Frank was then taken: Ibid.
587 "He looked up at me": Kelley, *His Way*, p. 336.
587 "It was like, 'Hey' ": Bill, discussion.
587 "SINATRA NEARLY": Associated Press, May 11, 1964.
587 "was rescued in a matter": United Press, May 11, 1964.
587 Two other people: Ibid.
587 "Brad Dexter, an actor": Associated Press, May 11, 1964.
587 "It was such a strange": Kelley, *His Way*, p. 336.
587 "Frank appeared uptight": Ibid., pp. 336–37.
588 "It could be that Mr. S": Jacobs and Stadiem, *Mr. S*, p. 212.
588 "tried to treat": Ibid.
589 "Oh, I just got a little": Kelley, *His Way*, p. 336.
589 "Frank would go get": Dick Bakalyan, in discussion with the author, Jan. 2007.
589 over a hundred times: Friedwald, *Sinatra!*, p. 411.
590 "He said, 'Hey, Q' ": Quincy Jones, in discussion with the author, Feb. 2013; Jones, *Q*, p. 179.
590 "In the middle of our": Jones, discussion.
590 "It started out with seven": Jones, *Q*, p. 180.
590 "Partied our brains": Jones, discussion.
590 Quincy quickly got to work: Friedwald, *Sinatra!*, p. 410.
590 "At around 6:30": Jones, *Q*, p. 180.
591 "He was a brother": Ibid.
591 "I'm not crazy": Jones, discussion.
591 "Frank was my style": Jones, *Q*, p. 179.

592 The publishers then passed: Friedwald, *Sinatra!*, p. 413.

592 "Frank was lazy": Jones, discussion.

593 as recently as December: Alex Freman, *Phoenix (Ariz.) Republic,* Dec. 1, 1963.

594 The Manhattan Post Office forwarded: Furia, *Skylark,* p. 230.

594 "When he told me that Tony": United Press, March 13, 1963.

596 And he had the last laugh: Friedwald, *Sinatra!*, p. 412.

596 "Beautiful. Beautiful": "The Hollywood Palace, Season 1, Episode 24," TV.com, www.tv.com /shows/the-hollywood-palace/host-dean-martin-the-rolling-stones-144861/recap.

597 "were a stupid fad": Jacobs and Stadiem, *Mr. S,* p. 216.

597 "I thought, 'Fuck you' ": http://entertainment.ca.msn.com/music/photos/rolling-stones-50th -anniversary?page=10.

597 He made nice: Marcucci, *Where or When.*

597 "an artless and obvious": *New York Times,* Aug. 6, 1964.

597 The picture did a little: Daniel O'Brien, *Frank Sinatra Film Guide,* p. 160.

597 "youth A&R man": Cornyn, *Exploding,* p. 62.

598 "Jimmy never cared": Lee Herschberg, in discussion with the author, May 2006.

598 " 'Listen, if you're going' ": Friedwald, *Sinatra!*, p. 420.

598 To that end, Bowen: Ibid.

598 "Nashville rock-style": Ibid., p. 421.

598 "heard two flutists": Cornyn, *Exploding,* p. 63.

599 "When we finished cutting": Friedwald, *Sinatra!*, p. 421.

599 "Softly, as I Leave You," with: O'Brien and Sayers, *Sinatra,* p. 266.

601 The Beatles, and other alien sounds: Bronson, *Billboard Book of Number One Hits,* p. 154.

601 "be in charge of": Earl Wilson, syndicated column, Aug. 11, 1964.

601 "Priding himself": Daniel O'Brien, *Frank Sinatra Film Guide,* p. 167.

601 When the director failed: Kelley, *His Way,* p. 339.

602 Sinatra took his posse: Ibid., p. 340.

602 "Between takes": Jacobs and Stadiem, *Mr. S,* pp. 216–17.

602 Romantically speaking: Harrison Carroll, syndicated column, June 25, 1964.

603 "One weekend": Jacobs and Stadiem, *Mr. S,* p. 217.

603 "What are you being": Kelley, *His Way,* p. 338.

603 The makeup artist covered: Server, *Ava Gardner,* p. 442.

604 He had planned to come: Ibid.

604 She writes in her memoirs: Gardner, *Ava,* p. 287.

604 He showed up for work: Taraborrelli, *Sinatra,* pp. 323–24.

604 "Frank was affectionate": Server, *Ava Gardner,* p. 443.

604 "She's the only woman": Ibid.; Taraborrelli, *Sinatra,* p. 324; Summers and Swan, *Sinatra,* p. 312.

604 In early September: Kelley, *His Way,* p. 340.

604 The next morning, in the lobby: Bob Thomas, syndicated column, Sept. 28, 1964.

605 The following morning: Ibid.

605 "spic faggot": Jacobs and Stadiem, *Mr. S,* p. 219.

605 "I'll never go back": Kelley, *His Way,* p. 341.

605 Even Ava was beginning: Server, *Ava Gardner,* p. 448.

605 Both *Von Ryan*: Aubrey Solomon, *Twentieth Century Fox,* p. 254; David Kamp, "When Liz Met Dick," *Vanity Fair,* April 2011.

605 Among the TV series: Lev, *Twentieth Century-Fox,* p. 258.

605 Tough blonde: Newcomb, *Encyclopedia of Television,* p. 1,754.

606 "He was an intelligent": Lloyd Shearer feature on Mia Farrow, Jan. 3, 1965.

606 "a mean and lecherous": Server, *Ava Gardner,* p. 243.

606 María de Lourdes Villiers Farrow: Taraborrelli, *Sinatra,* p. 327.

606 "I was the loner": Bob Thomas, syndicated column, Dec. 13, 1964.

606 "every once in a while,": Farrow, *What Falls Away,* p. 57.

606 "I discovered that only": *Life,* May 5, 1967.

607 With the exception of a bit: Farrow, *What Falls Away,* p. 48.

607 Her first movie role: Ibid., pp. 78–79.

607 "I want a big career": Hedda Hopper, syndicated column, Sept. 13, 1964.

608 Restless during a long: Farrow, *What Falls Away,* p. 86.

608 "I can say it now": Levy, *Rat Pack Confidential,* p. 271.

608 She also fails to note: Taraborrelli, *Sinatra,* p. 326; Kelley, *His Way,* p. 342; Jacobs and Stadiem, *Mr. S,* p. 219.

608 she told *Life*: *Life,* May 5, 1967.

608 "googly eyes": Kelley, *His Way,* p. 344.

608   As she was watching: Farrow, *What Falls Away*, p. 87.

609   The lights went down: Ibid., p. 88.

609   She has never listened: Ibid., p. 97.

609   "Sometimes I think I'd like": Kelley, *His Way*, p. 344.

609   Who has a sense: Farrow, *What Falls Away*, p. 89.

610   She has a three-room: Ibid., p. 84.

610   And, with honest: Ibid., p. 89.

610   Thus she finds: Ibid., p. 90.

610   "It wasn't that Mia": Jacobs and Stadiem, *Mr. S*, p. 226.

610   Years later: Farrow, *What Falls Away*, pp. 96–97.

611   "There was one of Ava": Kelley, *His Way*, p. 346.

611   He bought her: Farrow, *What Falls Away*, p. 95.

611   Thus, he had not been: Ibid., pp. 95–96.

612   As late as 1988: "Sinatra, Van Heusen, and a Piano in the Desert," The Jonathan Channel, July 23, 2014; Rob Fentress, e-mail to author, July 23, 2014.

612   Sometimes, as they strolled: Farrow, *What Falls Away*, p. 96.

612   "that stuffy, older crowd": Kelley, *His Way*, p. 346.

612   where he ordered her: Ibid., p. 344.

612   "no one, absolutely": Jacobs and Stadiem, *Mr. S*, p. 227.

612   "Mia was a very clever": Kelley, *His Way*, p. 345.

613   Miller, who had desperately: United Press, Nov. 10, 1964.

613   Frank would find: Gay Talese, "Frank Sinatra Has a Cold," *Esquire*, April 1966.

613   "Bill didn't really": Peggy Connelly, in discussion with the author, May 2006.

613   "Bill always took": Friedwald, *Sinatra!*, p. 39.

613   "And now, the mother": Marcucci, *Where or When*; Shaw, *Sinatra*, p. 342.

613   "Jack Entratter said": Jones, discussion.

614   "I can still hear": Taraborrelli, *Sinatra*, p. 331.

614   "the maddest, merriest": Reuters, Dec. 1, 1964.

614   "I have been meeting": Bob Thomas, syndicated column, Dec. 13, 1964.

614   "I don't believe it": Louella Parsons, syndicated column, Dec. 7, 1964.

614   "an obvious blockbuster": *Variety*, Dec. 2, 1964.

614   "took us over to the table": Havers, *Sinatra*, p. 289.

CHAPTER 22

615   "America in 1964": Dwight Garner, "Cigarettes, Coffee, a Stop at the Liquor Store," *New York Times*, Aug. 9, 2014, www.nytimes.com/2014/08/09/books/frank-oharas-lunch-poems -turn-50.html.

615   He was speaking of far: "Number of Color TV Households and Percentage of USA Homes with Color Television, 1964 to 1978," Television History—The First 75 Years, www.tvhistory .tv/Color_Households_64-78.JPG.

615   "It [rock 'n' roll] belongs": *Variety*, Nov. 6, 1964.

616   "Look at that": Havers, *Sinatra*, p. 291; O'Brien and Sayers, *Sinatra*, pp. 265–66.

616   "Mia Farrow and Frank Sinatra": Mike Connolly, syndicated column, Jan. 22, 1965.

616   A $250 one-time membership fee: *Time*, April 23, 1965.

616   (later raised to $1,000): *Sports Illustrated*, July 10, 1967.

616   who was said to own: *Time*, Sept. 27, 1963.

616   "has some of the most": *Time*, April 23, 1965.

617   "What in your profession": Larry King, in discussion with the author, Nov. 2012.

618   where, in the days: Lloyd Shearer feature on Mia Farrow, Jan. 3, 1965.

618   "New York's swinging": Alex Freeman, syndicated column, Feb. 7, 1965.

619   "I think they had": Christopher Cerf, in discussion with the author, June 2006.

619   after Hart's untimely: United Press, Dec. 23, 1961.

620   Once, in the summer of 1964: *New York Times*, May 25, 1964.

620   "I'm sure we'd all had": Cerf, discussion.

620   "Provocative and engrossing": Daniel O'Brien, *Frank Sinatra Film Guide*, p. 165.

621   "If the threat of Frank Sinatra": *New York Times*, Feb. 25, 1965.

622   "I'm well aware": Peter Bart, *New York Times*, April 18, 1965.

622   He might have been out: *Billboard*, Nov. 20, 1965.

623   "Four years from now": *Show Business Illustrated*, Sept. 5, 1961.

623   he livened up: Daniel O'Brien, *Frank Sinatra Film Guide*, p. 172.

624   She'd thought that her marriage: Nancy Sinatra, *American Legend*, p. 191.

624   "He chewed up scenery": Tony Bill, in discussion with the author, May 2006.

624 "PJ's and all those clubs": Quincy Jones, in discussion with the author, Feb. 2013.
624 He was enraged: Taraborrelli, *Sinatra: Behind the Legend*, p. 337.
624 "I remember coming home": Tina Sinatra, *My Father's Daughter*, pp. 131–32.
625 "He's awful": Jonathan Schwartz, in discussion with the author, Sept. 2011.
625 "Gordon had his identity": Friedwald, *Sinatra!*, p. 349.
625 "Jenkins relied on the most": Ibid., p. 348.
626 "I could have stayed": Stan Cornyn, in discussion with the author, Feb. 2006.
626 "Tonight will not swing": *September of My Years* liner notes.
627 "the same seat": David Bianculli, "CBS Replays Vintage Sinatra '48 Hours' Airing Cronkite Interview & Profile from '65," *New York Daily News*, May 21, 1998, www.nydailynews.com/ archives/entertainment/cbs-replays-vintage-sinatra-48-hours-airing-cronkite-interview- profile-65-article-1.786751.
627 "Tommy was the kind": Fifi Booth, in discussion with the author, April 2012.
627 "He kept hopping up": *Life*, April 23, 1965.
627 The moment was invariably: John Dominis, in discussion with the author, Jan. 2006.
628 "He was having an all-night": *Life*, April 23, 1965.
628 "I became fascinated": Ibid.
628 "He is a man who will": Ibid.
628 "Sinatra is rich": Ibid.
631 "Women are constantly": Ibid.
633 "The era of *cool* jazz": Ibid.
634 But her brilliance: Ed O'Brien, e-mail to author, Dec. 21, 2011.
635 Surprisingly, he gave: Jacobs and Stadiem, *Mr. S*, p. 216.
635 "sings well": *Life*, April 23, 1965.
636 In the November *Variety*: *Variety*, Nov. 6, 1964.
637 "Even though I've been singing": *Life*, April 23, 1965.
637 She was shocked when: Farrow, *What Falls Away*, pp. 98–99.
638 She discovered that: Ibid., p. 100.
638 Basie simply charged: Rob Fentress, in discussion with the author, June 2011.
639 He'd come east: Sun Lakes Aero Club, "Frank Sinatra and His Lear Jet N175FS."
639 "to Detroit or Chicago": Earl Wilson, syndicated column, June 10, 1965.
639 "We now have two": Bob Thomas, syndicated column, May 1, 1965.
639 The answer incorrectly: TV Scout, syndicated column, April 19, 1965.
639 "When Mia Farrow first": Dorothy Kilgallen, syndicated column, May 27, 1965.
640 "My son is just": Kelley, *His Way*, p. 347.
640 "She is not as fragile": Bob Thomas, syndicated column, May 1, 1965.
640 "The La Rue crowd": Walter Winchell, syndicated column, June 7, 1965.
640 In 1960, the National Guard: Rampersad, *The Life of Langston Hughes*, pp. 314–15.
640 That same year: Morton, *Backstory in Blue*, p. 260.
641 "the only time I've ever": Quincy Jones, in discussion with the author, Feb. 2013.
641 The silly subject: Friedwald, *Sinatra!*, p. 405.
641 "bland, banal": *New Yorker*, July 17, 1965.
642 In fact, $35,000: Wein, *Myself Among Others*, p. 248.
642 Yet Balliett somehow failed: Shaw, *Sinatra*, pp. 349–50.
642 "When the dual aircraft": Wein, *Myself Among Others*, p. 246.
642 "a glorious performance": Ibid., p. 250.
643 Among the numbers: Quincy Jones, e-mail to author, Aug. 26, 2014.
643 "Many believe [Jones's]": Fuchs and Prigozy, *Frank Sinatra*, p. 35.
643 "There have been many": Shaw, *Sinatra*, p. 349.
643 "Sinatra's festival": *Variety*, July 7, 1965.
643 At 10:25 p.m.: Ibid.
643 "As he left the stage": Wein, *Myself Among Others*, p. 250.
644 "The audience was made up": Shaw, *Sinatra*, p. 350.
644 Gross ticket sales: "Live: Shea Stadium, New York," The Beatles Bible, www.beatlesbible .com/1965/08/15/live-shea-stadium-new-york.
645 The A-group: Farrow, *What Falls Away*, p. 101.
646 Equally strange: Ibid.
646 Her television series: Ibid., p. 104.
646 "If Mia decided to marry": Associated Press, Aug. 5, 1965.
646 "the coven of golden oldies": Jacobs and Stadiem, *Mr. S*, p. 225.
646 This cruise was far more: Ibid., p. 228.
646 Not even Frank: Farrow, *What Falls Away*, p. 104.
647 Almost at once: Ibid., pp. 104–05.

647 Rather pathetically: Jacobs and Stadiem, *Mr. S*, p. 225.
647 A measure of relief: Farrow, *What Falls Away*, p. 105.
647 His image as: Ibid., p. 99.
647 Amid the constant: Ibid., p. 106.
647 She also writes: Ibid., p. 104.
648 The denial only fanned: United Press, Aug. 6, 1965.
649 Grimes and Goldfarb got: Associated Press, Aug. 11, 1965.
649 "the most closely watched": *Time*, Aug. 20, 1965.
649 "10 other persons": United Press, Aug. 26, 1965.
649 As the whole table: Farrow, *What Falls Away*, p. 101.
649 Typical nights in Vegas: Ibid., p. 102.
649 At 3:00 a.m., after: United Press, Aug. 26, 1965.
649 the program took: *Lethbridge Herald*, Sept. 18, 1965.
650 "If it's not Reprise": https://www.youtube.com/watch?v=FgcCfMo1HcY.
650 An added bonus: Daniel O'Brien, *Frank Sinatra Film Guide*, pp. 173–74.
650 the film lost $1.2 million: Balio, *United Artists*, p. 171.
651 "a lackluster nautical": Daniel O'Brien, *Frank Sinatra Film Guide*, p. 175.
651 "*Assault on a Queen* was a B-picture": Evans, *Kid Stays in the Picture*, p. 122.
651 "It's a good story": Bob Thomas, syndicated column, Oct. 15, 1965.
652 "CBS insisting on": *New York Times*, Nov. 5, 1965.
652 "We were getting along": Cronkite, *Reporter's Life*, pp. 343–44.
653 "You broke all": Hewitt, *Tell Me a Story*, p. 102.
654 "Cronkite's doing this thing": Gay Talese, in discussion with the author, May 2007.
655 "Watching him at recording": Talese, *Fame and Obscurity*, p. 12.
656 "security guards, Budweiser": Talese, "Frank Sinatra Has a Cold."
657 "What I do with my life": "Sinatra," transcript, CBS News, Nov. 16, 1965.
657 "The fact that I used": Ibid.
658 "This is the great age": Scott Raab, "The Graceful Exit," *Esquire*, May 2000.
659 "a nice little": Cynthia Lowry, syndicated column, Nov. 17, 1965.
659 "*Sinatra* wasn't authorized": Shaw, *Sinatra*, pp. 352–53.
659 "Although it seemed": Ibid., p. 352.
659 "His daughter Nancy's": Ibid.
659 "struck marinara": Nancy Sinatra, *My Father*, p. 196.
660 "Like a fourteen-year-old": Ibid., p. 198.
660 "a sixteen-year-old": Lee Hazlewood obituary, *The Guardian*, April 6, 2014.
660 "An hour of consummate": Rick DuBrow, syndicated column, Nov. 25, 1965.
660 and the ratings were: *Billboard*, Nov. 13, 1965.
660 "When Frank Sinatra drives": Talese, "Frank Sinatra Has a Cold."
661 "'Vicenzo,' Sinatra said": Ibid.
661 "After Sinatra had kissed": Ibid.
663 "This is the Month": Shaw, *Sinatra*, p. 353.
663 Two compilation albums: Ibid., pp. 353–54.
663 Tony Bennett sang with: Ibid., p. 354.
663 "Who in the forties": Tina Sinatra, *My Father's Daughter*, pp. 136–37.
663 "If Frank Sinatra had": Dorothy Manners, syndicated column, Dec. 17, 1965.
664 "Mia threw a fit": Jacobs and Stadiem, *Mr. S*, pp. 228–29.
664 Overjoyed, she bought: Taraborrelli, *Sinatra*, p. 345.
664 On opening night, he informed: Earl Wilson, syndicated column, Dec. 10, 1965.
664 Dorothy Manners's happy: Jacobs and Stadiem, *Mr. S*, p. 229.
664 "horror of vanity": Farrow, *What Falls Away*, p. 107.
665 "She didn't cut it": Taraborrelli, *Sinatra*, p. 346.
665 "Now I really will": Jacobs and Stadiem, *Mr. S*, p. 229.

CHAPTER 23

669 "The showmanship vibrations": *Variety*, Jan. 12, 1966.
669 Lacking a string section: Quincy Jones, in discussion with the author, Feb. 2013.
669 On their first Christmas: Farrow, *What Falls Away*, p. 108.
669 "Mia, Mia": Taraborrelli, *Sinatra*, p. 347.
670 "At 5 a.m. you": Hedda Hopper, syndicated column, Jan. 17, 1966.
670 Mia wrote of her alienation: Farrow, *What Falls Away*, pp. 108–9.
670 Frank's love of hosting: Ibid., p. 109.
670 In the first week: Dorothy Manners, syndicated column, Feb. 12, 1966.

670 "Now and then she": Dorothy Manners, syndicated column, Feb. 12, 1966; Wilson, *Sinatra*, p. 224.

671 Sinatra hired two: Leonard Lyons, syndicated column, Feb. 28, 1966.

671 "Don't get a headache": Dorothy Manners, syndicated column, Feb. 21, 1966.

671 She told Frank to leave: Taraborrelli, *Sinatra*, p. 348.

671 "were absurdly insignificant": Farrow, *What Falls Away*, p. 111.

671 "delightful": Ibid.

672 "With a week's": Harrison Carroll, syndicated column, April 15, 1966.

673 "I said, 'Man, get'": Friedwald, *Sinatra!*, p. 422.

673 "I don't want to": Summers and Swan, *Sinatra*, p. 334.

673 His last number 1: O'Brien and Sayers, *Sinatra*, pp. 264–65.

673 "I must have turned": Bowen, *Rough Mix*, p. 98.

673 "I don't give a damn": Ibid., p. 99.

674 "set up an all-night": Cornyn, *Exploding*, p. 63.

674 "He thought it was about": Havers, *Sinatra*, p. 296.

674 Singing it for audiences: Friedwald, *Sinatra!*, p. 423.

675 "Here's a song that I cannot": Recording of Nov. 27, 1975, Jerusalem concert.

675 In the U.K., it sat: Havers, *Sinatra*, p. 296.

675 "Just as predicted": Jack O'Brian, syndicated column, May 10, 1966.

675 "That's not so good": Taraborrelli, *Sinatra*, p. 349.

675 The night she came back: Farrow, *What Falls Away*, pp. 111–12.

676 "There is no particular": Friedwald, *Sinatra!*, pp. 271–72.

677 "looking madly": Earl Wilson, syndicated column, June 2, 1966.

678 "You're out of line": Kelley, *His Way*, p. 353.

678 "one of the phones": Jacobs and Stadiem, *Mr. S*, p. 230.

678 And years later: Summers and Swan, *Sinatra*, p. 329.

678 "Sinatra has been": Associated Press, June 10, 1966.

678 "Now I've gone": Taraborrelli, *Sinatra*, p. 353.

678 "That's the only time": Kelley, *His Way*, p. 354.

679 and, according to one source: Ibid., p. 355.

679 "millions": Jacobs and Stadiem, *Mr. S*, p. 231.

679 "There's nothing to settle": Kelley, *His Way*, p. 355.

679 "In the closing space between us": Farrow, *What Falls Away*, p. 112.

679 He went to Billy: Taraborrelli, *Sinatra*, p. 353.

679 As they flew: Farrow, *What Falls Away*, p. 112.

679 "I don't have a recollection": Christopher Cerf, in discussion with the author, June 2006.

680 "countless Mia-like waifs": Jacobs and Stadiem, *Mr. S*, p. 231.

680 On July 7, she finally: United Press, July 7, 1966.

680 Her asking price: Florabel Muir, syndicated column, July 9, 1966.

680 she'd cut her leg: Wilson, *Sinatra*, p. 221.

680 "It's a friendship": Kelley, *His Way*, p. 355; United Press, July 13, 1966.

680 "If Mr. Sinatra is going to marry": Kelley, *His Way*, p. 347.

680 Mia could announce: Ibid., p. 355.

680 "I couldn't be more": Associated Press, July 14, 1966.

681 "Let's get married": Farrow, *What Falls Away*, p. 112.

681 "It's too big": Kelley, *His Way*, p. 356.

681 Dexter then told: Summers and Swan, *Sinatra*, p. 316.

681 "He went crazy": Ibid., p. 329.

681 "the ceremony would": Associated Press and United Press, July 19, 1966.

681 The next day: Farrow, *What Falls Away*, pp. 112–13.

682 "looked grim": Jacobs and Stadiem, *Mr. S*, p. 235.

682 "a close friend": Taraborrelli, *Sinatra*, p. 354.

682 But on one fact: Ibid.; Server, *Ava Gardner*, p. 448.

682 "had just shot": Farrow, *What Falls Away*, p. 113.

682 "accidentally discharged": United Press, July 19, 1966.

682 "I've never seen such": Kelley, *His Way*, p. 357.

682 "Mr. S looked nervous": Jacobs and Stadiem, *Mr. S*, p. 235.

683 "This is the happiest": Kelley, *His Way*, p. 357.

683 He took his new wife: Taraborrelli, *Sinatra*, p. 354.

683 Someone noticed that: Wilson, *Sinatra*, p. 222.

683 "How are you, baby": Associated Press, July 20, 1966.

683 "This is a big day": Kelley, *His Way*, p. 357.

684 "My mother was stunned": Tina Sinatra, *My Father's Daughter*, pp. 140–41.

684 "My brother Patrick": Farrow, *What Falls Away*, p. 113.
685 Sinatra slugged him: United Press, July 27, 1966.
685 "This one don't talk": Kelley, *His Way*, p. 358.
685 "She's a little nothing": Jacobs and Stadiem, *Mr. S*, p. 236.
685 "She was a voracious": Tina Sinatra, *My Father's Daughter*, p. 142.
685 who felt threatened: Taraborrelli, *Sinatra*, p. 356.
686 "Mia knew far more people": Jacobs and Stadiem, *Mr. S*, p. 236.
686 "shiny green silks": Farrow, *What Falls Away*, p. 113.
686 His boss seemed testy: Jacobs and Stadiem, *Mr. S*, p. 237.
686 Aboard Loewe's yacht: Nancy Sinatra, *American Legend*, p. 200.
687 Dexter had to use: Daniel O'Brien, *Frank Sinatra Film Guide*, p. 179; Kelley, *His Way*, p. 360.
687 Equilibrium had been: Daniel O'Brien, *Frank Sinatra Film Guide*, p. 180.
687 "He hated the guy": Kelley, *His Way*, p. 361.
687 "I couldn't stand listening": Ibid.
687 "swore he'd move": Ibid.
687 "then received a communication": Daniel O'Brien, *Frank Sinatra Film Guide*, p. 180.
688 "How are you?": Kelley, *His Way*, p. 363.
688 "Questioned about the incident": Daniel O'Brien, *Frank Sinatra Film Guide*, p. 180.
688 "He was the producer": Kelley, *His Way*, p. 363.
689 "a straggly line": San Mateo Times, Sept. 8, 1966.
689 The newlyweds: Farrow, *What Falls Away*, p. 114.
689 "It was a five-bedroom": *Spy*, Sept. 1988; "209 Copa de Oro Rd, Los Angeles, California," the Movieland Directory, www.movielanddirectory.com/tour-location.cfm?location=20620&address=209%20Copa%20De%20Oro%20Rd&city=Los%20Angeles&state=california.
689 Dick Powell and June Allyson had: Lewis and Kaplan, *Dean and Me*, p. 87.
689 "If I could have one": Tina Sinatra, *My Father's Daughter*, p. 140.
690 "Sinatra?": Hayes, *Smiling Through the Apocalypse*, p. 314.
690 "A slow count": Ibid.
690 "I always knew Frank": Summers and Swan, *Sinatra*, p. 503.
690 And according to two: Earl Wilson, syndicated column, Oct. 4, 1966.
690 "I think we ought": Bowen, *Rough Mix*, p. 101.
691 "James," he said: Ibid., pp. 102–4.
692 A month later, the song: "The Hot 100: Week of November 19, 1966," *Billboard*, www.billboard.com/charts/1966-11-19/hot-100.
692 It was Sinatra's twenty-eighth: *Variety*, Nov. 4, 1966.
692 Then Lefty delivered: Marcucci, *Where or When*.
692 She knew the lyrics: Farrow, *What Falls Away*, pp. 102–3.
692 "Believe it or not": Earl Wilson, syndicated column, Nov. 8, 1966.
692 Half a dozen songs later: Ibid.
692 "Smokey the Bear": Kelley, *His Way*, p. 364.
693 Though the riots: Associated Press, May 27, 1966; United Press, Oct. 30, 1966.
693 "But Sammy's okay": Kelley, *His Way*, p. 364.
693 "he stopped at a blackjack": Earl Wilson, syndicated column, Nov. 8, 1966.
693 "she touched his craps-swinging": Graham, *Confessions of a Hollywood Columnist*, p. 48.
693 "We can't do just": Friedwald, *Sinatra!*, p. 425.
694 "That was Mia's": Rob Fentress, in discussion with the author, June 2011.
694 The air was crisp: Earl Wilson, syndicated column, Dec. 1, 1966.
694 He'd invited everyone: United Press, Nov. 29, 1966.
694 "a black-and-white blur": Cerf, discussion.
694 Farrow's eye mask: United Press, Nov. 29, 1966.

CHAPTER 24

696 "It's an honor": Castro, *Bossa Nova*, p. 327.
697 "On the night of Thursday": Wilson, *Sinatra*, p. 223.
697 The couple's Caribbean: Associated Press, Jan. 20, 1967.
697 they stayed at Claudette: Earl Wilson, syndicated column, Jan. 21, 1967.
698 "When he picked up": Claus Ogerman, in discussion with the author, Feb. 2013.
698 He also went into: Per Ed O'Brien: Rob Fentress, e-mail to author, Feb. 2, 2015.
698 On January 26, he took: Associated Press, Jan. 27, 1967.
699 Sinatra's remarks: Nancy Sinatra, *American Legend*, p. 201.
699 "this slight and tousled": O'Brien and Sayers, *Sinatra*, p. 131.

699 "He was in awe": Lee Herschberg, in discussion with the author, May 2006.
699 "Maybe too much": Ogerman, discussion.
700 "like the World Soft": *Francis Albert Sinatra & Antonio Carlos Jobim* liner notes.
700 "Very gentle": *Inside Sinatra-Jobim,* song outtake.
700 "The arrangements were just": Herschberg, discussion.
700 "were running like": Ogerman, discussion.
700 "gold cuff-links": *Inside Sinatra-Jobim,* song outtake.
700 "What was nice there": Ogerman, discussion.
700 On that last night: Nancy Sinatra, *American Legend,* p. 201.
700 The love duet: Ostin, discussion.
701 Released on March 18: O'Brien and Sayers, *Sinatra,* p. 266.
701 *That's Life,* which had: Ibid., p. 261.
701 "They were model": Tina Sinatra, *My Father's Daughter,* pp. 142–43.
701 "It'll be the first real": Earl Wilson, syndicated column, Feb. 16, 1967.
702 "Frank didn't seem": Farrow, *What Falls Away,* p. 114.
702 Jackie Mason, born: Finkelstein, *Jewish Comedy Stars,* p. 51.
702 which began not long after: Summers and Swan, *Sinatra,* p. 304.
702 were an open secret: Lloyd Shearer, article, Sept. 3, 1967.
702 "Frank soaks his dentures": Kelley, *His Way,* p. 364.
702 "I really came in": Earl Wilson, syndicated column, Nov. 8, 1966.
702 "Nah, I'm just kidding": Kelley, *His Way,* p. 364.
702 The bullets lodged: United Press, Nov. 8, 1966.
702 The Clark County sheriff's: Kelley, *His Way,* p. 364; Walter Winchell, syndicated column, Nov. 23, 1966.
702 "I have no idea": *Variety,* Feb. 15, 1967.
702 "I was warned": Kelley, *His Way,* p. 364.
703 "all of a sudden": Summers and Swan, *Sinatra,* p. 330.
703 He sustained multiple: *Variety,* Feb. 15, 1967.
703 "This is not the worst": Summers and Swan, *Sinatra,* p. 330.
703 The work in London: Farrow, *What Falls Away,* pp. 114–15.
703 "I never had an act": Shecky Greene, in discussion with the author, Nov. 2012.
704 "Fear," he said: Ibid.
705 Joe Fischetti, still nominally: Summers and Swan, *Sinatra,* p. 330.
705 "We're sitting in": Ibid.
706 "No better evidence": Harrison Carroll, syndicated column, March 14, 1967.
707 "The persona of a private": Santopietro, *Sinatra in Hollywood,* p. 388.
707 Having just been forced: Drosnin, *Citizen Hughes,* p. 52.
707 "He had not come": Ibid., p. 106.
708 "make Las Vegas as": Ibid., p. 108.
709 The Clark County Gaming: Associated Press, April 2, 1967.
710 "It was really enjoyable": Gena Rowlands, in discussion with the author, Jan. 2013.
711 "The air was volatile": Kelley, *His Way,* p. 368.
711 "Everybody wants to see": Dan Lewis, syndicated column, Aug. 9, 1967.
711 "Frank had so many": Kelley, *His Way,* p. 368.
711 The two were closely: Taraborrelli, *Sinatra,* p. 361.
711 "I have some hot": Leonard Lyons, syndicated column, April 16, 1967.
711 and at least one: Leonard Lyons, syndicated column, May 20, 1967.
711 Frank had become close: Jacobs and Stadiem, *Mr. S,* p. 3.
711 "Frank Sinatra has given": Sheilah Graham, syndicated column, March 10, 1967.
712 She turned around: Taraborrelli, *Sinatra,* p. 361.
712 On April 15: Bronson, *Billboard Book of Number One Hits,* p. 222.
712 As Reagan strolled: Shecky Greene, in discussion with the author, Nov. 2012.
713 "had one hell": Tiffany Bolling, in discussion with the author, Oct. 2012.
714 "Shecky, stick with me": Kelley, *His Way,* p. 368.
714 "Fischetti, that fuckin' moron": Greene, discussion.
714 "I said, 'I'm gonna' ": Ibid.
715 "I flew to New York": Bolling, discussion.
715 "Francis called me and said": Ibid.
716 "I said to him": Greene, discussion.
716 In early May, the American-Italian: United Press, May 4, 1967.
716 "The Frank Sinatra–Italian": Jack O'Brian, syndicated column, May 9, 1967.
716 "hardly matches the image": *New York Times,* May 12, 1967.
716 "It is this kind of": Ibid.

717 "It was obvious": Nancy Sinatra, *American Legend*, p. 202.
717 "There would be no point": Kelley, *His Way*, p. 369.
717 "I don't think a man": Jack Bradford, syndicated column, March 13, 1967.
717 "I've got to do things": Kelley, *His Way*, p. 369.
717 "There's talk that Mia": Marilyn Beck, syndicated column, May 19, 1967.
717 Two days later: Leonard Lyons, syndicated column, May 21, 1967.
717 "I don't want any trouble": Kelley, *His Way*, p. 370.
718 "Frank Sinatra may have": Sheilah Graham, syndicated column, June 4, 1967.
718 She writes of how stressful: Farrow, *What Falls Away*, pp. 117–18.
719 "We needed to protect": Ed Walters, in discussion with the author, Sept. 2013.
719 "I'm not sure when I got": Tina Sinatra, *My Father's Daughter*, pp. 144–45.
720 "groundbreaking, earthshaking": Farrow, *What Falls Away*, p. 137.
720 "She is just run down": Reuters, June 17, 1967.
720 "She was bruised": Kelley, *His Way*, p. 370.
720 "the references [in Kelley's *His Way*]": *Los Angeles Times*, Sept. 26, 1986.
720 "a creative genius": Jacobs and Stadiem, *Mr. S*, p. 245.
721 She passionately wanted: Ibid., p. 244.
721 "Maybe it bothered him": Kelley, *His Way*, p. 379.
721 "Dad wearing a Nehru": Tina Sinatra, *My Father's Daughter*, p. 143.
721 "Mia Farrow was dancing": Summers and Swan, *Sinatra*, p. 317.
721 That was the summer: Jacobs and Stadiem, *Mr. S*, p. 7.
721 He began making: Friedwald, *Sinatra!*, p. 433.
722 But Kaempfert, Bowen: Hyatt, *Billboard Book of Number One Adult Contemporary Hits*, p. 58.
722 "as written": Jonathan Schwartz, in discussion with the author, March 2015.
722 the tour would be: Marcucci, *Where or When*.
722 also on the bill: *Variety*, July 12, 1967; Nancy Sinatra, *American Legend*, p. 203.
723 "I remember how he played": Marcucci, *Where or When*.
723 "the timing . . . was": Farrow, *What Falls Away*, p. 118.
723 She and Frank discussed: Ibid.
723 As the talks proceeded: Kelley, *His Way*, pp. 371–72.
723 In the wake of the Giancana: *Variety*, Sept. 3, 1967.
724 Then, on July 22: United Press, July 26, 1967; Drosnin, *Citizen Hughes*, p. 473.
724 "We are buying": United Press, July 23, 1967.
724 But *The Detective* had: Earl Wilson, syndicated column, July 20, 1967.
724 The timetable dovetailed: Daniel O'Brien, *Frank Sinatra Film Guide*, p. 188.
724 For all her ambivalence: *Long Beach (Calif.) Press-Telegram*, Aug. 16, 1967.
724 "Frank Sinatra, still": *Variety*, Sept. 1, 1967.
725 "You're wondering why": Drosnin, *Citizen Hughes*, p. 125.
725 "The Sands' owners got": Ed Walters, *The Pit Boss* posting, Dec. 19, 1997.
725 "I'm here to buy": Earl Wilson, syndicated column, Sept. 8, 1967.
725 And he was furious: *Variety*, Sept. 13, 1967.
725 secure in his new five-year: Earl Wilson, syndicated column, July 27, 1967.
725 and rolling in the nearly: United Press, July 23, 1967.
725 and still Mob-run: Walters, discussion.
725 One of his conditions: Wilson, *Sinatra*, p. 234.
726 He stomped around: Drosnin, *Citizen Hughes*, p. 126.
726 "Like somebody deranged": Wilson, *Sinatra*, p. 234.
726 Entratter's assistant, Eleanor: Nancy Sinatra, *American Legend*, p. 203.
726 "He just shook his head": Walters, discussion.
726 When the show was over: Nancy Sinatra, *American Legend*, p. 203.
726 Mia Farrow's account: Farrow, *What Falls Away*, pp. 110–11.
727 "The cocktail waitresses": Walters, discussion.
727 "For two successive nights": Drosnin, *Citizen Hughes*, pp. 125–26.
728 "A spokesman for the Sands": United Press, Sept. 11, 1967.
728 her new beau: Farrow, *What Falls Away*, p. 120; Bowen, *Rough Mix*, p. 109.
728 They all chatted: Farrow, *What Falls Away*, pp. 120–21.
728 The next morning: Ibid., p. 121.
729 "He threatened to kill": Drosnin, *Citizen Hughes*, p. 126
729 "I built this hotel": Kelley, *His Way*, p. 372.
729 "When Carl is mad": Levy, *Rat Pack Confidential*, p. 295.
729 "You didn't fight": Walters, discussion.
729 "You son of a bitch": Ibid.; Levy, *Rat Pack Confidential*, pp. 295–96; Kelley, *His Way*, pp. 372–73; Summers and Swan, *Sinatra*, pp. 331–32.

730 Frank's people tried: *Variety*, Sept. 13, 1967.
731 "We can't deny any": United Press, Sept. 13, 1967.
731 as Frank's friend Kirk Douglas: Nancy Sinatra, *My Father*, p. 147.
731 "Kirk, I learned one thing": Ibid.
731 "Never fight a Jew": Anka, *My Way*, p. 214.
731 "Cohen was . . . treated": Kelley, *His Way*, p. 374.
731 "Carl was not a hero": Ed Walters, *The Pit Boss* posting, Dec. 19, 1997.
731 "Sinatra's fight": Leonard Lyons, syndicated column, Oct. 2, 1967.
731 "I regret the termination": Levy, *Rat Pack Confidential; Variety*, Aug. 7, 1970.
732 "Out of friendship": *Variety*, Sept. 13, 1967.
732 "Frank stopped by": Kelley, *His Way*, p. 377.
732 But he badly missed: Jacobs and Stadiem, *Mr. S*, p. 237.
733 "I think I hurt": https://www.youtube.com/watch?v=mQwRhMn6D2U.
733 "a quality that makes": Gardner, *Ava*, p. 139.
733 For this reason: Farrow, *What Falls Away*, p. 119.
734 "SINATRA APPROVES MIA": Earl Wilson, syndicated column, Oct. 11, 1967.
734 "returned to the void": Farrow, *What Falls Away*, pp. 129–30.
735 "unmoored in some nightmare": Ibid., p. 131.
735 Frank was puzzled: Ibid., pp. 122–23.
735 "While she's working": Kelley, *His Way*, p. 378.
735 "a gay, fast-paced romp": Associated Press, Nov. 14, 1967.
736 then production shut down: United Press, Nov. 30, 1967.
736 Made out in her name: Farrow, *What Falls Away*, p. 123.
736 "sobbing her heart out": Kelley, *His Way*, p. 379.
736 "I had nothing": Taraborrelli, *Sinatra*, p. 367.
736 "Frank Sinatra and Mia Farrow": United Press, Nov. 24, 1967.
737 "no one, nothing": Jacobs and Stadiem, *Mr. S*, p. 247.
737 Soon after the Warner-Reprise merger: Cornyn, *Exploding*, p. 56.
737 Though Frank had lost: Teachout, *Duke*, p. 337.
737 "that his music was no longer": Ibid., p. 323.
737 Much to Duke's annoyance: Friedwald, *Sinatra!*, p. 303.
738 "Jesus, the rehearsal": Granata, *Sessions with Sinatra*, p. 189.
738 "they [had] never touched the charts": Friedwald, *Sinatra!*, p. 306.
738 "He was very quiet": Herschberg, discussion.
738 And understandably: Granata, *Sessions with Sinatra*, p. 189.
739 The great alto: Friedwald, *Sinatra!*, p. 308.
739 He wasn't in the mood: Earl Wilson, syndicated column, Dec. 12, 1967.
739 "He wasn't really thrilled": Friedwald, *Sinatra!*, p. 306.
739 "Somebody, Jilly": Herschberg, discussion.
739 In a perfectly poignant moment: Farrow, *What Falls Away*, p. 124.
739 "I begged him": *Photoplay*, Feb. 1968.
740 "I would have taken": Kelley, *His Way*, p. 379.
740 Frank had invited: Ibid.
740 twenty-seven people: Harrison Carroll, syndicated column, Dec. 29, 1967.
740 "It was a fun crowd": *Photoplay*, Feb. 1968.
740 "withdrawn and stern": Farrow, *What Falls Away*, pp. 124–25.
740 "Your are a stupid, rude": Ibid., p. 125.
741 She had gone to considerable trouble: Ibid., p. 126.
741 The guests had gone silent: Ibid., pp. 126–27.
741 He hated it: Jacobs and Stadiem, *Mr. S*, p. 244.
741 "dressed to the nines": Farrow, *What Falls Away*, p. 127.
741 She was transported: Ibid.

CHAPTER 25

742 "Evening, Mrs. S.": Farrow, *What Falls Away*, pp. 128–29.
742 She writes that in her fog: Ibid., p. 127.
742 Then Frank himself arrived: Ibid., p. 128.
742 "Frank called me": Taraborrelli, *Sinatra*, p. 369.
742 "The New Year's reconciliation": Florabel Muir, syndicated column, Jan. 12, 1968.
743 a former crime reporter: Weller, *Dancing at Ciro's*, p. 227.
743 "I want to be a better": Associated Press, Jan. 25, 1968.
743 He was booked: *Variety*, Dec. 18, 1967.
744 Welch, so intimidated: Daniel O'Brien, *Frank Sinatra Film Guide*, p. 193.

744 "forced to bow out": *Variety*, Feb. 19, 1967.
744 which he'd originally set: Earl Wilson, syndicated column, Feb. 1, 1968.
744 Not only had his wife: *Variety*, Feb. 14, 1968; Earl Wilson, syndicated column, Feb. 14, 1968.
744 "causing talk in Miami Beach": Earl Wilson, syndicated column, Feb. 9, 1968.
744 "It wasn't true at all": Earl Wilson, syndicated column, Feb. 14, 1968.
745 "Sinatra wasn't ill": *Variety*, Feb. 14, 1968.
745 At Sammy, for unspecified reasons: Ibid.
745 She flew to Miami: Kelley, *His Way*, p. 381.
745 "She was taken": Server, *Ava Gardner*, pp. 451–52.
746 "She walked right into": Taraborrelli, *Sinatra*, pp. 371–72.
746 "I was very worried": Jacobs and Stadiem, *Mr. S*, p. 249.
746 "Frank Sinatra remains": Earl Wilson, syndicated column, Feb. 28, 1968.
746 "The Jet Set rush": Earl Wilson, syndicated column, March 1, 1968.
746 "for a fast weekend trip": Wilson, *Sinatra*, p. 239.
746 "Frank Sinatra refused": *Variety*, March 4, 1968.
746 "Frank didn't like": Wilson, *Sinatra*, p. 237.
747 "Did he like the way": Ibid., p. 240.
747 "SINATRA COMES ON": Ibid., p. 241.
748 Up till now: Farrow, *What Falls Away*, p. 137.
748 The group had turned to: *Washington Post*, Sept. 16, 1967.
748 "Whenever I meditate": Farrow, *What Falls Away*, p. 137.
748 "They seemed beautiful and fearless": Ibid., p. 138.
748 Then, one day: Ibid., p. 141.
749 From Miami: Ibid., pp. 145–46.
749 "If you kill yourself": Ibid., p. 146.
749 "Near the end, when": Hal Bates, syndicated column, April 7, 1968.
750 According to the Associated: Associated Press, March 11, 1968.
750 "He was sad": Nancy Sinatra, *American Legend*, p. 205.
750 He was determined: Earl Wilson, syndicated column, Feb. 20, 1968.
750 "He was real upset": Kelley, *His Way*, p. 380.
750 "refusing to do more than": Ibid.
751 "Gadge said": Raquel Welch, in discussion with the author, March 2010.
751 After the broadcast, Nancy: Nancy Sinatra, *American Legend*, p. 205.
752 The less sober: Roy Newquist, *Park Forest Star*, April 4, 1968.
752 "Sinatra played fast": *Variety*, April 10, 1968.
752 "Margulies said": Ibid.
752 "We're having a wonderful": Ibid.; Summers and Swan, *Sinatra*, p. 342.
753 "The Miami Herald reported": Associated Press, April 10, 1968.
753 But the Miami–Dade County: *Variety*, April 24, 1968.
753 "We are of the opinion": Ibid.
754 Pearson failed to mention: Drew Pearson, syndicated column, May 1, 1968; Betty Beale, syndicated column, May 5, 1968.
754 President Johnson, hearing: Pilat, *Drew Pearson*, p. 282.
754 "To meet Frank Sinatra": Ibid.
754 "I don't think Bobby": Maxine Cheshire, syndicated column, May 3, 1968.
754 "I'm really going to": Ibid.
754 Allen Dorfman, officially: Jeffrey Goldberg, "Hoffa Lives!" *New York* magazine, July 31, 1995.
754 Frank had flown: Kelley, *His Way*, p. 384.
754 "While Sinatra and several": Cheshire, *Maxine Cheshire, Reporter*, p. 106.
755 "was tight-lipped": Maxine Cheshire, syndicated column, May 3, 1968.
755 "Sinatra, wearing the gold": Betty Beale, syndicated column, May 12, 1968.
756 "It was the first really": Ibid.
756 At the same dinner: Cheshire, *Maxine Cheshire, Reporter*, p. 107.
756 "bring Drew around": Pilat, *Drew Pearson*, p. 283.
757 A splinter group of stars: Kelley, *His Way*, p. 385.
757 "The King of the World": *Oakland Tribune*, May 24, 1968.
758 "We were in the back": Nollen, *Jilly!*, pp. 70–71.
758 "no sense of satisfaction": Jacobs and Stadiem, *Mr. S*, p. 249.
759 Her father was quiet: Nancy Sinatra, *American Legend*, p. 206.
759 "Ava Gardner, who is": Walter Winchell, syndicated column, Aug. 2, 1968.
759 "An examination at the Chelsea": Server, *Ava Gardner*, p. 448.
759 "I was lying in bed": Evans and Gardner, *Ava Gardner*, p. 41.
760 To crown the indignity: Server, *Ava Gardner*, pp. 450–51.

760 "Critics praised the movie": Nancy Sinatra, *American Legend,* p. 205.

760 "a film that haphazardly": *New York Times,* May 29, 1968.

761 She took no pleasure: Farrow, *What Falls Away,* pp. 148–49.

762 "Peter Sellers is in town": Dorothy Manners, syndicated column, July 27, 1968.

762 "even want to dial up": Jacobs and Stadiem, *Mr. S,* p. 10.

762 Frank junior, touring: *Janesville (Wis.) Daily Gazette,* Aug. 2, 1968.

763 "in a coma": Nancy Sinatra, *My Father,* p. 270.

763 Not many nightspots: Jacobs and Stadiem, *Mr. S,* p. 11.

763 "I was just hanging out": Ibid., p. 13.

764 The floor itself seemed: Farrow, *What Falls Away,* pp. 149–50.

764 "Dressed in slacks": Vernon Scott, dispatch, Aug. 17, 1968.

764 "lean and sleepless": Associated Press, Aug. 17, 1968.

764 Nancy Sinatra recalled going: Nancy Sinatra, *My Father,* p. 208.

765 "Let's go with the dress": Ibid.

765 "It was as if someone": Ibid.

765 The wire services reported: Associated Press, Aug. 17, 1968; Vernon Scott, dispatch, Aug. 17, 1968.

765 When she arrived: Farrow, *What Falls Away,* p. 150.

765 She refused any financial: Kelley, *His Way,* p. 381.

765 "Frank Sinatra is rather": *Wall Street Journal,* Aug. 19, 1968.

766 "These reports are rumors": Ibid.

767 "Before Mr. Sinatra sold": Ibid.

767 Gage had managed: Nancy Sinatra, *American Legend,* p. 207.

767 "My father had known": Tina Sinatra, *My Father's Daughter,* p. 73.

767 "There is a good chance": *Madison Capital Times,* Aug. 21, 1968.

768 When Humphrey's special counsel: Kelley, *His Way,* p. 387.

768 Soon Humphrey stopped: Taraborrelli, *Sinatra,* p. 376.

768 "The maid came to me": Kelley, *His Way,* p. 382.

768 "Everyone around the old man": Ibid., pp. 382–83.

768 "After fourteen years together": Ibid., p. 382.

769 "Oh, man, I had": George Jacobs, in discussion with the author, May 2009.

770 "pressing recording": Wire-service report, Aug. 26, 1968.

770 In truth, he had nothing: Dorothy Manners, syndicated column, Aug. 28, 1968.

771 "Frank Sinatra, who receives": Sheilah Graham, syndicated column, Sept. 27, 1968.

771 Sinatra's excuse for quitting: Florabel Muir, syndicated column, Nov. 6, 1968.

771 One would think: Associated Press, Oct. 10, 1968.

771 He was dating again: Muir, syndicated column, Nov. 6, 1968.

771 "Frank Sinatra's name": *Chicago Tribune,* Sept. 27, 1968.

772 On the day Diane McCue: Giordmaina, *Sinatra and the Moll,* p. 68.

772 Like a number of other women: Ibid.; Associated Press, Aug. 31, 1971.

772 There is also evidence: http://www.intelius.com/Find-Phone-Address/Las+Vegas-NV/Diane-Giordmaina.html.

772 He was also a romantic: *Tonight Show* appearance with Johnny Carson and Don Rickles, Nov. 12, 1976.

772 "On October 15, 1968": Giordmaina, *Sinatra and the Moll,* p. 85.

772 "[Schwartz] and his wife": Robin Orr, *Oakland Tribune,* Oct. 18, 1968.

773 Diane McCue did not ride: *Baytown (Tex.) Sun,* Oct. 31, 1968.

773 "hated with a deep": MacLaine, *My Lucky Stars,* p. 86.

773 The following week: Marcucci, *Where or When.*

773 "My Way of Life" and: O'Brien and Sayers, *Sinatra,* p. 267; figures are from the *Cash Box* singles chart; "Cycles" hit number 23 on the *Billboard* Hot 100.

773 "Toward the end": Friedwald, *Sinatra!,* p. 267.

773 The two songs recorded: O'Brien and Sayers, *Sinatra,* p. 136.

774 "How do you do it": *Kingston (Jamaica) Daily Gleaner,* Dec. 6, 1968.

775 "such a perfect blending": *New York Times,* Nov. 21, 1968.

775 "He projects the ex-cop": *Los Angeles Times,* Nov. 8, 1968.

776 "As he has proved": *New York Times,* Nov. 21, 1968.

776 "Frank Sinatra has had it": Dorothy Manners, syndicated column, Nov. 7, 1968.

776 In early November: United Press, Nov. 6, 1968.

776 "The most surprising": Joyce Haber, syndicated column, Nov. 24, 1968.

777 "The Nehru jacket seems": Jack O'Brian, syndicated column, April 19, 1968.

777 "Nobody would explain": *El Paso Herald Post,* Nov. 23, 1968.

777 "And don't look now": https://www.youtube.com/watch?v=sC6-TlT1JJg.

777 Two days before Thanksgiving: *Variety,* Nov. 27, 1968.
777 After purchasing the Desert Inn: Drosnin, *Citizen Hughes,* p. 473.
777 "Vegas in the old days": Polly Bergen, in discussion with the author, Jan. 2011.
778 "When Frank went": Rob Fentress, in discussion with the author, June 2011.
778 "Frank Sinatra's return": *Variety,* Nov. 27, 1968.
778 "The electricity of the Sands": Fentress, discussion.
778 "I was like eighteen": *Rolling Stone,* June 25, 1998.
778 "The little Arab": Summers and Swan, *Sinatra,* p. 335.
778 "Frank Sinatra, Dean Martin": Anka, *My Way,* p. 2.
779 "and a couple of mob": Paul Anka, interview by Neil McCormack, *Daily Telegraph,* Nov. 8, 2007.
779 "I thought it was": Ibid.
779 "all him": *Newsweek,* May 25, 1998.
779 "I've got something really": Ibid.
779 "really had nothing": Frank Sinatra, interview by Sid Mark, WWDB (Philadelphia), Dec. 31, 1979.
779 "I know it's a very big hit": Granata, *Sessions with Sinatra,* p. xvii.
779 Still, his inner circle: Lee Herschberg, in discussion with the author, May 2006.

CHAPTER 26

783 "Just before Christmas": Suzy Knickerbocker, syndicated column, Jan. 10, 1969.
784 "Sinatra is much much": Ibid.
784 "Out in the garden": Ibid.
785 Pleasantly surprised to see: Nancy Sinatra, *My Father,* p. 225.
785 Anthony Martin Sinatra: Summers and Swan, *Sinatra,* p. 401.
785 "Sometimes I'd be lying awake": Hamill, *Why Sinatra Matters,* p. 84.
785 Her grandfather's funeral: Nancy Sinatra, *My Father,* p. 225.
785 "pure bedlam": Ibid.
785 "Frank was pissed": Taraborrelli, *Sinatra,* pp. 379–80.
786 Twenty-five limousines: Kelley, *His Way,* p. 389.
786 "Marty, Marty": Taraborrelli, *Sinatra,* p. 380; Nancy Sinatra, *My Father,* p. 226.
786 Back at her grandmother's: Nancy Sinatra, *My Father,* p. 226.
786 "But when his father died": Ibid.
786 "I don't want to move": Kelley, *His Way,* p. 391.
786 "He became a little": Tina Sinatra, *My Father's Daughter,* p. 153.
786 "In his down periods": Wilson, *Sinatra,* pp. 250–51.
787 "had charted quite respectably": Friedwald, *Sinatra!,* pp. 430–31.
788 "Somebody didn't like": Lee Herschberg, in discussion with the author, May 2006.
789 "Paul told me": Granata, *Sessions with Sinatra,* p. 190.
789 "Putnam will publish": Jack O'Brian, syndicated column, Sept. 23, 1968.
789 Putnam refused: Puzo, *Godfather Papers,* p. 53; *Variety,* Sept. 25, 1968.
789 "*The Godfather* is a work": *Winona (Minn.) Daily News,* April 27, 1969.
790 The public had also bought: Friedwald, *Sinatra!,* p. 438.
790 "Edgar Guest with": "Notable New Yorkers: Bennett Cerf," Columbia University Libraries Oral History Research Office, www.columbia.edu/cu/lweb/digital/collections/nny/cerfb /transcripts/cerfb_1_21_1024.html.
790 "the most important guest": Ibid.
790 "I had tried for years": Friedwald, *Sinatra!,* pp. 437–38.
791 One source says: Marcucci, *Where or When.*
792 "Sinatra had watched": Mo Ostin, in discussion with the author, Aug. 2012.
792 The 45 rpm single: Marcucci, *Where or When.*
792 The man who had once been: Cornyn, *Exploding,* pp. 128–29, 137.
792 "When he started chasing": Ostin, discussion.
792 *My Way,* the album: Havers, *Sinatra,* p. 309.
793 The LP, released: O'Brien and Sayers, *Sinatra,* p. 261.
793 Both the single: Havers, *Sinatra,* p. 309.
793 "I met Barbara": Betsy Hammes, in discussion with the author, June 2011.
793 "a $150-a-week": Barbara Sinatra, *Lady Blue Eyes,* p. 37.
793 "she was stunningly": Ed Walters, in discussion with the author, Dec. 2014.
794 "a well-tailored": Barbara Sinatra, "Sinatra, My Jekyll and Hyde Husband: His Fourth Wife Lays Bare His Terrifying Mood Swings and Sadistic Manipulation," *Daily Mail,* June 6, 2011, www.dailymail.co.uk/news/article-1394161/Frank-Sinatra-Jekyll-Hyde-husband-4th-wife -Barbara-sadistic-manipulation.html.

794 Zeppo was also a gifted mechanic: Homer, *Born in the USA,* pp. 176–77.
794 Despite Zeppo's ingenuity: Kelley, *His Way,* p. 434.
794 "She was like a racehorse": Hammes, discussion.
794 "was an inveterate card player": Kelley, *His Way,* pp. 433–34.
794 "were always sharing": Hammes, discussion.
795 "nod a hello": Barbara Sinatra, *Lady Blue Eyes,* p. 68.
795 "Then, one day": Barbara Sinatra, "Sinatra, My Jekyll and Hyde Husband."
795 "On Saturday evening": *Fremont (Calif.) Argus,* Dec. 13, 1968.
795 "those who drank": Barbara Sinatra, "Sinatra, My Jekyll and Hyde Husband."
795 "who liked to turn": Barbara Sinatra, *Lady Blue Eyes,* p. 69.
795 "I was on the opposing": Ibid., pp. 3–4, 99.
796 "He hated her": Summers and Swan, *Sinatra,* p. 358.
796 "Zeppo was in his sixties": Jacobs and Stadiem, *Mr. S,* p. 255.
796 once more at a Circus: Dorothy Manners, syndicated column, Nov. 11, 1968.
796 "no longer lean": *Variety,* May 12, 1969.
797 "McKuen was a star": Gay Talese, in discussion with the author, May 2007.
797 From June through: Marilyn Beck, syndicated column, Aug. 12, 1969.
797 He watched the *Apollo 11:* Drew Pearson, syndicated column, July 21, 1969.
797 he took the Cerfs: *Lowell (Mass.) Sun,* July 25, 1969.
797 he sailed back: *Fort Pierce (Fla.) News-Tribune,* Aug. 12, 1969.
797 He had Mickey: Associated Press, Oct. 15, 1969.
797 Two days later: O'Brien and Sayers, *Sinatra,* p. 267.
798 "For the second time": Tina Sinatra, *My Father's Daughter,* pp. 153–54.
798 "He told Sinatra they": Friedwald, *Sinatra!,* p. 440.
798 The LP was a resounding: Warner, *True Story of the Jersey Boys,* pp. 29–30.
798 "And then": *Watertown* liner notes.
798 "Jake and I discussed": Ibid.
799 "In a series of soliloquies": Ibid.
799 "I don't think he was": Ibid.
800 "The only album we ever did": Herschberg, discussion.
800 "He didn't know the songs": Friedwald, *Sinatra!,* p. 441.
800 The LP was a worthy try: Ibid., p. 443.
800 "That was unheard-of": Ostin, discussion.
801 "Mr. Sinatra left": Associated Press, Oct. 15, 1969.
801 "He went yachting": Associated Press, Oct. 16, 1969.
801 The commission rattled: United Press, Oct. 29, 1969.
801 "For many years every": Associated Press, Oct. 24, 1969.
802 Actually it was only three: Nancy Sinatra, *American Legend,* p. 212.
802 On October 19: Ibid., pp. 212–13.
802 Around the same time: United Press, Oct. 14, 1969.
802 "But don't get your": Norma Lee Browning, syndicated column, Nov. 8, 1969.

CHAPTER 27

803 Not long afterward: *Film Bulletin,* Vol. 38, 1969, p. 63.
804 Instead, a few days: Santopietro, *Sinatra in Hollywood,* p. 410.
804 "Frank took such good care": Kelley, *His Way,* pp. 431–32.
804 Then, one night: "Part III: Hollywood Lives, The Sisters Final Installment," *New York Social Diary,* www.newyorksocialdiary.com/legacy/socialdiary/2005/08_17_05/socialdiary08_17_05 .php.
805 In January 1970: United Press, Feb. 4, 1970.
805 "organized crime had": *New York Times,* Feb. 4, 1970.
805 "shortly after he flew": *New York Times,* Feb. 18, 1970.
805 Though the hearing: Nancy Sinatra, *American Legend,* p. 214.
805 "Under questioning": *New York Times,* Feb. 19, 1970.
805 Though nothing of what Frank: *New York Times,* Feb. 18, 1970.
806 "Q: Do you know": Kelley, *His Way,* pp. 393–94.
807 Nancy Sinatra wrote that: Nancy Sinatra, *American Legend,* p. 214.
807 "a high [commission]": *New York Times,* Feb. 19, 1970.
807 "he had an engagement": *Oakland Tribune,* Feb. 12, 1970.
807 "bipartisan, short on speeches": Associated Press, Feb. 28, 1970.
808 "He appeared tired": *Arizona Republic,* April 19, 1970.
810 "FRANK SINATRA, FOREIGN": Kuntz and Kuntz, *Sinatra Files,* pp. 209–10.
810 "Sinatra's affiliation over": Ibid., pp. 210–11.

811 "As a cabaret blockbuster": *Variety,* April 23, 1970.

811 "Frank Sinatra at Caesars": *Las Vegas Sun,* April 24, 1970.

811 It was all true: *Variety,* May 6, 1970.

812 "They applauded": *New York Times,* May 9, 1970.

812 It should be rerecorded: www.watertownology.com/forum.html.

813 "I have a funny feeling": Marcucci, *Where or When.*

813 "There are few occasions": Ibid.

813 "It is my duty": Associated Press, July 9, 1970.

813 "He made it clear": *Oakland Tribune,* July 9, 1970.

814 But for Frank to join: Jacobs and Stadiem, *Mr. S,* p. 238.

814 "The divine Francis": Joyce Haber, syndicated column, July 14, 1970.

814 Two weeks earlier: Associated Press, June 29, 1970.

814 "It looks like I held": Joyce Haber, syndicated column, July 14, 1970.

814 At the end of July: Norma Lee Browning, syndicated column, July 23, 1970.

814 "Dad's convalescence": Tina Sinatra, *My Father's Daughter,* p. 154.

815 "the topper on Saturday": *Variety,* Aug. 10, 1970.

815 "Miss Sinatra is an uneven": Ibid.

815 "Dear Frank": Steve Allen, *But Seriously . . . ,* p. 378.

816 "Only a few thousand": Ibid., p. 379.

816 "Wherever Frank is": Norma Lee Browning, syndicated column, Dec. 2, 1970.

816 "When he arrived": George Schlatter, in discussion with the author, May 2006.

816 "GUESS WHO": Nancy Sinatra, *American Legend,* p. 209.

817 In the summer of 1970: *Variety,* Oct. 1, 1969.

817 Jerome Zarowitz: Ed Walters, in discussion with the author, Dec. 2014.

817 When Zarowitz left the job: *New York Times,* Sept. 28, 1980.

817 In case the name: United Press, April 25, 1956.

817 "a major guy in New York": Ed Walters, in discussion with the author, Dec. 2014.

818 "That's when we knew": Kelley, *His Way,* p. 398.

818 "We were concerned": Ibid.

818 They said Sinatra was losing: *Los Angeles Times,* Sept. 8, 1970.

818 In 1970, the U.S. median: web.stanford.edu/class/polisci120a/immigration/Median%20 Household%20Income.pdf.

818 "What's the matter": Kelley, *His Way,* p. 398.

819 her father reacted coolly: Nancy Sinatra, *American Legend,* p. 215.

819 "If Sinatra comes back": *Los Angeles Times,* Sept. 8, 1970.

819 "He was coming right": Ibid.

820 Sinatra had witnesses: *Los Angeles Times,* Sept. 11, 1970.

820 "As for the remarks": Vernon Scott, syndicated column, Sept. 21, 1970.

820 "I wasn't in the baccarat game": Ibid.

820 According to Joyce Haber: *Los Angeles Times,* Sept. 17, 1970.

820 Never was a long time: Marcucci, *Where or When.*

820 "I just believed he was": Puzo, *The Godfather Papers,* p. 53.

821 "However, the movie": Ibid., pp. 53–54.

821 "a famous millionaire": Ibid., pp. 54–56.

823 "Francis, I'd play": Ibid., p. 57.

823 "The audience at": Associated Press, Oct. 5, 1970.

823 "he won't stand still": Norma Lee Browning, syndicated column, Oct. 24, 1970.

824 But he developed cold feet: Marilyn Beck, syndicated column, July 27, 1970.

824 "I still want to make": Dorothy Manners, syndicated column, Nov. 20, 1970.

824 a story in which: Dorothy Manners, syndicated column, Feb. 25, 1969.

824 a Sinatra and Goldie: Dorothy Manners, syndicated column, Aug. 5, 1969.

824 even a picture: Sheilah Graham, syndicated column, Feb. 24, 1969.

825 For one reason: Marcucci, *Where or When.*

826 "one of the best love songs": *Concert for the Americas* (Shout Factory, 2010), DVD.

826 This was nice of him: Schneider, *Long and Winding Road,* p. 122.

828 " 'Dirty Dingus Magee' is as shabby": *Chicago Tribune,* Nov. 23, 1970, www.rogerebert.com/ reviews/dirty-dingus-magee-1970.

828 referring to *The Stranger Returns*: Lang Thompson, "The Stranger Returns," www.tcm.com/ this-month/article/91156%7C0/The-Stranger-Returns.html.

828 "youth wig": *New York Times,* Nov. 19, 1970.

828 "He needed this silliness": Nancy Sinatra, *American Legend,* p. 214.

828 "Frank Sinatra also admired": Malatesta, *Party Politics,* p. 15.

829 "pusillanimous pussyfooters": Safire, *Before the Fall,* p. 323.

829 "These two gentlemen": Malatesta, *Party Politics,* p. 16.
830 "He said he would like": Ibid., pp. 17–18.
830 "Although long ago": Ibid., p. 18.
830 "DIRTY DINGUS MAY": Norma Lee Browning, column, Dec. 2, 1970 (first published in late November elsewhere).
831 "Schwartz is now": Ibid.
831 "He may become more": Ibid.
831 "since Daddy likes": Associated Press, Dec. 14, 1970.
831 The area's Mexican-American: Nancy Sinatra, *American Legend,* pp. 216–17.
832 When Frank learned: Ibid.
832 "What they saw": Joyce Haber, syndicated column, Dec. 27, 1970.
832 But Wagner: Marilyn Beck, syndicated column, Feb. 11, 1972.
832 "There were four": Joyce Haber, syndicated column, Dec. 27, 1970.
832 "where agents arrested": Associated Press, Dec. 13, 1970.
832 Upon opening: United Press, Feb. 23, 1971; *New York Times,* Sept. 28, 1980.
833 Peter Malatesta knew: Malatesta, *Party Politics,* pp. 21–22.
833 "a private world": Ibid., p. 32.
833 Ava had been sighted: Norma Lee Browning, syndicated column, Dec. 15, 1970.
833 "Says Suzy": Norma Lee Browning, syndicated column, Dec. 11, 1970.
833 "strolling into": Marilyn Beck, syndicated column, Dec. 19, 1970.
833 And though Frank: Bailey, *Cheever,* p. 435.

CHAPTER 28

834 "a Leviathan": *Oakland Tribune,* Jan. 5, 1971.
834 That night, Frank dined: *Oakland Tribune,* Jan. 4, 1971.
834 After Jimmy Stewart: Marcucci, *Where or When.*
834 a woman he had once: Jacobs and Stadiem, *Mr. S,* p. 238.
835 She beamed: Gloria Vanderbilt, in discussion with the author, April 2011.
835 "He's here": Norma Lee Browning, syndicated column, Jan. 22, 1971.
835 "Frank is married": Dorothy Manners, syndicated column, Feb. 3, 1971.
835 "As you will recall": Kuntz and Kuntz, *Sinatra Files,* pp. 212–13.
836 Nancy wrote that she felt: Nancy Sinatra, *My Father,* p. 228; Nancy Sinatra, *American Legend,* p. 217.
836 On Monday evenings: Nollen, *Jilly!,* p. 81.
837 In mid-February: Norma Lee Browning, syndicated column, Feb. 11, 1971.
837 "Everything we have done": *Life,* March 19, 1971.
839 Jim Mahoney had massaged: Jim Bishop, syndicated column, April 5, 1971.
839 "It didn't surprise me": Nancy Sinatra, *American Legend,* p. 219.
839 "His record history": Mo Ostin, in discussion with the author, Aug. 2012.
839 "You read it here first": Associated Press, March 24, 1971; Norma Lee Browning, syndicated column, March 31, 1971.
839 "I look forward to enjoying": Associated Press, March 24, 1971.
839 "His fade-out": Browning, syndicated column, March 31, 1971.
839 Starlets wore hot pants: Associated Press, April 18, 1971.
839 "Sinatra, Frank": https://www.youtube.com/watch?v=V_dGbyb7poo.
841 Coretta Scott King: Associated Press, April 18, 1971.
842 Some said he was quitting: Jim Bishop, syndicated column, April 5, 1971.
842 others, that he was secretly: *Life,* June 25, 1971.
842 "There are people": Paul Corcoran, syndicated column, April 7, 1971.
842 "He was nervous": *Life,* June 25, 1971.
843 "Everybody wants to be Cary Grant": *Newsweek,* March 12, 1990.
843 "We warmed 'em up": Ibid.
844 "when the vibrato": Ibid.
844 "Somebody help": Ibid.
844 "So I figure": Associated Press, June 14, 1971.
845 "Jump on it": Ibid.
847 "I'm tired": *Life,* June 25, 1971.

CODA

849 "Barbara had a fetching": Tina Sinatra, *My Father's Daughter,* pp. 146, 151–52.
850 "relentless strategist": Ibid., p. 150.

850 "I don't want no": Ibid., p. 152.
850 "From Jilly came a story": Ibid., pp. 152–53.
850 "appeared to be": Kuntz and Kuntz, *Sinatra Files*, p. 213.
851 "It is apparent": Ibid., p. 216.
851 "Bravo": Ibid., p. 220.
851 "by invitation, not demand": Kelley, *His Way*, p. 409.
851 "My hair was on fire": Tina Sinatra, *My Father's Daughter*, pp. 141–42.
852 "You know Miss Cheshire": Kelley, *His Way*, pp. 412–13; Cheshire, *Maxine Cheshire, Reporter*, pp. 123–25.
852 At the end of the night: Nancy Sinatra, *American Legend*, p. 219.
852 "Mr. President," Sinatra replied: Ibid.
852 "hinted that he might": Malatesta, *Party Politics*, p. 88.
854 Three days after: *Los Angeles Herald Examiner*, April 20, 1973.
854 Reprise's art director: *Los Angeles Times*, Aug. 21, 2006.
854 "I said, 'You're kidding'": Nancy Sinatra, *American Legend*, p. 230.
854 Along with Watergate: Ibid., p. 322.
855 "record an album every": Havers, *Sinatra*, p. 323.
855 Along with "Come Fly with Me": Marcucci, *Where or When*.
855 "Congress should give": Kelley, *His Way*, p. 423.
856 "You're the heavyweight champion": Weintraub, *When I Stop Talking*, p. 110.
856 "We will now do": Ibid., p. 326.
856 "Ah, Frankie": *New York Times*, Oct. 13, 1974.
856 "That style he set": *Rolling Stone*, June 6, 1974.
857 "There's nothing worse": Tina Sinatra, *My Father's Daughter*, p. 145.
857 "Marry me or lose me": Barbara Sinatra, *Lady Blue Eyes*, p. 166.
858 "My dad's inner life": Tina Sinatra, *My Father's Daughter*, p. 156.
858 "a brand-new profile": Ibid., p. 155.
858 "an enormous pear-shaped": Barbara Sinatra, *Lady Blue Eyes*, p. 170.
858 "Is this for me": Ibid.
858 it stipulated that none: Tina Sinatra, *My Father's Daughter*, p. 197.
858 "When the judge asked": Ibid., p. 157.
860 "He lied": Hewitt, *Tell Me a Story*, p. 103.
860 At the last minute: Tina Sinatra, *My Father's Daughter*, p. 163.
861 Though Barbara Sinatra wrote: Barbara Sinatra, *Lady Blue Eyes*, p. 198.
861 it has been suggested: Kelley, *His Way*, p. 441.
861 "Life went on": Barbara Sinatra, *Lady Blue Eyes*, p. 201.
861 "It turned out": Tina Sinatra, *My Father's Daughter*, p. 165.
862 "Sinatra and I were in": Granata, *Sessions with Sinatra*, p. 194.
862 "Fuck him": Vincent Falcone, in discussion with the author, Nov. 2012.
863 Barbara Sinatra writes that: Barbara Sinatra, *Lady Blue Eyes*, pp. 212–13.
863 "They were playing": Rob Fentress, in discussion with the author, June 2011.
863 "They were averaging": Tina Sinatra, *My Father's Daughter*, pp. 174–75.
864 He had been complaining: Anka, *My Way*, p. 214.
864 According to talk: Disclosed to the author by a physician who wished to remain anonymous.
864 Not long after Sinatra produced: Kelley, *Nancy Reagan*, pp. 311–12.
864 Tina Sinatra writes of: Tina Sinatra, *My Father's Daughter*, p. 178.
864 "During long-distance": Barbara Sinatra, *Lady Blue Eyes*, p. 269.
864 "Francis, this woman": Tina Sinatra, *My Father's Daughter*, pp. 178–79.
864 "If I would have left it": Ibid., pp. 176–79.
865 Mr. and Mrs. Sinatra: Ibid., pp. 180–81.
865 He did more than a thousand: Summers and Swan, *Sinatra*, p. 360.
865 Except in Atlantic City: Bob Eckel, in discussion with the author, May 2006.
865 "I travel with him": Associated Press, April 6, 1983.
865 "I vocalize an hour": Marcucci, *Where or When*.
866 "I was with him": Peter Bogdanovich, e-mail to author, Dec. 27, 2014.
866 Frank sent her: Cannon, *Grabtown Girl*, p. 103.
866 "I'm one hell": Server, *Ava Gardner*, p. 486.
867 "With her green eyes": *New York Times*, Feb. 25, 1985.
867 "Frank would call": Server, *Ava Gardner*, p. 488.
867 "He was utterly humiliated": Anka, *My Way*, p. 214.
868 "Frank refused to let": Barbara Sinatra, *Lady Blue Eyes*, pp. 276–77.
868 "as well as my hand": Nancy Sinatra, *My Father*, p. 280.
868 "I saw his memory": Falcone, discussion.

869 "Dean was half alive": Anka, *My Way,* p. 214.

869 "the spontaneity of phrasing": *New York Times,* May 17, 1990.

870 "Dear Daniel": Courtesy of Daniel Okrent.

870 "he was distraught": Tina Sinatra, *My Father's Daughter,* p. 214.

870 His manager, Eliot Weisman: Ibid., p. 230.

871 "I truly didn't know": Nollen, *Jilly!,* pp. 164–67.

871 Three days later: Marcucci, *Where or When.*

871 "Rock 'n' roll people": https://www.youtube.com/watch?v=PdRk2003jRg.

872 "There was one giant": Jim Snidero, in discussion with the author, Nov. 2014.

873 "What happened?": Tina Sinatra, *My Father's Daughter,* p. 240.

873 A waiter in the restaurant: https://www.youtube.com/watch?v=EGSb99HwcwU.

873 "May you all live": Marcucci, *Where or When.*

873 After his medication: Tina Sinatra, *My Father's Daughter,* p. 241.

873 He wound up the year: Marcucci, *Where or When.*

873 "We had been in the air": Cole, *Angel on My Shoulder,* p. 289.

873 Sinatra sang as well: Summers and Swan, *Sinatra,* p. 381.

873 "High notes, fine": Jonathan Schwartz, in discussion with the author, Dec. 2011.

874 "When are we going": Tina Sinatra, *My Father's Daughter,* p. 244.

874 "Sitting at the bar": Ibid., p. 245.

874 He stared at the TV: Ibid., p. 228.

874 "got on like a house": Barbara Sinatra, *Lady Blue Eyes,* p. 342.

874 As for the show: Tina Sinatra, *My Father's Daughter,* p. 247.

875 He was admitted to Cedars-Sinai: Associated Press, Nov. 5, 1996.

875 "His geography was limited": Tina Sinatra, *My Father's Daughter,* p. 260.

875 "It's sad to see": *Lawrence (Kans.) Journal World,* Nov. 27, 1996.

875 "I don't know how": Tina Sinatra, *My Father's Daughter,* pp. 276–77.

876 "I don't want to live": Ibid., p. 279.

876 It was a line: Barbara Sinatra, *Lady Blue Eyes,* p. 354.

876 "He was in his wheelchair": Ibid., pp. 354–55.

877 "I have bad news": Tina Sinatra, *My Father's Daughter,* p. 280.

877 "You'd better come": Barbara Sinatra, *Lady Blue Eyes,* pp. 356–57.

878 It was orange: Tina Sinatra, *My Father's Daughter,* pp. 280–81.

BIBLIOGRAPHY

Allen, Steve. *But Seriously . . . : Steve Allen Speaks His Mind*. Amherst, N.Y.: Prometheus, 1996.

Andersen, Christopher. *These Few Precious Days: The Final Year of Jack with Jackie*. New York: Gallery Books, 2013.

Anka, Paul. *My Way: An Autobiography*. With David Dalton. New York: St. Martin's, 2013.

Anthony, Carl Sferrazza. *The Kennedy White House: Family Life and Pictures, 1961–1963*. New York: Lisa Drew, 2001.

Bacall, Lauren. *By Myself*. New York: Ballantine, 1993.

Baggelaar, Kirstin. *Images of America: The Copacabana*. Charleston, S.C.: Arcadia, 2006.

Bailey, Blake. *Cheever: A Life*. New York: Vintage, 2009.

Balio, Tino. *United Artists, Volume 2, 1951–1978: The Company That Changed the Film Industry*. Madison: University of Wisconsin Press, 2009.

Barlett, Donald L., and James B. Steele. *Howard Hughes: His Life and Madness*. New York: Norton, 2004.

Basinger, Jeanine. *The Star Machine*. New York: Vintage, 2008.

Belafonte, Harry. *My Song: A Memoir of Art, Race, and Defiance*. With Michael Shnayerson. New York: Vintage, 2012.

Berg, A. Scott. *Goldwyn: A Biography*. New York: Riverhead, 1998.

Birkbeck, Matt. *Deconstructing Sammy: Music, Money, and Madness*. New York: Amistad, 2008.

Blair, Joan, and Clay Blair Jr. *The Search for JFK*. New York: Berkley, 1976.

Bogdanovich, Peter. *Who the Devil Made It: Conversations with Legendary Film Directors*. New York: Alfred A. Knopf, 1997.

———. *Who the Hell's in It: Conversations with Hollywood's Legendary Actors*. New York: Ballantine, 1998.

Bosworth, Patricia. *Marlon Brando*. New York: Viking, 2001.

Bowen, Jimmy, and Jim Jerome. *Rough Mix: An Unapologetic Look at the Music Business and How It Got That Way: A Lifetime in the World of Rock, Pop, and Country as Told by One of the Industry's Most Powerful Players*. New York: Simon & Schuster, 1997.

Braden, Joan. *Just Enough Rope*. New York: Villard, 1989.

Britt, Stan. *Frank Sinatra: A Celebration*. New York: Schirmer Trade Books, 1995.

Bronson, Fred. *The Billboard Notes of Number One Hits*. New York: Billboard Books, 2003.

Brownstein, Ronald. *The Power and the Glitter: The Hollywood-Washington Connection*. New York: Vintage, 1992.

Cahn, Sammy. *I Should Care: The Sammy Cahn Story*. New York: Arbor House, 1974.

Cannon, Doris Rollins. *Grabtown Girl: Ava Gardner's North Carolina Childhood and Her Enduring Ties to Home*. Asheboro, N.C.: Down Home Press, 2001.

Capra, Frank. *The Name Above the Title: An Autobiography*. Boston: Da Capo, 1997.

Capua, Michelangelo. *Janet Leigh: A Biography*. Jefferson, N.C.: McFarland, 2013.

Carlson, Peter. *K Blows Top: A Cold War Comic Interlude, Starring Nikita Khrushchev, America's Most Unlikely Tourist*. New York: PublicAffairs, 2009.

Caro, Robert A. *The Passage of Power*. Vol. 4 of *The Years of Lyndon Johnson*. New York: Alfred A. Knopf, 2012.

Castro, Ruy. *Bossa Nova: The Story of the Brazilian Music That Seduced the World*. Chicago: A Capella Books, 2000.

Cerf, Bennett. *At Random: The Reminiscences of Bennett Cerf*. New York: Random House, 1977.

Cheshire, Maxine. *Maxine Cheshire, Reporter*. With John Greenya. Boston: Houghton Mifflin, 1978.

Chung, Su Kim. *Las Vegas: Then and Now*. San Diego: Thunder Bay Press, 2007.

Clarke, Donald. *Billie Holiday: Wishing on the Moon*. Boston: Da Capo, 2002.

———. *Penguin Encyclopedia of Popular Music*. New York: Penguin Books, 1990.

Clarke, Gerald. *Get Happy: The Life of Judy Garland*. New York: Random House, 2000.

Clooney, Rosemary. *Girl Singer: An Autobiography*. With Joan Barthel. New York: Doubleday, 1999.

Cole, Natalie. *Angel on My Shoulder: An Autobiography*. With Digby Diehl. New York: Warner Books, 2000.

Cornyn, Stan. *Exploding: The Highs, Hits, Hype, Heroes, and Hustlers of the Warner Music Group*. With Paul Scanlon. New York: HarperCollins, 2002.

Cramer, Richard Ben. *Joe DiMaggio: The Hero's Life*. New York: Simon & Schuster, 2000.

Cronkite, Walter. *A Reporter's Life*. New York: Ballantine, 1997.

Crystal, Billy. *700 Sundays*. New York: Warner Books, 2005.

Curtis, James. *Spencer Tracy: A Biography*. New York: Alfred A. Knopf, 2011.

Dallek, Robert. *An Unfinished Life: John F. Kennedy, 1917–1963*. New York: Back Bay Books, 2004.

Damone, Vic. *Singing Was the Easy Part*. With David Chanoff. New York: St. Martin's, 2009.

Dannen, Fredric. *Hit Men: Power Brokers and Fast Money Inside the Music Business*. New York: Vintage, 1991.

Davidson, Bill. *The Real and the Unreal*. New York: Harper, 1961.

Davis, Miles. *Miles: The Autobiography*. With Quincy Troupe. New York: Simon & Schuster, 2011.

Davis, Sammy, Jr., Jane Boyar, and Burt Boyar. *Sammy: An Autobiography*. New York: Farrar, Straus & Giroux, 2000.

———. *Why Me? The Sammy Davis Jr. Story*. New York: Farrar, Straus & Giroux, 1989.

Decker, Todd. *Who Should Sing "Ol' Man River"? The Lives of an American Song*. New York: Oxford University Press, 2015.

Denton, Sally, and Roger Morris. *The Money and the Power: The Making of Las Vegas and Its Hold on America, 1947–2000*. New York: Alfred A. Knopf, 2001.

Douglas-Home, Robin. *Sinatra*. New York: Grosset & Dunlap, 1962.

Drosnin, Michael. *Citizen Hughes*. New York: Broadway Books, 2004.

English, T. J. *Havana Nocturne: How the Mob Owned Cuba . . . and Then Lost It to the Revolution*. New York: Harper, 2008.

Epstein, Daniel Mark. *Nat King Cole*. New York: Farrar, Straus & Giroux, 1999.

Evans, Peter, and Ava Gardner. *Ava Gardner: The Secret Conversations*. New York: Simon & Schuster, 2013.

Evans, Robert. *The Kid Stays in the Picture*. New York: Hyperion, 1994.

Exner, Judith. *My Story*. As told to Ovid Demaris. New York: Grove, 1977.

Falcone, Vincent, and Bob Popyk. *Frankly, Just Between Us: My Life Conducting Frank Sinatra's Music*. Milwaukee: Hal Leonard, 2005.

Farrow, Mia. *What Falls Away: A Memoir*. New York: Doubleday, 1997.

Finkelstein, Norman H. *Jewish Comedy Stars: Classic to Cutting Edge*. Minneapolis: Kar-Ben Publishing, 2010.

Finstad, Suzanne. *Natasha: The Biography of Natalie Wood*. New York: Three Rivers Press, 2001.

Fischer, Steve. *When the Mob Ran Vegas: Stories of Money, Mayhem, and Murder*. Omaha: Berkline Press, 2007.

Frank, Gerold. *Judy*. Boston: Da Capo, 1999.

Freedland, Michael. *All the Way: A Biography of Frank Sinatra, 1915–1998*. New York: St. Martin's, 2000.

Friedwald, Will. *A Biographical Guide to the Great Jazz and Pop Singers*. New York: Pantheon, 2010.

———. *Sinatra! The Song Is You*. Boston: Da Capo, 1997.

Fuchs, Jeanne, and Ruth Prigozy. *Frank Sinatra: The Man, the Music, the Legend*. Rochester, N.Y.: University of Rochester Press, 2007.

Furia, Philip. *Skylark: The Life and Times of Johnny Mercer*. New York: St. Martin's, 2003.

Gardner, Ava. *Ava: My Story*. New York: Bantam, 1992.

Giancana, Antoinette, and Thomas C. Renner. *Mafia Princess: Growing Up in Sam Giancana's Family*. New York: William Morrow, 1984.

Giancana, Sam, and Chuck Giancana. *Double Cross: The Explosive, Inside Story of the Mobster Who Controlled America*. New York: Warner, 1992.

Giordmaina, Diane. *Sinatra and the Moll*. Bloomington, Ind.: iUniverse, 2009.

Giuliano, Geoffrey, and Brenda Giuliano. *The Lost Lennon Interviews*. Avon, Mass.: Adams Media, 1996.

Glatt, John. *The Prince of Paradise: The True Story of a Hotel Heir, His Seductive Wife, and a Ruthless Murder*. New York: St. Martin's, 2013.

Goldstein, Norm. *Frank Sinatra: Ol' Blue Eyes*. Boston: Holt McDougal, 1983.

Goodman, Ezra. *The Fifty-Year Decline and Fall of Hollywood*. New York: Simon & Schuster, 1961.

Goodman, Wendy. *The World of Gloria Vanderbilt*. New York: Harry N. Abrams, 2010.

Gosch, Martin A., and Richard Hammer. *The Last Testament of Lucky Luciano*. New York: Little, Brown & Company, 1975.

Gould, Jonathan. *Can't Buy Me Love: The Beatles, Britain, and America*. New York: Three Rivers Press, 2008.

Graham, Sheilah. *Confessions of a Hollywood Communist*. New York: William Morrow, 1969.

Granata, Charles L. *Sessions with Sinatra: Frank Sinatra and the Art of Recording*. Chicago: A Capella Books, 1999.

Guralnick, Peter, and Ernst Jorgensen. *Elvis Day by Day: The Definitive Record of His Life and Music*. New York: Ballantine, 1999.

Hamill, Pete. *Why Sinatra Matters*. New York: Little, Brown, 1998.

Hamilton, Nigel. *JFK: Reckless Youth*. New York: Random House, 1992.

Havers, Richard. *Sinatra*. New York: DK, 2004.

Hayes, Harold, ed. *Smiling Through the Apocalypse: Esquire's History of the Sixties*. New York: McCall, 1970.

Haygood, Wil. *In Black and White: The Life of Sammy Davis Jr*. New York: Billboard, 2005.

Hersh, Burton. *Bobby and J. Edgar: The Historic Face-Off Between the Kennedys and J. Edgar Hoover That Transformed America*. New York: Carroll & Graf, 2007.

Hersh, Seymour M. *The Dark Side of Camelot*. Boston: Little, Brown, 1997.

Hershorn, Tad. *Norman Granz: The Man Who Used Jazz for Justice*. Berkeley: University of California Press, 2011.

Hewitt, Don. *Tell Me a Story: Fifty Years and 60 Minutes in Television*. New York: PublicAffairs, 2002.

Hoffman, William, and Lake Headley. *Contract Killer: The Explosive Story of the Mafia's Most Notorious Hit Man, Donald "Tony the Greek" Frankos*. New York: Thunder's Mouth Press, 1992.

Homer, Trevor. *Born in the USA: The American Book of Origins*. New York: Skyhorse Publishing, 2009.

Hotchner, A. E. *Doris Day: Her Own Story*. New York: Bantam, 1976.

Hyatt, Wesley. *The Billboard Book of Number One Adult Contemporary Hits*. New York: Billboard Books, 1999.

Ingham, Chris. *The Rough Guide to Frank Sinatra*. London: Rough Guides, 2005.

Jacobs, George, and William Stadiem. *Mr. S: My Life with Frank Sinatra*. New York: HarperCollins, 2003.

Jenkins, Bruce. *Goodbye: In Search of Gordon Jenkins*. Berkeley, Calif.: Frog, 2005.

Jones, Quincy. *Q: The Autobiography of Quincy Jones*. New York: Harlem Moon, 2002.

Jordan, Mearene. *Living with Miss G*. Smithfield, N.C.: Ava Gardner Museum, 2012.

Kaplan, James. *Frank: The Voice*. New York: Doubleday, 2010.

Kelley, Kitty. *His Way: The Unauthorized Biography of Frank Sinatra*. New York: Bantam, 1986.

———. *Nancy Reagan: The Unauthorized Biography*. New York: Simon & Schuster, 1991.

Keogh, Pamela Clarke. *Elvis Presley: The Man, the Life, the Legend*. New York: Atria, 2010.

Kibbey, Richard D. *Pat Boone: The Hollywood Years*. Mustang, Okla.: Tate Publishing, 2011.

Klein, Edward. *All Too Human: The Love Story of Jack and Jackie Kennedy*. New York: Pocket Books, 1997.

Knight, Timothy. *Sinatra: Hollywood His Way*. Philadelphia: Running Press, 2010.

Kraft, James P. *Vegas at Odds: Labor Conflict in a Leisure Economy, 1960–1985*. Baltimore: Johns Hopkins University Press, 2010.

Kuntz, Tom, and Phil Kuntz. *The Sinatra Files: The Life of an American Icon Under Government Surveillance*. New York: Three Rivers Press, 2000.

Lawford, Patricia Seaton. *The Peter Lawford Story: Life with the Kennedys, Monroe, and the Rat Pack*. With Ted Schwarz. New York: Carroll & Graf, 1990.

Leaming, Barbara. *Marilyn Monroe*. New York: Crown, 1998.

———. *Mrs. Kennedy: The Missing History of the Kennedy Years*. New York: Free Press, 2001.

Lev, Peter. *Twentieth Century–Fox: The Zanuck-Skouras Years, 1935–1965*. Austin: University of Texas Press, 2013.

Levinson, Peter J. *September in the Rain: The Life of Nelson Riddle*. New York: Billboard, 2001.

———. *Tommy Dorsey: Livin' in a Great Big Way*. Boston: Da Capo, 2009.

Levy, Shawn. *Rat Pack Confidential: Frank, Dean, Sammy, Peter, Joey, and the Last Great Showbiz Party*. New York: Broadway Books, 2001.

Lewis, Jerry, and James Kaplan. *Dean and Me: A Love Story*. New York: Three Rivers Press, 2007.

Lewisohn, Mark. *The Complete Beatles Chronicle: The Definitive Day-by-Day Guide to the Beatles' Entire Career*. Chicago: Chicago Review Press, 2010.

———. *Tune In*. Vol. 1 of *The Beatles: All These Years*. New York: Crown Archetype, 2013.

Loesser, Susan. *A Most Remarkable Fella: Frank Loesser and the Guys and Dolls in His Life*. Milwaukee: Hal Leonard, 2000.

MacLaine, Shirley. *My Lucky Stars: A Hollywood Memoir*. New York: Bantam, 1996.

Mailer, Norman. *Mind of an Outlaw: Selected Essays*. New York: Random House, 2013.

Malatesta, Peter. *Party Politics: The Confessions of a Washington Party-Giver*. Englewood Cliffs, N.J.: Prentice-Hall, 1982.

Martin, Ralph G. *A Hero for Our Time: An Intimate Story of the Kennedy Years*. New York: Scribner, 1983.

McBrien, William. *Cole Porter: A Biography*. New York: Alfred A. Knopf, 1998.

McClintick, David. *Indecent Exposure: A True Story of Hollywood and Wall Street*. New York: HarperBusiness Essentials, 2002.

McDougal, Dennis. *The Last Mogul: Lew Wasserman, MCA, and the Hidden History of Hollywood*. Boston: Da Capo, 2001.

Minnelli, Vincente. *I Remember It Well*. With Hector Arce. London: Angus and Robertson, 1975.

Morton, John Fass. *Backstory in Blue: Ellington at Newport '56*. New Brunswick: Rutgers University Press, 2008.

Munn, Michael. *John Wayne: The Man Behind the Myth*. New York: New American Library, 2005.

Mustazza, Leonard, ed. *Frank Sinatra and Popular Culture: Essays on an American Icon*. Westport, Conn.: Praeger, 1998.

———. *Ol' Blue Eyes: A Frank Sinatra Encyclopedia*. Westport, Conn.: Praeger, 1999.

Nasaw, David. *The Patriarch: The Remarkable Life and Turbulent Times of Joseph P. Kennedy*. New York: Penguin, 2012.

Navasky, Victor S. *Kennedy Justice*. New York: Scribner, 1971.

Newcomb, Horace. *Encyclopedia of Television*. New York: Routledge, 2004.

Nollen, Scott Allen. *Jilly! Sinatra's Right-Hand Man*. Henderson, Nev.: Vegas Broom Press, 2009.

O'Brien, Daniel. *The Frank Sinatra Film Guide*. London: Batsford, 1998.

O'Brien, Ed. *Sinatra 101: The 101 Best Recordings and the Stories Behind Them*. With Robert Wilson. New York: Boulevard, 1996.

O'Brien, Ed, and Scott P. Sayers Jr. *Sinatra: The Man and His Music*. Austin, Tex.: TSD Press, 1992.

O'Brien, Michael. *John F. Kennedy: A Biography*. New York: Thomas Dunne, 2005.

Parker, Robert, and Richard Rashke. *Capitol Hill in Black and White*. New York: Dodd, Mead, 1986.

Payn, Graham, and Sheridan Morley. *The Noël Coward Diaries*. Boston: Da Capo, 2000.

Petkov, Steven, and Leonard Mustazza, eds. *The Frank Sinatra Reader*. New York: Oxford University Press, 1995.

Pietrusza, David. *1960: LBJ vs. JFK vs. Nixon: The Epic Campaign That Forged Three Presidencies*. New York: Union Square Press, 2010.

Pilat, Oliver. *Drew Pearson: An Unauthorized Biography*. New York: Harper's Magazine Press, 1973.

Preminger, Otto. *Preminger: An Autobiography*. New York: Doubleday, 1977.

Puzo, Mario. *The Godfather*. New York: Signet, 1978.

———. *The Godfather Papers, and Other Confessions*. Greenwich, Conn.: Fawcett, 1972.

Quirk, Lawrence J. *The Kennedys in Hollywood*. Lanham, Md.: Taylor Trade, 2004.

Rampersad, Arnold. *The Life of Langston Hughes: Volume II: 1914–1967, I Dream a World*. New York: Oxford University Press, 2001.

Rappleye, Charles, and Ed Becker. *All American Mafioso: The Johnny Rosselli Story*. New York: Doubleday, 1991.

Reeves, Richard. *President Kennedy: Profile of Power*. New York: Simon & Schuster, 1994.

Reid, Ed, and Ovid Demaris. *The Green Felt Jungle*. New York: Pocket Books, 1964.

Richards, Keith. *Life*. New York: Back Bay, 2011.

Richmond, Peter. *Fever: The Life and Music of Miss Peggy Lee*. New York: Macmillan, 2007.

Rickles, Don. *Rickles' Book: A Memoir*. With David Ritz. New York: Simon & Schuster, 2008.

Riddle, Nelson. *Arranged by Nelson Riddle: The Definitive Study of Arranging by America's #1 Composer, Arranger, and Conductor*. Miami: Warner Brothers, 1985.

Ringgold, Gene, and Clifford McCarty. *The Films of Frank Sinatra*. London: Virgin, 1990.

Ritter, Scott. *Dangerous Ground: America's Failed Arms Control Policy, From FDR to Obama*. New York: Nation Books, 2010.

Roberts, Jerry. *The Great American Playwrights on the Screen: A Critical Guide to Film, TV, Video and DVD*. Milwaukee: Hal Leonard Corporation, 2003.

Roemer, William F., Jr. *Man Against the Mob*. New York: Donald I. Fine, 1989.

Rose, Frank. *The Agency: William Morris and the Hidden History of Show Business*. New York: HarperBusiness, 1996.

Russo, Gus. *The Outfit: The Role of Chicago's Underworld in the Shaping of Modern America*. New York: Bloomsbury, 2001.

———. *Supermob: How Sidney Korshak and His Criminal Associates Became America's Hidden Power Brokers*. New York: Bloomsbury, 2007.

Safire, William. *Before the Fall: An Inside View of the Pre-Watergate White House*. New York: Doubleday, 1975.

Santopietro, Tom. *Sinatra in Hollywood*. New York: Thomas Dunne, 2008.

Saunders, Frank. *Torn Lace Curtain*. With James Southwood. New York: Holt, Rinehart and Winston, 1982.

Schlesinger, Arthur M., Jr. *Robert Kennedy and His Times*. Boston: Houghton Mifflin, 1978.

———. *A Thousand Days: John F. Kennedy in the White House*. Boston: Mariner, 2002.

Schneider, Matthew. *The Long and Winding Road from Blake to the Beatles*. New York: Palgrave Macmillan, 2008.

Schwartz, Jonathan. *All in Good Time: A Memoir*. New York: Random House, 2004.

Sengstock, Charles A. *That Toddlin' Town: Chicago's White Dance Bands and Orchestras, 1900–1950*. Champaign: University of Illinois Press, 2004.

Server, Lee. *Ava Gardner: "Love Is Nothing."* New York: St. Martin's, 2006.

———. *Robert Mitchum: "Baby, I Don't Care."* New York: St. Martin's Griffin, 2002.

Shaw, Arnold. *Sinatra: Twentieth-Century Romantic*. New York: Holt, Rinehart and Winston, 1969.

Sheed, Wilfrid. *The House That George Built: With a Little Help from Irving, Cole, and a Crew of About Fifty*. New York: Random House, 2007.

Shirpser, Clara. *Behind the Scenes in Politics: The Memoirs of Clara Shirpser*. Portola Valley, Calif.: American Lives Endowment, 1981.

Sinatra, Barbara. *Lady Blue Eyes: My Life with Frank*. With Wendy Holden. New York: Crown Archetype, 2011.

Sinatra, Frank. *A Man and His Art*. New York: Random House, 1991.

Sinatra, Nancy. *Frank Sinatra: An American Legend*. Santa Monica, Calif.: General Publishing Group, 1998.

———. *Frank Sinatra, My Father*. New York: Doubleday, 1985.

Sinatra, Tina. *My Father's Daughter: A Memoir*. With Jeff Coplon. New York: Simon & Schuster, 2000.

Smith, Sally Bedell. *Grace and Power: The Private World of the Kennedy White House*. New York: Random House, 2005.

Solomon, Aubrey. *Twentieth Century–Fox: A Corporate and Financial History*. The Scarecrow Filmmakers Series. Lanham, Md.: Scarecrow Press, 1989.

Spada, James. *Peter Lawford: The Man Who Kept the Secrets*. New York: Bantam, 1991.

Sperber, A. M., and Eric Lax. *Bogart*. New York: William Morrow, 1997.

Spoto, Donald. *Marilyn Monroe: The Biography*. New York: Cooper Square Press, 2001.

Summers, Anthony, and Robbyn Swan. *Sinatra: The Life*. New York: Alfred A. Knopf, 2005.

Talese, Gay. *Fame and Obscurity*. New York: Dell, 1981.

Taraborrelli, J. Randy. *Sinatra: Behind the Legend*. Secaucus, N.J.: Birch Lane Press, 1997.

Teachout, Terry. *Duke: A Life of Duke Ellington*. New York: Gotham, 2013.

Thomas, Evan. *Robert Kennedy: His Life*. New York: Simon & Schuster, 2002.

Tosches, Nick. *Dino: Living High in the Dirty Business of Dreams*. New York: Dell, 1992.

Tuohy, John William. *The Mob Files: The Illustrated Guide to the Mob in Vegas*. Lexington, Ky.: CreateSpace, 2013.

Vanderbilt, Gloria. *Black Knight, White Knight*. New York: Ballantine, 1988.

———. *It Seemed Important at the Time: A Romance Memoir*. New York: Simon & Schuster, 2004.

Van Meter, Jonathan. *The Last Good Time: Skinny D'Amato, the Notorious 500 Club, and the Rise and Fall of Atlantic City*. New York: Three Rivers Press, 2003.

Wagner, Robert J. *Pieces of My Heart: A Life*. With Scott Eyman. New York: It Books, 2009.

Waldron, Lamar, and Thom Hartmann. *Ultimate Sacrifice: John and Robert Kennedy, the Plan for a Coup in Cuba, and the Murder of JFK*. Berkeley, Calif.: Counterpoint, 2006.

Warner, Jennifer. *The True Story of the Jersey Boys: The Story Behind Frankie Valli and the Four Seasons*. Anaheim, Calif.: BookCaps Study Guides, 2014.

Wein, George. *Myself Among Others: A Life in Music*. With Nate Chinen. Boston: Da Capo, 2004.

Weintraub, Jerry. *When I Stop Talking, You'll Know I'm Dead*. New York: Twelve, 2010.

Weller, Sheila. *Dancing at Ciro's: A Family's Love, Loss, and Scandal on the Sunset Strip*. New York: Macmillan, 2004.

White, Mark. *Kennedy: A Cultural History of an American Icon*. New York: Bloomsbury Academic, 2013.

White, Theodore H. *The Making of the President, 1960: A Narrative History of American Politics in Action*. New York: Atheneum, 1962.

———. *The Making of the President, 1968*. New York: Atheneum, 1969.

Wilder, Alec. *American Popular Song: The Great Innovators, 1900–1950*. New York: Oxford University Press, 1990.

Wills, Garry. *The Kennedy Imprisonment: A Meditation on Power*. Boston: Mariner, 2002.

Wilson, Earl. *The Show Business Nobody Knows*. Spokane: Cowles, 1971.

———. *Sinatra: An Unauthorized Biography*. New York: Macmillan, 1976.

Winspur, Ian, and Christopher B. Wynn Parry. *The Musician's Hand: A Clinical Guide*. Abingdon, Oxford, UK: Taylor & Francis, 2005.

Zehme, Bill. *The Way You Wear Your Hat: Frank Sinatra and the Lost Art of Livin'*. New York: William Morrow, 1999.

Zoglin, Richard. *Hope: Entertainer of the Century*. New York: Simon & Schuster, 2014.

Zook, Lynn M., Allen Sandquist, and Carey Burke. *Las Vegas, 1905–1965*. Charleston, S.C.: Arcadia, 2009.

INDEX

Page numbers in *italics* refer to illustrations.

ABOUT THE AUTHOR

James Kaplan has been writing about people and ideas in business and popular culture, as well as notable fiction (*The Best American Short Stories*), for more than three decades. His essays and reviews, as well as more than a hundred major profiles, have appeared in many magazines, including *The New Yorker*, the *New York Times Magazine*, *Vanity Fair*, *Esquire*, and *New York*. His novels include *Pearl's Progress* and *Two Guys from Verona*, a *New York Times* Notable Book for 1998. His nonfiction works include *The Airport*, *You Cannot Be Serious* (coauthored with John McEnroe), *Dean & Me: A Love Story* (with Jerry Lewis), and the first volume of his definitive biography of Frank Sinatra, *Frank: The Voice*. He lives in Westchester, New York, with his wife and three sons.